GROLIER
ENCYCLOPEDIA
OF KNOWLEDGE

Grolier Incorporated
Danbury, Connecticut

ISBN 0-7172-5300-7 (complete set)
ISBN 0-7172-5315-5 (volume 15)

Printed and manufactured in the United States of America.

This publication is an abridged version of the *Academic American Encyclopedia.*

Picabia, Francis [pee-kah'-bee-ah] A founder of DADA and one of its most colorful exponents, the French painter Francis Picabia, b. Jan. 22, 1879, d. Nov. 30, 1953, began his career painting in the impressionist style. By 1913, when he took part in the famous Armory Show in New York, he had turned to cubism, but this seemed to be too confining for Picabia's playful, self-assertive temperament. Soon he began to produce such mechanthropomorphic images as *Universal Prostitution* (1916–17; Yale University Art Gallery, New Haven, Conn.), in which human figures are represented by machinelike objects. His later works were painted in a more conventional manner.

Picardy [pik'-ur-dee] Picardy is a historic region in northern France that is now within the departments of Aisne, Oise, Pas-de-Calais, and Somme. AMIENS was the region's capital. On Picardy's fertile soils wheat, sugar beets, and fodder crops are grown. Dairy and beef cattle are raised, and intensive vegetable cultivation takes place in the valley of the SOMME RIVER.

Occupied by the Franks during the 5th century, Picardy was divided among six feudal counts. It became a French province in 1477 and was the target of numerous invasions from the Netherlands. During World War I it was the scene of protracted trench warfare.

picaresque novel [pik-uh-resk'] In the picaresque novel, a lower-class hero or heroine wanders from place to place, suffering hunger and humiliation before learning to survive by his or her cleverness and adaptability. In 16th-century Spain, where the style became popular, this sort of roguish hero was called a *pícaro*. Picaresque adventures were usually humorous, the tone of voice mock-innocent and satirical, and the hero or heroine was almost always the narrator.

Even before the terms *pícaro* and *picaresque* achieved popularity, the anonymous *Lazarillo de Tormes* (1554; Eng. trans., 1586) contained many picaresque characteristics—a ragged young boy without a respectable genealogy leaves home; experiences a painful initiation into a harsh, deceptive world; and ultimately conforms to its hypocritical standards of behavior. Similar features appear in Mateo ALEMÁN's lengthy, didactic *Guzmán de Alfarache* (2 parts, 1599, 1604; trans. as *The Rogue*, 1622).

This format was adopted by numerous Spanish authors, including Francisco Gómez de Quevedo y Villegas, whose *El Buscón* (1626; Eng. trans., 1657) brilliantly reduces the *pícaro* to a one-dimensional comic caricature. In the 18th century the genre flourished outside Spain in such works as Hans von Grimmelshausen's *The Adventurous Simplicissimus* (1669), Alain Lesage's *The Adventures of Gil Blas* (1715–35), Daniel Defoe's *Moll Flanders* (1722), Henry Fielding's *Tom Jones* (1749), and Tobias Smollett's *The Expedition of Humphrey Clinker* (1771). The 19th century's outstanding picaresque work in English may well be Mark Twain's *Huckleberry Finn* (1884).

Picasso, Pablo [pee-kah'-soh] Pablo Ruiz y Picasso, b. Malaga, Spain, Oct. 25, 1881, d. Apr. 8, 1973, was the most influential and successful artist of the 20th century. Painting, sculpture, graphic art, and ceramics were all profoundly and irrevocably affected by his genius.

For Picasso, the meaning of art was to be derived from other works of art, and not directly from nature. Henri de Toulouse-Lautrec's work had a significant impact on his early paintings, as did the work of Paul Cézanne. Their influence, among others', can be detected in the paintings of Picasso's "blue period" (1901–04), which was stimulated by his exposure to life and thought in Paris, where he made his home after 1904. In works such as *The Old Guitarist* (1903; Art Institute, Chicago) he created evocative portrayals of blind, impoverished, or despairing people in a predominantly blue palette. His use of blue as a motif was apparently derived from the symbolic importance of that color in the contemporary romantic writings of Maurice Maeterlinck and Oscar Wilde, whose work often derived its force from depictions of madness or illness. Although his palette and subject matter changed when he entered (1904) what is called his "rose period," during which he painted harlequins and circus performers in a lighter and warmer color scheme, an underlying

Picasso's "rose period," exemplified by Artists *(1905), was characterized by scenes from the circus world. (Staatsgalerie, Stuttgart, Germany.)*

In Guernica *(1937), Picasso fused elements of the surrealism and symbolism seen in his earlier work. This painting, 3.5× 7.8 m (11.5× 25.67 ft) was inspired by the April 1937 bombing of a town in northern Spain. (Prado, Madrid.)*

mood of spiritual loneliness and lyrical melancholy that marked his "blue" paintings was retained. These paintings, however, do display a classical calm that contrasts clearly with the nervous expressionism of the blue period.

The lyricism of Picasso's blue and rose periods vanished abruptly in the next phase of his career, during which he and Georges BRAQUE independently laid the foundations for CUBISM. Struck by the compelling simplicity of pre-Christian Iberian bronzes and of African sculpture, he and Braque began to work in a consciously primitive and monumental style that Picasso explored in sculpture as well as in painting. By amalgamating the simplified iconic forms of Iberian and African art with Cézanne's reduction of the underlying structure of nature to a few basic shapes, Picasso produced *Les Demoiselles d'Avignon* (1907; Museum of Modern Art, New York City), which prefigured cubism.

After 1908, Picasso joined with Braque and other like-minded artists to explore the representation of three-dimensional objects on a two-dimensional surface by means of overlapping planes. This early phase of the cubist movement, often called analytical cubism, is exemplified in the painting *Ambroise Vollard* (1909–10; Pushkin Museum, Moscow) and the sculpture *Woman's Head* (1909; Museum of Modern Art, New York City). By 1912, Picasso, Braque, and Juan GRIS were introducing real materials such as chair caning and wallpaper—actual materials or painted facsimiles—into their works in what came to be known as COLLAGE. This synthesis or reconstitution of reality, called synthetic cubism, proved to be of fundamental importance to the development of modern art.

Theoretical cubism soon became too formalized and dogmatic for Picasso. During the 1920s he alternated cubist-inspired works such as *The Three Musicians* (1921; Philadelphia Museum of Art) with depictions of monumental and classically modeled figures such as his *Mother and Child* (1921–22; Hillman Collection, New York City). Subsequently, through the 1930s, he added certain aspects of SURREALISM to his work, including the use of the double image to create a shifting frame of reference and the idea of one object being metamorphosed into another. The tenets of surrealism also suggested to Picasso the use of symbolic archetypes (see SYMBOLISM, art) such as the minotaur, the horse, and the bull. All these qualities were fused in his famous *Guernica* (1937; from 1981, the Prado Museum, Madrid). Also during the 1930s, Picasso accomplished his most important work in sculpture; dating from this period are numerous influential works, including welded pieces composed of found objects, bronzes cast from plaster, and maquettes for monumental outdoor sculptures.

Picasso executed less fanciful still lifes, urban views, and portraits while remaining in Paris during World War II. After the war he moved to the south of France, where he became interested in the classical cultural tradition of the Mediterranean. Mythological daydreams of nymphs, satyrs, fauns, and centaurs soon filled his works, as epitomized in *La Joie de Vivre* (1946; Musée Picasso, Antibes). The postwar years also marked a period of daring experimentation in lithography and ceramics. Although he had made prints throughout his career, he did not concentrate on that field until the late 1940s, when he embarked on a series of innovations that resulted in a reevaluation of printmaking as a means of expression. He gave a similar impetus to contemporary ceramics; his unconventional handling of the medium opened up possibilities that are still being explored.

Picasso's work of the 1950s and '60s consisted for

the most part of a reiteration of the themes and styles he had developed previously, although he never stopped experimenting with new materials and forms of expression. At the time of his death, he was universally recognized as the foremost artist of his era.

Piccard, Auguste [pee-kahr']   The Swiss-born stratosphere and deep-ocean explorer Auguste Piccard, b. Jan. 28, 1884, d. Mar. 24, 1962, with his associate Paul Kipfer, made (May 27, 1931) the first manned balloon flight into the stratosphere, setting a new altitude record of 15,781 m (51,775 ft). For this flight he designed the first pressurized cabin. Hampered by equipment failures, the flight ended on an Austrian glacier after 17 hours aloft. The following summer the same balloon took Piccard and Max Cosyns to an altitude of 16,201 m (53,153 ft). Piccard continued to make flights (27 in all) until 1937, when his interest turned toward exploring the ocean bottom.

Piccard took ten years to build his first BATHYSCAPHE, a free-moving vehicle for deep-sea descents. An unmanned dive to 1,388 m (4,554 ft) proved the basic design. Financed by private industry, Piccard and his son, Jacques (b. July 28, 1922), built a second bathyscaphe, the *Trieste*, and in 1953 successfully dived 3,150 m (10,330 ft). Between 1954 and 1956, Jacques Piccard made six more dives, gathering valuable data and descending more than 3,700 m (12,000 ft). In 1958 the U.S. Office of Naval Research bought the *Trieste*. Two years later Jacques Piccard and Lt. Don Walsh of the U.S. Navy descended 10,920 m (35,800 ft) in it to the bottom of the Marianas Trench, the deepest place known on Earth.

At the time of his death Auguste Piccard was designing a new vehicle, the mesoscaphe, to range at 1,500 to 4,600 m (5,000 to 15,000 ft) and collect specimens. His son completed the project and launched the *Auguste Piccard* in 1964. A second mesoscaphe, built in 1968, traveled the Gulf Stream from Florida to Cape Cod to study the current's marine life.

Auguste Piccard climbs into the pressurized gondola he designed to attempt the first manned stratospheric flight. Borne aloft by balloon, Piccard ascended to an altitude of 15,790 m (51,804 ft) in 1931.

piccolo [pik'-uh-loh]   The piccolo, a transverse flute pitched an octave above the concert, or standard, flute, is a development of the late 18th century. Its range is nearly three octaves, reaching the highest pitches in the modern orchestra. It has a bright sound that can be heard easily, even in thickly scored orchestral passages. Used for special effects in orchestras, it has a more prominent place in concert and marching bands. Although most modern flutes are built of metal, the preference for wooden piccolos persists among some older players.

Pichegru, Jean Charles [peesh-groo']   Jean Charles Pichegru, b. Feb. 16, 1761, d. Apr. 5, 1804, French revolutionary general, became a royalist conspirator against the DIRECTORY and NAPOLEON I. Promoted to general in 1793, he conquered the Low Countries (1794–95). In 1795, Pichegru began contacting royalist exiles. Suspected by the Directory, he resigned his commission in 1796. He was elected president of the Council of Five Hundred in 1797 by its royalist majority. Deported to Guiana after the September 1797 antiroyalist coup, Pichegru escaped in 1798. He returned secretly to Paris in January 1804 to plot against Napoléon, but he was arrested and several weeks later was found strangled in prison.

pickerel [pik'-uh-rul]   Pickerels are two species of long-bodied, broad-snouted fishes in the same genus, *Esox* (family Esocidae), as the northern pike and the muskellunge. The pickerels generally can be distinguished both by their smaller size and by the presence of scales covering the whole of the cheeks and gill covers: the northern pike lacks scales on the lower halves of the gill covers; the muskellunge lacks scales on the lower halves of both cheeks and gill covers. The redfin pickerel, *E. americanus*, which includes the smaller variety known as the grass pickerel, reaches about 35 cm (14 in) in length; the chain pickerel, *E. niger*, grows to about 65 cm (26 in). Both species are broadly distributed in eastern North America, where they inhabit shallow, weedy ponds and lakes.

The chain pickerel, a carnivorous North American freshwater fish, is named for the dark, chainlike markings on its sides. With its wide mouth, strong jaws, and sharp teeth, it can eat relatively large prey, including frogs, birds, and small mammals.

Pickering, Timothy   Timothy Pickering, b. Salem, Mass., July 17, 1745, d. Jan. 29, 1829, was an American revolutionary soldier and U.S. secretary of state (1795–1800). An early leader of revolutionary protest in Massachusetts, he was adjutant general (1777–78) and quartermaster general (1780–85) of the Continental Army. After the war he moved to Pennsylvania. Under President George Washington, Pickering served as postmaster general (1791–95), secretary of war (1795), and then secretary of state, replacing the Democratic-Republican Edmund Randolph (see RANDOLPH family), whose dismissal he had engineered. In 1800, President John Adams summarily dismissed Pickering, a member of the Hamiltonian wing of the FEDERALIST PARTY, for his concealed opposition to the president's policy of conciliation with France. Pickering became the leader of the extreme Federalists, serving in the U.S. Senate (1803–11) and House of Representatives (1813–17).

Pickett, George E.   George Edward Pickett, b. Richmond, Va., Jan. 25, 1825, d. July 30, 1875, a Confederate general in the U.S. Civil War, is remembered for Pickett's charge at the Battle of Gettysburg (see GETTYSBURG, BATTLE OF). He graduated from West Point in 1846, served in Mexico (1848), and remained in the U.S. Army until 1861, when he resigned to join the Confederate forces. A division commander at Gettysburg, on July 3, 1863, he led his troops as the spearhead of an attack on Cemetery Ridge that was designed to break through the center of the Union line. The desperate assault has been called the Confederacy's high-water mark. The attack was repulsed, and Pickett faded from prominence.

Pickford, Mary [pik'-furd]   Mary Pickford, stage name of Gladys Mary Smith, b. Toronto, Apr. 8, 1893, d. May 29, 1979, became one of the world's first film stars after

Mary Pickford, Hollywood's first female screen idol, appears in a scene from one of her silent films. Aided by her youthful appearance and diminutive stature, Pickford starred in children's roles well into her adult career, earning the sobriquet "America's Sweetheart."

beginning her cinema career in 1909 under the tutelage of D. W. Griffith. Together with her second husband, Douglas Fairbanks, and Charlie Chaplin, she founded United Artists in 1919. Despite considerable business acumen, her career faltered with the advent of talkies. Her best-known films include *Rebecca of Sunnybrook Farm* (1917), *Pollyanna* (1920), *Little Lord Fauntleroy* (1921), and *Little Annie Rooney* (1925). She received an Academy Award for *Coquette* (1929) and a special Academy Award in 1976.

pickling   The process of preserving food in vinegar or salt brine, or sometimes with added sugar, is known as pickling. Not only does the use of vinegar provide an acidic environment that prevents food spoilage that results from the growth of undesirable microorganisms, but vinegar is also inexpensive, plentiful, and flavorful. Salt brine or a sugar solution dehydrates microorganisms and thus preserves food from spoilage and contamination. Spices are usually added to enhance flavor.

Fruit pickles are made by a process similar to that of CANNING, except that the liquid covering the fruit ordinarily is a sweetened vinegar solution with a spice, such as cloves, added for flavor. Some vegetable pickles are produced by fermentation: the vegetable is placed in a covered crock and allowed to ferment in a brine solution for a period of time ranging from a few days to several weeks.

Vegetables, fruit, meat, eggs, and even nuts can be pickled; some fairly well-known pickled foods are sauerkraut (cabbage fermented in brine), dill or sweet pickles made from cucumbers, peach pickles, and pickled watermelon rind.

Pico della Mirandola, Giovanni, Conte [pee'-koh del'-lah mee-rahn'-doh-lah]   Giovanni Pico della Mirandola, b. Feb. 24, 1463, d. Nov. 17, 1494, was a well-known philosopher of the Italian Renaissance. Marsilio FICINO converted him to NEOPLATONISM. In 1486, Pico published *Conclusiones nongentae in omni genere scientiarum* (900 Conclusions in Every Kind of Science), covering logic, natural philosophy, metaphysics, theology, ethics, and the Kabbalah.

Pico's thought is an eclectic attempt to reconcile Judaism, Christianity, and Greek philosophy. He classifies all things in three categories: the *super-celestial*, God and the angels; the *celestial*, the Sun, Moon, planets, and stars; and the *terrestrial*, material things below the Moon. Mediating all categories is humankind, "the Divine Masterpiece," whose special dignity is in its freedom and its power to shape its own destiny.

Picts [pikts]   The Picts, a people of obscure origin, were the ancient inhabitants of northern Scotland. The name was first used in Roman sources in AD 297 and referred to all the northern tribes that raided the Roman province of Britain. They apparently spoke a form of Celtic akin to Welsh.

By the 6th century the Picts were organized in at least two kingdoms north of the River Forth. They were converted to Christianity as a result of the efforts of Saint NINIAN (4th century) and Saint COLUMBA (6th century). In the 7th century the Picts recognized a single king, Brude, who stopped the encroachments of the Scots from the kingdom of Dalriada (Argyll). They reached the peak of their power under Angus, who established ascendancy over the Scots in 740. Kenneth I of Dalriada (r. 843–58) united the Scots and Picts to form the kingdom of Alba (the nucleus of the kingdom of Scotland).

---

pidgin [pij'-in] A pidgin is a reduced and rudimentary variety of speech arising in a situation of limited social interaction between groups not sharing a common language. Pidginization happens whenever a language is learned in the absence of social integration with native speakers and whenever communicative pressures diminish the importance of accurate reproduction. It involves the combination of vocabulary and grammatical features from different languages and the reduction of the functions for which language is used.

In phonology, pidginization leads to a reduction in the number of distinctive sounds and a modification of the forms of words. Grammatical categories are often represented by function words rather than by inflectional endings—for example, Cameroon Pidgin English *a di tok*, "I'm talking," *a bin tok*, "I talked," *a go tok*, "I'll talk," and *a bin don tok*, "I have talked." Other characteristics include invariant word order, the elimination of redundant grammatical categories such as gender and number, and the use of juxtaposition instead of function words.

Pidginization produces highly variable and evanescent speech varieties that crystallize into stable pidgins only in those rare cases where the learners' version of the target language serves as a LINGUA FRANCA for the different groups in contact. When it is acquired by children and becomes the primary language of a linguistic community, a pidgin becomes a CREOLE and takes on all the characteristics of normal language.

Pied Piper of Hamelin [pyd py'-pur, ham'-lin] The Pied Piper of Hamelin is a figure of German legend. He supposedly appeared at Hamelin, Westphalia, in 1284, when the town was infested with rats, and offered to rid the town of the vermin for a handsome fee. Upon agreement, he played his magic pipe and lured the rats into the Weser River. When the townspeople reneged on the payment, the Pied Piper lured all their children into a mountain cave, and they never returned. Robert Browning popularized the legend in his poem "The Pied Piper of Hamelin" (1842).

Piedmont [peed'-mahnt] The Piedmont (Italian: Piemonte) is a region in northwest Italy covering 25,399 km² (9,807 mi²) and bordering on France in the west and Switzerland in the north. It has a population of 4,365,911 (1989 est.). Almost totally encircled by mountains (Piedmont means "foot of a mountain"), the region is dominated by the PO RIVER. TURIN is the regional capital. The Piedmont forms part of Italy's main industrial area and is divided into the provinces of Alessandria, Asti, Cuneo, Novara, Torino, and Vercelli. Factories produce motor vehicles (chiefly at Turin), textiles, clothing, chemicals, and office machines. In the Po Valley grains, vegetables, and fruits are grown, and dairying and winemaking are carried on.

The Piedmont area was under Roman rule from the 1st century BC and was composed of free communes and feudatories in the Middle Ages. By the 15th century Piedmont was dominated by the dukes of Savoy, who in 1720 became kings of Sardinia (see SARDINIA, KINGDOM OF; SAVOY, dynasty). Piedmont was under French rule from 1798 to 1814 but thereafter became the center of the Italian unification movement, or RISORGIMENTO. Victor Emmanuel II of Sardinia-Piedmont became (1861) the first king of united Italy.

Piedmont Plateau The Piedmont Plateau is a geographical area of the United States that lies between the APPALACHIAN MOUNTAINS to the west and the Atlantic Coastal Plain to the east. It extends from Alabama north to the Hudson River. The boundary between the plateau (whose name, Piedmont, means "foot of a mountain") and the coastal plain is marked by a shift from hard to soft rock. Although the exact boundaries are obscured by earth and vegetation, the FALL LINE indicates the change in the composition of underlying rock.

Piedras Negras [pee-ay'-drahs nay'-grahs] Piedras Negras, overlooking the Central Usumacinta River in Guatemala, is the site of an ancient MAYA city. Its well-preserved stone stelae with ruler portraits and long hieroglyphic inscriptions provided Tatiana Proskouriakoff with material she used in 1960 to demonstrate that Maya writing and calendars were a record of the history of the ruling nobility, not, as was once believed, a list of calendrical incantations.

Various Piedras Negras kings claimed military victories over Yaxchilán, an upstream power, until the end of the 7th century, when an important foreign dynast, Lady Ahau Katun, married into the Piedras Negras lineage. After a war with Pomona, a downstream city, Piedras Negras was abandoned about 800.

Pierce, Franklin Franklin Pierce, the 14th president of the United States (1853–57), served during a time of worsening sectional controversy that was exacerbated by the passage (1854) of the KANSAS-NEBRASKA ACT.

Early Life and Political Career. Pierce was born on Nov. 23, 1804, in Hillsborough (now Hillsboro), N.H., the son of Benjamin and Anna Kendrick Pierce. His father, a veteran of the American Revolution, later rose to a militia generalship and served two terms as governor of New

FRANKLIN PIERCE
14th President of the United States (1853–57)

Nickname: "Young Hickory of the Granite Hills"
Born: Nov. 23, 1804, Hillsborough (now Hillsboro), N.H.
Education: Bowdoin College (graduated 1824)
Profession: Lawyer, Public Official
Religious Affiliation: Episcopalian
Marriage: Nov. 19, 1834, to Jane Means Appleton (1806–63)
Children: Franklin Pierce (1836); Frank Robert Pierce (1839–43); Benjamin Pierce (1841–53)
Political Affiliation: Democrat
Died: Oct. 8, 1869, Concord, N.H.
Buried: Old North Cemetery, Concord, N.H.
Vice-President: William R. King

Hampshire. After an academy education, Franklin entered Bowdoin College in Brunswick, Maine. He graduated in 1824, studied law, and in 1827 began practice in Hillsborough.

In 1829, Pierce was elected to the state House of Representatives, and he served as its speaker in 1831 and 1832. Like his father, Franklin joined the ranks of the Jacksonian party and soon emerged as a state leader. He then served two terms in the U.S. House of Representatives (1833–37) and took his seat in the U.S. Senate in 1837 as the youngest member of that body. His wife, the former Jane Means Appleton, whom he had married in 1834, detested Washington, D.C., and in 1842 convinced him to resign from the Senate.

For a decade after 1842, Pierce served as a Democratic political manager in New Hampshire while building up a successful law practice. President James K. Polk appointed him U.S. district attorney in 1845. When the Mexican War broke out, Pierce volunteered and was commissioned first a colonel and then a brigadier general. In 1847, Pierce, with his brigade of 2,500 men, joined Gen. Winfield Scott in his campaign against Mexico City. A painful injury resulting from a fall off his horse prevented Pierce from taking part at Contreras, and illness kept him out of action at Chapultepec.

After his return to civilian life, Pierce's endorsement of the Compromise of 1850, including the Fugitive Slave Law, won him favorable attention in the South. Prior to the Democratic convention of 1852, some of his New Hampshire friends and fellow Mexican War officers pro-

posed him for the presidency. After Stephen Douglas, James Buchanan, Lewis Cass, and William Marcy fell shy of the votes needed to win, Pierce, the compromise candidate, gained support, and he won on the 49th ballot. Though a "dark horse" presidential aspirant, he took all but four states, soundly defeating his Whig opponent and former commander, General Scott.

Presidency. Pierce created a sectionally balanced cabinet and planned an aggressive foreign policy in hope of quieting the slavery controversy. He was persuaded, however, to endorse the Kansas-Nebraska Bill, which dealt with the explosive issue of slavery in the new territories of Kansas and Nebraska, leaving the decision as to whether slavery should be permitted to the settlers themselves. The measure encountered great opposition in the North. Following its passage, the Republican party was formed, and the Democrats suffered heavy losses in the elections of 1854.

Virtual civil war erupted (1856) in the Kansas Territory between proslavery and free-soil settlers. Pierce recognized the proslavery territorial government at Lecompton, chosen by fraudulent electoral practices, and sent troops to the territory; at the end of his administration, however, the Kansas question was far from resolved.

Despite some successes, the administration's record in foreign affairs was also disappointing. Through the GADSDEN PURCHASE, the United States acquired land from Mexico that made feasible a southern railroad route to the Pacific, and a treaty was signed with Great Britain that obtained fishing rights for Americans off Newfoundland.

The administration failed in its efforts to acquire Cuba; the OSTEND MANIFESTO, in which three overseas American ministers urged that if necessary that island should be wrested from Spain, aroused further controversy over the extension of slavery.

Few favored his renomination, and Pierce retired from public life after fellow Democrat James Buchanan succeeded him in March 1857. During the Civil War, Pierce's opposition to President Abraham Lincoln's war measures made him extremely unpopular in the North. He died Oct. 8, 1869.

Piero della Francesca [pee-ay'-roh del'-lah frahnches'-kah]

Piero della Francesca, b. c.1420, d. Oct. 12, 1492, now one of the most highly acclaimed Italian Renaissance artists, has been rediscovered only in the past 100 years. His works—a total of only about 16 extant paintings or sets of paintings—were based on the humanistic philosophy that later gave rise to the glorious

The Baptism of Christ (c.1450), by Piero della Francesca, demonstrates the artist's ability to use the newly discovered laws of perspective in compositions that are both naturalistic and rigorously composed. (National Gallery, London.)

achievements of the Florentine Renaissance. He absorbed the newly emerging ideals of human dignity and the majesty of nature, which he sought to express visually by applying the laws of perspective as set forth by Leon Battista Alberti.

Piero's oeuvre is difficult to date precisely, but scholars generally agree that his first mature work was The Baptism of Christ (c.1450; National Gallery, London), done for the Priory of Saint John the Baptist in Borgo Sansepolcro. In projecting an idealized humanity, this work demonstrates the artist's mastery of the new Renaissance style. The forms are based upon a geometry that governs humanity as well as other natural phenomena: the tree covering the foreground figures is of the same cylindrical shape as Christ. Piero used geometry in his paintings, but his framework is balanced by the naturalistic rendering of the landscape.

Piero's major undertaking was a fresco cycle (1452–66) in the Church of San Francesco in Arezzo, filling the three walls of the choir with narrative scenes. The subject is the Legend of the True Cross, a medieval legend tracing the history of the wood on which Christ was crucified from its first form as a branch of the Tree of Knowledge. Piero's handling of the complex tale includes the Discovery of the Wood of the True Cross and the Meeting of Solomon and the Queen of Sheba. He shows the Queen kneeling in adoration of the sacred wood; on the right she tells Solomon of her premonition that Christ will be nailed to it. Piero's tectonic composition gives an illusion of simplicity while also providing inexhaustible variation by juxtaposing the harmony of the natural setting with the classical ordering of the architecture. For Piero, life contained mathematical harmonies that represented the secrets of the universe and permitted humanity to see into the mind of God.

Piero di Cosimo [pee-ay'-roh dee koh'-zee-moh]

The Florentine artist Piero di Cosimo, c.1462–c.1521, is known as a painter of charming mythological scenes, such as the haunting Death of Procris (n.d.; National Gallery, London), in which the sentiment is enhanced by studies of bird and animal life. In his day Piero was also famous as a designer of accessories for the colorful public events and processions favored by Lorenzo de'Medici.

The artist adopted the Christian name of Cosimo Roselli, his master, whom he assisted in painting frescoes in the Sistine Chapel (1481–82; Rome). Many of Piero's mythological conceptions take the form of poetic idylls, and others—such as the Fight between the Lapiths and the Centaurs (n.d.; National Gallery)—exhibit an energetic urgency reminiscent of Luca Signorelli. In his later paintings the influence of Leonardo da Vinci, among others, is evident; however, a uniquely personal imaginative vision and love of visual incident distinguish all Piero's work.

Pierpont, Francis Harrison [peer'-pahnt]

Francis Harrison Pierpont, b. near Morgantown, Va. (now W.Va.),

Jan. 25, 1814, d. Mar. 24, 1899, was known as the father of West Virginia. When Virginia seceded from the Union, Pierpont organized (1861) Unionists in the western part of the state. The Wheeling Convention named him to head the provisional government there. He was later (1863–65) governor of the "restored" state of Virginia and (1865–68) governor of Virginia.

Pierre [peer]   Pierre (1990 pop., 12,906), the capital of South Dakota and the seat of Hughes County, is situated on the east bank of the Missouri River in the center of the state. Pierre is a trade center for area farms and ranches, as well as a center of government. The Aricara Indians had a fort on the site of Pierre. During the early 19th century, Fort Pierre, across the river, served the early fur traders, and during the gold mining boom in the Black Hills, it became (1876–85) a steamboat head for miners. The city's growth continued with the arrival of the railroad in 1880. Pierre became the state capital in 1889.

Piers Plowman [peerz plow'-muhn]   A late-14th-century work probably written by the cleric William LANGLAND, *Piers Plowman* (full title: *The Vision of William Concerning Piers the Plowman*) is one of the greatest religious poems written in English. It takes the form of a series of dream visions described in the first person by the Dreamer, whom the reader identifies with the poet. The poem concerns the poet's quest for Truth, the true nature of Christ's love, and man's relationship with God. A spiritual history of humanity provides a brilliant satire on the society of the time. The poet's genius is particularly evident in the great emotional and technical range of his work.

Pietermaritzburg [pee-tur-mair'-its-boorg]   Pietermaritzburg, the provincial capital (since 1856) of Natal, South Africa, has a population of 133,809 (1985). The city lies in the Drakensberg foothills on the Durban-Johannesburg railroad, 64 km (40 mi) west of the Indian Ocean. Pietermaritzburg's diversified light industries (furniture, aluminum ware) depend on local forest and agricultural resources and inexpensive African labor.

The city was founded in 1838 and named for Pieter Retief and Gerrit Maritz, pioneer Afrikaners who defeated the Zulus at the Battle of Blood River the same year. From 1839 to 1843, Pietermaritzburg was the capital of the Boer Voortrekker Republic of Natal.

pietism [py'-uh-tizm]   Originally a German Lutheran religious movement of the 17th and 18th centuries, pietism emphasized heartfelt religious devotion, ethical purity, charitable activity, and pastoral theology rather than sacramental or dogmatic precision. The term now refers to all religious expressions that emphasize inward devotion and moral purity. With roots in Dutch precisionism and mysticism, pietism emerged in reaction to the formality of Lutheran orthodoxy. In his *Pia Desideria* (1675), Philipp Jakob SPENER proposed a "heart religion" to replace the dominant "head religion." Beginning with religious meetings in Spener's home, the movement grew rapidly, especially after August Hermann Francke (1663–1727) made the new University of Halle a Pietist center. Nikolaus Ludwig, Graf von ZINZENDORF, a student of Francke's and godson of Spener, helped spread the movement. His MORAVIAN CHURCH promoted evangelical awakenings throughout Europe and in North America in the 18th and 19th centuries. John Wesley (see WESLEY family) and METHODISM were profoundly influenced by pietism.

piezoelectricity [py-ee'-zoh-ee-lek-tris'-i-tee]   An electric voltage is produced by certain crystals and by a number of ceramic materials when they are subjected to pressure. This voltage is called piezoelectricity. That is, when certain crystals, such as quartz, are compressed in certain directions, an electric polarization (and a corresponding voltage) is induced due to the displacement of charged atoms along the same axis. This voltage is directly proportional to the amount of strain and changes sign when the compression is replaced by an elongation. Piezoelectricity ("pressure-electricity") was discovered in 1880 by Pierre and Jacques Curie.

The piezoelectric effect has many applications. The conversion of mechanical vibratory energy into electric signals and vice versa can be achieved by this effect, and so piezoelectric crystals are used in microphones, sonar transducers, and ultrasonic sound generators. In a record player, a crystal can be used to convert the mechanical vibrations of the phonograph needle into easily amplified electrical oscillations. Perhaps the most important use of piezoelectricity is the quartz oscillator, which is used to regulate radio transmitters and precision timepieces. In this device, the extremely regular mechanical vibrations of a quartz crystal control corresponding electrical oscillations in a coupled electronic circuit, in a way analogous to the regulation of a mechanical clock by the oscillation of its pendulum.

pig   The pig, or SWINE, both wild and domesticated, is a cloven-hoofed mammal of the family Suidae (order Artiodactyla). The domesticated pig is believed to have descended principally from the Eurasian wild boar, *Sus scrofa*. No *Sus* species are native to the New World, although the related PECCARY is indigenous to Central and South America.

Pigs were probably domesticated first in China about 7000 BC. Their domestication in the West came later and independently. The domesticated pig was brought to the New World by Columbus in 1493 and to the North American mainland by DeSoto in 1539. DeSoto's original herd of 13 pigs developed into the American Razorbacks, some of which now roam wild in the U.S. Southeast. Early settlers in America imported pigs from England. By the late 1800s pig farming had become an important agricultural industry in the American corn belt.

Characteristics

The pig has a stout, medium-sized body and a thick hide blanketed with coarse hair; a large head, which tapers down to a mobile, disklike snout; a short tail; four-toed feet; and canine teeth, which grow outward and upward like tusks. The hoelike snout enables pigs to root in the ground for food. The animal has a keen sense of smell, is a strong swimmer, and can trot, canter, and run fast. Despite their reputation, pigs are clean and wallow in mud to protect themselves from the Sun's heat and from lice and other parasites. They are among the most intelligent of domesticated animals, and their adaptability and trainability have encouraged their use as household pets. The miniature Vietnamese potbellied pig (35 cm/14 in high; about 18 kg/40 lb—although it can grow to 59 kg/130 lb) is the pet pig of choice.

The Domestic Pig

The prolificacy of pigs and their ability to grow fat from table scraps and gleanings have encouraged their rearing even in areas that practice subsistence agriculture. Their ability to convert high-energy feeds into meat quickly and efficiently has made them an important farm enterprise in large-scale, intensive-production systems. They are produced in large numbers throughout the world. (The Jewish and Islamic religions consider pigs unclean and therefore inedible, and they are not raised in regions such as the Middle East, where these religions predominate.)

Breeding and Rearing. Continuing efforts by breeders to improve their stock and the selection of commercial breeding stock for systematic crossbreeding have led to the introduction of several new breeds in recent years and to the development of special breeds that are notable for meat production. Yorkshire, Hampshire, Duroc, Spotted, Chester White, Poland China, Berkshire, and Landrace are among the most popular breeds in the United States and Canada; they are raised primarily for meat. Pigs raised for bacon include Tamworth, Lacombe, and Large Black. Bacon-type pigs are fed primarily dairy by-products. The most recent attempts to improve U.S. pig breeds have involved crossbreeding with Chinese strains, which are notable for their early sexual maturity, large litter sizes, and superior disease resistance.

Pigs are prolific, farrowing from 6 to 15 young twice each year. Weaning age varies from 3 to 8 weeks. Sows can usually be bred a few days after weaning and have a gestation period of 114 days. Sexual maturity varies from 4 to 6 months of age, depending on breed and nutritional level.

Pigs are more dependent than other types of livestock on feed provided by the farmer. Commonly used rations are based on corn as an energy source, soybean meal as a protein source, and supplements of vitamins and minerals.

Diseases. Of the many parasites and diseases to which the pig is subject, one of the most serious is hog cholera, or swine fever. Caused by the virus *Pestivirus*, it is highly infectious and is nearly always fatal. Although it has been eradicated in the United States by strict federal pro-

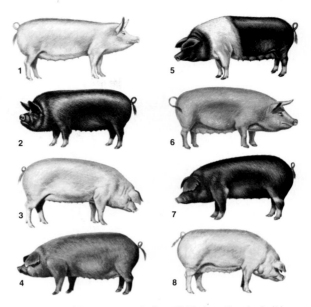

The pig is one of the most economically profitable domestic animals: it is omnivorous, matures quickly, and is a prolific breeder. Virtually all parts of a pig are used commercially: its flesh is marketed as ham, bacon, sausage, pork chops, and spareribs; it yields lard; and other parts of its body are used in soap, glue, brushes, medicine, and fertilizer. Above are eight sows representing popular breeds: Yorkshire (1); Berkshire (2); Landrace (3); Duroc (4); Hampshire (5); Tamworth (6); Poland China (7); Chester White (8).

grams, it remains endemic in many regions of the world. Transmissible gastroenteritis, another viral disease, is highly fatal to newborn pigs, but sows that recover from the disease transmit immunity to their young. Erysipelas, or infectious swine arthritis, is a bacterial disease that also occurs in other livestock and in humans. Pigs can transmit a number of other diseases to humans as well, including ASCARIASIS, BRUCELLOSIS, and TRICHINOSIS. For this reason, pork should always be well cooked.

Uses. Almost every part of the pig carcass is usable and marketable. The flesh provides meat; trimmings are made into sausage and headcheese. Stomachs are used for tripe, and intestines for casings in processed meats. Fat provides lard, and blood is used in some processed foods and in the production of fertilizer. Hides are tanned for leather, bristles are sold for the manufacture of brushes, and glands are used for hormones and other pharmaceutical products.

---

pigeon   Pigeon is an inclusive name for birds of the family Columbidae, a cosmopolitan group with about 300 species. Generally, larger species are called pigeons and smaller ones are known as doves, although there is no technical distinction.

Almost all species lay two eggs (usually white) in a weak nest of twigs and rootlets. Both male and female

Pigeons and doves are common inhabitants of North American cities, suburbs, and farmland. The band-tailed pigeon (left) *summers in western forests, whereas the mourning dove* (center) *and the rock dove, or common pigeon* (right), *are found in all areas of the United States. About 300 species of pigeons are known throughout the world.*

produce a nutritious "pigeon milk" that is fed by regurgitation to the young. This secretion is remarkably similar to mammalian milk, being rich in proteins (15%) and fats (10%). The pigeon milk is produced in the adult by the sloughing of layers of cells lining the crop, the rapid growth of these cells being controlled by the endocrine system. The principal hormone involved in the milk production is prolactin, as in humans.

Courtship behaviors of pigeons typically include various cooings or booming calls, with stereotyped bowing postures. Some species have courtship-display flights as well. Pigeons are often quite social, with some species breeding colonially and others simply congregating in flocks during the nonbreeding seasons. The diets of pigeons consist mainly of vegetable substances such as fruits, seeds, and berries. The muscular gizzard of the pigeon is usually well developed, and many species add small invertebrate animals, such as snails, to their diets. Pigeons are among the few groups of birds that drink directly, by immersing the bill and sucking.

The various forms within the pigeon family include brightly colored tropical species, several giant pigeons from islands, long-tailed African species, and many breeds of domesticated pigeons. A noteworthy extinction within the family was the passenger pigeon, *Ectopistes migratorius*, which occurred in flocks of millions throughout eastern North America. Slaughter for sport and food led to their demise by the end of the last century, with a single zoo bird remaining alive until 1914.

Breeds of the domestic or common pigeon, *Columba livia*, include more than 150 varieties with numerous patterns of coloration, feathering, and body form. Among the more striking breeds are the trumpeter, pouter, fantail, and Jacobin pigeons. For eating, the white king, a popular commercial breed, provides excellent squabs, which are young pigeons almost ready to leave the nest.

The most famous breed is the homing or carrier pigeon, known for its remarkable homing ability. Carrier pigeons have been used to send messages since the time of Christ; even during the two world wars, the communications corps kept these pigeons in mobile lofts. Today homing pigeons are maintained by racing enthusiasts and entered in races over distances of 800 km (500 mi) or more. The homing pigeon can fly at an average speed of 72 km/h (45 mph).

In cities the overabundance of domestic pigeons can present public-health problems because of the birds' droppings. Pigeon-control programs in urban areas have been attempted but are for the most part unsuccessful.

pigment   Pigments are a group of finely pulverized or processed chemicals, organic or inorganic, that are employed to color and opacify materials as well as to protect or regulate product performance, quality, and appearance. Dispersed as solids, they differ from DYES, which are used in solubilized form. They are classified as either prime pigments or extenders.

Prime pigments are used to impart color or opacity or to perform specific functions. Their color is a result of selective absorption and reflectance of visible light. Black pigments totally absorb light, whereas white pigments reflect all wavelengths.

Hiding, or the absence of transparency, is dependent upon differences in the refractive indices (see REFRACTION) between prime pigments and the vehicle. Titanium dioxide is valued as an inert, white pigment with a high refractive index (2.76). A pigment provides total hiding when all incident light is refracted or diverted before penetrating the pigmented film or object. Pigments for coatings and inks are useful to the extent that they can hide surfaces in relatively thin films.

Extenders, also called inert pigments, are almost exclusively mineral salts or oxides added to provide bulk volume, to thicken and fortify amorphous binders, or to influence such properties as gloss, hardness, and permeability. Because they are totally encapsulated in the binding media, they have a negligible effect on hiding and color.

See also: PAINT.

pigment, skin Differences in SKIN color between animal species, individuals within species, and human races occur because of differences in the amount and kind of skin pigment. Functions of pigmentation include protection against predators or from solar radiation, the use of solar radiation to raise body temperature, and the signaling of reproductive readiness between mating pairs in breeding season.

Pigments that contribute to skin color are carotene (yellowish), hemoglobin in blood vessels (pink-red), and melanin (black, brown, and red). Darker skins are dominated by melanin, which is produced from the amino acid tyrosine by pigment cells (melanocytes) in the skin. In mammals and birds, melanin is dispersed throughout each melanocyte and is also transported to nearby skin cells. Skin color can darken temporarily by increased production of melanin; conversely, it can lighten because of loss of melanin. Increased melanin results if melanocytes are stimulated by solar (ultraviolet) radiation; by the pituitary hormones melanocyte-stimulating hormone or adrenocorticotropin; or by high blood levels of the sex hormone estrogen, which occurs during pregnancy.

Reptiles, amphibians, and fishes can respond adaptively to environmental cues by moving melanin back and forth within each melanocyte, causing darker shades by dispersing pigment and lighter shades by concentrating it at one point. Certain reptiles and fishes can change to different colors by manipulating pigment cells that specialize in red, yellow, orange, blue, green, and white (or light-reflecting) pigments.

Pigmy see PYGMY

pika [py'-kuh] Pikas are small mammals related to rabbits and hares, order Lagomorpha. All 14 living species are classified in the genus *Ochonta* in the family Ochotonidae. Also called conies, rock rabbits, and other local names, pikas are found in Asia and western North America. They range from 12.5 to 30 cm (5 to 12 in) in length and from 110 to 400 g (4 to 14 oz) in weight. The animals have short legs, rounded ears, no visible tail, and dense, soft, usually grayish brown or reddish fur.

Pikas commonly live in colonies. They have evolved an interesting way of surviving the winter without hibernating. In mid- or late summer they begin to gather grasses and other plants and spread them to dry. The vegetation is then piled into "haystacks" for food during the winter.

pike Pike is the common name for either of two long-bodied, flat-snouted fishes: *Esox lucius*, popularly known in North America as the northern pike, and *E. reicherti*, the black-spotted pike of eastern Siberia. Both are members of the family Esocidae, which contains three other species: the muskellunge, the chain pickerel, and the redfin, or grass, pickerel. The northern pike is widely distributed in the Northern Hemisphere north of 40° north latitude. It grows to about 1.4 m (4.5 ft) long and 23 kg (50 lb) in weight; Eastern European and Asiatic specimens are claimed to have exceeded 70 kg (150 lb). The walleye, *Stizostedion vitreum*, often called the walleyed pike, is a member of the perch family, Percidae.

The northern pike is a popular sports fish that has a larger range of distribution than any other freshwater game fish. It reaches a maximum length of 1.4 m (4.5 ft) and a weight of 23 kg (50 lb).

Pike, James Albert Episcopal bishop James Albert Pike, b. Oklahoma City, Okla., Feb. 14, 1913, d. 1969, was one of America's most controversial religious leaders. Pike held various posts, among them dean of the Cathedral of Saint John the Divine in New York City, before his appointment as bishop of California in 1958.

Although he began his church career with fairly traditional theological views, Pike began to question much of the standard church doctrine in the 1960s. In 1966 his fellow bishops censured him for his "irresponsibility in an office of public leadership." In the spring of 1969 he announced he was leaving the church. That fall he became lost while on a hike in Israel and, on September 8, was found dead.

Pike, Zebulon Montgomery An American soldier and explorer, Zebulon Montgomery Pike, b. Lamberton (now part of Trenton), N.J., Jan. 5, 1779, d. Apr. 27, 1813, is best known for his expeditions in the American West. As a young army officer, he was dispatched (1805–06) to the upper Mississippi to buy fort sites from the Indians and to explore the sources of the river. In 1806 he was sent westward by Gen. James WILKINSON and instructed to explore the headwaters of the Arkansas and descend the Red River. Because the region had never been accurately mapped and because Pike was ill equipped for the rugged journey, he and his men became lost and suffered from cold and hunger. In southeastern Colorado they made an unsuccessful attempt to scale the snow-covered peak that now bears Pike's name. Pike strayed up and down the Arkansas, missed the Red River, and in January 1807 encamped on a branch of the Rio Grande in Spanish territory. He was arrested by a Spanish detachment, sent to Chihuahua for questioning, then escorted to the U.S. border near Natchitoches, La. Although he was suspected of conspiring with General Wilkinson and Aaron BURR in a private scheme to create an empire in the Southwest, there is no evidence that Pike was anything but a loyal officer whose luck was bad. He was killed in the War of 1812.

Pikes Peak   Pikes Peak is a 4,301-m (14,110-ft) mountain in the Front Range of the southern ROCKY MOUNTAINS, in central Colorado 16 km (10 mi) west of Colorado Springs. In 1859, "Pikes Peak or Bust!" was the cry of westward-bound pioneers, because of the gold and other minerals discovered in the vicinity such as the Cripple Creek gold area to the southwest. Today, the mountain's snow-covered summit and steep sides are more valued by skiers and tourists. A cog railway and toll road lead to the summit. The first successful ascent was made by three members of an expedition led by Maj. Stephen H. LONG.

Pilate, Pontius [py'-luht, pahn'-shuhs]   Pontius Pilate, the fifth Roman procurator (governor) of Judea (AD 26–36), condemned Jesus Christ to death. Appointed under Emperor Tiberius, he also had jurisdiction over Samaria and part of Idumea. Pilate's years in office were marked by conflict with the Jews. At one point he is reported to have introduced votive images of the emperor into Jerusalem; he also executed a large number of Samaritans in crushing a prophetic movement. Outrage against the latter act resulted in his removal from office.

In the Gospels, Pilate is portrayed as officiating at the trial of Jesus. Although believing him innocent, he yields to the desires of the crowds, releasing BARABBAS and sending Jesus to his execution. According to Christian tradition, Pilate and his wife were later converted to Christianity and martyred. Another version holds that he committed suicide in Rome.

piles   see HEMORRHOIDS

pilgrimage   Pilgrimage is the practice, common to most world religions, of journeying to a holy place or sacred shrine to obtain special blessings from God or as an act of devotion, penance, or thanksgiving. In the Judeo-

Christian tradition the practice is very ancient and is referred to in the Old Testament. In the Christian era there is written record of a pilgrimage as early as 217—that of the Cappadocian bishop Alexander to Jerusalem. The Holy Land remains the most popular place of pilgrimage to this day. JERUSALEM, the holy city of Jews and Christians, also contains important Islamic shrines. MECCA, however, remains the true focal point of Muslim pilgrimage or *hajj*. Islamic law prescribes that every Muslim who is physically and financially able must make the *hajj* at least once. In India, VARANASI is the most important of the many Hindu pilgrimage sites. Among the most popular Christian sites, in addition to Jerusalem and Rome, are SANTIAGO de Compostela in Spain and LOURDES in France.

At least since Saint Augustine's *City of God* (early 5th century) Christian thought has considered life in this world to be a pilgrimage, a journey to God.

Pilgrims   The Pilgrims were English Separatists who founded (1620) PLYMOUTH COLONY in New England. In the first years of the 17th century, small numbers of English Puritans broke away from the Church of England because they felt that it had not completed the work of the Reformation. They committed themselves to a life based on the Bible. Most of these Separatists were farmers, poorly educated and without social or political standing. One of the Separatist congregations was led by William BREWSTER and the Reverend Richard Clifton in the village of Scrooby in Nottinghamshire. The Scrooby group emigrated to Amsterdam in 1608 to escape religious persecution. The next year they moved to Leiden, where, en-

This painting portrays the Pilgrims departing from Plymouth, England, in 1620. They had originally set sail from Southampton on two ships, the Mayflower *and the* Speedwell. *When the latter proved unseaworthy, the expedition put into Plymouth to regroup aboard the* Mayflower.

joying full religious freedom, they remained for almost 12 years.

In 1617, discouraged by economic difficulties, the pervasive Dutch influence on their children, and their inability to secure civil autonomy, the congregation voted to emigrate to America. Through the Brewster family's friendship with Sir Edwin Sandys, treasurer of the LONDON COMPANY, the congregation secured two patents authorizing them to settle in the northern part of the company's jurisdiction. Unable to finance the costs of the emigration with their own meager resources, they negotiated a financial agreement with Thomas Weston, a prominent London iron merchant. Fewer than half of the group's members elected to leave Leiden. A small ship, the *Speedwell*, carried them to Southampton, England, where they were to join another group of Separatists and pick up a second ship. After some delays and disputes, the voyagers regrouped at Plymouth aboard the 180-ton MAYFLOWER. It began its historic voyage on Sept. 16, 1620, with about 102 passengers—fewer than half of them from Leiden.

After a 65-day journey, the Pilgrims sighted Cape Cod on November 19. Unable to reach the land they had contracted for, they anchored (November 21) at the site of Provincetown. Because they had no legal right to settle in the region, they drew up the Mayflower Compact, creating their own government. The settlers soon discovered Plymouth Harbor, on the western side of Cape Cod Bay, and made their historic landing on December 21; the main body of settlers followed on December 26.

Pilgrim's Progress   see ALLEGORY; BUNYAN, JOHN

Pillars of Hercules   see GIBRALTAR

pillbox   see FORTIFICATION

pillory

A means of punishing petty offenders in Europe and in colonial America, the pillory was a wooden frame, with holes in it, mounted on a post upon a platform. It was clamped over the stooped offender's neck and wrists, usually for several hours in a public place. A similar framework with holes for the offender's feet was called the stocks. The pillory was abolished in England in 1837 and in Delaware, the last U.S. state where it was legal, in 1905.

pilot fish

The pilot fish gains its name from its behavior of swimming along with slow-moving ships or large fishes, such as sharks, apparently guiding them. Why the larger fishes do not attack the pilot fish remains a mystery. The common belief is that pilot fish associate with the larger fishes to obtain left-over scraps of food and possibly the parasites on the larger fish's body, but the correct explanation may be that pilot fish swim with large objects, including driftwood and floating weeds, to obtain a traveling, protective cover. The pilot fish, *Naucrates ductor*, is a member of the jack family, Carangidae. It oc-

curs in all warm seas and grows to a length of about 60 cm (2 ft). It is bluish in color, with five to seven darker blue vertical bands.

Pilsen   see PLZEŇ

Piłsudski, Józef

[pil-sud'-skee] Józef Klemens Piłsudski, b. Dec. 5, 1867, d. May 12, 1935, was a Polish statesman and revolutionary leader. After five years in Siberia for allegedly conspiring to assassinate the Russian emperor Alexander III, he joined (1892) the Polish Socialist party, but Polish independence was always his first goal. During the Russo-Japanese War (1904–05) he offered military intelligence on the Russian army to Japan, hoping to secure Japanese aid for a Polish revolution. From 1910 he stressed military training to develop officer cadres for a Polish army.

Foreseeing an initial German-Austrian victory over Russia in World War I, Piłsudski led (1914–17) his Polish legions on the Austro-German side, against Russia, hoping to lay the foundations of a Polish state and army before the ultimate defeat of the Central Powers. He resigned when Germany refused to create a Polish government. After imprisonment in Germany he returned (November 1918) to Warsaw to become head of the restored Polish state and commander in chief of its army. To secure Poland against renewed Russian domination he aimed at a Polish-Lithuanian state allied with Ukraine. Although this attempt failed, he defeated the Red Army on the Vistula in August 1920, saving Poland from Soviet domination. Believing that the unstable Polish parliamentary system endangered Poland, he seized power (May 1926) and developed an authoritarian government. Piłsudski worked for good relations with both Germany and Russia but alliance with neither.

Piltdown man

One of the most famous hoaxes in the history of science surrounds the discovery of Piltdown man (*Eoanthropus dawsoni*), the name given a forged skull fragment made to simulate early human fossil material. In 1912, Charles Dawson, an amateur naturalist, announced the discovery of fossil bones and tools in gravels of great antiquity at Piltdown, in Kent, southern England. In 1915, Dawson allegedly found additional bones of another individual at a nearby site.

As reconstructed, the Piltdown fossils exhibited a large, apparently modern brain, but the jaws and teeth of an ape. This combination of features was accepted by scholars of the time as evidence of the long-sought missing link between the apes and humans in the evolutionary chain. In 1953 fluorine testing and a variety of analyses finally uncovered the forgery. The jaw of a modern orangutan and a 600-year-old human skull had been prepared cleverly enough to fool science for almost 40 years. Dawson is the main suspect as the perpetrator of the hoax. He is generally assumed to have had a collaborator, however. Several candidates have been put forward, but the case remains unsolved.

Pima [pee'-muh]   The Pima are a North American Indian tribe in Arizona linguistically related to their Aztec-Tanoan–speaking neighbors, the PAPAGO. Believed to be descendants of the prehistoric HOHOKAM CULTURE, the Pima in 1775 numbered about 2,500.

The Pima had plenty of water available in the Gila River for irrigating their fields and were able to live a settled life in villages near the river. Because of frequent APACHE attacks, they concentrated their numbers under an elected chief and developed a degree of tribal solidarity.

From the beginning of the gold rush to California in 1849, hundreds of white Americans followed the Gila River westward, obtaining from the Pima food and protection from the Apache. Settlers soon followed, diverting water from the Pima fields. By 1870 tribal life was disintegrating. In a few decades the Pima were thoroughly Christianized and acculturated; little remains of their traditional culture. They live with the Maricopa Indians on reservations near Phoenix, Ariz., with a joint population of about 16,800 in 1989.

Pinchback, Pinckney Benton Stewart   Pinckney Benton Stewart Pinchback, b. Macon, Ga., May 10, 1837, d. Dec. 21, 1921, was an African American who achieved political prominence during the Reconstruction era. Pinchback, whose mother was an emancipated slave and whose father was white, attended high school in Ohio. In 1862 he ran a Confederate blockade and reached New Orleans, which was in Union hands during the Civil War. There he enlisted and raised a company of black volunteers called the Corps d'Afrique. Pinchback, a Republican, was elected to the Louisiana Senate, served (1871) as its president pro tempore, and became lieutenant governor on the death of the incumbent.

Pinchot, Gifford [pin'-shoh]   The American public official Gifford Pinchot, b. Simsbury, Conn., Aug. 11, 1865, d. Oct. 4, 1946, made his greatest contributions to the U.S. conservation movement during the presidency (1901–09) of Theodore Roosevelt. He served (1898–1910) as chief of the Department of Agriculture's Division of Forestry (renamed the U.S. Forest Service from 1905). Here he implemented the concept of conservation for use—as opposed to preservation—and with Roosevelt spearheaded government regulation of natural resources. He was dismissed from his post by President William Howard Taft after a controversy with Secretary of the Interior Richard A. BALLINGER over the Taft administration's conservation policies.

Founder of the National Conservation Association, Pinchot was instrumental in congressional passage of a measure (1911) that expanded the nation's forest reserve and the Waterpower Act (1920); the latter initiated federal control of private power companies. He also served two terms (1923–27, 1931–35) as governor of Pennsylvania and founded the school of forestry at Yale University.

Pinckney (family) [pink'-nee]   The Pinckney family played a leading role in the politics of South Carolina and the nation during and after the American Revolution. After being educated in England, **Eliza Lucas Pinckney**, b. Antigua, c.1722, d. 1793, went to South Carolina, where she managed large plantations and introduced indigo cultivation in the South. She married Charles Pinckney; their sons had distinguished military careers during the Revolution, and both became leading Federalists. **Charles Cotesworth Pinckney**, b. Charleston, S.C., Feb. 25, 1746, d. Aug. 16, 1825, was appointed minister to France in 1796, but the French refused to receive him. In 1804 and 1808 he was the unsuccessful Federalist presidential candidate. **Thomas Pinckney**, b. Charleston, Oct. 23, 1750, d. Nov. 2, 1828, was governor of South Carolina (1787–89) and minister to Great Britain (1792–95). As special envoy to Spain he negotiated (1795) the Treaty of San Lorenzo, known as Pinckney's Treaty, which opened the Mississippi to American navigation. He served in the House of Representatives (1797–1801) and held the rank of major general during the War of 1812.

Thomas Pinckney's son **Henry Laurens Pinckney**, b. Charleston, Sept. 24, 1794, d. Feb. 3, 1863, was a prominent newspaper editor in Charleston and a leading champion of nullification. He was a member of Congress (1833–37) and for many years mayor of Charleston. A second cousin of Charles Cotesworth and Thomas Pinckney, **Charles Pinckney**, b. Charleston, Oct. 26, 1757, d. Oct. 29, 1824, was the youngest member of the Constitutional Convention of 1787. As minister to Spain (1802–05) he persuaded the Spanish government to recognize the Louisiana Purchase. An ardent Jeffersonian Republican, he led the fight against the Missouri Compromise in Congress.

Pindar [pin'-dur]   A Boeotian noble and the major lyric poet of ancient Greece, Pindar, c.518–c.438 BC, composed poetic songs for a variety of occasions such as weddings, funerals, and religious festivals. What survives are the epinicia, triumphal ODES written to celebrate athletic victories. Pindar also associated the occasion with a myth and used it as a basis for religious and moral statements.

Structurally, Pindar's poems, composed for a chorus, were written in stanzas called strophes. Sometimes the strophes repeated the same metrical pattern; sometimes they were in threes (a triad), consisting of strophe, antistrophe, and epode. Pindar was much imitated by ancient poets, and in later times by Abraham Cowley, John Milton, John Dryden, Thomas Gray, and Gerard Manley Hopkins.

Pindar derived much of his vocabulary and his interest in heroic values from Homer. From Hesiod, he adopted a strong moral and religious tone, the use of proverbs and aphorisms, and a didactic manner. His contemporaries Aeschylus and Bacchylides wrote choruses in a similar fashion. Pindar differs from them, however, in his density, his determined obscurity, and his willingness to allow sound and individual images to take precedence over rhetorical continuity.

Pindar was a political conservative who celebrated the values of an aristocratic, traditional society. He took the commonplace Homeric celebration of competition and raised it to a primary moral commitment, the pursuit of excellence. Each poem contains topical references to the event at hand; his praise is intimate and specific. In an age that had begun to rationalize myths and gods, Pindar was a religious conservative and took the Olympian gods seriously. He presented the myths in a manner that restored their sanctity and beauty, and he showed the gods as awesome, morally good forces.

pine   Pines, genus *Pinus*, comprise 90 to 100 species of evergreen, cone-bearing trees and a few shrubs in the pine family, Pinaceae. Worldwide in distribution, they are the most important conifers that grow in the Northern Hemisphere. Pines extend as far south as Nicaragua, northern Africa, Anatolia, Malaysia, and Sumatra.

Pines are of primary importance in lumber production and are also grown as ornamentals. Several pine species—for example, the long-leaf pine, *P. palustris*—are a source of turpentine, resin, pitch, tar, and oils. Most pine wood is also suitable for pulp and paper manufacture. Pines are often used for reforestation because they grow well on land that is open and windswept, well drained, and depleted of nutrients.

Pine trees usually have a thick, furrowed bark, resinous wood, and an upright trunk from which extend circles (whorls) of spreading branches. The needles are produced in groups of two, three, or five encased in a sheath. Needles persist from 2 to 12 years, depending on the species. The woody cones are egg-shaped or cylindrical, and the same tree may bear both male cones (POLLEN CONES) and female cones (SEED CONES). The ovules on the scales of the latter, when fertilized by pollen, become seeds. The

cones mature at the end of the second year. They may then drop from the tree or remain attached, shedding their usually winged seeds.

Pines can be separated into two major groups or subgenera. The soft or white pines, subgenus *Haploxylon*, have mostly softwood and needles commonly in clusters of five, with one vascular bundle in cross section. The hard pines, subgenus *Pinus* or *Diploxylon*, have mostly hardwood, and needles are commonly in clusters of two or three, with two vascular bundles in cross section.

Hard Pines. The species *P. palustris*, long-leaf pine in America and pitch pine in Europe, is native to eastern North America, where it forms forests in the Atlantic and Gulf states from Virginia to Florida. Cuban pine, *P. caribaea*, is found in subtropical parts of the southeastern United States and also in Cuba and Honduras. Scotch pine, *P. sylvestris*, has the widest distribution of any pine and is found throughout Europe and western and northern Asia. The red pine, *P. resinosa*, is native to eastern North America from Nova Scotia to Pennsylvania. It is intolerant of shade and must be grown in pure pine stands, or with slower-growing trees so that it can dominate. Black pine, *P. thunbergiana*, is native to Japan, where it has long been widely cultivated. It is used for reclaiming sand dunes.

Soft Pines. The eastern white pine, *P. strobus*, is a native of North America, where it has wide distribution in Canada and the northeastern United States. It is the tallest conifer occurring east of the Rocky Mountains. Records describe trees up to 78 m (260 ft) in height and 6 m (20 ft) in girth. Western white pine, *P. monticola*, is also native to North America, where it extends from southern British Columbia to the western slopes of the Rocky Mountains in northern Montana, the coast region of Washington and Oregon, and the Cascades and Sierra Nevada ranges in California. Sugar pine, *P. lambertiana*, native to Oregon and California, is one of the most prominent species of the timber belt of the Sierra Nevada.

The eastern white pine (left), *native to North America, is valued for its softwood timber. The red pine* (right) *is a quick-growing hardwood pine. It is also known as the Norway pine; the name refers to Norway, Maine.*

Pine Bluff   The city of Pine Bluff is the seat of Jefferson County; it is located in south central Arkansas, on a bluff overlooking the Arkansas River, about 65 km (40 mi) southeast of Little Rock. Pine Bluff has a population of 57,140 (1990). Cotton and grain fields stretch to the east and southeast, pine and oak forests to the west. The city's industries use these natural resources to manufacture paper and pulp products, furniture, and textiles, as well as metal and electrical goods. The U.S. Army maintains a center for chemical research there. The city's civic center was designed by Edward Durell STONE. The city grew around a trading post established on the river in 1819.

pine cone   SEE POLLEN CONE; SEED CONE

pine nut   Pine nuts—small, edible seeds extracted from the cones of various PINE species—have been eaten worldwide as a flavorful, protein- and oil-rich food. They are expensive, however, because they are difficult to extract from the resinous cone and also because their hard shells must be removed by hand. Unshelled pine nuts have a long storage life because of their low moisture content.

European pine nuts, commonly called pignolia nuts, are obtained primarily from the stone pine, *Pinus pinea*, native to northern Mediterranean regions. These seeds are 1 cm (0.4 in) in length and are rich in oil. Piñon nuts of the southwestern United States and northern Mexico are gathered from several pine species, including the pinyon pine, *P. edulis*, and the single-leaf pinyon, *P. monophylla*. Similar in quality to pignolia nuts, piñons have a rich, slightly sweet taste.

pineal gland [pin'-ee-ul]   The pineal gland is a small organ attached by a stalk to the posterior wall of the third ventricle of the BRAIN in vertebrate animals. Lying above the cerebellum, it is richly supplied with blood vessels and nerve fibers. In certain fishes, frogs, and lizards, the gland is associated with a well-developed light-sensitive organ, or so-called "third eye," and in all species the pineal is affected by light. The gland produces a hormone (see HORMONE, ANIMAL), called melatonin, from the neurotransmitter serotonin. This hormone is associated in varying and not yet well-understood ways with a number of biorhythms (see BIOLOGICAL CLOCK), including such long-term ones as the onset of puberty, and appears to be particularly important in animals that display seasonal behavior.

pineapple   A popular tropical fruit, the pineapple, *Ananas comosus*, of the Bromeliaceae family, originated in South America, perhaps in the Parana-Paraguay basin, and spread through much of the continent's lowlands and other tropical areas. After Amerindians domesticated the plant, the Spanish and Portuguese spread its cultivation

The pineapple plant grows up to 1.2 m (4 ft) tall and has 30–40 bladelike leaves. Flowers form on a stalk and fuse to form the fleshy center of the fruit (detail).

throughout the tropics, aided by the fact that it is propagated readily from parts of the fruit.

Like many plants brought from the New World, pineapple became a greenhouse curiosity in 18th-century England and France, and attempts were made to improve the basic stock. Using European cultivars, the imperial powers established pineapple plantations in their tropical colonies. In 1896 improved English plants were introduced from Australia into Hawaii, where they have grown very successfully ever since. China is the world's largest pineapple producer, followed by the United States, Thailand, Brazil, the Philippines, Mexico, Zaire, Ivory Coast, and Malaysia.

The pineapple plant has fleshy, overlapping leaves, sometimes with spiny margins, and an extensive root system. The leaves store water absorbed by specialized hairs on their clasping bases. The fruit, crowned by a cluster of leaves, is sweet and succulent when ripe. Most pineapple types produce seedless fruit that requires pollen from other plants to form seed. Varieties can be interbred. The derivatives of the cultivar "Cayenne," originating in Venezuela and improved in Europe, are the basis of most commercial crops.

Three or four years after the seed-grown plant germinates, it forms a fruit at the top. When the fruit is cut off, smaller fruits grow on lower branches. Further cutting produces another crop of yet smaller fruits; these are usually used for juice, crushing, or dicing. New seed must be sown after this "last" crop. Vegetative propagation from the fruit-crown or from suckers yields two crops in three years.

pinecone fish   Pinecone fish comprise two species of globular, marine fishes in the family Monocentridae. The Japanese pinecone fish, *Monocentrus japonicus*, is found in the deep water of the Indo-West Pacific Ocean; the Australian pinecone fish, *M. gloriaemaris*, is found off Australia. The Japanese pinecone fish is yellow with long dorsal and pelvic spines and large, bristling, overlapping scales resembling a pinecone. The underside of the small mouth possesses luminescent organs.

Pinero, Sir Arthur Wing [pi-nair'-oh]   With *The Second Mrs. Tanqueray* (1893), the drama of a woman with a disreputable past, English playwright Arthur Wing Pinero, b. May 24, 1855, d. Nov. 23, 1934, performed two valuable services for the English theater: he started the vogue for "problem plays" and launched the career of his leading lady, the soon-to-be-famous actress Mrs. Patrick Campbell. A master of the well-made play who began his career writing frivolous comedies, Pinero later wrote such serious plays about women as *The Notorious Mrs. Ebbsmith* (1895), *Iris* (1901), and *Mid-Channel* (1909). He is also known for *Trelawny of the Wells* (1898), a popular sentimental comedy, and *The Gay Lord Quex* (1899), his best comic work. He was knighted in 1909.

Ping-Pong   see TABLE TENNIS

pink   Pink, genus *Dianthus*, is the common name of about 300 species of flowering plants of the pink family,

Among the pinks are a number of popular ornamentals. Shown here are (1) the florist's carnation, prized for its beauty and fragrance; (2) sweet William; (3) the China pink; and (4) the maiden pink.

Caryophyllaceae. Native to the mountains of Eurasia, pinks are easily cultivated as ornamentals in mild climates. They have opposite, grasslike leaves and swollen stem joints. The flowers have tooth-edged petals, and some species have a clovelike fragrance; colors range from white to pink, lilac, and red. Well-known pinks include the CARNATION, *D. caryophyllus*, and SWEET WILLIAM, *D. barbatus*. The grass pink, *D. plumarius*, has gray leaves and one to three fragrant flowers on a stem. The maiden pink, *D. deltoides*, has clusters of tiny flowers, and the China pink, *D. chinensis*, has large flowers with no fragrance.

Pinkerton, Allan [pink'-ur-tuhn]   Allan Pinkerton, b. Glasgow, Scotland, Aug. 25, 1819, d. July 1, 1884, was an American detective and founder of the Pinkerton National Detective Agency. Pinkerton emigrated to the United States in 1842, settling in Illinois, where he became a deputy sheriff. In 1850, Pinkerton founded his agency to investigate cases of freight theft on the railroads. During the Civil War he was active in the Union cause, heading an organization engaged in spying on the Confederacy. When the war ended, Pinkerton resumed control of his agency and was instrumental in breaking strikes and in crushing the MOLLY MAGUIRES. After his death the agency he had founded continued to be active in combating the then-fledgling American labor movement, and Pinkerton agents were widely criticized for their part in such labor disturbances as the PULLMAN STRIKE (1894) and the Ludlow Massacre (Ludlow, Colo., 1914).

pinkeye   see CONJUNCTIVITIS

Pinkiang   see HAERBIN

pinniped   see SEA LION; SEAL; WALRUS

Pinocchio [pi-noh'-kee-oh]   A children's classic by Carlo COLLODI, pen name of Carlo Lorenzini, *The Adventures of Pinocchio* first appeared in book form in 1883 (Eng. trans., 1892; animated film, 1940). A wooden puppet, Pinocchio is distinguished by a nose that grows longer every time he tells a lie; his improved behavior eventually transforms him into a real, live boy.

Pinochet Ugarte, Augusto [pee-noh-chet' oo-gahr'-tay]   The Chilean army general Augusto Pinochet Ugarte, b. Nov. 25, 1915, was president of Chile (1974–90). He had led the right-wing military coup that deposed President Salvador ALLENDE in September 1973. As leader of the ruling junta, he instituted conservative economic policies and presided over massive violations of human and civil rights in efforts to suppress dissent. In 1981, Pinochet was sworn in as president under a new constitution. In October 1988 he lost a plebiscite that would have allowed him to continue as president beyond the end of his term in March 1990.

pinochle [pee'-nuh-kuhl]   Pinochle—sometimes spelled pinocle, penuchle, or binocle—is a trump card game derived from BEZIQUE. Pinochle is played with a deck of 48 cards, 12 in each suit—two each of the ace, king, queen, jack, 10, and 9, in each suit. The ace is the highest-ranking card, followed by the 10, king, queen, jack, and 9. Two, three, four, or more persons may play. If four play, partnerships are formed. If more than four play, only three players may actively participate at any one time.

Pinter, Harold [pin'-tur]   Harold Pinter, b. Oct. 10, 1930, one of England's leading playwrights, studied acting at the Royal Academy of Dramatic Art and began his theatrical career as an actor. He wrote his first play, *The Room*, in 1957, but first established himself as a highly original talent in 1960 with *The Caretaker*, a characteristic Pinteresque drama in its evocation of terror amid farcical "business" and sometimes fanciful dialogue. Typically, Pinter's characters seek security, self-identification, and verification of truth but find communication virtually impossible. Instead, there are pathetic games, clichés, long silences, and sinister threats, all presented in suspenseful plots.

In Pinter's first full-length play, *The Birthday Party* (1958; film, 1969), for instance, two gangsters interrogate and terrorize a nervous young pianist. *The Caretaker* (1960; film, 1962) centers on an old derelict who intrudes on two mysterious brothers and is ultimately thrown out by them. Pinter's reputation as an allusive and controversial dramatist grew significantly with *The Homecoming* (1965), in which a married couple visits the lower-class father and brothers of the husband, now a philosophy professor in the United States, and the wife finally remains in England to serve the family as a prostitute. Two later plays, *Old Times* (1971) and *No Man's Land* (1975), deal, respectively, with a middle-aged couple, their mysterious visitor (who once knew the wife), and the power of memory to wound; and the curious relationship between two elderly writers, one a success, the other a failure. More recent plays include *Betrayal* (1979; film, 1983), *Family Voices* (1982), and *One for the Road* (1984).

Pinter has directed a wide range of contemporary plays and has written screenplays for several of his own stage dramas and for such memorable films as *The Servant* (1963), *Accident* (1967), and *The Go-Between* (1971)—all directed by Joseph Losey—and for *The French Lieutenant's Woman* (1981) and *Turtle Diary* (1985).

pinto   see HORSE

pinworm   The pinworm, or threadworm, *Enterobius vermicularis*, is a tiny, parasitic nematode that infects children in temperate climates. As many as 5,000 worms may inhabit a child's rectum. Female worms creep through the anus to lay thousands of eggs on the skin and then die. An itch in the perianal region may result in the child's scratching and distributing the eggs; in this manner eggs may get into the mouth and be swallowed, spreading the infection. Infected persons often feel no symptoms or signs, and the parasitic relationship is seldom harmful, although it may cause diarrhea.

Pinyin   see CHINESE LANGUAGE

Pinza, Ezio [peen'-tsah]   The Italian-born operatic bass Ezio Pinza, b. May 18, 1892, d. May 9, 1957, was noted for his flowing, full-bodied voice, impeccable musicianship, and commanding characterizations. After his debut in Rome, in 1920, he quickly achieved leading status at La Scala, in Milan. He first sang at the Metropolitan Opera in 1926 and remained on the staff for 22 years. Among his 82 roles, his Figaro, Don Giovanni, and Boris Godunov were especially admired. In 1949 he left the Metropolitan to begin a new career, appearing for more than a year in the Broadway musical *South Pacific* and then in films.

Pinzón, Martín Alonso [peen-thohn']   The Spanish navigator Martín Alonso Pinzón, c.1441–93, commanded the *Pinta* during Christopher COLUMBUS's first voyage to the New World in 1492–93. Pinzón was probably part owner of both the *Pinta* and the *Niña*.

During a storm on the return trip to Spain the *Pinta* became separated from Columbus's ship, the *Niña* (the third ship, the *Santa María*, having been wrecked off Hispaniola). Some evidence suggests that Pinzón hoped to reach home ahead of Columbus, thereby winning royal favor, but Columbus arrived in Palos, Spain, a few hours before Pinzón.

Two of Pinzón's brothers, Francisco Martín Pinzón (fl. 1492) and Vicente Yáñez Pinzón (c.1460–c.1523), were also members of Columbus's first expedition. The latter explored (1500) the coast of Brazil, became (1505) governor of Puerto Rico, and sailed (1508–09) along the coast of Central America.

pion   see MESON

Pioneer   Pioneer is a long-running series of U.S. space probes that have included three basic types of missions: lunar, solar/interplanetary, and planetary.

Lunar Missions. Although a third-stage rocket failure on Oct. 11, 1958, limited *Pioneer 1* to a distance of about 113,000 km (70,000 mi) from Earth, the probe did send back information on radiation, magnetic fields, and micrometeroids near the planet. Like their predecessor, *Pioneers 2* and *3* (launched Nov. 8 and Dec. 6, 1958) failed to approach the Moon, but *Pioneer 3* made a major contribution with the discovery of the outer portion of the Van Allen radiation belts. The only one of the lunar series to approach its objective was *Pioneer 4*, which was launched on Mar. 3, 1959. This 6-kg (13-lb) probe passed within about 60,000 km (37,000 mi) of the Moon.

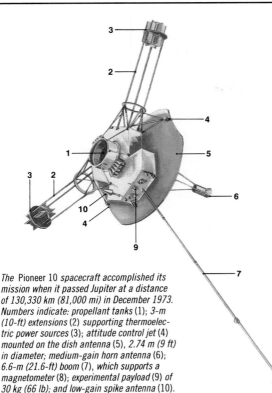

The Pioneer 10 *spacecraft accomplished its mission when it passed Jupiter at a distance of 130,330 km (81,000 mi) in December 1973. Numbers indicate: propellant tanks* (1)*; 3-m (10-ft) extensions* (2) *supporting thermoelectric power sources* (3)*; attitude control jet* (4) *mounted on the dish antenna* (5)*, 2.74 m (9 ft) in diameter; medium-gain horn antenna* (6)*; 6.6-m (21.6-ft) boom* (7)*, which supports a magnetometer* (8)*; experimental payload* (9) *of 30 kg (66 lb); and low-gain spike antenna* (10)*.*

Solar/Interplanetary Missions. *Pioneer 5,* launched Mar. 11, 1960, was the first truly deep-space probe launched by the United States. About seven times the weight of *Pioneer 4,* it carried a variety of sensors that reported on the interplanetary magnetic field and the solar wind out to more than 36 million km (22 million mi) from Earth.

More than 5 years passed before the Dec. 16, 1965, launching of *Pioneer 6.* The National Aeronautics and Space Administration considered it the first in a virtually new series of probes; each craft weighed more than 60 kg (130 lb) and was instrumented to monitor solar flares, cosmic rays, charged particles, and other phenomena. *Pioneers 7, 8,* and *9* were launched on Aug. 17, 1966, Dec. 13, 1967, and Nov. 8, 1968, respectively. All of the probes far outlasted their planned 6-month lifetimes.

Planetary Missions. The first two spacecraft to be sent to one of the solar system's large outer planets were *Pioneers 10* and *11,* which were launched on Mar. 2, 1972, and Apr. 5, 1973. Unlike previous Pioneers, *10* and *11* were powered by nuclear generators rather than solar cells, because their paths would take them away from the Sun.

En route to Jupiter, *Pioneer 10* became the first spacecraft to pass through the asteroid belt between Mars and Jupiter. As it flew by Jupiter on Dec. 3, 1973, the craft's instruments probed the planet's intense radiation belts; took numerous photographs, including several of

the Jovian satellites; established that electron bursts detected near Earth were actually coming from Jupiter; and mapped the planet's huge magnetic field (which expands and contracts in response to varying pressure from the solar wind). As it left the known solar system in 1983, *Pioneer 10* reported that various solar phenomena remained detectable even in interstellar space.

Pioneer 11 also survived passage through the asteroid belt and passed within 43,000 km (26,700 mi) of the Jovian cloud tops on Dec. 2, 1974. It took the first pictures of Jupiter's polar regions and returned much other data.

Pioneer 11 used Jupiter's gravitational acceleration as a boost on the way to a Sept. 1, 1979, rendezvous with the planet Saturn. *Pioneer Saturn* (as it was renamed) traversed the ring plane outside the edge of the outermost A-ring, from there passed underneath the rings at distances ranging from 2,000 to 10,000 km (1,200 to 6,200 mi), and then came within 21,400 km (13,300 mi) of Saturn's cloud tops. It took the first closeup pictures of Saturn. *Pioneer Saturn* indicated that the planet has a rocky inner core about the size of the Earth (or about one-ninth of Saturn's diameter) but with a mass three times as great, and that it has a magnetic field that is weaker than the Earth's. The spacecraft discovered new rings and satellites. *Pioneer Saturn's* instruments made photometric and polarization measurements of the Saturnian satellites Japetus, Rhea, Dione, and Tethys and also studied the temperature distribution, composition, and other properties of the clouds and atmospheres of Saturn and the satellite Titan.

Two further Pioneer spacecraft, bound for the inner planet Venus, were launched on May 20 and Aug. 8, 1978. The first one launched, *Pioneer Venus 1,* began orbiting Venus on Dec. 4, 1978. The second, *Pioneer Venus 2,* ejected a large probe and three small probes in mid-November; all of these probes, plus their transporter bus (which was also instrumented), descended into Venus's atmosphere on December 9 and returned important information.

pioneers   see FRONTIER

pipe   The tobacco pipe—consisting of a bowl for tobacco and a stem through which smoke is drawn—was introduced into Europe from the New World along with tobacco itself. Pipes of wood, clay, and bone have been found in Indian mounds of the Mississippi Valley dating from as early as 600 BC. Maya and Aztec priests used pipes in rites. North American Indians employed ceremonial pipes, such as the CALUMET, or peace pipe, which had a bowl of marble or pipestone.

As tobacco use spread to Europe, Africa, and Asia, designs and materials proliferated. At the end of the 16th century in England long-stemmed clay pipes became popular. The meerschaum pipe, probably invented in Hungary, had a bowl made of meerschaum, a light porous mineral from Asia Minor. Other materials used in pipes were wood, bone, horn, iron, glass, porcelain, gourd, and, in the United States, corncob. India and the Far East contributed the water pipe—the nargileh or hookah—which cooled and cleansed the smoke by drawing it through water.

In the 19th century, briarwood, from the roots of a species of Mediterranean tree heath (in French, *bruyère*) came to be valued for pipes because of its lightness, toughness, and heat resistance.

---

pipe and pipeline   A pipeline is a closed conduit system for conveying materials, usually fluid, in bulk. Most pipelines are underground; PUMPS placed at intervals along the line keep the cargo moving. Modern pipelines carry most of the energy supplies for the industrial nations. Among the pipeline's advantages are its low impact on the environment, its reliability, its low labor cost after installation, and its durability.

Pipeline Improvements.   The Bessemer process for wrought iron made possible the first big improvement in the construction of pipe. Wrought-iron pipe had lap-welded seams and threaded ends to fit collars and couplings.

The steel industry introduced a uniform seamless steel pipe in Philadelphia in 1899. Large-diameter seamless steel pipe appeared in 1925, and by 1927 the first electrically welded pipe was in use (see WELDING AND SOLDERING).

Hydraulically expanded pipe became universal in industrialized nations after World War II. In 1947 the American Petroleum Institute (API) began to standardize pipe specifications and introduced API standards for line pipe. Later in the 1940s, the American Society of Mechanical Engineers (ASME) established its codes, and the Canadian Standards Association adopted comparable codes in 1967. As metallurgy improved, pipe became stronger.

Pipe Laying.   The total length of pipeline systems increased as the construction of pipelines became more efficient. The first successful ditching machine was a 1912 ladder-type unit. During the 1920s a wheel ditcher used to install field drains on farms was adapted for pipeline trenching; with some improvements, it is still in use.

The backhoe was developed by reversing the "shovel" used in mining for hard digging and extra depth. Pipe had been bent by pulling the heated pipe's ends against a fulcrum, or "shoe." During the 1950s, hydraulic stretch-bending machines permitted uniform bends.

Pipelining boomed during the mid-1920s, when oil and natural gas were discovered in the southwestern United States. Pipeline contractors expanded rapidly in order to deliver gas from the new fields to large U.S. cities in the late 1920s and 1930s. In Canada, gas lines were built into Calgary and Edmonton (both in Alberta) during this period. The World War II–era pipelines "Big Inch" and "Little Big Inch" were built across the eastern half of the United States to free tankers from the job of hauling Gulf Coast crude oil to the East Coast. After the war these lines were converted to transporting natural gas. Other wartime projects were the Portland-Montreal Pipeline and the Trans-Isthmian pipelines in the Canal Zone.

Steel pipelines abroad were rare before World War I. Three exceptions were the 1935 line from Iraq to the Mediterranean and the Colombian (1938) and Venezue-

lan (1939) lines. The Trans-Arabian Pipeline (1950) was the forerunner of other lines in oil-producing countries that would bring crude oil to the port from which tankers could be loaded most efficiently. By the 1990s most countries had pipeline systems that distributed refined petroleum products to their major markets.

Another pipeline boom occurred during the late 1940s. Large gas lines were built to the Pacific and the Atlantic coasts of both the United States and Canada. By 1969 the ton-miles of commodities transported by pipeline in the United States had surpassed that transported by rail.

The energy crunch of the mid-1970s spawned another pipeline boom. In the United States the 1,300-km (800-mi) TRANS-ALASKA PIPELINE was finished in 1977. Coal "slurry" pipelines, which carry pulverized coal mixed with water, have been built to connect western coal mines with often distant power plants.

Other pipelines of major importance include a gas line across Australia and a line running under the Mediterranean from Algeria to Europe. In the 1980s, Canada built an oil pipeline from its vast petroleum deposits in the arctic Beaufort Sea down the Mackenzie River valley to northern Alberta. The immense pipeline from Soviet Siberia to the Trans-European Pipeline Network, which transports gas to West European nations, runs about 5,900 km (3,700 mi).

Workers prepare a section of the Trans-Alaska Pipeline for installation of a thick layer of insulation. At Arctic temperatures, oil tends to flow sluggishly. It is therefore heated, and the insulation prevents heat loss as the oil travels through the pipe.

The water pipit is a bird commonly found on shores and in fields. Like wagtails of the same family, pipits walk rather than hop.

pipit [pip'-it] Pipit is the common name for the small (13–20 cm/5–8 in) ground-dwelling birds of the genus *Anthus* in the family Motacillidae, which also includes the wagtails. Pipits are brownish above, lighter below, and have white outer tail feathers, long hind claws, and thin bills. Most are Old World species, but two occur in the Western Hemisphere: water pipit, *A. spinoletta,* and Sprague's pipit, *A. spragueii.*

Pippin, Horace [pip'-in] Horace Pippin, b. West Chester, Pa., Feb. 22, 1888, d. July 6, 1946, was a major African-American artist. He painted places he knew, as in the illustrations for a diary he kept as a soldier in World War I, and those he imagined, as in the scenes from the last raid, trial, and death of John Brown at Harpers Ferry, such as *John Brown Going to His Hanging* (1942; Pennsylvania Academy of the Fine Arts, Philadelphia). Pippin, who also painted landscapes and religious subjects, used large areas of flat color and infused them with emotional intensity. His style, generally termed naive rather than primitive, recalls at times that of Henri Rousseau.

piracy Piracy is the seizure of a ship or an airplane by an armed force that holds no commission from a sovereign state. Because piracy interrupts commerce between nations, it has traditionally been considered an offense against international law. Pirates are also called buccaneers (after *boucon,* the smoked meat of cattle slaughtered by West Indian pirates), corsairs (pirates operating from the Barbary States in North Africa), sea rovers, and freebooters. They are often confused with privateers (see PRIVATEERING), who have a national license or commission to seize enemy property. In contrast, pirates plunder the shipping of all nations indiscriminately, disrupting trade and preventing orderly commercial growth. In the early modern era the prevalence of privateering and piracy indirectly encouraged the rise of capitalism and modern corporate organizations, fostering the growth of insurance systems and partnerships to divide risk.

Ancient and Medieval Periods. Piracy dates from the time of the Phoenicians, the world's first seafaring people. A large Roman fleet led by Pompey the Great finally cleared the eastern Mediterranean of pirates in 67 BC after years of torment.

During the medieval era piracy again became a scourge. In northern Europe, VIKINGS raided continuously along the coasts from the Baltic Sea to the Strait of Gibraltar. With the rise of Turkish power in the East, several small autonomous provinces, known as the BARBARY STATES, developed along the North African coast under a vague Turkish suzerainty. The crews of their ships engaged in military activities of a piratic nature. The infamous Barbarossa (or Khair al-Din) was a 16th-century leader of these corsairs.

As the European economy expanded, efforts were made both in the Mediterranean and in northern waters to suppress piracy. In the Baltic and North seas, the HANSEATIC LEAGUE attacked and defeated the powerful Vitalean Brethren in the 15th century. Less success was achieved in the Mediterranean, where Christian pirates entered an arena already teeming with Muslim raiders.

Privateering, which originated in the Mediterranean during the 13th century, arose in response to piracy: governments commissioned ships to make reprisal raids on enemy ships in an attempt to recoup earlier losses. These privately armed vessels, their crews operating on a "no prize, no pay" basis, were often tempted into piracy.

The 16th–17th Centuries. The Elizabethan wars led to a new outbreak of piratic violence in the 16th century. Galleons carrying treasure from America to Spain were tempting targets for seafaring raiders. Pirates and privateers—such as the Sea Dogs of England, the Sea Beggars of the Netherlands, and the Sea Wolves of France—intercepted countless Spanish vessels. By the late 16th century, tempted by the booty available, some sea rovers—including Sir John HAWKINS and Sir Francis DRAKE—attacked Spanish colonies in America. By the 17th century

Edward Teach, better known as Blackbeard, battles Lt. Robert Maynard as British seamen rush to aid their officer. Blackbeard, who terrorized the Atlantic coast of the American colonies during the early 1700s, was killed by Maynard's crew during this battle off the coast of North Carolina.

Anne Bonny (left) and Mary Read were among the most formidable crew members sailing with Jack Rackam, who preyed on merchant shipping throughout the West Indies during the early 18th century.

pirates had established Caribbean bases at Saint Christopher's, Jamaica, Tortuga, and other points. Sir Henry MORGAN, a well known English pirate of this era, sacked and pillaged along the Spanish Main, although later, as governor of Jamaica, he tried to control piracy. Women were also attracted to pirate life; Anne Bonney and Mary Read participated in many coastal raids.

Decline of Piracy. By the end of the 17th century, governments no longer closed their eyes to piratic raids by their seamen, as evidenced in 1701 by the trial and execution of Capt. William KIDD. When Red Sea pirates began to prey on the rich East Indian trade, antipirate forces in England united to bring an end to freebooting. Naval squadrons suppressed piracy and strictly monitored privateering, confining the unlawful seizure of ships to a few sectors of the maritime world, such as the Barbary States of Tripoli, Tunis, Algiers, and Morocco. These states warred with weak nations while exacting tribute from the larger European states in return for leaving their ships and crews unmolested. After the United States warred with Tripoli (1801–05) in the TRIPOLITAN WAR, however, the power of the corsairs declined rapidly.

Pirates operated along the North American coast in the 17th and 18th centuries. The bloodthirsty BLACKBEARD (Edward Teach) was captured along the Carolina coast, and other pirates were seized and executed in America. The pirate Jean LAFITTE assisted the American army at the Battle of New Orleans (1815). Piracy waned considerably in the Atlantic area after 1815, but mercantile raids continued in the East Indies and along the China coast into the 20th century. Pirate activity increased in the waters off Southeast Asia following the Vietnam War.

Piraeus [py-ree'-uhs]   Piraeus (Greek Peiraiéus), the port city of Athens, Greece, is the largest port in the eastern Mediterranean. It lies on the Saronic Gulf, 8 km (5

mi) southwest of Athens. Piraeus has a population of 196,389 (1981). The city is an important fishing center, and the Greek shipping industry is concentrated there. The industries of Piraeus manufacture machinery, chemicals, cigarettes, textiles, and paper.

Themistocles was responsible for selecting Piraeus as the port of Athens in the early 5th century BC. After the completion of the harbor, the fortifications connecting the port with Athens—the Long Walls—were erected. After its destruction by Rome in 86 BC, Piraeus was a small fishing village for many centuries. Modern development began in 1833, when Athens became the capital of Greece.

Pirandello, Luigi [pee-rahn-del'-loh]   One of the 20th century's leading playwrights, the Italian Luigi Pirandello, b. June 28, 1867, d. Dec. 10, 1936, though also an accomplished novelist and short-story writer, is still known primarily for his teasing existentialist dramas in which he probed the nature of illusion and reality.

In 1921 the success of Six Characters in Search of an Author brought Pirandello international fame, and in 1925, with aid from Mussolini, he founded the Teatro d'Arte di Roma, whose ensemble he also directed on several tours abroad. After the venture failed in 1928, Pirandello lived for long periods abroad, notably in Paris and Berlin. In 1929 he was elected to the newly founded Accademia d'Italia, and in 1934 he was awarded the Nobel Prize for literature.

Analytical in nature and for the most part lacking in action, Pirandello's plays examine illusion and reality and the problems of personal identity and communication. Because he conceived of his writing as a process of unmasking, he published his collected plays under the title Maschere nude (Naked Masks, 1918–20; 1933–38). As his investigations also extended to the art form of theater itself, the story in his plays is often of only circumstantial

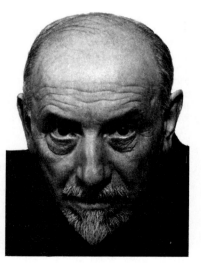

Luigi Pirandello, one of the foremost dramatists of the 20th century, was the recipient of the 1934 Nobel Prize for literature. Pirandello's work, including poetry, novels, and plays, of which Six Characters in Search of an Author (1921) is perhaps best known, explores the conflicts between appearance and reality and the fluctuating perceptions of identity.

importance. This is particularly evident in his analytical theater-within-the-theater trilogy *Six Characters in Search of an Author* (1921; Eng. trans., 1922), *Each in His Own Way* (1924; Eng. trans., 1923), and *Tonight We Improvise* (1930; Eng. trans., 1932), which he regarded as his best work. Most of Pirandello's later drama is concerned with implications of the concept of the mask, as in *Henry IV* (1922; Eng. trans., 1922) and *Naked* (1922; Eng. trans., 1930); displays his relativist convictions, as in *Right You Are If You Think You Are* (1917; Eng. trans., 1922); or centers on the life-versus-form concept so dear to him in his later years, as in *Diana and Tuda* (1927; Eng. trans., 1950), *As You Desire Me* (1930; Eng. trans., 1931), *To Find Oneself,* (1932; Eng. trans., 1943), and *When Someone Is Somebody* (1933; Eng. trans., 1958). To this period also belongs his trilogy of "modern myths"—*The New Colony* (1928; Eng. trans., 1958), *Lazarus* (1929; Eng. trans., 1952), and the unfinished *The Mountain Giants* (1938; Eng. trans., 1958).

Piranesi, Giovanni Battista [pee-rahn-ay'-zee]   The Venetian Giovanni Battista Piranesi, b. Oct. 4, 1720, d. Nov. 9, 1778, was a major Italian printmaker, architect, and antiquarian. The son of a master builder, he studied architecture and stage design, through which he became familiar with ILLUSIONISM. During a visit (1740) to Rome, which was then emerging as the center of European neoclassicism, Piranesi began his lifelong obsession with the visual diversity of the city's architecture. He began to etch views of Roman architecture that reflected his deeply felt emotional response to the surviving remnants of ancient grandeur.

Piranesi's etchings, executed in prodigious numbers from the 1740s onward, are technically masterful evocations of ancient buildings that are simultaneously schol-

Prison (1750), by the Italian artist Giovanni Piranesi, is one of a series of etchings of architectural fantasies inspired by the artist's interest in classical architecture. (Bibliothèque Nationale, Paris.)

arly inquiries and fanciful essays in space, light, and scale. When collected and published (1756) in *Antichità Romane* (Roman Antiquities) the 135 etchings created a sensation throughout Europe. Equally stimulating are the superb architectural fantasies depicted in his *Carceri d'Invenzione* (Imaginary Prisons, begun *c.*1745, reworked 1761).

piranha [puh-rah'-nuh]   The powerful jaws and sharp teeth of the piranha (family Characidae), combined with its usual attacks in overwhelming schools, make it a dangerous and feared fish. The more than a dozen species, of which at least four are dangerous, live in the waters of northern South America, particularly the Amazon Basin. The largest species, *Serrasalmus piraya,* reaches a length of 60 cm (24 in). The piranha's normal diet consists of small fish; schools are attracted by splashing or other commotion, however, and often attack and kill large animals. Aquarium species, fed regularly and not in schools, do not display the same aggressive tendencies. Piranhas make an excellent food fish.

The piranha is one of the most feared of predatory fish. A school of red piranhas can tear a victim to pieces in seconds.

Pisa [pee'-zah]   Pisa is a city in the Tuscany region of north central Italy, on the Arno River 10 km (6 mi) inland from the Ligurian Sea; it has a population of 104,364 (1987 est.). An important rail junction, Pisa has light industries producing glass, textiles, pharmaceuticals, and ceramics. The city is famous for its landmarks and art treasures—above all, the Leaning Tower. The 8-story, 54.5-m (163-ft) cathedral bell tower, built 1174–1350, deviates 5 m (16.5 ft) from the perpendicular and moves an average of 1.1 mm (0.043 in) per year; Galileo is said to have conducted experiments on gravity from there. (The tower was temporarily closed for repairs in 1990.) Other noted landmarks include the Pisan-Romanesque cathedral (1063–1118), the baptistery (1152–1278), and the medieval Camposanto Cemetery. The National

Museum of San Matteo has an outstanding collection of 12th-to-15th-century Tuscan sculpture and paintings. The University of Pisa (1343) is one of Europe's finest.

An important naval city under the Romans, Pisa was one of the major maritime republics of medieval Italy. Its age of glory—marked by economic and military dominance of the Ligurian Sea—was in the 11th to 13th centuries. Pisa's defeat by Genoa at the Battle of Meloria (1284) began its decline. It fell to Florence in 1406, became part of the grand duchy of Tuscany, and joined unified Italy in 1860.

Pisa, Council of

The Council of Pisa, a general assembly of the Roman Catholic church, was called (1409) by a group of church leaders from both the Avignon and Roman factions in an attempt to terminate the Great SCHISM that had divided Latin Christendom since 1378. When neither papal claimant, Gregory XII nor BENEDICT XIII, recognized the council, the churchmen present enunciated the theory that councils are superior to the pope (see CONCILIARISM). They thereupon deposed both popes as heretical and schismatic and elected another, Alexander V. Far from ending the schism, this move complicated it by adding a third claimant. Nonetheless, the conciliar theory elaborated at Pisa proved efficacious in finally ending the Great Schism at the Council of Constance (1415).

Pisanello, Antonio

[pee-zah-nel'-loh]   Antonio Pisanello, b. Antonio Pisano, c.1395–c.1455, was one of the most renowned painters and medalists of the early Renaissance period in northern Italy. He worked extensively for the courts of powerful ruling families such as the Gonzaga of Mantua, the Visconti of Milan, and the Este of Ferrara, as well as for Pope Eugenius IV.

Of the group of frescoes that he executed, only three major pictorial schemes have survived, along with a large number of drawings—well represented in the Vallardi Codex (Louvre, Paris)—and an important body of portrait medals. Pisanello's painting style, as represented in his elegantly decorative *Saint George and the Princess* (c.1437–38; Sant' Anastasia, Verona, Italy), clearly recalls the International Style in Gothic art of Gentile da Fabriano, his mentor, in its emphasis on visual splendor and detailed observation. In his drawings, Pisanello explored the effects of three-dimensional space and foreshortening, which paralleled the preoccupations of contemporary Florentine artists.

Pisano, Andrea

[pee-zah'-noh]   Andrea Pisano, c.1290–1348 or 1349, whose real name was Andrea da Pontedera, was an Italian Gothic sculptor best known for the pair of bronze doors (1330–36) that he created for the south portal of the Baptistery in Florence. After 1337, Pisano sculpted some of the marble reliefs surrounding the bell tower of the Florence Cathedral. The bulky rendition of his figures reflects the influence of painter and

sculptor Giotto, whom he succeeded on this project. From 1347 until his death Pisano was in charge of the construction and decoration of Orvieto Cathedral.

Pisano, Nicola and Giovanni

Nicola Pisano and his son Giovanni were the principal Gothic sculptors in Italy. The first known work of **Nicola Pisano**, c.1220–1284, is a hexagonal pulpit for the baptistery at Pisa (completed 1259); its reliefs and single figures reveal the influence of classical sculpture. He was one of the first sculptors before the Renaissance to turn to antique sources. A classical spirit also invests his pulpit for the cathedral at Siena (1265–68), on which Giovanni also worked. The Siena pulpit reflects the intrusion of softer and more flowing forms that can be attributed to the influence of French Gothic art. Father and son also collaborated on a fountain (completed 1278) for the main square in Perugia that again reveals both classical and Gothic influences.

Giovanni Pisano, b. c.1250, d. after 1314, was solely

Nicola Pisano's marble pulpit in the baptistery of Pisa Cathedral (1259) is one of the finest achievements of Gothic sculpture in Italy.

responsible for two other pulpits, one for the church of Sant' Andrea at Pistoia (completed 1301) and the other for the cathedral at Pisa (completed 1310). The relief panels of the Pistoia pulpit are crowded with moving figures executed in a sinuous and lyrical style derived from French Gothic sculpture. The Pisa pulpit, in contrast, reflects a subtle balance between the classical and Gothic styles. Among Giovanni's finest works are the sculptures that he carved (c.1284–96) for the facade of the Siena Cathedral, on which he also worked as supervising architect. The figures have a vigor and movement that achieve an entirely different effect from that of northern European art.

Piscator, Erwin [pis-kah'-tohr] An innovative German director and producer, Erwin Piscator, b. Dec. 17, 1893, d. Mar. 30, 1966, was a leading force in the Berlin "political theater" of the 1920s. Together with Bertolt Brecht he developed the concept of an EPIC THEATER, based on the use of films, slide projections, and new staging techniques. He presided over the League of Workers' Theaters (1931–36) in the Soviet Union and the Dramatic Workshop (1939–51) at the New School in New York City. In 1962, Piscator became artistic director of the Frei Volksbühne (Free People's Theater) in West Berlin, where he collaborated in the production of the new documentary drama.

Pisces [py'-seez] The constellation of "the fishes," Pisces is a group of faint stars representing two fish linked by a V-shaped chain. The group fits around the southwest corner of the constellation Pegasus. Although Pisces is regarded as the twelfth constellation of the zodiac, precession has brought the vernal equinox from Aries into Pisces, so that technically it is the first constellation. The Sun enters the sign of Pisces on February 19 and enters the constellation itself on March 11.

Pissarro, Camille [pee-sah-roh'] The French painter Camille Pissarro, b. July 10, 1830, d. Nov. 13, 1903, was one of the founders of IMPRESSIONISM. He exhibited at the Salon des Refusés (1863), and his link with such impressionists as Claude Monet and Auguste Renoir grew closer in the 1860s.

After encountering the work of the English painters J. M. W. Turner and John Constable while in London (1870–71), Pissarro lightened his palette and formulated a technique of applying strokes of bright color to the canvas to create luminous effects. These experiments did not meet with public or official approval, and Pissarro helped organize the first independent impressionist show of 1874. Pissarro never completely abandoned an underlying sense of solid form and contour. In such works as *Peasant Woman with a Wheelbarrow* (1874; Nationalmuseum, Stockholm), freely applied touches of broken color and the play of light transform ordinary settings with an

Camille Pissarro's Red Roofs *(1877) reflects the clear structure and delicate brushwork typical of his work, which was mainly landscape painting. (Musée d'Orsay, Paris.)*

atmosphere that softens and brightens forms without dissolving them.

Pissarro had great influence on the impressionists and their followers, including the neoimpressionist Georges Seurat, whose pointillist technique the older painter emulated after 1886. In his later years Pissarro returned to an impressionistic rendering of rural life, harbor views, and urban scenes, as in *Boulevard Montmartre in Paris* (1897; Hermitage Museum, Leningrad).

pistachio [pis-tash'-ee-oh] The edible nut pistachio is the seed of the tree *Pistachia vera*, of the family Anacar-

The pistachio tree is a warm-climate tree with simple leaves on spreading branches. Its valuable nuts grow in clusters.

diaceae. Native to central Asia, the pistachio is grown to-day mainly in Mediterranean and Middle Eastern countries, and the nut has become an important product in California.

Although pistachios grow best in deep, well-drained soils with a high lime content, they are also cultivated on shallow, rocky sites. Long, hot, dry summers are necessary to ripen the nuts and to prevent serious foliage diseases. The greenish seed is eaten roasted and salted and is used in many dishes that originate in the Middle East. The nuts are sold both in their natural color, a light beige, and dyed a bright red.

This brass-barreled English flintlock pistol (c.1780) was used for dueling. Its relatively long barrel provided accuracy while the butt fitted the hand comfortably, with enough curve to level the barrel at the target with the ease of pointing a finger.

Pistoia [pee-stoh'-yah]   Pistoia is a city on the Ombrone River in north central Italy, south of the Apennine Mountains and about 32 km (20 mi) northwest of Florence. The population is 83,600 (1981). Pistoia is a railroad junction and agricultural trade center and produces shoes, glass, lace, leather goods, and railroad machinery. Medieval landmarks include the Pisan-style cathedral (12th–13th century), the baptistery (1337–59), the Church of San Giovanni Fuorcivitas (12th–14th century), and the Pisan-Romanesque Church of Sant' Andrea (12th century). A free commune after 1085, Pistoia reached its economic and cultural zenith as an important banking center in the 13th century. It was subjugated by Florence in the early 14th century and became part of the duchy of Tuscany in 1530.

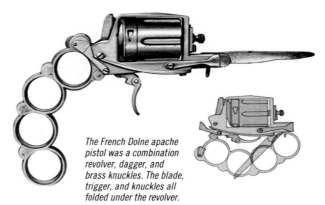

The French Dolne apache pistol was a combination revolver, dagger, and brass knuckles. The blade, trigger, and knuckles all folded under the revolver.

pistol   A pistol is a small, portable firearm that is held, aimed, and fired with one hand and has a short barrel and a breech lock-and-load firing mechanism. Designed for short-range use, it is inaccurate at long range except in the hands of an expert or when fired at a stationary target. The origin of the word *pistol* is not known for certain, although some historians believe that it may have been derived from Pistoia, an Italian city and province in Tuscany once famous for its ironworks and an area where primitive handguns were fabricated during the early years of the 14th century.

Handguns did not become practical FIREARMS until the 16th century, when wheel-lock and flintlock pistols, which could be fired with one hand, were introduced. The percussion-cap pistol was developed in the 19th century. The first practical REVOLVER was Samuel Colt's six-shooter (1836). Semiautomatic pistols were introduced in the 1890s. Utilizing late-19th-century improvements already made in the loading and firing of the RIFLE and the first truly automatic gun, the Maxim machine gun, the semiautomatic pistol is self-loaded from a magazine in the gun's handle, using the forces generated by firing and recoil gases to move bullets into the firing chamber and to cock the hammer. The machine pistol, like the machine gun, can fire in bursts, and is often equipped with a long, folding metal butt that makes it resemble a military assault weapon.

The Borchardt pistol, patented in 1893, was the first mass-produced and commercially successful automatic repeating pistol. Self-loading and carrying eight shots, it was technically semiautomatic because its trigger had to be used to fire each shot.

The Luger Model 1908, one of the most famous automatic pistols ever produced, was designed by German engineer Georg Luger. The 9-mm-weapon remained in use as the official military sidearm of the German armed forces until shortly before World War II.

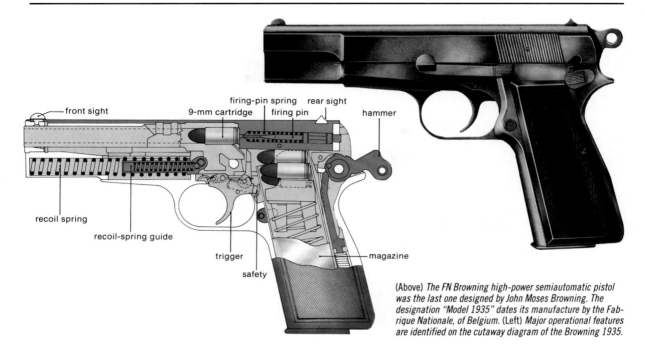

front sight

firing-pin spring   rear sight
9-mm cartridge   firing pin   hammer

recoil spring

recoil-spring guide

trigger

safety

magazine

(Above) *The FN Browning high-power semiautomatic pistol was the last one designed by John Moses Browning. The designation "Model 1935" dates its manufacture by the Fabrique Nationale, of Belgium.* (Left) *Major operational features are identified on the cutaway diagram of the Browning 1935.*

Piston, Walter   Walter Piston, b. Rockland, Maine, Jan. 20, 1894, d. Nov. 12, 1976, was a highly respected American composer and teacher. After graduating from Harvard University, he, like many American composers of his generation, studied (1924–26) with Nadia Boulanger in Paris. During the years he taught (1926–59) at Harvard, he influenced many younger composers by emphasizing perfect craftsmanship, which led to his being labeled a "classicist." His textbooks on various aspects of music, particularly *Harmony* (1941; 4th ed., 1978), are among the most widely used in American colleges.

Virtually all of Piston's music is instrumental, and his eight symphonies are regarded as the core of his production. He won Pulitzer Prizes for his third and seventh symphonies (1948 and 1961). His ballet *The Incredible Flutist* (1938) has become well known because of the popular suite (1940) derived from it.

pit bull   The term *pit bull* refers to a kind of compact, muscular, smooth-coated dog with powerful jaws derived from a bulldog-and-terrier cross. Originally bred to bait bulls and bears and to engage in the now illegal but still popular sport of dogfighting, pit bulls are noted for their strength and tenacity. The American pit bull terrier (registered by the United Kennel Club), the AMERICAN STAFFORDSHIRE TERRIER, the STAFFORDSHIRE BULL TERRIER, and sometimes the BULL TERRIER (all registered by the American Kennel Club), and crosses thereof, are generally considered pit bulls. Attacks on human beings by pit bulls, and the widespread publicity these attacks received, led

numerous localities to pass ordinances banning pit bulls in the 1980s. Many of these ordinances have been struck down on constitutional grounds. The American Kennel Club and other groups advocate legislation that imposes strict restrictions on vicious dogs but does not single out any specific breed.

pit viper   Pit vipers are venomous snakes having a pair of heat-sensing pits in the front of the head, and hollow, erectile fangs used to transmit venom. These snakes characteristically have broad, lance-shaped heads and vertical pupils. Terrestrial species are typically stout-bodied and marked with patterns of brown, gray, yellow, pink, or black; tree-dwelling species are generally more slender in shape and often green in color, with markings of yellow, red, or black. The pit vipers are closely related to the true vipers and are usually classified as a subfamily, Crotalinae, of the viper family, Viperidae.

The pit organ is located between the nostril and the eye on each side of the head. It is supplied with nerves and blood vessels and is partially enclosed in a cavity in the side of the maxillary, a bone of the upper jaw. The pit has a thermoreceptor function and is sensitive to infrared radiation; it is capable of responding to changes in temperature of only fractions of a degree. Thus pit vipers can detect the presence of animals with body temperatures only slightly different from that of the environment.

In North America, pit vipers are represented by about 31 species of RATTLESNAKE (genera *Crotalus* and *Sistrurus*) and by the COPPERHEAD and WATER MOCCASIN, or cottonmouth (*Agkistrodon*). The greatest diversity of pit vi-

Like all pit vipers, the eastern diamondback rattlesnake has a deep sensory pit between its nostril and eye, which detects warm-blooded animals up to 50 cm (20 in) away.

pers occurs in Central and South America, with 2 or 3 species of rattlesnakes, about 60 species of lance-heads, such as the FER-DE-LANCE (*Bothrops*), and the BUSHMASTER (*Lachesis*). In the Old World, pit vipers occur from the north Caspian region of Europe, across Asia to Japan and the Malaysian Archipelago.

Pitcairn Island [pit'-kairn]   Pitcairn is a mountainous, volcanic island in the South Pacific Ocean, about 2,170 km (1,350 mi) southeast of Tahiti. Since 1970 it has been administered—along with the neighboring islands of Ducie, Henderson, and Oeno—by the British high commissioner in New Zealand. Adamstown on the north coast is the administrative center and principal settlement. The wooded island has an area of 5 km² (2 mi²) and a population of 65 (1985). It rises to 335 m (1,100 ft), and sheer cliffs along all its coast make it almost inaccessible except by local longboats. The natives, almost all descendants of mutineers from the BOUNTY, support themselves by fishing, farming, and the sale of postage stamps.

Once probably inhabited by Polynesians, the island was discovered by Robert Pitcairn, sailing with Philip Carteret in 1767. In 1790 it was chosen by Fletcher Chris-

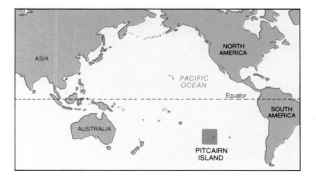

tian and 8 other mutineers from the Bounty as their refuge. Along with 6 men and 12 women from Tahiti, they remained isolated; by 1800 only one male was alive. U.S. whalers made contact with the islanders in 1808. In 1831 and in 1856 the British forced inhabitants off the island due to overpopulation; most eventually returned. Pitcairn was made a British colony in 1838.

pitch   In music, pitch is the property of tones according to which they sound high or low in relation to each other. Pitch is determined by the number of times a sound-producing medium vibrates per second; the result is recognized by the ear as the position of that sound in the audible high-low range. An international standard adopted in 1939 places *a'* (*A* above middle *C*) at 440 double vibrations per second. This placement is generally accepted by instrument makers, although some exceptions continue to be made. In the past a variety of pitch levels existed. The baroque era had different standard pitches for secular vocal music, church music, and chamber music. Instrumental pitch in the 18th and early 19th centuries was a half-step lower than at present. Therefore we now often hear the symphonies of Haydn, Mozart, and others at a different pitch from that originally intended.

pitchblende   see RADIUM; URANIUM

Pitcher, Molly   see MOLLY PITCHER

Pitman, Sir Isaac   see SHORTHAND

Pitt, William (the Elder)   William Pitt the Elder, 1st earl of Chatham, b. Nov. 15, 1708, d. May 11, 1778, is perhaps the most eulogized of all British prime ministers. He led the nation during the SEVEN YEARS' WAR (1756–63), which culminated in the capture of Quebec in 1759.

Elected to Parliament in 1735, Pitt bitterly opposed Sir Robert WALPOLE and then participated in Henry PELHAM's administration. In December 1756 he became secretary of state in the administration of William Cavendish, 4th duke of Devonshire, but opposition from King GEORGE II resulted in Pitt's dismissal in April 1757. Public pressure led to Pitt's reinstatement that June, and he formed a ministry with Thomas Pelham-Holles, 1st duke of NEWCASTLE. Three years of unchallenged primacy came to an end with the accession of George III in 1760, and Pitt resigned (1761) after a dispute with the new king's favorite, John Stuart, 3d earl of Bute.

The popular Pitt—dubbed the Great Commoner—incurred public wrath by his acceptance of a pension (1761) and a peerage (1766). A proud, theatrical man, he returned to office at the king's behest in 1766, but his triumph was ruined by a complete, though temporary, mental collapse.

Pitt resigned his office in 1768 and spent his remaining years in opposition to the crown, urging in particular a peaceful settlement with the American colonies. Pitt's

William Pitt the Elder, British prime minister, directed the nation's military efforts during the Seven Years' War, which established Britain's empire in Canada and India. He supported the American colonies and worked to prevent the outbreak of revolution.

As prime minister, Pitt passed through two distinct and superficially contradictory phases. In the 1780s he became known as a liberal reformer whose financial and commercial measures revived the economy and restored British prestige in Europe after the disaster of the American Revolution. Throughout the next decade, however, in the wake of the French Revolution, his name was a byword for repressive and reactionary policies, including the persecution of reforming groups. During the Anglo-French wars, which began in 1793, Pitt displayed considerable skill in marshaling the nation's resources, but he possessed little capacity for strategic military planning. Distracted from the war effort by the Irish rebellion of 1798, Pitt pressed for the union of the Irish and British parliaments (achieved by the Act of Union, 1800) and for CATHOLIC EMANCIPATION. When the king refused to grant Catholic Emancipation, Pitt resigned (1801), but he returned to office in 1804. He died 20 months later, after receiving word of Napoleon's defeat of Britain's allies at Austerlitz.

record as wartime minister testifies to his grasp of strategy as well as his political courage and immense popular appeal.

Pitt, William (the Younger)   William Pitt the Younger, b. May 28, 1759, d. Jan. 23, 1806, was one of Britain's most accomplished and enigmatic prime ministers. The second son of William Pitt, 1st earl of Chatham, he was educated privately and at Cambridge. His precocious ability in debate and his political inheritance from his father made him an influential figure in British politics during the early 1780s, leading GEORGE III to name him prime minister in December 1783, when Pitt was only 24. In the House of Commons, Pitt proved himself equal to such prominent opponents as Edmund BURKE; Frederick, Lord NORTH; and Charles James Fox. He garnered the support of both the crown and the electorate, winning a parliamentary majority in the election of 1784.

William Pitt the Younger inherited his father's great powers of statesmanship and oratory. As prime minister, he steered Great Britain through the crises brought on by the French Revolution, the Irish rebellion, and the Napoleonic Wars.

Pittsburgh   Pittsburgh, the second largest city in Pennsylvania and the seat of Allegheny County, is located in the western part of the state where the Monongahela and Allegheny rivers flow together to form the Ohio River. Pittsburgh has a population of 369,879 (1990); that of its metropolitan area is 2,056,705. The city covers 145 km² (56 mi²).

Contemporary City. Pittsburgh, built over a rich bituminous coal seam, was long one of the great U.S. industrial centers, particularly identified with steel. By the end of the 1980s, however, the last of the city's outmoded steel plants had closed. Pittsburgh's economic growth is now fueled by the service, education, and technology sectors. The city is also a transportation hub.

Pittsburgh's leading educational institutions are CARNEGIE-MELLON UNIVERSITY, the University of Pittsburgh (1787), and Duquesne University (1878). The Pittsburgh Symphony Orchestra, which performs in Heinz Hall, is one of the country's major orchestras. The Benedum Center (1987) is home to the city's opera company and ballet troupe. The Pittsburgh Public Theater presents plays. The Carnegie Institute incorporates both art and natural history museums. The city supports professional baseball, football, and ice hockey teams.

History. A fur-trading post was established at the site of modern Pittsburgh in the 17th century, and in 1749 the Virginia-based Ohio Company attempted to establish Fort Prince George there. The settlers were driven out in 1754 by the French, who built Fort Duquesne. The English captured it in 1758 and renamed it Fort Pitt in honor of the British statesman William Pitt (the Elder). Fort Pitt (later Pittsburgh) thrived, and the city of Pittsburgh was incorporated in 1816. By 1850 the city was the leading maker of American glassware. Pittsburgh's first blast furnace was opened in 1859, and within a decade the city was the iron and steel center of the nation.

Pittsburgh continued to prosper through the late 19th

century, when such industrialists as Andrew Carnegie, Henry Clay Frick, Andrew W. Mellon, and George Westinghouse made their fortunes there. The area was the scene of some of the bloodiest labor wars in U.S. history, including the Homestead Strike of 1892.

Because of its concentration of heavy industry, Pittsburgh gained the reputation of being one of the dirtiest and smokiest cities in the country. In the late 1940s, however, a massive urban-redevelopment project began, which included strict air-purification standards. In 1957, Pittsburgh became the first U.S. city to use atomic energy for generating electricity. The heart of the city, the Golden Triangle, at the confluence of the Allegheny and Monongahela, has been completely rebuilt.

Pittsfield   Pittsfield (1990 pop., 48,622), seat of Berkshire County in west central Massachusetts, is a city on the upper Housatonic River in the BERKSHIRE HILLS about 11 km (7 mi) east of New York State. An industrial center producing primarily electrical and electronic equipment, Pittsfield is also a resort community. The TANGLEWOOD FESTIVAL, in nearby Lenox, is a major summer attraction. The town, named for William Pitt, was settled in 1752 and incorporated in 1761.

pituitary gland [pi-too'-i-tair-ee]   The gland of the ENDOCRINE SYSTEM known as the pituitary, or hypophysis, is situated at the base of the brain and is connected to the hypothalamus by a stalk. It has three lobes.

The anterior lobe secretes six protein hormones (see HORMONE, ANIMAL): growth hormone, which promotes body growth; prolactin, which stimulates the production of milk; adrenocorticotropic hormone (ACTH), which stimulates the adrenal cortex; thyroid-stimulating hormone, or thyrotropin (TSH); and two gonadotropic hormones, follicle-stimulating hormone (FSH) and luteinizing hormone (LH). The latter two control the maturation and function of the ovaries and testes. The lobe is connected by blood vessels to the hypothalamus, which secretes hormones that regulate the release of these six hormones.

The intermediate lobe secretes melanocyte-stimulating hormone (MSH), which temporarily darkens the skin of cold-blooded animals for camouflage and for aggressive and mating behaviors. It has little, if any, significance in humans.

The posterior lobe has direct nerve connections with the brain. It stores and releases two peptide hormones produced by the hypothalamus: oxytocin, which stimulates uterine contractions during childbirth and initiates the milk letdown response in nursing mothers; and vasopressin, an antidiuretic hormone (ADH) that acts on the kidneys to prevent excess loss of body water. An insufficiency of ADH results in DIABETES insipidus.

Removal or destruction of the pituitary or, conversely, excessive secretion of the pituitary abnormally alters the function of the adrenals, the thyroid, and the gonads.

See also: ENDOCRINE SYSTEM, DISEASES OF THE.

Pius II, Pope [py'-uhs]   Pius II, b. Oct. 18, 1405, d. Aug. 15, 1464, was pope from Aug. 19, 1458, until his death. Named Enea Silvio de'Piccolomini, he distinguished himself as a diplomat and humanist scholar early in his career. At the Council of Basel (1432; see BASEL, COUNCIL OF), which he attended as a layman, he was a leading spokesman for CONCILIARISM. By the time he became a priest (1446), however, he had renounced this position. His reputation rests instead on his literary achievement—his celebrated *Tale of Two Lovers*, his valuable history of the Council of Basel, and above all, his *Commentaries*, which contain both an autobiography and a history of his pontificate.

Pius IV, Pope   Pius IV, b. Mar. 31, 1499, d. Dec. 9, 1565, was pope from 1559 until his death. His name was Giovanni Angelo de'Medici, but he was not related to the Medicis of Florence. He reconvened and presided (1562–63) over the conclusion of the Council of TRENT, whose decrees he confirmed in the bull *Benedictus Deus* (1564). Later in 1564 he published the Tridentine Profession of Faith, a summary of doctrine, and imposed it on the bishops. Under the guidance of his nephew Charles BORROMEO, Pius restored good relations between the papacy and the Habsburg dynasty.

Pius V, Pope   Saint Pius V, b. Jan. 17, 1504, d. May 1, 1572, was pope from 1566 until his death. He was named Antonio or Michele Ghislieri. Pius was made a cardinal in 1557. His subsequent role as a member of the Roman INQUISITION and his continued support of its activities, even while pope, indicate the often intransigent mentality of this saint of the COUNTER-REFORMATION.

During his pontificate Pius saw to the publication of revised liturgical texts, of the catechism decreed at the Council of TRENT, and of an edition of the complete works of Thomas Aquinas. An unsuccessful diplomat, he blundered dramatically in his excommunication of Elizabeth I of England in 1570. He was, however, instrumental in organizing the league of Christian princes, whose fleet defeated the Turks at Lepanto in 1571. He was canonized in 1712. Feast day: Apr. 30 (formerly May 5).

Pius VI, Pope   Pius VI, b. Dec. 25, 1717, d. Aug. 29, 1799, was pope from 1775 until his death. His name was Giovanni Angelico Braschi. Pius failed to dissuade Holy Roman Emperor JOSEPH II from his attempt to assert government control over the church, as part of the policy called Febronianism. Febronianist policies were also adopted in Italy, and in 1794, Pius condemned them in the bull *Auctorem Fidei*. His opposition to the French Revolution was also ineffective. In 1791 he condemned the Civil Constitution of the Clergy, which subordinated the French clergy to the state. In 1796 a French army occupied the Papal States, and in 1798, Rome was occupied and declared a republic. Pius was taken as a prisoner to Valence, France, where he died.

Pius VII, Pope

Pius VII, b. Aug. 14, 1742, d. Aug. 20, 1823, was pope from 1800 until his death. Named Barnabo Chiaramonti, he was born at Casena and became a Benedictine monk, professor, and abbot. Pius VI made him bishop of Tivoli (1782) and then bishop of Imola and a cardinal (1785). Pius VI died while being held prisoner by the French in 1799, and in March 1800, Chiaramonti was elected pope under Austrian protection in Venice.

Pius depended heavily on Enrico Consalvi, whom he created cardinal and secretary of state. Consalvi negotiated the CONCORDAT of 1801, which settled the status of the church in France. Pius VII was flexible enough to travel to Paris and assist at NAPOLEON I's self-coronation (1804), but he would not become a French ally. Napoleon forced Consalvi's temporary resignation (1806) and invaded papal territory, taking Rome in 1808 and formally annexing the Papal States in 1809. Pius excommunicated Napoleon, who imprisoned the pope for five years. Pius returned to Rome in 1814, while the allies defeated Napoleon. In 1814, Pius reestablished the Jesuit order, which had been suppressed in 1773.

Pius IX, Pope

Pius IX, b. Giovanni Maria Mastai-Ferreti, May 13, 1792, d. Feb. 7, 1878, had the longest pontificate (1846–78) in Catholic history. During the Revolutions of 1848 a mob forced him to flee Rome. He returned 17 months later after a French army occupied the city. The politically naive pope steadfastly refused to yield his temporal authority, but Sardinia-Piedmont nonetheless seized the Papal States in the period 1859–60, and the renamed Kingdom of Italy took Rome for its capital in 1870. Pius thereafter became the "prisoner of the Vatican," refusing to accept the Italian government's Law of Guarantees (1871), which offered an indemnity in return for the pope's disavowal of temporal authority.

Pius proclaimed the dogma of the IMMACULATE CONCEPTION of Mary on Dec. 8, 1854. His encyclical Quanta cura (1864) and its attached Syllabus of Errors condemned many modern ideas that the pope associated with secularization and anticlericalism. He summoned the First VATICAN COUNCIL (1869–70), which endorsed papal infallibility. Pius's reactionary reign consolidated ultramontane (see ULTRAMONTANISM) authority and bureaucratized it in the Curia.

Pius X, Pope

Pius X, b. Giuseppe Melchiorre Sarto, June 2, 1835, d. Aug. 20, 1914, was pope from 1903 to 1914. He was canonized in 1954.

At the conclave of 1903, Sarto reluctantly accepted election to succeed Pope Leo XIII. As pope he continued his pastoral interest in the poor, in promoting the Gregorian chant and Thomistic theology, and in the religious instruction of children, adults, and seminarians. The Vatican's rigid position in the face of French plans to abolish the Napoleonic Concordat compounded the trauma for the church when the French government separated church and state, sequestering church property in 1905. More pastor than intellectual or statesman, Pius disapproved of the "heresy" of MODERNISM, a movement that attempted to harmonize Catholic belief with critical biblical exegesis. He combated the movement with excommunications, a seminary purge, listings on the Index, a syllabus of modernist errors (Lamentabili sane exitu), and the encyclical Pascendi dominici gregis. Ironically, the Biblical Institute established at Rome under Pius X has now resumed this method of inquiry. Pius initiated a codification of canon law, completed in 1917, and encouraged frequent reception of communion. Feast day: Aug. 21.

Pius XI, Pope

Pius XI, b. Archille Ratti, May 31, 1857, d. Feb. 10, 1939, was pope from 1922 until his death.

The deadlocked conclave of 1922 chose Ratti as pope on the eve of Benito Mussolini's March on Rome. Facing a choice between the right and the left, the Vatican decided that fascism seemed the lesser of two evils. The Lateran Treaty of 1929, negotiated by Cardinal Gasparri, resolved the Roman Question with a financial settlement and restored papal sovereignty over Vatican City. This modus vivendi asserted the Catholic character of the Italian state and allowed a nonpolitical role for Catholic Action, a lay movement founded by Pius in 1923. Violation of the treaty terms by Mussolini provoked an encyclical, Non abbiamo bisogno (1931), which denounced the claims of the totalitarian state. In 1933 the papacy negotiated a concordat with Nazi Germany; later, however, Pius condemned the Third Reich's "aggressive neopaganism" in the encyclical Mit brennender Sorge (1937). The encyclical Divini redemptoris (1937) condemned communism.

Forty years after Leo XIII's encyclical on the social question, Pius XI issued Quadragesimo anno (1931), which elaborated the church's position on social and eco-

Pope Pius XI's humanism distinguished his 17-year reign (1922–39) between world wars. In his many encyclicals he denounced racism and totalitarianism and urged social reform. In 1929 he signed the Lateran Treaty with the government of Benito Mussolini, pledging papal neutrality in military conflicts.

nomic reform; it called for justice and charity in all endeavors and stressed Christian social action. As pastor, Pius XI appointed native bishops to many of the Asian hierarchies and founded colleges at Rome for the Eastern Rites.

Pius XII, Pope

Pius XII, b. Mar. 2, 1876, d. Oct. 9, 1958, was named Eugenio Maria Giuseppe Giovanni Pacelli. He helped Cardinal Gasparri codify canon law, aided prisoners of war during World War I, and represented the Holy See in Germany from 1917 to 1929. He became a cardinal (1929) and PIUS XI's secretary of state (1930). On Mar. 2, 1939, he was elected to succeed Pius XI as pope.

The last absolute monarch of the Holy See, Pius considered the Curia "not collaborators but executors." He held the Catholic line against divorce, contraception, and abortion. The encyclical *Mystici corporis* (1943) characterized the universal church with a tolerant reference to non-Catholics. In the encyclical *Divinio afflante spiritu* (also 1943), Pius opened the way to critical biblical studies. He considered calling an ecumenical council but feared a too-rapid pace of change.

In 1950, Pius issued an *ex cathedra* proclamation defining the dogma of the ASSUMPTION OF MARY. The encyclical *Humani generis*, of the same year, reasserted Catholic tradition and rejected modern theories such as existentialism. Condemnation of the French worker-priest experiment (1953) and the canonization of Pius X (1954) reflected a similar conservatism. At the same time, however, Pius gave the College of Cardinals a non-Italian majority, including several East Europeans. He replaced colonial bishops with native hierarchies, approved the "Dialogue Mass," and relaxed communion fast rules. Naturally ascetic, Pius became an isolated figure before his death.

Pizarro, Francisco

[pee-thahr'-oh] Francisco Pizarro, b. *c.*1475, d. June 26, 1541, was the Spanish conquistador who secured Peru for Spain. Shortly after the discovery of the New World, Pizarro went to Hispaniola with Hernán CORTÉS, a relative. In 1510, Pizarro participated in an expedition to the Gulf of Urabá in north Colombia, and he was second in command when Vasco Núñez de Balboa discovered the Pacific Ocean in 1513. Nine years later Pizarro formed a partnership with Diego de ALMAGRO and cleric Hernán de Luque to explore lands to the south. Their first expedition reached the San Juan River in Colombia; the second expedition (1526–28) reached the Santa River in Peru and returned to Panama with gold, cloth, and llamas.

When the governor of Panama refused permission for further exploration, Pizarro went (1528) to Spain to appeal directly to the king. The agreement reached gave the king of Spain all of Peru, its subjects, and its wealth. Pizarro was made (1529) a knight of Santiago and governor and captain general of the conquered lands. After returning to Panama, Pizarro and several of his brothers set sail (June 1530) with 180 men, 30 of whom were cavalry. The explorers sacked Tumbes, Peru, and then met ATAHUALPA, the INCA ruler, at Cajamarca on Nov. 15, 1532. Seizing Atahualpa, Pizarro demanded a huge ransom in gold and silver in exchange for Atahualpa's life. Once the ransom was paid, however, Atahualpa was promptly strangled (Aug. 29, 1533). After an unsuccessful last-ditch effort by Manco Capac, the son of Atahualpa, to recover CUZCO, the Inca capital, in 1536–37, a dispute broke out between Pizarro and Almagro, and the latter was executed. For the remainder of his life, Pizarro, now the marquis of Atavillas, organized his conquest, distributing lands and Indians to his followers and establishing new settlements. Lima was founded (1535) as the new capital of Peru. Pizarro was assassinated by followers of Almagro.

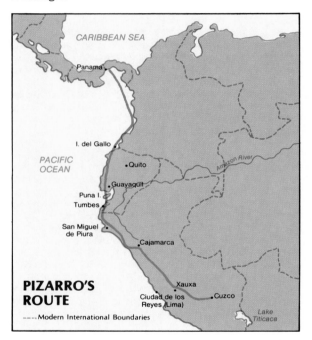

Pizarro's third expedition, which brought about the conquest of Peru, set out for the Peruvian coast from Panama in 1530. The fall of Cajamarca (1533) signaled the end of Inca rule, and Spanish forces quickly moved inland to claim the Inca capital of Cuzco (1534).

placebo

[pluh-see'-boh] A placebo is an inert substance made to appear indistinguishable from an authentic drug. An inactive component such as sugar is substituted for the active drug. The most common use of a placebo is in the testing of new drugs to provide an evaluation by comparison. Also, a placebo may be prescribed when there is no apparent organic basis for an illness. The "placebo effect" is attributed to psychological factors. In conditions involving the central nervous system, such as pain or anxiety, placebo effects often mimic the effects of an active drug.

placer deposit [plas'-ur]   Placers are an important type of ORE DEPOSIT formed by the mechanical concentration of heavy, durable minerals, principally by water and especially by rivers. Placers also can form on beaches or by wind blowing away lighter grains.

Placer minerals are chemically inert, physically stable, and heavier than the common rock-forming minerals. Thus most placer minerals have a specific gravity greater than 3. When river discharge is greatest, during floods and storms, placer minerals are the last to be eroded and the first to be deposited. This circumstance explains why they tend to be concentrated on the surface of the bedrock.

Most of the world's tin, diamonds, and titanium minerals come from placers, as have most of its gold and platinum. Today about two-thirds of the world's gold comes from the Witwatersrand conglomerates of South Africa, which are now thought to have formed as Precambrian beach placers. (This type of conglomerate also is a major source of uranium in Canada and South Africa.) Historically, the common way of recovering placer gold was with a gold pan. Prospectors would pan upstream until they found the bedrock source, or mother lode, of the gold. The bedrock source of placer minerals may or may not be economic to mine and commonly has a lower assay than individual placer deposits. Today the usual way to mine large placer deposits is with dredges.

Placid, Lake [plas'-id]   Lake Placid, approximately 6–8 km (4–5 mi) long and 2 km (1.5 mi) wide at its greatest extent, is located in the Adirondack Mountains of northeastern New York. Its altitude is 567 m (1,860 ft) above sea level. The lake was formed by glaciers during the Ice Age. The center of a winter sports resort of the same name, Lake Placid was the site of the 1932 and 1980 Winter Olympic Games. Abolitionist John Brown is buried near the village of Lake Placid.

plague   see BUBONIC PLAGUE

plaice [plays]   Plaices are flatfish that belong, with other right-eyed FLOUNDERS, to the family Pleuronectidae. The two species of North American pleuronectids are the American plaice, *Hippoglossoides platessoides*, an Atlantic species; and the Alaskan plaice, *Pleuronectes quadrituberculatus*, a Pacific species. The European plaice, *P. platessa*, is one of the more important food fishes in the northeastern Atlantic. It matures at 17.5–37.5 cm (7–15 in) in length and may grow to a length of 90 cm (3 ft).

plainsong   Plainsong is the name given to the monodic (single melodic line) vocal liturgical music of the Christian Catholic churches. It is unaccompanied and is usually in rhythm that is free, not divided into a regular measure. As commonly used, the terms *plainsong, plainchant*, and *Gregorian chant* are synonymous.

History

The music of early Christian worship derived from a sophisticated tradition of Jewish cantorial song. By the 4th and 5th centuries, as the church spread, different traditions of chant had arisen, the most important being Byzantine, Old Roman, Gallican, and Mozarabic. The chant of Rome had developed by the time of Pope Gregory I (Gregory the Great; 590–604), after whom the whole body of Roman chant is named.

Under the reign of a Byzantine pope, Vitalian (657–672), the liturgy and chant of Rome underwent a thorough reformation. It was this chant that Charlemagne, about 150 years later, spread throughout the Frankish Empire. Vitalian (or Carolingian) chant, although highly ornamented, was characterized by great clarity of melodic line. Melodies were written in a free rhythm using notes of long and short duration in proportion of two to one.

Largely because of the rise of POLYPHONY, by the 11th century the subtleties of Vitalian chant were lost. All notes were given the same basic duration, and thus rhythm was no longer proportional but equalist (hence the term *cantus planus* or *plainsong*), and ornamentation gradually disappeared. Beginning in the 12th century the melodic notes themselves were tampered with, and by the early 16th century the melodies had been ruthlessly truncated.

Notation

No notated examples exist of the Roman chant as it was heard during Gregory's reign. There is every reason to believe, however, that the tradition of 7th-century Vitalian chant is faithfully preserved in 9th- and 10th-century manuscripts, the earliest actual sources of chant. The musical signs therein are not written notes but rather depictions of the melodic shapes to be traced in air by the hand of the conductor, whose direction reminded the singers (schola cantorum) of the correct notes and indicated both rhythm and ornamentation. The notational shapes were called neumes.

Various attempts were made in the 11th and 12th centuries to notate melodies exactly: sometimes alphabetical letters indicating precise pitches were written above the text's syllables; in so-called diastematic notation, simplified neumes were written on from one to four pitch lines.

During the last hundred years, monks of the French Abbey of Solesmes, by comparing old sources, restored and corrected the notes of the melodies; however, they retain the equalist rhythm of the 11th and succeeding centuries, treating the neumatic rhythmic indications merely as nuances. The Dutch musicologist Jan Vollaerts (1901–56) developed a system for the proportional interpretation of neumes, thus clearing the way for a complete reconstruction of Vitalian chant.

Forms and Liturgical Use

Chant plays an integral role in the Mass and divine office. Certain parts in simple, set formulas are assigned to the ministers; ordinary parts are sung by the congregation in simple melodies; complex chants proper to the feasts of the liturgical calendar are sung by the schola of trained singers. It was the propers of Mass and office that were notated in the neumatic manuscripts. Two basic forms exist: ANTIPHON and responsory. Both have an *ABA* structure, the *B* section being an inserted solo; musically, the responsory is the more complex and ornate.

The proper parts of the Mass include: (1) the introit antiphon, or processional entrance song, which announces the feast being celebrated that day; (2) the gradual, a response to the Old Testament prophetical reading; (3) the alleluia, a response to the New Testament lesson and introduction to the reading of the Gospel; (4) the offertory, a processional piece in modified responsory form having from two to four highly ornate solo verses; and (5) the Communion antiphon. The ordinary parts of the Mass sung by the congregation include the petition *Kyrie Eleison*; the *Credo*, or statement of beliefs; the *Sanctus*; *Pater Noster* (The Lord's Prayer); the petition *Agnus Dei*; and the hymn of praise *Gloria in Excelsis*.

The office, or "canonical hours," is a set of eight prayer hours spread throughout the day. Psalms are sung, each preceded and followed by an antiphon proper to the feast or day, with hymns and orations. The two main hours are lauds (6 AM) and vespers (6 PM); the nocturnal hour of matins includes sung prophecies and lessons, with proper responsories.

planaria

planaria [pluh-nair'-ee-uh]   Planaria is the common name formerly given to almost any freshwater FLATWORM of the class Turbellaria characterized by a three-branched digestive tract. Some of these small, soft-bodied, unsegmented animals are included in the genus *Planaria,* and thus the term *planarian* is still used; however, *turbellarian* is more accurate. A majority live in shallow water, but a few live on land in regions where the air is humid (even in greenhouses). They range in size from 0.5 to 150 mm (0.02 to 6 in) long.

Planarians glide on a ciliated undersurface or swim with up-and-down movements. They resemble a flattened arrow, and their organs of touch, the auricles, are the side projections of the head. Between the auricles are two eyespots that detect the intensity and direction of light. Most planarians have a mouth and sucking pharynx located on the ventral (lower) surface near the middle of the animal. They take in minute particles of organic matter. Some planarians show a spectacular ability to repair the body after it has been cut.

Planck, Max

Planck, Max [plahnk]   The German physicist Max Karl Ernst Ludwig Planck, b. Apr. 23, 1858, d. Oct. 3, 1947, developed the concept of the quantum, or fundamental increment of energy—basic to QUANTUM MECHANICS, and a cornerstone of modern physics. After receiving his Ph.D. from the University of Munich in 1879, Planck taught at the University of Kiel (1885–89) and the University of Berlin (1889–1926). His appointment at the latter institution included the directorship of the Institute

Max Planck, a German physicist, revolutionized physics in 1900 with his discovery of the quantum, or fundamental unit of energy. In 1918, Planck received the Nobel Prize for physics for this breakthrough.

of Theoretical Physics that was newly founded for him.

Planck began studying BLACKBODY RADIATION in 1897 and discovered that at long wavelengths it did not obey the distribution laws given by Wilhelm Wien. This discovery led him to announce (1900) his revolutionary idea that an oscillator could emit energy only in discrete quanta, contrary to classical physical theory. The quantum theory—which gained Planck the Nobel Prize for physics in 1918—was used by Albert Einstein to explain (1905) the photoelectric effect and by Niels Bohr to propose (1913) a model of the atom with quantized electronic states; the theory was later developed into quantum mechanics.

Planck's constant

Planck's constant   Planck's constant, *h,* was introduced in 1900 by Max Planck in his equation that described BLACKBODY RADIATION. According to his theory, radiation of frequency v comes in quanta, or packages, with an energy E determined by $E = hv$. In meter-kilogram-second (mks) units, h is about equal to 6.6261×10^{-34} joule-sec, an extremely small quantity. The constant appears in every description of matter and radiation. Planck's constant measures the size of the quantum effects in the system, which are large if the system is small. The equations for many physical properties can be expanded in powers of h as if it were a variable. Classical physics assumes h is zero, so that quanta can have zero energy and radiation can have any energy whatsoever.

See also: ATOMIC CONSTANTS; QUANTUM MECHANICS.

plane (mathematics)

plane (mathematics)   A plane is a flat or level surface that has no thickness and has infinite length and width. It is a mathematical idealization, because any real surface does have thickness and a finite length and width. In GEOMETRY the plane is usually accepted as one of the undefined terms, along with the point and the line. Any three noncollinear points (points that are not all on the same line) determine a unique plane. A plane figure is a figure that lies entirely in a plane, and plane geometry is the study of plane figures.

plane tree   Plane trees, genus *Platanus,* also known as sycamores, are deciduous hard·wood trees that belong to the family Platanaceae. About seven species are distributed throughout north temperate regions. They are characterized by a whitish bark that flakes in large, thin patches, exposing brown, green, and gray inner bark. The alternate long-stalked leaves are 3- to 7-lobed and often toothed. Drooping, spherical fruit matures in the fall. The London plane, *P. acerifolia*, a hybrid, has been planted extensively in the United States as a street tree but is often attacked by a fungus that causes a canker-stain disease. The American sycamore, *P. occidentalis*, is a common stream-bank tree east of the Great Plains. These trees are often attacked in the spring by a leaf disease called anthracnose. The California sycamore, *P. racemosa*, is confined to stream banks and moist canyons of California.

The American sycamore, a plane tree often used as a shade tree in U.S. cities, has leaves with three to five shallow lobes. The spherical fruit breaks apart when ripe.

Planet X   The SOLAR SYSTEM, which consists of the Sun and the objects in orbit around it, is known to contain nine planets. It has been conjectured, however, that a possible 10th planet remains to be discovered beyond Pluto, the planet whose orbit extends farthest from the Sun. This hypothetical planet is referred to as Planet X, and the reasons for the conjecture are as follows.

For many centuries Uranus was the outermost known planet. Observations of Uranus in more recent times, however, revealed certain irregularities in its orbit that astronomers thought must be caused by the gravitational pull of some large and still more distant body. The search

for this unknown body led to the discovery of Neptune in 1846, and irregularities in Neptune's own orbit led in turn to the discovery of Pluto in 1930. Pluto was far too small, however, to cause the irregularities. Hence some scientists think that one or more planet-size bodies remain to be found. Others believe that the calculations of the irregularities, which date back into the 19th century, are themselves at fault, and that no Planet X is needed to account for the orbits now known.

Various attempts have been made at predicting the size and distance of any possible Planet X. Some astronomers suggest that it would have a mass of three to five Earths, and a highly elliptical orbit so distant that the planet would need about 1,000 years to complete one trip around the Sun.

planetarium [plan-uh-tair'-ee-uhm]   A planetarium is a device that demonstrates the apparent motions of the Moon, the Sun, the planets, and the stars. The name is also given to the building that houses such a device. In the most elaborate modern installations, the stars are shown in correct colors; other phenomena, such as the solar corona, eclipses, gegenschein, twilight, aurorae, Van Allen radiation belts, variable stars, and the Milky Way, are also demonstrated. Audio effects, such as thunder to accompany lightning storms, may also be added to the program.

The first planetariums were orreries—mechanical models of the solar system which were perfected by George Graham (*c.*1674–1751).

The Modern Planetarium. The mechanical orrery has been replaced by a system of light projection introduced (1923) by Carl Zeiss at the Deutsches Museum in Munich. The original equipment provided a representation of the sky from only one latitude, but modern installations go far beyond this. The projector is placed at the center beneath a white dome in a room that can be darkened and furnished with seating. In these surroundings the illusion is given of being out-of-doors under a starlit sky. Auxiliary projection systems for movies and color slides are usually provided.

In its most complete form the projector assembly consists of two spherical housings at opposite ends of the assembly from which light spots of correct relative intensity, corresponding to the brighter stars, are projected on the dome. Each sphere projects half of the sky. The central part of the assembly carries the equipment for producing enlarged images of the Moon and planets in correct positions and phases of illumination. Other projectors permit superposition of various coordinate grids, such as altazimuth and ecliptic systems.

The projector assembly may be tilted to represent the sky as seen from any terrestrial latitude and rotated to represent the diurnal motion of the sky due to the Earth's rotation. The complex mechanical gearing used in early versions of the planetarium is now often replaced by stepping motors under control of a computer program.

Locations of Major Planetariums. Installations with domes larger than 15 m (50 ft) in diameter and accom-

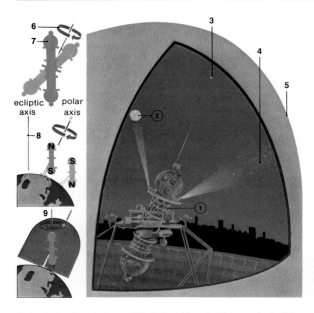

A planetarium is an instrument (1) designed to project images of celestial objects (2, 3, 4) on a large domed ceiling (5). A star's daily motion (6) about the celestial pole can be depicted for any latitude by tilting the projector (7) about a horizontal axis. A view of the night sky as seen from the polar regions (8) is obtained by turning the planetarium to a vertical position. One project for (N) depicts the stars visible at the North Pole; the opposite project for (S) shows those seen at the South Pole. Changes (9) in the pole star (arrow) resulting from precession of the Earth's axis are duplicated by moving the planetarium about a specifically designed axis.

modations for large audiences are usually associated with museums or science centers. For many years planetarium projectors were constructed only by Zeiss, but since World War II, Spitz in the United States and Goto in Japan have become important builders. Among the earliest and best-known large planetariums are the Morrison in San Francisco (the first to be constructed in the United States), the Griffith in Los Angeles, the Adler in Chicago, the Hayden in New York City, and those in Moscow and London. Many large cities throughout the world now have full-scale planetariums. In addition, several hundred educational institutions in the United States have smaller planetariums that are used for astronomical aspects of instruction.

planetary nebula   see NEBULA

planetoid   see ASTEROID

---

planets and planetary systems   A planet is a celestial body that revolves around a central star and does not shine by its own light. A group of such bodies is called a planetary system. The only planetary system yet understood in any detail is the SOLAR SYSTEM, so named because its star is our own Sun, or Sol. It contains nine

major known planets. In order of increasing distance from the Sun, they are MERCURY, VENUS, EARTH (Terra), MARS, JUPITER, SATURN, URANUS, NEPTUNE, and PLUTO. (Some scientists conjecture the possible existence of a 10th planet; see PLANET X.) Many minor planets also orbit the Sun, but they are more commonly called ASTEROIDS. Other objects in solar orbit, such as comets, meteors, and tiny grains or molecules of interplanetary dust and gas, are by convention not considered planets, and bodies that directly circle the planets and only secondarily orbit the Sun are called satellites, or moons, of the objects they orbit.

These various terms for star-orbiting bodies are at present of practical use only in describing the solar system. Systems of some sort have been observed around a number of other relatively nearby stars, but the objects they might contain are not yet known. Calling such systems planetary systems does not imply the existence of planets like those in the solar system.

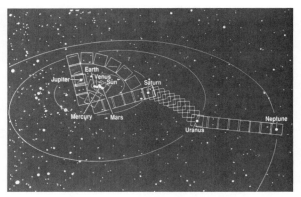

When Voyager 1 *left the solar system, its cameras were turned to take photographs of the Sun's family, as indicated by white frames (above). Even at that relatively near distance, the spacecraft could detect only six planets (below). At greater depths in space, all members of the system except the Sun itself would be invisible to observers.*

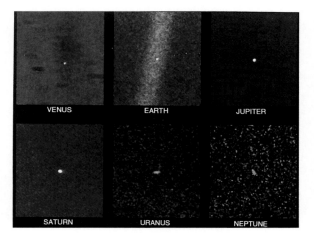

Kinds of Planets The solar system's major planets vary greatly in nature, from the rocky bodies of the inner system (Mercury through Mars) to the giant, mainly gassy planets of the outer system (Jupiter through Neptune). The minor planets are tiny lumps of rock and ice. The known planets are similar, then, only in being nonluminous, shining by the reflected light of their star and radiating no light of their own.

Possible planets could range still more greatly in size, the one limitation being their MASS. That is, when a celestial body contains more than a certain critical mass, internal forces of heat and compression initiate the thermonuclear reactions that turn it into a STAR (see STELLAR EVOLUTION). This critical mass is about one-fiftieth the mass of the Sun. Jupiter, the largest planet in the solar system, has a mass of only about one-thousandth the solar mass. Even so, it is large enough to radiate a greater amount of heat than the heat it receives from the Sun. Objects intermediate in size between Jupiter and the critical mass would similarly radiate heat. Such objects are conjectured to exist and have been called BROWN DWARFS. A few possible brown-dwarf candidates have been detected.

Other Planetary Systems. Beyond these possible sightings, other planetary systems have long been conjectured to exist. Most astronomers believe that the planets of the solar system were formed as a by-product of the formation of the Sun by condensation from INTERSTELLAR MATTER. On this basis other stars should also have planetary systems. In addition, most of the ANGULAR MOMENTUM in our own system resides in the planets, rather than in the Sun. Other relatively cool stars, like the Sun, have also been observed to have small angular momenta compared to hotter stars. Thus these cooler stars may have lost much of their angular momentum to their own planets.

The most promising Earth-based technique for discovering planetary systems is to photograph a likely star repeatedly and to look for apparent anomalies in its motion. Such anomalies could be caused due to gravitational perturbations by an unseen planet or planets orbiting it. Another method makes use of an occulting disk to block out the bright light of a central star so that the fainter, infrared light of cooler orbiting objects might be detected (see INFRARED ASTRONOMY). The latter method was used successfully in 1984 to photograph a possibly evolving planetary system around the star Beta Pictoris. In addition, the INTERFEROMETER technique known as speckle interferometry has revealed other stars surrounded by dust halos that could be planetary systems in the making.

---

plankton [plank'-tuhn] Plankton comprises those plants and animals of the aquatic environments which drift with the currents. The term is derived from the Greek *planktos*, or "wanderer." Planktonic life-forms are distinguished from members of the nekton (active swimmers) and from attached or sedentary members of the benthos, or seafloor—for example, clams, burrowing worms, and large seaweeds. Plankton constitutes more than 90% of the total productivity of the sea and of large lakes, and forms the basis of virtually all major food chains there.

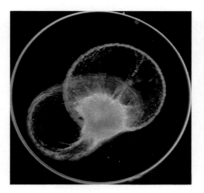

A major constituent of marine phytoplankton are the dinoflagellates, unicellular organisms possessing two flagella—one that propels the organism and another that causes it to spin. Many are bioluminescent, including Noctiluca.

Phytoplankton and Zooplankton

Phytoplankton includes most photosynthetic (plant) members of the plankton (see PHOTOSYNTHESIS), mainly unicellular ALGAE. In the oceans these are principally the golden or brown pigmented diatoms and dinoflagellates, their green CHLOROPHYLL masked by yellow or orange accessory pigments (CAROTENOIDS). These groups have freshwater representatives, but the phytoplankton of lakes and streams is more likely to be dominated by green or blue-green algae.

Planktonic animals, the zooplankton, are divided into two groups: holoplankton, which spend their entire life cycle in the plankton; and meroplankton, which have planktonic larval forms but which are nektonic or benthic as adults. The most significant members of the holoplankton are the small crustaceans that function as grazers on the phytoplankton and thus serve as the first link in planktonic food chains. The meroplankton includes many important marine fish—for example, herring, cod, and anchovy—and the larval forms of most shellfish. Meroplankton are less common in fresh water.

Copepods are microscopic crustaceans such as the freshwater Cyclops. They feed primarily on phytoplankton and are, in turn, a major part of the diet of larger aquatic animals.

Adaptations for Planktonic Existence

All planktonic organisms are somewhat denser than water and thus tend to sink. This tendency, however, can be slowed appreciably through a number of adaptations. For instance, the organisms' small size increases the cellular surface-to-volume ratio and therefore the relative degree of drag encountered while sinking. Phytoplankton cells are seldom larger in diameter than a few tenths of a millimeter, and large copepods, a type of zooplankton, are rarely greater than 5 mm (0.2 in) in total body length unless they are relatively strong swimmers. (The "giant" plankters, such as the larger jellyfish, have delicate, gelatinous bodies with a density very closely approaching that of water, and most also possess accessory flotation mechanisms.) The smaller plankters increase their surface area even further through the possession of long spines. Healthy diatoms also often contain intracellular oil vacuoles that reduce the cellular density. Many freshwater blue-green algae produce intracellular gas vacuoles and are thus capable of staying at the water's surface for prolonged periods.

Phytoplankton Productivity

Ecologically, the most important function of phytoplankton is its primary production: using solar energy and CO_2 in the synthesis of biologically useful carbohydrates by the process of photosynthesis. The overall productivity of the oceans is somewhat over half that of all the land-based ecosystems combined, and more than 90% of the marine production represents phytoplankton activity. Two major factors influence the distribution of phytoplankton primary production: light and inorganic micronutrient supply. Light is absorbed as it penetrates water. Below the depth where the light intensity has dropped to about 1% of its intensity at the surface, the rate of algal photosynthesis drops below the level needed to sustain cell growth. The column of water between this depth and the surface is called the photic zone. In clear tropical waters, the photic zone may extend as far down as 100 m (328 ft), but in more turbid coastal seas and in most lakes, depths of 5–20 m (16.5–66 ft) are the norm.

The important micronutrient requirements of phytoplankton include: nitrogen (as nitrates or ammonium), phosphorus (as phosphates), silicon (required in quantity only by diatoms for their siliceous cell walls), and various metals such as iron and copper in trace amounts. Nitrogen and phosphorus are in the shortest relative supply in most waters, and their relative lack sets the limit on phytoplankton growth. Thus when nitrate or ammonium is added to a body of water by sewage or by runoffs from agricultural land, the result is a sustained bloom of phytoplankton (see BLOOM, ALGAL). Such blooms are the most visible aspect of this form of pollution (see POLLUTION, ENVIRONMENTAL; EUTROPHICATION).

In unpolluted waters, micronutrients are supplied by the introduction of deeper, nutrient-rich water into the photic zone. In coastal marine waters at the latitudes of the United States and Canada, sufficient mixing of the water column to effect this introduction normally occurs

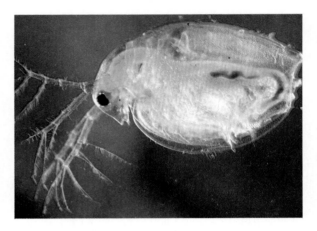

Water fleas, such as Daphnia, *are often the primary components of freshwater zooplankton. Named for their mode of swimming, which resembles leaping through the water, most water fleas feed on phytoplankton.*

during late winter storms. This leads to a pronounced diatom bloom and an analogous and somewhat later peak in meroplankton activity, as the larvae take advantage of the increased availability of food.

In tropical seas and in clear open-ocean waters the photic zone is deeper, and storms that mix the water column to greater depths are less common. Also, in these areas light and temperature do not fluctuate as much. The seasonal cycle of plankton productivity is therefore much less pronounced, and levels tend to be low and constant.

By far the most productive areas of the ocean are those very limited regions where the direction of prevailing surface currents leads away from continental landmasses, where the water so displaced is replaced by upwelling from below the photic zone. The two most famous locations lie off the coast of Ecuador and Peru (Humboldt Current) and off western Africa (Benguela Current). These waters support an immensely productive planktonic ecosystem.

Planktonic Food Chains

In all ecosystems, the first step in a food chain—the first trophic level—is occupied by herbivores, those animals which graze on the primary producers. In planktonic ecosystems the primary producers are microscopic plants. Their herbivores, such as copepods and meroplanktonic larvae, are also small in order to be able to harvest them efficiently. These grazers are preyed upon by somewhat larger zooplankters (for example, predatory copepods, and fish larvae) of the second trophic level. In a planktonic food chain there may be three or four trophic levels before fish of commercially useful size (cod or tuna) become involved. Only 10% of the energy of one trophic level is passed on to the next higher one.

Planned Parenthood Federation of America

The Planned Parenthood Federation of America was organized by Margaret SANGER in 1916 to provide the general public with information on family planning. Its headquarters is in New York City, and its 172 affiliates and 879 clinics in communities throughout the United States conduct research and offer medical services, including BIRTH CONTROL information and devices, ABORTION, and sterilization.

plant   The significance of plants is all-pervasive. The energy obtained from food is first converted from sunlight to usable, transferable energy by green plants. The oxygen supply in the Earth's atmosphere is a result of PHOTOSYNTHESIS by green plants. Fossil fuels come from plant material. Plants also create and modify local environmental conditions on which many species of animals and other plants depend.

Historically, plants have been considered one of the two kingdoms of living things, the other being animals. Plants, kingdom Plantae, are broadly distinguished from animals, kingdom Animalia, by being stationary, by manufacturing their own food, by having a continuous type of growth that is readily modified by the environment, and in possessing a less definite form when mature. Possibly 300,000 species of plants exist, however, and many do not fit well into either kingdom. The recent trends are to recognize five kingdoms of living things based on evolutionary origins and relationships: Monera, the bacteria and blue-green algae; Protista, including all other algae and the protozoans; Fungi, such as mushrooms and molds; Plantae, or plants, containing the mosses, ferns, seed plants, and several minor groups; and Animalia, or animals.

Classification of the Plant Kingdom

In the five-kingdom system, a plant is defined as being multicellular and eukaryotic, that is, having a membrane around the nucleus of each cell. It has a life cycle consisting of alternating sexual and asexual generations. A plant also contains special types of light-absorbing molecules called chlorophyll *a* and chlorophyll *b* as well as a number of carotenoid pigments; it stores food in the form of starch. A plant has cell walls composed mostly of cellulose and develops a separation layer (cell plate) during cell division; it lacks centrioles, which are structures involved in cell division in animals.

Under the traditional two-kingdom system, organisms having only several, or even just one, of the foregoing characteristics are considered plants. The two-kingdom system includes the prokaryotic bacteria, the single-cell algae, and the fungi—which lack chlorophyll—in addition to those defined as plants according to the five-kingdom system. Although the two-kingdom system is broader and more inclusive, the five-kingdom system will be followed here.

Thallophytes. The thallophytes are classified in three different kingdoms, not as part of the plant kingdom. Thallophytes have a simple plant body (thallus) without roots, stems, or leaves. They may be unicellular, filamentous, or of simple structure and live in or near water.

The green (photosynthetic) thallophytes are the algae, and the nongreen thallophytes are the fungi and bacteria (although some bacteria are photosynthetic). When these plants reproduce sexually, the zygote (fertilized egg) develops directly into a new plant or into spores and does not go through an embryonic stage as do the zygotes of plants in the subkingdom Embryobionta. The gametes, or sex cells, are produced within single cells. For the most part the plants are haploid; that is, they have a single set of chromosomes.

Embryophytes. The embryophytes, or true plants, develop from an embryo and have multicellular reproductive

Tropical rain forests, such as this one in Costa Rica, are the most species-rich habitats on Earth. Plants in rain forests and other natural habitats are among the most important resources available to humankind, providing food, medicine, and other commercially valuable products. For example, the rosy periwinkle contains substances effective against certain cancers. The babassú palm produces fruit from which oil for cooking and other purposes is extracted. In recent years, however, deforestation is reducing rain-forest cover at an alarming rate. This activity has had a devastating effect on plant and animal species diversity. In addition, it is considered a major contributor to the greenhouse effect.

PLANT CLASSIFICATION*

Rank	Name	Number of Species
Phylum	Bryophyta	23,600
Class	Hepaticae (liverworts)	9,000
Class	Antherocerotae (hornworts)	100
Class	Musci (mosses)	14,500
Phylum	Tracheophyta (vascular plants)	
Subphylum	Lycophytina (club mosses)	1,000
Subphylum	Sphenophytina (horsetails)	12
Subphylum	Pterophytina	261,600
Class	Filicineae (ferns)	11,000
Class	Coniferinae (conifers)	550
Class	Cycadinae (cycads)	70
Class	Gingkoinae (gingko)	1
Class	Angiospermae (flowering plants)	250,000
Subclass	Dicotyledonae (dicots)	190,000
Subclass	Monocotyledonae (monocots)	60,000

*A number of different systems of classification have been proposed by various authorities. Those which may agree on groupings and rankings may differ on the names applied to these groupings and rankings or on the spellings of the same names. This classification is based on Whittaker's five-kingdom system.

structures. Chlorophyll *a* is the primary photosynthetic pigment, and chlorophyll *b* and carotenoids are the principal accessory ones. All divisions after the mosses and other bryophytes have specialized fluid-conducting, or vascular, tissues containing elongated, hollowed tracheid cells and thus are known as tracheophytes. The more primitive vascular plants lack seeds and instead utilize spores in their dispersal.

The phylum Bryophyta includes the mosses, liverworts, and hornworts. These plants are fairly small, multicellular plants that usually occur in moist, shaded places. They may have stemlike and leaflike structures but actually lack true roots, stems, and leaves. They also may have an elementary water-conducting system of simple cells but not the advanced xylem and phloem tissues of the higher, vascular plants.

The phylum Tracheophyta comprises all vascular plants. The subphylum Rhyniophytina is an extinct group of primitive plants without roots or true leaves, and the apparent ancestors of the other vascular plant groups. The subphylum Psilophytina is a primitive group that includes the living "whisk fern." They lack roots and leaves and have a forked shoot with spore sacs. The lycopods (subphylum Lycophytina), or club mosses, are another ancient group; they have simple, primitive leaves. Also primitive are the horsetails (subphylum Sphenophytina), which are characterized by jointed stems and the presence of silica in the walls of the outer cells.

The subphylum Pterophytina includes true ferns, gymnosperms, and flowering plants. The ferns (class Filicineae) possess large, much-divided leaves (fronds). The

spore sacs, or sporangia, are clustered on the underside of the leaf in various patterns. The leaves arise from an underground stem (rhizome). The conifers (class Coniferinae), cycads (class Cycadinae), and ginkgoes (class Ginkgoinae) are gymnosperms: their seeds lie exposed, typically at the base of scales (which are actually modified leaves) in a cone. The gymnosperms have no flowers; they lack the specialized water-conducting vessels of flowering plants but have tracheids, tubular cells that serve both as support and for water transport. The cycads are an ancient group of tropical plants with a short, stout trunk that is unbranched and also with palmlike leaves.

The class Angiospermae are the flowering plants, in which the seeds are enclosed in a dry or fleshy fruit that develops from the ovary of the flower. Angiosperms are the most diverse and successful of plant groups, with well-developed vessels in the xylem and other adaptations to a variety of land habitats. Angiosperms are divided into two subclasses: Dicotyledonae and Monocotyledonae. The dicotyledons have two seed leaves (cotyledons) in the embryo; typically netted, or branched, leaf veins; flower parts in multiples of four or five (such as four stamens or ten petals); and a cambium (the cell-producing growth layer), which often develops secondary growth. The monocotyledons have one seed leaf, parallel leaf veins, flower parts in threes, and no cambium.

Evolution of Plants

The earliest known forms of life date back to about 3.5 billion years ago. These organisms were apparently BACTERIA and BLUE-GREEN ALGAE. Photosynthesis almost certainly first developed in bacteria, but the release of oxygen into the atmosphere was first accomplished by the photosynthetic green ALGAE, which appeared about 1 billion years ago along with the FUNGI. The earliest land plants occurred a little more than 400 million years ago, during the Late Silurian Period, and were similar to the "whisk fern," *Psilotum*, of today. The first seed plants appeared about 350 million years ago, during the Late Devonian Period, and are referred to as seed ferns because of the large fernlike leaves. The flowering plants date back to about 120 million years ago, in the Early Cretaceous Period, and today total about four-fifths of all plants.

Structure and Function

A green plant's physiological processes are functions adapted to fulfilling its needs for energy, nutrients, water, reproduction, and dispersal. It accomplishes these by the processes of photosynthesis (the manufacture of carbohydrates from carbon dioxide and water using light as an energy source), assimilation, respiration, and growth. A plant's structural features, although markedly diverse in the various groups, are each specially adapted for carrying out these functions.

The algae, living in water, directly absorb the water and nutrients into the cells. Reproduction is accomplished by division and by motile gametes and spores. In the semiterrestrial mosses and other bryophytes, water and nutrients are absorbed from the soil through rootlike hairs (rhizoids), which also serve to anchor the plant. Ma-

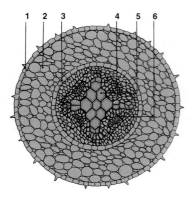

A cross section of an angiosperm root reveals several distinct tissue layers. The epidermis (1) absorbs water and minerals through root hairs. Cells of the cortex (2) store starch and other substances. A thin endodermis (3) encloses the vascular cylinder, which contains food-conducting phloem (4), water-conducting xylem (5), and a region of dividing cells (6).

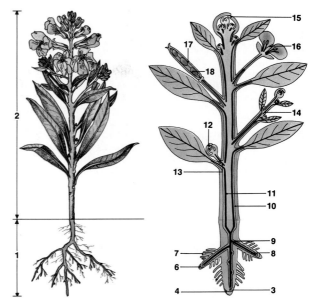

A typical flowering plant consists of a root (1) and shoot (2). The root grows from an apical meristem (3), which is protected by a root cap (4). Both primary (5) and branch (6) roots develop absorptive root hairs (7) and contain water-conducting xylem (8) and food-transporting phloem (9). In dicots these conducting tissues form a ring of bundles that divides the shoot into cortex (10) and pith (11). Leaves and axillary buds (12) are found at nodes (13) of the stem. Branch stems (14) arise from axillary buds if the terminal bud (15) is damaged. The flower (16) is the reproductive structure that develops, when fertilized, into a fruit (17) that bears seeds (18).

terials move directly from cell to cell. Photosynthesis is concentrated in the thin leaflike structures, which, without efficient means of preventing water loss, merely curl up when conditions are dry. Reproduction and dispersal involve motile gametes and small wind-borne spores. The vascular plants on land have more complex structures that allow them to survive away from a permanently wet habitat. The typical flowering plant consists of roots, stems, leaves, and flowers.

The Root. The functions of the root are to anchor the plant, to absorb and transport nutrients and water, and sometimes to store food and serve in asexual reproduction. Root systems may consist of one major root (taproot) or of a profuse mass of similar-sized branches. Penetration into the soil is accomplished by cell division and, largely, by the elongation of cells just behind the tip. A protective cap covers the tip. Just behind the region of elongation are the root hairs, myriad small projections of the epidermal cells that are responsible for absorption. Once absorbed, water and minerals pass through the cortex, or root wall, into the center of the root, called the vascular cylinder; there these substances are conducted upward through the xylem.

The Stem. The functions of the stem include production and support of new leaves, branches, and flowers,

and placing them in positions where they can function most efficiently. Support is provided by various thick-walled cells found in the xylem or in strands outside the xylem. In herbaceous stems, turgor, or internal water pressure, is also important, as evidenced by the limp shape of a wilted plant.

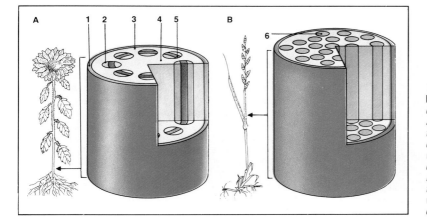

The stem of a typical dicot, such as the sunflower Helianthus (A), is surrounded by epidermis (1) and contains bundles of vascular tissue (2) arranged in a ring. This ring separates the outer cortex (3) from the inner pith (4). A layer of dividing cells, the vascular cambium (5), produces more vascular tissue, which increases the thickness of the stem. A typical monocot, such as grass (B), has its vascular bundles (6) scattered throughout the stem. No distinction exists between pith and cortex, and the vascular bundles, which lack a cambial layer, are closed to further growth.

Another stem function is to transport materials to and from the roots. Water and minerals are carried in the xylem, and manufactured food in the phloem. Frequently, stems also serve to store food, photosynthesize, or reproduce new plants.

The Leaf. The leaves intercept light, exchange gases, and provide a site for photosynthesis. Some leaves also store food and water, provide support, or form new plants.

A flat, broad, thin structure gives more surface area for light interception and penetration. Gas exchange, including intake of carbon dioxide and release of oxygen and excess water, occurs through small pores (stomata) in the leaf surface. When the humidity is so high that minimal amounts of water can be lost through evaporation, water is forced out of the leaves through specialized structures (hydathodes), in a process called guttation.

Flowers, Fruits, and Seeds. The FLOWER is the sexual reproduction unit that functions to produce and house gametes (sex cells). The male gametes are contained within pollen, which must be transferred to the female structure of the flower, where the seeds will develop. Flowers utilize a variety of agents to ensure that this transfer, called POLLINATION, occurs.

The female structure, or pistil, has an enlarged ovary containing ovules, where the female gametes are produced and where fertilization takes place. Upon fertilization, the ovary begins to develop into a fruit and the ovules into seeds. The function of the fruit is to aid in the

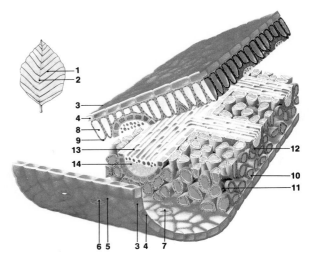

A typical angiosperm leaf is a flat blade supported by a network of veins (1) that branch from a midrib (2). The leaf is covered by a waxy cuticle (3) secreted by the single layer of epidermal cells (4). Guard cells (5) can open (6) or close (7) small pores, or stomata, which regulate gas exchange. The epidermis protects the palisade cells (8), which contain numerous chloroplasts (9), the sites of photosynthesis. Spongy mesophyll cells (10), surrounded by air spaces (11), have fewer chloroplasts. A vein, enclosed by a bundle sheath (12), consists of xylem (13), which brings water and minerals to the leaf, and phloem (14), which carries food to other parts of the plant.

Leaves vary widely in form. The broad leaf of the English oak (A) and the needles of the Scots pine (B) are simple leaves, with a single leaf blade. The horse chestnut (C) bears palmately compound leaves, with leaflets radiating from one point. The leaf of Polypodium *(D), a fern, has segments arranged pinnately along a main stalk. The garden pea (E) has leaflets modified as coiling tendrils. Leaves of* Mammillaria *(F) and other cacti are modified as spines.*

dispersal of the seeds (see FRUITS AND FRUIT CULTIVATION). The SEED, containing the embryo, serves as the unit of dispersal for the new plant. It also provides some protection from injury and drying and some nourishment for the young plant until it can make its own food.

Reproduction in Plants

Plants may reproduce either sexually or asexually, with many utilizing both modes. Sexual reproduction involves two important processes: the fusion of reproductive cells—sperm and egg, collectively referred to as gametes—and a reduction division (meiosis) to halve the number of chromosomes present in each gamete. The zygote that results from the fusion of the sperm and egg, therefore, contains twice the chromosome number of either gamete. The zygote divides and develops into an embryo, which grows into the new plant.

Asexual reproduction involves no change in chromosome number. Vegetative cells or organs may become separated from the parent plant and continue to grow and develop into a new plant. Only mitosis, or cell division that retains the full number of chromosomes, is involved. The new plants have a genetic structure identical to that of the parent. In some plants embryos and seeds are formed asexually from an unfertilized egg cell (parthenogenesis or apomixis).

The life cycle of plants that reproduce sexually involves an alternation of two phases, or generations: the gamete-producing phase (the gametophyte plant) and the

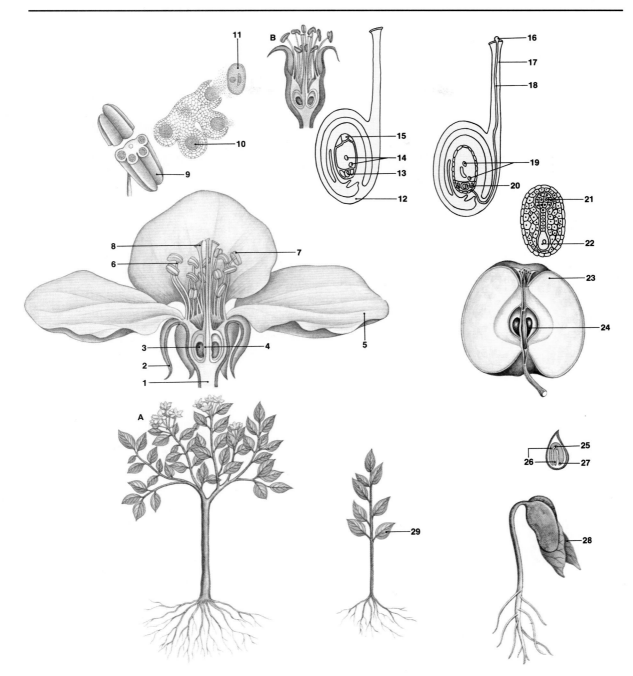

A mature apple tree (A) *bears flowers, which contain sepals* (2); *petals* (5); *male filaments* (6) *and anthers* (7); *and a compound ovary* (4), *with ovules* (3) *and stigma* (8)—*all attached to a receptacle* (1). *Anthers* (9) *consist of pollen sacs* (10), *which release pollen grains* (11) *that are carried to another flower* (B). *Within the ovary* (12) *of this flower the ovule contains three antipodal cells* (15), *two polar nuclei* (14), *an egg* (13), *and two other cells. A pollen grain* (16) *reaching the stigma* (17) *produces a pollen tube* (18), *which grows into the ovule. Two male nuclei enter: one fuses with the egg* (20) *to form the embryo* (22), *and the other fuses with the polar nuclei* (19) *to form food-storage tissue* (21). *The receptacle* (23) *grows around the seed* (24) *to form the apple fruit. The seed, with cotyledons* (26) *and potential shoot* (25) *and root* (27), *germinates in the soil. The cotyledons* (28) *eventually wither as the true leaves* (29) *develop.*

Plant succession is the replacement of one plant community by another on the same site over a period of time. Each series of successional stages is termed a sere. These plants of the northern temperate zone illustrate a typical xerosere, which originates on a dry site, and hydrosere, which starts in water. As each successive community becomes established, mineral and organic matter accumulate and the habitat changes. Habitats become less extreme than those of the initial stages; in the xerosere the soil layer becomes deeper and richer; in the hydrosere the lake or pond is eventually filled in. Theoretically, under similar climatic conditions, the different seres should lead toward the same vegetational climax (in this example, deciduous forest). Actually, the process is more complex and variable; successional stages usually overlap; a given stage may vary in species composition on different sites; such disturbances as fire, erosion, and agriculture may interrupt or reverse the succession.

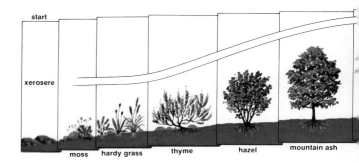

start

xerosere

moss   hardy grass   thyme   hazel   mountain ash

spore-producing phase (the sporophyte plant). In the bryophytes the gametophyte is the dominant generation, being the green structure readily visible; the sporophyte consists of a small capsule at the tip of a stalk. In the vascular plants the sporophyte is the larger, dominant generation; in seed plants the gametophyte develops in place within the flower or cone of the sporophyte. (See ALTERNATION OF GENERATIONS.)

Growth and Development

One of the general characteristics of plants, compared to animals, is that they tend to grow continuously throughout their lives. Growth serves not only to increase a plant's size but also to provide the plant with a limited means of movement and orientation for placing itself in a more favorable position with regard to light, nutrients, reproduction, and dispersal.

There are two aspects of plant growth: primary and secondary. Primary growth takes place in young, herbaceous organs, resulting in an increase in length of shoots and roots. Secondary growth follows primary growth in

some plants and results in an increased girth as layers of woody tissue are laid down.

The important factors affecting plant growth and development include heredity, hormones, nutrition, and environment. Hereditary, or genetic, factors control the general species characteristics of the individual and set limits on size and rate of growth. The genetic structure, through DNA and RNA patterns, acts by regulating protein synthesis, especially the manufacture of enzymes, as well as cell division, cell enlargement, the incorporation of substances into the cell walls, and the production and activity of the hormones. The gene action, in turn, is controlled by various growth regulators, particularly hormones and nutrients.

So-called plant hormones are organic chemicals that occur in plants and have definite physiological effects, although their precise roles in plant biochemistry are still little understood. Such chemicals include the auxins, cytokinins, gibberellins, abscisic acid, and ethylene. Cytokinins are present in cell division, as are auxins and gibberellins in elongation. Auxins are also associated with

An aggregate fruit, such as that of the sugar apple (A) develops from separate carpels of a single flower and contains many fruitlets. Simple fruits, derived from one or several united carpels of a flower, include fleshy fruits, usually animal dispersed, and dry forms. Drupes, such as the fruits of the cherry (B) and walnut (C), have a fleshy outer layer (not shown for walnut) and stony interior. Berries of the orange (D) and tomato (G) are also fleshy fruits. The fruit of most grasses, including wheat (E), is a dry, one-seeded caryopsis, or grain, in which the seed coat adheres to the fruit wall. Verbena (F) bears a dry fruit that separates into four nutlets at maturity.

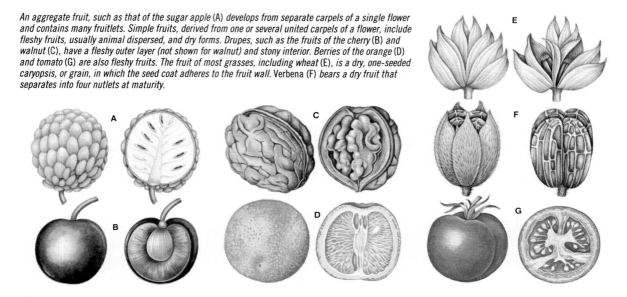

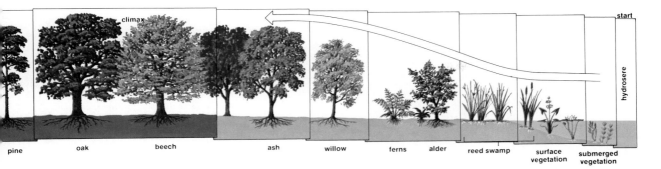

pine   oak   beech   ash   willow   ferns   alder   reed swamp   surface   submerged
                                                                                                                   vegetation   vegetation

TROPISM processes such as the bending of stems toward light. Other growth-related activities regulated by hormones include seed germination, flower and fruit development, and leaf enlargement.

Plants require all the essential ingredients of photosynthesis to construct the necessary compounds and structures. Water is especially important, because cell enlargement is a result of internal water pressure (turgor) extending the walls. In periods of drought plants tend to have smaller leaves. Calcium interacts with auxins and cytokinins in regulating cell divisions and elongation. Nitrogen is involved in the structure of chlorophyll, proteins, auxins, and cytokinins.

Many activities are affected greatly by the external en-

Plant growth originates in regions of undifferentiated tissue called meristems. In vascular plants, cells of the apical meristem (2) of the shoot rapidly divide and give rise to the procambium, ground meristem, and protoderm. Procambial strands (3) are present in rudimentary leaves, or leaf primordia (1), and the stem. Just beneath the apical meristem, cells produced by the meristem enlarge (4) and cause the stem to grow in length. The protoderm develops into epidermis (5); the ground meristem forms ground tissue, such as cortex (6) and pith (7); and the procambium differentiates into phloem (8) and xylem (10), with a cambial layer (9) between them.

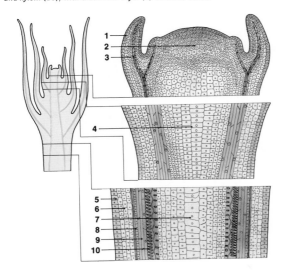

vironment, particularly light and temperature. Certain wavelengths of light affect the activity of a pigment called phytochrome, which in turn interacts with hormones in regulating flowering, leaf expansion, and other processes. Warmer temperatures are favorable to more growth; cold temperatures are needed for some seeds to germinate, some buds to begin growing, and some plants to flower.

Roles of Plants

Green plants, because of their photosynthetic processes, form the base of the food chain and thus the beginning of the energy flow through an ecosystem. They are also the only important organisms able to assimilate inorganic elements and incorporate them into organic compounds in living tissues, and they therefore form a vital link in the cycling of nutrients. Bacteria and fungi serve as the other major link in the cycling process because they decompose organic tissues and release the elements to the soil or water (see NITROGEN CYCLE). The energy that is not used by the plant in carrying out its life processes goes into the production of new tissues, which can then be used by other organisms as a food source.

Edible, concentrated portions of various plants—such as seeds, fruits, and tubers—are used as a food source not only for the human populations of the world but also for livestock feed (see AGRICULTURE AND THE FOOD SUPPLY). The most important food plants are the GRAINS of the grass family, particularly wheat, rice, corn, sorghum, and barley. In many tropical countries the higher-protein cereal grains do not grow well, and the basic foods are the starchier root crops, such as yams, sweet potatoes, and manioc (cassava).

Certain plants also provide the major beverages of the worlds, including coffee, tea, maté, and fruit juice. Beer is usually brewed from fermented barley and hops; wines, from grapes; and such spirits as whiskey and vodka, from grains or potatoes. Many textile fibers are derived from plants, including cotton, flax, and hemp. The wood of trees is used to make tools, furniture, and houses; such chemicals as acetic acid, methanol, and turpentine are obtained from trees. Oils, stored as food reserves in the seeds and fruits of many plants, are used as human food and in industry.

Plants also contain medicinally useful chemicals. Some of these chemicals are the antimalarial quinine

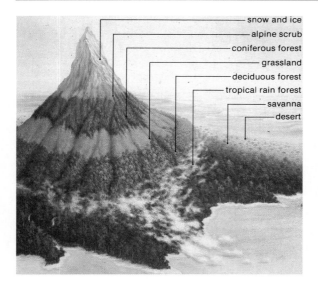

snow and ice
alpine scrub
coniferous forest
grassland
deciduous forest
tropical rain forest
savanna
desert

Plant communities vary with both latitude and elevation. This hypothetical mountain located in a tropical region illustrates the change from tropical rain forests at the base to alpine scrub and snow that reflect the cold, dry conditions at the summit. A similar series of vegetation zones occurs as one travels poleward from the equator.

from cinchona bark, the heart-stimulant digitalis from foxglove leaves, the antispasmodic atropine from belladonna (nightshade), and rauwolfia tranquilizers from the genus *Rauwolfia.*

Plants can also be harmful to humans, especially bacteria and fungi. Parasitic plants such as dodder and broom rape can seriously damage plants valued by humans.

Geographical Distribution and Plant Communities

Few places on the Earth can be found where at least some of the 300,000 species of plants are not adapted to live. Only the polar zones, the highest mountains, the deepest oceans, and the driest deserts are devoid of plants (other than bacteria). A given plant species has a limited distribution, however, depending on its own particular requirements. Some species are broadly distributed, being tolerant of a wide range of conditions. Narrowly restricted species have limited tolerance to a specific factor, such as soil type.

Climate is the major factor affecting the distribution of plants and determining their structural adaptations. The greatest number of species are found near the equatorial regions in tropical climates, where moisture and temperature are seldom limiting. The number of species per area decreases toward the poles.

plant, woody   see BARK; SHRUB; TREE; WOOD

---

plant breeding   Plant breeding is the deliberate attempt to change the genetic architecture of a plant spe-

cies and is now considered to be an applied branch of the field of GENETICS, although significant improvements were made in all the important crop plants long before anyone had an understanding of genetic principles. About 200 species of plants have been domesticated (see AGRICULTURE, HISTORY OF), and plant breeding has been practiced, directly or indirectly, on all of them.

History. Einkorn and emmer WHEAT kernels—in which the grains are firmly enclosed in the glumes—that date back to 6750 BC have been found in Iraq. The primitive hulled wheats were largely replaced by the naked durum and poulard wheats in the Mediterranean region during the period 500 BC to AD 500, and the common and club bread wheats were beginning to replace durum toward the end of this span. CORN was used as food in Mexico as early as 5000 BC; although primitive, this corn was unquestionably domesticated. RICE sowing was an important religious ceremony in China by 3000 BC, and differences among rice varieties were recognized as early as 1000 BC in India.

The primary objectives of early cultivators appear to have been to increase grain size and ease of harvesting and threshing, but indirect selection for yield and resistance to disease must also have been practiced. These objectives changed very little during the Middle Ages.

A number of discoveries reported in the 18th and 19th centuries revolutionized procedures and firmly established plant breeding as a scientific discipline in the early part of the 20th century. Chief among these were Joseph Koelreuter's observations (1763) that plant hybrids often possessed unusual vigor; Charles DARWIN's publications on evolution, inbreeding, and natural selection, which influenced plant breeder Luther BURBANK; and Gregor MENDEL's discovery of the basic laws of HEREDITY. The realization that yield and quality of plant products are quantitatively inherited—that is, a large number of genes contribute to these characteristics—and that controlled hybrids could be produced led to the basic procedures that constitute modern plant breeding. One of the first researchers to apply these breeding theories was the American botanist George Shull; from two pure strains of corn he developed (1909) a hybrid corn whose yield was enormously greater than those of pure strains.

Modern Practices and Factors. Yield, which is still the primary selection criterion, is affected by almost all factors that influence the growth and health of a plant, including such inherited characteristics as nutrient uptake, photosynthetic efficiency, rate and period of growth, and the number, size, and density of seeds produced. Diseases, insects, and weather conditions can seriously affect yield, and a breeding program must consider resistance or avoidance of these external factors. Cultural practices and user requirements must also considered. Mechanized agriculture, for instance, requires that all plants in a field mature virtually simultaneously.

Modern plant-breeding programs generally are conducted by teams of scientists that may include plant breeders, geneticists, statisticians, plant pathologists, plant physiologists, biochemists, and nutritionists. Hybridization and selection remain the principal tools; but the potential hybrid parents are carefully chosen for their

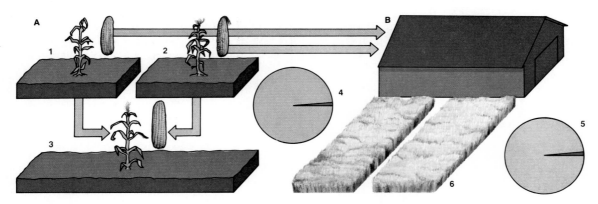

The production of high-yielding strains of corn is one of the most successful applications of scientific plant breeding. Superior plants are selected and, over several generations, are self-pollinated to produce inbred lines, which are then hybridized (A). Once the two inbred lines (1 and 2) that produce the best hybrid (3) are identified, seeds from the parent lines are stored in germ-plasm banks (B). Hybrid vigor is reduced in the next generation, however, and seeds from the parent lines are used to produce each new crop. If the germination rate of the stored seeds falls below a certain value (4 and 5), the seeds are planted out (6) and new plants selected to renew the stock.

specific genetic contributions, and the evaluation criteria that form the basis for selection have become quite sophisticated. GENE BANKS have been established as vital repositories of plant seeds; a large genetic pool is thus available to the research teams.

Most plant breeding is now conducted by commercial seed companies, governmental agencies, and international organizations. The success of the International Maize and Wheat Improvement Center in Mexico and the International Rice Research Institute in the Philippines resulted in the GREEN REVOLUTION of the 1960s, delaying the situation predicted by Thomas MALTHUS—that populations would exceed the amount of food available (see AGRICULTURE AND THE FOOD SUPPLY).

Trends. Recent developments in plant-tissue culture and molecular genetics promise to bring about a second revolution in plant-breeding methodology before the end of the 20th century. Individual cells of some plant species now can be cloned—that is, cultured, caused to differentiate, and grown to maturity. Some foresters are using CLONING techniques to produce genetically identical trees that grow faster or are resistant to disease, insect pests, or ACID RAIN. Researchers are culturing cells of the vanilla plant in the hope of producing vanilla flavoring commercially.

GENETIC ENGINEERING—the transfer of small segments of DNA containing specific genes from one cell to another using gene-splicing techniques—is now being practiced in plant breeding. Although it is unlikely that significant increases in crop yield can be engineered, the quality or quantity of specific plant products can be modified. Being tested, for example, are tomatoes that ripen but will not rot and soybeans that resist disease and tolerate pesticides.

plant distribution Plant life is distributed throughout the world in definable patterns. The factors controlling these patterns are climatic, physical, and biological and include light, temperature, soil, moisture, wind, competition with other plants, parasites and diseases, plant dispersal and adaptability, and many others. All these factors interact and cannot truly be isolated. For example, the tolerance of certain grasses to low levels of moisture is influenced by the amount of nitrogen in the soil. For analytical purposes, however, controlling factors have been judiciously separated, and two major principles applicable to plant distribution have been formulated: Liebig's law of the minimum and Shelford's law of tolerance.

The law of the minimum, proposed by Justus von Liebig, states that a plant requires certain materials for survival, growth, and reproduction and that of these materials the one that is least available will exert the greatest effect. The closer this material comes to the absolute minimum required for survival, the more significant become small differences in its amounts. Thus in a desert, where moisture may be scarce, small variations in moisture can result in marked differences in habitat. The law of tolerance, proposed by Victor Shelford, may be interpreted as the law of the maximum; that is, too much of a certain material may limit a plant's survival, growth, or reproduction. The range between minimum and maximum levels is called the limits of tolerance.

Climate is the primary influence on plant distribution, and plants reflect the climatic characteristics of a region, its geologic history, and the influence of its landforms. Vegetative types form broad but discernible patterns, which have been classified on both a worldwide and a more local basis.

Floristic regions are a worldwide classification, with each region characterized by a broadly distinctive complex of plant species. The floristic regions are the boreal, which comprises North America, Europe, and Asia; paleotropical, which covers Africa, southeastern Asia, and Polynesia; neotropical, which extends from South America into Mexico; South African; Australian; and Antarctic.

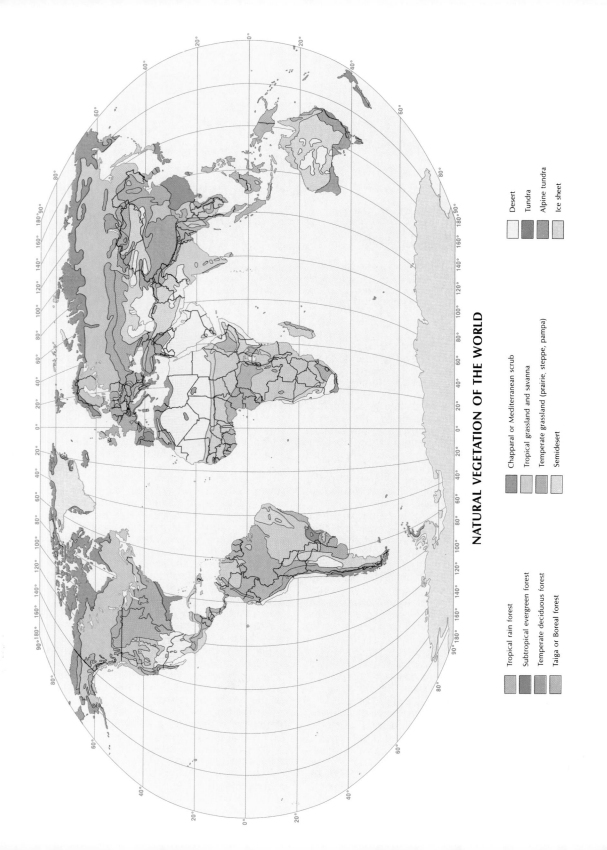

NATURAL VEGETATION OF THE WORLD

Tropical rain forest

Subtropical evergreen forest

Temperate deciduous forest

Taiga or Boreal forest

Chapparal or Mediterranean scrub

Tropical grassland and savanna

Temperate grassland (prairie, steppe, pampa)

Semidesert

Desert

Tundra

Alpine tundra

Ice sheet

BIOMES are a worldwide classification based on climax vegetation, that is, long-persisting types of vegetation that are characteristic of a given climatic area. The species may change across large distances, but the plant types remain the same, as in the grassland or desert biomes. Other biomes include the tundra, northern coniferous forest, and tropical rain forest.

Classification of vegetative patterns also may be based on the ranges of certain plants. At the intercontinental level four main patterns of distribution are recognized. (1) Cosmopolitan distribution: no plant is truly cosmopolitan and can live anywhere. Those most closely approaching cosmopolitan distribution are some of the lower plants, such as mosses, and the weeds of cultivation that tend to follow humankind. (2) Circumpolar distribution: these plants are distributed around the North and South poles. A number of plants are circumpolar, such as the purple saxifrage, *Saxifraga oppositifolia*, and Edward's eutrema, *Eutrema edwardsii*. (3) Circumboreal and circumaustral distributions: the boreal and austral zones lie next to the Arctic and Antarctic, respectively, and extend to the borders of the subtropics. Examples of plants with this type of distribution are the currants and gooseberries, genus *Ribes*. (4) Pantropic distribution: the pantropic region extends throughout the tropics and subtropics of the world. A number of palms are pantropically distributed.

plant hopper

Plant hoppers are small, jumping insects of the order HOMOPTERA, related to the leafhoppers, aphids, and cicadas. Originally considered one family, they are now classified as the superfamily Fulgoroidae and are divided into 11 to 18 families and more than 5,000 species. Most plant hoppers are less than 15 mm (0.6 in) long, but some tropical species may exceed 50 mm (2 in). Plant hoppers are characterized by the antennae arising on the sides of the head below the eyes, and the front of the head is often elongated into a "snout" or a still more unusual shape. Plant hoppers feed on plant juices.

plant propagation

In horticulture, plant propagation is the controlled REPRODUCTION of plants, carried out to increase plant numbers or to preserve their desirable characteristics.

Seed Propagation. SEED propagation is the most widely practiced method of plant increase, because seeds offer an easy way to reproduce plants and a convenient way to store them. Plant progeny from the seeds of self-pollinated plants, such as wheat and tomato, normally do not vary significantly from the parent plants. Many cultivated plants, however, must be cross-pollinated by other genetically different plants. The plants grown from seeds that are the result of cross-pollination will not be identical to either of the parent plants. With many species, plant uniformity can be achieved through controlled fertilization over several generations of parent plants selected for the characteristics desired in their progeny. To grow trees and

certain other plants from seed, however, takes many years. For such crops, vegetative reproduction is more economic.

Vegetative Propagation. Vegetative propagation exploits the facility of a plant to regenerate and replicate its entire structure from an individual plant part (see CLONING). Methods of vegetative propagation include the planting of specialized storage or reproductive structures such as tubers, bulbs, and corms; the cutting off and replanting of runners and offshoots; and techniques using cuttings, grafting, and tissue culture.

Plant cuttings—pieces of stem, leaves, or roots—may be induced to re-create the entire plant. In GRAFTING, a stem piece or a bud (scion) is joined to a root or a root-bearing stem (stock). The generation of tissues in the graft union forms a new, living connection between stock and scion. Many fruit trees are propagated by grafting, which produces an individual that is identical to the scion.

Some plants may also be propagated by the culture of small pieces of shoot tips or callus (scar) tissue on an artificial medium. The tips form multiple shoots, and each shoot will grow into a separate plant after roots are formed.

Plantagenet   see ANGEVINS

Plantago

[plan-tay'-goh]   The genus *Plantago* in the plantain family, Plantaginaceae, comprises more than 200 species of primarily stemless, perennial or annual herbs commonly called plantains. They should not be confused with the banana plantain, *Musa paradisiaca*. Plantains are distributed worldwide, mostly in temperate regions, and several are well-known lawn weeds. Their leaves, which may be erect or supine and are up to about 30 cm (1 ft) long, are produced in a rosette at the base of the plant. The tiny and usually greenish white flowers are borne on a leafless stalk in clusters or in conical heads.

plasma, blood   see BLOOD

plasma physics

Plasma physics is the branch of science that studies the properties and applications of plasma. A plasma is an assemblage of positive ions and unbound electrons in which the total number of positive and negative charges is almost exactly equal. In general, the plasma will also contain some proportion of neutral atoms or molecules. The properties of plasma are sufficiently different from those of solids, liquids, and gases for it to be considered to be a fourth state of MATTER.

Historical Development

Electrical discharges in gases were studied as early as the 1830s by the English physicist Michael Faraday and later by Sir William Crookes, who first suggested (1879) that the ionized gas in the discharge constituted a fourth state of matter. In 1926, radio-frequency oscillations were discovered in a low-pressure discharge in mercury vapor. These oscillations were further studied by American chemist Irving Langmuir and coworkers. In 1929, Langmuir applied the term *plasma* to the regions of the discharge in which the oscillations occurred. The terminology was derived from a belief that the ions acted like a rigid jelly through which the electrons were free to move. Using electrostatic-probe techniques that now bear his name, Langmuir established that the electrons pervading the plasma had a characteristic temperature. Since the 1920s the study of the plasma state has grown into a major research discipline.

Occurrence of Plasma

Near the Earth's surface, gaseous plasmas either are transient natural phenomena, such as LIGHTNING, or they occur in the operation of certain devices such as fluorescent tubes and electric arcs. Beyond the Earth's dense lower atmosphere, however, more than 99% of the matter in the universe appears to exist as plasma. In the upper atmosphere the ionosphere contains plasma that reflects terrestrial radio transmissions.

Driven from the surface of the Sun, the SOLAR WIND is a hydrogen plasma having a density of 10 particles per cm^3. This plasma sets up a bow shock wave, known as the magnetopause, upon encountering the Earth's magnetic field. Within that field, plasma from the solar wind is confined within bands known as the VAN ALLEN RADIATION BELTS at distances up to several Earth radii. At high latitudes, where these belts approach the upper atmosphere, they give rise to the AURORA.

The Sun and STARS are dense, highly ionized plasmas that have central temperatures in excess of 10,000,000 K and central densities of 10^{25} particles per cm^3. The vast space between stars is filled with a tenuous, weakly ionized plasma that may range in density from about 1 particle per cm^3 near stars to about 10^{-5} particles per cm^3 in intergalactic space (see INTERSTELLAR MATTER). Thus most of the universe exists in plasma form. Some plasma physicists, such as Hannes ALFVEN, have proposed a plasma-based cosmological theory to replace the currently dominant BIG BANG THEORY. According to these scientists, gravity together with the electromagnetic forces of plasmas were sufficient to shape the universe as it is now known, with no need for an initiating event (see COSMOLOGY).

Plasmas can also exist in solids. For example, the fixed ions and free electrons in an electrically conducting METAL constitute a plasma, as do the free electrons and mobile positive "holes" in a SEMICONDUCTOR.

Properties of Plasma

The electric field of an isolated charged particle diminishes as the square of the distance from the particle. In a plasma, however, this field is modified because the electrons are free to move into the vicinity of positive ions and away from other electrons. The field of each isolated particle is thus partially shielded by its immediate neighbors. Over a sufficiently large distance—wherein the fields of many individual charges are able to cancel each other—this shielding becomes complete. This distance, called a Debye length, is a measure of the distance over which an individual charged particle can exert an effect. For a body of particles to behave as a plasma, its dimensions must be large compared to the Debye length.

Any displacement of the electrons relative to the ions over a distance of the order of a Debye length gives rise to strong electric fields that accelerate the electrons back toward the ions. Upon reaching their original positions the electrons will have kinetic energy equal to the potential energy acquired in their displacement and will consequently overshoot, continuing to oscillate about an equilibrium position until this energy is dissipated. This simple harmonic oscillation is common to all plasmas.

Another important property of a plasma is its electrical conductivity. Because of its large number of free electrons, a gaseous plasma generally offers little resistance to the passage of an electric current. The resistance that does occur arises from the collisions of electrons with each other and with ions. Because the probability of such collisions occurring decreases with increasing electron velocity, the electrical resistance of a plasma decreases at higher temperatures—exactly opposite to the behavior of a metal. This characteristic has profound effects when attempts are made to heat a plasma by passing a current through it. As the plasma gets hotter, there is a proportional decrease in the power input. Thus it is very difficult to raise the temperature of a hydrogen plasma much above 10,000,000 K by this method (called ohmic heating).

Plasmas are also characterized by waves—collective phenomena in which many particles oscillating about their equilibrium positions interact through collisions and fields. Some of the simplest types of waves occur when a magnetic field line is disturbed (see MAGNETOHYDRODYNAMICS). Charge displacements excite electrostatic waves at the plasma frequency discussed earlier. Electromagnetic waves, such as light or microwaves, can propagate through a plasma so long as the wave frequency is higher than the plasma frequency.

Production of Plasmas and their Applications

In the laboratory, most plasmas are produced by applying an electric field to a gas in order to accelerate free electrons. The free electrons are supplied either by an electron-emitting cathode, by photoionization (a process in which a light is used to excite an atom to emit an electron), or by the passage of ionizing cosmic rays. Through collisions these electrons impart energy to the gas atoms, releasing more electrons. When the rate of free-electron production equals or exceeds the rate of electron loss, a plasma is formed.

Plasmas have come to play an important role in processing materials in the semiconductor industry. Ions supplied by plasmas are used to etch surfaces and are deposited in materials to alter their physical properties. Plasmas also have many potential applications, of which the most significant is controlled nuclear FUSION. If certain light nuclei can be held together in a plasma for a sufficient time at high enough temperatures and densities, enormous amounts of energy will be released as light nuclei fuse to form heavier ones.

Plasma thrusters for propulsion in space can eject their propellant at much higher velocities than can chemical rockets, so that less mass need be expended. One type of thruster uses pulsed magnetic fields, while another accelerates the ions through electrostatic lenses and then adds electrons to the beam to maintain overall neutrality.

A potentially important application of plasma physics, and one that has been the subject of much research, involves the direct conversion of thermal energy to electricity without steam turbines or other moving mechanical parts. One such device is the thermionic converter, which consists of a cathode heated by the energy source so that electrons are emitted from its surface; a cooled anode; and an intervening cesium plasma that allows large currents to flow by neutralizing the space charge of the emitted electrons. Another possibility is the magnetohydrodynamic generator. In this device, a plasma is heated by the energy source and allowed to expand through a channel located in a magnetic field perpendicular to the direction of expansion; this produces an electromotive force perpendicular to the directions of both the magnetic field and the expansion. This electromotive force can drive an electric current (the field of which decelerates the plasma) across the plasma, converting part of the plasma's thermal energy of expansion into electricity.

plasmid [plaz'-mid]   Plasmids are small, circular molecules of double-stranded deoxyribonucleic acid (DNA) that exist in the cytoplasm of many bacteria. Plasmids carry genes for several different properties, including resistance to various drugs and chemicals, as well as the ability to synthesize toxins that adversely affect foreign species of bacteria. In some cases, plasmids can be rapidly transferred from cell to cell by means of hairlike structures, called sex pili, that project from the cell surface. The information for synthesis of the pili is carried in the plasmid, but it is not clear how pili actually carry out plasmid transfer. Cell-to-cell plasmid transfer can result in various properties carried on a transmissible plasmid being rapidly disseminated throughout an entire population of bacteria. This property has been responsible for the appearance of various bacterial populations that are resistant to common antibiotics.

Recently, research involving plasmids has been directed toward gene-splicing techniques in the field of GENETIC ENGINEERING. Plasmid DNA is isolated from bacteria, and its circular structure is broken by specific enzymes. A foreign DNA segment is then inserted in the plasmid, and the circle is resealed by other enzymes. This reconstructed plasmid, which contains an extra gene, can be replaced in the bacterial cell. Under the proper conditions the cell will synthesize the product of the foreign gene as well as those coded by its own DNA.

Plasmodium   see MALARIA; SLIME MOLD

plastic surgery   Plastic surgery is the branch of surgery concerned with the correction of physical deformities and disfigurements caused by birth defects, injuries, or disease. It is also known as reconstructive surgery. Examples of such operations include the rebuilding of lost or deformed ears, noses, or jaws; the repair of cleft lip or cleft palate; the reconstruction of a breast after mastectomy; the repair of damage after burns; the correction of birthmarks or scars; and the implantation of material to give a normal appearance to the body where a part was absent at birth—for example, a missing chest muscle.

Transplantation, which includes the grafting of skin, bone, muscle, cartilage, tendons, and nerves, is an important technique in plastic surgery (see also TRANSPLANTATION, ORGAN). The tissue to be transplanted is obtained from the patient whenever possible or from a genetically compatible donor. Cartilage from a rib is often used to reconstruct missing or damaged ears or noses. Bone from a rib or the hip can be used to reconstruct the lower jaw. Transplanted tendons, nerves, and muscles can restore function to a hand that has been damaged by injury.

Skin grafts are used to replace skin that has been destroyed by severe burns (see BURN). The usual procedure, called the split-thickness graft, involves cutting a section from the donor that is sufficiently thick to contain enough living cells to grow on the damaged area. At the same time, enough live dermal tissue is left behind at the donor site for healing to occur. Another skin-grafting technique, called a skin flap or pedicle flap, involves leaving one end of the donor skin attached to its original site—such as a cheek, to cover a nose wound—so that the blood supply is maintained until the area being repaired begins to heal and to establish its own supply of blood.

Another area of plastic surgery, called aesthetic (or cosmetic) surgery, is intended to improve a patient's self-image by correcting a feature that the person finds objectionable although it is not an actual deformity. This kind of surgery also includes minimizing age-related features such as wrinkles.

Common types of aesthetic surgery include rhinoplasty, to reduce the size of a nose; otoplasty, to correct prominent ears; blepharoplasty, to remove drooping skin from around the eyes; rhytidectomy (commonly called a facelift), to tighten skin and remove facial wrinkles; reconstructions of receding or prominent chins; and breast augmentation, using implants to enlarge the breasts. Lipectomy—the removal of adipose tissue (fat) by suction—is used particularly on the abdomen and thighs. Chemical face peeling removes fine wrinkles and minor skin blemishes, and dermabrasion (abrasion of the skin) is employed to remove acne scars. Plastic surgeons also perform hair transplants to correct baldness.

plastics   The plastics are a very large group of synthetic materials whose structures are based on the chemistry of carbon (see ORGANIC CHEMISTRY). Plastics are also called polymers because they are made of extremely long chains of carbon atoms. An important characteristic of plastics is that they can be readily molded into finished products by the application of heat. The group has now become so diverse that some polymers, such as SILICONES, do not conform comfortably to this definition. Since the 1940s many outstanding and indispensable plastics have been developed, and these have been used in a wide range of critical applications, including machine gears, artificial hearts, and bonding cements for such things as aircraft structures.

History

The first synthetic plastic was CELLULOID, a mixture of cellulose nitrate and camphor, invented in 1856 by Alexander Parkes. In 1909 the second synthetic plastic, phenol-formaldehyde (also called Bakelite), was invented by Leo Baekeland when he simply heated a mixture of phenol and formaldehyde. Shortly before World War II a number of synthetic polymers were developed, including casein, NYLON, POLYESTERS, polyvinyl chloride (see VINYL), polystyrene, and polyethylene. Since then the number as well as the types and qualities of plastics have greatly increased, producing superior materials such as epoxies, polycarbonate, TEFLON, silicones, and polysulfones.

Two modern trends in the development of plastic materials are the increased number of foamed plastics—plastics that are imbedded with gas—and the custom designing of plastics to satisfy particular service requirements.

Chemical Structure of Plastics

The bonding properties and chemical versatility of carbon account for the great number of plastics. Although carbon is the backbone of polymer chains, other elements are included, to varying degrees, in the chemical structures of plastics. These include hydrogen, oxygen, nitrogen, chlorine, fluorine, and occasionally other elements, such as sulfur and silicon.

High-molecular-weight polymer molecules are built up by joining together into chains repeating chemical units called monomers. Monomer molecules may be either gases or liquids. In the case of polyethylene the monomer unit is ethylene, C_2H_4, which is obtained from the dehydrogenation of ethane, C_2H_6. With the aid of a catalyst, ethylene molecules attach to each other in a process known as POLYMERIZATION. The lengths of the resulting polymer chains, that is, the average number of monomer units, and the average molecular weight, can be controlled. This is important, because large variations in chain lengths can result in variations in properties. In the case of polyethylene, longer chains create plastics that are harder and stronger, but more difficult to shape. Although polymer chains are, for the most part, linear, they may include side branches. In addition, although chains are often shown as straight lines in diagrams, they actually tend to twist around each other in a random manner.

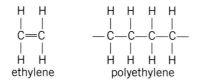

ethylene   polyethylene

Linear polymers such as polyethylene that can be re-

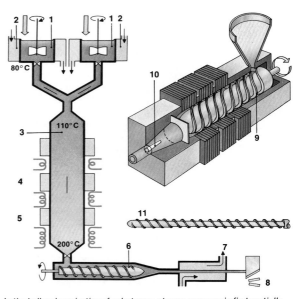

In the bulk polymerization of polystyrene, styrene monomer is first partially polymerized in mixing tanks (1), which are water cooled (2) to remove excess reaction heat. The reaction is then completed in a cylindrical reactor (3). As the reaction mass moves downward, its temperature is controlled by cooling coils (4) and by heating coils (5). The fluid polystyrene product is extruded (6) into a rod shape, which is solidified by water cooling (7) and cut into chips (8). The chips are later formed into various articles by screw extrusion (9) through a die (10). One type of extrusion screw (11) is thicker at the extrusion end to promote compression and melting of the polymer.

peatedly softened or melted by heating are called thermoplastics. Plastics that cannot be softened by heating are called thermosetting plastics or thermosets. For structural reasons, Teflon and a few more complex thermoplastics cannot be softened by heat, and in this respect they resemble thermosets. Thermosets are set or hardened by heat during the molding operation and thereafter cannot be reshaped. Wood is an example of a natural thermoset. In a thermosetting plastic a cross-linking agent joins one linear chain to another, thereby creating a three-dimensional network. Oxygen atoms are the most commonly used cross-linking agents. Because cross-linking reduces the mobility of polymer chains, the thermosets are more brittle than the thermoplastics.

It is not necessary for all the monomer units in a polymer to be identical. Two kinds of monomers may be blended into a polymer chain, as in the case of styrene and butadiene. Such plastics are called copolymers. ABS plastic is a copolymer of the monomers acrylonitrile, butadiene, and styrene. Copolymerization of two or more monomers is analogous to the alloying of two or more metals. Pure polystyrene is brittle, but if a percentage of butadiene monomers is incorporated into the chain of styrene monomers, a high-impact grade of polystyrene results. Polybutadiene is too soft to be used in the tires of vehicles but can be modified with styrene monomers to create a suitable synthetic rubber.

Thermoplastics

Ethylene-Based Plastics. The simplest structure among the many thermoplastics is that of polyethylene. Addition polymerization is the name given to the process in which each ethylene monomer opens up at a double bond and joins to the end of the lengthening chain. The earliest thermoplastics to be developed had the basic structure of polyethylene and were made by addition polymerization. These polymers could be created simply by substituting other atoms or groups of atoms for one or more of the four hydrogen atoms in the ethylene monomer. For example, polyvinyl chloride is made from an ethylene monomer in which one chlorine atom has replaced one hydrogen atom.

Except for the fluorinated polymers and the acrylic polymers, thermoplastics must be protected from destruction caused by ultraviolet radiation. Carbon black provides such protection in polyethylene pipe, but other additives must be used if the product must be white or pigmented.

The consumption of polyethylene exceeds that of any other plastic. This soft, flexible, waxy material is produced in five grades: low density, medium density, high density, ultrahigh molecular weight (UHMW), and irradiated (cross-linked by radiation). It is also made into a flexible foam. The differences in density result from differences in the degree of crystallinity. When the long polymer chains are ordered in a parallel arrangement like the atoms in a metal crystal, the result is a higher density than would be possible in a random or disordered distribution. The branching of polymer chains also leads to lower densities. Although low-density polyethylene has the highest vapor transmission rate, it is the least expensive of the five grades and is used as a vapor barrier in buildings. High-density polyethylene is used in blown bottles and pipes. The UHMW grade is a harder, stronger material.

Polypropylene is hard and strong, and has a higher useful temperature range than polyethylene, polyvinyl chloride, and polystyrene. It is highly crystalline. At low temperatures it becomes brittle, but this is overcome by copolymerization with ethylene or other monomers.

Polymethyl methacrylate (PMMA), also called acrylic, is known by its trade names Lucite and Plexiglass. Its monomer contains a complex side group, which prevents crystallization. PMMA has outstanding resistance to outdoor environments, including ultraviolet radiation. It has excellent optical properties and unlimited coloring possibilities. It is also harder and stronger than the plastics previously mentioned, although it is brittle. PMMA is familiar in lighting fixtures, outdoor signs, aircraft windows, and automobile taillights.

The fluorocarbon group consists of several polymers, all containing fluorine. The presence of fluorine makes these polymers nonflammable. The carbon-fluorine bond is extremely stable and provides chemical and heat stability and low surface tension, thus leading to low friction and nonwetting, nonstaining, nonsticking properties. New resins called Teflon AFs are also amorphous, enhancing their physical properties and making them of potential great usefulness in optical and electronic circuits for computers and instruments.

Polyvinyl chloride (PVC) is a stiff plastic made soft and flexible by adding plasticizers. It is used as shower curtains, hoses, and electrical insulation. Polystyrene is a clear, hard, brittle plastic that is easily damaged by many solvents.

Engineering Plastics. The so-called engineering plastics, those with superior properties that make them suited to such applications as machine parts, do not have the straight carbon chain. The first of these to be developed were the nylons, a group of polymers that incorporate nitrogen into the chain along with carbon. The nylons are crystalline, strong, abrasion resistant, and white in color. Their property of low friction accounts for their employment in such machine parts as noiseless small gears, bearings, slides, rollers, and aerosol valves.

Although the incorporation of the phenyl ring as a side attachment to the polymer chain in polystyrene results in no favorable properties, the incorporation of a phenyl ring into the chain itself produces dramatic results. In polycarbonates the incorporation of the phenyl ring in the chain leads to properties of transparency, heat resistance, flame resistance, dimensional stability, and remarkable toughness. Polycarbonates have been used as vandal-proof glazing and in hard hats, nails, screws, and power-tool housings. The sulfone plastics are similar to polycarbonate, with phenyl rings as well as sulfur atoms in the chain. They too are tough, and resistant to heat and flame. They are commonly used in the housings of smoke detectors attached to ceilings. Poor resistance to sunlight confines them to indoor applications.

Thermosets

The thermosets, such as wood, wool, Bakelite, epoxy, polyurethane, and paints, cannot be softened following polymerization and cross-linking. Because the thermosets do not offer the wide range of properties found in the thermoplastics, fewer thermosets are in use. In general, they are harder and more brittle than thermoplastics.

The polymerization of a thermoset is a more complex chemical process than the addition polymerization of a thermoplastic. It frequently proceeds by the process called condensation polymerization, in which a compound reacts with itself or another compound and in the reaction releases, or "condenses" some small molecule such as water. In the case of phenol-formaldehyde (Bakelite), phenol and formaldehyde molecules attach to each other in an alternating-chain fashion, releasing water molecules in the process.

It was noted above that cross-linking reduces the freedom of movement of polymer chains under stress, resulting in brittleness. Rubbers, however, though cross-linked, are not brittle even though they are thermosets. Common cross-linking agents include sulfur for rubbers, styrene for polyesters, and oxygen for linseed oil and many paints and varnishes. Polymer paints are obtained in the thermoplastic condition. After paint is brushed onto a surface, it cross-links by means of oxygen in the air or other agents, be-

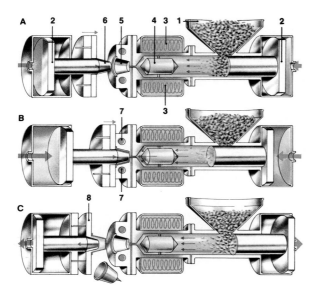

A machine (A) for injection molding thermoplastic resins consists of a feed hopper (1), hydraulic pistons (2), electric heating coils (3), a double-coned cylinder known as a torpedo (4), a fixed mold (5), and a movable mold (6). In molding a cup (B), plastic pellets are poured through the hopper into the machine chamber and forced by the piston around the torpedo, the purpose of which is to ensure uniform melting. The melted plastic flows into the closed mold, and water is circulated through cooling coils (7) to solidify the resin. The mold is opened (C), and an ejection plate (8) pushes out the finished cup.

coming thermosetting and brittle. To counter shrinkage that occurs during molding and to improve properties such as impact resistance and tensile strength, thermosets are usually compounded with fillers such as wood flour, minerals, or glass fiber. The epoxies undergo very little shrinkage, however, and are rarely compounded with fillers.

Phenol-formaldehyde is commonly used in pot handles, bottle caps, wall switches, and other electrical hardware and as a plywood adhesive. It is available only in black and brown colors. When a differently colored formaldehyde is needed, as in countertops and tabletops, urea-formaldehyde or melamine-formaldehyde are commonly chosen. Urea-formaldehyde is not suited to outdoor exposure, however.

The superior properties of the epoxy thermosets are in part accounted for by oxygen atoms and carbon rings in the polymer chains. Epoxies are usually supplied as two components to be mixed and set. These are strong, corrosion-resistant materials that adhere well to most materials, including metals. Their low shrinkage and high strength make them the preferred filler-adhesive in demanding applications such as aircraft structures.

Polyesters are thermosetting plastics familiar as fiberglass-reinforced materials in boats, fishing rods, and furniture. There are also thermoplastic polyesters. Polyesters are synthesized in a wide range of reactions involving complex organic acids and alcohols. By suitable selection

of the acid and alcohol, specific properties such as flexibility and heat resistance can be obtained. Styrene is commonly used as a cross-linking agent for polyesters; methyl methacrylate is used when improved color and weatherability are needed. Because neither heat nor pressure is required for the production of polyesters, there is almost no limit to the size of the part that may be produced. With glass as a reinforcement, polyesters can be created with strengths equal to those of metals.

Composites

Most plastics are manufactured as composite materials: fiberglass-reinforced polyester; phenol-formaldehyde compounded with wood flour to reduce mold shrinkage; polyvinyl chloride floor tile with clay filler to reduce moisture absorption and improve surface gloss; polyethylene compounded with carbon black for ultraviolet protection; epoxies filled with aluminum for ease of machining; plastic foams, which are composites of plastic and gas cells. These examples indicate the wide range of advantages that filler materials give to plastics.

To obtain strength in a plastic comparable to that of metals, reinforcing fibers must be used. The strength of the reinforced composite is proportional to the weight percentage of the reinforcing fiber. Strength is also influenced by the orientation of the fibers.

Foams

The first of the foamed plastics to be developed was polystyrene (styrofoam). It is commonly used as building insulation and in flotation devices. Polystyrene foams are either extruded with a blowing agent or created in a mold by using expandable beads. The latter method is used to make the familiar white coffee cup. Like solid polystyrene, the foam version is low in cost, brittle, and attacked by solvents and ultraviolet radiation.

Although most plastics have been foamed, only polystyrene, ABS, polyethylene, polyvinyl chloride, urea-formaldehyde, and polyurethane have found extensive applications. These foams have three principal uses: thermal insulation, cushioning materials, and structural materials. Insulating foams must be of low density, whereas structural foams must have high density to obtain strength and hardness.

See also: EPOXY RESINS; MATERIALS TECHNOLOGY; PETROCHEMICALS; RESIN.

Plata, Río de la   see RÍO DE LA PLATA

Plataea [pluh-tee'-uh]   Plataea was an ancient Greek city in southern Boeotia; it allied with Athens from about 519 BC to resist efforts by Thebes to force it into the Boeotian league. During the PERSIAN WARS the Plataeans came to the aid of Athens and fought (490) at Marathon. The city was later the site of the great victory of the Greeks under ARISTIDES and PAUSANIAS over the Persian forces in 479. Plataea was besieged and sacked (429–427) by the Spartan alliance in the PELOPONNESIAN WAR and destroyed by Thebes in 373. The Macedonian kings Philip II and Alexander the Great rebuilt the city.

plate tectonics Plate tectonics is an all-embracing concept that has revolutionized the Earth sciences in the 20th century. It posits that the LITHOSPHERE, or outermost shell of the Earth, is divided into a number of rigid plates that float and drift on a viscous underlayer in the mantle. The generation of new crust between diverging plates accounts for the relative recency of the world's ocean basins, and collision of converging plates explains the formation of the world's mountain belts.

The Plates

Six major plates and a host of smaller ones have been distinguished. The Alpine fold belt extending from Gibraltar to the Middle East is made up of many miniplates. Plates are either solely oceanic (for example, Cocos and Nazca), solely continental (for example, Iranian), or both (for example, North American). In the case of North America, new oceanic crust has been welded onto older continental crust. Thus the margins of some continents, such as the western side of South America, are occupied by an active compressional plate boundary, whereas other continental margins, such as the western side of Africa, lie within a plate and are tectonically passive.

The plates consist of lithosphere, which includes oceanic and continental crust plus the upper part of the mantle. They are about 70 to 80 km (40 to 50 mi) thick under the oceans and about 100 to 150 km (60 to 90 mi) thick under the continents.

Most of the world's earthquakes occur along plate boundaries. Three types of boundary have been distinguished: MID-OCEANIC RIDGES, along which new oceanic lithosphere is created; convergent zones, such as OCEANIC TRENCHES (where one plate is bent under or subducted beneath another and consumed) or sutures (where two continental plates have collided); and TRANSFORM FAULTS, where two plates slide passively past each other, and crust is neither created nor destroyed.

Continental Rifting

At the inception of the plate-tectonic scheme of events, the continental crust splits into a series of rifts and grabens (see HORST AND GRABEN). First, a domal uplift forms (probably because of mineral changes in the Earth's mantle) and, ideally, three RIFT VALLEYS develop that symmetrically meet at the center of the dome. Such domes and rift valleys are clearly seen today in Africa, especially in the northeast where the Ethiopian Rift meets the Red Sea and the Gulf of Aden (both of these have opened into narrow seas) at the triple junction at Afar. The three rifts may all widen and become narrow seas that will eventually grow into an ocean as wide as the Atlantic. Alternatively, it is common for only two rifts to develop into oceans, the third being left as a failed rift arm extending into the continent. Examples of rifts that failed to become oceans are the East African Rift System, the Midland Valley of Scotland, and Scandinavia's Oslo Graben. If the ocean reaches a mature stage, it may begin to contract by subduction, and eventually the subduction zone bordered by a continent may collide with the original continental margin, leaving the failed rift as a sediment-filled trough that intersects a mountain belt.

Rifts such as these are sites of marked heat flow and magma injection, phenomena that commonly give rise to VOLCANOES and dikes of basic igneous rock. After a rift has evolved into an ocean, some of the early lavas and dikes may be preserved on the facing continental coasts. For example, Triassic rifts filled with continental sediments and volcanic rocks occur along the eastern coast of the United States, and Early Jurassic, basic-dike swarms occur parallel to the coast in southwestern Greenland and Liberia. All of these examples date from the incipient stage of the development of the Atlantic Ocean.

Ocean Opening and Closure

The way in which two plates move apart and a new ocean is created can be demonstrated by the structure and mode of evolution of the oceanic crust on either side of a mid-oceanic ridge. Seafloor spreading takes place when magma wells up from the upper mantle and forms a new ocean-floor layer at such a ridge. Seafloor spreading takes place symmetrically, with the result that older lavas with

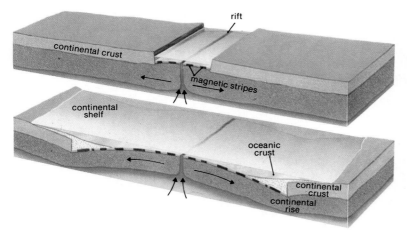

(Top) *Tensional forces may tear apart a continent and develop a rift through which molten lava from the mantle can rise. As the magma pours out on both sides of the rift and hardens, it pushes apart the two parts of the fractured continent and forms a new ocean basin. As it hardens, the lava takes on the Earth's prevailing magnetic polarity. Because the field reverses at intervals, lava stripes of alternating polarity form over long periods of time. (Bottom) As seafloor spreading continues in an old ocean basin, the abutting edges of the continental crust and oceanic crust continuously subside. The sinking results from the weight of sediments transported by inland streams to the continental margin and deposited along the continental shelf and continental rise. The boundary between the continental and oceanic crusts is eventually concealed by the deep deposits of accumulated sediment.*

a recognizable magnetic polarity are carried away equal distances on each side of the ridge, and a symmetrical pattern of magnetic stripes is created about the ridge axis (see PALEOMAGNETISM). Thus the ocean crust contains a magnetic record of its own formation. These magnetic patterns demonstrate that the ocean floors of the world have all been created since the Early Jurassic, less than 190 million years ago. Formation of the ocean basins in this manner requires that the continents move apart to accommodate creation of new oceanic crust.

The world's oceans are in different stages of opening and closure. The Red Sea is in a narrow, embryonic stage. The Atlantic Ocean is still spreading on both sides. The Indian Ocean is opening on the west but subducting on the east side. The Pacific Ocean is being subducted on both sides and will probably disappear as Asia collides with the Americas.

The rate of plate movement away from a mid-oceanic ridge, which is half of the rate at which an ocean expands, varies from 1 cm/yr (0.4 in/yr) in the North Atlantic and the Red Sea to 4.4 cm/yr (1.7 in/yr) in the East Pacific.

Continental Drift

In addition to seafloor-spreading data, much geologic and geophysical evidence from continental rocks corroborates the CONTINENTAL DRIFT theory—that the present-day continents, originally part of a single supercontinent, separated and drifted aboard lithospheric plates to their present positions. Paleomagnetism provides a major quantitative confirmation of continental drift. By carefully measuring the declination and inclination of the magnetic field built into oriented rock samples when they formed, geologists can calculate the paleolatitude of the rocks and the location of the paleopole at a given time. The paleolatitudes can be used in the construction of paleographic maps, and the paleopoles in the construction of apparent POLAR WANDERING paths.

If the paleopole positions are determined for a sequence of North American rocks of different ages ranging from the Early Mesozoic to the present, these positions can be plotted on a map to define a polar-wandering curve for that continent. When the paleopoles of rocks from Europe of a similar age range are also calculated and plotted, the two separate curves clearly converge on the present pole. This convergence strongly suggests that the polar-wandering paths do not represent a true wandering of the poles but rather the drift of the two continents.

Paleogeographical maps have now been constructed for all the continents for all the periods of the Phanerozoic Eon by using a combination of paleomagnetic, geometric-fit, and oceanic-magnetic data. These maps demonstrate how widely dispersed the continents were during the Cambrian Period, gradually moving together during the Paleozoic Era and colliding to form mountain belts, and eventually forming the Pangea supercontinent during the Permian and Triassic periods, then drifting during the Mesozoic and Cenozoic eras (see PALEOGEOGRAPHY).

Mountain Building

Mountain building, or orogeny, results from the conver-

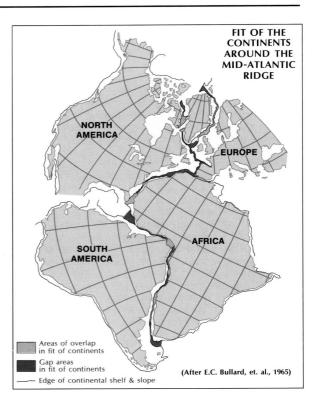

FIT OF THE CONTINENTS AROUND THE MID-ATLANTIC RIDGE

NORTH AMERICA

EUROPE

SOUTH AMERICA

AFRICA

Areas of overlap in fit of continents

Gap areas in fit of continents

—— Edge of continental shelf & slope

(After E.C. Bullard, et. al., 1965)

During the early 1960s several Cambridge University scientists led by Sir Edward Bullard determined by use of computer techniques that the continental edges on opposite sides of the Atlantic Ocean could be fitted together along the continental slope. Except for a few small gaps and overlapping areas, the fit was nearly perfect.

gence and collision of two plates. The three basic types of plate interaction are oceanic-oceanic, oceanic-continental, and continental-continental. These three types can be regarded, in essence, as a progressive developmental sequence.

Island Arcs. The island arc represents the incipient stage (oceanic-oceanic plate interaction) in mountain building. The inner wall of the oceanic trench contains a complex zone where wedges of a mélange of oceanic crust are thrust under older rocks so that the youngest material continually occupies the base of the tectonic pile. This underplating tends to raise the evolving arc margin. High-pressure–low-temperature metamorphism in this zone causes the formation of glaucophane (a sodic amphibole) and a rock called eclogite. Otherwise, the arc-trench gap is the site of deposition of flat-lying, shallow-water, shoreline sediments.

The arc is characterized by three features. First, intense volcanic activity is caused by magmas derived from the melting of the subducted lithospheric slab. Young arcs, such as the Tonga and the South Sandwich, have tholeiitic BASALTS; more mature arcs such as Japan, the

Aleutians, and Indonesia have more highly evolved calc-alkaline ANDESITES. Second, volcanic tuffs, ash flows, and turbidites are deposited in intraarc basins. Third, low-pressure–high-temperature metamorphism occurs; it is related to the high heat flow and the rise of magma deep in the arc, where GRANITES may be intruded. The high-pressure–low-temperature and low-pressure–high-temperature belts of metamorphism make up paired belts.

Behind the arc, a small basin—floored by oceanic crust that has formed by a process of seafloor spreading roughly analogous to that which created the main oceanic crust—often develops. Extension in the back-arc basin separates the growing arc from a formerly adjoining arc or continent. Examples are the Sea of Japan, the Aleutian basin, and the Tasman Sea.

Cordilleran Mountain Belts. The next stage in mountain building is represented by Cordilleran mountain belts, which are caused by subduction of an oceanic plate beneath a continental plate. Much of what can be said about island arcs also applies to the Cordilleran mountain belts, because both are developed at subducting plate margins. For example, they both ideally have a trench, an arc-trench gap, an arc and back-arc basin structure, paired metamorphic belts, underthrusting in the trench, and andesitic volcanism in the arc.

The development of a Cordilleran mountain belt on a subducting continental margin, such as the Pacific margin extending from Alaska to Chile, can be superimposed on an Atlantic-type trailing continental margin. A classic modern example of the latter extends along the eastern United States, where two main tectonic environments are present. The Bahama Banks represents a shallow-water carbonate succession developed on the continental shelf; to its east, a deepwater sequence, consisting of shales and of graywackes deposited by turbidity currents, has developed on the continental rise. Such an Atlantic-type continental margin can become a Cordilleran-type margin if the oceanic crust-mantle breaks or decouples from the continental rocks and begins to descend beneath the continental rise.

A trench develops at the mouth of the subduction zone as oceanic material is underthrusted to form mélanges. After the downgoing slab reaches depths of 100 to 150 km (60 to 90 mi), magmas released by partial melting well up and are either extruded as lavas in the arc (for example, the andesites of Oregon) or intruded as granitic batholiths (as in the Sierra Nevada, Southern California, and Peruvian batholiths). The heated arc core expands and rises with appropriate low-pressure metamorphism and at a high level becomes the site of erosion and an axis of sedimentary transport. Flysch sediments are transported on one side over the arc-trench gap toward the trench and on the other toward the continent into the back-arc trough that develops from the sagging continental shelf. Gradually the arc rocks are thrust toward the continent over the back-arc trough, which is eventually filled with postorogenic sandstones and conglomerates.

Collisional Mountain Belts. The final stage in the plate-tectonic scenario occurs when an oceanic plate is totally consumed by subduction. Two continental plates collide to give rise to a new collisional mountain belt that will probably be superimposed on a Cordilleran-type belt. The prime example is the Himalayas, caused by the northward drift and collision of India against Asia. The formation of the Alpine fold system extending from Gibraltar to the Middle East is in general attributed to the collision of Africa with Europe and the destruction of the intervening Tethyan oceanic plate. The fold belt consists of a large number of small plates that have shuffled about with respect to each other, many colliding and giving rise to narrow collisional mountain belts, such as the French, Swiss, Austrian, and Dinaric alps; the Apennines; the Taurus Mountains; and the Zagros Mountains.

A mountain belt that marks the collision of two plates may contain a zone of complex thrusts and nappes, the formation of which tends to thicken the evolving continental crust as splinters of one plate are stacked above those of another. Such stacking is clearly seen in the Swiss Alps.

The northward movement of India into Asia is an example of indentation tectonics, analogous to driving a wedge into a sheet of plastic. The effects of stress release, which can be modeled, are seen not only in the thrust sheets of the collisional mountain belt but also in transcurrent faults that occur widely throughout China and southern Siberia more than 3,000 km (1,900 mi) north of the Himalayas.

Mineral Deposits

During the evolution of new oceanic plates and mountain belts by plate tectonics, a large number of mineral deposits with vast accumulations of minerals form, particularly in association with plate boundaries. Many of these deposits may be economic for mining purposes (see ORE DEPOSITS). Specific types are diagnostic of different plate regimes.

The Oceanic Crust. Sediments from certain areas of seafloor spreading, such as the East Pacific Rise and the Red Sea contain high enrichments of iron and manganese (see OCEANIC MINERAL RESOURCES). Similar metal-enriched sediments occur in remnants of oceanic crust called ophiolites. Copper ores occur in or above the basaltic pillow lavas in ophiolites in Cyprus, Turkey, and the Philippines. Chromite deposits are common in the lower, serpentinized, ultramafic rocks of many ophiolites in Turkey, Greece, and Yugoslavia. Similar deposits are likely to be found on mid-oceanic ridges and in marginal basins.

Island Arcs and Cordilleran Mountain Belts. The new magmas that are generated by partial melting of a subducting lithospheric plate arise in the main arc of Cordilleran mountain belts and island arcs. Fractional crystallization of these magmas gives rise to volcanic and plutonic rocks and associated ore deposits. The lavas and granitic rocks change systematically in composition on passing inland from the trench, and the mineral deposits also have a zonal distribution. A general sequence (passing inland from the trench) of iron, gold, copper, molybdenum, gold, lead, zinc, tin, tungsten, antimony, and mercury occurs across the American Cordilleran margin and the arcs of the western Pacific.

Collisional Mountain Belts. Little is known about the

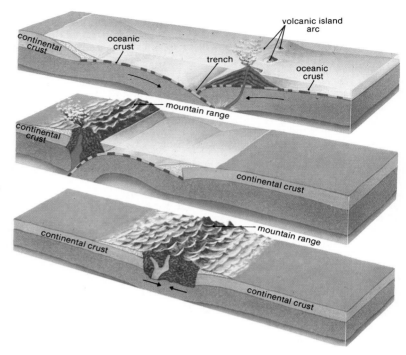

(Top) *When two moving oceanic plates converge, a trench is created where one plate is pushed down, or subducted, under the other plate and is absorbed into the Earth's mantle. Such trenches are often associated with the ocean side of island arcs, or chains of islands, such as the Aleutians or the islands of Japan. Intense volcanic activity and earthquakes occur in the subduction zones as a result of the plates' grinding past each other. (Center) In the convergence, or collision, of an oceanic plate with a continental plate, the thinner oceanic plate generally plunges under the thicker continental plate along a line of subduction marked by an oceanic trench. The impact often folds and uplifts the edge of the continental land-mass into a mountain range. The Andes Moun-tains, for example, were pushed up by a collision of the Nazca oceanic plate with the South American plate. (Bottom) Continents cannot be subducted into trenches because they are lighter than the mantle and float on it. The result is that the collision of two lithospheric continental plates create major mountain systems. Thus the collision of India with Asia millions of years ago thrust up the Himalayan Mountains as India underthrust Asia. The Alps were formed when Africa collided with Europe and lifted part of the overriding Eurasia plate.*

mineralization of collisional mountain belts. Having been through a stage involving subduction of an oceanic plate, these belts should contain many of the Cordilleran-type ore deposits, such as, in particular, all the types of ores found in ophiolite complexes like those in the Indus su-ture of the Himalayas and in the eastern Mediterranean. Tin is widely thought to occur in granites derived directly by the continental collision process; an example may be the Permian tin ores associated with the granites of Corn-wall in England.

The Driving Mechanism

Although the relative distribution of rocks and structures with regard to plate boundaries is increasingly well un-derstood, the underlying driving force responsible for the motion of plates is still the subject of debate.

The most favored hypothesis is based on two consid-erations. First, more than 50 percent of the heat escaping from the Earth's interior does so via plate boundaries (see EARTH, HEAT FLOW IN). Thermal energy derived at depth by the decay of radioactive materials is thus probably one fundamental driving force. Second, seafloor spreading and continental drift can best be explained by the action of convection currents operating in the uppermost 500 km (300 mi) of the mantle. The basic idea is that hot, partially molten materials well up beneath the early rifts and the developing mid-oceanic ridges. The mantle ma-terials are carried by convective currents horizontally away from the ridges. The materials gradually cool and become denser as they pass toward the continents, where they

sink back into the deeper mantle below subduction zones. Recent seismic studies of the mantle, however, somewhat complicate this picture by suggesting that such heat flow may be confined to the upper mantle.

Undoubtedly, many other variables affect or assist the process. Oceanic crust, for example, is denser than conti-nental crust—a density difference that would facilitate the sinking of the subducted plate. Computer and experi-mental models corroborate the convection-cell hypothesis.

History of the Concept

The concept of plate tectonics has evolved over a period of many years. Early geological ideas were qualitative and speculative and were not widely accepted, but geophysi-cal data obtained from the ocean floor in the 1950s and '60s enabled construction of a quantitative model that has since emerged as the main conceptual framework for the Earth sciences.

The ideas of continental drift, seafloor spreading, and plate tectonics developed sequentially. The first major protagonist of continental drift was Alfred WEGENER, who suggested as early as 1912 that one supercontinent, called Pangea, had broken up during the Early Mesozoic and that the separate continents had then drifted to their present positions. He collated evidence to support his theory, such as the similarity of fossil fauna and flora in different continents and the continuity of geological structures and paleoclimatic belts.

Similar geological correlations between South America and Africa were advanced (1927 and 1937) by Alexander

L. du Toit, who suggested the existence of two supercontinents—Laurasia in the north and Gondwanaland in the south—separated by the long-vanished Tethys Sea. In 1929, Arthur HOLMES envisaged that subcrustal convection currents were dragging two continents apart with consequent mountain building at the margin of a trench. Apparent confirmation of continental drift came in 1956, when Stanley Keith Runcorn and his colleagues established that the polar-wandering paths for North America and Europe diverge progressively from the present to the Triassic.

Beginning in the late 1950s, oceanographers began to discover magnetic anomaly stripes in the ocean floor; the significance of these features, however, was not initially understood. The first major breakthrough came in 1960, when H. H. HESS suggested that new ocean floor was created at the mid-oceanic ridges and that the ocean evolved by seafloor spreading. The second came in 1963, when D. H. Matthews, F. J. Vine, and Lawrence Whitaker Morley proposed that the alternating magnetic anomalies in the ocean floor were caused by regular reversals in the Earth's magnetic field. Such geomagnetic reversals were previously known only in continental rocks. A further advance came in 1965, when J. Tuzo Wilson advocated the transform-fault mechanism to explain how oceanic plates slide laterally past each other.

The concept of plate tectonics came to fruition by 1970. The tectonic plates of the world were tentatively defined, along with their relative directions of movement and the rates of extension and compression at their boundaries. Major earthquake zones were correlated with the boundaries, and schematic models were developed for the evolution of island arcs, Cordilleran mountain belts, and Himalayan belts. The foundations of such mountain building were located at subducting and collisional plate boundaries.

Although plate tectonics remained somewhat controversial for a number of years, by the 1980s the actual movement of plates had been recorded by means of very long baseline interferometry (see RADIO ASTRONOMY). Mechanisms of plate movement remain a subject of intense geophysical research, however, and the continental-drift aspect of plate movement continues to be controversial. Some researchers, for example, point out that studies indicating the depth of continental roots in the mantle rule out any simple linkage between plate activity and the actual form and movement of the continental bodies.

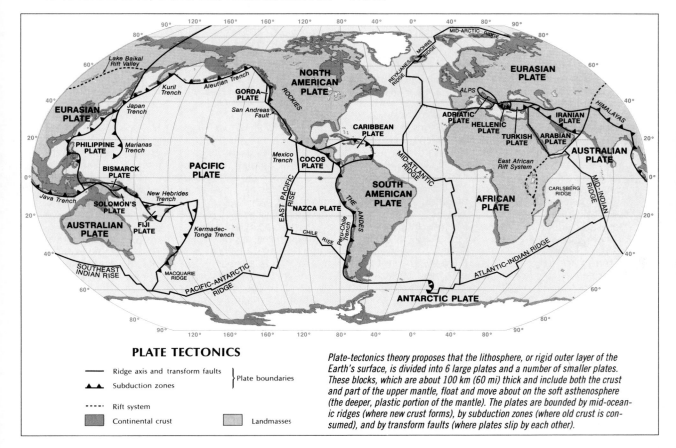

PLATE TECTONICS

— Ridge axis and transform faults } Plate boundaries

▲▲ Subduction zones

---- Rift system

Continental crust

Landmasses

Plate-tectonics theory proposes that the lithosphere, or rigid outer layer of the Earth's surface, is divided into 6 large plates and a number of smaller plates. These blocks, which are about 100 km (60 mi) thick and include both the crust and part of the upper mantle, float and move about on the soft asthenosphere (the deeper, plastic portion of the mantle). The plates are bounded by mid-oceanic ridges (where new crust forms), by subduction zones (where old crust is consumed), and by transform faults (where plates slip by each other).

plateau   A plateau is a tableland, an uplifted area of comparatively level land. It is characteristically underlain by essentially horizontal rock layers, either sediments or lava flows. With continued erosion such areas become deeply dissected by river valleys. In arid areas, this may isolate large, uneroded tracts (mesas) or leave smaller, isolated hills called buttes.

platemaking   A printing plate is made of a metal, plastic, or rubber material upon which an ink-receptive image is etched or engraved. Positioned in a printing press, the plate receives ink from an ink roller system and transfers the image to paper.

Toward the end of the 19th century the perfection of photomechanical imaging techniques made it possible to convert virtually any text or image into a form suitable for one of the three main printing processes—letterpress, gravure, or offset lithography. Each requires a different kind of plate.

Letterpress. On the LETTERPRESS plate, the image to be printed is raised above the nonprinting areas. Once the dominant printing process, letterpress printing gave rise to a huge PHOTOENGRAVING industry. In its simplest form, a photoengraving is a thin metal plate coated with a photosensitive material called a resist and exposed to light through a film negative of the image to be engraved. The resist becomes hard and insoluble where light hits it, while the nonimage area, protected from the light, can be washed away, exposing the bare metal. The plate, with its image area protected by the resist, is placed in an etching bath where the bare metal portions of the plate are eaten away, leaving the image area standing in relief. Mounted on a wood, metal, or magnetic base to bring it up to the level of the letterpress type, the plate is ready to run on a press. (See also ELECTROTYPE; STEREOTYPE.)

Halftones. With the exception of gravure presses, most printing presses lay down a film of ink that is uniform in thickness and in density of color. The printed reproduction of a continuous tone image—one that, as in a photograph, has a range of light and dark values—is created by patterns of minute dots too small for the human eye to resolve individually, but which together appear as tonal gradations. Dot patterns are created using a special halftone screen of clear glass or plastic, closely ruled with two sets of opaque lines at right angles to each other. These dots are reproduced on a film negative of the original. The negative, in turn, is exposed to a sensitized plate to form a positive halftone printing image.

Gravure. The gravure press uses plates whose image areas are etched or engraved below the plate surface. The image area is broken up into minute ink-holding cells of varying depth or area. In printing, the gravure plate is covered with ink. Excess ink is wiped from the plate surface by a "doctor blade," leaving ink only in the cells.

To make a gravure plate, a photosensitive resist material is exposed to a cross-ruled screen that controls the uniformity of cell size, and to a continuous-tone photographic positive of the image, which controls cell depth.

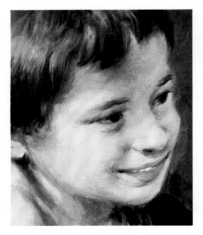

This reproduction (left) *of* A Peasant Boy, *by the Spanish artist Bartolomé Murillo, was made by four-color lithographic printing. The enlargement* (above) *shows how the four colors were combined in a dot pattern to obtain the final tones.*

(Below) *In the four-color photolithographic process for printing full-color illustrations, four separate plates are used to print yellow, magenta, cyan, and black images over one another in sequence. The images on each plate are produced by a photographic etching process in a specific dot pattern. The dot pattern is set at a different angle for each color to obtain a sharper color reproduction.*

The resist is developed and affixed to a copper-coated cylinder, which is then bathed in an etching solution, reproducing the image in the copper surface. In conventional ROTOGRAVURE, only the cell depth varies. In halftone gravure, achieved by exposing the resist to a halftone screen positive, the cell area varies, while the depth remains constant. High-quality gravure printing uses a hybrid process in which cells that vary in both area and depth are produced.

With the perfection of computer-controlled optical scanning and engraving devices, an electronic scanner analyzes an original image and converts it into signals that are transmitted to a diamond stylus, which engraves up to 4,000 cells per second on a copper cylinder.

Offset Lithography. More than any other kind of image carrier, a lithographic plate—on which image and nonimage areas are on the same plane—depends on the achievement of precise chemical balances, both during its preparation and while it is on press. The image areas must be made ink-attracting, while the nonimage areas must repel ink. The offset plate is made of a base material—aluminum, stainless steel, or, for very short runs, paper—coated with a photoreactive substance. After exposure, the plate is developed and then treated to enhance its ink-attracting or water-repelling properties. For extremely long print runs, bimetal plates are sometimes used: typically, copper forms the image area, while aluminum or chromium is used for nonimage areas. (See OFFSET LITHOGRAPHY.)

Color Separation. Any color in an original colored image can be reproduced by creating a specific halftone dot pattern from three different ink colors, cyan, magenta, and yellow. A fourth color, black, is used to intensify shadow areas and to help print greys. Each of the four colors requires its own printing plate. A set of separation negatives is prepared by photographing the original color image through a halftone screen and, successively, through red, green, and blue filters. Plates are then prepared from the four separation negatives.

Most separations are now made on color scanners. The original image, or a positive transparency of it, is placed on a drum, and a laser light beam moves rapidly back and forth over it. The reflected (or, in the case of a transparency, transmitted) light is divided into three separate beams that pass through red, green, and blue filters, activating extremely sensitive photocells. Laser light generators automatically expose a set of separation negatives by emitting precisely controlled bursts of light.

plateosaurus [plat-ee-uh-sohr'-uhs]   The best-known dinosaur of the infraorder Prosauropoda (suborder Theropoda, order Saurischia) is *Plateosaurus*, which is widely viewed as the archetypal prosauropod. The prosauropods were the ancestors of the gigantic sauropods, such as *Apatosaurus* (*Brontosaurus*) and *Diplodocus*, of the following Jurassic Period. The *Plateosaurus* is known from

The Plateosaurus, *which flourished about 200 million years ago, was among the earliest large-sized dinosaurs. It may have been an ancestor of such later giant sauropods as* Brontosaurus *and* Diplodocus.

dozens of European specimens from the Late Triassic Period, about 200 million years ago. Its teeth and its heavy-bodied shape and stout limbs indicate that, like most other prosauropods, it was essentially herbivorous, but it may have occasionally supplemented its diet with animal food. Its forelegs, although much smaller than the hind legs, were still relatively large and heavy, with broad forefeet that were somewhat modified for grasping; it was apparently capable of moving either on all fours or on its hind legs. The *Plateosaurus* measured more than 6 m (20 ft) long, was about 5 m (16.5 ft) high when standing erect, and weighed perhaps 1,000 kg (2,200 lb); it was the largest reptile of the Triassic Period.

platform tennis   Platform tennis is a racquet-and-ball game, usually for doubles competition, that is particularly popular in the northeastern United States. The game is derived from lawn tennis and PADDLE TENNIS and takes most of its rules from those games. Like tennis, 6 games win a set and 2 out of 3 sets win a match. Only one serve per point is allowed, however.

The game is played on a wood surface that is 60 ft (18.3 m) long and 30 ft (9.1 m) wide, stands above the ground on supports, and is completely enclosed by a steel mesh fence 12 ft (3.7 m) high. A net divides the court. The oval racquets used are slightly larger than table-tennis racquets, and the official ball is bright yellow in color, 2.5 in. (6.4 cm) in diameter, and made of sponge rubber. The major factor in platform tennis is the fence, and the proper play of balls that rebound from it must be mastered in order to progress in the game.

Plath, Sylvia [plath]   One of the finest American poets of her generation, Sylvia Plath, b. Boston, Oct. 27, 1932, d. Feb. 11, 1963, achieved technical mastery in her first volume of verse, *Colossus* (1960), but it was only after the publication of *Ariel* (1965), two years following her suicide, that she became the most celebrated poet of her generation and assumed the status of a cult figure. Two other posthumous collections, *Crossing the Water* (1971) and *Winter Trees* (1971), also show Plath's control of sound and rhythm, as well as her remarkably sharp, sometimes savage, imagery. Her semiautobiographical novel, *The Bell Jar* (1963), is an account of a young woman's mental breakdown. Plath's reputation is based on intense descriptions of extreme states of mind whose violence has led to the assumption that she was a martyr to her own creative introspection.

platinum   Platinum is a silvery metallic chemical element, a member of the six TRANSITION ELEMENTS in Group VIII of the periodic table known collectively as the platinum metals (ruthenium, rhodium, palladium, osmium, iridium, and platinum). Platinum's symbol is Pt, its atomic number is 78, and its atomic weight is 195.09. The name is derived from the Spanish *plata*, meaning "silver." The element was discovered in South America independently by Antonio de Ulloa in 1735 and by N. Wood in 1741, but it had been used earlier by Indians.

Occurrence. The platinum metals are extremely rare elements; platinum is the most common, with an abundance in the Earth's crust of about a millionth of 1 percent, whereas the others of the group have abundances of about one ten-millionth of 1 percent. Platinum occurs in nature as the pure metal and also in alloys with other metals of the group, principally in the alluvial deposits of the Ural Mountains, of Columbia, and of some parts of the western United States. In addition, the element occurs in the mineral sperrylite ($PtAs_2$) and in the nickel ores of Ontario in Canada. The large-scale production of nickel makes it feasible to recover the small amounts of platinum in the ore (only 1 part of platinum to 2 million parts of ore). The recovery of the individual platinum metals from the natural alloys is a complex process that depends on the distinct properties of the individual elements.

Properties. Platinum is an attractive silvery white metal with a melting point of 1,774° C, a boiling point of 3,827° C, and a density of 21.45 g/cm^3 at room temperature. It has a coefficient of thermal expansion close to that of soda-lime-silica glass and is consequently used to make sealed electrodes in soft-glass systems.

Platinum is chemically inert and will not oxidize in air at any temperature. It is resistant to acids and is not attacked by any single mineral acid but dissolves readily in aqua regia. In keeping with the other members of the platinum group, the metal shows a fairly strong tendency to form complex ions such as $PtCl_6^{2-}$, $Pt(NH_3)_6^{4+}$, and $Pt(NH_3)_4^{2+}$.

Uses. Because of its inertness and attractive appearance, one of the major uses of platinum is in the manufacture of jewelry. Gold-platinum alloys, referred to as white gold, are widely used in dentistry and in the making of jewelry. Platinum and its alloys are used in the manufacture of crucibles and evaporating dishes for chemical analyses. Other applications include the formation of thermocouple wires, the production of electrical contacts and corrosion-resistant apparatuses, and the manufacture of platinum resistance thermometers used in the temperature control of furnaces. The alloy consisting of 76.7% platinum and 23.3% cobalt by weight forms a powerful magnet.

Catalysis. Along with palladium, the metal absorbs large volumes of hydrogen, retaining it at ordinary temperatures but desorbing it at red heat. The fact that the absorbed hydrogen is extremely reactive suggests that it is present either as atomic hydrogen or as a very reactive platinum-hydrogen compound or complex. In finely divided form platinum is an excellent catalyst; about half of the annual production of the metal serves this purpose, most of it in the petrochemical industry. It is also used as a catalyst in the contact process for the manufacture of sulfuric acid from sulfur dioxide and oxygen. There is much current interest in the application of the metal as a catalyst in fuel cells and in catalytic converters as antipollution devices for automobiles. In the latter instance a suitable form of platinum will catalyze the oxidation of carbon monoxide to carbon dioxide and will convert nitric oxide to nitrogen and water. Fine platinum wire glows

when placed in methyl alcohol vapor, where it acts as a catalyst, converting the alcohol to formaldehyde. This effect is used commercially to produce cigarette lighters and hand warmers.

▬

Plato   The Greek philosopher Plato was among the most important and creative thinkers of the ancient world. His work set forth most of the important problems and concepts of Western philosophy, psychology, logic, and politics, and his influence has remained profound from ancient to modern times.

Life

Plato was born in Athens in *c.*428 BC. Both his parents were of distinguished Athenian families, and his stepfather, an associate of Pericles, was an active participant in the political and cultural life of Periclean Athens. Plato seems as a young man to have been destined for an aristocratic political career. The execution (399) of SOCRATES, however, had a profound effect on his plans.

After Socrates' death Plato retired from active Athenian life and traveled widely for a number of years. In *c.*388 he journeyed to Italy and Sicily, where he became the friend of Dionysius the Elder, ruler of Syracuse, and his brother-in-law Dion. The following year he returned to Athens, where he founded the Academy, an institution devoted to research and instruction in philosophy and the sciences. Most of his life thereafter was spent in teaching and guiding the activities of the Academy. When Dionysius died (367), Dion invited Plato to return to Syracuse to undertake the philosophical education of the new ruler, Dionysius the Younger. Plato went, perhaps with the hope of founding the rule of a philosopher-king as envisioned in his work the *Republic*. The visit, however, ended (366) in failure. Plato died in 348 or 347 BC.

Writings

Plato's published writings, of which apparently all are preserved, consist of some 26 dialogues on philosophical and related themes, in which the discourse is placed in the mouths of characters who may or may not be based on historical persons; Socrates is a focal character in all but a few of the dialogues.

Early Dialogues. Stylistic and thematic considerations suggest a rough division of the dialogues into three periods. The earliest dialogues, begun after 399 BC, are seen by many scholars as memorials to the life and teachings of Socrates. Three of them, the *Euthyphro, Apology,* and *Crito,* describe Socrates' conduct immediately before, during, and after his trial. The early writings include a series of short dialogues that end with no clear and definitive solution to the problems raised. Characteristically, Plato has Socrates ask questions of the form "What is X?" and insist that he wants not examples or instances of X but what it is to be X, the essential nature, or Form, of X.

Socrates holds that an understanding of the essential nature in each case is of primary importance, but he does not claim himself to have any such understanding. A formal mode of cross-examination called elenchus, in which the answers to questions put by Socrates are shown to result in a contradiction of the answerer's original statement, reveals the ignorance of the answerer as well. Although the dialogues appear to end in ignorance, the dialectical structure of each work is such that a complex and subtle understanding of the concept emerges.

Middle Dialogues. The dialogues of the middle period were begun after the founding of the Academy. Here more openly positive doctrines begin to emerge in the discourse of Socrates. The dialogues of this period include what is widely thought to be Plato's greatest work, The Republic. Beginning with a discussion on the nature of justice, the dialogue articulates a vision of an ideal political community and the education appropriate to the rulers of such a community. Justice is revealed to be a principle of each thing performing the function most appropriate to its nature, a principle of the proper adjudication of activity and being. In political terms this principle is embodied in a society in which citizens perform the tasks for which they are best suited; in the individual human soul the principle is to be discovered when each part of the soul performs its proper and appropriate function. Reason in both instances is to rule, but in both the political community and the individual soul, justice is ideally coupled with the virtue of temperance, the harmony and self-mastery that results when all elements agree as to which should do what. Thus the rule of reason is not a tyranny but the harmonious rule of the happily unified individual and society.

Late Dialogues. In the dialogues of the later period, begun after Plato returned from Syracuse, the figure of Socrates recedes into the background. The *Sophist* shows how a proper understanding of appearance depends on an account of being and nonbeing and of the relation between particulars and Forms, principles explaining individual things. In the *Parmenides* the theory of Forms comes under exacting scrutiny, and arguments are presented to show that the Forms cannot be entities of the same sort as those whose being they explain. The *Timaeus* presents a semimythical description of the origin and nature of the universe, and the *Philebus* considers the place of pleasure in the good life. In the *Laws*, Plato's longest and last work, a model constitution for an ideal city is considered.

Thought

Central to Plato's thought is the power of reason to reveal the intelligibility and order governing the changing world of appearance and to create, at both the political and the individual level, a harmonious and happy life. Socrates' view that virtue is a form of understanding and that the good life must consequently be grounded in knowledge is refined into the view that philosophical education is to effect a harmony between reason and passion, a life of self-mastery in which reason governs the will not as something alien to it but as its natural guide and source. The doctrine of recollection, according to which learning is the remembering of a wisdom that the soul enjoyed prior to its incarnation, is a mythical statement of this view that neither reason nor the intelligible order that it reveals is

The Greek philosopher Plato, portrayed in this copy (3d century AD) of a 4th-century BC bust, remains one of the most influential thinkers in Western civilization. Plato's dialogues, in their exploration of the basic questions raised by philosophical inquiries, were seminal works in the history of thought. (Louvre, Paris.)

alien to the human soul.

This order—seen by Plato as providing an account both of the being and of the intelligibility of the world of appearance—is articulated in the theory of Forms. Forms are the principles of being in the world, of the fact that the world presents itself as instances of being this or that, as well as the principles of human understanding of those instances of being. The nature and intelligibility of the world of appearance can thus be accounted for, in Plato's view, only by recognizing it as an "image" of the truly intelligible structure of being itself, which is the world of Forms. The relationship between Forms and particulars, or between the world of being and the world of appearance, was recognized by Plato to be deeply problematic. He remained clear, however, that no theory could fail to recognize both features of the world without falling prey to either the relativism of Heraclitus or the monism of Parmenides, both of which destroy the very possibility of being and understanding.

The world of being, itself governed by the Form of the good, is seen by Plato as also the source of value and the object of proper desire. The philosopher is thus pictured as in love with the Forms, that is, in love with the world as it truly is. The philosopher's wish to see through the world of flux to the true principles of its being is thus basically an act of love. This love is not simply an attraction to the good but a creative force for the procreation of the good. Directed toward others, it is the power of education, the bringing to birth of understanding and virtue through the process of dialectic, as portrayed in Socrates' relation to the youths about him.

Reason for Plato, as for the Greek tradition in general, is most clearly manifest in LOGOS, the word, and language, as the medium in which reason articulates being, is a central topic throughout the dialogues. Plato was impressed by the fact that language has the capacity both to articulate the intelligibility of the world and to belie the world's true being. He constantly addresses the question of how to purge language of its potential deceptiveness, how to win the fidelity of words to the world. Bad poetry and bad rhetoric alike are pathological forms of the inescapable dissociation of word and world; the Platonic question is how to make this dissociation benign. The central vehicle that Plato envisions for this purpose is dialectic, the dialogue that refines and articulates the true shape and tendency of speech and understanding. This dialectic is presented mimetically in the dialogues themselves, which are thus not simply presentations of philosophical views but representations of philosophy at work, of human beings engaged in the distinctively human and highly civilized activity of rational conversation.

Platt, Thomas Collier Thomas Collier Platt, b. Owego, N.Y., July 15, 1833, d. Mar. 6, 1910, was an American political boss who ruled New York state Republican politics in the 1890s. Platt served (1874–78) in the U.S. House of Representatives and, in 1881, was elected to the Senate. He feuded with President James Garfield over patronage, however, and resigned almost immediately. He served (1897–1909) again in the Senate. In 1898, Platt helped Theodore Roosevelt become governor of New York, but in 1900 he sought the vice-presidency for Roosevelt in order to remove the independent governor from state politics. Roosevelt's sudden succession to the presidency the next year, however, sealed the decline of Platt's political power.

Platt Amendment The Platt Amendment defined the relationship between Cuba and the United States from 1901 to 1934 and continues to influence it today. At the end of the SPANISH-AMERICAN WAR, U.S. military forces under Gen. Leonard WOOD occupied Cuba in order to maintain stability there after Spain's withdrawal. When the newly independent Cubans drew up a constitution in 1900, U.S. Secretary of War Elihu ROOT informed them that certain provisions were a necessary condition for U.S. withdrawal from the island. These provisions were incorporated into a rider attached to the Army Appropriations Bill of 1901 that was sponsored by U.S. Senator Orville H. Platt. The amendment made Cuba, in effect, a U.S. protectorate. It limited Cuba's treaty-making capacity, restricted its right to contract public debt, and gave the United States the right to maintain naval bases in Cuba and to intervene in Cuban affairs in order to preserve order or Cuba's independence. These provisions were appended to the Cuban constitution in 1901, and U.S. forces withdrew the next year.

The Platt Amendment formed the basis for U.S. reoccupation of Cuba in 1906–09 following an uprising led by Juan Vicente GÓMEZ and for various other instances of U.S. interference in Cuba's affairs. Long regarded as a symbol of "Yankee imperialism," it was repealed by the United States on May 29, 1934. The Americans retained their naval base on GUANTÁNAMO BAY, however.

Platte River [plat]   The Platte River is a 500-km-long (310-mi) tributary of the MISSOURI RIVER formed by the confluence of the North Platte and South Platte rivers and flowing across central and southern Nebraska. The 1,095-km (680-mi) North Platte begins in the Rocky Mountains of north central Colorado and flows north into Wyoming before entering Nebraska. The South Platte, 712 km (442 mi) long, rises in central Colorado. The branches join at the city of North Platte in central Nebraska, and the Platte River flows east to join the Missouri River at Plattsmouth, just south of Omaha. Its principal economic value is as a source of irrigation water. The Platte system drains an area of about 233,000 km^2 (90,000 mi^2).

Explored as early as 1739 by the French and in 1820 by Stephen H. LONG, the river valley was one of the main routes for pioneers using the Oregon and Mormon trails. The Union Pacific Railroad, the first rail link between the eastern and western United States, ran through the valley as well.

platypus   see DUCK-BILLED PLATYPUS

Plautus [plawt'-uhs]   Titus Maccius Plautus, c.254–184 BC, the greatest comic dramatist of ancient Rome, wrote in the style of Greek New Comedy and exercised an abiding influence on the development of COMEDY and romantic drama in the West from the Renaissance to the present. Of the approximately 130 plays he wrote, only 21 survive in whole or part. All of these are based on the Greek models provided by MENANDER, Philemon, and Diphilus, although Plautus also borrowed extensively from the Atellan farces of Italy. Making inventive use of colloquial Latin—the spoken parts alternating with lyrical passages expressed in song—and of puns, allusions, and asides to the audience, Plautus created witty comedies that were a unique blend of farce, music, and dance. Only two of his plays can be assigned definite dates: *Stichus* (200 BC) and *Pseudolus* (191 BC). Others include *Mercator, Miles Gloriosus, Captivi*, and *Menaechmi*.

play (in behavior)   In the 20th century play has usually been defined as a voluntary, fun-filled activity carried on for its own sake. This definition, however, is more a description of what people would want play to be than what it always is. Children, for example, may often join in play in order to be with others, and the activity is not always entirely pleasurable.

When one looks at animals at play, one notices that they give very clear-cut communications to each other. They signal the message "This is play" by wagging their tails, jumping up and down, or doing some other thing to indicate that what they are about to do is not to be taken for real. Their bite is a playful bite, not a real bite. Current studies of human players show that they are also very careful to let others know they are playing, in much the same way animals do. They announce that "This is only a game," or they laugh, nudge, or do something odd to show their intent.

Play, then, is a primitive kind of communication in which the players engage in behaviors that mimic reality but do not threaten it. It is primitive because it is a way of sharing that animals are capable of and that precedes the use of language. Not surprisingly, children who as yet have few other ways of communicating use play as their major technique for self-expression and social behavior.

Children's Play. Much of a child's first two years is occupied with exploring objects and toys in order to learn how they work. Typically, this kind of serious learning precedes the child's play with the same object. Having soberly dropped a block on the floor a number of times, an infant may subsequently mimic his or her own block-dropping in a gleeful manner, laughing while doing so. From this, one sees how play always contains some imitation of sober life activities, and is accompanied by a degree of mockery, parody, or exaggeration.

By two years of age children have learned how to play imaginatively, and much of their time in the next two years will be spent in negotiating with other children about pretending. "Is that a bunch of sand?" "No, it's a birthday cake." Between four and seven years children develop an interest in organized group play with rules.

Play does not cease in adulthood. Rather, it is institutionalized in the forms of sports, entertainments, spectator events, and social occasions and thus becomes a part of sober cultural reality. Because children are childlike, adults tend to think of children's activities as more playful than the play of adults, but for much of the time children go about their play with all the earnestness with which adults go about their sports and amusements. (See also GAMES.)

Theories of Play. All modern theories of play claim that it is useful. Evolutionary theories at the turn of the century contended that play was a preparation for life and itself a kind of growth: one had to be young in order to play. Between the world wars most attention was given to the emotional aspects of play, and important new discoveries were made of the part that play could have in therapy and the way it could be used to diagnose conflicts in children who could not otherwise put feelings into words. In more recent years the focus has shifted to the ways in which children learn to solve intellectual and social problems while they play. Video games bring the promise of many discoveries of this sort. The latest trend, however, is to see play as most fundamentally a way in which one expresses his or her inner self and communicates it to others.

play (theater) see DRAMA

▬

playa [ply'-uh] *Playa* (Spanish for "shore" or "beach") is the name given by U.S. geologists and geographers to a dry lake bed in a desert region. Playas occupy the lowest portions (generally 2% to 5% of the area) of closed drainage basins in desert regions. Playas are drainage sumps—almost level vegetation-free flats of clay, salt, or both. Most playas are remnants of larger pluvial lakes (see LAKE,

GLACIAL) that existed during wetter periods thousands of years ago, as manifested by gravel-sand embankments and other shore features that surround the present playas. Playas are inundated occasionally after exceptionally severe storms by a thin sheet of water that rarely remains more than a few weeks. True playas are without an outlet, losing their water entirely by evaporation. Some desert basins, however, have semiplayas, which are clay flats that have sluggish drainage to lower areas—an ocean, in some cases.

Playas—some containing valuable EVAPORITE mineral deposits—are restricted to semiarid and arid regions between 10° and 50° latitude. In North America they are numerous in the BASIN AND RANGE PROVINCE (especially the Great Basin) and the Southern High Plains.

▬

Player, Gary The South African golfer Gary Jim Player, b. Nov. 1, 1935, was a professional player by the time he was 17 years of age. After winning several minor tournaments, he attracted wide attention with victories in the Australian Professional Golfers Association tournament (PGA; 1957), the Australian Open (1958), and the British Open (1959); he won the Masters in 1961. Player is one of only four golfers to have captured all 4 titles in the modern Grand Slam, the others being Gene Sarazen, Ben Hogan, and Jack Nicklaus. He won the British Open 3 times (1959, 1968, 1974); the Masters 3 times (1961, 1974, 1978); and the PGA tournament twice (1962, 1972); in 1965 he became the first non-American player to win the U.S. Open since Ted Ray of England in 1920.

▬

player piano The player piano (also called pianola) is a PIANO fitted with a mechanism for automatic playing of the instrument. The development of a pneumatic action in the middle of the 19th century made the self-playing piano a mechanical and commercial success. The basis for most of the ensuing patent mechanisms is as follows: a roll of paper with perforations corresponding in position and length to the pitches and durations of musical tones is drawn over a cylinder with a row of holes, connected by pipes to the piano's action; when a perforation passes over a hole in the cylinder, a stream of air is allowed to pass through the pipe, activating the hammer for the corresponding note. The player piano was immensely popular in the late 19th and early 20th centuries; in the 1920s, about 360,000 were sold each year. The electronic player piano gained favor during the late 1970s.

playing cards see CARD GAMES

plea bargaining see CRIMINAL JUSTICE

▬

plebeians [ple-bee'-uhnz] The plebeians, or plebs, a majority of the free citizens of ancient Rome, were originally denied most of the rights accorded the privileged, hereditary PATRICIAN class. At first barred from public office, they began electing their own TRIBUNES about 494 BC. In 445 BC the plebeians won the right to marry patricians. Gradually succeeding in their lengthy fight for equality, by about 300 BC they were eligible to hold all major political and religious posts. In 287 BC the laws passed by the plebeian assemblies became binding on patricians.

plebiscite [pleb'-is-yt]   The plebiscite is a political instrument that allows voters to express their will on a specific issue directly at the polls, instead of through their elected representatives. The holding of a plebiscite usually implies that the issue being decided by the voters is of the utmost importance. The plebiscite was used by Napoleon I to lend legitimacy to his annexation of certain territories. A plebiscite in 1852 confirmed the coup d'état that made Napoleon III emperor. Following World War II, plebiscites have been held to allow colonial territories to decide whether they wanted to become independent.

Plecoptera   see STONE FLY

Pledge of Allegiance   "I pledge allegiance to the flag of the United States of America and to the Republic for which it stands, one Nation under God, indivisible, with liberty and justice for all." This pledge is recited by schoolchildren in classrooms throughout the United States. It was originally printed (1892) in the magazine *Youth's Companion*; the question of its authorship was in dispute for many years and was resolved only in 1939 when authorship was officially attributed to Francis Bellamy, who had been on the staff of the magazine. The original text has been altered twice. In 1923, the words *the flag of the United States of America* were substituted for the words *my flag,* and in 1954 an act of Congress added the words *under God.*

The pledge was once an obligatory public school ritual, but state laws no longer require students to recite it. A 1943 ruling by the U.S. Supreme Court (*West Virginia State Board of Education* v. *Barnette*) reversed a previous decision that had justified the expulsion of students who refused on religious grounds to pledge themselves to (in effect, to swear by or take an oath on) a flag. Nevertheless, the custom persists, usually as part of opening school exercises.

Pleiades (astronomy) [plee'-uh-deez]   The Pleiades, also called the Seven Sisters, is a galactic star cluster (M45) about 415 light-years away, in the constellation Taurus. Of its approximately 400 stars that lie within a 25-light-year radius, at least six are visible to the naked eye. The stars are surrounded by nebular dust and gas, from which they originally condensed; the nebula glows by their reflected light. The cluster is named after seven nymphs of Greek mythology: Alcyone (the brightest, magnitude 3), Celaeno, Electra, Maia, Merope, Sterope, and Taygete.

Pleiades (mythology)   In Greek mythology the Pleiades were seven nymphs, the daughters of ATLAS and Pleione: Maia, Electra, and Taygete, each of whom bore a child to Zeus; Celaeno, who bore Poseidon's child; Merope, wife of Sisyphus; Sterope, who bore Ares' child; and Alcyone. While hunting with ARTEMIS they encountered ORION, who pursued them until Zeus engineered their escape by turning them into a constellation. In Roman mythology they were called the Vergiliae.

Pleistocene Epoch   see EARTH, GEOLOGICAL HISTORY OF; EVOLUTION; GEOLOGIC TIME

Plekhanov, Georgy Valentinovich [pli-kah'-nuhf]   Georgy Valentinovich Plekhanov, b. Dec. 11 (N.S.), 1856, d. May 30 (N.S.), 1918, was the father of Russian Marxism. After studying for a military career, he joined the populist NARODNIKI in the 1870s. He was a leader of the Land and Freedom organization, but, becoming disillusioned with its growing use of terror and with the peasants' conservatism, he formed (1883) the Marxist Liberation of Labor group in Geneva. In exile from 1880 until 1917, he wrote influential tracts that helped develop the Marxist revolutionary movement.

At first close to V. I. LENIN, Plekhanov saw a progressive role for Russian liberals and came to value political liberty as much as social democracy. He also opposed a Marxist revolution before the workers had gained political maturity. He therefore split with the Bolsheviks and organized his own social democratic group. A supporter of the Russian war effort during World War I, he returned to Russia during the March Revolution of 1917 but later opposed the Bolshevik Revolution. He died in exile.

plesiosaur [plee-see-uh-sohr']   Plesiosaurs are an extinct group of large aquatic reptiles that ranged through the oceans of the world from the Late Triassic until the end of the Cretaceous, or from about 195 million to 65 million years ago. The plesiosaurs make up the suborder Plesiosauria in the order Sauropterygia and are usually divided into the superfamilies Plesiosauroidea, or long-necked plesiosaurs, and Pliosauroidea, or short-necked plesiosaurs. The number of neck bones, or vertebrae, in these differing forms varied from as few as 13 in *Brachauchenius* to 76 in *Elasmosaurus*, whose neck was twice as long as its body.

Plesiosaurs ranged in length from about 2.5 to 14 m (8 to 46 ft). As larger forms evolved, the necks of the long-necked forms tended to get even longer, whereas in the short-necked forms the skulls increased in length. The short-necked, 12-m (40-ft) *Kronosaurus* had a skull 3 m (10 ft) long. Both types had broad, flat, apparently inflexible bodies; large, strong front and hind flippers; medium-length tails; and relatively small, flat heads. Sharp, needlelike teeth indicate that they were predators.

A plesiosaur had flippers like those of a turtle and a long, snakelike neck. A slow swimmer, the plesiosaur probably caught prey with a forward snap of its head.

The apparent inability of plesiosaurs to scull with their tails or perform swimming movements with their bodies led to the image of the animals "rowing" about in the sea. Whereas long-necked forms could feed on fish and squid by means of rapid head thrusts, short-necked forms lacked this option. More recent studies, however, have indicated that the large flippers of plesiosaurs were probably used in an up-down, winglike stroke and that the animals "flew" through water much as modern penguins do.

Plessy v. Ferguson [ples'-ee]   The case of *Plessy* v. *Ferguson* (1896) involved the constitutionality of a Louisiana law that required separate accommodations for white and "colored" passengers on railroads in the state. Homer Plessy, a citizen of Louisiana, had been arrested for refusing to sit in the car designated for blacks. After his conviction in the state courts Plessy appealed to the U.S. Supreme Court, claiming that the statute was contrary to the 13th and 14th amendments.

For a majority of seven, Justice Henry Brown delivered the opinion upholding the Louisiana law. Interpreting the 14th Amendment, Justice Brown declared: "The object of the Amendment was undoubtedly to enforce the absolute equality of the two races before the law, but in the nature of things it could not have been intended to abolish distinctions based upon color, or to enforce social, as distinguished from political, equality, or a commingling of the two races upon terms unsatisfactory to either."

pleurisy   see RESPIRATORY-SYSTEM DISORDERS

Pliny the Elder [plin'-ee]   Gaius Plinius Secundus, called Pliny the Elder, AD *c.*23–79, is known for his one surviving work, the monumental *Natural History* (*c.*77), a source of much ancient scientific and technical lore. An encyclopedia devoted to the Earth and planetary sciences, it deals with zoology, anthropology, psychology, pharmacology, and metallurgy. Pliny's scientific curiosity led to his death by asphyxiation when he approached too close to Mount Vesuvius on its eruption in 79.

Pliny the Younger   Gaius Plinius Caecilius Secundus, or Pliny the Younger, *c.*61–*c.*112, became a Roman senator *c.*90 and served as consul in 100. As governor of Bithynia (*c.*111–112), he corresponded with the emperor Trajan on such questions as the treatment to be given Christians within the province. Ten books of epistles (100–112) provide an informal account of the daily life of a rich and cultured Roman gentleman and are a valuable source of historical information.

Pliocene Epoch   see EARTH, GEOLOGICAL HISTORY OF; EVOLUTION; GEOLOGIC TIME

Plisetskaya, Maya Mikhailovna [plee-set'-sky-ah]   Prima ballerina assoluta of the Bolshoi Ballet, Maya Plisetskaya, b. Nov. 20, 1925, is a dancer of great dramatic range and power. She is most famous for her interpretation of Odette-Odile in *Swan Lake* and for her Carmen in the ballet by Alberto Alonso. Plisetskaya has appeared internationally, frequently with the Paris Opéra and Maurice Béjart's Ballet du XXe Siècle. She became artistic director of the National Ballet of Spain in 1987 and in 1988 danced her *Anna Karenina* (1972) in its U.S. premiere in Boston.

PLO   see PALESTINE LIBERATION ORGANIZATION

Ploiești [plo-yesht']   Ploiești, a city in south central Romania, lies in the foothills of the Transylvanian Alps, about 65 km (40 mi) north of Bucharest. Its population is 234,886 (1986 est.). One of Europe's richest petroleum fields is near the highly industrialized city, which has large oil refineries, storage tanks, petrochemical plants, and many varied manufactures. Ploiești is also a railroad and petroleum-pipeline hub. Founded in the 16th century, Ploiești gained in importance after the discovery of oil there in the 1850s. The city was heavily bombed by Allied forces during World War II and was occupied by Soviet troops in 1944.

plot   see NARRATIVE AND DRAMATIC DEVICES

Plotinus [ploh-ty'-nuhs]   Plotinus, AD 204–70, is generally considered the founder of NEOPLATONISM. Born probably in Egypt, he studied philosophy at Alexandria for

11 years. His ideas were recorded in six sets of discourses, each with nine sections (*The Enneads*). These were published posthumously by his pupil and biographer PORPHYRY.

Plotinus developed an interpretation of Plato's philosophy that changed the position of the Platonic Academy from one of skepticism into a new religious view. He agreed with the skeptics that knowledge is required in order to grasp the Platonic forms that are "beyond" the physical heavens. He argued, however, that in order to acquire it souls must somehow journey to this "transcelestial" place to see the forms there.

The system of Plotinus has as its highest form "the One," an indefinable ultimate principle. By an overflow (emanation) from itself, the One creates a second order, Reason and the Forms; this level, in its turn, generates the level of Soul. The final level, that of matter, is dark and unreal, and the goal of the human soul is to escape that level and return to the One. The return becomes possible through ascetic moral training and the contemplation of beauty; if these are practiced purely, one can reestablish the connection of the Soul with Reason and ultimately, through a mystical experience (which Plotinus described variously as "ecstacy," "self-surrender," and "flight yonder, of the alone to the Alone"), arrive at knowledge of, and therefore unification with, the One.

Plovdiv [plawf'-dif]   Plovdiv, a city in south central Bulgaria, lies on approximately 120-m-high (400-ft) cliffs above the Maritsa River, about 140 km (85 mi) southeast of Sofia. Its population of 364,162 (1989 est.) makes it Bulgaria's second largest city. Strategically important since ancient times because of its location, it is a railroad junction and a major industrial city. Landmarks include Macedonian remains, part of the Roman walls, and 15th- and 16th-century mosques.

The ancient Thracian settlement of Eumolpias, the city was captured by PHILIP II of Macedonia in 342 BC and named Philippopolis. In AD 46, as Trimontium, it became the Roman capital of Thrace. A succession of conquerors included Goths, Crusaders, Bulgarians, Greeks, and Turks, who took the city in 1364 and named it Philibé. The Russians defeated the Turks there in 1878, and the area including Plovdiv was annexed to Bulgaria in 1885. The city assumed the name Plovdiv after World War I.

plover [pluhv'-ur]   With few exceptions plovers belong to the family Charadriidae in the order of shorebirds, Charadriiformes. About 60 species of plovers are widely distributed throughout the world, including the Arctic and Antarctic.

Many plovers undertake spectacular migrations, the best known of which is that of the American golden plover, *Pluvialis dominica*. Adults of the eastern form make a nonstop, 3,900-km (2,400-mi) transatlantic flight from Nova Scotia to northern South America and then to the southern regions of South America. The young move at a more leisurely rate down the Mississippi Valley to Argentina. In the spring all the birds return north by way of the Mississippi Valley.

Plovers are small to medium-sized birds and have stout bodies with a short neck and tail. Bills in most species are short and stout and are swollen at the tip. Many species also have bands or rings around the neck. Plovers are swift in flight and forage for insects. They usually lay four large eggs.

Perhaps the most familiar New World plover is the killdeer, *Charadrius vociferus*. The family also includes dotterels, lapwings, and the unique wrybill of New Zealand, which has a laterally curved bill. What is known as an upland plover is actually a sandpiper, *Bartramia longicauda*.

plow   A plow is a farm implement used to till and turn over soil. Early farmers used the antlers of a deer, a crooked stick, or similar objects for tilling. The first true plow consisted of a pointed wedge of wood with a handle for guiding it and a beam to which humans or oxen could be tied to pull the plow over the soil. Early plows could cut into lightly sodded soils, but they could not turn the

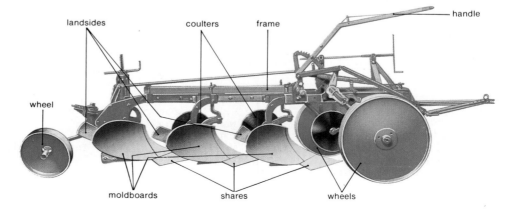

landsides   coulters   frame   handle

wheel

moldboards   shares   wheels

A gang plow can plow more than one furrow at a time. Most often drawn by tractor, it is sometimes pulled by draft animals. The type seen here has moldboard bottoms for throwing the soil to one side.

soil over. A significant innovation was the use of metal to reinforce the front cutting edge, or share, of the plow. The Greeks and Romans used the ard, or scratch plow, a metal-tipped but lightweight implement that was pulled by oxen. Although plows became larger and heavier, were occasionally mounted on wheels, and eventually were pulled by horses rather than oxen, their basic design was little changed until the early Middle Ages, when a metal colter, or cutting blade, was added to the front of the plow to slice into the ground ahead of the plowshare.

In contrast to the soils of the Mediterranean region, the soils of northern Europe are heavy and difficult to till. As more agricultural land was opened in northern Europe, plows necessarily became heavier, and the use of iron for plow parts increased. In about the 11th century the mold-board—the curved surface of the plow behind the plow-share—was invented in Europe (although it had been known in China for a millennium). A moldboard-equipped plow could lift and turn over the soil, digging deeper than could the older plows.

The first U.S. patent for a solid cast-iron plow was granted to Charles Newbold in 1797. Thomas Jefferson designed moldboards, and in 1819, Jethro Wood patented a cast-iron plow that used a Jefferson-designed mold-board. With its interchangeable parts, it was considered the best plow of its time. The 1868 plow designed by James Oliver was made by a process of molding iron and chilling it to produce a plow that was stronger and that scoured cleaner.

The opening of the Midwest to agriculture presented new problems, because soils there were thickly sod-covered and far loamier than the soil of the East. John Lane and John DEERE, both Illinois blacksmiths, independently devised plows made of saw-blade steel in the 1830s. These horse-drawn plows were both strong and durable and were ideal for turning tough sod. Two- and three-wheel steel plows became common in the late 1800s, and gang plows—which mounted four or more plowshares and were pulled by several teams of horses—came into use in the 1890s.

As tractor power was augmented and traction improved by using dual sets of tires with four-wheel drive, gang plows were enlarged. Some modern tractors can pull twenty-one 40-cm (16-in) moldboard plows that can till 64 ha (160 acres) in 12 hours. Contemporary designs of plows, either pulled or mounted on tractors, include shallow plows, subsoil plows, and disk plows.

See also: AGRICULTURE, HISTORY OF; TECHNOLOGY, HISTORY OF.

plum   Plum is the name given to various small trees of the genus *Prunus*, family Rosaceae, that have been cultivated for centuries for their lovely ornamental blossoms and their smooth-skinned fruit. The fruit is called a drupe because it has one seed surrounded by a stony endocarp. Plum trees are wide-spreading and low, seldom reaching 9 m (about 30 ft) in height. Approximately 100 species are known. The most important for commercial

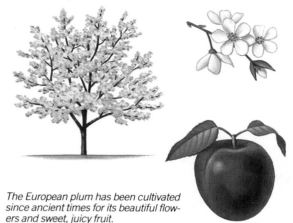

The European plum has been cultivated since ancient times for its beautiful flowers and sweet, juicy fruit.

growing purposes is the common, or European, plum, *P. domestica*—probably introduced into North America by the Pilgrims—which today produces most of the dessert plums and all of the prune plums in the United States. The Japanese plum, *P. salincina*, believed to be native to China, was introduced into the United States by way of Japan in 1870.

plumbing   In a house or building, plumbing provides water for consumption, cleaning, and waste disposal. In general, plumbing uses two pipe systems—one to convey clean water into a building and another to carry away waterborne wastes.

The need for a convenient means of water distribution is as old as the existence of cities. Urban areas have used masonry conduits to transport water since the time of ancient Egypt. The Romans developed complex plumbing systems that used AQUEDUCTS to bring water into the city and lead pipes to distribute the water into buildings. (The word *plumbing* is derived from the Latin *plumbum*, "lead.")

Pipe. Pipe must be made of material that will not be corroded by water. Copper is one of the most resistant pipe materials. Cast iron, an iron alloy with corrosion-resistant properties, or steel with a galvanized zinc coating is often used. Lead pipe has virtually disappeared since the discovery that the lead "migrates" into water and can cause lead poisoning. Nonmetallic pipes may be made of clay, concrete, or a plastic material such as polyvinyl chloride.

Water Distribution. A typical water distribution system starts with cold water from a municipal water supply system or a private well. Supply water must be provided in adequate volume and pressure to deliver water to the topmost fixtures in a building. In multistory buildings, pressure from a municipal system is seldom enough to meet this requirement, and it must be boosted by pumps that are part of the building's mechanical equipment.

Plumbing in a typical house includes metal pipes that permit clean water from water-supply systems to flow under pressure to various fixtures and soiled water to drain away to waste-disposal systems. Some of the inflowing water is diverted to a water-heating system. Used water drains into a vertical soil stack, into which flows air from a vent pipe in order to prevent a vacuum that might slow the water flow.

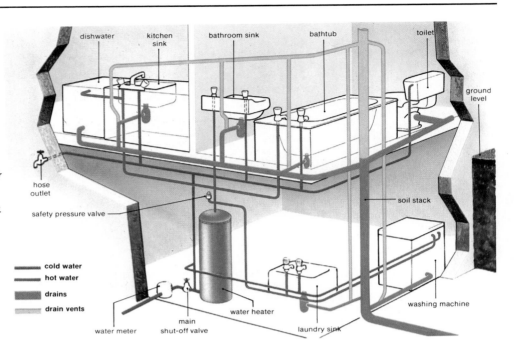

dishwater
kitchen sink
bathroom sink
bathtub
toilet
ground level
hose outlet
safety pressure valve
soil stack
cold water
hot water
drains
drain vents
water meter
main shut-off valve
water heater
laundry sink
washing machine

Heating. A portion of a building's water is diverted for heating. Hot water used for cleaning and cooking is usually supplied at a temperature of 46° to 60° C (110° to 140° F). Water may be heated by the same system that heats the building or by independent heaters designed for water only. In most buildings the need for hot water varies during the day. The heater may be designed for requirements of the highest-demand period, or a storage tank may act as a bank to help supply those periods, permitting a smaller heater to be used at somewhat greater energy efficiency.

Drainage. Drainage pipe must also resist corrosion from water and wastes. Materials commonly used are cast iron, copper, galvanized steel, and polyvinyl chloride for aboveground lines, along with concrete pipe and vitrified clay-tile pipe for underground use.

Like water lines, drainage piping extends from each fixture in the building and joins into one or more major conduits called house drains, which conduct the sewage to a private disposal system or municipal sewer. Drainage from sanitary fixtures is called sanitary waste and goes to a sanitary sewer or disposal system.

Sewer Gases. Direct connection of sanitary fixtures to a sewer or private disposal system would not be possible without a means of preventing sewer gases, bacteria, or vermin from entering the building through the pipes. A water trap near the outlet of each fixture contains a short column of water that isolates the incoming water from contamination. As sanitary wastes pass through the piping system, they cause changes in air pressure that can siphon water away from the traps, leaving the fixtures open. A relief piping system, which includes at least one

major conduit to the atmosphere, prevents such changes in pressure.

In the design of buildings, economy of construction and simplicity of maintenance dictate that fixtures be placed in relationship to each other so that water, waste, and vent piping is as simple and direct as possible. In multistory buildings, plumbing fixtures are placed in tiers so they can be served by common vertical pipes called stacks (wastes and vents) or risers (water).

pluralism Pluralism is a theory or system of thought that recognizes more than one (MONISM) and generally more than two (DUALISM) ultimate principles. The elements in metaphysical pluralisms are quite varied: from the earth, air, fire, and water of EMPEDOCLES, and the mercury, sulfur, and salt of PARACELSUS; to the Chinese water, fire, wood, metal, soil, and Yin and Yang; to the mind, matter, and God of William JAMES. Epistemological pluralism, presented in William James's PRAGMATISM, maintains that there is no single meaning or truth; meaning varies as the consequences vary for the individual, and truth is the expedient way of thinking. Attributive monisms, such as Gottfried Wilhelm von LEIBNIZ's monadology, have also been considered pluralisms because they talk of many elements of the same type.

In political theory pluralism is a concept that describes the heterogeneity of groups that share power in public policymaking. The theory of democratic pluralism asserts that the public interest emerges from the democratic competition of diverse and changing elite groups, none of which are able to become dominant.

Plutarch [ploo'-tahrk]   The most important Greek writer of the early Roman period, Plutarch, c.46–c.120, is primarily known for his *Parallel Lives* (c.100) of Greek and Roman political and military leaders. This work consists of 50 biographies: 23 of Greek leaders, matched by an equal number of Romans, and 4 separate lives. Nineteen of the parallel sets are accompanied by short comparative essays. Based on wide and careful reading, the *Lives* were intended to bring out the virtues and vices of great men as seen through their actions. Plutarch's emphasis is therefore on character, moral choice, and anecdote, although historical information is also included. The *Lives* are among the most popular works of all time. The English translation by Sir Thomas North (1579) was one of the earliest English versions of a classical text and furnished Shakespeare with the plots for *Coriolanus, Julius Caesar,* and *Antony and Cleopatra.* Plutarch's philosophical views were based on those of PLATO. Although a Greek, Plutarch admired the achievements and qualities of the Romans and accepted their rule over Greece without question.

Pluto (mythology) [ploo'-toh]   In Greek mythology Pluto, or Pluton (also known as HADES), was a god both of death and of fertility or abundance. The name Pluto means "rich one," and the Romans derived Dis (from *dives,* "rich"), their god of the dead, from Pluto. Pluto helped his brothers ZEUS and POSEIDON depose their father, CRONUS, as the ruler of the universe, which they then divided among themselves. Pluto's realm, the house of Hades, is usually located beneath the earth, though sometimes in the west.

Pluto (planet)   Pluto, the ninth planet from the Sun, is the smallest and most remote planet known in the SOLAR SYSTEM. The astronomer Percival Lowell, at his private observatory in Flagstaff, Ariz., instituted a search for another planet that eventually resulted in the discovery of Pluto by Clyde W. TOMBAUGH on Feb. 18, 1930. It was named for the PLUTO of mythology.

Orbit. Pluto's average distance from the Sun is 5.9 billion km (3.66 billion mi, or 39.44 astronomical units), but because of a high orbital eccentricity (0.249), it comes as near as 4.42 billion km (2.75 billion mi) and travels as far as 7.40 billion km (4.60 billion mi) from the Sun. This unusual orbit brings Pluto inside the orbit of planet Neptune during its close approach to the Sun, as, for example, during the current period between Jan. 23, 1979, and Mar. 15, 1999. The actual orbital paths do not cross, however. Pluto's orbit is inclined an unusually high 16° to the ecliptic, or Earth-Sun orbital plane. The planet revolves around the Sun once every 248.4 years. In 1988 a computer simulation revealed that the orbit of Pluto is chaotic, that is, not completely predictable.

Physical Characteristics. With a visual magnitude of 15.3, Pluto appears only as a faint point of light in even the largest telescopes. Through various types of studies made of the planet and its known moon, Charon, in the

On Feb. 18, 1930, Clyde W. Tombaugh discovered Pluto while comparing photographic plates taken on Jan. 23 (left) and Jan. 29 (right), 1930, at the Lowell Observatory in Arizona. Pluto is seen as a dot of light (arrows) moving slowly.

late 1980s, it was determined that Pluto may have a diameter of about 2,284 km (1,416 mi). The planet's methane atmosphere may lie many kilometers deep, however, making the diameter figure uncertain. In addition, the atmosphere apparently varies seasonally in thickness according to the planet's distance from the Sun. Spectroscopy indicates that Pluto's mantle of ices is covered at the surface with methane frost, which is redder toward the equator and bluer at the poles. Pluto's core—perhaps of silicate rock—may be relatively large, with a radius of nearly 885 km (550 mi). This would help to account for Pluto's apparent high density of about 2.1 g/cm^3 (131 lb/ft^3).

Satellite. Charon, Pluto's grayish satellite, was discovered by American astrophysicist James W. Christy on June 22, 1978. Its average orbital path lies 19,000 km (11,800 mi) from the center of Pluto at an inclination of 55° to the ecliptic. It lacks an atmosphere and is about 1,160 km (721 mi) wide. Charon completes one revolution in 6.39 days, the same as Pluto's rotation period. The two objects always present the same face toward each other.

plutonium [ploo-toh'-nee-uhm]   Plutonium is a radioactive chemical element, the fifth member of the ACTINIDE SERIES and in Group IIIB of the periodic table. Its symbol is Pu, its atomic number is 94, and its atomic weight is 239.13 (physical scale) for the isotope ^{239}Pu. The stablest plutonium isotope is ^{244}Pu. The name is derived from the planet Pluto.

Plutonium was the second TRANSURANIUM ELEMENT (after neptunium) of the actinide series to be discovered. In 1940, Glenn T. SEABORG and his associates created the isotope ^{238}Pu by bombarding uranium with deuterons in the cyclotron at Berkeley, Calif. Seaborg's group synthesized ^{239}Pu in 1941. Subsequently, trace quantities of natural plutonium have been found in uranium ores. Of the 15 known isotopes, ^{239}Pu is the most important because it is used as a fuel in nuclear-fission reactors (see BREEDER REACTORS) and in nuclear weapons (see ATOMIC BOMB).

Properties. Plutonium is a metal that is silvery in appearance but becomes yellowish when exposed to air. It exists in six structural forms, or allotropes, which vary according to temperature. Large pieces of the metal are warm to the touch due to the release of energy from alpha-particle decay. The pure metal is prepared by the reduction of plutonium trifluoride by alkaline-earth metals.

Plutonium is chemically reactive and will dissolve in concentrated hydrochloric acid, hydriodic acid, or perchloric acid. This chemical reactivity is characteristic of all elements of the actinide series.

Uses and Dangers. Besides being used for explosives in nuclear weapons, the isotope ^{239}Pu has been proposed for use as an explosive in mining and oil-drilling projects. Nuclear reactors, particularly in France and the USSR but not in the United States, create electrical power using ^{239}Pu as fuel. Various isotopes of plutonium are starting materials in the synthesis of other transuranium elements and the manufacture of radioactive isotopes for medical research and industrial purposes. The isotope ^{238}Pu powers such devices as batteries in implanted heart PACEMAKERS.

Because the element is specifically absorbed by bone marrow in humans and because it emits alpha particles at a high rate, plutonium is an extremely dangerous radiological poison. For this reason, the possibility of plutonium contamination of water near nuclear-power plants has caused public concern.

Plymouth (England) [plim'-uhth] Plymouth is a port city of 258,100 (1988 est. pop.) on the south coast of Devon, England. It is built around the combined estuaries of the Tamar and Plym rivers, which provide a natural harbor. Much of the industry is located in Devonport, the western part of Plymouth. Factories produce soap and chemicals, and there are fisheries, but Plymouth is best known as a naval base. Ships are guided into the harbor by Eddystone Lighthouse. Plymouth has undergone substantial reconstruction since the bombing destruction of World War II. Saint Andrew's parish church and the guildhall have been remodeled, and other buildings, such as the Roman Catholic cathedral, have been added.

The original site of the city is believed to be a group of 15th-century fortifications, including a wall, standing on a hill above the harbor. Plymouth's fame as a naval dockyard began in the 17th century, but it had long been associated with sailing. It was the base for such explorations as those of Sir Francis DRAKE and for the fleet that defeated the SPANISH ARMADA (1588). The Pilgrims sailed (1620) from Plymouth on the *Mayflower*.

Plymouth (Massachusetts) Plymouth (1990 pop., 45,608) is a city in southeastern Massachusetts, on Plymouth Bay, about 55 km (34 mi) southeast of Boston. The seat of Plymouth County, it was the site of the first permanent European settlement in New England; it is now a fishing and tourist center with ship-related industries and packinghouses for cranberries. Plymouth Rock, a tourist attraction, is on the shore under a granite canopy; re-creations of Plimoth Plantation and the MAYFLOWER are also there. The PILGRIMS founded Plymouth on Dec. 21, 1620, establishing a settlement that became the seat of PLYMOUTH COLONY in 1633 and a part of Massachusetts Bay Colony in 1691.

Plymouth Brethren The name Plymouth Brethren identifies several small Christian sects of common origin—found in Britain, Europe, and the United States—that are conservative in theology and millenarian in outlook. The movement had its beginning in Ireland and England in the 1820s, Plymouth being a main center of activity. The most prominent early leader was John Nelson Darby (1800–82), who taught that Christ might return at any moment and in a "secret rapture" would take away the members of the true church to dwell in heaven. The polity of the Plymouth Brethren is congregational. At their services there is neither a presiding minister nor a set form of devotions. In the absence of centralized authority there have been recurrent splits within the body, most notably in the Exclusive Brethren and the Open or Christian Brethren.

Plymouth Colony Plymouth Colony, the first permanent Puritan settlement in America, was established in December 1620 on the western shore of Cape Cod Bay by the English Separatist Puritans known as the PILGRIMS. Although their small and weak colony lacked a royal charter, it maintained its separate status until 1691. The Pilgrims secured the right to establish an American settlement from the LONDON COMPANY. The landfall (Nov. 19, 1620) of their ship, the MAYFLOWER, at Cape Cod put the settlers far beyond that company's jurisdiction, provoking mutinous talk. To keep order, the Pilgrim leaders established a governing authority through the Mayflower Compact (Nov. 21, 1620). The 41 signers formed a "Civil Body Politic" and pledged to obey its laws.

To finance their journey and settlement, the Pilgrims had organized a joint-stock venture. Capital was provided by a group of London businesspeople who expected—erroneously—to profit from the colony. During the first winter, more than half of the settlers died, as a result of poor nutrition and inadequate housing, but the colony survived due in part to the able leadership of John CARVER, William BRADFORD, William BREWSTER, Myles STANDISH, and Edward WINSLOW. SQUANTO, a local Indian, taught the Pilgrims how to plant corn and where to fish and trap beaver. Without good harbors or extensive tracts of fertile land, however, Plymouth became a colony of subsistence farming on small private holdings. In 1627 eight Pilgrim leaders assumed the settlement's obligations to the investors in exchange for a six-year monopoly of the fur trade and offshore fishing.

Plymouth's government was initially vested in a body

New England's first Thanksgiving celebration (1621) marked the gathering of Plymouth Colony's first harvest and culminated in a feast shared by the colonists and neighboring Indians. (National Collection of Fine Arts, Washington, D.C.)

of freemen who met in an annual General Court to elect the governor and assistants, enact laws, and levy taxes. By 1639, however, expansion of the colony necessitated replacing the yearly assembly of freemen with a representative body of deputies elected annually by the seven towns. The governor and his assistants, still elected annually by the freemen, had no veto. At first, ownership of property was not required for voting, but freemanship was restricted to adult Protestant males of good character. Church membership was required for freemen in 1668 and, a year later, the ownership of a small amount of property as well.

Plymouth was made part of the Dominion of New England in 1686. When the Dominion was overthrown (1689), Plymouth reestablished its government, but in 1691 it was joined to the much more populous and prosperous colony of Massachusetts Bay to form the royal province of Massachusetts. At the time Plymouth Colony had between 7,000 and 7,500 inhabitants.

plywood   see WOOD

Plzeň [pul'-zen]   Plzeň (or Pilsen), an industrial city and regional capital of western Bohemia, Czechoslovakia, lies about 90 km (55 mi) southwest of Prague. The population is 174,765 (1987 est.). The city is surrounded by fertile valleys in which sugar beets, grains, and hops are grown and cattle are raised. Pilsner beer, brewed since the Middle Ages, is internationally famous. Plzeň is also a center of heavy industry. The Škoda Engineering Works, the largest engineering complex of the country, manufactures armaments, automobiles, locomotives, and machine tools. (Founded in 1869, the Škoda Works was long one of Europe's largest armament industries.) Other industries include paper mills, sugar refineries, and distilleries. Some anthracite coal is mined in the nearby hills. The city has a medical school, a technical college, and art and historical museums. Landmarks include the 15th-century Church of Saint Bartholomew and the 16th-century town hall.

First chronicled in the 10th century, Plzeň was chartered in 1292 by King Wenceslas II of Bohemia, who built its first fortifications. During the Hussite wars in the early 15th century the city was a Roman Catholic stronghold.

pneumatic systems [noo-mat'-ik]   Pneumatic systems, in the most general sense, involve the use of gas—most commonly air—under pressure. Because electricity is not needed to operate pneumatic tools, such tools can be used in wet or explosive environments such as mines without presenting a hazard. Pneumatic devices include construction tools, shock-absorbing devices, tools used in metals processing, sprayers (such as the AIRBRUSH), and tube delivery systems. The ancestor of today's pneumatic devices is the hand bellows.

A typical pneumatic system has a compressor that produces air under pressure, tubes and pipes to convey the pressurized air to the work site, and a tool with which to perform the work. The two major types of pneumatic compressor are the positive-displacement type, and the velocity or dynamic type. In positive-displacement systems, successive volumes of air are confined in a closed space and pressurized by reducing the volume of the space. The simple hand PUMP used to inflate tires is a positive-displacement device. Such systems may also involve motion in a circular path (rotary motion).

The simplest form of dynamic compressor is the propeller-type fan. Dynamic compressors may be of the centrifugal, axial-flow, or fluid-jet types. Centrifugal compressors have a rotating impeller with fixed vanes surrounded by a casing. The air enters at one end, is made by centrifugal force to flow perpendicular to the axis of rotation, and is thus pressurized against the vanes. Axial-flow compressors normally employ several stages of

When the control lever (1) of a pneumatic hammer is pressed, compressed air enters the inlet (2) and flows into the inner chamber (3), forcing the piston (4) down against the tool bit (5). The diaphragm valve (6) reverses airflow; air enters the outer chamber (7), forcing the piston up. The cycle repeats when airflow is reversed.

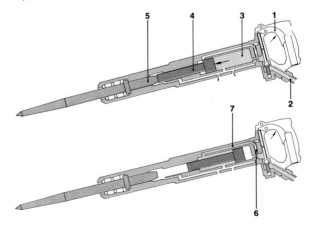

blades attached to a rotor that rotates inside a casing. In fluid-jet compressors, air is pressurized as it is forced through constricted channels by a fluid such as steam.

Pneumatic tools employ a rotor or a piston drive. Rotor tools have a rotor, with blades, inside a casing. Compressed air enters the tool; as it flows past the blades, it exerts a force on them, causing them to turn along with the shaft to which they are attached. Rotor tools include pneumatic buffers, drills, screwdrivers, and impact wrenches. Piston or percussion tools have a hollow shaft that contains a piston. The familiar jackhammer has a throttle that admits pressurized air to a cylinder; this causes the piston to deliver successive blows to the chisellike device at the tool's lower end.

pneumococcus   see STREPTOCOCCUS

pneumonia [noo-mohn'-yuh]
Pneumonia is an inflammation of the LUNGS caused by a wide variety of agents, including viruses, bacteria, microorganisms known as *Mycoplasma* and *Rickettsia*, and fungi. Inflammation also occurs with the inhalation of various dusts or gases and with the aspiration of food or stomach acid as a result of vomiting during an unconscious state. The pathological process consists of irritation of lung tissue. The walls of air sacs (alveoli) swell or are destroyed, and plasma, red blood cells, and white blood cells from lung capillaries fill the alveolar spaces. The portion of the lung involved becomes relatively solid and basically is rendered temporarily nonfunctional. Typical symptoms include fever, chills, cough, chest pain (pleurisy), increased production of sputum, sweating, aching, expectoration of blood, and difficulty in breathing.

Viruses are believed to cause about half of all pneumonias. These infections range from mild (walking pneumonia) to severe and rapidly fatal. The most common form of bacterial pneumonia is caused by the pneumococcus *Streptococcus pneumoniae*. It is often referred to as lobar pneumonia because it frequently spreads in a lobar, or segmented, manner throughout the lung. (Double pneumonia refers to the simultaneous inflammation of both lungs.) Other causative bacteria include *Staphylococcus*, *Bacteroides*, *Klebsiella*, and HEMOPHILUS *influenzae*. These types of pneumonia can be treated successfully with antibiotics. Vaccines against pneumococcal pneumonia are available.

Primary atypical pneumonia is a special type of pneumonia that occurs frequently in children and young adults. It is caused by the microorganism *Mycoplasma pneumoniae*. Another microorganism, *Pneumocystis carinii*, causes pneumonia in persons with depressed immune systems, as in leukemia. A preventive drug, trimethoprim sulfamethoxazole, is available for leukemia patients.

Po River [poh]
Italy's longest river, the Po flows approximately 650 km (405 mi) across the northern part of the country. From its source in the Cottian Alps in northwestern Italy, the Po flows northeast past Turin, Pavia, Piacenza, Cremona, and Ferrara to its delta on the Adriatic Sea, south of Venice. In all, the river drains an area of about 70,000 km^2 (27,000 mi^2). The Po's tributaries—the Dora Baltea, Tanaro, Ticino, and Adda—bring water from both the Alps and the Apennines. Seasonal flow variations prevent the river's use by regular shipping. The densely populated Po valley, with such manufacturing centers as Turin, Milan, and Brescia, is both an agricultural region and Italy's industrial center. The Po valley probably has been settled since the 3d millennium BC, and Etruscan settlements there date back to the 6th century BC.

Pocahontas [poh-kuh-hahn'-tis]
An American Indian princess, Pocahontas, b. *c*.1595, d. Mar. 21, 1617, supposedly saved the life of Capt. John SMITH and befriended the English colony at Jamestown, Va. She was a daughter of Powhatan, chief of the POWHATAN confederacy of Virginia. Her personal clan name was Matoaka.

In 1608, Smith, who had helped establish the English settlement at Jamestown, was captured by the Indians and brought to Pocahontas's village, about 24 km (15 mi) from Jamestown. According to Smith's account in his *Generall Historie of Virginia* (1624), he was set before an altar stone to be killed but was spared when Pocahontas threw herself over his body. Many historians have been skeptical about Smith's story. Pocahontas then reportedly persuaded Powhatan to bring food to the starving colonists.

In 1613, Pocahontas was seized by Capt. Samuel Argall and taken to Jamestown and then to the new community of Henrico. She learned the elements of Christianity and became a convert. Pocahontas also learned the ways of the English, and in 1614, with her father's approval, she married John ROLFE, a successful tobacco planter. The marriage initiated an eight-year period of peaceful relations between Indians and settlers. A boy, christened Thomas, was born to the couple in 1615. The following year Pocahontas (now Lady Rebecca Rolfe), her family, and an Indian retinue voyaged to England. Pocahontas charmed London society and was entertained at the royal

Pocahontas, portrayed here as Lady Rebecca, was an American Indian woman of the 17th century. The daughter of Chief Powhatan of Virginia, she reputedly saved Capt. John Smith's life in 1608. In 1616, Pocahontas and her husband, John Rolfe, visited England; she was received at court and met the poet Ben Jonson. (National Gallery of Art, Washington, D.C.)

palace at Whitehall. While preparing to return to the New World, she was overcome by illness and died.

Pocatello [poh-kuh-tel'-oh] A city in southeastern Idaho and the seat of Bannock County, Pocatello has a population of 46,080 (1990). On the Portneuf River near its junction with the Snake, the city is a processing center for farming and livestock and has a phosphate-mining industry. Idaho State University (1901) is there. Settled in the 1880s, Pocatello was named for a Bannock Indian chief.

pocket gopher Pocket gophers are about 30 species of burrowing rodents making up the family Geomyidae and found from southwestern Canada to Panama. They are thickset animals, with large, flattened heads, barely distinct necks, small eyes and ears, and usually a short tail that is either sparsely haired or naked. They are characterized by an external opening in the skin of each cheek that leads into a fur-lined pouch, the "pocket," used to transport food. Pocket gophers range up to 30 cm (12 in) long, plus a 14-cm (5.5-in) tail, and up to 900 g (2 lb) in weight. They feed primarily on the underground portions of plants but also eat succulent stems.

podiatry [puh-dy'-uh-tree] Podiatry, also known as chiropody, is a specialty concerned with the medical and surgical care of human feet. Podiatrists are licensed to make independent judgments in the care of patients. Admission to the profession requires four years of advanced education in a school of podiatry, leading to the degree of doctor of podiatric medicine.

podocarp [pahd'-uh-kahrp] Podocarp is the common name of evergreen coniferous trees and shrubs of the genus *Podocarpus* in the family Podocarpaceae. The name refers to the characteristic fruit, which is a round, fleshy seed on a thick stalk. This single seed represents a primitive form of a seed-bearing cone. Pollen is borne in yellow catkinlike cones. Most species have flat, narrow leaves, but some have broader leaves. Podocarps are native to the higher elevations of tropical and subtropical regions of the Southern Hemisphere and are found in the West Indies and Japan. A few species are used for timber, known as yellowwood. Certain tree and shrub species are used as ornamentals, for yewlike hedges, or as greenhouse plants.

podzol see SOIL

Poe, Edgar Allan [poh] Edgar Allan Poe, b. Boston, Jan. 19, 1809, d. Oct. 7, 1849, produced some of the most enduring literary criticism of his time and some of the most musical poetry, but his reputation rests primarily on his contributions to fiction.

Early Life. Orphaned before he was 3, Poe was taken into the Richmond, Va., home of a childless, well-to-do couple, John and Frances Allan. He accompanied them to England 3 years later, studying for the last 2 of 5 years there in the suburban London boarding school described in his tale "William Wilson." Poe's education continued in Richmond and then for one year at the new University of Virginia. He proved a good student, especially in languages, but he ran up a gambling debt, and Mr. Allan prevented his return to college. Poe had seen before him a career appropriate for a Southern gentleman—perhaps politics, perhaps a commission in the army—but suddenly his prospects appeared bleak. Mrs. Allan's death prompted a change of heart in her husband, and he secured Poe an appointment at West Point. The reconciliation proved short-lived, however, and when it became clear that his foster-father would not contribute to his support, Poe arranged to be dismissed from West Point. At age 22 he found himself disinherited, destitute, and without a profession.

Artist and Critic. Poe had published by that age three dozen poems, including "Romance" (1829), in which the influence of Byron is apparent; "Fairy Land" (1829), which makes fun of the style of Thomas Moore; and "Israfel" (1831) and the 15-line "To Helen" (1831), pure poems that are distinctly his own. Poe would leave only about 50 poems, published (many more than once) in the volumes *Tamerlane and Other Poems* (1827), *Al Aaraaf, Tamerlane, and Minor Poems* (1829), *Poems by Edgar A. Poe... Second Edition* (1831), and *The Raven and Other Poems* (1845).

Fiction promised greater rewards, and the young poet turned to the short story, a genre still in its infancy, which he, more than any other writer, would shape and perfect. Recent critics have found more "literature" than "life" in Poe's early tales: like "Fairy Land," they were written as imitations or parodies of prevailing literary styles. Indeed, this creative genius who worked as a magazine editor and book reviewer (Richmond, 1835–36; New York City, 1837, 1844–49; Philadelphia, 1838–44) never recognized the boundary between fiction and criticism. Thus "How to Write a Blackwood Article" and the attached tale "A Predicament" (1838) make fun of overwritten stories in which narrators narrowly escape death; in "The Pit and the Pendulum" (1842), however, he produced what might be called the greatest "Blackwood article" ever written. "The Masque of the Red Death" (1842) is among Poe's most effective serious tales; yet it appeared in the same issue of *Graham's Magazine* in which Poe as book reviewer first praised Hawthorne as "original in *all* points" and then charged that the idea for Hawthorne's "Howe's Masquerade" (1838) was stolen from Poe's own "William Wilson" (1839). In fact, Poe had stolen—or expropriated—the idea for "The Masque of the Red Death" from "Howe's Masquerade."

Poe virtually invented detective stories. He called them "tales of ratiocination," for such stories as "The Murders in the Rue Morgue" (1841) and "The Purloined Letter" (1844) focus attention not on a criminal or a crime but on the mental processes of a brilliant detective, C. Auguste Dupin. Another of his contributions to fiction is closely related. "Ligeia" (1838), "The Fall of the

One of the great figures of American literature, Edgar Allan Poe displayed a fascination with the mysterious and the horrific in much of his work. His short fiction, such as "The Mystery of Marie Rogêt" (1842), one of the first detective stories, features shrewd analysis and subtle characterization.

House of usher" (1839), "William Wilson," and "The Tell-Tale Heart" (1843) are tales told by "unreliable narrators." The reader must assume the role of detective, and the act of reading becomes a major focus. The key to such enigmatic tales lies in style. The agitation and convolution of the language of the narrator of "Ligeia" warns the reader to regard his story with skepticism. The narrator is a maniac, probably homicidal. In "The Fall of the House of Usher" the narrator's language degenerates from clarity to confusion. By the end of the tale he has come to share mad Roderick's hallucinations.

Reputation. "I desire," Charles Baudelaire wrote in 1856, "that Edgar Poe, who is no great thing in America, should be a great man in France." His idolizing essays on Poe and his pellucid translations of the prose, together with Stephane Mallarmé's translations of the poems, made the neglected American just that—a major figure in French literature. Poe's direct influence on American literature was to prove negligible, but through his influence on the great French symbolists he has come to have a profound effect on world literature, American literature included. Baudelaire's translations, however, missed the key variety of Poe's styles, thus inviting readers to confuse the writer with his narrators. Moreover, Baudelaire's interpretation of Poe the man as the poète maudit, the poet condemned (to drunkenness, addiction, evil) by a society that could not understand him, perpetuated a dark myth scholars and biographers have striven with incomplete success to dispel.

The fault here is not Baudelaire's: he derived virtually all his information from a tainted source. When Poe died, he left instructions that the Reverend R. W. Griswold serve as his literary executor. Griswold published an admirable edition of the works, but he included a long biographical essay that represented Poe as a drunkard (he seldom drank), a negligent journalist (he was an energetic and productive editor), and an envious, conniving fraud whom none could admire (he was respected by a wide circle of friends). Griswold even intimated sexual misconduct. (Poe's marrying his 13-year-old cousin Virginia when he was 27 raises questions, but he proved a good

and faithful husband.) To support his calumnies, Griswold resorted to innuendo and outright fabrication. Friends who knew the truth rose to Poe's defense, but Griswold's lies were believed and Poe was condemned—or by some admired—for faults that were never his.

poet laureate The term *poet laureate* refers to those poets appointed by the monarchs of Great Britain to provide poems commemorating historic or official occasions. John Dryden was the first such poet officially named (1668), but the term *laureate* had been previously used in association with such poets as Geoffrey Chaucer and Ben Jonson. In 1985 the U.S. Congress added the title of poet laureate to the already-existing position of consultant in poetry at the Library of Congress. The appointment is made yearly but may be renewed.

poetry The term *poetry* is usually associated with artificial or highly refined language, whereas *prose* is regarded as the natural medium of communication. It appears, however, that the literature of all cultures began with poetry, whose rhythmic and sensuous qualities satisfy a fundamental human need.

Poetry generally differs from other kinds of literature in its reliance on the techniques of prosody and VERSIFICATION, and the term *poetry* is often equated with *verse*. A poem, in this partial and inadequate sense, is any metrical and rhymed composition. It is clear, however, that *poetry* carries a further range of meaning because it often suggests a value judgment: *verse* may imply a mechanical jingle; *poetry*, a form of verbal art capable of eliciting an emotional response from the reader. The ambiguity of the term is allowed by its origin. Etymologically, *poetry* is derived from the Greek work *poiein*, "to make," and the poet is therefore one who invents, or makes things up. For the ancient Greeks this word signified any artist—writer, painter, or musician—who made forms that did not previously exist in nature.

Poetry is closely allied with other forms of language but differs from them in that it exploits the shapes and sounds of words as well as their meanings. Poetic form, however mysterious its final effect, can be investigated through the language from which it is created. Such an inquiry can usefully include the common parts of speech as well as the more elusive qualities of METAPHOR, SYMBOLISM, and imagery. Poetry may also alter the normal relations between the words of a prose sentence by manipulating syntax, changing their sequence and, therefore, their meaning. Meaning itself can be modified and made sensuous by meter and other devices, such as alliteration and assonance, that are apprehended by the ear.

Poetry, an art form that depends on sensuous immediacy, cannot be fully explained by abstract concepts, but it can be divided into its various GENRES—kinds of compositions that are distinguished according to formal characteristics. Among these genres are EPIC, a narrative of heroic actions and events of more than personal significance; LYRIC, mellifluous verses originally intended to be sung; and SATIRE, moral censure of evil, pretension, or anti-social behavior. The primary genres, distinguished by Aristotle according to their manner of presentation as epic, DRAMA, and lyric, have in turn given rise to other kinds of poetry such as the BALLAD, ELEGY, ODE, and SONNET.

Classical attempts to explain the nature of poetry were made in spiritual terms. Homer and Hesiod claimed that their writings were inspired by the MUSES, who were, in Greek mythology, the daughters of the goddess of memory. Plato, the first literary critic of importance, wrote numerous discussions of poetry, all of which describe it as the outpouring of a supernatural force that binds the poet to the audience by an irrational attraction. The association of poetry with madness, which has greatly affected attempts to estimate its social value, was long current throughout western European culture. Shakespeare's celebrated description of poetic imagination in *A Midsummer Night's Dream* is characteristically ironic in its grouping of the poet with the lunatic and the lover.

Recognition of the power of poetic imagination is made ambiguous by the suggestion that poetry may, after all, consist of "nothing." This attitude was already evident in the poems of Hesiod, who acknowledges that the muses may tell lies and make them seem like truth, and is amplified by Plato, who banishes poets from his utopian state, The REPUBLIC, on the moral grounds that poetry is a counterfeit creation that appears to be true but merely mimics the misleading appearance of the physical world. From the European Renaissance through the 19th-century romantic movement the argument about the nature of poetry and its moral and aesthetic utility revolved about the issues raised by Plato. Sir Philip Sidney, in his *Apology for Poetry* (1595), saw the poetic imagination as an afflatus that gave access to truth beyond the scope of reason; for Wordsworth, writing two centuries later, poetry still claims to be a realm of knowledge quite separate from rational inquiry but no less accurate and true.

Aristotle was less concerned with the psychology of poetic composition and the abstract question of what poetry is than with pragmatic analysis of how poetry affects its audience. He explained that poetry was the outcome of humanity's desire to imitate life. Plato believed that poetry is to be valued only insofar as it imitates ideal truth; Aristotle asserts that imitation is valuable in itself. Plato objects to poetry because it excites emotion; Aristotle says that this has a beneficial, cathartic effect. More important still, Aristotle rebuts Plato's stricture that poetry is a third-hand copy of ideal truth by claiming that, in its concern for what is universally true in human nature, it is more valuable than other kinds of writing, such as history, which is confined to mere fact. It was Aristotle who first expressed and discussed poetry's claim to represent a separate reality—not a microcosm of the real world but an independent realm subject to its own laws.

Moralists have always argued that poetry is false, and philistines have dismissed it as useless. Poetry, however, was originally intended to teach and was therefore functional. It probably originated in the magical incantations and formal storytelling of preliterate societies, in which it played an important civic and religious role. All societies once valued poets as preservers of tradition. Homer, Vergil, Ovid, Firdawsi, and the anonymous authors of *Beowulf*, the *Edda*, and the *Mahabharata* were celebrators of cultural traditions that they idealized, stressing the connections between past and present and between humanity and the gods.

Such poetry was transmitted orally (see ORAL LITERATURE), perhaps by professional poets, and it is thought that Homer composed his poems before the invention of a writing system. Even after the invention of writing, the Greeks consulted Hesiod for information on agriculture, and in Roman times Lucretius set down scientific knowledge in verse. Horace said that poetry should both please and instruct and could be both beautiful and useful. The idea that the hedonistic and the practical functions of poetry are allied was long-lived, and this notion was not dispelled until the 20th century. Many Renaissance humanists, such as Sidney, regarded moral profit as the aim of poetry, and the most forceful critic in the age of neoclassicism, Samuel Johnson, wrote that "it is always the writer's duty to make the world better."

The legend of the poet Archilochus, whose imprecations drove his enemies to suicide, suggests some of the functions that poetry originally served and the reverence with which the poet was regarded. It could placate and invoke spiritual powers in poems that were the remote ancestors of odes, hymns, and panegyrics, and it could expel evil influences by violently abusive verses that were the earliest satire. These functions are now so weakened that they have virtually disappeared, but poems in praise of public acts are still written, especially in totalitarian states, and satirists are still capable of inducing fear and hatred. Rhythm and meter, which give words an appeal to the ear regardless of their meaning, made poetry a useful means of instruction. Versification was then a mnemonic device—and it remains so in advertising jingles and in verses such as "30 days hath September...."

It seems likely that the growth of literacy reduced poetry's didactic purpose because that function was then assumed by prose. Poetry nonetheless continued to play a public role—as panegyric, history, and satire—until well into the 19th century in Europe, and the British monarch still appoints a POET LAUREATE. The last major poet to believe that poetry could influence political events was perhaps W. B. Yeats, who feared that his poems had helped to incite the bloodshed of the Irish Rebellion.

Pogonophora [poh-guh-nahf'-uh-ruh]   Pogonophora is a phylum of wormlike marine animals commonly known as beardworms. Pogonophorans, first dredged up from deep water in Indonesia in 1900, are now thought to be common and widespread in the deep-sea environment. Two orders—Thecanephria and Athecanephria—and about 100 species are recognized. Pogonophorans typically live in upright chitinous tubes, which they secrete in soft bottom ooze, usually at depths of 1 km (3,000 ft) or more. They commonly range from 6 to 36 cm (2.5 to 14 in) and may reach 85 cm (33.5 in) in length, but are less than 2 mm (8/100 in) in diameter. The body consists of a short front region bearing from 1 to about 250 tentacles (hence the name beardworm) and tube-secreting glands; a long mid-region; and a short end region used to anchor the animal in its tube. Pogonophorans lack a mouth, digestive system, and anus, and it is not known exactly how they obtain their food. Suggested modes of nutrition include the external digestion and absorption of organic debris, and the direct absorption of amino acids produced by microorganisms. In sulfide-rich habitats near HYDROTHERMAL VENTS, scientists have found SYMBIOSIS between tube worms and sulfide-oxi-dizing bacteria. The bacteria inhabit and obtain the hydrogen sulfide they need from the worms, in turn providing nutrients for the worms.

pogrom [puh-grahm'] *Pogrom,* the Russian word for riot involving destruction, is the name that came to be applied to the mob attacks on Jews and Jewish property, primarily in Russia between 1881 and 1921. The tsars indirectly encouraged pogroms by their anti-Semitic policies and their unwillingness to act against the assaults. Among the more notorious incidents were those at Kiev and more than 200 other sites, mostly in the Ukraine, in 1881; at Kishinev in 1903; and at Odessa, Yekaterino-slav, and hundreds of other locations, primarily in the Ukraine and Bessarabia, in 1905. The worst pogroms took place during the tumultuous period of the Russian Revolutions and Civil War (1917–21). They were perpetrated by the White Russian forces, independent anti-Bolshevik bands, and to a lesser extent by some Red Army units; more than 60,000 Jews were killed.

Pohl, Frederik [pohl] An American writer, editor, and anthologist of science fiction, Frederik Pohl, b. New York City, Nov. 26, 1919, is known for satires of present follies extrapolated into the future. In collaboration with Cyril Kornbluth he wrote *The Space Merchants* (1953), a satiric prediction of the ultimate triumph of advertising. Writing on his own or in collaboration with Kornbluth and Jack Williamson, Pohl has dealt with such themes as overpopulation, air pollution, and computerization. Pohl's works, which have won four Hugo awards, include both novels and short-story collections, such as *Day Million* (1970), *Gateway* (1977), *JEM* (1979), and *The Years of the City* (1985).

Poincaré, Henri [pwan-kah-ray'] Jules Henri Poincaré, b. Apr. 29, 1854, d. July 17, 1912, was one of France's greatest theoretical scientists. His contributions to mathematics, mathematical physics, and celestial mechanics were often basic, profound, and highly original. His interest in the foundations and philosophical issues of the fields in which he worked were also influential.

In mathematics, Poincaré can be said to have been the originator of algebraic topology and of the theory of analytic functions of several complex variables. He also made fundamental advances in the theory of Abelian functions and in algebraic geometry. Moreover, as a student of Charles Hermite, Poincaré was interested in number theory; his major contribution was related to a problem in the theory of Diophantine equations.

Poincaré was deeply involved in the mathematics relevant to problems of celestial mechanics, the THREE-BODY PROBLEM, and theories of light and electromagnetic waves. He is credited by many as a codiscoverer (with Albert Einstein and Hendrik Lorentz) of the special theory of relativity. He helped place celestial mechanics on a rigorous basis in two major works: *New Methods of Celestial Mechanics* (3 vols., 1892–99; Eng. trans., 1967) and *Leçons de mécanique céleste* (Lessons of Celestial Mechanics, 1905–10).

Poincaré, Raymond Raymond Poincaré, b. Aug. 20, 1860, d. Oct. 15, 1934, French premier (1912–13, 1922–24, 1926–29) and president (1913–20), advanced policies leading to France's entrance into World War I. Between 1887 and 1912 he sat in the Chamber of Deputies and in the Senate and held several cabinet posts. In 1912, Poincaré became premier and foreign minister. As a conservative, stubborn patriot, he wanted to prepare France in the event of war with Germany. During his first ministry he reinforced the Franco-Russian and Anglo-French ententes. As president in 1913, with World War I threatening, Poincaré secured a law extending conscription to three years.

Seeking to maintain national unity, Poincaré allowed a personal enemy, Georges CLEMENCEAU, to become leader of the government in 1917; he believed that Clemenceau alone could secure a victory. After World War I he supported a hard line against the Germans at Versailles, and in 1923 he ordered the occupation of the Ruhr to force the Germans to continue reparation payments. During his last years as premier, Poincaré won great popularity by stabilizing the franc.

poinsettia [poyn-set'-ee-uh] The poinsettia, *Euphorbia pulcherrima*, is a showy flowering plant belonging to

The poinsettia shrub is a favorite decorative plant during the Christmas season. Its small, winter-blooming flowers are usually surrounded by large, bright-red or white leaves.

the SPURGE family, Euphorbiaceae. It is particularly popular at Christmastime as a potted houseplant. The poinsettia "flower" actually is bracts, or modified leaves, which usually are red but also may be white or pink. At the center of the bracts are the tiny true flowers. The poinsettia thrives outdoors in subtropical and tropical regions, where it can reach heights of more than 3 m (10 ft). Native to Mexico and South America, it must be grown indoors in cold climates; it is a popular garden shrub in southern states and California.

point   The term *point*, an undefined element in GEOMETRY, may be interpreted or described in several ways. In elementary-school geometry a point is considered to be a position in space and is usually represented by a dot. Points and lines are the basic undefined elements of geometry. A point is a zero-dimensional figure; a line is a one-dimensional figure. Two points determine a unique line (the line that connects them). Two distinct coplanar lines that are not parallel determine a unique point (the point of intersection). Points (x, y) on a coordinate plane and points (x, y, z) in coordinate space are determined by their coordinates. Euclid described a point as "that which has no part," the ultimate indivisible geometric element.

Point Four Program   Point Four, an American foreign-aid program, was proposed by President Harry S. TRUMAN as the fourth point in his Jan. 20, 1949, inaugural address and was approved by Congress in June 1950. A technical-assistance program designed to improve living standards by helping people in underdeveloped countries acquire industrial and agricultural equipment and skills, Point Four was intended as a bulwark against Communism. Its funds were administered by several U.S. agencies and by the United Nations.

pointer   The origin of the pointer, a type of hunting dog, is uncertain. The consensus is that it was derived

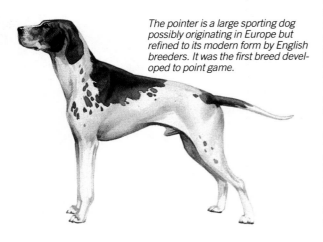

The pointer is a large sporting dog possibly originating in Europe but refined to its modern form by English breeders. It was the first breed developed to point game.

from the Spanish pointer, which is said to have been brought to England in 1713. Others believe that the Italian pointer or the French pointer was a major contributor to the breed. Whatever the pointer's ancestry, its development was entirely British. It was developed from hounds that showed a tendency to pause before concealed game rather than flushing and chasing it. In the 1700s the pointer was crossed with foxhounds and other breeds, among the most likely being the greyhound.

The pointer has a long, rectangular head, hanging ears, and a long tail. Its coat is short, hard, and glossy and may be liver, lemon, black, or orange, either solid or mixed with white. The breed stands from 58.5 to 71 cm (23 to 28 in) high at the shoulder and weighs from 20.5 to 34 kg (45 to 75 lb). Most pointers are registered with the Field Dog Stud Book, a hunting- and field-trial–oriented registry, rather than with the American Kennel Club.

poison   A poison is a chemical that produces a harmful effect on a living organism. Almost any substance has the potential of being poisonous in humans if a substantial amount gains entry into the body or if the substance enters the body by way of the wrong route. As a result, a variety of poisons exist in solid, liquid, gaseous, or vaporous form. Naturally occurring poisons are used by POISONOUS PLANTS AND ANIMALS to prevent predation or to capture prey. Synthetic poisons range from certain types of pharmaceuticals (used other than as directed) or household cleaning products to waste products of industrial and nuclear-energy plants and chemicals deliberately used as weapons (see CHEMICAL AND BIOLOGICAL WARFARE).

Dosage, route of entry, and potency (strength) determine if a substance is poisonous. For example, if water is accidentally inhaled into the lungs instead of being swallowed, it becomes an asphyxial poison. Whereas a specific dose of a prescription drug may be safe and effective for a 45-year-old man who weighs 82 kg (180 lb), the same dose may prove fatal for an 85-year-old woman weighing 45 kg (100 lb).

Poisons can enter the body in many ways, depending on their chemical and physical properties. Gases such as methane, carbon monoxide, and hydrogen sulfide are inhaled. Some chemicals can penetrate the skin, and others can be poisonous if injected into the body. Most poisons, however, enter the body by way of the mouth, and the greatest number of poisonings in the United States occur as a result of oral ingestion. There are approximately 13,000 deaths each year in the United States as a result of poisonings, and more than 80 percent of these are accidental.

Most poisonings are of the acute type, occurring in a short period of time, such as FOOD POISONING AND INFECTION. Treatment for most acute poisoning consists of supportive therapy and ridding the body of poison. Depending on the type of poison swallowed, emergency treatment may involve inducing vomiting with syrup of ipecac. In some cases, antidotes are available that counteract the effects of poison, such as nalorphine for narcotic poisonings and desferokamine for iron poisoning.

Chronic poisonings are often brought about by environmental or occupational exposure to such substances as LEAD or MERCURY compounds, which accumulate in the body. RADIATION INJURY from nuclear accidents, such as the one that occurred in 1986 in Chernobyl in the Soviet Union, is another example of chronic poisoning. Treatment for chronic poisoning is limited to removing the patient from exposure to the poisoning agent and providing therapy to relieve symptoms.

poison gas   see CHEMICAL AND BIOLOGICAL WARFARE

---

poison hemlock   Poison hemlock, *Conium maculatum*, a biennial herb of the carrot family, Umbelliferae, is very poisonous and is the plant associated with the death of Socrates. It is native to Europe but now grows wild throughout the New World. Poison hemlock reaches 3 m (10 ft) tall and has a smooth, hollow stem that is spotted or striped with purplish color. Its root is white and carrot-like. The leaves, which may exceed 30 cm (12 in) in length, are divided into many fine-toothed segments. The tiny white flowers are formed into small clusters, which themselves are grouped into multiple dome-shaped clusters about 5 cm (2 in) across.

Common poison hemlock is a powerfully aromatic, notoriously poisonous biennial herb. A drink made from the plant was used by the Athenians to execute the philosopher Socrates.

A twining plant, poison ivy, the scourge of campers and hikers, is easily recognized by its three shiny leaflets. It also produces clusters of tiny flowers that develop into gray berrylike drupes.

southern Canada to Guatemala and in Bermuda, the Bahamas, and parts of Asia. Contamination can occur through direct or indirect contact with the plants or by exposure to smoke from burning plant parts. The resulting DERMATITIS, which may spread from the site of contact, can range from itching and inflammation to severe swelling with oozing blisters. Treatment with cortisone creams and ointments helps.

---

poison oak   The name poison oak is often applied to the shrublike forms of poison ivy and to at least two similar plants that are usually considered separate species of the cashew family, Anacardiaceae. The poison oak of the southeastern United States, *Rhus quercifolia*, has leaves divided into three hairy leaflets that generally have three to seven distinct lobes. The poison oak of the U.S. Pacific coast, *R. diversiloba*, is a shrubby or sometimes climbing plant; its three-leaflet leaves are toothed or lobed and are hairless. Both species contain poisonous substances that are believed to be identical or closely related to that found in poison ivy.

---

poison sumac [soo'-mak]   Poison sumac, *Rhus vernix*, of the eastern United States, is a shrub or small tree of the cashew family, Anacardiaceae. It grows to 6 m (20 ft) or more in height and has a smooth, gray, black-speckled bark. Its leaves, divided into 7 to 13 smooth-margined leaflets, are from 15 to 38 cm (6 to 15 in) long and have bright red stalks.

The small, greenish white or yellowish green flowers are borne in drooping clusters on purplish stalks, followed

---

poison ivy   The classification of poison ivy, a member of the cashew family, Anacardiaceae, is confused because of the plant's highly variable growth forms. Some authorities recognize at least two species of poison ivy, *Rhus radicans* and *R. toxicodendron*, whereas others consider these a single species. (The confusion is added to by referring to the shrubby forms of these plants as POISON OAK.) Poison ivy is a trailing or climbing woody vine or a shrublike plant containing a poisonous, oily substance called urushiol or toxicodendrol. The leaf consists of three leaflets, which are commonly dark glossy green above and slightly hairy below. Small, yellowish or greenish flowers are followed by berrylike drupes. Poison ivy is native to eastern North America but is now found from

Poison sumac is more of a skin irritant than poison ivy. In fall it has scarlet leaves and white berrylike drupes.

by hanging clusters of small, grayish white berrylike drupes. The poison, considered more toxic than that of poison ivy, can cause serious skin reactions.

poisonous plants and animals POISONS, or toxins, substances that chemically interfere with the normal physiology and behavior of organisms, are pervasive in nature. Some form of poison is produced by almost every major group of organisms. Because plants do not have the option of running, hiding, or fighting to avoid being eaten, many plant species have developed some form of chemical deterrent to prevent their being fed upon by herbivores. Chemical weaponry appears in all major animal groups with the exception of the vertebrate class Aves, the birds. Toxins manufactured by animals are called VENOMS, plant-synthesized poisons are collectively known as secondary substances, and the toxins generated by microorganisms (algae, bacteria, and fungi) are technically referred to as ANTIBIOTICS, which have proved useful in the development of drugs.

Natural poisons are usually complex chemicals, many with highly specific modes of action that have evolved by natural selection in the contexts of defense, competition, and exploitation. In most cases, these substances confer advantages on their producers. Natural poisons function in three ways: to prevent predation, to protect resources, and to capture prey.

Kinds of Poisons. Natural poisons may be classified in several ways: by their chemical composition, by how they are produced or acquired, by the organisms they affect, by their mode of action, and by their method of delivery.

Natural toxins are found in all four of the major classes of organic compounds: carbohydrates, lipids, proteins, and nucleic acids. They range in molecular complexity from cyanide (HCN), a simple compound produced by

certain millipedes and found in peach pits, to complex protein molecules containing scores of carbon atoms.

Toxins are synthesized directly from raw materials by both plants and animals, selectively concentrated from the soil by plants, or sequestered from plants by herbivores. Soil nitrates in toxic concentrations are accumulated from the soil by many plant species. The monarch butterfly, *Danaus plexippus*, is noted for its larvae having the ability to sequester cardiac glycosides contained in the milkweed plants (*Asclepias*) upon which they feed. This provides a chemical defense for the larva, the pupa, and the adult butterfly.

Natural poisons directed against animals are called zootoxins; those active against plants are called phytotoxins. Most phytotoxins are fungicidal, defending plants against parasitism by fungi. Mature creosote bushes produce toxins that inhibit the growth of and prevent the establishment of competitive seedlings in their vicinity.

Natural poisons range in effect from mild to severe, and are sometimes fatal. They include skin irritants, emetics (vomit-inducing agents), proteolytic (protein-digesting) agents, hemotoxins (blood poisons), neurotoxins (nerve poisons), muscle contractants and relaxants, and physiological regulators. Some of these toxins affect specific organs, such as cardiac glycosides that impinge on the heart, and others interfere with critical life processes, such as molting in insects. Some poisons may have long-term effects and may result in the development of cancerous growths.

Passive Poisoners. Any poisonous species that requires an action by the target organism to dispense its poison is called a passive poisoner. Virtually all plants that produce toxic secondary substances are passive poisoners because they must be ingested in order for their poisons to have an effect. The addictive alkaloid drugs—such as nicotine from tobacco, cocaine from the coca plants, opium from poppies, and psilocybin from certain mushrooms—belong in this category.

Some animals are passive poisoners. Puffer fishes in the family Tetrodonidae are considered a delicacy in Japan and Southeast Asia, although the viscera of these fish contain tetrodoxin, an extremely potent poison.

Other types of passive poisoners that require only animal contact in order to transmit poison include poison oak, poison ivy, and poison sumac, and the skin of bufonid toads, *Bufo*, which all exude toxic substances that cause irritation of the epidermal tissues of animals that contact them. Certain Central and South American tree frogs produce a poison from skin glands whose toxicity is so severe that small amounts are used to tip darts and arrows for hunting.

Some poisonous plants and animals that use passive poisoning either to secure prey or for defense deliver their noxious chemicals when an offending animal punctures itself with sharp spines or triggers an otherwise static delivery mechanism. In nettles tiny spinose hairs inject the plant's poison, as do the urticating (stinging) hairs of certain caterpillars. Lion fish and scorpion fish in the family Scorpaenidae are some of the most venomous fish; if ap-

Venomous snakes include the black mamba (A) and puff adder (B), both of Africa; the Indian cobra (C) of southern Asia; and the sea snake (D), of Indo-Pacific waters. The stonefish (E), stingray (F), and Portuguese man-of-war (G) inject venom into their victims by means of fin spines, a tail spine, and stinging cells on the tentacles, respectively. Plants that are toxic when eaten include the buttercup (H); deadly nightshade (I); and parts of rhubarb (J), and pokeweed (K). The fly agaric (L) is a poisonous mushroom.

proached in a contentious manner, they present their venomous spines and invite the aggressor to bump them. Coelenterates such as jellyfish, sea anemones, and stinging corals have tiny barbed darts called nematocysts, which inject venoms when triggered by contact.

Active Poisoners. The overwhelming majority of venomous animals are active poisoners, with aggressive behavior patterns or mechanisms specifically evolved to dynamically deliver their venoms. Active poisoners employ three basic methods of dispensing their venoms: biting, stinging, and squirting. Biting includes piercing, stabbing, and chewing. Piercing involves highly specialized mouthparts through which sharp stylets pierce the skin of the victim; these parts are found in the insect orders Hemiptera (the true bugs) and Diptera (the flies). Salivary or associated glands produce the venom, and ducts transport it to the tubelike mouthparts through which it is injected into the victim. Stabbers include all hollow-fanged species such as spiders, centipedes, and rattlesnakes. These creatures employ hypodermic injection directly analogous to what is accomplished by a hypodermic needle and syringe.

Stinging species that are active poisoners include the sting rays, the scorpions, and the ants, wasps, and bees. The barb at the tip of the scorpion tail injects venom produced in the last tail segment. Ants, wasps, and bees have posterior abdominal stingers that are hollow. These inject venom from special glands and storage sacks in the abdomen.

Venom squirters are a remarkable group that includes the whip scorpions, *Uropygi*, which spray acetic acid on their antagonists, and the bombardier beetles, *Brachinus*, which create a small explosion in a specially designed abdominal chamber such that a caustic liquid at a very high temperature blasts from the insect's posterior. The marksmanship of the spitting cobra, *Naja nigricollis*, is such that it can project its venom up to 3 m (9.8 ft) and hit the eyes of its victim. This feat is surpassed by skunks, *Mephitis*, which can disable enemies up to 9 m (30 ft) away with a fine spray of butyl mercaptan.

Evolution. Many natural poisons are believed to have begun their evolution as metabolites, mildly toxic intermediate or waste products of essential metabolic processes. This has often been the point of departure in the development of most plant poisons. ENZYMES, proteins essential to the control of the chemistry of life, were the likely starting compounds for the development of many animal venoms. For example, the digestive enzymes found in animal saliva have been modified to produce venoms in spiders, true bugs, flies, snakes, and shrews. Accessory glands associated with the female reproductive system of wasps, ants, and bees have evolved the secondary function of venom production, and the ovipositor has been modified through evolutionary time to produce the stinger.

Most animals learn from unpleasant experiences to avoid negative circumstances. Therefore it is not surprising that many animals with particularly punishing chemical defenses have developed bright colors and distinctive behavioral displays that become recognizable to potential victims. Some species mimic others to avoid predation.

Natural Poisons and Humans. Although toxins from plants and animals kill few people in the United States each year, they kill many thousands worldwide. In North America, poisoning by rattlesnakes (*Crotalus*), coral snakes (*Micrurus*), widow spiders (*Latrodectus*), brown spiders (*Loxosceles*), and scorpions (*Centruroides*), may be life-threatening if untreated. Poisoning from plants (excluding plant-derived narcotic drugs) amounts to less than 2,000 cases annually, and the number of human deaths attributable to plant poisons is insignificant. The most common plant poisonings of humans are by common ornamental and house plants—such as holly (*Ilex*), pyracantha (*Pyracantha*), philodendron (*Philodendron*), and dieffenbachia (*Dieffenbachia*)—consumed by children. Any plant or animal toxin can cause severe allergic reactions in persons who have a tendency to be allergic to various substances. Anaphylaxis (a severe reaction to specific substances such as wasp venom or penicillin) is the life-threatening manifestation of this condition; it kills far more people than the direct effects of all natural toxins combined. Most U.S. states have poison-control centers that are operated 24 hours a day to provide information on all kinds of poisoning.

The benefits of natural toxins enormously outweigh their negative impact on humans. These compounds, in regulated doses, have great utility as drugs for managing and treating human and domestic animal disease and as research tools to enhance the understanding of life processes. For example, digitalis, a substance obtained from the common foxglove, *Digitalis purpurea*, is used as a drug to regulate heartbeat rate; quinine, an alkaloid from the bark of the cinchona, *Cinchona officinalis*, was the first drug to be used successfully to treat malaria. In addition, plants supply commercial insecticides, such as rotenone and pyrethrum. The genes for thousands of compounds may be inserted into the major food and fiber crop plants using GENETIC ENGINEERING to protect them against insects and disease.

Poitier, Sidney [pwah'-tee-ay]

Sidney Poitier, b. Miami, Fla., Feb. 24, 1924, was the first black to play a leading role in an American movie without reference to his race. *The Blackboard Jungle* (1955), *The Defiant Ones* (1958), *Lilies of the Field* (1963; Academy Award, best actor), *The Bedford Incident* (1965), *Guess Who's Coming to Dinner* (1967), and *In the Heat of the Night* (1967) are among his key films. He both starred in and directed *A Patch of Blue* (1973) and directed *Stir Crazy* (1980) and *Traces* (1981). He returned to the screen in *Little Nikita* (1987). Poitier portrayed (1991) Thurgood Marshall as a young lawyer in the actor's first television-movie role.

Poitou [pwah-too']

Poitou is a historic region in west central France. Wheat, corn, and cattle are raised there, and industries produce machinery, chemicals, and dairy products.

Poitiers, the former capital of the region, is its chief city. Called Limonium by the Romans, Poitiers has been occupied since prehistory. Roman baths and amphitheaters, the Baptistery of Saint John (4th–12th century), the Cathedral of Saint Pierre (12th–14th century), the palace of the counts of Poitou, and the University of Poitiers (1431) are there.

The region's first known inhabitants, the Pictavi, a Gallic tribe, were conquered in 56 BC by the Romans, who incorporated the area into Gaul as part of the province of Aquitania. The Visigoths seized the region in AD 418, but it passed to the FRANKS in 507. In 732 or 733, CHARLES MARTEL ended the Muslim invasion of western Europe by his victory in the Battle of Poitiers. From the 10th to the mid-12th century, the counts of Poitou were also the dukes of AQUITAINE, and the city of Poitiers grew in importance. In 1152, Poitou came under English control through the marriage of ELEANOR OF AQUITAINE to Henry II (later king of England). The region was reunited with the French crown in 1416 and was a province of France until the Revolution (1789–95), when it was divided into three departments, Vienne, Deux-Sèvres, and Vendée.

poker

Poker, originally a card game for unprincipled gamblers only, is now played for amusement or stakes at home or exclusively for stakes in gambling establishments. There are two basic forms of the game: draw, or closed, poker, in which all players' cards are unknown to the other players until the showdown; and stud, or open, poker, in which some or all cards are exposed as play progresses.

Most poker games require a standard 52-card deck. The object of all poker games is to have a better five-card hand than any other player or to win by bluffing the other players into believing that one has a better hand and thus causing them to fold, or drop out, from that particular hand.

Draw poker is the most commonly played variant. Five-card draw poker, also known as jacks or jackpots, is best played by two to six persons. Each player is dealt five cards, face down and one at a time. Each player then places a set number of chips or money, called the ante, on the table to form the pot. The player who opens the betting must hold a pair of jacks or a better hand. Then each player, in clockwise order, may fold, call (that is, match) the bet in order to remain in play, or raise the stakes. Once this round of betting is over, the players remaining in the hand may draw up to three new cards in an attempt to improve their hands. Players who elect to draw new cards must have discarded previously a like number of cards. After all players have drawn, the player who opened the first round of betting reopens the betting, whereupon the other players, in turn, may check (momentarily pass the turn), call, fold, raise, or reraise. When the betting is over, players who have not folded reveal their hands in the showdown, and the player with the high hand wins the pot.

The most popular form of stud poker in the United States is seven-card stud. It is best played by two to eight persons. Each player is dealt two cards face down, called the hole cards, and one card face up. The players then bet. The subsequent cards are all dealt face up; in some versions the last card is dealt face down. Players continue

These poker hands, shown in ascending order of value, are nine of the 2,598,960 poker hands possible with a 52-card deck. Although various ways to play the game exist, these combinations are the same everywhere: one pair (1), two pairs (2), three of a kind (3), straight (4), flush (5), full house (6), four of a kind (7), straight flush (8), and royal flush (9).

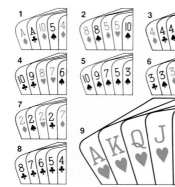

to bet as each new round is dealt. In the showdown each player selects the best five cards of the seven held.

Poker hands are listed here in descending order of value. A royal flush is the ace, king, queen, jack, and 10 of the same suit. A straight flush is any sequence of five cards in the same suit. Four of a kind is any four cards of the same denomination. A full house is any three cards of one denomination and any two cards of another. A flush is any five cards of the same suit. A straight is any five cards of more than one suit in sequence. Three of a kind is any three cards of the same denomination, plus any other unmatching cards. Two pairs is any two cards of the same denomination, plus two cards of another denomination, plus any fifth card. One pair is any two cards of the same denomination, plus any three other cards.

Some authorities trace poker to the Persian game *as nas*. Most experts, however, believe that poker may be more directly traced back to the old Italian game of primero and the French game of gilet, which became brelan during the reign (1550–74) of Charles IX. Brelan evolved into bouillotte, which flourished during the French Revolution. It is from this game that the betting techniques of poker are derived. Brelan also gave rise to ambigu, which included the draw feature, and the English game of brag, which incorporated bluffing.

pokeweed   The pokeweed family, Phytolaccaceae, includes about 25 species of perennial herbs. *Phytolacca americana*, native to the United States and Mexico, is commonly known as poke or pigeonberry. Its deep purple berries, when ripe, are a source of red dye. Young stalks, when cooked, are edible, but the bitter roots and the mature stalks, leaves, and berries are poisonous.

Pol Pot   [pawl paht]   The Cambodian communist leader Pol Pot, b. May 19, 1928, became prime minister of Democratic Kampuchea (now Cambodia) in April 1976. He joined Ho Chi Minh's Indochinese Communist party in the 1940s and became the leader of the KHMER ROUGE movement that overthrew the American-backed govern-

ment of Lon Nol in 1975. Pol Pot's regime allegedly caused the deaths of more than 1,000,000 Cambodians in an attempt to build a purely agrarian-based Communist society. In January 1979, Vietnamese forces invaded Cambodia and overthrew the Pol Pot government. Pol Pot retreated to the hills bordering Thailand. In 1982 he formed the coalition government of Democratic Kampuchea with non-Communist partners. His retirement as head of the Khmer Rouge was announced in 1985, but he retained a military advisory role.

Poland   Poland is a nation in east central Europe. It borders on the Baltic Sea and the USSR in the north, the USSR in the east, Germany in the west, and Czechoslovakia in the south. The dominant power in eastern Europe from the 14th to the 17th century, Poland was divided up by its neighbors in the 18th century and ceased to exist until 1918. Again partitioned by Germany and the USSR at the beginning of World War II, it was reestablished as a Soviet satellite in 1945 and remained a Communist-dominated "people's republic" until 1989. Poland is now an emerging liberal democracy that is moving toward a market economy. The capital is WARSAW.

Land and Resources

Poland's principal topographical characteristic is the North European Plain, which extends across most of the country. Along the Czechoslovak border in the south are the CARPATHIAN and SUDETEN mountains. The highest elevation is Rysy (2,499 m/8,200 ft) in the High Tatra range of the Carpathians.

Soil and Drainage. Poland's highest-quality soils are in the central and southern areas. The two principal river systems flowing northward into the Baltic Sea are the ODER, which forms the border with Germany, and the VISTULA in central Poland.

Climate. The country's climate is continental, moderated by maritime weather from the Atlantic. The mountain regions can suffer extreme cold in the winter, as well as sudden *föhns*—dry south winds sweeping the northern side of the ranges. Average annual precipitation in Warsaw is 635 mm (25 in); the mountain resort of Zakopane has twice as much.

Flora and Fauna. Poland's forestlands, which account for about one-quarter of its territory, contain pine, spruce, fir, oak, elm, poplar, and the indigenous Polish larch. The Bialowieza forest on the Soviet border is unique in Europe not only for its primeval nature but as the home of the European bison. Animals commonly found in deciduous and mixed forests include deer and wild boar. More typical of the taiga are elk and mountain hare, while fauna found in the mountains include the lynx and the brown bear.

Natural Resources. Coal is the most important mineral resource. The hard (or bituminous) coal mined around Katowice in Upper SILESIA is of high quality, but Poland also produces brown coal (lignite). Upper Silesia contains significant deposits of lead ore and zinc, while Lower Silesia has some of Europe's largest copper deposits.

REPUBLIC OF POLAND

Land: Area: 312,683 km² (120,727 mi²). Capital and largest city: Warsaw (1989 est. pop., 1,651,000).

People: Population (1990 est.): 38,064,000. Density: 122 persons per km² (315 per mi²). Distribution (1990): 61% urban, 39% rural. Official language: Polish. Major religion: Roman Catholicism.

Government: Type: republic. Legislature: Sejm. Political subdivisions: 49 provinces.

Economy: GNP (1989): $172.8 billion; $4,560 per capita. Labor distribution (1988): agriculture—28%; industry and mining—27%; commerce—8%; construction—8%; transportation and communications—7%; services and other—22%. Foreign trade (1987): imports—$22.8 billion; exports—$24.7 billion. Currency: 1 zloty = 100 groszy.

Education and Health: Literacy (1989): 99% of adult population. Universities (1989): 11. Hospital beds (1989): 217,470. Physicians (1989): 78,662. Life expectancy (1990): women—77; men—68. Infant mortality (1990): 13 per 1,000 live births.

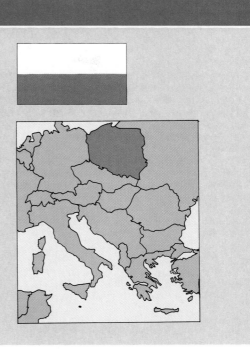

People

Prior to World War II, Poland had sizable German, Ukrainian, Belorussian, and Jewish minorities. Polish Jewry was largely destroyed in the HOLOCAUST; after the war most of the Germans of western Poland were expelled, and the Ukrainian and Belorussian districts of eastern Poland were transferred to the USSR. As a result, 98% of the present population are ethnic Poles. Roman Catholicism, the predominant religion, is closely identified with Polish national feeling. The Polish language serves as the first language for nearly the entire population. In the freer atmosphere that has followed the end of Communist domination in 1989, the minority groups that remain (Silesians of German descent and Ukrainians) have become more assertive.

Urbanization accelerated during the Communist period, the urban population exceeding the rural component for the first time. Aside from Warsaw, the largest cities are ŁÓDŹ, KRAKÓW, WROCŁAW, POZNAŃ, GDAŃSK, SZCZECIN, BYDGOSZCZ, KATOWICE, and LUBLIN.

Education and Health. Compulsory elementary education together with a two-track secondary system of academic and vocational schools have produced a well-educated population. The coalition government that took office in 1989 has encouraged the establishment of private schools and private medical care.

The Arts. Poland's literary tradition is covered in the article POLISH LITERATURE. In music and the visual arts, as in literature, Poland's heritage is linked to the countries of Western Europe.

Polish avant-garde art can be dated to the early-20th-century dramatists and painters Stanisław WYSPIAŃSKI and Stanisław Witkacy. The most noteworthy figures of the post–World War II period include the sculptor Władysław Hasior, the poster artists Franciszek Starowieyski and Waldemar Swierzy, and the experimental theater directors Jerzy GROTOWSKI, Adam Hanuszkiewicz, Tadeusz Kantor, and Józef Szajna. The Łódź film school's most renowned graduate is the contemporary director Andrzej WAJDA. Contemporary Polish composers include Witold LUTOSŁAWSKI and Krzysztof PENDERECKI.

Economic Activity

The deterioration of the Polish economy in the 1980s was a major factor in the crisis that forced the Polish United Workers' (Communist) party to surrender its monopoly of power in 1989. Heavy borrowing from Western banks in the 1970s left Poland saddled with an unmanageable debt. In 1987 the Polish government reached an agreement with its creditors on restructuring the debt, with payments extended over a period of 15 years. Western aid to Poland increased substantially after the political revolution of 1989.

The new non-Communist government sought to bring about economic reform through "shock therapy" in a scheme devised by Finance Minister Leszek Balcerowicz. Price subsidies on foodstuffs and manufactured goods were removed, and many state-owned industries were sold to private owners, work-force collectives, and foreign companies. At first the results were chaotic. Inflation and unemployment rose dramatically, industrial production fell, and the currency lost much of its value. The situation was eased by the inflow of foreign credits and foreign investments. By the summer of 1990 the currency had stabilized, and although prices remained high, the shops were filled with an abundance of consumer goods.

Manufacturing. In line with Communist policy emphasizing heavy industry, iron and steel production—largely based in the Katowice region—was at the heart of the manufacturing sector between 1945 and 1989. The chemical industry was developed in the same period. The chief light industry was textiles, based in Łódź. Beginning in the 1970s, greater attention was given to production for the consumer market, for example, motor vehicles, food processing (especially fish), and electronics.

Agriculture. Temperate-zone grains produced in Poland include barley, oats, rye, and wheat. The country's production of potatoes and sugar beets is among the world's highest. Pork has been the traditional animal stock bred on Polish farms, but cattle and sheep farming increased in the 1980s. Pasture land represents 20% of agricultural land use. The most productive farm sector, even under Communist rule, was the family farm. The Communist government's approach to agriculture was to maintain large-scale private ownership, in contrast to neighboring Communist countries.

Transportation. Extensive rail and road systems span the country. The major ports—equipped with modern shipyards and container terminals—are Gdańsk, Gdynia, and Szczecin. Lot, the Polish national airline, provides regular flights between all major Polish cities.

Trade. As a member of the COUNCIL FOR MUTUAL ECO-

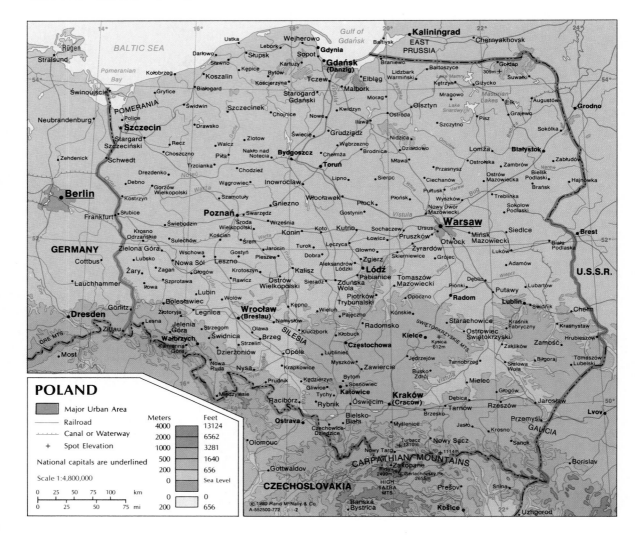

NOMIC ASSISTANCE (Comecon), Poland's trade was principally with the USSR and other Communist countries, but both Comecon exports and imports showed a steady decline from the early 1970s. By the mid-1980s nearly a third of Poland's foreign trade was with developed capitalist states. The principal exports are coal, machinery, and agricultural products, and the major import commodities are petroleum and natural gas.

Government and Politics

The so-called "roundtable agreement," worked out in 1989 between Communist leaders and SOLIDARITY, the previously outlawed opposition movement, established the basis for a new political system with a powerful presidency. The president is elected by the National Assembly for a six-year term. In the roundtable agreement the presidency was entrusted to the head of the previous Communist regime, Gen. Wojciech JARUZELSKI.

The National Assembly consists of two houses: the Sejm (or Diet), which has 460 seats based on electoral districts, and the Senate, whose 100 members represent the country's 49 provinces. The Senate, which serves as a check on the Sejm, has limited powers. Members of both houses serve four-year terms.

The first elections for the Assembly were held in June 1989, and in August Tadeusz Mazowiecki, representing the Solidarity-backed Civic Committees, was installed as prime minister. His government was composed mostly of non-Communists. Although he did not hold any government or parliamentary office, Lech WAŁESA, founder and head of Solidarity, played a major role in the political process.

The party system continued to evolve following the official dissolution of the Polish Communist party in early 1990. In May 1990 the first elections to local councils were held throughout the country, and Solidarity candidates won overwhelmingly. The Citizens' Committees increasingly moved away from the trade-union part of Solidarity. By the summer of 1990, Wałesa's supporters had organized into the Center Bloc, while his rivals in Solidarity had formed the Citizens' Democratic Action Movement.

Other political parties in Poland include a peasants' party that invokes the legacy of the interwar party headed up to 1948 by Stanisław Mikołajczyk. Two other peasant parties are Rural Solidarity and the previously pro-Communist Peasant party (now called Renewal). Other noteworthy parties include the nationalist right-wing Confederation for Independent Poland, the Christian Democratic party, the formerly pro-Communist Democratic party, a new Socialist party, and, further on the left, the Social Democratic Union and, successor to the Communist party, Social Democracy of the Polish Republic. Most parties claim to base political programs on the social teachings of the Catholic church, thus seeking the support of the ecclesiastical establishment headed by the primate Józef Glemp and the former Polish cardinal Karol Wojtyla, now Pope JOHN PAUL II.

The presidential election in November–December 1990 was a three-way race between Wałesa, Mazowiecki, and Stanisław Tyminski, a Polish-born emigré busi-

The Old City, dating from medieval times, forms the nucleus of Gdańsk (Danzig), one of Poland's principal ports. Gdańsk formerly had a large German population, and Hitler's desire to annex the city was one of the main causes of war between Germany and Poland in 1939. More recently, Gdańsk was the birthplace of the Solidarity movement.

nessperson from Canada. Mazowiecki was eliminated in the first round, and Tyminski in the second, Wałesa winning with nearly 75% of the vote.

History

The name *Poland* is derived from that of the Polanie, a Slavic people that settled in the area, probably in the 5th century AD. Polish history begins with the conversion of the Polish nation to Christianity in 966 under Prince Mieszko I. Mieszko's son, BOLESŁAW I, was crowned as the first king of Poland, establishing the PIAST dynasty. The last of the dynasty was CASIMIR III, crowned in 1333. He extended Polish influence eastward into Lithuania and Russia and acquired POMERANIA from the TEUTONIC KNIGHTS in the west. During his 37-year reign a university was established, law was codified, castles were fortified, and minority groups were given protection.

In 1386, 16 years after Casimir's death, the Polish nobility selected a grand duke of Lithuania, Jagello (see JAGELLO dynasty), to rule by arranging his marriage to the Polish queen JADWIGA. The initial personal union with Lithuania, formalized only two centuries later by the Union of Lublin in 1569, produced a state that extended from the Baltic Sea in the north to the Black Sea in the south. Poland's Golden Age had begun, symbolized by the Polish victory over the Teutonic Order at the Battle of Tannenberg in 1410.

The Polish Renaissance of the 16th century produced a flourishing of the arts and intellectual life, exemplified by the scientific work of COPERNICUS. Protestantism gained adherents in Poland during this period, and the Jewish community, which had prospered in Poland since the 14th century, won the right of self-government. The country's economic wealth was based on grain exports to western Europe.

In 1572 the Jagello dynasty ended with the death of SIGISMUND II, and power was transferred from the aristocracy to the broader class of the nobility called the *szlachta.* From 1573 to the last partition of Poland in 1795 the Republican Commonwealth was organized around a system of elective monarchy and of a Sejm in which each of the nobles had a vote. The kings Stephen Báthory (r. 1575–86; see BÁTHORY family) and SIGISMUND III (r. 1587–1632) sought greater influence abroad by intervening in Russia, and Sigismund even succeeded briefly in installing his son on the Russian throne during MUSCOVY's TIME OF TROUBLES.

During a war-torn decade beginning in 1648, Poland was attacked by Ukrainian Cossacks, marauding Tatars, Turks, and Russians. The Swedes laid to waste virtually the entire country in 1655. King JOHN III Sobieski's victory over the Turks at Vienna in 1683 recovered some of Poland's prestige as a European power, but he could not stop further loss of the eastern territories. During the reign (1697–1733) of AUGUSTUS II, who was also elector of Saxony, Poland was involved in the Great Northern War. Austro-Russian intervention in Poland in support of the second Saxon king, AUGUSTUS III, triggered the War of the POLISH SUCCESSION (1733–35).

The last king of Poland, STANISŁAW II (r. 1764–95), was a puppet of Catherine II of Russia. Anti-Russian feeling led to the formation (1768) of the Confederation of Bar, a French-supported alliance of Polish nobles, but this was unable to prevent the dismemberment of Poland

Lech Wałesa, shown here addressing a group of his followers, was the founder of Poland's Solidarity movement. Jailed by the Polish Communist regime in 1981, Wałesa reemerged as a leader of democratic reform and was elected president in 1990.

by Russia, Prussia, and Austria (see POLAND, PARTITIONS OF). Even as its fate was being decided by the great powers, the country plunged forward with radical new experiments in democracy and reform, culminating with the constitution of May 3, 1791, which granted political rights to the burghers and peasants. The defeat of Tadeusz KOŚCIUSZKO's national insurrection of 1794 was followed by the partition of 1795.

Foreign Rule. A short-lived Polish state reemerged when Napoleon I established the Grand Duchy of Warsaw in 1807, but in 1815 the Congress of Vienna once more divided the country among Russia, Prussia, and Austria. In the Russian sector, Tsar Alexander I established the Congress Kingdom of Poland with himself as monarch. The bloody Polish uprising of 1830 was put down after a nine-month struggle, and a second abortive nationalist uprising occurred in 1863. In the 1870s the German chancellor Otto von Bismarck sought to eliminate Polish culture in the Prussian-occupied lands. In Austrian-controlled GALICIA, on the other hand, the Poles enjoyed considerable autonomy.

At the beginning of the 20th century, Polish leaders were divided over the means to employ to regain independence. The most notable representative of the political right was Roman DMOWSKI, who headed the National Democracy movement. He believed that an ethnically homogeneous Polish nation, free of Ukrainian and Jewish influence, had the best chance to regain a political identity. On the Left, Rosa LUXEMBURG and Feliks DZERZHINSKY believed that nationalism was anachronistic. Others, including Józef PIŁSUDSKI, argued that the Polish workers' movement should not be subordinated to any other movement.

Independence. When independence finally came in 1918, it was the result of the dissolution of the Russian, German, and Austrian empires at the end of World War I; the ideological foundation of the reborn Polish state owed more to Woodrow Wilson's Fourteen Points than to the arguments of the Polish right or left. Piłsudski became the dominant political figure in interwar Poland until his death in 1935. In 1920 he led Polish legionnaires against the Russian Bolsheviks in the Polish-Soviet War with considerable success, winning boundary concessions favorable to Poland in the Treaty of Riga (1921). It did not matter to Piłsudski that 60% of the population in the territories regained from Russia were non-Polish. In 1926, Piłsudski staged a coup d'état and established a thinly disguised personal dictatorship. The "colonels' regime" that followed Piłsudski was not able to meet the threat posed by Nazism in Germany and failed to conclude defensive security agreements with the other European powers.

World War II. In September 1939 the German army attacked Poland from the west and the Soviet army from the east. Hitler and Stalin had agreed in the NAZI-SOVIET PACT to carve up Poland once again, and after a six-week struggle the nation capitulated. German occupation led to the extermination of Polish Jews at the AUSCHWITZ, TREBLINKA, and Majdanek death camps, and the slaughter of 3 million ethnic Poles in summary street executions, gas chambers, labor camps, and the WARSAW UPRISINGS.

The Poles suffered at the hands of Russian forces too. Close to 2 million Poles were removed from territories east of the Bug River and sent to Kazakstan, Siberia, and the Soviet Far East, many to die in the harsh gulags. The massacre of at least 10,000 Polish officers at Katyn and elsewhere by the Soviet secret police further showed the brutality of the Stalinist regime. By July 1944, Soviet forces had begun to drive the Germans out of eastern parts of Poland, and a pro-Soviet provisional government was established in Lublin.

Communist Poland. Agreements among the victorious Allied powers had placed Poland in the Soviet orbit; by 1948 anti-Communist resistance had been overcome, and the country was firmly in the hands of the Polish United Workers' party, which established a rigid police state. Redrawn boundaries had deprived Poland of its eastern lands but compensated it with former German territories in the west. Hopes for greater freedom rose in 1956 when Władysław GOMUŁKA came to power in the liberal atmosphere of the "Polish October." Gomułka quickly shut the door on political pluralism, however, and his attacks on the church, the cultural intelligentsia, and protesting students in 1968 were greatly resented.

Edward GIEREK, who replaced Gomułka as party chief in 1970, helped modernize the Polish economy, but he also countenanced widespread corruption, graft, and waste. Gierek's overthrow was accomplished by the Solidarity-inspired strikes in the Gdańsk shipyards during the summer of 1980. The Solidarity labor union created the first independent social and political movement in postwar Eastern Europe. Its demands for democratic reforms led to the imposition of martial law (December 1981) by Wojciech Jaruzelski, who had taken over leadership of the party and government. The Solidarity movement went underground, and for the rest of the 1980s, Polish society manifested both battle fatigue from the lost political struggle and renewed determination to live as much of its life as possible free from Communist dictates. Mikhail Gorbachev's appointment as Kremlin leader in March 1985 was the signal that the Polish opposition had been waiting for. Exploiting the new liberalization in the region, Lech Wałesa and Solidarity, Pope John Paul II and the church hierarchy, and ordinary citizens stung by the deepening economic recession combined to force the Communists to sit down at roundtable talks in 1989, and finally drove them from power.

___

Poland, Partitions of The Partitions of Poland (1772, 1793, 1795) divided the Polish kingdom among its three powerful neighbors, Russia, Austria, and Prussia. By the First Partition (1772), which was designed to meet Russian demands for additional territory, Russia took part of northeast Poland. To maintain the balance of power, Austria annexed Galicia, and Prussia took Polish Pomerania and Ermeland. Humiliated by these encroachments, the Poles began to reform and strengthen their central government. A constitution adopted May 3, 1791,

PARTITIONS OF POLAND

1772	1793	1795	To Russia	■ 500,000 people
1772	1793	1795	To Brandenburg-Prussia	—— Boundary in 1770
1772	1775	1795	To Austria	

Cartographic Production by Lothar Roth & Associates.

replaced the elective monarchy with hereditary kingship and introduced liberal reforms abolishing feudal legal and social practices.

Fearing that a revived Poland might recover its lands, Russia intervened militarily and with Prussia arranged a Second Partition (1793), giving the former most of eastern Poland and the latter Gdańsk and Great Poland. In 1794, Tadeusz KOŚCIUSZKO led a national revolt in Poland, which, although initially successful, was crushed by Russia and Prussia. This defeat resulted in the Third Partition (1795), in which Russia, Austria, and Prussia absorbed the remainder of Poland. The Polish state was not restored until 1918.

___

Polanski, Roman [poh-lan'-skee] The Polish film director and actor Roman Polanski, b. Paris, Aug. 18, 1933, was a student (1954–59) at the Polish State Film School at Łódź. His first feature film, *Knife in the Water* (1962), a subtle treatment of sexual tension, presaged more explicit treatments of sexuality in *Repulsion* (1965) and *Cul-de-Sac* (1966). With *Rosemary's Baby* (1968), Polanski established himself as a master of macabre horror. After the 1969 murder of his wife, the actress Sharon Tate, by the Charles Manson gang, he moved to France to become a French citizen, but returned to the United States to make *Chinatown* (1974). Indicted for a sexual offense in Los Angeles in 1977, he returned to France, where he made *Tess* (1980) and *Frantic* (1988).

polar bear   see BEAR

polar climate   Polar climates are confined to high latitudes and are characteristically too cold to support the growth of trees. Over large parts of the continents, the poleward limit of tree growth coincides approximately with the 10° C (50° F) isotherm, or line of equal temperature, for the warmest month. The average location of the arctic front (the boundary between air masses of Arctic and polar origin) over North America and Eurasia in July also corresponds with this boundary.

During much of the winter, the Sun is constantly below the horizon in polar regions, and thus the incoming solar radiation is zero. Because the terrestrial radiation is outgoing, the radiation budget is negative. In summer the Sun never sets, and the incoming radiation greatly exceeds the outgoing radiation, but temperatures remain low because of the high reflectivity (ALBEDO) of clouds and snow and ice surfaces. Furthermore, because the melting of the snow-and-ice cover consumes considerable energy, the surface temperature is usually held close to freezing.

The Arctic is a region of frequent cyclonic activity. Antarctic weather is complicated by elevation above sea level. Weather disturbances occur frequently at the margins of the continent, but the interior core region is rarely affected, and precipitation there is meager.

polar wandering   Polar wandering is the apparent movement of the Earth's magnetic poles over long periods of geologic history (see EARTH, GEOMAGNETIC FIELD OF). This motion has been charted by studying the magnetic fields "frozen" into ancient rocks to determine their latitude at the time of their formation (see PALEOMAGNETISM). A polar-wandering curve shows the apparent migration of the poles as seen from a particular continent. Each continent exhibits a unique curve. This suggests that the continents themselves have moved, not the poles, supporting the theory of CONTINENTAL DRIFT. The latitudes of the continents as they have moved can be mapped in this way. This is not the case for longitudes, however, because polar-wandering charts do not distinguish between east-west motions and rotations of a continent. The charts support the assumption that the magnetic poles have always nearly coincided with the Earth's axis of rotation.

polarimeter [poh-luh-rim'-uh-tur]   The polarimeter is an optical instrument used to determine the chemical concentration of certain chemical substances by observing the interaction of these materials with polarized light. The same basic principles that are used in the POLARISCOPE apply to the polarimeter (see OPTICAL ACTIVITY).

In a simple visual polarimeter, the elements of the light path, starting from its source, are: (1) a light source, such as a sodium, mercury, or cadmium arc; (2) a filter to isolate a narrow band of wavelengths; (3) a polarizer prism system, usually a Nicol prism; (4) a sample tube in which the unknown solution is placed; and (5) a rotatable analyzer system (essentially identical with the polarizer) equipped with a graduated circular-reading scale. Con-

centration is determined by the amount of rotation, which can be read with a precision of 0.002 degrees.

Polaris (astronomy) [poh-lair'-is]   Polaris, also called the North Star, is a second-magnitude star that remains in a nearly fixed position; the other Northern Hemisphere celestial objects appear to rotate about it. Polaris will be the pole star for only a few hundred more years, because precession of the Earth's axis (see PRECESSION OF THE EQUINOXES) causes Polaris to drift slowly away from the north celestial pole. The brightest star in the constellation Ursa Minor (see LITTLE DIPPER), Polaris is about 680 light-years distant from Earth.

Polaris (missile)   Polaris, a submarine-launched ballistic missile (SLBM), was the first nuclear missile developed by the U.S. Navy in conjunction with its development of a nuclear deterrent force. The Polaris program began in 1957; the first submerged firing of the missile occurred in 1960. Among its innovations, the Polaris had a two-stage solid propulsion system, an inertial navigation guidance system, and a miniaturized nuclear warhead. Production ended in 1968, after more than 1,400 missiles had been built. The last version, the A-3, had an increased range (4,700 km/2,900 mi compared with 2,700 km/1,700 mi for the A-2 model) and multiple-warhead capability (see MIRV MISSILE). The missile was replaced by the POSEIDON SLBM, and later by the TRIDENT.

The British Royal Navy had (1990) a fleet of four nuclear submarines, each carrying 16 Polaris A3TK missiles, which are British-designed adaptations of the U.S. Polaris. They will be replaced by Trident II missiles by the mid-1990s.

polariscope [poh-lair'-uh-skohp]   The polariscope is an optical instrument for demonstrating and studying the interaction of various materials and phenomena with polarized light. The basic operations that occur in the polariscope are: a parallel beam of polarized light is produced; the state of polarization of the light beam is transformed (its plane is rotated or its ellipticity changed) by the material or experiment under investigation; and the new state of polarization is analyzed. The basic concept of the polariscope dates back to the early 1800s.

polarized light   A normal beam of light consists of many individual waves, each vibrating in a direction perpendicular to its path. Normally, the vibrations of each ray have different orientations with no favored direction. In some cases, however, all the waves in a beam vibrate in parallel planes in the same direction. Such light is said to be polarized, that is, to have a directional characteristic. More specifically, it is said to be linearly polarized, to distinguish it from circularly and elliptically polarized light, to be discussed later.

Light from familiar sources such as a light bulb, the

Sun, or a candle flame is unpolarized but can easily become polarized as it interacts with matter. Reflection, refraction, transmission, and scattering all can affect the state of polarization of light. The human eye cannot distinguish polarized from unpolarized light, so objects illuminated by both kinds of light appear the same to it. This is not true of all animals. In fact, light from the sky is considerably polarized, as a result of scattering, and some animals, such as bees, are able to sense the polarization and use it as a directional aid.

Production of Polarized Light. Any device that is used to produce polarized light is called a polarizer. Most of the methods of producing polarized light involve splitting a beam of unpolarized light according to the direction of the electric vector of the waves (see ELECTROMAGNETIC RADIATION) and separating the polarized portion from the remainder. The simplest and earliest method of achieving this was by reflection of the beam from a dielectric (nonmetallic) surface. The reflected light is always partially polarized and, at a particular angle of incidence, is completely polarized. This angle, called Brewster's angle, is named for Sir David Brewster, who discovered that at this polarizing angle the reflected and refracted rays are 90° apart. Using Snell's law of REFRACTION, Brewster's angle can be correlated with n, the index of refraction of the medium, as $\tan \phi = n$.

Early experimenters also made extensive use of natural crystals that had the property of double refraction, or birefringence. These materials, such as calcite and quartz, can split an incident light beam into two beams linearly polarized at right angles to each other.

Light can be polarized by materials exhibiting the property of dichroism, the ability of the material to absorb light of one electric-vector orientation much more strongly than light vibrating at right angles. Tourmaline is a natural dichroic crystal that has been long used as a polarizer.

Quinine crystals can also completely absorb one component of polarization, but it is very difficult to grow crystals of sufficient size for optical work. The problem was solved in 1928 when E. H. LAND invented the Polaroid sheet polarizer. These are sheets of plastic in which are embedded microcrystals of a dichroic material, such as quinine iodosulfate, that are aligned as the viscous plastic is extruded through a slit. Other forms of sheet polarizers similarly depend on a uniform molecular alignment. These are widely used in many optical instruments, as well as in sunglasses, because they are cheaper than crystals, commercially available, and can be obtained in large sheets.

Circular and Elliptical Polarization. For linearly polarized light, the electric vector is confined to a plane, specifically one containing the direction of propagation. There are types of polarization in which the plane of polarization is not fixed, but rather the electric vector traces out a spiral as the wave moves through space. Circularly polarized light has an electric vector that remains constant as it rotates, whereas in an elliptically polarized wave the electric vector is greater in one direction than in another, so that the tip of the vector describes an ellipse when viewed in the direction of propagation. Rotation can be either clockwise or counterclockwise.

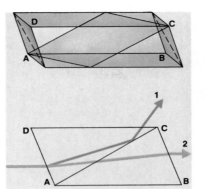

A Nicol prism, for producing polarized light, is made by cutting a calcite crystal in half along the diagonal plane AC and cementing the two pieces back together with Canada balsam. A beam of light entering the end surfaces is split into two plane polarized beams. Beam 1 is internally reflected along AC, beam 2 is transmitted through the prism.

Analyzers. An analyzer is any device that can determine the nature and orientation of polarized light. Linearly polarized light can be detected by any linear polarizer; the light will be transmitted when the orientation of the polarizer matches the plane of polarization of the light, and will be extinguished when the polarizer is turned at right angles. This can be demonstrated with two Polaroid sunglasses, one held in front of the other; the first acts as a polarizer and the second as an analyzer. When they line up, light is transmitted through both; rotating either one prevents the passage of light.

Uses. A major industrial use of polarized light is in stress analysis. Models of mechanical parts are made of a transparent plastic, which becomes birefringent when stressed. Forces are applied to the model, which is then examined in a polariscope between crossed polarizers. Unstressed regions remain dark; regions under stress rotate the polarization of light from the first polarizer so that some can get through the second. When white light is used, each wavelength is affected differently; the result is a highly colored contour map showing the magnitude and direction of the stresses.

Polarized light plays an important role in analytical chemistry. Many compounds are optically active; that is, they have the ability to rotate the plane of plane-polarized light. This property can be used to measure the concentrations, in solution, of such compounds.

Polaroid sunglasses and camera filters are designed to reduce glare. Sunlight reflected off dielectric surfaces is partially polarized, usually in the horizontal plane. The sunglass lenses are oriented to transmit only vertically polarized light, thus eliminating the harsh glare from reflections.

polarography [poh-luh-rahg'-ruh-fee] Polarography is a technique for the identification of chemical species through the use of an electrochemical apparatus known as a polarographic analyzer. The analyzer consists of two electrodes, a source of a highly accurate voltage, and a means of recording the current flowing between the electrodes. The cathode consists of a fine capillary that is filled with mercury. As an analysis proceeds, drops of mercury slowly form at the capillary tip and fall to the bottom of the testing vessel, thus providing a clean, constantly renewed electrode surface. The other electrode, the anode, consists of a pool of mercury in the bottom of the vessel. Voltage through the test solution is gradually increased. The voltage at which current increases serves to identify the chemical species, and the magnitude of the increase compared to a standard serves to quantitate it.

polder   see LAND RECLAMATION

pole, magnetic   see EARTH, GEOMAGNETIC FIELD OF

Pole, Reginald   A major figure in the early Counter-Reformation and the last Roman Catholic archbishop of Canterbury, Reginald Pole, b. Mar. 3, 1500, d. Nov. 17, 1558, reconciled England with the Holy See during the reign of MARY I. Although he was a cousin of Henry VIII, he opposed the Reformation in England. When he defied Henry by not supporting his divorce from Catherine of Aragon, his brother was executed and his mother was imprisoned in the Tower of London and later beheaded. Upon the accession (1553) of Mary Tudor, Pole returned to his homeland to become a close advisor to the queen and, in 1556, archbishop of Canterbury. He died on the same day as Mary.

pole vault   SEE TRACK AND FIELD

polecat   Polecat is the common name for some members of the WEASEL family, Mustelidae. The European polecat, *Mustela putorius*, is found in Europe, Asia, and North Africa and has been introduced into New Zealand; the common European FERRET is a domesticated form. The animal is about 46 cm (18 in) long, plus a 19-cm (7.5-in) tail, and weighs up to 1.5 kg (3.3 lb). Its coat is dark brown to black, with yellowish markings on the head and ears. The lighter-colored Turkestan polecat of the Asian steppes is sometimes classified separately, as *M. eversmanni*. The marbled polecat, *Vormela peregusna*, found from southeastern Europe into Central Asia, has a white or yellowish back with reddish brown mottling. The striped polecat, or zorilla, *Ictonyx striatus*, of Africa,

With its elongated body and short legs, the European polecat resembles the common weasel. This nocturnal predator sometimes preys on poultry and other livestock.

somewhat resembles the spotted skunk. In the United States, skunks are often called polecats.

police   The police are government agents charged with maintaining order and protecting persons from unlawful acts. In most modern democratic nations the police provide a variety of services to the public, including: law enforcement (the detection of CRIME and the apprehension and arrest of criminals), the prevention of crime, and the maintenance of order. In the United States (and in many other countries around the world) the police are the largest and most visible component of the CRIMINAL JUSTICE system.

History. Most developed societies have had some kind of law-enforcement agency. In the English-speaking world—and beyond—police practices are based on English models. Beginning in colonial days, Americans have adopted the English criminal justice system, particularly the law-enforcement pattern. During the 17th and 18th centuries, colonial America relied on the sheriff, the constable, and the night watch for police protection.

The sheriff, appointed by the governor of a colony, was the most important law-enforcement officer in the county. His duties included law enforcement, tax collection, and the maintenance of public facilities. The constable had similar responsibilities, although his jurisdiction was limited to towns and cities. The night watch was charged with the responsibility of protecting the municipality from fires, crime, and suspicious persons.

By the mid-19th century increasing crime rates in Boston, New York, and other large cities resulted in the establishment of new police forces. These new police differed from the old in that the new officers worked both day and night, wore uniforms, carried firearms, and patrolled the streets in an attempt to prevent crime and maintain order. During this period the patterns of basic, present-day urban police operations were set.

In the late 19th and early 20th centuries inefficiency and corruption dominated police work. The primary source of the problems was the political machines that controlled most city governments. By the 1920s a campaign to "professionalize" the police began to emerge. With professionalization came demands for better selection of police officers, centralization of commands, more technology for aiding crime prevention, and the elimination of politics from policing. These reforms slowly occurred during the 20th century.

Agencies. The U.S. police establishment operates at several levels. A number of federal law-enforcement units exist in different U.S. government agencies. The FEDERAL BUREAU OF INVESTIGATION (FBI) is the largest and most important. Other prominent federal units include those of the Drug Enforcement Agency, Immigration and Naturalization Service, SECRET SERVICE, Internal Revenue Service, and Customs Service.

All states except one (Hawaii) have state highway patrols or state police. Highway patrols direct their efforts to highway, motor vehicle, and traffic-safety functions. State-police authority includes jurisdiction over many types of criminal activity as well as traffic services.

Virtually all of the nation's 3,000 counties have police forces, with most of these directed by an elected sheriff.

Municipal police departments constitute the largest number of police agencies in the country. Nearly three-quarters of all full-time police employees work for municipal agencies.

The U.S. police system differs substantially from those of other democratic nations. In European countries, Canada, and Japan police forces are highly centralized. Great Britain, for example, with a population of approximately 46 million people (about one-fifth that of the United States), has a total of 39 law enforcement agencies (compared to some 20,000 in the United States). The London Metropolitan Police Department, with its headquarters at SCOTLAND YARD, is the largest agency in the country.

The Canadian police system bears some resemblance to the U.S. system. The ROYAL CANADIAN MOUNTED POLICE (RCMP) is the counterpart of the FBI. It is mandated to enforce federal laws. The RCMP differs from the FBI in that it has responsibility for law enforcement in provinces that do not have provincial (state) police. Canada also has municipal police departments.

On the international level the United States is a member of the International Criminal Police Organization (INTERPOL). This is a mutual-assistance group that exchanges information among its police members about criminals who operate in more than one country, whose crimes affect other countries, or who have fled from one country to another to escape prosecution.

Operations. Police operations involve the actual work of law-enforcement agencies. The range of police activities is quite broad. It includes areas of patrol, detective work, TRAFFIC CONTROL, vice, crime prevention, and special tactical forces.

The patrol function has three basic components: answering calls for assistance, maintaining a police presence, and probing suspicious circumstances. The object of the patrol function is to disperse the police in ways that will eliminate or reduce the opportunities for lawbreaking and to increase the likelihood that a criminal will be caught while committing a crime, or soon thereafter.

Detectives are primarily concerned with law-enforcement activities after a crime has been reported. They are involved in an investigative function, relying on criminal-history files, laboratory technicians, and forensic scientists for help in apprehending criminals.

Specialized operations units are set up to deal with particular types of problems. Traffic, vice, juvenile, and special weapons and tactics (SWAT) units are often created in larger departments to deal with such problems.

Enforcement of laws against vice—prostitution, gambling, narcotics—is the area that involves undercover work and informers. Juvenile divisions work on processing youth arrests, prepare and present court cases in which a juvenile is involved, and often divert juvenile offenders out of the criminal justice system. The special weapons and tactics (SWAT) units are trained in marksmanship and equipped with shotguns, sniping rifles, automatic weapons, climbing gear, and other specialized equipment useful in dealing with snipers, barricaded persons, or hostage-takers.

Selection and Training. Police agencies use a number of criteria to pick the best-qualified applicants. The most prominent selection methods include a written examination, a background investigation, an oral interview, a medical examination, and possibly psychological testing.

Virtually all departments have minimum requirements for age, height, weight, and visual acuity. Standards vary for each of these categories. Most departments require only a high school diploma as the minimum level of educational attainment.

The formal training for a police recruit involves primarily the technical aspects of police work: the details of criminal law and procedure; internal departmental rules; and the care and use of firearms.

—

poliomyelitis [poh'-lee-oh-my-uh-ly'-tis]   Poliomyelitis, or infantile paralysis, is an acute viral infection caused by any one of three polioviruses. The infection is spread through contact with a polio patient or with human feces. Young children are the most susceptible and the most effective spreaders of the disease, but older persons can also be stricken. The virus enters the body through the mouth and invades the bloodstream. If it enters the central nervous system, it attacks motor neurons and can cause lesions that result in paralysis. The arms and legs are most often affected.

Most instances of contact with polioviruses result in no clinical symptoms or only mild symptoms, such as headache, sore throat, and slight fever; complete recovery occurs in 1 to 3 days. In cases of major illness (when the nervous system is invaded), 50 percent of the patients also recover fully. Of the rest, about half suffer mild disability and the others sustain severe permanent disability, sometimes requiring the use of devices such as the IRON LUNG. The disease can be fatal in bulbar poliomyelitis, when paralysis develops in the throat muscles and can cause respiratory failure through the swallowing of gastric contents; about 80 percent of the patients so stricken, however, can recover through treatment.

In the United States, development by Jonas SALK and Albert SABIN in the 1950s of a vaccine for all three strains of poliovirus brought about a dramatic reduction in the incidence of the disease. In the 1980s, however, concern was aroused when long-term survivors of the disease began reporting various symptoms of joint and muscle pain, fatigue, respiratory problems, and sometimes an increasing loss of muscle strength (postpolio muscular atrophy). Such symptoms are apparently related to a destabilizing of overburdened motor neurons. Therapy for this condition includes carefully paced exercise programs.

—

Polish Corridor   The name *Polish Corridor* was commonly used between 1919 and 1939 for Polish Pomerania (*Pomorze* in Polish), a narrow neck of territory separating East Prussia from the rest of Germany. The area had once belonged to Poland but was seized in 1772 by

Prussia in the First Partition of Poland. It was awarded to the reconstituted Polish state by the Versailles Treaty (1919) at the end of World War I because of its preponderantly Polish population and because it would give Poland direct access to the Baltic Sea. GDAŃSK (or Danzig), a Baltic port east of the corridor, was made a free city. When the German-controlled legislative assembly at Gdańsk limited Polish use of this port, the Poles developed a port at Gdynia, to the northwest. In 1938 the German dictator Adolf HITLER demanded the return of Gdańsk to Germany; his demands for Gdańsk and the Polish Corridor formed the pretext for Germany's invasion of Poland in September 1939.

Polish language   see SLAVIC LANGUAGES

Polish literature   The first important writer to use the Polish vernacular, rather than Latin, was the moralist Mikołaj Rej (1505–69), who produced (1543) a satire on contemporary social and religious affairs. The greatest writer of the Polish Renaissance was the lyric poet Jan Kochanowski (1530–84). Polish baroque literature of the late 16th and 17th centuries includes the lyrics of Jan Andrzej Morsztyn (1620–93) and the emblematic poetry of Zbigniew Morsztyn (c.1628–89). Polish neoclassicism derived its form from the work of the poet and first Polish novelist, Ignacy Krasicki (1753–1801).

Adam MICKIEWICZ, the foremost nationalist poet of the 19th century, is credited with launching Polish romanticism. After the disastrous January Insurrection (1863), positivist writers predominated. These include Bolesław Prus (1847–1912), famous for his panoramic novel of contemporary Warsaw, *The Doll* (1890), and the great historical novelist Henryk SIENKIEWICZ, who won the Nobel Prize in 1905. The loose grouping of neoromantic writers known as Young Poland—including such novelists as Władysław REYMONT, the Nobel Prize winner in 1924, and Stefan Żeromski (1864–1925)—dominated Polish literature from the late 1880s until World War I. Stanisław WYSPIAŃSKI was the principal dramatist of the period, and Jan Kasprowicz (1860–1926) was a leading poet. Avantgarde writers such as dramatist Stanisław WITKIEWICZ, Kafkaesque short-story writer Bruno SCHULZ, and novelist Witold GOMBROWICZ were active between the wars.

Following the ouster of the Stalinist regime in 1956, a range of literature was published, including the work of Czesław MIŁOSZ (1980 Nobel Prize winner, writing from exile since 1951), science-fiction writer Stanisłav LEM, playwright Sławomir MROZEK, poet Tadeusz Rosewicz, and novelist Tadeusz Konwicki. With the imposition of martial law in 1981, a large underground press developed, which began publishing the officially banned work of newer writers like poet Stanisław Baranczak, who became Poland's favorite contemporary poet, and the no-longer-printed works of popular older writers like Maria Dabrowska and Kazimierz Brandys. The liberalization that began in 1989 has seen the virtual ending of censorship, and the works of such authors as emigré novelist Jerzy KOSINSKI are available to Polish readers for the first time.

Polish Succession, War of the   The pretext for the War of the Polish Succession (1733–35) was Austro-Russian intervention in Poland in support of Frederick Augustus II of Saxony, who was elected (1733) king of Poland (as AUGUSTUS III) by a minority of the Polish nobles. His rival was STANISŁAW I, who was elected king by most of the nobles and was supported by LOUIS XV of France.

The war ended with a series of settlements finalized in the Treaty of Vienna (1738). Lorraine was given to Stanisław for life in return for abdicating the Polish throne and was to revert to France after his death. Francis Stephen, duke of Lorraine (later Holy Roman Emperor FRANCIS I), was compensated with Tuscany, added to Austrian possessions because he had married (1736) the Austrian archduchess MARIA THERESA.

With Francis Stephen removed from Lorraine, France recognized the PRAGMATIC SANCTION that made Maria Theresa heir to Holy Roman Emperor CHARLES VI. The War of the Polish Succession also established Russia as a dominant influence in Polish affairs.

Politian [poh-lish'-uhn]   The Italian poet and humanist Politian, or Poliziano, b. July 14, 1454, as Angelo Ambrogini, d. Sept. 24, 1494, was a protégé of Lorenzo de'Medici and the tutor of his sons. Famous for his literary polemics and his translation of the *Iliad* into Latin, Politian also wrote *Orfeo* (1475; Eng. trans., 1921), the first secular Italian drama, which was later turned into an opera (1607) by Monteverdi.

political action committee   In the United States, political action committees (PACs) are organizations established by private groups to support candidates for public office. Labor unions began forming PACs during the 1940s, but corporations were barred from doing so until the passage of the Federal Campaign Act of 1971 (FECA). By lifting the prohibition against using corporate money to set up PACs, the FECA and its 1974 and 1976 amendments legitimized a new and much larger role for trade associations and corporations in politics. Thus, the FECA spawned a dramatic change in the way political money is raised and fostered an enormous growth in the numbers of PACs and in the amount of PAC money spent in elections. The millions of dollars contributed by PACs to congressional candidates underscored concern about the influence of SPECIAL-INTEREST GROUPS. Some members of Congress have created their own PACs, to sway their colleagues. In 1989, President George Bush proposed abolishing most PACs in a plan to reform campaign-financing. (See also POLITICAL CAMPAIGN.)

political campaign   A political campaign consists of activities, by a political party or a candidate for public office, designed to attract voter support in an approaching ELECTION. Such campaigns are an important part of the political process in democracies that allow free competition among political groups.

Political Campaigning in the United States. The traditional American political campaign developed in local, state, and federal elections during the period before the Civil War. It involved visits by candidates to local communities, addresses to public meetings, and the stimulation of popular enthusiasm by means of political pamphlets, slogans, songs, and parades. Many of the classic American campaigning techniques originated in the presidential campaign of 1840, in which the Democratic incumbent Martin Van Buren was opposed by the Whigs under William Henry Harrison (known as Old Tippecanoe) and his running-mate, John Tyler. The Whigs represented Harrison as a man of the people, symbolized by a frontier log cabin and a cider barrel, and made effective use of the slogan (and song) "Tippecanoe and Tyler too." The practice of influencing voters or candidates by bribery was common enough to inspire the passage, beginning about 1890, of laws regulating campaign expenditures.

During the age of railroad travel, presidential aspirants made extensive "whistlestop" tours, pausing at small towns along the way to make speeches from the back of the train. With the coming of radio and television, the electronic media began to play a major part in exposing candidates to the electorate. At the same time, public opinion polls came to be used widely as a means of predicting the vote.

Historically, political campaigns in the United States have been conducted by political parties in contests for control of PATRONAGE and political jobs. Party ideology was usually less important than the struggle for the "perquisites of office." Candidates were nominated by party caucuses, and voters tended to cast their ballots for the party rather than for the candidate.

In recent decades, however, parties have declined in importance, and U.S. politics has been characterized by candidate-centered rather than party-centered campaigns. Campaigns for major offices are now managed, not by party leaders, but by paid professionals who are the equivalent of public relations consultants in the business world. Below them are unpaid but trusted friends of the candidate who provide advice and money. Last come the volunteers who do the basic jobs (mailing campaign literature and ringing doorbells) and work for the candidate because they believe in him or her.

The decline of party influence is associated with the increasing use of the PRIMARY ELECTION as a means for choosing candidates for office, such elections allowing voters to exercise a power formerly held by party officials.

Campaigning has also been affected by changes in the financing of candidates and political parties. The Federal Election Campaign Act of 1971, as amended subsequently, introduced federal financing of candidates in presidential elections, restricted private fund raising, and allowed the formation of POLITICAL ACTION COMMITTEES (PACs) to raise funds for any candidate, thus freeing candidates from financial dependence on their parties. Through PACs, congressional candidates increasingly obtain funds from SPECIAL-INTEREST GROUPS, which may also spend money to defeat candidates they oppose. These changes in nominating and funding candidates have resulted in much longer campaigns, especially those for the presidency, and in much more expensive campaigns.

Campaigns in Other Political Systems. Campaigns in Britain and other parliamentary democracies differ from those in the United States in a number of ways. The number of elected officials, for example, is much smaller. A British voter will typically vote for one member of Parliament and a local councilman. In the United States voters elect the president, U.S. senators and representatives, state legislators, city or town council members, and occupants of many minor offices. Another difference is in the length of campaigns. In parliamentary democracies, the election takes place shortly after it is announced, leaving only about a month for campaign activities.

A third difference between the U.S. campaigns and those in other democracies is in the role of parties. In most democratic societies, elections are still party centered rather than candidate centered. One reason for this is the absence of the primary election. In parliamentary systems, the choice of candidates is usually made by the party organization at the constituency level and ratified by the national-party executive.

In European democracies voter turnout typically exceeds 70 percent of the electorate, whereas in the United States it has not been much above 50 percent in recent presidential elections.

---

political convention Political conventions are meetings at which parties select their leaders, decide on their programs, and organize for election campaigns (see POLITICAL CAMPAIGN). In the United States national party conventions are held during PRESIDENTIAL ELECTION years. Party conventions are also conducted at the state and local levels.

Delegates to the turbulent 1968 Democratic national convention in Chicago celebrate the nomination of Hubert H. Humphrey, Jr., as their party's candidate for president.

A delegate to the 1988 Republican National Convention in New Orleans wears a hat decorated with an elephant, symbol of the GOP. The Republican nominees, George Bush and Dan Quayle, defeated their Democratic opponents, Michael Dukakis and Lloyd Bentsen, by a comfortable margin.

Before the 1830s, U.S. presidential candidates were selected by caucuses of the parties' members in Congress and the state legislatures, or in state conventions. The first national convention was that of the ANTI-MASONIC PARTY in September 1831. Soon afterward the National-Republican (later WHIG) and DEMOCRATIC parties met in respective conventions to nominate Henry Clay and Andrew Jackson for the presidency in 1832. Since then conventions have been held every four years to name candidates for president and vice-president.

Aside from nominating candidates, the party conventions perform three other functions. A convention can establish rules for the selection of delegates, for internal organization, and for membership. It also provides an opportunity for the party to reach the electorate and to attempt to win votes for the campaign. Finally, the conventions decide on the party's platform.

The principal business of conventions, however, remains the selection of national candidates. Traditionally, candidates have been chosen through bargaining among state delegations. In the past this process often led to the selection of relatively unknown, "dark horse," compromise candidates after many ballots had failed to nominate one of the leaders. Thus, Warren G. Harding became the REPUBLICAN PARTY nominee in 1920 through a meeting of ten major politicians in a "smoke-filled room." In recent conventions, however, the presidential nominee has usually become apparent before the convention assembled.

The vice-presidential candidate is chosen on the last day of the convention, usually by the presidential candidate after consultation with other party leaders.

The decisive time for winning a presidential nomination is now long before the convention meets. A president who is completing his first term is usually assured renomination. In a party out of power or a party with a second-term president, the campaign for the nomination begins in January of the election year. Recent evidence indicates that the candidate holding first place in opinion polls at this time is most likely to win the nomination. This outcome can be changed, however, by a candidate's performance in state PRIMARY ELECTIONS that are held to select delegates to the national conventions or to give voters a chance to indicate their personal preferences among the presidential candidates.

Convention delegates are chosen on the basis of guidelines established by the parties' national committees. Recently, both parties have attempted to increase the proportions of women, young people, and minority group members at their conventions.

The basic purpose of the convention is to unify the party behind an acceptable pair of candidates and an agreed-upon platform. A party's appeal must be broad to win votes from diverse groups and to achieve the required electoral votes.

Conventions are common at the state level. Because the nomination of candidates for state offices is usually decided in direct primaries, the conventions normally are confined to writing platforms, establishing party rules, and, in a few cases, endorsing candidates of their party who are entered in the primaries.

In other nations, party conventions or conferences have more limited functions. In Great Britain, annual party conferences do not choose the party leaders because these are elected by the parliamentary party memberships; the conferences largely confine themselves to debating party policy and determining campaign issues. In Canada, conventions are held at irregular intervals to choose a new party leader when the existing leader retires.

political parties Political parties are groups of people who come together out of a desire to obtain political power. The obvious way to obtain such power is to gain control of the government, but political parties also exercise power by influencing the policies of governments not under their control. Actual control, however, is the primary aim, and political parties are oriented toward that goal and attempt to realize it by legal means (elections), extralegal means (picketing and demonstrations), or illegal means (revolution). The purposes behind the desire for power are as varied as the individuals belonging to parties. Parties exist, however, for several basic discernible— and often overlapping—purposes: to promote an ideology, such as fascism and communism; to promote an individual or a family, such as Peronism; and to promote a special interest (see SPECIAL-INTEREST GROUPS) or section of a nation, such as the Parti Quebecois or the Prohibition party. Some parties are also job oriented and serve as mechanisms by which individuals may enjoy the perquisites of power, such as the Democratic and Republican parties in the United States.

Competitive political parties are widely regarded as indispensable to the proper functioning of a democratic society. The functions assigned political parties in democratic societies such as the United States and Great Britain include the nomination of candidates for the offices of government; the presentation of alternative sets of policies to cope with the major problems of the nation; the political education of the electorate by means of the ventilation of these alternatives through public debates; and the mobilization of the electorate behind one or the other of the parties, thereby securing broad popular participation in determining who shall rule. The party that wins the election is usually responsible for running the government for a specific period of time until the next election; and the parties that lose the election are responsible for organizing a loyal opposition.

History of Political Parties

The modern party systems have their origins in the constitutional and religious struggles of 17th-century England. A central issue in contention was whether affairs of state were exclusively the province of the crown. The supporters of the Stuart monarchs claimed that sovereignty resided solely in the crown; they were called Tories (see TORY PARTY) and their opponents were called Whigs (see WHIG PARTY, England). The Tories had the support of the landed gentry and Anglican clergy (an important political force at that time). The Whigs had the support of the great landholders, the mercantile and financial interests, and the rising class of factory and mill owners. The lower classes, completely disenfranchised, had no support for (or from) either party. Since the 17th century the Tories have evolved into the CONSERVATIVE PARTY. The Whigs gave way to the LIBERAL PARTY in the 19th century. It, in turn, was replaced by the LABOUR PARTY as one of today's two major British parties.

The framers of the U.S. Constitution had hoped to avoid the factionalism of political parties and wrote no role for them into the Constitution. Nevertheless, party divisions began during the administration of the first president, George Washington. The Federalists coalesced around John Adams and the Democratic-Republicans around Thomas Jefferson. The Jeffersonians became the Democratic party, and the Federalists were succeeded by the National Republicans in the 1820s and then by the WHIG PARTY in the 1830s. The Whigs, in turn, were replaced by the Republican party in the 1850s. Since then, the DEMOCRATIC PARTY and the REPUBLICAN PARTY have been the two major parties.

Party Structure

Political parties can be categorized in terms of two broad— and not entirely clear-cut—types of party structure: cadre parties, such as the political parties in Canada and the United States; and mass-membership parties, such as the Communist party in China and the Labour party in Great Britain.

Cadre Parties. In the United States and Canada only a small fraction (between 2 and 5 percent) of the population formally belong to one of the political parties in the sense of actually being members of one of the local clubs or organizations. Most of the remainder of the population do, in fact, identify with one of the parties and call themselves (in the United States) Democrats or Republicans; they may even be formally registered as Democrat or Republican and vote in party PRIMARY ELECTIONS. The work and the financing of the party, however, is left to a small elite group of political activists.

The organization of the cadre parties in Canada and the United States is heavily influenced by the federal form of government that prevails in both countries. In the United States, separate Democratic and Republican parties exist in each of the 50 states, and they are largely organized around the state governments. These 50 state parties convene every 4 years to nominate a presidential and vice-presidential candidate and to endorse a platform. Otherwise, they interact little with each other, although there is a permanent national committee that coordinates the activities of the state parties. A similar situation prevails in Canada.

Another important influence on party organization is the relation between the executive and legislative branches of government. In the United States a separation of power has been established between the president and the Congress. The national party nominates only the president and vice-president and has little influence in the choice of nominees for the legislative branch of government. As a consequence each state party plays a role in nominating and electing members of the Congress with little or no reference to the national party. In Canada, however, a parliamentary system of government prevails wherein the chief executive (the prime minister) is the leader of the majority party in Parliament. The constituency parties in each province are therefore organized around obtaining a parliamentary majority.

Mass Parties. Typically, mass-membership parties are more issue oriented than cadre parties. An issue-oriented party system consists of competing groups of people whose participation in politics derives in the main from their desire to translate certain policy preferences into public policy. One of the motives, however, for joining a mass-membership party is a desire for job preferment and other advantages that may accompany membership. This is particularly true of mass-membership parties in one-party nations. In such countries party membership often carries such benefits as preference in government housing and school acceptance for their children.

In states with more than one political party, however, the party activists are not primarily oriented toward political jobs or privileges, although they may also seek these ends. Frequently they are representative of interest groups. The Labour party in Great Britain is a coalition of trade unions and a variety of socialist and cooperative organizations. The Conservative party primarily represents the interests of the land-owning, financial, and commercial sectors. Both, however, are mass-membership parties and include in their ranks many members from almost every class of the society, who enlist in the party out of agreement with its principles, and who pay party dues, providing a mass base for financing.

Organization and Discipline. The structure and discipline of a particular party depends on whether it is a cadre or a mass-membership party; whether the nation has a federal or unitary system of government; and whether the national government has a presidential or parliamentary system. In turn, the clout of the party when in power depends on all of these factors.

The U.S. political parties are cadre parties, with a highly decentralized structure and little internal discipline. When in power, therefore, these parties are less likely to enact broad coherent legislative packages than are centralized parties in parliamentary systems. In competitive systems such as that in Great Britain, where the parties are both mass-membership and highly organized and disciplined, the ruling party may be able to translate into public policy much of what it advocates in the general elections. Members of Parliament, for example, are expected to vote with the party on virtually every issue. U.S. senators and representatives are under no such compulsion.

In one-party systems, such as in China, the single party in power has virtually complete control over who is to occupy the offices of government, over the policies they propose, and frequently over the press and other news media as well.

Party Systems

Party systems are typically categorized according to the number of parties that participate meaningfully in the struggle for power. Some Communist states have one-party systems; fascist states, such as pre–World War II Italy, have one-party systems; many developing countries in Africa, the Middle East, and Latin America also have one-party systems. English-speaking states typically have two-party systems, for example, Great Britain, the United States, Canada, Australia, and New Zealand. France, Italy, and other Western European nations tend toward multiparty systems. These categories of party systems are fluid and often overlap.

One-Party Systems. In general a one-party system is the vehicle by which a dominant group excludes or attempts to exclude political competition from participating in the struggle for power; for example, during the first half of the 20th century in the American South, one-party politics was a means of excluding blacks.

Communist or fascist one-party states usually emerge out of a REVOLUTION in which the party is triumphant. Thereafter, the party proceeds to eliminate competition. Emerging or developing countries also tend to have one-party systems. Many of these countries must move quickly to stimulate and direct economic development. This intention may require efforts aimed at limiting consumption, encouraging capital development, and various types of economic redistribution. Because many of these decisions are unpopular politically, the governments usually claim that they cannot permit the luxury of competing political parties.

Two-Party Systems. The two-party form exists in nations such as Germany, where competition between the Christian Democratic and Social Democratic parties is continual. This party system, however, had its roots in the British political system and remains one of the distinctive features of the political culture in Great Britain (Labour party versus Conservative party), the United States (Democratic versus Republican), Canada (Liberal versus Progressive Conservative), New Zealand (Labour versus National), and Australia (Australian Labor versus a semi-

permanent coalition of the Liberal and Country parties).

Many theorists have indicated what they believe to be the virtues of a two-party system. One of the more important is that there is almost always a majority party, and when there is, the majority party rules. According to democratic theory, this mathematical majority legitimizes all the constitutional actions of the majority party. More practically, in a parliamentary system it means that one party has a majority of the seats and, therefore, can direct political and governmental activity, because leaders and laws are adopted by majority vote.

Another strength of the two-party system is that the political parties, of necessity, are umbrella parties embracing virtually every element of the society. The parties are forced, therefore, to aggregate and synthesize the demands of all these elements in developing and proposing a program for election.

Multiparty Systems. Three broad categories of multiparty systems may be distinguished. The first is the classical variety, where many small parties exist that are highly competitive and represent very particular points of view, such as communist, fascist, Catholic, Protestant; and where no one of the parties is large enough to command a majority of the vote or a majority in the legislature. The classic example is France's Fourth Republic (1946–58). In the various elections no party ever came close to obtaining a majority in the National Assembly. Therefore, governments were always the result of coalitions of many parties. These governments would last only so long as they avoided important and contentious issues. When such issues arose they would tear the coalition apart and force the resignation of the government. The net result was a government that was incapable of addressing itself to the most pressing problems facing the society. In 1958 the French, under Charles de Gaulle, ratified the Fifth Republic, which provided for a cross between a presidential and a parliamentary system and gave the president a specified term of office and extensive powers.

A second broad category of multiparty system exists where one party constitutes a sizable proportion of the voters and the remainder of the electorate is divided among several small parties. This type of multiparty system may resemble the one-party system. Examples include India, where the Congress party—in power for most of the period since 1948—has ruled with about half the vote and the remaining vote was divided among radical parties on the left and religious parties on the right.

A third category of multiparty system prevails where coalitions of parties are successfully formed after or before elections, enabling one coalition to rule. Examples include the French Fifth Republic and the Netherlands. In the Netherlands there are about ten parties represented in the Dutch States-General. Coalition cabinets, however, representing primarily the center and moderate left parties are able to rule reasonably firmly and successfully. In France the creation of a strong president and reformed or revised election laws in 1958 have resulted in the formation of workable coalitions that provide reasonably stable and effective governments.

political science Political science is the systematic study of politics. The field of political science is a wide one, ranging from political parties and elections to ideas and ideologies, among many other topics. The Greek philosopher ARISTOTLE, considered politics to be "the master science," because it studies the state (or government), which to him was the most comprehensive of human associations. Since Aristotle's day the forms of political association have grown in size, scale, variety, and complexity. Accordingly, modern political scientists study a wide variety of activities and institutions, including local ward politics, political parties, state and national governments, and international organizations.

Because of its varied and complex subject matter, political science is divided into different branches or subfields. Political theory analyzes and traces the evolution of political thought and concepts such as power, authority, freedom, DEMOCRACY, and REPRESENTATION, as these have been developed by thinkers from PLATO and Aristotle to the present. Comparative politics classifies, compares, and analyzes political systems in different parts of the world. International relations is concerned with relations between and among nation-states and with international organizations such as the United Nations. Closely related to this is the field of INTERNATIONAL LAW (see also FOREIGN POLICY). Political behavior is the study of the actions and motivations of people participating in politics. Public administration is the study of BUREAUCRACY and other means by which government policies are implemented and regulations enforced. In many countries, study of the national political system is treated as a separate field. The field of American politics, for example, is concerned specifically with U.S. political behavior and institutions.

Each of these subfields is further divided into more specialized areas. In the field of political behavior, for example, some students investigate the formation and manipulation of public opinion, others examine political socialization (the ways in which political attitudes and beliefs are inculcated), and still others study voting behavior.

Polk, James K. [pohk] James Knox Polk was the 11th president of the United States (1845–49). During his term the nation expanded to the Pacific Ocean as a result of the Oregon Treaty and the Mexican War.

Early Life. Polk was born on Nov. 2, 1795, in Mecklenburg County, N.C. As a boy he moved to what is now Maury County, Tenn., with his parents, Samuel and Jane (Knox) Polk. He entered the University of North Carolina in 1815 and graduated in 1818 at the top of his class. After studying law in Nashville, Tenn., he was admitted to the bar in 1820. On Jan. 1, 1824, he married Sarah Childress (1803–91) of Murfreesboro, Tenn.

Political Career. Polk was soon devoting more time to politics than to law. He served as a member of the Tennessee legislature from 1823 to 1825 and in the U.S. House of Representatives from 1825 to 1839. A leader of the Democratic party, he loyally supported the adminis-

tration of Andrew JACKSON, particularly in the war against the Bank of the United States. In the controversy over the succession to the presidency, he supported Jackson's choice of Martin VAN BUREN, thus breaking with a majority of the Tennessee delegation. Polk was Speaker of the House from 1835 to 1839.

Leading Democrats, believing that a Polk candidacy would strengthen the party in Tennessee, urged him to run for governor. Polk won the election in 1839, but for the next few years his political career was stymied because of the growing strength of the Whig party in the state. He was defeated for reelection in 1841 and 1843; nevertheless, he was still regarded by Democrats as a likely vice-presidential candidate in 1844 on a ticket that they expected to be headed by former president Van Buren.

A letter from Van Buren opposing the annexation of Texas was published shortly before the Democratic convention; it drastically changed the political situation. Expansionists prevented the selection of Van Buren at the convention. Polk, who had earlier backed the U.S. claims to Texas and Oregon, won the party's endorsement on the ninth ballot, thereby becoming the first "dark horse" presidential nominee.

Running on a platform that called for "the reoccupation of Oregon and the reannexation of Texas," Polk won a narrow victory in the general election, edging out his Whig opponent, Henry Clay, by 38,000 votes. Polk received 170 electoral votes to Clay's 105. Just before Polk's inaugural in March 1845, Congress fulfilled one of the Democratic campaign pledges by passing a joint resolution offering terms of annexation to the Texas republic.

Presidency. The first president to commit himself to a single term, Polk resolved to govern independently. He also had definite goals for his administration: a reduced tariff; reestablishment of the INDEPENDENT TREASURY SYSTEM; settlement of the OREGON QUESTION; and the acquisition of California.

Polk's domestic program was enacted at the cost of much dissension within his own party. In 1846 the Walker Tariff provided for substantial reductions of import duties (see TARIFF ACTS). It pleased southern Democrats but met with bitter resistance from Pennsylvania protectionists. The Independent Treasury Act of that same year displeased probanking elements of the party. Seeking to reduce federal expenditures for internal improvements, Polk also angered northwestern Democrats by his veto of a rivers-and-harbors bill popular in that section.

In accomplishing his foreign policy objectives, Polk also dissatisfied many northern Democrats. Although he publicly reaffirmed the U.S. claim to the entire Oregon Territory up to 54°40' north latitude, he ultimately submitted to the Senate a British offer to settle along the 49th parallel. Polk's earlier stand had encouraged the "All of Oregon" men in his party to adopt the cry of "Fifty-four Forty or Fight," however, and they denounced his acceptance of compromise.

While reaching a settlement with Britain, Polk adopted a bellicose stand against Mexico that led to the MEXICAN WAR. After the congressional action providing for the annexation of Texas, Mexico had broken off diplomatic rela-

AT A GLANCE

JAMES KNOX POLK
11th President of the United States (1845–49)

Nickname: "Young Hickory"

Born: Nov. 2, 1795, Mecklenburg County, N.C.

Education: University of North Carolina (graduated 1818)

Profession: Lawyer

Religious Affiliation: Presbyterian

Marriage: Jan. 1, 1824, to Sarah Childress (1803–91)

Children: None

Political Affiliation: Democrat

Writings: *The Diary of James K. Polk* (4 vols., 1910), ed. by Milo M. Quaife; *Correspondence of James K. Polk* (6 vols., 1969–83) ed. by Herbert Weaver

Died: June 15, 1849, Nashville, Tenn.

Buried: State Capitol Grounds, Nashville, Tenn.

Vice-President: George M. Dallas

tions with the United States. Polk sent John SLIDELL to Mexico to propose that the United States would assume the claims of American citizens against Mexico in exchange for recognition of the Rio Grande as the southern boundary of Texas. Polk was also prepared to offer $15–40 million for the cession of California and New Mexico. When the Mexican government refused even to receive Slidell, Polk made plans to ask for a declaration of war on the grounds that Mexico refused to pay the claims of American citizens. Before such a war message could be prepared, however, it was learned that a Mexican force had crossed the Rio Grande and had attacked U.S. soldiers under the command of Gen. Zachary TAYLOR. On Polk's recommendation, Congress passed a declaration of war in May 1846.

Having failed to achieve his aims by diplomacy, Polk set out to obtain them by conquest. As commander in chief he personally planned U.S. strategy during the war. Lacking confidence in Taylor's ability to force the Mexicans to sue for peace, he sent an army under Gen. Winfield SCOTT to land at Veracruz and march on Mexico City, which the Americans occupied in September 1847. The Treaty of GUADALUPE HIDALGO of February 1848, which ended the war, recognized the U.S. claim to Texas and provided for the cession of California and New Mexico.

Polk's acquisitions from Mexico had dangerous consequences for the Union, however. The efforts of antislavery

forces to bar slavery from the Mexican cession reopened the sectional controversy that led to the Civil War. Divisions within the Democratic party, for which Polk was significantly responsible, helped bring the defeat of Lewis CASS by his Whig opponent, General Taylor, in the presidential election of 1848. Polk died June 15, 1849, in Nashville, Tenn., three months after leaving the White House.

Polk, Leonidas   An Episcopal bishop, Leonidas Polk, b. Raleigh, N.C., Apr. 10, 1806, d. June 14, 1864, was a Confederate general during the U.S. Civil War. He graduated from West Point in 1827 but left the army to enter the ministry. Ordained a priest in 1831, he became bishop of Louisiana in 1841. He was active in establishing the University of the South at Sewanee, Tenn. In 1861 he entered the Confederate army as a major general at the behest of President Jefferson Davis and was promoted to lieutenant general in 1862. He was killed in action at Pine Mountain in Georgia.

poll tax   A poll, or head, tax is a uniform amount levied against each adult person within a jurisdiction. Known throughout history and originally used strictly as revenue producers, poll taxes sometimes have been used to keep certain people from voting. The U.S. poll tax, which a person had to pay in order to vote, was at one time used to disfranchise poor blacks. The 24th Amendment (1964) to the Constitution forbade using a tax as a requirement to vote in federal elections. In 1966 the Supreme Court (in *Harper* v. *Virginia State Board of Elections*) outlawed it in state elections as well.

Pollaiuolo (family) [pohl-ly-woh'-loh] **Antonio Pollaiuolo**, b. *c.*1432, d. Feb. 4, 1498, and his brother, **Piero Pollaiuolo**, *c.*1443–*c.*1496, were Italian painters, sculptors, and goldsmiths whose work played an important role in the development of Early Renaissance art. Antonio presided over one of the most prestigious art studios in Florence; Piero largely served as his brother's assistant on their collaborative projects. Antonio was the creative genius; his powerfully modeled pictorial and sculptural figures exerted a great influence on contemporary and subsequent Italian Renaissance artists.

Although Antonio originally won renown as a goldsmith, his paintings and engravings constitute his most important work. His principal interest lay in exploring the anatomy of male bodies in motion, as the varied poses of the characters in *The Martyrdom of Saint Sebastian* (1475; National Gallery, London) demonstrate clearly. The awesome muscularity of his figures owes some debt to the powerful forms favored by Andrea del Castagno, but Antonio's figures are far more animated than his predecessor's. His studies of nudes in violent motion, such as the engraving titled *Battle of the Ten Nudes* (*c.*1475; Bargello, Florence), represent one of the finest figural achievements of the Early Renaissance and directly foreshadow the monumental figures of Michelangelo.

Antonio's sculptures generally mirror his pictorial works in emphasizing the human form extended in strenuous activity. Perhaps his best-known sculpture, the bronze *Hercules and Antaeus* (*c.*1492; Bargello, Florence), is in fact a three-dimensional interpretation of the poses depicted in a now-destroyed fresco (*c.*1460) executed for the Medici Palace.

pollen   Plants characteristically undergo a cyclic alternation of generations in which a spore-producing generation, called the sporophyte (spore plant), is followed by a gamete (sex cell)-producing generation, called the gametophyte (gamete plant), and so on. In evolutionarily higher plants the gamete-producing generation has been progressively reduced in size and in the duration of its existence; in seed plants the male gametophyte has been diminished to the tiny pollen grain.

Pollen grains (male gametophytes) are produced on highly modified leaves called microsporophylls (megasporophylls produce female gametophytes). In conebearing plants, such as pine trees, the microsporophyll is a scale of a male cone. In flowering plants the microsporophyll is the stamen of the flower. A stamen consists of a pollen-producing section, called the anther, and a stalk. As the anther matures, four groups of specialized cells develop within it; these specialized

cells are called microspore mother cells (or pollen mother cells, or microsporocytes). Each of the four groups of microspore mother cells is surrounded by nutritive tissue and supporting cells and is collectively referred to as an anther sac, a pollen sac, or a microsporangium. Each microspore mother cell divides to form four microspores, which is why the flower-bearing plant is called the sporophyte. While still in the anther sac and shortly before being released, each microspore begins to germinate; that is, its nucleus divides into two nuclei, the generative nucleus and the tube nucleus. The two-nuclei structure is the pollen grain, or male gametophyte. The pollen grain's generative nucleus will later divide into male sex cells, or gametes, which is why the pollen grain is called the gametophyte. The two male sex cells are known as sperm nuclei and correspond to the sperm of animals.

Pollen may be produced in relatively small amounts, as few as several dozen grains per anther sac, or in tremendous numbers, as in the wind-pollinated coniferous trees, where a single cone may produce millions of grains. Pollen grains are commonly yellow in color but may also be orange, green, or other colors; they range from about 2 microns (8/100,000 in) to several hundreds (1/1,000 in) or more. Pollen grains contain proteins and sugars and serve as an attractant to insects and other animals, which aid in POLLINATION. Because pollen grains are distinctive in shape and structure, their plants of origin can be identi-

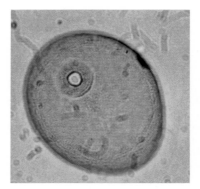

Pollen grains of all grasses, including wheat (left), *have a distinct pore, or aperture, in the outer layer, or exine, of the wall. Wheat pollen is nearly spherical and measures about 50 microns (2/1,000 in) across.*

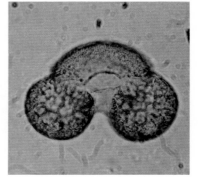

Protruding air sacs characterize the pollen grains of the pine genus (right), *and certain other gymnosperms. It has been estimated that a single pine tree may produce several billion pollen grains in 1 year.*

fied from them; a branch of botany, called palynology, specializes in this study.

pollen cone

pollen cone A cone, botanically called a strobilus (plural, strobili), is the characteristic reproductive structure of conifers, such as the pine tree. There are two types of cones: male and female. Male cones are staminate, or pollen-producing; female cones are ovulate, or seed-bearing, and commonly develop into hard, woody "fruits." Both types are characteristically a collection of overlapping scales spirally arranged around a central stalk, or axis. The scales are actually sporophylls, which are highly modified, spore-bearing leaves. A sporophyll of a male cone consists of a short, flattened leafstalk (petiole) and a midrib (middle vein of a leaf blade), the latter bearing two spore sacs, also called pollen sacs or microsporangia. The pollen sacs contain microspore mother cells, which divide to form microspores; the microspores later develop into pollen grains. Male cones are generally small, averaging about 13 mm (½ in) or less in length and 6 mm (¼ in) in width. They may be yellow, scarlet, or another bright color and are usually produced in clusters. Male cones are typically short-lived; female cones may persist for a year or more.

See also: POLLEN; SEED CONE.

pollen stratigraphy

pollen stratigraphy Pollen stratigraphy involves the identification and study of fossil pollen in soils and rock formations. Because the outer walls of pollen grains are quite resistant to chemical decomposition, the grains can serve as valuable microfossils. Fossil pollen was originally identified in 1836. Lennart von Post made (1916) the first application of pollen stratigraphy in studies of peat bogs in Sweden.

Fossil pollen is most often associated with sedimentary rocks and in particular with lake, swamp, or bog deposits. It can also be found in deltaic, estuarine, nearshore-marine, and even deep-ocean deposits. The most suitable deposits for pollen preservation are fine-grained sediments that have been subjected to little distortion, compaction, or oxidation. Pollen is not as common in limestone or other deposits having a high pH. Pollen is extracted from sediments by the use of acid or by flotation of the grains in a heavy liquid, such as zinc chloride. The latter process involves the separation by froth of materials of differing specific gravity.

The plant assemblage that contributed pollen to a deposit at a specific time is called a pollen spectrum. A pollen curve can be created by plotting and connecting successive spectra on a graph. A pollen diagram—a plot of a series of pollen curves versus soil or core depth—provides an indication of the changes in vegetation type that occurred in a particular locality over a period of time.

A pollen count may not provide a true picture of a former vegetative habit if individual plant types are not proportionately represented in the count. Such a misrepresentation may result because some plants produce or release more pollen than others. Variations in the trans-port mechanisms, such as changes in wind speed, wind direction, or stream velocity, also affect the distribution of pollen. Another assumption is that past plant assemblages lived under the same climatic conditions as similar existing plant assemblages do today.

The chronologic and areal distribution of pollen in geologic deposits can be used to reconstruct past climates (see PALEOCLIMATOLOGY) and environments (see PALEOECOLOGY) and is also used as a method of stratigraphic correlation. Pollen stratigraphy is better adapted to identifying ecotones—the boundaries between different plant communities—than to indicating changes within a plant community. Pollen data can be used to determine former environments on a larger scale than can most other fossils, which tend to reflect only the immediate surroundings of the former organism (see FOSSIL RECORD). Other uses of pollen stratigraphy include the location of ancient shorelines and identification of the impacts of human settlement in an area, such as those caused by the introduction of agriculture.

pollination

pollination Pollination is any process in seed plants by which pollen grains are transferred from their production site in pollen sacs on male structures to a receptive site on or near an ovule, the future seed, in female structures. Cross-pollination is essentially pollination between two plants. Self-pollination occurs in both flowering plants, within a single flower or between two flowers on the same plant, and in gymnosperms, the naked-seeded plants.

A pollen grain is a mature small spore that is partially developed into a male gametophyte. Gametophytes are haploid plants that produce gametes, or sex cells (sperm and eggs), as contrasted with sporophytes, or diploid plants that produce spores. The pollen tube produced by the pollen grain grows to the ovule, where it ultimately deposits the male gametes (sperm cells).

Spores are produced in a structure called a sporangium. In flowering plants the male sporangium (the microsporangium) is known as the pollen sac, or anther sac, and is located in the anther, a part of the flower's stamen. In gymnosperms, such as the conifers, the male sporangium is located on a microsporophyll of a male cone, or male strobilus.

The female sporangium (the megasporangium) of flowering plants is called an ovule. One of its large spores (megaspores) matures into the female gametophyte, also called the embryo sac, which produces the female gamete (egg cell). The ovules are located within the ovary at the base of the flower's pistil. In gymnosperms the ovules are not enclosed within an ovary but are borne on a scale of a female cone.

Pollination in Gymnosperms

Gymnosperms have ovules or developing postfertilization seeds borne somewhat exposed to the environment. Familiar gymnosperms include not only conifers (cedars, larches, pines, spruces) but also cycads and gnetopsids. Pollination in gymnosperms, according to all current information, is strictly by wind and is termed anemophily. Some authorities, however, hold that insects may play a part in the pollination of some gymnosperms. Mature pollen is released from male sporangia and is carried by air currents to female cones on the same or different plants. The pollen is deposited in a droplet of sugary water exuded from a tiny opening in the ovular coat. The physiological properties of the pollen and the chemical constituents of the pollination droplet and ovular tissues determine whether the pollen will germinate successfully.

Pollination in Flowering Plants

Pollination in flowering plants varies markedly, but there is a fundamental difference between gymnosperm and flowering-plant pollination: because flowering-plant ovules are enclosed in an ovary, pollen is not transferred to the ovule directly but rather to a specialized and somewhat distant receptive surface termed the *stigma*.

Biological Agencies

Insects (Entomophily). Insects appear to be attracted to flowers by color and scent; the insect, once it is on or within the flower, obtains food in the form of either nectar or nutrient-rich pollen, or both. Among insects the most common pollinators are beetles, flies, butterflies, moths, and bees.

Birds (Ornithophily). A bird's special adaptations for carrying out pollination may include its size and weight; the ability to hover in one spot; a long bill and tongue; the ability to locate nectar without tongue guides; sensitivity to colors, especially red; and a near lack of a sense of smell.

Bats (Chiropterophily). A relatively specific relationship exists between bats and bat flowers. Features of bat flowers include stiffness or strength of flower; a large floral opening; drab coloring; flowers that open at night; a strong nighttime odor; large quantities of pollen and nectar; and flowers that are often situated away from the leaves. Attributes of bats that can be related to those of bat flowers are color blindness; nocturnal activity; an acute sense of smell; a high metabolic rate requiring much food consumption; and the existence of an echolocation, or sonar, system (if the flowers were situated among foliage leaves, such leaves would interfere with the ability of the bat to locate the flower).

Primates. At least six species of nocturnal monkeylike lemurs in Madagascar may be significant pollinators of the flowers they visit for nectar and other food material.

Nonbiological Agencies

Wind. Although anemophily has been described in gymnosperms as an apparently nonspecific, primitive mode of pollen transfer, in flowering plants it appears to be an advanced form of pollination. Within the beech family, for example, certain more-primitive members are insect-pollinated, whereas more-advanced members exhibit anemophily. Anemophily occurs mostly in areas such as cool, dry grasslands with a relative scarcity of animal pollinators.

Water (Hydrophily). Hydrophily is considered to be an advanced form of pollination relatable to specialized

(Left) *Simple, unspecialized flowers such as those of the brambles, are often pollinated by beetles and flies. These flowers tend to be open, rather than tubular, and attract insects primarily by means of odors.*

(Right) *Bee-pollinated flowers, including gorse, are commonly tubular and brightly colored. Bees, which coevolved with these flowers, possess long tongues for reaching nectar inside the flower, pollen-collecting bristles on their legs, and the ability to recognize colors.*

(Left) *Bird-pollinated flowers, such as hibiscus (shown with ruby-throated hummingbird), occur mainly in tropical regions. Birds, which have keen vision but a weak sense of smell, are attracted by large, brightly colored flowers.*

(Right) *Wind-pollinated flowers are inconspicuous and usually have their stamens exposed so that the pollen can be easily scattered by the wind. The catkins of hazel are typical wind-pollinated flowers.*

plant habitats, such as that of the hornwort, *Ceratophyllum*, which grows submerged in shallow, quiet waters. The flowers have either male sporangia or ovules; the ovulate flowers remain below water. Hornwort pollen has the same density as water and remains dispersed near the plant. Pollen ultimately contacts the stigmatic area of the female flower, where it may germinate and develop a pollen tube.

Self-Pollination

Self-pollination may simply result from accidental transfer of pollen from male to ovulate structures on the same plant, or it may result from organized and complex events relating to floral morphology and physiology. Self-pollination of the latter type probably developed, as did nonbiological pollination types, as a partial compensation for the lack of pollinators in specialized habitats.

Pollock, Jackson [pah'-luhk]   The controversial painter Jackson Pollock, b. Cody, Wyo., Jan. 28, 1912, d. Aug. 11, 1956, was a central figure of American ABSTRACT EXPRESSIONISM. His art was intensely personal and at times violently emotional and anarchic.

By the mid-1930s he had developed a dark style, possibly influenced by the Mexican muralists, a style he used while working (1938–42) on the Federal Art Project. His first one-person show (1943), at Peggy Guggenheim's gallery in New York City, included paintings representative of his increasingly vivid style, such as *The She Wolf* (1943; Museum of Modern Art, New York City). By 1947, Pollock relied more and more on the

Reflection of the Great Bear *(1947) shows the swirling energy of Jackson Pollock's abstract expressionist style. Pollock's work, created by a drip technique, was initially a source of heated controversy. (Stedelijk Museum, Amsterdam.)*

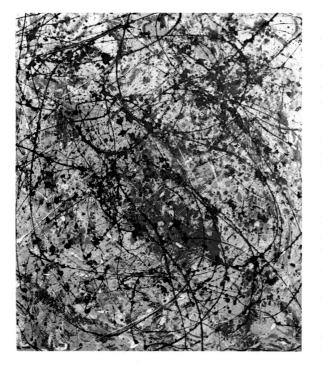

unconscious mind to prompt his art. He perfected new techniques of application, dripping paint from cans and pouring and hurling paint onto unstretched canvases placed on the floor, as in *Full Fathom Five* (1947; Museum of Modern Art).

In his final years Pollock drew on the various innovations he had pioneered, occasionally using human and anatomical imagery and ranging from dynamic swirled and dripped color paintings to smaller black-and-white studies. After his death he came to be recognized as a seminal influence on American art, having opened new boundaries of texture, line, and expression.

pollutants, chemical   Chemical pollutants are substances that enter the environment through industrial, agricultural, and other human-generated processes and pose a hazard to human, plant, and animal health and life. In the largest sense almost any manufactured substance present in excess can be considered a pollutant. This discussion, however, will be limited to those chemicals which have been discovered to be hazardous or toxic, which are produced in quantity, and which are difficult or impossible to remove from the environment.

Major Classes of Chemical Pollutants

Heavy Metals. Although heavy metals exist in nature, when concentrations of such metals as mercury, cadmium, and lead build to higher-than-normal levels, they become potentially hazardous. Major sources of heavy-metals pollution include mineral and metal processing, manufacturing of inorganic products, and use of coal in power production.

About half of the mercury mined each year is lost into the environment. Mercury poisoning has occurred in the United States and in other countries. The most notorious episode occurred in the 1950s at Minamata Bay in Japan, where mercury in the effluent from a plastics factory was ingested by fish and, ultimately, by people in the communities on the bay.

Cadmium, used in metal plating and in batteries, vaporizes when it is smelted; heavy concentrations can cause kidney and bone-marrow diseases and emphysema. Airborne lead from automobile and industrial emissions is absorbed into the body through the lungs. Residues from lead-based paints (banned since 1977) can cause lead poisoning in children.

Aromatic Hydrocarbons. Polycyclic aromatic hydrocarbons (PAH) are formed by industrial processes and during the burning of gasoline, waste materials, and many other substances. Some PAHs have been found to be highly carcinogenic.

Organic Solvents. Organic solvents, vital to many industrial processes, are often toxic. After use they have often been stored for disposal in steel drums, which eventually corrode and leak. Organic solvents may enter waterways in factory effluent. In Europe such effluents have been largely responsible for the pollution of the Rhine River and the Mediterranean Sea. Many aromatic hydrocarbons (benzene, toluene, xylene) and organochlorine compounds (carbon tetrachloride, trichlorethylene) are used as organic solvents. Benzene has been causally linked with leukemia and central-nervous-system disorders.

Organo-Halogen Compounds. Organo-halogen compounds are compounds of chlorine, bromine, or fluorine with organic chemicals. They are useful as solvents, pesticides, and fire retardants and raw materials for some plastics. Many of them, however, have extremely toxic effects.

The pesticide kepone contaminated Virginia's James River in the early 1970s, and both the river and parts of the Chesapeake Bay were closed to fishing from 1975 through 1980. Polychlorinated biphenyls (PCBs), used in the manufacture of electrical appliances, were dumped as effluent into the upper Hudson River in New York and the Housatonic in Massachusetts over many years. Commercial fishing is now impossible in portions of both rivers. PCBs are so widespread that trace amounts have been detected in mothers' milk.

Polybrominated biphenyl (PBB) is used as a fire retardant. In 1973 in Michigan it was accidentally mixed with animal feed that was subsequently fed to farm animals, necessitating the destruction of thousands of cattle and chickens and causing extended illness and long-term contamination of many Michigan residents.

Dioxin. The DIOXIN group of chemical compounds are unwanted by-products occurring in the manufacture of certain organo-halogens that are used in making herbicides, wood preservatives, and many other products.

A member of the dioxin family, tetrachlorodibenzo-p-dioxin, or TCDD, is a contaminant in the widely used herbicide 2,4,5-T. This herbicide was originally developed as a chemical-warfare agent during World War II and was an ingredient in the defoliant Agent Orange, used in Vietnam in the late 1960s. Since the mid-1960s it has been suspected that TCDD may be the causative agent for a number of diseases. U.S. Army veterans who were exposed to Agent Orange in Vietnam have brought suit against the federal government and the chemical companies that produced the herbicide, charging that TCDD is responsible for the illnesses they experience, including cancer, and for genetic disorders among their children.

Since 1979 a federal ban has eliminated some uses of herbicides containing 2,4,5-T. Other dioxin compounds, however, have been found in many industrial waste products. Dioxins have also entered the environment through the use of tainted oil as a roadway dust suppressant. The town of Times Beach, Mo., was abandoned in 1983 because tests indicated that highway spraying had left high levels of dioxin in the soil.

Other Important Pollutants. Arsenic, a by-product of zinc, copper, and lead smelters—and possibly also produced through the large-scale burning of coal—poisons both livestock and humans. The fluorosis of cattle is caused by the presence on forage of fluoride, a by-product of aluminum manufacturing and inorganic-fertilizer production. Sulfites and other wastes from paper mills are often serious local pollutants of streams and rivers. ASBESTOS is a widely distributed pollutant in U.S. cities, where older buildings often contain considerable amounts as fireproofing. Asbestos dust causes various lung diseases, including cancers (see DISEASES, OCCUPATIONAL).

Government Regulation

The U.S. ENVIRONMENTAL PROTECTION AGENCY is charged with controlling the use and disposal of toxic chemicals in the United States. The EPA decides, for example, whether a new pesticide may be registered for use. If it is considered likely to cause excessive environmental damage or to be carcinogenic, the EPA can refuse to allow the product to be marketed. Many of the new pesticides and hundreds of other new compounds marketed each year are never intended to enter the environment, although through waste and accidents most eventually do.

New Products. In 1976, Congress passed the Toxic Substances Control Act, which requires the EPA to be informed of the estimated production volume, uses, and any existing health-related studies for every new commercial chemical. If the data indicates that a substance causes cancer or genetic or birth defects, it is designated a "substantial risk" and may be regulated or banned.

Toxicity Studies. Toxicity studies are conducted mainly by private companies, often hired by firms that wish to market the test substances. Tests that appeared to show the safety of a given compound have often proved faulty. When maximum permissible levels of exposure for humans are established, those levels have often proved to be too high.

Waste Disposal

The EPA is responsible for ensuring the safe disposal of hazardous waste. As required by the 1976 Resource Conservation and Recovery Act (amended in 1984), it regulates the handling of substances listed as toxic or hazardous. Their movement must be documented from production through ultimate disposal. Disposal sites must meet certain standards and be monitored and maintained.

Long-term contamination was involved in the Love Canal in Niagara Falls, N.Y. A chemical dump and LANDFILL used by the Hooker Chemical Corporation, once filled, became the site (1953) for a school and housing tract. In 1971 toxic liquids began leaking through the clay cap that sealed the dump, and the tract was declared an official disaster area. About 1,000 families had to be relocated.

The EPA has compiled an inventory of 32,000 sites that may contain hazardous wastes. (In addition to the known dumps and landfills, such as Love Canal, there are undoubtedly numerous sites where chemical wastes have been illegally dumped.) Beginning in 1980 congressional appropriations to a "Superfund"—money to be used by the EPA for hazardous-waste cleanup—have totaled $8.64 billion, of which the EPA has spent $6 billion (1990), and has completed work on only 52 sites from a national priority list of 1,218 sites.)

International Control Efforts

Attempts are being made internationally to monitor the release of toxic chemicals into the environment. An agreement to control the release of pollution into the Rhine River—and another to attempt the reduction of pollutants poured into the Mediterranean Sea—have been signed by the countries that use these waters. An International Registry of Potentially Toxic Substances has been established by the United Nations to provide computer data concerning the environmental hazards of a wide variety of substances.

pollution, environmental Environmental pollution is any discharge of material or energy into water, land, or air that causes or may cause acute (short-term) or chronic (long-term) detriment to the Earth's ecological balance or that lowers the quality of life. Pollutants may cause primary damage, with direct identifiable impact on the environment, or secondary damage in the form of minor perturbations in the delicate balance of the biological food web that are detectable only over long time periods.

Until relatively recently, environmental pollution problems have been local and minor because of the Earth's own ability to absorb and purify minor quantities of pollutants. The industrialization of society, the introduction of motorized vehicles, and the explosion of the human population, however, have caused an exponential growth in the production of goods and services. Coupled with this growth has been a tremendous increase in waste by-products. The indiscriminate discharge of untreated industrial and domestic wastes into waterways, the spewing of thousands of tons of particulates and airborne gases into the atmosphere, the "throwaway" attitude toward solid wastes, and the use of newly developed chemicals without considering potential consequences have resulted in major environmental disasters, such as the formation of smog in the Los Angeles region since the late 1940s and the pollution of large areas of the Mediterranean Sea. Technology has begun to solve some pollution problems (see POLLUTION CONTROL), and public awareness of the extent of pollution may eventually force governments to undertake more effective environmental planning and adopt more effective antipollution measures.

Water Pollution

Water pollution is the introduction into land or ocean waters of chemical, physical, or biological material that degrades the quality of the water. This process ranges from simple addition of dissolved or suspended solids to discharge of the most insidious toxic pollutants (such as pesticides, heavy metals, and bioaccumulative chemical compounds) that persist and pervade the environment.

Conventional. Conventional or classical pollutants are generally associated with the direct input of (mainly human) waste products. Rapid urbanization and rapid population increases have produced sewage problems because treatment facilities have not kept pace with need. Untreated and partially treated sewage from municipal wastewater systems and septic tanks in unsewered areas contribute significant quantities of nutrients, suspended solids, dissolved solids, oil, metals (arsenic, mercury, chromium, lead, iron, and manganese), and biodegradable organic carbon to the water environment.

Although essential to the aquatic habitat, nutrients such as nitrogen and phosphorus may also cause overfer-

An oil-soaked bird is among the victims of an oil spill. Such spills result from tanker accidents or offshore well eruptions. Some 10-12 million tons of oil are added to the world's waters each year.

tilization and accelerate the natural aging process (EUTROPHICATION) of lakes. This acceleration in turn produces an overgrowth of aquatic vegetation, massive algal blooms, and an overall shift in the biologic community—from low productivity with many diverse species to high productivity with large numbers of a few species of a less desirable nature. Bacterial action oxidizes biodegradable organic carbon and consumes dissolved oxygen in the water. In extreme cases where the organic-carbon loading is high, oxygen consumption may lead to an oxygen depression: less than 2 mg/l (compared with 5 to 7 mg/l for a healthy stream) is sufficient to cause a fish kill and seriously disrupt the growth of associated organisms.

Nonconventional. The nonconventional pollutants include dissolved and particulate forms of metals, both toxic and nontoxic, and degradable and persistent organic carbon compounds discharged into water as a by-product of industry or as an integral part of marketable products. More than 13,000 OIL SPILLS of varying magnitude occur in the United States each year. Thousands of environmentally untested chemicals are routinely discharged into waterways; an estimated 400 to 500 new compounds are marketed each year. In addition, coal strip mining releases acid wastes that despoil the surrounding waterways. Nonconventional pollutants vary from biologically inert materials such as clay and iron residues to the most toxic and insidious materials such as halogenated hydrocarbons—DDT, kepone, mirex, and polychlorinated biphenyls (PCBs). The latter group may produce damage ranging from acute biological effects (complete sterilization of stretches of waterways) to chronic sublethal effects that may go undetected for years. The chronic low-level pollutants are proving to be the most difficult to correct and abate because of their ubiquitous nature and chemical stability.

Thermal Pollution

Thermal pollution is the discharge of waste heat via energy dissipation into cooling water and subsequently into nearby waterways. The major sources of thermal pollution are fossil-fuel and nuclear electric-power generating facilities and, to a lesser degree, cooling operations associated with industrial manufacturing, such as steel foundries, other primary-metal manufacturers, and chemical and petrochemical producers.

The discharge temperatures from electric-power plants generally range from 5 to 11 C degrees (9 to 20 F degrees) above ambient water temperatures. An estimated 90% of all water consumption, excluding agricultural uses, is for cooling or energy dissipation.

The discharge of heated water into a waterway often causes ecologic imbalance, sometimes resulting in major fish kills near the discharge source. The increased temperature accelerates chemical-biological processes and decreases the ability of the water to hold dissolved oxygen. Thermal changes affect the aquatic system by limiting or changing the type of fish and aquatic biota able to grow or reproduce in the waters. Thus rapid and dramatic changes in biologic communities often occur in the vicinity of heated discharges.

Land Pollution

Land pollution is the degradation of the Earth's land surface by mining, industrial waste dumping, and indiscriminate disposal of urban wastes.

In the United States in 1988, municipal wastes alone—that is, the solid wastes sent by households, businesses, and municipalities to local landfills and other waste-disposal facilities—equaled 163 million metric tons (180 million U.S. tons), or 18 kg (40 lb) per person, according to figures released by the Environmental Protection Agency. Additional solid wastes accumulate from mining, industrial production, and agriculture. Although municipal wastes are the most obvious, the accumulations of other types of waste are far greater, in many instances are more difficult to dispose of, and present greater environmental hazards.

The most common and convenient methods of solid-waste disposal are landfills and open dumps. These cause primarily aesthetic problems, or eyesores, in the country-

A huge garbage dump on the Island of New Dreams in Tokyo Harbor illustrates the solid-waste disposal problems of many large cities.

side. Open dumps may cause environmental-health problems because of their large population of rodents and other pests. Sanitary landfills, which are now more common, provide better control aesthetically, but often industrial wastes of unknown content commingle with domestic wastes. Groundwater infiltration and contamination of water supplies with toxic chemicals have recently led to more active control of landfills and industrial waste disposal. Careful management of sanitary landfills, such as providing for leachate and runoff treatment as well as daily coverage with topsoil, has alleviated most of the problems of open dumping. In many areas, however, space for landfills is running out and alternatives must be found. RECYCLING OF MATERIALS is practical to some extent for much municipal and some industrial wastes, and a small but growing proportion of solid wastes is being recycled.

Pesticide Pollution

Pesticides (see PESTICIDES AND PEST CONTROL) are organic and inorganic chemicals originally invented and first used effectively to better the human environment by control-

Persistent pesticides, such as DDT, remain in the bodies of organisms and accumulate in successive levels of a biologic food chain. When sprayed (A), the pesticide reaches plants as well as insects. With leaf fall (B), pesticide-bearing vegetation reaches the soil. As worms eat decaying leaves (C), as small birds feed on worms (D), and as predators prey on small birds (E), the food material is metabolized but the pesticide is retained. In top predators, such as the peregrine falcon (F), the pesticide reaches high levels. This affects the bird's metabolism and causes it to produce thin-shelled eggs that tend to break prematurely, resulting in high mortality.

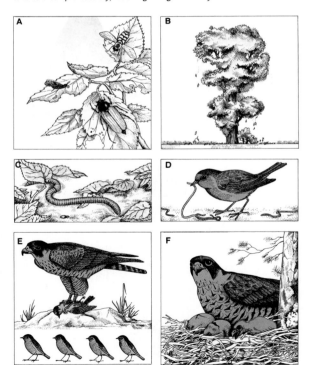

ling undesirable life-forms such as bacteria and insect pests. Their effectiveness, however, has caused considerable pollution. The persistent, or hard, pesticides, which are relatively inert and nondegradable by chemical or biologic activity, are also bioaccumulative; that is, they are retained within the body of the consuming organism and are concentrated with each ensuing level of the biologic food chain. DDT provides an excellent example of cumulative pesticide effects. (Although DDT use has been banned in the United States since 1972, it is still a popular pesticide in much of the rest of the world.) DDT may be applied to an area so that the levels in the surrounding environment are less than one part per billion. As bacteria or other microscopic organisms ingest and retain the pesticide, the concentration may increase several hundredfold to a thousandfold. Concentration continues as these organisms are ingested by higher forms of life—algae, fish, shellfish, birds, or humans. The resultant concentration in the higher life-forms may reach levels of thousands to millions of parts per billion.

The long-term (chronic) effects of persistent pesticides are virtually unknown, but many scientists believe that they are as much an environmental hazard as are the acute effects. Nonpersistent (readily degradable) pesticides or substitutes, male sterilization techniques, hormone homologues that check or interfere with maturation stages, and the introduction of animals that prey on the pests currently present a brighter picture for pest control with significantly reduced environmental consequences.

Radiation Pollution

Radiation pollution is any form of ionizing or nonionizing RADIATION that results from human activities. The most well-known radiation results from the detonation of nuclear devices and the controlled release of energy by nuclear-power generating plants (see NUCLEAR ENERGY). Other sources of radiation include spent-fuel reprocessing

At a toxic waste dump in New Jersey a technician takes a sample of water, which will be tested to determine the levels of chemical toxins it contains. According to studies released by the Environmental Protection Agency, New Jersey has the highest number of toxic dumps in the United States.

plants, by-products of mining operations, and experimental research laboratories. Increased exposure to medical X rays and to radiation emissions from microwave ovens and other household appliances, although of considerably less magnitude, all constitute sources of environmental radiation.

Another source that became a matter of concern only in the 1980s is RADON, a radioactive gas that is released during the breakdown of the miniscule uranium deposits present in many types of rocks and in the decomposition of radium and uranium. The gas seeps into homes through basements and foundations and, if allowed to build up in poorly ventilated houses, over a long term may cause diseases such as lung cancer. Areas of radon-generating rock occur throughout the United States.

Public concern over the release of radiation has greatly increased following the disclosure of possible harmful effects from nuclear-weapons testing, the accident (1979) at the Three Mile Island nuclear-power generating plant near Harrisburg, Pa., and the catastrophic 1986 explosion at CHERNOBYL, a Russian nuclear-power plant. In the late 1980s, revelations of major pollution problems at nuclear-weapons reactors in South Carolina and Washington State raised apprehensions even higher (see NUCLEAR WASTE).

Noise Pollution

Noise pollution has a relatively recent origin. It is a composite of sounds generated by human activities ranging from the blasting of stereo systems to the roar of supersonic-transport jets. Although the frequency (pitch) of noise may be of major importance, most noise sources are measured in terms of intensity, or strength of the sound field. The standard unit, one decibel (dB), is the amount of sound that is just audible to the average human. The decibel scale is somewhat misleading because it is logarithmic rather than linear; for example, a noise source measuring 70 dB is 10 times as loud as a source measuring 60 dB and 100 times as loud as a source reading 50 dB. Noise may be generally associated with industrial society, where heavy machinery, motor vehicles, and aircraft have become everyday items. Noise pollution is more intense in the work environment than in the general environment, although ambient noise increased an average of 1 dB per year during the 1980s. The average background noise in a typical home today is between 40 and 50 db. Some examples of high-level sources in the environment are heavy trucks (90 dB at 15 m/50 ft), freight trains (75 dB at 15 m/50 ft), and air conditioning (60 dB at 6 m/20 ft).

The most readily measurable physiological effect of noise pollution is damage to hearing. The effect is variable, depending on individual susceptibility, duration of exposure, nature of noise (loudness), and time distribution of exposure (such as steady or intermittent). The psychological side effects of increased noise levels may include irritability, lower productivity, increased incidence of ulcers, migraine headaches, and fatigue.

Air Pollution

Air pollution is the accumulation in the atmosphere of substances that, in sufficient concentrations, endanger

Smog, a dense mixture of smoke and moisture, can damage important crops as well as produce respiratory and eye irritations. One variety, photochemical smog, results largely from the interaction of sunlight with chemicals emitted in automobile exhaust.

human health or produce other measurable effects on living matter and other materials. Among the major sources of pollution are power and heat generation, the burning of solid wastes, industrial processes, and, especially, transportation. The six major types of pollutants are carbon monoxide, hydrocarbons, nitrogen oxides, particulates, sulfur dioxide, and photochemical oxidants.

Local and Regional. Smog has seriously affected more persons than any other type of air pollution. It can be loosely defined as a multisource, widespread air pollution that occurs in the air of cities. Smog, a contraction of the words *smoke* and *fog,* has been caused throughout recorded history by water condensing on smoke particles, usually from burning coal. The infamous London fogs—about 4,000 deaths were attributed to the severe fog of 1952—were smog of this type. Another type, ice fog, a combination of smoke particles and ice crystals, occurs only at high latitudes and extremely low temperatures.

As a coal economy has gradually been replaced by a petroleum economy, photochemical smog has become predominant in many cities. Its unpleasant properties result from the irradiation by sunlight of hydrocarbons (primarily unburned gasoline emitted by automobiles and other combustion sources) and other pollutants in the air. Irradiation produces a long series of photochemical reactions (see PHOTOCHEMISTRY). The products of the reactions include organic particles, ozone, aldehydes, ketones, peroxyacetyl nitrate, and organic acids and other oxidants. Sulfur dioxide, which is always present to some extent, oxidizes and hydrates to form sulfuric acid and becomes part of the particulate matter. Furthermore, automobiles also emit carbon monoxide, one of the most toxic constituents of smog, and are responsible for much of the particulate material in the air.

All types of smog decrease visibility and, with the possible exception of ice fog, are irritating to the respiratory system. Statistical studies indicate that smog is a contributor to malignancies of many types. Photochemical smog produces eye irritation and lacrimation and causes severe damage to many types of vegetation, including important crops. Acute effects include an increased mortality rate, especially among persons suffering from respiratory and coronary ailments.

Air pollution on a regional scale is in part the result of local air pollution—including that produced by individual sources, such as automobiles—that has spread out to encompass areas of many thousands of square kilometers. Meteorological conditions and landforms can greatly influence air-pollution concentrations at any given place, especially locally and regionally. For example, cities located in bowls or valleys over which atmospheric INVERSIONS form and act as imperfect lids are especially likely to suffer from severe smog. Oxides of sulfur and nitrogen, carried long distances by the atmosphere and then precipitated in solution as ACID RAIN, can cause serious damage to vegetation, waterways, and buildings.

Global. Humans also pollute the atmosphere on a global scale, although until the early 1970s little attention was paid to the possible deleterious effects of such pollution. Measurements in Hawaii suggest that the concentration of carbon dioxide in the atmosphere is increasing at a rate of about 0.2% every year. The effect of this increase may be to alter the Earth's climate by increasing the average global temperature (see GREENHOUSE EFFECT). Certain pollutants decrease the concentration of OZONE occurring naturally in the stratosphere, which in turn increases the amount of ultraviolet radiation reaching the Earth's surface. Such radiation may damage vegetation and increase the incidence of skin cancer. Nitrogen oxides emitted by supersonic aircraft and chlorofluorocarbons used as refrigerants and aerosol-can propellants are the major stratospheric contaminants. It is believed that these chemicals were responsible for the noticeable loss of ozone over the polar regions during the 1980s.

Abatement. Numerous and often ingenious methods have been proposed for removing pollutants from the atmosphere once they have been emitted. All have proved impracticable, primarily because of the huge mass of air that must be treated. Introduction of substances into city air to prevent the occurrence of reactions producing photochemical smog has also been suggested but not implemented, in part because of a reluctance to introduce still more foreign substances into the air. Thus control at the source has so far been the only effective means of decreasing air pollution.

Because the complete elimination of air pollution would be impractical for economic and other reasons even if it were technically feasible, compromises must be made. In the United States the federal government has established both pollutant-emission-rate standards and ambient air-pollutant concentration standards. Various emission-control measures can be taken to meet these standards. For example, today's automobiles are equipped with catalytic devices to decrease the emission of hydrocarbons, nitrogen oxides, and carbon monoxide. Attempts to wean people away from their automobiles have been at best only partially successful (see TRANSPORTATION). Electrostatic precipitators and filters are used in power plants to meet particulate-emission standards, and low-sulfur-content fuels can be used to limit sulfur-dioxide emissions.

See also: CONSERVATION; ENVIRONMENTAL PROTECTION AGENCY; SEWERAGE; WASTE DISPOSAL SYSTEMS.

pollution control   Pollution control is the management of waste materials in order to minimize the effects of pollutants on people and the environment. The quality of human health and of the natural environment depends on adequate pollution control. In the United States much has been done to control the more noticeable pollutants since 1965; more subtle yet still hazardous pollutants, however, remain to be adequately controlled.

Four general approaches to pollution control are: the intermittent reduction of industrial activities during periods of high air-pollution conditions; wider dispersion of pollutants using such devices as taller smokestacks; reduction of emission to air and water by removing pollutants from waste flows; and change of an industrial process or activity in order to produce less pollution. Taller smokestacks may reduce the concentrations to which local people are exposed, but they are ineffective in reducing overall pollution. The fumes from these stacks have also caused a noticeable increase in ACID RAIN—rain in which pH has been lowered because of the presence of atmospheric sulfuric acid, formed from sulfur dioxide.

Pollutants removed from waste flows to reduce emissions to air and water may be disposed of by burial or storage on land, practices that pose potential hazards.

The fourth approach—changing a manufacturing process or activity in order to produce less pollution—may involve either the production of fewer residuals, by means of an improved process, or the separation and reuse of materials from the waste stream. This method of pollution control is the most effective and, as the costs of pollution control and waste disposal increase, is considered one of the most efficient.

Regulations

Federal air- and water-pollution-control laws of the late 1960s and the 1970s established standards and goals to be met by certain deadlines. Subsequent bills have extended the standards and goals, and sometimes changed existing regulations—by either tightening or relaxing them.

The Clean Air Act of 1970 established air-quality standards for six major pollutants: particulate matter, sulfur oxides, carbon monoxide, nitrogen oxides, hydrocarbons, and photochemical oxidants. Under this federal law, each state was required to develop plans to implement and maintain these standards. The Clean Air Act also set standards for automobile emissions—the major source of carbon monoxide, hydrocarbons, and nitrogen oxides. The ENVIRONMENTAL PROTECTION AGENCY (EPA) has also tightened rules regulating the amount of lead added to gasoline.

The Water Pollution Control Act of 1972, as amended in 1977, set a national goal of waters fit for swimming

and fishing by 1983 and of no pollutant discharge into these waters by 1985. The Marine Protection, Research, and Sanctuaries Act (1972) empowered the EPA to control the dumping of sewage wastes and toxic chemicals in the oceans. In 1987 the United States ratified an amendment to the Marine Pollution Treaty of 1973 (Marpol), prohibiting ocean dumping of plastic materials. The states of New York and New Jersey agreed in 1988 to halt the dumping of sludge—the settled material from wastewater treatment—in the Atlantic Ocean by the end of 1991.

Treatment Systems for Water

Primary wastewater treatment involves such physical techniques as screening large debris, skimming off floating materials, and settling out suspended material in tanks. These techniques remove about 60% of solid waste and 35% of biodegradable organic material in municipal sewage as well as in comparable industrial wastewater. Secondary treatment biologically breaks down organic matter remaining from the primary treatment by using microorganisms to decompose the wastes. This method increases the total removal of solid wastes and biodegradable organics to 90%. As a final step, municipal sewage is chlorinated to kill any pathogenic microorganisms.

Sludge can be reduced in volume by digestion in special airtight tanks, composting (an oxygen-requiring digestion), dewatering, or incineration. Energy or materials recovery may accompany these techniques and may even replace final disposal in LANDFILLS or the ocean. For example, some sludges may be applied to the land, recycling their plant nutrients.

Advanced treatment of waste involving biological, chemical, and physical methods of disposal is used either to remove nutrients that promote excessive growth of algae or to remove industrial pollutants, such as heavy metals and nonbiodegradable organic chemicals.

Treatment Systems for Air

Treatments for air pollution from stationary sources either remove particulate matter or remove gases. Four techniques, varying in cost and efficiency, for removing particulates are the cyclone separator, the wet scrubber, the electrostatic precipitator, and the baghouse. The cyclone separator causes air emissions to whirl around, forcing heavy particles to the outside and ultimately to removal below. The wet scrubber essentially washes particulates out of the exhaust. The electrostatic precipitator electrically charges the particles and attracts them to charged plates, thereby removing them. The baghouse operates like a vacuum cleaner, trapping particles in fabric filters placed in the exhaust stream.

Gaseous emissions are in general more difficult to control than particulates. Automobile emissions have been reduced by lowering engine combustion temperatures and by completing the oxidation of unburned gases by means of a CATALYTIC CONVERTER in the exhaust system.

One of the most difficult air pollutants to control is sulfur dioxide, which is given off in the combustion of sulfur-containing fuels, particularly coal in power plants. The projected increasing reliance on coal because of dwindling oil supplies makes this a critical problem. Removal of sulfur dioxide from exhaust gases can be accomplished with devices called scrubbers. Limestone scrubbers, for example, can remove up to 90% of the sulfur dioxide. They are, however, very expensive; they consume about 5% of a power plant's output; and they create massive amounts of calcium sulfite sludge, which must be disposed of as waste. The placement of strict emission controls on coal-burning plants has stimulated research on improved scrubbing devices.

Problems in Pollution Control

Pollution-treatment systems have been effective in reducing the massive quantities of water and air pollutants that are produced. The costs of pollution control—resulting from capital, maintenance, and labor costs, as well as from the cost of additional residuals disposal—generally go up rapidly as a greater percentage of residuals is removed from the waste stream. Damage from pollution, however, goes down as more contaminants are removed.

In addition, extensive treatment may result in more residuals and may involve a trade-off of one form of pollution for another. Because of the economic and residual–trade-off problems associated with the more advanced treatment systems, complete reliance on them to meet federal goals may not be appropriate. In many cases the development of processes that either reduce residuals or convert them into usable products can extensively reduce the cost of treatment.

See also: CONSERVATION; POLLUTANTS, CHEMICAL; SEWERAGE; WASTE DISPOSAL SYSTEMS.

▬

polo   Polo is a fast-paced game played on a turf field by teams of 4 players on horseback. Each team attempts to drive a small wooden ball through the opposing team's goalposts with a special mallet. The polo field is 300 yd (274.3 m) long and 160 yd (146.3 m) wide and enclosed by wooden sideboards. Indoor polo, which is played mainly in the United States, is played by teams of 3 on a smaller field. In either game the winning team is the one that scores the most goals within the allotted playing time.

Polo is believed to have originated in ancient Persia; the first written account describes a game between the Persians and the Turkomans that took place in about 600 BC. The name polo comes from the Persian word for willow root, *pulu,* the material from which the balls were made.

The game of polo was seen by British soldiers in 19th-century India and quickly spread to other English-speaking countries. In the 1870s, Gordon Bennett introduced the game to the United States; today there are approximately 3,000 registered U.S. polo players.

Players are required to wear hard hats, and the fetlocks of all horses, usually called ponies, must be covered with protective material to prevent injury. The polo ball—traditionally made of solid willow, ash, or bamboo root—is now almost always made of solid plastic. It is painted white, measures 3.0–3.5 in (7.6–8.9 cm) in diameter, and weighs 3.5–4.5 oz (99.2–127.6 g). The game is usually divided into 4 to 8 chukkers, or periods, of 7 minutes each. Penalties for various infractions are assessed by two mounted officials and may include free goals and free shots at the goal, depending on the severity of the infraction.

The quality of the horse is largely responsible for success or failure in a contest. Many of the best horses, which can take 2 to 3 years to train, come from Argentina, which has dominated polo since 1945. The Cup of the Americas, between Argentina and the United States, though only occasionally contested, is considered the premier polo tournament in the world. It occurs whenever either country decides to mount a challenge for it.

▬

Polo, Marco [poh'-loh]   Marco Polo, *c.*1254–1324, was a Venetian explorer and merchant whose account of his travels in Asia was the primary source for the European image of the Far East until the late 19th century. Marco's father, Niccolò, and his uncle Maffeo had traveled to China (1260–69) as merchants. When they left (1271) Venice to return to China, they were accompanied by 17-year-old Marco and two priests who quickly deserted them.

Traveling across central Asia, the Polos arrived (1275) in Shandu, the summer capital of Kublai Khan, the Mongol emperor of China. Marco soon became a favorite of the khan and for 17 years roamed through China in his service.

Toward the end of this time the Polos increasingly desired to return home, but the khan was reluctant to part with them. In 1292 he allowed them to sail to Persia on a diplomatic mission; they were finally able to reach Venice in 1295.

The Venetian traveler Marco Polo wrote an invaluable account of his journeys in Asia during the late 1200s. This miniature shows Marco (kneeling, right), with his father and uncle, presenting the pope's letter to Kublai Khan.

Shortly thereafter Marco was captured by the Genoese in a naval battle and imprisoned for a short time. In prison he dictated an account of his experiences to Rustichello, a well-known writer. Although full of systematic detail, *The Travels of Marco Polo* was received with astonishment and disbelief. After reports by other travelers to China verified portions of the tales, they stimulated Western interest in Far Eastern trade and influenced people like Christopher Columbus. Marco's account stood virtually alone as a description of the Far East until supplemented by the chronicle of the Jesuit missionary Matteo RICCI, which appeared in 1615.

polonaise [pahl-uh-nayz'] The polonaise is a Polish national dance of folk origins. Its music is in triple meter in moderate tempo and is characterized by sharply articulated rhythms. The polonaise had emerged as a stylized courtly dance by the 18th century; early examples may be found in the music of Johann Sebastian Bach, François Couperin, Handel, and Mozart. In the late 18th century it was cultivated as a nationalistic expression, and dozens of Polish composers in the early 19th century produced countless works in the form. The polonaise would today be considered little more than a provincial curiosity, however, were it not for the 13 examples by Frédéric Chopin, the masterpieces of the genre. Chopin cast his polonaises in heroic form, and in using them to symbolize his ties to his homeland, he followed the example of his Polish predecessors.

polonium [puh-loh'-nee-uhm] Polonium was the first radioactive element to be isolated; its discovery in 1898 by Marie and Pierre CURIE marks the beginning of the atomic age. The name is derived from Mme. Curie's homeland, Poland. The chemical symbol of polonium is Po, and the element's atomic number is 84.

In the periodic table polonium is classified among the Group VIA elements—oxygen, sulfur, selenium, and tellurium. It differs from these in being a metal (m.p. 254° C, b.p. 962° C) and in behaving chemically more like lead or bismuth. All polonium isotopes are radioactive. There is only a tiny amount of naturally occurring polonium present in the Earth's crust; it is found in uranium-ore deposits, having been formed there as part of the natural decay sequences of heavier unstable elements.

Exposure to polonium is an extreme health hazard. The emitted radiation energy is so great that even minute samples ionize the surrounding air, causing it to glow; these samples will also heat themselves to temperatures substantially higher than their surroundings. The polonium-210 isotope is used as an alpha-particle source and as a heat source for generating electricity aboard space satellites.

Polonnaruwa [pahl-uh-nuh-roo'-wuh] Polonnaruwa was the administrative and royal capital of ancient Lanka (Ceylon: modern Sri Lanka) from the 10th through the 13th century. The period of its greatest creative activity occurred during the reigns of Parakrama Bahu I (1153–86) and Nissanka Malla (1187–96). Extensive ruins of royal and ecclesiastical structures bear witness to the brilliant civilization that then flourished. The most spectacular remains are numerous colossal images of the Buddha, rock-cut and built up of brick and stucco; gigantic image halls; and enormous palaces of multiple stories. The Hindu temples at the site were constructed during the 11th-century occupation of the city by the Cholas of South India.

Poltava [puhl-tah'-vah] Poltava (1984 est. pop., 296,000) is the capital of Poltava oblast in Ukraine, a republic of the USSR. It is situated in rich Ukrainian farm country along the Kharkov-Kiev highway. Industry there is limited to light manufacturing and food processing. One of the oldest cities in Ukraine, Poltava is best known as the site of a major battle in 1709 in which the Russians under PETER I defeated the army of CHARLES XII of Sweden.

polyandry see POLYGAMY

Polybius [poh-lib'-ee-uhs] Polybius, c.200–c.118 BC, was a Greek historian of Rome. One of 1,000 hostages taken to Rome in 168 BC, he befriended the Roman general Scipio Aemilianus (SCIPIO AFRICANUS MINOR) and accompanied him to Spain and Africa, where they witnessed the destruction of Carthage in 146. His major historical work contained 40 books, of which the first five are extant (in addition to large fragments of the remaining volumes). His main purpose was to present the facts and causes of Rome's swift rise to world mastery from 221 to 168, with an introduction describing Roman history from 264 to 220 and a conclusion summarizing events from 168 to 146. The Romans, he believed, prevailed over their opponents because of a superior constitution and military organization.

Polycarp, Saint [pahl'-uh-kahrp] Polycarp, c.69–c.155, bishop of Smyrna, was a living link between the Apostles and the church of the later 2d century. As a leader of the church in Anatolia, he visited (155) Rome to discuss with its bishop the disputed date for the celebration of Easter. It was agreed that the Eastern and Western churches would continue their divergent usages. After his return to Smyrna, Polycarp was arrested and burned to death. A letter from the church of Smyrna, the oldest known narrative of a Christian martyr, gives an account of his trial and death. Feast day: Jan. 25 (Eastern); Feb. 23 (Western).

Polychaete [pah'-lee-keet] Polychaetes are mostly marine, bristly worms constituting the class Polychaeta in the phylum Annelida. The polychaetes are the largest and most diverse class of annelids, comprising about 5,000 species. They range in length from 2 mm to 3 m (8/100 in. to 10 ft), with most measuring between 5 and 10 cm (2 and 4 in) long. Among the better-known polychaetes are the clamworms, or sandworms, *Nereis*; the lugworms, *Arenicola*; and the fanworms, families Sabellidae and Serpulidae. A primitive, or unmodified, polychaete consists of a long, cylindrical body composed of externally identical segments, except for the two-part head and the posterior tip. Each identical body segment bears two fleshy, lobed, paddlelike appendages called parapodia, which aid in locomotion. Bundles of firm, bristly setae project from each parapodium and are used for movement, for defense, or for holding the worm within its shelter. The head bears antennae, eyes, and various fleshy projections. Polychaetes may be filter feeders, scavengers, or predators. Reproduction is usually sexual.

Polyclitus [pah-luh-kly'-tuhs]   Polyclitus, one of the foremost Greek sculptors of the 5th century BC, was noted for his statues of athletes, particularly the *Doryphorus* (spear bearer). One of his creations—the cult statue of Hera, produced for the temple of the goddess in his native Argos and acclaimed in the ancient world for its beauty—was made of gold and ivory.

None of Polyclitus's original works has survived; the *Doryphorus* is preserved only in Roman copies, the best of which is in the Museo Nazionale, Naples. The statue is an excellent example of contrapposto composition, with a supporting leg and idle arm on one side and a receding leg and active arm on the other to suggest movement. The statue illustrates the principles of human proportion that Polyclitus recorded in his book, the *Canon,* which unfortunately is now lost. Because it embodied the ideal classical human figure, the *Doryphorus* itself came to be called the *Canon.*

polycythemia [pah-lee-sy-thee'-mee-uh]   Polycythemia describes an abnormally increased concentration of blood cells. Polycythemia rubra vera is a primary defect in the mechanism that regulates the rate at which all blood cells are produced in bone marrow. Symptoms are headache; ruddy coloration of the skin, nail beds, and lips; fatigue; generalized itching; and visual disturbances. Hypertension, strokes, clotting of various major blood vessels, and gout may be secondary complications, and the spleen often becomes enlarged. After 10 to 15 years, polycythemia rubra vera may evolve into chronic or acute myeloid LEUKEMIA; treatment involves the periodic removal of blood or the suppression of red-blood-cell production by means of chemotherapy or radiation therapy. Secondary polycythemia, more properly called secondary erythrocytosis, may be a compensatory response to inadequate oxygenation of blood, resulting from a wide variety of cardiac or pulmonary diseases.

polyester   Polyesters are a class of long-chain polymers (see POLYMERIZATION) characterized by formation through ESTER groups. There are four major classes of polyesters, each with its specific composition and applications: alkyds, unsaturated polyesters, polyethylene terephthalates, and aromatic polycarbonates.

Alkyds are coating polymers that, when fully polymerized, are cross-linked from one chain to another. The hard, brittle properties of alkyds are modified for use in most oil-based paints. Unsaturated polyesters were developed during World War II and used in combination with fiberglass for boat hulls, protective armor, and other military uses. Polyethylene-terephthalate polyesters are often spun into SYNTHETIC FIBERS—notably Dacron, Fortrel, and Kodel—and stretched into films, all of which have remarkable strength and resistance to heat, chemicals, mildew, and pest damage. Photographic film, electrical components, laminates, and sails are made of these polyesters. Aromatic polycarbonate polyesters often replace glass and metals because they are less prone to shape distortion. They are also used in photographic film.

polygamy   Polygamy is a type of MARRIAGE in which a person may legally have several spouses concurrently, as opposed to MONOGAMY, marriage to only one spouse at a time. It may take the form of polygyny, the marriage of a man to more than one woman, or polyandry, the marriage of a woman to more than one man. Both systems seem to arise from special local conditions.

Polyandry is by far the rarer form of polygamy. Few societies sanction it. Among those that have traditionally done so are the Toda and Nayar of India and some Tibetan groups. It occurs in matrilineal societies (see LINEAGE), in which a woman remains a member of her mother's household and kin group after marriage, and in which her children are considered as belonging exclusively to her kin group, rather than to that of their father or to those of both parents. Among the Nayar, however, the child had to have an acknowledged father to be fully entitled to membership in its mother's lineage, an acknowledged father being one who was within the woman's appropriate marriage group and who had paid part of the expenses connected with childbirth. In polyandry, no one husband has exclusive sexual rights to his wife. In traditional Sinhalese practice, the first husband has priority, and later husbands must obtain his consent for sexual relations with the common wife. All children share equally in the mother's property, and the children of each father share in their father's property.

Polygyny is found in many parts of the world, but it is most frequent among African peoples, such as the MENDE of Sierra Leone and Liberia, the Nupe of Nigeria, and the Serer of Senegal and Gambia. Among the many customs contributing to polygyny in various societies is the *levirate,* according to which a man is obliged to marry the widow of a brother. Where the custom of the *sororate* is observed, if a wife fails to bear children the husband marries her sister; some or all of the children of this union are considered as belonging to the barren wife. Concurrent marriage with up to four wives is permitted by the tenets of ISLAM, with the stipulation that each wife be treated equally. Polygyny was formerly practiced in the United States under MORMONISM by members of the Church of Jesus Christ of Latter-Day Saints.

polygon A polygon is a simple closed plane figure that is bounded by a finite number of intersecting line segments (at least three segments are required). More precisely, the union of *n* segments is an *n*-sided polygon, provided that: (1) each endpoint (vertex) lies on exactly two segments, (2) no three consecutive endpoints lie on the same line, and (3) no segments intersect except at the endpoints. A polygon is convex if all of the interior angles are less than 180 degrees; it is concave if at least one of its interior angles is greater than 180 degrees. A regular polygon (see examples illustrated above) is one that is both equilateral (all sides of the same length) and equiangular (all angles the same).

A polygon can be classified according to the number of its sides or the number of its angles. Polygons with, respectively, 3, 4, 5, 6, 7, 8, 9, or 10 sides are called TRIANGLES, QUADRILATERALS, pentagons, hexagons, septagons (or heptagons), octagons, nonagons, and decagons. A regular triangle is called an equilateral triangle, and a quadrilateral that is regular is known as a SQUARE.

The sum of the angles of an *n*-sided polygon is $(n - 2) \times 180°$. For example, $n = 3$ in a triangle, and the sum of the angles equals $180°$. Each angle of a regular *n*-sided polygon is $(n - 2) \times 180°/n$.

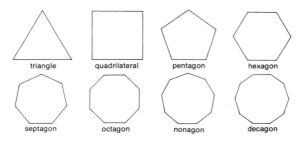

triangle	quadrilateral	pentagon	hexagon

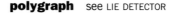

septagon	octagon	nonagon	decagon

polygraph see LIE DETECTOR

polyhedron [pah-lee-hee'-druhn] A polyhedron is a three-dimensional figure bounded by plane polygonal regions. A polygonal region consists of a POLYGON and its interior points. The polygonal regions are the faces of the polyhedron; the edges of the polygons are the edges of this polyhedron; and the vertices of the polygons are the vertices of the polyhedron. If the faces of the polyhedron are all congruent regular polygons, then the polyhedron is called a regular polyhedron. There are only five regular polyhedrons: the regular tetrahedron (triangular PYRAMID), which has 4 equilateral triangles as faces; the cube, with 6 squares as faces; the regular octahedron, with 8 equilateral triangles as faces; the regular dodecahedron, with 12 regular pentagons as faces; and the regular icosahedron, with 20 equilateral triangles as faces. Any regular polyhedron may be inscribed in (have its vertices on) or circumscribed about (have its faces tangent to) a sphere. For any polyhedron the numbers of vertices, *V*, edges, *E*, and faces, *F*, are related by Euler's theorem: $V - E + F =$

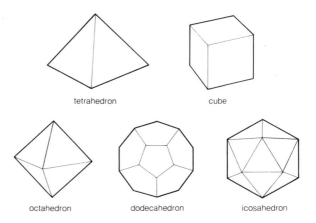

tetrahedron	cube

octahedron	dodecahedron	icosahedron

2. For a tetrahedron, $V = 4$, $E = 6$, and $F = 4$, which agrees with Euler's theorem.

polymerase chain reaction The polymerase chain reaction (PCR) is a genetic-engineering technique developed as a way to obtain in quantity some specific sample of genetic material for research purposes. The three-step PCR process was originated in the late 1980s by the Cetus Corporation of California. First the desired sample—a tiny fragment of the nucleic acid DNA—is heated to separate the two strands of the molecule. Segments of DNA called primers are then attached to each strand to identify them for copying. Copying, the third step, is accomplished by adding the natural enzyme called DNA polymerase. A given sample can be increased a millionfold within hours by repeating these steps about 20 times.

PCR is useful in many areas of medical research. The investigation of genetic disorders, for example, must often make use of tiny samples of DNA. PCR can also enhance investigations of remaining genetic samples from earlier life-forms.

polymerization [pahl'-uh-mur-uh-zay'-shuhn] Polymerization is a chemical reaction in which a large number of small molecules, known as monomers, react to form large molecules, called polymers, that contain many identical repeating units (*poly* = many, *mer* = units). Polymers are widely used as plastics, synthetic fibers, and finishes. To form a polymer, a monomer must have at least two reactive sites.

Condensation Polymerization. The monomers in condensation polymerization are difunctional molecules that react with the loss of a small molecule, such as water. For example, the −OH group of the hydroxy acid $HOCH_2CH_2COOH$ reacts with the −COOH group of another monomer to give an ester dimer:

$$2\ HOCH_2CH_2COOH \rightarrow HOCH_2CH_2\overset{\displaystyle O}{\overset{\|}{C}}-OCH_2CH_2COOH + H_2O$$

The ester dimer is also difunctional and may react further to form the polyester

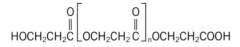

$$HOCH_2CH_2C \left[OCH_2CH_2C \right]_n OCH_2CH_2COOH$$

which contains a large number (n) of the repeating unit shown in brackets. Polyesters may also be formed by the reaction of a difunctional alcohol with a difunctional acid. Dacron is produced in this manner from ethylene glycol, $HOCH_2CH_2OH$, and terephthalic acid, $HOOCC_6H_4COOH$. Reactions in which a small molecule is split off are known as condensations, and polymers formed in this way are known as condensation polymers. Other important condensation polymers are polyamides such as nylon, made by condensation of diamines with dicarboxylic acids, and polyurethanes, made from diisocyanates and dialcohols.

Addition Polymerization. The monomers in addition polymerization contain carbon-carbon double bonds ($C = C$), which can react at both carbon atoms. The polymers formed in this way contain all the atoms that were present in the reactant monomers and are known as addition polymers. The addition polymerization of ethylene gives polyethylene.

$$nCH_2{=}CH_2 \xrightarrow{\text{catalyst}} \left[CH_2{-}CH_2 \right] n$$

The reaction occurs in the presence of a suitable catalyst—free radicals, acids, or bases (see CHAIN REACTION). Other important addition polymers include polyacrylonitrile, also known as Orlon; polymethyl methacrylate, marketed under the trade names Lucite, Plexiglas, and Perspex; polyvinyl chloride, commonly called PVC; and polytetrafluoroethylene, sold under the trade name Teflon.

In 1983 workers at the DuPont company announced a new addition polymerization technique called group transfer polymerization. The process involves an initiator molecule containing an activating group. Individual monomers insert themselves inside the activating group, so that the group continuously gets transferred to the end of the growing polymer chain. Benefits of this new method include precise control of the chain length and flexible use of different monomers.

See also: PLASTICS; RUBBER; SYNTHETIC FIBERS.

Polynesia [pah-luh-nee'-zhuh] Polynesia, one of the three groups of Pacific islands (the other two being Melanesia and Micronesia), lies in a triangle between Hawaii and Easter Island, both included in the area, and New Zealand. Although the water area is about 39,000,000 km² (15,000,000 mi²), the land area is only about 294,000 km² (114,000 mi²), consisting of mountainous volcanic islands and low coral atolls. In addition to Hawaii and Easter Island, the major island groups are Samoa, Tonga, and the islands of French Polynesia, including Tahiti and the Society Islands.

The peoples of the area, known as Polynesians, speak various Malayo-Polynesian languages and number about 1 million. The mythical homeland of their ancestors was Hawaiki, near Tahiti. Current views suggest that they came to Polynesia from the direction of Asia. An agricultural and fishing people, Polynesians developed intricate patterns of conduct, elaborate mythology and religion, art, and song-poetry. MANA and TABOO strengthened sociopolitical relationships. In early times the island and lagoons were divided among kin groups. Kinship ties weakened, and warfare became more frequent as the population increased. Secular leaders arose, although traditional chiefs kept their religious role.

Polynesian language see MALAYO-POLYNESIAN LANGUAGES

polynomial see EQUATION

---

polyp [pah'-lip] In medicine a polyp is a tumor that usually occurs on mucous membranes and is characteristically attached to underlying tissues by means of a stalk. It thus resembles somewhat the animal known as a polyp. Medical polyps typically occur in the nose, stomach, large intestine, bladder, and uterus. They can be malignant or benign.

Polyphemus [pah-luh-fee'-muhs] In Greek mythology Polyphemus was a CYCLOPS, a one-eyed giant, who lived in a cave on Sicily. According to Homer's *Odyssey,* Polyphemus imprisoned Odysseus and 12 of his men. After the monster had eaten 6 men, Odysseus contrived to make him drunk and to blind him with a burning pole. He then tied Polyphemus's sheep 3 abreast, and when the giant let his flock out to graze, Odysseus and his men escaped the cave, each suspended below a group of sheep. Thus, Odysseus earned the hatred of POSEIDON, Polyphemus's father.

---

polyphony [puh-lif'-uh-nee] *Polyphony* is a term derived from Greek ("many sounds") and is applied to music in which several melodic parts proceed simultaneously, as opposed to homophony—music with one melody and with chords underneath. The term is used in a specific way to refer to music of the Middle Ages and the Renaissance with a strong contrapuntal interest (see COUNTERPOINT). In fact, the definition need not be so narrow, for it would be equally correct to describe a motet by Heinrich Schütz or an orchestral suite by J. S. Bach as polyphony, and if this is so there is no point in denying the term to music of more recent periods. The earliest surviving polyphony in Western music dates from the 8th century, since which time it has grown constantly in complexity and sonority, sometimes reaching an astonishing number of real and independent parts, as in the motet *Spem in alium* for 40 voices (8 five-part choirs), by Thomas TALLIS.

polysaccharide [pah-lee-sak'-uh-ryd]   Polysaccharides are organic compounds that occur widely in plants and animals. Most natural CARBOHYDRATES occur in the form of polysaccharides. As their name indicates, they are polymers of the monosaccharides, or simple SUGARS. The most common polysaccharides are CELLULOSE, the structural material of plants, and the nutrients known as plant STARCH and animal starch, or GLYCOGEN. The polysaccharide CHITIN is a structural material in arthropods. Molecules of these compounds have straight chains and are not water-soluble, but some branched polysaccharides are, such as the GUMS.

polysilane [pah-lee-si'-layn]   Polysilanes are synthetic polymers made up of long chains of SILICON atoms rather than the carbon atoms that make up most polymers (see PLASTICS). Silicon is in the same chemical family as carbon, and its atoms can also bear two side groups while linked in a chain. Differences in bonding, however, give polysilanes special properties. Some, for example, are very sensitive to ultraviolet light and have great potential value in the preparation of integrated circuits by means of ultraviolet laser light. The first polysilanes were prepared in the late 1940s, but their more extensive development began with the discovery of soluble polysilanes in 1978.

polytheism [pah'-lee-thee-izm]   Polytheism is the belief in and worship of many gods. It contrasts with MONOTHEISM, belief in one god, and PANTHEISM, identification of God with the universe. In polytheism the gods are personified, distinguished by functions, related to one another in a cosmic family, and the subjects of myths and legends.

Pombal, Sebastião José de Carvalho e Melo, Marquês de [pohm-bahl']   The marquês de Pombal, b. May 13, 1699, d. May 8, 1782, chief minister of Portugal (1756–77), instituted many reforms but was hated for his dictatorial rule. Sebastião de Carvalho began his career as a historian and diplomat and in 1750 was appointed minister of war and foreign affairs. In 1756, Joseph, an indolent monarch, made him chief minister. Carvalho attacked the powers of the church, restricted the Inquisition, and expelled (1759) the Jesuits from Brazil and Portugal. A mercantilist, he set up monopolistic companies for the production of wine, for fishing and colonial trade, and for glass and textile manufacturing.

Carvalho reduced the power of the nobility, modernized the university curriculum (1772), and abolished slavery in Portugal (1773). His opponents were jailed, tortured, and executed, but he enjoyed the support of the king, who made him marquês de Pombal in 1769. After Joseph died in 1777, Pombal was exiled from Lisbon.

pomegranate [pahm'-uh-gran-it]   The pomegranate, *Punica granatum*, a deciduous tree or large shrub and its fruit, originated in the Middle East and has long been cultivated throughout the Mediterranean world. The plant bears white or bright red flowers followed by seedy, red fruits that may reach 13 cm (5 in) in diameter. Thriving on a wide range of soils in warm climates, the pomegranate produces excellent fruit under semiarid conditions, as in parts of California and Israel.

The fruit was associated with both fertility and death in classical mythology. The goddess Aphrodite was said to have planted it on the island of Cyprus. The Romans, who believed that the best pomegranates came from Carthage, called the fruit *punicum*, the Latin for Carthage. The fruit's Spanish name is *granada*, and the fruit appears on that city's seal.

The pomegranate is eaten as a fresh fruit, and the dark red, acid juice is used as a flavoring and is the principal ingredient of the red flavoring syrup grenadine.

The pomegranate shrub bears flamboyant flowers and glossy leaves that are red when young. Its many-seeded fruit has a thin, leathery rind and a red, translucent pulp.

Pomerania [pahm-uh-ray'-nee-uh]   Pomerania (German: Pommern), a historic region on both sides of the ODER RIVER, is bounded by the Baltic Sea in the north and the Vistula River in the south. Occupying the historically shifting border area between Poland and Germany, the region is now divided between northeastern Germany and northwestern Poland. Most of Pomerania is a low-lying, glaciated, coastal plain, poor in resources except for peat. Potatoes, rye, and hay are raised there, and pasturelands support cattle. Tourism is also important.

The region was named for the Slavic Pomerani tribe, which settled there during the 5th century. At various times independent, Pomerania was split during the 12th century. The western part became tied to the Holy Roman Empire; the eastern part, which became known as Pomerelia, was taken from Poland by the Teutonic Knights in 1308 but returned in 1466. Pomerelia became part of West Prussia in 1772, and in 1919 part of it was given to Poland. Seized by Germany in 1939, Pomerelia was returned to Poland in 1945. Western Pomerania had an equally confused history. Part of the Holy Roman Empire until 1637, although ruled by Polish dukes, it was divided between Prussia and Sweden in 1648. In 1720, Sweden returned some of its territory to Prussia, and after 1815, Prussia gained the rest. Thus Prussia (which had gained control of eastern Pomerania in 1772) held all of Pomerania from 1815 to 1919, when most was lost to Poland. In 1945 part of western Pomerania was incorporated into East Germany.

pomeranian [pah-mur-ay'-nee-uhn]   The pomeranian, a toy breed but a member of the SPITZ group of dogs, was bred down from the German grosspitzen (great spitzes). In the northern German state of Pomerania, mainly the white variety was bred to a smaller size. It was these smaller "pomeranians" that were taken to England, where the present toy breed was developed. The breed came into prominence in 1888, when one was acquired by Queen Victoria. By 1900 the small variety then known as the miniature pomeranian was shown in two categories: more than and less than 3.5 kg (8 lb). These early dogs, however, lacked the profuse coat seen in today's breed.

The modern pomeranian is a short-bodied dog with a foxy head, a double coat, and a profusely feathered tail. The coat may be any of a number of colors, including sable, black, and parti-color. Pomeranians range from 1.4 to 3.2 kg (3 to 7 lb) in weight and ideally should be between 1.8 and 2.3 kg (4 and 5 lb) and about 15 to 18 cm (6 to 7 in) high at the shoulder.

The pomeranian is a toy dog that resembles the larger Arctic sled dogs from which it is descended. Originally used as a sheep-herding dog in central Europe and standing 46 cm (18 in) at the shoulder, the pomeranian has been bred down to an average height of 15 cm (6 in).

Pomo [poh'-moh]   The Pomo are a North American tribe of central Californian Indians noted for their highly developed BASKETRY arts. Their lands once extended from the shores of Clear Lake, north of San Francisco, westward to the coast. Speakers of a Hokan language with seven dialectic divisions, the Pomo traditionally inhabited about 50 autonomous villages, each housing 100–300 persons and with designated territories for the gathering of wild plant foods and for hunting and fishing. Each village had at least one large semisubterranean earth-covered structure for major ceremonials. In 1989 about 4,700 Pomo lived on or near reservations in California.

Pompadour, Jeanne Antoinette Poisson, Marquise de [pohm-pah-door', zhahn ahn-twah-net' pwah-sohn']   The talented and beautiful Jeanne Antoinette Poisson, the marquise de Pompadour, b. Dec. 29, 1721, d. Apr. 15, 1764, as mistress of LOUIS XV of France from 1745 to 1750 and thereafter as his close friend, exerted a strong cultural, intellectual, and political influence at the French court. Married to the financier Charles le Normant d'Étoiles, she moved in fashionable and Enlightenment-oriented Parisian circles. The king installed her as his official mistress in September 1745 and gave her the marquisate of Pompadour. She arranged the king's entertainment and helped design many public buildings and mansions, defended Denis Diderot's *Encyclopédie*, and influenced the appointment of the duc de CHOISEUL and other ministers.

The marquise de Pompadour, mistress and confidante of Louis XV of France, greatly influenced the king's cultural undertakings and political appointments.

pompano [pahm'-puh-noh]   Pompanos are relatively deep-bodied, fast-swimming marine fishes of the genus

Trachinotus in the jack family, Carangidae. Most attain sizes of 30 to 60 cm (1 to 2 ft). Pompanos are found worldwide in shallow to middle depths of tropical and warm-temperate seas. Many species inhabit the sandy areas of the surf zone, where they feed on crustaceans and other organisms. The Florida pompano, *T. carolinus*, is found from Brazil to Massachusetts. The European pompano, *T. glaucus*, occasionally wanders as far north as Scandinavia.

Pompeii [pohm-pay'-ee]   Pompeii, an ancient Roman city on the Gulf of Naples, in southern Italy, was buried under a thick layer of lava and ash by the sudden, violent eruption of Mount VESUVIUS in AD 79. The remains unearthed in the course of the first systematic excavations there (1738–56) exerted a major influence on neoclassical art during the 18th century. Continuing excavations at the site have provided a unique picture of daily life in a provincial Roman city.

History. Pompeii was originally founded in the 8th century BC by the Oscans, an Italic tribe. The settlement was controlled by the Greeks and the Etruscans before coming under the influence of the Samnites toward the end of the 5th century BC. After being conquered (89 BC) by the Roman general Sulla, Pompeii was given the status of a Roman *municipium*. It flourished as a prosperous Roman port and resort town, with roughly 20,000 inhabitants and an urban area of 66 ha (163 acres) at the time of the eruption of Vesuvius.

The Romans regarded Vesuvius as an extinct volcano, and the destruction by earthquake of parts of Pompeii and nearby HERCULANEUM in AD 62 was not interpreted as a sign of its renewed activity. Reconstruction was still in progress when, 17 years later, on the morning of Aug. 24,

79, the great eruption took place that destroyed Pompeii, Herculaneum, Stabiae, and a number of smaller settlements. When the eruption ceased on the second day, more than 2,000 inhabitants of Pompeii had perished, and the city lay covered under a layer of ash and volcanic debris about 6 m (20 ft) deep. An eyewitness account of the calamity is given in two letters written to the historian Tacitus by the Roman author Pliny the Younger, whose uncle lost his life at Pompeii.

As soon as the ashes had cooled, survivors attempted to dig out their possessions, but Pompeii was later all but forgotten. The buried city was rediscovered late in the 16th century in the course of work on an underground water line; not for another 150 years, however, were systematic excavations undertaken at the site. These were begun in 1738 at neighboring Herculaneum, where marble statues had earlier been unearthed (1709), and in 1748 at Pompeii itself. Excavations were conducted intermittently in the 18th and 19th centuries and have continued to the present. About 65 ha (160 acres) of Pompeii—more than half of the original city—have now been uncovered.

The Excavated City. Pompeii was roughly oval, had a regular grid layout, and was surrounded by a wall 3,120 m (10,236 ft) in length with 11 towers and 7 gates. The rectangular forum (marketplace), which was surrounded by columns, formed the center of the city. It was the site of the principal temple, dedicated to the three deities Jupiter, Juno, and Minerva, and other public buildings, including the curia (council chamber) and the comitium (municipal assembly hall) as well as the basilica (covered market and courthouse) and the macellum, where food was sold. The southern part of the city contained the so-called Triangular Forum, consisting of a Doric temple dating from the 6th century BC, a Hellenistic columned

Ritual dancing and scourging are depicted in this detail from a fresco in Pompeii's Villa of the Mysteries. The fresco shows the initiation of a bride into the mystery cult of Dionysus.

The ruins of Pompeii, formerly hidden under volcanic ash, offer a detailed picture of life in a prosperous Roman city of the 1st century AD. Since Pompeii's rediscovery, excavations have uncovered houses, temples, shops, public offices, baths, and theaters.

hall with a palaestra (wrestling school), an open-air theater, an odeum (concert hall), and gladiators' barracks.

The interior walls and floors of the houses were often richly decorated with mural paintings and mosaics. Much of what is known of Greek and Roman painting in the period 300 BC to AD 79 is based on the well-preserved discoveries made in houses at Pompeii.

See also: ROMAN ART AND ARCHITECTURE.

Pompey the Great [pahm'-pee] Gnaeus Pompeius, known as Pompey the Great, b. Sept. 29, 106 BC, d. Sept. 28, 48 BC, was Julius CAESAR's most powerful rival in the waning days of the Roman republic. Having helped put down a revolt by Rome's allies (89–88 BC) and the siege of Rome (87) by Gaius MARIUS and Lucius Cornelius CINNA, Pompey threw in his lot with Lucius Cornelius SULLA against Marius's successors in 83, using his three private legions to drive them from Sicily and Africa. Always opportunistic, Pompey intrigued to join METELLUS PIUS against Sertorius's rebellion in Spain. After the revolt was crushed (72) he brought his army home to Italy, where he cashed in on the victory of Marcus Licinius CRASSUS over SPARTACUS by annihilating some fugitive slaves.

As joint consuls (70 BC), Pompey and Crassus helped restore powers to the tribunes, revived the dormant censorship, and at least permitted reform of the jury courts. Subsequent tribunes obtained commands for Pompey against the Mediterranean pirates, whom he quickly suppressed (67), and against the powerful MITHRADATES VI of Pontus. He not only defeated Mithradates (66–63) but also reorganized the administration of Anatolia and other areas of the Near East so as to secure Rome's eastern frontier.

Pompey's military exploits won him great power and wealth, but he encountered strong opposition within the senate. His opponents, led by Lucius Licinius LUCULLUS and CATO the Younger, forced him into the First Triumvirate (60 BC) with Crassus and Caesar, whose daughter, Julia, he married (59).

The coalition was renewed (56) at Luca, and Pompey again became (55) consul with Crassus and received the

Pompey the Great, an outstanding Roman general and statesman, was the last obstacle in Julius Caesar's rise to power. Defeated in a civil war, Pompey fled to Egypt, where he was murdered.

governorship of the Spanish provinces. After the deaths of Julia (54) and Crassus (53), however, Pompey joined his former enemies and opposed Caesar. The dominant oligarchs, regarding Pompey as the lesser threat to the status quo, chose (52) him as sole consul; he restored order at Rome and introduced reforms that undermined the absent Caesar's position. Early in 49 BC, attempts to avert civil war failed. Caesar crossed the Rubicon and forced (49) Pompey's retreat to Greece. Though Pompey was victorious at Dyrrhachium (Durazzo, 48), he was finally beaten at Pharsalus (Aug. 9, 48), after which he fled to Egypt, where he was assassinated.

Pompidou, Georges [pohm-pee-doo'] Georges Pompidou, b. July 5, 1911, d. Apr. 2, 1974, a close associate of Gen. Charles DE GAULLE, was premier (1962–68) and president (1969–74) of France's Fifth Republic. Pompidou served (1944–46) as an aide on de Gaulle's staff, and from 1946 to 1957 he was a member of the council of state, a key administrative-judicial body. He joined the Rothschild bank in 1955. Pompidou became de Gaulle's personal advisor in 1958, when the general assumed the presidency of the new Fifth Republic. Pompidou was rewarded in 1962 with the premiership, but de Gaulle did not reappoint him in 1968.

After de Gaulle resigned in 1969, Pompidou was elected president. As president, he gave greater attention than de Gaulle had to domestic problems. Although he continued the general's independent foreign policy, Pompidou dropped the opposition to British entry into the European Economic Community. He died in office following a protracted illness.

Pompidou Center, Paris   see BEAUBOURG

Ponce [pohn'-say] Ponce, the second largest city and the chief commercial center of Puerto Rico, has a population of 187,749 (1990). Ponce lies 5 km (3 mi) from the south central coast of the island. Its port, Playa de Ponce, handles tobacco, coffee, rum, and sugarcane. Its principal industries produce cement and textiles. One of the oldest cities in the New World, Ponce was founded in the 17th century and named for Juan Ponce de León, first governor of Puerto Rico. The Catholic University of Puerto Rico (1948) is located there.

Ponce de León, Juan [pohn'-say day lay-ohn'] The Spanish explorer Juan Ponce de León, c.1460–1521, is credited with the discovery of Florida. In 1493 he accompanied Christopher Columbus on his second voyage to America. Ponce de León helped crush Indian revolts on the island of Hispaniola, and he conquered Puerto Rico, serving as its governor from 1509 to 1512. King Ferdinand II granted (1512) Ponce de León a patent to discover and settle the "island of Bimini." His three ships reached land near the site of Saint Augustine during the Easter season of 1513. Because of the holiday *Pascua*

Florida or because of the profusion of flowers, he named the land Florida. According to legend he was seeking the Fountain of Youth—a rejuvenating, tonic spring that Caribbean natives had described. He explored the Florida Keys and part of the west coast of the peninsula before returning to Puerto Rico by way of Cuba. In 1514, Ponce de León received a royal commission to colonize the "isle of Florida," but he did not return to Florida until 1521. In July he was mortally wounded by an Indian arrow.

Ponchielli, Amilcare [pohn-kee-el'-lee, ah-meel-kah'-ray]　The Italian composer Amilcare Ponchielli, b. Aug. 31, 1834, d. Jan. 6, 1886, is today remembered for a single work, the opera *La Gioconda.* He was trained at Milan Conservatory, where he later taught. As a composer he devoted himself mostly to operas, writing nine between 1856 and 1885. The first, *I Promessi Sposi*, based on Alessandro Manzoni's novel, won Ponchielli belated acclaim in Milan in 1872. Only his sixth opera, however, has endured—*La Gioconda*, with libretto by Arrigo Boito, after a drama by Victor Hugo, first produced at Milan's La Scala in 1876. Its ballet episode, *The Dance of the Hours*, is famous as a concert piece.

pond turtle　Members of the genus *Clemmys*, in the family Emdidae, are sometimes collectively called pond turtles, but in the United States this name refers specifically to only one species, *C. marmorata*, the Pacific, or western, pond turtle. It is one of the few species of turtles encountered on the Pacific coast of North America. The Pacific pond turtle is generally less than 180 mm (7 in) in length. It has a broad, flattened, upper shell, which may be black, dark brown, or olive, and usually has dark lines or dashes radiating from the center of each of its scales, or shields; the lower shell is yellow, with blackish blotches. This species is quite aquatic, preferring bodies of water that have muddy bottoms and an abundance of aquatic vegetation. It feeds primarily on animal prey but may eat water plants or scavenge. Nesting occurs from late April through August; from 3 to 11 eggs are laid.

The western, or Pacific, pond turtle is the only freshwater turtle native to western North America.

Pondicherry [pahn-di-chair'-ee]　Pondicherry (French: Pondichéry) is a union territory of India situated on the Coromandel coast of the Bay of Bengal. The population is 604,471 (1981). The city of Pondicherry is the capital. The manufacturing of cotton textiles; trade in peanuts, oilseeds, and cotton cloth; and the cultivation of rice are the principal economic activities. Aurobindo Ashram, a devotional retreat in the city of Pondicherry established by the philosopher Sri Aurobindo before World War II, attracts visitors from all over the world. The city of Pondicherry was established by the French as a trade center in 1674. During the 18th century the British frequently disputed French control, but Pondicherry remained a French possession until 1954, when it became part of India.

Pons, Lily [pahnz]　Lily Pons, coloratura soprano, b. France, Apr. 12, 1904, d. Feb. 13, 1976, first played ingenue roles in Paris, making her operatic debut in Delibes's *Lakmé* in 1928. She became a leading singer with the Metropolitan Opera in 1931, remaining there until 1940. In the late 1930s she appeared in several Hollywood movies and during World War II entertained troops. So great was her appeal that the citizens of a Maryland town renamed it Lilypons.

Ponselle, Rosa [pahn-sel']　The operatic soprano Rosa Ponselle, b. Meriden, Conn., Jan. 22, 1897, d. May 25, 1981, was the first singer born and trained in the United States to appear at the Metropolitan Opera House. Caruso heard her and recommended her engagement by that company in 1918. She first sang Bellini's *Norma*, considered her greatest role, in 1927. She retired only ten years later, at the height of her powers, and then became active in the musical life of Baltimore, Md., where in 1950 she was appointed artistic director of the Baltimore Civic Opera.

Pontchartrain, Lake [pahn'-chur-trayn]　Lake Pontchartrain is a large, shallow tidal lagoon in southeastern Louisiana. The Inner Harbor Navigation Canal connects the lake and the Mississippi River; New Orleans lies between the lake and the river. Formed by shifting of the Mississippi River Delta, the lake is connected to the Gulf of Mexico by Lake Borgne. Lake Pontchartrain is 64 km (40 mi) long, 40 km (25 mi) wide, and has a depth of 3–5 m (10–16 ft). Its brackish waters teem with game fish. Two causeways span it. Floodwaters of the Mississippi River enter the lake through the Bonnet Carre Spillway.

Pontiac's Rebellion　In 1763, following the British defeat of French forces at Quebec in 1760, a group of American Indians—suspecting, correctly, that British expansionism posed a greater threat to their survival than the presence of the French—launched an uprising known as Pontiac's Rebellion.

In 1760, British commander Jeffrey AMHERST abruptly ordered an end to the distribution of gifts to the Indians, a French practice that the Indians had come to rely on. Pontiac, an OTTAWA chief born about 1720 near present-day Detroit, assumed leadership of a loose confederation of tribes and directed attacks on all British forts in the Great Lakes area in the spring of 1763. Eight outposts were overrun, and English supply lines across Lake Erie were severed, but assaults on Fort Detroit and Fort Pitt failed. At this point news arrived of the complete French capitulation and withdrawal from North America, and the uprising collapsed in the fall of 1763. Pontiac was assassinated (1769) by a Peoria Indian at Cahokia, Ill.

Pontius Pilate   see PILATE, PONTIUS

Pontormo, Jacopo Carucci da [pohn-tohr'-moh] The Florentine painter Jacopo Carucci, b. May 24, 1494, d. Jan. 1, 1557, called Pontormo for his birthplace, developed an unorthodox and agitated style that made him one of the founders and principal exponents of MANNERISM.

By 1518, Pontormo had broken completely with the classical style. In such works as *Joseph in Egypt* (1518–19; National Gallery, London), he created an asymmetric, complex spatial network that dislocated the perspective logic of the High Renaissance. To divide the three sequential scenes depicted, theatrical staircases and bizarre landscape elements were introduced.

Pontormo's unsettling manipulation of space and figures is epitomized in the cycle of paintings he executed (1525–28) for the Capponi Chapel in the church of Santa Felicità, Florence. The central altarpiece of the program is the entombment, a traditional theme in Christian art. Pontormo transformed it into what is considered one of the most disturbing pictorial images ever created. Although Pontormo's dead Christ is consciously modeled after the sinuously sculpted Christ in Michelangelo's Vatican *Pietà*, the vision is one of wildly colored figures floating in a swirl of tormented faces and contorted poses. Pontormo even included himself as witness in the face of the bearded young man in the upper right. This painting is among the most expressive visual documents of the Mannerist style in painting.

Pontus [pahn'-tuhs]   In ancient times Pontus was a maritime region of northeastern Anatolia (now part of Turkey) abounding in thick forests and deposits of iron, copper, and silver. The region was isolated from the civilized centers of Anatolia until about the 6th and 5th centuries BC, when colonization by Greek cities of Anatolia, especially MILETUS, opened up the coastal areas to Hellenic influence. During the 4th century BC the Greek seaports, such as Sinope and Amisus, came officially under Persian rule, though they often remained autonomous in practice.

The Pontic kingdom reached the height of its strength and influence under MITHRADATES VI, but following his defeat in 66 BC by POMPEY THE GREAT was divided and absorbed into the Roman Empire.

pony   see HORSE

pony express   The pony express (1860–61) was a brief but spectacular experiment in rapid mail delivery from Missouri to California. Hoping to win a government contract, the freighting and express firm of Russell, Majors, and Waddell promised to carry letters the almost 3,200 km (2,000 mi) between Saint Joseph, Mo., and Sacramento, Calif., in 10 days. This was half the time taken by the Overland Mail Company, which followed a longer route through the Southwest. To provide fresh mounts for riders, the company established 190 way stations 16–24 km (10–15 mi) apart along a route through Nebraska, Wyoming, and Nevada. The riders, who traveled about 120 km (75 mi) each in a relay system, carried the mail at a cost of $5 an ounce, continuing even through the winter months. Unsuccessful financially, Russell, Majors, and Waddell went bankrupt. Pony-express service ended after 18 months, in October 1861, when overland telegraph connections were completed.

poodle   The poodle became the most popular dog breed in the United States in 1960 and has retained that position ever since. The dog has a long muzzle and hanging ears; its tail is docked. The coat is long, profuse, and harsh. Three varieties are recognized for show purposes: in the United States and Britain, standard poodles are more than 38 cm (15 in) high at the shoulder; miniature poodles, from just over 25 to 38 cm (10 to 15 in); and toy poodles, 25 cm (10 in) and under. Standard poodles, however, are usually taller than the minimum, and in other countries the divisions may differ. Poodles with more than one color are disqualified from show competition and are usually killed as puppies, but efforts have been made to remove parti-color from the list of disqualifications.

The poodle may have been developed as a retriever of waterfowl in France, where the breed was popularized; or

The poodle is among the most intelligent of all dogs. The standard (left), *the largest and oldest form of the breed, was originally used as a waterfowl retriever. The miniature* (center), *bred from the standard, was used to produce the still smaller toy* (right).

in Germany, which gave it its name, *pudel*, referring to water; or even in Italy or Denmark. Its ancestors may have included the French barbet and the Portuguese water dog. Toy poodles were probably created by crosses of the miniature with the little bichon frise.

pool see BILLIARDS

Poona [poo'-nuh] Poona (also Pune) is a city in Maharashtra state, western India, situated 120 km (75 mi) southeast of Bombay on the Deccan Plateau. Its population is 1,203,351 (1981). Poona is a gateway to the Bhor Ghat pass, leading south to India's western coast. It has cotton and paper mills, metallurgy plants, distilleries, and an ammunition factory. The city is the center of Maratha culture. Poona University (1949) and the headquarters of the Indian army's southern command are there. It is also a popular resort.

Poona became important when Balaji Baji Rao (Peshwa) made the city capital of the Maratha confederacy in 1750. The British took Poona in 1817.

poor laws Poor laws provided the basis for relief and welfare payments in England from the 16th until the 20th century. Legislation in 1572 authorized each parish to levy a rate, or tax, for relief of the poor if charitable contributions proved insufficient. The Elizabethan Poor Law Act of 1601 provided that overseers of the poor be appointed in each parish; they were to give relief to those unable to work and to set up workhouses for the able-bodied unemployed. Those unwilling to work were to be punished severely as vagabonds. In the 18th century temporary relief for unemployed persons outside of the workhouses was set up, and relief payments were also given to some employed persons who did not receive a living wage. This so-called Speenhamland system was abolished by the Poor Law Amendment Act of 1834, which required able-bodied unemployed to enter workhouses in order to receive assistance. Charles Dickens gave a bleak description of such a workhouse in his novel *Oliver Twist* (1838). Criticism of the poor-law system by social reformers such as Sidney and Beatrice WEBB led to reforms under the Local Government Act of 1929. After World War II the poor laws were largely replaced by the social legislation of the WELFARE STATE.

Poor Richard's Almanack Benjamin FRANKLIN's compilation of practical information, anecdotes, maxims, and proverbs, *Poor Richard's Almanack* appeared annually between 1732 and 1757. Franklin founded and owned the almanac and did much of the writing before 1748. He sold it in 1757, and it continued under an altered title until 1796. The almanac contained such improving maxims as, "God helps those who help themselves" and "A penny saved is two pence clear." Issues of Franklin's almanac have been republished countless times in whole or in part.

Roy Lichtenstein's Maybe *(1965) epitomizes the comic-strip style, clichéd subject matter, and pseudomechanical execution typical of his pop art work during the 1960s. (Wallraf-Richartz Museum, Cologne.)*

pop art The term *pop art* was first used in the 1950s in London by the critic Lawrence Alloway to describe works by artists who combined bits and pieces of mass-produced graphic materials to enshrine contemporary cultural values. Richard HAMILTON's *Just What Is It That Makes Today's Homes So Different, So Appealing?* (1956; private collection), a typical photomontage, exemplifies the values of pop art.

Subsequently, the materials and techniques long used by abstract, or action, painters—acrylic paints, stencils, silk screens, spray guns—were applied to figurative uses by pop artists. These artists emphasized contemporary social values: the sprawl of urban life, the transitory, the vulgar, the superficial, and the flashy. Seeking cultural resources, pop artists reworked such industrial products as soup and beer cans, American flags, and automobile wrecks. They turned images of hot dogs and hamburgers into gigantic blowups or outsized vinyl monsters.

Most prevalent in the United States and the United Kingdom, pop artists appeared in all highly industrialized countries, notably in France, Italy, Japan, and Sweden. In America the leading pop artists included Roy LICHTENSTEIN, Claes OLDENBURG, James ROSENQUIST, George SEGAL, and Andy WARHOL. The major British pop artists were Peter Blake and Richard Hamilton.

Pop Warner Football Pop Warner Football is the organization that oversees a football program for boys and girls aged 7 to 15 in the United States (primarily), Mexico, England, and Japan. The goal of the organization is to teach cooperation, teamwork, and basic football skills. Pop Warner Football was started in 1929 in Philadelphia—still its headquarters—by Joseph J. Tomlin and was named for the college coach Glen Scobey "Pop" WARNER.

Because injuries are more likely among players of unequal size and development, eight age and weight divisions are observed. They are, in order of increasing age and weight: Mitey-Mite, Junior Peewee, Peewee, Junior Midget, Midget, Senior Midget, Junior Bantam, and Bantam. For the four divisions of greatest participation (Junior Peewee through Midget), U.S. national championship competition is held in sites that change periodically.

Popé [poh-pay'] Popé, c.1630–c.1690, a celebrated medicine man of the Tewa PUEBLO Indians at San Juan, N.Mex., instigated a successful rebellion against the Spaniards in 1680. Preaching resistance to the Spanish and restoration of the traditional Pueblo culture and religion, Popé led his people in an attempt to obliterate all Spanish influence. On Aug. 10, 1680, the Indians under his leadership killed about 400 missionaries and colonists and drove the other Spaniards south to El Paso, Tex. Popé and his followers then proceeded to destroy Christian churches and other evidences of the Spanish presence in Pueblo territory. Thereafter, as the head of several Tewa villages, Popé exerted what many considered increasingly harsh rule. Dissension arose, weakening Pueblo unity, and in 1692, two years after Popé's death, the Spaniards regained control.

pope see PAPACY

Pope, Alexander The most accomplished verse satirist in the English language, Alexander Pope, b. May 21, 1688, d. May 30, 1744, was the preeminent poet of the AUGUSTAN AGE. Pope's life, which he ironically described as "this long disease," was shaped by two great disadvantages: he was crippled from his earliest years by a deformity of the spine, and as a member of the Roman Catholic church he was excluded from the public life of his time and denied a university education.

Pope showed an early aptitude for verse; he wrote his earliest surviving poem when he was about 12. His first published works, the *Pastorals* (1709), was an imitation of Vergil; it was followed by *An Essay on Criticism* (1711) and *The Rape of the Lock* (1712). His *Essay*, an imitation of Horace's *Art of Poetry* (c.19 BC), is a summary of neoclassical literary doctrine. *The Rape of the Lock*, a MOCK EPIC poem, relates a trivial incident in a courtship and is one of the most exquisite comic poems in English literature. Pope turned next to translating Homer; his versions of the *Iliad* (1720) and the *Odyssey* (1725–26),

Although Alexander Pope showed a precocious talent for poetry, composing his Pastorals *at 14 years of age, it was his earliest ambition to become a painter. This portrait of him as a young man was executed about 1720. (National Portrait Gallery, London.)*

in heroic couplets, rank among the greatest translations in the English language.

His early poems earned Pope the friendship of Jonathan Swift, with whom he, John Gay, John Arbuthnot, and Thomas Parnell founded (1714) the Scriblerus Club, whose purpose was to satirize bad poetry and pedantry. The club was short-lived, but Pope carried out its objective in his prose treatise *Peri Bathous, or The Art of Sinking in Poetry* (1728) and in The DUNCIAD (1728), a mock epic that ironically celebrated the achievements of inept and morally corrupt writers.

At the height of his career Pope addressed questions of metaphysics and ethics and wrote the didactic poem for which he was best known in his time, *An Essay on Man* (1733), expressing 18th-century perceptions of the universe and humanity's place in God's scheme. Pope's concern with ethics also found expression in his four *Moral Essays* (1731–35). Satire, however, remained the vehicle in which he excelled. Along with many of his contemporaries, Pope saw in the government of Sir Robert Walpole a source of infection that threatened the nation's morality. In defense of public and private virtue Pope wrote a series of satires, *Imitations of Horace* (1733–38). The finest of his satires, written as a prologue to the *Imitations*, is *Epistle to Dr. Arbuthnot*, a moving defense of his work from malicious interpretation. Pope's last work was *The New Dunciad* (1743), in which, elevating satire to prophecy, he foretells the cultural extinction of England.

Pope, John John Pope, b. Louisville, Ky., Mar. 16, 1822, d. Sept. 23, 1892, was a Union officer in the U.S. Civil War. In 1862, as a major general, he commanded the Army of the Mississippi, securing the Union access to the Mississippi River almost as far south as Memphis. Promoted to brigadier general, he commanded the Army of Virginia, suffering defeat at the Second Battle of BULL RUN. Relieved of his command in September 1862, Pope served in the West and headed several military departments.

Pope, John Russell John Russell Pope, b. New York City, Apr. 24, 1874, d. Aug. 27, 1937, was among the most eminent and successful of American architects trained in the eclectic tradition of the École des Beaux-Arts in Paris. For the residences of his wealthy clients he chose English Tudor or Georgian, Italian Renaissance, or French manorial; for Yale University, Gothic; for Dartmouth College, American colonial. For institutions and monuments in Washington, D.C., he selected classical forms: the Temple of the Scottish Rite (1916), the National Archives Building (1935), the National Gallery of Art (completed 1939), and the Jefferson Memorial (completed 1941). His works exude a sense of luxury and imperial grandeur that earlier critics found at odds with the American democratic spirit.

Popish Plot see OATES, TITUS

The white poplar (left) *and the Lombardy poplar* (right) *are two stately Eurasian trees widely used for landscaping. Poplars bear male and female flowers that hang in catkins on separate trees.*

poplar [pahp'-lur] Poplars are deciduous hardwood trees of the genus *Populus* in the willow family, Salicaceae. The name poplar is applied collectively to the 35 or more species in the genus, which includes the aspens and cottonwoods. The leaves are usually long-stalked and broad, with coarsely toothed or nearly smooth margins. The overwintering leaf buds are covered by several overlapping scales, which are larger toward the tip of the bud. Poplars are dioecious, separate male and female flowers being borne on different trees. The flowers are small and closely packed into soft, drooping, tassellike clusters called catkins or aments. The fruits are small, flask-shaped capsules containing a number of cottony-tufted seeds.

Poplars are widely distributed throughout the northern temperate region. They thrive in moist soil and are often found along stream banks. The quaking aspen, *P. tremuloides*, the most widely distributed tree in North America, forms large forests up to the timberline. The European aspen, *P. tremula*, ranges across Eurasia into northern Africa. Ten or possibly more species of poplars are native to North America, and several species have been introduced. With the exception of the balsam poplar, *P. balsamifera*, also known as the tacamahac or hackmatack, native North American species are generally called aspens or cottonwoods. Aspens have 6 to 12 stamens in each male flower, thin-walled capsular fruits, nonsticky (nonresinous) winter leaf buds, and oval or nearly round leaves. Cottonwoods (and the balsam poplar) have 12 to 60 or more stamens, thick-walled capsular fruits, a sticky (resinous) coating on the winter leaf buds, and usually triangular leaves.

Poplars are exceptionally fast-growing trees. For this reason they have been planted extensively as street trees and used for reforestation. The eastern cottonwood, *P. deltoides*, grows wild east of the Great Plains from the Canadian border to the Gulf of Mexico. The plains cottonwood, confined to the Great Plains area, is variously regarded as a separate species, *P. sargentii*, or as a variety of the eastern cottonwood, *P. deltoides* var. *occidentalis.* These cottonwoods may exceed 30 m (100 ft) in height and 1.2 m (4 ft) in trunk diameter and are used for pulpwood, as ornamentals, and for other purposes. The black poplar, *P. nigra*, native to Eurasia, grows to 27 m (90 ft) tall. A variety of black poplar, the Lombardy poplar, *P. nigra* var. *italica*, has a distinctive tall, narrow shape and is commonly grown as fencing and screening.

Popocatépetl [poh-poh-kah-tay'-pet-ul] Popocatépetl, a quiescent volcano in central Mexico, rises 5,452 m (17,887 ft) on the border between the states of Puebla and Mexico, 72 km (45 mi) southeast of Mexico City. The second highest peak in Mexico (after Orizaba), Popocatépetl has a symmetrical cone, forested at the base; the summit is covered by snow all year. The brilliantly colored crater, 152 m (500 ft) deep and 823 m (2,700 ft) wide, contains immense reserves of pure sulfur, which was used by the Spanish to make gunpowder. Eruptions were recorded in the 16th and 17th centuries, but since 1802 the volcano, whose Nahuatl name means "smoking mountain," has emitted only smoke and sulfurous gases.

Popper, Sir Karl Raimund [pahp'-ur] Sir Karl Raimund Popper, b. Vienna, July 28, 1902, is a highly influential philosopher who gained fame as a philosopher of science through his *Logic of Scientific Discovery* (1939; Eng. trans., 1959). He claimed that science is characterized by its aggressive attempt to falsify its conjectures. Popper was an early critic of certain assumptions of LOGICAL POSITIVISM and other philosophical movements that focused on how language has meaning. His work helped move philosophy of science from a focus on the logical relations among scientific statements to studies of the process of inquiry.

In *The Open Society and Its Enemies* (1945) and *The*

Poverty of Historicism (1957), Popper vigorously attacked historicism, the view that there are general laws of historical development that make history predictable.

poppy

poppy Poppy is the common name for several hundred species of plants in about 13 of the 26 genera making up the poppy family, Papaveraceae. These include the California poppies, *Eschscholtzia*; the plume poppies, *Macleaya*; the bush poppies, *Dendromecon*; and the Mexican poppies, *Hunnemannia*. The genus *Papaver* consists of about 100 species of annual, biennial, or perennial herbs native to the Old World, with a few from western North America.

Poppies of the genus *Papaver* contain a white, milky sap and have lobed or deeply dissected leaves and mostly long-stalked, large, showy flowers of red, white, violet, or yellow. The flower buds are generally nodding, or bent downward, due to the rapid growth of one side of the flower stalk. The flowers have an outer layer of two sepals, which drop off as the bud opens, and an inner layer of usually four but sometimes five or occasionally six petals. The flower's stamens are numerous and surround the pistil, which consists of a many-celled ovary capped by a multilobed, pollen-receiving stigma. The ovary develops into a short capsular fruit with an upper row of windowlike pores (a poricidal capsule), roofed over by the dried, lobed stigma. The tiny seeds escape through the pores when the capsule is shaken.

Poppies are grown for their narcotic content. The opium poppy, *P. somniferum*, is an annual herb, about 1.2 m (4 ft) tall, with white, pink, red, or purple flowers. It is native to southeastern Europe and western Asia but is now grown throughout much of the world, except in the United States, where it is illegal. OPIUM is generally obtained from the latex, or milky sap, of the unripened fruit capsule.

Poppies may also be grown for food. The small seeds are used as bird food and, especially those of the opium poppy, as flavoring in breads, rolls, and cakes. (The seeds have no drug properties, because the narcotic al-

Ornamental poppies include the oriental poppy (center) *and the California poppy* (bottom left).

kaloids are present only in the milky sap of the unripened fruit capsule, before the seeds develop.) The seeds also can be pressed to extract their oil, which is used in cooking and in food preparation, in artist's colors, and in soap. The pressed seed cake can be fed to livestock. The seed oil of the prickly poppy, *Argemone mexicana*, is used medicinally (as a purgative) in parts of Africa and India.

Poppy-seed oil has been linked in India to epidemics of dropsy and to glaucoma. The principal injurious ingredient is believed to be an alkaloid, sanguinarine, though researchers are not certain how the oil causes its damaging effects. Poppy-seed oil is also ingested in Europe and the Americas, either directly in poppy-seed flavoring or indirectly—for example, in. the milk of cows that have grazed on *Papaver* or *Fumaria* plants.

popular music SEE BLUES; COUNTRY AND WESTERN MUSIC; GOSPEL MUSIC; JAZZ; RAGTIME; ROCK MUSIC; SWING

popular sovereignty In the years before the U.S. CIVIL WAR, the term *popular sovereignty* (literally "rule by the people") referred to a controversial political doctrine—that the people residing in a new federal territory had the right to decide whether to permit slavery in that territory. Although the idea that local communities were best able to decide on the nature of their local governing institutions was an old one, U.S. senator Lewis CASS of Michigan made the first clear statement linking the concept to new territories, which he said should be organized without mention of slavery so that they could regulate it themselves.

By the COMPROMISE OF 1850 the principle of popular sovereignty was applied to New Mexico and Utah territories. Although it worked in these former Mexican provinces, the doctrine broke down when Illinois senator Stephen A. DOUGLAS sponsored legislation that applied it to Kansas and Nebraska territories. The KANSAS-NEBRASKA ACT of 1854 repealed that section of the MISSOURI COMPROMISE of 1820 which prohibited slavery north of latitude 36°30'; the act permitted the new territories to decide the slavery issue themselves. Settlers poured into the border territory of Kansas, and in 1856 violence erupted between proslavery and antislavery forces that were competing for political control and the power to decide the slavery issue in their own favor.

population A population is a grouping of individuals subject to the processes of birth, death, and migration. Human populations are usually defined territorially, such as those of the United States or of the Maldive Islands, but such nonterritorial groups as the female or African-American inhabitants of the United States may also be described as populations.

Population Growth

During the first 2 million or so years of its history the human population was a minor element in the world ecosystem, with at most 10 million members. The rough equilibrium maintained before Neolithic times gave way when the human population developed agriculture and animal husbandry and no longer had to spread out in search of game. With the abandonment of a hunting-gathering way of life and the rise of permanent settlements and eventually cities, the human population underwent dramatic growth. By the beginning of the Christian era it had reached 250 million, and by 1650, half a billion.

In various parts of the world, plagues and epidemics appeared and reappeared, usually spreading from populations habituated and at least partly immune—especially in East Asia—to hitherto untouched populations in Europe and the Americas. The Black Death in the 14th century wiped out a third of the population of Europe. In the 17th century the plagues stopped in Europe, but the emigration of Europeans to the Americas gave old diseases a new life; they decreased the Indian populations, who were not biologically immune.

Triumph over disease on a worldwide scale came during the 20th century with antibiotics and DDT; all continents showed a striking fall in death rates. But birthrates did not go down in proportion. Populations with birthrates continuing at the base level of 45 per 1,000 people per year, and whose death rates have fallen well below 20 per 1,000 people per year, are growing by as much as 3.5% per year and thus doubling over 20 years.

People and Subsistence. The vast population increases of the 20th century have been accompanied by advances in agriculture. Domestic animals supply about 145 million metric tons (1980–87 average) of meat each year; this, with about 495 million metric tons of wheat and a somewhat smaller quantity of rice, provides the main sustenance for humans.

Populations tend to grow rapidly to the highest level at which the available technology can provide sustenance and then remain constant. As technology becomes more sophisticated, population increases. Thomas MALTHUS, the British economist and student of population, failed to predict technological change and consequently underestimated future growth in both populations and their incomes. The 38 million British counted in the census of 1901 were far better off than the 12 million counted in 1801 soon after Malthus wrote *An Essay on the Principle of Population, As It Affects the Future Improvement of Society*.

Karl Marx claimed that each society has its own law of population growth. Because ancient Rome was constantly conquering and settling foreign lands, it never experienced overpopulation. During the 19th century the expansion of industry required people, as Scottish economist Adam SMITH discerned, and population grew in accord with this need. By contrast, in the 20th century population growth has tended to be independent of political or economic factors.

Much contemporary discussion of population is framed in terms of a demographic model in which deaths decline from a level of about 30 per 1,000 each year to about 10 per 1,000; after a longer or shorter lag the decline in deaths is followed by a decline in births from about 45 per 1,000 or higher to about 20 per 1,000 or

lower. The time lag separating the fall in births from the fall in deaths is of crucial importance; with a delay of 45 years the population can multiply fourfold; with a delay of 75 years it can multiply ninefold. What is certain is that if no fall in birthrate occurs, the death rate will inevitably rise in countries that are technologically backward; only a certain number of people will be able to support themselves within a given territory through subsistence agriculture.

Current Population Figures. In 1990 the total world population was estimated at about 5.3 billion. The most significant world trend is that death rates are currently falling in poor and rich countries alike, while birthrates remain high in most poor countries and low in most rich ones. Exceptions are the generally higher death rates of Africa and the high birthrates of the rich oil-producing countries.

The four most populous countries, in descending order, are China, India, the USSR, and the United States. The U.S. population was 249,632,692 in 1990. Each year about 3.8 million children are born in the United States, and 2 million persons die. The greater number of births is due to the high proportion of young couples—themselves the product of the high birthrates of the 1950s. Once these couples have passed through their childbearing years, births will be fewer than deaths, unless a considerable rise in average family size occurs. International immigration is another major element in U.S. population growth. Legal immigration has recently amounted to more than 600,000 per year; illegal immigration is probably even greater.

For China, only the roughest indications of even the most basic facts are available. The 1953 census counted 584 million in mainland China; the population in 1990 was estimated at nearly 1.2 billion. China's annual increase is thought to be about 1.4%. India's population of more than 853.4 million (1990 est.) is increasing faster than China's, and if present trends continue it will catch up with or surpass China in the early decades of the 21st century. The USSR has about 291 million people (1990 est.). Its overall rate of increase corresponds with that of other industrialized societies, although differentials in its birthrate are large: the birthrate of European USSR is comparable to rates in the United States and Western Europe, whereas birthrates in parts of Soviet Central Asia are higher. Indonesia, Brazil, and Japan rank 5th, 6th, and 7th, respectively, in order of total population.

Population Control

With luck, population stabilization will be brought about through a falling birthrate. In some parts of the world, however, malnutrition and such diseases as malaria are actually on the increase, and population control may occur through a rise in the death rate.

Projections. Presuming that birthrates and death rates coincide in all parts of the world by the end of the century, demographers estimate that the world population will level off at between 8 and 9 billion about the year 2075. This figure includes China at 1.5 billion and India at 1.6 billion. For the developed countries the same assumptions show a smaller change from present levels. Japan

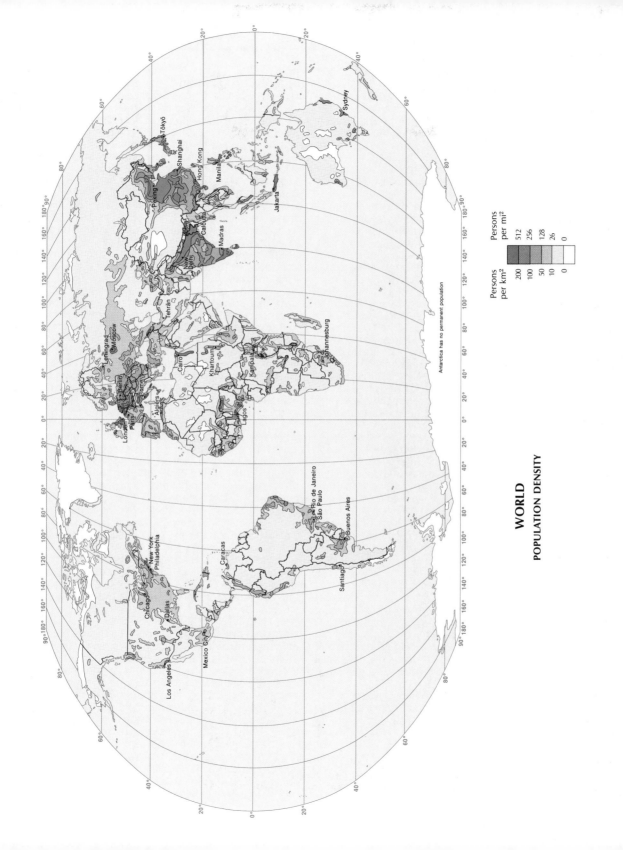

WORLD

POPULATION DENSITY

Persons
per km²

	200
	100
	50
	10
	0

Persons
per mi²

	512
	256
	128
	26
	0

Antarctica has no permanent population

Los Angeles
Chicago
Dallas
New York
Philadelphia
Mexico City
Caracas
Santiago
Buenos Aires
São Paulo
Rio de Janeiro
London
Paris
Algiers
Berlin
Rome
Lagos
Cairo
Khartoum
Kampala
Johannesburg
Leningrad
Moscow
Tehrān
Madras
New Delhi
Calcutta
Peking
Shanghai
Tōkyō
Hong Kong
Manila
Jakarta
Sydney

would increase from 123.6 (1990 est.) million to 143 million in 2075; the United Kingdom, from 57.4 to 69 million; the United States, from 251.4 to 292 million; and the USSR, from 291 to 354 million.

Certain features generally accompany the stabilization or slowdown of population growth. Slowing means proportionately more old people and fewer young people in the society; less-rapid promotion of individuals within organizations; a possibly slower rate of innovation resulting from the higher average age; and probably a less optimistic culture.

Population Policy. Population has been a perennial preoccupation of government policy. Rome rewarded mothers and taxed bachelors, as the USSR began to do in Stalin's time; abortion and even contraception were made illegal in 19th-century France and in many other countries; Sweden provided government housing at low rents; many countries, including Canada, have directly subsidized children by providing family allowances. The effectiveness of such pronatalist measures in raising the birthrate has, however, never been clearly demonstrated.

Any effect that such measures may have is largely swamped by contemporary social changes that governments cannot control. These include the liberation of women from subservient roles, the increasing involvement of women in work and careers, and rising DIVORCE rates.

Birth-Control Programs. Lowering births is the unambiguous object of government policy in many developing countries. Increasing populations press on the environment and its resources, take away from the capital available for new investment, crowd cities with people for whom jobs are not available, upset the balance of payments, and cause political turmoil. After a period of uncertainty, during which the ancient idea that population is a source of national power prevailed, governments have become aware that national power—not to mention individual welfare—is more likely to be attained with fewer people.

Contraception is freely available in most countries and is actively promoted in many. Such promotion has little effect when people want large families, but when the other forces of modernization have come into play, and the birthrate has started to fall spontaneously, promotion of birth control speeds the decline. Typically, the better-off take up family limitation first; governmental sponsorship of BIRTH CONTROL and foreign aid that makes contraceptives available to the poor apparently help to spread the practice of family limitation among ever-wider strata of the population. Surveys in places with active programs point to a more rapid decline in birthrates than had previously been thought possible.

Such government action is more likely to be effective when it accompanies social and economic changes, such as the equalizing of incomes. Those countries where income inequality is slight and declining have shown the greatest fall in birthrates; apparently people are most likely to limit family size when they see a chance of rising out of poverty.

See also: AGRICULTURE AND THE FOOD SUPPLY; CITY; DEMOGRAPHY.

population, stellar   Stars are placed in two classifications based on the age, composition, and position of the stars in a galaxy (see EXTRAGALACTIC SYSTEMS). Stars in the arms of a spiral galaxy are called population I and are generally hot, young, blue stars, often associated with interstellar clouds and nebulae. Population II stars, which include cooler, older stars, are found in the nucleus of a galaxy and in the globular clusters in the halo that may surround it. The distinction was first made in 1945, when Walter BAADE at the Mount Wilson Observatory observed systematic differences between stars in the arms and stars in the nucleus of distant spiral galaxies. The same distinction was soon found to apply to stars in our own Milky Way Galaxy.

The significance of population I and population II stars lies in their relation to theories of the evolution of stars and galaxies. The existence of two populations of stars can be explained by assuming that each galaxy started as a cloud of hydrogen and helium in which small, local concentrations condensed by gravitational attraction to form stars. The larger concentrations (10 or 20 solar masses) formed giant blue stars that quickly evolved to explode as novae and supernovae, blowing out most of their mass as dust and gas containing heavier elements formed by nuclear reactions in their cores. From this "interstellar stuff" a new generation of stars was formed. While this STELLAR EVOLUTION was going on, each galaxy also evolved from a ball of gas and stars to an ellipsoid or a disk, depending on how much angular momentum (rotation) the original gas had. With a large quantity of angular momentum, the original ball of gas and stars condensed to a spiral disk, and the interstellar gas and dust resulting from stellar evolution was pulled into the disk plane. This "disk population," where stars continue to be formed from INTERSTELLAR MATTER, contains those relatively young stars called population I; the stars in the halo and nucleus, known as population II, are uniformly older because they lack the interstellar matter necessary for the formation of new stars.

Although astronomers eventually found that the population I and population II categories are not as cleanly divided as Baade thought, the distinction is still an important one for discussions of stellar evolution.

population biology   Population biology is the study of factors involved in the stability, variability, and density of populations of plants or animals. Among such factors are predator-prey relationships, birthrates, death rates, food supply, migration patterns, age and sex distribution, relationships between members of different species living in the same area, cooperation and competition among members of the same species, genetically controlled behavior patterns, and environmental influences. Population biologists attempt to develop general mathematical models that incorporate the many factors regulating the size and density of a population. The equations are useful for predicting the effects of changing one or more such factors in a given population.

population dynamics Population dynamics seeks to describe changes in population densities and to explain these changes in terms of underlying biological forces. It is the basis of all ecological patterns and is also necessary to solve problems of human economy, such as biological conservation, pest management, and optimal harvesting of wildlife populations. A population comprises the organisms of a single species in a defined region—for example, the yellow-fever mosquitoes *Aedes aegypti* in Singapore. For meaningful scientific analysis, the region over which the population is defined should be small enough that all of the organisms have the potential to interact; for example, they could interact sexually or by fighting.

Density. The first problem addressed in population study is the measurement of density. Only a few populations, such as humans and large mammalian grazers, can be counted completely, but often a complete census can be taken of some life stage or subclass of a population. Normally some kind of statistical sampling of small areas within the region is required. Finally, for some species, such as those which live in or under the ground or which are active at night, only a relative index of density can be obtained. These estimates can be made from the various products of their activity—tracks, excrement, pelts of kills, discarded shells, tailings from burrows, and vocalizations.

Growth. Organisms may enter a population by birth or immigration and may leave it by death or emigration. The nature of population growth may be understood by considering a closed population with constant per capita birthrates and death rates. The growth rate of the population, called the intrinsic growth factor, is the birthrate minus the death rate. The number of organisms added per time period is the growth rate times the current population size. The growth is thus a constant percentage of the population. It is known as exponential growth.

Thomas MALTHUS in his *Essay on the Principle of Population* (1798; rev. 1803) was the first to notice that human population growth is exponential. Because he believed that the growth in the food supply must be arithmetic (a constant absolute increase per time period), he argued that the human population density must eventually outstrip its food supply and thus be held in check by starvation or by warfare or disease that food shortages might cause. (In his second edition he allowed the possibility of natural restraint.) Charles DARWIN realized that the same truth held for all biological populations and that their densities should be held in check by limited resources, disease or predation, or fighting. He reasoned that individuals with traits that enabled them to face these pressures would leave behind the greatest number of descendants, thus causing the gradual evolution of the population and the species.

Since the time of Malthus, however, the human food supply has also been growing at an exponential rate, mainly through the application of technology. Moreover, all primitive human groups have practiced population restraint, sometimes including infanticide, and were thereby able to hold their densities at an optimal level relative to their food supply.

Controlling Forces. All populations can grow exponentially, but environmental forces under particular conditions act to limit the potential of the population. This process is termed the carrying capacity. Three general patterns of population density result from the action and interaction of these forces. Population density may grow and remain relatively constant, may oscillate in a regular fashion, or may fluctuate irregularly with unpredictable eruptions or outbreaks. One common oscillation is the annual cycle that is caused by birth in the spring and summer and heavy mortality in the winter.

The weather acts independently of the density of a population. A night of $-10°$ C ($14°$ F) might kill 30% of a population regardless of its total density. The chance pattern of local weather is responsible for irregular population fluctuation, particularly for small animals, such as insects, that cannot regulate their body temperatures. Outbreaks occur only when the temperature, humidity, and rainfall during the spring and summer precisely follow the required pattern.

Larger animals typically have behaviors and morphological features that make them relatively insensitive to the chances of weather; thus the weather-caused irregularities of population density are minor. These populations are restricted by factors that are related to density. Limited resources such as food, space, or nesting sites are examples of density-dependent factors. They become steadily scarcer as the population density increases. Predation, parasitization, and disease can increase with density.

Sometimes the density-limiting forces arise from within a population. Fighting may increase, adults may kill the juveniles of other families when nest sites are too close, or they may actually cannibalize any juvenile they encounter. Territorial systems are an extremely widespread form of density limitation, even among insects. A male, a mated pair, a group, or a colony holds a defined region from which are excluded all other members of the species.

Oscillations. Lemmings and voles (rodents) exemplify population oscillations. Over a 3- to 4-year period their densities may go from 2 to 200 per acre. As densities increase, the animals overeat their vegetation. This triggers mass migrations that usually end in death. Because the most aggressive animals remain behind, the rate of reproduction remains low until stable families can reform and initiate the next cycle.

population genetics Population genetics describes, in mathematical terms, the consequences of heredity on a population (rather than on an individual). The system by which individuals mate determines how genes are combined to form the genetic makeup of certain traits.

Hardy-Weinberg Equilibrium

Populations evolve by responding to changing environments through natural selection. The evolutionary response results from a change in the frequency of alleles. (An allele is one of a group of genes that determines a specific trait, such as a gene for red flowers and one for white flowers.) A change in the frequency of alleles is initiated by a mutation that produces a new gene in one individual. This new gene affects evolution in the population, however, only if its frequency increases in successive generations and becomes spread throughout the population. Three researchers—William E. Castle (1903), an American scientist, Geoffrey Hardy (1908), a British mathematician, and Wilhelm Weinberg (1908), a German physician—independently found that the frequencies of genes in a population remain constant and their proportions stay the same unless certain evolutionary forces affect the population. An equation, known as the Hardy-Weinberg Equilibrium Equation or the Hardy-Weinberg law, was developed to determine the frequency and proportion of any given allele in a population whose members are randomly breeding. This equation forms the mathematical basis of population genetics.

Evolutionary Factors

Forces that change allele frequencies in a population include mutation, selection, migration, and drift. The importance of MUTATION for the evolutionary process lies in its producing individuals with new structural and functional traits. These individuals, as is true of all other members of the population, are exposed to NATURAL SELECTION, which determines whether the new alleles will increase or decrease in frequency in future generations.

Selection reflects the total of all the environmental challenges that an organism must overcome in order to survive and reproduce. It determines the relative reproductive success of the various competing genotypes in a population.

Individuals migrating from one population to another will change the allele frequencies of the recipient population if the migrants have allele frequencies different from those of the recipient group.

Drift refers to the situation in which, by chance alone, the allele frequencies found in offspring are different from those in their parents. For example, with two alleles (*A* and *a*) at a particular chromosomal locus, only three possible genotypes can be formed: *AA*, *Aa*, and *aa*. If in a family both parents are *Aa* and they have only two children, both children may possibly be *AA*. Thus the *a* allele would be lost from the next generation of that particular family.

See also: EVOLUTION; GENETIC DISEASES; GENETICS; HEREDITY.

Populist party

The Populist party was formed in the 1890s at the culmination of a period of agrarian discontent in the United States. The party traced its roots to the farmers' alliances, loose confederations of organizations that had formed in the South and West beginning in the late 1870s and expanded rapidly after about 1885. The alliances advocated tax reform, regulation of railroads, and FREE SILVER (the unlimited minting of silver coins). In 1890 many candidates who supported alliance objectives were elected in state and local contests. Encouraged by these results, alliance leaders formed a national political

party, officially the People's party, but usually called the Populist party. At a convention in Omaha, Nebr., in 1892, the Populists nominated James B. WEAVER of Iowa as their presidential candidate. Hoping to unite Southern and Western farmers with industrial workers of the Northeast, the party adopted a platform calling for government ownership of the railroads and the telephone and telegraph systems; free silver; a graduated income tax; a "subtreasury" plan to allow farmers to withhold crops from the market when prices dipped; the direct election of U.S. senators; immigration restriction; an eight-hour day for industrial workers; and other reforms. In the election of 1892, Weaver received more than a million popular votes and 22 electoral votes, but the Democratic candidate, Grover Cleveland, won the election. Several Populist candidates won election to Congress that year and in 1894.

In 1896 the Populist party was overshadowed by the Democrats, who took up the issue of free silver and other Populist goals and nominated William Jennings BRYAN of Nebraska. The Populists supported Bryan but substituted their own candidate, Thomas E. WATSON of Georgia for the Democratic vice-presidential nominee. The Republican candidate, William McKinley, won the election. As farm prices rose, agrarian protest was defused. The Populist party, unable to broaden its base by winning the votes of industrial workers, split in 1900 over the issue of fusion with the Democrats. Although Watson ran as the Populist candidate in 1904 and 1908, the party's significance all but disappeared after 1908.

The term *populism*, however, continued to be used to refer to the grass-roots movements claiming to represent the "common people" against big business and industry. Huey Long of Louisiana was a notable populist, in this sense.

---

porcelain   SEE POTTERY AND PORCELAIN

---

porcupine   Porcupines are large, spine- or quill-bearing rodents in the families Hystricidae (Old World) and Erethizontidae (New World) of the mammalian order Rodentia. The often large spines, or sharp hairs, which act as defense organs, are controlled by erectile muscles in the skin. The arboreal North American porcupine, *Erethizon dorsatum*, ranges across Canada and most of the United States into northern Mexico. It is about 58 cm (23 in) long, weighs up to 18 kg (40 lb), and eats bark, buds, twigs, and leaves. The prehensile-tailed porcupines, genus *Coendou*, of Mexico and Central and South America, com-

The North American porcupine defends itself by raising its barbed quills and thrashing its tail to drive them into an attacking animal.

prise about 20 species. The spines are shorter but denser than those of the North American porcupine. The Old World porcupines include the common or crested porcupine, *Hystrix cristata*, found in southern Europe and Africa. A large nocturnal rodent, about 61 cm (2 ft) long, it has a crest of white-tipped quills. After a gestation period of nearly four months, the female gives birth to two or three young, which initially have soft fur rather than quills.

porcupine fish Porcupine fish are about 15 species of PUFFER-related fishes that constitute the family Diodontidae and occur worldwide in shallow, tropical seas. When a porcupine fish is threatened it swallows water or air to inflate itself, producing a bristling ball of spines; in some smaller species, called burrfish, the spines are permanently erect. Most species are about 30 cm (1 ft) long, but some may reach 90 cm (3 ft). The fused teeth form a beaklike mouth, and the body is usually light-colored with dark spots.

The porcupine fish Diodon holacanthus, *a feeder on small mollusks, is seen in normal and inflated form.*

porgy [por'-gee] Porgy, or sea bream, is the common name for about 200 species of important food and sport

The northern porgy, or scup, has powerful jaws and strong, sharp teeth capable of breaking the shells of mollusks and crustaceans.

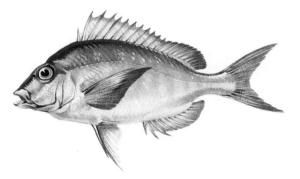

fishes constituting the family Sparidae. Porgies occur in warm to cooler waters, with a wider range of species found in the Atlantic than in the Pacific Ocean. Names for individual species include the gilthead, gunner, jolthead, musselcracker, pandora, pinfish, scup, and sheeps-head. Porgies have laterally flattened bodies and strong jaws and teeth; they are omnivorous and usually travel in schools. Many species average less than about 0.5 kg (1 lb) in weight, but some may weigh up to 90 kg (200 lb).

Porgy and Bess The most popular of all American operas, *Porgy and Bess* was composed by George Gershwin in collaboration with lyricist Ira Gershwin (see GERSHWIN, GEORGE AND IRA) and writer DuBose Heyward, from whose novel, *Porgy* (1925), the story came. Set in Catfish Row, an impoverished but idyllic black community in the South, the plot involves the crippled Porgy and his true love, Bess, who is pursued by the gambler Crown—eventually murdered by Porgy—and the cocaine-sniffing Sportin' Life. Drawing heavily on black musical idioms, as well as on Gershwin's own ability to synthesize "operatic" with popular music, the work opened on Broadway in 1935 and has since been performed throughout the world. It was filmed in 1959 and received its Metropolitan Opera premiere in 1985.

pork see MEAT AND MEAT PACKING; PIG

pornographic literature see EROTICA

pornography Pornography, or obscenity (which is the legal term), is any material, pictures, films, printed matter, or devices dealing with sexual poses or acts considered indecent by the public. Traditionally, the distribution and sale of pornography has been illegal in most countries. Only in Denmark have all restrictions on pornography been withdrawn (since 1969).

Although Massachusetts had antiobscenity laws in colonial times, federal antipornography legislation in the United States was not passed until 1842. Sending such matter through the mails became illegal in 1865. Late in the century enforcement of the laws was vigorous, due largely to the efforts of Anthony Comstock and the Committee for the Suppression of Vice. In Great Britain the first antipornography legislation, the Obscene Publications Act, was passed in 1857.

Defining pornography has from the beginning proved to be a complex legal problem because public attitudes change; materials considered pornographic in Victorian society may not be considered remarkable today. Thus the enforcement of the antipornography laws has involved suppression of several works of literature currently regarded as masterpieces, including the novels *Ulysses*, by James Joyce, and *Lady Chatterley's Lover*, by D. H. Lawrence. Several obscenity cases have been brought before the U.S. Supreme Court. In *Roth* v. *United States* (1957), the Court affirmed for the first time the traditional position that pornography was "not within the area of constitutionally protected speech" and evolved a three-part definition of obscenity: matter that appeals to prurient interests, offends current standards, and has no redeeming social value. In 1973 (*Miller* v. *California* and four companion cases) the Court reversed earlier decisions, ruling that the matter could be left to the discretion of individual states, where "contemporary community standards" were to be applied in judging whether or not material is pornographic. In 1982 the Court upheld a New York statute prohibiting the production and sale of materials depicting children in sexually explicit situations. Child pornography was thus added to the category of "speech" that is not protected by the 1st Amendment.

The huge increase in the quantity and types of pornography that have become available since the 1960s, however, has left many people uneasy. Although the national Commission on Obscenity and Pornography in 1970 could find no link between the consumption of pornography and antisocial behavior, the depiction of violence directed against women in pornographic material was then comparatively rare. Recently, psychologists have begun to establish connections in some men between exposure to such violence—usually in films, and often in films without overt sexual content—and both sexual stimulation and negative changes in attitudes toward women. Even if a decisive link between pornography and violent behavior is eventually proved, it is difficult to see how a definition of pornography could be drawn that would not abridge free-speech guarantees. (See also CENSORSHIP; EROTICA.)

porphyria [por-feer'-ee-uh]   Porphyria refers to any of a number of hereditary diseases characterized by the body's excessive production of porphyrins, an important class of biological molecules that includes HEMOGLOBIN. Forms of porphyria are manifested by acute abdominal pain, gastrointestinal dysfunction, neurologic disturbance, skin lesions, or combinations of these symptoms. Depending on the version of the disease, excessive amounts of porphyrin molecules are found in the urine, feces, bone marrow, or liver. Some types of porphyria are transmitted as a dominant trait, some as a recessive trait, and one type is associated with alcoholism.

porphyrin   see HEMOGLOBIN

Porphyry [pohr'-fir-ee]   Porphyry, AD *c*.232–*c*.305, was a philosopher who helped found NEOPLATONISM. He studied in Rome under PLOTINUS, whose writings he edited and whose biographer he was. Porphyry saw philosophy as a means to salvation and emphasized purification through asceticism. His commentaries on Aristotle's *Categories*, particularly the introduction (*Isagoge*), became the standard text on logic in the Middle Ages.

porphyry   Porphyry is an igneous rock of any composition in which relatively large crystals are surrounded by a groundmass of fine-grained crystals. Porphyries occur in dikes and sills or in border zones of plutons that may have cooled more rapidly than the more coarsely and uniformly crystalline material inside the pluton. A compositional name must be appended to describe the rock fully (for example, syenite porphyry). The difference between granite porphyry and porphyritic granite lies in the size of groundmass crystals: fine grained in porphyry and coarser grained in porphyritic granite.

porpoise [pohr'-puhs]   Porpoises, small- to medium-sized whales, have a rounded rather than a beaked snout but are often mistaken for the Atlantic bottle-nosed DOLPHINS, the beaked, small whales that perform in oceanariums. In addition, porpoises have a triangular rather than a hooked dorsal (top) fin and usually a smaller, stouter body than dolphins. Both animals are classified in the family Delphinidae, order Cetacea.

Porpoises are either entirely black, or black above and whitish below. They eat shrimp, fish, squid, and other sea animals. Porpoises mate in the summer, and gestation lasts about 1 year. Their life span is about 30 years.

The common, or harbor, porpoise, genus *Phocaena*, is 1.2 to 1.8 m (4 to 6 ft) long and weighs 49 to 74 kg (110 to 165 lb). It is the most widely distributed porpoise, inhabiting almost all Atlantic and Pacific waters. The common porpoise travels in large schools and sometimes enters rivers, but avoids ships. The dall and true porpoises, genus *Phocoenoides*, are 1.2 to 1.65 m (4 to 5.5 ft) long and weigh up to 124 kg (275 lb). They are gregarious, often playing about ships and leaping out of the water. Their range is from Siberia and Alaska to California waters.

The common porpoise is a marine mammal of the whale family. Like other mammals it is warm blooded, and it breathes air by swimming to the surface about four times each minute.

port (harbor)   see HARBOR AND PORT

port (wine)   Port, a slightly sweet after-dinner WINE, is made from grapes grown in the Douro valley of Portugal, near the city of Oporto. This wine is fortified—brandy is added to halt fermentation when the process is half complete and much of the grape sugar remains. Port is then aged in oak casks and usually is blended from wines of different vintages.

Ruby port, fruity tasting and named for its color, is aged for 2 to 5 years. Tawny port, named for its pale color, is a smooth, dry port that has been aged between 15 and 20 years. Vintage port, from grapes of a single, exceptionally good year, is aged in casks for 2 years and, without blending, is bottled and aged for 15 or more years until mature. It is sweeter and more full-bodied than ruby or tawny port, has a deep color, and requires decanting because it forms a crusty sediment.

Port Arthur (China) see LUSHUN

Port Arthur (Texas)   Port Arthur (1990 pop., 58,724), a city in southeastern Texas, is a deepwater port of entry on the Sabine-Neches and Gulf Intracoastal waterways. Petroleum, first discovered (1901) at Spindletop, several kilometers away, is the city's economic mainstay. Port Arthur has shipyards, refineries, and chemical plants; manufactures include oil-drilling equipment and other metal products. Settled as Aurora c.1853, the city began to grow in 1895, when Arthur E. Stilwell designated it a port-terminus for the Kansas City Southern Railway.

Port-au-Prince [pohrt-oh-prans']   Port-au-Prince, the capital of Haiti, lies on the west coast of the island of Hispaniola on a well-protected bay. The population is 514,438 (1989 est.). To the north of the city is the fertile central plain of Haiti. To the east and south are hills and mountains. Port-au-Prince is the commercial and transportation center of Haiti, handling half of Haiti's foreign trade. Main exports are coffee and sugar. Industries include cotton ginning, textile and cement manufacture, and the production of sisal and wood handicrafts. The National Palace, rebuilt in 1918, the modern cathedral (built 1915), and the Iron Market are notable points of interest. The University of Haiti (1944) is located in the city.

In 1749, Port-au-Prince was settled by the French, who named it L'Hôpital. It replaced Cap-Haitien as the capital in 1770 and remained the capital when Haiti became independent in 1804. The city was occupied by U.S. troops from 1915 to 1934.

Port Elizabeth   Port Elizabeth, a major seaport and the largest city in South Africa's Cape Province, has a population of 272,844 (1985). It is located on Algoa Bay of the Indian Ocean. Principal exports are iron ore, manganese, wool, and citrus fruits. The metropolitan area produces automobiles, tires, textiles, leather goods, and chemicals. The University of Port Elizabeth (1964) is there. Nearby are Addo Elephant National Park and

Snake Park, with about 2,000 reptiles. Because of its fine beaches, the city is a popular resort. After the British built Fort Frederick on the site in 1799, the city was settled in 1820. It grew rapidly after its rail connections with Kimberley's diamond mines were completed (1873).

port of entry   A port of entry is a coastal, lake, or river port, an airport, or some other site at which a nation's customhouse admits imported goods and collects customs duties on them. Customs officers verify the amount and kind of goods offered for import and determine the amount of tariff or tax to be paid. They also enforce navigation laws relating to the entry and clearance of ships. A person who unloads forbidden or dutiable goods of another nation at a port that has no customhouse is liable to prosecution for SMUGGLING.

Port Louis   Port Louis is the capital and largest city of Mauritius. Located on the northwestern coast facing the Indian Ocean, it is a busy commercial port. The population of 141,870 (1990 est.) is mostly Indian and Chinese. Sugar processing, light industries, and tourism are important. A citadel (1838) overlooks the city, founded by the French in about 1735. Before the opening of the Suez Canal in 1869, the city was an important port of call for ships sailing between Europe and Asia.

Port Moresby [mohrz'-bee]   Port Moresby (1987 est. pop., 152,100), the capital of Papua New Guinea, lies on the Gulf of Papua in the southeastern part of the country. Exports include rubber, coconuts, coffee, and timber. The first European visitor was Adm. John Moresby in 1873. The capital of the former British New Guinea, the city was an Allied base during World War II and developed rapidly after Papua New Guinea gained independence in 1975.

Port Said [sah-eed']   Port Said, a port city in northeastern Egypt, is located on the Mediterranean seacoast at the northern entrance to the SUEZ CANAL, about 175 km (110 mi) northeast of Cairo. Port Said has a population of 374,000 (1985 est.) and is the administrative headquarters of the Suez Canal. Its deepwater outer harbor is the principal fueling station for ships using the canal. Port Said handles a large part of Egypt's export trade in cotton, rice, and salt. The principal industries are fishing, fish processing, and the manufacture of chemicals and tobacco products. The city is also a summer resort.

Port Said was built in 1859 on a narrow sandspit between Lake Manzala and the Mediterranean Sea, its foundations buttressed partly with material dredged from the canal, then being dug. It was named for Said Pasha, the khedive of Egypt at the time. Because of Arab-Israeli hostilities, the harbor was closed from 1967 until 1975.

Port of Spain   Port of Spain is the capital, principal commercial port, and trade center of Trinidad and Tobago. It is located on the Gulf of Paria in western Trinidad and has a population of 58,300 (1987 est.). The city exports rum, foodstuffs, plastics, lumber, and textiles. Tourism is also important. Port of Spain, settled about 1560, was under Spanish rule from 1595 to 1797. The city was made the national capital upon independence from the United Kingdom in 1962.

portative organ   [pohr'-tuh-tiv]   The small, portable organ (Italian, *organetto*) of the late Middle Ages, supported by the left arm and knee, or slung from a strap when carried in processions, was called the portative. The right hand alone played the keyboard, while the left hand worked the bellows. The blind composer Francesco LANDINI was its most famed player. It should not be confused with the positive, or "chamber," organ, which could not be moved while being played.

Porter (family)   Members of the Porter family played a prominent role in U.S. military history. **David Porter**, b. Boston, Feb. 1, 1780, d. Mar. 3, 1843, was a naval officer who raided British commerce during the War of 1812. In 1811 he was given command of the frigate *Essex*. Accompanied by David Glasgow FARRAGUT, whom he had adopted, Porter ravaged British maritime activity in the Pacific until he was captured off Chile on Mar. 28, 1814.

Porter served (1815–22) on the Board of Navy Commissioners. He subsequently fought pirates in the Caribbean but was court-martialed (1825) for causing a confrontation with Spanish officials in Puerto Rico. Resigning his U.S. commission, he became chief of the Mexican navy (1826–29). He later served (1839–43) as U.S. minister to the Ottoman Empire.

David's son, **David Dixon Porter**, b. Chester, Pa., June 8, 1813, d. Feb. 13, 1891, also a naval officer, served under Farragut at the capture (1862) of New Orleans during the U.S. Civil War. As commander of the Mississippi River squadron, he joined Gen. Ulysses S. Grant during the VICKSBURG CAMPAIGN and was promoted to rear admiral. On Farragut's death, in 1870, he was promoted to admiral and remained the senior officer in the U.S. Navy for 21 years.

David Dixon Porter's cousin, **Fitz-John Porter**, b. Portsmouth, N.H., Aug. 31, 1822, d. May 21, 1901, served in the Civil War as a Union general. He was court-martialed for failing to obey orders at the Second Battle of Bull Run but was exonerated.

Porter, Cole   Cole Porter, b. Peru, Ind., June 9, 1892, d. Oct. 15, 1964, was an American lyricist and composer of popular songs for stage and screen. A graduate of Yale College, he attended Harvard School of Arts and Sciences for two years and later studied under the French composer Vincent d'Indy. Both his lyrics and music have a witty sophistication, technical virtuosity, and exquisite sense of style that have rarely been paralleled in popular music. He contributed brilliant scores to numerous Broadway musicals, such as *Anything Goes* (1934) and *Kiss Me, Kate* (1948), and to motion pictures. His best songs have become classics; these include "Begin the Beguine," "Night and Day," and "I Love Paris."

Porter, Eliot   Known for his color photographs of birds and the American wilderness, Eliot Furness Porter, b. Winnetka, Ill., Dec. 6, 1901, d. Nov. 2, 1990, contributed to both the cause of conservation and the art of photography. The realist painter Fairfield Porter was his brother. A research physician at Harvard, Eliot Porter did not take up photography until 1939. He was among the first photographers to use color. His publications include *Appalachian Wilderness* (1970), *Birds of North America—A Personal Selection* (1972), *Intimate Landscapes* (1979), *Eliot Porter's Southwest* (1985), and, with text by his son Jonathan, *All under Heaven: The Chinese World* (1983).

Porter, Katherine Anne   The American short-story writer and novelist Katherine Anne Porter, b. Indian Creek, Tex., May 15, 1890, d. Sept. 18, 1980, was greatly admired for her short fiction, whose fame has outlived that of her novel, *Ship of Fools* (1962; film, 1965). Born into a distinguished Southern family, Porter worked as a journalist in Chicago and Denver before traveling (1920) in Mexico, the setting of her first published story, "María Concepción" (1923). In 1931 she received a fellowship to work in Germany and sailed from the Mexican port of Veracruz. This 27-day voyage formed the basis of *Ship of Fools*, an allegorical novel alluding to the 15th-century satire of the same title by Sebastian Brant. In Porter's novel a group of Germans return home on the eve of the rise of the Nazis. The work was a best-seller, but it is on the stories in her first collection, *Flowering Judas* (1930), and in *Pale Horse, Pale Rider* (1939) and *The Leaning Tower* (1944), that her reputation as one of the most accomplished stylists of her time rests. The *Collected Short Stories of Katherine Ann Porter* (1965) won the Pulitzer Prize for fiction in 1966.

Porter, William Sydney   see O. HENRY

Portland (Maine)   Portland, the seat of Cumberland County and the largest city in Maine, has a population of 64,358 (1990), with 215,281 persons in the metropolitan area. Its position on two peninsulas jutting into Casco Bay gives Portland a large deepwater harbor and makes it the economic center of the state. Portland's diversified industries include foundries, shipyards, lumber and textile mills, printing and publishing firms, and food-processing plants. It is the eastern terminus of the Portland-Montreal oil pipeline. The University of Maine at Portland (1878) is located in the city. Landmarks include the birthplace of Henry Wadsworth Longfellow, museums of art and natural history, and the Portland Head Light, erected in 1791 on orders of George Washington.

Settled in 1623, Portland (known variously as Machigonne, Indigreat, Elbow, Casco, and Falmouth) was sacked by Indians in 1676. The area remained abandoned until 1716. The new town built on the site was burned by the British in 1775. In 1866 an Independence Day fire again destroyed much of the city. Portland served as state capital from 1820 to 1831.

Portland (Oregon)   Portland, one of the principal cities of the Pacific Northwest, the largest city in Oregon, and the seat of Multnomah County, is located in the northwestern part of the state. The city straddles the Willamette River just above its confluence with the Columbia. The city has a population of 437,319 (1990), and the metropolitan area, 1,239,842.

Although Portland has some important manufacturing establishments, notably those turning out wood products and processed foods, its economy is primarily commercial. The port is used by both barges carrying grain and ores downstream through the Columbia Gorge and oceangoing vessels, which can navigate the Columbia as far upstream as Portland. Culturally, the city is served by the University of Portland (1901), Reed College (1909), and several other colleges, as well as a symphony orchestra, a civic theater, and an art museum. Mount Hood and its large national forest are nearby.

Settled in the early 19th century, the city was named for Portland, Maine. By 1860 it was the largest city in the Pacific Northwest, a distinction it held until it was surpassed by Seattle, Wash., at the turn of the century. The world's first long-distance electric transmission line brought power to the city in 1889, and hydroelectricity (especially from the nearby Bonneville Dam) has been a major influence in the city's economy. Portland was a shipbuilding center during World War II, and it has maintained a rapid rate of growth ever since.

Porto [pohr'-toh]   Porto (Oporto) is a major port city in northern Portugal. Located on steep slopes overlooking the Douro River, 5 km (3 mi) from the Atlantic Ocean, Porto has a population of 347,300 (1986 est.); it is Portugal's second largest city. The city has been famous since the 17th century for its PORT wine. Fruit, cork, olives, lace, silver-filigree jewelry, and textiles are also exported from its suburban port, Leixões. Fishing and tourism are important. Landmarks include the 12th-century Romanesque cathedral and several museums. The University of Porto (1911) is there. Three large bridges span the Douro at Porto, including one designed by Alexandre Gustave Eiffel.

Located in an area settled as early as 2000 BC, Porto became the Roman town of Portus Cale in the 3d century BC. It passed to the Moors in 716, who held it until the end of the 10th century. By the 12th century it was regarded as the northern capital of Portugal. The British took the city from the French during the Peninsular War (1809).

Pôrto Alegre [pohrt'-oh ah-leg'-ree]   The largest city in southern Brazil and the capital of the state of Rio Grande do Sul, Pôrto Alegre has a population of 1,272,121 (1985). It lies at the northern end of the 275-km-long (171-mi) freshwater lagoon, Lagoa dos Patos. The city is one of Brazil's most important industrial centers. Factories produce woolen textiles, leather goods, chemicals, beer, and wine, which are then transported across the Lagoa dos Patos to the cities of Pelotas and Rio Grande at its southern end and transferred to ocean vessels. Pôrto Alegre has two universities and an important publishing industry. The city was founded in the 1740s by Portuguese settlers. Germans arrived in the area in the 1820s and were followed by Italian immigrants.

Porto-Novo [pohrt'-oh-noh'-voh]   Porto-Novo (1982 est. pop., 208,000), the capital city of Benin, lies on a lagoon on the west central coast of Africa, about 90 km (55 mi) west of Lagos, Nigeria. Cotonou, the nation's major industrial and transportation center, is located nearby. Porto-Novo's economy depends on palm oil produced in the surrounding agricultural area. Porto-Novo was the center of the YORUBA Toffa dynasty. In the 17th century the Portuguese developed it into a flourishing slave-trade port.

Portolá, Gaspar de [pohr-toh-lah']   Gaspar de Portolá, c.1723–c.1784, commanded the expedition (1769–70) that took possession of Upper California for Spain. Accompanied by the Franciscan missionary Junípero SERRA, Portolá set out from Baja California in May 1769 and explored as far north as San Francisco Bay, founding the first European settlements at San Diego (1769) and Monterey (1770), Calif.

Portrait of the Artist as a Young Man, A
James JOYCE wrote the first draft of his autobiographical novel *A Portrait of the Artist as a Young Man* in various stages between 1904 and 1914. After serialization in *The Egoist*, it appeared in book form in 1916. The book is a BILDUNGSROMAN; the novel describes the hero's search for identity. Each chapter is written in a different style, reflecting Stephen Dedalus's progress toward maturity, and each is part of a dialectic in which apparent triumph is undermined by actual experience. At the conclusion, Dedalus discovers his identity as a writer and leaves Ireland for the greater freedom of Europe.

Death mask of Amenhotep III *(c.1379 BC; Staatliche Museen, Berlin)*

Portrait of a Young Girl *(1st century AD; Museo Nazionale, Naples)*

Domenico Ghirlandaio, Portrait of an Old Man and His Grandson *(c.1480; Louvre, Paris)*

Raphael, Portrait of Baldassare Castiglione *(1514–15; Louvre, Paris)*

Thomas Gainsborough, Blue Boy *(c.1770; Huntington Art Gallery, San Marino, Calif.)*

Rembrandt, Self Portrait *(1657; Kunsthistorisches Museum, Vienna)*

J. A. D. Ingres, Mademoiselle Rivière *(1805; Louvre, Paris)*

Vincent van Gogh, Self Portrait *(1890; Musée d'Orsay, Paris)*

Pablo Picasso, Portrait of the Art Dealer Vollard *(1910; The Hermitage, Leningrad)*

portraiture [pohr'-truh-chur] Portraiture is the art of depicting specific human individuals as themselves. The ability or desire to portray the features of a particular person in a convincing way has not been universal in the arts. It is even more rare to capture the personality of an individual, the goal of the portrait in its truest sense. Images that seek to show only the physical form of an individual are termed *effigies*, such as the tomb figures of the Egyptian pharaohs.

Portraits in the fullest sense were created first by the Greeks in the late classical period (4th century BC). The earliest certain example is a head of Aristotle (c.320 BC; Kunsthistorisches Museum, Vienna), which conveys not only a convincing sense of physical reality but a broader feeling of personality as well. The portraits of Alexander the Great by artists such as LYSIPPUS and APELLES began a tradition of heroic-ruler imagery that dominated the official art of the Greeks, Romans, and their medieval followers. Among the early Romans a tradition of ancestor effigies involving death masks evolved into a highly realistic portraiture by the 1st century BC, at the same time that increased contact with Greek art encouraged a contrasting fashion for idealized likenesses, especially of political leaders.

Medieval portraits were more concerned with spiritual likeness but never completely lost their Greco-Roman heritage of accuracy. Individuals tended to be portrayed as standardized, recognizable images. In the late Middle Ages realistic portraits appeared in works in which the identity of the subject was particularly important—tomb figures and donor portraits.

The first great northern Renaissance portraitist was the Flemish painter Jan van EYCK, who endowed his subjects with life and personality and introduced the portrait as a secular art form to Europe. The conflict between idealism and realism was characteristic of the High Renaissance. Many of the great 16th-century masters treated portraiture as a sideline (RAPHAEL), submerged individuality in atmospheric effects (LEONARDO DA VINCI), or ignored likeness altogether (MICHELANGELO).

Using a suggestive rather than a detailed technique, the Venetian painters led by TITIAN achieved a dramatic portrait style that became popular throughout Europe and influenced generations of artists. In the hands of Peter Paul RUBENS, the heroic-ruler imagery of baroque Europe was continued; Sir Anthony VAN DYCK introduced the style to England. More sharply focused realism evolved from the Venetian tradition in other countries; Diego VELÁZQUEZ created powerful portraits at the Spanish court. Outside court circles, this realistic style was popularized in France by the LE NAIN BROTHERS and affected the portraits of the Dutch artists Frans HALS and REMBRANDT.

Portraiture was the most popular art form in England at the time of Sir Joshua REYNOLDS. It was virtually the only one in the American colonies until after the Revolution, and was practiced by the early LIMNERS. Even after the Revolution, American artists, including the PEALE family and Gilbert STUART, were rarely able to support themselves except by portraiture. The neoclassical move-

ment produced a generation of brilliant portraitists led by J. A. D. INGRES; at the same time, the romantic painter Eugène DELACROIX used a purely atmospheric approach.

In the 19th century the photograph rapidly supplanted the paintbrush in satisfying mass demand for commemorative portraiture. Only at the level of high society was portraiture still important, as in the work of John Singer SARGENT. Among the founders of modern art, portrait subjects were likely to be treated freely, as in Vincent VAN GOGH's vivid likenesses of his friends. In the 20th century serious portraiture has been of interest primarily to expressionists concerned with psychological insights—Oskar KOKOSCHKA, Chaim SOUTINE, and, more recently, Francis BACON.

Portsmouth (England) [pohrts'-muhth] Portsmouth is an English Channel port city in Hampshire, England. Its population is 179,419 (1981). The city encompasses Portsea, the site of the United Kingdom's largest naval base; Southsea, a residential and resort area; and the old town of Portsmouth. Shipyards and aircraft factories contribute to the local economy, as does tourism. Portsmouth was the birthplace of the novelist Charles Dickens. The city has a 12th-century cathedral, and Lord Nelson's ship the *Victory* is preserved in the harbor.

The present city was founded in 1194 by Richard I, who chose the site because of its strategic location. It rapidly eclipsed the older settlement of Portchester, with its Roman and medieval castle, as the sea receded from that site. Portsmouth's first dry dock was constructed in 1496.

Portsmouth (New Hampshire) The city of Portsmouth is a port of entry in southeastern New Hampshire, at the mouth of the Piscataqua River opposite Kittery, Maine, on the Atlantic Coast. Portsmouth has a population of 25,925 (1990). The city's economy depends on trade, light industry, tourism, and the Portsmouth Naval Yard (actually located in Kittery) and Pease Air Force Base. Of historical interest are houses of the colonial and federal periods, Saint John's Episcopal Church (1807), and the Strawbery Banke restoration project, a 4-ha (10-acre) site of more than 30 buildings dating from 1695 to 1865.

Settled in the early 1600s on a natural harbor, the settlement (called Strawbery Banke until 1653) flourished as the seat of colonial government, with a thriving shipbuilding industry and import-export trade. A decline set in, however, as Massachusetts ports won much of the city's early trade, and the state capital was moved to Concord in 1808.

Portsmouth (Virginia) Portsmouth (1990 pop., 103,907) is a seaport city in southeastern Virginia across the Elizabeth River from NORFOLK. Manufactures include chemicals, fertilizers, and plastics. Portsmouth is the site of the Norfolk Naval Shipyard (1801). The city was founded in 1752.

PORTUGUESE REPUBLIC

Land: Area: 92,389 km² (35,672 mi²). Capital and largest city: Lisbon (1986 est. pop., 829,600).

People: Population (1990 est.): 10,388,000. Density: 112 persons per km² (291 per mi²). Distribution (1989): 30% urban, 70% rural. Official language: Portuguese. Major religion: Roman Catholicism.

Government: Type: parliamentary democracy. Legislature: Assembly of the Republic. Political subdivisions: 18 districts, 2 autonomous regions.

Economy: GNP (1989): $44 billion; $4,260 per capita. Labor distribution (1987): agriculture—21%; industry—23%; services—21%; trade—13%; other—22%. Foreign trade (1988): imports—$17.7 billion; exports—$11.0 billion. Currency: 1 escudo = 100 centavos.

Education and Health: Literacy (1990 est.): 83% of adult population. Universities (1989): 13. Hospital beds (1988): 48,838. Physicians (1988): 26,381. Life expectancy (1990): women—78; men—71. Infant mortality (1990): 14 per 1,000 live births.

Portugal   Portugal, an independent nation along the Atlantic Ocean at the southwestern edge of Europe, occupies about one-sixth of the Iberian Peninsula, which it shares with Spain, its only neighbor. The AZORES and MADEIRA ISLANDS are Portuguese autonomous regions.

The name *Portugal* is probably derived from the Roman settlement of Portus Cale, located on the present site of Porto. One of the oldest nations in Europe, Portugal became independent of both Moorish and Castilian control in 1143, when Alfonso I was proclaimed king. The original kingdom was located north of the Douro River, but it expanded southward along the coast by driving the Moors from Lisbon and Alentejo and Algarve, south of the Tagus River, by 1252. In the 15th and early 16th centuries Portugal created a large overseas empire. A period of Spanish control (1580–1640) contributed to the subsequent decline of Portugal's influence and commercial prosperity. A republic from 1910, Portugal was under a dictatorial government from the late 1920s until 1974; António de Oliveira SALAZAR was the dominant figure until 1968. With the establishment of democratic government in 1974, Portugal granted independence to its African colonies. Its sole remaining overseas colony, the enclave of MACAO, will be ceded to China at the end of the century.

Land and Resources

Portugal is composed of the mountainous Meseta in the interior and a coastal plain in the west that widens significantly from north to south. The highest mountain, Estrella (1,993 m/6,539 ft), is in the Serra da Estrela ridge in central Portugal. The TAGUS RIVER flows across Portugal from east to west. The Meseta north of the Tagus is high, with summits exceeding 1,200 m (4,000 ft). South of the river the land is lower and more gently rolling, with only 3% of the land higher than 400 m (1,300 ft) above sea level and peaks in the Serra de Monchique, the highest mountains in the south, under 915 m (3,000 ft).

Soils.   The most fertile soils occur on alluvium in the main river valleys. Uplands in the north have peaty, usually infertile soils on wetter summits and soils of moderate fertility in better-drained areas. Soils deficient in lime predominate in some northern areas, especially where underlain by schistose rock or sandstones. Thin, dry soils are common in the hilly country near Lisbon and in Algarve.

Climate.   Portugal has a unique variant of the typical Mediterranean climate, the northern areas being wetter than average with only a short dry season and the south approaching subtropical, semiarid conditions. Along the coast the mean monthly temperatures range from 9° to 12° C (48° to 54° F) in January and from 20° to 24° C (68° to 75° F) in July. Winds from the Atlantic moderate temperatures throughout the year. Frosts are rare in the north and virtually unknown in the south. Inland, mean temperatures fall by 3° or 4° C (5° or 7° F) in winter and rise appreciably in summer.

The average yearly precipitation decreases from between 1,000 and 1,300 mm (40 and 51 in) in the north to between 400 and 600 mm (16 and 24 in) in the south. During spring and fall cloudy and sunny spells alternate, whereas in summer, the Azorean high pressure area dominates, bringing a period of dry, sunny weather

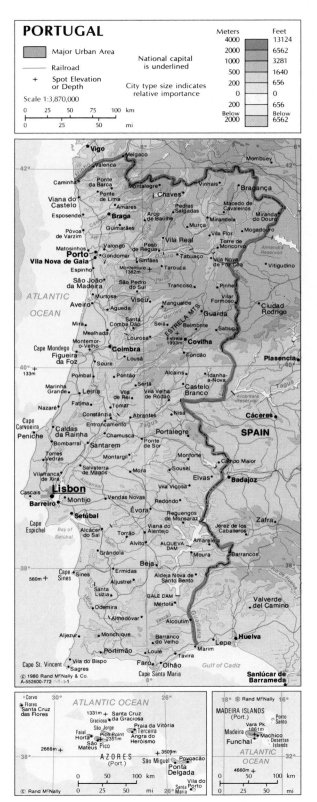

PORTUGAL

Major Urban Area

—— Railroad

+ Spot Elevation
or Depth

National capital
is underlined

City type size indicates
relative importance

Scale 1:3,870,000

| 0 | 25 | 50 | 75 | 100 km |
| 0 | | 25 | | 50 mi |

Meters	Feet
4000	13124
2000	6562
1000	3281
500	1640
200	656
0	0
200	656
Below 2000	Below 6562

© 1980 Rand McNally & Co.
A-552600-772 -1-1-1

that lasts an average of two months at Porto and three months at Lisbon.

Drainage. Portugal's four largest rivers are the Minho, DOURO, Tagus, and the Guadiana; all rise in Spain and, with the exception of the Guadiana, flow from east to west across Portugal. The principal Portuguese tributary of the Tagus is the Zezere, which rises in the Serra da Estrela and is an important source of hydroelectric power. All Portuguese rivers have low water flow in summer, and in the extreme south many watercourses almost dry up during this season. The country abounds in hot mineral springs (*caldes*), which are popular for medicinal reasons.

Vegetation and Animal Life. More than 2,700 species of plants are known to occur in Portugal. Of these, only 90 are unique to the country, and the remainder is a mixture of European and African species and exotic elements introduced since the 15th century from the New World and the Far East. About 31% of Portugal is forested: oaks, deciduous in the north and evergreen in the south, cover about one-third of all timberland, and pines cover about one-half. Wolves survive in remote mountain areas, and wild boars are protected by law.

Resources. Portugal is Europe's leading producer of tungsten ore and also possesses important deposits of coal and copper pyrites. Some kaolin, hematite (iron ore), cassiterite (tin ore), and gold also occur. About 48% of the land is cultivated; 6% is in meadows and pasture, and 15% is in heathland, swamp, and other waste. Hydroelectric power is the principal energy source.

People

The original Portuguese stock was Iberian. Celtic invaders added other physical characteristics during the 1st millennium BC; as did the Romans after 137 BC; Visigoths and Suevi, who settled north of the Douro in the 4th century AD; and the Moors, after 711 AD. A Jewish community flourished in Portugal under the Moors, but the Jews were expelled or absorbed during the *Reconquista* (Christian Reconquest) of Muslim areas in the 12th and 13th centuries. Blacks were freely imported from Africa as slaves and were also absorbed into the Portuguese population. Despite such complex origins, the population today is one of Europe's most homogeneous. The approximately 10,000 black colonial refugees from Africa make up the only important minority.

Language and Religion. The Portuguese language is one of the ROMANCE LANGUAGES, with an admixture of Arabic and other foreign idioms. It is related to and similar to Galician, a Spanish dialect. About 97% of the population are Roman Catholic.

Demography. Population densities are highest in the northern coastal areas and in the Douro River valley and decrease inland and toward the south. About 80% of the population are concentrated north of the Tagus River, where habitable areas are densely settled with towns, villages, and farmsteads. By contrast, except for a densely settled strip along the Algarve coast, areas south of the Tagus are sparsely populated.

Only one-third of the total population is officially classified as rural, but many of the two-thirds listed as urban

(Above) *Wheat is one of Portugal's primary cereal crops. Although traditional farming methods prevail in most parts of Portugal, large farm machinery has been successfully introduced in some areas.*
(Right) *Lisbon, situated on the Tagus River, was established as Portugal's capital in 1256. The waterfront Praça do Comércio, a square bordered by government buildings, was constructed on the site of the former Terreiro do Paço following the 1755 earthquake.*

dwellers live in small towns and villages rather than large urban centers. The two largest cities are LISBON, on the mouth of the Tagus; and PORTO, on the north bank of the Douro River. Lisbon, with well over 1,000,000 inhabitants in its metropolitan area, is the capital and the main industrial, commercial, and financial center. Porto, the principal town in the north, has the second largest metropolitan area. Of the other major cities, BRAGA, COIMBRA, ÉVORA, Setúbal, and Faro are important regional centers; FUNCHAL is the capital of the Madeira Islands.

Portugal's birthrate and death rate, once among the highest in Europe, have fallen significantly in the last 25 years and are now close to the Western European average.

Traditionally, Portuguese have emigrated from overpopulated Portugal in large numbers since the 15th century; many still leave permanently for Brazil, the United States, and Canada, but increasing numbers now seek temporary employment in Germany and other European Community (EC) countries. Conversely, about 1,000,000 Portuguese of European and black-African descent were forced to return to Portugal when Angola, Mozambique, and other African colonies became independent in the 1970s.

Education and Health. Education has been free and compulsory since 1911, and all children over the age of 7 must attend school for 6 years. The first 4 years are spent in primary schools, and secondary education takes place in either state-run lyceums and other high schools or in a variety of professional and technical institutions. The government also sponsors an adult-education program. Several hundred private, mostly church-run, schools provide an alternate education system. The five major universities are at Coimbra (1290), Lisbon, Porto, Aveiro, and Braga.

Health care has improved significantly in recent years. A national health service was established in 1979, and infant mortality rates declined by nearly 50% between the mid-1970s and the mid-1980s. Doctors are paid by the state and must reside in the areas to which they are appointed.

Arts. The 16th century was the Golden Age of Portuguese literature. Its luminaries included the dramatist Gil VICENTE and the poet Luís de CAMÕES, author of Portugal's great epic *The Lusiads* (see PORTUGUESE LITERATURE).

PORTUGUESE ART AND ARCHITECTURE reached its peak in the 16th century during the reign of MANUEL I (r. 1495–1521). During this period, the golden age of Portuguese maritime expansion, a new Manueline style was developed; its reliance on marine and overseas motifs can be seen at the monastery at Batalha. Music traditions include the celebrated fado (an urban folk song), and each major region has its traditional folk music, songs, and musical instruments.

Economic Activity

In the 15th and 16th centuries Portuguese navigators brought great wealth into Portugal from their command of the profitable spice trade and the import of luxury items from India and the Far East. After 1600, command of world sea routes passed to the Dutch and the English, but Portugal continued to profit from development of the agricultural and mineral wealth of its overseas colonies. The economy of the mainland remained tied to agriculture and fishing, the main exports being sardines, wine, and cork. Industrial development has been emphasized since the 1960s.

Manufacturing. Manufacturing provides less than one-third of the national income, but its share is growing, and it employs a continuously increasing percentage of the labor force. Most manufacturing is concentrated in and around Lisbon and Porto. The metallurgical industry remains small, despite efforts to enlarge it, and the Siderugia Nacional, established in 1961 at Seixal, supplies much of the nation's pig iron and most of its steel. Shipbuilding and repair yards are located in Lisbon and Setúbal; most of the nation's production of armaments, agricultural implements, general hardware, and textile machinery is located in Lisbon. Textiles are especially important at Porto. Ceramics, based on kaolin quarried in plateaus near the course of the Douro River, are also widely produced, the products ranging from industrial ceramics to decorated tiles (*azulejos*). Leiria specializes in the manufacture of glass, and Barreiro in the production of fertilizers, insecticides, and other chemicals. Other important products, all processed from local raw materials, include wines, cork, pulpwood, and canned sardines.

Energy. Production of electricity increased more than tenfold from 1955 to 1985. About one-half of all electricity is derived from hydroelectric installations; the remainder is produced in thermal electric stations, fueled with imported petroleum. A nuclear-power station is in operation at Sacavém, just north of Lisbon.

Agriculture. Farming is an important part of the economy. Cereal crops predominate and occupy two-thirds of all cultivated land; corn is the principal crop north of the Tagus River, and wheat the principal crop in the south. Beans, a staple food in the Portuguese diet, are both in-tercropped and rotated with cereals, the beans supplying the soil with a natural source of nitrogen. The major cash crops are grapes and olives. Livestock includes sheep, pigs, cattle, goats, donkeys, and mules. Farms in the north are generally less than 12 ha (30 acres). In the south, large estates (*latifundia*) predominate; used mainly for wheat, many of these units were owned by absentee landlords before the land reforms of 1974–75, and farm employment drops drastically after the wheat harvest.

Forestry and Fishing. Pine trees covering half the timbered areas are cut for lumber and pulp and also supply large quantities of resin and turpentine for export. An additional one-third of the timberland bears cork oak, which supplies about one-half of the world's total cork supply. Fishing employs about 30,000 persons in coastal regions. The most valuable fish caught are sardines, mackerel, hake, haddock, cod, and tunny.

Transportation and Trade. High-speed motorways are rare in Portugal. Most of the roads, though surfaced, are winding, and minor roads are often unsuitable for motor traffic. The rail system is state owned. Except on the Tagus, river traffic is of minor importance and restricted to shallow vessels. The main ports are Lisbon, Setúbal, and Leixões (the port for Porto).

Portugal has an unfavorable balance of trade. The principal imports, by value, are petroleum, iron and steel, sugar, motor vehicles, cotton, oilseeds, and wheat. The main exports are wines, cork, pulpwood, sardines, resin and turpentine, and wolframite. Most imports come from Germany, the United Kingdom, and the United States; most exports are destined for the United Kingdom. In 1986, after years of difficult negotiations, Portugal became a member of the EC and withdrew from the European Free Trade Association.

Government and Politics

A new constitution, Portugal's fifth, was promulgated in 1976. It vested legislative power in a unicameral legislative assembly, with 263 members elected every 5 years. Executive authority rests with the president, also elected for a 5-year term. The principal political groups are the Socialist party, led by Mário SOARES, who was elected president in 1986 and reelected in 1991; the Communist party, led by Álvaro Cunhal; and the Democratic Alliance, a coalition of center-right political parties.

History

Much of Portugal's early history was shared with Spain, its neighbor on the Iberian peninsula. Portugal did not develop a distinct identity until the Middle Ages.

Ancient and Medieval Portugal. Celts settled in the area after 1000 BC. A Celtic federation, the Lusitani, resisted the advance of the Romans until *c*.140 BC; afterward, the Romans imposed their administration and language on the conquered region, which they called Lusitania. Christianity was introduced in the 3d century AD.

After the disintegration of the Roman Empire in the West in the 5th century AD, two Germanic tribes, the Suevi and the Visigoths (see GOTHS), vied for control of Lusitania. Muslims (Moors) invaded (711) from North

Fishing is one of Portugal's oldest industries, and fish products are still a major export. Fishing villages, such as Nazaré, proliferate on the country's Atlantic coastline. Sardines, cod, and shellfish constitute the bulk of the catch.

Africa but concentrated their settlements south of the Tagus River. In the 10th century, Portugal was attached to the kingdoms of León and Castile, whose ruler, ALFONSO VI, named Henry of Burgundy, the husband of his daughter Teresa, as count of Portugal in 1095. In 1128 their son, Alfonso Henry, began calling himself King ALFONSO I. His kingship was recognized by the pope in 1179. During his long reign Alfonso pushed the frontiers of his kingdom south to the Tagus River.

The war against the Muslims as well as conflicts with the papacy continued under Alfonso's successors, Sancho I (c.1154–1211; r. 1185–1211) and ALFONSO II. Alfonso II was excommunicated, and the chaotic reign of his son Sancho II (c.1209–48; r. 1223–45) ended when Sancho was deposed by Pope Innocent IV.

ALFONSO III, brother of Sancho II, conquered the southernmost province of Algarve in 1249, ending the Portuguese reconquest from the Moors. His son DINIS developed the country's agriculture and founded the first university (1290; at Lisbon, later at Coimbra). Portuguese replaced Latin as the court's written language. At the same time, however, unsuccessful wars with Castile gave the Castilians a claim to the Portuguese throne.

The House of Avis (1385–1580). In 1383 a war broke out between John of Avis, illegitimate son of King PETER I of Portugal, and John I of Castile and León (1358–90; r. 1379–90), who claimed the throne by marriage. The support of the people of Lisbon and the military victory of Nuno Álvares PEREIRA at Aljubarrota (1385) gave the throne to John of Avis (as JOHN I). The house of Avis was soon recognized by Burgundy and by England.

John's successors included the remarkable JOHN II, who curbed the power of the great nobles, promoted maritime expansion, and sought to maintain good relations with Spain. Manuel I reaped the benefits of Portugal's new empire in the East. During his reign culture flourished, and Lisbon became a great city. Manuel's son, JOHN III, established an INQUISITION and encouraged the Society of Jesus (JESUITS). The closer ties with Spain culminated in a dynastic union. In 1580, PHILIP II of Spain, claiming the Portuguese throne by marriage to John III's daughter, Maria, became King Philip I of Portugal.

The Discoveries and the Empire. Portugal's leadership in Europe's overseas expansion was a remarkable achievement for so small and poor a country. The reconquest of Moorish-held lands supplied an initial impulse for discovery and trade. Eventually the Portuguese combined a scientific interest in maritime exploration with a desire to capture the SPICE TRADE of the East Indies, spread Christianity, and exploit islands in the Atlantic for profit.

Prince HENRY THE NAVIGATOR, a son of John I was the first guiding spirit of the Portuguese discoveries. In 1434, Gil Eanes passed Cape Bojador. In the 1440s a new ship, the caravel, allowed Portuguese seafarers to sail to Senegal; by 1460 they had reached Sierra Leone.

In the 1480s, King John II took up the cause of exploration. Diogo Cam reached the Congo in 1482, and in 1488, Bartholomeu DIAS rounded the Cape of Good Hope. In 1494 a treaty with Spain (see TORDESILLAS, TREATY OF) confirmed Portugal's rights to lay claim to

The port of Lisbon bustles with international commerce in this engraving from the 16th century, when Portugal reached its height as a colonial power.

lands to the east of a line running north and south through the bulge of South America. Vasco da GAMA reached India in 1498; and in 1500, Pedro Álvares CABRAL discovered Brazil, claiming it for Portugal. Soon large Portuguese fleets were sailing yearly into the Indian Ocean and contact was made with China. Francisco de ALMEIDA and Afonso de ALBUQUERQUE established fortified trading stations from Ormuz to Malacca. The superiority of Portuguese ships and guns and the daring of their sailors allowed them to dominate the Indian Ocean and the spice trade. In the 16th century they were Europe's leading dealers in the products of the Orient. In the Atlantic, meanwhile, they pioneered the slave trade from Africa to America. The great discoveries quickly enriched Lisbon and the court but depopulated the countryside as generations of hardy men ventured out, never to return.

The Old Regime (1580–1811). Union with Spain dragged Portugal into Spain's wars after 1580. The Dutch proceeded to usurp Portuguese control of the eastern trade, to take some of the colonies in the East Indies, and to occupy parts of Brazil. Eventually, Portuguese resentment of Spanish wars and taxes resulted in the national revolution of 1640, during which the Spanish were expelled and the duke of Bragança became King JOHN IV. Spain recognized Portuguese independence in 1668.

During the 18th century relative peace and prosperity returned. The discovery of large reserves of gold and diamonds in Brazil enriched the monarchy and reinforced its absolutist tendencies. The Methuen Treaty (1703) marked the beginning of Portugal's political subordination to England. In 1755 a terrible earthquake destroyed Lisbon. The task of rebuilding the city concentrated extraordinary powers in the hands of King Joseph's (1750–77) minister, Sebastião José de Carvalho Melo, later marquês de POMBAL, who ruled Portugal with an iron hand until the king's death.

Despite some popular sympathy for the French Revolution, the government of the melancholic Maria I (1734–

1816; r. 1777–1816) joined (1793) England and Spain against the revolutionary power. After the Spanish made peace with the French, they invaded (1801) Portugal. Napoleon then pressured the Portuguese to end their alliance with England, and in 1807 his armies invaded the country (see NAPOLEONIC WARS). The British evacuated the royal family and court and transported them to the Portuguese colony of Brazil.

The Constitutional Monarchy (1811–1910). The French withdrew from Portugal in 1811, but King John VI did not return from Brazil until 1821. One year after his arrival, Brazil declared its independence under one of his sons, who became Emperor PEDRO I. At the same time John had to accept (1822) a liberal constitution.

After John VI's death (1826), Pedro (Peter IV of Portugal) passed the Portuguese throne to his daughter, MARIA II. Her reign (1826–53) was marked by popular uprisings, but by mid-century, Portugal had achieved some stability under a succession of short-lived parliamentary governments.

After 1880, Portugal turned its attention to Africa, trying to connect its possessions in Mozambique and Angola. The British blocked these ambitions, but Portugal still acquired more territory than either Germany or Italy. Colonial adventures helped to exhaust the treasury and contributed to the rise of republican sentiment. In 1908, King CHARLES I was assassinated, and two years later a republican uprising of civilians and soldiers forced his son and successor, Manuel II (1889–1932), into exile.

The Republic: Salazar and After. The republican politicians expelled the monarchy, introduced wide-ranging anticlerical legislation, and wrote a new democratic constitution. From 1910 to 1926, Portugal experienced political violence and a procession of short-lived governments, from radical-democratic to dictatorial. Portugal, loyal to its English alliance, joined the Allies in World War I but gained little from its participation.

In 1926, President António Oscar de Fragoso Carmona called on an economics professor, António de Oliveira SALAZAR, to solve a financial crisis. Salazar–who was officially minister of finance (1928–40) and premier (1932–68)—received virtual dictatorial powers and proceeded to balance the budget and reform the administration. His government, known as the New State, was an expression of Catholic-corporatist principles.

In the 1960s, Portugal lost its enclaves in India, and insurrections broke out in its African possessions. Salazar was replaced by Marcello Caetano (1906–80), and in April 1974 a revolution brought independence for the colonies and the return of democracy under a military junta. The constitution of 1976 committed the country to socialist goals, and from July 1976 to July 1978 a minority socialist government under Mário SOARES was in power. From December 1979 until the end of 1982 the country was governed by the Democratic Alliance, a right-centrist coalition. Led first by Francisco Sá Carneiro and later (after Sá Carneiro's death in December 1980) by Francisco Pinto Balsemão, the coalition was frequently in conflict with President António dos Santos Ramalho EANES. The Socialists returned to power under Soares from 1983 to 1985. They were replaced by a new coalition under the right-of-center Social Democrat Aníbal Cavaço Silva, who won a second victory at the polls in 1987, capturing more than 50% of the vote, the first time any party had done so since the restoration of democracy. Soares succeeded Eanes as president in 1986 and was reelected in 1991.

Portuguese art and architecture   The history of Portuguese art, and of the nation itself, began in 1128 when Alfonso I revolted against Castilian rule to establish an independent kingdom ruled by the Burgundian dynasty. This link with France partially explains the strong French influence on Portuguese Romanesque art. Coimbra was a major center of Romanesque Portugal; its churches, including the 12th-century Old Cathedral, are noted for their solid granite construction and sober, sparsely decorated facades.

The first great monument of the Portuguese Gothic was the Cistercian monastery of Alcobaça (begun 1178). Other monuments of the 12th and 13th centuries were hybrids of the International Gothic and late Romanesque styles with Romanesque proportions and Gothic buttress and vault systems.

Among the finest examples of Portuguese medieval sculpture are the mid-14th-century tombs of Peter I and Inés de Castro at Santa Maria in Alcobaça. The figures lie stiffly on sarcophagi decorated with Gothic ornamentation.

The Manueline style, named for King Manuel I (r. 1495–1521), blended naturalistic and bizarre architectural and sculptural forms, as in the Jesus church (1492–98), Setúbal, and the monastery of the Hieronymites (1502–19) at Belém. Manueline doors and windows were richly surrounded by shell and coral motifs, as at the

The monastery of the Hieronymites at Belém (1502–19) represents the culmination of Manueline style. This style combined Gothic architectural principles with the ornamentation characteristic of early Renaissance decoration.

Nuno Gonçalves's mastery of form and composition is seen in the Panel of the High Constables, *one of the panels constituting the polyptych of Saint Vincent (c.1467–70). (Museu Nacional de Arte Antiga, Lisbon.)*

Christ Church (1510–14), Tomar, with its fantastic encrusted windows designed by Diogo de Arruda.

Portuguese painting produced its greatest master in the mid-15th century in the figure of Nuno GONÇALVES (fl. 1450–71), whose works contain realistic portraits of 15th-century political figures as well as saints but show little regard for a naturalistic setting. Other Renaissance painters were Vasco Fernandes ("Grão Vasco"), Cristóvão Figueiredo, and Gregório Lópes.

Classicism played an important role in Portuguese architecture from the 16th to the 18th century. Donato Bramante's project for Saint Peter's, Rome, probably inspired João Tinoco's Santa Engrácia (1682–1730), Lisbon, a Greek-cross plan church with rounded arms framed by four square towers. The great 18th-century monastic complex at Mafra (1717–70), by João Pedro Frederico Ludovice, was also the result of close study of classical principles.

Portugal was under Spanish domination from 1580 to 1640, and Spanish influence was strongly felt in painting. Josefa d'Ayala (c.1630–84) painted scenes of religious life, often concentrating on female saints, in the style of Francisco de Zurbarán. The great baroque portraitist Domingos Vieira displays his characteristic sober style in his *Portrait of Isabel de Moura* (c.1635; Museu Nacional). Fresco painting became popular in the 18th century; the ceiling at the entrance of São Vicente de Fora (1710), Lisbon, by Vincenzo Bacherelli, introduces baroque illusionism into Portuguese decoration. Late baroque style combined with French rococo inspiration in the work of Pedro Alexandrino de Carvalho (1730–1810).

The French artist Nicolas Chanterene (fl. c.1516–50) dominated 16th-century Portuguese sculpture; his reputation was established by his portal sculpture (c.1517) at

Belém and the royal tombs (c.1518–21) at Coimbra. Manuel Pereira was Portugal's greatest baroque sculptor, although most of his work, such as the famous *Saint Bruno* (c.1632–35; Monastery of Miraflores, Burgos), was done in Spain. Queluz Palace (1747–60) is a charming rococo complex in a style that would soon be abandoned in favor of neoclassical forms. Neoclassicism in painting was exemplified by Domingos António de Sequeira in such works as his *Allegory of João VI* (1810; Museu Nacional). From this time onward Portuguese art acquired an increasingly international flavor, with the exception of the decorative arts, which have preserved their autochthonous character to this day.

Portuguese Guinea   see GUINEA-BISSAU

Portuguese language   see ROMANCE LANGUAGES

Portuguese literature   Often innovative, Portuguese literature has influenced such diverse writers as Lord Byron, Lope de Vega, and Herman Melville.

Central to its early Middle Ages are the poems called cantigas ("songs"), the most noteworthy being the lyrical *cantigas de amigo* and *cantigas de amor* ("lovers' songs"). King DINIS (r. 1279–1325) was the best-known writer of this period. The later Middle Ages are memorable for the surprisingly modern historiography of Fernão Lopes (c.1378–1459).

A principal Renaissance figure was the great poet playwright Gil VICENTE. The poet Luís de CAMÕES gave Portuguese poetry its highest expression, culminating in the national epic *The Lusiads* (1572; Eng. trans., 1655).

Annexation by Spain (1580–1640) confirmed the neoscholasticism of the baroque. The period's greatest poet and spokesperson for poetic theory was Francisco Rodrigues Lobo (1579?–1621). A significant prose stylist was António VIEIRA.

The Enlightenment in Portugal dates approximately from the founding of the Lusitanian Arcadian Society in 1756. It was primarily a poetical movement—one of whose outstanding figures was Antônio Dinis da Cruz e Silva (1739–99).

João Baptista de Almeida Garrett (1799–1854) was a prominent 19th-century dramatist. Eça de Queiroz (1845–1900) became the finest 19th-century Portuguese novelist. Through the end of the 19th and well into the 20th century, poetry was shaped by French literary trends, although the avant-gardist Fernando Pessoa (1888–1935) also brought English influences to bear.

Since the revolution of 1974 contemporary Portuguese writers have turned to questioning the myths of Portuguese history. Once suppressed works are now published, and the new freedom has encouraged the publication of writings by Portuguese-Africans, such as the Angolan José Luandino Viera, and by many women writers, of whom novelist Olga Gonçalves is the most prominent. José de Almeida Faria's trilogy about the past two decades, and especially its final volume, *Lusitânia* (1981), is an important recent work of fiction.

Portuguese man-of-war   A striking marine animal, the Portuguese man-of-war, genus *Physalia*, is characteristically found in tropical and subtropical waters, particularly the open waters of the Atlantic Ocean. The animal is actually a floating colony of several functionally distinct individuals. Such colonies are termed polymorphic and are members of the phylum Coelenterata, class Hydrozoa, order Siphonophora.

The most conspicuous portion of the Portuguese man-of-war colony is a blue, oval, gas-filled float, up to 30 cm (12 in) in length, with a crest that serves as a sail. The organism is thereby passively moved about by the wind. The float prevents the colony of individuals from sinking. Specialized individuals suspended from the float are the feeding gastrozooids and the reproductive members. Also suspended are short tentacles and "fishing" tentacles several meters in length, with poisonous stinging cells (cnidocytes). Long tentacles immobilize and grasp prey, even medium-sized fish, and contract to a fraction of their length, bringing victims to the numerous feeding zooids. This beautiful and bizarre organism can inflict painful and serious injury to humans.

The Portuguese water dog is an adept swimmer and diver. These dogs are now few in number. Most are found along the Portuguese coast.

curly, and is either black or brown, usually with white front feet. The Portuguese water dog was developed along the coast of Portugal; it was used by fishermen to retrieve lost nets and tackle and to guard the boats in harbor. The breed was recognized by the American Kennel Club in 1983.

Posada, José Guadalupe   [poh-sah'-duh]   José Guadalupe Posada, b. Feb. 2, 1852, d. Jan. 20, 1913, a popular Mexican caricaturist and graphic artist, played a significant role in the founding of the so-called Mexican Renaissance of the 20th century. After illustrating many broadsides and small popular books, Pasada then turned from lithography and wood and metal cuts to drawing directly on zinc plates with acid-resistant inks. Using the latter method, he produced more than 20,000 illustrations that document and satirize the political and social events of his time. Works of great originality, his prints illustrate many popular songs, sayings, and stories and depict crimes, disasters, and national events. Most famous are his *calaveras*, or scenes from everyday life peopled with skeletons or clothed figures with skull faces. Posada's vigorously expressionistic style profoundly influenced such later artists as Diego RIVERA and José OROZCO, among others, who led the brilliant outpouring of Mexican art in the 1930s and '40s.

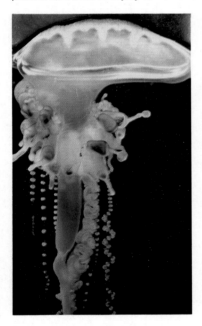

The Portuguese man-of-water floats above water, its transparent body filled with gas. Its tentacles, which hang underwater, have a paralyzing sting used to capture prey. Humans are advised to avoid this organism either in the water or on the beach. Its sting is very painful and can cause shock, fever, and heart and respiratory distress.

Portuguese Timor   see TIMOR

Portuguese water dog   The Portuguese water dog is a medium-sized, curly-coated breed standing 50–56 cm (20–22 in) high and weighing 19–25 kg (42–55 lb). It has a wiglike topknot and a long, curled tail and resembles a cross between a standard poodle and an Irish water spaniel, both of which probably contributed to the breed. The dog has two coat varieties, long and wavy or short and

Poseidon (missile) [puh-sy'-duhn]   Poseidon, a submarine-launched ballistic missile (SLBM), provides a portion of the U.S. Navy's nuclear deterrent force. Poseidon is a two-stage, solid-propellant, inertially guided strategic weapon with a range of 4,700 km (2,900 mi) and a weight of 29,500 kg (65,000 lb). It succeeded the PoLARIS A-3—the missile was accommodated in Polaris submarine launch tubes without major modification—and its considerably increased nuclear payload consists of multiple warheads (see MIRV MISSILE) that enable a single Poseidon missile to attack a number of separate targets. An improved guidance system provides double the accuracy of earlier SLBMs. The first Poseidon launch took place on Aug. 16, 1968, and the weapon system became operational on Mar. 31, 1971, when the fleet ballistic submarine U.S.S. *James Madison* left on patrol from Charleston, S.C. In the 1970s, 31 U.S. Navy submarines were outfitted with Poseidons. By the end of the 1980s, however, U.S. ballistic missile submarines were being armed with the TRIDENT missile, which would, it was planned, eventually replace the Poseidon:

Poseidon (mythology)   In Greek mythology Poseidon was the god of the sea and of earthquakes. Son of CRONUS and Rhea and brother of Zeus, he has been portrayed as a violent and powerful god who was involved in many battles. His chief weapon was the trident, a three-pronged spear, and he was closely associated with bulls, horses, and dolphins. Although married to Amphitrite, granddaughter of Oceanus, Poseidon was renowned for his many love affairs. One of his conquests was MEDUSA, when she was still a beautiful woman. After he made love to her in one of Athena's temples, the virgin goddess turned Medusa into a hideous creature and helped Perseus to slay her. PEGASUS, who sprang from Medusa's blood, was Poseidon's issue. The Mycenaeans worshiped Poseidon as their principal deity.

Posidonius [poh-see-doh'-nee-uhs]   The Greek philosopher Posidonius, *c.*135–*c.*51 BC, was a member of the Stoic school (see STOICISM) who taught at Rhodes and in Rome and was heard by the young CICERO. He wrote extensively on natural science and in defense of divination. Posidonius combined Stoic doctrines with ideas drawn from Plato and Aristotle. In particular, he modified the Stoic view of the human soul by accepting a Platonic-Aristotelian division within it into "rational" and "irrational."

positivism [pahz'-i-tiv-izm]   Positivism is a philosophical movement characterized by an emphasis on science and scientific method as the only sources of knowledge, a sharp distinction between the realms of fact and value, and a strong hostility toward religion and traditional philosophy—especially metaphysics. An outgrowth of the empirical tradition (see EMPIRICISM), positivism was first introduced into the philosophical vocabulary in the early 19th century by the comte de SAINT-SIMON. As developed by Auguste COMTE, Ernst MACH, and others, the movement had great influence in philosophy well into the 20th century.

Hostility toward traditional thought was especially strong in Comte, who denied the possibility of metaphysical knowledge, which he held to be a stagnant and useless branch of inquiry. He demanded a "sociocracy" ruled by scientists for the unity, conformity, and progress of all humanity. Mach's interest, on the other hand, was in physics, which he regarded as the paradigm of knowledge, since he believed it to be based on sensations and abstractions from sensations. He was suspicious of any thought (including scientific hypotheses) that was incapable of being reduced to direct observation. Positivism thus redefined the purpose of philosophy, limiting it to the analysis and definition of scientific language. It was a logical and historical ancestor to contemporary LOGICAL POSITIVISM and ANALYTIC AND LINGUISTIC PHILOSOPHY.

positron [pahz'-i-trahn]   The positron, also called a positive electron, is a subatomic particle most commonly formed by a process in which a proton within the nucleus of an atom is transformed to a neutron. The positron is the antiparticle of the electron and has the same mass but opposite electric charge.

See also: ANTIMATTER; FUNDAMENTAL PARTICLES.

positron emission tomography   Positron emission tomography (PET) is a diagnostic imaging technique used to evaluate many body organs, particularly the brain and related structures. Unlike traditional RADIOLOGY methods, it reveals the biochemical status as well as the structure of tissues. In a PET brain scan, the patient is injected with glucose (the primary energy source for brain activity) that is treated with radioactive tracers. These tracers emit radioactive particles called positrons that are monitored by the PET scanner. Computer processing produces false-color images of the glucose metabolism levels in the brain, indicating varying degrees of biochemical activity. Used to diagnose brain tumors and strokes, PET is also being used to study mental illnesses, such as schizophrenia, as well as how the brain processes words that are spoken or read.

Post, Emily   Emily Post, b. Baltimore, Md., Oct. 3, 1873, as Emily Price, d. Sept. 25, 1960, was one of America's foremost authorities on ETIQUETTE. Her first books—such as *The Flight of a Moth* (1904)—were fictional. It was not until 1922 that she published her famous *Etiquette in Society, in Business, in Politics, and at Home.* Later known as *Etiquette: The Blue Book of Social Usage,* the book was reprinted more than 90 times and led to Post's nationally syndicated newspaper column and radio show.

post and lintel   The post-and-lintel, or trabeated, system of construction involves the use of vertical members, or posts, to support horizontal beams, or lintels. As a simple construction requiring neither cement nor arches, the post-and-lintel system was one of the first methods used by ancient architects to solve the problem of supporting the upper structures of monumental buildings (see STONEHENGE).

The principal drawback to trabeated design is that if stone members are used, the posts must be very closely spaced to compensate for the tendency of stone lintels to sag in the middle, as a result of their lack of tensile strength. The Egyptians accepted this deficiency and built stone temples with many-pillared interior spaces; the Greeks, in their early wooden temples, opened up the interiors by using wooden lintels. When the Greeks subsequently built stone temples, they retained the use of wooden interior crossbeams to support the roof. With the widespread Roman use of the ARCH AND VAULT, the post-and-lintel system was largely superseded as the principal structural element of monumental buildings.

post-traumatic stress disorder

post-traumatic stress disorder Post-traumatic stress disorder (PTSD) is a STRESS-related psychological disorder that can cause its victims great problems in coping with daily life. PTSD may develop in any person who undergoes a major traumatic experience such as an accident or a battle. Known as shell shock during World War I and as battle fatigue during World War II, PTSD gained prominence in the United States in the 1970s as the mental-health community sought to ameliorate the extreme postwar readjustment difficulties experienced by some Vietnam War veterans. PTSD was listed as a diagnostic category by the American Psychiatric Association in 1980.

The victim of PTSD typically experiences an initial state of numbness while trying to assimilate the traumatic experience. Later symptoms, which may not appear for months, or even years, include irritability, depression, an unreasoned sense of guilt for having survived, and difficulties in relating emotionally to other people. Nightmares, flashbacks to the traumatic scene, and overreactions to sudden noises are common, and outbursts of violence may occur. Even in relatively stable individuals, the condition may reactivate earlier emotional problems. Modes of therapy used to deal with PTSD include behavioral techniques, administration of sedating drugs, group therapy, and individual psychotherapy. Their common aim is to help the individual to understand and accept the traumatic experience and to restore self-esteem.

postal services

postal services A postal service is responsible for the collection and distribution of the mail. It is financed largely through the sale of postage stamps to those who use its services and by various other fees. In almost every country the postal service is operated, and often subsidized, by the government. In the United States, however, the U.S. Postal Service, which was established under the Postal Reorganization Act of 1970, is an independent, nonprofit corporation.

Origins

As early as the 2d millennium BC in Egypt and the 1st millennium in China, relay systems were developed using messengers riding on horseback and relay stations situated along major roads.

The Persian Model. The Persians inaugurated a postal service under Cyrus the Great (d. 529 BC) that still ranks as a major achievement. The Greek historian Herodotus enumerated 111 relay stations for mounted couriers on the Sardis-Susa road alone, a route of about 2,575 km (1,600 mi). The Romans patterned their postal organization on the Persian model. Their extensive highway system facilitated postal communications.

Renaissance Postal Systems. The introduction of paper just prior to the advent of the Renaissance in western Europe sparked a boom in correspondence, making it necessary to rehabilitate and extend the postal systems. The University of Paris established one of the first postal services in western Europe. In 1477 the French king Louis XI established a nationwide network of relay stations serviced by mounted couriers. England opened a similar service in 1481.

Developments in North America

Early colonial mail service was irregular, haphazard, and for the most part in private hands. For a fee of one penny, colonists in seaport towns could post letters to relatives abroad with the captains of merchant ships. Incoming mail from Europe was left at seaport taverns and coffeehouses for pickup.

The first attempt to regulate foreign mail was made in 1639, when Massachusetts designated Richard Fairbanks's tavern in Boston as the official repository for overseas mail. Similar enactments were soon made elsewhere. After the English seized New Amsterdam from the Dutch, the second English governor of New York, Francis Lovelace, established an overland postal service between New York and Boston in 1672. It was the first intercity service in colonial America. Mounted courier service was soon instituted between other cities.

The Administration of Benjamin Franklin. After serving as Philadelphia's postmaster from 1737, Benjamin Franklin was appointed by the British government as deputy postmaster general for America in 1753. Franklin made many fundamental improvements in the colonial postal services. He mapped shorter routes for faster deliveries between stations and introduced the use of stagecoaches as mail carriers. In 1755, packet service was launched from England both to New York and to Charleston, S.C.

On July 26, 1775, Benjamin Franklin was appointed postmaster general by the Continental Congress. He served in this capacity until Nov. 7, 1776, when his talents were needed elsewhere.

The U.S. Postal System. The Constitution of 1789 mandated the establishment of post offices and post roads.

A commemorative stamp dated 1847 bears the portrait of Benjamin Franklin, the first postmaster general of the United States. Franklin reorganized the system, restored its finances, and improved and extended its network of routes.

The first regular airmail service was instituted between Washington, D.C., and New York City, in 1918. Until 1924, planes carried mail only during daylight hours.

Congress made the U.S. Post Office an organ of the federal government, and the first postmaster general, Samuel Osgood of Massachusetts, was appointed by President George Washington in 1789. When Osgood took office, the 13 states had only about 75 post offices.

Rates of postage—except for newspapers—had always been high. Postage for a single-sheet letter sent more than 650 km (400 mi), for example, was 25 cents (1816–45). Letter carriers earned no salaries but were paid 2 cents by the recipients for each letter they delivered. In the populous East, private letter companies began challenging the federal postal monopoly in the 1830s and '40s by providing low-cost service within and between cities.

Rowland Hill's Postal Reforms. The English educator Rowland Hill published his recommendations for post office reform in 1837. Among his innovative ideas were the ending of postage charges based on the distance letters traveled, the establishment of a uniform postage rate, and the prepayment of postage through the sale of adhesive-backed stamps sold at post offices (see PHILATELY). Hill's recommendation for the basic letter rate was one penny for each half-ounce (the average charge for letters was sixpence). Hill's reforms were adopted in England in 1840. The U.S. Congress authorized the use of adhesive postage stamps in 1847 and gradually adopted more of Hill's suggestons.

The Growth of the Postal System. The reduction of postal rates in the United States (by 1863, letter rates had shrunk to 3 cents per half-ounce) and the gradual broadening of service allowed the federal postal monopoly to grow, and by the time of the Civil War, most private posts were closed. The California Gold Rush (1849) precipitated an immediate need for transcontinental mails. Steamships provided service by way of Panama; improved overland coach routes reduced transcontinental transit to 20 days. The PONY EXPRESS (1860–61)—a private venture—offered 10- to 6-day horse courier service between Saint Joseph, Mo., and San Francisco. The transcontinental railroad (1869) provided 7-day mails between New York and San Francisco.

Established in 1863, the Railway Mail Service remained the most valued postal innovation until shortly after World War II. Day and night mails were sorted, picked up, and dropped off by clerks in special postal cars while trains sped between thousands of towns.

Rural Free Delivery became permanent in 1896 on a nationwide basis. Canceling machines (1876) and mechanical sorting devices (1907 and 1915) were introduced into various U.S. cities. Airmail was first tried in 1911. After World War II the rapid expansion of airmail service and the reduction of railway mail service drastically changed mail transportation in the United States.

New postal facilities serving an urbanized American society without railroads proved extremely costly. With virtually no mail sorted in transit, burdens in fixed post offices mounted. ZIP codes (introduced 1963) became adjuncts to key-punch sorting machines and automatic address-reading machines.

Postal Reorganization Act of 1970

On Aug. 12, 1970, President Richard M. Nixon signed into law the Postal Reorganization Act of 1970, which changed the federal Post Office Department into the U.S. Postal Service, an independent agency within the executive branch. Its purpose was to enhance the self-financing potentialities of the postal service, to increase its efficiency, to reduce the public tax burden, and to remove the service from political control. The U.S. Postal Service (USPS) often operated at a deficit, however. Despite postage-rate hikes in 1985 and 1988, there were deficits. By 1988, faced with finding ways to help cut the overall federal deficit, the USPS cut back on some services. Nonetheless, in 1990 the USPS sought and was granted another rate increase.

New Postal Service Technology

Recognizing that the utilization of electronic automation could help contain rising costs while helping to meet increasing public demands for faster delivery services, the USPS has conducted feasibility studies on available technologies. To pave the way for such improvements, it developed the "ZIP + 4," the nine-digit code system that began, with congressional authorization, in October 1983.

Postal Union, Universal The Universal Postal Union (UPU) was established in 1875 under the Universal Postal Convention of 1874 and became a specialized agency of the United Nations in 1948. The UPU's permanent headquarters is at Bern, Switzerland. It provides information and technical advice to assist cooperating nations in improving their postal services. In 1990 it had 169 members. Each country, under the postal convention, pays transportation charges to members who carry international mail across their borders. The charges are determined by the UPU. The UPU's governing body is the Universal Postal Congress, which meets every 5 years.

---

poster The term *poster* was originally used (c.1838) in England to refer to a printed sheet of paper that com-

This advertisement for a railroad company is typical of the Art Nouveau posters of Alfons Mucha, who specialized in drawing idealized women with long hair, flowers, and flowing dresses, all done in elaborate detail.

bined text and illustration. Posters were displayed in public places as announcement or advertisement. The design of these early utilitarian posters gradually became more ambitious as they began to compete with one another to catch the public's eye for commercial, promotional, or political reasons.

By 1845 gifted French artists such as Paul GAVARNI were designing elaborate posters. The mass production of posters was aided by such developments as the power press—which by 1848 could print as many as 10,000 sheets an hour—and by improvements in color lithography.

The first to take advantage of these inventions was the French artist Jules Chéret (1836–1932). While working in England, he saw and admired American circus posters, which, although crudely designed and garishly colored, had the animation and vividness of folk art. From about 1866, Chéret tried to bring into his designs some of this zest, and by the mid-1870s his work had persuaded both the public and the critics that a new art form had been created.

In the 1890s such major artists as Aubrey BEARDSLEY, Pierre BONNARD, and Henri de TOULOUSE-LAUTREC brought their genius to poster design; some Paris-based artists, including Alfons MUCHA, are almost exclusively remembered for their posters. Such artists as Maxfield Parrish, Will Bradley, Edward Penfield, M. Louise Stowell, and Ethel Reed continued the lively American tradition that had originally inspired Chéret. Germany and Austria produced excellent designers, including Gustav KLIMT, Oskar KOKOSCHKA, and Egon SCHIELE.

The outbreak of World War I in 1914 challenged poster designers on both sides to meet propaganda requirements. Alfred Leete's British recruiting poster of General Kitchener, *Your Country Needs You!* (1914), inspired the famous American imitation by James Montgomery Flagg; his stern Uncle Sam design *I Want You!* (1917) is one of the best-known posters.

The period between 1918 and the outbreak of World War II is remarkable for the inventiveness with which designers adapted the avant-garde experiments of cubism, expressionism, and surrealism into poster art. In Germany and the USSR posters became propaganda weapons, produced by such artists as El LISSITSKY. World War II revived the need for patriotic posters, and many excellent ones were designed despite the serious paper shortages that curtailed their production.

Poster art has become widely appreciated and avidly collected, partly due to the realization that the work of major artists may be bought inexpensively and—unlike reproductions of paintings, for example—as art that has been explicitly designed for its medium. Contemporary artists who contributed significantly to poster art include Saul STEINBERG and Andy WARHOL, such graphic artists as Saul Bass, Milton Glaser, Seymour Chwast, and Peter Max, and illustrator Tomi Ungerer.

This famous U.S. Army recruiting poster by James Montgomery Flagg was derived from a British poster of Lord Kitchener by Alfred Leete. Flagg appears in self-portrait as Uncle Sam. The poster, drawn to encourage Army enlistment during World War I, has been reproduced an estimated 5 million times.

postimpressionism   *Postimpressionism* is an art-historical term coined (1910) by British art critic Roger FRY to describe the various styles of painting that flourished in France during the period from about 1880 to about 1910. Generally, the term is used as a convenient chronological umbrella covering the generation of artists who sought new forms of expression in the wake of the pictorial revolution wrought by IMPRESSIONISM. Among the principal figures in this group were Pierre BONNARD, Paul CÉZANNE, Paul GAUGUIN, Odilon REDON, Georges SEURAT, Henri de TOULOUSE-LAUTREC, and Vincent van GOGH.

Although their individual styles differed profoundly, all of these artists moved away from the aesthetic program of impressionism and, in particular, from the impressionists' emphasis on depicting a narrow spectrum of visual reality. It would be a mistake to view the postimpressionists as simply rejecting their impressionist heritage; rather, they accepted the revolutionary impact of impressionism and went on to explore new aesthetic ideas, many of which

The Circus *(1887) by Georges Seurat demonstrates the artist's use of pointillism, a technique employing "points" of color to achieve luminosity. (Louvre, Paris.)*

grew out of concepts implicit in impressionism. Another connecting link between most of the postimpressionists—with the notable exception of Cézanne—was a common emphasis on surface pattern, a trait that led many con-

Paul Gauguin's Parau Parau *(1891) was painted in Tahiti after he renounced impressionism in favor of the flat shapes and pure colors of primitive art. (Hermitage, Leningrad.)*

temporary critics to use the term *decorative* to describe postimpressionist pictures. Aside from a general dissatisfaction with impressionism and a widely shared interest in surface pattern, however, the postimpressionists displayed few stylistic or thematic similarities.

postmodern architecture   Postmodern architecture developed in the 1960s in reaction to the dominant modern movement. By the mid-1970s postmodern designers were deliberately rejecting contemporary versions of modernist design, especially the corporate glass boxes of the INTERNATIONAL STYLE that had filled American cities in the post-World War II period.

The American architect Robert VENTURI first pointed the way toward a postmodern style in *Complexity and Contradiction in Architecture* (1966; rev. ed. 1977), in which he lamented the loss of traditional compositional strategies and intention to the abstract geometries of modernism. Soon, in drawings and urban and architectural designs, postmodernists staked out positions radically opposed to the modern movement. Practitioners bypass the taut austerity of modernism to inform their work with styles and techniques from the past, especially classicism, so that color, texture, monumental axes, and decoration reappear. After the initial critical polemics over Philip JOHNSON's AT&T Building in New York (1978–84) and Michael GRAVES's Portland Building in Oregon (1980–82) subsided, popular postmodernism became the style of choice for developers of commercial buildings large and small.

Johnson's AT&T tower broke with the corporate modern tradition in several ways, and even before it was finished it became the most prominent postmodern skyscraper. Clad in granite rather than glass, bedecked with arcades, arches, and even rustication, the AT&T Building reintroduced the old base-shaft-crown scheme. Its most conspicuous feature, however, was the crowning pediment with an opening (orbiculum). Suddenly major corporations and developers vied for the most striking skyline signature.

A second major icon of postmodern office space is Graves's Portland Building. Graves broke open the color field and the possible historical sources an architect might appeal to in design. A green tile base and a small rectangular crown frame a garlanded, cream shaft, which in turn contains sets of six-story groups of concrete pilasters topped by huge capitals and a massive reddish brown keystone, with the rest of the shaft punctuated by windows.

Both the Portland and the AT&T buildings pale by comparison with Charles MOORE's contribution to New Orleans, the Piazza d'Italia (1975–78). Moore gives colonnades of the five Roman orders surrounding the fountain a sixth "Delicatessen" order, from which point the Piazza descends into an unrestrained spoof of classicism.

The work of a number of important architects, including Richard MEIER (United States), James STIRLING (Britain), and Aldo Rossi (Italy), is sometimes classified as postmodern. While these architects loosen the constraints of the narrow functionalism of postwar design, however, none decorates in the manner of Johnson, Graves, and

Charles Moore's Saint Joseph's Fountain, *a profusion of classical forms at the center of Piazza d'Italia (1975–78) in New Orleans, characterizes the eclecticism of Moore's postmodernism.*

Moore. One of the few postmodern designers of residences is Robert A. M. STERN, who presented the style in the PBS television series, "Pride of Place" (1986).

Paolo Portoghesi (Italy) introduced postmodernism on an international scale in the 1980 Venice Biennale, where the streets of facades by various designers aptly conveyed the emphasis on surface manipulation upon which this style depends. Significantly, beneath their newly decorative skins of granite and stucco still beat the hearts of traditional modernist reinforced steel-and-concrete structures. Postmodernists explore neither structural innovation nor social and political purpose, perhaps here most definitively departing from the premises of modernism.

postmortem examination   see AUTOPSY

postulate   see AXIOM

potash   see POTASSIUM

---

potassium [puh-tas'-ee-uhm]   The chemical element potassium is a soft, light, silver white metal. It is one of the ALKALI METALS of Group IA of the periodic table. Its chemical symbol is K (from *kalium*, the Latinized version of the Arabic word for "alkali"), its atomic number is 19, and its atomic weight is 39.098.

Potash, or potassium carbonate (K_2CO_3), was well known and had important industrial uses in glass manufacture well before 1700; it was often mistaken, however, for sodium carbonate (Na_2CO_3), and only their decidedly different sources prevented total confusion. Sodium carbonate (soda) is most often found as a mineral; potash was originally derived from the ashes of vegetable materials. Even before the discovery and differentiation of potassium and sodium, potash and sodium carbonate could be identified by their crystal structures. On Oct. 6, 1807, Sir Humphry Davy connected a piece of solid potash to the poles of a battery and caused the release of a new metal at the negative pole. He named it potassium, from potash, and within a short time had determined many of its physical and chemical properties.

Occurrence. In cosmic abundance potassium is the 20th most common element; in solar abundance, 17th; and in the Earth's crust, 7th. About 2.6% of the Earth's crust consists of potassium. It is far too reactive to exist in the free state and thus occurs combined as compounds such as carnallite ($KMgCl_3 \cdot 6H_2O$), orthoclase feldspar [$KAl(Si_3O_8)$], leucite [$KAl(SiO_3)_2$], potash mica [$KH_2Al_2(SiO_4)_3$], and kaolin. Commercial quantities of potassium oxide are found in Searle's Lake, Calif.; Carlsbad, N.Mex.; and other sites in Europe and Canada. Potassium can be recovered from the ashes of plants, which remove it from the soil, and from seawater.

Chemical Properties. Potassium, as an alkali metal, is one of the most reactive metals and forms only ionic bonds. It readily reacts with the halogens to form potassium halides and with oxygen to form potassium oxide (K_2O) and potassium peroxide (K_2O_2).

Potassium reacts with sodium to form an intermetallic compound, KNa_2. It reacts violently with water and explosively both with acids and with liquid bromine and forms an explosive carbonyl, $K_2(OC\equiv CO)$, with carbon monoxide. An intimate mixture of 75% potassium nitrate (KNO_3), 15% carbon (charcoal), and 10% sulfur is the "black powder" used as gunpowder for more than 2,200 years.

Biological Role. Potassium, like sodium, is essential to all life. Involved in ACTIVE TRANSPORT, the process of moving substances in and out of cells, it constitutes about 0.06 percent of the atoms in the human body. Whereas sodium ions are found primarily in intercellular fluids, about 99 percent of the body's potassium lies within the cells. Together, these ions help to regulate cellular osmotic pressure and acidity, or pH, levels. Potassium plays a key role in muscle activity and the transmission of nerve impulses. It is also involved in cellular enzyme functions. An abnormally low level of potassium in blood serum causes cardiac abnormalities, and an abnormally high level leads to a heart attack. Such changes in level, which are controlled by the kidneys, can result from various diseases. Potassium is present in most food substances, so a diet deficient in the substance is unlikely.

Production. Except for its greater reactivity, potassium is similar to sodium. It can be produced by electrolytic reduction of fused potassium hydroxide (KOH) or fused potassium chloride (KCl). Although this method is occasionally used to make laboratory quantities of the metal, the energy requirements are too great for commercial production of the metal.

Commercial uses of potassium are most often also satisfied by the more easily recovered sodium. Therefore only modest amounts of the former metal are produced. One industrial method of production uses sodium vapor to reduce molten potassium chloride at 880° C. The potassium vapor formed is drawn off and condensed to liquid metal.

Important Compounds and Uses. When dispersed on supports of carbon or potassium carbonate (K_2CO_3), metallic potassium is used as a catalyst for various reactions, such as the dimerization of propene to 4-methyl-1-pentene. Dissolved in mercury to form an amalgam, potassium metal yields a liquid reducing agent. Dissolved in alcohols it gives alkoxides, which are reducing agents and also a source of nucleophilic ions. Potassium alkyls can be used for metallation reactions and when dispersed on an inert support may act as a catalyst in the polymerization or isomerization of alkenes.

Because potassium is vital to plant growth, large quantities are annually used in the form of KNO_3. Until World War I the United States imported most of its potassium nitrate from the mines in the prehistoric seabeds of Europe. When these sources became unavailable during the war, the brines of Searles Lake, Calif., became the principal source of this chemical. Until the improvement (1919) of equipment and methods, however, separation methods were inefficient.

Potassium phosphate (K_3PO_4) is also an important potassium salt. For many years large quantities of potassium phosphate have been used as "builders" in enhancing surfactant performance of detergents. This use is now decreasing in response to the need to remove phosphates from the environment.

Potassium carbonate (K_2CO_3) is a third important potassium compound. It is prepared by the Leblanc process from potassium chloride (KCl) and magnesium carbonate ($MgCO_3$). Its principal use is in the manufacture of glass.

---

potato White potatoes are edible tubers that grow at the end of underground stems of the plant *Solanum tuberosum*, a member of the NIGHTSHADE family. Above ground, the plant has a stem and coarse, dark green leaves resembling those of the tomato. Its flowers range from white to purple, and occasionally fruits develop that resemble small green tomatoes. Like the berries of the nightshade, these fruits are poisonous. The tuber's skin ranges from tan to purple, and its flesh is usually white or light yellow, although in some Andean varieties it is purple. The tuber has external buds, or "eyes," that can sprout into new plants. These eyes, rather than the seeds of the fruit, are planted to grow a new crop.

Food Value. According to food experts, a diet of potatoes and milk will supply all the nutrients the human body needs. Potatoes contain plentiful carbohydrates and

The white potato is a herbaceous plant with stems that grow up to 1 m (3 ft) long, odd-pinnate compound leaves, and clusters of white to purple flowers that grow to 2.5 cm (1 in) across. The edible portion of the plant is a tuber with tan to purple skin.

some protein, calcium, and niacin. They also contain a considerable amount of vitamin C. They are cooked fresh and can also be frozen or dried. They are processed into flour, starch, and alcohol and are used as fodder, especially in Europe. In the United States, annual per-capita consumption is 19 kg (42 lb) of fresh potatoes and 13 kg (30 lb) of processed potatoes, such as frozen french fries and potato chips.

Cultivation. Potatoes are the fourth largest world crop, surpassed only by wheat, rice, and corn. The leading potato-growing countries in 1990 were the USSR, China, Poland, and the United States. The leading U.S. states, in order of production, were Idaho, Washington, Maine, Oregon, and Colorado.

History. The potato plant, native to the Peruvian Andes, was, along with maize, a staple of the Inca diet. It was introduced into Europe by 16th-century Spanish explorers. Because the potato is a nightshade, it was at first shunned as a food by Europeans. It was supposedly endowed with powers such as the ability to cure impotence, and so long as the plant remained rare in Europe, its price often reached astronomical heights. By 1573, however, it was being grown in Spain, and shortly thereafter in the Low Countries and in Switzerland.

The English were familiar with the potato by 1586, but only in the mid-18th century was it first planted as a food crop there. Because the plant grows well in cool, moist areas and is a reliable, uncomplicated crop, potatoes soon became a major food staple, particularly in Ireland. (Today the vegetable is often called the "Irish" potato, to distinguish it from the unrelated sweet potato.) When a potato blight caused the crop to fail (1845–47), about 1 million people perished in Ireland and an equal number emigrated. Immigrants had already brought the potato to North America by then, and it was first grown in volume in Londonderry, N.H., in 1719.

Potawatomi [paht-uh-waht'-uh-mee] The Potawatomi, an Algonquian tribe of North American Indians, showed great skill in adapting to the fur trade and early Euro-American intrusions in their territory; they negotiated more treaties with the British and Americans than any other tribe. By the late 1640s they had been driven out of their villages and maize fields in lower Michigan into a refuge in northeastern Wisconsin, which was the base for their territorial expansion.

In the 1760s the Potawatomi started abandoning the use of birchbark canoes in favor of horses, which they obtained primarily through raids on American settlements. By 1812 they had expanded their tribal lands to include much of present-day Wisconsin, Michigan, Illinois, and Indiana. When they surrendered their Great Lakes lands to the United States in the 1830s, the tribe's members divided. Some moved into northern Wisconsin and Michigan, others migrated west to Iowa, Oklahoma, and Kansas, and about one-third of the population fled to Ontario. In 1989 the Potawatomi population on or near U.S. federal reservations was about 6,350.

Potemkin, Grigory Aleksandrovich [poh-tem'-kin] Grigory Aleksandrovich Potemkin, b. Sept. 24 (N.S.), 1739, d. Oct. 16 (N.S.), 1791, as a young Guards officer, helped CATHERINE II seize power in 1762. One of Catherine's "official favorites," or lovers (1774–76), and her most trusted and powerful advisor and minister until the late 1780s, he became the richest man in Russia.

An empire builder, Potemkin organized the war against Turkey (1768–74; see RUSSO-TURKISH WARS), which brought the southern steppes bordering the Black Sea under Russian control, and then administered and organized these territories of "New Russia." He built the Russian naval base at Sevastopol on the Black Sea and the city of Ekaterinoslav on the Dnepr River. In 1787, Potemkin arranged a triumphant tour into the region for Catherine, who was accompanied by Holy Roman Emperor Joseph II.

potential, electric Electric or electrostatic potential, often confused with voltage, is the capability of doing electrical work as a result of the separation of electrical charge. In theory, the potential at a point in space is the work done against the electric forces in bringing a test charge to that position. The actual calculation follows directly from COULOMB'S LAW. Essentially, then, the electric potential is the energy the test charge possesses in the electrostatic force field of all the electric charges that influence it. The analogy to the Earth's gravitational field is the increased gravitational potential a mass acquires by moving to a higher position. In practice, potential may be calculated from the physical and electrical properties of a system, such as a capacitor.

potential energy see ENERGY

potlatch [paht'-lach] The potlatch was an institutionalized procedure of North American Indians of the Northwest Coast for formally assuming hereditary rights and ceremoniously distributing valuables. Social status and its symbols were hereditary. Honorific names, crests, ceremonial paraphernalia, songs, and dances were considered property, to be transmitted according to fixed rules of descent. The inheritance had to be claimed before guests to whom gifts were given. Subsequently, guests validated claims by inviting their host by the name he had claimed and seating him in the claimed place in a formal seating order. Thus the purpose of potlatching was not to achieve status but rather to assume an inherited status.

Among the HAIDA, TSIMSHIAN, and TLINGIT, major potlatches were part of a chief's mortuary observances for investiture of his recognized heir; among the KWAKIUTL, a chief normally potlatched to transfer his position to his heir. "Rivalry potlatches" occurred when, with no living direct heirs, remote relatives claimed the right to the vacant status. The term *potlatch* comes from traders' Chinook jargon; each Northwest Coast language had its own term.

Potomac River [puh-toh'-mik] The 459-km-long (285-mi) Potomac River is formed southeast of Cumberland, Md., by the confluence of its north and south branches. The river flows northeast, then southeast to Harper's Ferry, W.Va., where it is joined by its largest tributary, the SHENANDOAH RIVER. The Potomac empties into Chesapeake Bay. The river is navigable by large ships upstream to Washington, D.C.

Potosí [poh-toh-see'] The city of Potosí lies in the Andes mountains of south central Bolivia. It has a population of 103,183 (1982 est.). Situated at the base of the Cerro Rico ("rich hill"), one of the world's richest ore mountains, Potosí is also one of the world's highest cities. The Cerro Rico is a source of tin, silver, tungsten, and copper. Potosí also manufactures mining and electrical equipment.

Potosí was founded by Spaniards in 1545 after the discovery of silver in the area. During the early silver-mining boom, the town's population grew rapidly, reaching 160,000 by 1645. Isolation, silver-ore exhaustion, and floods led to the city's decline in the 18th century. Improved mining technology and the discovery of tin in the area led to Potosí's rebirth in the late 19th century. Many of the old Spanish colonial buildings have been restored, including the Royal Mint House and the Royal Treasury. Tomás Frías University was founded there in 1892.

Potsdam [pohts'-dahm] The German city of Potsdam lies to the southwest of Berlin on the Havel River. Its population is 141,662 (1987 est.). Locomotives, boats, electrical equipment, drugs, musical instruments, textiles, and foodstuffs are produced there. Among the city's landmarks are Sans Souci Palace (1745–47), the New Palace (1763–69), the Garrison Church (1731–35), the Brandenburg Gate (1770), and the Church of St. Nicholas (1830–49).

Potsdam was probably settled by Slavs in the 10th century. Albert I, margrave of Brandenburg, fortified the town during the 12th century. Potsdam grew rapidly in importance after Frederick William, elector of Brandenburg, took up residence there in 1660. Many of the city's landmarks date to the reign (1740–86) of Frederick II of Prussia, who chose Potsdam as his chief residence. It was a favored residence of later Prussian kings, and their successors, the German emperors, also lived in Potsdam. The city was heavily bombed during World War II. In 1945 the Potsdam Conference was held there to determine the future government of defeated Germany.

Potsdam Conference The Potsdam Conference, July 17–Aug. 2, 1945, at Potsdam, Germany, was the final Allied summit meeting of WORLD WAR II. Delegations were led by U.S. President Harry S. TRUMAN, Soviet leader Joseph STALIN, and British Prime Minister Winston CHURCHILL, whose place was later taken by his successor, Clement ATTLEE. They dealt with issues arising from the defeat of Germany and the war against Japan.

The conference established machinery for drafting peace treaties with Italy and the minor Axis nations and solidified plans for the military occupation of Germany. It agreed upon German disarmament and the punishment of leading Nazis as war criminals. The USSR renewed a pledge to declare war against Japan.

Foreshadowing the COLD WAR, the USSR and the Western nations disagreed on several major issues—the amount of German reparations, the ultimate boundaries and political unification of Germany, the future governments of Eastern Europe, and Soviet demands in the Mediterranean region.

Potter, Beatrix The English author Helen Beatrix Potter, b. July 28, 1866, d. Dec. 22, 1943, wrote and il-

Beatrix Potter, an English author and illustrator of children's fiction, is portrayed at Hill Top Farm, Westmoreland, the setting for many of her stories. Potter, whose single most memorable work remains The Tale of Peter Rabbit *(1901), also executed the watercolor illustrations for her stories.*

lustrated about 28 children's stories, all with animals as characters. Her first books, some of which evolved out of letters she had written to children, include *The Tale of Peter Rabbit* (1901) and *The Tailor of Gloucester* (1902). The original illustrations for all of her works are now in the Tate Gallery in London. In 1905, Potter became engaged to Norman Warne, the publisher of most of her books, but he died before they could be married.

See also: CHILDREN'S LITERATURE.

potter's wheel A potter's wheel is a revolving disk on which clay may be shaped into dishes, vases, and other round forms. The modern wheel is turned by a motor, or by a weighted kickwheel that is mounted at the base of the device and revolves at a push from the potter's foot. Among the oldest of mechanical devices, early forms of the wheel—hand-turned *tournettes*, or turntables—date from about 3250 BC in the Middle East. In China, similar wheels were in use by the 2d millennium BC. In ancient Greece such turntables were large and heavy enough to revolve for some time by themselves, once they had been given sufficient momentum. The kickwheel did not come into wide use until much later—in Egypt, for example, only in late dynastic times, around 300 BC.

pottery and porcelain The production of pottery is one of the most ancient arts. Excavations in the Near East have revealed that primitive fired-clay vessels were made there more than 7,000 years ago. In the Far East ancient Chinese potters had developed characteristic techniques by about 5000 BC. In the New World many pre-Columbian American cultures developed highly artistic, unique pottery traditions. After general sections on basic pottery types and decorating techniques, this article focuses on the development of Western pottery since the beginning of the Renaissance. For detailed treatment of ancient Western and non-Western pottery, see CHINESE ART AND ARCHITECTURE; EGYPT, ANCIENT; GREEK ART; ISLAMIC ART AND ARCHITECTURE; JAPANESE ART AND ARCHITECTURE; KOREAN ART; MESOPOTAMIA; PERSIAN ART AND ARCHITECTURE; and PRE-COLUMBIAN ART AND ARCHITECTURE. For detailed treatment of manufacturing techniques, see CERAMICS.

Types of Wares

Pottery comprises three distinctive types of wares. The first type, earthenware, has been made following virtually the same techniques since ancient times; only in the modern era has mass production brought changes in materials and methods. Earthenware is basically composed of clay—often blended clays—and baked hard, the degree of hardness depending on the intensity of the heat. After the invention of glazing, earthenwares were coated with GLAZE to render them waterproof; sometimes glaze was applied decoratively. It was found that, when fired at great heat, the clay body became nonporous. This second type of pottery, called stoneware, came to be preferred for domestic use.

The third type of pottery, porcelain, is a Chinese inven-

These earthernware vessels from the 3d millennium BC were excavated from megalithic burial sites in Denmark. A bowl (top) found in northern Jutland features impressed geometric patterns typical of late Neolithic pottery. Two pottery vessels (center, bottom) from a tomb in west Jutland display decorations characteristic of the Schnurkeramik ("corded ware") culture of northern Europe. (Nationalmuseet, Copenhagen.)

tion that appeared when feldspathic material in a fusible state was incorporated in a stoneware composition. The ancient Chinese called decayed feldspar *kaolin* (meaning "high place," where it was originally found); this substance is known in the West as china clay. "True" porcelain consists of a kaolin hard-paste body, extremely glassy and smooth, produced by high-temperature firing. Soft porcelain, invariably translucent and lead glazed, is produced from a composition of ground glass and other ingredients including white clay and fired at a low temperature. The latter was widely produced by 18th-century European potters. Porcelain was probably first made by Chinese potters toward the end of the Han period (206 BC–AD 220), when pottery generally became more refined in body, form, and decoration.

Basic pottery techniques have varied little except in ancient America, where the potter's wheel was unknown. Among the requisites of success are correct composition of the clay body by using balanced materials; skill in shaping the wet clay on the wheel or pressing it into molds; and, most important, firing at the correct temperature.

Decorating Techniques

In the course of their long history potters have used many decorating techniques. Ancient potters in Egypt, Mesopotamia, Greece, northern India, and the high regions of Central Asia (where primitive TERRA-COTTA figures associated with religious cults were produced) frequently decorated wares with impressed or incised designs. A notable incising technique developed more recently was that of Korean potters working in the Koryo period (918–1392). These artisans began by ornamenting their CELADON wares with delicately incised and impressed patterns and later developed elaborate inlay by filling incised lines with colored slip (semiliquid clay). Black and white slip was used most effectively for inlaying colored porcelains.

The sgraffito, or "scratched," technique used by Italian potters before the 15th century was first used during the Song dynasty (960–1279) in China. By the 16th century Italian potters working mainly in Padua and Bologna were incising designs on red or buff earthenware that had been coated with ordinary transparent lead glaze. After firing, the wares were dipped into white clay slip; by cutting through the white slip, the artist produced a design on the exposed red or buff body. Pigments were also sometimes applied. After a further coating of lead glaze the ware was fired a second time.

The origin of glazes and glazing techniques is unknown, but the fine lustrous glazes developed in China surely began with a simple glaze that served to cover earthenware and render it watertight. Under the Han emperors the use of lead glaze increased, and wood ash was incorporated in its composition, imparting a dullish brown or gray green coloring, somewhat blotchy and occasionally iridescent. Colored glazes were developed and used to brilliant effect by Tang and Song potters. Many connoisseurs, however, feel that the pure white porcelain, called blanc de chine, which first appeared during the Ming dynasty, is the most serenely beautiful of all Chinese ceramics. Dehua potters in Fujian province, working during the 17th century, produced their blanc de chine masterpieces in the purest white porcelain coated with a thick white glaze.

Salt glaze, used by English potters during the early 1700s, may well have been known to the Chinese but was not used by them. Near Eastern potters glazed wares in ancient times. Potters in Mesopotamia and Iran commonly used an alkaline glaze made of quartz mixed with sodium and potassium. An admixture of colored metallic oxides, mostly lead, was introduced later.

Painting on pottery and porcelain became richly colorful in many regions and periods. Decorative brush painting directly on the baked clay reached its zenith in China during the Ming dynasty (1368–1644). It is believed that the appearance in China of 13th-century brush-decorated wares from Persia, painted in blue cobalt under the glaze, inspired the so-called blue-and-white style that prevailed for a long time. The overglaze enamel decorations executed during the reign of Zheng Hua (1465–87), which were

This Ming jar dating from the Xuande period (1426–35) of the Ming dynasty was created at the imperial porcelain factory at Jingdezhen. It was during this period that the distinctive blue-and-white ware characteristic of the Ming period attained its highest degree of perfection. (Metropolitan Museum of Art, New York City.)

never surpassed in China, incorporated flowers, foliage, and figure subjects against backgrounds of arabesques and scrollwork. Designs enclosed within dark blue outlines were filled in with brilliant color. Enamel decoration of superb quality was also executed in Japan during the Edo period (1615–1868).

In the ancient Aegean, the potter's art developed continuously from the Neolithic period and through the periods of the Minoan and Mycenaean civilizations. In ancient Greece it reached its height between the 6th and 4th centuries BC. The finest Greek pottery, especially Attic vases, was exquisitely proportioned and often decorated with finely painted relief work. Unlike artisans in Egypt, Mesopotamia, and Persia, the Attic potters did not apply heavy glaze to their wares. Neither a glaze nor a varnish, the unique gloss commonly seen on Attic pottery and similar wares made elsewhere in Greece still baffles those who have tried to determine its formula and method of application.

In the Islamic world, ceramic decorative art flowered with the creation of a great diversity of painted wares. Painted luster decoration on pottery originated in Mesopotamia and spread to ancient Egypt; later, under Islam in Persia, this type of decoration on white-glazed wares became incredibly brilliant. Islamic luster-painted wares were later imitated by Italian potters during the Renaissance.

Major Traditions in the West

After the fall of the ancient Roman Empire, potters in Europe produced little other than repetitive utilitarian wares until the end of the Middle Ages.

Earthenware. A distinctive type of earthenware known as MAJOLICA, which was derived from Chinese porcelain, appeared in Italy during the last quarter of the 14th century, probably inspired by the Hispano-Moresque luster-decorated ware of Spanish origin and introduced into Italy by Majorcan seagoing traders. Whether thrown on the wheel or pressed into molds, majolica ware was fired once to obtain a brown or buff body, then dipped in glaze composed of lead and tin oxide with a silicate of potash. The

A 17th-century Japanese porcelain Kakiemon jar displays the brilliant enamel overglaze technique characteristic of Kakiemon ware. The Kakiemon family began producing a high-quality porcelain ware near Arita, on the island of Kyushu, soon after a clay suitable for porcelain was discovered there in 1616. (Smithsonian Institution, Freer Gallery of Art, Washington, D.C.)

(Below) *A Greek red-figure Attic calyx-krater (c.515 BC) shows a scene from the* Iliad. *In red-figure ware, black pigment is applied to the ground, leaving the figures the color of the red clay. (Metropolitan Museum of Art, New York City.)*

(Below) *This detail is from a tile wall panel (1600–50) thought to have been part of the Chihil Sutun, Isfahan. In Persia, tile replaced mosaic as the primary form of architectural decoration during the 16th century. (Metropolitan Museum of Art, New York City.)*

(Above) *This Meissen porcelain figure, representing Africa, was part of a continent series designed (1746–59) by Johann Joachim Kändler. (Cooper-Hewitt Museum, New York.)*

(Below) *Sumptuous gilt vases and a jardiniere, manufactured at Sèvres during the late 18th century, are decorated with delicate miniatures and the brilliant colors that distinguish much Sèvres ware. (Frick Collection, New York City.)*

opaque glaze presented a surface that was suitable to receive decoration. A second firing after decoration fixed the white glaze to the body and the pigments to the glaze, so that the colors became permanently preserved. Application of metallic luster pigments required great skill because these colors were extremely volatile.

Luca della Robbia (see DELLA ROBBIA family) did not, as has been held, invent the enamel tin-glazing process; nevertheless, his work raised majolica production from a craft to high art in Italy. Not only did he use blue-and-white enamels in decorative work, but, as a sculptor, he also used the majolica technique to add brilliance to the surface of his productions. By the beginning of the 15th century a revolution in style and techniques was underway, and Faenza became the thriving center of a reinvigorated pottery industry in Italy. A new, rich decorative style, known as *istoriato*, reached its zenith in the workshops of Urbino.

In early-17th-century England, attractive slipwares were produced, including the slip-decorated earthenware that was a speciality of the Toft family of potters. A kind of tin-glazed earthenware was also produced in the Netherlands, principally at Delft, beginning in the mid-17th century. Termed DELFTWARE, it was among the first European wares to be decorated with motifs inspired by Chinese and Japanese models.

Continental Porcelains. Eventually, European potters, who much admired the porcelain of the Far East, attempted to imitate it, but the formula remained elusive. In March 1709, Augustus II of Saxony announced that his ceramist Jöhann Böttger (1682–1719) had discovered how to make porcelain, and the first European royal porcelain manufactory was consequently established at Meissen, near Dresden, Germany. Throughout the century following the discovery of the porcelain formula many rival factories were set up in Germany, Austria, Italy, France, and England.

Porcelain figures were first produced in Meissen as table ornaments; the earliest examples were formed as part of sweetmeat dishes. German porcelain figures were usually produced from molds, which, in turn, were cast from an original master model made of wax, clay, or, occasionally, wood. The use of molds facilitated unlimited reproduction.

Europe's second hard-paste porcelain factory began commercial operations at Vienna in 1717. In the late 1700s at the royal Sèvres factory in France, potters experimented until they developed a remarkably white, finely textured body. Sèvres wares were painted in unique colors that no other European factory could duplicate. The bleu de roi and rose Pompadour of Sèvres wares captivated all Europe and, with the products of Meissen and Vienna, inspired English potters.

English Wares. The finest English porcelain—both soft- and hard-paste—was made between about 1745 and 1775. The first English porcelain was probably produced at Chelsea (see CHELSEA WARE) under Charles Gouyn, but his successor Nicholas Sprimont, a Flemish silversmith who took over management in 1750, was responsible for the high-quality wares, especially the superb figures for which the factory became famous. Factories at Worcester, Bow, Derby, and elsewhere also produced wares that rival those of the Continent.

Led by the ambitious, energetic, and enterprising Josiah WEDGWOOD and his successors at the Etruria factory, English potters in the late 18th and early 19th centuries became resourceful and inventive. Wedgwood's contributions consisted mainly of a much improved creamware, his celebrated jasperware, so-called black basalt, and a series of fine figures created by famous modelers and artists.

This Wedgwood jas-perware teapot (c.1785–1800) displays the simplicity and elegance of the unglazed stoneware created by the English potter Josiah Wedgwood in Etruria, Staffordshire. This type of fine-grained stoneware was ornamented with classical scenes executed in cameo-like relief.

After Wedgwood, other potters of the first half of the 19th century developed a number of new wares. Of these, Parian ware was the most outstanding and commercially successful. The name of this ware was derived from Paros, the Greek island from which sculptors in ancient times obtained the creamy or ivory-tinted marble that Parian ware resembled. The first examples of this new product, described as "statuary porcelain," issued from Copeland and Garret's factory in 1842. Pâte-sur-pâte was a paste-on-paste technique devised sometime after 1870 by Marc-Louis Solon (1835–1913) of Minton's in England. Involving both modeling and painting techniques, pâte-sur-pâte was stained Parian ware decorated with reliefs in translucent tinted or white slip, the colors being laid one upon the other. Minton wares decorated with pâte-sur-pâte became the most costly and coveted ceramic ornaments produced in England in the last quarter of the 19th century.

A superbly crafted vase (1904) of the Rookwood Potteries, a world-renowned American firm, combines a rich surface of subtly blended color and extraordinary detail with a simple, curving form. The glazed art pottery of this firm was produced until the early 1940s. (Cooper-Hewitt Museum, New York City.)

20th-Century Developments. By the late 19th century, with the development of machinery and the introduction of new technologies, the age of mass production dawned and the potter's art consequently suffered. Not until the 1930s were signs of revival in the form and decoration of ceramics discernible, principally in the productions of artist-potters who were active in Western Europe and the United States. Since the end of World War II the design and decoration of ceramics, especially ornamental wares, has been largely influenced by individual artist-artisans.

potto [paht'-oh]   The potto, *Perodicticus potto*, of western Africa, is a slow-moving, compactly built primate with a dense, woolly, brownish coat and a short tail. Pottos reach about 40 cm (16 in) in head and body length and about 1.5 kg (3.3 lb) in weight. Spines from the backbone project through the skin at the base of the neck, but their function is uncertain. Related to the lorises, pottos are nocturnal and arboreal and feed on fruits, nuts, and small animals.

The potto, a primitive primate of Africa, moves slowly along tree branches at night, searching for insects and other food with its large eyes.

Poulenc, Francis [poo-lahnk']   The French composer Francis Poulenc, b. Paris, Jan. 7, 1899, d. Jan. 30, 1963, was a prominent member of the group of postimpressionist composers known as *Les Six*. Influenced by Erik Satie, Poulenc's earliest music revealed the wit, humor, and directness that would be characteristic of all his work.

Poulenc first attracted public attention with his *Rhapsodie nègre* (1917) for baritone, string quartet, piano, flute, and clarinet, in which he used pseudo-African nonsense syllables to satirize the Parisian interest in African art. In 1936 he began composing sacred music, and in 1944 he began writing operas, an endeavor that occupied much of his later creative effort. His most successful opera, *Dialogue of the Carmelites*, received its premiere in Milan's La Scala in 1957. He was working on his fourth opera, a setting of Jean Cocteau's *La Machine Infernale*, at the time of his death. A masterful creator of melody, Poulenc composed about 50 solo songs as well as concertos, chamber music, incidental music for the theater, ballet music, sacred choral works, and short piano pieces.

poultry   Poultry is a broad classification, covering the species of domesticated birds that are raised to provide food for humans. These include the CHICKEN, TURKEY, DUCK, and GOOSE; and the GUINEA FOWL, PIGEON, PHEASANT, and other game birds. Among these food-providing birds, chickens are the most important because they are a source both of meat and of eggs. Next in importance are turkeys and ducks, which are raised commercially in the United States solely for their meat. Guinea fowl, pigeons, pheasants, and other game birds are farm raised in smaller numbers for specialized markets.

Chickens. Although an estimated 375 million chickens are raised and processed every year on general farms, the largest sources of production are commercial broiler farms. In the late 1980s these specialized farms raised, dressed, and marketed about 5.5 billion broiler chickens in the United States annually. Raised for their heavy meat content, broilers are 7- to 8-week-old chickens marketed at approximately 1 to 2.5 kg (2 to 5 lb) liveweight.

The commercial rearing of chickens, whether for meat or for EGG PRODUCTION, involves several steps. The first of these takes place at the breeding farm, where carefully bred and fed chicks are raised to lay eggs for incubation in commercial hatcheries. When the eggs from the breeding farm are hatched, the newborn chicks may be separated according to gender. With broiler-type birds both male and female chicks are reared for meat. With egg-

American-class chickens include the New Hampshire, Plymouth Rock, and Rhode Island Red. The English class includes the Australorp, Cornish, Dorking, and Sussex. The Leghorn is an important Mediterranean breed. Domestic ducks include the meat breeds White Pekin and Aylesbury and the egg breeds Khaki Campbell and Indian Runner. Domestic geese raised for meat include the Toulouse and Embden. The Small White Beltsville and the Broad-Breasted Bronze are important domestic turkey breeds.

production strains the females are reared, but the males are sacrificed at the time of sex determination. Because chickens are highly susceptible to infectious diseases, broiler chicks, in particular, are bought by the growing farm in bulk at one time, housed together in one place, and then sold together at one time to help break any potential disease cycles. They are fed a scientifically prepared mash consisting of ground corn, meat meal, fish meal, soybean meal, minerals, and vitamins. Feed additives commonly used in large-scale chicken production include antibiotics and arsenicals, which have a growth-stimulating effect; drugs to prevent specific diseases; and antioxidants, which prevent rancidity in feed.

Growing farms are an important sector of the poultry industry, and many of them are equipped with ten or more chicken houses, each of which can accommodate more than 40,000 chicks. Broiler production and processing is a highly integrated business. Processors contract with growers for most of their chickens. These are processed and sold to retail outlets and fast-food service stores.

Most breeders of poultry in the United States subscribe to the National Poultry Improvement Plan sponsored by the United States Department of Agriculture and administered by official state agencies. Under this federal program, chicken houses and hatcheries must conform to sanitary standards; blood tests on flocks are periodically conducted as a safeguard against pullorum and other diseases, pedigreed male breeding stocks are determined, and pullets are trapnested to ascertain their egg-laying performances. As a result of such measures and also of selective breeding and careful feeding, the flesh of the modern chicken is healthy and more tender than its range-raised predecessor. Moreover, chickens today mature faster and, consequently, the cost of feeding them is low in comparison to other kinds of farm-raised livestock.

Turkeys. Descended from the wild turkey, which is native to America and flourishes in some sections of the United States, the domesticated turkey is second in importance to the chicken in both Canada and the United States. A land bird capable of flight unless wing-clipped, it is bred and raised mainly for its meat. Turkeys are bred, raised, and processed very much like chickens and are ready for marketing at 18 to 22 weeks.

Ducks. Ducks are web-footed waterfowl. Like chickens, they may be bred and raised for egg-laying as well as for meat. The Khaki Campbell breed, for example, which is raised only for egg production, can actually lay just as many eggs as any breed of hen raised for the same purpose.

The most popular duck in the United States is the White Pekin. A meaty bird, the average weight of the adult male is about 4 kg (9 lb). The ducks are usually marketed at lesser weights, however. Their profit-earning potential is enhanced by the demand for duck feathers and down among manufacturers of bedding materials.

Ducks are slaughtered, bled, scalded, and rough-picked in one continuous machine operation. To remove the ducks' valuable feathers, their carcasses must be dipped in a hot, resinous wax, which is cooled to harden and then removed by machine with all feathers intact.

Geese. Geese are restless, aggressive, and intelligent birds. Also waterfowl, they are much larger in size than ducks, with adult ganders often reaching more than 12 kg (approximately 26 lb) in liveweight. Geese are bred and raised for their meat and feathers. Because their egg-laying capabilities are much less than those of chickens and ducks, their eggs are reserved for incubation to assure reproduction of the species.

Geese graze for most of their food. For this reason, most of the world's goose population is concentrated in areas where grain is in short supply and where herders are available to watch over the flocks. In some European countries these domesticated waterfowl are sometimes force-fed, or hand-stuffed, with rinsed kernels of corn to fatten their livers, which are prized as a delicacy.

Other Poultry Breeds. A few other species of poultry are raised for food, as game, or for ornamental purposes. Domesticated guinea fowl are often reared for their meat, which tastes like that of a game bird. Pheasants, quail, and grouse are raised for food and for stocking preserves. Ornamental birds include peacocks and swans.

pound The pound (lb) is a unit of weight, mass, or force in the U.S. customary system of English units and the English gravitational system. The standard avoirdupois pound, equal to 16 avoirdupois ounces, is equivalent to 0.45359237 kg. A one-pound force is equal to 4.4482 newtons. The troy pound, used for weighing precious metals, is equal to 12 troy ounces (1 troy ounce = 1.097143 avoir ounce), which is equal to 0.8228571 lb avoir or 0.3732417216 kg.

Pound, Ezra The American poet Ezra Loomis Pound, b. Hailey, Idaho, Oct. 30, 1885, d. Nov. 1, 1972, was one of the most important literary figures of the 20th century. Pound grew up in the Philadelphia suburb of Wyncote, receiving his Ph.B from Hamilton College (N.Y.) in 1905 and an M.A. from the University of Pennsylvania in 1906.

In 1908, Pound moved to Europe, not to return for decades. In 1909 he was in London, drawn by William Butler YEATS, whom he judged the greatest living poet and whose verse he helped tighten. He married the English artist Dorothy Shakespear in 1914. Early during his stay in London (which lasted until 1921), Pound was friendly with novelist Ford Madox FORD, who published some of Pound's work, and philosopher and poet T. E. HULME, who influenced Pound's ideas concerning poetic imagery. In 1912, Pound founded IMAGISM, whose tight expression and crystalline images dovetailed with his interest in Chinese poems and ideograms. With painter and writer Wyndham LEWIS, Pound also founded VORTICISM and contributed to its magazine, *Blast* (1914–15). During this time Pound launched the literary careers of T. S. ELIOT and James JOYCE—helping to edit texts, fostering publication of their work, and even arranging financial assistance for them.

Though he had been publishing collections of poems since 1908, Pound first achieved a truly individual note with *Ripostes* (1912). In 1915 he published *Cathay*, a sequence of adaptations from the ancient Chinese, mediated by the notebooks of 19th-century American orientalist Ernest Fenollosa, who had coerced cribs from Japanese instructors. In 1917 he wrote *Homage to Sextus Propertius*, a sequence of 12 adaptations from the 1st-century BC Roman poet, whose compliments to the imperial ventures of the emperor Augustus Pound read as ironic. The poem implies a comparably ironic view of British imperial-minded self-esteem.

Despite complaints about inaccuracies, Pound was arguably the most accomplished verse translator of his time. The *Cathay* and *Propertius* sequences illustrate his developing view of translation as a means, not as an end: a device for using one age or culture to highlight another. That would be the method of his lifelong work in progress, *The Cantos*, which he was starting at about this time.

Another concept important to Pound's thought was that of "sequences." Long poems—the *Iliad*, the *Aeneid*, the *Divine Comedy*—had typically been held together by a narrative. After the invention of the novel, however, prose had come to seem a more efficient form for narratives; a modern long poem seemed more workable as a sequence of shorter poems in various meters, creating and examining a common theme. The work of Yeats offers many examples. The century's best-known sequence poem, Eliot's The WASTE LAND (1922), is inestimably indebted to Pound, who helped identify inert material in a 1921 draft. His own *Cantos*, which he called "a poem including history," was a 50-year effort to test the limits of the form.

Also while still in London, Pound wrote his famous sequence *Hugh Selwyn Mauberley* (1920), a quasi-autobiographical account of a young American poet's quest to locate himself within, and simultaneously to help affect, the English literary tradition. The poet is seen as hero, and the value placed on words, on language, by a society is seen as a signpost to the health of that society.

Pound collected his shorter works in *Personae* (1926), and thereafter his efforts in verse were with The CANTOS, which appeared in successive volumes from 1926 until 1968. In 1921 he and Dorothy moved to Paris, where he aided and encouraged Joyce (who was working on *Ulysses*) and Ernest Hemingway, among many others. In 1925 the Pounds moved to Rapallo, Italy. By then he had fathered a daughter, Mary, by the American violinist Olga Rudge. Omar, his son by Dorothy, was born the following year.

Pound had meanwhile grown preoccupied with economics as seen by Maj. C. H. Douglas. The quest for foreign markets puts nations on a collision course, according to Douglas's theory, and hence, wars are inevitable. This theme winds through *The Cantos*, where many villains are international bankers. Enough of those were Jewish to fuel what would flare in the 1940s as a ruinous episode of anti-Semitism. By the time Pound repudiated (1967) that as "stupid, suburban," it had helped destroy his credibility.

In January 1941, supporting Mussolini, Pound commenced recording talks for broadcast over Rome Radio.

Ezra Pound, whose poetry, criticism, and editorial work had a profound impact upon William Butler Yeats and T. S. Eliot, left the United States in 1908 and became a central figure in the European literary avant-garde. Pound's imagist writings did much to introduce a strain of terse but evocative symbolism into modern literature.

In 1943 he was indicted for treason, and in May 1945 he was arrested and confined at the Detention Training Center, near Pisa. There, in the summer and fall, he managed to write *The Pisan Cantos*. Back in Washington, D.C., in February 1946 he was judged unfit to stand trial and confined to St. Elizabeth's Hospital. Released in April 1958 as "incurable," he returned to Italy.

The Pisan Cantos was awarded the Bollingen Prize in 1949, a year after publication. Two further sequences, *Rock-Drill* (1955) and *Thrones* (1959), followed. The 20th century's most expansive epic poem was abandoned with the 1968 *Drafts and Fragments*.

Pound, Roscoe The American educator and jurist Roscoe Pound, b. Lincoln, Nebr., Oct. 27, 1870, d. July 1, 1964, became well known for his view of law, known as "sociological jurisprudence." Approaching law as a system of social engineering, he asserted the law's need to change with changing social conditions, a view that was influential in the New Deal. Pound attended (1889–90) Harvard Law School and became a professor of law there in 1910.

pound sterling The monetary unit of Great Britain, the pound sterling was originally equal in weight to 1 pound of silver and was divided into 20 shillings of 12 pence (or pennies) each. (The penny was further divided into 4 farthings.) In 1971, Britain went on the decimal system, and the pound was divided into 100 pence (also called new pence). In the 19th and early 20th centuries, the pound sterling served as the principal medium of international payments. The pound, which is denoted in the United Kingdom by the symbol £ before the numeral, is also used by a number of other countries, chiefly members or former members of the British Commonwealth.

Poundmaker Poundmaker, b. 1826 or 1842 in the Northwest Territories of Canada, d. June or July 1886, was chief of a band of the Plains CREE Indians in southern Manitoba. His name alludes to the Plains Cree buffalo-hunting technique of creating a surround, or "pound." In 1881 he guided the Marquis of Lorne on a tour across the prairie to Calgary. With another Cree chief, Big Bear, Poundmaker was persuaded by the Canadian insurgent Louis RIEL to participate actively in the Half-Breed, or Northwest, Rebellion of 1885. He led his Cree warriors in the fights at Batouche and Cut Knife Creek in Saskatchewan. When Riel was captured, Poundmaker surrendered to Canadian authorities, who tried him and convicted him of insurrection. After a year's imprisonment he was released.

Poussin, Nicolas [poo-san']

Nicolas Poussin, b. June 1594, d. Nov. 19, 1665, a French painter who spent most of his career in Rome, was renowned as the great painter-philosopher of the baroque age. His career in Paris, where he developed his early style, is known only in brief outline, because some of the more important commissions have been lost. Poussin is documented as having been in Rome by 1624. By about 1630 he was admired for such works as *The Death of Germanicus* (1627; Minneapolis Institute of Arts) and *The Triumph of Flora* (1627; Louvre, Paris); had executed the important commission for an altarpiece for Saint Peter's Basilica, *The Martyrdom of Saint Erasmus* (1629); and with his reputation firmly established, took his place as the rival of the architect and painter Pietro da Cortona.

Although the chronology of individual works is difficult to establish, it is clear that the decade of the 1630s represented an especially fruitful and progressive stage in Poussin's development as a painter. He withdrew from competition for large, demanding public commissions and devoted himself to easel pictures on themes of his own choice. He studied ancient statuary, painting, mathematics, and optics and gave new importance to the role of landscape in his compositions: *The Adoration of the Golden Calf* (c.1633–34; National Gallery, London), *The Triumph of Neptune* (c.1636; Philadelphia Museum of Art), and *Venus Bringing Arms to Aeneas* (c.1639; Art Gallery of Toronto).

In 1640, Poussin went to France at the invitation of Louis XIII, where he was received with great enthusiasm and given the title First Painter. The demanding and critical atmosphere at court, as well as his expected role as creator of large-scale official projects, proved uncongenial to Poussin's contemplative nature, and he returned to Rome permanently in 1642.

Again Poussin dedicated himself almost exclusively to a studio practice devoted to the contemplation and resolution of self-imposed problems. He worked, for approximately a decade, in a severe and monumental style—evident in *Holy Family on the Steps* (1648; National Gallery of Art, Washington, D.C.) and *Achilles among the Daughters of Lycomedes* (1648–50; Boston Museum of Fine Arts). He also created a type of "heroic landscape" that was remarkable for its depiction of figures and architecture in dramatically rendered landscapes—as, for exam-

Summer, or Ruth and Boaz *(1660–64), an idealized biblical landscape, was painted by Nicolas Poussin, foremost French painter of the 17th century. The rational, ordered composition and heroic theme of this work reflect Poussin's conception of painting as an image of humankind's nobility. (Louvre, Paris.)*

ple, *Saint John on Patmos* (*c.*1643–44; Art Institute of Chicago) and *The Body of Phocion Carried from Athens* (1648; Collection of the Earl of Plymouth, Oakley Park, Shropshire).

In his last period, after about 1654, Poussin was plagued by ill health and became increasingly introspective. A heightened interest in human emotion was added to the statuesque monumentality of his designs, often resulting in works charged with great power of mood and psychological drama, such as *The Arcadian Shepherds* (*c.*1656; Louvre, Paris) and *The Birth of Bacchus* (1657; Fogg Art Museum, Cambridge, Mass.). The mythological landscapes created during this period rank among Poussin's most visionary and imaginative productions; they include *Landscape with Orion* (1658; Metropolitan Museum of Art, New York City) and *The Four Seasons* (1660–64; Louvre).

Despite Poussin's commanding reputation, his austere, severely classical style had little immediate influence in Italy, where the vogue was for the bold and energetic art of the Roman baroque. In France, however, Poussin's ideas were enthusiastically received and became the basis of teaching at the Académie Royale de Peinture et Sculpture under the directorship of Charles Le Brun.

poverty Poverty is the lack of goods and services necessary to maintain a minimal adequate standard of living. The definition of the word *adequate* varies, however, with the general standard of living in a society and with public attitudes toward deprivation. In poor countries it means living at subsistence level. In the United States few impoverished families face starvation, but many suffer from undernourishment.

No society distributes income evenly, but some reasons for the inequality are acceptable to a society and others are not. During the 1970s and '80s the income distribution among American families became more unequal, with the share of income received by the lowest 20% of families declining from 5.6% to 4.6%. In 1988 the top 5% of families received 3.7 times the money income of the poorest 20%, compared with 2.8 times 20 years earlier.

Measuring Poverty

The U.S. government has devised a poverty index that reflects the different consumption requirements of families depending on their size and composition, on the sex and age of the family head, and on whether they live in rural or urban areas. The designers of the poverty index determined that families of three or more persons spend approximately one-third of their income on food; the poverty level for these families was, therefore, set at three times the cost of the economy food plan. For smaller families and persons living alone, the cost of the economy food plan was multiplied by higher factors in order to compensate for the larger fixed expenses of smaller households. The poverty thresholds are updated every year to reflect

changes in the CONSUMER PRICE INDEX but not overall rises in living standards. The estimated poverty threshold based on 1989 prices was as follows:

U.S. POVERTY THRESHOLD INDEX, 1989

Family Members	Income
1	$ 6,314
2	8,075
3	9,890
4	12,675
5	14,994
6	16,927

SOURCE: U.S. Department of Commerce.

The poverty index has several flaws: (1) it does not allow for regional variations in the cost of living or for higher costs in central-city areas, where many of the poor are concentrated; (2) government poverty statistics fail to take into consideration nonmonetary benefits and assets, such as food stamps, in determining the number of poor, which if counted would reduce the numbers in the official poverty ranks; and (3) the poverty index was calculated at three times the food budget because in the 1950s the average consumer spent one-third of his or her income for food, but as this proportion has since fallen to one-sixth, the food budget should now be multiplied by a higher figure.

The growing gap between the poverty level and median family income demonstrates the inaccuracy of adjusting a poverty level for price increases but not for rising living standards and productivity gains. In 1960 the poverty threshold was nearly half the median income of a four-person family, but by 1988 the ratio had dropped to 30%. Median family income for four persons in 1960 was 1.9 times the poverty level; in 1988 it was 2.7 times the poverty level.

Alternative definitions and concepts have a major impact on poverty estimates. The Congressional Budget Office has estimated that if transfer payments—income-support programs such as SOCIAL SECURITY—are not counted, then about 20% of all Americans lived in poverty during 1988. Government income transfers are, however, included in the official poverty index, and this fact reduced the number of destitute Americans to 13.1%. If in-kind programs such as MEDICAID, subsidized housing, and food stamps were also included, then the percentage in poverty might have been reduced to 10.5%.

Identifying the Poor

Counting only cash income and excluding in-kind assistance, poverty declined substantially in the 1960s. Almost 40 million persons, or 22% of the population, were classified as poor in 1960. By 1978 the figure had fallen to approximately 24 million, or 11.7%. Special governmental efforts, such as the WAR ON POVERTY, were responsible for part of the reduction. By 1988, however, the number of poor Americans had risen to 31.9 million, or about 13%.

Blacks are three times as likely to be poor as whites. Families headed by women are nearly five times more likely to be poor than other households. Families where the head has no more than eight years of schooling are nearly five times as likely to be poor compared with families headed by a college-educated person. Minority- and female-headed units are less likely to escape from poverty than other family groups.

The Elderly. In 1988, 12% of people aged 65 or older lived in poverty, compared with 10.5% of younger adults. A drop in the number of aged poor—from 4.3 million (about 20%) in 1971 to 3.5 million in 1988—was due largely to more generous social-security benefits, private pensions, and veterans' pensions.

Few elderly people hold jobs, and that is the main cause of poverty among this group. As the elderly live longer, meeting their income needs, especially for health care, becomes increasingly burdensome. Often the only practicable way to help the aged poor is to give them income support.

Children. Two of five persons classified as poor in 1988 were children under 18 years of age. Low-income families are often driven into poverty by the birth of additional children. In 1988, 48.2% of families with five or more children lived in poverty, compared with 14.1% of two-children families.

In 1988, 3.6 million poor families (including 12.6 million children) were headed by females. More than half of all poor families are now headed by women, and female-headed households with children are six times more likely to be poor than two-parent families. The feminization of poverty threatens to create a permanent dependent underclass.

The Working Poor. Although the problem is often overstated, unemployment remains a major cause of poverty. Being employed, however, does not in itself guarantee an adequate income. In 1988, 1.9 million persons, or 40% of the poor, worked full-time year-round and still remained poor. The working poor also experience other labor-market difficulties. Many leave the work force voluntarily because of illness or disability or because they become discouraged about finding a job and stop looking. A greater number of the working poor are employed at low-paying jobs.

The problems for the working poor are frequent joblessness, low wages, deficient education, and inadequate skills. The plight of the working poor can be alleviated by employment programs that streamline the operation of the labor market, increase the productivity of low-income workers, and create opportunities for employment and advancement.

The Unemployed. Many of the unemployed poor of working age cannot find jobs because of such factors as personal handicaps or a scarcity of jobs. Illness and family responsibilities are the main reasons poor people do not work. In 1988, 11% of poor family heads did not work at all because they claimed to be ill or disabled. Another 39% were keeping house, unable to find work, or going to school. Children not only increase income requirements but also keep mothers from working and thereby limit available income.

Strategies for Helping the Poor

Many basic needs of the poor cannot be filled simply by increasing their incomes. Young people and family heads require both daily subsistence and help in acquiring work skills. Medical care and nursing homes are key concerns for the aged. Children also require health care and education. For all poor people, income support can be supplemented by direct provision of housing, medical services, food, and other goods and services.

Since the NEW DEAL in the 1930s, the United States has developed an intricate series of programs to help the economically disadvantaged. Four types of programs exist: cash support; direct provision of such necessities as food, shelter, and medical care; preventive and compensatory help for children and young people; and attempts to restructure existing institutions or to help the poor cope with their problems.

Cash Support. Income-support programs are the main form of assistance to the poor. One problem with cash subsidies is that payments to employable persons may diminish their incentive to work; another is that income subsidies may not be used to provide basic sustenance as intended. Public opinion may also be averse to paying allowances to poor people who are idle.

Cash-income support programs include UNEMPLOYMENT INSURANCE; WORKERS' COMPENSATION; old age, survivors', and disability insurance; public assistance (welfare); and veterans' PENSIONS. These programs aim primarily at persons outside the work force or those who cannot find employment. More comprehensive programs, such as a guaranteed income, a negative income tax, and family allowances, have also been proposed to distribute income subsidies according to need rather than labor-force status.

Direct Provision of Necessities. Programs provide goods and services directly to the needy to supplement their cash income. Whatever the merits of helping the poor with cash or in-kind income, public attention must usually be focused on a specific problem in order for it to receive political attention, as with increased food appropriations for the poor in the late 1960s.

Sometimes, because the necessary goods and services are not available on the market, direct provision is the most effective way of supplying essential aid. Low-cost housing, for example, desperately needed to combat HOMELESSNESS, is not profitable to construct and will not be provided by the private sector without direct government action.

Services to Help Children and Youth. Helping families to avoid having more children than they desire is one of the most productive ways of eliminating poverty. Proper care for mother and child ensures that the young will be healthy. The federal government also provides some compensatory education from preschool (see HEAD START) to college for children of the poor.

Restructuring Institutions. Programs intended to restructure institutions or to improve the ability of the poor to work with existing institutions are meant to attack the causes of poverty rather than merely its symptoms. Such programs are generally aimed at offering more opportunities to the employable poor. They fall into three groups: (1) programs to give the individual a competitive edge in the labor market through training, placement, and rehabilitation and through incentives to private employers to hire the disadvantaged; (2) programs to restructure the labor market by establishing a minimum wage, offering public employment, and combating discrimination; and (3) programs to redevelop depressed urban and rural areas suffering from chronic unemployment.

The Scale of Antipoverty Efforts

In 1987, U.S. programs for the poor carried an estimated price tag of $165 billion, 13% of the federal budget and 7% of total state and local budgets. In 1988 the federal government spent about $3,500 per poor person, while state and local governments spent an additional $1,350. Adjusted for inflation, the annual per capita federal outlay for the nonaged poor declined by more than a fifth between 1980 and 1988, from $2,300 to $1,800. The difference between the family income of the poor and the poverty line—the poverty gap—shows that the poor have become poorer since the 1970s.

See also: EMPLOYMENT AND UNEMPLOYMENT; SOCIAL AND WELFARE SERVICES.

▬

Powell, Adam Clayton, Jr.   Adam Clayton Powell, Jr., b. New Haven, Conn., Nov. 29, 1908, d. Apr. 4, 1972, was a minister, civil rights leader, and controversial Democratic U.S. representative (1945–67, 1969–71) from New York City. A graduate (1930) of Colgate University, Powell entered the ministry and succeeded his father as pastor of Harlem's Abyssinian Baptist church. Using it as a political base, he won election to Congress in 1944. He had numerous legislative successes, especially in equal-employment opportunity. Powell became chair of the House Committee on Education and Labor in 1961. In 1967 the House of Representatives stripped him of his seat in Congress because of a number of dubious practices, including misuse of public funds and ignoring a court order. The House readmitted him in Janu-

Adam Clayton Powell, Jr., represented Harlem in the U.S. Congress for almost 25 years. The charismatic Powell never lost the support of his constituents, even when he underwent censure for misuse of funds.

ary 1969 after he won a special 1967 election and the regular 1968 election, but he was stripped of his seniority and chairmanship. In June 1969 the Supreme Court declared his expulsion unconstitutional.

▬

Powell, Anthony [pohl]   Anthony Dymoke Powell, b. Dec. 21, 1905, an English novelist, won critical acclaim for his 12-volume novel cycle, *A Dance to the Music of Time*. Starting in 1951 with *A Question of Upbringing* and ending in 1976 with *Hearing Secret Harmonies*, the novels constitute a 60-year social history of the author's own generation and class, in which an extended gallery of upper- and middle-class characters are followed from World War I to the present. Powell's prewar comedies of manners include *Afternoon Men* (1931), *Agents and Patients* (1936), and *What's Become of Waring?* (1939).

▬

Powell, John Wesley   An American geologist and ethnologist, John Wesley Powell, b. Mount Morris, N.Y., Mar. 24, 1834, d. Sept. 23, 1902, was the first to classify American Indian languages. Powell taught at Illinois Wesleyan University (1865) and Illinois Normal College (1867). In 1869 he and 11 others—financed by the Smithsonian Institution—explored the Green and Colorado river canyons. His further explorations, conducted for the federal government in the 1870s, added to the information on public lands in the Rocky Mountains area and laid the groundwork for irrigation and conservation projects. Powell's expeditions sparked interest in and study of the American Indians, which led to his classification of their languages. He was appointed the first director of the U.S. Bureau of Ethnology in 1879 and also served as director of the U.S. Geological Survey from 1881 to 1892.

▬

Powell, Lewis F., Jr.   Lewis Franklin Powell, Jr., b. Suffolk, Va., Sept. 19, 1907, was a U.S. Supreme Court justice (1972–87) known as a moderate conservative who often cast decisive votes. After earning law degrees from Washington and Lee University and Harvard, Powell began the practice of law in Richmond, Va., in 1932. He came to be widely respected for his legal acumen and in 1964 was elected president of the American Bar Association. In 1971, President Richard Nixon appointed Powell to the Supreme Court. During a period when the Court was frequently split, Powell's vote was often pivotal—in favor of affirmative action, the right to abortion, and church-state separation as well as of capital punishment.

▬

Powell v. Alabama   The U.S. Supreme Court case of *Powell* v. *Alabama* (1932) set the stage for the development of the rule that the right to counsel in all state criminal cases is inherent in DUE PROCESS of law. The case arose out of the notorious Scottsboro incident in which seven young black men were convicted of raping two white women on a freight train on its way through Alabama. As the train approached Scottsboro, a sheriff's posse seized the seven blacks and charged them with rape. They were indicted on Mar. 31, 1931, and tried a few days later in three groups, each trial lasting a single day. The juries found the defendants guilty and imposed the death penalty on all.

On appeal to the Supreme Court the convicted prisoners alleged that they (1) had been denied the right to counsel; (2) had not been given a fair and impartial trial; and (3) had been tried before juries from which blacks were systematically excluded. They argued that these constituted a denial of due process of law and equal protection of the laws under the 14th Amendment. Speaking for a majority of seven, Justice George Sutherland declared that the Alabama trial court had failed to give the defendants reasonable time to secure counsel—a denial of due process.

power   Power, in physics, is the rate at which WORK is done. A given amount of work done over a longer period of time represents less power than that work done over a short period of time. The average power required to accomplish a certain amount of work is found by dividing the work by the time period during which it is done. The instantaneous power requirement at any moment during the job may be found from the time derivative of the work function, a concept of calculus. For example, the ¼-horsepower electric motor in many household appliances may deliver several horsepower just after it is turned on; its average power output over a longer period is likely to be somewhat less than ¼ horsepower. Units of power are properly expressed in terms of work per unit time. In the international metric (SI) system, power is expressed in joules per second or watts (W). A machine capable of delivering 746 W of continuous power is rated at one HORSE-POWER in the English system of physical units. Other units of power include the Btu/h and the foot-pound/sec.

power, generation and transmission of   Electric power is an indispensable form of energy throughout much of the world. Even systems that use forms of energy other than ELECTRICITY are likely to contain controls or equipment that run on electric power. For example, modern home heating systems may burn natural gas, oil, or coal, but most systems have combustion and temperature controls that require electricity in order to operate. Similarly, most industrial and manufacturing processes require electric power, and commercial establishments are usually paralyzed when electric service is interrupted.

During the first part of the 20th century, only about 10% of the total energy generated in the United States was converted to electricity. By 1990 electric power accounted for about 40% of the total. Developing countries are usually not as dependent on electricity as are the more industrialized nations, but the growth rate of electricity use in some of those countries is comparable to the rate of growth in the early years of electricity availability in the United States.

Edison's first direct-current generator was displayed at the Paris World Exhibition in 1881. A year later Edison set up a commercial electric generating station in New York City. He used a generator of this type to provide power for the first electric streetlights.

Growth of the Electric Power Industry

The first commercial electric-power installations in the United States were constructed in the latter part of the 19th century. The Rochester, N.Y., Electric Light Company was established in 1880. In 1882, Thomas A. Edison's Pearl Street steam-electric station began operation in New York City and within a year was reported to have had 500 customers for the lighting services it supplied. A short time later a central station powered by a small waterwheel began operation in Appleton, Wis.

In 1886 the feasibility of sending electric power greater distances from the point of generation by using ALTERNATING CURRENT (AC) was demonstrated at Great Barrington, Mass. The plant there utilized transformers to raise the voltage from the generators for a high-voltage transmission line.

The electric power industry of the United States grew from small beginnings such as these to become, in less than 100 years, the most heavily capitalized industry in the country. It now comprises about 3,100 different corporate entities, including systems of private investors, federal and other government bodies, and cooperative-user groups. Less than one-third of the corporate groups have their own generating facilities; the others are directly involved only in the transmission and distribution of electric power.

For several decades electric power use in the United States grew at an average annual rate of about 7%, a rate that results in a doubling every 10 years. The rate of growth remained constant, with only minor year-to-year variations, until the early 1970s, when fuel shortages and rising concern over possible environmental damage, together with reduced expansion of the U.S. economy, slowed the expansion. In the period from 1974 to 1985 the annual increase in electricity use varied between 1.7% and 6.2%. Although total energy use in the United

States has either declined or remained unchanged since 1973, electricity use has continued to grow.

Standard Electric Generating Plants

Virtually all commercial electric energy is now produced by generators driven by steam from the burning of fossil fuels or from nuclear sources or by hydropower. Developed nations depend mainly on fossil fuels, but some countries now depend more heavily on NUCLEAR ENERGY produced by materials such as uranium. France, for example, generates about 70% of its electricity from nuclear power plants; power costs in that nation are the lowest in Europe.

A basic steam-power plant includes a furnace or reactor for raising the temperature of the water in a BOILER, or steam GENERATOR, until it changes into steam, and a TURBINE, which drives the generator to produce electric power. Throughout the history of the electric-power industry, improvements in design, metallurgy, fabrication techniques, and control systems have permitted continual increases in the size, operating temperatures, pressures, and efficiencies of electric generating units. These improvements and increasing demands for electric power have led generating facilities to develop from the early steam-engine–driven generator, which could produce a few kilowatts (kW), to today's giants, with outputs as high as 1,300,000 kW. Hydroelectric, or waterpower, generators have grown from the 12-kW machines of 1882 to the 600,000-kW units at the Grand Coulee station in Washington State (see HYDROELECTRIC POWER).

New Forms of Electric Generation

A continued search has gone on for many years to find new forms of electric power generation that would be suitable for electric-utility use, provide higher efficiencies, and reduce damage to the environment. The key issue is whether alternative systems can produce power at an acceptable cost. Thus far no new methods have been developed sufficiently to be practical for large-scale utility use other than those which depend on rotating machinery to convert input energy into mechanical energy that is then converted into electrical energy. However, the power industry is examining other possibilities.

In *magnetohydrodynamics* (MHD) an ionized gas or liquid metal is passed through a magnetic field to generate electricity. Electrogasdynamics (EGD) utilizes a gas stream to carry charged particles through an electric field. Neither method is yet capable of substituting for conventional generators. Generators working on the principle of THERMOELECTRICITY or of THERMIONIC EMISSION are static devices that can convert heat directly into electricity without converting it into mechanical energy first. Both have been used in some small applications with low power requirements, but neither seems promising as a source of large amounts of utility power in the near future.

Fuel cells are thought by some to have a bright future as sources of electric power for some industries and remote residential areas, but so far none is competitive with conventional utility-electric service. Interest in SOLAR ENERGY has grown in recent years as the public has become increasingly aware that fossil fuels such as oil and coal cannot be replaced as they are consumed and as concern increases over air pollution and environmental effects of the normal combustion processes. Producing electric power from solar energy is still costly, but research continues. Wind energy has received considerable attention in recent years as a method of electricity production (see WINDMILLS AND WIND POWER). Wind power, however, is intermittent in places where power is needed most. The difficulties in constructing long-lived turbines that can withstand strong winds and the high cost of wind power are the two main reasons why wind power will probably

(Above) *Each generator at the Snowy Mountains plant in New South Wales is powered by a water turbine.* (Left) *The Flevo power plant in Holland, contains 3 turbogenerators that can develop 856 million W of electricity.*

play only a small role in power production in the future.

Pockets of heat inside the Earth have been tapped as GEOTHERMAL ENERGY sources for electric-power generation in California, Italy, Iceland, Mexico, New Zealand, the United Kingdom, and a few other locations, and more may be developed if increased costs of other processes make the geothermal alternatives more economically competitive. TIDAL ENERGY plants have been constructed in a few places outside the United States, but none has yet produced spectacular results. No such installations have been built in the United States. In several cities in the United States and elsewhere in the world, energy-recovery plants with massive incinerators convert municipal solid waste into electricity for sale to electric power utilities.

Fuel Use for Power Generation in the United States

The central-station generating plants built throughout the United States were generally designed to use the most accessible and economical fuels. Hydroelectric plants were constructed at locations where dams could be built to impound the water needed to supply the hydraulic energy for the turbogenerators. Power plants near coalfields were likely to have coal-fired furnaces, whereas others were more likely to utilize oil or natural gas as the primary fuel. In time the price of fuel became an important factor in the generating process as fuel transportation systems developed. Many coal-burning plants were converted to use either oil or gas as competition between the fuels and fuel suppliers increased.

Air pollution from coal-fired plants became a major issue in some parts of the country in the 1960s and '70s, leading more utilities to switch to gas or oil. Later, however, shortages of oil and gas required some plants to be converted back to coal, either because high costs or uncertain supplies of the desired fuel meant that it was not available or because of governmental regulatory action. To reduce pollutants to within new statutory limits, some utilities shifted to new—and frequently distant—sources of coal, and some installed sophisticated and expensive devices to cleanse pollutants from plant emissions.

The locations for power plants run by nuclear energy are usually determined not by the source of their fuel but by land availability, access to suitable sources of cooling water, and other physical considerations. At one time the BREEDER REACTOR, a nuclear reactor that makes more fuel than it uses, was looked upon as a major potential source of energy for electric power production in the United States, but the determination that uranium supplies will be adequate for some time to come and recent concern about the spread of plutonium have resulted in a de-

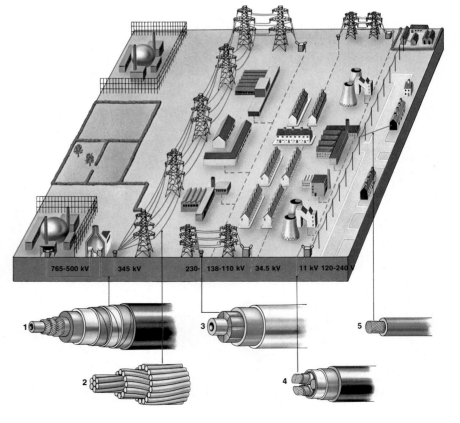

Most electric-power transmission circuits in the United States involve alternating currents and operate at voltages ranging from 11 to 765 kV, depending on the amounts of power to be transferred and on the transmission distances. Because power losses decrease with increased voltages, large amounts of electricity are transmitted over long distances at as high a voltage as possible. Generally, the electricity is carried by overhead lines in rural areas and by underground lines in densely populated urban areas. At consumer locations, substations equipped with step-down transformers lower the high voltages to usable levels in the 11.0– 34.5 kV range for further distribution. The actual voltage utilized by a consumer is obtained from secondary transformers connected to the primary line systems. Thus the voltage is further reduced for use in homes. Metal-sheathed oil- or gas-insulated cables (1 and 3) are used for high-voltage transmission underground, whereas bare conductors (2) are employed on overhead lines. Power from the high-voltage lines is conducted through plastic-sheathed cables (4) to the substations. A covered, twisted multiwire strand (5) leads current into residences.

765-500 kV 345 kV 230- 138-110 kV 34.5 kV 11 kV 120-240 V

This giant heat exchanger is one unit in a solar-electric generation plant in California's Mojave Desert. Fluid heated by a huge array of solar collectors is piped to the exchanger, where it produces steam to drive the steam-turbine generators.

creased interest in breeder-reactor power plants. Sharp differences of opinion exist concerning the safety of nuclear plants, and safety has become a growing public concern, particularly since the reactor accident (1979) at Three Mile Island in Pennsylvania and the nuclear disaster (1986) at CHERNOBYL in the Soviet Union. As a result the future of nuclear power in the United States appears uncertain. Increasing concern about the contribution of the burning of fossil fuels to the GREENHOUSE EFFECT has led to a reevaluation of nuclear power, however. Nuclear power plants do not emit "greenhouse gases" such as carbon dioxide (CO_2).

In 1987, production of electric energy by utilities in the United States totaled 2,570 billion kilowatt-hours (kW h). Of this, 56.9% was produced by coal-burning plants, 4.6% by oil, 10.6% by gas, 9.7% by hydroelectric plants, and 17.7% by nuclear plants. The remainder came from geothermal, wood, waste, and solar plants. This distribution of sources represents a significant decrease in oil use by utilities and an increase in coal and uranium use.

The highly industrialized nature of the United States, together with its population, economic development, and overall size, have made it the world's largest user of electric energy. In 1988, about 35% of the total electricity sold in the United States was used for residential purposes, 35% for industrial activities, and 27% for commercial purposes. The remainder was used for farm purposes and miscellaneous uses, and some was lost in the generation, transmission, and distribution system.

Electric Power Transmission

Electric power transmission systems consist of step-up transformer stations to connect the lower-voltage power-generating equipment to the higher-voltage transmission facilities; high-voltage transmission lines and cables for transferring power from one point to another and pooling generation resources; switching stations, which serve as junction points for different transmission circuits; and step-down transformer stations that connect the transmission circuits to lower-voltage distribution systems or other user facilities. In addition to the transformers, these transmission substations contain circuit breakers and associated connection devices to switch equipment into and out of service, lightning arresters to protect the equipment, and other appurtenances for particular applications of electricity. Highly developed control systems, including sensitive devices for rapid detection of abnormalities and quick disconnection of faulty equipment, are an essential part of every installation in order to provide protection and safety for both the electrical equipment and the public.

Many transmission circuits utilize underground CABLES, although these installations have been limited largely to locations where rights-of-way for overhead lines could not be obtained or where overhead lines were not feasible because they would have interfered with other activities. In general the costs of underground circuits are several times those of comparable overhead circuits.

Future Needs and Considerations

Researchers in both government and industry are seeking new technology, methods, and equipment for the years ahead. Among the issues under investigation are the more efficient use of power during peak periods, and the development and greater utilization of power-saving devices, such as high-efficiency fluorescent light bulbs. The search for economic methods of SYNTHETIC FUEL creation continues, as well as experimentation in such promising areas as the use of hydrogen for fuel. In addition, recent discoveries of higher-temperature superconducting materials that present lower resistance to current flow may open up important new approaches (see SUPERCONDUCTIVITY).

As awareness grows of the need to conserve energy resources, increasing interest also is being shown in the development of small-scale hydroelectric power plants. In the United States, legislation now favors the development of such plants. The Public Utilities Regulatory Policies Act (1978) states that utilities must buy electric power fed into their lines from small, privately owned generators. Such small-scale facilities can make more efficient use of power resources.

In the 1990s, faced with the possibility of government deregulation and increasing energy costs, the electric power industry in the United States is seeking more economical ways to generate electricity.

See also: ENERGY SOURCES; FUEL.

Powers, Hiram   The American neoclassic sculptor Hiram Powers, b. Woodstock, Vt., July 29, 1805, d. June 27, 1873, worked as a model maker in Cincinnati until a Prussian sculptor taught him to model heads. His rugged portrait of Andrew Jackson (1835; Metropolitan Museum of Art, New York City) established Powers's reputation in Washington, D.C., and enabled him to settle in Florence, Italy. The stance of his *Fisherboy* (1859; Metropolitan Museum of Art) is modeled after Praxiteles' *Hermes,* but the figure has natural proportions as well as Powers's characteristic meticulously rendered, fleshlike surface. His *Greek Slave* (1851; Yale University Art Gallery, New Haven, Conn.) introduced the female nude to American sculpture.

Powhatan   [pow-uh-tan']   Powhatan, c.1547–1618, the leading chief of the Powhatan Confederacy, was the father of POCAHONTAS and an intimate friend of Capt. John SMITH and John Rolfe. At the time of the English settlement of Jamestown (1607), the all-powerful Powhatan was consolidating the 30 or more tribes of the confederacy. He was initially friendly to the English colonists, but upon learning that John Smith was interested in metals and in finding a waterway leading to the western ocean, Powhatan perceived the English as dangerous and decided to remove them from his territory.

When Smith was captured (c.1608) by the Indians, Powhatan left his fate in the hands of his warriors. Pocahontas, Powhatan's favorite daughter, is said to have saved Smith's life, in all probability saving thereby the life of the Jamestown colony. In 1614, with Powhatan's approval, Pocahontas married the Englishman John Rolfe. The marriage inaugurated a period of peace between the Indians and whites, which lasted until Powhatan's death.

powwow   [pow'-wow]   A powwow is a communal celebration among North American Indians. Lasting from one day to a week or more, the powwow is characterized by dancing, displays of crafts and arts, and traditional tribal dress.

The derivation of *powwow*—from the Algonquian "he dreams," suggesting communication with the dream or spirit world—shows that powwows had their origin in religious ceremonies, and some religious powwows are still held. In times of crisis or on other important occasions, powwows were held to unite minds and spirits for the common good. Prayer, dance, and song commemorated the dead, sought to expel sickness, celebrated manhood, renewed friendships, or expressed hope for a lasting peace. Speeches, games, pipe smoking, and gift giving also characterized these councils.

The dispersion, decimation, and restriction of American Indians during the 19th century, and the consequent lapsing of traditional ways, resulted in secularization of powwows. As a united Indian movement, or Pan-Indianism, began to emerge among the Plains Indians, their powwows served as unifying mechanisms. Today powwows continue to reinforce tribal identity and promote Pan-Indian solidarity.

Powys   [poh'-is]   A county in east central Wales, Powys was established in 1974 by the merger of the counties of Montgomery, Radnor, and part of Brecon. It has a population of 114,900 (1988 est.). Llandrindod Wells (1981 pop., 4,186) is the administrative center. The county, which covers 5,077 km² (1,960 mi²), consists mostly of highlands, dotted with lakes. Mountain chains traverse the county, including the Plynlimon and Berwyn ranges, the Brecon Beacons, and the Black Mountains. Health spas in the area have mineral springs. The chief rivers are the SEVERN, Wye, and Usk. Livestock raising and freshwater fishing are the mainstays of the economy. Industry is limited to the main towns of Welshpool, Brecon, and Newtown. Tourism is also important. Evidence exists of settlement from the Bronze and Iron ages. Several Roman ruins have also been found.

Poznań   [pawz-nan']   Poznań (Posen), one of Poland's largest commercial and industrial cities, lies in the western part of the country, about 300 km (190 mi) west of Warsaw on the Warta River. Its population is 585,900 (1988 est.). The economy is based on metalworking, textile and furniture production, and food processing. A Gothic cathedral (begun 966) was rebuilt following its destruction during World War II. Several universities, theaters, and museums are located there.

Poznań, founded in the 9th century, served as the residence of the first Polish kings from the 10th century until 1296. By the 16th century it had become a prosperous trade and cultural center. In 1793, Poznań was annexed to Prussia. Since 1918, Poznań has been a part of Poland. It was heavily damaged by the Germans during World War II.

Prado   [prah'-doh]   The Prado Museum in Madrid, which houses one of the world's most important collections of Western European painting and classical art, was begun during the reign (1759–88) of King Charles III. Designed by Juan de Villanueva, it is one of the finest examples of Spanish neoclassical architecture. The building consists of two long gallery wings ending in pavilions and connected by a central structure; the pavilions are faced in the severe style of a Spanish 16th-century palace. The relief carvings of the west and north facades were executed by the 19th-century masters Ramón Barba, Valeriano Salvatierra, and Jerónimo Suñol. More than 6,000 paintings, drawings, sculptures, and other objects are now kept in the museum, which was inaugurated on Nov. 19, 1819, and enlarged several times.

Praetorian guard [pree-tohr'-ee-uhn] The Praetorian guard was the privileged, politically influential imperial bodyguard of ancient Rome established in 27 BC by Augustus (see ROME, ANCIENT). Commanded by a prefect, it numbered up to 16,000 men who attended the emperor constantly. The guard often determined the imperial succession. Constantine I disbanded it in AD 312.

Praetorius, Michael [pree-tohr'-ee-uhs] Michael Praetorius, b. Feb. 15, 1571, d. Feb. 15, 1621, was a German organist, theorist, and composer. Entering (1604) the service of Bishop Heinrich Julius of Halberstadt (later duke of Brunswick), Praetorius devoted his time to the composition of church music, publishing his first important collection in 1605. He proved to be an indefatigable composer, as is demonstrated by the 22-volume modern edition of his works; his psalms, hymns, motets, masses, and Magnificat settings offer abundant proof of his contrapuntal ability, and his splendid collection of French dance music, *Terpsichore* (1612), is still popular. His great musical treatise, the *Syntagma Musicum*, in three volumes (1615; modern facsimile, 1958–59), concerns the history of church music and the entire range of musical instruments in addition to useful material on performance practice and musical theory.

Pragmatic Sanction [prag-mat'-ik] In European history an official proclamation by a sovereign ruler on a subject of great political significance was sometimes called a pragmatic sanction. Two of these formal decrees were especially important. The first, known as the Pragmatic Sanction of Bourges (July 7, 1438), was issued by France's King CHARLES VII following an assembly of the French clergy that he had convened. It set forth a policy known as GALLICANISM, asserting the independence of the French church from papal jurisdiction except in matters of doctrine. It also extended the powers of the French monarch over clerical appointments and taxation within his kingdom. The second document was devised by Holy Roman Emperor CHARLES VI to ensure an undivided succession to the lands of the HABSBURG dynasty. Issued on Apr. 19, 1713, it stipulated that without a male heir all of Charles's dynastic possessions should pass to his daughter MARIA THERESA. When Charles died (1740), however, FREDERICK II of Prussia invaded Silesia, and the War of the AUSTRIAN SUCCESSION ensued.

pragmatism [prag'-muh-tizm] Pragmatism is a philosophical movement, developed in the United States, that holds that both the meaning and the truth of any idea are functions of its practical outcome. Fundamental to pragmatism is a strong antiabsolutism: all principles are to be regarded as working hypotheses.

Charles Sanders PEIRCE is considered the founder of pragmatism. He developed it as a theory of meaning in the 1870s, holding that an intrinsic connection exists between meaning and action—that the meaning of an idea is to be found in its "conceivable sensible effects" and that humans generate belief through their "habits of action." William JAMES developed it as a theory of truth. True ideas, according to James, are useful "leadings"; they lead through experience in ways that provide consistency, orderliness, and predictability. The classical American pragmatists are, in addition to Peirce and James, John DEWEY, George Herbert MEAD, and Clarence Irving LEWIS.

The influence of Darwinism on pragmatic thought is seen in its evolutionary approach, which holds that what is true for one time or place may not be true for another—that reality, as well as human knowledge of it, is constantly evolving, as is morality. What is good or evil, as well as what is true or false, is dependent on its practical outcome—in the case of ethics, its effects on human behavior. Pragmatists do not regard this relativism, whether in epistemology, ethics, or metaphysics, as subjective. Real, true, or good ideas, they maintain, have developed in the course of humanity's interactions with the environment, emerging because they work to lead humans successfully through their experiences. One major pragmatic criterion for truth is agreement on the part of the community of investigators in the long run. Truth tends to be that which gets accepted in the free competition of ideas. Politically, pragmatists usually advocate democracy as the system best suited to change with the needs of the majority.

Prague [prahg] Prague (Czech: Praha) is the capital and largest city of Czechoslovakia. Its population is 1,211,307 (1989 est.). The city is situated along both banks of the Vltava (German: Moldau) River and covers an area of 496 km² (192 mi²). Prague has traditionally been one of the principal intellectual and artistic centers of central Europe.

The Hradčany Castle complex overlooks Prague, located on the Vltava River in west central Czechoslovakia. Prague is a major cultural center of central Europe and has been Czechoslovakia's capital since 1918.

Contemporary City. Prague is the political, administrative, financial, and commercial heart of Czechoslovakia. It is also an industrial city, producing goods ranging from machinery, rolling stock, and chemicals to textiles, furniture, foodstuffs, and beer. The city is a rail junction and a terminus of the Elbe-Vltava waterway.

The importance of the theater in Prague is symbolized by the fact that it was a playwright, Václav Havel, who became the first president of post-Communist Czechoslovakia in 1989. Music has played an equally prominent role in Prague's tradition. It has two major orchestras—the Prague Symphony and the Czech Philharmonic. The annual Prague Spring Music Festival is world renowned. The largest of its many art galleries and museums is the National Museum (1818). The city's institutions of higher learning include the prestigious Charles University (1348), the oldest in central Europe. The writers Franz Kafka and Jaroslav Hašbek, who lived in Prague, epitomize for many the spiritual character of the city.

Dating from medieval times, the old center of Prague consists of five sectors. The Old Town, the New Town, and the Josefov (once a Jewish ghetto) are on the eastern bank of the river. On the western bank are the Lesser Quarter and the Hradčany, which surround the Hradčany Castle—former residence of the Czech kings and since 1918 the seat of Czechoslovakia's presidents. Despite gradual modernization, Old Prague has retained much of its original appearance. Prague suffered little damage in World War II and has about 1,700 officially designated historic monuments. Industrial and residential sections fan out from the center.

History. Dating from the 9th century, Prague has been for most of its history the political heart of BOHEMIA. In the 14th century the city experienced unprecedented prosperity when the Bohemian king became Holy Roman emperor as CHARLES IV and chose Prague as capital of the empire. In the 15th century Prague was the hotbed of early Protestantism, triggered by the fiery preaching of the Czech reformer John HUSS. In 1618 the Czech Protestant nobles signaled their rebellion against Habsburg rule by throwing three royal councillors out of a window in Hradčany Castle, precipitating the THIRTY YEARS' WAR. After the 1620 victory of the Habsburg armies over the Czechs at White Mountain near Prague, the city fell into political obscurity. The Czech national revival in the 19th century restored Prague's political and cultural prominence. In 1918 the city became the capital of newly independent Czechoslovakia. It was occupied by the Germans from 1939 to 1945, and in 1968 by Soviet troops moved in to oust the reformist government of Alexander Dubček. In 1989, Prague was the scene of the persistent demonstrations that brought the downfall of Czechoslovakia's Communist regime.

prairie chicken   SEE GROUSE

---

prairie dog
Prairie dogs are stout-bodied, ground-dwelling members of the squirrel family, Sciuridae, native to prairies and other open, grassy areas in western North America from Canada to northern Mexico. They are called prairie dogs because one of their calls is a barklike yip. The five species, all in the genus *Cynomys*, are similar in appearance, with short legs, short tail, small ears, and a

Prairie dogs live in highly organized towns. The entrance to each burrow is marked by a mound of earth (1) that keeps rainwater out. It is deliberately formed into shape (2) and constantly maintained. The entrance tunnel may lead to a guard post (3) and then to several rooms, 3-5 m (10-16 ft) below ground. There nests may be constructed (4) and pups raised (5). Typical behavior in colonies includes the "kiss greeting" (6), grooming (7), and loud barking (8) to warn against enemies. Other animals, such as the burrowing owl (9), may inhabit vacant burrows.

grizzled, yellowish to reddish gray or brown coat. Prairie dogs range from 28 to 42 cm (11 to 16.5 in) in length and from 700 g to 1.4 kg (1.5 to 3 lb) in weight. Prairie dogs live in groups called coteries. A breeding coterie contains one male, one to four females, and the young of the past two years. Several coteries are formed into wards, which are united into a town—a complex system of underground, interconnecting burrows and many entrances. Towns may cover 65 ha (160 acres, or about ½ mi on each side) and contain thousands of individuals. Because prairie dogs compete with livestock for food, they were subjected to mass extermination. Today they exist largely within national parks.

prairie school *Prairie school* is the name given to a group of Chicago-based architects who produced numerous residences, banks, and libraries in the Midwest between 1895 and 1917. Louis SULLIVAN and Frank Lloyd WRIGHT, founders of the school, devised an alternative to the standard "box" house by using open cruciform floor plans, deeply overhanging roofs, and massive low chimneys, all with a strong horizontal emphasis. The "prairie house," exemplified by Wright's Robie House (1909) in Chicago, was ideally suited to the climate and topography of the Midwest and was popularized by followers of the founders, including Walter Burley Griffin, Barry Byrne, William Drummond, and George Grant Elmslie. It was one of the most influential styles in American domestic architecture.

prairie schooner see CONESTOGA

praseodymium [pray-zee-oh-dim'-ee-uhm] Praseodymium is a chemical element, a silvery white metal of the LANTHANIDE SERIES of the periodic table. Its symbol is Pr, its atomic number is 59, and its atomic weight is 140. Pure praseodymium was first obtained in 1885 by C. A. von Welsbach. The name is derived from the Greek for "leekgreen," referring to the color of the element's salts. Praseodymium salts are used to color glass and ceramic glazes, and its oxide is used, along with other rare-earth metal oxides, as a core material for carbon arcs.

Pravda [prahv'-duh] The official newspaper of the Central Committee of the Soviet Communist party, *Pravda* (meaning "truth") has one of the world's largest circulations—nearly 10 million in 44 cities of the USSR. It was founded in 1912 as the organ of the Bolshevik wing of the Communist party, with Joseph Stalin as editor. Its editorials are regularly transmitted by TASS, the Soviet international news agency.

Praxiteles [prak-sit'-uh-leez] An Athenian and the presumed son of the sculptor Cephisodotus, Praxiteles (fl. 370–330 BC) was renowned in ancient times for the grace and beauty of his figures and for the skill with which he

expressed emotions in marble. His most famous work was a statue of the goddess Aphrodite, which was bought by the city of Cnidus in Anatolia. The *Cnidian Aphrodite*, much admired by contemporaneous writers, has survived only in Roman copies. One of the most complete (Vatican Museums) follows the overall composition depicted on coins of Cnidus: Aphrodite, standing nude in a languorous pose, lets her drapery fall on a water jar. This statue had a great influence on later representations of the goddess. Most scholars believe that *Hermes and the Infant Dionysus* (*c.*340 BC; Museum, Olympia) is an original work by Praxiteles. The sinuous curve of the body and the fine finish of the marble conform to what is known of the style of the master.

prayer Prayer is the process of addressing a superhuman being or beings for purposes of praise, adoration, thanksgiving, petition, penitence, and so on. Prayer is a part of every culture and does not belong to any particular religious tradition. The foundations for prayer, however, differ according to the understanding of God's relationship to human beings and to the world. In the Judeo-Christian tradition, prayer is based on the belief that God is both transcendant and personal, an active agent in human history.

Prayer may be communal, as in public worship, or private; vocal, as in prayer said aloud by individuals or groups, or mental, as in MEDITATION and contemplation. Popular forms of prayer include litanies (see LITANY) and prayers for the dead (for example, the Jewish Kaddish). Jesus taught his disciples the LORD'S PRAYER.

praying mantis Praying mantises, or mantids, large predatory insects of the order Orthoptera, are so named because the spiny forelegs appear to be folded in an attitude of prayer. The uppermost leg segment (the coxa), usually small in other insects, is greatly elongated, providing greater reach and allowing the next two segments, the femur and tibia, to be snapped closed against one another as an insect trap. The front portion of the thorax (prothorax), the region just behind the head, is also greatly elongated, forming a necklike structure; mantises are the only insects that can turn their heads to look directly behind them. As the mantis moves its head to keep its prey in sight, its head stimulates special receptors that

The common praying mantis, shown grasping prey with its forelegs, is legally protected in some areas as a destroyer of insect pests.

send out nerve impulses that automatically and instantly adjust the distance and angle of the mantis's strike. In captivity the female mantis may kill and eat the male immediately after or even during mating, but this behavior is not common in the wild. Mantis eggs are laid in a frothy egg case in fall and hatch in spring.

pre-Columbian art and architecture

The shining cities of the AZTEC and the INCA encountered by Hernán CORTÉS and Francisco PIZARRO in the 16th century were the latest products of pre-Columbian art and architecture. Its highest achievements were centered on the 6,400-km (4,000-mi) Pacific coast and parallel mountain ranges extending from present-day Mexico to Peru. A number of distinct cultures developed there before the arrival in the Caribbean of Christopher Columbus in 1492. The impact the Europeans had on the native civilizations was so devastating that the region's history has been divided into pre-Columbian (before Columbus and other Europeans) and post-Conquest periods.

The true civilizations of pre-Columbian America were in MESOAMERICA (the valley of Mexico south to Honduras and parts of Nicaragua) and in the region of the central Andes; between them an intermediate area of high chiefdoms stretched from Nicaragua south to Ecuador. Pre-Columbian MAYA cultures in Mesoamerica have three chronological periods: Preclassic (2000 BC–AD 300), Classic (300–900), and Postclassic (900–1540). Although other Mesoamerican cultures, such as the Olmec, do not fit well within this dating scheme, the same terms are often used with their chronologies. The central Andean region has its own time division based on the seven "horizon" cultures that spread over the entire region.

Some prominent Andean cultures were the Chavín (900–200 BC), the Huari (AD 600–900), and the Inca (1450–1540). The central Andes was as separate from Mesoamerica as India was from Europe during the same long period from 1600 BC to AD 1500. Only after European contact did the entire area fall under the control of one culture, that of Spain. (For art and architecture of the post-Conquest periods, see LATIN AMERICAN ART AND ARCHITECTURE; for the pre-Columbian art of North America, see INDIANS OF NORTH AMERICA, ART OF THE.)

Mesoamerica

Preclassic Period (2000 BC–AD 300). In Mesoamerica, figurines and fine ceramics fill the ruins of early-Preclassic villages from Ocós, in Guatemala, to Tlatilco, next to modern Mexico City. In the far western part of Mesoamerica, around the present-day states of Nayarit, Jalisco, and Colima, lively hand-modeled figurines remained an important tradition after the Preclassic period. Surface painting became increasingly important in representing details, whereas modeling and incising fell into relative disuse. Artistically the western Mexican culture was exhausted before it received a new wave of ideas and forms from central Mexico during the TOLTEC expansion in the 10th century AD.

The OLMEC, often considered the mother culture of Mesoamerica, arose in about the 12th century BC. A civilization with kings, professional specialization, and writing, Olmec culture transformed the individual village-centered cultures of Mesoamerica into a network dominated by advanced centers, such as SAN LORENZO and LA VENTA. The art in those centers was enormously difficult to produce. Masses of people had to be organized, first to locate the rare types of stone demanded by the Olmec rulers, then to transport the stone to their capitals,

(Above) *A colossal basalt head (2.4 m/7.9 ft high) from La Venta, an Olmec site in Tobasco, Mexico, represents one of two major artistic traditions that flourished there during the Preclassic period.* (Right) *Representing the second major tradition is this group of incised jade steles and male figurines (15-25 cm/6-10 high).* (Museo Nacional de Anthropologia, Mexico City.)

then to spend the thousands of hours needed to shape and finish the work, and finally to install the art where the rulers and their religious consultants ordained that it be placed.

Two characteristic types of stone objects were produced: small jade carvings and colossal basalt monuments. Neither type of stone was available in the coastal plain of the Gulf of Mexico, where the Olmec centers were built. The blue green jade favored by the Olmec could be found only far to the northwest, in the state of Guerrero, and far to the southeast, in Guatemala and Costa Rica. The basalt blocks, each of which weighed several tons, came from the Tuxtla volcanic range, located far north of the Olmec sites. They were transported partially by rafts but were also dragged many kilometers overland by platoons of laborers.

The Olmec probably settled widely in Mesoamerica to supervise their extensive trade network; low reliefs carved on rock outcroppings in Morelos, Chiapas, and El Salvador attest to their presence, as do paintings deep within caves in Guerrero. Relief carvings on stone stelae (upright slabs) commemorate the lord-and-vassal relationship between the Olmec and other groups. The image of the jaguar is everywhere in Olmec art, depicted either as a naturalistic pouncing animal or as an abstract face.

Between 100 BC and AD 300, Olmec innovations were developed in distinctively varying ways in the different regions of Mesoamerica. In central Mexico, the local Nahuatl-speakers focused on architecture: earthen mounds were faced with stone and terraced. In the Maya-speaking southeast (Chiapas and Guatemala), the IZAPA culture of the Preclassic stressed the stela cult: low-relief carvings on the stelae depict not only standing personages in ceremonial attire but also rich mythological scenes with sacred trees and animal divinities, all bordered by monster-mouth bands. Around the 1st century AD, the lords of TEOTIHUACÁN erected what was to be the largest pyramidal structure for more than a millennium.

Classic Period (AD 300–900). During the Classic period all the arts of Teotihuacán have severe geometric forms. The sculpture is broad and blocklike. Mural paintings in temples and palaces represent divine idols, priests making offerings, and armed warriors surrounded by their animal symbols: eagles, jaguars, and coyotes. Teotihuacán motifs spread widely through Mesoamerica during the early Classic period. Stone stelae show standing figures in elaborate costumes carved in relief with astonishing delicacy. These figures represent the rulers; glyphs tell their ancestry and the key dates of their lives. In the great mural cycle at BONAMPAK, battle and prisoner scenes shatter the earlier notion that peaceful theocracies existed during the Classic Maya period.

Maya pyramids, four-sided, stepped structures, had two specialized forms: the twin-pyramid complex and the mortuary pyramid. The former, known from TIKAL, consisted of identical flat-topped and stepped pyramids facing each other across a plaza lined by plain stelae and low altar stones. Mortuary pyramids known so far at Tikal and at PALENQUE have nine stages, symbolizing the nine levels of the underworld.

(Left) *Elaborate high-relief ornamentation and glyphic inscriptions frame a naturalistic portrait of a Maya ruler on this stone stele (dated AD 782) at Copán, Honduras.*

(Below) *A judgment scene in which prisoners are led before Maya rulers appears in this reconstruction from the monumental Bonampak mural series (AD 800) in Mexico. (Peabody Museum, Cambridge, Mass.)*

In the Maya area and in adjoining Veracruz, mold-made ceramic figurines often accompanied the dead. Some images are stiff, clothed in elaborate ornaments of a god; others are naturalistic, molded and adorned in life-like fashion. Classic Veracruz art includes images of giggling children with dimples and broad grins.

The need to struggle against insurmountable odds, even resulting in one's own sacrifice, is a central concept of Mesoamerican philosophy that finds clear expression in the Classic ball courts. The players struggled to keep the solid rubber ball, a symbol of the Sun, in motion by hitting it with their hips. Heavy belts, shaped like yokes and perhaps constructed of wood and leather, protected the players and increased the ball's momentum; these belts were often carved with images of death and the under-

(Left) *The intricacy of this funerary urn depicting the fertility god Xipe-Totec exemplifies the pottery style that evolved during the Classic phase of Zapotec culture. (Museo Nacional de Anthropologia, Mexico City.)* (Above) *This turquoise mosaic snake (15th century) reveals the technical skill and sophistication of Aztec mosaic work. (British Museum, London.)*

world. A relief from the south ball court at El Tajín depicts the final punishment of the loser in this game: the player was stretched back over a stone and his heart cut out as an offering to try to bring the Sun back from the underworld. In late Classic Maya art (AD 500–900), such mythological scenes were painted in many colors on funerary vases and plates. The finesse of the brushstrokes proves that many vase painters were full-time professionals; their literacy, as revealed in the surrounding bands of hieroglyphic (pictorial) writing, suggests that they numbered among the intellectual elite of Maya society.

Postclassic Period (900–1540). Early in the Postclassic era the Toltec, formerly a nomadic people, settled at Tula, northwest of Teotihuacán, and soon extended their control over long-settled peoples. The Maya had recently abandoned their older cities and increased the population of their northern Yucatán cities, such as UXMAL. With the

The radial symmetry of the Castillo, a temple-pyramid at Chichén Itzá, reflects the hydridization of Maya-Toltec style that occurred in northern Yucatán cities during the Postclassic period.

same fine artisanship typical of their southern contemporaries, the Toltec cut and fit stones into palace and temple facades and clay vessels before firing. At CHICHÉN ITZÁ this so-called Puuc style was supplanted by an art that was uniquely Toltec in form: inverted serpent columns, colonnaded halls, low banquettes with carved processions, human forms supporting roofs and tabletops, and a new emphasis on death motifs. The Toltecs also built, at Chichén Itzá, the largest ball court (150 m, or 492 ft, long) in Mesoamerica.

Painted screenfold books were perhaps the major way that the angular Toltec style was spread. These books were of two kinds: ritual, representing the deities controlling the various days and time periods; and genealogical, recording the evolution of the ruling houses (preserved only from the MIXTEC, a people of western Oaxaca). Polychrome pottery based on this codex style was found not only where the Mixtec lived, but also in the valley of Puebla-Tlaxcala. Murals and goldworking, recently acquired from lower Central America, supplied intricate media in which to execute Mixteca-Puebla subjects. Beautiful ceramics, some in cloisonné technique, reflect the same subjects and style throughout western Mexico.

The Aztec, the dominant political power in Mesoamerica when the Spaniards arrived (1519), had been northern nomads like the Toltec, whose culture they copied. In the island capital of TENOCHTITLÁN, Aztec temples had colossal statues of their deities, in front of which black-painted priests placed offerings, from sacrificed quails to human hearts. Far more than any previous sculpture except that of the Olmec, Aztec statuary was carved in the full round. All other Aztec arts continued, and were really a part of, the Mixteca-Puebla tradition: precious-stone carving, metalsmithing, manuscript illustration, mural painting, relief carving, and ornamental featherwork. Such objects, sent to Spain by the conquistadors, amazed European artists by the skill and ingenuity they displayed.

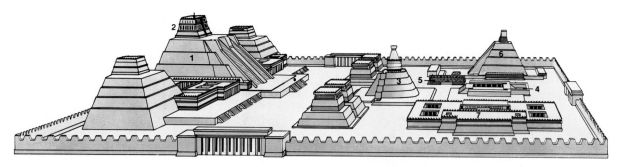

The ceremonial precinct of Tenochtitlán, the Aztec capital, is depicted in this reconstruction. The site was dominated by a great pyramid (1), upon which stood two temples (2) dedicated to the Aztec deities Tlaloc and Huitzilopochtli. A round pyramid (3), sacred to Quetzalcoatl, was located before the ballcourt (4). A sacrificial skull rack (5) and the temple of the Sun (6) flanked one side of the ballcourt, and the priests' living quarters (7) were on its other side.

Intermediate Area and Central Andes

South of Mesoamerica, the art of the so-called Intermediate Area specialized in small objects made of gold or *tumbaga* (an alloy of gold with copper) and ceramics, with occasional work in fine stone and bone. Because this area was divided into small chiefdoms, its art never achieved the integration of the civilizations to the north or the south.

Earliest Andean Art. The earliest artistic tradition appeared along the coast and foothills of the northern Andes. There Indians manufactured containers of clay fired at high temperatures. Although the earliest pottery may have come from Puerto Hormiga, Colombia, before 3000 BC, the richest and most expressive ceramics and figurines are known from villages such as Valdivia in Ecuador. The early artists there expressed themselves not only in the variety of proportions of their pots but also in the small figures they modeled on the pots' handles, rims, and shoulders.

In villages along the north coast of Peru, the earliest art, dating from before 2000 BC, resembled the art of Valdivia but lacked ceramics. Instead, at Huaca Prieta art concentrated on burning squared figures into the surface of gourds and weaving cotton textiles, Peru's most distinctive art form. A few of these coastal villages have impressive public architecture of adobe in the form of a coherent sequence of large plazas with centralized depressions and raised platforms. The early dates of these centers, before 1600 and possibly as early as 2800 BC, indicate that large-scale construction occurred there far earlier than in Mesoamerica.

Chavín Style (900–200 BC). The central Andeans adopted ceramics from the Ecuadoreans about 1200 BC, and by 900 BC the Chavín art style had become the first widespread art style in the Andes. It apparently radiated

(Below) *This hammered gold pectoral (400–700) is designed in the Calima style that flourished (300 BC–AD 700) in southwestern Colombia. Calima goldsmiths were especially famed for their breastplates. (Museo de Oro, Bogotá.)*

This incised granite slab (c. 1200–1000 BC) portraying a warrior formed part of the retaining wall of a temple platform at Cerro Sechín, in the Casma valley on the northern coast of Peru. Cerro Sechín is one of the oldest coastal sites associated with the Chavín style. (Museo Arqueólogico, Lima.)

This detail from an embroidered burial cloak (300–200 BC) exhibits the mastery of textile production achieved by the Paracas culture of Peru. Hundreds of these shrouds, woven from finely spun thread and colored with dyes, were wrapped around mummies discovered in the Paracas burial grounds. (Museum of Fine Arts, Boston.)

from the cut-stone temple at CHAVÍN DE HUÁNTAR, in the north central highlands. Honeycomb passages in its U-shaped mass led to a shaped stone, incised and carved in low relief with the body of a jawless monster whose single row of teeth curves up in a smile.

On the north coast, several temples constructed of plaster and adobe were decorated with reliefs of jaguar faces. Monochrome ceramics represent realistically modeled jaguars as well as humans and houses. No architecture of the Chavín period has been discovered on the southern Peruvian coast, but ceramics named for the PARACAS peninsula repeat the Chavín theme of the smiling god and the feline face abstracted in flat, geometrically linear designs painted in many colors after firing.

Immediately following the end of Chavín influence a style of brilliantly patterned textiles, named Necropolis for the cemetery area in which they were found, appeared (300–100 BC) in Paracas. Large mantles wrapped around the mummified bodies of important Indians present mythological and human images in as many as 12 colors of threads embroidered onto the wool-and-cotton cloth.

Nazca (200 BC–AD 600) and Mochica (100 BC–AD 700) Styles. During the NAZCA period many of these same mo-

The techniques developed in the Nazca-style pottery of Peru, exemplified by this double-spouted vessel (100 BC–AD 300), involved firing the piece after it was painted to intensify the coloration. (Musée d'Ethnographie, Geneva.)

tifs are transferred to brilliant polychrome ceramics, which were painted before the clay was fired to increase their brightness and to seal the color under a burnished surface that looks glazed (although no pre-Columbian potters used true glaze). Extraordinarily large versions of these Nazca designs, plus long radiating and crisscrossing lines, were scraped on the faces of high desert mountains overlooking the valleys of the south coast.

During the same period on the north coast, the culture known as MOCHICA created the most humanistic statements in art found south of Mesoamerica. Mochica ceramicists modeled remarkably realistic animals with turned heads, alert eyes, and heavy bodies. Humans, in various positions and degrees of dress and undress, are also portrayed with powerful realism, including true portrait head jars of the nobility.

The excavation in 1987–88 of a Moche warrior priest's tomb north of Trujillo, Peru, was of crucial importance to pre-Columbian archaeology. The tomb yielded gold, silver, and jeweled ornaments in quantity and quality unknown before. This revolutionized the understanding of New World metallurgy. A wealth of ceramics also came from this tomb.

During the flowering of regional styles like the Mochica and the Nazca, which in some ways parallel the Mesoamerican Classic period, the powerful cult center of TIAHUANACO was built in the southern highlands in Bolivia, near Lake Titicaca. A high pyramidal mound stands opposite a semisubterranean depression, the huge spaces punctuated by standing human figures cut in single square-sectioned blocks of stone incised with delicate patterns. Space flows through small freestanding gateways; the finest one, called the Gate of the Sun, probably represents the Andean lunar calendar. Carved in relief in the center of the lintel, a frontal figure stands on a stepped mountain and holds serpent staffs. He wears a sunburst headdress like the Mochica solar god. Around him winged human- and bird-headed figures kneel on one leg. Beneath him are 12 disembodied heads, also with radial headdresses, linked together by a celestial serpent with multiple heads.

Huari (600–900) and Chimú (1000–1450) Styles. The images depicted on the Gate of the Sun at Tiahuanaco appear on pottery, textiles, and metalwork throughout the central Andes during the Huari period, which marks the second area-wide civilization of Peru. The rulers of the city of HUARI, in the central highlands, apparently became enthusiastic converts to the religion embodied in the images of Tiahuanaco, an especially important pilgrimage center. South-coast artists applied the bright colors and linear stylization of the earlier Nazca pottery and textiles to the Tiahuanaco images and lent their technique to the central coast, where the important shrine and oracle of PACHACAMAC later eclipsed Tiahuanaco itself.

After the decline of Huari influence, the royal lineages, first of Lambayeque and then of CHIMÚ, emerged on the northern Peruvian coast. Known from accounts made shortly after the Spanish conquest, the Chimú kings built impressive citadels for themselves at CHAN CHAN, with

This 16th-century wood kero is an example of the traditional Inca drinking vessel. (Musée d'Ethnographie, Geneva.)

ceremonial courts, royal apartments and workshops, a water reservoir, and a large cemetery. The graves contained a rich supply of Chimú gold and silver work, feather clothing and wall hangings, figures and masks, and a lustrous black pottery with modeled figures and relief scenes reminiscent of the Mochica.

Inca Culture (1450–1540). Inca art tended to be monotonous in its decorative objects such as textiles and pottery, in which purely geometric patterns abound. Favored forms found throughout the Andean highlands included the ceramic *aryballos,* a curving, long-necked vessel, and the wooden *kero,* a drinking cup with straight or slightly flaring sides. In architectural and engineering feats, however, the Inca achieved far more than their predecessors: paved roads spanned the empire; extensive terracing and irrigation systems were developed; and enormous, thick walls were constructed of perfectly fitted stones such as those at the renowned lost city of MACHU PICCHU. The hilltop fortress and ceremonial center of SACSAHUAMAN, which overlooked the Inca capital city of CUZ-

The Inca city Machu Picchu, famed for its carefully fitted walls of white granite, was designed on terraced levels. Located in the Peruvian Andes, Machu Picchu was discovered in 1911.

CO, was surrounded by zigzag tiers of walls formed of massive irregular stones fitted with such precision that a knife blade cannot be inserted between them. The hillside opposite was carved with stepped seats for the Inca ruler and his court to observe the glittering ceremonies, which were resplendent with gold, silver, brightly colored costumes, and brilliant plumage from birds of the Amazon.

Preble, Edward [preb'-ul] Edward Preble, b. Falmouth (now Portland), Maine, Aug. 15, 1761, d. Aug. 25, 1807, was an American naval officer who, as commander of the Mediterranean squadron in the TRIPOLITAN WAR, ordered the blockade of Tripoli. Preble served in the Massachusetts navy during the American Revolution and in the U.S. Navy during the Quasi-War (1798–1800) with France. As captain of the frigate *Essex,* he escorted (1800) a convoy of American merchant ships to the East Indies; this cruise marked the first appearance of a U.S. warship in the waters east of the Cape of Good Hope. Appointed Mediterranean commander in 1803, Preble energetically prosecuted the war against Tripoli. He endorsed Stephen DECATUR's bold plan to enter Tripoli harbor and burn the captured U.S. frigate *Philadelphia.*

Precambrian time see EARTH, GEOLOGICAL HISTORY OF; GEOLOGIC TIME

precession Precession is the motion of the end of the axis of a spinning object, if it is free to move, so that the axis traces out the surface of a cone. The torque on a spinning top due to gravity, for example, produces a change in the top's ANGULAR MOMENTUM, which previously had been only along the axis; the additional angular momentum adds to the original in such a way that the free end of the top moves slowly in a horizontal circle rather than falling down.

precession of the equinoxes The Earth's axis slowly precesses, or changes its direction, over a period of about 26,000 years. The north celestial pole describes a small circle with a radius of 23.5° around the north ecliptic pole, with a consequent westward drift of the equinoxes—the two points where the celestial equator crosses the ecliptic (see COORDINATE SYSTEMS). (Irregularities in addition to this motion are called NUTATIONS.) The effect was first noticed by Hipparchus in about 130 BC. At that time the vernal equinox was in the constellation Aries (from which it received its name, "the first point of Aries"). As a result of precession, the vernal equinox is now in the constellation Pisces and is approaching Aquarius.

Precession, explained by Isaac Newton, can be understood through the analogy of the Earth spinning like a top, with the Sun and Moon pulling on the Earth's equatorial bulge—hence the phrase *lunisolar precession.* Planetary precession is the result of changes in the ecliptic caused by perturbations in the orbit of the Earth caused by other

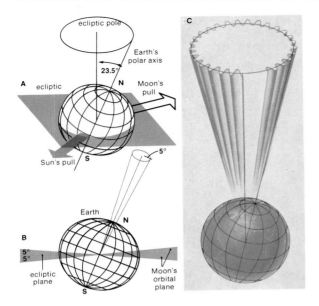

The Earth's equator bulges slightly and is tilted about 23.5° to the ecliptic plane. The Sun's gravitational force (A) tends to pull the bulge into the ecliptic plane, whereas that of the Moon tends to pull it into the Moon's orbital plane. The action of these two forces causes the Earth's polar axis to precess, or turn, in a circle about the ecliptic pole every 26,000 years. The Moon also precesses (B), such that the opposite sides of its orbital plane move above and below the ecliptic plane with a period of 18.5 years. This periodic change causes nutation, or a slight nodding of the Earth's pole, which appears as a small wave (C) superimposed on the precessional circle.

planets; its effects are less than 1% of the lunisolar precession. The combination of these two effects is called general precession. Geodesic precession is an effect due to general relativity.

precious stone   see GEMS

precipitation (chemistry)   In chemistry, precipitation occurs when dissolved substances are modified in some way to form an insoluble product. This may occur when two solutions containing two different soluble substances are mixed; if a chemical reaction takes place such that a new substance is formed that is relatively insoluble, it will precipitate as a fine, solid powder. A precipitate will also appear, in general, when a supersaturated solution eliminates excess solute from solution.

Precipitates are classified by their appearance; they are described according to their texture as milky, gelatinous, or crystalline. Precipitation is used in identification tests for many ions in inorganic QUALITATIVE CHEMICAL ANALYSIS. An example is the addition of chloride ion to a solution containing silver ion, or vice versa. In either case, the formation of a white precipitate (silver chloride, $AgCl$) indicates the presence of the suspected ion.

precipitation (weather)   Precipitation in meteorology refers to all forms of liquid or solid water particles that form in the ATMOSPHERE and then fall to the Earth's surface. Types of precipitation include hail (see HAIL AND HAILSTONES), sleet, snow (see SNOW AND SNOWFLAKE), rain, and drizzle. Frost and dew are not classified as precipitation because they form directly on solid surfaces.

Formation

The formation of precipitation may occur at temperatures above or below freezing. Precipitation that is formed at temperatures entirely above freezing is called warm precipitation; cold precipitation involves ice at some stage of the process.

Warm Precipitation. Nearly all precipitation begins with the condensation of water vapor about microscopic particles called cloud condensation nuclei. Condensation may occur at relative humidities less than 100% for hygroscopic particles (those having an affinity for water) or may be delayed until the relative humidity exceeds 100% if the particles are hydrophobic (lacking an affinity for water). Sea-salt particles left behind when sea spray evaporates are particularly effective nuclei.

Saturation of air occurs when rising air currents cool adiabatically (that is, without loss of heat) by expansion. Because the saturation vapor pressure of water decreases exponentially with decreasing temperature (a property often summarized by the statement "Cold air can hold less water vapor than warm air"), cooling of a moist air mass by rising is an efficient mechanism for producing saturation and condensation.

The condensation processes are efficient in producing only cloud drops that are too small to have an appreciable fall velocity relative to the air. In order to produce precipitation particles that are heavy enough to fall to the ground, a cloud drop with a radius of 0.001 cm (0.0004 in) must increase its radius by a factor of 10 and its volume by a factor of 1,000. In clouds with temperatures above freezing, the growth occurs by coalescence, which is simply the merging of water drops that collide.

Cold Precipitation. Whereas collision and coalescence are efficient means for producing precipitation in the warm, humid tropical regions, the formation of precipitation in middle latitudes usually involves ice. Because the vapor pressure at saturation is less over ice than over water, ice crystals will grow at the expense of water drops when both exist together in a supercooled cloud (which contains liquid drops at temperatures below freezing).

Although most precipitation in middle latitudes begins as snow at altitudes above the freezing level (about 3 km/1.8 mi), the form of the precipitation reaching the surface depends on the temperature structure of the atmospheric layers through which the precipitation falls. If the temperature near the ground is warm enough, the snow has time to melt and reaches the ground as rain. A warm layer aloft and a subfreezing layer at the surface may produce sleet (ice pellets) or freezing rain (rain that freezes immediately on contact with surface objects). Hail occurs when alternating strong updrafts and downdrafts cause

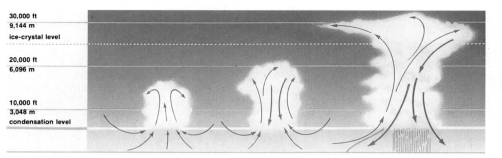

Moisture-laden warm air rises above the condensation level, cools, and forms a cumulus cloud. As the air continues to rise, cloud particles condense into water droplets. The falling rain brings down cold air. Droplets at the top of the cloud freeze and flatten the head into the shape of an anvil.

ice crystals to pass repeatedly through layers that contain supercooled water. The frequent passage through these layers allows the water to freeze around the growing hailstone in layer after layer.

Occurrence

Precipitation is produced whenever moist air rises sufficiently to produce saturation, condensation, and the growth of the precipitation particles. THUNDERSTORMS, with updraft wind components of more than 30 m/sec (67 mph), carry moist, low-level air to the tropopause, the upper boundary of the TROPOSPHERE, and hence can produce heavy precipitation in short amounts of time. Rainfall rates of 10 cm/hr (4 in/hr) are not uncommon in thunderstorms.

Less intense rainfall occurs over much larger scales (horizontal distances of 1,000 km/620 mi or more) when warm, moist air is lifted over a frontal surface or put in circulation around extratropical cyclones (those poleward of the tropical easterlies). In the Northern Hemisphere the favored location for this frontal type of precipitation is

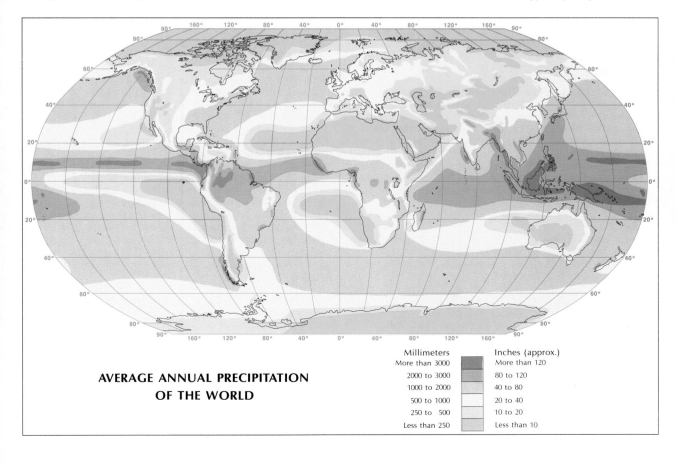

AVERAGE ANNUAL PRECIPITATION OF THE WORLD

Millimeters	Inches (approx.)
More than 3000	More than 120
2000 to 3000	80 to 120
1000 to 2000	40 to 80
500 to 1000	20 to 40
250 to 500	10 to 20
Less than 250	Less than 10

north of the surface warm FRONT and north of the track of an eastward-moving cyclone (see CYCLONE AND ANTICYCLONE).

Orographic precipitation is produced when air flowing over mountainous terrain is forced to rise. An example is the heavy precipitation that falls on the Sierra Nevadas in western North America. Moist Pacific air forced over the mountains produces up to 250 cm (100 in) of liquid precipitation annually. As the air descends over the lee slopes and warms adiabatically, the rainfall decreases abruptly. This rain shadow effect can produce extreme variability in rainfall over short horizontal distances.

Geographical Distribution

Because the annual distribution of precipitation depends on small-scale factors such as topographic variations as well as the vertical branches of the average global circulations (the general circulation), the geographic distribution of precipitation is not simple. In general, the average rising branch of the general circulation that occurs in a band between latitudes 15° S and 15° N results in heavy equatorial rainfall. Sinking motion occurs on the average over a band approximately 15° of latitude wide centered at 20–25° north and south, and rainfall is at a minimum near these latitudes (see DROUGHT). A second rainfall maximum occurs between 40° and 50° latitude because of the high frequency of traveling cyclones there. Finally, the annual precipitation drops off sharply toward both poles because the cold air cannot contain enough moisture for heavy precipitation.

---

precocial animal [pree-koh'-shul]   Precocial animals are animals that can function with little parental aid soon after they are born. They are contrasted with altricial animals, which require complete parental care; intermediate conditions, usually designated as semialtricial, also exist. The terms are commonly used in reference to the young of birds, but they are also applicable to mammals. The hare, born fully furred, with its eyes open, and able to hop about, is precocial. The rabbit, which is naked, blind, and helpless at birth, is altricial.

---

predestination   Predestination is a Christian doctrine according to which a person's ultimate destiny, whether it be salvation or damnation, is determined by God alone prior to, and apart from, any worth or merit on the person's part. In some cases, it is claimed that God determines only those to be saved; in others, that he determines those to be saved and those to be condemned. The latter teaching is called double predestination.

Predestination has roots in the Old Testament concept of an elect people. Hints of the doctrine appear in the New Testament, especially in Romans 8:28–30 and 9:6–24. It does not appear in full form, however, until the 5th century in the writings of Saint AUGUSTINE. Opposing PELAGIANISM, which held that humans can merit salvation by good works performed by application of their own will, Augustine insisted that humans require the help of God's GRACE to do good and that this grace is a free gift, given by

God without regard to human merit. Augustine's teaching was generally upheld by the church, but the further idea that some are predestined to condemnation was explicitly rejected at the Council of Orange (529).

The doctrine of predestination again became important in the late medieval period and passed into the theology of the Protestant reformers, especially John CALVIN. Calvin also insisted, against other forms of Christian theology, that grace is a gift and that a person cannot earn salvation. In the course of subsequent controversies, Calvin's doctrine of double predestination was strongly affirmed by the Synod of Dort (1619) in Holland and in the Westminster Confession (1647) in England. Until recently, it has remained a characteristic teaching of churches in the Calvinist tradition (see CALVINISM; PRESBYTERIANISM). In other branches of Christianity, however, it has received only limited support.

Preemption Act [pree-emp'-shuhn]   The Preemption Act, a statute passed by the U.S. Congress in 1841, allowed Western settlers to preempt public lands on which they had settled. It marked an end to the policy that gave speculators advantage over squatters in competition for land. No longer was revenue from the public domain considered more desirable than actual settlement of it. Before the act's passage, squatters, who usually had cleared their land and made various improvements, were often forced to forfeit it to claim-jumpers when it went on sale at public auction. The act, popularly known as the Log Cabin Bill, gave squatters exclusive rights to purchase 160 acres (64.7 ha) at the minimum price of $1.25 per acre. Largely superseded by the HOMESTEAD ACT of 1862, the Preemption Act was repealed by Congress in 1891.

---

prefabrication   Prefabrication is an approach to construction that employs precut and preassembled components that are assembled on-site. The housing industry prefers the names "industrialized construction" or "factory-built housing" because of the poor reputation of "prefab" homes, a result of the necessarily hurried and sometimes shoddy efforts of builders during the 1940s. Consumer antipathy was not reversed until the housing shortages of the late 1960s increased demand; improvements in quality resulted from government regulations enacted in 1976.

The mobile home, which is usually mobile only in the sense that it can be trucked from factory to site, is true prefabricated housing. Built and even furnished in a factory, it requires only a concrete pad and utility hookups at its final site. Mobile homes are cheap and quickly built but are often inferior in construction quality to conventional homes.

At another level of prefabrication is the panelized home package. Prefabricated wall panels, roof trusses, joists, and associated components are trucked to the site for assembly into frame homes that can be assembled in as little as a day, by crews with minimal carpentry skills, on properly prepared sites. Such homes equal in quality most conventionally built homes, but they are also comparable in price, because the home manufacturer's profit absorbs much of the builder's saving in labor.

pregnancy and birth   Pregnancy is a normal physiologic process that begins with conception, follows through development and growth of the fetus and delivery, and ends with return to a fully normal state approximately 6 weeks after birth. Pregnancy causes physiologic changes in the mother's bodily functions to allow for growth and development of the fetus. For the fetus, pregnancy is a time of dependency on the mother for nutrition and, thus, exposure to whatever agents to which the mother is exposed. Although a healthy pregnancy is normal for the majority of women, for some there may be complications that can lead to adverse outcome for the mother or the fetus.

The average biological length of human gestation, from conception to delivery, is 266 days. Due to the difficulty in assessing the exact date of conception, however, the clinical length of pregnancy is considered to be 280 days, or 40 weeks, calculated from the last normal menstrual period before the cessation of menses, or menstrual flow. This calculation assumes that ovulation occurs 14 days after the last menstrual period. Human gestation is further divided into trimesters, each of which lasts slightly more than 13 weeks.

Fetal Development

After the ovum, or egg, is fertilized by a sperm (see FERTILIZATION; REPRODUCTIVE SYSTEM, HUMAN), the fertilized ovum becomes implanted in the uterus.

First Trimester. Most fetal development, with the exception of such complex functions as brain development, occurs in the first trimester. The heart begins to beat after 4 weeks. By 8 weeks, the eyes, ears, nose, mouth, fingers, and toes are easily recognizable, and male and female reproductive systems have differentiated.

By 12 weeks, all of the recognizable organs have developed. During these first weeks the fetus is most vulnerable to potential teratogenic, or birth-defect–inducing, agents, such as drugs, radiation, and viruses. Drugs taken in by the mother during the first weeks can be of particular harm.

Second Trimester. During the second trimester, thin-walled skin develops, organs begin to function, and blood begins to be formed in the bone marrow. In addition, scalp hair appears, subcutaneous fat increases, and bones start to harden. The fetus begins to move in the first trimester, and at about 20 weeks gestation the mother can perceive the movements, the onset of which is called "quickening."

Third Trimester. The majority of fetal weight gain occurs in the third trimester. Ear lobes begin to develop cartilage, testes start to descend into the scrotum, nails begin to grow over the tips of the digits, and creases develop over the soles of the feet. In addition, the fetus begins to demonstrate coordinated patterns of behavior.

The mother and fetus are physiologically connected

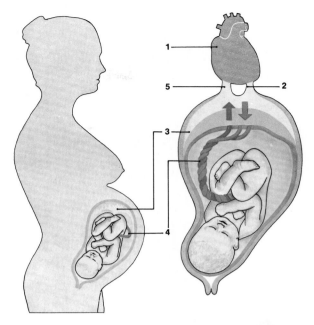

The growing fetus depends on its mother for nutrients and removal of wastes. The mother's heart (1) pumps blood through uterine arteries (2) into the placenta (3). Nutrients and oxygen (red arrow) diffuse through the placental membranes into the fetal bloodstream by way of the umbilical cord (4). Wastes (blue arrow) pass in the reverse direction to the maternal bloodstream through the uterine veins (5).

via the placenta, which filters oxygen and nourishment from the mother's blood to the baby via the umbilical cord. It also removes waste products from the fetus to the mother.

The Pregnant Body

A woman's body undergoes a variety of changes to prepare for the growth, nourishment, and birth of a child.

First Trimester. An early sign of pregnancy is the cessation of menses, which occurs due to the rising levels of human chorionic gonadotropin (HCG), a hormone produced by the placenta (see PREGNANCY TEST). This trimester is characterized by various discomforts, including nausea and vomiting, (so-called morning sickness), increased frequency of urination due to pressure of the enlarging uterus on the bladder, and breast soreness or tingling due to hormonal stimulation.

Second Trimester. Increasing abdominal girth and pressure from the growing uterus can lead to constipation. Normal intermittent uterine contractions, called Braxton-Hicks contractions, may occur. The mother may experience lightheadedness and may even faint due to the effects of the hormones on the blood vessels and the amount of blood diverted to the uterus, placenta, and fetus. Heartburn becomes an increasing problem because of the increasing pressure on the stomach by the enlarging uterus and delayed emptying of the stomach.

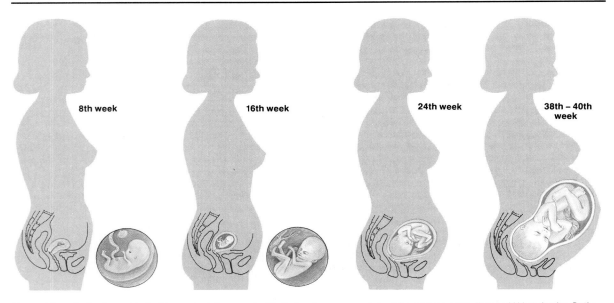

The most dramatic development in the fetus occurs between weeks 4 to 8 when the nervous and circulatory systems, lungs, liver, and kidney develop. By the end of week 8 the fetus is about 3.75 cm (1.5 in) long, fingers, toes, and eyelids are evident, and the bones are beginning to develop. By week 16 the fetus weighs about 168–224 g (6–8 oz) and measures 20–25 cm (8–10 in). The head and neck are more fully developed, and the sexual organs are formed. At 24 weeks the fetus is about 30 cm (12 in) long and weighs about 0.67 kg (1.5 lb). The inner ear is completely developed, and a loud noise may cause noticeable movement from the fetus. By 38 to 40 weeks, some light filters into the uterine cavity through the abdominal wall. The fetus's eyes are fully developed and respond to bright light by increasing fetal movement. Although there is wide variation in birth size in healthy babies, the average weight is 3.38 kg (7.5 lb), and length is about 50 cm (20 in).

Third Trimester. The last weeks of pregnancy become increasingly uncomfortable. Headaches, hemorrhoids, varicose veins, and swelling of the legs may occur. Shortness of breath is common due to the enlarged uterus, which prevents full expansion of the lungs. In the last days of gestation increased pelvic discomfort develops, caused by the dropping of the fetal head into the pelvis. False labor pains, or contractions of the uterus that do not lead to progressive dilatation, or opening, of the cervix, often occur.

Prenatal Care

Women who receive prenatal care have fewer complications of pregnancy and birth and have healthier babies. Also, the earlier and more consistently the care is received, the better the outcome. Education about pregnancy and child rearing is an important part of prenatal care, as are detection and treatment of abnormalities. Assessment and reassessment of risk to the mother and fetus are inherent in the provision of prenatal care. In fact, the best time to assess many of these risks is before a woman conceives. Therefore, it is becoming popular for women to receive preconception care while still planning a pregnancy.

Special Problems in Pregnancy

Although it is a normal process, some women have severe problems during pregnancy. The maternal mortality rate is the number of maternal deaths occurring per 100,000 live births. In many Western countries this number is lower than 10 deaths per 100,000 live births. In developing countries, however, maternal mortality rates can be as high as 1,000 per 100,000 live births. It is estimated that in the 1980s, approximately 500,000 women worldwide died every year from pregnancy-related causes. These deaths were related to either direct causes where the pregnancy itself or pregnancy complications led to maternal complications; or indirect causes where the pregnancy aggravated a maternal condition such as diabetes or heart disease. Problems of pregnancy include the following.

Spontaneous Abortion. Anywhere from 10% to 40% of human pregnancies end in miscarriage, or spontaneous abortion. Often, increased vaginal bleeding and cramping occurs around the time of a normal menstrual period and may go unnoticed by the woman. At least 50% of these spontaneous miscarriages appear to be due to major chromosomal abnormalities in the fetus.

Ectopic Pregnancy. A pregnancy that occurs at a site other than inside the uterus, such as in the fallopian tube, is termed ectopic. Such pregnancies are generally not viable and can in fact be life-threatening to the mother.

Infectious Diseases. A variety of infectious diseases, especially GERMAN MEASLES (rubella), TOXOPLASMOSIS, and CHICKEN POX, can lead to abnormalities of fetal growth and development. Some sexually transmitted diseases can be transmitted to the fetus, particularly gonorrhea, syphilis, and acquired immune deficiency syndrome (AIDS). Routine tests are conducted before and during pregnancy to test for these infections and, if possible, treat them before harm is done to the fetus.

Rh Disease. The RH FACTOR is a specific antigen located on red blood cells. If a mother has Rh negative blood and carries an Rh positive child, it is possible that the child's Rh positive blood cells will cross the placental barrier, triggering antibody production to the Rh factor in the mother. The maternal antibodies may attack the blood of a subsequent Rh positive fetus, causing a severe and often fatal type of anemia. Rh disease can be prevented with a vaccine.

Diabetes. DIABETES, or glucose intolerance, is a common complication of pregnancy. Diabetic women develop an increase in their insulin requirements when pregnant, which often makes their diabetes difficult to control. Labor and delivery of these mothers and babies may put them at risk for complications. In cases where diabetes is advanced, kidney and placental impairment may occur, which may lead to fetal growth problems. Glucose intolerance that develops during pregnancy is called gestational diabetes. It can be managed with diet alone, or in combination with insulin.

Hypertension. Women who have chronic hypertension, or high blood pressure, have an increase in complications of pregnancy, particularly kidney disease. In addition, certain hypertension diseases can develop during pregnancy. The causes of these diseases are poorly understood; they are characterized by protein in the urine and swelling, or edema, that can lead to seizures, liver and kidney damage, bleeding abnormalities, and poor fetal growth and outcome.

Anemia. Anemia, or a low blood-cell count, is common during pregnancy. Women often have a chronic iron-deficiency anemia before pregnancy due to monthly blood loss from menstruation. During pregnancy this is compounded by the increased nutritional requirements to support the fetus. Other problems, such as folate deficiency, can also cause anemia.

Pregnancy over Age 35. Generally, women over age 35 who become pregnant do well if they were in good health prior to the pregnancy. Certain conditions are more common in older pregnant women, however, such as hypertension and gestational diabetes. In addition, for each year over the age of 35, there is an increased risk of giving birth to a child with chromosomal anomalies, such as DOWN'S SYNDROME.

Poor Nutrition. It is ideal for the growing fetus if the mother gains at least 11.3–13.6 kg (25–30 lb) during her pregnancy. Low prepregnancy weight or low weight gain, particularly if food is low in protein, vitamins, and minerals, can impair fetal growth, including brain-cell development.

Smoking, Alcohol, Drugs. Smoking during pregnancy affects fetal growth and development due to increased carbon monoxide and decreased oxygen in the blood. Heavy drinking of alcohol impairs the mother's nutrition and can cause damage to her liver. In addition, the fetus can develop FETAL ALCOHOL SYNDROME, a cluster of mental and physical birth defects. The use of such drugs as mar-

ijuana, amphetamines, cocaine, and heroin all adversely affect the fetus. Babies are smaller, more sickly, and more likely to be stillborn. In addition, babies born to women who used drugs during pregnancy may be addicted to the drug at birth. (See also BIRTH DEFECTS.)

Tests of Fetal Well-Being

Valuable prenatal tests of fetal well-being range from basic techniques, such as the mother counting fetal movements, to highly technical tests, such as electronic fetal monitoring.

Amniocentesis. During an AMNIOCENTESIS, a sample of the amniotic fluid surrounding the fetus is obtained. This fluid contains cells from the fetus that can be cultured, or grown, to determine chromosomal makeup, fetal lung maturity, and other information about the fetus. Amniocentesis carries a risk of fetal death of less than 1%.

Chorionic Villus Sampling (CVS). In this procedure, a small amount of tissue is removed from the fetus at 9–10 weeks gestation. The genetic material of the tissue sample is tested for chromosomal abnormalities. The risks of fetal death due to the procedure are about the same as those from amniocentesis, or about 1%.

Percutaneous Umbilical Blood Sampling. During this procedure, also known as cordocentesis, blood is obtained directly from the umbilical cord. Chromosomal and biochemistry tests can be performed on this pure fetal blood sample. This procedure carries a higher risk of fetal loss than those above, somewhere in the range of 2% to 5%.

Fetal Monitoring Techniques. Electronic fetal monitoring has become commonplace in the evaluation of fetal well-being. Tracings of the fetal heart rate and uterine activity are used to evaluate the response to contractions, fetal movement, or external stimuli. These tests are begun after 28 weeks gestation, the time when a fetus has a reasonable chance of living outside the uterine environment, if that environment is deemed to be potentially dangerous. The nonstress test, which evaluates the fetal heart-rate response to fetal movement, is the most common method of antepartum (prebirth) screening for well-being. If the fetus is in some jeopardy, there will be no characteristic accelerations of the fetal heart rate accompanying fetal movement.

Ultrasound. When high-frequency sound waves are passed over the maternal abdomen, images of the fetus and surrounding tissues are produced, which can be observed on a viewing screen. Ultrasound monitors the growth of fetal structures. The technique is also used to evaluate fetal movement, breathing, the amount of amniotic fluid, the condition of the placenta, and other factors.

Fetal Surgery. Fetal surgery has been performed to correct fetal kidney obstruction, fetal hydrocephalus, and diaphragmatic hernia. The procedure, still considered experimental, is beneficial to only a small number of fetuses.

Birth

The onset of labor is a complex event involving the release of the hormone oxytocin from the baby's pituitary gland into the maternal circulation, stimulating uterine contraction.

Labor is divided into three stages. The first stage begins at the onset of regular contractions, which cause progressive dilatation of the cervix. The latent phase of this stage is from the start of labor to approximately 4 cm (1.6 in) dilatation, and the active phase is from the end of the latent phase to approximately 10 cm (3.9 in) dilatation. At the end of this stage, the baby's head begins to move down the birth canal, accompanied by a bloody discharge from the vagina and a marked change in contractions. This transition stage may last from a few minutes up to an hour. The second stage of labor begins at the onset of complete dilatation (cervix is dilated to 10 cm) and continues until birth. The third stage of labor begins at the birth of the baby and continues through the expulsion of the placenta.

Complications of Birth

Most often, pregnancy and birth results in an uncomplicated spontaneous vaginal delivery. Complications of labor and birth may occur, however, many of which can pose serious problems for the mother or the fetus or both.

Premature Labor and Birth. Premature labor is defined as labor that begins before the 37th week of pregnancy. Warning signs include mild menstruallike cramps, low backache, pelvic pressure, increased vaginal discharge or light bleeding, and diarrhea. A prompt exam will determine if preterm labor exists and if it should be treated with medications in an attempt to stop labor. Depending on gestational age, preterm birth frequently leads to respiratory distress, leading to a large proportion of neonatal (newborn) deaths; therefore, every attempt is made to recognize and stop preterm labor.

Premature Rupture of the Membranes. Rupture of the amniotic fluid sac prior to the onset of labor is considered premature rupture of the membranes. This may pose danger to the mother and baby due to the possibility of infection and preterm birth. Labor is sometimes induced if the pregnancy is far enough along; at other times the woman is placed at rest to reduce the risk of infection and prematurity.

Malpresentation. About 96% of babies are born head first. About 3% are born breech, with the buttocks and legs appearing first; they may be delivered vaginally or by CESAREAN SECTION. About 1% are born in a sideways position and must be delivered by cesarean. Malpresentations pose added risk to the mother and fetus.

Disorders of Labor. Deviation from the expected progress of labor may result in abnormal patterns of labor contraction, dilatation of the cervix, or descent of the fetus through the pelvic passage. Many disorders are treated with a contraction-inducing drug. Other ways of managing labor disorders include maternal rest, maternal and fetal position change, and administration of anesthesia. If treatment is unsuccessful, operative delivery is almost always necessary.

Pregnancy-Induced Hypertension (PIH). PIH is also known as preeclampsia or toxemia of pregnancy. The symptoms include swelling or edema, high blood pressure, and protein in the urine. When unrecognized or untreated in pregnancy, it can be life-threatening to the mother and the fetus.

Placenta Previa. The placenta normally implants itself at the top of the uterus. When it implants lower in the uterus, near or over the cervix, it can cause mild to severe bleeding during the last half of the pregnancy or during labor or both. If the placenta covers the entire cervix at the time labor begins, a cesarean delivery is necessary.

Multiple Births. Twins occur once in 80 births, triplets once in 10,000, and quadruplets almost once in 1 million. Multiples are more likely to be born prematurely, and these pregnancies are consequently at higher risk for complications compared to single-infant births. (See MULTIPLE BIRTH.)

Chorioamnionitis and Endometritis. Chorioamnionitis is an infection of the chorion of the placenta that may spread to surrounding maternal and fetal tissues. It is characterized by maternal fever, increased maternal and fetal heart rate, and uterine tenderness. In almost all cases, the infection affects the fetus and can be life-threatening. Endometritis is an infection of the uterine lining and is the most common cause of postpartum infection. It is common in women with chorioamnionitis and in women delivered by cesarean. Both conditions are very serious but, if recognized promptly, can be effectively treated with antibiotics.

Emergencies can also occur during labor, such as placental detachment before birth, problematic changes in the fetal heart rate, and the umbilical cord slipping in front of the fetal head—any of which may lead to an operative birth.

Operative Delivery. A cesarean section—the surgical delivery of a baby through the maternal abdomen—when needed, can be a lifesaving measure for the mother or the baby. Reasons for a cesarean include: cephalopelvic disproportion (baby is too large for mother's pelvis), transverse lie, fetal distress, prolapsed cord, failure to progress in labor, active genital herpes, and maternal diseases such as preeclampsia, diabetes, or heart disease.

Other operative deliveries can be conducted using forceps or a vacuum extractor. These techniques are used most often to "lift" the baby out of the birth canal during the very last stages of labor.

Modern Birth Practices

A variety of health-care professionals are involved in providing care to women during pregnancy. These include nurses, nurse-practitioners, nurse-midwives, family physicians, obstetricians, and perinatologists. There is no doubt that some women who are at very high risk for pregnancy complications must be under the care of a physician. Most pregnant women who are healthy with normal pregnancies, however, can receive care from nurse-midwives with appropriate consultation from physicians. The role of other health professionals such as dieticians and social workers is also valued in providing a safe and healthy pregnancy and birth.

Birth can now safely take place outside the hospital, depending on a woman's risk for complication and the training and expertise of the care providers. Approximately 90% of all births in the United States occur in the hospital. Birthing centers that create a homelike atmosphere and home birth sites for very low-risk women account for most of the remaining births.

Natural Childbirth. Natural childbirth is based on the belief that fear of anticipated pain of childbirth creates body and muscle tensions that in turn make the process more difficult and unnecessarily painful. It is very common for women to attend some type of childbirth-preparation class during the latter weeks of pregnancy. Many techniques are available, but three that are the most common are the Lamaze Method, or psychoprophylaxis technique; the Leboyer Technique, or gentle-birth technique; and the Bradley Method, or "husband-coached" technique.

Pain Relief. When pain of labor requires pharmocologic treatment, or when an operative birth is required, several methods of analgesia and anesthesia are available. Narcotics and sedatives are used to reduce anxiety and give some pain relief at certain times in labor. Regional anesthesia is becoming increasingly popular. General anesthesia used for obstetrics includes various combinations of barbiturates, narcotics, and muscle relaxants.

Postpartum Maternal and Child Care

The length of the postpartum period is traditionally 6 weeks. This is the length of time required for the mother's reproductive tissues to return to their former condition. It may take this number of weeks for the woman to return to her previous emotional state and her previous level of vigor as well.

During the first weeks of life, the baby adjusts to conditions outside the mother's body. The neonatal period, which extends from birth to 28 days of life, is the time when the baby's feeding (either breast or bottle) and sleep patterns are established. At 28 days of life, the newborn enters the period of INFANCY, which extends throughout the first year.

pregnancy test   A pregnancy test determines if a living embryo or fetus is present within a woman's body. It is often used in conjunction with such presumptive signs of pregnancy as cessation of menstrual periods, morning sickness, breast tenderness, and urinary frequency. Pregnancy tests generally measure a circulating hormone, human chorionic gonadotropin (HCG), produced by pregnancy tissues and present in the urine and blood of pregnant women.

Early tests were based on the injection of urine potentially containing HCG into frogs or rabbits to determine any effects of HCG. Such biologic assays have been replaced by more accurate methods that measure HCG levels in urine or blood. The urine pregnancy test (immunoassay) determines if the level of HCG is consistent with known pregnancy levels and is usually positive two weeks after conception or several days after a missed menstrual period. Widely available home pregnancy tests use an im-

munoassay for HCG with generally accurate results. A blood test (radioimmunoassay) is a more sensitive test that can detect minute quantities of HCG. This test can be positive within days of conception and before a missed period.

Pregnancy tests, in addition to diagnosing pregnancy, are also used to assess the viability of pregnancy, or the presence of tubal pregnancy. HCG can also be produced by some tumors, in which case pregnancy tests can be used as a marker of tumor activity.

With new radioimmunoassay techniques, false-negative tests are uncommon. The most common cause of false-negative tests is advanced pregnancy, because HCG values tend to decrease during the course of gestation. False-positive tests may occur, possibly due to certain medications, or by such clinical situations as incomplete miscarriage, ectopic pregnancy, and tumor.

prehistoric animals   see EARTH, GEOLOGICAL HISTORY OF; EVOLUTION; FOSSIL RECORD

prehistoric art   The term *prehistoric art* refers generally to the paintings, engravings, and sculptures created from about 35,000 to 12,000 years ago during the last ice age in Eurasia. The term is also often applied to the art of the succeeding Mesolithic and Neolithic cultures in this area, as well as to the rock art produced by various nonliterate cultures from later periods.

Paleolithic Art

The earliest stone tools date from more than 2 million years ago, but prehistoric art is a relatively recent development; it first appeared during the Upper PALEOLITHIC PERIOD, the last division of the Old Stone Age. It is associated with the remains of CRO-MAGNON MAN (*Homo sapiens sapiens*), who appeared in Europe about 35,000 years ago, having gradually replaced the NEANDERTHALERS. So far no direct evidence of Neanderthal art has been found.

The Venus of Willendorf (c.30,000–25,000 BC), discovered (1908) in Austria, represents one of the earliest forms of statuary art. The exaggerated form of the Venus figurine emphasizes her power of fertility. The limestone statuette is one of a group of distinct types of prehistoric goddess figurines. (Naturhistorisches Museum, Vienna.)

Types of Art. Paleolithic art appeared in the form of either (1) pictorial images or markings engraved, carved, or painted on the walls and roofs of rock-shelters or caves; or (2) portable works engraved or painted on stone, bone, or ivory or carved in the round on soft stone or ivory. In eastern Europe, as at the Czechoslovakian site of DOLNÍ VĚSTONICE, figurines were modeled in clay, placed in the ashes near a fire, and hardened by heat. Although wood may also have been used, no examples have survived.

Portable art includes figurines, necklaces, or bracelets, as well as decorated tools like spear-throwers or harpoons. The engravings seen on these objects often closely resemble those on cave walls and are useful for dating mural art. The cave at ALTAMIRA, Spain, provides an example. There, at a level containing Solutrean artifacts, engraved stone slabs were found. The finely hatched hinds with which these slabs were decorated proved to be identical in technique with the figures seen on the walls.

The first report of cave art was in 1879, when the painted ceiling at Altamira was discovered. The claim that this represented Stone Age art, however, aroused general disbelief; it seemed impossible that art of such sophistication and excellence should have been the work of primitive people. New finds were made, some of them in caves that had been sealed since the Stone Age. Finally, at the beginning of this century, Paleolithic art was recognized as authentic. To date, about 230 caves containing cave art are known; the great majority are in France and Spain, although a number have also been found in Italy, Portugal, and the USSR. One of the reasons for the concentration of cave art in western Europe may be the presence there of many limestone cliffs containing caves and rock-shelters. The geographical range of portable art is much wider; indeed, a great number of the so-called Venus figurines—small, highly stylized statuettes of nude, usually obese women—come from the USSR, where they were made before 25,000 BC.

Periods. Characteristic tool traditions serve to label periods and styles of prehistoric art. The earliest representative style is the AURIGNACIAN I (c.30,000 BC). Art associated with this culture typically appears in the form of animals engraved in rigid outline or painted black or red, finger drawings on clay, imprints of hands, and engravings—chiefly representing abstract symbols—on slabs. During the late Aurignacian and Perigordian (also sometimes called Gravettian) periods (c.29,000–c.20,000 BC) the quality of art improved, and the animals are sometimes shaded—although they are still shown isolated, with little sense of composition. Symbols, often ambiguous in meaning, become numerous and complicated. The succeeding Solutrean culture (c.19,000–c.15,000 BC) is known mainly through large bas-relief friezes like those at the French site of Cap-Blanc; the monumental paintings at the Pech-Merle cave, France, are also ascribed to this period. Solutrean portable art is represented mainly at the cave of Parpallo, near Valencia in Spain, with its thousands of engraved or painted limestone slabs. The high point of Paleolithic art dates from the period of Magdalenian culture (c.15,000–10,000 BC), to which belong the majority of the finest cave paintings, including those of LASCAUX and Altamira.

Techniques. Sculpted cave art is generally found in shallow rock-shelters or at the entrances of caves; it was probably executed by daylight. Most cave art, however, is found deep inside the caves. The distance from the cave mouth to the great fish at La Pileta, Spain, is about 1,190 m (1,300 yd). To work inside the caves, Cro-Magnon artists used torches; the smudges caused by these can still be seen on the walls.

Although many symbols and some masked human fig-

The elaborate cave paintings (c.19,000–15,000 BC) at Pech-Merle, in France, are characterized by animal and hunting motifs. The horses are shown in foal and are framed by painted silhouettes of hands, believed to have possessed magical significance.

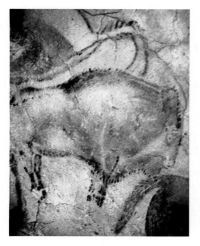

The cave paintings at Lascaux, France (below), and Altamira, Spain (left), are representative of late Ice Age higher hunting culture art. These details from Lascaux and Altamira, respectively, portray a cow with small horses and a standing bison. Various techniques, including outlining and coloring with charcoal and mineral pigments, were used by Paleolithic painters.

size of the animals may violate the rules of realism, the drawing is always naturalistic and accurate.

To date, no wholly satisfactory theories as to the meaning and interpretation of cave art have been offered. Much of it is hidden in dark and barely accessible places where it never could have been seen by more than one or two people at a time. Perhaps such art served a ritual function in connection with passage rites, like those of primitive peoples living today. Although some figures of wounded animals may hint at hunting magic, many of the portable artworks appear to have been primarily decorative; others, notably the female figurines, such as the famous VENUS OF WILLENDORF, suggest a fertility cult.

Mesolithic Art

At the end of the Paleolithic Period the climate grew milder, and caves were deserted both as dwelling places and as sanctuaries. The MESOLITHIC PERIOD, or Middle Stone Age, began about 9000 BC and lasted until about 4000 BC in western Europe, although it was much shorter in such regions as the Near East. The tradition of cave art survived in the Levant rock art of eastern Spain and in the Scandinavian and Russian rock engravings, whereas portable art was replaced in many areas by the Azilian painted or engraved pebbles.

The rock art of eastern Spain is generally found in shallow rock-shelters where access is difficult. Painted representations at Dos Aguas, Gasulla, and Polvovín, among other important Spanish sites, depict people tracking, hunting singly or in groups, doing battle, dancing, and gathering honey or fruit. These complex artistic representations often reveal some idea of perspective and composition, although various styles recalling Magdalenian traditions are also recognizable.

In Mesolithic Scandinavia and northern Russia the Paleolithic rock art tradition was maintained in the form of huge animal engravings, mainly on cliffs, showing reindeer, elks, bears, and fish, notably whales. These works, dated at about 5000 BC, may in fact have been executed by late Magdalenians who followed the dwindling herds of reindeer to their present habitat.

Neolithic, Bronze, and Iron Age Art

The NEOLITHIC PERIOD, or New Stone Age, began in the Near East by about 8000 BC; within several millennia it had spread throughout Anatolia and eastern Europe. Neolithic rock art is characterized by marked simplification and schematization; the figures grow progressively coarser and heavier. The scenes depict mainly domestic activities, with little indication of hunting or gathering. This schematic rock art is well represented in Spain, with a large concentration in the area of Ciudad Real, as well as in southern France and Italy; such art dates from c.4000 to c.2000 BC.

Also produced during the Neolithic Period were a variety of portable clay statuettes of female figures apparently related to some form of fertility cult centered on a MOTHER GODDESS. Numerous figurines dating from the 4th to the 2d millennium BC have been found at sites in eastern Europe and in the USSR. The Neolithic statuettes

ures have been found, animals are the chief subject of Paleolithic art. They may be carved in high or low relief, modeled in clay, or engraved either deeply or finely and then hatched. The paintings exhibit various techniques: they may be done in outline only, filled in with flat wash, or shaded in one or several colors. Finger drawings were made by either impressing the fingers on wet clay or dipping them into paint. Hand imprints, sometimes considered the earliest art, may be positive, executed by applying the paint-daubed hand against the wall, or negative, as when pigment is applied around the outline of the hand. The natural mineral pigments included yellow ocher, red ocher, manganese, and iron oxide; charcoal was also sometimes used as a colorant. The colors were ground and mixed with animal fat, vegetable juices, water, or blood and then applied with a stick or brush. The often-seen spray effects may have been obtained by blowing pigments through a hollow reed.

Subject Matter. The animals depicted are mostly mammoths, bison, horses, deer, wild cattle and goats, and wild boars. Although the reindeer was an important food source, it is very seldom pictured. Although the relative

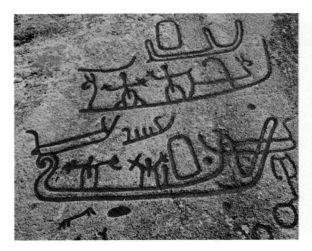

A schematized style of representation characterizes this Bronze Age rock engraving of boats (c.1000 BC), discovered near Borge, Norway. Bronze and Iron Age artists depicted a variety of themes not seen in earlier rock art traditions.

Tassili n'Ajjer, in Algeria, is one of the richest sites of neolithic rock art in the Sahara region. The naturalistic rendering of this animal possesses the numinous quality that pervades prehistoric animal portraits.

generally appear far less stylized than the carved Venus figurines of the preceding Paleolithic Period.

Beginning in the 4th millennium BC the cultures associated with the erection of megalithic monuments often decorated their large burial chambers and alignments of standing stones with engraved symbols (see MEGALITH). Some of the most impressive examples are found in Malta, northern France, and Ireland, where decorated megalithic monuments date from c.3500 BC. Menhirs—single, freestanding megalithic stones—are also sometimes carved, with notable examples in Portugal, Spain, and Corsica.

During the BRONZE AGE, schematic figures and symbols dating from c.2000 BC were superimposed on earlier works of rock art in Spain, Scandinavia, and the Lake

This ornamental stone (c.3000–1800 BC) marked the entrance to a passage grave at Newgrange, Ireland. It exemplifies one of the most elaborate Neolithic carving techniques, which included polishing the finished grooves.

Onega region of Karelia, USSR. The last prehistoric rock art of Europe is that of the IRON AGE, in which chariots and ploughs are often depicted.

Other Traditions of Prehistoric Rock Art

Africa. The Saharan and Libyan deserts of Africa may constitute the world's largest repository of open-air art. Various styles have been recorded in North Africa, the most ancient being that of the engraved or painted wild cattle, which may date from as far back as 6500 BC; scenes that include hunters or herdspeople, as at Tassili n'Ajjer in the Algerian Sahara, are more recent. Several links between the Saharan rock drawings and early dynastic Egyptian art have been found; scenes with charioteers and horses may be as recent as 500 BC.

The nomadic SAN (Bushman) people of Tanzania, Zimbabwe (Rhodesia), South Africa, and South West Africa have also left paintings and engravings. Depicting scenes of warfare, the hunt, and mythological subjects, they are characterized by subtle shading and naturalistic modeling of the figures. Some date from as early as 15,000 BC; the outstanding scene of animals from Philipp's Cave, South Africa, is dated c.1500 BC. More recent painting often shows European traders with stovepipe hats (see AFRICAN ART).

The Americas. A large area of the Americas contains rock art; the largest concentrations are on the northwest coast, the Great Basin area, and in the southwestern United States, as well as in Mexico, Venezuela, and Colombia. Stenciled hands and footprints are frequent motifs. Indian rock art may be naturalistic, symbolic, or schematic. Although a carved animal head from Tepexpan, Mexico, is dated c.9000 BC, many examples of prehistoric Indian art are dated to the recent past; the intricate, mazelike Chibcha rock drawings from Colombia, for example, are ascribed to the 12th century AD. Some North American rock art may date from as far back as 2000 BC, but the frequent representations of figures on horseback could not be earlier than AD c.1550. (See also INDIANS OF NORTH AMERICA, ART OF THE.)

Australia. The Australian ABORIGINES developed a highly original tradition of rock art. The principal preoccupation is with spirits, usually represented by anthropomorphic figures, and with mythical ancestors and the creation of the world. Another original feature is the "X-ray figure," or animal outline within which the internal organs are shown. The origins of aboriginal rock art are very ancient; a hearth from Koonalda that includes some finger engravings is dated 17,000 BC. (See also OCEANIA, ART OF.)

This rock painting has been executed in the "X-ray" style of the Australian aboriginal painters, revealing the animal's internal organs. Aboriginal rock paintings, which belong to a distinctive artistic tradition, possess profound magicoreligious significance. (Städtisches Museum für Völkerkunde, Frankfurt am Main.)

---

prehistoric humans   Prehistoric humans may be defined as the prehistoric populations of the living human species, *Homo sapiens*, together with other, ancestral species of the genus *Homo*. Paleoanthropologists are concerned with reconstructing the evolutionary history and ways of life of prehistoric *Homo sapiens* and of the extinct human species HOMO ERECTUS and HOMO HABILIS. They seek the origin of the genus *Homo* among the early hominids, or prehumans, and the origin of the hominids among still earlier hominoid, or apelike, PRIMATES.

History of Paleoanthropology

Paleoanthropology originated with the recognition that the oddly shaped stones found in the 18th and 19th centuries in certain ancient river gravels of Europe were in fact artifacts—tools made by humans—rather than natural phenomena. With the growth of scientific GEOLOGY in the 19th century, most biologists came to accept a time scale of Earth history running into millions of years. Along with this theory grew the notion of a stage in human history, before the invention of metalworking, when stone tools alone were used. The discovery by the Western world of "stone age" peoples still living in places such as Australia reinforced the idea that human society and technology had developed, or evolved, through a series of stages. The idea, however, that the human species had itself evolved physically from a nonhuman species was not generally acknowledged until the last quarter of the 19th century, when biologists began to accept the evolutionary theories of Charles Darwin (see EVOLUTION). Darwin and his colleagues Thomas Henry Huxley and Ernst Haeckel showed that humans share many anatomical features with chimpanzees, gorillas, and orangutans, and they argued that *Homo sapiens* probably evolved from a more primitive species that resembled these apes in many respects.

During the past century numerous human, prehuman, and hominoid fossils were discovered that in a general way linked the modern human species to its apelike ancestors (see ARCHAEOLOGY). At the same time, ideas of human cultural evolution also became more refined. Excavations and discoveries enabled archaeologists to recognize additional stages in human PREHISTORY. The "stone age" was subdivided into the PALEOLITHIC PERIOD, or Old Stone Age, preceding the invention of agriculture, and the NEOLITHIC PERIOD, or New Stone Age, which succeeded it. The Paleolithic was subdivided into lower, middle, and upper divisions, defined by the invention of new techniques of stone working, mainly in Europe. Again using evidence mainly from Europe, the later stages of prehistory were distinguished as the BRONZE AGE and the IRON AGE. As archaeological research has been applied to regions outside Europe, some of these stages have been found to be inappropriate (Africa, for instance, had no Bronze Age), and modern archaeologists are more concerned with local sequences of cultural evolution than with universal stages.

The Pleistocene Setting of Human Evolution

Fossil evidence indicates that the earliest true humans (members of the genus *Homo*) appeared close to the end of the Pliocene Epoch, about two to three million years ago. Most of human evolution therefore occurred during the Pleistocene Epoch, which stretches from about 2.5 million years ago to the present. The Pleistocene has been a time of unusually great environmental variation. Comparatively short warm periods have alternated with periods of glaciation, when the climate cooled and ice sheets spread from the poles (see ICE AGES).

By the time of the appearance of *Homo*, glaciers had formed on the higher mountains in mid-latitudes. During the past 2.5 million years the cooling trend culminated in continental glaciations, in which sheets of ice, hundreds of feet thick, blanketed much of Europe and North America. During glacial episodes plants and animals that had adapted to warm climates were replaced by arctic plants and animals such as the reindeer. Although the climate was harsh, the plains of glacial Europe and North America supported large herds of game and were therefore rich hunting grounds for any human populations hardy enough to inhabit them.

Climatic variation during the Pleistocene also occurred in the tropics. Evidence exists, especially in Africa, that cool, moist periods, when forests spread, alternated with drier intervals, when forests retreated before dry grasslands and desert. The relationship between rainy periods in the tropics and glaciations in mid-latitudes is not clear. An important side effect of glaciation was to alter the level of the oceans. With much of the Earth's water frozen, the oceans shrank, exposing the continental shelves and providing new dry-land corridors, notably between Asia and North America by way of Siberia and Alaska (see BERING LAND BRIDGE).

Human Origins

The human species is a member of the mammalian order Primates. It is related, in descending order of closeness, to apes, monkeys, tarsiers, and lemurs. The earliest traces of fossil primates are found in rocks about 70 million years old; by about 45 million years ago a side branch of this primitive ancestral group had given rise to more advanced primates that were quite similar to modern lemurs. Among this group can be seen characteristics that are distinctive of modern primates: relatively large brains, a well-developed visual sense, and nails rather than claws. All of these characteristics were evidently adapted for life in the trees.

Early Ancestral Forms. About 35 million years ago appeared the first evidence of primitive monkeylike primates. True monkeys and apes appeared about 22 million years ago, at the beginning of the long geological epoch known as the Miocene. From rocks of this age have been found the earliest fossils representing the primates of sub-Saharan Africa, the probable place of origin of the human family.

Early Miocene apes and monkeys probably behaved and looked not unlike their living relatives. Among the apes was the group called *Dryopithecus*, believed to include the evolutionary ancestor of both hominids and apes such as the chimpanzee and gorilla. For most of the Miocene, *Dryopithecus* was widespread and successful. However, as the climate grew drier, *Dryopithecus* disappeared from the fossil record. Presumably, it retreated with the forests to the tropical regions where the great apes still survive.

For many years anthropologists assumed that the origin of hominids as a group separate from apes must have occurred in Europe between 14 and 10 million years ago. Most anthropologists now believe that the split occurred much later and that it occurred in Africa. *Oreopithecus*, an apelike primate that lived in Europe about 10 million years ago, was proposed as the first hominid, but it is now believed that this primate died out completely without leaving descendants. Likewise, *Ramapithecus* and its close relative *Sivapithecus* were once championed as the first hominids. It was argued that *Ramapithecus*, in com-

mon with the hominids, had adapted to life outside the forest and lived off the hard, tough vegetable foods of the grasslands. It is, however, highly unlikely that *Ramapithecus* walked upright or used tools more than living apes. Moreover, most anthropologists now feel that its early origin rules out the possibility that it was a hominid. Pointing to the remarkable similarity in blood chemistry and genetics between chimpanzees and humans, they maintain that the earliest hominids originated from an apelike stock no more than 8 million years ago. In this case, the earliest true hominid is probably AUSTRALOPITHECUS.

Australopithecus. The genus *Australopithecus*, first described on the basis of a single skull from South Africa, is now represented by many fossils from several areas of the African continent. Important sites include OLDUVAI GORGE, Tanzania; Lake Rudolf (Turkana), Kenya; and Hadar, Ethiopia. The genus appears to have been confined to Africa, where it existed during the time range between 5.5 and 1 million years ago.

Although primitive in some respects, *Australopithecus* is classified within the human family, Hominidae, because it shares with humans certain significant advances over earlier forms. In particular, its leg bones show that it walked upright; its brain, although still within the ape range, was relatively larger than that of most apes; and neither sex had the projecting canine teeth (fangs) that are used by apes in fighting. Presumably, *Australopithecus* used simple clubs or threw stones to defend itself. *Australopithecus* varied considerably in size—from less than 1.2 m (4 ft) to about the size of a modern human.

Three species are generally distinguished (although some classification schemes list five): *Australopithecus africanus*, the smallest and earliest, which may have been ancestral both to humans and to later *Australopithecus*, and two larger, more specialized and robust species (*A. robustus* and *A. boisei*), which overlap in time with early members of the genus *Homo* and which evidently became extinct. An australopithecine fossil known as the "black skull," similar to *A. boisei*, is thought by some to represent a new species.

All species of *Australopithecus* lived in open woodland and grassland rather than in forests as had the apes, and the ways in which they differ physically from apes can be seen as adaptations to the new habitat. Whereas their front teeth were quite small, their back, grinding teeth (molars and premolars) were huge—evidently an adaptation to hard chewing. Studies of minute scratches on their dental enamel suggest that their diet consisted largely of hard, chewy seeds and berries. Although *Australopithecus* probably ate small animals, as do chimpanzees, most scientists consider it unlikely that *Australopithecus* was a systematic hunter, or "killer ape," as this species used to be depicted.

Whether *Australopithecus* regularly made and used tools is a matter of debate. Some paleoanthropologists have suggested that the broken bones and tusks found at *Australopithecus* cave sites may have been used as tools and weapons; other paleoanthropologists consider it more likely that the broken animal bones were the leavings of

In this artist's rendering, members of the genus Australopithecus *are portrayed near a rock-shelter on the African savanna. The australopithecines probably used stones, bones, and sharp sticks as simple tools and weapons. Food sharing and a division of labor are thought to have existed among these humanlike creatures, whose diet consisted of gathered plant foods and meat acquired through hunting and scavenging.*

leopards and hyenas that also frequented the caves. Although some sites with *Australopithecus* fossils have also yielded well-made stone tools, these tools are more likely to be the handiwork of early, true humans, whose remains are also found at these sites. If, as seems probable at present, *Australopithecus* was no more of a hunter and toolmaker than the modern chimpanzee, why did it, unlike the apes, develop two-legged locomotion, or bipedalism? The reasons for this development, too, are debated.

One theory is that *Australopithecus* babies were more helpless and had to be carried in the arms of their mothers. Another emphasizes the importance of free hands to an animal that had no large fangs to defend itself. Yet another sees the advantage of bipedalism as freeing the hands to gather the small, scattered vegetable foods on which *Australopithecus* usually fed. These ideas are not mutually exclusive. The brain of *Australopithecus*, although less than half the size of a modern human's, was relatively larger than that of an ape. Brain expansion may have been favored by a more complex social organization, perhaps one in which "families" of one adult male and one or more females and their young clustered in troops for protection.

Early Humans

From deposits dating from about 2 million years ago have emerged the first direct evidence of behavior that decisively separates the species *Homo* from other animals. This behavior includes the regular use of stone tools and other artifacts and the life-style called hunting and gathering. In contrast to the foraging of nonhuman primates, the hunting and gathering of the first humans involved a division of labor. Some group members (probably males) hunted animals for meat, whereas the rest searched for small game and wild vegetable foods. All shared the food they collected. This cooperative way of life strongly favored the evolution of technology (cutting tools and containers, especially).

Additionally, there is evidence that these early humans meticulously planned their hunts. So the human capacity for abstract thought, foresight, and adaptation to local conditions of life also apparently improved. The evidence for these changes is seen in the gradually increasing size of the brain, the development of increasingly complex technology (represented by stone working), and the rapid geographical spread of the human species.

Homo Habilis. After the extinction of *Australopithecus*, no more than one hominid species existed at any time. However, the single human species is given different names at different stages of its evolution. The earliest humans are known as *Homo habilis*. Physically, they were much like *Australopithecus*, apart from the larger size of

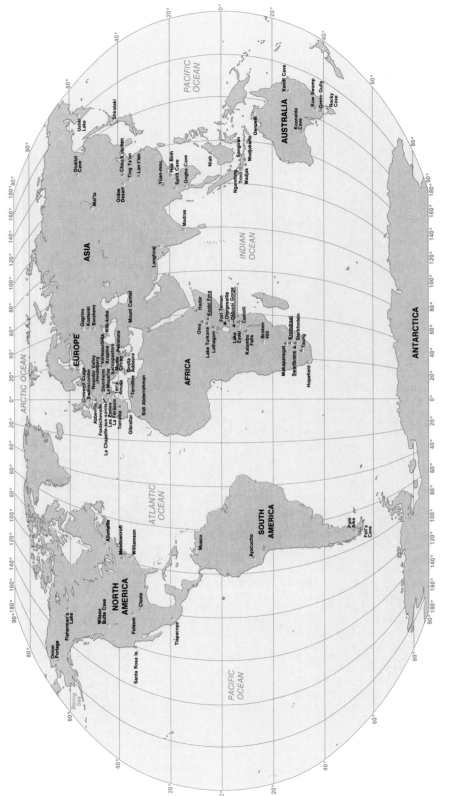

PREHISTORIC HUMANS: 14,000,000 TO 10,000 YEARS AGO

▲ Ramapithecus (14 to 8 million years ago)

▲ Australopithecus afarensis (4 to 3 million years ago)

▲ Australopithecus africanus (3.5 to 2.5 million years ago)

▲ Homo habilis (2 to 1.5 million years ago)

▲ Australopithecus robustus and Australopithecus boisei (1.5 to 1 million years ago)

▲ Homo erectus (1.5 million to 300,000 years ago)

▲ Neanderthal man and other archaic Homo sapiens (250,000 to 40,000 years ago)

▲ Modern man (Homo sapiens sapiens) (40,000 to 10,000 years ago)

NORTH AMERICA

Onion Portage
Fisherman's Lake
Allumette
Meadowcroft
Williamson
Wilson Butte Cave
Clovis
Folsom
Santa Rosa Is.
Tlapacoya

SOUTH AMERICA

Muaco
Ayacucho
Palli Aike
Fell's Cave

EUROPE

Creswell Crags
Swanscombe
Neander Valley
Heidelberg
Steinheim
Vértesszöllös
Krapina
Abbeville
Fontéchevade
LeMoustier
Les Eyzies
Saccopastore
La Chapelle-aux-saints
La Ferrassie
Grotte Petralona
Terra Amata
Circeo
Torralba
Gibraltar
Ternifine
Addaura
Sidi Abderrahman

ASIA

Diuktai Cave
Ushki Lake
Shiraताki
Chou-K'ou-tien
Ting Ts'un
Lan-t'ien
Yüan-mou
Mal'ta
Ordos Desert
Madras
Langhnaj
Mount Carmel
Gagarino
Kostenki
Borshevo
Klik-koba
Hoa Binh
Spirit Cave
Ongba Cave
Niah
Ngandong
Trinil
Wadjak
Sangiran
Modjokerto
Oenpeli

AFRICA

Omo
Hadar
Lake Turkana
Lothagam
Koobi Fora
Fort Ternan
Olorgesailie
Olduvai Gorge
Laetolil
Lake Eyasi
Kalambo Falls
Broken Hill
Makapansgat
Swartkrans
Kromdraai
Sterkfontein
Taung
Hopefield

AUSTRALIA

Kenfit Cave
Koonalda Cave
Kow Swamp
Green Gully
Rocky Cove

ANTARCTICA

PACIFIC OCEAN
ATLANTIC OCEAN
INDIAN OCEAN
ARCTIC OCEAN
Bering Sea

their brains. Most *Homo habilis* fossils have been discovered in East Africa. They are often found with simple implements, including stone choppers, cores, and sharp-edged flakes, called the Oldowan tool industry. At some sites evidence exists that animals up to hippopotamus size were butchered and eaten, but whether the meat was obtained by hunting or by scavenging the carcasses of dead animals has not been determined.

Homo Erectus. As well as favoring the evolution of the brain, the early development of technology and culture also affected the evolution of the teeth and jaws. As tools (and later fire) were used to prepare and soften food, the teeth of early humans became smaller and the jaws less robust. By about 1.6 million years ago, these trends had produced a mentally and physically more advanced population called *Homo erectus*. At about the same time, the hand ax, a finely chipped, versatile, two-edged stone implement first appeared. Hand axes typify the Acheulean tool industry, which also included a variety of pounders and flakes.

Although first recognized in Asia (see JAVA MAN and PEKING MAN), *Homo erectus* populations also lived throughout the warmer parts of the Old World. In Europe the jaw of HEIDELBERG MAN and many scattered hand axes attest to their presence (although some researchers consider this fossil to belong to an archaic *Homo sapiens*). In

Africa both fossil remains and habitation sites have been found throughout the length of the continent. On the whole, *Homo erectus* seems to have preferred open or lightly wooded country, where game would have been most plentiful. Although the colder regions of the far north were not inhabited, *Homo erectus* was sufficiently adaptable to survive in a variety of habitats, from tropical Africa to chilly central China. Undoubtedly, the more rigorous climate of the north stimulated technological inventions. One of the most important of these was the use of fire, in cooking, for warmth, and in the hunt. This vital step probably occurred about 500,000 years ago.

Archaic Homo Sapiens and the Neanderthalers. By about 250,000 years ago humans had become sufficiently advanced to be assigned to *Homo sapiens*. However, until about 40,000 years ago, they were not identical to modern humans. They retained many ancestral features recalling *Homo erectus*: a large face with big teeth and a low skull with heavy brow ridges and little or no forehead. In brain size, however, they were within the modern range, which distinguishes them from the small-brained *Homo erectus*. Fossils of these archaic humans have been found at many sites: among the best-known early specimens are the skulls from Steinheim, Germany, Swanscombe, England, and Broken Hill, Zambia.

An important sign of technological advance was the

The Hortus cave, near Montpellier in southern France, was used as a summer shelter about 40,000 years ago by the prehistoric human population known as the Neanderthalers. The reconstruction shows a hunter sharpening a wood spear. Behind him a young man is making fire with the help of an elder, and a woman is scraping hides. The Mousterian tool kit in the foreground includes points, scrapers, and backed blades.

invention, about 100,000 years ago, of the Levallois technique of stone working, in which a large thin flake is struck from a core and used as a blank for making more specialized tools such as knives and scrapers (see LEVAL-LOISIAN). As human populations began to exploit a wider variety of habitats, new, local tool traditions appeared: the Fauresmith on the plains of South Africa, the Sangoan on the fringes of the African forest, and the MOUSTERI-AN in the frigid plains of glacial Europe.

The makers of the Mousterian tools were the NEAN-DERTHALERS (*Homo sapiens neanderthalensis*), who flourished between 100,000 and 40,000 years ago. Far from being the brutish "apemen" of popular imagination, the Neanderthalers were an advanced human group whose ingenuity enabled them to wrest a living from the most challenging habitat then occupied by humankind. Mousterian tools were adapted to a wide variety of tasks: cutting and preparing meat, scraping hides, working wood, and many others. Evidence of rituals—and careful burial of the dead—suggests the existence of religious beliefs. Given the evidence for ritual and complex beliefs, it is likely that the brain of archaic *Homo sapiens* was sufficiently evolved to permit the use of true language.

About 40,000 years ago humans of modern type replaced the archaic humans such as the Neanderthalers. Some anthropologists believe that only a very few archaic populations evolved directly into *Homo sapiens sapiens* (the taxonomic classification of fully modern humans), the rest being displaced as the moderns expanded their range. Others hold that archaic groups everywhere became "modern" by evolutionary change. Both ideas are probably to some extent correct; evolution of archaic populations into the modern human type probably occurred in many regions, but in other regions, such as western Europe, the archaics may have been absorbed and displaced by invading modern populations.

Upper Paleolithic and Mesolithic Populations. In Europe and elsewhere in the Old World the remains of the earliest physically modern humans occur with tools that attest to the invention of new techniques of manufacture, especially the production of long, narrow flake tools, called blades. These innovations define a new period of prehistory, the Upper Paleolithic. In the Old World this period began about 40,000 years ago, in the middle of the last glaciation. In the Americas the comparable stage, the Paleo-Indian, began at least 12,000 years ago with the migration of people across the Bering Strait from Siberia (see NORTH AMERICAN ARCHAEOLOGY).

In both continents culture based on hunting and gathering reached its peak of development during this period. Hunters became more expert, devising sophisticated techniques that involved large numbers of people working in cooperation to kill whole herds of game. In areas such as west and central Europe, where game was most plentiful, permanent communities sprang up, and the population rose in numbers and density. Besides the stone blade, which could be fashioned into any one of a variety of handy small tools, technical innovations included tools made of bone and ivory, clothing sewn together and decorated with beads, and among some groups a system of

reckoning time by the Sun and Moon.

Among the finest productions of the Upper Paleolithic are the paintings and engravings (mostly animal representations) executed on stone slabs or ivory or on the walls of caves. Their function is still obscure, but some are thought to have involved hunting magic or a ritual use (see PREHISTORIC ART).

About 10,000 years ago the ice sheets and tundra vegetation in the north gave way rapidly to coniferous and hardwood forest. The great herds of bison, horses, reindeer, and mammoths were replaced by more elusive, hard-to-hunt animals such as moose and elks. Human society and technology evolved in adaptation to the changing conditions. The resulting cultures are called Mesolithic in the Old World and Archaic in North America. New tools included microliths, tiny stone blades that were hafted in wood or antler handles. New weapons such as the bow and arrow enabled hunters to pursue solitary game. Ingenious traps, snares, and nets enabled people to exploit resources such as wildfowl and fish. Settlements became smaller, more dispersed, and less permanent (see MESOLITHIC PERIOD).

Food Production and Urbanization. In the land to the east of the Mediterranean some populations began to concentrate on exploiting wild sheep and goats and a few species of wild grasses that produced edible seeds. Gradually, as revealed in the archaeological record, a mutual dependence developed between the human populations and the animals and plants they exploited and protected: the people became farmers, and the animals and plants, domesticates.

Western Asia is the best-known, and perhaps the earliest, center of domestication, but several other early centers existed in various parts of the world. In Mexico an agriculture was developed on the basis of maize, beans, and squash. Other centers of plant and animal domestication existed in Southeast Asia, China, and probably tropical Africa.

Contrary to a common notion, prehistoric villagers did not live more easily than hunters. Villagers tended to eat a poorer diet, work harder, and suffer from more diseases. However, they also tended to produce more offspring and thus built up a much denser population. Moreover, primitive agriculture and herding often exhausted the soil in a few seasons, forcing the early farmers to move on and wrest new territory from the hunters. Within a few thousand years most hunting-and-gathering peoples had been replaced by cultivators or herders in all continents except Australia.

Along with their tendency to expand, food-producing societies are distinguished from hunter-gatherer societies by their emphasis on property. A farmer owns wealth in the form of land, herds, and the right to call on the labor of his friends and kinfolk. By passing his wealth to his heirs, he can create a family of hereditary "notables" or headmen. In this way a stratified society emerges. Unmistakable indications of social stratification appeared within a few thousand years of the beginnings of agriculture. Within a few centuries more the process had culminated, in a few favored centers, in the appearance of complex societies in which specialist artisans and merchants plied their trades, a priestly elite presided over religious ceremonials, and a bureaucratic organization commanded the labor of the landless. Thus the appearance of CIVILIZATION ended two million years of human prehistory.

prehistory   Prehistory refers to periods of remote antiquity before the appearance of written records. For more recent prehistoric periods, especially for periods such as the Celtic Iron Age—when Europe, although itself nonliterate, was described in the contemporary literatures of Greece and Rome—the alternative term *protohistory* has sometimes been adopted. The first usage of the term has commonly been attributed to Daniel Wilson, who claimed to have coined it in the title of *The Archaeology and Prehistoric Annals of Scotland* (1851), although it had in fact been used before.

For many scholars the term *prehistory* is virtually synonymous with *prehistoric archaeology*, representing that branch of ARCHAEOLOGY in which the principles and techniques of the discipline have been developed without reference to texts, epigraphy (the study of inscriptions), or numismatics (the study of coins).

prejudice   see DISCRIMINATION

prelude   Before the 19th century, the prelude (German, *Vorspiel*) was an instrumental piece played as a preliminary either to an event, such as a liturgical ceremony, or to another composition. Most preludes were composed for keyboard or lute. The combination of prelude and fugue was common, becoming fully established by J. S. Bach. In the 19th century, Chopin wrote characteristic piano pieces under the name prelude, a practice continued by Debussy and others. Opera composers such as Puccini have often replaced the opera overture with a shorter prelude.

premature baby   see PREGNANCY AND BIRTH

premenstrual syndrome   Premenstrual syndrome (PMS) is a common name for a wide variety of recurring psychological and physical symptoms experienced by some women in the week or two before menstruation. Some common symptoms include sudden episodes of tearfulness, irritability, or depression; fatigue; water retention; headaches; and joint or muscle pain. Twenty to 50 percent of all women are believed to experience at least one symptom of PMS regularly; only 5 percent of these women are estimated to have symptoms severe enough to interfere with normal activity.

PMS can begin with puberty but is most common in women over age 25. The cause is still unknown, but one theory proposes that low progesterone levels in the second half of the menstrual cycle may be responsible. There is no cure for PMS, but oral-contraceptive use or diet and exercise programs may alleviate some symptoms.

Preminger, Otto   [prem'-in-jur]   An American film director whose reputation was elevated by the admiration of French critics during the mid-1950s, Otto Preminger, b. Vienna, Dec. 5, 1906, d. Apr. 23, 1986, began his career in Germany as an assistant to Max Reinhardt. After teaching at Yale University from 1938 to 1941, Preminger went to Hollywood (1943), where he enjoyed almost immediate success with the subtle mystery *Laura* (1944). Preminger's subsequent work ranged from musicals such as *Carmen Jones* (1954) and Westerns such as *River of No Return* (1954) to such lavish productions of best-sellers as *Exodus* (1960), *Advise and Consent* (1962), and *The Cardinal* (1963). His strongest suit probably lay in the melodrama of *Laura* and such films as *Fallen Angel* (1945), *Where the Sidewalk Ends* (1950), and the taut thriller *Anatomy of a Murder* (1959).

Prendergast, Maurice   [pren'-dur-gast]   Maurice Prendergast, b. St. John's, Newfoundland, Canada, Oct. 10, 1859, d. Feb. 1, 1924, was the first American painter to fully understand and apply the ideas of the French postimpressionist movements. Brought up in Boston, Prendergast went to Europe for the first time in 1886 and studied in Paris for three years (1891–94), where he absorbed the techniques of the Nabis, the neoimpressionists, and the symbolists. By 1900 he had established his reputation in the United States as an innovative painter. Prendergast helped to organize the ARMORY SHOW, held in New York City in 1913, which introduced avant-garde American and European art to a broad public.

Central Park *(1901), with its open-air subject, strong linear composition, and rich color, is typical of the work of Maurice Prendergast. (Whitney Museum of American Art, New York City.)*

preparatory school   see PRIVATE SCHOOLS

Pre-Raphaelites   The Pre-Raphaelites were a coalition of British artists united in their distaste for formal academic art and the neoclassical style dominating the art of the early 19th century. The principal members of the movement were Holman HUNT, John Everett MILLAIS,

(Right) *The annunciation scene* Ecce Ancilla Domini *(1848–50), an early work by Dante Gabriel Rossetti, exhibits the psychological and mystical intensity that distinguishes much of his later work. (Tate Gallery, London.)*

(Below) *John Everett Millais's* Christ in the House of His Parents *(1849) combines exacting and detailed realism with the symbolism that pervades Pre-Raphaelite painting. (Tate Gallery, London.)*

and Dante Gabriel ROSSETTI. Founded in 1848, the Pre-Raphaelite Brotherhood also included James Collinson, William Michael Rossetti, Frederic George Stephens, and Thomas Woolner.

The group selected the name Pre-Raphaelite because of their belief that Raphael was the source of the academic tradition they abhorred. Like the early-19th-century NAZARENES, the Pre-Raphaelites felt that art should return to the purer vision of Gothic and Early Renaissance art. They looked to the past for inspiration, dealing primarily with religious, historical, and literary subjects. Their work was characterized by vivid color, rich detail, elaborate symbolism, and moral fervor. The group shared a predilection for sweeping curves and arabesques as well as an ideal of feminine beauty exemplified by Rossetti's *Beata Beatrix* (1868; Tate Gallery, London). Their personal stylistic distinctions can be seen by comparing the strong frontal symmetry and direct realism of Millais's *Christ in the House of His Parents* (1849; Tate Gallery) with the dreamlike vision of Rossetti's *Ecce Ancilla Domini* (1848–50; Tate Gallery) and the colorful agitation of Hunt's *The Scapegoat* (1854; Lever Gallery, Port Sunlight, England).

The initial negative response to the group was overcome mainly by the critic John RUSKIN, who helped to make Pre-Raphaelitism a dominant force in English art. Although the brotherhood disbanded about 1854, its ideas attracted many talented adherents, including Ford Madox BROWN, the visionary painter Sir Edward BURNE-JONES, and William MORRIS, the founder of the Arts and Crafts Movement. The Pre-Raphaelite movement was particularly important to the development of Art Nouveau and the European symbolist movement.

Presbyterianism [prez-buh-tir'-ee-uh-niz-uhm]   Presbyterianism is the form of church government in which elders, both lay people and ministers, govern. The name derives from the Greek word *presbuteros*, or "elder." Substantial numbers of Presbyterians are found in Scotland, Northern Ireland, England and its former colonies, the Netherlands, Switzerland, Hungary, France, South Africa, Indonesia, and Korea. The Church of Scotland (see SCOTLAND, CHURCH OF) is the only Presbyterian body that retains a governmental connection. The largest Presbyterian body in the United States is the Presbyterian Church (U.S.A.), formed in 1983 by the union of the United Presbyterian Church and the (Southern) Presbyterian Church in the United States. A number of other Presbyterian and Reformed denominations in America trace their origins to Europe or to secessions from the larger American bodies. (The older name REFORMED CHURCHES remains prevalent among groups of continental European origin; "Presbyterian" is generally used by churches of British origin.)

Presbyterianism emerged in the 16th-century REFORMATION as an effort by Protestant reformers to recapture the form as well as the message of the New Testament church. Lutherans were content to adapt the Roman Catholic episcopacy and medieval connections between church and state to their Protestant needs. Other reformers in Switzerland, the Netherlands, and south Germany were more radical. They noted that in the New Testament "elders" had been appointed to rule the early churches (Acts 14:23) and that the term *elder* had been used interchangeably with the word *bishop*, Greek *episcopos* (Acts 20:17, 28; Titus 1:5–7). These reformers argued that although a hierarchy among elders could be observed in New Testament times (1 Tim. 5:17), it was not the sharp division between bishop and priest (a contraction of presbyter) that characterized the Roman Catholic church. From his study of the Bible, John CALVIN, the Reformed leader in Geneva, concluded that Jesus Christ himself is the sole ruler of the church and that he exercises that rule through four kinds of officers: preachers (to exhort, admonish, and encourage), doctors or teachers (to instruct), deacons (to aid the poor), and lay elders (to guide and discipline the church).

When Calvin's Genevan church order was carried to Scotland by John KNOX, it evolved into the Presbyterianism that, in essentials, is still practiced today. Individual local congregations elect their own elders, including the minister, who together govern the church as a session (or consistory in certain Reformed churches). The minister (or teaching elder), who is called by the local church and who usually serves as moderator of the session, is, however, ordained and disciplined by the next level of church organization, the presbytery (or classis), which administers groups of churches in one area. Presbyteries select delegates to regional synods, which in turn select representatives to the General Assembly (or General Synod), a national body, the final judiciary of the church.

Presbyterian worship is simple and orderly. It revolves around preaching from the Scriptures. Presbyterian hymnody is indebted to the Calvinistic tradition of singing paraphrased Psalms. Two sacraments are recognized: the Lord's Supper, which is usually celebrated monthly or quarterly; and baptism, which is administered to the infant children of church members as a sign of God's covenant of mercy.

—
preschool education   Preschool education refers to the education of children prior to the first grade. The overwhelming majority of children in such classes in the United States are between the ages of three and five. The programs that serve them include kindergartens, nursery schools, DAY-CARE CENTERS, Montessori schools, and programs for children with special-educational needs.

Preschool programs in general are designed to support the development of children during their early years. They serve to increase children's intellectual and language competence and to provide them with the skills of self-expression. They act as socializing agents, preparing children for the world of the elementary school as well as for participation in society at large. A number of special programs serve children whose parents work, as well as those of single-parent families and families that need additional social support to maintain themselves. HEAD START and similar programs supported under Title I of the Elementary and Secondary Education Act provide education, health, and social services for children from low-income families.

Many communities have also begun to provide preschool education for children with special problems—visual, auditory, linguistic, emotional, mental, and orthopedic—or learning disabilities through programs designed to help them cope with their difficulties and to learn to use their potential abilities to their maximum. In many cases preschool programs provide extended services both for the children enrolled and for their families.

Preschool Programs

Kindergartens, serving five-year-olds, are part of the public elementary school in most communities. Some younger children—primarily those in special educational programs and those from low-income families—are also enrolled in public school programs. Many private kindergartens also exist in the United States, especially in communities whose public schools do not have kindergartens. Nursery schools, Montessori schools, and day-care centers are usually run by private agencies, nonprofit community agencies, or profit-making institutions that are owned by individuals or corporations. Franchise nursery schools and day-care centers and parent-organized cooperative nursery schools also operate.

In many countries day-care services are supported by government funds and are widely available. In the United States, although limited federal and some state funds are available to purchase day-care services for needy children, legislative bills in support of comprehensive child-development programs including day-care services have not met with success.

History

Although the various forms of preschool programs have much in common, they have different roots and have evolved independently. The kindergarten, originating in Germany about 1835, was developed by Friedrich Wilhelm August FROEBEL, who designed a program for young children to help them understand the unity of Man, God, and Nature through a set of symbolic activities. Froebel's ideas were brought to the United States by German immigrants and soon reached English-speaking American communities as well, so that by the early 20th century private kindergartens existed in many areas. A number of settlement houses offered kindergarten education to children from poor and immigrant families. Some public schools also experimented with kindergartens.

With the advent of the field of child study and the PROGRESSIVE EDUCATION movement, kindergarten programs departed from the original Froebelian activities and became more responsive to the needs of American society and the new knowledge that was being generated about young children.

The nursery school was first developed (1911) by Rachel and Margaret McMillan in England. It was designed to serve the needs of the poor, and health, nutrition, and social services were provided along with an educational program. When nursery schools were introduced in the United States in the 1920s, they were organized as private schools and university laboratory schools, catering to the needs of more affluent children for whom extended services were not needed. Programs became more education-oriented, supporting the development of the young child through play activities.

The MONTESSORI METHOD developed in Italy in the early 20th century and originally served poor children. Unlike the nursery school's emphasis on play, Montessori programs focused on reading and writing instruction and exercises in practical life designed to help children become more independent.

Day nurseries were established in the United States as early as the 1850s, primarily as custodial institutions for children of working mothers. In time they became social agencies supporting families in trouble or helping single-parent families. In recent years the needs of working mothers have again become a concern of these programs.

Educational components were added as the idea of nursery education was disseminated in the 1920s. Although the day-care center has an educational program like that of a nursery school for part of the day, it must also cater to the child's need to eat, rest, and play.

Learning in Preschools

Preschool programs are built on the concept of play as an educational medium. Through play children are expected to learn about themselves and the world around them, to organize what they learn into conceptual schemes, and to express what they come to know. A blockbuilding area allows children to create wooden constructions and to use various toy accessories. A housekeeping area provides opportunities for children to act out various adult roles. An arts-and-crafts area allows children to paint, draw, build, and shape both two- and three-dimensional projects. An area is set aside to allow children to work with puzzles, parquetry blocks, pegboards, Cuisinaire rods or other mathematical materials, and construction materials. A music area provides musical instruments for children to explore, records to listen to, and a place to move to music. A library area provides a quiet space where children can begin to acquaint themselves with printed materials. Outdoor space is provided nearby for children to play in more active ways.

Play activities alternate with quieter, sometimes structured activities, such as listening to stories, participating in discussions, watching films, or engaging in teacher-directed projects. Cleaning up the classroom and self-care help the children learn to become more responsible and independent. Field trips may be used to extend the child's experiential world.

As children move through nursery school and kindergarten there is increasing emphasis on required work activities to prepare them for learning the basic academic skills that are introduced in the primary grades.

In recent years a range of preschool program alternatives has been developed, especially for children from low-income families. These program models differ both in the techniques of teaching used and in the purposes assigned the preschool. Some programs focus essentially on preparation for primary school instruction, whereas others attempt to support a broader intellectual and personal development. Some programs are built on particular psychological theories, such as the behavior theory of B. F. SKINNER or the cognitive theory of Jean PIAGET.

Parents and Teachers in Preschool Education

The involvement of parents in the education of preschoolers is important, for they are actually their children's first teachers. Early American kindergartens included parents' clubs, and parent-cooperative nursery schools have evolved into centers where parents are involved in both policymaking and classroom teaching activities. Head Start programs are required to involve parents on advisory committees, to engage them in classroom activities, and to provide some form of parent education.

Teachers in preschool programs differ widely as to the kind and depth of their preparation. Kindergarten teachers in public schools are expected to be prepared in early-childhood or elementary education. Most often this preparation comes in a 4-year college program. Such teachers are required to maintain a teaching certificate from the education agency in their state. Nursery-school teachers and day-care practitioners may be prepared in early-childhood programs or in child-development programs, available in 2- or 1-year community college programs, but some personnel in preschools have no formal preparation.

The requirements for working in a nursery school or day-care center are set by the state agency that licenses preschool centers. Often the main concern of such licensing is the basic protection of children rather than the quality of education they receive. In some states early-childhood or nursery-school teaching certificates are issued. Sometimes licensing requirements do not require schools to hire certified or degreed teachers. The Child Development Associate Consortium issues a credential for a child-development associate to those who work with young children, but this credential has not yet found nationwide acceptance.

The primary issue in preschool education today concerns its availability. Kindergarten is still not universal in all states, and many educators feel that it should be. Educators also feel that nursery schools and day-care centers should be available to all children, not just to those whose parents can afford to pay the tuition. To make it universally available, government support would be required. There is also the question of whether preschool education should be provided within the public school system or through private agencies.

Another issue relates to its content. There is as yet no agreement on the proper goals of preschool education or the best method of teaching young children. Both the amount and content of preparation that should be required of practitioners are also at issue. Moreover, the quality of teacher preparation bears on the cost of preschool education. Requiring higher standards will necessarily lead to staffing of centers by higher-paid personnel.

See also: PLAY (in behavior); PRIMARY EDUCATION.

Prescott [pres'-kuht]   Prescott (1990 pop., 26,455), the seat of Yavapai County in central Arizona, is located 120 km (75 mi) northwest of Phoenix. The town's economy depends on livestock raising and the mining of gold, silver, copper, lead, and zinc in the surrounding region. Prescott National Forest is nearby. Founded in 1864, Prescott was the capital of Arizona Territory from 1864 to 1867 and from 1877 to 1889.

Prescott, William H.   William Hickling Prescott, b. Salem, Mass., May 4, 1796, d. Jan. 28, 1859, one of the greatest American historians, was a specialist on the Spanish conquest of the New World. His vivid style made him popular with the reading public, while his careful work based on archival sources made him one of the first American historians to use a more scientific approach. *A History of the Conquest of Mexico* (3 vols., 1843) and its sequel, *A History of the Conquest of Peru* (2 vols., 1847), remain classics in American historical writing.

preservatives, food see CANNING; DEHYDRATION (food) ; FOOD ADDITIVES; FOOD PRESERVATION

president A president is an officer elected or appointed to preside over an organized body, such as a political state, a business corporation, a university, or some other type of organization. In politics the president is the head of a republic, with powers that vary from country to country. In Germany, Italy, and India, for example, the president is largely a ceremonial figure, with the actual governing power residing with the chancellor or prime minister. In the United States and France, on the other hand, the president has extensive powers.

president of the United States The president of the United States functions in many capacities: head of state, head of government, commander in chief of the armed forces, and leader of the president's political party. The president is thus the most unifying force in a political system in which power is highly dispersed, both within the government and between government and the people.

The President as Head of State

The president's unifying influence is exerted through the position of head of state. Like traditional European monarchs, the president is the ceremonial head of the government. The president receives representatives of other governments and performs a variety of ceremonial duties such as holding state dinners and bestowing the Medal of Honor.

Activities as head of state are not limited to the White House and Washington, D.C. The president is expected to travel within the country occasionally. Today presidents also travel extensively abroad. As head of state, the president symbolizes the sovereignty and power of the United States; presidential words and acts radiate an aura of significance that no other American can command.

The President as Head of Government

As head of the government the president rules as well as reigns. The president is chief executive, chief diplomat, commander in chief, and chief policymaker.

Chief Executive. As chief executive the president appoints the heads of the government departments (who constitute the CABINET) and the heads of agencies, subject to the Senate's approval, and supervises the work of the executive branch.

The president also provides leadership in legislation. More than anyone, the president establishes the agenda for Congress. The heart of the president's legislative program is conveyed in messages to Congress each January, beginning with the State of the Union address—a general, wide-ranging treatment of national problems and policies. The Economic Report follows, accompanied by the massive, detailed budget document itself; this contains the financial work plans for reaching the president's pre-

President Dwight D. Eisenhower, in his 1957 State of the Union address, asked Congress to pledge military aid to Middle East nations as a means of resisting Soviet aggression. Congress agreed to provide the funds for this policy.

viously announced general objectives.

Subsequently, the president sends special messages to Congress, each devoted to a single topic such as foreign aid, welfare, or agriculture. Accompanying or soon following the special messages are drafts of legislation that the president urges Congress to pass. The president and the various cabinet secretaries work to persuade Congress to enact as much of the proposed legislation as possible. The president, however, can also be a constraining force on Congress. Recent presidents have tried to curb congressional spending. Congress and the presidency, particularly when controlled by opposing parties, may disagree regarding their priorities. Recent presidents have frequently used the constitutional power to veto.

President Richard M. Nixon dined with Zhou Enlai, premier of the People's Republic of China, in Shanghai in 1972. Nixon's diplomatic mission opened the way for U.S.–Chinese trade and cultural and scientific exchanges.

President Harry S. Truman (right) talked with Gen. Douglas MacArthur after revoking MacArthur's command of U.S. troops in Korea on grounds of insubordination. In firing the general, Truman exercised his constitutional rights as commander in chief of the armed forces.

Chief Diplomat. The president is the nation's chief diplomat. Success in waging major wars such as the two world wars has enlarged the presidency's prestige and power. The unpopularity of the Vietnam War, however, an undeclared war, caused Congress to adopt the War Powers Act (1973), which bars long-term wars without congressional approval.

As chief diplomat, the president deals directly with the heads of foreign governments. Presidents preside over the negotiation of major treaties with other countries, oversee ARMS CONTROL negotiations with the USSR, and endeavor to work out international agreements for handling such problems as inflation, recession, energy, and hunger.

Commander in Chief. As commander in chief of the armed forces, the president is responsible for the nation's security. The president deploys troops abroad and sometimes orders them into combat. Presidents have also used the armed forces within the United States to maintain domestic peace, and they are empowered to impose MARTIAL LAW, as Lincoln did in the Civil War. The president is custodian of the country's nuclear weapons; under law the president is the only person who can order their use, and the "Black Box" through which that order can be sent accompanies the president at all times.

As a civilian commander in chief, the president embodies the principle of civilian supremacy over the military. The president appoints the Joint Chiefs of Staff and other military commanders, oversees the military budget, and passes on the development of new weapons systems. The president also directs the country's participation in military alliances.

The powers of the chief executive may extend even further in time of war. The president may find it necessary to establish wide-ranging controls on the economy, as in World War II. A president may even interfere with civil lib-

erties, as Franklin D. Roosevelt did in approving the forced relocation of thousands of Japanese-Americans on the Pacific coast in World War II.

Policymaker. The president is the single most potent policymaker in economic and social affairs. Recent presidents have been concerned with such problems as energy, inflation, unemployment, the U.S. balance of payments, the strength of the dollar abroad, and the mounting budget deficit.

The president and advisors also establish and administer national policies in such areas as social security, education, health, CIVIL RIGHTS, and air and water pollution.

The President as Political Leader

Because the presidency is the foremost prize of American politics, the president is also normally the nation's principal political leader and regarded as the leader of his political party. The president chooses the chairperson of the party's national committee and oversees the national committee and the national party bureaucracy. The president seeks to win and maintain the support of state and local party organizations, which in turn can aid in obtaining congressional enactment of the president's programs.

The president manages PATRONAGE for the party—that is, rewarding supporters with jobs. The president appoints cabinet and subcabinet officers, federal judges, U.S. attorneys, and ambassadors to important foreign countries and fills several thousand other jobs of varying importance. The president also administers an executive pork barrel—the distribution of federal funds to be spent on public works, military installations, and social programs.

If presidential legislative requests are to thrive in Congress, the president must exert political leadership on Capitol Hill, inducing legislators to support presidential policies. The president accomplishes more on Capitol Hill when successful as a public leader. Presidents who excel at public leadership skillfully employ the dominant communications media of their day.

President Lyndon B. Johnson signed the Civil Rights Act of 1964, outlawing many forms of discrimination.

President John F. Kennedy (left) *confronted Soviet foreign minister Andrei Gromyko* (right) *during the Cuban Missile Crisis in 1962. In response to the installation of Soviet missile bases in Cuba, Kennedy ordered a naval blockade to halt all weapons shipments to the island.*

The president gains special credentials as a political leader by winning election to office, a supreme political test. Beyond satisfying constitutional requirements (the president must be 35 years old, a "natural-born citizen," and a U.S. resident for 14 years prior to election), most contemporary presidential candidates must also undergo the physically exhausting test of entering up to 30 PRIMARY ELECTIONS in various parts of the country. Both in the primaries and in the national convention, in which nomi-

nation is won, a candidate must avoid embittering other candidates and their followers whose support is valuable in the postconvention campaign.

The person running for president must also formulate a strategy that will win a majority of the electoral votes (see ELECTORAL COLLEGE). Because PRESIDENTIAL ELECTIONS are often close, the candidate's strategic choices as to the states in which to make the greatest efforts can be crucial to victory or defeat.

Presidential Remuneration. For the many presidential duties, the president receives (as of 1991) $200,000 a year in salary and $50,000 for expenses, an additional $100,000 for travel expenses, and handsome retirement benefits.

Organization of the Executive Office

Personal Staff. The president's personal staff, which works in the White House Office, includes a score of top assistants—such as the press secretary, the appointments secretary, the special counsel, the assistant for national security affairs, the cabinet secretary, the staff secretary, the assistant for congressional liaison, and various administrative assistants—aided by a sizable junior staff. The White House staff totals several hundred.

Institutional Staff. In addition to personal staff, the president commands a large institutional staff concerned with managing the executive branch and with policy development. The principal managerial arm is the Office of MANAGEMENT AND BUDGET (OMB), which prepares the budget of the executive branch, among other duties.

Prominent among the president's policy advisory organs is the NATIONAL SECURITY COUNCIL (NSC). It is con-

EXECUTIVE BRANCH OF THE UNITED STATES

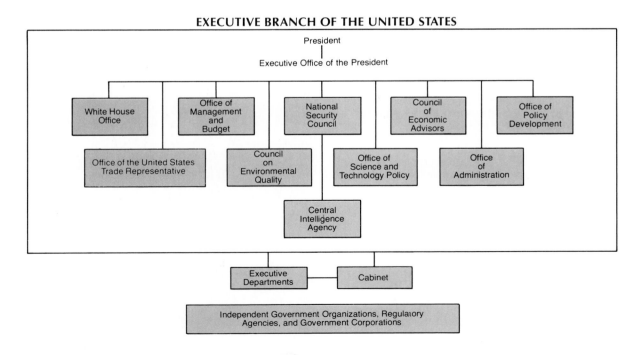

In September 1990, George Bush's cabinet included (front row, left to right) Elizabeth Dole, Labor; Richard Cheney, Defense; James A. Baker III, State; Nicholas F. Brady, Treasury; Richard Thornburgh, attorney general; Manuel Lujan, Jr., Interior; (back row) Clayton Yuetter, Agriculture; Louis W. Sullivan, Health and Human Services; Richard Darman, Management and Budget; Lauro F. Cavazos, Education; Samuel K. Skinner, Transportation; the president; Vice-President J. Danforth Quayle; Carla Hills, trade representative; James D. Watkins, Energy; Robert Mosbacher, Commerce; Edward Derwinski, Veterans Affairs; Jack Kemp, Housing and Urban Development.

cerned with the whole gamut of foreign policy, including military strategy. From the COUNCIL OF ECONOMIC ADVISERS (CEA) the president secures professional economic advice. The Office of Policy Development (OPD) assists the president in formulating and evaluating long-range economic and domestic policy.

Other units of the Executive Office include the Council on Environmental Quality, the Office of the United States Trade Representative, the Office of Science and Technology Policy, and the Office of Administration.

The Cabinet. The cabinet is not part of the Executive Office but exists independently. Consisting of the heads of government departments, the cabinet is used irregularly by presidents, largely because cabinet members' administrative duties and loyalties to their own departments often preclude a close working relationship with the president.

Occasionally, the VICE-PRESIDENT becomes important in an administration, although the Constitution does not allot the vice-president any responsibilities other than to "preside over the Senate." Usually the vice-president is remote from the circles of power.

Presidential Transitions. When a new president is elected, a delicate and often cumbersome 10-week process of transition begins. The president-elect appoints teams of academic, business, and political people to gather information, prepare reports, and make recommendations on policies and appointments. Outgoing staff members brief the newcomers. The Senate begins confirmation hearings to advise and consent on cabinet-level appointees well in advance of inauguration day, so that the new administration can take power smoothly.

Growth of the Presidency

The establishment of the presidency in 1789, by the framers of the U.S. Constitution, was an act of political creativity. The presidency had no real counterpart in historical experience. The framers aimed to have a strong, but responsible, chief executive, and to this end the office was made to consist of a single incumbent whose power would not be shared with a cabinet or council. The president would be elected by a source outside the legislature—the electoral college—and thus could govern without being indebted to Congress. The president gained strength from a fixed, substantial term of office and was originally eligible for reelection indefinitely. (Presidential tenure of office has since been limited to two terms by the 22d Amendment and otherwise affected by the 20th Amendment and the 25th Amendment.)

The Constitution granted the presidency powers of its own, such as the power of commander in chief. Believing, however, in balanced government, the framers created a strong Congress and a judiciary to check the chief executive.

The first incumbent of the office, George Washington, interpreted his powers broadly and defended them against congressional encroachment. Thomas Jefferson exploited the presidential role of party leader and won exceptional congressional support. Under his weaker successors, however, the office was eclipsed by Congress.

Andrew Jackson revived the presidency by reinterpreting it as an organ of popular leadership. Abraham Lincoln, in the crisis of the Civil War, largely on his own claimed authority, expanded the armed forces, imposed a

Franklin D. Roosevelt, calling Dec. 7, 1941, the day of the Japanese attack on Pearl Harbor, "a date which will live in infamy," asked Congress for a declaration of war.

The continued bombing of North Vietnam by the United States was the subject of consultation between Lyndon B. Johnson and congressional leaders at the White House in January 1966.

naval blockade, and used funds from the Treasury without congressional appropriation. Congress soon reacted against the expanded power that he had given the presidency, and through the remainder of the 19th century the office's impact remained modest.

Theodore Roosevelt, the first 20th-century president and an extraordinarily gifted politician and popular leader, was the principal architect of the office's modernization. Woodrow Wilson was also a vigorous president; he led the country into World War I, but after his failure to secure Senate approval of the League of Nations, another reaction against the presidency set in. His Republican successors, Warren Harding, Calvin Coolidge, and Herbert Hoover, interpreted presidential power much more modestly.

The DEPRESSION OF THE 1930s, followed by World War II, produced an enormous expansion of presidential activity under Franklin Delano Roosevelt. This expansion continued during the COLD WAR and the KOREAN WAR, when Harry S. Truman used the presidential powers fully. Although Dwight D. Eisenhower restored peace, the troubled relations with the USSR required him to maintain the armed forces and the nuclear arsenal at high levels. John F. Kennedy successfully managed the first nuclear confrontation with the USSR in the 1962 CUBAN MISSILE CRISIS while at the same time guiding the nation through a domestic crisis over civil rights. Lyndon Johnson's Great Society program enlarged the presidency's commitment to the welfare state, but this expansion was limited by the financial demands of the escalating VIETNAM WAR.

Richard Nixon ended that war and inaugurated a policy of détente toward the USSR. He clashed with Democratic Congresses, and the threat of IMPEACHMENT for his implication in the WATERGATE break-in and related scandals forced him to resign. Gerald Ford and Jimmy Carter struggled to restore popular confidence in the office and to cope with a reassertive Congress. Carter's difficulties in charting a decisive course and obtaining congressional cooperation during his single term in office helped reestablish public desire for a strong presidency and pave the way for public and congressional acceptance of many of Ronald Reagan's economic initiatives. George Bush's speedy and successful conclusion of the GULF WAR dramatically increased the prestige of the presidency.

Powers of the President

The executive-power clause of Article II, Section 1, of the Constitution states merely that "The executive Power shall be vested in a President of the United States of America." The executive-power clause has been used by presidents to justify a broad range of actions. For example, presidents have claimed the power to remove officers of the executive branch. In 1935, however, the Supreme Court ruled that the president could not remove an officer engaging in "quasi-legislative" and "quasi-judicial" duties except for cause provided for in the statute establishing the position.

A companion constitutional power to which presidents have given vast scope is the commander-in-chief power (Article II, Section 2). One of the freest interpretations of this power was Lincoln's, who—after the Civil War erupted, and while Congress was not in session—called up 75,000 men and waged war for 12 weeks, relying on his independent authority. The commander-in-chief power has been cited to justify commitment of the armed forces to scores of short-term hostilities. A notable example was the intervention in Vietnam. Critics contended that the Vietnam War could be legally sustained only by a congressional declaration of war, which was never made.

Although the Constitution specifies that the president can make treaties, the requirement that they be approved by a two-thirds vote of the Senate has often driven presidents to use executive agreements instead. Presidents have used them to annex territory, to settle border disputes, and to determine the armistice terms of major wars. For authority to make such agreements presidents cite the executive-power clause and the commander-in-chief power.

Presidents have, by constitutional interpretation, enlarged their powers in relations with Congress. Early presidents, for example, employed the veto only when they considered legislation unconstitutional, but Jackson extended it to legislation he considered objectionable on policy grounds, as presidents have continued to do. After Congress appropriates funds, the president may impound them, or delay their expenditure. But President Richard Nixon enormously expanded the practice by impounding billions of dollars of appropriations. Subsequently, both

President Gerald R. Ford appeared before a congressional committee in 1974 to explain his pardon of former president Richard M. Nixon. The pardon prevented Nixon's prosecution on criminal charges.

the judiciary and Congress acted to limit the president's power to impound appropriations.

Tenure of office confers power. Presidential tenure is protected by a rigorous impeachment procedure. Conviction requires a two-thirds vote of the senators present. President Andrew Johnson escaped conviction by a single vote. In 1974, President Nixon, facing impeachment and almost certain conviction, became the first president to resign. President Ford, exercising the president's pardoning power, pardoned Nixon for all federal crimes that he "committed or may have committed or taken part in."

Executive Privilege. Presidents also claim to possess EXECUTIVE PRIVILEGE, or the right to withhold information from Congress and the public. President Eisenhower employed it in denying executive papers and testimony to Senator Joseph McCarthy's investigation of Communist infiltration of the government. In court proceedings concerning Watergate, President Nixon sought to withhold tapes and transcripts of White House conversations, but in *United States* v. *Nixon* (1974) the Supreme Court ruled that executive privilege did not immunize him from judicial proceedings.

Presidential Power and the Supreme Court. Although the Supreme Court determines presidential power by its interpretation of the Constitution, the Court has seldom directly checked the exercise of presidential power. In many cases, the Court has affirmed it. In *United States* v. *Curtiss-Wright Export Corporation* (1936), for example, the Court acknowledged a broad presidential power to make executive agreements. The Court's rulings against the president have occurred mainly in civil liberties cases. In 1952, Truman's seizure of steel mills on his own authority was held unconstitutional.

Actual Presidential Use of Power. Presidents have employed their powers most fully in visible major crises, such as the Civil War and the world wars, and in grave economic emergency such as the Great Depression of the

1930s. When crises are less obvious, as in the energy crisis of the 1970s, the president may have difficulty impressing the public and Congress of the necessity for serious action.

The powers presidents can actually employ also depend heavily on their political skills and on their own conception of the office. Some presidents, such as James Buchanan or William Howard Taft, have interpreted their powers narrowly. At the other extreme are the presidents who, like Theodore Roosevelt, feel constrained in their "stewardship" only by what is expressly forbidden by the Constitution.

The Current Issue of Executive Power. After the unpopular Vietnam War and the excesses of Watergate, the presidency passed into an era of criticism and reassessment. The office was seen to have become inordinately powerful and to be threatening or violating civil liberties. It was viewed as having placed the political system in disequilibrium by drawing excessive power to the presidency at the expense of the other branches.

Congress became more assertive after Watergate, passing the War Powers Act and other measures to control presidential abuses. It also created its own Budget Office to sharpen its annual review of the budget. Congress employed the appropriations power to constrain presidential initiatives in foreign affairs.

In the late 1970s and 1980s, however, public sentiment called for a more assertive presidency that could provide greater leadership to a fragmented and interest-ridden Congress and that could act decisively on the array of stubborn problems that troubled Americans.

presidential elections   The election of the president of the United States every 4 years is the focal point of the American political process. Because of the preeminent role of the president as the national leader in domestic and foreign policy and as the only elected official with a national constituency, the presidential contest receives the greatest attention from voters, politicians, and the mass media. Furthermore, because of the importance of the United States in international affairs, the U.S. presidential elections are followed with interest all over the world.

Qualifications for Candidacy. The formal qualifications for presidential candidacy are spelled out in Article II, Section 1, of the Constitution, which limits the presidency to natural-born citizens who have lived in the United States at least 14 years and who have reached the age of 35. The 22d Amendment (ratified in 1951) to the Constitution limits presidents to two terms in office.

Although the formal qualifications are straightforward and few in number, there have been many practical constraints on who may actually be considered a serious presidential aspirant. For example, no woman, black, or Jew has ever been the presidential nominee of a major political party. Only one Roman Catholic—John F. Kennedy in 1960—has been elected president.

In addition to primarily being white male Protestants, most presidential candidates have had extensive political experience. Despite this, from the first president, George

Hard cider and log cabins were symbols of the Whig party in the 1840 presidential election. This appeal to the hardworking common man won a victory for William Henry Harrison over the incumbent, Martin Van Buren.

Washington, there has been a recurring tendency for the nation to elect war heroes. These include Andrew Jackson, William Henry Harrison, Zachary Taylor, Ulysses S. Grant, and Dwight D. Eisenhower. During much of U.S. history the office of state governor was the major springboard to a presidential nomination. Between the death of Franklin D. Roosevelt in 1945 and the election of former Georgia governor Jimmy Carter in 1976, however, no former governor served as president.

The eclipse of the governorship as the main breeding ground of presidents was accompanied by a rise in the importance of the Congress (especially the Senate) and the vice-presidency. Between 1945 and 1989, five vice-presidents with backgrounds in the Congress became president: Harry S. Truman, Lyndon B. Johnson, Richard M. Nixon, Gerald R. Ford, and George Bush. In addition, John F. Kennedy's political background was entirely congressional.

The election of Jimmy Carter in 1976 and Ronald Reagan in 1980 may have served to turn attention once again to state governors (and former governors) as potential presidential aspirants, but Gov. Michael Dukakis of Massachusetts decisively lost the 1988 election.

Development of Presidential Campaigning. Traditionally, the presidential campaigns have been the responsibility of the party organizations. Today, however, presidential candidates rely heavily on their own special campaign organizations and on various ad-hoc citizens' groups. Special attention is devoted to the mass media, particularly television, to bring campaigns to the voters. Media experts and marketing and public-relations specialists have taken key roles in the planning and conduct of a campaign.

The PRIMARY ELECTION system, increasingly important in choosing presidential nominees, is widely covered by the media and offers successful candidates the advantage of being already known to the television public by the time the campaign proper begins. Television-dominated campaigns have, however, hurt political parties in a number of ways. The media specialists who run such campaigns tend to be loyal to a candidate and not to the candidate's party. In addition, the heavy reliance on television allows a candidate to reach voters directly, thereby weakening the traditional function of the party as an information-providing intermediary between the candidate and the voters.

Other developments have served to weaken the role of the political party in the presidential campaign. The growth of computerized direct-mail fund-raising techniques and computerized mail and telephone appeals have encroached on activities traditionally performed by the political party. Recent reforms in the areas of campaign financing and delegate selection to the nominating conventions (see POLITICAL CONVENTION) have made the party less significant with the respect to fund raising and candidate selection.

The widespread use of television has had some positive consequences for campaigns; it certainly allows many more citizens to follow the campaign directly and perhaps get more of a personal insight into the candidates. Nevertheless, observers worry whether the prominence of television converts the campaign into a public-relations effort to package or market a candidate to the detriment of a serious discussion of the issues.

Election Outcomes. There have been many amazingly close races for the presidency—the Garfield-Hancock contest in 1880, for example—and several landslides—as in the Roosevelt-Landon contest of 1936—as well. Since 1956 election outcomes have swung dramatically, with landslides for Republicans (1956, 1972, 1980, and 1984) and Democrats (1964).

Republicans in the Wide Awake movement paraded through New York City by torchlight during the 1860 presidential election in support of Abraham Lincoln and Hannibal Hamlin.

A cartoon from the presidential race of 1900 shows incumbent president William McKinley overshadowed by his running mate, Theodore Roosevelt. The president stayed home while Roosevelt toured the country as a war hero, rousing enough voter enthusiasm to defeat Democrat William Jennings Bryan.

With the presence of serious third- and fourth-party challengers, such candidates as Abraham Lincoln in 1860, Woodrow Wilson in 1912, and Harry Truman in 1948 have been elected president by less than a majority of the popular vote. Because of the operation of the ELECTORAL COLLEGE, Rutherford B. Hayes in 1876 and Benjamin Harrison in 1888 were elected president even though they received fewer popular votes than their leading challengers.

Campaign Debates. From time to time in U.S. history, presidential nominees of the major parties engage in debates. The most famous debates in American political history, those between Abraham Lincoln and Stephen A. Douglas in 1858, occurred when the two were candidates for the Senate from Illinois. Douglas won the Senate seat, although the debates served to create a national reputation for Lincoln and propelled him toward the presidential nomination in 1860, when Douglas again was his opponent.

In 1960, John F. Kennedy and Richard M. Nixon met for four debates that were a milestone in presidential politics, primarily because of their vast television audiences. More than 70 million Americans saw the first debate, and audiences of greater than 50 million people witnessed the other three. Probably the greatest consequence of the debates was to assure voters that the relatively young and inexperienced Senator Kennedy was capable of being president.

Although it is rare for an incumbent president to provide a forum and publicity for his challenger, Presidents Ford in 1976, Carter in 1980, and Reagan in 1984 debated their challengers. In 1976 and 1980 polls showed the incumbents behind their opponents. In 1976 the televised debates probably had little effect on the election outcome. In 1980, Carter met Republican candidate Ronald Reagan in debate one week before Election Day; Reagan's reassuring manner probably contributed to his electoral victory. In 1988, Democrat Michael Dukakis and Republican George Bush held two debates; observers generally agreed that they "won" one each.

Campaign Issues. The issues that have dominated presidential campaigns have varied dramatically over time. Certainly, the state of the economy and the nature of economic relationships are such themes. Wars, their conduct, and their avoidance have also been critical issues in many elections.

At times specific issues and slogans may dominate the presidential campaign, as slavery and related economic issues did in 1860. In more recent times the New Deal programs of Franklin D. Roosevelt and the Fair Deal of Harry S. Truman, along with Truman's attacks on the "do-nothing" Republican Congress, helped to keep the Democrats in power from 1932 to 1952. The Republicans were finally victorious with Eisenhower in 1952, emphasizing the Democrats' "Korea, Corruption, and Communism." In 1960, Kennedy propounded the New Frontier and talked of getting the "country moving again"; Lyndon B. Johnson spoke of the Great Society in 1964 and proposed comprehensive social-welfare programs. In 1980, Republican candidate Ronald Reagan made persistent inflation and the perceived decline of U.S. military might and international prestige the major issues.

Neither candidate in 1988 stressed crucial issues such as the budget and trade deficits. So much attention was devoted to matters like crime and patriotism that many voters considered it a "no-issue" campaign.

Campaign Financing. The cost of presidential campaigns rose so sharply between 1952 ($12 million) and 1972 ($114 million) that public financing of presidential campaigns was instituted for the 1976 election. A major reason for the increased cost was the heavier reliance on television and on computer technology. Convinced that Federal Corrupt Practices Act of 1925 and the HATCH ACT of 1939 were inadequate to deal with this situation, Congress passed amendments (1974 and 1976) to the Federal Election Campaign Act of 1971. These provided partial public funding during the primary season for candidates who met certain criteria and full public funding for the general election if candidates opted for public funding. The law also included tighter reporting provi-

President Harry S. Truman displays a premature newspaper headline on the morning after his reelection in 1948. Public-opinion polls had predicted a landslide victory for Thomas E. Dewey.

Richard M. Nixon and John F. Kennedy debated on television during the 1960 presidential campaign. The debate gave national exposure to Kennedy, until then a relatively unknown senator, who went on to win the election by a narrow margin.

sions for contributions, limitations on individual and organizational contributions, funds for the parties' national nominating conventions, and the establishment of a Federal Election Commission (FEC) to enforce the law. The source of all public funds spent on the campaign is the Presidential Election Campaign Fund, which consists of moneys designated by citizens on their income-tax returns to be used for presidential elections. Although the FEC obliges presidential candidates to forego private fund raising and abide by spending ceilings to qualify for public money ($46.1 million each in 1988), both parties have used state party funds, technically allowed for "party building," to circumvent the restriction.

Presidential Succession. The 25th Amendment to the Constitution details procedures for presidential and vice-presidential succession when there is a vacancy in either office or in the event that the president becomes incapacitated. When Vice-President Spiro T. Agnew resigned in 1973, President Richard M. Nixon nominated as vice-president Gerald R. Ford, who was subsequently confirmed by majority vote in both the House and the Senate. When Nixon also resigned, Ford succeeded to the presidency and designated Nelson A. Rockefeller to be vice-president; he also was confirmed by both houses of Congress. Should the presidency and the vice-presidency become vacant simultaneously, the Speaker of the House and the president pro tempore of the Senate, in that order, are next in the line of succession, followed by members of the cabinet in a specified order.

Presley, Elvis [prez'-lee]   Although Elvis Aaron Presley, b. Tupelo, Miss., Jan. 8, 1935, d. Aug. 16, 1977, did not invent rock 'n' roll, he did more than anyone to popularize it, and he was rock's most powerful performer. From the mid-1950s, Presley's vocal mannerisms, sideburns, and attitude—a combination of sex and sneer—made the "King" an international hero of the young.

Presley's success began with his recording of the blues song "That's All Right, Mama," written by the black singer Arthur Crudup. Presley's rendition combined his potent, shouted vocal style with a fast, hard, country-and-western-music instrumental backing. It won considerable attention and eventually a recording contract with RCA Victor. With national promotion, Presley's subsequent recordings became instant hits: "Heartbreak Hotel" in 1956, followed by "Hound Dog," "Don't Be Cruel," "Love Me Tender," and "All Shook Up." His concerts and television appearances drew huge audiences, and his 33 movies, which were minor films at best, increased his fame.

Even after his death, Presley's cult continues, and Graceland, his mansion in Memphis, Tenn., where he is buried, has become a place of pilgrimage.

Elvis Presley, seen performing in June 1956, was rock 'n roll's biggest star and the person most responsible for its emergence in the 1950s as both a musical and a wider cultural phenomenon. Presley sold more records (over 500 million), had more top-ten hits (39), and had more gold records (28 – each signifying sales in excess of 1 million) than any individual or group in history.

pre-Socratic philosophy   The pre-Socratics were Greek philosophers who lived in Ionia (on the southwest coast of modern Turkey), Greece, and southern Italy in the 6th and 5th centuries BC. They are considered the founders of Western philosophy because they were the first thinkers to explain reality in natural rather than supernatural terms. These philosophers did not form a systematic school of thought, however, and are called pre-Socratics only because Socrates, who lived in the late 5th century BC, is the earliest Greek philosopher of whom any detailed information exists. What is known about pre-Socratic thought comes from fragments preserved in the writings of Plato, Aristotle, and later authors.

Before the rise of philosophy Greek thought was religious and mythological. Questions about the origins of things and workings of nature were answered by reference to the activities of the gods. The pre-Socratics tried to answer these questions by citing natural processes, such as the motion of whirlpools, or rarefaction and condensation, of which the workings of nature are instances.

The earliest pre-Socratics were Ionians from the city of Miletus, an Aegean port that carried on a busy trade with the older civilized countries of the Near East. The Milesians' familiarity with Egyptian and Babylonian learning and their city's atmosphere of intellectual freedom may explain why philosophy began there.

The philosophers of the MILESIAN SCHOOL—THALES OF MILETUS, ANAXIMANDER, and ANAXIMENES—speculated about the origin and composition of the world and sought to explain the mechanisms by which change is possible. Another school, the PYTHAGOREANS of southern Italy, was more concerned about the fate of the soul and the kind of life one ought to live. Both of these tendencies can be found in HERACLITUS of Ephesus, who asserted that everything is constantly changing and that all things are composed of opposites. Reacting to Heraclitus's assertions, PARMENIDES and ZENO OF ELEA in Italy (see ELEATIC SCHOOL) argued that change and a plurality of existing things were impossible because they necessitated a passage from nonbeing to being, and nonbeing, they said, is a meaningless concept.

The Parmenidean critique brought a variety of responses. The pluralists tried to preserve the reality of change while taking Parmenides' logic into account. EMPEDOCLES claimed that all transitory things were mixtures of four elements: earth, water, fire, and air, which themselves were everlasting and unchanging. ANAXAGORAS argued for the unchanging status of a class of things all of whose parts were like the whole: divide gold and one still has gold; split a person and one does not get more persons. The atomists, LEUCIPPUS and DEMOCRITUS, posited the everlasting existence of atoms—indivisible units possessing only size, shape, and perhaps weight—and empty space, in which the atoms move.

The mutually incompatible alternative theories of the other pre-Socratics were exploited by the SOPHISTS. PROTAGORAS, the most famous Sophist, argued that all beliefs are equally correct and that all moral and political norms are the products of human custom and convention.

The impact of the pre-Socratics on subsequent Greek thought was considerable. Socrates was particularly concerned to defeat the relativism and conventionalism of the Sophists.

press, freedom of the　see FREEDOM OF THE PRESS

—

press agencies and syndicates　Press agencies and syndicates are organizations whose function is to gather and distribute news to NEWSPAPERS, radio and television stations, and other subscribers. News-gathering services began in the 19th century with the formation (1835) of Havas in France, followed by the opening (1849) of the first telegraphic news agency in Berlin and the foundation (1851) of the London agency, Reuters. The news supplied by these agencies, and by the smaller agencies that soon opened in the capitals of Europe, was primarily commercial. As the telegraph system expanded, however, they began to wire their clients newspaper stories of major events around the world.

The first U.S. news agency was the N.Y. Associated Press (AP; 1848), a cooperative endeavor of six New York City newspapers, begun because of the expense of sending a reporter from each newspaper to cover the Mexican War. During the Civil War, 43 daily newspapers in the South pooled their resources to establish the Press Association of the Confederate States of America (PA), whose reporters supplied Southern newspaper readers will well-written, relatively objective news stories that were transmitted over the Confederate Army's Military Telegraph Lines.

After the Civil War, various regional newspaper groups joined the AP, and by 1900 it had become a nationwide cooperative that distributed foreign as well as U.S. news. In the early 1900s, newspaper magnates E. W. SCRIPPS and William Randolph HEARST challenged the AP's near monopoly. Scripps established the United Press Association in 1907; Hearst founded the International News Service in 1909. In 1958 the two agencies merged to form United Press International (UPI).

Today the AP is still operated as a cooperative by a large group of U.S. newspapers and is the largest of the international news agencies. UPI, which has been bought and sold several times since 1958, is the second largest.

AP, UPI, Reuters, Agence France-Presse (the successor to Havas), and TASS, the Soviet-government news agency, are the five major news services for the Western press. Other important news agencies include the Japanese agency Kyodo and the Press Trust of India. All use telephone wires, communications satellites, teleprinters, and other telecommunications technologies. They also contribute information to computer databases, which is transmitted to terminals in subscribers' offices and to home screens.

Newspaper-owned syndicates offer their subscribers news stories and features that are generated by the staffs of the newspapers themselves. Among the largest are those of the *New York Times* and the *Los Angeles Times/Washington Post*. Feature syndicates provide newspapers with non-news material: articles, comics, cartoons, pictures, and fillers. The syndicates began as a 19th-century service to small weekly newspapers, supplying them with pages preprinted on one side or with stereotyped plates of articles that could be cut apart to fit the newspaper page. Major 20th-century syndicates include William Randolph Hearst's King Features Syndicate, United Features, and the *Chicago Tribune–New York News* Syndicate.

—

pressure　In physics, pressure is FORCE measured in terms of its distribution over an area of opposing force. This is expressed as force F divided by unit area A of the surface area to which the force is applied. Pressure most commonly refers to a force exerted uniformly in all directions. Absolute pressure is pressure measured with respect to zero pressure, whereas gauge pressure is pressure measured with respect to air pressure (the pressure exerted by the weight of the atmosphere). In the International System of Units (see UNITS, PHYSICAL), pressure is given as kilograms per square meter (1 kg/m^2 = 0.20481614 lb/ft^2). In the centimeter-gram-second (cgs) system, it is given as DYNES per square centimeter

(1 kg/m^2 = 98.0665 dyne/cm^2). Other units may also be used, as in the expression of air pressure, where BAROMETER and manometer readings are commonly given in terms of the height of a column of mercury.

Prester John [pres'-tur]

From the era of the Crusades, Europe's Christian rulers sought to form an anti-Muslim alliance with the realm of Prester (or Prebyster) John, a legendary Christian king whose domain was believed to be somewhere in southwest Asia or northeast Africa, just beyond the Islamic empire. Accounts of his heroic struggles against the Muslims were first recorded by Bishop Otto of Freising in 1145. About 1165 a letter was circulated in Europe in which "Prester John" addressed various European rulers. Early missions from Portugal sought to find the kingdom of Prester John. When Ethiopia was reached in 1493 by Pero da Covilha, its rulers, Coptic Christians, were quickly identified with Prester John. Portuguese missions to Ethiopia in the 16th century reinforced the legend, but it subsequently died out.

Pretoria [pri-tohr'-ee-uh]

Pretoria is the administrative capital of South Africa and the provincial capital of the Transvaal. Situated 48 km (30 mi) north of Johannesburg, Pretoria is the gateway to the northern Transvaal and the nation of Zimbabwe and lies on the Apies River in a small basin in the Magaliesberg Range. Its population is 822,925 (1985). Besides the state-owned iron and steel works, Pretoria's industries include railroad workshops, auto-assembly plants, and food-processing plants. Pretoria has some of South Africa's most magnificent public and private gardens and several architectural landmarks—the Union (government) Buildings, Voortrekker Monument, and the historic government offices facing Church Square. The residence of former president Paul Kruger is now a museum. The city is the seat of the University of South Africa (1873) and the University of Pretoria (1908).

The townsite was selected by Marthinus Pretorius in 1855, and the town was named for his father, Voortrekker hero Andries Pretorius. In 1860, Pretoria was designated capital of the Transvaal, and in 1881 it became the capital of the South African Republic. It was made the administrative capital of the new Union of South Africa in 1910.

Pretorius, Andries [pray-tohr'-ee-uhs]

Andries Wilhelmus Jacobus Pretorius, b. November 1789, d. July 23, 1853, an Afrikaner statesman and a military leader, was instrumental in establishing the Natal and Transvaal republics. A farmer, he took part in the GREAT TREK and settled (1838) in Natal, where he was elected leader by the Afrikaners. In the Battle of the Blood River that year he inflicted a decisive defeat on the Zulu in Natal. He failed, however, to prevent the British from annexing Natal, and in 1848 he emigrated to Transvaal, where he became one of four commandants general. In 1852 he negotiated the Sand River Convention, whereby the British acknowledged the independence of Transvaal.

Pretorius, Marthinus Wessel

Marthinus Wessel Pretorius, b. Sept. 17, 1819, d. May 18, 1901, was a leader of the Afrikaners, or Boers, and the first president (1857) of the South African Republic (Transvaal). The son of Andries Pretorius, whom he succeeded (1853) as a commandant general in Transvaal, he labored to establish a central government in Transvaal to unite all the Boer settlers under one flag. He founded (1855) the city of Pretoria. Elected president of Transvaal in 1857, he also became president of the Orange Free State in 1859 but failed in his attempt to unite two adjoining states. He resigned from the presidency of the Orange Free State in 1863 and was forced out of his Transvaal presidency in 1871.

Previn, André

André George Previn, b. Berlin, Apr. 6, 1929, is a multitalented conductor, composer, and pianist. His family fled Nazi Germany in 1938, settling in Los Angeles in 1939. He worked as a jazz and concert pianist and as a writer and arranger of film scores, for which he won four Oscars. He later focused on classical composition and on conducting, leading the Houston (1967–69), London (1968–79), Pittsburgh (1976–84) and Los Angeles (1984–89) symphonies. In 1985 he was designated music director of London's Royal Philharmonic.

Prévost, Abbé [pray-voh']

The French novelist Antoine François Prévost, better known as the Abbé Prévost, b. Apr. 1, 1697, d. Nov. 23, 1763, is best remembered for the novel *Histoire du chevalier des Grieux et de Manon Lescaut* (1731; trans. as *Manon Lescaut*, 1738). The story, which recounts the degradation of a youth in love with a glamorous but inconstant woman, inspired the 19th-century operas *Manon* (1884) by Jules Massenet and *Manon Lescaut* (1893) by Giacomo Puccini.

Prevost, Sir George [prev'-oh]

Sir George Prevost, b. New Jersey, May 19, 1767, d. Jan. 5, 1816, was governor in chief and commander in chief of the Canadas (Lower and Upper Canada) from 1812 to 1815. A British army officer, he was governor of Saint Lucia (1798–1801) and Dominica (1802–08), lieutenant-governor of Nova Scotia (1808–11), and administrator of Lower Canada (1811–12). Although successful as a conciliator of French Canadians, he was blamed for two military errors in the War of 1812: the withdrawal after a successful attack on Sackett's Harbor (1813) and the defeat at Plattsburgh (1814). He died a week before he was to face a court-martial.

Priam [pry'-uhm]

In Greek legend Priam was king of Troy during the TROJAN WAR. He was portrayed in Homer's *Iliad* as a gentle, revered old man, the father of many sons and daughters, whose most famous act was the attempt to ransom the body of his son HECTOR, slain by ACHILLES. Moved by Priam's grief, Achilles yielded the body. When the Greeks sacked Troy, Priam was killed by NEOPTOLE-MUS, Achilles' son.

priapism [pry'-uh-pizm]   Priapism is prolonged penile erection, usually without any sexual desire. The onset is usually sudden and very painful. Thrombosis (obstruction) of the pelvic veins is thought to be the most common cause, but priapism may involve both vascular and neurological abnormalities. Priapism sometimes occurs secondary to leukemia or sickle-cell disease, as well as after injuries to the spinal cord or brain (or as a result of tumors or other lesions there), and after infection and inflammation of the genitals. Urination may be very difficult or impossible. Treatment is difficult, and permanent impotence is a frequent consequence; often the only measure that can be taken is to drain blood from the penis.

Priapus [pry-ay'-puhs]   In Greek mythology Priapus was the son of APHRODITE and DIONYSUS. Portrayed as a grotesque little man with a huge phallus, he was associated particularly with fertility rites and also protected crops and gardens.

Pribilof Islands [prib'-uh-lawf]   The Pribilof (Fur Seal) Islands lie in the Bering Sea about 290 km (180 mi) north of the Aleutians and 470 km (290 mi) west of mainland Alaska. Saint Paul, the largest island, has an area of 91 km^2 (35 mi^2) and a population of 763 (1990).

In 1786, Gerasim Pribilof, a Russian sea captain, sighted the islands and claimed them for Russia. They were acquired by the United States as part of the purchase of Alaska in 1867. In the 1880s a dispute known as the Bering Sea controversy arose between the United States and Canada over pelagic sealing in the area. An international arbitration on Aug. 15, 1893, led to the regulation of pelagic sealing but fined the United States for interfering with Canadian sealers outside territorial waters. By the early 20th century hunters had nearly destroyed the huge seal herds. International conventions of 1911 and 1957 limited the annual catch, and the seal herd had greatly increased by the 1990s.

Price, Leontyne [lee'-uhn-teen]   The American operatic soprano Leontyne Price, b. Laurel, Miss., Feb. 10, 1927, achieved international renown for her brilliant voice and sensitive musicality. She attended (1948–52) the Juilliard School on a scholarship. In 1952 she sang the role of Mistress Ford in Verdi's *Falstaff,* took the lead in Virgil Thomson's *Four Saints in Three Acts,* and toured the United States as Bess in George Gershwin's *Porgy and Bess.* Her important debuts include: Town Hall (1954), in the New York premiere of Samuel Barber's *Hermit Songs*; television (1955), with the NBC Opera

Company, in Puccini's *Tosca*; the Vienna Opera (1958), in Verdi's *Aïda*; La Scala (1960), in *Aïda*; and the Metropolitan Opera (Jan. 27, 1961), in Verdi's *Il Trovatore.* She gave her farewell performance (Jan. 3, 1985) from the Metropolitan in *Aïda*.

Price, Sterling   Sterling Price, b. Prince Edward County, Va., Sept. 20, 1809, d. Sept. 29, 1867, was a Confederate general in the U.S. Civil War. After moving to Missouri he entered politics, serving as a state legislator, member of the U.S. House of Representatives, and governor. He was a general in the Mexican War. Initially a Unionist, he joined the secessionist forces in Missouri in May 1861. After notable victories against the Union army, he joined (March 1862) the regular Confederate army. He spent most of the war west of the Mississippi, struggling unsuccessfully to win Missouri for the Confederacy.

Price, Sir Uvedale   see LANDSCAPE ARCHITECTURE

price system   The price system, in economics, is the basic mechanism through which the decisions of consumers, businesses, government, and resource suppliers are communicated and synchronized in a free-enterprise economy. It is primarily through the price system that a capitalistic economy determines what goods and services are to be produced, what productive techniques are to be employed, and how total output or income is to be distributed. Determined by the interaction of SUPPLY AND DEMAND, prices are measures of the relative economic value of both products and resources. Prices provide the necessary information upon which producers and resource owners act in seeking to further their own self-interests. Hence, resource owners will attempt to have their resources (land, labor, and capital) employed where the economic rewards or incomes are highest. Business executives in turn rely on prices in determining what products can be profitably produced and what productive techniques (combinations of resources) will yield maximum PROFITS.

prickly heat   Prickly heat, or heat rash (miliaria rubra), is a disorder characterized by an acute inflammation of the skin and, specifically, the formation of small, reddish bumps. It usually occurs with exposure to high temperatures and humidity, and is caused by clogging of the ducts of sweat glands. In another disorder, miliaria crystallina, sweat accumulates under the skin, forming small blisters.

prickly pear   About 300 members of the cactus family that belong to the genus *Opuntia* are grouped under the name prickly pear. Although native to the Western Hemisphere, some species now grow throughout the world. Some have a tall, treelike growth habit, and others are shrubs; most have visible spines. Flowers may be red, purple, or yellow. *O. ficus-indica,* the Indian fig or Indian tuna, is widely grown in tropical regions for its edible fruit, which is pear shaped and spine covered and has a sweet, red flesh. Other species are used for forage. In many areas where species of *Opuntia* have been introduced, they have become serious weed pests.

See also: CACTI AND OTHER SUCCULENTS.

Pride and Prejudice Originally entitled *First Impressions* and rejected for publication, the revised *Pride and Prejudice* (1813) became Jane AUSTEN's most popular novel. A portrait of English provincial society, enlivened by skillfully varied dialogue and ironic narration, *Pride and Prejudice* focuses on the spirited and witty Elizabeth Bennet and her relationship with the proud Mr. Darcy. In the course of the novel, both characters learn much about themselves and the society in which they live. Elizabeth's initial adverse reaction to Darcy yields to respect, and Darcy also casts off his supercilious pride.

priest The office of a priest is essentially that of a mediator; he interprets God (or the gods or other supernatural forces) to the adherents of a religion and represents them before God, usually as the one who offers sacrifice on their behalf. All ancient religions had their priests, and these priests exercised great influence, not only as custodians of the sacred mysteries but often as the only literate members of society. Many present-day religions such as Buddhism, Hinduism, and Shinto have priests, but others, notably Islam, do not. Judaism had priests until the destruction of the Temple.

In Christianity the word *priest* comes from two distinct Greek terms, one meaning elder or presbyter and the other meaning priest in the traditional sense of mediator. Roman Catholics, Anglicans (Episcopalians), and Eastern Orthodox commonly refer to as priests those who have been ordained (see HOLY ORDERS); these priests correspond roughly to those whom Protestants call ministers or sometimes presbyters (see MINISTRY, CHRISTIAN).

Priestley, J. B. John Boynton Priestley, b. Sept. 13, 1894, d. Aug. 14, 1984, was a prolific and popular English novelist, dramatist, and essayist. Priestley left school at age 16. After serving in the army in France for 5 years during World War I, he attended Cambridge University and then began the writing career that brought him almost immediate success and that continued into the 1970s. Many of his works express his concern with the nature of time. *The Good Companions* (1929) is Priestley's fourth, but first major, novel and one of his best; others include *Angel Pavement* (1930), *Bright Day* (1946), and *Lost Empires* (1965). Some of his plays have been published in the three-volume *Collected Plays* (1948–52); *Time and the Conways* (1937) and *An Inspector Calls* (1946) are among the best of them. A selection of his essays—on literature, the arts, and travel—appears in *Essays of Five Decades* (1968).

Priestley, Joseph Joseph Priestley, b. Mar. 13, 1733, d. Feb. 6, 1804, achieved fame as a radical theologian and as a scientist. He was a founder of English Unitarianism and of chemistry.

Priestley's avocation was science. He discovered several gases, the most important being oxygen (later named by Lavoisier). The work that earned him election to the Royal Society, however, was his *History and Present State of Electricity* (1767). He spent his most productive years of scientific work while in the service (1773–80) of William Petty, 2d earl of SHELBURNE, in whose household he served as librarian and tutorial advisor. He traveled with Shelburne in Europe and met a number of scientists there. Priestley published a six-volume account of his work, *Experiments and Observations on Different Kinds of Air* (1774–86). His studies of plant respiration anticipated the concept of photosynthesis.

Because of Priestley's positions as a minister and teacher, his strongly expressed opinions led to controversy. Much of his influence derives from his books, which total more than 70. His *History of the Corruptions of Christianity* (1782)—in which he not only attacked Roman Catholicism as a chief repository of error but also maintained that any departure from the original faith of Christ and the apostles was corrupt—caused an uproar. Moreover, Priestley attempted to prove that Apostolic Christianity was Unitarian. This book was officially burned in Dort, the Netherlands, by the public executioner. Eventually, a mob destroyed (1791) Priestley's church, house, and laboratory. In 1794 he fled England to settle in the United States.

Joseph Priestley was an 18th-century British scientist and theologian. Priestley's study of gases led to his discovery of oxygen, and he was elected to the Royal Society in 1766 for his work on electricity. Priestley's Unitarian religious convictions forced him to flee from England to the United States in 1794.

Prigogine, Ilya [pree-goh'-zheen] The Belgian chemical physicist Ilya Prigogine, b. Jan. 25, 1917, initiated the application of thermodynamics to irreversible processes. He discovered that, contrary to the second law of thermodynamics (see ENTROPY), there are reactions in biochemistry (formation of amino acids from "primordial soup") and other systems that increase in complexity rather than decrease. Such systems are maintained at the cost of energy and are called "dissipative" structures, the latter providing a theoretical framework for the origin of life. Prigogine was awarded the 1977 Nobel Prize for chemistry.

Prim, Juan [preem]   Juan Prim, b. Dec. 6, 1814, d. Dec. 30, 1870, a Spanish general and liberal revolutionary, led the uprising that overthrew Queen ISABELLA II in 1868. He gained fame as a courageous officer, an able administrator, and a dangerous political conspirator. After the expulsion of Isabella, he served as prime minister in the provisional government. He tried to establish a liberal constitutional monarchy but was thwarted by social unrest and the difficulty of finding a new king. Finally in 1870, Amadeus of Savoy, son of King Victor Emmanuel II of Italy, accepted the Spanish throne. Prim was assassinated before the new king was established.

primary education   All societies establish systematic methods of teaching young children to perpetuate their society and its traditions and to equip them for survival. In PRIMITIVE SOCIETIES children acquire an education by observing or assisting adults in life's basic tasks. As a society becomes more complex, education becomes a formal process, although it does not always occur in a school; PRESCHOOL EDUCATION and primary education have more usually been the responsibility of the FAMILY. Only in the mid-19th century did most Western societies accept the notion that it was the state's responsibility to provide education for all children.

History. Public education in the American colonies began in 1647 when the General Court of the Massachusetts Bay Colony required towns of 50 or more households to select a person to teach all children to read and write and towns of 100 or more households to establish a grammar school (see SECONDARY EDUCATION). This type of law was not the rule for all the colonies at this date, however. Some New England children learned the rudiments of reading from dame schools, conducted by women in their own homes. In the Southern colonies, families more often employed a tutor or assigned a servant to teach their own and neighboring children.

After the Revolution a number of distinctively American school texts were produced, including Noah WEBSTER's *American Speller* (1783). It had a syllabary and a pronunciation key geared to the language as spoken in America, and it included many moral admonitions, scriptural passages, and a "moral catechism."

During the 1830s and '40s a movement for the establishment and reform of common schools developed. Its leaders, Horace MANN and Henry BARNARD, argued that it was in the interest of the state to educate all children at public expense so as to maintain social order, which increasing immigration and industrialization had put in doubt. They also argued that state control of schooling was necessary to eliminate unfair local variations in quality. Their efforts resulted in the formulation of education law by states, rather than by federal or local authorities.

By the end of the 19th century these reformers had introduced graded schools and established schools for the training and certification of teachers. About the same time, the Reverend Dr. William Holmes McGUFFEY published his *First Reader* and *Second Reader* (1836), the first two of a set of six graded texts—The McGuffey Eclectic Readers, which within 50 years swept the country.

Three European theorists—Johann Heinrich PESTALOZZI, Johann Friedrich HERBART, and Friedrich Wilhelm August FROEBEL—offered ideas that changed traditional views of education. Pestalozzi emphasized that children learn through all their senses and urged that they study objects as well as books. He claimed that appeals to their natural instincts would engage them in learning more effectively than threats of punishment. Herbart taught that interest is the basis of learning and that teachers should relate their lessons to the ideas children have already learned through a five-step approach. Froebel developed the kindergarten because he believed that children should have the opportunity to develop through play, self-expression, and the manipulation of objects. His ideas helped move primary education from its traditional stress on discipline and reading and writing toward schooling that was concerned with natural development.

The last quarter of the 19th century witnessed the beginnings of scientific child study and EDUCATIONAL PSYCHOLOGY, as pioneered by G. Stanley HALL. Building on this, the philosopher John DEWEY argued that learning would not occur without effort and that effort would not occur without interest. To test his theories he opened a laboratory school in 1896 where children were taught by undertaking a series of occupations. The occupations were designed to teach children how civilization developed, the need for social cooperation, and how various branches of learning related to each other. Dewey's ideas spurred the PROGRESSIVE EDUCATION movement.

Under Hall, Arnold Gesell, and the Swiss psychologist Jean PIAGET, DEVELOPMENTAL PSYCHOLOGY became an important influence on education in the first half of the 20th century. They identified the stages of human growth and the norms for those stages, giving rise to the idea of "reading readiness," which maintained that children would learn to read (or undertake other learning tasks) only when they had reached the appropriate stage in intellectual development. Lewis TERMAN developed the STANFORD-BINET TEST during World War I and encouraged the growth of EDUCATIONAL MEASUREMENT AND TESTING. Edward L. THORNDIKE, in developing tests to measure children's intelligence, stressed the necessity of finding intrinsic rather than extrinsic rewards to promote learning.

Students of BEHAVIORISM, such as John B. WATSON and B. F. SKINNER, placed an exclusive emphasis on environmental factors in learning. Watson's influence was at its greatest in the 1920s and '30s. Those who applied his theories stressed the importance of developing learning procedures and paid much less attention to affective considerations. During the 1960s and subsequently, Skinner's theories of operant conditioning (see LEARNING THEORY) were applied to the problems of classroom management.

Contemporary Primary Education. The varying approaches to primary education include the belief that the school should concentrate on skill acquisition and cognitive development; that emphasis should be placed on the development of the "whole child," with special attention to social and emotional adjustment; that children should be trained to serve the needs of society; that children should be equipped for economic and social progress; and that schools should attempt to resolve social inequalities.

Project HEAD START (1965) showed that preschool experiences had a positive influence on the intellectual development of children. Whereas formal schooling usually begins at age 5 or 6, educators and parents now view the earlier years of childhood as an essential part of primary education.

Primary education usually ends after 6 or 8 years of schooling, depending on the organization of the local school system. From there children go to MIDDLE SCHOOLS AND JUNIOR HIGH SCHOOLS, or the high school. Nearly all developed countries provide public primary education and require attendance, as do all 50 states of the United States. About three-fourths of the world's 6- to 11-year-old children attend school.

primary election

A primary election, also called a direct primary in the United States, is an election process whereby a political party chooses its candidates for public office by a direct polling of party members. It is contrasted with the party caucus or convention, where party candidates are chosen by party leaders and activists. Winners in primary elections go on to run in the general election against candidates of the other parties.

Types of Primary. Primary elections were first provided for by state laws early in the 20th century, and nearly all nominations are now made in primaries. A majority of states use what is known as a closed primary, whereby the voter must have previously declared himself or herself a member of the party before he or she can vote in that party's primary. Other states have open primaries, which means that members of one party may cross over and cast their votes in another party's primary. In either the closed or open primary, a voter may vote in only one party's primary.

Presidential Primaries. Candidates for president of the United States are not nominated in a direct primary but in national conventions of their political parties. Most of the delegates to those conventions, however, are picked in primaries (other delegates are chosen through caucus systems). A majority of states use presidential primaries in which voters take part either by electing delegates on a given candidate's slate to the national conventions or by voting their preference for the candidates listed on the state ballot.

The presidential primaries are spread over a period of months because each state selects its own date. Consequently, the candidates journey from state to state campaigning. In an unprecedented experiment in 1988, 16 states, mostly in the South, held primaries on the same day (four others had caucuses). Critics of this "super" primary maintained that it made systematic campaigning impossible and pushed candidates to spend large sums for television commercials.

Presidential primaries have become crucial in the nomination of candidates, but there are serious objections to them. One emphasizes the physical strain on the candidates and the large amounts of money involved—contributed in many cases by special-interest groups. A second objection is that presidential primaries have become media events, detracting from serious discussion of issues and placing too much emphasis on the personalities of the candidates.

Despite the objections to presidential primaries, they are unlikely to be abandoned because they are popular with the media, with much of the public, and with those candidates who have a better chance to be nominated this way.

primate

Primates are the order of mammals containing monkeys, apes, humans, and other similar forms. Nearly 200 living species, grouped into more than 50 genera, are usually recognized, and almost 100 extinct genera are also known. Although the primates cover a wide array of adaptive modifications in size, structure, and habits, the group's unifying feature is its common evolutionary descent. The features discussed below serve to characterize the order in a general way.

Most of the principal features associated with the primates have arisen as a result of an arboreal, or tree-living, mode of life. Agility in trees demands good vision, and consequently one evolutionary trend has been the development of large, forward-directed eyes. The optic nerve fibers of each eye run to both halves of the brain, resulting in a superimposed, or double, image and an associated sense of depth. A bony ring around each eye socket helps support the eyes, and in the higher primates this support has become a complete bony wall behind the eye. This emphasis on vision led to the enlargement of the occipital lobe—that part of the brain which deals with vision—and to the relative reduction of structures associated with the decreasingly important sense of smell.

Most primates climb by grasping with their hands. The grasp of most primates has evolutionarily been improved by the development of a big toe or thumb, which is set apart from the other digits but which can be moved toward the tips of at least two of them. This ability is called opposability; it also provides primates with capabilities such as holding objects close for examination, eating with one hand, and so on. Opposability, manipulative skills, and the muscular coordination necessary for rapid movement through the trees evolved along with enlargement of the motor, or movement, areas of the brain, thus contributing to the continuing increase in primate brain size.

Because claws were no longer needed for climbing, the primates evolved flat nails as protection and support for the tactile tips of the digits. Clawlike structures are still present among a number of primates, including the marmosets, the lorises, and lemurs (grooming claw), but argument continues as to whether these structures are clawlike nails, intermediate stages between claws and nails, or true claws.

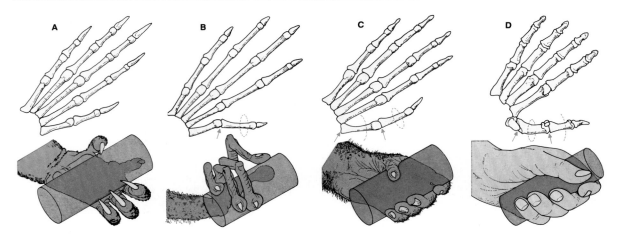

Primate hands show an evolutionary trend toward increased opposability of the thumb. The tree shrew (A) has clawed digits and nonopposable thumbs—unable to rotate in their sockets—that provide minimal grasping ability. The tarsier (B), a leaping primate, has disks on the fingertips that help it cling to tree trunks. Hands of the macaque (C), an Old World monkey, can lift objects between the thumb and fingers. In humans (D), whose thumbs are set at a wider angle from the hands, manipulative ability is even more precise.

Other features of the primates include the presence of a clavicle, or collarbone, which serves as a connecting support between the shoulder and the trunk of the body and helps reduce muscle strain in an animal often suspended by its arms. In addition, primates, along with only bears and bats, have pendant penises; that is, the penis is not permanently positioned along the abdomen. Reproductive cycles are also different. In most primates other than the lemurs and lorises, there are no definite breeding seasons. Instead, the female primate passes through a regularly recurring menstrual cycle, with sexual drive generally at its highest just prior to ovulation, or release of the egg from the ovary. Male higher primates are generally capable of breeding at any time.

Variation of Types

Living primates vary vastly in size, from the mouse lemur, *Microcebus*, which weighs as little as 60 g (2 oz), to the gorilla, exceeding 180 kg (400 lb) in the wild. Gestation periods vary accordingly, from the 2 months of the mouse lemur to the approximately 9 months of the gorilla, orangutan, and human. Natural longevity is difficult to estimate, but some captive chimpanzees and capuchin monkeys have lived more than 40 years. Locomotor, or movement, patterns are highly variable, from the forelimb-dominated arm-swinging (brachiation) of the gibbon to the hind-limb–dominated locomotion of galagos (clinging to and leaping between vertical supports) and humans (terrestrial bipedalism). Many types of quadrupedal, or four-legged, movement exist.

Primates feed on leaves, fruit, insects, buds, flowers, seeds, bark, roots, and other items. Some feed regularly, if infrequently, on birds and other small animals, and a few, such as baboons, occasionally kill and eat larger animals.

All primates are social, even those, such as the lorises, which lead mostly solitary lives. Social units of the more gregarious types vary greatly in size, composition, and or-ganization, from the family unit consisting of an adult pair and their immature offspring to large multimale aggregations numbering in the hundreds. Even within a species, social units may vary with environmental circumstances, emphasizing the fact that a great deal of primate behavior is learned.

Indeed, highly developed capacities for learning and for problem solving are primate characteristics. Most primate learning is social; young primates learn those things which they must know to survive within the context of their social group and its specific environment. Systems of social communication among primates are complex and varied and include scent, vocal, and visual signals; even "solitary" primates constantly employ scent marking to communicate with neighbors with whom they rarely come into physical contact.

Evolution

Primates are assumed to have originated from insectivorelike ancestors during the Cretaceous Period, possibly between 100 million and 65 million years ago. The first great increase in primate types occurred during the Paleocene Epoch, between 65 million and 54 million years ago. Fairly typical was *Plesiadapis*, known from both North America and Europe. *Plesiadapis* had clawed, nongrasping paws, a small brain, and a long snout; it lacked the bony ring around the eye.

Primates of the Eocene Epoch, from 54 million to 38 million years ago, were considerably more "modern," possessing grasping extremities and most closely resembling certain of the Madagascan lemurs. Bony eye rings appeared, as did shortened faces, which reflected an emphasis on vision at the expense of the sense of smell.

Old World higher primates first appear in the fossil record during the Oligocene Epoch, from 38 million to 26 million years ago. During the Miocene Epoch, from 26 million to 12 million years ago, a variety of apes were

galago

mouse lemur

indri

potto

aye-aye

lemur

marmoset

tarsier

howler monkey

vervet monkey

langur

chimpanzee

gibbon

Oreopithecus *is an extinct primate known from fossils in Late Miocene (ended 12 million years ago) deposits of East Africa and the Early Pliocene of southern Europe. Although it had some features similar to those of the Old World monkeys and others like those of humanlike apes, dental details suggest that* Oreopithecus *represents a line of apes that evolved separately from other primate families.*

present in Africa, Asia, and Europe, although it is not yet clear whether any of these was directly ancestral to any living ape. It is also from the Miocene that the earliest potential human relative, *Ramapithecus*, is known (see AFRICAN PREHISTORY; PREHISTORIC HUMANS). Old World monkeys are known from Miocene deposits in Africa and Eurasia, and during this epoch the two modern subfamilies (Cercopithecinae and Colobinae) became differentiated. A substantial increase in types of Old World monkeys occurred on these continental masses during the Pliocene, about 12 million to 1.7 million years ago, and the Pleistocene, about 1.7 million to 10,000 years ago.

Paleontologists assume that South American monkeys are descended from earlier forms discovered in North America. In the 1980s a new wave of conjecture followed the discovery of a fossil primate in Wyoming dating from 53 million years ago and appearing to be ancestral to both lemurs and tarsiers. The primate, named *Cantius torresi*, was more primitive than other fossil species from either North America or Europe, raising the possibility that primates spread from Asia into North America earlier than they reached Europe.

Classification

The classification of living primates is currently a matter of some dispute. Most authorities, however, would provisionally accept the following simplified arrangement.

ORDER PRIMATES

Suborder Strepsirhini
　　Family Lemuridae (true lemurs)
　　Family Indriidae (sifakas, indris)
　　Family Daubentoniidae (aye-aye)
　　Family Cheirogaleidae (mouse and dwarf lemurs)
　　Family Lorisidae (lorises, pottos, angwantibos)
　　Family Galagidae (galagos)

Suborder Haplorhini
　　Infraorder Tarsiiformes (tarsier)
　　Infraorder Platyrrhini (New World monkeys)
　　　　Family Callitrichidae (marmosets, tamarins)
　　　　Family Cebidae (capuchins, howlers)
　　Infraorder Catarrhini (Old World higher primates)
　　　　Superfamily Cercopithecoidea (Old World monkeys)
　　　　　　Family Cercopithecidae
　　　　　　　　Subfamily Cercopithecinae (vervets, baboons)
　　　　　　　　Subfamily Colobinae (leaf monkeys)
　　　　Superfamily Hominoidea (apes and humans)
　　　　　　Family Hylobatidae (gibbons and siamangs)
　　　　　　Family Pongidae (great apes)
　　　　　　Family Hominidae (humans)

Primaticcio, Francesco [pree-mah-teet'-choh]
The Bolognese Mannerist architect, decorator, painter, and stuccoist Francesco Primaticcio, b. Apr. 30, 1504, d. 1570, was one of the masters of the FONTAINEBLEAU SCHOOL. He was particularly skilled in combining paintings with stucco work. In 1531, Primaticcio was called to France by Francis I to assist in the decorations of the château at Fontainebleau; in 1541 he became the head of the workshop there.

The influence of PARMIGIANINO led Primaticcio to develop the ideal of elegant feminine beauty, which was most often expressed in elongated nude figures. These figures became dominant in French taste during the Mannerist period (see MANNERISM). Unfortunately many of Primaticcio's most important works at Fontainebleau, such as the Galerie d'Ulysse (begun *c.*1452), have been destroyed, but the Chambre de la Duchesse d'Étampes (*c.*1541–45) and Galerie Henri II (1552–56) survive, if in somewhat altered form.

prime meridian　The prime, or Greenwich, meridian is that LONGITUDE line designated 0° 00' 00". It passes through the old Greenwich Observatory in London. An 1884 international treaty made it the line on which global TIME ZONES are based.

prime minister　A prime minister, or premier, is the chief member of the cabinet in a parliamentary government and, as such, the head of government. A prime minister is not the head of state. In a republic, that position is held by the PRESIDENT; in a monarchy, by the sovereign.

The prime minister is normally chosen by the head of state from among elected members of the legislature; this choice is usually limited to the leader of the party in control of the legislature. The prime minister, who continues to serve in the legislature, selects a CABINET, formulates and administers government policy, and dispenses party patronage. Prime ministers are generally chosen for an indefinite term, and in democratic countries the support of the legislative body is required. Should this support be withdrawn, the resignation of the prime minister and the cabinet is in order. The prime minister has the right to call for the resignation of a cabinet member at any time.

In Great Britain the prime minister may call for a general election by asking the sovereign to dissolve PARLIAMENT and is required to do so if ruling policies have met with decisive defeat in the House of Commons. The prime minister there is by modern convention a member of the House of Commons.

Historically, the office of prime minister developed from the growing power of Parliament in the 17th and 18th centuries. The monarchs, who had previously depended on their own courtiers for political advice, found it advantageous to have a supporter in Parliament. Robert WALPOLE is generally regarded as the first prime minister. The power of the office grew during the 19th century, as the power of the crown declined.

prime number   A prime number is any integer larger than 1 such that the only positive integers dividing evenly into it are itself and 1. (This means that all prime numbers, except for 2, are odd numbers.) The first few primes are 2, 3, 5, 7, and 11. The primes are the building blocks of the positive integers, because every positive integer is a product of prime numbers in one and only one way, except for the order of the factors. For example, $22,891,869 = 3 \times 3 \times 3 \times 7 \times 7 \times 11 \times 11 \times 11 \times 13$. This fact is very useful in finding common denominators and in performing other arithmetic operations. Prime numbers have found use in codes in computer technology; because they are difficult to discover, primes improve the security of computer installations (see CRYPTOLOGY).

The distribution and determination of primes has puzzled mathematicians since ancient times. The earliest efficient method of finding primes was given (c.240 BC) by ERATOSTHENES OF CYRENE and is called the Sieve of Eratosthenes. To obtain a list of all the primes less than or equal to N, one makes a list of all the integers less than or equal to N and strikes out the multiples of the primes that are less than or equal to $\sqrt{N}$. For example, to find all the primes less than or equal to 100, one need only strike out the multiples of 2, 3, 5, and 7.

If a number is large enough, deciding whether or not it is prime is difficult. Large primes in recent years have been so-called Mersenne primes, which take the form of $2^m - 1$—that is, a power of 2, minus 1, where m is itself a prime. The largest Mersenne prime yet known, $2^{216,091} - 1$, was found in 1985. A somewhat larger prime, $(2^{216,193} \times 391,581) - 1$, found in 1989, is of interest because it is not a Mersenne prime, and because the ALGORITHMS involved in the work have wider applications in science and computer technology. The 1989 prime, if written out, would contain 65,087 digits.

There are many unsolved problems concerning primes. One of them is the Goldbach conjecture: Is every even integer greater than 4 a sum of two odd primes?

primitive arts   Primitive arts are the various arts produced by nonliterate societies. Also called tribal, exotic, traditional, or preliterate art, primitive art is distinct from European FOLK ART, the art of Western primitives (artists working in naive styles), and archaeological cave art (see PREHISTORIC ART). The term *primitive* refers to the small-scale nonurban nature of the society producing the arts, rather than the forms of the arts themselves. The major areas are covered in such articles as AFRICAN ART; AFRICAN MUSIC; INDIANS OF NORTH AMERICA, ART OF THE; INDIANS OF NORTH AMERICA, MUSIC AND DANCE OF THE; OCEANIA, ART OF; and PRE-COLUMBIAN ART AND ARCHITECTURE. Primitive arts were traditionally important to the functioning of the society itself. Such primitive art today, however, is often made for sale to outsiders and has lost many of its former functions.

primitive religion   *Primitive religion* is a name given to the religious beliefs and practices of those traditional, often isolated, preliterate cultures which have not developed urban and technologically sophisticated forms of society. The term is misleading in suggesting that the religions of those peoples are somehow less complex than the religions of "advanced" societies. In fact, research carried out among the indigenous peoples of Oceania, the Americas, and sub-Saharan Africa have revealed rich and very complex religions, which organize the smallest details of the people's lives.

The religions of archaic cultures—the cultures of the Paleolithic, Mesolithic, and Neolithic ages—are also referred to as primitive.

Theories of Primitive Religion

Edward B. TYLOR based his intellectual-rational interpretation of primitive religion on the idea that primitive people make a mistaken logical inference—an intellectual error. He thought that they confuse subjective and objective reality in their belief that the vital force (soul) present in living organisms is detachable and capable of independent existence in its own mode. Dreams, he thought, might be a basis for this error. Tylor's definition of primitive religion as ANIMISM, a belief in spirtual beings, expresses his interpretation that the basis of primitive religion is the belief that detached and detachable vital forces make up a suprahuman realm of reality that is just as real as the physical world of rocks, trees, and plants.

An opposing interpretation of primitive religion comes from an experimental and psychological approach to the data. R. H. Codrington's study *The Melanesians* (1891), in which he described the meaning of MANA as a supernatural power or influence experienced by the Melanesians, has provided a basis for other scholars to explain the origin and interpretation of primitive religion as rooted in the experience by primitive peoples of the dynamic power of nature.

(Above) *A West African shaman, or witch doctor, wears an elaborate mask during the performance of a ritual. Masks, a common feature in the magicoreligious practices of many primitive societies, are used to enhance the power of the wearer.* (Right) *Wooden effigies are an integral part of the traditional funerary customs of many indigenous Melanesian cultures. The animist religion practiced by these peoples focuses on the veneration of the spirits of the dead.*

Another intellectual-rationalist approach to primitive religion is exemplified by Émile DURKHEIM, who saw religion as the deification of society and its structures. The symbols of religion arise as "collective representations" of the social sphere, and rituals function to unite the individual with society. Claude LÉVI-STRAUSS moved beyond Durkheim in an attempt to articulate the way in which the structures of society are exemplified in myths and symbols. Starting from the structural ideas of contemporary linguistics, he argued that there is one universal form of human logic and that the difference between the thinking of primitive and modern people cannot be based on different modes of thought or logic but rather on differences in the data on which logic operates.

Rituals

One of the most pervasive forms of religious behavior in primitive cultures is expressed by rituals and ritualistic actions. The forms and functions of rituals are diverse. They may be performed to ensure the favor of the divine, to ward off evil, or to mark a change in cultural status. In most, but not all, cases an etiological myth provides the basis for the ritual in a divine act or injunction.

Generally, rituals express the great transitions in human life: birth (coming into being); puberty (the recognition and expression of sexual status); marriage (the acceptance of an adult role in the society); and death (the return to the world of the ancestors). These passage rites (see PASSAGE, RITES OF) vary in form, importance, and intensity from one culture to another, for they are tied to several other meanings and rituals in the culture. For example, the primitive cultures of south New Guinea and Indonesia place a great emphasis on rituals of death and funerary rites. They have elaborate myths describing the

geography of the place of the dead and the journey of the dead to that place. Hardly any ritual meaning is given to birth. The Polynesians, on the other hand, have elaborate birth rituals and place much less emphasis on funerary rituals.

Almost all primitive cultures pay attention to puberty and marriage rituals, although there is a general tendency to pay more attention to the puberty rites of males than of females. Because puberty and marriage symbolize the fact that children are acquiring adult roles in the KINSHIP system in particular, and in the culture in general, most primitive cultures consider the rituals surrounding these events very important. Puberty rituals are often accompanied with ceremonial CIRCUMCISION or some other operation on the male genitals. Female circumcision is less common, although it occurs in several cultures. Female puberty rites are more often related to the commencement of the menstrual cycle in young girls.

In addition to these life-cycle rituals, rituals are associated with the beginning of the new year and with planting and harvest times in agricultural societies. Numerous other rituals are found in hunting-and-gathering societies; these are supposed to increase the game and to give the hunter greater prowess.

Another class of rituals is related to occasional events, such as war, droughts, catastrophes, or extraordinary events. Rituals performed at such times are usually intended to appease supernatural forces or divine beings who might be the cause of the event, or to discover what divine power is causing the event and why.

Rituals are highly structured actions. Each person or class of persons has particular stylized roles to play in them. Whereas some rituals call for communal participation, others are restricted by sex, age, or type of activity.

Thus initiation rites for males and females are separate, and only hunters participate in hunting rituals. There are also rituals limited to warriors, blacksmiths, magicians, and diviners.

Divine Beings

Divine beings are usually known through the mode of their manifestation. Creator-gods are usually deities of the sky. The sky as a primordial expression of transcendence is one of the exemplary forms of sacred power. Deities of the sky are often considered to possess an ultimate power.

Allied to and existing within the same sphere as the sky-god are the manifestations of divine presence in the Sun and the Moon. The symbolism of the Sun, while sharing the transcendent power of the sky, is more intimately related to the destiny of the human community and to the revelation of the rational power necessary to order the world. Sun-deities are creators by virtue of their growth-producing powers, whereas the sky-god creators often create *ex nihilo* ("out of nothing"); they do not require human agency in their creative capacities, and in many instances they withdraw and have little to do with humankind.

The manifestation and presence of the deity in the Moon is different from that of the Sun. Moon-deities are associated with a more rhythmic structure; they wax and wane, seeming more vulnerable and more capable of loss and gain. Moon-deities are often female in form and associated with feminine characteristics. The moon-goddess is the revelation of the vulnerability and fragility of life, and unlike solar gods her destiny is not the historical

The Calendar Stone of the Aztecs, who worshiped a solar deity, is carved with reliefs depicting the history and eschatology of the five sequential worlds, or suns, of the universe. (Museo Nacional de Antropologia, Mexico City.)

destiny of powerful rulers and empires, but the destiny of the human life cycle of birth, life, and death. Other places where deities show themselves are in the natural forms of water, vegetation, agriculture, stones, human sexuality, and so on.

The pattern of deities, of course, varies markedly among different types of societies. Hunting-and-gathering cultures, for example, not only have language and rituals related to hunting but also often have a Lord, Master, or Mistress of Animals—a divine being who not only created the world of humans and animals but who also cares for, protects, and supplies the animals to the hunters.

A somewhat more complex religious culture is found in early agricultural societies. It is commonly accepted that the earliest form of agriculture was both a feminine rite and a female right. This means that the gift and power of agriculture provided a means by which the sacredness of the world could be expressed in the femininity of the human species. Agricultural rituals became a powerful symbolic language that spoke of gestation, birth, nurture, and death. This development does not imply an early MATRIARCHY or the dominance of society by females. In agricultural societies males dominate in the conventional sense of the term, but the power of women is nevertheless potent and real.

Sacred Personages

Just as sacredness tends to be localized in the natural forms of the world in primitive religious cultures, sacred meaning is also defined by specific kinds of persons. On the one hand, sacredness may be located in and defined by office and status in a society. In such cases the role and function of the chief or king carries a sacred meaning because it is seen as an imitation of a divine model, which is generally narrated in a cultural myth; it may also be thought to possess divine power. Offices and functions of this kind are usually hereditary and are not dependent on any specific or unique personality structure in the individual.

On the other hand, forms of individual sacredness exist that do depend on specific types of personality structures and the calling to a particular religious vocation. Persons such as SHAMANS fall into this category. Shamans are recruited from among young persons who tend to exhibit particular psychological traits that indicate their openness to a more profound and complex world of sacred meanings than is available to the society at large. Once chosen, shamans undergo a special shamanistic initiation and are taught by older shamans the peculiar forms of healing and behavior that identify their sacred work. Given the nature of their sacred work, they must undergo long periods of training before they are capable practitioners of the sacred and healing arts. The same is true of medicine men and diviners, although these often inherit their status.

Each person in a primitive society may also bear an ordinary form of sacred meaning. Such meaning can be discerned in the elements of the person's psychological structure. For example, among the ASHANTI of Ghana, an individual's blood is said to be derived from the goddess of the earth through that individual's mother, an individual's destiny from the high-god, and personality and temperament from the tutelary deity of the individual's father. On the cosmological level of myths and rituals all of these divine forms have a primordial meaning that acquires individual and existential significance when it is expressed in persons.

Summary

Underlying all the forms, functions, rituals, personages, and symbols in primitive religion is the distinction between the sacred and the profane. The sacred defines the world of reality, which is the basis for all meaningful forms and behaviors in the society. The profane is the opposite of the sacred. Although it has a mode of existence and a quasi-reality, the profane is not based on a divine model, nor does it serve as an ordering principle for activities or meanings. For example, the manner in which a primitive village is laid out in space imitates a divine model and thus participates in sacred reality. The space outside of the organized space of the village is considered profane space, because it is not ordered and therefore does not participate in the meaning imparted by the divine model.

This characteristic distinction between the sacred and the profane is present at almost every level of primitive society. The tendency to perceive reality in the terms provided by the sacred marks a fundamental difference between primitive and modern Western societies, where this distinction has been destroyed. The openness to the world as a sacred reality is probably the most pervasive and common meaning in all forms of primitive religion and is present in definitions of time, space, behaviors, and activities.

The sacred is able to serve as a principle of order because it possesses the power to order. The power of the sacred is both positive and negative. It is necessary to have the proper regard for the sacred; it must be approached and dealt with in very specific ways.

A kind of ritual behavior defines the proper mode of contact with the sacred. Failure to act properly with respect to the sacred opens the door to the negative experience and effects of sacred power. The specific term for this negative power among the Melanesians is TABOO. This word has become a general term in Western languages expressing the range of meanings implied by the force and effects of a power that is both negative and positive and that attracts as well as repels.

—

primitive societies Primitive societies, as contrasted with so-called civilized societies, include those peoples of the world who live in nonurban, nonindustrialized, nonstate societies. As formerly applied, the term connoted illiterate, backward, inferior groups of "natives," as they were often referred to during the colonial era—peoples who had halted at a point in the process of cultural evolution. That idea sprang from the evolutionary theories of the 19th century, which assumed that primitive peoples were the "living ancestors" of modern industrialized

peoples. Scientists today recognize that so-called primitive peoples have continued to evolve but have adapted in ways different from "civilized" peoples to their particular social and ecological environments.

Except in unusual cases, such as that of the polar Eskimo, primitive societies have not been isolated from other groups; most conduct interethnic relationships involving mutual respect, trade, or warfare. Although rates of infant mortality and death from accidents or combat are high, these societies generally have fewer communicable diseases. Daily tasks are rigorous, but probably less time is spent in actual work than among industrialized peoples. Work is mainly associated with hunting, fishing, herding, and the gathering of wild foods or with nonmechanized agriculture and crafts. Some trade in valuables may be conducted, but these valuables are hand processed.

The security of a close community is balanced by the tight social controls typical of such groups. Primitive societies may be egalitarian, or they may be ranked but without sharp class or caste divisions. They are rarely communistic in the modern sense. Personal property may include tools and utensils, magic, and songs. Basic resources—such as hunting and fishing grounds, pastures, waterholes, woods, and fields—are usually owned by families or clans and in some cases by the entire community. The society may be organized into permanent villages or into nomadic bands. Social relations are usually based on kinship, and social roles on age, lineage, and gender. All primitive societies relate to the supernatural through some form of religion, such as ANIMISM, shamanism (see SHAMAN), totemism (see TOTEM), or ANCESTOR WORSHIP.

Most primitive societies have been changed or engulfed as a result of the colonial expansion of the past few centuries. Technologically less powerful groups have generally been forced to become more similar to the societies around them, or they have been absorbed by those societies, disappearing as separate entities.

—

Primo de Rivera, Miguel [pree'-moh day ree-vay'-rah] Miguel Primo de Rivera y Orbaneja, b. Jan. 8, 1870, d. Mar. 16, 1930, a Spanish general, was dictator of Spain from 1923 to 1930. In 1922, when the Spanish government was paralyzed by labor unrest, defeat in Morocco, and rumors of scandal at court, Primo de Rivera was appointed captain general of Barcelona. With the enthusiastic support of King ALFONSO XIII, Primo de Rivera overthrew the government, dissolved the Cortes, and proclaimed himself dictator, taking immediate steps to suppress social unrest and political liberties.

Primo de Rivera's government achieved victory in Morocco in 1927, supported labor arbitration, built public works, and stimulated tourism, commerce, and industry. In his efforts to substitute order and prosperity for democracy, he modeled his government after that set up in Italy by Benito Mussolini. After 1927, however, Primo's arbitrary decisions, his rough handling of intellectuals, and his mounting budget deficits alienated many of his supporters. When his fellow generals refused to support him in January 1930, he retired to Paris. His son José Antonio Primo de Rivera was the founder of the Falange, the Fascist-style party that was used by Francisco FRANCO in his rise to power.

primogeniture [pry-moh-jen'-i-chur]   Primogeniture is the preference given to the eldest son and his descendants in the INHERITANCE of property or position or both. It may occasionally involve preferential inheritance by the eldest child, regardless of sex, or by the eldest daughter. Ultimogeniture is the preferential inheritance by the youngest son or child.

Where land ownership was the basis of an aristocracy, as in much of medieval Europe, the practice of primogeniture preserved aristocratic status by maintaining estates whole and intact. In addition, the ownership of land often carried with it military and other obligations that could not be vested in more than one heir. In peasant societies with limited land, primogeniture serves to prevent the division of land into insignificant plots. In many nonliterate societies, however, strict primogeniture is not the custom. Often, the eldest son or brother inherits as a trustee and manages the estate on behalf of his brothers and their families.

primrose   Primrose is the common name for the at least 400 species of mostly perennial herbs constituting the genus *Primula* in the family Primulaceae. Most primroses are native to Europe, Asia, and North America, and in the wild they are often found in hilly areas. Primroses grow best in shady sites having a deep, moist, loamy soil. They die back each winter but renew themselves from

The English primrose and the showy primrose are perennial herbs native to Europe. The former has been cultivated in many color varieties.

buds on the rootstock (rhizome) each spring. Primroses have dimorphic flowers—that is, some plants within a species have flowers with long pistils (the female structures) and short stamens (male structures), whereas others have flowers with short pistils and long stamens. This arrangement increases the likelihood of cross-pollination, because each kind of insect pollinator tends to enter a flower in the same way and to the same depth each time.

The genus contains a large assemblage of common perennial garden flowers, generally about 30 to 120 cm (1 to 4 ft) tall, with showy clusters of trumpet-shaped flowers of yellow, white, pink, blue, red, or purple borne at the top of a long stem. The leaves are mostly at ground level and may be wrinkled or smooth in texture. Primrose seed may not reproduce parental characteristics, and special or diverse varieties are thus obtained by divisions of the root crowns.

prince   see TITLES OF NOBILITY AND HONOR

Prince, The   Nicolò MACHIAVELLI's *The Prince*, written in 1513 and published in 1532, was one of the most controversial works of the Italian Renaissance. Having observed Cesare Borgia's totalitarian government in Florence and the confusion that followed its demise, Machiavelli argued that an effective ruler should be pragmatic rather than virtuous in his use of power. His argument was partly based on his reading of classical historians, but *The Prince* was the first work to deal openly with the use of force in the STATE and to claim that the pursuit of stable government condoned amoral actions. These views, and Machiavelli's defense of republicanism, opposed the traditional order and caused his name to become synonymous with cynical brutality and atheism. The villainous character of Machiavel in Christopher Marlowe's *The Jew of Malta* (*c.*1589) typifies the popular image of Machiavelli in 16th-century Europe.

Prince Albert   Prince Albert is a city in central Saskatchewan, Canada, on the North Saskatchewan River. It has a population of 33,686 (1986). The city's industries include pulp and paper milling, oil refining, and food packaging. The city is the gateway to Prince Albert National Park. Several Indian reservations are nearby. In 1776 a fur-trading post was built in the area, and in 1866, Scottish missionaries established a Presbyterian mission on the site. Lumbering was the main activity during the early 20th century.

Prince Edward Island   Prince Edward Island, Canada's smallest and least populated province, lies in the Gulf of St. Lawrence on the east coast of Canada. It is separated from New Brunswick to the west and Nova Scotia to the south by the Northumberland Strait.

Prince Edward Island has played an important role in Canadian history. In September 1864 the "founding fathers" met at Charlottetown to lay the foundation for the

PRINCE EDWARD ISLAND

Land: Area: 5,660 km² (2,185 mi²); rank: 10th. Capital and largest city: Charlottetown (1986 pop., 15,776). Municipalities: 39. Elevations: highest—142 m (466 ft), in Queens County; lowest—sea level.

People: Population (1990 est.): 130,400; rank: 10th; density: 23 persons per km² (59.7 per mi²). Distribution (1986): 38.1% urban, 61.9% rural. Average annual change (1981–86): +0.68%.

Government (1991): Lieutenant Governor: Marion L. Reed. Premier: Joe Ghiz, Liberal. Parliament: Senate—4 members; House of Commons—4 Progressive Conservatives. Provincial legislature: 32 members. Admitted to Confederation: July 1, 1873, the 7th province.

Economy (monetary figures in Canadian dollars): Total personal income (1987): $1.7 billion; rank: 10th. Median family income (1987): $30,929. Agriculture: net income (1986)—$50.6 million. Fishing: value (1986)—$51.9 million. Forestry: lumber production (1985)—4.7 million board feet. Mining: value (1986)—$1.7 million. Manufacturing: value added (1986)—$107 million.

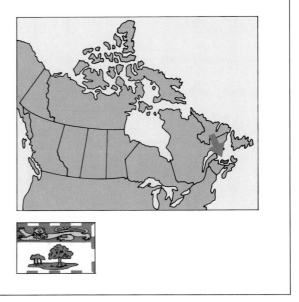

Confederation of Canada. The island, however, did not join the Confederation until 1873. In 1969 the federal and provincial governments jointly entered a 15-year comprehensive development plan for the province designed to solve the major provincial problems: high unemployment, low per capita income, high power costs, and lack of industrial development.

Land and Resources

Prince Edward Island is part of a plain that stretches into eastern New Brunswick and northern Nova Scotia. Most of the landscape is gently rolling with some flat lowlands. Iron compounds in glacial deposits have given rise to a striking feature of the island, its red soil, which is generally fertile and productive. The most important river is the Hillsborough; CHARLOTTETOWN, the capital, is on its branching estuary.

During the long, cold winters, Arctic air covers the island, and the coasts are icebound from January to April. Spring arrives late. In the summer, waters surrounding the island are much warmer, as are the prevailing southern winds. Yearly temperatures average –7° C (20° F) in January and 18° C (65° F) in July. Mean annual precipitation is about 1,060 mm (42 in), of which more than one-third falls as snow.

Most of the island's wooded areas are in the western and eastern extremities. The mixed forest is dominated by red spruce and balsam fir, with sugar maple the most widely distributed deciduous species. The island is lacking in mineral resources except for some gravel pits. Oil and gas exploration is taking place offshore. The surrounding seas provide a variety of finfish and shellfish. In March and April seal herds are found on the ice fields offshore.

People

The island's population, mostly of English ancestry, includes discrete groups of French, Scottish, and Irish descent. Roman Catholics form the largest religious denomination, followed by the United Church of Canada. Prince Edward Island is the most densely populated but the most rural of Canada's provinces. Only about 38% of the population lived in towns in 1986. Charlottetown and Summerside are the only major urban centers. Historically, the province has been an area of net out-migration. This trend has reversed in recent years, but the percentage of the population over age 65 has steadily increased.

The school population is almost entirely registered in the public school system. Charlottetown is the major cultural center. It has the only university—the University of Prince Edward Island—and the Confederation Centre of the Arts, which hosts the annual Charlottetown Summer Festival. Of historic interest is Fort Amherst National Historic Park, the site of the former French capital, Fort La Joye (established 1720), in Charlottetown. Prince Edward Island National Park is located on the north shore.

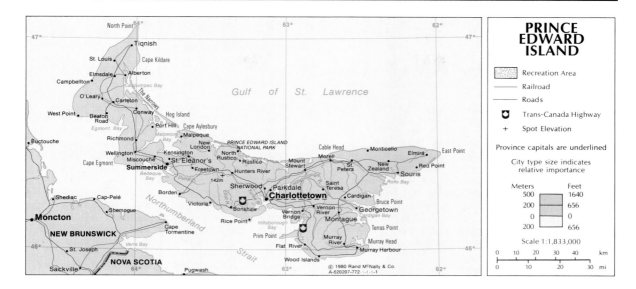

PRINCE EDWARD ISLAND

▒ Recreation Area
— Railroad
— Roads
🅐 Trans-Canada Highway
+ Spot Elevation

Province capitals are underlined

City type size indicates
relative importance

Meters	Feet
500	1640
200	656
0	0
200	656

Scale 1:1,833,000

Economic Activity

Much of Prince Edward Island's gross domestic product has been dependent on federal and provincial government spending. Agriculture is the cornerstone of the economy. High-quality seed potatoes are the island's major export, primarily to the United States. The north shore in Queens County around Cavendish, Rustico, and the national park is the major focus of a lucrative tourist trade. Efforts have been made to encourage tourism in Kings County in the east and Prince County in the west.

Lobsters, oysters, herring, redfish, cod, and mackerel are found offshore and support the fishing industry. Fishing and agriculture give rise to most of the island's small-scale manufacturing industry, which is primarily concerned with canning, bottling, freezing, or packing produce for export.

Government

The government consists of a lieutenant governor, an executive council headed by a premier, and a legislative assembly. The province is divided into 16 electoral districts;

Charlottetown, an important port and the capital of Prince Edward Island, is situated on Hillsborough Bay, along the southern coast of the island. The site was first settled in 1720 by the French, who named it Fort La Joye. After Great Britain took formal possession of Prince Edward Island in 1763, the town was renamed in honor of the royal consort of King George III.

each elects 2 assembly members for terms of no more than 5 years.

History

The Micmac Indians were the island's only inhabitants when the first European, Jacques Cartier, discovered the island in 1534. Europeans did not begin to settle the island until 1713, when French emigrants and Acadians from nearby Nova Scotia and New Brunswick arrived. In 1763 the island formally passed to the British. In 1764 it was divided into 3 counties and 67 lots, or townships, that still exist. These lots were granted to landlords in Britain, who remained there and rented their lots to Loyalist settlers from New England and to Scottish, Irish, and English emigrants. In 1875 the provincial government bought back the land and sold it to the tenant farmers. Since Prince Edward Island joined (1873) the confederation, its economic problems have been partially offset by temporary booms—including shipbuilding and silver-fox fur farming—and federal aid.

▬
Prince George   Prince George (1986 pop., 67,621) is a city in central British Columbia. The city serves as the processing and distribution center for the region's lumber, stock-raising, and mining activities. A fur-trading post was established near the present city in 1807 by Simon Fraser. The railroad arrived in 1914.

▬
Princeton   Princeton (1990 pop., 12,016) is a town in central New Jersey, located about 80 km (50 mi) southwest of New York City. It is the seat of Princeton University, the Institute for Advanced Study, and Princeton Theological Seminary. It was settled in 1689. George Washington defeated (1777) the British there, and it served (1783) briefly as the nation's capital.

▬
Princeton University   Established in 1746 as the College of New Jersey by a charter from King George II and given its present name in 1896, Princeton University is a private, coeducational, liberal arts institution in Princeton, N.J. A member of the IVY LEAGUE, it has a graduate school, schools of engineering and applied sciences and of architecture, and the Woodrow Wilson School of Public and International Affairs (1930). Research in plasma physics, aerospace and mechanical sciences, meteorology, and oceanography is carried out at the James Forrestal campus. The Office of Population Research is a division of the institution. Facilities of the university, the INSTITUTE FOR ADVANCED STUDY, and Princeton Theological Seminary are reciprocally available. Nassau Hall, the administration building, was briefly the seat of the Continental Congress (July to November 1783). The library's special collections include the John Foster Dulles Library of Diplomatic History. The Marquand Art Museum and the Guyot Hall Museum have, respectively, art and archaeological, and geological and biological collections.

Principia   see NEWTON, SIR ISAAC

Principia Mathematica   see RUSSELL, BERTRAND

▬
printed circuit   A printed circuit is a rigid or flexible board on which an electrical circuit is etched, and to which electronic components can be attached, eliminating the need for complex wiring. The idea was developed in 1940 by the Viennese scientist Paul Eisler, who wanted to simplify the manufacture of radio circuitry. The use of printed circuits became widespread after World War II, as they became prized for their reliability, their space-saving quality, and the ease with which they could be mass-produced. Printed circuits are now used in a wide range of equipment, including digital watches, electronic cameras, radios, and digital computers.

In a printed circuit, electrical conductors are formed on an insulating substrate in order to interconnect various electronic components. The most widespread method for forming the conducting paths makes use of a rigid or flexible plastic, phenolic, masonite, or glass baseboard (the substrate) that is coated on one or both sides by a thin layer of copper foil. The copper foil is sprayed with a light-sensitive film called the resist. An exact rendition of the desired interconnections, called a mask, is photographically reproduced on a transparent overlay. This overlay is then placed directly over the light-sensitive resist, and the substrate is briefly exposed to light. The substrate is immersed in a developer solution, which dissolves the resist that has not been exposed to light. The substrate is then placed in a bath of etchant, which dissolves all portions of the copper foil not protected by the resist. After the etching is complete, the resist is removed from the resulting copper-foil pattern.

A working electronic circuit is produced by inserting ("stuffing") the wire leads of components into holes in the board. The leads are then manually soldered in place one at a time—or simultaneously, by passing the copper side of the board over a protruding wave of molten solder in an automatic solder machine.

▬
printer, computer   A printer is a computer output device that records information on paper (see INPUT-OUTPUT DEVICES). The information can be in the form of written script, numerical data, or graphics. There are two main types of printers: impact printers, which employ a physical hammering device to impart images on paper, and ink-jet printers, which fire small bursts of ink at the paper. Formed-character printers are impact printers containing fixed characters on the ends of metallic or plastic arms that are forced against an inked ribbon and paper, producing a sharp image. An example is the daisy wheel, a flat, rotatable wheel with individual characters at the ends of spokes. Formed-character printers can produce letter-quality print, like a typewriter. The dot-matrix printer is also of the impact type. It employs a matrix of small pegs that, hit from behind, impart a series of dots on paper. The dot-matrix printer is more flexible than the

individual-character types in that combinations of dots can form a wider variety of characters, as well as graphics. Ink-jet printers share the flexibility of dot-matrix printers and operate more quietly. In addition, ink-jet printers can be adapted to complex color printing.

A third category of printers includes the electrostatic printer (see ELECTROSTATIC PRINTING) and the laser printer; in these, output is formed on a selenium-coated drum by, respectively, a cathode-ray tube and a laser beam. As with an ordinary copier, the output is then transferred from drum to paper.

printing   Printing, in its broadest sense, is any process whereby one or more identical copies are produced from a master image. The master image can range from an inscription engraved in stone to an illustration cut into a wood block or a text stored in a computer. Image transfer, from master to copy, is usually accomplished with ink, and the transferring agent is most often the printing press. The development of new technologies has blurred traditional definitions of printing, however: office copiers, for example, reproduce master images using electrostatically charged graphite toner (see ELECTROSTATIC PRINTING).

The routine, though rudimentary, reproduction of textual matter first occurred early in the 8th century AD, when the Chinese began to experiment with the printing of relief, or raised, images cut in wood blocks. During the 11th century both the Koreans and the Chinese experimented with the manufacture of movable type made from clay and wood and, later, from bronze and iron. Although the notion of movable type was a major advance in printing technology, the complex characters that formed the written Korean and Chinese languages were too difficult to produce as individual pieces of type.

The German Johann GUTENBERG, working 400 years later with a simple alphabet, developed a method of casting type and printing so successful that its fundamental principles were not improved until well into the 19th century.

The modern age of printing began in the mid-15th century, when Johann Gutenberg devised a method for making movable type and printed copies of the Bible.

Printing Presses. The essential features of Gutenberg's invention included lead-alloy type cast in an adjustable mold, oil-based inks, and a wooden printing press in which a large screw moved the upper part, the platen, up or down against paper laid over type on the lower surface, the bed. Later improvements to Gutenberg's screw press were largely devoted to increasing impression power, improving the clarity of the printed image, and devising a return mechanism for the press handle. About 1800, Charles, 3d Earl Stanhope, developed an all-metal press, and in 1813, George Clymer dispensed with the screw, substituting instead a system of power-multiplying levers. Although 19th-century designers continued to improve the efficiency of the handpress, its practical limits were soon reached. Until recently, though, small-job printers continued to use the platen press, invented in the early 19th century, in which the flatbed was vertically positioned and power was supplied by a foot treadle or by steam (see LETTERPRESS).

In 1811, Friedrich Koenig patented the first flatbed cylinder press, using a revolving cylinder instead of a flat platen to press sheets of paper against a flatbed of type. The bed moved under inking rollers between each cylinder impression. A steam-powered Koenig press installed by the *Times* of London could print over 1,000 sheets an hour. In 1835 the Englishman Rowland Hill patented a "web fed" press, one that printed a continuous reel of paper. His press was never built, but in the United States a web-fed rotary press was built in 1837. The U.S. firm of Richard Hoe became the preeminent manufacturer of rotary presses. Hoe's rotary was faster than the older cylinder press, because he replaced the flatbed with a second cylinder, or drum, to which the type was attached.

The difficulty of making curved relief printing plates slowed the acceptance of the rotary press. By the 1870s curved STEREOTYPE plates could be accurately cast, and they replaced Hoe's metal type. From that point until well into the 20th century, the press of choice—especially for newspaper publishers—became the automatic rotary cylinder press, printing both sides of a continuous web of paper. Steam provided power for the early machine presses; electric power was used from the end of the 19th century.

Lithography. Most printing technology was based on letterpress, the printing of images that projected above nonprinting areas. In 1796, Aloys Senefelder invented a planographic, or flat-plane, printing process later called lithography. He found that an image, no matter how detailed, that was drawn with a greasy substance on the face of a water-absorbent stone and then inked could be printed onto water paper with absolute fidelity. Lithography was ideally suited for illustration and enjoyed a phenomenal popularity during the 19th century, especially for color printing, which required a separate stone to print each color. Eventually, it was found that the image on the stone could be transferred, using a special starch-coated transfer paper, from the stone to a metal plate that was used for the actual printing.

Photoengraving. Early in the 19th century it was discovered that certain materials hardened and became in-

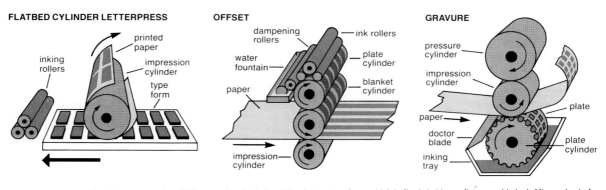

FLATBED CYLINDER LETTERPRESS

OFFSET

GRAVURE

(Left) *In the flatbed cylinder letterpress, the printing area is raised above the plate or type form, which is firmly held on a flat, movable bed. After a sheet of paper is printed, by being rolled between the impression cylinder and the type form, the form moves under the inking rollers, receiving ink to print the next sheet. (In all the presses illustrated here, the impression cylinder acts to press the paper against the printing surface.) (Center) In offset, where image and nonimage areas are on the same level of the plate, the image areas are grease-receptive and water-repellent. The plate cylinder revolves, contacting dampening rollers that wet the nonimage portions of the plate and prevent them from holding ink. The inked image is transferred, or "offset," to the blanket cylinder, which is the actual printing agent. (Right) The thousands of tiny cells that make up the gravure plate are filled with ink as the plate cylinder rotates in the inking tray. Excess ink is wiped off by the doctor blade. The ink left within the cells is transferred directly to the paper. In gravure, two impression cylinders provide extra pressure of paper against plate.*

soluble in direct proportion to the amount of light exposure they received. By the 1880s it had become possible to expose a metal plate, coated with a light-sensitive substance, to a photographic negative, creating a positive image that could be engraved in relief on the plate (see PLATEMAKING). Early PHOTOENGRAVINGS were linecuts: they could reproduce only in black and white. The invention of the halftone screen in the 1880s made it possible to reproduce a continuous tone image, one in which a range of blacks and grays was present.

Offset Lithography. Lithographic metal plates had only rarely been used for commercial printing, in part because the image on the plate was often worn through by the printing paper. In 1904 an American printer, Ira W. Rubel, accidentally discovered that the lithographic image could be transferred, or offset, to a rubber cylinder that could then print as perfectly as the plate and would last indefinitely. Rubel's three-cylinder offset press was the first in the field of OFFSET LITHOGRAPHY, which would become the most popular OFFSET printing process because of its economy, long plate life, and ability to print on many different textures.

Gravure. Although intaglio techniques, such as etching and engraving, had long been used as printing methods by artists, the development of an intaglio printing plate—one whose image was incised below the plate surface—was developed only late in the 19th century for commercial printing. The Czech artist Karl Klič used a gelatin-coated, light-sensitive tissue to transfer a grid pattern onto a copper cylinder, together with the image to be printed. When the cylinder was etched and inked, it printed an image whose varying tones were achieved by the varying depth of the ink-filled cells that the grid pattern had produced. Klič's process gave rise to the field of gravure printing, which includes ROTOGRAVURE, a high-speed, high-volume technique—essentially the same process used by Klič—that today prints magazines and newspa-

per color sections, as well as a huge variety of packaging materials.

Other Printing Processes. Flexography, a relief process utilizing flexible rubber or plastic plates, is particularly well suited for printing on many kinds of nonpaper packaging materials and, recently, has been used successfully to print newspapers. Screen process printing (SILK-SCREEN PRINTING) makes use of a finely woven metal or synthetic mesh to which a nonporous stencil is mechanically or photographically fixed, blocking the mesh except where the image is to be printed. Applications of screen printing include the printing of posters, fabrics, and electronic circuit boards.

Color Printing. Halftone color printing, the process still used today to reproduce full color, was introduced in the 1890s, but many years passed before its full potential was realized. Although color reproduction theory was fairly well understood, the lack of color film restricted color work to studios where the necessary separation negatives had to be made directly from the subject, under the most exacting conditions. Reliable color film became available in the 1930s and '40s, and color reproduction grew both more common and more accurate.

Type. Throughout the 19th century, attempts to mechanize the processes of typemaking (casting) and composition (typesetting) resulted in a number of ingenious inventions, some incorporating both casting and composing operations. The LINOTYPE machine of Ottmar MERGENTHALER and the MONOTYPE invented by Tolbert Lanston, both introduced by their American inventors in 1887, proved to be so clearly superior to rival devices that no better mechanical systems for letterpress composition were ever developed. The Linotype was a keyboard-operated machine that composed and cast a justified line of type and was particularly suitable for newspapers. The Monotype's keyboard produced a punched tape that instructed a separate typecaster to produce individual characters in complete, justified lines. The Monotype was used largely for book printing.

The type used to make offset lithographic plates originally came from proofs taken from letterpress type. As offset printing grew in popularity, a more efficient method was sought. In 1954 the Photon machine became the first commercially successful electronic photocomposition system. Its key elements, which were used by later machines as well, were a stroboscopic light source and a spinning film matrix disk through which photographic film was exposed with images of type previously composed on a keyboard. More recent generations of typesetters have done away with the film matrix. Some employ type characters produced on cathode ray tubes from master images stored as digital information. Others make use of a laser that scans digitally stored type and reproduces it on photographic film.

Computer Printing. Computers play a vital role in nearly every area of printing, from typesetting to on-press control of the many variables subject to change during a print run. Digital storage and manipulation of text, whether at a word-processing station or a typesetting terminal, were early computer-printing operations. When paired with long-distance digital transmission technology, numerous possibilities became evident. For example, reporters in the field can now send word-processed copy via phone lines to the editorial offices of newspapers and magazines. When an issue is ready for printing, a central production facility can electronically transmit the entire contents to regional printing plants, speeding up both printing and distribution. Increasingly powerful systems can now provide the vast storage required for very high-resolution graphics, as well as providing methods for sophisticated image manipulation. The operator of a typical system can scan a color photograph into the computer memory, then call the image up to a display screen where a number of editing processes can be employed: rotation of the image, increased shading, color correction or color changing, the moving of parts of the image or its entire deletion. The accompanying text can also be called up to

These high-speed rotary letterpress machines can spew out more than 50,000 finished multipage copies per hour. A typical newspaper plant installation with four presses in tandem is capable of printing both sides of a continuous roll, or web, of paper four pages wide and of automatically cutting, folding, and combining the different pages, delivering a finished copy at the exit end. A continuous supply of paper is ensured by a device that automatically pastes the end of an exhausted roll of paper to the beginning of a full roll.

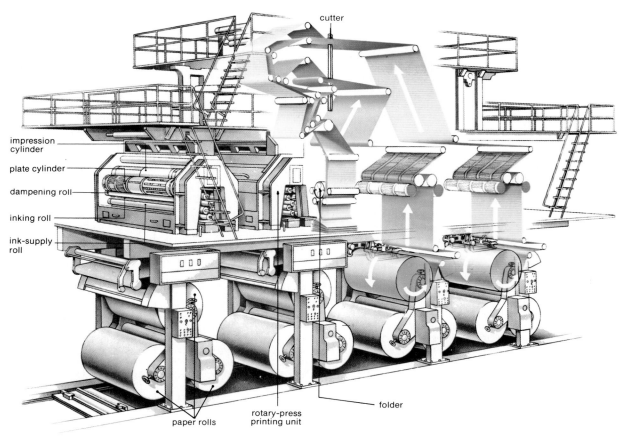

cutter

impression cylinder

plate cylinder

dampening roll

inking roll

ink-supply roll

paper rolls

rotary-press printing unit

folder

the screen for copyfitting and layout experimentation. The final, edited image is sent to an output laser scanner, which produces a set of color film separations that will be used to make the printing plates.

Recent developments in platemaking technology suggest that film may no longer be needed to produce printing plates. Instead, a scanning device may one day expose the printing plate with images generated by a computer.

prion [pry'-ahn] Prions are small protein particles that have been implicated in a number of human and animal diseases. The name *prion*, which derives from "proteinaceous infectious particle," was coined by American neurologist Stanley Prusiner in the 1980s. His controversial proposal that the particles were somehow infectious and self-replicating within an organism has generally not been accepted by other scientists. The apparent association of prions with certain neurological diseases, however, continues to be a subject of scientific investigation.

Among the infectious diseases of the nervous system are a few whose causative agents reproduce very slowly in their host, producing symptoms months or even years after the initial infection. In animals these disorders include a fatal disease in sheep called scrapie (see DIS-EASES, ANIMAL). In humans they include a degenerative disease called kuru, observed in New Guinea highlanders, and Creutzfeldt-Jakob disease, a progressive presenile dementia (see NERVOUS SYSTEM, DISEASES OF THE). Various causative agents have been suggested, including viruses (see VIRUS, SLOW). A study of the brain tissues of victims of the above diseases has revealed the presence of abnormal patches or flat areas (plaques) of protein. Analysis of plaques from the brains of sheep that died of scrapie led to isolation of protein particles only one-hundredth the size of the smallest known viruses. These particles, infectious or not, are now known as prions.

Prior, Matthew [pry'-ur] The English poet Matthew Prior, b. July 21, 1664, d. Sept. 18, 1721, excelled in writing epigrams and humorous verse. He is also remembered for *Alma; or, The Progress of the Mind* (1716, 1718), a satire of contemporary philosophy, and for *The Country Mouse and the City Mouse* (1687), a burlesque of John Dryden's *The Hind and the Panther*, written in collaboration with Charles Montagu. A diplomat, Prior was the chief negotiator of the Treaty of Utrecht (1713).

Pripet Marshes [prip'-et] The Pripet Marshes, also known as the Pinsk Marshes or Polesye, are a vast forested swamp along the Pripyat River and its tributaries in the European USSR. The largest marshland in Europe, it covers about 100,000 km² (38,600 mi²) within a triangle formed by the cities of Brest, Kiev, and Mogilev. Crisscrossed by rivers and streams at an elevation of less than 165 m (540 ft) above sea level, the area has sandy soils and abundant precipitation. Thick peat deposits near Mozyr are the main resource. Since the late 19th

century, drainage systems have been built; grains and potatoes are grown in reclaimed areas.

prism [pris'-uhm] In optics, *prism* refers to any transparent medium having two or more plane surfaces. A familiar example is the triangular prism, usually made of glass, used to split a beam of white light into its component colors. The ability of the prism to do this stems from the fact that the INDEX OF REFRACTION of any optical medium depends on the wavelength (color) of the light, a property called dispersion. In all ordinary media—glass, water, and so on—the refractive index increases as the wavelength becomes shorter. Thus the rays in the violet end of the visible spectrum (corresponding to the shorter wavelengths) are more sharply refracted by a prism than are the longer wavelengths, in the red end of the spectrum.

Another common type of prism is the right-angle, total-reflecting prism. This prism does not disperse light into its colors; rather, it reflects the light by what is called total internal reflection (see REFRACTION). Retroreflecting prisms are used in the making of binoculars and other optical instruments.

See also: OPTICS.

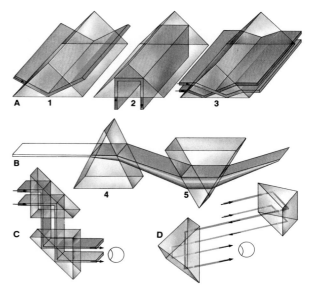

(A) *Light entering a right-angle total reflecting prism* (1) *is bent toward the normal, then reflected internally at an angle equal to the angle of incidence, and then bent away from the normal as it emerges. The direction of light entering perpendicular to the hypotenuse face* (2) *is reversed; the direction of light traveling parallel to that face* (3) *is unchanged.* (B) *White light dispersed into colors by a triangular prism* (4) *can be recombined by an inverted prism of slightly greater angle* (5). *Prisms are used in periscopes* (C) *and in binoculars* (D), *where they reverse the initially inverted image.*

prison Prisons are facilities maintained for the confinement of convicted felons. Until the 18th century, exile, execution, and various forms of corporal punishment were the most common penalties for criminal acts. Although jails were commonplace, imprisonment was viewed as a temporary restriction rather than the prescribed penalty for crime. Prisons ranged from workhouses for debtors to institutions for incorrigible boys. Retribution was acknowledged as the prime motivation for official punishment.

Under the influence of the 18th-century Enlightenment, the extreme harshness of most punishment was questioned. Attempts were made to fit the severity of the punishment to the severity of the crime, in the belief that clearly articulated and just penalties would act as deterrents to crime. Thus deterrence superseded retribution as a leading principle of penology.

Development of U.S. Prisons. Early U.S. prisons were viewed as mechanisms to instill discipline, remove temptation, and rehabilitate the offender. Systems were based on the premise that isolation, the substitution of good habits for sloth and crime, and a regimen of silence, penitence, and labor would return the offender to society cured of vices and ready to become a responsible citizen.

Because it was an effective way of harnessing the labor power of prisoners and was thus less costly to adopt, the Auburn, N.Y., system (1817) in which prisoners worked together during the day became the dominant method of confinement in the United States. The goal of reformation was eventually shunted to the background, however, as prisons became holding operations, designed to promote a respect for order and authority.

The National Prison Conference in 1870 was the first signal of reform. Encouraged by the recent development of PROBATION and PAROLE, the conference called for the establishment of the indeterminate sentence, which allows a court to specify, within statutory limits, the minimum and maximum length of sentence for a particular offense. It was believed that this type of sentence would give offenders an incentive for rehabilitation, for they would be released only when it was determined that satisfactory change had taken place.

In recent years, however, rising crime rates have thrown into question the effectiveness of prison rehabilitation, and several states have returned to mandatory sentencing laws whereby the convict must serve a term of specified length.

The U.S. Prison System Today. By the late 1980s the total number of convicted criminals in U.S. federal and state prisons was the largest in the nation's history, having nearly doubled in the space of a decade. To a large degree, the national drug problem contributed to this growth. As a result, overcrowding is common in all correctional institutions and a big factor in the high levels of tension and aggression that lead to prison riots. There is little doubt that conditions in most prisons are a threat to the safety of inmates and prison staffs alike.

The cost of maintaining prisons is staggering: depending on the type of prison and the state where it is located, an annual $14,000–30,000 per prisoner. The cost of new construction averages almost $54,000 per bed. In 1989, 43 states were under court order to correct overcrowding in their prisons. A few of these states have turned to private companies, which build and administer new prisons at lower costs than those the states can obtain.

The most familiar type of correctional institution is the large, fortresslike maximum-security prison. Such structures as San Quentin in California are characterized by their massive size, thick stone walls, gun towers, steel doors, multitiered cell blocks, large populations, and rural locations. By contrast, medium- and minimum-security institutions are identified by their openness and the absence of strict security procedures. Persons held in such facilities are judged to be less dangerous and therefore better security risks. Various correctional programs and a wide range of counseling programs are offered in many prisons, but their extent is limited by their cost, the size of the prison population, and the expertise of the staff.

Prison work programs have existed since colonial times, although often under rigid restrictions intended to limit their competing with outside industry. Recent attempts to bring outside work into the prison have demonstrated the productive potential of prison labor. Under one such program, businesses are offered financial inducements to enter the prison. Inmates are paid the market wage for their labor, with deductions made for room and board, family support, union dues, taxes, restitution, and savings. Fewer than 10 percent of inmates are assigned to prison industry programs, however.

Medical care is another urgent inmate need, especially with the growing presence of AIDS in the prison population. Many prisoners suffer from the ravages of drug and alcohol abuse. In addition, the population of medically vulnerable elderly prisoners will increase as inmates serve longer sentences. Despite the need, regular medical services are costly to provide and difficult to maintain. Many institutions have attempted to provide care by contracting for medical services rather than maintaining full-time facilities.

The Swedish Prison System. The Swedish system contrasts significantly with that of the United States and has been praised for its humanitarian use of imprisonment and its innovative treatment programs. Policy is guided by the recognition that crime is often socially produced, that criminals suffer from "problems in living," and that only truly dangerous offenders should be incarcerated. Sweden therefore offers alternatives to prison, such as fines. The correctional system features facilities specializing in psychiatric treatment, an industrial prison, and a university release program. Despite these innovations, recent evidence indicates that Sweden, like the United States, now suffers from high rates of recidivism.

Prison Life. Among the pains faced by prisoners are the loss of liberty and the loneliness and boredom of imprisonment; the deprivation of all goods and services from the outside world; the absence of heterosexual relationships; and subjection to a vast body of institutional regulations designed to control every aspect of behavior.

The male inmate is thrown into prolonged intimacy with other men and is forced to assume an aggressive posture and to maintain a constant wariness for his personal safety. Homosexual rape is a common occurrence in male prisons, with attacks generally made on vulnerable new inmates. Solidarity among prisoners, where it exists, helps reduce the pains of imprisonment. Thus gangs attempt to define and control the prison experience.

In U.S. female prisons, inmate society is generally made up of informal pseudofamilies, and almost all inmates define their relations in kinship terms. The pseudofamily provides a predictable and stable structure of social relations—including homosexual relations—to which a female inmate can turn for support and help. It is not uncommon, however, for different "families" to come into conflict.

Women are held in smaller prisons with fewer programs and recreational opportunities, and the programs that are offered reflect stereotyped female roles, with emphasis on housekeeping, sewing, clerical and typing skills. Because female prison populations are growing at a faster pace than male populations, living conditions have grown even more onerous than conditions for men. Overall, women enter prison with more serious health problems than men, and mothers may have the burden of concern about the care of their children while they are in prison.

Given the problems engendered by prison itself, it is not surprising that rehabilitation programs have failed to reduce recidivism in the United States, now estimated at 60 percent.

Legal Rights of Prisoners. Early U.S. court decisions ruled that prisoners had forfeited all of the rights enjoyed by free citizens. Eventually, the courts recognized certain rights and legal remedies available to prisoners, who may now file their own suits, have direct access to the federal courts, and file writs of HABEUS CORPUS and MANDAMUS. (Under habeus corpus the prisoner may request release, transfer, or another remedy for some aspect of confinement. Mandamus is a command issued by a court, directing a prison administrator to carry out a legal responsibility or to restore to the prisoner rights that have been illegally denied.) Prisoners have sought relief from unreasonable searches, release from solitary confinement, and the procuring of withheld mail. Recent decisions have indicated, however, that the courts are now willing to limit legal suits by prisoners.

Probation and Parole. Probation is a conditional sentence imposed on a convicted offender by the court, which requires supervision by a probation officer in lieu of incarceration. Parole, the early release of an offender after the completion of a portion of the sentence, is a key factor in the indeterminate sentence. Like probation, release on parole is conditional, and if the offender violates the conditions or commits a new crime, the parole can be revoked and the offender returned to prison to complete the sentence. The parole decision is made by a parole board, an administrative body consisting of persons who usually have a background in criminal justice and have been appointed for a fixed term. Criticism of these practices have led to laws that forbid the imposition of probation when offenders are convicted of violent crimes and that limit the use of parole.

Prison Improvements and Alternatives. Attempts to aid the prisoner's return to society have led to the develop-

ment of several innovative programs. The goal of conjugal visitations is to keep marriages intact by permitting social and sexual contact between prisoners and wives. Furloughs provide home visits of 48–72 hours for prisoners nearing their release dates and are intended to aid in restoring family ties and in job seeking. Work-release programs permit inmates to test their work skills and earn money outside the institution for the major part of the day. The supervised halfway house is designed to help the parolee make the transition from prison to community.

First-time youthful offenders may be sentenced to short-term "shock incarceration units," which function like marine boot camps. Offenders convicted of nonviolent crimes may receive probation rather than a prison sentence and must report to a probation officer at regular intervals. They may be required to perform community service, and to pay restitution to their victims. "House arrest" offenders wear devices that send electronic signals notifying probation officers of their whereabouts.

See also: CRIME; CRIMINAL JUSTICE.

prisoner of war   A prisoner of war (POW) is a member of the military captured by the enemy during combat. According to international law, prisoners of war are entitled to special protections not provided captured civilians. POWs are protected by international treaties from mental and physical torture or coercion and are required to give their captors only their name, rank, service number, and date of birth. They are entitled to adequate food and medical treatment and can receive mail and parcels. Most nations claim to adhere to the rules regarding POWs, which are overseen by the International Red Cross. Nevertheless, every war in this century has seen numerous infractions.

Captured combatants were once executed or sold into slavery; prisoners of high rank might be held for ransom. The movement to give special protection to captured military personnel had its beginnings in the 18th century. It was not until the 20th century, however, that any appreciable progress was made. The Hague Conventions of 1899 and 1907 and the GENEVA CONVENTIONS of 1929 and 1949 all contained provisions governing the treatment of POWs.

Pritchett, V. S.   A master of the short story, the British author Victor Sawdon Pritchett, b. Dec. 16, 1900, is known for novels and nonfiction as well. Pritchett earned a scant living as a free-lance writer before taking a job as a correspondent (1922–27) for the *Christian Science Monitor*. He achieved his first critical success with the novel *Nothing Like Leather* (1935); later novels include *Mr. Beluncle* (1951) and *The Key to My Heart* (1963). He has also written literary essays, biographies of Turgenev and Balzac, numerous travel books, and several autobiographical works. His short stories, known for their craftsmanship and comic irony, have been compared with those of Chekhov and Maupassant. They appear in *Complete Collected Stories* (1991).

Pritzker Architecture Prize   Considered the most prestigious architecture award, the international Pritzker Architecture Prize is given annually to an architect whose work is a "significant contribution to humanity and the environment." The prize, established in 1979, was named for Jay A. Pritzker, president of the Hyatt Foundation, which administers and funds the prize. Winners are selected by jury. They receive $100,000 tax free and a bronze sculpture, *Ode to Architecture*, designed by Henry Moore. The first Pritzker laureate was Philip JOHNSON (1979).

privacy, invasion of   Invasion of privacy is generally defined as interference with the private sphere of a person's affairs. Under law it can be warranted or unwarranted, depending on the means employed and the information sought. Unlike freedom of speech, press, and religion, protection against invasion of privacy is not specifically guaranteed by the U.S. Constitution. Nevertheless, the right of individuals to their privacy has become an accepted part of TORT and U.S. constitutional law.

In the case of *Griswold* v. *Connecticut* (1965), the Supreme Court ruled that a state law prohibiting the use of contraceptives or advice on their use by a third party invaded the privacy of the individual and was therefore unconstitutional. Justice William O. Douglas said in his decision that the "right to privacy is older than the Bill of Rights." He reasoned that it existed in the penumbra, or shadow, of other constitutional guarantees. The right of association, for instance, can be derived from the 1ST AMENDMENT; the right to privacy in a person's own home and the prohibition against unlawful searches and seizures are protected by the 3d Amendment and the 4th Amendment; the 5th Amendment protects individuals from testifying against themselves (see SELF-INCRIMINATION); and, finally, the 9th Amendment states that the enumeration of certain rights in the Constitution "shall not be construed to deny or disparage others retained by the people." The 4th Amendment has been the most frequently cited procedural protection against governmental invasion of privacy.

In two 1973 cases, ROE V. WADE AND DOE V. BOLTON, the Court struck down two state laws prohibiting abortion. It held that the right to privacy was "broad enough to encompass a woman's decision whether or not to terminate her pregnancy." At the same time, however, the Court noted that the right to privacy is not absolute but is subject to certain governmental limitations. As if to emphasize that point, the Court has refused to rule unconstitutional state laws prohibiting certain sexual acts performed privately by consenting adults. In general the Court has moved cautiously in the area of invasion of privacy, often deferring to laws passed by the elected legislatures of federal and state governments.

One reason for acting with caution has been the problem of defining the concept of privacy. In *Olmstead* v. *United States* (1928), Justice Louis Brandeis called privacy the right "to be let alone." In *Roe* v. *Wade*, on the other hand, privacy has been imbued with notions more appropriate to autonomy—the right to do as an individual wishes. In his book *Privacy and Freedom* (1967), the political scientist Alan Westin suggested that privacy be defined as the right of persons to control the distribution of information about themselves. Using this definition, invasion of privacy becomes the attempt to gather information about a person (and sometimes making that information public) that the person expects to be disclosed, if at all, only as he or she wishes. For example, according to this definition, secretly taping another person's telephone or other private conversations would clearly be an invasion of privacy; so would be the opening of another person's mail. In 1967 the Supreme Court ruled in *Katz* v. *United States* that telephone and other private conversations are protected by the 4th Amendment. As a result, WIRETAPPING and other forms of electronic surveillance must be authorized by a court warrant if they are to be legal.

Individuals may wish to protect their secrets from a variety of organizations, such as newspapers, credit bureaus, and universities. Much recent discussion of invasion of privacy has focused on the right of the press to gather and print personal information. In a 1975 case, *Cohn* v. *Cox Broadcasting Co.*, the Supreme Court ruled unconstitutional, because of the 1st Amendment's guarantee of FREEDOM OF THE PRESS, a Georgia law prohibiting the publication of names of rape victims. The Court emphasized that the name was taken from an otherwise public record, the criminal indictment; it did not clarify the question about newspaper publication of personal information derived from nonpublic sources.

Congress legislates in the area of privacy rights, although changing circumstances and political pressures often act to transform its work. As an example, the Privacy Act of 1974 was intended to protect citizens from privacy invasions by the federal government. Among its provisions, the act prohibits the exchange between agencies of personal information about individuals that is kept in government agency records. The Paperwork Reduction Act (1980), however, in effect allowed all personal data gathered by government to be made available to any agency. The subsequent profusion of computer databanks encouraged "computer matching"—cross-checking licensing applications with drug abuse convictions, for instance. The 1988 Computer Safeguards Bill then imposed new limits on the government's use of computer records.

Because each of the 50 states has had its own set of laws regarding privacy, no single set of protections against invasion of privacy existed other than those inferred from the U.S. Constitution, applying only against agencies of government. But the age of computerized information has brought new urgency to privacy issues.

private schools   Private, or nonpublic, schools are elementary and secondary schools operated under private auspices for fees charged to the students attending them. Private schools have existed in the United States since colonial times, and, until the rise of the public school system in the mid-19th century, they provided virtually all educational facilities through the secondary level. In 1986 there were about 25,600 private schools with more than 5.2 million students (more than 12% of the nation's total) and about 404,000 teachers.

Although private schools offer educational opportunities similar to those available in public schools, they also offer a variety of other experiences based on the schools' affiliation or commitment to particular special purposes or methods of teaching—for example, military academies, Montessori schools, and schools for the disabled. Private schools vary considerably, too, in their governance, some being integral parts of school systems, some loosely associated, and some autonomous. The extent of these options with regard to church affiliation, educational program, and governance—and the freedom of a private school to determine its special character—explains the great diversity in the schools.

The issue of granting tuition tax credits—federal income tax credits for private-school tuition costs—was renewed in the 1980s. Adding to the controversy was a U.S. Supreme Court decision, *Mueller et al.* v. *Allen et al.* (1983), that upheld a Minnesota law allowing state tax deductions for both private and public elementary and secondary school expenses.

Roman Catholic Schools. About 38% of the private schools in the United States are affiliated with the Roman Catholic church, and of the 5.2 million students in private schools, about 2.5 million attend Catholic schools. About 35% of these schools offer programs for the gifted, and a majority offer remedial programs in reading and mathematics. The schools, which for the most part provide programs concentrating on the liberal arts, are governed by one of four bodies: a diocese, a parish, a religious order, or a lay Catholic board of control. In general, these schools serve communities in which they are located and usually accept all students who do not have exceptional problems, although some schools conducted by religious orders or by lay boards have academically selective admissions policies.

Other Church-Related Schools. About 40% of U.S. private schools are related to religious bodies other than Roman Catholic. About a third of these schools offer programs for the gifted, while about 60% offer remedial reading and 40%, remedial mathematics. Virtually every Protestant denomination sponsors some schools for its children. The Lutherans, Seventh-Day Adventists, Baptists, Episcopalians, and Evangelicals run the largest number of schools.

The Lutheran schools generally offer conservative, traditional, academically oriented programs. They strive to serve students of as broad a range of academic aptitude as possible. The Seventh-Day Adventists conduct schools offering conservative, traditional academic programs and vocational programs featuring productive work experiences. Their admissions standards, also, are designed to serve students of a broad range of academic aptitude. Schools run by Evangelical church groups are conservative and staunchly independent.

Within the Jewish community the Hebrew day-school

movement has become significant since World War II. The greatest growth has occurred in Orthodox Jewish communities, but a significant number of schools serve Conservative communities, and Reform Jews have shown interest in establishing schools. For the most part, they provide demanding programs stressing academic and religious subject matter.

Independent Schools. Independent schools, whether for day students or boarders, are free of the control of any organization or group. Each school is separately owned and conducted. Some are church-related, and some are nonsectarian. They include the oldest schools in the United States, which provided the greater part of American elementary and secondary education until the mid-19th century. More than 4,900 of these schools exist in the United States today. They offer a variety of programs; most are college preparatory, and some are academically demanding. Admissions standards can be selective, stressing academic aptitude and achievement. Many schools offer scholarship programs to assist families of limited means, and some are heavily financed by endowment and gift income.

privateering   Privateering was the practice by which governments employed privately owned vessels to capture enemy commerce during wartime. Motivated by the profits made by such captures, privateers held licenses, called letters of marque and reprisal, and their attacks were limited to vessels of nations at war with the country issuing their commissions. Privateering differed from PIRACY mainly because of those licenses and limitations. Although privateers existed from at least the 13th century and into the 19th, the heyday of privateering was from the 16th to the 18th century.

As regular navies assumed a more important place in the military posture of nations, their reliance on privateers lessened. The major European powers (excluding Spain) outlawed privateering by the Declaration of Paris (1856); at the Second Hague Conference (1907) it was finally abolished. Most nations still appropriate private vessels into their navies during wartime, however.

privet [priv'-it]   Privets are about 50 species of deciduous or evergreen shrubs and some trees constituting the genus *Ligustrum* in the olive family, Oleaceae. These Old World plants, native mostly to eastern Asia, grow rapidly and are well suited for ornamental plantings. The evergreen species, however, are not hardy. Some privets can be trimmed into tight hedges.

The common privet, *L. vulgare*, native to the Mediterranean region and cultivated as a hedge for centuries, is a deciduous shrub growing to 4.5 m (15 ft) high; it has neat, green foliage, white flowers in the summer, and blackish berries in winter.

Privy Council [priv'-ee]   The Privy Council, in Great Britain, is a governmental body whose purpose is to advise the sovereign. The council has about 300 members. Membership includes all current and most former cabinet ministers, as well as eminent persons from all segments of public life. Most council work is done through its various committees; they primarily deal with those few powers still under the prerogative of the crown. The whole council is called only when a sovereign dies or announces his or her intention to marry.

The Privy Council evolved from the Norman *curia regis*, which developed into the king's council of the Middle Ages. At first composed of persons close to the monarch, it was enlarged in the 15th century and played a prominent role under Elizabeth I. Its influence began to decline under the Stuarts. As the strength of Parliament grew, the powers of the council were gradually assumed by the CABINET.

prizefighting   see BOXING

probability
Probability is a branch of mathematics that deals with the likelihood of observing one of several possible outcomes that can occur in an event. In probability, an event is a single happening—sometimes called a trial—and an outcome is one of several possible results. For example, one toss of a coin is an event, whereas a head or a tail is an outcome. The determination of probabilities is important in many practical activities. For example, manufacturers need to know the likelihood that a randomly selected product is flawed; personnel managers need to know the likelihood that a person hired for a job will be successful; insurance companies need to know the likelihood that a client will have an accident in a given year.

In the 17th century the Swiss scholar Jacob Bernoulli showed how to make predictions involving combinations of events for which there are two possible outcomes, as in the tossing of three pennies, with each landing heads or tails. In that century two French mathematicians, Blaise PASCAL and Pierre de FERMAT, also discussed probability theory as it related to games of chance. In the 18th century Abraham de Moivre studied games of chance and developed the distribution of possible outcomes known as the bell-shaped curve or normal distribution. This curve was also independently developed in the 18th century by the French mathematician Pierre Simon de LAPLACE, who applied it to astronomical observations. Adolphe Quetelet, a 19th-century Belgian scientist, fostered the idea that the normal curve could be applied in many fields, and in this way he introduced the use of probabilistic models into most sciences. In 1929, Russian mathematician A. N. Kolmogorov gave the science of probability a rigorous foundation when he published a set of axioms that could be used to develop theories of probability.

In the most straightforward case probability theory deals with a set of outcomes that are equally likely to occur. For example, if a card is drawn from a deck (a random event), it is equally likely to be a heart, a spade, a diamond, or a club. In this case probability is found by dividing the number of outcomes of a given kind (say hearts) by the total number of possible outcomes. An outcome is called a sample; all possible outcomes are called the sample space.

Probability can also be viewed as the relative frequency of an outcome in a very long sequence of events. This view is often called the empirical approach to probability, because probabilities are based on data accumulated from a number of random samples from a defined population. For example, in calculating the probability that, in a group of 20 first-grade children, 3 or more have blue eyes, a number of random groups of 20 first-grade children can be examined. The central limit theorem refers to the fact that sums of large samplings of random, independent variables approximate a normal distribution (see RANDOM VARIABLE). The law of LARGE NUMBERS implies that as samplings become larger, observed frequencies of events approach theoretical probabilities.

The expected value, or expectation, quantifies the concept of "average value over the long run." The expected value (X) is given by $X = p_1x_1 + ... + p_nx_n$, where p is the probability of an event occurring, and x represents a specific value of that event.

probate
[proh'-bayt]   Probate, in law, is the act or legal proceeding by which the validity of a WILL is established. The right of probating wills and administering estates belongs to a civil court, called a probate court in many jurisdictions or an orphans' or surrogate court in others.

After the fact of a person's death has been proved, the person who has been designated executor presents the deceased's will to the court with a petition for probate. The court then sets a date for the probate hearing, allowing enough time for all interested parties, including possible heirs, to examine the will and decide whether they want to object to any of its provisions.

At the probate hearing anyone who thinks the will is not genuine may contest it on the grounds that the testator (the deceased) did not sign it and the signature is that of another person; that the witnesses did not actually observe the testator signing the will; or that the testator was unaware of signing it because of illness or was coerced into signing it. Unless affirmative proof is presented showing the will to be invalid, however, the court usually admits it to probate even if one or both of the witnesses to the will is dead or cannot be found.

probation
Probation, in law, is a suspension of sentence for a person convicted of a minor offense. First offenders, particularly juvenile offenders, are often granted probation in the belief that society is better served if they are given another chance. The court determines probation after an investigation of the offender's personality and background, usually by a social worker. If the court approves, the offender is allowed to continue his or her normal life, upon promise of good behavior, and is placed under the supervision of a probation officer. The aim is to help offenders rehabilitate themselves without the stigma of a sentence or contact with hardened criminals in prison. Another advantage is that society is spared the expense of maintaining a prisoner.

problem solving A problem exists when an individual has a goal and a choice of means by which it might be achieved but does not know how to proceed immediately. The psychology of problem solving deals primarily with intellectual problems: those which can be solved mentally or by manipulating symbols. It uses three principal methods: (1) examining what scientists, mathematicians, and others have said about their own activities; (2) presenting test problems to experimental subjects, noting the effect of various conditions on the likelihood that the problems will be solved; (3) asking individuals to "think aloud" as they solve problems, and devising theoretical models to explain the sequence of steps that typically appears in such reports.

The first important experimental studies of problem solving were carried out by the Gestalt psychologists. GESTALT PSYCHOLOGY emphasized the difference between solving a problem by really understanding its structure and finding the solution by a blind application of rules. In problems requiring a genuine search for a solution, Karl Duncker noted that every phase of a solution is essentially a productive reformulation of the original problem. He also coined the term *functional fixedness* to describe a common source of difficulty in problem solving. If the solution requires that some object or concept be used in an unfamiliar way, a fixation on the common usage may prevent the new one from being seen.

The mathematician Gyorgy Polya introduced the idea that there are general techniques for solving problems, which he called *heuristics:* procedures that often help though they cannot guarantee success. One useful heuristic is working backward from the solution: if the answer were known, what characteristics would it have to have? Another important heuristic is to establish subgoals: think of some situation from which the solution might be easier to obtain, and work toward that situation first. Still another is means-end analysis: establish lists of methods that are useful for attacking various kinds of goals or subgoals, and work through the list systematically.

Recent research on problem solving has involved computer programs that enable a computer to solve difficult problems. If the sequence of steps taken by the machine is similar to the sequence reported by human subjects who think aloud, the program itself can be regarded as a theory of the problem-solving process. The programs developed go through the same sequences of steps (and make the same sorts of errors) as people who are thinking aloud; thus they probably incorporate many of the principles that govern human problem solving.

See also: ARTIFICIAL INTELLIGENCE; COGNITIVE PSYCHOLOGY; REASONING.

proboscidean   see ELEPHANT

procaine [proh'-kayn]   Procaine hydrochloride, the generic term for the drug Novocain, is a local anesthetic used frequently in dentistry and minor surgery. Its anesthetic properties resemble those of cocaine, but it does not cause the euphoria that may lead to cocaine abuse. It has no chemical resemblance to cocaine.

procaryote   see PROKARYOTE

process control *Process control* is a general term applied to describe the many methods of regulating the values of variables involved in industrial operations. These variables are parameters such as fluid pressure, temperature, and flow rate of raw materials. In fact any quantity that requires regulation in an industrial process can be treated as a variable for process control.

An integral part of the Industrial Revolution and the ensuing manufacturing innovations was the necessity to control—that is, to automatically regulate—the values of many different production parameters. For example, to manufacture plastic it may be necessary to maintain the temperature of a reaction vessel at a constant value. If the process were not controlled, the temperature of the vessel might vary radically and create a poor-quality product or even a dangerous situation. Procedures have been

Computer operators monitor a completely automated casting plant from a master control room. The plant can be seen through the glass windows at the back of the room and is schematically illustrated on the backlit panel to the right. Because microprocessor-based process control systems can precisely monitor dozens of manufacturing variables—such as heat, pressure, and rate of water flow—and display the information graphically on the computer screens, the operators can make minute adjustments in the process with ease. This particular plant produces a variety of castings, from automobile transmission and clutch housings to sewer grates and manhole covers.

developed to provide such regulation. Regulation was accomplished manually at first—through measurement, evaluation, and adjustment of the variable. Later, automatic systems were developed that could measure, evaluate, and adjust without direct human interaction. Automatic regulation of this type makes use of the FEEDBACK of the value of a variable in order to effect necessary adjustments of the process involving that variable (see AUTOMATION).

The complete assembly of the three elements—measurement, evaluation, and adjustment—constitutes what is called a process-control loop, where the word *loop* conveys the idea of feedback of adjustments to the process following measurements in the process. Most industrial operations involve many variables to be regulated and thus many such process-control loops. Sometimes the loop variables interact with each other so that adjustments for one variable affect a second variable, and so on. The overall process-control system is the assemblage of all these loops.

Since the late 1970s, microprocessor-based process-control systems have come into wide use. Depending on the user's need, such systems use an array of microprocessors to control from one to hundreds of variables. Further, these microprocessors are "cross-coupled," or connected, with each other in such a way that complex adjustments can be made across a series of variables based on information traded between microprocessors.

See also: COMPUTER-AIDED DESIGN AND COMPUTER-AIDED MANUFACTURING.

process philosophy The concept of process in contemporary philosophy arises from the view that any understanding of change or development that begins with discrete or atomistic units is inadequate. The starting point in process is continuity. Continuity is ultimate, both temporally and spatially. Time is duration as opposed to the fictional "instant moment." There is no discontinuity of externally related units, and no infinite series of discrete points can make a true continuum.

In process philosophy, then, the focus may be on the concretely experienced, continuous "stream of thought" as opposed to the level of conceptualization, or on a metaphysics of a durational flow of events as opposed to a metaphysics of discrete, unchanging, or permanent substances.

An emerging span of duration brings with it an aspect of creativity. A developing process contains both a continuity with what has been and an emerging novelty. Process philosophy rejects the understanding of either the physical universe or humanity in terms of a deterministic system.

Process philosophy is usually associated with the philosophers Henri BERGSON and Alfred North WHITEHEAD.

Proclus [proh'-kluhs] Proclus, c.410–85, was a Neoplatonist philosopher (see NEOPLATONISM) who succeeded Syrianus as head of the Platonic Academy in Athens. Proclus gave a new logical dimension to Neoplatonist thought, introducing a detailed schematization of the levels of reality between "the One," which is beyond and yet the source of knowing and being, and the world of appearances. His writings, many of which are extant, include commentaries on Plato's dialogues and on Euclid's *Elements* and formal expositions of Platonic theology.

Proconsul [proh-kahn'-sul] First discovered by the British anthropologists Mary and Louis Leakey in the 1930s, fossil bones of the extinct ape Proconsul have since been recovered from several sites in East Africa. Proconsul is believed to have lived 17 to 21 million years ago, during the Miocene Epoch. The remains show many anatomical similarities to the chimpanzee and gorilla, leading many scientists to consider Proconsul as the direct ancestor of the African apes. Anatomical studies also reveal a close resemblance between the Proconsul fossils and the jaws of another, later-occurring Miocene ape, *Dryopithecus*. This suggests that the two may be related. Proconsul was a fruit eater that lived in tropical forests.

Procopius of Caesarea [proh-koh'-pee-uhs] The works of the Byzantine historian Procopius, b. c.500, d. after 555, are the primary source of knowledge of the reign of Emperor JUSTINIAN I. Born in Caesarea, Palestine, and trained in law, Procopius was attached (c.527) to the general BELISARIUS as legal advisor and accompanied his campaigns in Syria, North Africa, and Italy. After Belisarius's disgrace in 548, Procopius probably lived in Constantinople. His major work, the *Wars,* narrates Justinian's achievements to 553. The *Buildings* (c.554–55) further eulogizes Justinian for his public works. In the *Secret History* (published posthumously) Procopius claims to reveal information about the emperor's personality and policy that he did not dare present in the earlier books; this scurrilous account is the source of the scandals attributed to Justinian's wife, Empress THEODORA.

profit Profit is the excess of revenues over costs. It is also referred to as net earnings or income; its opposite is loss. As net income, profit is computed before taxes and dividends are disbursed. In a corporate operation it is customary to disburse only an established percentage of the profits as dividends to the shareholders. The rest is retained by management to meet financial contingencies, to finance capital improvements, and to finance expansion and diversification (all aimed at eventually increasing profits). In the free-enterprise, or capitalistic, system, profit is the major economic motivation. In such a capitalist economy, profit provides the incentive for individuals and corporations to make innovations and to take risks with their capital or services.

The characterization of the role of profit—and the profit motive—has been a major difference between traditional, free-enterprise economists and Marxists. In Marxist theory, profit is regarded as the difference between what the laborer is paid and what his or her services are worth. According to MARXISM, the value of goods is determined by the amount of labor that goes into them (the labor theory of value). Pursuant to this theory, workers in a capitalist economy are paid subsistence wages, far lower than the value their labor actually adds to the goods. The difference—or "surplus value"—is skimmed off as profit by the capitalist, whose motive always is to increase the difference by paying the workers as little as possible.

Profumo scandal [pruh-fue'-moh]   The Profumo scandal of 1963 seriously damaged the reputation of the British security system and nearly destroyed the government of Harold MACMILLAN. John Profumo was secretary for war (1960–63) in Macmillan's Conservative government. In June 1963 it became known that Profumo had earlier lied to the House of Commons when he had denied a sexual relationship with Christine Keeler, one of a ring of expensive call girls. Keeler had also been intimate with Captain Ivanov, a naval attaché of the Soviet embassy in London and probably a secret agent. Profumo had to resign from the government and the House of Commons, the secret service was accused of incompetence in failing to inform the prime minister of a potential security risk, and Macmillan was attacked for trying to protect Profumo and other colleagues. An official investigation revealed that many prominent persons were involved in illicit sex, pornography, and drugs. Profumo later became active in the social rehabilitation of juvenile offenders.

progesterone   see SEX HORMONES; STEROID

programmed learning   Programmed learning, or programmed instruction, given impetus by behavioral psychologist B. F. SKINNER in the 1950s, refers to a process of education that permits self-instruction by means of algorithms, TEACHING MACHINES, instructional textbooks, radio, television, or computers. The purpose of testing and revision is to ensure that an instructional program will enable students of a certain age, background, and ability to achieve measurable learning objectives. Programmed texts or simple teaching machines that use a linear sequence of presentations (frames) involving questions and feedback to check the student's answers are only one of several methods of programmed learning. Audiotapes and videotapes and discs, interactive lessons on computers, instructional games and simulations, and a wide variety of printed materials have also been developed.

Programmed learning lost favor somewhat during the late 1970s, when empirical research failed to uphold its early promise. Educators felt that many of the programs did not provide enough variables to meet the needs of individual students. One type of program that is well adapted to individual students, however, is the "branching" program, which allows for the presentation of different material depending on responses to earlier material and adjusts the difficulty of the material to the skill level displayed by the user. This technique is especially useful in computer-assisted instruction (see COMPUTERS IN EDUCATION).

programming, computer   see COMPUTER PROGRAMMING

progression   In mathematics, a SEQUENCE is a SERIES of numbers, or terms, in which each term is related to the preceding one according to some prescribed rule of mathematical operation. Three particular sequences are by convention known as progressions: the arithmetic, the geometric, and the harmonic. They are useful in various fields of science and technology.

In an arithmetic progression, the difference between terms remains constant. For example, 2, 4, 6, 8, and so on is a progression in which the difference between terms is always 2. In a geometric progression, the ratio between terms remains constant. For example, in the progression 2, 4, 8, 16, and so on, each term is found by multiplying the preceding one by 2. In a harmonic progression, the reciprocals of the numbers (the numbers divided into 1) proceed as in an arithmetic progression. Thus $\frac{1}{2}$, $\frac{1}{4}$, $\frac{1}{6}$, $\frac{1}{8}$, and so on is the harmonic counterpart to the arithmetic example above.

Progressive Conservative party   see CONSERVATIVE PARTIES

progressive education   The term *progressive education* refers to a diverse group of theories and practices that took shape in Europe and the United States during the late 19th century. Progressive educational theory comprises beliefs that are alike only in their opposition to traditional schooling, which emphasizes mastery of an academic curriculum within a disciplinary system, and in their concern for the emotional and physical well-being of the child. In the United States the term is applied to a movement whose intellectual leader was the philosopher John DEWEY.

The intellectual origins of progressive education may be traced to Jean Jacques ROUSSEAU, whose treatise *Émile* (1762) advocated the natural development of children, free from the restraints of social conformity; Friedrich Wilhelm August FROEBEL, founder of the first kindergarten in 1837, who encouraged young learners to engage in self-initiated activities; Johann Friedrich HERBART, whose theory of mental development centered on interests and needs; Herbert SPENCER, who applied evolutionary theory and the doctrine of utilitarianism to education; and Johann Heinrich PESTALOZZI and Maria MONTESSORI, who created educational environments in which children were encouraged to develop their abilities through sensory experience. The principal forerunner of progressive education in the United States was Francis Wayland PARKER, who in Massachusetts and Chicago replaced the formal curriculum with a flexible program geared to the individual abilities, needs, and interests of children.

John Dewey's philosophy of PRAGMATISM and numerous books on educational method shaped the progressive education movement in the 20th century. Dewey recommended that instruction focus on social activities through which children learn to solve problems cooperatively and deal with a changing world. He wished to make education a democratic process that prepared children for participation in a democratic society. His ideas were put into practice in the Laboratory Schools of the University of Chicago, which Dewey founded in 1896.

The cause of progressive education was furthered in the United States by the Progressive Education Association (PEA; 1919–55) and by TEACHERS COLLEGE of Columbia University, New York City, which became an important center for the dissemination of progressive ideas, especially after the appointment of William Heard KILPATRICK to the faculty in 1909. By the 1930s, progressive educational practices had given rise to experimental schools throughout the world, including A. S. Neill's SUMMERHILL in England.

By the 1950s, when the ideas of progressive education had become assimilated into most educational systems in Europe and the United States in the form of student participation in school government, VOCATIONAL EDUCATION as practical preparation for adult life, the OPEN CLASSROOM, and other common features, the movement fell into disfavor. Although a study published by the PEA in 1942 showed that students from progressive schools were more successful in later life than their counterparts from traditional institutions, progressive education has recently been criticized for its alleged neglect of the basic skills of literacy and numeracy. Many of the liberal educational policies of recent decades, however, such as HEAD START, COMPENSATORY EDUCATION, and early-childhood schooling, draw extensively on progressive assumptions and methods, which remain a major influence on educational thought.

Progressive Era   The Progressive Era, in U.S. history, refers to the period from 1900 to World War I. It was an age of reform (trust-busting, railroad legislation, pure food and drug acts), dominated by President Theodore ROOSEVELT.

Progressive party   The Progressive party was the name for three separate political organizations in U.S. history. Although the 1912, 1924, and 1948 organizations were all concerned with social reform and were generally opposed to excessive corporate power, they differed substantially in their emphases.

The Progressive party of 1912 grew out of former president Theodore ROOSEVELT's drive for the Republican presidential nomination. Foiled by the incumbent, William Howard Taft, who controlled the convention machinery, Roosevelt led his supporters into his BULL MOOSE PARTY (another name for the Progressives). The party's 1912 platform called for numerous social and political reforms, including the conservation of natural and human resources, women's suffrage, popular election of U.S. senators, and the initiative, referendum, and recall. Roosevelt campaigned zealously but could not defeat the progressive Democratic candidate, Woodrow Wilson; still, Roosevelt polled 4.1 million votes—about 600,000 more than Taft received.

In 1924 the Committee of 48, custodians of the Progressive party label, united with the SOCIALIST PARTY, the railroad unions, and the American Federation of Labor behind the independent candidacy of Robert M. LA FOLLETTE. Remembering the divisive 1912 strategy, they did not oppose Progressive candidates from the two major parties. La Follette ran on a plank that was largely antimonopoly, although large corporations were of little concern to Socialists and organized labor. The American economy improved, however, the Republicans minimized the scandals of Warren Harding's administration, and La Follette was short of funds and smeared as an unpatriotic, red demagogue. As a result, the Republican candidate, Calvin Coolidge, won a landslide victory.

In 1947–48 the cold-war policies of President Harry S. Truman caused a major break within the left wing of the Democratic party. The defectors, who favored more cooperative relations with the USSR, organized as the Progressive party and nominated Henry A. WALLACE for president in 1948. The party advocated such programs as repeal of the Taft-Hartley Act and the reestablishment of price controls and won the endorsement of the U.S. Communist party. Wallace insisted that prosperity required peace and the tacit recognition of respective spheres of influence. Undermined by Communist actions in Czechoslovakia and Berlin, Wallace received less than 3 percent of the votes cast.

prohibition   [proh-uh-bish'-uhn]   In U.S. history the era of prohibition was the period (1920–33) when the 18th Amendment to the U.S. Constitution forbade the manufacture, sale, and transportation of alcoholic bever-

The destruction of liquor barrels by ax-wielding federal agents was a common occurrence during the prohibition era in the United States. Although the 18th Amendment was intended to promote moral virtue, it led to the rise of illegal saloons and an organized black market.

ages. Known as the Noble Experiment, national prohibition was the product of a century-long reform movement. Prohibitionists, who viewed alcohol as a dangerous drug that destroyed lives and disrupted families and communities, argued that it was the government's responsibility to free citizens from the temptation of drink by barring its sale.

Organized by the Woman's Christian Temperance Union (see WCTU), the Anti-Saloon League of America (see TEMPERANCE MOVEMENT), and the National Prohibition party, prohibitionists pressed for an amendment to the federal Constitution. The 18th Amendment was finally ratified in January 1919, and nine months later Congress passed the Volstead Act, which provided for the enforcement of the amendment. The law, which was enforced sporadically at best, met with widespread opposition. BOOTLEGGING, speakeasies (illegal saloons), and smuggling (known as rum-running) all flourished, largely under the control of gangster elements. Opponents, known as "wets," claimed that not only was prohibition ineffective but also that it represented an unnecessary restriction on personal choice. They mounted a campaign to annul the law and were successful in 1933, when the 21st Amendment was ratified. It repealed the 18th Amendment and negated the Volstead Act, although prohibition remained a local option and was retained in some areas.

projection Projection is a psychological DEFENSE MECHANISM. Of the three types of projection that have been identified, attributive projection is the most well documented. In this type of projection, a person attributes the same negative traits they see in themselves to others they like or admire. In complimentary projection, a person has a negative feeling, such as fright, and believes incorrectly that another person is the cause of that feeling. In similarity or classical projection, a person is unaware of possessing the same negative traits he or she attributes to another person.

projective geometry Projective geometry is the study of properties of figures that are unchanged when the figures are transformed in certain ways (transformed by finite sequences of perspectivities). Projective geometry may also be considered as a very general GEOMETRY of points, lines, and planes—the geometry that is obtained when the requirements of preserving area, shape, and parallelism are removed from Euclidean geometry.

The axioms of projective geometry are few in number and inherently simple. Relative to a Euclidean plane, a projective plane includes—in addition to the Euclidean plane—a line that corresponds to the horizon line associated with that Euclidean plane. On a Euclidean plane any two distinct lines either intersect or are parallel. The parallel lines have a point of the horizon line of the plane in common. Thus on a projective plane any two distinct lines have one and only one point in common. Also, on a projective plane any two distinct points have one and only one line in common. Each of the last two statements in projective geometry may be obtained from the other by

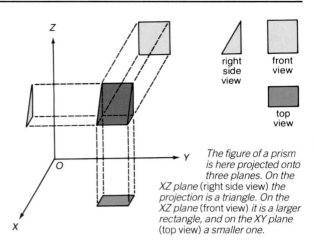

The figure of a prism is here projected onto three planes. On the XZ plane (right side view) the projection is a triangle. On the XZ plane (front view) it is a larger rectangle, and on the XY plane (top view) a smaller one.

interchanging the words *point* and *line*. Such statements are called plane duals. Each statement in projective plane geometry has a plane dual statement, and the two statements are either both true or both false.

Projective geometry and descriptive geometry both arose from the efforts of artists and mathematicians to represent three-dimensional figures on a plane. Descriptive geometry has two essential features. First, any object in space may be projected parallel to the coordinate axes onto the coordinate planes. Second, the images obtained may be represented on a single plane. If there are edges that cannot be seen from a particular point of view and are not behind other edges, the hidden edges are indicated by dashed lines. Descriptive geometry probably originated with Albrecht DÜRER and was given a sound mathematical basis by Gaspard MONGE.

projective tests Projective tests are techniques in psychology that rely on ambiguous stimuli to assess an individual's personality structure as a whole. Projec-

This image is one of the ten inkblots constituting the Rorschach Inkblot Test, one of the most famous projective tests of personality. The Rorschach test is administered by allowing the subject to view each card and describe whatever he or she perceives.

This picture is from the Thematic Apperception Test (TAT), a series of 30 black-and-white scenes portraying ambiguous situations. The subject is required to create a story for each picture. Pervasive themes are assumed to reflect the subject's past experiences and concerns.

tive tests are unstructured. Their lack of structure is due to the underlying projective hypothesis that behavior is indicative of personality structure. Projective tests are therefore designed to be ambiguous and vague in order to enhance the likelihood that a person's response is determined by internal ways of structuring and perceiving the world rather than by the objective demands of the situation.

The Rorschach Inkblot Test is perhaps the most well-known and widely used projective test. Developed from 1911 to 1921 by Hermann Rorschach, a Swiss psychiatrist, the Rorschach test consists of ten bisymmetrical inkblots, five in black and white and five in color. The subject is asked to say what the inkblots look like. Traditionally, the content of the response has been assumed to reveal the most about an individual's personality; that is, the individual's description of the inkblot was the major factor taken into account in diagnosis. Later, formal analysis came into vogue. A subject's style of response—such as reacting to color or shading, describing an object in motion, placing an object within a specific location, or making a wholly original observation—also became an important determinant of personality.

The Thematic Apperception Test (TAT) is the next most common projective instrument. Devised by Henry A. Murray at Harvard, it consists of 30 pictures about which the subject must tell a story. Traditionally, the test has been thought to assess an individual's more conscious attitudes, moods, and interpersonal orientation in contrast with the deeper structures of the personality tapped by the Rorschach test. Efforts are currently under way, however, to use the TAT as a means of assessing the structure of the individual's object relationships. Although early research on the reliability and validity of projective tests was pessimistic, some recent investigators have suggested that these findings were the result of poorly designed experiments. Recent research by clinicians sensitive to the clinical uses of projective tests has demonstrated their efficacy and reliability. Projective tests are also currently being explored as measures of the effectiveness of psychotherapy. They have traditionally been used only in the psychiatric diagnostic process.

projector The projector, an optical device involving, primarily, a light source and a lens, is used to transmit an enlarged image from a small piece of photographic material onto a large surface such as a screen. The image is either transmitted through a transparent object (film), or reflected off an opaque object (photograph), and through a LENS. The size of the projected image depends on the distance between projector and screen and the focal length of the lens.

Motion picture projectors, which must move a long strip of film through a gate that sits between light source and lens, are more complex than still projectors, but the basic principles are the same. Although there had been various early efforts at projecting moving pictures, it was the development of flexible transparent film by George Eastman in the 1880s that produced the motion picture projector of today. In 1889, Thomas Edison cut this film into 35-mm widths, perforated its edges, and used it in a working motion picture camera called the Kinetograph. These earliest films were first seen by the public in 1893 via a coin-operated machine called the Kinetoscope. The Cinématographe, invented in 1895 by Louis and Auguste

Movie projectors are capable of handling both 35-mm and 70-mm films, as well as magnetic and optical sound tracks. Most projectors use high-intensity carbon arc light sources. Many are equipped with special anamorphic lenses for projecting panoramic Cinemascope film images onto a wide, curved screen. A typical projector includes a hot-air flue (1); shield for protecting the film from excessive heat during initial sparking of the arc (2); double-sided magnetic pickup (3); film guide (4); an anamorphic lens (5); standard lens (6); focus drive (7); intermittent sprocket (8); revolving drum-type shutter (9); take-up reel (10); optical sound track scanning drum (11); carbon rod drives (12), positive and negative carbon rods (13, 14); flame shield for mirror protection during arc start-up (15); and ellipsoid mirror (16).

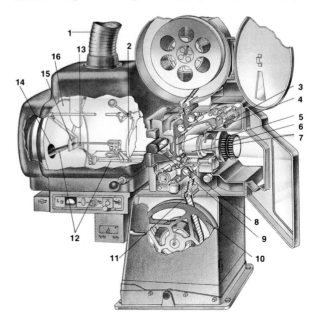

Lumière, incorporated a claw mechanism to move the film. A year later T. H. Blair developed a registration device that produced a much steadier image.

The most significant advance has been the addition of sound to the motion picture film, and the wide-screen image obtained with 70-mm film. Probably the most advanced example of the projector art can be seen in PLANETARIUMS. These complex instruments can project the position of the stars and planets in our solar system for any given date.

---

prokaryote [proh-kair'-ee-uht] Prokaryotes, or procaryotes, which include bacteria, blue-green algae, spirochetes, rickettsiae, and mycoplasma organisms, are very small living cells that reproduce asexually by a process that does not involve mitosis. They have no membranes, except the cell membrane, and no cytoplasmic organelles such as vacuoles, mitochondria, endoplasmic reticulum, or photosynthetic plastids. Prokaryotes have a single chromosome consisting of a tightly coiled molecule of deoxyribonucleic acid (DNA) that is not associated with protein and is not separated from the cytoplasm by a membrane. Prokaryotes are thought to be the first cells that arose in evolution. (See also EUKARYOTE.)

Prokofiev, Sergei [proh-kawf'-ee-ef, sir-gay'] The Russian composer Sergei Sergeyevich Prokofiev was born in the Ekaterinoslav Province of Ukraine. His birth certificate lists the date as Apr. 15 (O.S.), 1891, although he always gave it as Apr. 23 (N.S.), 1891. In 1904, after lessons from Reinhold Glière, Prokofiev entered the Saint Petersburg Conservatory, studying with Rimsky-Korsakov, Liadov, N. Tcherepnin, and Anna Essipov. He had already made his mark as an innovator when he graduated in 1914. He resisted the trends in Russian music represented by Rachmaninoff and Scriabin, evolving a novel style distinguished by emotional restraint, sharply motoric rhythms, and harmonic clarity in a context of abrupt and unpredictable tonal shifts defined by neoclassical cadential gestures. Although he was aware of the innovative power of his brilliant contemporary Stravinsky, Prokofiev's personal idiom remained remarkably consistent throughout his life.

Prokofiev left Russia in 1918, settling finally in France. His association with Diaghilev's Ballets Russes led to *Chout* (1921), *The Steel Step* (1927), and *The Prodigal Son* (1929). The premieres of two of his most successful works were held in Chicago in 1921—the Third Piano Concerto and the opera *Love for Three Oranges*, which was commissioned by the Chicago Opera Association. Despite fame as a composer, his livelihood came from concert tours, which sapped his energy. In 1932, Prokofiev reached an understanding with Soviet authorities that allowed him more time for composing, and in 1936 he left Paris and resettled permanently in the USSR. Even before returning, his style had mellowed. He embraced the idea that as an artist supported by Soviet

Sergei Prokofiev, a 20th-century Russian composer, combined lyrical beauty and dramatic dissonance in such works as the opera Love for Three Oranges (1921), the ballet Romeo and Juliet (1938), and the symphonic tale Peter and the Wolf (1936). Prokofiev also wrote concertos, symphonies, and piano sonatas.

society he must address a wide public. Not only the *pièces d'occasion* (the cantatas *Twentieth Anniversary of October* and *Ode to Stalin*) but such works as the ballet *Romeo and Juliet* (1938), *Peter and the Wolf* (1936), and the Fifth Symphony (1945) reveal his mastery of an original, professionally adroit, yet highly accessible style. Through his film scores—among them, *Alexander Nevsky* (1939) and *Ivan the Terrible* (1945)—Prokofiev's work became known to a wide public. His operas include *The Fiery Angel* (1927) and *War and Peace* (1953), and his total opus includes seven symphonies (among them, the *Classical* Symphony, 1918), five piano concertos, two violin concertos, and chamber music.

In 1948, Prokofiev and other leading Soviet composers were severely criticized by Communist party spokespersons for "ideological laxity." Prokofiev's last years were shadowed by illness and frustration, the latter from petty bureaucrats appointed to verify the ideological soundness of Soviet music. He died of a stroke in Moscow on Mar. 5, 1953, on the same day as Soviet dictator Joseph Stalin.

prolactin see HORMONE, ANIMAL

---

proletariat [proh-luh-tair'-ee-at] The proletariat, in Marxist economic theory (see MARXISM), is that portion of society which owns little property or capital and lives by selling its labor for the purposes of industrial production. It is also called the industrial working class. According to Marxist theory the proletariat is continually exploited by capitalists, the owners of the means of production. As a result of this exploitation, the proletariat grows larger, poorer, and more desperate until it revolts, seizes the means of production, and establishes a state in which all economic classes are eliminated.

Prometheus [proh-mee'-thee-uhs] In Greek mythology Prometheus ("Forethought") was the TITAN who stole fire from the gods and gave it to humans, along with all human arts and civilization. He was also variously regarded as the creator of man (from clay), the first mortal man (along with his brother Epimetheus), and humanity's preserver against the threats of Zeus, whom he greatly offended by his actions. In Hesiod's version, Zeus's punishment was the creation of PANDORA, the first woman, who unleashed on the world all its woes. In *Prometheus Bound*, a tragic play by AESCHYLUS, Zeus had Prometheus chained to a rock on Mount Caucasus, where an eagle ate at his liver, starting afresh each day after the liver had grown back during the night. One source has Prometheus eventually freed by Hercules and brought to Olympus to join the gods.

promethium [proh-mee'-thee-uhm]   Promethium is a radioactive chemical element, a metal of the LANTHANIDE SERIES of the periodic table. Its symbol is Pm, its atomic number is 61, and its atomic weight is 147 (most commonly isolated isotope). Promethium is one of the fission products of uranium, thorium, and plutonium. Some scientists claim to have discovered promethium in nature by spectral analysis, but it has not been isolated from natural materials. First produced artificially in 1945, it is used in the preparation of PHOSPHORS and in the manufacture of nuclear-powered batteries for use in space.

pronghorn   The pronghorn, *Antilocapra americana*, the only living member of the family Antilocapridae, in the mammalian order Artiodactyla, is often called pronghorn antelope, although it is not a true antelope. It has pronged, or branching, hollow horns with a permanent bony core, covered with an outer sheath that is shed annually after the breeding season. The pronghorn is 1½ m (5 ft) long and may weigh 60 kg (135 lb). One of the fastest of New World mammals, it can run up to 72 km/h (45 mph). Pronghorns live on grasslands and deserts from northern Mexico to southwestern Canada.

The pronghorn, a mammal related to deer and antelope, once lived in vast numbers on the North American plains. Like the bison, the pronghorn was greatly overhunted in the 19th century.

pronunciation   see PHONETICS; PHONOLOGY AND MORPHOLOGY

proof, mathematical   A proof is an argument that conclusively establishes the truth of a statement or that establishes the conclusion only on certain assumptions or hypotheses.

A mathematical proof has a definite structure and can be divided into steps: initial steps are hypotheses or assertions supposed to be evident without proof or to have been previously proved; otherwise a statement is inferred or deduced from statements made at earlier steps (see DEDUCTION).

Because it is not possible always to return to statements that have been previously proved, mathematical proofs must be representable as consisting of inferences from statements assumed without proof. Such statements are called AXIOMS, and a codification for a given subject matter is called an axiomatization; an example of the latter from antiquity is Euclidean geometry. Ideally, inferences should proceed by logic alone, but this procedure was not carried out until the 20th century.

If axioms and rules of inference are codified exactly, then proofs can be represented as sequences of signs and become objects of mathematical study. Such a codification is called formalization. The mathematical study of formal proofs is called proof theory. Proof theory has shown that formalized axiom systems containing arithmetic are necessarily incomplete; in any such system, some statements can be neither proved nor refuted. This is known as Gödel's theorem, named for the mathematician and logician Kurt GÖDEL.

Increasingly, mathematicians have used powerful computer systems to generate complex proofs. The solution of the FOUR-COLOR THEOREM in 1976 is a famous example of a computer-assisted proof. In 1988, Canadian mathematicians used computers to develop a proof for a problem in PROJECTIVE GEOMETRY that involved reviewing trillions of possible solutions. Some mathematicians have argued that solutions too complicated to be comprehended by the human mind cannot be considered valid mathematical proofs.

propaganda   Propaganda is the systematic attempt to manipulate the attitudes, beliefs, and actions of people through the use of symbols such as words, gestures, slogans, flags, and uniforms. Ideas, facts, or allegations are spread to further a cause or to damage an opposing cause. The factor that distinguishes propagandizing from educating and informing is deliberate selectivity and manipulation. In modern history, the propaganda machine of the German Nazis under Joseph GOEBBELS is especially infamous.

Propaganda ranges from overt attempts to influence the public to covert means of persuasion. Psychological warfare is a form of propaganda employed to confuse and demoralize enemy populations. BRAINWASHING is the prac-

Germany Lives!, a Nazi propaganda poster from the 1930s, uses quasi-religious imagery to glorify the Nazi program of national supremacy and race hatred. Adolf Hitler is portrayed as a messianic savior.

paigns, and other efforts at mass persuasion frequently rely on emotional shock to motivate people to carry out preventive measures or to support policies designed to avert potential dangers.

The larger the propaganda enterprise, the more important are such mass media as television, newspapers, and radio for reaching the widest audience. Mass-communication studies that investigate the relative effectiveness and credibility of the various media are frequently used by propagandists when selecting a means of reaching the public.

The Impact of Propaganda. Early studies of the effects of propaganda on public opinion and behavior suggested that people in modern society were highly gullible. More recent review indicates that mass communications generally fail to produce marked changes in social attitudes or actions. Numerous factors limit the effectiveness and impact of propaganda within democratic societies. Because people can belong to any number of groups with differing goals and values, it becomes difficult for the propagandist to appeal to all these group interests simultaneously. A free and competitive press makes possible the presentation of information from every side of an issue. Existing laws require that equal media time be given to all major contenders in political campaigns.

Government regulations also protect the consumer from marketing propaganda by insisting on truth in advertising. Moreover, as the level of education increases worldwide, the public is becoming more capable of questioning and evaluating the arguments and symbols that propagandists use.

tice of subjecting individuals to intensive political indoctrination and depends on methods aimed at breaking down the subject's resistance.

ADVERTISING, too, has been regarded as propaganda. Information on consumer sentiments toward various products, their packaging, and sales and advertising techniques is obtained through market research. The information is then used to mount advertising campaigns making one-sided appeals to consumer preferences.

Propaganda Techniques. Among the techniques employed by propagandists to achieve their aims are scapegoating, the displacement of guilt for some action or circumstance on others; presentation of an individual or social group as morally superior; and coordination of symbol manipulation with acts of violence and bribery. Emotional appeals, especially to popular fears, are also often used. Antiwar propaganda, public-health cam-

Bad propaganda is easily recognized. In 1990, Iraqi television showed a smiling Saddam Hussein chatting with tense British hostages (whom he called "guests") trapped in Iraq after the invasion of Kuwait.

An American propaganda poster from World War I, painted by James Montgomery Flagg, aroused the loyalties, fears, and protective impulses of the American public by portraying the nation as a sleeping woman oblivious to outside dangers. American propaganda was dominated by the graphic arts until World War II, when radio, films, and television assumed a more important role.

propane Propane, chemical formula C_3H_8, is a HYDROCARBON of molecular weight 44.09 and boiling point $-42.1°$ C ($-43.8°$ F) at atmospheric pressure. Like ethane and methane, propane is a member of the ALKANE series of hydrocarbons. It is an important fuel gas and chemical feedstock and is a major constituent of liquefied petroleum gas (see PETROLEUM INDUSTRY). The net calorific value of propane is about 12,000 cal/g (21,600 Btu/lb). When used as a fuel, 23.8 m³ of air are required for the combustion of 1 m³ of propane gas, with the products of combustion being CO_2 and H_2O. The ignition temperature is 466° C, and the flame temperature is 1,970° C.

propeller   A propulsion device used primarily on ships and airplanes, a propeller is a series of blades on a hub that is mounted on an engine-driven shaft. The rotation of the blades in air or water produces a forward thrust.

Marine Propeller. The first type of propeller was the marine screw propeller, invented by JOHN ERICSSON in the 1830s. It gradually replaced the paddle wheel in steam-driven SHIPS. Modern marine propellers are usually large castings in manganese-bronze. The blades may be three to six in number and are roughly circular in shape. The Kort propeller is enclosed by a short cylindrical shell, which increases thrust by 15–25% and also protects the blades against damage. The Voith-Schneider design is one in which the propeller rotates about a vertical axis with the blades projecting downward; the blades can be adjusted to provide thrust in any direction. Large ships often have small ducted propellers at the bows to create side thrust for better control in a harbor.

Aircraft Propeller. The earliest AIRCRAFT propellers had two or four thin blades carved from hardwood or shaped from laminated wood. Later, metal blades were made of aluminum fastened to a steel hub, or both hub and blades were pressed from a single steel sheet. Today's airplanes use propellers made of aluminum or steel alloys. Most are equipped with variable-pitch capacity, allowing the blade angle to be altered to provide more efficient propulsion. The earliest variable-pitch propellers had only two blade positions and were set on the ground by hand. Modern propellers on large aircraft change pitch automatically and continuously, according to varying wind and speed conditions. For takeoff, the blades are set at a low (or fine) pitch. As speed increases, the pitch is inclined more sharply into the airflow (high or coarse pitch).

proper motion   The proper motion of a star is the apparent speed at which a star moves against a fixed background. The effect was first discovered in 1718 by Edmond HALLEY, who noticed that the positions of some stars had changed since they were catalogued by Hipparchus about 20 centuries before. The position of Arcturus, for instance, had changed by about 1°.

The proper motion of a star, usually denoted by the symbol μ, is measured in seconds of arc per year. The largest known is for BARNARD'S STAR for which $\mu = 10.3$ seconds of arc per year. Today proper motions are measured photographically and are referred to the background of distant galaxies for which proper motion is insignificant. A star's proper motion depends on the star's distance from the Sun and on the transverse component (at a right angle to the line of sight) of its velocity. For complete information about a star's velocity relative to the

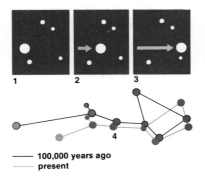

The relative positions of stars change with time. Barnard's Star has the fastest rate of change of position, or proper motion. Photographs taken in 1894 (1), 1916 (2), and 1947 (3) reveal its rapid proper motion. The appearance of a group of stars, such as the Big Dipper (4), can change markedly with time as a result of proper motions.

—— 100,000 years ago
—— present

Sun, its velocity in the line-of-sight radial velocity must be known. This is measured spectroscopically.

Propertius, Sextus [proh-pur'-shuhs]   Sextus Propertius (c.55–16 BC), a Roman elegiac poet noted for his celebration of love, was a contemporary of Horace and Vergil and a follower of Catullus. Propertius confesses himself, in the manner of Catullus, to be a slave to love, and his poems are passionate accounts of love's vicissitudes. Propertius was admired and imitated by Ezra Pound in his *Homage to Sextus Propertius* (1917).

property   Property is anything that can be possessed and disposed of in a legal manner. Running water in a stream is not anyone's property, because no one possesses it. If one takes water from a stream in a container, however, the water in the container becomes property. In a legal sense property is the aggregate of legal rights of individuals with respect to objects and obligations owed to them by others that are guaranteed and protected by the government. Ownership of property is classified as either private or public. Private property is ownership by an individual or individuals, whereas public ownership implies possession by some kind of a governmental unit. In another sense property is classified as either real or personal. Real property, also known as realty, is land, any buildings that may be on the land, any mineral rights under the land, and anything that is attached to the land or buildings with the intention that it remain there permanently. Personal property, also known legally as personalty (and sometimes as chattels), is simply defined as any property that is not real property.

Although private ownership of land is a relatively recent development, during most of human history real property—the land itself—was considered the greatest source of wealth. With the coming of the Industrial Revolution, however, personal property—especially in the form of STOCKS and BONDS—gradually outstripped land as the basis of the industrial nations' wealth.

Real Property. When a house is bought the purchase includes, as real property, the land, the buildings on the land, and such items as are permanently attached to the buildings. Known legally as fixtures, these items include the heating system, built-in kitchen cabinets, attached plumbing appliances, and fitted carpets. Mineral and timber rights may or may not be included with the land; some jurisdictions permit landowners to sell or lease their mineral and timber rights to an outside party, a contract that continues in effect when the land is sold to another party.

Two basic instruments of transfer are used for real property: the DEED and the WILL. (The government may cause land to pass from some form of public ownership to private ownership by a grant, and may reclaim private land for public use by EMINENT DOMAIN. Much of the land in the American West, for example, was granted by the government to the original settlers.) When the owner of real property sells to another person, the instrument of transfer is the deed, and the transfer by deed must be recorded by the county clerk or registrar (see TORRENS SYSTEM). Deeds may contain restrictions on how the purchaser may use the real property.

When an owner chooses to leave his or her property to another person upon death, a will effects the transfer. Where property is in the names of two or more persons with the right of survivorship or in the names of a husband and wife, the property must pass to the survivor or survivors. In most modern jurisdictions, however, owners of real property are free to will it to whomever they choose (although in the United States spouses are protected against total disinheritance; see INHERITANCE).

Personal Property. Personal property is classified as tangible or intangible. Tangible personal property is any physical object (other than real property) with intrinsic value—an automobile, for example. Intangible personal property includes COPYRIGHTS, FRANCHISE agreements, PATENTS, stocks, bonds, personal annuities, leases, and business goodwill. The transfer of ownership of personal property is generally quite simple; the most common transfer of personal property is the retail sales transaction. The transfer of intangible property often requires the formal reregistration of the property in the new owner's name. Personal property may also be transferred by will.

property tax   Property tax is a tax that is levied by a governmental unit on various kinds of property. Real-property tax, the most common form, is levied on land and buildings. Personal-property tax is assessed on such items as machinery, merchandise, furniture, automobiles, and equipment. Intangible-property tax is levied on such assets as bank savings, notes, stocks, bonds, and other securities. In the United States, use of property taxes is limited to state and local governments. The property-tax revenue may be used to support local education and other community services.

The reliance of school systems on property-tax revenues has come under strong criticisim in recent decades. Lawsuits have claimed that students in the poorer districts are denied equal protection of the law because lower revenues from property taxes result in inferior school systems. The U.S. Supreme Court rejected this contention, however, in *San Antonio Independent School District* v. *Rodriguez* (1973).

prophet   In the Old Testament of the BIBLE the prophets were a succession of men whose inspired utterances molded the shape of Israelite history. Chronologically, the prophets, and the Old Testament books of, may be divided into four groups: (1) AMOS, HOSEA, MICAH, and ISAIAH, of the 8th century BC; (2) NAHUM, ZEPHANIAH, HABAKKUK, and JEREMIAH, immediately preexilic (late 7th to early 6th century); (3) EZEKIEL and Second Isaiah, exilic period; and (4) the postexilic prophets—JOEL, OBADIAH, JONAH, HAGGAI, ZECHARIAH, and MALACHI. The prophetic tradition, however, goes back at least as far as SAMUEL and includes such early figures as ELIJAH and ELISHA.

All together the Old Testament prophets voiced a particular way of looking at history and world events. They spoke as the mouthpieces of God, addressing his people and revealing to them his divine plan. They relate the address of God to his people through the processes of history. In admonishing the Israelites, calling them to repentance and redemption, the prophets stressed monotheism, morality, and messianism—themes carried forward into Christianity.

The Old Testament prophets are similar to figures in other cultures of the ancient Near East. In the earlier texts, figures such as Samuel are called not only prophet but seer. The seer knew the technical skills of divination and could predict the course of future events; the trade appears in various surrounding cultures.

Old Testament prophets expressed their perception in a number of stereotyped forms of speech. A typical form of prophetic speech is the oracle, or word from God, in which the expression of divine judgment is prefixed by an indictment that the prophet understands as his own explanation of cause for the divine judgment. In addition to the oracle of judgment, the prophet employs a divine promise for deliverance.

In Christian belief the Holy Spirit "spake through the [Old Testament] prophets." Prophesying was accorded great respect until the rise of MONTANISM in the 2d century AD discredited it in the eyes of the orthodox. Thereafter, it was associated primarily with mystics and millenarians, people and sects that were often (but by no means always) labeled as heretical. Among Protestants the Anabaptists and Quakers stress the gift of prophecy. In Islam, MUHAMMAD is believed to be "the Seal of the Prophets," the last and greatest of God's human messengers.

See also: ORACLE; SHAMAN.

propionates   see FOOD ADDITIVES

proportional representation   Proportional representation is an electoral system by which each party has members in the legislature in proportion to the number of votes it received in the election. Proportional representation contrasts with the more common single-member district system wherein the candidate receiving the most votes in the district wins the seat and the voters for the losing parties are in effect unrepresented in the legislature. Various proportional representation systems were put forward in the late 19th century as a corrective to the "winner-take-all" method of electing legislators. Opponents of proportional representation, however, claim that it promotes political instability by encouraging the proliferation of minority parties. Proportional representation is considered a threat to the two-party system and therefore has never had wide acceptance in the United States.

prosecuting attorney A prosecuting attorney (often called a district attorney) is an elected or appointed public official who institutes and conducts criminal proceedings on behalf of the state or public against a person accused of a crime and represents the government at all levels of appeal. In a TRIAL, the prosecuting attorney (or an assistant) makes an opening statement explaining the case to the jury, then presents the state's witnesses, cross-examines the defense's witnesses, and at the conclusion of the trial sums up the state's case to the jury.

See also: CRIMINAL JUSTICE.

prostaglandins [prahs-tuh-glan'-duhnz] Prostaglandins are hormonelike substances that occur in various tissues and organs of the human body. At least 16 prostaglandins have been isolated. They affect several body systems, including the central nervous, cardiovascular, gastrointestinal, urinary, and endocrine systems. Their effects on the ENDOCRINE SYSTEM include stimulating the release of growth hormone by the pituitary gland, mediating the effects of luteinizing hormone on the ovary, stimulating the dissolution of the corpus luteum, and altering steroid hormone synthesis by the adrenal cortex. One of the prostaglandins has been found to be a powerful stimulant of uterine contractions and may prove useful for inducing labor. It is used in France, in conjunction with the ABORTION-inducing drug RU-486, to encourage the womb to contract and expel its contents. (See HORMONE, ANIMAL.)

prostate gland [prahs'-tayt] In males the prostate gland surrounds the part of the urethra that is located just below the urinary bladder. Prostatic secretions pass into the urethra through several ducts and are believed to increase the motility and fertility of spermatozoa. This gland may enlarge in old age and obstruct the urethra, making surgical removal (prostatectomy) necessary. Cancer of the prostate is the second most common cancer in men, after skin cancer, occurring in about 1 of every 11 U.S. men.

See also: REPRODUCTIVE SYSTEM, HUMAN.

prosthetics [prahs-thet'-iks] Devices such as ARTIFICIAL LIMBS, ARTIFICIAL ORGANS, and false teeth are examples of prostheses—artificial devices that replace a missing part of the body. Prosthetics is the surgical and dental specialty concerned with such replacements. Prostheses may be functional, cosmetic, or both.

prostitution Prostitution is the sale of sexual services, which may consist of any sexual acts, including those not involving copulation. Payment most commonly is in the form of money. Although the majority of prostitutes have been women, male prostitution and prostitution of prepubescent children also occur. In general, prostitutes are drawn from segments of society that are economically and politically marginal.

History of Prostitution in Western Societies. Probably the earliest form of the institution was temple, or religious, prostitution. The factors contributing to independent, nonreligious prostitution were increasing urbanization, the growth of a money-based economy, and the displacement of persons from a traditional, village-centered way of life.

Solon (*c*.639–559 BC) established state brothels in Athens, the employees of which came from the lowest strata of society. Later, independent prostitutes were regulated and taxed. The hetaerae were courtesans who provided various kinds of entertainment including music, poetry, and intellectually stimulating conversation and companionship.

In ancient Rome, prostitutes were licensed by the state and taxed. Patrician women were forbidden to engage in prostitution. Women who were neither patricians nor slaves but relied on other means of income (for example, actresses, musicians, dancers), were free to sell sexual services without registration or taxation. Male prostitutes were also numerous in Rome but were not regulated by the state.

The early Christian church excommunicated (AD 305) all prostitutes on moral grounds. Prostitution, nevertheless, remained a well-established institution, and it provided an important source of tax revenue to the imperial state.

In the High Middle Ages, prostitution came under the protection and regulation of municipal governments. The crackdown against prostitution in early modern Europe coincided with the outbreak of a syphilis epidemic and the repressive stance toward sexuality of Reformation morality.

Female prostitution greatly expanded in modern Europe, while its practice was increasingly condemned. Beginning in the 19th century, the rise of capitalism brought increasing numbers of women into the labor force at the lowest possible wages, and many turned to occasional prostitution to supplement their incomes. In the cities many became involved in regular prostitution either through forcible recruitment or as an alternative to unemployment.

Prostitution in Non-Western Cultures. Both secular and sacred prostitution have coexisted in India since classical Hindu times. Lay prostitutes were a recognized caste. The Muslim invasions (AD *c*.1000) of India resulted in official pronouncements against the institution, but in practice the Muslims did little to discourage it. Temple prostitution, in which girls are dedicated to a deity, has continued into the 20th century.

In China, prostitution was a well-established institution by the 7th century BC. The predominant form was in brothels of female slaves. After slavery was officially ended, the sale of wives, concubines, and daughters into prostitution remained a common practice. Since the Communist revolution, prostitution has greatly diminished.

The well-known role of the GEISHA in Japan is of relatively recent origin, dating from the 18th century. This institution resembles that of the classical Greek hetaerae.

Prostitution in Contemporary Societies. In contemporary, technologically developed societies, the vast majority of acts of prostitution are carried out by people who use it to supplement low incomes. Men and women who rely on prostitution as their primary source of income typically have left their natal families in adolescence. Without education or work skills, and often prevented from employment by child labor laws, such runaway children resort to prostitution as their only means of survival.

Some Western governments combine regulated prostitution with public-health measures to control VENEREAL DISEASE. Otherwise, prostitution is illegal in most developed countries. Enforcement is left up to municipal authorities, who usually direct their police efforts against the most visible practitioners of prostitution. Customers are rarely arrested, and although pandering is also illegal, most pimps are not subject to arrest.

Drug addiction is prevalent among prostitutes, as are a variety of chronic and infectious nonvenereal diseases. Recent concern about the spread of AIDS has stimulated educational campaigns to help control venereal disease among prostitutes.

protactinium [proh-tak-tin'-ee-uhm] Protactinium is a shiny, malleable radioactive metal chemical element of the ACTINIDE SERIES of the periodic table. Its symbol is Pa, its atomic number is 91, and its atomic weight is 231 (stablest isotope). The first isotope identified, ^{234}Pa, was discovered in nature by Kasimir Fajans and O. H. Göhring in 1913. The chemical properties of the metal are similar to those of its neighboring element thorium. Protactinium is the most expensive naturally occurring element and is not used commercially.

Protagoras [proh-tag'-uh-ruhs] Protagoras, *c.*490–*c.*420 BC, was one of the leading Greek professional teachers called SOPHISTS. He taught rhetoric and law and introduced the "adversary system," in which a student argues both sides of a case, into legal training. Protagoras was particularly famous for his urbane religious skepticism and his relativism; "man," he said, "is the measure of all things." Through his friend Pericles, he influenced contemporary political thought in Athens. Plato, in his dialogue the *Protagoras*, created an imaginary conversation between Protagoras and Socrates.

protectionism Protectionism refers to the theory and practice of insulating a nation's firms or workers from foreign competition. (In contrast, FREE TRADE allows open-market access to foreign industry.) Protectionism can be implemented through taxes on imports (TARIFFS) or with quantitative limits (quotas) or other devices that discriminate against foreign products. Trade protection can generate tax revenue; increase national economic self-sufficiency; offset competitive advantages of foreign producers, such as lower wages; and enhance the welfare of labor and management in protected industries. With these benefits, however, come higher consumer prices and, in most instances, lower welfare for the nation as a whole, because inefficient domestic industries are favored and gains from international trade are reduced.

History. The early 19th century saw the death of MERCANTILISM, an extreme form of protectionism practiced by European governments in their colonies as well as their home countries. In the United States, however, protectionism in the form of tariff restrictions had been the prevailing trade doctrine from the beginning of nationhood. The policy reached a climax in 1930, when Congress passed the Smoot-Hawley Act (see TARIFF ACTS) setting tariff rates averaging 60 percent. Other nations raised tariffs in response, and exports shrank dramatically, deepening the DEPRESSION OF THE 1930s.

The administration of Franklin D. Roosevelt inaugurated (1934) a trade-expansion policy, negotiating mutually advantageous tariff-reduction agreements with other countries. After World War II, the United States led in the establishment of the GENERAL AGREEMENT ON TARIFFS AND TRADE (GATT), aimed at limiting and regulating import barriers. Successive negotiations under GATT auspices reduced U.S. tariffs to less than one-tenth of the Smoot-Hawley level. International trade expanded enormously, contributing to unparalleled Western prosperity.

Protectionism in the 1990s. Today protectionism remains out of favor as a general doctrine in major industrial countries, although selective protection continues through a variety of means. Government procurement can favor products made at home: the Japanese government, for example, has purchased satellites and supercomputers from domestic suppliers. Product standards, ostensibly designed for health and safety purposes, can keep imports out. Also, a nation can press another to restrict its exports—as the United States has done with non-European countries on textiles and apparel—through so-called orderly marketing agreements that enforce quota limits.

Trade Relief Procedures. Domestic producers who claim injury from imports can petition the U.S. International Trade Commission to recommend protection. Those who allege unfair practices on the part of foreign governments (who may subsidize exports) or firms (which "dump" products on export markets at prices below the cost of production) can ask the Department of Commerce to impose offsetting duties. Workers who lose jobs because of trade competition can seek adjustment assistance, including unemployment benefits and job retraining.

Those hurt by imports can also seek restrictive legislation. When, for example, the U.S. textile industry did so, Congress responded with a new trade law (1988) that called for aggressive efforts to get other nations to open their markets to U.S. products.

protein   Proteins are molecules essential to maintaining the structure and function of all living organisms. The term *protein* is derived from the Greek word *proteios*, meaning "primary." Proteins have many different properties and function in a variety of ways. For example, ENZYMES; HEMOGLOBIN; the COLLAGEN of bones, tendons, and skin; and certain HORMONES all are proteins.

Amino Acids. Proteins exist in diverse, complex structures that specify their particular function. Despite the variety of structures, however, all proteins comprise about 20 AMINO ACIDS. Each amino acid is composed of an amino group and a carboxyl group as well as a carbon side chain, which specifies the characteristics of the particular amino acid. A primary protein is simply a long chain of amino acids linked together by a peptide bond between the amino group of one and the carboxyl group of another. In addition, the sequence of the amino acids in the chain varies with each type of protein.

The amino acids constituting a protein are arranged in such a way as to give rise to periodic secondary structures. The way in which a protein folds into its final conformation, or shape, is vital to its function.

Special Chemical Groups. Most proteins are polymers of amino acids, but some have other chemical groups attached to them. Lipoproteins contain lipid subunits in addition to the amino acids, glycoproteins contain carbohydrate subunits, phosphoproteins contain phosphoric acid, and nucleoproteins contain nucleic acids. Some proteins have important smaller molecules, known as prosthetic groups, attached to their surfaces; heme, a porphyrin ring containing an iron atom, is an example. It gives hemoglobin and myoglobin the ability to transport and store oxygen.

Protein and Diet. Protein is a critically important part of the diet. Plants synthesize all the amino acids required for building all the necessary proteins. Animals, however, cannot synthesize eight essential amino acids and therefore depend on food to obtain them.

Dietary protein is broken down into amino acids during digestion. These amino acids are absorbed into the bloodstream, where they travel to tissues throughout the body. Cells build up new proteins from these amino acids to serve a specific function. Proteins play a role in virtually every cellular function. For instance, proteins regulate muscle contraction, antibody production, and blood-vessel expansion and contraction to maintain normal blood pressure. Generally, a lack of protein in the diet retards growth in children and causes a decrease in energy. A protein-deficiency disease common in developing countries of Asia, Africa, and South America is KWASHIORKOR, which afflicts children of ages 1 to 4 who are being weaned on starchy food.

In general, however, the average daily protein intake by adults in the United States exceeds the 0.8 to 1.6 gram per kilogram of body weight recommended by the National Academy of Sciences. Excess protein intake puts a strain on the liver and kidneys during excretion, and increased risks of certain cancers and coronary heart disease have been associated with high-protein diets.

See also: DIET, HUMAN; METABOLISM; NUTRITION, HUMAN.

proteins and protein synthesis   see GENETIC CODE

Protestant ethic   The Protestant ethic, also called the work ethic, is a code of morals based on the principles of thrift, discipline, hard work, and individualism. The adjective *Protestant* is explained by the fact that these qualities were seen to have been especially encouraged by the Protestant religion, especially those denominations based on the tenets of CALVINISM. The major formulators of the concept of the Protestant ethic were the German political philosopher and sociologist Max WEBER and the English historian Richard H. Tawney. Both men saw a close relationship between the Protestant ethic and the rise of capitalism.

Protestantism   Protestantism is a movement in Western Christianity whose adherents reject the notion that divine authority is channeled through one particular human institution or person such as the Roman Catholic pope. Protestants look elsewhere for the authority of their faith. Most of them stress the BIBLE—the Hebrew Scriptures and the New Testament—as the source and the norm of their teaching.

The Reformation. Although reform movements have been a feature of the Christian church throughout its history and were particularly evident in the 14th and 15th centuries (see HUSS, JOHN; HUSSITES; LOLLARDS; WYCLIFFE, JOHN), most Protestants date the beginning of their movement to 1517, when the German monk Martin LUTHER posted for debate a series of theses that challenged Roman Catholic teaching. Protestantism took its name from the "Protestatio" issued by reformers at the Diet of Speyer in 1529. Within two decades the REFORMATION had spread through most of northwest Europe. In England, King HENRY VIII repudiated papal authority over the church, and the Church of England (see ENGLAND, CHURCH OF) was set on a course of reform that made it essentially a Protestant body (although Anglicans, also called Episcopalians, are often classified separately). In Switzerland, France, parts of Germany, Scotland, and the Netherlands, a second style of non-Lutheran reform, influenced chiefly by the French-turned-Genevan John CALVIN and the Swiss leader Ulrich ZWINGLI, began to take shape. At the same time, a more radical style of Protestantism appeared on the left wing of the movement. ANABAPTISTS, MENNONITES, and others rebaptized Christians and initiated them into a movement that drastically rejected Catholic practices even where LUTHERANISM, CALVINISM, and Anglicanism did not. The Reformation spread from these bases into Scandinavia, central Europe, and—in the 17th century—North America.

The Authority of the Bible. Protestants have always made much of the Bible, but acceptance of its authority has not led to unanimity among them. Differing interpretations of the same Bible have produced the most divided movement of any in the great world religions, as hundreds of sects in at least a dozen great Protestant families of churches (Anglicanism, CONGREGATIONALISM, METHODISM, PRESBYTERIANISM, Lutheranism, the BAPTIST churches, and the like) compete in free societies. Attitudes toward the Bible in contemporary Protestantism range from belief in its literal truth on the fundamentalist end of the spectrum (see FUNDAMENTALISM) to extremely free interpretations among liberal Protestants.

Justification by Faith. Second only to belief in the Bible as a mark of Protestantism is the conviction that humans are not saved by their merits or good works, as the 16th-century reformers heard Catholics claiming, but only "by grace, through faith." According to Protestants, God took the initiative in saving the world from sin through his activity in Jesus Christ, and even the faith that led people to believe in this activity was a gift, not an achievement. Nonetheless, however consistent Protestant teaching on this subject may be, Protestant cultures have often produced earnest strivers after God—sober and hard-working people who try to prove that they are God's elect (see PREDESTINATION) and preachers or other leaders who seem as legalistic in their approach to church life as the 16th-century Catholics were.

Sacraments. Most Protestants share faith in the divine Trinity—God the Father, Son, and Holy Spirit; most of them keep alive the ancient creedal witness to the fact that Jesus Christ was and is both divine and human; most of them celebrate two SACRAMENTS (sacred acts they believe were instituted by Christ): baptism and the Lord's Supper. They are divided over whether to immerse the baptized in water or to apply water in other ways; over the age at which to baptize people, although most practice infant baptism; over whether baptism imparts grace or is a sign of response and obedience. Some Protestants believe that Jesus is somehow really present in the bread and wine of the Lord's Supper (see EUCHARIST), whereas others consider this sacrament an act of remembrance and obedience. In their worship Protestants more than most other Christians stress the preaching of the Word of God as an agent for building faith.

Church Polity. Protestants allow for many styles of church government, from the episcopal, where bishops rule, to the congregational, which acknowledges no earthly authority beyond the local. Accenting "the priesthood of all believers," they have assigned an important role to the laity, although in practice many Protestant churches are quite clerical in outlook. Increasingly during the past century and especially in recent decades, Protestant churches have ordained women to the ministry and have encouraged them to take lay leadership roles.

Protestantism, more than Roman Catholicism and Orthodoxy, has faced two recurrent problems. The first relates to the internal unity of the movement. From the Reformation until the present, Protestants have sought concord but more often than not have remained in dispute. In the 20th century, however, the ECUMENICAL MOVEMENT has gathered strength. In addition to the organic mergers of separate bodies that have taken place, movements of federation, councils for cooperation, and coalitions for common tasks have been formed (see, for example, NATIONAL COUNCIL OF CHURCHES; WORLD COUNCIL OF CHURCHES).

The second problem involves civil authority. Orthodoxy and Catholicism found alliances with the throne congenial, but Protestants were restless about their early decisions to keep such alliances. Movements for religious toleration were most aggressive and successful in Protestant countries. The act of separating church and state (in most countries) has made it difficult for Protestants to produce coherent views of how Christians should live with both spiritual and civil responsibilities. This problem was presented in its most acute form in the dilemma of the Confessing church in Nazi Germany (see BONHOEFFER, DIETRICH).

Cultural Impact. The rejection of the Catholic tradition and in some instances a tendency toward iconoclasm militated against the development of a specifically Protestant style in the visual arts, although many great artists have been Protestants. In general the Protestant contribution has been a simplicity, even austerity, of design and decoration. This is particularly true of the Calvinist tradition.

In music and literature the Protestant contribution has been enormous. The vernacular versions of the Bible, such as Luther's and the King James Version, played a formative role in the development of modern German and English literature. A strong musical tradition developed out of the encouragement of hymn singing and the use of the organ and other instruments, reaching its pinnacle in the work of Johann Sebastian Bach.

The lack of central authority and thus the acceptability of divergent views has also borne fruit in a rich theological tradition, which embraces such figures as Karl BARTH, Rudolf BULTMANN, and Paul TILLICH in the 20th century.

Proteus [proh'-tee-uhs]   In Greek mythology Proteus was a sea god, the keeper of the seals of Poseidon, with the ability to assume various shapes. Whoever could bind him during his noontime sleep to keep him from changing shape could oblige him to foretell the future. In Homer's *Odyssey*, Menelaus held onto Proteus until he informed him how to return to Sparta. The word *protean* is derived from his name.

Protista [pruh-tis'-tuh]   The kingdom Protista comprises perhaps nine phyla, which include the one-celled heterotrophs (PROTOZOA); eukaryotic algae, including some that are multicellular; and SLIME MOLDS. The term *protista* was proposed by Ernst H. Haeckel in 1868 in order to unite the Protophyta (one-celled plants) and the Protozoa (one-celled animals) into a third "neutral kingdom," along with Metazoa (animals) and Metaphyta (plants). The five-kingdom classification system introduced by R. H. Whittaker in 1969 includes the kingdoms Monera and Fungi, in addition to Protista, Plantae, and Animalia.

Many protists characteristically have flagella or cilia, which if present have a 9 + 2 structural configuration. This refers to the microtubules within the flagella or cilia, which are organized in a circle of nine surrounding two. Others move by pseudopodia (extensions of cytoplasm) or are nonmotile. The eukaryotic cell contains a membrane-bound nucleus; complex membrane-bound organelles, such as mitochondria, and chloroplasts in photosynthetic protists; and DNA combined with protein in chromosomes that are within the nuclear envelope. Protists reproduce both sexually and asexually.

The varied unicellular heterotrophic (incapable of producing food) organisms that make up the Protozoa have been divided into four main groups. The Mastigophora have one or more flagella, and some are parasitic, such as *Trypanosoma gambiense*, which causes African sleeping sickness. The Sarcodina are amoebalike organisms that lack a cell wall and move and feed by pseudopods. The Ciliophora, or ciliates, have cilia of the 9 + 2 structure and include *Paramecium* and *Stentor*. The Sporozoa are parasitic, such as the species of *Plasmodium*, several of which cause malaria.

As many as seven phyla of algae are included in the kingdom Protista, depending on the classification system followed. Algae are differentiated by their accessory photosynthetic pigments, the presence or absence of a cell wall, and the composition of the cell wall if present. Accessory pigments that mask the green of the chlorophyll are responsible for the characteristic colors of many phyla.

Organisms of the phylum Myxophyta, the slime molds, resemble algae, but they are multicellular or are multinucleated in all or most of their life cycle. They reproduce asexually by means of spores.

Protoceratops [proh-toh-sair'-uh-tahps]   *Protoceratops* is the oldest of the horned dinosaur group, the suborder Ceratopsia in the order Ornithischia. Known from a great many skeletons collected in the Gobi Desert of Mongolia from Late Cretaceous strata, about 90 million years old, it is one of the few dinosaurs whose young and near-hatching stages are known. The dozens of fossil eggs attributed to *Protoceratops* were the first dinosaur eggs to be discovered (1922). *Protoceratops*, a herbivore, was about 2 m (6.5 ft) long and weighed 140 kg (300 lb) or more. It had a large turtle-beaked head, almost as long as the trunk of the body, and the flattened parietal and squamosal bones at the rear of the skull were flared out to form a crest, or frill; unlike its descendants, it had no

Protoceratops is an early primitive horned dinosaur, one of a group of herbivorous reptiles with heavily armored heads. More than 80 specimens of Protoceratops have been found.

horns. *Protoceratops* has been found only in Asia, but all of its descendants are known only from North America (see TRICERATOPS).

Protocols of the Elders of Zion   *The Protocols of the Elders of Zion* was the title of a forged treatise purporting to outline the plans of a late-19th-century council of Jews to subvert Christianity and seize control of the world. The treatise first appeared in its entirety in Russia in 1905 but was apparently written in France in the 1890s by members of the Russian secret police. They based their contents on Maurice Joly's satire on Napoleon III—*Dialogue aux Enfers entre Machiavel et Montesquieu* (A Dialogue in Hell between Machiavelli and Montesquieu, 1864). Although the *Times* (London) revealed the forgery in 1921, the *Protocols* was translated into many languages and circulated widely in Europe and the United States during the 1920s and '30s. It was cited as the classical defense for anti-Semitism, especially by the National Socialists in Germany.

Proton [proh'-tahn]   The Proton rocket is a Soviet space launch vehicle intermediate in size between the U.S. Saturn IB and Saturn V. Proton has been developed in several versions since it was first introduced in 1965 to launch the 12.2-metric ton (11.1-U.S. ton) high-energy-particles satellites, also known as Proton.

As originally introduced, the vehicle, designated by U.S. experts as Proton D, had two stages that could lift a payload of about 18,000 kg (40,000 lb). The first stage comprised six strap-on boosters that jettisoned after use; the engines operated at a high combustion pressure. The second stage comprised the propulsion element of the central core, which ignited at a given altitude. Engine details of this stage have not been revealed. This combination was used to launch *Protons 1, 2*, and *3* (1965–66) and another research satellite of the same type that failed to reach orbit. The heavier *Proton 4* (1968) weighed 17 metric tons (15.5 U.S. tons) and required the addition of a third stage attached to the top of the sustainer core. An added fourth stage resulted in the D-1-E launcher, which sent new-generation space probes to the Moon, Mars, and Venus. All four stages used liquid propellants.

A further development of the three-stage launcher, the Proton D-1-H, is responsible for launching the heavy COSMOS modules and the 18.5-metric-ton (16.8-U.S.-ton) SALYUT space stations into orbit. Liftoff thrust is approximately 1,360,800 kg (3,000,000 lb).

proton [proh'-tahn]   The proton was the second subatomic FUNDAMENTAL PARTICLE to be identified. Long before the nuclear structure of the atom was determined, William Prout conjectured (1815) that all ATOMS were complexes of hydrogen, the lightest atom then known. When the hydrogen atom was recognized as a combination of an electron and a positive nucleus and when protons ("H rays") were observed ejected from atoms by alpha particle bombardment, the Prout hypothesis was adopted, temporarily, in a modified form. Ernest RUTHERFORD discovered (1919) the proton as a product of the disintegration of the atomic nucleus.

In modern physics the positively charged proton, with its uncharged NEUTRON partner, provide the basic constituents for the interpretation of the structure and interactions of atomic nuclei. As an elementary particle it is the most stable of all the BARYONS, with a mass 1,836.11 times the electron mass—approximately 2.5 electron masses lighter than the neutron. The proton may well have an infinite lifetime; the inability to observe proton decay indicates a lifetime longer than 10^{28} years, a period much greater than the age of the universe. The proton's electromagnetic behavior, when probed at high energy, indicates a complex structure. The behavior of the proton is essentially that of a system of three QUARKS, two of which have a positive electric charge equal to $2/3$ of the electron's charge, and the other having a negative charge of $1/3$ of the electron's charge. The proton cannot divide into separate quarks. Although some scientists have predicted proton decay, it has never been observed.

proton-proton reaction   see STAR

---

protoplasm   The term *protoplasm* was first used in the 19th century to describe the thick, translucent matter found in living cells. This substance, basic to life activities, is a complex solution of such materials as salts and simple sugars, with other molecules, mostly proteins and fats, in a colloidal state, that is, dispersed but not dissolved in one another. Carbon, hydrogen, oxygen, and nitrogen constitute more than 90 percent of protoplasm. Knowledge of the intricate structure of the cell has reduced use of the general term *protoplasm*.

Protozoa   [proh-tuh-zoh'-uh] The Protozoa (Latin: *proto*, "first"; *zoa*, "animals") are a diverse collection of microscopic organisms. Most protozoans qualify as animals because, unlike pigmented plants—to which some Protozoa are otherwise nearly identical—they cannot live on simple organic compounds. Some protozoologists recommend that the classification group Protozoa, as the term is commonly used, should be spelled with a small "p." The reason they give is that modern evidences, both structural and biochemical, indicate that the designation "protozoa" is a term of convenience rather than a genuine classification group, or taxon.

Classification problems have arisen with such genera as *Euglena*, which has chloroplasts and is photosynthetic but ingests food in the dark, and *Astasia*, which is similar to *Euglena* but lacks chloroplasts. Some biologists claim that such genera are protozoans, whereas others consider them to be ALGAE. Some scientists favor using the single kingdom PROTISTA, subdivided into groups, one of which is Protozoa. In this system Protozoa contain all unicellular animals that do not resemble plants. In the kingdom Protista other phyla are set aside for unicellular plants and those organisms which exhibit both animal and plant characteristics.

A problem also arises when defining Protozoa as unicellular organisms. In fact, the growing opinion among protozoologists is that so-called single-celled animals and plants are not genuinely single celled. There is increasing evidence that many, if not all, of the EUKARYOTE cell's organelles were originally free-living, non–organelle-bearing PROKARYOTE cells. In some way as yet unknown, these original prokaryote cells were incorporated into other prokaryote cells, thus giving rise to eukaryote cells.

Many species of Protozoa exhibit individuality at the multicellular level. In some, such as the ciliated protozoans *Carchesium* and *Zoothamnium*, various members of the cell progeny (zooids) of a single cell remain together as a colony, physically connected to each other and, in some species, reacting simultaneously as a unit to a stimulus applied to any one cell of the colony. Such colonies commonly have a specific form. Within a colony, all cells of zooids may be alike in form or structure, or some may be visibly differentiated to function as migrators, or generative cells that leave the colony to found new colonies.

A second form of higher-order individuality is shown by certain amoeboid Protozoa, such as the SLIME MOLD *Dictyostelium*. (Some systems classify slime molds with the kingdom FUNGI.) The amoebas feed and reproduce asexually, as separate individuals. When the food supply (bacteria) is exhausted, however, neighboring amoebas aggregate into a mass that moves as a unit and develops into an erect structure in which some cells form a stalk and others, at the top, form a capsule in which each amoeba transforms into a spore, later to be blown about to find food and repeat the cycle.

Another form of individuality in the life cycle appears in the ciliated protozoan *Paramecium*. A fertilized cell asexually produces a large clone by repeated cell division. Changes occur in the character of the cells, such that those produced in earlier generations are unable to conjugate, whereas later generations can conjugate with compatible mating types.

Classification

All schemes for classifying the approximately 40,000 known protozoan species recognize four main classes, based on modes of locomotion. The Mastigophora use principally flagella for locomotion. The Sarcodina move mainly by means of temporary extensions of the cell in the form of pseudopodia. The Ciliophora move by means of cilia. The Sporozoa lack flagella, cilia, and pseudopodia. Many species of Protozoa have both pseudopodial and flagellated stages.

Structure and Function

Some types of Protozoa, such as some amoebas, are minute, formless, and seemingly simple and homogeneous in structure. Others, such as radiolaria, possess shells of amazing intricacy and beauty. Still others, such as *Stentor* and *Paramecium,* are large and among the structurally most complex cells known. The largest, a fossil marine Protozoa of the order Foraminifera, exceeds 19 cm (7.6 in) in diameter.

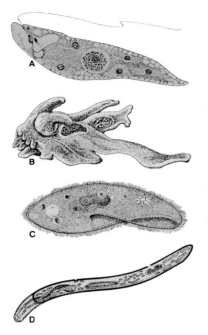

Protozoans can be classified in four main groups on the basis of type of locomotion. The Mastigophora, which include Euglena (A), *move by means of flagella. Sarcodines, such as* Amoeba proteus (B), *possess flowing extensions of the cell known as pseudopodia, which are used for both locomotion and capturing food. The Ciliophora, including* Paramecium aurelia (C), *move by ciliary action. The malaria-producing* Plasmodium (D) *belongs to the Sporozoa, a class of parasitic protozoans that lack specialized organelles of motion.*

under the electron microscope to be quite similar, with similar arrangements of microtubules.

Reproduction

Most protozoans reproduce asexually, and in some species this is the only means of REPRODUCTION. Fission is the division of the cell into two similar daughter cells. Multiple fission occurs in some protozoans. After a varying number of nuclear divisions, the cell divides into a number of daughter cells.

Sexual reproduction may involve fusion of identical gametes or differing gametes (anisogametes). In the latter case the differences range from slight variations in size to well-differentiated sperm and eggs. In ciliated protozoans, distinct gametes are not formed. The two animals adhere to each other and exchange nuclei, a process termed conjugation. Each migrating nucleus fuses with a stationary nucleus to form a zygote nucleus (synkaryon).

The life cycle of many protozoans, especially freshwater species, includes encystment. Protozoans form cysts by secreting envelopes around themselves and become

The protozoan cell shows all the main features of the cells of higher animals. The body is usually bounded by only a membrane. Nonliving coverings, ranging from simple cellulose to shells, are found in some groups. The many functions in protozoan cells take place by means of organelles, specialized parts of the protoplasm. The nucleus may be densely packed, or contain a large amount of nucleoplasm and one or more nucleoli. Many protozoans have one or more contractile vacuoles, which act as pumps to remove excess water. Tubules and vesicles, in the cytoplasm, empty their contents into the main vacuole during its filling stage. The vacuoles periodically collapse, releasing fluid to the outside.

Within food vacuoles, the contents are digested by enzymes in an alkaline fluid that originates from the cytoplasm. Products are absorbed and the undigestible waste is egested. During digestion and absorption, small vesicles surround the outer membrane of the vacuole. They are believed to aid the transfer of material to the cytoplasm.

Gas exchange occurs by diffusion of oxygen across the cell membrane. Many protozoans live in other animals or in water. They can exist on little or no oxygen. Some are facultative anaerobes, using oxygen when present but also capable of respiration without oxygen. Ammonia is the major waste.

Motility of these organisms may be accomplished, generally, in two ways: either by the formation of pseudopodia or by the possession of one or sometimes many FLAGELLA and cilia. For example, *Chlamydomonas* is flagellated, whereas *Paramecium* is heavily ciliated. The eukaryotic cilium and flagellum, although they appear different when observed under a light microscope, are seen

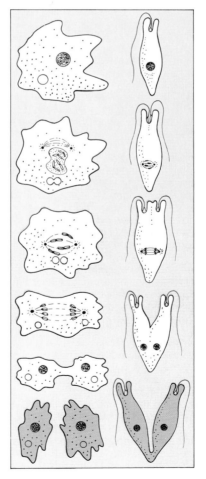

Protozoans most commonly multiply by binary fission—the splitting of one cell into two similar "daughter" cells. Before dividing, Amoeba (left) *withdraws its larger pseudopodia, and the chromosomes in the nucleus separate. As the nucleus divides, the cell stretches and constricts in the middle, and the two daughter cells begin to pull apart.* Euglena (right) *and other flagellates split lengthwise from front to back, forming two approximately equal cells. The euglena begins to separate at the anterior end as the bases of the flagella also divide. As the cell continues to split, the nucleus divides and new organelles are formed. The beating of the new flagella pulls the two daughter cells completely apart.*

inactive. This action protects the organism from unfavorable environmental conditions. Protozoans may be dispersed a great distance by water current, wind, and other animals.

Importance

The existence of protozoans remained unrecognized until the development of crude compound light microscopes and, especially, certain types of magnifying glasses. Among the latter the foremost were those built and used by the 17th-century Dutch scientist Antoni van LEEUWEN-HOEK, who has come to be considered the father of protozoology. Since that time, Protozoa have come to be one of the most studied groups of animals. Few, if any, aspects of biology are without important contributions from the study of Protozoa.

Protozoa were found first in lake water, then in a wide range of other habitats, including moist earth, air, and plants and animals. Explorations of ocean life revealed thousands of species of shelled Protozoa, Foraminifera and Radiolaria, that were preserved as fossils in sedimentary rocks. Eventually it was realized that the presence of certain species of protozoan fossils indicated the proximity of oil deposits. In a sense, another use of Protozoa is in the building-stone industry: the pyramids in Egypt and many other structures in the world have been built with stone that consists largely of protozoan shells.

The Protozoa played a role in advancing the germ theory of disease. In 1870, Louis PASTEUR succeeded in demonstrating that a disease of silkworms, which was threatening the silk industry, was caused by a protozoan, the cnidosporidian, *Nosema*. This was the first study of a parasitic protozoan that resulted in effective practical control.

Of the nearly 30 species of Protozoa occurring in human beings, the most medically important are the several species of *Plasmodium* that cause malarias; the species of *Trypanosoma* that cause African sleeping sickness, Chagas' disease, and other diseases; and the amoeba (*Entamoeba histolytica*) that causes dysentery. The most common protozoan parasite in humans is the Sporozoan, *Toxoplasma*, but it rarely produces disease.

Other species of Protozoa parasitize plants, insects, worms, snails, and all kinds of vertebrates. It has been suggested that insects and many other multicellular animals are parasitized by at least one species of Protozoa that normally parasitizes no other species. If this is the case, the number of species of parasitic Protozoa may well be in the millions.

Beginning in the late 19th century fundamental advances in biology were made that led to vast new areas of knowledge about the Protozoa. Some Protozoa, especially *Paramecium* and other ciliates, were among the organisms first examined (1888–89) by scientists for nuclear division, meiosis, and fertilization. Among the distinctive 20th-century contributions to the knowledge of Protozoa is the analysis of their behavior.

Another area of increasingly important study is genetics. H. S. Jennings (1868–1947) at Johns Hopkins University initiated studies of heredity in Protozoa; his most

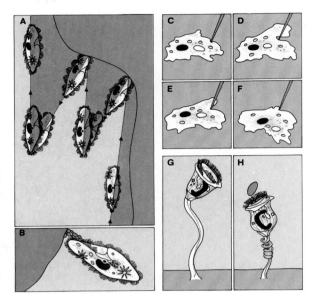

Protozoans respond to mechanical stimuli. If Paramecium *meets an obstacle (A), it normally backs up, turns about 30° to the side, and starts forward again; this process repeats until a free path is found. In a bacteria-rich culture,* Paramecium *may cling to an object (B), an action believed to facilitate food capture.* Amoeba *reacts (C, D, E, F) to harmful objects by retracting its pseudopodia and changing direction.* Vorticella, *a stalked ciliate, is usually extended (G) but contracts its stalk like a corkscrew (H) after contact with an object.*

important result was the discovery of the genetic constancy of the asexually produced progeny of a single cell, the clone. This discovery was formulated as the Pure Line Theory for Asexual Reproduction, which is the basic theory or law underlying all cell heredity in all organisms. Mating types were later discovered in *Paramecium*, and for the first time Protozoa could be crossbred in the way higher organisms are crossbred. This discovery led to the modern genetics of Protozoa.

---

protozoal diseases [proh-tuh-zoh'-ul]   Protozoal diseases are parasitic infectious diseases caused by the single-celled Protozoa. In general, these diseases are widespread, especially in the warmer climates. Some require intermediate hosts, such as mosquitoes, for transmission. Most of the diseases are associated with poor socioeconomic conditions.

A variety of protozoal diseases commonly affect humans. African forms of TRYPANOSOMIASIS are caused by the parasitic flagellates *Trypanosoma brucei gambiense* and *T. b. rhodesiense*, which invade the central nervous system. The organisms are transmitted to humans by the bite of tsetse flies (genus *Glossina*). Chagas' disease, or South American trypanosomiasis, is caused by *T. cruzi* and occurs primarily in young children. The intermediate host is a blood-sucking insect (triatome). LEISHMANIASIS is a group of diseases affecting different tissues and caused by several species of *Leishmania*, which are related to trypanosomes and are transmitted by sand flies.

Giardiasis is an infection of the intestinal tract caused by the flagellated protozoan *Giardia lamblia* (see GIARDIA). It is transmitted directly from person to person by fecal contamination. AMEBIASIS, also known as amoebic dysentery, is caused by an amoeba, *Entamoeba histolytica*. It is also transmitted by fecal contamination of food and water.

MALARIA, characterized by chills, fever, sweating, and anemia, is caused by *Plasmodium vivas, P. falciparum, P. malariae*, and *P. ovale*. These parasites are transmitted to humans by the bite of the anopheles mosquito.

Protura [pruh-tue'-ruh]   The order Protura comprises minute insects that live in moist soil, humus, and leaf mold, where they use their suctorial mouthparts to feed on decomposing plant matter. They are pale and 0.6–1.5 mm (0.024–0.06 in) long, with cone-shaped heads that lack eyes and antennae. The first pair of legs is usually raised and serves primarily as a sensory structure. The order consists of 4 families, and about 20 species are known in North America.

Proudhon, Pierre Joseph [proo-dohn']   French social philosopher Pierre Joseph Proudhon, b. Jan. 15, 1809, d. Jan. 19, 1865, was an anarchist and writer whose work contributed to radical thought in mid- and late-19th-century France and Germany and influenced the French syndicalists (see SYNDICALISM). Born to a working-class family in Besançon, Proudhon, largely self-educated, learned Latin, Greek, and Hebrew and earned (1838) a scholarship to study in Paris. There he wrote *What Is Property?* (1840), an indictment of the abuses of concentrated wealth that included the famous statement "property is theft." Acquitted (1843) of charges relating to his book *Property, Warning to Proprietors*, Proudhon fled to Lyon but returned to Paris as an active participant in the Revolution of 1848. He was elected to the Constituent Assembly but was later imprisoned (1849–52) because of his radical sympathies. His *Philosophy of Poverty* (1846) is his most famous work.

Proust, Marcel   Marcel Proust, b. July 10, 1871, d. Nov. 18, 1922, was a French writer whose seven-volume work *À la Recherche du temps perdu* (1913–27; trans. as *Remembrance of Things Past*, 1922–31) is among the few novels that have radically changed the genre. It concerns the narrator's attempt to recapture the past through a sustained effort of memory, whose re-creations of experience are based on trains of association sparked by chance events.

Proust was born in Paris, the elder son of a wealthy Roman Catholic doctor and his cultivated Jewish wife. Extreme sensitivity and a Jewish background separated Proust from his schoolmates, and early in life he sought to leave his solid, middle-class milieu for the world of

The French novelist Marcel Proust's multivolume Remembrance of Things Past *(1913–27) is an exploration of the power of memory to preserve experience and conquer the passage of time. This semiautobiographical work is among the most extraordinary works of modern fiction.*

aesthetic sensation. Never robust, Marcel suffered frequent severe attacks of asthma from the age of nine. He was nevertheless a brilliant student, mastering law and political science as well as literature. In his youth Proust often contributed criticism and reviews to leading periodicals. This, plus a delicate wit and a gift for conversation, gained him entry to many of the exclusive salons of Paris. There Proust mingled with high society, gaining many of the impressions that would later be transmuted into the fictional world of his novel.

In 1896, Proust published *Les Plaisirs et Les Jours* (trans. as *Pleasures and Regrets*, 1948), a volume of short stories, social vignettes, and poems that reflected the snobbish concerns and elegant tastes of the aristocratic world. At about this time Proust also announced his support for Captain Dreyfus, a Jewish army officer accused of treason (see DREYFUS AFFAIR), taking an unpopular stand that placed him squarely in opposition to the aristocrats he numbered as friends.

In 1895, Proust began a rambling, impressionistic novel dealing with personal experiences in Paris and Normandy, the summer retreat of his childhood. Here again his characteristic preoccupations are evident, as are the shadowy forms of characters that would eventually be realized in *Remembrance of Things Past*. This work was put aside in 1899 and forgotten until it was discovered among the author's papers and assembled under the title *Jean Santeuil* (1952; Eng. trans., 1955).

What probably deflected Proust from his first attempt at fiction was a translation of the works of the English writer John Ruskin, the leading aesthetician of Proust's day, and one whose sensibilities and attitudes toward art Proust vehemently upheld. With the help of his mother, Proust translated Ruskin's *Bible of Amiens* (1885) in 1904 and *Sesame and Lilies* (1865) in 1906, adding lengthy prefaces to both. During this period Proust continued to write his society notes, portraits, and reviews for

Parisian periodicals and newspapers. Some of these were published in *Pastiches et Mélanges* (Pastiches and Miscellanies, 1914); others were gathered in *Textes retrouvés* (Rediscovered Writings, 1968).

Proust's asthma had grown so severe by 1902 that he was forced to curtail his social life. The death of his mother in 1905 marked the beginning of his total withdrawal from society. In the year following her death, he had the walls of his room lined with cork to shut out light and sound. There he retreated to think and write, sleeping during the day and venturing forth at night, much in the manner of the fictional Marcel who narrates *Remembrance of Things Past.* Although he published little of importance until 1913, Proust was engaged in making notes and jotting down observations on his favorite subjects—painting and literature.

In 1908 he began an extended essay in opposition to Charles Augustin SAINTE-BEUVE's critical method, which approached a work through its author's biography. Proust rejected biographical criticism and stressed the importance of dealing with the literary text on its own terms. This essay, fragments of which are known today as *Contre Sainte-Beuve* (1954; Eng. trans., 1958), included dialogues between a narrator and his mother that dealt with a variety of writers and literary problems and soon grew to vast length. The fictional framework eventually submerged the literary essay, and by 1910, Proust was intensely involved in writing what became *À la Recherche du temps perdu.* Originally conceived in three parts, the first, *Du côté de chez Swann* (trans. as *Swann's Way,* 1934), appeared late in 1913, but the death of his beloved chauffeur Alfred Agostinelli and the outbreak of the war in 1914 halted publication of the other two volumes. During the war years Proust continued to work on his novel, increasing its size to the present seven volumes. The Goncourt prize, awarded to Proust for the second section, *À l'Ombre des jeunes filles en fleurs* (trans. as *Within a Budding Grove*), in 1919 brought him to public attention.

In declining health and isolated from the outside world, Proust literally wrote himself to death. When he died, his novel was two-thirds published; the remainder was in rough draft form. Later writers, confronted by Proust's achievement, have been obliged either to follow Proustian themes or techniques or to reject his particular solution to the problems of narration and develop entirely different conceptions of the novel.

Provençal language   see ROMANCE LANGUAGES

Provençal literature [proh-vahn-sahl']   Provençal literature, which has exercised an immense influence on Western literature from medieval times, was inaugurated in southern France in the 11th century by the appearance of poems in the vernacular. Alternatively known as Provençal, or *langue d'oc*, this tongue had long been in everyday use, but until the troubadours (see MINSTRELS, MINNESINGERS, AND TROUBADOURS) adopted it for the works they performed at the courts of the southern French aristocracy, Latin had been the language favored by writers and poets.

These wandering troubadours composed splendid political, religious, and satiric verse, but their greatest works were their love lyrics, which generally celebrated the virtues of COURTLY LOVE. In the 10 or 11 surviving works of Guillaume IX, duke of Aquitaine (1071–1127), nearly all the distinctive traits of Provençal poetry are already developed: the theme of the ennobling effect of love; religious and political concerns; the singer's boastful pride in the craft; and the technical virtuosity of lyrics that made use of difficult rhyme schemes, complex strophic forms, and a rhetoric capable of both the highest refinement and the coarsest outbursts.

The next generation of troubadours included Jaufré Rudel (fl. mid-12th century), celebrated for his lyrics on the theme of "distant love," and Marcabrun (fl. *c.*1130–48), who attacked the profligacy of the courtly class. Among the greatest poets of 12th-century Provence were BERNART DE VENTADORN, who distinguished himself at the court of ELEANOR OF AQUITAINE; Peire Vidal (*c.*1180–1206), the most personal and self-assertive of the troubadours; Peire Cardenal (*c.*1225–72), a master of satiric poetry; Arnaut DANIEL; and Guiraut Riquier (*c.*1230–92), known as "the last troubadour."

In the period 1208–29, the Albigensian Crusade crushed most of the southern courts, depriving the troubadours of their support. A popular, somewhat debased Provençal literature nevertheless survived for another six centuries. With the founding (1854) of the Félibrige movement by such poets as Frédéric MISTRAL, Théodore Aubanel (1829–86), and Joseph Roumanille (1818–91), Provençal literature underwent a significant revival in the 19th century, and similar efforts at renewal are in progress today.

Provence [proh-vahns']   Provence is a historic province in southeastern France along the Mediterranean Sea. AIX-EN-PROVENCE was its capital. The area is now divided into the departments of Alpes-de-Haute-Provence, Alpes-Maritimes, Bouches-du-Rhône, Hautes-Alpes, Var, and Vaucluse.

Colonies of Greeks developed in Provence from the 6th century BC, including Massalia—now MARSEILLE. In 125 BC, Rome came to the defense of Massalia against invading Celts; by 121 BC the Romans had established Transalpine Gaul, the first Roman province. After the decline of the Roman Empire, Visigoths, Burgundians, and Ostragoths invaded the region. After *c.*536, the Franks controlled the area. Subjected to frequent invasions by Moors in the 8th century, the area was defended by the Frankish king CHARLES MARTEL. From 855 until 863 it was part of the First Kingdom of Provence, and from 879 until 933 the area was part of the Kingdom of Arles. In 1032, Provence was absorbed by the Holy Roman Empire. A local dynasty ruled until 1113, when the House of Barcelona gained control and brought about the highest period of Provençal literature and culture. The ANGEVIN dynasty of

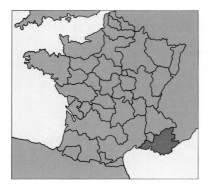

The shaded portion of the map indicates the location of Provence, a historic region in southeastern France bordering Italy. During the medieval period, Provence developed a distinctive literary tradition based on its unique language (Provençal).

Naples ruled most of the area after 1246; the popes took up residence at AVIGNON in 1309, remaining until 1376. In 1481, Provence was willed to the French crown.

proverb   Proverbs are usually homely, witty, and colorful statements of general truth and wisdom, especially of a moral nature. They are often stated in an alliterative or rhymed form, as in Benjamin Franklin's "Early to bed, early to rise, makes a man healthy, wealthy, and wise." Along with aphorisms (from the medical *Aphorisms* of Hippocrates) and maxims, they express their truths in pithy, concise, memorable forms.

Proverbs, Book of   The Book of Proverbs, in the Old Testament of the Bible, is a grouping of wisdom sayings and longer, connected poems composed from the 10th to the 4th century BC and finally collected about 300 BC. The sayings are either statements that provoke further thought or admonitions to behave in particular ways. The longer poems celebrate wisdom, encourage its observance, and personify it as a woman who at God's right hand assisted in creation. Egyptian wisdom is evident in Proverbs, making it possible to date the nucleus of the book to preexilic times. The book is conventionally attributed to Solomon as the prototype of Israelite wisdom, but many sages had a hand in composing and collecting the subsections.

Providence   Providence is the capital and largest city of Rhode Island. Located in the northeastern part of the state on the Providence River at the head of Narragansett Bay, it has a population of 160,728 (1990) and is the seat of Providence County. Providence is primarily a manufacturing city noted for its silverware, jewelry, and electronic equipment. It is also the state's commercial and transportation center and is one of New England's largest seaports. A historic city, Providence contains the Providence Athenaeum library (1753) as well as the Stephen Hopkins House (completed 1755) and the First Baptist Meetinghouse (1775). BROWN UNIVERSITY and the Rhode

Island School of Design (1877) are there.

The site of the present city was purchased from the Narragansett Indians by Roger WILLIAMS in 1638 and developed as a refuge for religious dissenters. Burned by the Indians during King Philip's War (1675–76), Providence began to exploit its harbor 4 years later and flourished as a center for the rum, slave, and molasses trade. Industrialization was swift following the American Revolution, during which it was headquarters for American and French soldiers. The Rhode Island Independence Act was signed in the city on May 4, 1776. Providence became the state's sole capital in 1900.

Provincetown   Provincetown is a town in Barnstable County, Mass., at the tip of Cape Cod. Its population is 3,561 (1990). Provincetown is a commercial fishing center and—in the summer—a tourist center and art colony. The Provincetown Players, a theatrical group, was founded in 1915. The site was the first landing place of the Pilgrims in the New World (1620). Province Lands, to the north of the present town, was settled before 1700; it prospered as a fishing, whaling, and salt-making center. Provincetown harbor was used by the British as a base during the American Revolution and the War of 1812.

Provo   [proh'-voh]   A city in north central Utah and the seat of Utah County, Provo is 61 km (38 mi) southeast of Salt Lake City on the Provo River. It has a population of 86,835 (1990). Provo's industries manufacture steel, iron, and metal products, and the city is also a marketing and distribution center for the area's farms and mines. BRIGHAM YOUNG UNIVERSITY (1875) is located there. Provo was settled in 1849 by Mormon pioneers.

Proxima Centauri   see CENTAURUS

Proxmire, William   [prahks'-myr]   Edward William Proxmire, b. Lake Forest, Ill., Nov. 11, 1915, became the

William Proxmire, a Wisconsin Democrat, was first elected to the U.S. Senate in 1957. Proxmire conducted a much-publicized campaign against excessive government spending, instituting an award called the Golden Fleece for projects he deemed especially wasteful of taxpayers' money.

Democratic U.S. senator from Wisconsin in 1957. After studying at Yale and Harvard universities, he moved to Wisconsin, where he served (1951–52) in the state assembly. In 1957 he won a special election to fill the unexpired term of Sen. Joseph R. McCarthy. He was reelected to five more terms and retired in 1989.

In the Senate he became known as an opponent of waste in government, while voting as a liberal on issues supported by environmentalists and consumer groups. He served as chairman of the Banking, Housing, and Urban Affairs Committee from 1975 to 1981 and from 1987 to 1989.

Prudhoe Bay [prood'-oh]   Prudhoe Bay is an inlet of the Arctic Ocean on the northern coast of Alaska. The bay is closed by ice for much of the year. Lying north of the Brooks Range, Prudhoe Bay borders Alaska's petroleum-rich North Slope. The explorer Sir John Franklin reached the bay in 1826, but the area remained barren and deserted until 1968, when petroleum was discovered there. At the outlet of the Sagavanirktok River lies the town of Prudhoe Bay. The Trans-Alaska Pipeline, from Prudhoe Bay to Valdez, Alaska, now permits the transport of crude petroleum throughout the year.

Prud'hon, Pierre Paul [proo-dohn']   Pierre Paul Prud'hon, b. Apr. 4, 1758, d. Feb. 16, 1823, was a leading French romantic painter of portraits and subject pictures. Prud'hon was greatly influenced by the delicate and charming neoclassicism of the sculptor Antonio Canova, and by the works of Correggio and Leonardo da Vinci, whose soft modeling he attempted to emulate. In contrast to the clarity of Jacques Louis David's painting style, Prud'hon developed a more poetic technique that soon found favor. The distinctly different styles of the two great romantic artists made them competitors for Napoleonic commissions. At his best, as in his portrait of Empress Josephine (1805; Louvre, Paris), Prud'hon combined an air of mystery and vague melancholy with an almost sentimental seductiveness to create images of great charm and grace. In his subject paintings Prud'hon tended to avoid heroic and tragic themes, concentrating instead on the more domestic ideals of happiness, love, and friendship.

prune   see PLUM

Prusser, Gabriel   see Gabriel (slave)

Prussia [pruh'-shuh]   *Prussia* was the name used for the region on the southeast coast of the Baltic Sea that the Hohenzollern dynasty organized into a hereditary duchy under Polish suzerainty in 1525. When it became a kingdom, with its capital at Berlin, in 1701, its territories stretched from the Rhine to the Niemen River. Prussia was the state around which modern Germany was unified in 1871. After World War I, Prussia continued to exist as the largest *Land* (state) within the Weimar Republic and Adolf Hitler's Third Reich. After World War II it was dissolved by decree of the Allied Control Council in 1947.

EXPANSION OF BRANDENBURG – PRUSSIA, 1415-1815

The original Prussians were pagan peoples who were conquered by the TEUTONIC KNIGHTS in the mid-13th century. Two centuries later the knights succumbed to the growing power of Poland-Lithuania. Under terms of the second Peace of Toruń (1466), they ceded their territories west of the Vistula River to the Poles; their eastern possessions became a fief of the Polish crown. In 1511 the knights elected as their grand master Margrave Albert of Ansbach from the Franconian line of the house of Hohenzollern (see ALBERT, 1ST DUKE OF PRUSSIA).

In 1611, Ducal Prussia passed to the Hohenzollern elector of Brandenburg, John Sigismund. His grandson, FREDERICK WILLIAM, known as the Great Elector, gained sovereignty over Ducal Prussia in 1660 and laid the foundations of a professional army and centralized bureaucracy, thus turning Brandenburg-Prussia into an ascendant European power.

The status of Prussia rose rapidly during the 18th century. In 1701, Frederick William's son secured the title King in Prussia from Holy Roman Emperor LEOPOLD I in exchange for Hohenzollern support in the War of the Spanish Succession. He ruled as FREDERICK I. Soon all of the Hohenzollern provinces were collectively called the Kingdom of Prussia. By building a strong army of 80,000 men and creating a tightly knit administrative system to sustain his troops, FREDERICK WILLIAM I (r. 1713–40) gave to the Prussian state a militaristic and bureaucratic character. He also acquired Swedish Pomerania, with the port city of Stettin, in 1720. Prussia's most celebrated ruler was FREDERICK II, known as Frederick the Great (r. 1740–86). He made Prussia a dominant European power when he wrested Silesia from the Austrians in 1740. By obtaining West Prussia in the first partition of Poland (1772; see POLAND, PARTITIONS OF), he at last linked Brandenburg and East Prussia.

Frederick the Great's nephew and successor, FREDERICK WILLIAM II (r. 1786–97), added the old family lands of Ansbach and Bayreuth to his kingdom in addition to extensive territories in the east through the second and third partitions of Poland (1793 and 1795). Prussia did not fare well in the era of the FRENCH REVOLUTIONARY WARS and NAPOLEONIC WARS. Compelled to surrender its provinces west of the Rhine in 1795, Prussia remained out of the wars until 1806, when it was badly beaten at the Battle of Jena-Auerstädt. By the Treaties of TILSIT (1807), Napoleon stripped away nearly half of Prussia's territory. Subsequently, however, Prussia played a prominent role in the liberation of Germany from French occupation. The Congress of Vienna (1814–15) awarded Prussia Posen, Swedish Pomerania, parts of Saxony, Westphalia, and the Rhineland.

During the first half of the 19th century, Prussia vied with Austria for influence in the GERMAN CONFEDERATION. Otto von BISMARCK, who became chief minister in 1862, provoked—and won—wars with Denmark (1864), Austria (1866), and France (1870–71), completing the unification of Germany under Prussian leadership. On Jan. 18, 1871, King WILLIAM I of Prussia was proclaimed German emperor (or kaiser). Although Prussia was now a federal state within the new empire, it comprised two-thirds of the population and land area and dominated German policy until the end of World War I.

The last Prussian monarch, German Emperor WILLIAM II, was forced to abdicate (1918) after the German defeat in World War I. Prussia was incorporated into the Weimar Republic, retaining its disproportionate size but without an overriding influence in political affairs. What remained of Prussian autonomy disappeared on Jan. 30, 1934, when Hitler eliminated the governments of the various German states. Thereafter, Prussia functioned as an administrative unit until the collapse of the Nazi regime in 1945.

Przewalski's horse [pshuh-vahl'-skee] Przewalski's horse, *Equus przewalskii przewalskii*, is the last surviving subspecies of the wild true HORSE. Remaining known specimens exist in zoos. The horse resembles a heavy-boned pony, standing about 12–14 hands (122–142 cm/48–56 in) tall. Its coat is reddish tan, and its mane and tail are dark. It has a whitish nose, a long face, and a strong lower jaw. It was discovered and identified near the Altai Mountains of Central Asia by Russian explorer Nikolai Przhevalsky (1839–88) about 1879. It has changed little since the time of its prehistoric depiction on cave walls in France and Spain.

Przewalski's wild horse was depicted in paintings and sculpture by early Stone Age humans. This horse is cautious near people; a stallion will warn his mares away from farms or towns.

Psalms, Book of [sahmz] The Book of Psalms, in the Old Testament of the BIBLE, is the largest collection of Hebrew religious poetry; it consists of 150 pieces divided

Flowing pen-and-ink drawings accompany the 52d Psalm in the Utrecht Psalter, a 9th-century manuscript of the Book of Psalms. (University Library, Utrecht, Netherlands.)

into 5 sections. Originally spoken or sung in various worship settings, the psalms were composed individually from the 10th through the 4th century BC and compiled in their present form by at least 200 BC. Tradition assigns the psalms to King DAVID, but the titles to particular psalms also name Moses, Solomon, Ethan, Asaph, and the sons of Korah as authors. The psalms are numbered differently in various versions of the Bible.

Like all Hebrew poetry, the psalms are written in parallel lines that balance word masses, images, and thoughts and have the effect of nuancing and emphasizing the sense through a skilled mixture of repetition and variation. The thought in parallel lines may be repeated, contrasted, or extended and qualified. The same literary devices appear also in Canaanite religious poetry from Ugarit in Syria. It is evident that Israel took over these forms and styles along with the Canaanite language. Babylonian, Assyrian, and Egyptian influences are also seen in the psalms.

Many psalms can be classified into major literary types: (1) laments for an individual or for the community that seek to overcome a real threat by direct address to the deity; (2) declarations of praise by an individual or community that may thank God for specific deliverance or more generally laud the divine majesty and goodness in hymns that celebrate his working in nature and in Israel's history; and (3) liturgical psalms that were composed for particular festival rites, such as those accompanying processions in the temple precincts, pilgrimages to Jerusalem, and the recitation of priestly blessings.

psaltery [sawl'-tuh-ree]   The psaltery is a class of instruments in which strings are stretched parallel to a flat soundboard. It is held either in one arm or on the lap and plucked with fingers or plectra. Throughout history it has been cast in various shapes—square, triangular, trapezoidal, winged (like a grand piano), or in the shape of a "pig's head" (*strumento di porco*).

The term *psalterion* was used by the ancient Greeks but probably referred to a HARP-type instrument. The Arabic *qanun*, a true trapezoidal psaltery, was introduced into Spain by the Moors in the 11th century, thereafter spreading throughout western Europe. Other forms of psaltery, however, had been present in Europe from at least the 10th century. The instrument remains in its purest form as the Russian *qusli*.

See also: DULCIMER; ZITHER.

Psamtik I, King of Egypt [sahm'-tik]   Psamtik I, d. 610 BC, king of Egypt (664–610 BC) and founder of the 26th dynasty, reunited Egypt after the longest period of decline in pharaonic history. Between 1069 and 664 BC, Egypt disintegrated into 11 petty kingdoms unable to resist conquest by the Cushites (*c.*730) and the Assyrians (671). In 664 the Assyrians made Psamtik vassal ruler of Saïs, a Delta kingdom. Later, with Assyria distracted elsewhere, Psamtik recruited Greek mercenaries and seized control of northern Egypt. In southern Egypt he used diplomacy to secure the loyalty of local rulers, then gradually replaced them with royal officials. A cultural and economic revival had begun by his death.

pseudepigrapha [soo-duh-pig'-ruh-fuh]   The word *pseudepigrapha*, meaning "books with false titles," refers to books similar in type to those of the Bible whose authors gave them the names of persons of a much earlier period in order to enhance their authority. Among the best known are 3 and 4 Esdras and the Prayer of Manasses, which are included in the APOCRYPHA.

The term is applied to many Jewish and Jewish-Christian books written in the period 200 BC–AD 200. The Jewish books include Jubilees, Enoch, Psalms of Solomon, Assumption (or Testament) of Moses, Testaments of the Twelve Patriarchs, the Sibylline Oracles, and the Apocalypse of Baruch. Fragments of the Damascus Document have been found among the DEAD SEA SCROLLS.

Other pseudepigrapha exist in Greek, Slavonic, and other languages, many of them revisions of Jewish books. These include the Apocalypse of Peter, the Shepherd of HERMAS, and the Ascension of Isaiah. The Gospel of Thomas and the Protoevangelium of James contain many legends about Jesus and Mary and show the influence of GNOSTICISM, as does the Apocalypse of Adam. The Gospel of Nicodemus is composed of the Acts of Pilate and the Harrowing of Hell.

psi   see PARAPSYCHOLOGY

psilocybin [sy-luh-sy'-bin]   The active substance contained in the fruiting bodies of the *Psilocybe mexicana* mushroom, among others, psilocybin is a potent HALLUCI-NOGEN. Taken orally or injected, it produces effects similar to those of the chemically unrelated LSD, and cross-tolerance has been experienced between psilocybin, LSD, and mescaline. The use of mushrooms in religious rituals—to induce visions—by the Indians of Mexico has been documented as far back as the 16th century. The use of psilocybin is illegal in the United States.

psittacosis [sit-uh-koh'-sis] Psittacosis, also called ornithosis or parrot fever, is an infectious form of PNEUMO-NIA caused by the bacteria *Chlamydia psittaci*. The disease is transmitted by various species of birds, although it was once believed that only birds of the parrot family could transmit the disease. When transmitted to humans, psittacosis can produce an infection without symptoms, a mild INFLUENZA-like illness, or a serious form of pneumonia with a mortality rate, if untreated, of up to 40 percent. Psittacosis is usually acquired by breathing the dust from feathers or dried excreta of infected birds. Transmission from person to person is rare. Treatment consists of the antibiotic tetracycline administered for several days.

Pskov [puh-skawf'] Pskov is the capital of Pskov oblast in Russia, a republic of the USSR. Situated on the Velikaya River in northwest European Russia, Pskov has a population of 202,000 (1987 est.). An important center of trade and artisan crafts before the Industrial Revolution, Pskov was largely bypassed by industrial development. Some light manufacturing is focused on ropemaking, electrical engineering, and electronics. Surviving fortress walls, towers, and churches are examples of a distinctive Pskov architectural style favored from the 12th to the 17th century. The ancient walled kremlin, or citadel, contains the Cathedral of the Trinity, dating in its present form from 1699.

Pskov is one of the oldest of Russian cities, first mentioned in historical chronicles of the year 903. It was under the control of Novgorod from the 11th to the 13th century. The city was independent from 1348 until 1510, when it passed to the Muscovite state. The railroad station at Pskov was the site of the abdication of Nicholas II in 1917.

psoriasis [suh-ry'-uh-sis] Psoriasis is a common, non-contagious skin disease characterized by bright red, sharply outlined dry plaques covered with silvery scales, primarily on the knees, elbows, scalp, and lower back. (Itching seldom occurs unless the disease is in an eruptive stage or the lesions are in skin folds.) It is typically accompanied by a stippled appearance of the nails, and sometimes by an arthritis called psoriatic arthritis, which is similar to rheumatoid arthritis. Psoriasis is usually chronic and difficult to treat; patients often experience regressions.

A genetic predisposition to psoriasis exists, but the factors involved are still uncertain. Onset is slow, and the disease can affect any age group. No cure is yet known,

but patients may experience improvement in a warm climate. Topical corticosteroids can reduce or eliminate symptoms for varying periods of time, as can the drug methotrexate combined with intervals of long-wave ultraviolet light exposure. The drug etretinate has been used for extreme forms of psoriasis, but it causes birth defects in the fetuses of pregnant women.

Psyche [sy'-kee] In Greek and Roman mythology Psyche was a beautiful maiden who won the love of Cupid (EROS). He visited her each night but made her pledge never to look upon his divine countenance. Overcome by curiosity, she shone a light on him while he slept. A drop of oil woke him, and he vanished. Psyche begged Venus for help in finding him, but Venus, jealous of Psyche's beauty, assigned her several impossible tasks. At last, with Jupiter's help, Cupid and Psyche were reunited and married, and Psyche became immortal. The story is told by Apuleius in *The Golden Ass*.

psychiatry Psychiatry is the area of medicine concerned with the diagnosis, treatment, and study of disordered behavior. After completion of medical training, physicians generally take a three-year residency in psychiatry to become qualified psychiatrists. Because psychiatry is an area of medicine, psychiatrists tend to view and conceptualize disordered behavior as types of mental illness. Within psychiatry there are a number of divergent schools and theoretical viewpoints, ranging from those which emphasize the biological and genetic factors in behavioral disorders to those which emphasize psychological or social factors. Consequently, particular treatment approaches vary with the orientation of the individual psychiatrist. Although some psychiatrists make use of any or all types of treatments as appropriate, some biologically oriented psychiatrists favor somatic therapies, such as drug treatment (see PSYCHOPHARMACOLOGY) or electric SHOCK THERAPY, whereas other psychiatrists may emphasize the various approaches of PSYCHOTHERAPY, such as psychoanalysis.

Modern psychiatry became an autonomous medical specialty in the early 19th century; Benjamin RUSH and his *Medical Inquiries and Observations upon the Diseases of the Mind* (1812) were highly influential in the United States. The forerunner of the *American Journal of Psychiatry*, the *American Journal of Insanity* began publication in 1844. By the late 1980s there were approximately 36,000 psychiatrists in the United States. For a historical overview of treatment techniques, see PSYCHOPATHOLOGY.

Psychiatry from its beginnings has dominated the field of disordered behavior, but in more recent times other professions, such as clinical PSYCHOLOGY, SOCIAL WORK, and nursing, have increasingly participated.

psychic research see PARAPSYCHOLOGY

psychoanalysis Psychoanalysis is a system of psychology originated by the Viennese physician Sigmund

Sigmund Freud believed psychoanalysis to be a scientific approach to the study of the mind. His research focused on the psychosexual origins of behavior, methods of exploring the unconscious mind, and the therapeutic use of these methods. His work now forms a cornerstone of contemporary thought.

FREUD in the 1890s and then further developed by himself, his students, and other followers. It consists of three kinds of related activities: (1) a method for research into the human mind, especially inner experiences such as thoughts, feelings, emotions, fantasies, and dreams; (2) a systematic accumulation of a body of knowledge about the mind; and (3) a method for the treatment of psychological or emotional disorders.

Psychoanalysis began with the discovery that HYSTERIA, an illness with physical symptoms that occurred in a completely healthy physical body—such as a numbness or paralysis of a limb, loss of voice, or blindness—could be caused by unconscious wishes or forgotten memories. (Hysteria is now commonly referred to as conversion disorder.) The French neurologist Jean Martin CHARCOT tried to rid the mind of undesirable thoughts through hypnotic suggestion, but without lasting success. Josef Breuer, a Viennese physician, achieved better results by letting Anna O., a young woman patient, try to empty her mind by just telling him all of her thoughts and feelings. Freud refined Breuer's method by conceptualizing theories about it and, using these theories, telling his patients through interpretations what was going on inside the unconscious part of their minds, thus making the unconscious become conscious. Many hysterias were cured this way, and in 1895, Breuer and Freud published their findings and theories in Studies in Hysteria.

Classic Psychoanalytic Theory

Traditional psychoanalytic theory states that all human beings are born with instinctual drives that are constantly active even though a person is usually not conscious of thus being driven. Two drives—one for sexual pleasure, called libido; the other called aggression—motivate and propel most behavior. In the infant the libido first manifests itself by making sucking an activity with pleasurable sensations in the mouth. Later similar pleasures are experienced in the anus during bowel movements, and finally these erotically tinged pleasures are experienced

when the sexual organ is manipulated. Thus psychosexual development progresses from the oral through the anal to the phallic stage. (Phallic, in psychoanalytic theory, refers to both male and female sexual organs.)

During the height of the phallic phase, about ages three to six, these libidinal drives focus on the parent of the opposite sex and lend an erotic cast to the relation between mother and son or between father and daughter, the so-called Oedipus COMPLEX. Most societies, however, strongly disapprove of these sexual interests of children. A TABOO on incest rules universally. Parents, therefore, influence children to push such pleasurable sensations and thoughts out of their conscious minds into the unconscious by a process called repression. In this way the mind comes to consist of three parts: (1) an executive part, the EGO, mostly conscious and comprising all the ordinary thoughts and functions needed to direct a person in his or her daily behavior; (2) the id, mostly unconscious and containing all the instincts and everything that was repressed into it; and (3) the superego, the conscience that harbors the values, ideals, and prohibitions that set the guidelines for the ego and that punishes through the imposition of guilt feelings.

Strong boundaries between the three parts keep the ego fairly free from disturbing thoughts and wishes in the id, thereby guaranteeing efficient functioning and socially acceptable behavior. During sleep the boundaries weaken; disturbing wishes may slip into the ego from the id, and warnings may come over from the superego. The results are intrapsychic conflicts, often manifested in dreams (see DREAMS AND DREAMING), sometimes even in frightening NIGHTMARES. Freud elucidated this concept in his first major work, The Interpretation of Dreams (1900; Eng. trans., 1913). Something very similar to the weakening of boundaries during sleep sometimes happens during ordinary daytime activities when some impulse from the id manages to cross the repression barrier to invade the ego and cause faulty actions such as slips of the tongue. Psychoneurotic symptoms occur if psychologically hurtful experiences during childhood have left the repression too weak or have distorted the ego, or if overstimulation has left the id wishes too strong, or if the delicate balance between ego, id, and superego has been upset by injury or other events. Any kind of psychic trauma may lead to the ego becoming an arena of intrapsychic conflict between the intruding id, the threatening superego, and the powerful influences emanating from the surrounding environment. Furthermore, the damage done to the basic psychological structures by traumatic experiences leaves those structures weakened and with defective functioning.

Such conflicts and defects can cause intense ANXIETY and severe DEPRESSION. In order to keep functioning effectively, the ego attempts to maintain control by achieving some sort of compromise between the contending forces. Often such compromises appear in the form of inhibitions or compulsions that affect behavior. Abnormal behavior and the anxiety, depressions, and PHOBIAS that go with it are called psychoneurotic symptoms in psychoanalytic theory. Neurotic character is the phrase used to designate a consistent pattern of neurotic behavior. When the damage abnormally distorts self-esteem, the resulting disturbance is called a narcissistic personality disorder, or a disorder of the self.

Treatment

Patients seek psychoanalytic treatment because they suffer from one or more of a variety of psychological symptoms such as anxiety, depression, sexual and other inhibitions, obsessive thoughts, compulsive actions, irrational angers, shyness and timidity, phobias, inability to get along with friends or spouses or coworkers, low self-esteem, a sense of feeling unfulfilled, nervous irritability, and blocked creativity. The defects and repressed conflicts that cause these symptoms are usually indicative of a psychoneurosis or a narcissistic personality disorder. Normal ego functioning and the joy of life that comes with easy relationship to others are seriously interfered with or sometimes lost altogether.

According to psychoanalysis, psychological maladaptations usually originate from painful misunderstandings or outright failures in the child's relationship to his or her parents. Even in adults there remain ever-present though usually unconscious fears that early hurtful experiences will now be repeated again with others. Transference is the unconscious expectation that old injuries and insults will now again be suffered, only this time at the hands of friends, spouses, children, bosses, just about anybody—as if transferred from the past into the present. Transference makes one have irrational expectations from the people with whom one lives and works. For example, one may feel a need to be appreciated by one's supervisors similarly to a child's needing approval from his or her parents. Frustration of these expectations may evoke rage or other immature behavior. Transference causes great distress but also makes treatment possible.

The method of treatment seems simple at first. The patient reclines on a comfortable couch in the analyst's

Freud's consulting room at Berggasse 19, Vienna, was filled with ancient paintings and sculpture. Patients who came for psychoanalytic treatment reclined on the couch while they described their dreams and free associations.

DIE

TRAUMDEUTUNG

VON

Dꝛ SIGM. FREUD.

«FLECTERE SI NEQUEO SUPEROS, ACHERONTA MOVEBO.»

LEIPZIG UND WIEN.
FRANZ DEUTICKE.
1900.

Die Traumdeuting (The Interpretation of Dreams), Freud's first major work and the foundation of psychoanalysis, was published in 1900. Freud regarded dreams as coded texts that, once deciphered, yield information about the mind of the dreamer.

office with the analyst seated behind the patient. The recumbent position, as well as not being able to see the analyst, minimizes distraction and allows concentration on inner experiences, thoughts, wishes, fantasies, and feelings. The patient is instructed to say absolutely everything that comes to mind without censoring anything, a technique that is called free association. This brings about a state of regression in which long-forgotten events and painful encounters are remembered, often with great clarity and intense emotions. At the same time, because of transference, the patient experiences the analyst as well, as if he or she were a figure from the past, perhaps resembling a parent.

The analyst often can trace the connection between the patient's current fantasies and feelings about the analyst and the origin of these thoughts and emotions in childhood experiences. The reexperienced conflicts and traumas, together with the accompanying fears and feelings, then are interpreted by the analyst. The patient learns to recognize the connections between the past and the present. The combination of insight together with the powerful emotional reexperience during the regressed state brought about by the analytic method causes a reorganization of the psychological structures into more healthfully adaptive patterns.

Typically, an analysis lasts for a few years, with four to five sessions per week of about 45 minutes each. In this way the psychoneuroses and the narcissistic personality disorders can be treated successfully in a majority of patients. Serious mental illnesses such as schizophrenia, manic-depressive illness, and the psychoses caused by organic malfunctioning of the brain cannot be cured by psychoanalytic treatment.

Training

In the United States most psychoanalysts are physicians who, after medical school, first specialized in PSYCHIATRY and who then were trained as psychoanalysts in an institute for psychoanalysis. Institute training typically takes from 5 to 7 years. Outside the United States many non-medical psychologists and other behavioral scientists have been trained as psychoanalysts, and recently non-medical candidates are being trained in increasing numbers by American institutes.

Post-Freudian Theory

Continuing research has discovered much evidence that the early relationships between children and parents, the so-called object relations, have the greatest impact on later psychological development. The influence of the caregivers, especially during infancy, leaves a lasting imprint on the personality. Emphasis on the object-relations theory developed by Melanie Klein characterizes psychoanalysis in much of Britain and Latin America. In the United States a particular aspect of object relations, namely their effects on the sense of self and on self-esteem, are being studied by a growing number of psychoanalysts.

Initiated by Heinz Kohut, self-psychology is being developed by his followers into one of the main concepts that make up the body of psychoanalytic theory. Self-psychology is a psychology of subjective experience. The self-psychologically oriented psychoanalyst, in addition to considering the usual psychoanalytic data of inner experiences such as dreams and free associations, emphasizes the use of empathic immersion by the analyst into the life experience of the patient as an essential source of data for treatment and for theorizing. Self-psychology postulates a nuclear self at the core of the individual. A cohesive, vigorous, and balanced self lends the person a sense of self and of well-being.

psychodrama   see GROUP THERAPY

▬

psychohistory   Psychohistory combines the techniques of history and psychology, especially PSYCHOANALYSIS, to provide insights into history and historical figures. Sigmund FREUD, the founder of modern psychoanalysis, wrote essays on Moses and Leonardo da Vinci that hinted at ways in which psychoanalysis might be used in historical research. Since World War I psychoanalytic concepts have often been used by scholarly and popular biographers. A landmark in the development of psychohistory was Erik ERIKSON's *Young Man Luther* (1958), a model study that Erikson followed with *Gandhi's Truth* (1969).

psychokinesis   see PARAPSYCHOLOGY

▬

psycholinguistics   The mutual relevance of PSYCHOLOGY—the study of mental and behavioral operations—and of LINGUISTICS—the study of language elements and structure—had long been recognized, but only recently has psycholinguistics become an accepted discipline.

Behaviorism. At one time, linguistics was restricted to the study of speech behavior. The linguist would construct a grammar of the language and try to formalize the native speaker's intuitive knowledge of his or her language. Thus linguistics was held to be independent of psychology. The task of the linguist was to analyze behavior. Mental operations were of no importance and in any event were not amenable to scientific study.

In 1957 the psychologist B. F. SKINNER, in his book *Verbal Behavior*, stated the relation between psychology and language in a much more sophisticated way. Skinner argued that the task of the psychologist of language was twofold: to describe the types of verbal utterances and to explain their occurrence. For example, a *mand* (coined on the basis of such terms as *command* and *demand*) was an utterance that was controlled by some drive state—an urgent requirement—and that specified a means of satisfying that drive, or controlling the behavior of the listener, or both. Similarly, a *tact* (coined on the basis of such terms as *contact*) was a response that labeled or named an object in the nonverbal world. A person would *tact* an object, such as water, because in the past such labeling behavior was reinforced, or rewarded.

The Generative-Transformational Approach. In the same year that Skinner's work appeared, Noam CHOMSKY published a brief book called *Syntactic Structures*. He argued that existing explanations of language did not account for the information that native speakers of a language had at their disposal. A totally different conception of language was needed, and since the 1960s that new approach to language—the generative-transformational approach—has been formulated, expanded, revised, and reformulated. The position of Chomsky and the generative-transformational grammarians is a mentalistic one and defines linguistics as a subdivision of cognitive psychology.

One of the major distinctions in psycholinguistics is that between performance and competence. Performance refers to the actual speaking and comprehending processes, which are influenced by such factors as fatigue, attention, and memory. Competence refers to the speaker-listener's knowledge of the language, uninfluenced by any psychological restraints. Language competence is the knowledge of a language that enables speakers to construct, or encode, and to understand, or decode, sentences.

Another distinction made in early psycholinguistic models was that between deep and surface structures. The surface structure of a sentence is close to what is spoken and heard; it is similar to the sentence as performed. Deep structure, however, represents the meaning elements and their relations and is a level of the sentence postulated to account for a wide variety of language phenomena.

Later models have challenged the original assumptions, and even Chomsky altered his views somewhat. The newer models theorize variously that surface and deep structures may be closer in meaning than previously thought, more levels of structure may be involved in language processing, other factors (such as the context in which a sentence is communicated) may be more important to meaning than structures, and deep and surface structures may simply be theoretical constructs with no basis in reality.

The Search for a Model. One of the major problems confronting early psycholinguistic research was the assumption that the psychological theory or model of language competence should be identical with the linguistic model. Early researchers assumed, for instance, that all sentences were formed from the simple, active, affirmative, declarative sentence by applying transformations—that is, linguistic rules by which additions, deletions, substitutions, or permutations are made in sentences. The derivational theory of complexity assumed that there was a one-to-one correspondence between linguistic complexity and psychological complexity. Thus sentences with a large number of transformations would be more difficult to comprehend, to judge as true or false, to recall, or to remember than sentences with fewer transformations. When empirical evidence accumulated to indicate that this correspondence did not always hold, psycholinguists began to search for a purely psychological model of language behavior.

Phonology. At the phonological level, contemporary psycholinguistic research has attempted to confront such issues as the apparent absence of a one-to-one correspondence between the acoustic signal and the perceived linguistic unit. Investigators are trying to learn why different acoustic signals are often perceived as the same sound.

Another issue is the relation between speech perception and speech production. The motor theory postulates that a listener, in perceiving speech, uses essentially the same mechanisms that are used to produce speech. Thus we perceive accurately what someone is saying because we ourselves imitate the sequences the speaker goes through. We know what the speaker is saying because we know what we would be saying with similar movements.

Semantics. At the semantic level, researchers are attempting to define the nature of meaning and its role in sentence encoding and decoding. One assumption is that word meanings are bundles of features. For example, the meaning of *wife* would consist of such features as human, female, and married. Under this assumption, psycholinguistic research at the semantic level is directed at discovering what the features are, the possible universality of the features across all languages, and their role in such psychological processes as recall, comprehension, and memory.

Other psycholinguists make the assumption that meaning is derived from the individual's attempt to fit linguistic information into his or her own cognitive system. Thus the meaning of a sentence is integrated with various other kinds of information—information from other sentences, from previously acquired knowledge, and generally from an understanding of the way things are related in the real world.

Syntax. Most psycholinguistic research has been directed at the syntactic level. Much attention has been given to the role of ambiguity—its effects on sentence comprehension and how ambiguities are decoded by a listener. Paralinguistic phenomena such as rhythm, intonation, and pauses have been investigated to determine their effects on sentence comprehension and their role in sentence production.

The Acquisition of Language. Prior to the development of contemporary psycholinguistics, language learning in the child was explained through a general process of imitation. One of the problems with such an approach, however, was the fact that the child hears numerous ungrammatical sentences yet somehow induces the correct rules of grammar. Furthermore, the child often will hear grammatical utterances yet will induce rules that are incorrect but regular. For example, the child will hear the past tense of *go* as *went*, and the plural of *mouse* as *mice*, and yet will say *goed* and *mouses*.

According to Chomsky, the child is born with a language-acquisition device that enables him or her to hear speech, analyze it, and derive the rules of the language.

---

psychological measurement Psychological measurement, assessment, or testing—also called psychometrics—refers to techniques or tests that seek to quantify a person's cognitive, emotional, or behavioral activities or abilities. An individual may undergo various tests and measurements during the course of psychological diagnosis, a job interview, or career counseling, or under other circumstances. At other times whole groups are tested to determine the placement of individuals within the group (see EDUCATIONAL MEASUREMENT AND TESTING).

History. British scientist Sir Francis GALTON, in an effort to demonstrate the role of heredity in mental ability, developed the first psychological tests in the late 1800s. The first generally useful psychological test, however, was the INTELLIGENCE test created by French psychologist Alfred BINET. Modified at Stanford University in 1916, the test and its various revisions (see STANFORD-BINET TEST) eventually became widely used as a standard test of intelligence in the United States.

During World War I, psychological testing became more important as the military attempted to measure its soldiers' intellectual aptitudes and emotional stability. World War II gave further impetus to psychological measurement, and a variety of new tests and techniques have been put into effect since the war.

Objective and Projective Tests. Psychological tests are customarily divided into two categories: objective and PROJECTIVE TESTS. Objective tests, sometimes called pencil-and-paper tests, allow a limited number of responses for each question on the test. Most intelligence tests, particularly those administered in a group setting, are of this nature. The Stanford-Binet and the Wechsler Adult Intelligence are two examples of intelligence tests commonly used in the United States. Both measure mental aptitude—that is, innate mental ability—rather than achievement, and both score results along a scale known as the intelligence quotient, or IQ, with an average IQ rated as 100 on the scale.

An example of an objective personality test is the widely used Minnesota Multiphasic Personality Inventory (MMPI), first published in 1943 and periodically revised. The most recent version of the MMPI, revised in the late 1980s, incorporates some 700 true-false questions about personal preferences and aversions. Its primary function is as a tool for the diagnosis of psychological disorders.

Projective tests or techniques are measurements in which there are no set answers. Rather, a person is presented with an ambiguous stimulus—an inkblot, a drawing, or an incomplete sentence, for example—and asked what that stimulus represents. The assessor looks for patterns in the responses to many such stimuli in order to make a psychological evaluation of the subject. Developed after World War I, the Rorschach Inkblot Test was one of the first projective tests.

Observations. Psychological observations have proved difficult to quantify because an observer's subjective perceptions can change the way those being observed act and can also get in the way of objective evaluations. Unobtrusive observation techniques stress hiding the observer from those being observed. A psychologist may observe family interactions through a one-way mirror or, from a distance, watch a child at play on a playground. Observations, though highly effective, can be costly and time consuming, which is why mental-health workers opt for testing whenever possible.

Reliability, Validity, and Norms. A test or measurement is considered reliable if it conforms to many criteria, of which three important ones are test-retest, inter-rater, and intratest reliability. If a test-taker achieves similar results taking the same test at two different times, the test has test-retest reliability. A test in which two or more evaluators reach similar conclusions over scoring has inter-rater reliability. A test has intratest reliability if it can be demonstrated that a test-taker's scores on similar sections of the test reflect the overall test score; such tests are said to be "homogeneous."

A test or measurement is considered valid if it actually measures what it is constructed to measure. One way to gauge validity is to administer the test to someone for whom the correct measurement is already known. Predictive validity is established if it is shown that a test predicts the future behavior or abilities of the test-taker.

Norms, or a scale, must be established for any psychological test or measurement so that individual scores can be compared against what is considered the normal range of test responses. Designers of psychological tests and measurements establish norms after testing a large-enough SAMPLING of the possible test-taking population.

Criticism. Psychological measurement and testing comes under fire mainly from people or groups who claim that a particular test lacks validity. For example, industry-administered IQ tests for potential workers were attacked in the United States in the 1960s as being culturally biased. It was argued that the tests measured achievement (acquired knowledge) rather than aptitude and were, therefore, discriminatory to culturally deprived minorities. Some test designers choose to answer criticism by improving their tests. The MMPI, for instance, has been revised partly to excise sexist and outdated language.

psychological testing   see PSYCHOLOGICAL MEASUREMENT

psychology   Psychology is the systematic study of human and animal behavior. Psychologists try to understand why living beings act the way they do, how they grow up, how they learn and change, how they differ from one another, and even how they get into trouble or become disturbed. Unlike PSYCHIATRY, which is a medical specialty devoted to the understanding and cure of mental disease, psychology has a broader task, ranging from the laboratory study of simple behavior in animals (insects, worms, rats, and pigeons have been commonly used in psychological experiments) to the examination of the complicated behavior of human beings in social groups.

To be sure, some psychologists—clinical psychologists—devote most of their efforts to helping disturbed, troubled, and mentally ill people; clinical psychologists often use techniques much like those employed by psychiatrists. Psychology is, however, far more than a set of therapies for the troubled.

In a sense, psychology can be best understood as a federation of interests: an alliance of scholars, scientists, and practitioners that is held together by a shared commitment to the systematic study of human and animal behavior. The present article introduces the varieties of psychology that make up this intellectual federation. The historical development of psychology is treated separately in the article on PSYCHOLOGY, HISTORY OF. What is important to note here is that about a century ago psychology became an independent field of study. With its roots in philosophy, physiology, and psychiatry, the relatively new field of psychology has maintained its breadth. It stretches from biological study at one border, through the examination of human beings in groups—which has much in common with sociology and anthropology—out to the edges of clinical psychiatry and general medicine.

About half of contemporary psychologists are in basic work and half are in applied psychology. Interaction can be seen in all fields. For the sake of economy and clarity, however, basic and applied psychology are separated here to give an overview of contemporary psychology.

Fields of Basic Psychology

Psychology as a Biological Science. Perhaps the oldest and longest thread in the growth of psychology as a research discipline ties psychology to biological study. Physiological and comparative psychology grew primarily from the evolutionary theories of Charles Darwin; learning was added as a major component of psychology near the beginning of the 20th century. These three fields are discussed below.

Physiological Psychology. Applying neuroanatomy and neurophysiology to the study of behavior, physiological psychology asks such questions as: Which structures of the brain and nerves grow and change in animal and human action? What are the neural networks that manage sensory experience? More recently, physiological psychologists have become especially interested in hormonal and biochemical changes in nerves, glands, and muscles—changes that may be closely related to human development, emotion, and learning. Much additional research is necessary before explicit links can be made between DNA and learning French, for example, but physiological psychologists are moving steadily toward a resolution of the ancient question of how the brain relates to behavior.

Comparative Psychology. Comparative psychology investigates animal behavior. More modest about the lessons of animals for human beings than their 19th-century forerunners, comparative psychologists continue to be interested in animal behavior in its own right and as a potential model for understanding human behavior. Ethology, a subgroup of comparative psychology, studies animals ranging from ducks and rats to baboons, in natural settings, and tries to draw general conclusions about patterns of mating, parental care, and adaptation. The articles ANIMAL BEHAVIOR and ETHOLOGY contain more information.

Learning. The study of learning is one of the central themes of psychology, with connections to child psychology, physiological psychology, education, and therapy. Learning psychologists examine simple behavior in animals—for example, pigeons learning which of several keys to peck for a reward. Learning psychologists also study human learning, design procedures and devices for educational application (such as TEACHING MACHINES), and develop programs for modifying problem behavior. In the history of psychology, learning psychologists—especially Ivan PAVLOV, John B. WATSON, Clark HULL, and B. F. SKINNER—have uniformly represented psychology as a science, subject to the same rules of evidence and inference that characterize physics or biology. They have also usually argued for simple and straightforward explanations of behavior and for the efficacy of reward and punishment in the modification of behavior. The articles LEARNING THEORY and BEHAVIOR MODIFICATION outline the key principles.

Cognitive Psychology. Among the first issues that excited the interest of psychologists in the early decades of the discipline were perception, memory, and language. How do people come to interpret sights and sounds as meaningful objects and events? How do people store evidence about what has happened in order to remember the past? How is speech acquired? These questions are still alive in psychology, and, together with inquiries about imagery and thinking, they make up the broad field called cognitive psychology. The field as a whole is discussed in the article COGNITIVE PSYCHOLOGY, and the separate component areas are outlined below.

Perception. Studies in perception investigate visual illusions, the recognition of depth and color, and, increasingly, the ways people put information together to make sense out of what they experience. Adult humans are able to move through a rich and complicated world of sensations and impressions; perceptual psychology examines how people group, categorize, and organize all the evidence their senses deliver. Greater detail can be found in the following articles: ILLUSIONS; PERCEPTION; and SENSES AND SENSATION.

Memory. The workings of the memory are akin to both perception and thinking. Recent research has demonstrated that people have several systems of memory: a short-term memory that holds images of sight and sound just long enough for people to see properly and to hear; a slightly longer-term memory that permits, for example, the storage of telephone numbers long enough to get them dialed; and a long-term memory that seems to hold the past almost indefinitely. Psychologists who study memory tackle the mechanisms of memory encoding and retrieval in all three forms. See the article MEMORY.

Psycholinguistics. A significant segment of cognitive psychology, psycholinguistics stretches from formal linguistics to social psychology. The articles SPEECH DEVELOPMENT and PSYCHOLINGUISTICS explore how language is acquired, used, and related to thinking and action.

Thinking. Cognitive psychologists study thinking from several points of view. Some investigators carry out experiments on problem solving, the making of inferences, and the use of analogies in thought; others examine real-life thought in games such as chess or in the making of complex decisions. Further information can be found in the articles PROBLEM SOLVING and REASONING. An exciting recent development in the study of thinking has been the attempt to mimic or simulate human thought with computer programs. The articles ARTIFICIAL INTELLIGENCE and PATTERN RECOGNITION address this line of investigation.

Imagery. After long neglect, imagery is a bright field in contemporary psychology. Researchers are studying imagery and creativity, fantasy, dreams—even the place of television in children's imagination. See the articles DREAMS AND DREAMING; FANTASY; and NIGHTMARES.

Emotion. Why are some people calm, effective, and surefooted when others are jumpy and scattered? What makes people courageous, sad, angry, or mean? The answers proposed to such questions have been various. Some psychologists are interested in the genetics of individual differences in emotion and personality; other researchers delve into the nature of emotion itself. The EMOTION article considers the various theories of emotion.

Motivation. Investigators work on the sources of action—motivation—to determine how much behavior can be accounted for by simple drives such as hunger, sex, or pain, and how much depends on complex social motivation such as the need to achieve or the desire to outpoint a rival. The MOTIVATION article goes into greater depth on this subject.

Personality. No part of psychology is more difficult and contentious than the study of personality. In recent years the very idea of stable personal characteristics has come under attack; some researchers have maintained that people behave more according to the requirements of the immediate social environment than according to persistent traits of personality such as good humor or irritability. Many tests of personality exist. See PERSONALITY; PROJECTIVE TESTS; and PSYCHOLOGICAL MEASUREMENT.

Abnormal Psychology. The study of abnormal behavior is a branch of personality psychology, and it is perhaps the kind of psychology that most often finds its way into the popular press, television, and imagination. Abnormal psychology includes the diagnosis of mental malfunction, often with tests of assorted kinds; the systematic description or taxonomy of abnormal behavior; and the study of the effectiveness of psychological and pharmacological (drug) therapies. The study of abnormal psychology, described in the article PSYCHOPATHOLOGY, touches closely on the applied field of clinical psychology.

Social Psychology. When a human being enters into an exchange with another human being, this interaction is a candidate for study in social psychology. Social psychologists study the normal, everyday actions of people—the developing social skills of children, for instance—as well as reactions to extraordinary events. For an outline of the field, see the article SOCIAL PSYCHOLOGY.

Developmental Psychology. The "general practitioners" of psychology, developmental psychologists study all aspects of behavior as it changes from birth to old age. The DEVELOPMENTAL PSYCHOLOGY article introduces the field, and the following articles give additional information: INFANCY; SPEECH DEVELOPMENT; CHILD DEVELOPMENT; PLAY (in behavior); SEXUAL DEVELOPMENT; ADOLESCENCE; MIDDLE AGE; OLD AGE; and SENILITY. The work of developmental psychologists borders on the applied fields of educational and school psychology covered below.

Fields of Applied Psychology

The practical, important, and demanding task of applied psychologists is to combine their own experience with their knowledge of basic psychology in order to solve everyday human problems. Applied psychologists may help a schoolchild to learn, an assembly line to move smoothly, a group of executives to reach a wise decision, an abusing parent to stop beating a child, or a patient in an institution to experience some relief from anxiety.

Educational Psychology. Educational psychologists usually work with teachers and with schoolchildren in an attempt to devise effective teaching procedures and to design classroom activities that lead to learning; they also counsel students about curriculum and personal problems. See the article EDUCATIONAL PSYCHOLOGY.

Industrial Psychology. Industrial psychology brings together information about perception, management, and social organization to make industries and businesses operate more efficiently and humanely. Some industrial psychologists are specialists in organizational behavior—how best to get people working together—and others concentrate on job satisfaction, public relations, incentives for work, and aspects of advertising. See the article INDUSTRIAL PSYCHOLOGY.

Psychometrics. This field lies between basic and applied psychology. Psychometricians (the term means "mind-measurer") invent and refine tests of competence and aptitude; give tests of various kinds to discover human talent, potentiality, or the need for special training; and examine verbal skills, aptitude for new jobs, personality characteristics, or the likelihood of emotional disturbance. The article PSYCHOLOGICAL MEASUREMENT gives details.

Clinical Psychology. The largest field of applied psychology, clinical psychology diagnoses mental distress and helps psychologically disturbed people find a more balanced way of living. Clinical psychology has, of course, affinities to psychiatry. Much of the therapy of clinical psychologists is carried out in person-to-person meetings, but, increasingly over the years, clinical psychologists have worked with larger groups, from two-person groups such as spouses or parent and child to a dozen or more residents of an institution. The PSYCHOTHERAPY article introduces and differentiates the bewildering variety of therapeutic techniques. When apt clinical psychologists diagnose and attempt to cure, they draw on all that is known of basic psychology.

Methods Psychologists Use

Just as the research and practical interests of psychologists are diverse, so are their methods. Some applied procedures—tests or therapy methods—have been mentioned earlier. The present section will focus on research methods.

Random-Assignment Experiment. The surest and most reliable way to find out the sources of behavior is to conduct an experiment. Two (or more) groups of subjects are selected randomly, so that there is no bias in their selection, and then each group is given a different experience. For example, one group of young sparrows is raised with adult sparrows, a second group with adult wrens. In this way one may learn something about transmission of species-specific birdsong. The random-assignment experiment permits strong inferences from its results. Its use is limited, however, by the fact that some important human behavior cannot be subjected to experimental study.

Contrasting Natural Groups. Since the mid-19th century a major method of psychological investigation has been to observe naturally occurring groups that differ in some important way. Often the comparison of natural groups is made more informative by giving the groups a planned common experience. Psychologists now know, for example, that mentally retarded children in institutions will not work as hard on their own in a laboratory task as will mentally retarded children (with the same test scores) raised at home.

A problem persists in comparing natural groups: the differences observed between groups may be related to the defining characteristic (such as IQ), but they may also be related to some other correlated factor that defines the groups. Some psychologists feel that serious misinformation has been written about racial differences in behavior because inadequate attention was sometimes given to factors other than ancestry—such as education or economic status—that separate minority groups in modern society.

Field Observation. Some animal and human action can be studied in its everyday setting. A group of European ethologists including Konrad LORENZ made many discoveries about the mating, parental, and fighting behavior of birds and small mammals. A number of studies have monitored a small group of children over the first years of their lives (a few for 40 years or longer) to understand the development of personality, intelligence-test performance, or other aspects of individual difference. Such longitudinal studies of development combine field observations in hospital, home, and school with laboratory tasks and with intricate batteries of tests.

The Case Study. Less widely used in research than either the experiment, comparison study, or field observation, the case study has been a significant source of new ideas for psychologists. A case study is the intensive study of a single person or of a few persons; it has been most influential in three fields of psychology—abnormal psychology, cognitive development, and language.

Sigmund FREUD's reconstructions of life histories stand as models for the application of the case study to abnormal psychology: he built an explanation of his patient's disorders from interviews, free association, and the analysis of dreams. Jean PIAGET has used the case study in a different, but equally productive, way: he studied his three children over the first three years of their lives to outline the course of early cognitive development. In language studies the case study has always been important. Case studies are, however, limited in their generality. Who can say for sure in what ways the person under study is typical or eccentric? Nevertheless, case studies remain a basic first step in psychologists' exploration of the human mind.

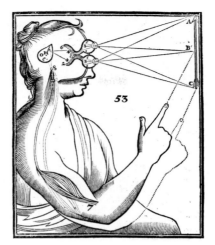

A woodcut diagram by the French Renaissance philosopher René Descartes illustrates his theory that sensory impressions are converted into motor impulses through the agency of the pineal gland in the brain. Descartes believed that the pineal gland was the habitation of the human soul.

psychology, history of

psychology, history of   This article briefly discusses the historical development of psychology and refers to the biographies of some of those people who played a part in this development. For a description of the fields of inquiry that make up contemporary psychology, and references to specific psychological topics, see the article PSYCHOLOGY.

The history of psychology may be traced to many sources. Often psychology has borrowed models from other sciences; its history reflects historical trends of science in general.

Early Models

The Greek views of human behavior focused on the fact that human beings are animals, and so are like other animals in many ways, but that humans are distinguished by their ability to reason. As in many other sciences, Aristotle's views provided the dominant structure for subsequent explanations until the scientific revolution. He held that people had a hierarchy of functions, from those shared by all living things, through those shared by all animals, to those unique to human beings. Feelings and sensations were common to all animals and were the result of external causes acting on the body. Mind, however, in directing actions to satisfy desires, worked by the processes of reason and thinking. It was an unmoved mover.

In the 17th century, René Descartes simplified this spectrum of functions into a DUALISM, in which all mental functions, including perception, were mechanically determined. The soul, however, was a nonmaterial spirit that interacted with the body through the pineal gland (an organ in the brain that is not duplicated on both sides). This view of the mechanical causation of ideas led to the theory of associationism, a theory of how sensations could be combined to form ideas.

Eventually a neural basis was sought for these processes, and—via studies of reaction time—this was one way psychological questions were moved into the laboratory. A second, more purely psychological route was through introspection.

Modern Experimental Psychology

The first purely psychological laboratory was founded at Leipzig, Germany, in 1879 by Wilhelm WUNDT. He experimented on sensation and perception using introspective analysis of the elements of experience. His contemporaries, such as Hermann EBBINGHAUS, Gustav Theodor Fechner (1801–87), and Hermann Ludwig Ferdinand von HELMHOLTZ, formulated and elaborated basic laws of perception and association.

Edward B. Titchener (1867–1927), an Englishman, studied under Wundt and brought the new psychology of introspection to the United States in 1892. For 35 years at Cornell University, Titchener taught that psychology represented the study of experience dependent on the experiencing individual. He felt that psychology should study general properties of adult human experience and not individual differences or nonverbal organisms.

Wilhelm Wundt established psychology as an independent academic discipline with the founding of the first psychology laboratory at the University of Leipzig in 1879. Wundt used introspective study to describe the elements of consciousness.

The American pragmatist philosopher William James, who founded functional psychology, viewed consciousness as a product of the evolutionary process, constantly adjusting to new requirements and motivations.

(Right) The American psychologist Clark L. Hull formulated a hypotheticodeductive framework that set forth his theories of cognition in symbolic, mathematical form. His experimental research on learning was directed toward greater understanding and better management of human behavior.

William JAMES is often referred to as the father of American psychology for the broad, inclusive summary presented in his *The Principles of Psychology* (1890). He is also known for the theory of emotion that holds that emotion results from physical responses. G. Stanley Hall (1844–1924), a contemporary of James, established the first true laboratory of psychology in the United States at Clark University in 1883, where he contributed to several areas of psychology, especially child study. Hall was instrumental in founding the American Psychological Association, of which he was the first president. James McKeen CATTELL studied individual differences in Wundt's laboratory but rejected the latter's introspectionist methods. Cattell was interested in individual differences in reaction times, mental tests, and studies of eminence and was among the first to apply statistical procedures to psychological data.

Psychology was moving in the direction of functionalism in the hands of the British and American schools and under the influence of Darwin's theory of evolution. The movement was crystallized into a more systematic statement in the late 19th century by John DEWEY and his colleagues at the University of Chicago. Functionalism, consistent with the American experience, stressed the utility of behavioral processes as opposed to mere description of mental structures.

One of the most influential of American psychologists was John B. WATSON, the popularizer of BEHAVIORISM in the early 20th century. Behaviorism holds that the relationships between objectively observable behavior comprise the only possible subject matter of psychology. Watson adopted the work of Russian physiologist Ivan Petrovich PAVLOV on the conditioned reflex as the unit for association. Theories and interpretations of learning were advanced by a number of influential researchers. Edward L. THORNDIKE, working with animals, developed a theory that emphasized reinforcement as the basis for learning in a kind of psychological hedonism. A more cognitive interpretation of learning was presented by Edward C. Tolman (1886–1959), whose purposive behaviorism postu-

In a landmark paper, "Psychology as a Behaviorist Views It" (1913), John B. Watson laid the groundwork for modern behaviorism. Watson criticized "mentalist" concepts of human psychology, which stressed theories of introspection. Watson felt that only a person's behavior—as opposed to thoughts—could be measured.

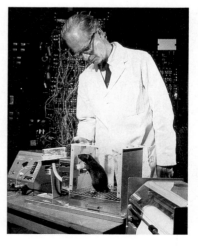

(Right) The American behaviorist B. F. Skinner conditions a rat to perform certain actions in exchange for food when a light is flashed. This form of training, called operant conditioning, is conducted in a soundproof, light-resistant experimental chamber known as a Skinner box.

lated cognitive intervening variables between stimulus and response. Clark HULL developed an elaborate theory of learning that was extended in the animal-learning area by Kenneth W. Spence (1907–67) and was applied to human personality by Neal E. Miller (1909–   ). The 20th century's best-known behaviorist was B. F. SKINNER, whose operant interpretation of learning stressed the idea that behavior is a systematic function of its antecedents and consequences in a form of radical behaviorism. Contemporary theories of learning reflect modern science. For example, William Kaye Estes (1919–   ) incorporated sampling concepts from statistics into his theory of learning.

A more cognitive alternative to behaviorism than Tolman's was the GESTALT PSYCHOLOGY brought to America by its founders, Max WERTHEIMER, Wolfgang KÖHLER, and Kurt KOFFKA. They emphasized the mental structure that organisms bring to their PERCEPTION and PROBLEM SOLVING, and the importance of meaning and understanding as opposed to reinforcement.

Computer models and information processing are also important current influences on experimental psychology. These approaches treat the senses as input devices and the mind as a collection of parts that analyze, store, recode, and use information. Researchers in COGNITIVE PSYCHOLOGY seek to uncover the nature and workings of these devices.

The role of heredity and subtle brain abnormalities in basic human psychology became important avenues of research in the 1980s. For example, a few studies have discovered consistent differences in particular chromosomes between groups of DEPRESSION sufferers and the normal population. CAT scans have revealed small, though potentially significant, structural abnormalities in the brains of those suffering from SCHIZOPHRENIA and other major mental disorders. Some theorists have suggested that even the emotional makeup of average people may be genetically predisposed. Others regard this notion as simplistic and continue to investigate the role of environmental factors on basic human psychology.

Clinical Psychology

Clinical psychology is concerned with methods of diagnosing and treating mental disorders. A historical look at the various methods of treating mental disorders is given in the article PSYCHOPATHOLOGY. In addition to its roots in experimental psychology, clinical psychology stems from several traditions. An assessment tradition is traceable to attempts in the late 19th century by Sir Francis GALTON to study individual variation. Differences in sensation and perception and their assessment by, for instance, reaction times were treated in Cattell's book *Mental Tests and Measurements* in 1890. Soon after, in France, Alfred BINET undertook the development of scales to predict school success, which were published in 1905. Lewis TERMAN, at Stanford University, extended earlier translations and standardized the instrument for the U.S. population in what are known as the Stanford-Binet scales. In 1939, David Wechsler (1896–1981) published his first version

Alfred Binet developed the first widely used scale of mental age and formulated standardized tests designed to measure a subject's ability to reason. Binet's was the first of many attempts to arrive at an objective method for determining intelligence and learning capacity.

of the Wechsler Adult Intelligence Scales. Both tests, in updated versions, are used currently. World Wars I and II gave impetus to the assessment movement as methods were needed to evaluate and assign a large number of recruits. Objective personality assessment developed later than intellectual assessment. The most-used instrument of this type is the Minnesota Multiphasic Personality Inventory.

The medical tradition in clinical psychology is traceable largely to the influences of Sigmund FREUD, who opened the area of psychopathology to psychological study. He was a physician and neurologist, and his psychodynamic theory of instinctual energies borrowed heavily from models of fluid dynamics current in turn-of-the-century physics. G. Stanley Hall invited Freud to speak at Clark University, and these lectures, published in 1910, served as the introduction of psychoanalysis to

Pioneers of the psychoanalytic movement gathered at Clark University in 1909 to attend lectures by Sigmund Freud. The group included (clockwise from top left) A. A. Brill, Ernest Jones, Sandor Ferenczi, C. G. Jung, G. Stanley Hall, and Freud.

Carl Rogers altered traditional psycho- therapy with his client-centered method.

the United States. The article PSYCHOANALYSIS contains more information about its historical development. Psychological assessment was also influenced by psychodynamic theories. Projective tests began with the use of word-association techniques and then became more popular in the 1920s with the publication of the inkblot technique developed by Hermann Rorschach (1884–1922).

The first psychological clinic in the United States was founded in 1896 at the University of Pennsylvania by Lightner Witmer (1867–1956). The clinic dealt primarily in the problems of schoolchildren, a basic focus of much of early clinical psychology. A child-guidance movement developed in this country as part of a larger reform effort that was known as the mental-hygiene movement. The opening of other clinics marked its progress.

Psychoanalytic theory dominated much of early clinical psychology, but other points of view were expressed as well. John Watson and some of his students were applying behaviorist learning principles to clinical problems in the late 1920s. In two now-famous cases, he demonstrated that a fear response could be conditioned in a small child through association and that a phobia could be diminished through application of the same principles. Gestalt psychology had an effect on clinical psychologists and formed the basis for a system of psychotherapy.

Carl ROGERS was one of those whose training in psychoanalytic theory and methods left him dissatisfied. He developed his own nondirective or client-centered approach to psychotherapy and counseling, which he first described in 1942. His systematic presentation of his ideas and subjection of them to empirical tests in the clinic were important steps in maintaining a research base for all psychological activity and in expanding the role of psychologists to include psychotherapy.

Modern clinical psychology continues to use a variety of scientific paradigms. In the 1960s and '70s a renewed interest in the application of learning principles and methods led to a major movement labeled behavior therapy or BEHAVIOR MODIFICATION. This movement was given an

initial impetus by a psychiatrist, Joseph Wolpe (1915–), who developed an effective procedure akin to Watson's for dealing with phobias. Based on associationist principles, the procedure, systematic desensitization, became the focus of much research that spawned many other behavioral therapies. In recent years behaviorism in clinical psychology has been tempered with cognitive models, as experimental psychology had been earlier. Therapies have been developed from these cognitive and behavioral models that are specific to various disorders, in contrast with the earlier generic forms of psychotherapy.

For more intractable psychological problems, other therapies have been devised. PSYCHOPHARMACOLOGY continues to develop an array of drugs for the treatment of mental illnesses. Other somatic therapies, such as SHOCK THERAPY, once widely employed, are used to a lesser extent today.

Since World War II, psychology as a profession has become formally recognized. Standards of training have been developed and promulgated by the American Psychological Association. Clinical psychologists and some social workers are trained to be scientist-professionals, meaning that professional practice is tied closely to theory, research, and evaluation of methods. Certification or licensing laws have been passed to regulate the practice of professional psychology.

Today there are many types of psychology and psychologists. These branches of psychology share many traditions and historical antecedents in their own unique blend. As a science and profession psychology has progressed from a branch of philosophy to the broad field of the study of human behavior.

psychometrics   SEE PSYCHOLOGICAL MEASUREMENT

---

psychopathology   Psychopathology, or mental illness, is illness that is revealed in impaired behavioral or psychological functioning or both. The term refers to a broad range of syndromes that involve abnormalities in sensations, cognition, and emotional states. A working assumption in the field is that psychopathological syndromes, or groups of symptoms, are not merely predictable responses to a specific stressful event—for instance, the death of a loved one—but rather a manifestation of a psychological or a biological dysfunction in the person. Psychopathologies range from relatively mild disorders, such as dysthymia (a form of DEPRESSION), to serious disorders that involve pervasive disability, such as schizophrenic disorders (see SCHIZOPHRENIA).

Modern Classification

The primary diagnostic system used in the United States today—and imitated in many other countries—is the *Diagnostic and Statistical Manual of Mental Disorders* (*DSM*), a publication of the American Psychiatric Association. The first *DSM* was published in 1952, and it has been revised and expanded three times—in 1968 (*DSM-II*), 1979 (*DSM-III*), and 1987 (*DSM-III-R*).

Therapists using the *DSM-III-R* employ several diagnostic criteria—such as psychological stress factors and an assessment of functional skills—in addition to delineating the various symptoms of each disorder. Extensive information is gathered in an interview with the patient and is augmented through PSYCHOLOGICAL MEASUREMENT, a physical examination, and interviews with family members. Listed below are the major categories of psychopathology contained in the *DSM-III-R*.

Schizophrenic Disorders. These disorders are characterized by the presence of psychotic symptoms (see PSYCHOSIS) during active, or heightened, episodes of the illness. Delusions, hallucinations, certain abnormalities in emotional expression, and thought disorder are among the primary defining features of schizophrenia.

Dissociative Disorders. These disorders involve a disruption of the patient's normal personality due to alterations in consciousness, identity, or memory for personal experiences. The most common type of dissociative disorder is psychogenic AMNESIA, which involves a total loss of memory for events associated with a traumatic experience. In the disorder known as psychogenic fugue, the individual loses all awareness of his or her own identity. Whereas both amnesia and fugue states are predominantly manifested in the patient's thinking, multiple-personality disorder (see PERSONALITY, MULTIPLE) involves more-pervasive behavioral changes.

Anxiety Disorders. These disorders include illnesses in which there is debilitating tension, ANXIETY, and avoidance. In phobic disorders (see PHOBIA) there is a specific source of anxiety, and negative feelings are controlled by the patient's efforts to avoid the feared object or situation. Another form of anxiety disorder is the panic attack—the sudden, overpowering feeling of terror that is experienced by about 1.5 percent of the population at some time in their lives. In contrast to the abrupt onset and dispersal of a panic attack is the constant state of tension associated with generalized anxiety disorders. OBSESSIVE-COMPULSIVE DISORDERS involve recurrent, unpleasant thoughts or repetitive behaviors, or both, that are presumed to reflect the patient's attempts to control anxiety.

Affective Disorders. These disorders are characterized by mood disturbances, and they generally occur when normal human emotions reach extremes. The affective disorders can be mild or severe and can sometimes require hospitalization. Similarly, the recovery rate for affective disorders varies from a few months to several years following an episode. One of the most common affective disorders is dysthymia, which involves long-standing (at least two years in duration) symptoms of depressed mood, disturbances in eating and sleeping, decreased energy, and feelings of hopelessness and low self-esteem. Major depressive disorder is characterized by these same symptoms but is typically of a more intense nature and with a shorter duration. People with bipolar affective disorder experience periods of depression as well as periods of mania, or extreme mood elevations. During manic episodes the individual may show high levels of activity, talk-ativeness, and elation. (See MANIC-DEPRESSIVE PSYCHOSIS.)

Psychosexual Disorders. These are disorders of sexual behavior in which psychological factors seem to be at the root of the problem. There are two general classses of psychosexual disorders: paraphilias and sexual dysfunctions.

The essential feature of the paraphilias is an intense and recurrent sexual urge involving nonhuman objects, or the suffering of oneself or one's sexual partner, or children or other nonconsenting persons. Transsexualism (see SEX REASSIGNMENT), EXHIBITIONISM, PEDOPHILIA, FETISHISM, sadomasochism, and VOYEURISM are among the most frequently diagnosed paraphilias. Transsexuals experience an incongruity between their biological sex and their subjective sense of gender identity. Individuals with a diagnosis of exhibitionism suffer from extreme urges to expose their genitals in inappropriate places. Pedophilia is characterized by sexual fantasies about, or sexual acts with, prepubescent children. Fetishism is a preference for the use of nonliving objects as the method of achieving sexual excitement. Sadomasochism is a preference for inflicting and receiving pain during sexual activity. Voyeurism is defined as a recurrent, intense desire to observe unsuspecting people who are disrobing or engaged in sexual activity. A diagnosis of exhibitionism, voyeurism, or pedophilia does not require that a person act on his or her impulses, but only that the abnormal sexual impulses are disturbing to the patient.

The sexual dysfunctions involve abnormalities in sexual appetite or psychophysiologic changes that characterize the complete sexual-response cycle. Included among these dysfunctions are premature ejaculation, male erectile disorder, and inhibited female orgasm.

Somatoform Disorders. These disorders involve physical symptoms that do not have demonstrable organic bases. There are two general types of somatoform disorders: those which are characterized by excessive concerns about physical conditions but are associated with no specific symptom, and those in which there is one or more identifiable physical symptoms. Hypochondriasis (see HYPOCHONDRIA), or exaggerated concerns and unrealistic fears about one's health, fall into the first group. Also included in this group is body dysmorphic disorder, which is characterized by a preoccupation with some imagined defect in physical appearance.

Conversion disorders constitute the second group of somatoform disorders. They involve actual physical disabilities without any physical basis. These disorders are typically easy to separate from organically based problems because the physical symptom usually appears suddenly during a period of extreme psychological distress and often tends to be psychologically symbolic, as when a person develops paralysis in a subconscious effort to avoid unpleasant situations.

Organic Mental Disorders. These disorders include mental disturbances in which intellectual functioning, emotional functioning, or both are impaired through an abnormality in brain functioning that can be either transient or permanent; they may be caused by injury, disease, the aging process, or drug abuse. DELIRIUM is an acute, temporary state of mental confusion, often accompanied by hallucinations and delusions. Dementia is a more permanent deterioration of intellectual functioning and behavioral capacities. This mental disorder is frequently caused by ALZHEIMER'S DISEASE, a degenerative disorder of the central nervous system.

Personality Disorders. These disorders entail inflexible, maladaptive personality traits that cause functional impairment or inner distress. These traits are presumed to be characteristic of a person's functioning since early adulthood. The *DSM-III-R* classifies personality disorders into three groups.

The first group includes paranoid, schizoid, and schizotypal personality disorders. In all of these disorders the patient appears excessively odd or eccentric to others. In addition, patients with paranoid personality disorder (see PARANOIA) show unwarranted suspicion, jealousy, and anger and, as a result, have recurring interpersonal conflicts. Schizoid personality disorder is characterized by marked indifference to social relationships and a restricted range of emotional expression. Essential features of schizotypal personality disorder are peculiarities of thought and behavior, and deficits in social skills. The abnormalities in the thoughts of schizotypal patients include paranoid tendencies and bizarre fantasies (such as a belief that others can read one's thoughts). These abnormalities, however, are much less severe and debilitating than those shown by patients with the similarly named schizophrenic disorders.

The second group comprises the antisocial, borderline, histrionic, and narcissistic personality disorders. Symptoms of these disorders can include dramatic, emotional, and erratic behaviors. Persons with antisocial personality disorder display a pattern of irresponsible, aggressive, and nonconformist behavior that extends from adolescence through adulthood. This disorder is more common in males than in females. In contrast, borderline personality disorder occurs more often in women and is characterized by emotional instability, confusions about identity, and unstable interpersonal relationships. Histrionic personality disorder involves a pervasive pattern of excessive emotionality and attention seeking. A preoccupation with the self and a lack of empathy for others are the chief features of narcissistic personality disorder.

The third class of personality disorders involves predominant symptoms of anxiety and fearfulness. These include avoidant, dependent, obsessive-compulsive, and passive-aggressive personality disorders. In avoidant personality disorder the individual shows extreme shyness and fear of being negatively evaluated by others. Submissiveness and a lack of initiative characterize patients with dependent personality disorder. Obsessive-compulsive personality disorder involves inflexibility and excessive concern with details and rules, as well as an inability to spontaneously express emotions (sufferers of this disorder, however, do not experience uncontrollable compulsive thoughts and purposeless repetitive behaviors in the way those who suffer from the similarly named obsessive-compulsive disorder do). In passive-aggressive personality disorder the patient does not openly defy laws or expecta-

tions, but rather resists influence indirectly by procrastination or intentional inefficiency.

Disorders Associated with Childhood and Adolescence. These disorders involve syndromes that tend to have their onset early in life. They cover a broad range of behavioral and cognitive disabilities and vary in severity and duration. Attention-deficit HYPERACTIVITY disorder affects as many as 5 percent of all elementary-school children and is more common in males than females. It is characterized by excessive movement or restlessness, and problems in maintaining attention. Pervasive developmental disorders are more serious and are characterized by extreme distortions in several functional domains, including language, perception, social and motor skills, and attention. AUTISM is one of the pervasive developmental disorders. Eating disorders, such as ANOREXIA NERVOSA and BULIMIA, also typically have their onset in childhood or adolescence.

History

The modern scientific study of psychopathology has evolved out of a long-standing search for the causes of abnormal tendencies in human behavior. The earliest explanations for abnormal behavior were based on beliefs in the supernatural. Demonology, or the belief that an evil supernatural being can control a person's body or mind, was the rationale that most ancient cultures used for explaining psychopathology. These ideas are apparent in the cultural artifacts of the Babylonians, Egyptians, Chinese, and Greeks. In biblical times it was believed that the evil beings had to be exorcised from disturbed persons in order to make them well. EXORCISM took many forms, including praying for the afflicted, administering brews, or, in extreme cases, flogging and starving the victim.

In the 5th century BC, HIPPOCRATES and other Greek philosophers developed ideas about the origins of mental illness that are compatible in many ways with current theories in the field. The Hippocratic school recognized the brain as the seat of emotion and intellectual life and considered—as do contemporary researchers—the possibility that brain damage acquired early in life could contribute to subsequent psychopathology. Although many of the

William Morris, a mental patient, was chained to the wall of a cell in London's Bethlehem Hospital for 10 years. The name of the notorious hospital has entered the English language as bedlam.

theories were insightful, Hippocratic biological theories were unsophisticated. They propounded, for instance, that imbalances of various bodily fluids determined individual temperament.

From time to time, religious beliefs regained dominance in society's response to psychopathology. Medieval views of mental illness were heavily influenced by religion, and belief in witchcraft was common from the 10th through the 18th century. The practice of witchcraft, which by definition involved dealings with the devil, was viewed as a denial of God and was punishable by torture and execution. Undoubtedly, many persons punished as witches were suffering from psychopathology.

Medieval society, however, was also characterized by some more-enlightened and more-sympathetic attitudes toward the mentally ill and by some modest advances in treatment. In 1243 the Priory of St. Mary of Bethlehem was established in London, and by 1403 its hospital routinely housed several mentally disturbed men. Eventually, it came to serve as the major institution for the mentally ill in London. A corruption of its name, *bedlam*, has passed into the language as a synonym for mad or chaotic conditions.

The number of asylums in Europe grew dramatically in the 15th and 16th centuries. As was the case with the Bethlehem hospital, however, the chief function of these institutions was behavioral control, and this often took the form of physical restraint. For example, at the "Lunatic's Tower" in Vienna, which was constructed in 1784, the inmates were not only confined to small cells but were also restrained with chains, straps, and locks. Even so, humanitarian approaches to treatment were soon to gain a foothold in Europe.

French physician Philippe Pinel (1745–1826) was one of the key figures in the quest for humane treatment for the mentally ill. He argued that they should be treated as sick individuals instead of as "wild animals." In 1793, after much resistance from authorities, Pinel was given permission to remove the chains of the patients under his charge at Bicetre Hospital in Paris. Some were subsequently allowed to move freely around the hospital grounds, and they improved markedly. Pinel fostered the belief that through purposeful activity and being comforted, the "insane" could be restored to reason. His reforms rapidly spread throughout France.

In the 19th century an important figure in reform advocacy was American schoolteacher Dorothea Dix. Her initial interest in psychopathology stemmed from her experience as a Sunday-school teacher for female convicts, many of whom suffered from mental disorders. Dix subsequently gathered information on the maltreatment of people in U.S. mental institutions and advocated her cause with legislators until the situation was improved through legal statutes. She then traveled around the country inspecting psychiatric facilities to ensure that her reforms were put into practice.

Enlightened attitudes toward the treatment of the mentally ill were accompanied by a more systematic, scientific study of mental disorders. In an 1883 textbook, German physician Emil KRAEPELIN advanced the first

Philippe Pinel orders (1793) the unshackling of mentally ill women in the Paris hospital of Salpêtrière.

classification of the various mental disorders based on their presumed origins.

Also in the 19th century, significant progress was made in research on the functioning of the nervous system. Some of the degenerative brain-cell changes accompanying senility and the structural pathologies associated with mental retardation were documented. Another discovery was the cause and consequences of the disease SYPHILIS. With the connection between syphilitic infection and the eventual mental deterioration (general paresis) that accompanies it identified, the link between central-nervous-system impairment and mental-illness symptoms was clearly established.

In the 20th century new discoveries in the fields of GENETICS and neurobiology emerged, as did new theories of the causes of mental illness. Gradually accumulating data on the occurrence of mental illness in the biological relatives of patients led to theories that posited a hereditary component in such disorders as schizophrenia and major depression. As knowledge of the neurochemistry of the brain expanded, biochemical theories of mental disorders were proposed. Among these was the still-prevalent theory that increased levels of the neurotransmitter dopamine (see NERVOUS SYSTEM) in the brain may be a factor in schizophrenic disorders.

Competing with the various biological approaches to mental illness were numerous theories of environmental causation. These are often referred to as psychogenic theories because they make the general assumption that conflict or emotional stress contributes to mental illness. Psychogenic theories set the stage for the development of therapies (see PSYCHOANALYSIS; PSYCHOTHERAPY) aimed at reducing dysfunction through psychological and environmental intervention.

Modern Treatment

The introduction in the 1950s of a class of drugs known as the neuroleptics marked a watershed in the treatment of mental disorders. These drugs are effective in reducing the psychotic symptoms associated with schizophrenia and some affective disorders. Significant progress has also been made in the development of antidepressant medications, and the drug LITHIUM has proved to be very effective in ameliorating the symptoms of bipolar disorder. As a result of the introduction of pharmacologic treatments, many patients who would have required hospitalization are now treated on an outpatient basis. This has contributed to a dramatic reduction in the number of hospitalized psychiatric patients. (See PSYCHOPHARMACOLOGY.)

A variety of psychotherapies are also currently used in the treatment of psychopathology. Approaches used include psychodynamic (concerned with cause and effect), cognitive (concerned with sensations and perceptions), and psychoeducational (concerned with educating sufferers about their disorders). Research has shown that psychotherapy is effective in treating major depression, especially when applied in conjunction with medication. For schizophrenics, the psychoeducational approach appears to be the most effective. Behavioral therapies, such as systematic desensitization and contingency management, are typically used to treat phobias, obsessive-compulsive disorders, eating disorders, and many childhood disorders.

Psychotherapy and behavioral therapy are often components of inpatient treatment programs. In addition, hospitalization for psychopathology frequently includes drug therapy, as well as recreational and occupational therapies. More-dramatic somatic therapies such as electroconvulsive SHOCK THERAPY, popular in the 1930s and '40s, are used on a much more limited basis today.

A psychologist monitors the electroencephalogram (EEG) of a patient receiving electroconvulsive shock therapy. Although controversial, shock therapy is sometimes prescribed for severe cases of depression.

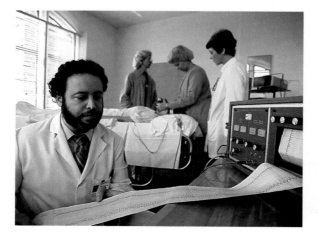

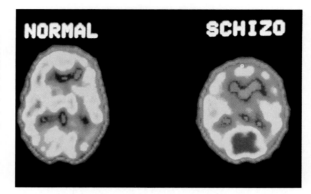

Positron emission tomography (PET) scans reveal differences in glucose metabolism (shown in yellow) between a normal and a schizophrenic brain.

Although the number and efficacy of available treatments have increased dramatically during this century, there is currently no "cure" for any of the psychopathologies. The neuroleptics, antidepressants, and lithium have all served to significantly improve the quality of life and prognosis for mental illness, yet none of these drugs completely restores the individual to mental health. Also, unfortunately, many very ill patients do not respond to medication.

Recent Research

The results of research on the nature and determinants of mental illness indicate that causes are diverse and often complex. As early theorists, such as Kraepelin, would have predicted, there is now evidence that many forms of psychopathology are biologically based. For example, CAT scans of the brains of patients with schizophrenic and affective disorders have revealed ·that some of these patients have abnormalities of the brain. There is also substantial evidence of biochemical imbalance in the central nervous systems of some patients with panic disorders and depression.

One potential source of such organic dysfunction is heredity. Research on genetics has revealed that vulnerability to psychopathology can be inherited. Up to this point, however, no specific genetic cause has been identified. Furthermore, genetic studies have demonstrated that heredity is not the sole determinant of mental illness. Monozygotic twins are genetically identical, yet it is often the case that one member of the twin pair will show a mental illness, such as schizophrenia or depression, whereas the other does not. This indicates that factors other than heredity are involved.

Numerous environmental factors have been studied to determine their relationship to mental illness. For instance, researchers recently have found evidence that obstetric complications and viral infections may have an adverse effect on the central nervous system of the newborn and lead to psychopathology. The role of other environmental factors, such as emotional conflict, in mental illness also continues to be the focus of much research.

psychopathy [sy-kahp'-uh-thee] Psychopathy consists of a particular cluster of personality traits and behaviors, including irresponsibility; impulsivity; hedonism; selfishness; egocentricity; low frustration tolerance; lack of guilt, remorse, or shame; and chronically unstable and antisocial life-style. Psychopaths are selfish, callous, and exploitative in their use of others, and often become involved in socially deviant behaviors. These traits and behaviors appear in psychopaths without the attendant signs of PSYCHOSIS, NEUROSIS, or mental deficiency found in most other mental illnesses. Psychopaths make up perhaps 15 to 20 percent of criminal populations but are responsible for a disproportionately higher number of crimes and violent acts.

The personality structure and life history of the psychopath are quite different from those of the person whose antisocial or criminal behavior is related to some underlying emotional disturbance or to an environment in which such behavior is expected or rewarded. Unlike the psychopath, these individuals may be capable of forming strong affectionate relationships and of experiencing concern and guilt over their behavior.

The causes of psychopathy are unknown, although investigators have shown increasing interest in the role of genetic factors in the development of criminality in general, and in psychopathy in particular. Some investigators have suggested that childhood HYPERACTIVITY may in rare cases lead to adult psychopathy.

Attempts to modify the behavior of psychopaths have not been successful, probably because psychopaths do not suffer from personal distress, see nothing wrong in their behavior, and are not motivated to change. Nevertheless, for reasons that are unclear, the behaviors of some psychopaths seem to become less grossly antisocial with age.

psychopharmacology Psychopharmacology is the study of DRUGS that affect mental and behavioral activity in some way. In general, any substance that affects psychic function or behavior is called a psychotropic drug. Those drugs with more or less specific medicinal functions are classified as psychotherapeutic. Many psychotropic drugs have been used to great benefit in psychotherapeutic treatment programs.

Historical Background. Psychotropic drugs are undoubtedly among the earliest types of drugs to be used by humans (see MEDICINAL PLANTS). They include such substances at OPIUM and COCAINE, which were used to help reduce a person's response to painful stimuli and to lessen fatigue. ALCOHOL has had similar uses. HALLUCINOGENS such as PEYOTE, which can induce some of the symptoms of psychosis, have been taken in conjunction with religious ceremonies (see FOLK MEDICINE).

As these substances indicate, psychotropic drugs were often taken in the past and continue to be taken today for reasons that are other than medicinal, although some were believed to be effective cures when in fact they only relieved symptoms. Actually, repeated administrations of many such drugs at sufficiently high doses can cause body damage or lead to dependence, or both (see DRUG ABUSE).

Modern psychopharmacology began in the early 1950s, ushered in by two events. First, the drug chlorpromazine, an antipsychotic agent, was synthesized in 1952. It was thereafter introduced widely into mental institutions, with the effect that the institutionalized population began to decrease. Second, important discoveries began to be made about the possible mode of action of psychotropic drugs on BRAIN chemistry and behavior. The coupling of these developments served to define psychopharmacology as a new discipline.

Classification. Psychotherapeutic drugs may be classified by the conditions under which they are most effective. Such classifications, however, are not mutually exclusive. Different groupings may have a good deal of overlap. These major groupings are indicated below, but this encyclopedia has many articles on individual drugs as well.

Psychomotor STIMULANTS are used in the treatment of fatigue, obesity, narcolepsy, and some forms of depression. They are also used to deal with hyperactivity. Effects of these drugs include appetite loss and mood elevation as well as fatigue reduction. In general, the drugs act through the NEUROTRANSMITTER dopamine in the brain. ANTIDEPRESSANTS similarly act through other such neurotransmitters. The drug LITHIUM, more specifically, is used to treat MANIC-DEPRESSIVE PSYCHOSIS.

Antianxiety drugs include the TRANQUILIZERS—formerly called "minor tranquilizers"—and the SEDATIVES, or sedative-hypnotics. They serve to reduce anxiety, tension, and agitation. Alcohol, although a much simpler chemical, may also be considered to act in this way, but it is not used medicinally for such purposes. The more powerful antipsychotic drugs, formerly called "major tranquilizers," include chlorpromazine and other drugs that are used to ease psychotic symptoms, manic-depressive illness, and SCHIZOPHRENIA.

In addition to these major drug categories, painkillers such as the ANALGESICS and ANESTHETICS may also be considered psychotropic because they act on the nervous system.

psychophysics Psychophysics is that branch of psychology which concerns the measurement of the psychological effects of sensory stimulation. The oldest branch of experimental psychology, it is usually said to have begun with the publication of Gustav Fechner's *Elemente der Psychophysik* (1860; Eng. trans., 1966).

See also: PERCEPTION.

psychosis [sy-koh'-sis] Psychosis is a severe mental disorder that involves a disruption in the individual's capacity to differentiate fantasy from reality. The symptoms of psychosis include disturbances in perception, thought content, and behavior. Perceptual abnormalities are referred to as HALLUCINATIONS; the patient experiences an auditory, visual, tactile, or olfactory sensation that has no basis in reality. For example, the patient might report hearing voices talking to him or her when there is no one else present, or claim to see objects that are not perceived by others. Delusions are unsubstantiated or incorrect beliefs about the self or others. For example, delusions of grandiosity, which often involve the belief that one has supernatural powers, are frequently manifested by psychotic patients. Other types include delusions of persecution, body deterioration, or nonexistence. The behavioral abnormalities associated with psychosis typically take the form of bizarre posturing, stereotyped movements of the face or limbs, or ritualistic behaviors.

The disorders classified as SCHIZOPHRENIA constitute the most commonly occurring psychotic illnesses; about 1 percent of the general population will be diagnosed as schizophrenic at some point in their lives. Psychotic symptoms can also be present in patients with major depressive disorder and bipolar disorder (see PSYCHOPATHOLOGY). Although psychotic symptoms can occur in children, they are relatively rare prior to adolescence. The onset of psychotic disorders generally occurs from ages 20 to 25.

The most effective pharmacologic treatment for psychotic symptoms are the neuroleptics, or "antipsychotic" drugs. These drugs are known to alter the biochemistry of the brain, and they seem to have an effect on dopamine, a neurotransmitter that may be overactive in psychotic patients.

psychosomatic medicine [sy-koh-suh-mat'-ik]
Psychosomatic medicine has been defined as that branch of medicine dealing with disturbances of body function that are caused at least in part by emotional or psychological factors. In the past a number of disorders such as migraine HEADACHES, peptic ULCERS, and ASTHMA have incorrectly been labeled psychosomatic, and physiological explanations for these conditions have since been defined or indicated. The concept that a group of diseases exists that are specifically psychosomatic is in fact generally outdated and should be discarded, although various STRESS-related disorders and those brought on by disturbances in eating patterns are still often considered primarily psychosomatic in nature. Psychosomatic medicine might now better be defined as a patient-oriented rather than a disease-oriented model of health, illness, and disease.

See also: BIOFEEDBACK; PSYCHOPATHOLOGY.

psychotherapy   Psychotherapy is a form of treatment for psychological disorders. In psychotherapy a patient or client talks with a therapist to obtain help in changing emotions, thinking, or behavior patterns that are distressing. Many types of human problems are treated in psychotherapy: disorders such as PHOBIAS, generalized ANXIETY, obsessions, compulsions, DEPRESSION, and psychosomatic and psychosexual disorders (see PSYCHOPATHOLOGY). In addition, psychotherapy may help patients and their families cope with severe disorders such as SCHIZOPHRENIA.

Psychotherapy also addresses interpersonal difficulties, such as unassertiveness, lack of interpersonal skills, and marital and family difficulties, as well as HABIT problems, such as drug abuse, excessive alcohol consump-

tion, tobacco smoking, and obesity. Psychotherapy may be used as an alternative to or in conjunction with medications and other somatic (physical) treatments on an inpatient or outpatient basis.

Therapists

Psychotherapy is usually offered by psychiatrists, clinical psychologists, and psychiatric social workers. Psychiatric social workers are trained in treatment methods and often work as part of a treatment team in hospitals or clinics. Today psychotherapy is being practiced more and more by paraprofessionals, who have less training but may be supervised by a professional or may be trained to work with specific problems using specific methods. In self-help groups therapists share the characteristics of their patients. Ex-alcoholics, for example, serve as therapists for alcoholics.

Formats of Therapy

Psychotherapy is conducted in several formats. Individual therapy refers to a therapist's work with one person on his or her unique problem; the relationship between client and therapist may be particularly important in producing change. In GROUP THERAPY, therapists meet with a group of patients, and the interactions between patients become an important part of the therapy process. Marital therapy focuses on the relationship between a husband and wife; often both a male and a female therapist are involved so as to provide both male and female perspectives. Family therapy brings all the members of one family into a therapy group, on the assumption that families operate as an interacting system and that one member's problems are only symptomatic of problems in the system.

Many different theories or schools of psychotherapy exist. They fall into the four broad classes covered in the remainder of this article: psychodynamic therapy, phenomenological therapy, cognitive therapy, and behavioral therapy.

Psychodynamic Therapy

Psychodynamic therapy makes the fundamental assumption that emotional disorders are merely symptoms of internal, unobservable, and unconscious conflicts between personality components. These conflicts result from unresolved family conflicts, experienced in early stages of childhood, that become reactivated in problem situations in adulthood. The aim of psychodynamic therapies is to revive the early conflict and to transfer it to the relationship with the therapist. The symptoms are removed when the therapist helps the patient to resolve the conflict in the transference relationship. The therapist interprets the transference to the patient and helps him or her overcome resistances to accepting the interpretation. Additional methods, such as dream interpretation or word-association techniques, are used to aid in uncovering unconscious material. Sigmund Freud's PSYCHOANALYSIS is the primary example of a psychodynamic therapy. Other variations include analytic psychology (Carl JUNG); will therapy (Otto RANK); holistic therapy (Karen HORNEY); individual psychology (Alfred ADLER); interpersonal psychiatry (Harry Stack SULLIVAN); and TRANSACTIONAL ANALYSIS (Eric Berne).

Phenomenological Therapy

Phenomenological approaches view people as naturally evolving in the direction of psychological growth and maturity. Society may hinder this process by imposing false values and causing the individual to distort his or her awareness of experience. Emotional disorder results from this distortion. The goal of therapy is to restore the patient's natural self-direction by helping him or her to become aware of distorted or denied feelings and emotions. The therapist attempts, as far as possible, to understand the subjective experience of the patient and to communicate back—and thus clarify—this experience. The therapist is an active, empathetic listener who provides an accepting atmosphere and helps the patient to regain awareness and thus control of his or her emotions and behavior. Emphasis is on present experience as opposed to recollections of early development. In some forms of phenomenological therapy the therapist may use various exercises to elicit emotional responses within the therapy session. The client-centered therapy of Carl ROGERS is a well-developed example of this type of approach. Fritz Perl's Gestalt therapy is a related technique that uses therapy exercises (see GESTALT PSYCHOLOGY). The existential approaches of Abraham MASLOW and Rollo May can also be grouped here.

Cognitive Therapy

Cognitive approaches to therapy assume that emotional disorders are the result of irrational beliefs or perceptions. Cognition is assumed to precede and determine emotion and behavior. Each person develops a complex set of categories (variously referred to as constructs, schemas, or plans) that is used to construe, or understand, events. The way in which an event is construed makes it frightening or calming, happy or sad. The emotionally disordered person distorts categorization (for instance, he or she sees all adverse events as personal failures) and has unrealistic beliefs about the world (for instance, he or she decides, "If I am not loved by everyone, I am worthless").

Cognitive psychotherapies attempt to make the patient aware of the occurrence and irrationality of these distortions and to substitute more rational and realistic evaluation. The therapist's role is to educate and to persuade logically. Examples of cognitive psychotherapies are personal construct theory (George Kelly); rational-emotive therapy (Albert Ellis); and cognitive therapy (Aaron T. Beck).

Behavioral Therapy

Behavioral approaches assume that all behavior is learned. Emotional disorders are considered to be conditioned responses or habits that can be modified by the same principles of learning that govern all behavior. From this perspective psychotherapy means providing corrective learning or conditioning experiences. Different therapy techniques are employed for remedying specific disordered behaviors (see BEHAVIOR MODIFICATION). Phobias, for instance, are treated by desensitization, in which the client is taught to relax while approaching the feared object in a gradual progression. In social-skill training, patients practice handling difficult interpersonal situations via role playing.

psychotropic drugs   see DRUG; PSYCHOPHARMACOLOGY

PT boat   Technically, the PT boat is a particular type of small, torpedo-armed motorboat used by the U.S. Navy in World War II. The designation stands for patrol torpedo. In common usage the term is equivalent to *torpedo boat* and applies to almost any small, fast vessel with powerful antiship armament. The classic PT boat was a plywood craft about 24 m (80 ft) long, displacing about 33 tons, and powered by 3 gasoline engines with a total of 4,500 horsepower. Originally armed with 4 torpedo tubes plus light cannon and machine guns, it had a top speed of about 40 knots, but overloading, heavy seas, damage, and plant life growing on the hull (in tropical waters) all reduced the available speed.

After the development of the first practical self-propelled TORPEDO by Robert Whitehead in the late 1860s, the idea of small, inexpensive vessels armed with a weapon capable of sinking the most powerful warships was appealing to the military, and the torpedo boat became an important component of many fleets around the turn of the century. The steam-powered torpedo boat, nevertheless, was no match for the DESTROYER, which soon replaced it. The appearance of the INTERNAL-COMBUSTION ENGINE, however, led to the construction of light vessels capable of higher speeds. Although they were hardly more seaworthy than their predecessors, their shallow draft and maneuverability made them valuable for inshore patrol and as raiding vessels in World War II.

The development of gas turbines after the war has made speeds of up to 60 knots possible, and the torpedo has been superseded by even more powerful weapons—antiship guided missiles. Light, fast motor vessels have consequently retained their importance and continue in use today, particularly in the fleets of smaller countries.

The PT boat, a variety of fast-moving motor torpedo boat used by the U.S. Navy during World War II, carried a crew of 14 and was capable of speeds up to 40 knots (46 mph). The vessels were heavily armed, bearing 3 antiaircraft guns of various caliber and 4 torpedo tubes.

Ptah [ptah]   In Egyptian mythology Ptah was the chief god of Memphis, who created the Moon, the Sun, and the Earth. One tradition held that he had created all things from mud; another, that he spoke the names of all things and his will created them from his words. Ptah was the patron of artisans and was identified by the Greeks with the god HEPHAESTUS.

The willow ptarmigan is an upland ground bird common to the colder regions of the Northern Hemisphere. During summer the male (left) *is generally red to brown with white wings and belly, and the female* (center) *is mottled brown with barred belly and white wings. Ptarmigans are the only genus of birds that molt into a white winter camouflage plumage* (right).

ptarmigan [tahr'-muh-guhn]   Ptarmigans, genus *Lagopus*, are stocky members of the GROUSE family that inhabit tundra, moors, and alpine areas of northern Eurasia and North America. All three of the species have short, rounded white wings, extensively feathered toes, and upper tail coverts that extend to the tip of the tail. Males have red "combs" above the eyes. Ptarmigans undergo seasonal color changes; in winter their white plumage matches the snow, and in summer their mottled brown plumage blends with the vegetation. They eat berries, buds, and leaves and fall prey to hunters, foxes, and owls.

pteridophyte [tuh-rid'-uh-fyt]   A pteridophyte (Greek: *pteris,* "fern"; *phyton,* "plant") is any member of a number of primitive plant groups, including the CLUB MOSSES, FERNS, HORSETAILS, and various fossil forms. In the Whittaker five-kingdom classification system, pteridophytes are placed in the phylum Tracheophyta, which includes all vascular plants. Many pteridophytes, which were the dominant plants in the Coal Age, are now extinct. Some were trees of considerable size, whereas living species are relatively small except for certain tropical tree ferns.

Pteridophytes contain a vascular system. Morphologically, these plants have the equivalent of roots, stems, and leaves. True seeds are not produced in these plants; however, a few species develop structures resembling seeds. These plants are mainly land plants, but water is required to complete the reproductive process; the sperm must move through water to reach the egg for fertilization. The sporophyte, the spore-producing stage in the life cycle, is the dominant generation. Except for the earliest stages of embryo formation, the sporophyte is completely independent of the gametophyte, the stage in which the sex cell (gamete) is produced.

pterosaur [tair'-uh-sohr]   Pterosaurs are a group of extinct flying reptiles that form the order Pterosauria. This order is usually divided into two suborders: the primitive Rhamphorhynchoidea, which lived during the Late Triassic and Jurassic periods (about 210 million to 135 million years ago), and the more advanced Pterodactyloidea, which lived from the Late Jurassic into the Late Cretaceous (about 160 million to 65 million years ago).

Pterosaurs had long, narrow wings constructed of a thin skin membrane supported by an elongated fourth finger of each front foot. Large extensions, or processes, on the upper-arm bones, and a large breast bone with a prominent keel for muscle attachment, are clear indications that these creatures were capable of active flight. Pterosaur remains are commonly found in sedimentary rocks of marine origin, leading to the conjecture that smaller species rested like gulls on the water and landed only to nest. Their pelvic structure suggests that they could walk, however. Evidence of a hairlike covering in a few specimens suggests that pterosaurs may have been warm-blooded, or endothermic, like mammals and birds.

Rhamphorhynchoids ranged from blue-jay size up to

Pterodactylus is a genus of flying reptiles, or pterosaurs, that existed during the latter part of the Mesozoic Era. These pterosaurs had heads nearly as long as their bodies, which ranged from sparrow to hawk size. Fossil remains have been found in East Africa and Europe.

that of large gulls; *Rhamphorhynchus* was about 60 cm (2 ft) long. Pterodactyloids varied from the size of a sparrow to such giants as *Pteranodon* and the recently discovered *Quetzalcoatlus*, with a wingspread of 15.5 m (51 ft).

Ptolemaic system   see GEOCENTRIC WORLD SYSTEM

Ptolemy [tahl'-uh-mee]   One of the most influential Greek astronomers and geographers of his time, Ptolemy, AD c.100–170, propounded the GEOCENTRIC WORLD SYSTEM that prevailed for 14 centuries. Little is known of Ptolemy's life, but he made astronomical observations from Alexandria, Egypt, during the years AD 127–41 and probably spent most of his life there.

Ptolemy's two major works, both extant, are the *Almagest* and the *Geography*. The *Almagest*, probably the earliest of his works, presents in detail the mathematical theory of the motions of the Sun, Moon, and planets. Ptolemy accepted the solar theory of his predecessor HIP-PARCHUS, improved on the lunar theory, and made his most original contribution by presenting details for the motions of each of the planets. Ptolemy's geometric models, used only to predict the positions of these bodies, employed combinations of circles known as epicycles, within the framework of the basic Earth-centered system supplied by ARISTOTLE.

The *Geography*, an early attempt to map the known world, drew on the work of Hipparchus, STRABO, and Marinus of Tyre.

Two relatively minor works, the *Optics* and the *Tetrabiblos*, dealt with ASTROLOGY and, respectively, with reflection and refraction. With the exception of the *Optics*, all of Ptolemy's works were immensely influential; the *Almagest* was not superseded until a century after Copernicus presented his heliocentric theory in the *De revolutionibus* of 1543.

Ptolemy, the Greco-Egyptian astronomer, geographer, and mathematician (fl. 2d century AD), is portrayed in this bas-relief from the Florence Cathedral in Italy. The Ptolemaic system of geocentric, or Earth-centered, planetary orbits dominated astronomy until the 16th century.

Ptolemy I, King of Egypt (Ptolemy Soter)   Ptolemy I, c.367–283 BC, created the political and military foundations of the Ptolemaic dynasty of Egypt (323–30 BC). When Alexander the Great died in 323 BC, Ptolemy, one

The head of Ptolemy I is printed on a silver coin. Ptolemy, a general under Alexander the Great, declared himself king of Egypt in 304 BC. He sought to counter Egyptian resentment of foreign domination by restoring the temples of the pharaohs and restoring traditional Egyptian religion.

of his leading generals, became satrap (governor) of Egypt and in 304 declared himself king.

Ptolemy's foreign policy was shrewdly designed to guarantee Egypt's security and trading advantages. He held Cyrenaica for most of his reign. His domination of Cyprus, Phoenicia, and Palestine was more intermittent, but all three were in his control by the end of the reign.

Ptolemy acquired great wealth through trading networks linking India, East Africa, and the Mediterranean. Taxes, dues, and monopolies further increased the royal treasury. Ptolemy depended on Greeks and Macedonians in government and the army, settling his veterans on farms throughout Egypt. Egyptians were resentful despite the prevailing prosperity. Ptolemy supported traditional Egyptian religion while both Greeks and Egyptians worshiped a Greco-Egyptian god, SERAPIS, and the king himself. Making ALEXANDRIA his capital, he founded the great library and museum there. Ptolemy abdicated for his son Ptolemy II in 284.

Ptolemy II, King of Egypt (Ptolemy Philadelphus) [fil-uh-del'-fuhs]   Ptolemy II, 308–246 BC, king of Egypt from 284 BC until his death, maintained an extensive empire. Cyprus, Phoenicia, and Palestine were Egypt's possessions for most of his reign, but control of Cyrenzica was partial and intermittent. Ptolemy developed contacts with Rome and extended his influence into Nubia and the Arabian peninsula. Ptolemy enhanced the efficiency of state exploitation of Egyptian agricultural labor. He also won renown as a great patron of the arts and sciences.

Ptolemy III, King of Egypt (Ptolemy Euergetes) [yoo-ur'-jit-eez]   Ptolemy III, c.280–221 BC, succeeded his father, Ptolemy II, as king of Egypt in 246 BC. By his marriage he reunited Egypt and Cyrenzica, and his wars against the Seleucid kings of Syria extended Egyptian territories in the Near East, although some of these were later lost. Ptolemy, whose reign was prosperous, began building the great temple at Edfu and reformed the Egyptian calendar, dating it from the start of the dynasty.

Ptolemy V, King of Egypt (Ptolemy Epiphanes) [ee-pif'-uh-neez]   Ptolemy V, c.210–180 BC, ruled as king of

Egypt from 205 until his death. Only a child when he succeeded his father, Ptolemy IV, he was an ineffectual ruler, and during his reign Egypt lost most of its foreign possessions to the Seleucid king ANTIOCHUS III. The domestic revolts of his father's reign continued. Ptolemy's concessions to the rebels and his suppression of them were inscribed on the ROSETTA STONE.

Ptolemy VI, King of Egypt (Ptolemy Philometor) [fil-uh-mee'-tur]

The reign of Ptolemy VI, king of Egypt from 180 until his death, in 145 BC, was marked by the problems of dynastic rivalry that would eventually destroy the Ptolemaic dynasty. Succeeding to the throne as a child, Ptolemy was well served by his mother as regent until her death in 176. From 170, Ptolemy uneasily shared the throne with a brother, Ptolemy VIII Euergetes, until Euergetes displaced him in 164. With Roman help, Ptolemy VI regained Egypt and Cyprus, although Euergetes retained Cyrenaica. When he died, he left a weakened monarchy to his young son, Ptolemy VII.

Ptolemy VIII, King of Egypt (Ptolemy Euergetes II) [yoo-ur'-jit-eez]

Ptolemy VIII, c.182–116 BC, presided over the accelerating decay of Ptolemaic Egypt. An unsavory intriguer, Ptolemy was coruler with his brother Ptolemy VI from 170 to 164 and king of Cyrenaica from 163 to 145. He assassinated (145) his nephew, Ptolemy VII, and was sole king of Egypt from 145 to 116. A long civil war (131–124) fought against one of his wives disrupted internal stability until 118 but left him in control of Cyprus and Cyrenzica. He also intervened in Syria. Ptolemy's mischievous will created conflict among his heirs.

Ptolemy XII, King of Egypt (Ptolemy Auletes) [aw-lee'-teez]

Ptolemy XII, c.112–51 BC, king of Egypt from 80 BC until his death, was an illegitimate son of Ptolemy IX (r. 107–88 BC), and his reign was heavily dependent on Roman support. Through bribery he prevented Roman annexation of Egypt, although Rome did seize Ptolemaic-ruled Cyprus, and won Roman recognition as ruler in 59 BC. The following year Ptolemy traveled to Italy, seeking aid against his rebellious subjects. After he had dispensed additional bribes, he was reinstalled (55) by a Roman army.

Ptolemy XIII, King of Egypt

Ptolemy XIII, 63–47 BC, ruled Egypt with his sister CLEOPATRA from the death of their father, Ptolemy XII, in 51 until his own death. Hoping to retain his father's Roman allies, Ptolemy supplied aid to the Roman general POMPEY THE GREAT. Increasingly suspicious of his sister, he expelled (48) her from Egypt. Cleopatra raised an army, however, and attacked the northeastern Egyptian city of Pelusium. After Julius CAESAR arrived at Alexandria with his army in search of the defeated Pompey, Ptolemy and Cleopatra were briefly reconciled. Cleopatra allied with Caesar, becoming his mistress, but the armies of Ptolemy and Caesar took up arms,

and the king was killed. His younger brother, Ptolemy XIV (c.59–44), subsequently became coruler with Cleopatra.

ptomaine poisoning [toh'-mayn]

Ptomaine poisoning is an archaic term reflecting an early belief that sickness occurring after eating was due to ptomaines—decomposition products (of proteins) that arise from the action of putrefying bacteria of the large intestine. The body has biochemical systems that detoxify ptomaines. Food poisoning actually is due to the toxins produced by certain bacteria that are growing in the food itself (see FOOD POISONING AND INFECTION).

puberty   see SEXUAL DEVELOPMENT

puberty rites   see PASSAGE, RITES OF

Public Broadcasting Service   see RADIO AND TELEVISION BROADCASTING; TELEVISION, NONCOMMERCIAL

public domain

The term *public domain* is used in two ways. First, it is the legal term that refers to products or processes unprotected or no longer protected by COPYRIGHT or PATENT and therefore freely available for appropriation or use by the public at large. Second, public domain refers to public land, that is, land owned by the U.S. government and not reserved for some specific use. The individual states do not own public lands, except for Texas, which agreed to join the Union in 1845 only if it retained its public lands.

public health

Public health is the effort organized by society to protect the health of its members. On all levels—local, national, and international—the major concerns of public-health agencies are the assurance of wholesome food and clean water, adequate sanitation systems, the prevention or control of epidemic and endemic diseases, the delivery of health care to needy population groups, and the formulation of laws regarding health.

Although the knowledge base of the field cuts across a number of disciplines (biomedical sciences, social sciences, engineering, law), public-health work relies heavily on specialized methods of quantitative analysis. The basic techniques for measuring and evaluating community-wide health problems are those of EPIDEMIOLOGY and biostatistics.

History. Concern with the regulation of diet, with the water supply, sewage disposal, and the isolation of the sick was already present in early civilizations. During the Middle Ages, efforts to fight epidemics of infectious diseases resulted in such practices as quarantine and sanitary cordons.

In 17th-century England, physician William Petty and John Graunt—considered the first demographer—developed a numerical method for studying the social phenomena that might provide the state with information on the number and "value" of people. The method required accurate statistical data on population, trade, manufacture, and education, as well as disease. This "political arithmetic" marked the beginning of quantitative studies of the health of populations.

VACCINATION, introduced (1798) by the English country physician Edward JENNER, was the first practical means to control and eventually to totally eradicate smallpox, as later it was to end the spread of other contagious diseases.

During the early 19th century, public-health focus shifted to the health problems associated with industrialization and urbanization, such as crowding in tenements, lack of a clean water supply, and poor food. In England recognition of these conditions gave rise to the sanitary movement, which was responsible for the passage of the Public Health Act of 1848, the first attempt to create an official body to supervise health-related public conditions.

The identification of microbes as causative agents of disease allowed public-health workers during the late 19th and early 20th centuries to develop specific methods of prevention. Antitoxins and vaccines were discovered and used, and mass immunization programs were initiated. Public-health laboratories were founded to test the purity of water, food, and milk, as well as to diagnose contagious diseases.

The new impetus given to public health by the application of bacteriology, coupled with the growing health needs of an industrial and urban United States, produced a rapid growth in state and municipal health departments, voluntary health agencies, public-health NURSING, maternal and child welfare programs, and school health programs.

The Modern Era. International conferences aimed at drafting sanitary conventions and quarantine regulations led first to the establishment (1909) of an international health organization based in Paris and ultimately to the founding of the WORLD HEALTH ORGANIZATION (WHO, 1942), an agency of the United Nations.

The health services of individual countries are organized in many different ways. In the Soviet Union, public health is the responsibility of the national government, and its administration is strongly centralized. The United Kingdom allows substantial autonomy to local governments. The United States, with its pluralistic approach to health services, gives local and state governments and the private sector large areas of responsibility. The Public Health Service, the principal health agency of the U.S. federal government, had its beginnings as the Marine Hospital Service (1798–1902), which provided medical relief to merchant seamen. It became the Public Health Service in 1912 and now operates as a division of the Department of Health and Human Services.

Of the many agencies making up the PHS, five are responsible for carrying out its major functions: the NATIONAL INSTITUTES OF HEALTH (NIH); the FOOD AND DRUG ADMINISTRATION (FDA); the CENTERS FOR DISEASE CONTROL (CDC); the Alcohol, Drug Abuse, and Mental Health Administration; and the Health Resources and Services Administration. Important functions of the PHS include medical research and dissemination of research results; the supply of health professionals and facilities to the public; the

provision of medical services to such special groups as American Indians; the investigation of the causes of epidemics; the testing of foods and drugs to ensure their safety; the development of treatment programs for alcohol and drug abuse and mental-health problems; and the collection and analysis of statistical health data.

public relations   *Public relations* is a general term describing a wide variety of techniques used by institutions such as corporations, government agencies, charitable foundations, and trade groups to present themselves in a favorable light to the general public and to specific audiences such as stockholders, the financial community, employees, customers or potential customers, and federal, state, and local legislators. Such groups frequently undertake research into public opinion before making decisions. Proposed actions of an institution may be reviewed by a public-relations specialist in order to assess their possible impact on public opinion. The day-to-day business of public-relations firms is to seek favorable publicity for the products, services, or personnel of client organizations within the editorial content of newspapers, magazines, television, radio, and major business and trade publications.

public television   see TELEVISION, NONCOMMERCIAL

public utility   A public utility is a business considered so important to the public welfare that it is subjected to some form of GOVERNMENT REGULATION or ownership. Often the business is a "natural monopoly," meaning that efficiency requires a single company (a monopoly) or, at most, relatively few companies in the industry. One example is the telephone industry: to have two or more companies with separate sets of telephone lines serving the same community has been traditionally viewed as both wasteful and unsightly. Other important public utilities include electric-power and gas companies, railroads, airlines, and waterworks.

Government intervention in such industries may take the form of regulation or ownership. In the United States, public utilities—other than waterworks and, recently, interstate railroad lines—are commonly regulated rather than owned by state and federal agencies. In other countries, public ownership is the usual approach.

In the United States the giant of public utilities until its breakup in the 1980s was the American Telephone and Telegraph Corporation (AT&T). Telephone service is regulated by the FEDERAL COMMUNICATIONS COMMISSION and state regulatory agencies. The largest publicly owned utility is the TENNESSEE VALLEY AUTHORITY (TVA). Cities or regional authorities usually own and operate their own water and sewer services and frequently their own transit systems, parking facilities, and electric-power systems.

Public Works Administration   Established as a NEW DEAL measure under Title II of the National Industrial Recovery Act of June 1933, the Public Works Administration (PWA) was designed to stimulate U.S. industrial recovery from the DEPRESSION OF THE 1930S by pumping federal funds into large-scale construction projects. President Franklin Delano ROOSEVELT placed the PWA under Secretary of the Interior Harold ICKES. Although Ickes established an enviable record for incorruptibility, his extreme caution in allocating funds did not stimulate the rapid revival of U.S. industry that New Dealers had hoped for. Initiating its own construction projects and funding similar ones started by federal agencies and state governments, the PWA spent $6 billion during the 1930s. Although it worked through private companies and was not conceived primarily as a relief agency, the PWA enabled building contractors to employ approximately 650,000 workers who might otherwise have been jobless. The PWA built courthouses and hospitals, schools and libraries, bridges and tunnels, roads and highways, and dams and levees. The agency also financed the construction of cruisers, aircraft carriers, and destroyers for the navy.

publishing   Originally the term *publishing* meant to make publicly known. Now it refers to the preparation and dissemination of written material for public consumption—including textbooks, works of nonfiction, newspapers, and periodicals as well as fiction, drama, and poetry.

Although PRINTING had developed in China about the 6th century AD, the invention of movable type by Johann GUTENBERG in Germany in the 15th century marks the beginning of modern publishing. Until that time publishing meant self-publishing, in which an author distributed handwritten manuscripts, or copying, from which the author's manuscript was laboriously transcribed. This article focuses on U.S. book publishing in a broad sense. Further information appears in more specialized articles: BOOK, JOURNALISM, NEWSPAPER, PERIODICAL, and RADIO AND TELEVISION BROADCASTING.

European Background. During the Renaissance and in the following centuries, spurred by Gutenberg's invention, publishing flourished in Europe and England as a result of the pioneering enterprise of Aldus MANUTIUS and Nicolas Jenson in Italy, Jean Dupré in France, William CAXTON in England, and several other publisher-printers.

Early U.S. Developments. In contrast to the publication of newspapers and journals, book publishing developed comparatively slowly in the United States. The new nation depended heavily on publishers in England. English books were either imported or reprinted in the American colonies. Nevertheless, an American publishing industry began to emerge on the East Coast during the 18th century.

J. B. Lippincott and Company, John Wiley, Harper (now HarperCollins), G. P. Putnam's Sons, and Charles Scribner's Sons, founded in the late 18th and early 19th centuries, were among the first U.S. publishers. Unlike the European publisher, whose profession gradually evolved from that of printer-publisher, the typical 19th-century U.S. publisher regarded the business as a comprehensive operation combining the functions of publisher and bookseller.

19th-Century Advancements. During the 19th century the attributes of the present-day publishing house emerged. Editors acquired or solicited manuscripts from authors. The editors then worked with authors to produce the best possible works. Marketing and sales forces managed the publicizing and advertising of books and placed copies for sale in bookstores. A production staff undertook designing, printing, and binding, making full use of increasingly sophisticated printing technology. With the cooperation of literary agents, who developed in England in the late 19th century and soon flourished in the United States, the publisher's subsidiary-rights department became an important source of income.

At the turn of the century marketing changes began to occur. Mail-order publishing grew in importance—an inevitable development in the United States, where many people live far from bookstores. Encyclopedias and expensively illustrated books became mail-order staples.

Prosperity after World War I and the rapid expansion of literacy set U.S. publishing on a course of steady growth, with only a comparatively brief setback during the Depression of the 1930s. Many new publishing houses, such as Random House (founded 1924) and Simon & Schuster (founded 1925), began publishing American authors. The 1920s also saw the birth of book clubs.

The Paperback Revolution. The next major development was paperback publishing. Inexpensive reprints had been published in the 19th century. Paperbacks, however, represented a major advance in the growth of publishing and literacy. Originally introduced in England by Allen Lane's Penguin Press in 1936, paperbacks quickly caught on in the United States. Further development of the paperback was interrupted by World War II, although the war paradoxically gave the industry its greatest impetus. The armed forces had a huge appetite for reading matter, and the book industry distributed large quantities of popular and classical works.

After the war publishing flourished as never before. College enrollment soared under the auspices of the G.I. Bill, creating a new market for college texts. Prosperity and leisure time also helped to expand readership. The number of new books—hardcover and paperback—published between 1945 and 1988 tells the story—1945: 6,548 titles; 1950: 11,022; 1962: 21,914; 1966: 30,050; 1974: 40,846; 1984: 51,000; 1988: 55,000. In 1989, however, the number decreased to 45,700 new titles, reflecting a decline in profits, especially in trade books. In the early 1990s mass-market paperbacks held more than 25% of the market.

Recent Developments. Most popular works of fiction and nonfiction appear in paperback about a year after hardcover publication. Although hardcover books get most of the reviewers' and advertisers' attention, a few paperback publishers have endeavored to find new writers of quality and to work with those they already publish in hardback.

Paperback rights for best-selling hardcover books commonly sell today for six figures, and some have even exceeded $2 million. Because books are advertised in the same style as Hollywood films—often, in fact, in conjunction with the film version—publishing has acquired a new image. Once regarded as a quiet, scholarly pursuit, it is now often seen as a branch of show business. The opportunity for huge profits from comparatively small investments has naturally attracted the attention of big business. Beginning in the mid-1960s, U.S. publishing gradually changed from the largely family-owned concerns to a corporate industry.

Recent developments include the expansion of bookstores from the city into the suburbs and innovations in computerized printing. Computers have made possible the almost immediate publication of current events in book form. New technologies also represent new markets for publishers, including audio versions of books. Electronic publishing features computerized texts (including reference works) available in on-line form through personal computers as well as on compact disc read-only memory (CD-ROM).

Giacomo Puccini, born into a family of operatic composers, was encouraged to study music at an early age. Puccini's gifts for melodrama and sentimental eroticism, displayed in such works as Tosca and La Bohème, have assured the continued popularity of his work.

publishing, desktop   Desktop publishing is a method for using a computer, a laser printer, and various software programs to prepare and print documents—anything from a single page of text to advertisements, pamphlets, books, and magazines. Although computer-aided publishing has been available since the early 1970s, the cost was initially quite high; in 1985 it became possible to perform desktop publishing with personal computers (PCs) and relatively inexpensive laser printers producing "letter quality" type and visuals (see COMPUTER, PERSONAL; PRINTER, COMPUTER).

A basic desktop publishing system allows its user to produce printed matter by employing a variety of type fonts and sizes, type justification, hyphenation, and other typesetting capabilities offered by various publishing software programs. Page layouts can be set up on the computer monitor and transferred to the printer. Many types of graphics can be created, and the system may also be able to incorporate art and photographs from sources outside the computer. The command codes for producing text and graphics are comparatively simple.

A basic system includes a microcomputer; a laser printer that is able to print at 300 or more dots per inch (dpi); word-processing software; and a page description language, a software program that enables its user to position, size, and manipulate blocks of type and pictures. In contrast to professionally printed matter, 300 dpi provides relatively low resolution. More complex laser printers or the use of an added phototypesetting unit produces finer quality print and illustrations. The addition of a computer-connected scanner allows the use of text and visual material from other sources.

Puccini, Giacomo [poo-chee'-nee]   Giacomo Puccini, the composer of some of the world's best-loved operas, was born into the fifth generation of a family of musicians in Lucca, Italy, on Dec. 22, 1858. Inspired by Verdi's Aïda, the young music student resolved to compose operas. Financial aid from family members and a

scholarship from Queen Margherita of Italy allowed him to enroll at the conservatory in Milan, where he spent three years (1880–83) working under Antonio Bazzini and Amilcare Ponchielli. Ponchielli introduced Puccini to the writer Ferdinando Fontana, the librettist of Le Villi, Puccini's first opera. Like Juno, Le Villi failed to win prizes but commanded public acclaim when produced in Milan in 1884. That success led the publisher Ricordi to commission a new opera from Puccini; five years later the composer delivered Edgar, again on a text by Fontana but to no great applause.

With his third and fourth operas, Manon Lescaut (1893) and La Bohème (1896), both first presented in Turin, Puccini won fame and fortune. His next two operas, Tosca (1900) and Madama Butterfly (1904), were greeted with less enthusiasm by opening-night audiences. The critics who damned Tosca, however, were eventually outvoted by the public, and after Puccini revised Madama Butterfly in the weeks following its La Scala premiere, that work, too, met with success. With this pair of operas, both notable for their beautiful and memorable melodies as well as for a heightened tension, the composer was hailed as the successor to Verdi—the highest acclaim he could have asked from Italian audiences.

Puccini was not the musical or dramatic innovator that Verdi was, but he nevertheless continued to enjoy tremendous international success. His next opera, La Fanciulla del West (The Girl of the Golden West), was written for the Metropolitan Opera, where it was first presented in 1910. There followed La Rondine (1917), Il Trittico (three one-act operas: Il Tabarro, Suor Angelica, and Gianni Schicchi, 1918); and Turandot, the last act of which was completed by Franco Alfano after the composer's death in Brussels, Nov. 29, 1924. Turandot received its premiere at Milan's La Scala in 1926.

Puck   In the folklore of England, Wales, and Ireland, Puck, also known as Robin Goodfellow, is a small hobgoblin who assists with household chores. Puck is also, however, addicted to practical jokes and is accused of responsibility for the mishaps of domestic life. His most famous literary personification is in Shakespeare's *Midsummer Night's Dream*, in which the dramatist merged classical myth with English rural lore to create an entire fairy kingdom in which Puck is the mischievous envoy of Prince Oberon and takes delight in the folly of human love. The adjective *puckish* aptly describes a whimsical delight in confusion.

pudelpointer   The pudelpointer, or poodle pointer, resembles the German wirehaired pointer and is believed to be the product of a cross by German sportsmen in the late 1800s of poodles with pointers in an effort to obtain an all-around gundog. There is some question, however, regarding the use of the poodle in this breeding. The old German word *pudel* referred to water, and the term may have been used to refer to any of several *pudel hunds,* or water dogs.

The pudelpointer's usually tan or brown coat consists of a woolly undercoat and a medium-length, dense, wiry outercoat, which becomes short on the legs and feet but forms a beard and bushy eyebrows on the head. The pudelpointer's ears hang close to its head, and its tail is docked to be 15 to 20 cm (6 to 8 in) long. Pudelpointers average 60 cm (24 in) high at the shoulder and 27 kg (60 lb) in weight.

Pudovkin, Vsevolod I.   [poo-dawf'-kin, fsev'-uh-luht]   Excited by D. W. Griffith's *Intolerance* when it was shown in Moscow in 1919, Soviet filmmaker Vsevolod Pudovkin, b. Feb. 28 (N.S.), 1893, d. June 30, 1953, abandoned a career in chemistry for the cinema. In 1922 he joined the experimental film workshop of Lev Kuleshov (1899–1970). The first films Pudovkin directed were *Chess Fever* (1925), a short, witty comedy; *Mechanics of the Brain* (1925–26), an instructional film on Pavlov's experiments; and *Mother* (1926), a worldwide success that dealt with the 1905 revolution. His best-known works were the admirably photographed and edited *The End of St. Petersburg* (1927) and *Storm over Asia* (1928).

Puebla (city) [pway'-blah]   Puebla (de Zaragoza, or Puebla de los Angeles) is the capital of Puebla state in central Mexico and the fifth largest city in the country (1990 pop., 1,054,921). It lies 130 km (80 mi) southeast of Mexico City. Puebla produces textiles and ceramics and is famous for its blue Talavera tiles. It is the seat of the Autonomous University of Puebla (1937). Among Puebla's 60 churches are a 16th-century cathedral and the 17th century baroque church of Santo Domingo. The city's theater, dating from 1550, is the oldest in the New World. Puebla was settled in 1532. It was the site of the 1862 battle in which Mexican troops under Ignacio Zaragoza defeated the French, although in the following year the city fell to the French after a long siege.

Puebla (state)   Puebla is a mostly mountainous state in east central Mexico, traversed by the Sierra Madre Oriental. It has an area of 33,902 km^2 (13,090 mi^2) and a population of 4,118,059 (1990). The capital is the important city of Puebla. The most famous peaks are the dormant volcanoes Popocatépetl and Ixtacihuatl. Agricultural crops include corn, wheat, and alfalfa. Stock is raised primarily in the southern part of the state. Numerous pre-Aztec ruins, including the famous pyramid at Cholula, attract tourists.

Pueblo (Colorado) [pweb'-loh]   Pueblo is a city located in south central Colorado, on the Arkansas River, along the eastern slope of the Rocky Mountains. The seat of Pueblo County, it has a population of 98,640 (1990). A network of highways and rail connections makes it a trade and shipping center for coal, timber, livestock, and farm products. Pueblo is Colorado's center of heavy industry, producing steel, wire, concrete, and lumber. The University of Southern Colorado (1933) is in the city.

The founding of Pueblo is credited to James P. Beckwourth, who arrived with his party in 1842 to set up a trading post for Rocky Mountain fur traders and trappers. With the arrival of the railroads in the 1870s and the discovery of coal nearby, the settlement grew rapidly. By 1882, Pueblo's first blast furnace and smelter had been built, and the city became one of the West's leading steel producers.

Pueblo (Indian tribes)   Pueblo (Spanish for "town") refers to the village-dwelling Indians of the southwestern United States, including the Hopi of northeastern Arizona, the Zuñi of western New Mexico, and the Rio Grande Pueblos. Descendants of the prehistoric Anasazi peoples, the Pueblo Indians on or near reservations numbered

Ancestors of the Pueblo Indians built hundreds of pueblos throughout the Four Corners region—where Arizona, Colorado, New Mexico, and Utah meet—in the period AD 900–1300. Among the most spectacular are the Cliff Palace ruins at Mesa Verde National Park in Colorado.

more than 48,000 in the late 1980s. Linguistically they are diverse. The Hopi and Tanoan Pueblos of the Rio Grande speak Aztecan-Tanoan languages; the languages of the Zuñi and of the Keresan-speaking Pueblos of New Mexico have not been clearly related to any existing linguistic family (see INDIAN LANGUAGES, AMERICAN).

The Western Pueblos—as the Hopi and Zuñi are called—were too remote to be brought under effective control by the religious and governmental authorities of Spain. Their comparative isolation, reinforced by deliberate resistance to acculturative pressures, enabled the Hopi and Zuñi to preserve more of their ancestral heritages than have any other Indian tribes in the United States. They still enact the pageants of their traditional ceremonial system and retain their indigenous social structure and much of their technology. The KACHINA cult is still followed by many Pueblos.

The Eastern Pueblos include the peoples of ACOMA and Laguna, in the high plateaus of west central New Mexico, as well as along the Rio Grande, including the villages of TAOS, Isleta, Jemez, Nambé, Picurís, Pojoaque, Santa Clara, San Ildefonso, San Juan, Sandia, and Tesuque. Historically, the Rio Grande Pueblos are noted for their resistance, both passive and overt, to alien encroachments (see POPÉ).

Pueblo Incident   On Jan. 23, 1968, a U.S. Navy intelligence-gathering ship, the *Pueblo*, was seized by the North Koreans in the Sea of Japan off the Korean coast. American claims that the vessel was in international waters were repudiated by North Korea, which declared that the *Pueblo* had intruded into that country's territorial waters and was conducting espionage. Negotiations between U.S. and North Korean representatives failed to secure the ship's release.

The *Pueblo*'s 82 surviving crew members, including its captain, Comdr. Lloyd M. Bucher, were detained for 11 months. They were freed only after U.S. officials signed a document apologizing for the alleged spying and promising that no such incident would recur. In a procedure unprecedented in international law, the United States branded the document false before signing it.

puerperal fever [pue-ur′-puh-rul]   A bacterial infection of the female genital tract following childbirth or abortion, puerperal fever, also known as childbed fever, was a common cause of death during the 19th century. It is usually caused by *Streptococcus pyogenes* (hemolytic streptococcus). Rapidly progressive high fever and weakness occur as the bacteria multiply in the lining of the uterus and enter the bloodstream through the large raw surface where the placenta was attached. This blood poisoning (septicemia) is rapidly fatal unless treated immediately with antibiotics. Bacteria often reach the patient's pelvic organs by way of the hands of infected persons doing manipulations during labor; the need for scrupulous cleanliness during childbirth was first advocated by Ignaz Semmelweis in Vienna in the 1840s.

Puerto Rico [pwair′-toh ree′-koh]   The island of Puerto Rico is located in the Caribbean Sea, east of the Dominican Republic and west of the Virgin Islands. A possession of the United States officially known as the Commonwealth of Puerto Rico, it encompasses 9,104 km^2 (3,515 mi^2). The population is 3,336,000 (1990 est.), with a density of 366 persons per km^2 (949 per mi^2). The population of its largest metropolitan area (and capital), SAN JUAN, is 431,227 (1986 est.). Until recently the economy of Puerto Rico was dominated by agricultural products, but at present, employment in manufacturing, the service sector, and tourism prevails. Juan PONCE DE LEÓN established a settlement on Puerto Rico in 1508, and it remained a Spanish possession until control passed to the United States in 1898.

Land and Resources

In addition to the main island, the commonwealth comprises several smaller nearby islands, including Culebra, Mona, and Vieques. Approximately three-fourths of the area is hilly or mountainous. The most prominent topographic feature is a central backbone of low mountains (called the Cordillera Central in the west and Sierra de Cayey in the east), which extends through the center of the island from the east to the west coast. Puerto Rico's highest peak is Cerro de Punta, with an elevation of 1,338 m (4,389 ft), north of the island's third largest city, PONCE.

Climate. The climate is tropical, with an annual mean temperature of 24° C (75° F). Annual temperature ranges are slight, resulting in a year-round growing season. The windward northeastern coast experiences approximately 1,524 mm (60 in) of precipitation annually, whereas the leeward southwestern coast receives an average of about 508 mm (20 in). Puerto Rico lies astride the Atlantic's major hurricane path.

Vegetation and Soil. Much of the original tropical vegetation and fauna have been removed by humans and replaced by exotic species. About 25% of the island is under forest cover. The Caribbean National Forest is a 116-km^2 (45-mi^2) tropical rain forest preserve in the Sierra de Luquillo. The dry extreme southwest is characterized by drought-resistant plants such as grasses and cacti. The soils, like those of most tropical areas, are generally poor for agricultural practices.

Drainage and Resources. Puerto Rico does not contain any notable rivers or large lakes. The deep tropical waters that surround it do not produce good commercial fisheries, and local fish production supplies only a small percentage of the island's consumption. Pleasant beaches, however, are important for the tourist industry. The most notable mineral resource is copper, which is found in large deposits located in a triangular area enclosed by the towns of Adjuntas, Lares, and Utuado.

People

Puerto Rico has a white majority, unlike most Caribbean islands. Approximately 2% of Puerto Rico's population are foreign born, coming mostly from Cuba and the Dominican

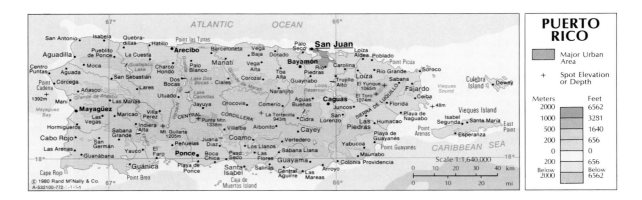

Spanish was the major language in Puerto Rico prior to U.S. acquisition in 1898. English is now taught as a required second language and is widely understood by the people of Puerto Rico, although only a minority speak it fluently. An overwhelming majority of the population are Roman Catholics, but religious practices have been influenced by traditional Caribbean beliefs.

From 1980 to 1990, Puerto Rico's population grew by only about 3%, and over the years many rural areas have experienced population declines as their residents moved to either Puerto Rican cities or the U.S. mainland. A large proportion of all Puerto Ricans live on the U.S. mainland.

One of the most dramatic changes in Puerto Rico over recent decades has been an improvement in health care. Between 1940 and 1989, average life expectancy rose from 46 to more than 70 years. A health-care system operated by the insular and municipal governments provides free medical and dental programs.

Puerto Rico is the only country in the Americas that allocates as much as one-third of its budget for education. The island's school system employs more people and spends more money than any other sector of the government. In 1940 about two-thirds of the population was literate; by the late 1980s the literacy rate had increased to about 90%, one of the highest in Latin America. The University of Puerto Rico provides higher education facilities at several campuses.

Puerto Rico has its own symphony orchestra and a conservatory of music. Each year in May it holds the world-famous Casals Festival, named for cellist Pablo Casals. The privately operated Ateneo Puertorriqueño (Puerto Rican Atheneum; founded in 1876), and the government-sponsored Institute of Puerto Rican Culture (opened in 1955) have provided the vital nuclei for the island's cultural expression.

Economic Activity

Per capita income in Puerto Rico is much lower than that of any of the 50 states, although it is higher than that of other Caribbean areas. The United States purchases about 85% of Puerto Rico's exports and provides about 60% of its imports.

Manufacturing. By 1955 manufacturing had surpassed agriculture as the major generator of income. The largest industrial sectors are textiles and apparel, electrical and electronic equipment, plastics, chemicals, petrochemicals, petroleum products, processed foods, metal, and leather. A huge integrated petroleum refinery and petrochemical complex operates on the southwest coast in the Guayanilla-Peñuelas area.

Agriculture. Sugar, once the principal agricultural product, now accounts for a relatively small part of the

Fort San Gerónimo, on one of the two islets of Old San Juan in San Juan Bay, was built in 1771. Originally called Puerto Rico ("rich port"), San Juan is the capital and largest city of Puerto Rico.

value of agricultural production. Coffee and tobacco also account for smaller percentages of the total agricultural output than formerly. The cultivation of rice, a staple on Puerto Rican tables, is being encouraged on former sugarcane lands.

Transportation and Tourism. Three well-developed maritime complexes are located in the ports of Ponce, Mayagüez, and most importantly San Juan, which alone accounts for the majority of the island's shipments. The major international airport is in San Juan. The network of paved roads is among the best-developed in Latin America. Tourism is one of Puerto Rico's leading sources of revenue.

Government and Politics

The Puerto Rican Constitution was approved in 1952, when the island was granted its present commonwealth status. The government has the ability to write and amend its own constitution, but it must not contradict the Constitution of the United States. Puerto Ricans do not pay federal income taxes, nor do they vote in U.S. presidential elections. They elect a resident commissioner, having only committee voting privileges, to the U.S. Congress.

Modeled after that of the United States, the Puerto Rican government has executive, legislative, and judicial branches. The legislature is bicameral with a 27-member Senate and a 51-member House of Representatives. The governor heads the executive branch and is elected every four years.

Puerto Rico's political status is controversial, and debate goes on among the commonwealth, statehood, and independence political factions. The island has three main political parties: the Popular Democratic party, which favors continued commonwealth status; the New Progressive party, which supports U.S. statehood; and the minority Independence party.

History

Originally named Boriquén by the Taino Indians, Puerto Rico was settled by several Indian groups long before it was visited (1493) by Christopher Columbus on his second voyage to the New World and renamed San Juan Bautista. It was given its present name, meaning "Rich Port," by Juan Ponce de León, who established a settlement inland from San Juan at Caparra in 1508. Although the dominant Taino then numbered about 30,000, the Indian population had virtually disappeared by 1582.

The Spaniards introduced sugarcane to the island in 1511, and the first black slaves arrived in 1518. In the centuries that followed the colony grew slowly, as the Spanish concentrated on the richer colonies of Mexico and Peru. During the late 16th century the island's strategic value was realized, and Spain began to fortify it, holding it against frequent English, French, and Dutch attacks into the 19th century.

Spain, which had granted Puerto Rico almost complete autonomy by 1897, ceded the colony to the United States in 1898 after the Spanish-American War; it was under U.S. military rule from 1898 to 1900. In 1917, the Jones Act made all Puerto Ricans U.S. citizens and created an elected senate. Puerto Rico did not elect its own governor until 1948; the Commonwealth of Puerto Rico was established in 1952.

In 1948, Luis Muñoz Marín initiated "Operation Bootstrap" to improve the economy. Tax incentives and low labor costs attracted large- and small-scale industries, providing the underpinnings for an economic transformation during the 1950s and '60s. An economic slump in the early 1980s increased demands for greater autonomy. Subsequently, the economy picked up. Hurricane Hugo in 1989, however, brought much damage and economic hardship. In 1990 the longstanding issue regarding Puerto Rico's political status was again considered, with legislation pending before the U.S. Congress that would authorize a plebiscite in which Puerto Rican voters could choose statehood, commonwealth status, or independence.

puff adder see VIPER

puffball see FUNGI

puffer Puffers, also called blowfish, globefish, or swellfish, are about 120 to 130 species of fishes with the ability to inflate their stomachs with water or air. The jaw teeth are fused into a small, hard, cutting beak useful for grasping and crushing hard-shelled prey. The fused teeth in both jaws are separated by a space, giving the puffer the appearance of having four large teeth; this is noted in the family name Tetraodontidae, meaning "four teeth." Considered a delicacy in Japan, puffers can be poisonous if prepared improperly. Most puffer species occur around coral reefs in tropical waters. Six or seven species of *Sphoeroides* live along the southeastern coast of the United States; *S. maculatus*, the northern puffer, found from Florida to Cape Cod, grows to about 35 cm (14 in) long.

Puffers inflate their large, distensible stomachs with air or water when threatened—a defensive device that may scare a predator or suggest that the puffer is too big to be swallowed. Illustrated here are a reticulated puffer (A), semi-inflated (1) and uninflated (2); and a freshwater puffer (B), uninflated (3) and fully inflated (4).

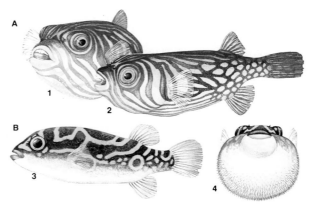

puffin Puffins, sometimes referred to as bottlenoses or sea parrots, comprise three species of birds (common, horned, and tufted puffins: *Fratercula arctica, F. corniculata,* and *Lunda cirrhata*) in the family Alcidae, order Charadriiformes. Their closest relative, the rhinoceros auklet, *Cerorhinca monocerata,* does not have the large, triangular-shaped, laterally compressed, and sculptured bill typical of puffins. Puffins are compactly built, about 30 cm (12 in) tall, and their three front toes are webbed. They feed by diving for marine organisms.

Puffins are found along seacoasts and on islands in the northern oceans, nesting in colonies of as many as 50,000 inhabitants. Total world population of the birds is about 15 million. The puffins usually nest in burrows or caves and lay a single white egg. Both eggs and adult birds are used as a human food resource.

The common Atlantic puffin is considered by sailors to be a land indicator; if three or more are sighted, land is likely within 240 km (160 mi). Once threatened by extinction in the United States, puffins from Canada have been used to reestablish breeding colonies in Maine.

pug The pug is a small, short-bodied dog with a rounded head, a short, wrinkled face, large eyes, and small ears; it has a short, smooth, soft coat and carries its tail curled tightly over the hip. The breed apparently originated in China and is related to the Pekingese. It probably reached Europe at least as early as the 1600s. The modern pug may be fawn or black, the former having a black face mask and black ears. The desirable size for pugs is between 25 and 28 cm (10 and 11 in) high at the shoulder and from 6 to 8 kg (14 to 18 lb) in weight, making them the largest of the toy breeds.

The pug has a shortened muzzle and a tail that curls over its back. It is thought to be of Chinese origin. Introduced into Holland by traders during the 17th century, the pug was a fashionable pet in England during the 1880s and '90s.

Pugachev, Yemelian Ivanovich [poo-gah-chawf', yim-il-yahn' ee-vahn'-uh-vich] Yemelian Ivanovich Pugachev, b. *c.*1742, d. Jan. 22 (N.S.), 1775, was a Russian Don Cossack who led the great peasant rebellion of 1773–74. In the late 18th century the DON COSSACKS, fiercely jealous of their traditional political autonomy, saw their position being weakened by the strong centralizing policies of Empress CATHERINE II. Although Catherine's husband and predecessor, PETER III, had been assassinated in 1762, it was widely rumored that he was still alive. In 1773, Pugachev declared himself to be Peter, abolished serfdom, and by December he was marching toward Moscow with an army of 30,000. Despite initial successes, the rebel force was eventually defeated by Catherine's army. Pugachev was captured, taken to Moscow in an iron cage, and later beheaded.

Puget, Pierre [pue-zhay'] Pierre Puget, b. Marseille, France, Oct. 16, 1620, d. Dec. 2, 1694, was among the greatest sculptors of the 17th century. Although he worked in Italy, the years from 1668 were spent in France, where he obtained several royal commissions but never received official success. His famous *Milo of Crotona* (1671–82; sculpted for Versailles, now in the Louvre, Paris) characterizes his baroque style, which was influenced by the works of Michelangelo and Bernini.

Puget Sound [pue'-jit] Puget Sound is a deep inlet of the Pacific Ocean in western Washington, extending south from the Strait of JUAN DE FUCA through the Admiralty Inlet. Hood Canal is its western arm. The Olympic Peninsula lies to the west. Deepwater ports are located at OLYMPIA, SEATTLE, and TACOMA; and Bremerton has a naval shipyard. The sound is the southern terminus for the Inside Passage to Alaska. Climate in the entire area is controlled by a warm current, resulting in mild winters, abundant precipitation, and frequent fogs. The British navigator George Vancouver explored Puget Sound in 1792.

Pugin, Augustus [pue'-jin] The British architect, decorator, archaeologist, and theorist Augustus Welby Northmore Pugin, b. Mar. 1, 1812, d. Sept. 14, 1852, was the foremost exponent of the GOTHIC REVIVAL style in mid-19th-century Britain. His most important and influential works were the books *Contrasts* (1836) and *The True Principles of Pointed or Christian Architecture* (1841), in which he argued that contemporary architects should return to the structural principles of Gothic architecture rather than simply emulate its outward forms.

Pugin pursued his theories in the churches he designed. For example, the plain exterior of Saint Giles's in Cheadle, Staffordshire (1841–46), reflects faithfully the late Gothic models studied by Pugin, who sumptuously decorated the interior with colorful and intricate patterns formed by the floor tiles, metalwork, woodwork, and stained glass. Pugin's best-known work is the richly ornamented interior of WEST-MINSTER PALACE in London (1840–65).

Puig, Manuel [pweek]   Among the most popular contemporary Latin American novelists, Manuel Puig, b. Argentina, Dec. 28, 1932, d. July 22, 1990, won international recognition with such novels as *Betrayed by Rita Hayworth* (1968; Eng. trans., 1971), *The Buenos Aires Affair* (1973; Eng. trans., 1976), *Blood of Requited Love* (1982; Eng. trans., 1984), and *Pubis Angelical* (1979; Eng. trans., 1986). For English-language readers, his best-known novel is *Kiss of the Spider Woman* (1976; Eng. trans., 1979; film, 1985), whose protagonists—a jailed homosexual and the political prisoner who is his cellmate—share with most of Puig's characters the compulsion to interpret their humdrum lives in the rich images of popular entertainment: the movies, radio drama, and the like.

Pujo, Arsène Paulin [poo-zhoh', ahr-sen']   Arsène Paulin Pujo, b. Lake Charles, La., Dec. 16, 1861, d. Dec. 31, 1939, a Louisiana Democrat, chaired (1912) a subcommittee of the U.S. House of Representatives that examined the financial dealings of the so-called money trust. Pujo, a member of Congress from 1903 to 1913, headed the Banking and Currency Committee from 1911; as chair of a subcommittee known as the Pujo Committee, he investigated J. P. Morgan and other leading financiers. The committee's findings aroused public opinion against the concentration of economic power in private hands and helped passage of the Federal Reserve Act (1913) and the Clayton Anti-Trust Act (1914).

Pula [poo'-lah]   Pula, a port in Croatia, Yugoslavia, lies on the Adriatic Sea at the southern tip of the Istrian peninsula, about 100 km (60 mi) south of Trieste. Its population is 77,278 (1981). The city has a naval base and shipyards. Machinery, cement, textiles, and glass are produced. Landmarks include the Arch of Sergius (29–28 BC), a Roman amphitheater (begun 30 BC), and a 5th-century Byzantine basilica.

Once a fishing village, Pula fell to Rome in the 2d century BC. The city passed to Venice in 1148 and was nearly demolished (1379) in wars between Venice and Genoa. Austria gained control in 1797, but between 1806 and 1814 the port came under French rule. After 1856, Pula became a major Austrian naval base. Italy held the city from 1920 until 1947, when it became part of Yugoslavia.

Puɫaski, Kasimierz [poo-lahs'-kee, kah-zee'-myersh]   The Polish patriot and soldier Kasimierz Puɫaski, b. c.1747, d. Oct. 11, 1779, was a cavalry officer in the service of the colonists during the American Revolution. A Polish aristocrat, he gained fame (1768–72) as a cavalry commander in the anti-Russian Confederation of Bar, becoming its commander in chief. When the Russians de-feated the confederation, he fled to Turkey, then to France. In 1777 he offered his services to Benjamin Franklin. He organized the first American cavalry unit, the Pulaski Legion. Puɫaski died from wounds sustained in a cavalry charge near Savannah, Ga.

puli [pue'-lee]   The puli (plural, pulik) is a small Hungarian herding dog distinguished by its soft, dense, wooly undercoat and long, thick, unkempt outer coat. Coat colors are solid dull black, rusty black, various grays, or white. The puli has a slightly domed, small head and a short muzzle; V-shaped, hanging ears; and usually a long tail carried either low or, when the dog is aroused or moving, curled over the back. Males are commonly between 43 and 48 cm (17 and 19 in) high at the shoulder and 13.5 and 16 kg (30 and 35 lb) in weight; females are slightly smaller.

Pulitzer, Joseph [pul'-it-sur]   A powerful editor and publisher in St. Louis, Mo., and in New York City, Joseph Pulitzer, b. Mako, Hungary, Apr. 10, 1847, d. Oct. 29, 1911, helped establish the foundations for the modern American newspaper. At his death he left funds to establish a school of journalism at Columbia University (opened in 1912) and to endow the Pulitzer Prizes for achievements in American journalism and letters, and later in music.

Pulitzer emigrated to the United States when he was 17 and served briefly in the Union Army during the Civil War. He then went to St. Louis, where he started (1868) his journalistic career with the *Westliche Post,* a German-language newspaper. Following the Civil War, Pulitzer bought and merged (1878) the *Dispatch* and the *Post* in St. Louis. The evening *Post-Dispatch* combined a crusading editorial page with thorough news coverage, augmented by sensationalism to boost circulation.

Pulitzer purchased the *New York World* in 1883 and repeated the *Post-Dispatch* formula—adding such new touches as sports, comics, women's fashions, and illustrations. Fierce competition from William Randolph

Joseph Pulitzer, an American journalist and newspaper magnate, established a national reputation through vigorous editorials and sensationalistic reporting. Pulitzer's will funded one of the first American schools of journalism and established the prestigious prizes that bear his name.

Hearst, owner of the *New York Journal,* led to the sensationalistic coverage of the Spanish-American War that came to be known as YELLOW JOURNALISM.

Pulitzer Prize   Awarded each spring in the United States for excellence in journalism, letters, and music, the Pulitzer Prizes are prestigious and highly coveted as symbols of success in the designated fields. First awarded in 1917, they were established by Joseph Pulitzer, who left in his will $2 million to Columbia University to establish a school of journalism, specifying that $500,000 should be used to maintain annual prizes for the advancement of journalism and letters. The awards are bestowed by Columbia's trustees and are administered by the Graduate School of Journalism.

Pulitzer had indicated four journalism awards and four for letters (novel, play, history, and biography). Over the years, however, the advisory board has added new categories and revised some of the wording; for example, awards are now given for "distinguished" rather than the "best" work in a particular category.

The journalism prizes are awarded for material that appears in U.S. newspapers during the previous calendar year. Each prize is $1,000, except for the public-service award, which is a gold medal. The categories are meritorious public service (by a newspaper), general news reporting, special local (investigative) reporting, national reporting, international reporting, editorial writing, explanatory journalism, specialized reporting, editorial cartooning, spot news photography, feature photography, commentary, criticism, and feature writing.

Six awards in letters and one in music, each $1,000, are given. The prizes are for works published by American authors during the calendar year. Those for drama and music are for the period from April 21 to March 31, the accepted opening and closing dates for the theater and music seasons in the United States. American themes are preferred. The categories in letters are fiction, poetry, drama, history, biography or autobiography, and general nonfiction.

---

pulley   A wheel used to transmit power or force by means of an encircling flat belt, V-belt, rope, or cable is called a pulley. In order for a pulley to accommodate a flat belt, which is often made of leather, the rim (periphery) of the pulley is made flat or slightly convex (crowned). For a V-belt, rope, or cable, the rim is grooved. For a treatment of power transmission by a belt, see MACHINE.

When used with ropes or cables, pulleys can be combined in a variety of arrangements to increase the mechanical advantage—the ratio of the load overcome to the effort expended. In figure 1, neglecting friction and the bending elasticity of the rope, the force F on the rope is constant, and the upward pull on the pulley B is $2F$, which is equal to the load W. This means that a person could lift a load of 20 kg by exerting a force of 10 kg on the rope.

In figure 2, making the same simplifying assumptions, the rope around pulley B still exerts an upward force of $2F$. This means, however, that the rope around pulley C

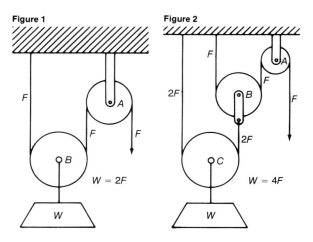

Figure 1

Figure 2

$W = 2F$

$W = 4F$

exerts a force of $2F$, so that W, the load lifted, is equal to $4F$. Other arrangements and numbers of pulleys are possible. One or more pulleys enclosed in a case is called a block, and pulley blocks together with the necessary rope are known as a block and tackle and are used for lifting and pulling heavy loads.

See also: SIMPLE MACHINES.

Pullman, George Mortimer   George Mortimer Pullman, b. Brocton, N.Y., Mar. 3, 1831, d. Oct. 19, 1897, was an American industrialist who developed the railroad sleeping car. Trained as a cabinetmaker, he moved to Chicago in 1855 and began to remodel old railroad coaches. In 1863 he built the first modern sleeping car, the *Pioneer,* which had a folding upper berth and seat cushions that could be extended to create a lower berth. In 1867, Pullman organized the Pullman Palace Car Company to manufacture his sleeping cars, and then developed other types of railroad cars, including the dining car (1868).

Pullman Strike   The Pullman Strike (May–July 1894) was a violent confrontation between railroad workers and the Pullman Palace Car Company of Illinois. In the wake of the Panic of 1893, the company cut wages but did not lower rents or other charges to employees in the company town of Pullman, now part of Chicago. When representatives of the American Railway Union protested (May 11), they were fired. Eugene V. DEBS, the head of the union, then called a boycott of all Pullman cars. On July 2, Att. Gen. Richard OLNEY obtained a court injunction to halt the strike, and federal troops arrived in Chicago on July 4. Rioting broke out and several strikers were killed, but by July 10 the strike had been broken. Debs and other top union officials were jailed for disobeying the injunction.

pulmonary artery   see CIRCULATORY SYSTEM; HEART; LUNGS

pulmonary embolism Pulmonary EMBOLISM is a blockage of an artery in the lungs, usually caused by the lodging of a detached blood clot from elsewhere in the body, often from the deep leg veins, but sometimes caused by air or detached particles of fat, bone marrow, or tumor tissue. Such blocking agents are called emboli. In about 10 percent of cases the interruption of blood flow causes areas of lung tissue to die (pulmonary infarction). Some 30 percent of pulmonary embolism cases suffer heart attacks. Pulmonary embolisms are treated with ANTICOAGULANTS. (See also CARDIOVASCULAR DISEASES.)

pulp magazines Inexpensive fiction magazines, printed on pulpwood paper, achieved mass circulation at the beginning of the 20th century and came to be called pulps. Sold only at newsstands, they featured stories of adventure and romance. The first pulp magazine, *Argosy,* was begun as an adventure-fiction anthology by Frank MUNSEY in 1896.

Pulp authors, who earned about 2 cents a word, had to write fast to earn a living, and for this reason they produced standardized stories. The result was fiction with highly predictable plots, long sections of stiff dialogue, and an emphasis on details describing physical action. Love stories were popular among women readers, but most pulps were written for a male audience and Westerns were the most popular; other types included detective, masked avenger, war, sports, and fantasy stories. The first major specialty magazine was *Detective Story* (1915).

Among the most famous pulp writers were Edgar Rice BURROUGHS, who created Tarzan in 1912, and Frederick Faust, who wrote under 20 pseudonyms, the best known of which is Max BRAND. Pulp magazines that made a contribution to literature include *Black Mask,* which developed the hard-boiled detective genre with such writers as Raymond CHANDLER and Dashiell HAMMETT, and *Astounding,* which in the late 1930s helped to develop modern science fiction.

pulsar [puhl′-sahr] Pulsars are older stars that give out regular pulses of electromagnetic radiation, mainly radio waves. They were discovered in 1967 by the radio astronomers Jocelyn Bell Burnell and Antony Hewish at Cambridge, England.

Hundreds of pulsars are now known. Their pulse periods range from 0.03 to 0.0015 sec. The periods are accurately maintained but show a slight slowing down in most cases. Pulsars are believed to be NEUTRON STARS that are rapidly rotating, the pulse period being the rotation period. The rotation is gradually slowing down because of loss of rotational energy. The best-known pulsar is situated in the CRAB NEBULA, where the loss of energy as the pulsar slows down provides the means of keeping the nebula radiating.

The pulses, while accurately periodic, are individually highly variable. For example, strong pulses may be followed by weak pulses. Sometimes a pulsar may spend some time not exhibiting pulses, and then resume puls-

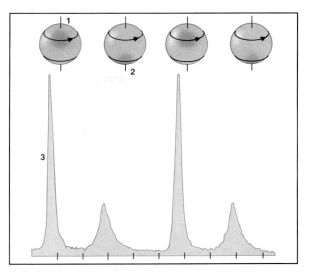

A pulsar, or pulsating radio star, is thought to be a rapidly rotating neutron star that emits radio waves from its magnetic polar regions (red). The star's magnetic field is tilted with respect to the axis of rotation, such that first one region (1) and then another (2) faces a terrestrial observer as the star rotates. Sharp radio pulses of varying intensity, depending on which region faces the Earth most directly, are detected at extremely regular intervals (3). The radio waves are emitted by charged particles moving in the magnetic field.

ing. When many individual pulses from a given pulsar are averaged, they show a characteristic pulse profile.

Pulsars appear to be located anywhere in our galaxy within a few hundred parsecs from the galactic plane. In 1984 the first pulsar to be discovered outside the Milky Way Galaxy was found in the nearby Large Magellanic Cloud.

The Crab and Vela pulsars show pulses at optical and gamma-ray frequencies, and X-ray pulses have been detected from the Crab pulsar. Binary radio pulsars have also been discovered. Another kind of pulsar, the binary X-ray pulsar, is thought to consist of a neutron star and a companion star revolving around one another. The X rays are believed to arise because of material being ejected from the companion star and landing on the neutron star.

pulsating stars SEE VARIABLE STAR

pulse (electronics) A pulse is a brief change in what is otherwise a reasonably stable electrical signal. Pulses may be irregular natural phenomena, such as a bolt of lightning, or they may be generated intentionally in virtually any number and sequence imaginable. A pulse may be characterized according to its rise, duration, and decay. The rise time is generally a measure of the time required for the pulse to rise from 10% to 90% of its full amplitude. The duration is the width of the pulse in units of time. The decay time is a measure of the time required for the pulse to fall from 90% to 10% of its full amplitude.

Many electronic circuits and components depend on single or multiple pulses for their operation. Often the pulses are very rapid and have rise and decay times measured in microseconds (1 μsec = 10^{-6} sec) or nanoseconds (1 nsec = 10^{-9} sec); the pulse frequencies range from fewer than one pulse per second to trillions per second. The most common example of an electronic circuit that is capable of accepting and emitting pulses is the gating circuit, or digital logic gate. In a digital COMPUTER a typical network of logic gates may accept, process, and transmit billions of pulses in a single second. The pulses are generally of the same amplitude and have similar rise and decay times. Their durations, however, may range from a few nanoseconds to well over a second. It is the presence or absence of pulses at any given time that controls the operation of both the individual logic gates and the circuit as a whole. Electrical pulses also find use in RADAR and in pulse modulation—the MODULATION of signals for the transmission of information.

pulse (medicine)   The human pulse results from the alternating expansion and contraction of artery walls as the heart varies the volume of blood (cardiac cycle) entering the arterial system. Thus it corresponds to the heartbeat. It can be counted by feeling points on the body surface where an artery lies close to the skin, such as the wrist or ankle. Artery walls are elastic, and they become distended when the heart contracts, termed *systole*, causing a surge of blood from the heart into the arteries. When the heart relaxes, termed *diastole*, the blood volume or BLOOD PRESSURE in the arteries is decreased and the walls contract, pushing the blood along. The normal pulse rate in healthy adults at rest ranges roughly from 70 to 90 pulsations per minute; in children the range is roughly from 90 to 120.

pulse, electromagnetic   see ELECTROMAGNETIC PULSE

pulse crop   Pulse crops, or grain LEGUMES, are various leguminous plants used as human foods and as forage plants and fodders for domesticated animals. The term *pulse* refers specifically to the seeds of these plants, but other plant parts are also often eaten. Pulse crops are a major source of dietary protein; many legumes also supply fats and oils. Most legumes can enrich soils through the action of nitrogen-fixing bacteria on their roots, and a number of pulse crops are used agriculturally for this purpose (see NITROGEN CYCLE).

Among the most commonly used grain legumes are the SOYBEAN, the PEANUT, and the many species of PEAS and BEANS (see also LIMA BEAN). Other pulse crops of more limited or geographically restricted use include the CAROB, CHICK-PEA, COWPEA, fenugreek, LENTIL, LUPINE, MESQUITE, and VETCH. Still other legumes grouped with the pulse crops, although some are cultivated only locally, are the catjang or pigeon pea (*Cajanus*), jack bean (*Canavalia*), guar (*Cyamopsis*), lablab (*Dolichos*), wild pea (*Lathyrus*), white popinac (*Leucaena*), velvet bean (*Mucana*), and Bambara groundnut (*Voandzeia*).

See also: AGRICULTURE AND THE FOOD SUPPLY; DIET, HUMAN.

puma [poo'-muh]   The puma, *Puma concolor*, in the cat family, Felidae, is also called mountain lion or cougar. Pumas range from British Columbia through South America; they prefer forested areas and jungles and can adapt to various climates. A male puma may grow to be 1.8 m (6 ft) long, plus a tail of 60–90 cm (2–3 ft), and may weigh more than 91 kg (200 lb). The coat ranges in color from reddish to brownish yellow or gray. Black stripes reach from the mouth to the eyes, and the tail tip is black. The head is small and round with a black spot over each eye. The puma usually hunts at night. It climbs well, is an excellent jumper, and often drops from limbs onto its prey. Its mating call is a harsh scream. Litters, which are born usually 2 years apart, contain from one to five young. The male does not aid in raising the young. Pumas usually live to be about 12 years old.

The puma, a large North American cat, ranges from southern Canada to South America. This solitary cat has been hunted by farmers and ranchers because it sometimes attacks livestock.

pumice [puhm'-is]   Pumice is a frothy volcanic glass, usually light in color and high in silica. It occasionally contains some crystals of quartz and feldspar. The froth, which forms during an eruption of a gas-rich magma because of the decrease in confining pressure, is similar to the bubbles formed in carbonated beverages when their containers are opened. The bubbles make pumice so light that it will float on water. Pumice may float for weeks before it becomes waterlogged and sinks. It has been found floating as much as 6,400 km (4,000 mi) from its source. Pumice is used primarily for abrasives, polishing compounds, insulators, and lightweight aggregates and in stucco, plaster, and cement.

pump A pump is a device used to move or compress liquids or gases. The syringe demonstrates its simplest form: a piston inside a cylinder. The Greek inventor HERO OF ALEXANDRIA's pump (1st century AD) had two cylinders, and the pistons and piston rods were formed as a single piece, their top ends coupled to the hand-worked rocking-beam. Force pumps, utilizing a piston-and-cylinder combination, were used in Greece to raise water from wells. Similar air pumps operated spectacular devices in Greek temples and theaters, such as the water organ. The Romans adopted and improved upon these useful devices.

In its simplest form the piston pump was made of wood, either square or circular, without any valve, the water being drawn up below the piston, which fitted tightly in the cylinder. By the Middle Ages the bilge or burr pump was used aboard ship. Typically it had one valve in the bottom and a conical leather piston that could collapse and open out on successive strokes of the piston.

With the dawn of the Industrial Revolution, pumps were increasingly needed for draining mines and for supplying power for cranes, hoists, and lifts. The centrifugal pump, developed by Denis Papin in 1689, proved to be the pump to meet this need. It and its many variants proved to be by far the most effective means for handling vast quantities of water continuously. By 1851 the centrifugal pump had become firmly established in most parts of the world.

Types of Pumps

Present-day pumps can be divided into two basic types: the positive-displacement, or static, type and the dynamic, or kinetic, type. In a positive-displacement pump the pumping action is a displacement produced by a decrease in volume in the working chamber of the pump. Examples of this type are reciprocating, rotary, gear, and vane pumps. In the dynamic type a dynamic (kinetic) action takes place between some mechanical element and a fluid. Centrifugal pumps and jet pumps are examples of this type.

The reciprocating pump is a simple type of plunger pump. A piston is made to move back and forth (reciprocate) inside a cylinder. The inlet and outlet parts have valves that limit the fluid to unidirectional (one-way) flow. During the intake stroke the inlet valve opens, allowing fluid to be drawn in, as the volume of the cylinder is increased. During the power, or output, stroke the inlet valve closes, the output valve opens, and the cylinder volume is decreased, forcing fluid through the outlet. This pump is best for low flow-rates and high-suction lifts but is not suitable for dirty or viscous fluids.

The rotary pump, or vane pump, also makes use of a varying volume in a cavity to force fluid in the desired direction. In this type the volume may be made to vary in a number of ways. Depending on the type of rotating impeller, a rotary pump may be a gear pump, a vane pump, or a piston-type rotary pump.

The centrifugal pump consists of a rotating impeller—a wheel fitted with vanes—and a stationary casing, or housing. The impeller imparts pressure and kinetic ener-

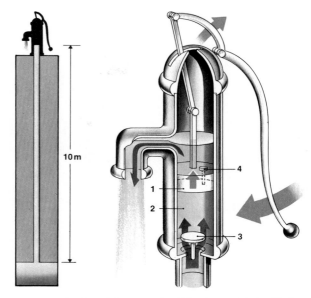

The lift pump is a form of piston pump in which a downward stroke of the lever moves the piston (1) upward, forming a vacuum in the cylinder (2). Atmospheric pressure—which, at sea level, can theoretically support a column of water as high as 10 m (33 ft)—on the surface of the water outside the pump forces water through the open valve (3) into the cylinder, filling the upper chamber. On the upward stroke of the lever the valve closes, and the piston valve (4) opens to allow the piston to move downward through the trapped water. On the next downward stroke of the lever the piston again moves upward, and the piston valve is closed by the water in the cylinder. The water is then discharged, and the cycle repeats.

gy to the fluid, and the casing guides the motion of the fluid. The centrifugal pump produces a flow that is smooth and steady and can handle sewage and water that contains grit, gravel, and small stones.

Applications

The use of pumps in the modern world is widespread. Pumps are used to deliver water in homes and in industry; to transport oil and other fluids; to circulate water, fuel, coolant, or working fluid, as in automobiles, aircraft, air conditioners, and refrigerators; and to drain coffer dams, quarries, and mine shafts. Another application is the use of fluids in power transmission, where mechanical work is transformed into fluid energy (see HYDRAULIC SYSTEMS; PNEUMATIC SYSTEM).

pumpkin Pumpkin is a name commonly given to fruit of the genus *Cucurbita* of the GOURD family, Cucurbitaceae. The name SQUASH is often interchanged with "pumpkin." Most varieties that are called pumpkin have orange fruit, very long vines, and stems that are firmer and squarer than those of other squashes. The most common pumpkin, a variety of *C. pepo,* has been cultivated for so long that a wild form no longer exists.

Pumpkins grow on trailing vines that bear broad, rough leaves and are punctuated by yellow flowers and tendrils (right). The gourdlike orange fruit has a smooth, thick, slightly furrowed rind.

Pumpkin seeds are planted in groups called hills. They are not harvested until the skin is tough, about 120 days after seeding. Pumpkins do not keep as long as winter squashes and must be picked before frosts occur.

pun   A pun, in which two disparate meanings are linked by a single sound, is often regarded as the most primitive form of humor. The very simplicity of the pun, however, may account for its long history and its frequent use, not only by subversive comedians such as Groucho Marx, but also by William Shakespeare, whose plays are replete with puns—not all of them comic (as in Mercutio's dying scene in *Romeo and Juliet*: "Ask for me tomorrow and you shall find me a grave man"). A pun may be an absurd practical joke played on language or it may, by taking advantage of a linguistic accident, extend the meaning of a word by bringing two or more of its meanings into simultaneous use.

Punch and Judy   Puppets from which a famous street show takes its name, Punch and Judy are an early-19th-century English development of characters imported from France and Italy in the latter part of the 17th century. Although the basic plot varies, it usually involves Punch's enraged bludgeoning of his wife, Judy, their child, and several lesser characters, followed by his imprisonment and escape. Often accompanied by his dog, Toby, Punch is a hook-nosed, long-chinned hunchback whose quick wit is triumphant even over the devil. The violence of the story is counteracted by slapstick action and humorous dialogue.

punched card   see COMPUTER

punctuation   The word *punctuation* is derived from the Latin *punctus,* "a point." It refers to the system of marks or points inserted in a text to clarify the meaning or signal a change in pitch or intonation. Ancient Greek grammarians used only three points, placed high, low, or at midline, to indicate grammatical units and subunits. Hebrew scribes marked vowel signs and accents above or below the lines of the Masorah, or sacred text. Medieval English scribes commonly used a medial point, a semicolon, an inverted semicolon (called a *punctus elevatus*), and a virgule [/]. William Caxton, the first English printer, used only a virgule, comma, and period.

Modern punctuation is, by contrast, complex. Some punctuation marks divide discourse according to a scale of grammatical relationships. The period [.] indicates completion of the largest punctuated unit, the sentence; next in rank, the colon [:] indicates major divisions within a sentence. In descending order follow the semicolon [;], which marks off minor sentence divisions; the comma [,], marking off groups of word units; and, finally, the apostrophe ['], denoting either possession, as in *John's coat*, or elision, as in *don't.* Other punctuation marks indicate the pauses, stresses, and changes of pitch in live speech. The interrogation point, or question mark [?], signals a question; the exclamation point [!] indicates emphasis; the dash [—] marks a break in the sentence; the hyphen [-] separates words or word elements, as in *vice-president*; ellipsis points [. . .] signify an omission; and quotation marks [" "] encompass the words of a speaker. Parentheses [( )] set off incidental explanatory material, and square brackets ([]) enclose editorial interpolations.

Punic Wars [pue'-nik]   The Punic Wars were three great confrontations between Rome and the North African city-state of CARTHAGE fought from 264 to 146 BC. At their conclusion, Rome was the greatest power in the West, and Carthage was totally destroyed.

The First Punic War (264–241 BC). In the 3d century BC, Carthage controlled several islands that allowed it to dominate the western Mediterranean. Its occupation of Messana (Messina), Sicily, in 264 and that city's request for Rome's intervention triggered the First Punic War. With the aid of HIERO II, tyrant of Syracuse, the Romans built a large fleet of ships to challenge Carthaginian naval supremacy and won major naval victories at Mylae (260) and Ecnomus (256). They were defeated, however, after besieging Carthage (256).

Holding Mount Eryx, HAMILCAR BARCA, the Carthaginian commander, harassed the Romans in Sicily and on the Italian coast. Rome desperately commissioned 200 new ships, and Gaius Lutatius Catulus defeated an unprepared Carthaginian fleet in 241. Rome granted peace to Carthage at the price of its abandoning Sicily and paying a huge indemnity.

The Second Punic War (218–201 BC). The most important of the three conflicts and one of the decisive wars of history, the Second Punic War was brought on by Carthaginian bitterness over its defeat and by Rome's seizure of Sardinia and Corsica in 238.

Hamilcar Barca's son, HANNIBAL, and son-in-law, HASDRUBAL, restored Carthaginian fortunes by conquering (237–219) part of Spain. The suspicious Romans negoti-

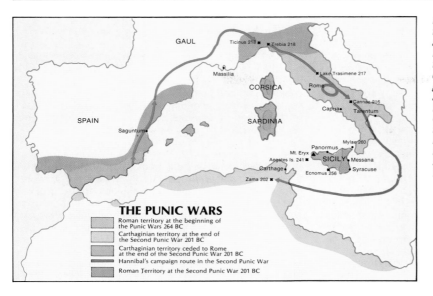

THE PUNIC WARS

Roman territory at the beginning of the Punic Wars 264 BC
Carthaginian territory at the end of the Second Punic War 201 BC
Carthaginian territory ceded to Rome at the end of the Second Punic War 201 BC
Hannibal's campaign route in the Second Punic War
Roman Territory at the Second Punic War 201 BC

In the three Punic Wars, fought between 264 and 126 BC, Rome defeated and ultimately destroyed the powerful North African city of Carthage. During the second war, however, Rome came close to defeat at the hands of the great general Hannibal, who invaded Italy and won a string of victories over the Romans, culminating in the Battle of Cannae (216). Later, Roman delaying tactics and insufficient support from home turned the tide against him. The initiative passed to the Roman general Scipio Africanus Major, who defeated Hannibal at Zama (202).

ated a treaty (c.226) with Hasdrubal that set the Ebro River as the Carthaginian boundary in Spain, but Roman failure to honor this agreement convinced Hannibal to challenge Rome at Saguntum in 219.

Fear of Carthage, aristocratic ambitions, growing commercial interests, and agitation by its ally Massilia (Marseille) all probably caused Rome to declare war (218). Hannibal unexpectedly crossed the Alps (somewhere between the Little Saint Bernard and Mount Genèvre passes) into the Po Valley. That crossing, with its elephant baggage train, is one of history's most celebrated military feats.

Despite an initial string of victories (Ticinus River, 218; Trebia River, 218; Lake Trasimene, 217), Hannibal subverted few Roman allies in northern Italy. In the south the Roman commander, Fabius Maximus (see FABIUS family), harassed (217) him with delaying tactics, but more impatient consuls lost four legions in Hannibal's trap at Cannae (216). Despite the defection of Capua and

A Spanish coin bears the likenesses of Carthaginian general Hannibal (obverse) and a war elephant (reverse) from the army that marched from Spain through the Alps to launch a surprise invasion of Italy.

Syracuse, Rome's other allies held firm, Roman armies continued to hold Spain, and the Roman fleet controlled the Mediterranean. After recapturing Capua (211), Syracuse (211), and Tarentum (209), the Romans defeated reinforcements brought from Spain across the Alps by Hannibal's brother Hasdrubal at the Metaurus River (207). The Roman general SCIPIO AFRICANUS MAJOR drove (206) the remaining Carthaginian forces from Spain, then boldly invaded (204) Africa, where, after attacking Carthage's Numidian ally Syphax, he defeated Hannibal at Zama (202) with the tactics learned at Cannae. Peace was granted (201) Carthage at the cost of Spain, another large indemnity, and reduction of the Punic fleet to ten ships. Carthage's power was effectively destroyed.

The Third Punic War (149–146 BC). The Third Punic War was declared in 149 when Carthage attacked Rome's ally, MASINISSA, king of Numidia. Rome quickly defeated Carthage, which surrendered conditionally. The Roman consuls immediately increased their demands, however, and decreed the complete abandonment of the city itself. The Carthaginians desperately renewed fighting and withstood siege for three years, until SCIPIO AFRICANUS MINOR captured the citadel after a week of house-to-house combat. The surviving Carthaginians were sold into slavery, and the Romans razed the city.

punishment   Punishment describes the imposition by some authority of a deprivation—usually painful—on a person who has violated a law, rule, or other norm. When the violation is of a society's criminal law there is a formal process of accusation and proof followed by imposition of a sentence by a designated official, usually a judge. Informally, any organized group—most typically the family, in rearing children—may punish perceived wrongdoers.

In Western culture, four basic justifications for applying punishment have been given: retribution, deterrence, rehabilitation, and incapacitation. The history of formal punitive systems is one of a gradual transition from familial and tribal authority to the authority of organized society. Although parents today retain much basic authority to discipline their children, physical beatings and other severe deprivations—once widely tolerated—may now be called CHILD ABUSE and result in criminal charges.

Most penal historians note a gradual trend over the last centuries toward more lenient sentences in Western countries. Capital and corporal punishment, widespread in the early 19th century, are today seldom invoked. Indeed, in the United States corporal punishment as such appears to be contrary to the 8th Amendment's restrictions on cruel and unusual punishment, yet the rate of imprisonment in the United States appears to be growing, as improved information and enforcement systems make criminal convictions more likely. Furthermore, since the mid-1970s, popular and professional sentiment has taken a distinctly punitive turn and now tends to see retribution and incapacitation—rather than rehabilitation—as the goals of criminal punishment.

See also: CAPITAL PUNISHMENT.

Punjab [puhn'-jahb] The Punjab is a semiarid plains region of northwestern India and northeastern Pakistan covering about 777,000 km^2 (300,000 mi^2) and roughly corresponding to the Indian states of Punjab and Haryana and the Pakistani province of Punjab. The Pakistani Punjab has a population of about 51 million (1983 est.); the population of the Indian Punjab is about 30 million (1981). The name is derived from *panca nada* ("five rivers") and refers to the SUTLEJ, the Jhelum, the Chenab, the Ravi, and the Beas, all of which are tributaries of the Indus. LAHORE is the capital of Pakistani Punjab, and CHANDIGARH is the capital of both Indian Punjab and Haryana. Principal crops include wheat, cotton, oilseeds, sugarcane, maize, and rice. Small-scale manufacturing is also important.

Excavations in the Punjab at Harappa (2500 BC) on the Sutlej River have revealed an advanced INDUS CIVILIZATION. Aryans (1500 BC), Greeks (326 BC), Scythians (1st century AD), and Muslims (11th century AD and after) crisscrossed the region as migrants, invaders, and rulers. Ranjit Singh, a leader of the Punjabi Sikhs, ruled a Punjabi kingdom from 1801 to 1839. The British occupied Punjab in 1849 and later designated it a province. In 1947 the Punjab was divided between India and Pakistan. Communal riots caused an exodus of Hindus and SIKHS from Pakistani Punjab and Muslims from Indian Punjab.

Wealthy Punjab state (India), the home of the Sikhs, has the holiest Sikh shrine—the Golden Temple at AMRITSAR. The predominantly Hindu state of Haryana, originally part of Punjab, was separated from it in 1966. After two years of increasingly violent agitation for greater autonomy for Punjab state, Indian troops stormed the Golden Temple in 1984 to oust Sikh militants headquartered there. Despite subsequent efforts to redress various Sikh grievances, violence by Sikh extremists continued.

Punta Arenas [poon'-tah ah-ray'-nas] Punta Arenas, the capital of Chile's Magallanes province and the southernmost mainland city in the world, lies on the Strait of Magellan (see MAGELLAN, STRAIT OF). The population is 111,700 (1987 est.). Sheep raising, lumbering, canning, coal mining, and petroleum shipping from TIERRA DEL FUEGO are the main economic activities. Founded in 1847 to strengthen Chilean claims to the strait, Punta Arenas became a coaling station for ships en route to California.

pupa [pue'-puh] A pupa is the intermediate stage between young and adult forms in those INSECTS which pass through a complete, or holometabolous, metamorphosis from larva (caterpillar, grub, maggot) to a radically different adult. Insects having a complete metamorphosis, and therefore also a pupal stage, include the butterflies, beetles, flies, and bees. Pupae are generally inactive and nonfeeding, and consequently the harsh, unproductive period of winter frequently serves as the time of pupation. The pupal stage is a time of breakdown of larval tissue and reorganization into adult form.

puppet A puppet, from Latin *pupa,* "doll," is usually a jointed representation of a human, an animal, or, more rarely, an abstract figure that can be manipulated to give an illusion of life. Performances using such figures have been part of the theater from early times.

Puppets are defined by their mode of operation. The hand, or glove, puppet, most familiar from PUNCH AND JUDY shows, fits directly over the operator's hand, so that its head and arms can be moved by the fingers. The shadow puppet is a flat cutout held against a screen and illuminated by a lamp from behind. The rod puppet is controlled from below by long, thin rods. The marionette is worked from above by strings connecting it to a complex control bar; its name, from French meaning "little Mary," is derived from the use of such figures in medieval sacred dramas.

The earliest recorded appearance of puppets is in religious rites, either as moving effigies of the gods or, possibly, as replacements for the original human sacrifices. Even in classical Greece puppets were already used regularly for entertainment. In the Far East puppetry has enjoyed continual prestige as a high dramatic art; Japan evolved the specialized form of BUNRAKU, which after reaching its height in the 17th century competed successfully with the live theater and produced many of the same plays.

In Europe puppetry has generally been considered as appealing to simpler tastes. The Greco-Turkish Karaghiozis SHADOW PLAYS offered robust, often obscenely satirical fare to village audiences. In Sicily and southern Italy, large, heavy marionettes dramatized medieval tales of heroic chivalry in serial form. In 17th-century England, the art degenerated into children's entertainment.

It is argued that puppets can provide a degree of abstractness and stylization unattainable by the human actor. In Eastern Europe puppets permit a freedom of satiri-

(Right) *The popular English hand puppets Punch and Judy were originally marionettes. The figure of Punch evolved from clown characters in early Italian farce. Judy was added during the 1660s, when the show was first taken to England.*

These mechanical marionettes are from the Puppet Theater of Munich. Refined techniques have produced marionettes capable of playing musical instruments, dancing ballets, and performing operas.

cal comment prohibited in other media. In the United States, the Bread and Puppet Theater has combined masks, puppets, and human actors in performances of politically oriented material.

Today the Salzburg Marionette Theater performs Mozart operas; a Russian state-supported puppet theater offers major works for adults. The most widely known puppets—through their exposure on television and in films—are Edgar Bergen's Charlie McCarthy and the MUPPETS.

Purcell, Henry   Henry Purcell, b. London, c.1659, d. Nov. 21, 1695, was the most eminent British composer of his time. Born into a distinguished musical family, he studied with his father and later with Henry Cooke, Pelham Humfrey, and possibly Matthew Locke, whom he succeeded in 1677 as composer for the royal string band. Two years later he was appointed organist of Westminster Abbey, and from 1682 onward he served as one of the organists of the Chapel Royal.

Purcell's sacred music includes organ voluntaries, services, motets, and religious songs for home use, but his greatest contributions were his numerous anthems, either full (for choir and occasional solos) or verse (in which small vocal ensembles tend to predominate). Many of the verse anthems call for a string orchestra in addition to ample vocal resources, as Purcell frequently had to provide music for important state occasions such as a coronation or a royal wedding.

The secular works are wide-ranging: more than 100 solo songs (some with chorus), compositions for small ensembles (including a choice collection of delightfully ribald catches), and—on a grander scale—occasional pieces written for the arrival, birthday, or marriage of royal or noble personages and for the perennial celebrations on Saint Cecilia's Day.

Purcell's chamber music is also richly varied. Although most of his string fantasias excel in contrapuntal and harmonic invention, the two sets of trio sonatas bal-

Henry Purcell, one of England's greatest composers, wrote a wide variety of choral, church, and dramatic works during his short lifetime. A superb organist, he was composer to the king and organist of Westminster Abbey during the last quarter of the 17th century. His works include the opera Dido and Aeneas *(1689) and his odes for Saint Cecilia's Day.*

ance lyricism and polyphony to perfection, whereas the solos and suites for harpsichord prove the composer's considerable competence as a keyboard player.

His operas, masques, and semioperas (in which speech alternates with music) demonstrate his instinctive feeling for drama, and even though he was to some extent hampered by theatrical conventions of the time, he often managed to triumph over their limitations and produce works of lasting beauty and persuasion, such as *Dido and Aeneas* (1689) and *The Fairy Queen* (1692).

pure food and drug laws   see FOOD AND DRUG ADMINISTRATION

Pure Land Buddhism   Pure Land Buddhism is one of the most influential forms of Mahayana BUDDHISM. According to some Mahayana schools, the cosmos contains many Pure Lands in each of which dwells one Buddha. The most popular of these is Sukhavati, the Land of Bliss of Amitabha, located in the West; it is on Sukhavati that Pure Land Buddhism focuses. Through devotion to Amitabha, it is claimed, Buddhists can be reborn and saved in his paradise.

Although the cult of Amitabha had its roots in India, it was developed and flourished in China and Japan. Hui Yüan founded the cult in AD 402, calling it the White Lotus sect. From the 5th century on, a succession of Chinese Pure Land masters, Shandao (613–81) foremost among them, attracted followers from all social strata. Gradually their emphasis shifted from devout contemplation or visualization of Amitabha and his Pure Land to a doctrine of salvation through faith and the devout recitation of Amitabha's name.

These Pure Land doctrines were first introduced into Japan within the Tendai sect. Honen (1133–1212), emphasizing them exclusively, broke with Tendai and founded the independent Jodo (Pure Land) sect.

purgatory   In Roman Catholicism purgatory (from the Latin *purgare*, "to cleanse") is the place or state after death where those who have died in a state of grace but not free from imperfection expiate their remaining sins before entering the visible presence of God and the saints; the damned, on the other hand, go directly to hell.

The living are encouraged to offer Masses, prayers, alms, and other acts of piety and devotion on behalf of those in purgatory. The suffering of purgatory is less a concept of physical pain than one of postponement of the "beatific vision." Purgatory will end with the Last Judgment at the close of the world.

The official Roman Catholic teaching on purgatory, defined at the councils of Lyon (1274) and Ferrara-Florence (1438–45), was rejected by leaders of the Reformation, who taught that persons are freed from sin through faith in Jesus Christ and go straight to heaven. The Orthodox church also rejects the theology of purgatory, although it encourages prayers for the dead in some undefined intermediate state.

purification, rites of   Rites of purification are common to all religions. Their purpose is to remove pollution and restore purity that has been lost because of some violation of religious law or injunction. Purification may also be required before initiation into religious secrets, mysteries, or societies within a culture. They may be required before the affected person can resume community life or engage in specific religious acts. Rites of purification are typically associated with birth, puberty, and death, as well as with the food cycle. They seek to remove impurity, to transfer it, or to destroy it as a means of preserving the proper relationship between humans and the divine. The practical means may be washing, sprinkling with blood, burning, fumigating with incense, cutting, beating, blowing, prayer and incantation, or killing or excluding the affected person. The rites of Yom Kippur in Leviticus 16 are classic examples. The Churching of Women, a form of prayer used in the Christian tradition when women return to worship after childbirth, based on Leviticus 12 and Luke 2, is a similar rite.

Purim   [poo'-reem]   Purim (Hebrew for "lots") is a minor Jewish festival in early spring, the 14th day of Adar in the Jewish calendar. It commemorates the deliverance of the Jews from a massacre in the Persian Empire, as told in the biblical Book of ESTHER. HAMAN, a malicious chief minister of Ahasuerus (probably Xerxes I), planned to exterminate all the Jews of the empire. He is reported to have cast lots to fix the date (Adar 13) of his projected massacre, hence the name Purim. Queen Esther, however, disclosed to Ahasuerus that she was a Jew and persuaded him to allow the Jews to defend themselves.

Purim is marked by a carnival atmosphere, with masquerades, farcical plays, and the giving of gifts, especially charitable gifts. In the synagogue, the chief observance is the reading of the Megillah (scroll) of Esther.

purine   see GENE

Puritanism   *Puritans* was the name given in the 16th century to the more extreme Protestants within the Church of England (see ENGLAND, CHURCH OF) who thought the English REFORMATION had not gone far enough in reforming the doctrines and structure of the church; they wanted to purify their national church by eliminating every shred of Catholic influence. In the 17th century many Puritans immigrated to the New World, where they sought to found a holy commonwealth in New England. Puritanism remained the dominant cultural force in that area into the 19th century.

English Puritanism. Associated exclusively with no single theology or definition of the church (although many were Calvinists), the English Puritans were known at first for their extremely critical attitude regarding the religious compromises made during the reign of ELIZABETH I. Many of them were graduates of Cambridge University, and they became Anglican priests to make changes in their local churches. They encouraged direct personal religious experience, sincere moral conduct, and simple worship services. Worship was the area in which Puritans tried to change things most.

After JAMES I became king of England in 1603, Puritan leaders asked him to grant several reforms. At the Hampton Court Conference (1604), however, he rejected most of their proposals, which included abolition of bishops. Puritanism, best expressed by William Ames and later by Richard Baxter, gained much popular support early in the 17th century. The government and the church hierarchy, however, especially under Archbishop William LAUD, became increasingly repressive, causing many Puritans to emigrate. Those who remained formed a powerful element within the parliamentarian party that defeated CHARLES I in the ENGLISH CIVIL WAR. After the war the Puritans remained dominant in England until 1660, but they quarreled among themselves (Presbyterian dominance gave way to Independent, or congregational, control under Oliver CROMWELL) and proved even more intolerant than the old hierarchy. The restoration of the monarchy (1660) also restored Anglicanism, and the Puritan clergy were expelled from the Church of England under the terms of the Act of Uniformity (1662; see CLARENDON CODE). Thereafter English Puritans were classified as NONCONFORMISTS.

American Puritanism. Early in the 17th century some Puritan groups separated from the Church of England. Among these were the PILGRIMS, who in 1620 founded PLYMOUTH COLONY. Ten years later, under the auspices of the MASSACHUSETTS BAY COMPANY, the first major Puritan migration to New England took place. The Puritans brought strong religious impulses to bear in all colonies north of Virginia, but New England was their stronghold, and the Congregationalist churches established there were able to perpetuate their viewpoint about a Christian society for more than 200 years.

Richard Mather (see MATHER family) and John COTTON provided clerical leadership in the dominant Puritan colony planted on Massachusetts Bay. Thomas HOOKER was an example of those who settled new areas farther west according to traditional Puritan standards. Even though he broke with the authorities of the Massachusetts colony over questions of religious freedom, Roger WILLIAMS was also a true Puritan in his zeal for personal godliness and doctrinal correctness. Most of these men held ideas in the mainstream of Calvinistic thought. In addition to believing in the absolute sovereignty of God, the total depravity of man, and the complete dependence of human beings on divine grace for salvation, they stressed the importance of personal religious experience. These Puritans insisted that they, as God's elect, had the duty to direct national affairs according to God's will as revealed in the Bible. This union of church and state to form a holy commonwealth gave Puritanism direct and exclusive control over most colonial activity until commercial and political changes forced the Puritans to relinquish it at the end of the 17th century.

Jonathan EDWARDS and his able disciple Samuel Hopkins revived Puritan thought and kept it alive until 1800.

CONGREGATIONALISM gradually declined in power, but Presbyterians under the leadership of Jonathan DICKINSON and Baptists led by the example of Isaac Backus (1724–1806) revitalized Puritan ideals in several denominational forms through the 18th century.

Purple Heart see MEDALS AND DECORATIONS

purpura [pur'-puh-ruh] Purpura is hemorrhaging, or bleeding, in the skin, mucous membranes, or serous membranes. The term (Latin for "purple") refers to the resulting discolored areas, which range from small dots (petechiae) to large patches. The condition can occur in drug or transfusion reactions and in disturbances that interfere with the blood-clotting mechanism. Idiopathic thrombocytopenic purpura is due to a reduction of the number of platelets needed for proper blood clotting in the blood and to increased capillary fragility.

The acute disease, which commonly affects children 2 to 6 years old and is often triggered by infections or allergies, normally clears up in about 2 weeks. The chronic disease, most common in young women, is usually preceded by a history of easy bruising and excessive menstrual flow; it is usually treated with hormones or by surgical removal of the spleen.

purslane [purs'-luhn] Purslane, *Portulaca oleracea,* or pusley, is a member of the purslane family, Portulacaceae, and is a common weed in gardens and cultivated fields. It is a creeping annual, with thick, succulent, reddish stems; fleshy, oblong leaves; and tiny, stalkless, yellow flowers often surrounded by a rosette of leaves. The flowers open only in the morning on warm, sunny days. Purslane seeds are tiny, black, and numerous and are produced in small, lidded capsules. The whole plant is edible when young.

Pusan [poo'-sahn] Pusan, South Korea, is a city with provincial status, located at the southeastern tip of the Korean Peninsula. It lies on a sheltered bay at the mouth of the Naktong-gang (river), on the Korea Strait. With a population of 3,825,000 (1990 est.), it is the nation's second largest city and its chief port. Fishing and foreign trade take place in different parts of the harbor. The city's industries include shipbuilding and the manufacture of chemicals and metals. Pusan is the terminus of a ferry to Japan and a railroad to China. Known since the Koryo dynasty (10th–14th century), it began its modern development under the Japanese (1910–45). During the Korean War it was the capital of South Korea.

Pusey, Edward Bouverie [pue'-zee] English theologian, educator, and preacher Edward Bouverie Pusey, b. Aug. 22, 1800, d. Sept. 16, 1882, was a leader of the OXFORD MOVEMENT within the Church of England. He was regius professor of Hebrew at Oxford University and canon of Christ Church from 1828 until his death. Eager to defend the Church of England against the assaults of liberals in theology and government, Pusey joined (1833)—and reinforced by his position and name—the Oxford movement and contributed essays on baptism, fasting, and the Eucharist to *Tracts for the Times.* When John Henry NEWMAN converted (1845) to Roman Catholicism, the leadership of the movement passed to Pusey.

Aleksandr Pushkin, the greatest Russian poet of the 19th century, established the modern Russian literary idiom in such works as Boris Godunov *(1831) and his masterpiece,* Eugene Onegin *(1823–31).*

Pushkin, Aleksandr Aleksandr Sergeyevich Pushkin, b. June 6 (N.S.), 1799, d. Feb. 10 (N.S.), 1837, was Russia's greatest poet. His use of the vernacular as the language of poetry freed Russian writing from the constraints of tradition and set new literary standards for novelists and poets, and his preference for subjects from history and folklore brought fresh vitality to Russian literature.

Pushkin studied at the lyceum in the town of Tsarskoye Selo, later renamed Pushkin, and after graduating (1817), was appointed to a post at the Ministry of Foreign Affairs in the capital city of Saint Petersburg (now Leningrad). Here Pushkin indulged in the glittering social life he would eventually satirize in *Eugene Onegin* (1823–31), a verse novel that describes a shallow, pleasure-loving man's insensitivity to the love of a noble woman. Despite the somewhat frivolous nature of his social pursuits, Pushkin remained deeply committed to social reform and gained the reputation of spokesperson for literary radicals. As a result, he angered the government and was transferred from the capital, first to Kishinev (1820–23) and then to Odessa (1823–24).

Pushkin again clashed with his superiors in Odessa and was again exiled, this time to his mother's rural estate. In 1826 he was recalled to Moscow under the tsar's protection, but his relations with the government always remained strained. He married Natalia Goncharova, a society beauty, in 1831. His wife's social ambitions caused Pushkin to become involved in a reckless social life, put him deeply in debt, and eventually killed him. In 1837 he was forced to fight a duel to defend Natalia's reputation and was mortally wounded.

Pushkin's early writing is mainly in the 18th-century classical tradition of light, frivolous verse. The verse fairy tale *Ruslan and Ludmila* (1820) is his first major attempt to use colloquial speech and themes from Russian folklore. This work and other exotic narratives written at that time were very much influenced by romanticism, and Pushkin was particularly drawn to the verse of Lord Byron, whose style he emulated in such poems as *The Prisoner of the Caucasus* (1822), *The Robber Brothers* (1827), and *Eugene Onegin.* In *Onegin,* however, the Byronic hero has been changed by Pushkin into a tragic figure. He disdains the love offered him by a naive and awkward provincial girl, only to fall in love with her later when he meets her in Saint Petersburg, now a poised, married woman prominent in society. Although she still loves him, she remains faithful to her husband and rejects Onegin. The plot is simple, but Pushkin has used it to convey his poignant central theme: the relentless passage of time and the irrevocable nature of past actions.

Pushkin's deep regard for his compatriots, his interest in history, and his distaste for the rigid class structure of his society are evident in most of his mature work. In *Wasteland Sower of True Freedom,* a political tract published in 1823, he deplores the cruelties of serfdom and warns prophetically that reform is necessary to avert revolution. Several of his major dramas recall great Russian heroes of the past, notably *Boris Godunov* (1831; Eng. trans., 1899), *Poltava* (1828–29; Eng. trans., 1899), and *The Bronze Horseman* (1837; Eng. trans., 1899), which depicts the legendary Peter the Great. In later years Pushkin frequently wrote prose. Two of his most widely read works are the novel *The Captain's Daughter* (1834; Eng. trans., 1846) and the short story "The Queen of Spades" (1834; Eng. trans., 1894).

pussy willow see WILLOW

Putnam, Israel [puht'-nuhm] Israel Putnam, b. Salem (now Danvers), Mass., Jan. 7, 1718, d. May 29, 1790, an American soldier, served in the French and Indian War and was a general during the American Revolution. A leader at the Battle of BUNKER HILL (1775), he supposedly gave the command "Men, you are all marksmen: don't one of you fire until you see the whites of their eyes." (Gen. William Prescott is credited with giving a similar command.) In 1776, Putnam's troops were routed by Sir William Howe in the Battle of Long Island (see LONG ISLAND, BATTLE OF). The following year he was reprimanded by George Washington for insubordination. He retired from active service in 1779.

Putnam, Rufus Rufus Putnam, b. Sutton, Mass., Apr. 9, 1738, d. May 4, 1824, played a prominent role in the early history of Ohio. He served in the American Revolution and, in 1786, helped organize the OHIO COMPANY

OF ASSOCIATES to promote the development of western lands. He founded MARIETTA, Ohio's first permanent settlement, in 1788. Putnam was later surveyor general of the United States (1796–1803) and a member of the Ohio state constitutional convention (1802).

Puvis de Chavannes, Pierre [poo-vee' duh shah-vahn'] Pierre Puvis de Chavannes, b. Dec. 14, 1824, d. October 1898, had great influence on mural painting during the late 19th century in Europe and the United States. His allegorical and religious subjects, expressed with classical order and serenity, were painted in light, cool colors and in flat decorative forms that were ideal for adorning wall surfaces without violating their architectural integrity. These features of his work, as in *Winter* (1889–93; Hôtel de Ville, Paris), were admired by conservative and avant-garde artists alike. The symbolist painter Alexandre Séon and such Nabis artists as Maurice Denis and Paul Gauguin saw the flat, decorative quality and the elegiac mood of *Winter* and Puvis de Chavannes's other work as moving in the antirealistic direction they felt art should be taking. On the other hand, Puvis de Chavannes's conservative colleagues respected the classical composition and subject matter of his work.

Puyallup [pue-al'-uhp] The Puyallup are a tribe of Coast SALISH Indians of North America, whose traditional homeland was in the Puget Sound area of Washington State. Their language is a dialect of the Nisqually linguistic group, a subdivision of the Algonquian-Wakashan language family. In their homeland, fishing, shellfishery, and sea hunting formed the foundation of their subsistence activities. The Puyallup lived in wooden houses in compact, densely populated, permanent villages. Society was organized into large extended families, kinship groups, and a system of clans. Societal classes consisted of hereditary nobles, commoners, and nonhereditary slaves. Local communities were politically independent, and chieftainships were not hereditary. The Puyallup were among the Salish who practiced artificial head-flattening for aesthetic reasons. They also participated in POTLATCH ceremonies.

By the 1854 Medicine Creek Treaty the Puyallup gave up their lands and moved onto a reservation; they numbered 1,725 in 1989. In 1990 a land-claims settlement valued at $162 million was negotiated between officials of the tribe; the federal, state, and local governments; and others.

Pygmalion (mythology) [pig-mayl'-ee-uhn] In Greek mythology Pygmalion was the subject of two separate legends. In one he was the king of Cyprus who sculpted an ivory statue of a woman and then fell in love with it. In answer to his prayers Aphrodite gave life to the statue, whom Pygmalion called Galatea. She bore him a son, Paphos. Ovid tells this story in *Metamorphoses.*

In Vergil's *Aeneid,* Pygmalion was the king of Tyre who murdered the husband of his sister DIDO to secure his

wealth. Dido, however, fled with the treasure to Africa, where she founded Carthage.

Pygmalion (play) A play written in 1912 by George Bernard SHAW, *Pygmalion* was first produced in 1914. One of the author's best-loved works, it describes the transformation of a Cockney flower girl into a fine lady at the hands of a cynical and slightly misanthropic phonetician. *Pygmalion* is based on the Greek legend of Pygmalion and Galatea. Frequently staged during Shaw's lifetime, it has remained popular and was filmed in 1938. In 1956 it was adapted on Broadway as *My Fair Lady,* which became one of the most successful musicals of all time. The film version was released in 1964.

Pygmy [pig'-mee] Pygmies, also called Negrillos, are a group of Central African peoples living in scattered parts of Zaire, Congo, Gabon, Cameroon, Rwanda, and Burundi. The name is also sometimes applied to the NEGRITOS of the Pacific, whose stature does not exceed about 150 cm (5 ft). African Pygmies are from 122 to 142 cm (4 ft to 4 ft 8 in) tall; some of the slightly taller groups are termed Pygmoid. The Mbuti of the Ituri forest of northeastern Zaire, numbering about 80,000, are a major subgroup of Pygmies, who speak the languages of Bantu and Sudanic tribes that have migrated into their territory. The total Pygmy population is estimated at more than 200,000.

Pygmy groups live in what has been described as a symbiotic relationship with neighboring sedentary farmers, with whom they trade and participate in social and ceremonial activities. As nomadic HUNTER-GATHERERS, Pygmies hunt, fish, and collect wild plant foods and insects in the forest. The basic social unit is the band of 20 or more persons, which moves about the forest living in temporary camps, with huts built of sapling frames thatched with leaves. Marriage is between bands, often by sister exchange, and is

In the Central African Republic, Pygmies inhabit the southwestern rain forest. Diminutive stature is one of the basic characteristics of the Pygmy peoples, who are descendants of the original population of central Africa.

usually monogamous. Pygmy religious beliefs center on the forest, considered their host and benefactor.

Pyle, Ernie [pyl]   The American journalist Ernest Taylor Pyle, b. Dana, Ind., Aug. 3, 1900, d. Apr. 18, 1945, was a noted war correspondent who became famous for his intimate accounts of soldiers at the front during World War II. After holding various newspaper office jobs, Pyle became a roving reporter for the Scripps-Howard newspaper chain and, with his wife, traveled throughout the Western Hemisphere. In 1940 he went to London as a war correspondent, and thereafter he accompanied the American troops on their campaigns in Europe. He was killed by machine-gun fire on the Pacific island of Ie Shima. Many of Pyle's columns have been published in book form, notably *Here Is Your War* (1943).

Pyle, Howard   Howard Pyle, b. Wilmington, Del., Mar. 5, 1853, d. Nov. 9, 1911, was a noted American illustrator and author whose work is characterized by an imaginative and colorful realism and a passion for historical detail. He illustrated numerous historical and adventure stories for such periodicals as *Harper's Weekly* and *St. Nicholas* as well as his own books for children, including *The Merry Adventures of Robin Hood* (1883) and *Otto of the Silver Hand* (1888). In his later years Pyle taught such outstanding illustrators of the succeeding generation of the American Brandywine school as Maxfield Parrish, Frank E. Schoonover, Jessie Wilcox Smith, and N. C. Wyeth.

Pylos [py'-lahs]   Pylos was an ancient Greek city located on the present-day Bay of Navarino in the southwestern Peloponnesus. The long-sought-after site of the so-called Palace of Nestor, the Homeric hero, has been located at modern Epano Englianos, about 17 km (10.5 mi) north of Pylos harbor. On a hilltop occupied since the Middle Bronze Age are remains of a palace erected in the 13th century BC and rivaling that at MYCENAE.

Pym, Barbara [pim]   English author Barbara Pym, b. June 2, 1913, d. Jan. 11, 1980, wrote novels of manners set in quiet English places and peopled, primarily, with women. Mildly successful during the 1950s (her *Excellent Women* appeared in 1952), Pym went unpublished during the 1960s and early 1970s but was rediscovered in 1977. By the time of her death three new novels had been published and all of her earlier work reprinted. Her posthumous publications include the autobiographical *A Very Private Eye* (1984) and *Civil to Strangers and Other Writings* (1988).

Pym, John   The English Puritan statesman John Pym, b. c.1583, d. Dec. 8, 1643, was a leader of the parliamentary opposition to King CHARLES I. Pym sat in every Parliament from 1621 until his death; during the 11-year period (1629–40) in which Charles ruled without Parliament, Pym was active in colonial enterprises. In the Long Parliament, Pym began the proceedings against the earl of Strafford and Archbishop Laud and was one of the authors of the Grand Remonstrance (1641). He was among the five members of Parliament that Charles tried personally to arrest in 1642. After the outbreak of the ENGLISH CIVIL WAR, Pym devised new methods of taxation to raise money for the parliamentarians and arranged (1643) the alliance with the Scots.

Pynchon, Thomas [pin'-chuhn]   Widely regarded as a major 20th-century novelist, Thomas Pynchon, b. Glen Cove, N.Y., May 8, 1937, established his reputation with three novels. *V.* won the William Faulkner Foundation Award for the best first novel of 1963; *The Crying of Lot 49* (1966), Pynchon's most accessible novel, won an award from the National Institute of Arts and Letters; and *Gravity's Rainbow* (1973), a vast and complex novel that has been compared with *Moby-Dick* and *Ulysses*, received the National Book Award and a nomination for the Pulitzer Prize. His fourth novel, *Vineland* (1990), is an amusing celebration of the sixties revolution and a lament for its aftermath.

Pynchon's first American ancestor was William Pynchon. Little else is known about the novelist except that he attended Cornell University and served briefly in the navy. All efforts to interview, photograph, or even find him have failed.

Pynchon's fiction is wildly comic, structurally complex, historically accurate, and astonishingly erudite. His most compelling theme is the dehumanizing effect of the modern obsession with order, certainty, and stability, as expressed through technology, bureaucracies, systems of formalized thought, and the manipulation of history itself. His novels expose the destructiveness of systems and contain so vast and diverse a sampling of disorderly life that they are practically impervious to systematic literary analysis.

Pynchon, William   William Pynchon, b. England, c.1590, d. Oct. 29, 1662, was a pioneer settler of western Massachusetts. A patentee and assistant of the Massachusetts Bay Company, he emigrated to New England in 1630 and founded (1636) the town of Springfield on the Connecticut River, dominating its government for the next 15 years. In 1651, Boston authorities publicly burned his theological tract on the atonement, *The Meritorious Price of Our Redemption*, and denounced him as a heretic. Pynchon returned to England in 1652.

Pyongyang [pyuhng-yahng]   Pyongyang (1986 est. pop., 2,000,000) is the capital and largest city of North Korea. It is situated on the Taedong River in west central North Korea, about 50 km (30 mi) east of the Yellow Sea. Steel and chemical industries dominate, but textiles, food products, sugar, ceramics, and rubber products are also manufactured.

Founded, according to legend, in 1122 BC, Pyongyang's recorded history began in 108 BC with the establishment of a Chinese colony on the site. In 300 BC it was made capital of the Choson kingdom. Its history has been punctuated with invasions by China, Japan, and contending Korean groups. During the Japanese occupation from 1910 to 1945, Pyongyang became an industrial center. Much of it was destroyed during the Korean War but has been rebuilt.

___

pyorrhea [py-uh-ree'-uh]   Pyorrhea is the infection of the gums and other tissues surrounding the teeth. Initially, the gums bleed. As the disease progresses, pus-filled abscesses may form in the gums and the disease may spread into the tooth socket, causing the teeth to loosen and fall out. The causes of pyorrhea include poor nutrition and poor oral hygiene (see PERIODONTICS).

___

pyramid   A pyramid is a special type of POLYHEDRON in which all the faces except possibly the base are triangles that meet in a common point called the vertex. The base is a polygon but not necessarily a triangle. (A polyhedron is a more general three-dimensional figure that is bounded by plane polygonal faces.) Pyramids may be classified according to the number of sides of the base. If the base is a triangle, the solid is called a triangular pyramid or a tetrahedron. A pyramid with a square base—for example, the famous Egyptian pyramids—is called a square pyramid.

___

pyramids   In architecture the term *pyramid* denotes a monument that resembles the geometrical figure of the same name. It is almost exclusively applied to the stone structures of ancient Egypt and of pre-Columbian Central America and Mexico.

Egypt. The Egyptian pyramids were funerary monuments built for the pharaohs and their closest relatives. Most date from the Old Kingdom (*c.*2686–2181 BC) and are found on the west bank of the Nile south of the delta, between Hawara and Abu Ruwaysh. Pyramids developed from the MASTABA, a low, rectangular stone structure erected over a tomb. The oldest pyramid known is the Step Pyramid of King Zoser at SAQQARA (*c.*2650 BC).

The next phase of development is represented by the 93-m-high (305-ft) pyramid at Maydum, built at the order of Snefru, founder of the 4th dynasty (*c.*2613–*c.*2498 BC). This structure was designed as a step pyramid; later the steps were covered with a smooth stone facing to produce sloping sides.

A characteristic feature of all classical Egyptian pyramids is a temple complex, comprising a lower or valley temple at a short distance from the pyramid and connected by a causeway with a mortuary temple, situated adjacent to the pyramid. The most elaborate example of the temple complex is found at Giza, near modern Cairo, where the 4th-dynasty pyramids of Kings KHUFU (Cheops), KHAFRE (Chephren), and MENKAURE (Mycerinus) lie in close proximity to each other. The pyramid of Khufu, erected *c.*2500 BC, is the largest in the world, measuring 230 m (756 ft) on each side of its base and originally measuring 147 m (482 ft) high.

The last great pyramid of the Old Kingdom is that of Pepi II of the 6th dynasty (*c.*2345–2181 BC). When King Mentuhotep II of the 11th dynasty attained power (*c.*2060 BC), pyramid construction resumed. During the 11th and 12th dynasties, until 1786 BC, pyramids continued to be built (at Dahshur and al-Faiyum), but later, rock-cut tombs were preferred.

Pre-Columbian America. All pre-Columbian pyramids are truncated, stepped pyramids and served as the foundations for temples. The largest ones usually slope less steeply than the Egyptian pyramids, but the smaller ones often have an even steeper incline. Stairways carved into one or more sides of the pyramid lead to the temple.

(Left) *The 4th-dynasty pyramids at Giza reflect the technical perfection achieved by Egyptian architects. The pyramids were originally covered with white limestone.* (Below) *The Step Pyramid (*c.*2650 BC) of King Zoser at Saqqara is the earliest pyramidal structure of the ancient world. It consists of six terraces of receding sizes.*

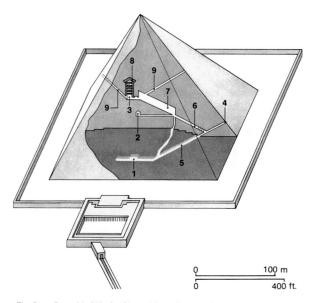

The Great Pyramid of Khufu (Cheops) is the largest of the three pyramids at Giza. Three separate, internal chambers were built within the pyramid. The construction of the original, underground chamber (1) and the so-called Queen's Chamber (2) was abandoned to commence work on the King's Chamber (3). The entrance (4) led to a corridor (5) that descended to the abandoned subterranean chamber. An ascending corridor (6) extended into a Grand Gallery (7) that led to the King's Chamber. The King's Chamber was covered with five tiers of stone beams (8) to buttress the weight of the pyramid upon it. Two ventilation shafts (9) led from the King's Chamber to the exterior.

Pyramids were erected by the ancient Mesoamerican cultures of the MAYA, TOLTECS, and AZTECS, and they are found in many areas of Mexico, Honduras, Guatemala, and El Salvador. Most were built during the Classic period (AD 300–900) and in the following Postclassic period (900–1542). The pyramid of EL TAJÍN, which was built between the 4th and 9th centuries in northern Veracruz, Mexico, is unique. On each of its terraces is a series of recessed niches in which sacrificial offerings were probably placed. In the pyramid of the Temple of the Inscriptions at PALENQUE, Mexico, which also dates from the Classic period, a passage beneath the floor of the temple leads to a richly furnished burial crypt deep within the pyramid. One of the largest pyramids in Central America is the 66-m-high (216-ft) Pyramid of the Sun (2d century AD) at TEOTIHUACÁN, Mexico. Temple-pyramid complexes at late civic-ceremonial centers such as CHICHÉN ITZÁ and UXMAL, dating from the Postclassic Maya-Toltec period, are generally lower in height, topped with a larger, flat platform; they therefore are generally not considered true pyramids.

See also: EGYPT, ANCIENT; PRE-COLUMBIAN ART AND ARCHITECTURE.

Pyramus and Thisbe [peer'-uh-muhs, thiz'-bee]   In classical mythology Pyramus and Thisbe, young Babylonian

lovers, were forbidden by their parents to meet. They nevertheless arranged a tryst under a mulberry tree at a tomb outside the city. Thisbe arrived first and saw a lion whose jaws were bloody from eating its prey. Terrified, she dropped her scarf and fled. When Pyramus arrived he saw the lion ripping the scarf and assumed that Thisbe had been devoured. Pyramus committed suicide, and Thisbe, returning, found him dead and killed herself with his sword. From that time the fruit of the mulberry tree was no longer white but turned dark red from the stain of the lovers' blood. The myth appears in Ovid's *Metamorphoses.*

Pyrenees [peer'-uh-neez]   The mountains of the Pyrenees form a physical border between France and Spain, stretching 435 km (270 mi) from the Bay of Biscay (part of the Atlantic Ocean) to the Mediterranean Sea. ANDORRA, wholly within the Pyrenees, straddles the French-Spanish border, which generally follows the crest of the range. The highest peak, 3,404 m (11,168 ft), is Pico de Aneto, on the Spanish side in the center of the chain. Many passes are more than 1.5 km (1 mi) high. Railroads cross the mountains at the ends of the range. Major rivers rising in the Pyrenees include the GARONNE and Adour of France and the EBRO of Spain.

Among the rocks forming the mountains are slate, limestone, sandstone, and granite. Marble is quarried, and iron ore, zinc, lead, magnesium, and coal are mined. The eastern section, which receives little rain, is somewhat barren, but the central and western sections are heavily wooded with beech, pine, oak, and boxwood. Mountain farmers

This agrarian community is situated in a valley of the Pyrenees in the Spanish region of Catalonia. The Pyrenees extend from the Atlantic Ocean to the Mediterranean Sea, forming a natural barrier separating the Iberian Peninsula from the rest of Europe.

raise tobacco, potatoes, corn, buckwheat, and livestock. Hydroelectric-power and industrial-development potentials remain to be exploited. Textiles and paper are now produced. Tourism is growing: winter sports, hunting, sightseeing, and fishing attract many visitors, and hot springs serve health spas, especially on the French side.

pyrimidine   see GENE

—

pyrite [py'-ryt]   The iron SULFIDE MINERAL pyrite (FeS_2) has been called fool's gold because of its pale, brass yellow color and glistening metallic luster. It is the most widespread and abundant sulfide mineral in rocks of all ages. The cubic, dodecahedral, and octahedral crystals and the fine-grained masses may be distinguished from gold by their higher Mohs hardness of 6 to 6½ and their lower specific gravity of 5.00 to 5.02; pyrite has a greenish black streak, conducts electricity, and generates a weak electric current when heated. Its darker-colored isometric crystals distinguish pyrite from the chemically identical marcasite, which has orthorhombic crystals.

Pyrite forms large bodies in moderate- to high-temperature hydrothermal deposits and in contact metamorphic ore deposits, is an accessory in many igneous rocks, and is common in sedimentary beds and metamorphosed sediments. It is mined as a source of sulfur and iron as well as of the impurities gold and copper. Pyrite is readily oxidized to create sulfuric acid, both commercially and naturally; in the latter case it helps form the enriched zone of ore deposits, especially of copper; oxidation also creates limonite, which forms the gossan, or iron capping, of sulfide ore deposits.

Pyrite, an iron sulfide, is the most widespread and abundant sulfide mineral. Called fool's gold because of its light brass yellow color and metallic luster, it is usually found as striated cubic, octahedral, and twelve-faced clusters.

pyrolusite   see MANGANESE

—

pyrolysis [py-rahl'-uh-sis]   Pyrolysis, or destructive distillation, is the decomposition of a substance by the action of heat alone, with no access to air or oxygen. The word is derived from the Greek *pyr* for "fire," and *lysis*, meaning a "loosening." The earliest use of pyrolysis was

to produce COKE by heating coal to a high temperature and distilling the volatile products known as coal tar from the coke. A now-obsolete method for making methyl alcohol (wood alcohol) was to pyrolyze wood chips and separate the volatile alcohol from the charcoal.

Pyrolysis is now the major step for cracking, a PETROLEUM INDUSTRY process in which large-molecular-weight PETROCHEMICALS are converted to smaller ones. One of the principal products of this process is ethylene ($CH_2{=}CH_2$), which can be used as a building block of polymers and for making synthetic chemicals. The hydrogen produced by cracking is used in the Haber-Bosch process to manufacture AMMONIA. In some pyrolysis reactions the hydrocarbon is diluted with steam, heated for a fraction of a second at 700°–900° C (370–465° F), and then cooled rapidly. This process is important in producing a number of alkene hydrocarbons, such as butadiene and isoprene, which are used in the production of synthetic rubbers. The most important products from petroleum pyrolysis, however, are low-molecular-weight hydrocarbons, which are suitable as motor fuels. Pyrolysis improves not only the quantity of gasoline-type hydrocarbons obtainable from crude oil but also the quality of the fuel.

—

pyroxene [py-rahk'-seen]   The pyroxenes are an important group of rock-forming SILICATE MINERALS that are characterized by a specific arrangement of atoms and similar physical, optical, and chemical properties. They occur as both major and minor constituents in a wide variety of igneous, metamorphic, and sedimentary rocks and are common in lunar rocks and stony meteorites. Although consisting of the same group of elements as the AMPHIBOLES, pyroxenes contain silica tetrahedra that are linked in single chains of SiO_3 composition.

The similarity in crystal structure throughout this group results in rather uniform physical properties. Hardness is 6 to 6½ on the Mohs scale, and cleavage is good in two directions parallel to the crystal faces and intersects at nearly right angles. Specific gravity varies between 3.1 and 3.9 and is generally indicative of iron enrichment. Pyroxenes may be colorless, white, gray, pink, blue, green, brown, or black; the darker colors tend to appear in the iron-rich varieties. The crystals are generally prismatic and square in cross-section, but most pyroxenes form irregular grains. The exceptions are aegirine, often in long, needlelike crystals, and spodumene, which can form giant crystals up to 3 m (10 ft) thick and more than 15 m (50 ft) long.

Magnesium-rich orthopyroxenes are common constituents of some ultrabasic igneous rocks and of olivine-rich inclusions in basalts. Orthopyroxene—pyroxene crystallizing in the orthorhombic system—is an essential mineral constituent of norite and frequently occurs in cumulate rocks of layered intrusions. Iron-rich orthopyroxenes are occasionally found in acidic (SiO_2-rich) rocks, such as granites.

Diopside ($CaMgSi_2O_6$) and hedenbergite ($CaFe^{2+}Si_2O_6$) are typical minerals of thermally metamorphosed limestones and iron-rich sediments. Hedenbergite is also characteristic of acidic igneous rocks such as quartz syenite and granite.

Augite [Ca(Mg, Fe, Al)(Si,Al)$_2$ O$_6$] and subcalcic augite, in which the chemical composition often varies systematically from the center to the edge of the crystal, are the most abundant of the pyroxenes and are essential minerals in basic igneous rocks such as gabbro and basalt. With higher pressures of formation, omphacite [(Ca, Na)(Mg, Fe^{2+}, Fe^{3+}, Al) Si$_2$O$_6$)] is the characteristic pyroxene of dense, green plutonic rocks such as eclogite. Jadeite (NaAlSi$_2$O$_6$), a form of precious JADE, is also characteristic of rocks that have been metamorphosed at high pressure and fairly low temperature.

Aegirine (NaFe^{3+}Si$_2$O$_6$) is generally found in alkaline igneous rocks, such as syenites and alkali granites. Spodumene (LiAlSi$_2$O$_6$), a commercial source of lithium, is a characteristic mineral of granitic PEGMATITES.

Pyrrho of Elis [peer'-oh, ee'-lis]   The Greek philosopher Pyrrho of Elis, c.365–c.275 BC, for whom Pyrrhonism is named, is considered the founder of SKEPTICISM. He believed that tranquillity and happiness result from the realization that all perceptions and judgments are relative and that genuine knowledge is unattainable.

Pyrrhus, King of Epirus [peer'-uhs]   Pyrrhus, c.318–272 BC, king of EPIRUS, was a brilliant general who won battles at such a high cost that the term *Pyrrhic victory* was coined to describe a ruinous victory. Driven from Epirus as a youth, he regained his throne in 297. He consolidated the Epirote monarchy and warred successfully with his eastern neighbor, Macedonia. He left Greece for Italy in 280, when the Greek colony Tarentum sought his aid against Rome. With about 25,000 men and 20 elephants he defeated the Romans twice in battle. When they refused to negotiate with him, he proceeded to Sicily, pushing back the Carthaginians, then Roman allies, from Syracuse. Returning to Italy, he fought an inconclusive battle at Beneventum in 275 and then withdrew to Epirus. Further conflict with Macedonia led to his death at Argos.

pyrrole   see HETEROCYCLIC COMPOUND

pyruvic acid [py-roo'-vik]   Pyruvic acid (CH$_3$COCOOH) occupies a central position in metabolism, linking the metabolic pathways of proteins, carbohydrates, and fats. The acid can be formed from proteins by deamination of certain amino acids and from glycogen and glucose by means of glycolysis; it also can give rise to glycogen by the reversal of glycolysis (gluconeogenesis). Through formation of acetyl coenzyme A, pyruvic acid can give rise to fats.

Pythagoras, theorem of [pi-thag'-uh-ruhs]   The theorem of Pythagoras is a statement that the square of the hypotenuse of a right triangle is equal to the sum of the squares of its other two sides. At the time of Pythago-

ras of Samos (6th century BC), the square of a number n was represented by the area of a square with side of length n. Using this representation, the Pythagorean theorem may be stated: The area of the square on the hypotenuse of a right triangle is equal to the sum of the areas of the squares on the legs.

Pythagoras, or perhaps one of his students, proved that if triangle *ABC* is a right triangle with a right angle at *C*, then $c^2 = a^2 + b^2$. The converse theorem (If $c^2 = a^2 + b^2$ in a triangle *ABC*, then the angle at *C* is a right angle) appears to have been used much earlier. For example, early Egyptian surveyors used knotted ropes to form triangles with sides 3, 4, and 5 units long. Because $5^2 = 3^2 + 4^2$, the angle opposite the side of length 5 was assumed to be a right angle. This surveying technique was useful for marking off the boundaries of fields after the annual flooding of the Nile River.

Pythagoras of Samos [say'-muhs]   Pythagoras of Samos, c.560–c.480 BC, was a Greek philosopher and re-

Pythagoras of Samos was a 6th-century BC Greek philosopher and mathematician. He is most famous for his ideas on astronomy and geometry, and he is credited with developing the theorem on right triangles that bears his name.

ligious leader who was responsible for important developments in the history of mathematics, astronomy, and the theory of music. He migrated to Croton and founded a philosophical and religious school there that attracted many followers. Because no reliable contemporary records survive, and because the school practiced both secrecy and communalism, the contributions of Pythagoras himself and those of his followers cannot be distinguished.

Pythagoreans

Pythagoreans [pi-thag-uh-ree'-uhnz] The Pythagoreans were a group of early Greek scientific and religious thinkers influenced by Pythagoras of Samos. Many lived in quasi-religious communities centered in Croton, southern Italy. Much of the information about Pythagoreanism, which existed as a school of philosophy from about 525 to the mid-4th century BC, comes from indirect or later sources. It is hard to decide how far back a particular view goes or how much comes from Pythagoras.

Pythagoreans believed that the soul is immortal and separable from the body; it is reincarnated in different animal bodies until it completes the cycle of all creatures (see TRANSMIGRATION OF SOULS). For this reason they practiced vegetarianism. By leading a pure life, an individual might secure the release of his or her soul from all flesh.

Most Pythagorean thought is concerned with numbers and mathematical practices. The universe was created when the One or the Limit "breathed" in some void and separate things were distinguished. The basic principles of things are the Limit and the Unlimited; the structure of the cosmos is based on the fundamental musical ratios 4:3, 3:2, and 2:1.

Some later Pythagoreans linked odd and even numbers, in tables of opposites, with good and bad, male and female; virtues were equated with numbers. Unlike Plato, however, Pythagoreans apparently never hypostatized numbers as existents separate from physical objects.

Pythian Games

Pythian Games [pith'-ee-uhn] The Pythian Games was one of the four great athletic and artistic festivals of ancient Greece. They were held at Delphi every 4 years halfway between Olympic Games. There were contests in running and throwing, as well as singing, music, poetry, and chariot racing. Winners were awarded crowns of bay leaves (sweet laurel), the plant thought to belong to the god Apollo, to whom the games were dedicated. The first Pythian Games, held in 582 BC, were open to all Greek citizens. Eventually, the games were opened to people of other civilizations. During the 4th century AD the games were abolished as Christianity became the dominant religion.

Python

Python [py'-thahn] In Greek mythology Python was a serpent that dwelt in the caves of Mount Parnassus and was slain by APOLLO, who then founded the sacred oracle at DELPHI or took it over from Python's guardianship. According to one version, a jealous Hera sent Python to harm LETO, impregnated by Zeus. Zeus helped Leto escape, and soon afterward she bore Apollo and Artemis. When Apollo was still an infant, he avenged the wrong done his mother by slaying Python with his arrows, which he had never before used against any but the most feeble animals. He then took the name Pythius and organized the Pythian Games to celebrate his victory.

python

python Pythons are 16 to 18 species of nonvenomous snakes of the family Boidae, which also contains the boas and other large constricting snakes. The python subfamily, Pythoninae, sometimes classified as a separate family, is composed of 6 or 7 essentially tropical genera distributed in Africa, Asia, and the Australian region. Some pythons are among the largest of snakes: the reticulated python, *Python reticulatus*, has reached lengths of more than 10 m (33 ft) and weights of approximately 140 kg (300 lb). Other species, however, such as the burrowing python, *Calabaria reinhardtii*, scarcely attain 1 m (3 ft) in length.

Pythons differ from most other snakes by having a pair of well-developed lungs rather than a much smaller left lung or no left lung at all. Both sexes have a short spur protruding from each side of the vent (anus). The spurs, which represent the last vestiges of the hind limbs, are larger in the males than in the females and are used in courtship. The male python vibrates his spurs against the female or uses them to stroke her flanks. This movement stimulates her and helps align her into a copulatory position.

All pythons lay eggs, which in larger species average 30 to 50 per clutch. Females of a few species, such as the Indian python, *P. molurus*, and the blood python, *P. curtus*, remain coiled around their eggs and can raise their body temperatures more than 7 C degrees (13 F degrees) by spasmodically contracting their muscles; thus the eggs are truly incubated. The eggs usually hatch in 60 to 80 days. In captivity pythons have lived for more than 20 years. Pythons feed primarily on mammals, which they kill by constriction. Death by constriction is due to suffocation rather than crushing.

The Asiatic reticulated python wraps around its prey and then constricts its body so that the animal cannot breathe. The python's specialized jaw hinge allows it to swallow large prey.

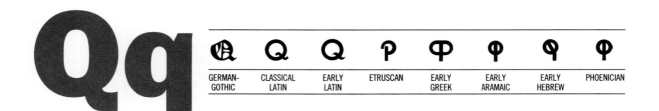

GERMAN-GOTHIC	CLASSICAL LATIN	EARLY LATIN	ETRUSCAN	EARLY GREEK	EARLY ARAMAIC	EARLY HEBREW	PHOENICIAN

Q *Q/q* is the 17th letter of the English alphabet. Both the letter and its position in the alphabet were derived from the Latin alphabet, which in turn derived it from the Greek by way of the Etruscan. The Greeks took the letter, which they called *koppa*, from the Semitic sign *qoph*, but it had disappeared by the time of the classical Greek alphabet. The Etruscans, however, used *Q/q* for the sound of *k* before *u*, a usage that was perpetuated in early Latin. In Latin the combination *qu* developed into a single sound, *kw*. As a result, in modern English, *Q/q* is always followed by *u* and is usually pronounced *kw* as in *quake, quick,* and *equal*. However, in some words, mostly taken from French, *qu* has the sound of *k*, as in *grotesque, oblique,* and *queue.*

Q fever Q fever, caused by *Coxiella burnetti*, is different from other rickettsial diseases of humans in that it is commonly acquired by inhalation of contaminated aerosols rather than from an insect bite. Ticks may also transmit the disease. The usual reservoir of infection is livestock—cattle, sheep, and goats. The disease normally begins abruptly about 9 to 20 days after respiratory exposure and is characterized by headache, fever, chills, cough, aching muscles, severe malaise, and, in about half the cases, pneumonia. Its duration ranges from a few days in young persons to one to three weeks in older persons. Fatalities are rare; antibiotics provide effective therapy.

Qaddafi, Muammar al- [kah-dah'-fee, moo-ahm-mahr' ahl] Muammar al-Qaddafi, b. June 1942, became head of state of Libya after leading a bloodless coup that overthrew the Libyan monarch King IDRIS I on Sept. 1, 1969. Since coming to power, he has led his country on a course of radical revolution at home and abroad.

Qaddafi, a devout Muslim, graduated from the Libyan Military Academy in 1965. Soon after the 1969 coup he undertook serious efforts to distribute the country's large oil revenues equitably and to assert Libya's independence and nonalignment. In the mid-1970s, however, Qaddafi embarked on a radical, utopian-socialist revolution at home. Qaddafi's commitment to unifying the Arab world, his opposition to Israel and the United States, and his efforts to export his idiosyncratic revolution met with little

After coming to power in 1969, Libyan leader Muammar al-Qaddafi negotiated the removal of U.S. and British military bases and took control of the Libyan assets of foreign oil companies. In 1973 he introduced a so-called cultural revolution in Libya and created workers' committees to supervise all aspects of economic and social life.

success, but he was accused of meddling in the internal affairs of other African nations and supporting various terrorist groups. Qaddafi's alleged support of international terrorism led the United States, on Apr. 15, 1986, to launch air attacks against Libyan targets it linked to terrorist activities.

Qatar [kah'-tahr] The sheikhdom of Qatar occupies a peninsula that juts into the PERSIAN GULF from the Arabian Peninsula (see ARABIA). On the south it shares an undemarcated border with Saudi Arabia and the United Arab Emirates (UAE). A former British protectorate, Qatar became independent on Sept. 1, 1971.

Land, People, and Economy

Qatar's terrain is barren, with low, sandy hills reaching a high point of only 105 m (345 ft) at Aba Al-Bawl Hill, in the south. Rainfall averages less than 127 mm (5 in) per year, and the average annual temperature is 24° C (75° F). The principal resources are petroleum and natural gas.

About 70% of Qatar's inhabitants live in DOHA, the capital. Less than 30% of the population are indigenous to Qatar, although the majority are Arabs. The nonindigenous population includes Palestinians, Indians, Paki-

AT A GLANCE

STATE OF QATAR

Land: Area: 11,000 km² (4,247 mi²). Capital and largest city: Doha (1986 est. pop., 217,294).

People: Population (1990 est.): 490,897. Density: 44.6 persons per km² (115.6 per mi²). Distribution (1989): 88% urban, 12% rural. Official language: Arabic. Major religion: Islam.

Government: Type: emirate. Legislature: none. Political subdivisions: none.

Economy: GDP (1987): $5.4 billion; $17,070 per capita. Labor distribution (1986): agriculture and fishing—3%; mining—2%; industry—7%; construction, public utilities, transportation, and commerce—40%; government and services—48%. Foreign trade (1988): imports—$1.0 billion; exports—$2.2 billion. Currency: 1 Qatar riyal = 100 dirhams.

Education and Health: Literacy (1986): 76% of adult population. Universities (1990): 1. Hospital beds (1989): 1,069. Physicians (1989): 752. Life expectancy (1990): women—73; men—69. Infant mortality (1990): 25 per 1,000 live births.

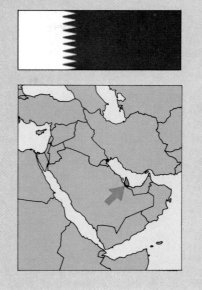

stanis, and Iranians. Almost all Qataris are orthodox Sunni Muslims of the Wahhabi sect (see WAHHABISM). Petroleum wealth has financed the expansion of health and education services. The University of Doha was founded in 1973.

Qatar, a member of the ORGANIZATION OF PETROLEUM EXPORTING COUNTRIES, derives 90% of its income from petroleum; the value of petroleum exports exceeds that of imports. Oil wealth has been used to establish fertilizer, flour, and cement industries. Natural gas, limestone, and clay are also exploited. About 85% of all jobs in the private sector are held by foreign nationals. Although only 1% of the land is cultivated, due to the lack of water, Qatar grows most of its own vegetables. The nation is largely self-sufficient in fish and exports small quantities of food to other Persian Gulf states.

Government and History

Qatar is a traditional monarchy, ruled by Emir Khalifa bin Hamad al-Thani. The Basic Law of 1970 allows for a council of ministers, led by an appointed prime minister. When it became independent in 1971, Qatar elected not to join the UAE. No legal political parties exist in the country.

Originally dominated by the nearby island of Bahrain in the Persian Gulf, Qatar fell under the rule of the Ottoman Turks from 1872 until World War I. It became a British protectorate in 1916, during the war, and began exporting petroleum in 1949. In 1971, Qatar became independent under Sheikh Ahmad bin Ali al-Thani. Five months later he was deposed in a bloodless coup by his cousin, Sheikh Khalifa bin Hamad al-Thani. In 1976 all petroleum interests were nationalized. Qatar is an active member of the Gulf Cooperation Council, and it signed a bilateral defense agreement with Saudi Arabia in 1982. Relations with Bahrain have been strained due to a territorial dispute. Qatar allied itself with the United States in the 1991 GULF WAR. After the war Qatar and other members of the Gulf Cooperation Council announced that they would no longer provide aid to Jordan or the PALESTINE LIBERATION ORGANIZATION.

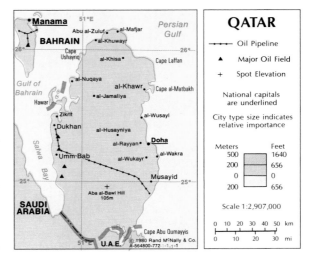

Qattara Depression [kah-tahr'-uh]   The Qattara Depression, an arid, sandy basin in the LIBYAN DESERT in northern Egypt, drops to Africa's second lowest point, 133 m (435 ft) below sea level. The eastern tip of the basin lies 56 km (35 mi) south of El Alamein on the Mediterranean coast. About 275 km (170 mi) long and 110 km (70 mi) wide, the basin has an area of about 19,500 km^2 (7,500 mi^2). It receives less than 50 mm (2 in) of rain annually, but any precipitation creates marshy conditions.

Qi Baishi (Ch'i Pai-shih) [chee-by-shih]   Qi Baishi, b. Nov. 22, 1863, d. 1957, was among the leading 20th-century traditional Chinese painters. Born into a humble peasant family, Qi became a carpenter and wood engraver. A self-taught artist, his mature style did not emerge until his later years. He is best known for his studies of flowers and small creatures, and his highly individualistic style is characterized by loose calligraphic brushwork.

Qianlong (Ch'ien-lung) [chee-en-lung]   Qianlong, b. Sept. 25, 1711, d. Feb. 7, 1799, was the fourth emperor of the Manchu, or QING, dynasty, which reached the peak of its power during his long reign (1735–96). In the so-called Ten Great Campaigns Qianlong's Manchu generals extended Chinese domination over Xinjiang and Tibet. Official projects for compiling and publishing dynastic histories and a series of encyclopedias on government, as well as a huge imperial manuscript library, drew to his court thousands of scholars from every part of the empire. An imperial art collection was assembled in the Beijing palace, and many new palaces and temples were built.

In Qianlong's reign, the population grew at a phenomenal rate, outstripping food production. Moreover, the cost of his military campaigns and the maintenance of his splendid court drained the treasury. The resulting weakness of the administration was aggravated in the final 20 years of his reign, when the aging emperor fell under the influence of a corrupt courtier, Heshen.

Qin (Ch'in) (dynasty) [chin]   The Qin dynasty, which ruled from 221 to 206 BC, established the first centralized imperial administration in China. From the dynasty is derived the name *China*. The Qin state, centered in present-day Shaanxi, emerged as the most powerful of the Warring Kingdoms, whose rivalry marked the decline of the ZHOU dynasty.

After the elimination of the Zhou in 256 and the conquest of the other feudal kingdoms from 230 to 221, the young Qin king adopted the title Shi Huangdi (First Emperor) of the Qin dynasty and began applying the centralized administrative system that had been a source of Qin strength to the whole empire. His adroit consolidation of Qin rule was probably due to his chief minister, Li Si (d. 208 BC). Besides effecting the division of China into non-feudal provinces with civil and military governors, Qin rule brought a new uniformity to weights and measures and coinage. Li Si standardized Chinese characters and literary composition, essentially as these are used today. He also tried to enforce uniformity of thought by proscribing philosophic debate and by burning most books. To secure the northern border of China, Shi Huangdi mobilized huge levies of laborers to connect sections of wall built by earlier states into the GREAT WALL OF CHINA. Strife erupted after his death in 210, and the dynasty soon collapsed. Excavation of the grave complex of Shi Huangdi in Xi'an in the 1970s yielded a magnificent pottery treasure of life-size men and horses.

Qing (Ch'ing) (dynasty) [ching]   The Qing, or Manchu, dynasty, founded by conquerors from Manchuria in 1644, was the last imperial dynasty of China. When it was overthrown in 1911, China became a republic. Under the Manchus the Chinese empire reached its greatest geographic extent, covering all of China proper, four outlying dependencies (Manchuria, Mongolia, Xinjiang, and Tibet), and several tributary states (chiefly Korea, Annam, Burma, and Nepal). The years of Qing rule also saw vigorous cultural and economic growth as the masterful emperors KANGXI (r. 1661–1722) and QIANLONG (r. 1735–96) preserved the institutions of neo-CONFUCIANISM while enlarging contacts with the West.

By the early 19th century the Qing dynasty began to weaken in the face of internal disorder and external aggression. This was evident after the First OPIUM WAR, when China signed the Treaty of Nanjing, ceding Hong Kong to Britain outright and opening the five so-called treaty ports of Guangzhou (Canton), Xiamen (Amoy), Fuzhou (Foochow), Ningbo (Ningpo), and Shanghai to foreigners. Official corruption and a general unease over foreign encroachments awakened latent anti-Manchu sentiment and eventually triggered the TAIPING REBELLION in 1850. The Taiping armies fought for more than a decade to overthrow the Manchu dynasty before being suppressed.

Cixi, dowager empress of China (1861–1908), acted as regent from 1861 to 1873 and 1898 to 1908, winning support from conservative Manchu factions. Cixi's failure to implement reforms led, in 1911, to the end of the Qing dynasty and of imperial rule in China.

In 1856, pressing the embattled Qing government for broader trade and diplomatic concessions, British and French warships bombarded Guangzhou. After taking the port in 1858, they sailed to Tianjin. When the Qing court balked at ratifying a new treaty, a larger European force stormed Beijing. The emperor fled while his brother, Prince Gong, exchanged ratifications and signed new conventions. A few days later Russia wrested a treaty ceding territory on the Pacific.

Succession of the young and weak Dongzhi emperor to the throne in 1862 led to a struggle for the regency ultimately won by Dowager Empress Cɪxɪ (Tz'u-hsi). Until she died (1908) the wily Cixi kept a ruthless hold on power, although her reign saw the death throes of the empire. The Europeans pushed inland, extracting further concessions. Japan defeated the Chinese in the First Sɪɴᴏ-Jᴀᴘᴀ-ɴᴇsᴇ Wᴀʀ (1894–95), acquiring Taiwan and later Korea. Overdue reforms, developed by Kᴀɴɢ Yᴏᴜᴡᴇɪ and Liang Qichao, were enacted in 1898 only to be annulled by Cixi, who then gave her support to the antiforeign Bᴏxᴇʀ Uᴘʀɪsɪɴɢ. Although she later allowed some reforms, the revolutionary movement gained momentum and overthrew the dynasty.

Qing Hai see Kᴏᴋᴏ Nᴏʀ

Qingdao (Tsingtao) [ching-dao] Qingdao, a city in northern China, is the largest industrial center in Shandong province. It is located on a hilly promontory on the southeast shore of Jiaozhou Bay, an inlet of the Yellow Sea. Its population is 1,300,000 (1988 est.). Qingdao is essentially an industrial port city. Cotton and silk fabrics, textile machinery, diesel locomotives, and railroad cars are among its manufactures. The city has an excellent natural harbor able to accommodate large oceangoing vessels. It is an important naval base and a popular health and summer resort. Shandong University (1926) is there.

Originally a small fishing village, Qingdao became a trade center during the Qing dynasty (1644–1911). Its history as a modern city dates from 1898, when it became a German leased territory. Japan occupied the city in 1914–22 and 1938–45.

Qinghai (Tsinghai) [ching-hy] Qinghai is a mountainous province in west central China, with an area of 721,000 km² (278,400 mi²) and a population of 4,456,946 (1990). The capital is Xining (1988 est. pop., 620,000). The province forms the northeastern section of the Tibetan plateau. The two largest Chinese rivers, the Huang He (Hwang Ho) and the Chang Jiang (Yangtze), have their headwaters there. The economy is based on the cultivation of spring wheat, barley, potatoes, and fruits and on sheep raising and horse breeding. Petroleum fields in the Qaidam Basin in the northwest have been worked since the late 1950s, and coal is mined in the northeast. Because of its remote location, Qinghai came under Chinese control as late as the 3rd century BC. It has been a province of China since 1928.

quadrant The quadrant has been used from medieval times to measure the altitude of the Sun or a star and for surveying. In its simplest form the quadrant is a flat plate in the shape of a quarter circle marked with a degree scale along the curved side; two sights are attached to one of the radial sides and a plumb bob hangs from the apex. Many sophisticated variants were developed by Arabic and medieval astronomers. On some the time could be read directly from the position of the Sun or specified stars.

Observatories used large wall-mounted quadrants for precise astronomical measurements from Ptolemaic times through the 1700s. The seaman's reflecting quadrant, invented by John Hadley (1682–1744) of England, was the precursor of the modern sextant (see ɴᴀᴠɪɢᴀᴛɪᴏɴ). The quadrant was brought to its greatest accuracy by London instrument maker John Bird about 1750–70.

quadrilateral A quadrilateral is a ᴘᴏʟʏɢᴏɴ formed by four intersecting line segments. The points of intersection of the segments are called vertices. A line segment connecting either pair of nonadjacent vertices is called a diagonal of the quadrilateral. The most general quadrilateral—in which no sides are parallel—is called a trapezium. Specific types include the ᴘᴀʀᴀʟʟᴇʟᴏɢʀᴀᴍ, the ʀᴇᴄᴛᴀɴɢʟᴇ, the sǫᴜᴀʀᴇ, and the ᴛʀᴀᴘᴇᴢᴏɪᴅ.

Quadruple Alliance Quadruple Alliance is the name of three European alliances formed in the 18th and 19th centuries. The first was formed (Aug. 2, 1718) by Austria, France, Britain, and the Dutch Republic to oppose Spain after the Spanish king Pʜɪʟɪᴘ V seized Sardinia and Sicily, violating settlements concluded (1713–14) at the end of the War of the Spanish Succession. The allies occupied Sicily and northern Spain and forced Spain to renounce all claim to Sicily and Sardinia. By the Treaty of The Hague (Feb. 17, 1720), Savoy surrendered Sicily to Austria in exchange for Sardinia.

The second Quadruple Alliance was formed toward the end of the Nᴀᴘᴏʟᴇᴏɴɪᴄ Wᴀʀs by Britain, Prussia, Austria, and Russia, each of which pledged (Mar. 9, 1814) not to conclude a separate peace with Napoleon. The alliance was renewed at the Congress of Vienna (1814–15; see Vɪᴇɴɴᴀ, Cᴏɴɢʀᴇss ᴏꜰ) after the final defeat of Napoleon. The parties then agreed to hold regular congresses to ensure the maintenance of the political status quo. The congress system collapsed after Britain withdrew from the alliance in 1822.

The last Quadruple Alliance was established in 1834 when Britain and France went to the aid of Isᴀʙᴇʟʟᴀ II of Spain and Mᴀʀɪᴀ II of Portugal, monarchs facing challenges from more conservative claimants to their thrones. The alliance defeated the pretenders in both countries.

quagga [kwag'-uh] The quagga, *Equus quagga*, a type of ᴢᴇʙʀᴀ once numerous in southern Africa, became extinct by 1883 because of a high demand for its hide. A

The quagga is an extinct zebra that once inhabited the steppes of southern Africa. Its stripes faded toward the rear of the body, so that the back was a solid yellowish brown. The last surviving quagga died in 1883.

member of the HORSE family, Equidae, it had typical zebra striping that was confined to the head, neck, and forequarters. Studies of protein and DNA fragments in quagga hides indicate that the animal was actually a variant of the plains zebra.

quail [kwayl]   The name *quail* designates birds belonging to two divisions of the pheasant family, Phasianidae: the New World quail, subfamily Odontophorinae; and the

The California quail (male, foreground, and female, background) ranges from Baja California to British Columbia.

Old World quail, subfamily Phasianinae, which also includes partridges.

Most New World quail are brightly marked and crested, and the two sexes are distinct in color. They lack spurs on their tarsi and have stronger bills than do Old World quail. About 30 species are distributed from southern Canada to northern Argentina, ranging from deserts (for example, the scaled quail, *Callipepla squamata*) to cloud forests (the bearded tree quail, *Dendrortyx barbatus*). None is migratory and most are considered game birds.

The bobwhite, *Colinus virginianus*, a North American game bird, measures up to 28 cm (11 in) in length; the male has a white throat and bands across each side of the head. It is considered beneficial to farmers because its diet includes a wide variety of agricultural pests.

The Old World common quail, *Coturnix coturnix*, domesticated in Japan and other countries, often migrates in dense flocks. The sparrow-sized Chinese painted quail, *Excalfactoria chinensis*, is the smallest known gallinaceous bird—that is, a bird related to the domestic fowl.

Quakers   see FRIENDS, SOCIETY OF

qualitative chemical analysis   Qualitative analysis is the branch of chemistry concerned with the identification of the components of chemical substances, either pure or present in a mixture. Qualitative analysis answers the question "what?" whereas QUANTITATIVE CHEMICAL ANALYSIS answers the question "how much?"

The methodology of qualitative analysis involves tests, which should be simple and direct and easily performed with readily available equipment, chemicals, and instruments. The results of the tests should be clear, reproducible, and easily interpreted.

Qualitative analysis frequently is used to identify a pure substance, usually an organic chemical. This procedure requires the determination of several chemical and physical properties of the "unknown," followed by a search of published chemical and physical properties of known compounds. Identification of the unknown is accomplished when a "known" is found with identical chemical and physical properties. If such a "known" is not found, the unknown must be a newly identified substance.

Test results may be a reading from a particular instrument, an observation of some physical property (for example, the temperature at which the substance melts), or a chemical reaction. Such reactions attempt to cause the appearance or disappearance of a characteristic color or precipitate, the evolution or absorption of a gas, or the formation of a characteristic odor. If the test indicates the presence of a substance, it is called a positive test; if it indicates that the substance is absent, it is a negative test. The tests must be specific (giving a positive test for the substance in a mixture of chemical compounds), sensitive (able to detect a small quantity of the substance in a mixture), and free from interference from related species.

Quanah   see PARKER, QUANAH

quantitative chemical analysis Quantitative analysis is that part of analytical chemistry which deals with determining relative amounts of one or more chemical constituents of a sample. In principle the analysis is simple; one measures the amount of each analyte (constituent of interest) in a known amount of sample. In practice, however, the analysis is often complicated by interferences among sample constituents, and chemical separations are necessary to isolate the analyte or remove the interfering constituents.

Quantitative analyses are carried out on small samples that are representative of larger amounts of the same material. Care must be taken to ensure that the small sample is representative of (identical in composition to) the larger amount.

A most demanding step in many analytical procedures is isolating the analyte, or separating from it those sample constituents which otherwise would interfere with its measurement. Some common separation methods are precipitation, distillation, extraction into an immiscible solvent, and various chromatographic procedures. Loss of analyte during separation procedures must be guarded against. The purpose of all earlier steps in an analysis is to make the final measurement a true indication of the quantity of analyte in the sample. Many types of final measurement are possible, including gravimetric analysis (based on weight measurements), volumetric analysis (based on volume measurements), and the use of sophisticated instruments to measure a wide variety of optical, electrochemical, and other physical properties of the analyte.

Quantrill, William C. [kwahn'-tril]   William Clarke Quantrill, b. Canal Dover, Ohio, July 31, 1837, d. June 6, 1865, was a Confederate guerrilla leader during the U.S. Civil War. His guerrilla bands burned and looted Union strongholds in Kansas and Missouri, diverting thousands of Union troops. On Aug. 21, 1863, Quantrill's Raiders pillaged Lawrence, Kans., killing more than 150 civilians. Mortally wounded by Union troops in May 1865, Quantrill died shortly thereafter in prison in Louisville, Ky.

quantum chromodynamics   In physics, quantum chromodynamics (QCD) is a theory that explains the strong nuclear force in terms of force carriers called GLUONS, acting between subatomic particles called QUARKS. Protons, neutrons, and other particles of the HADRON class are composed of quarks. In theory, there are six types, or "flavors," of quarks, further characterized by three indistinguishable qualities referred to as "colors." Color changes and quark grouping are manifestations of the strong nuclear force (see FUNDAMENTAL PARTICLES).

quantum electrodynamics   In physics, quantum electrodynamics (QED) is the theory that explains the electromagnetic force of electrons and other charged particles in terms of force carriers called photons. QED was developed in the 1920s and 1930s, based upon principles of electromagnetism, relativity, and quantum mechanics (see ELECTROMAGNETIC RADIATION).

quantum mechanics [kwahn'-tuhm]   Quantum mechanics is the fundamental theory used by 20th-century physicists to describe atomic and subatomic phenomena. It has proven very successful in tying together a wide range of observations into a coherent picture of the universe.

While quantum mechanics uses some of the concepts of Newtonian mechanics, the previous description of physical phenomena, it differs fundamentally from the Newtonian description. For example, in Newtonian physics, quantities were believed to be continuously variable, able to take on any value in some range. An example is angular momentum, which, for a particle revolving in a circular orbit about some center of attraction, is proportional to the speed multiplied by the distance from the center. Because that distance could have any value in Newtonian mechanics, so could the angular momentum. In quantum mechanics, on the other hand, angular momentum is always restricted to certain discrete values, whose ratios are simple rational numbers.

An even more fundamental difference between quantum mechanics and previous physical theories is that probability enters in a basic way into how quantum mechanics describes the world. This is made evident by the ways that quantum mechanics and Newtonian mechanics deal with predictions of the future. For something described by Newtonian mechanics, such as the solar system, it is possible, if sufficiently accurate measurements are made at one time, to predict the future behavior of the system to arbitrarily great accuracy. For systems de-

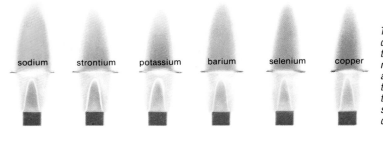

sodium   strontium   potassium   barium   selenium   copper

The occurrence of certain metallic elements in a material can be determined easily and quickly by means of a flame test. The flame test simply involves dipping a clean platinum wire loop into a solution of the material to be tested and then holding the loop in the nearly colorless upper portion of the flame of a Bunsen burner. A color is imparted to the flame that is characteristic for a given element and serves as a qualitative test for its presence. Typical colors obtained in flame tests of various elements are shown.

scribed by quantum mechanics, even one as simple as an atom with a single electron, precise prediction of future behavior is usually impossible. Instead, only predictions of the probability of various behaviors can be made. This can be illustrated by the description of an unstable radioactive nucleus. Quantum mechanics does not predict when the individual nucleus will decay, although if many similar nuclei are surveyed, one can predict what fraction will decay in any time interval. This novel feature of quantum mechanics, known as indeterminism, has been one of the things that has led some prominent physicists, such as Albert EINSTEIN, to resist it. Nevertheless, it appears to be an unavoidable feature of physics at the atomic and subatomic levels.

Early Historical Development

Planck's Work. Quantum mechanics was developed over a period of 30 years, during which it was successively applied to several physical phenomena. The first use of quantum ideas was made in the analysis of how electromagnetic radiation is produced. This was done by the German physicist Max PLANCK in 1900. Planck was trying to account for the distribution, among different frequencies, of the radiation emitted by a hot object, such as the surface of the Sun. He found that to obtain results in agreement with observation, he had to assume that the radiation was not emitted continuously, as was previously believed. Instead, it was emitted in discrete amounts, which he called quanta. For these quanta, there was always a relation between the frequency *f*, and the amount of energy emitted *E*, of the form $E = hf$. Here *h* is a universal constant introduced by Planck, and now named for him. Planck's constant has the units of energy multiplied by time, known as action. Its numerical value is approximately 6.63×10^{-34} joule-seconds. The specific result of Planck's analysis was a formula expressing the amount of energy radiated at any frequency as a function of the temperature of the emitting object. This relation, the blackbody distribution, agrees accurately with observation (see BLACKBODY RADIATION).

Photons. In Planck's work the nature of the quanta was rather mysterious. It was clarified by the work of Einstein, who in 1905 proposed that light itself was composed of individual packages of energy, which later came to be known as photons. Einstein also proposed that the frequency of the light is related to the energy of the photons composing it by Planck's formula. Einstein's theory of light quanta, which was rejected by many of his contemporaries, including Planck, was verified both by Robert Millikan's work on the PHOTOELECTRIC EFFECT, and by the discovery by Arthur Compton of the COMPTON EFFECT, or the scattering of photons by electrons.

Bohr's Theory. Another significant early use of quantum ideas was by Niels BOHR, who in 1913 showed that by assuming that the angular momentum of electrons in a hydrogen atom could only take on values that are an integer multiple of Planck's constant divided by 2π, he could derive accurate expressions for the frequencies of light emitted by the atom. Bohr's analysis implied that only certain energy values are possible for the electron in the atom, that there is a minimum value, and that in this minimum energy state, the electron cannot radiate energy. This result helped explain how the atom could be stable, and how all atoms of one element have the same chemical properties. However, it proved impossible to extend Bohr's ideas directly to atoms more complex than hydrogen. Also, the strange blend of Newtonian and quantum ideas left physicists uneasy about the supposedly basic principles of their science.

Forms of Quantum Mechanics

The development of actual quantum mechanics—the mathematical theory—took place in the years 1924–27. Initially there were two seemingly different approaches: matrix mechanics, invented by Werner HEISENBERG, and wave mechanics, invented by Erwin SCHRÖDINGER. However, it was soon shown that these were distinct aspects of a single theory, which came to be known as quantum mechanics. This unified version was invented by Paul DIRAC. In matrix mechanics, physical quantities such as the position of a particle are represented not by numbers, but by mathematical quantities known as matrices. Matrix mechanics is most useful in dealing with situations in which there is a small number of relevant energy levels, such as a particle with definite angular momentum in a magnetic field.

Wave Mechanics. Wave mechanics is more useful in a situation where the number of energy levels is infinite, as with an electron in an atom. It is based on the idea originally suggested by Louis DE BROGLIE, that particles such as electrons have waves associated with them. The wavelength, λ, of the wave is related to the mass, *m*, and speed, *v*, of the particle by the relation $\lambda=h/mv$. This implies that for electrons moving at 10% the speed of light, such as those produced by some television tubes, the wavelengths are about 10^{-10} meters, or about the distance between atoms in a crystalline solid. This prediction of de Broglie was verified by Clinton Davisson and by George Thomson, who were able to pass the electron waves through metallic crystals, and so produce diffraction patterns similar to those produced by X rays.

The Schrödinger Equation. In 1925, Erwin Schrödinger developed an equation, now bearing his name, that describes how a wave associated with an electron or other subatomic particle varies in space and time as the particle moves under the influence of various forces. This equation has many types of solutions, and Schrödinger imposed the condition that for a particle bound in an atom, the solution should be mathematically well defined everywhere. When applied to the case of an electron in a hydrogen atom, Schrödinger's equation immediately gave the correct energy levels previously calculated by Bohr. However, the equation could also be applied to more complicated atoms, and even to particles not bound in atoms at all. It was soon found that in every case, Schrödinger's equation gave a correct description of a particle's behavior, provided that the particle was not moving at a speed near that of light.

In spite of this success the meaning of the waves remained unclear. Schrödinger believed that the intensity of the wave at a point in space represented the "amount" of the electron that was present at that point. In other words the electron was spread out, rather than concentrated at a point. However, it was soon found that this interpretation was untenable, because even if a particle was originally concentrated on a small region, in most cases it would soon spread over an increasingly larger region, in contradiction to the observed behavior of particles.

Born's Probability Interpretation. The correct interpretation of the waves was discovered by Max BORN. While studying how quantum mechanics describes collisions between particles, he realized that the intensity of the de Broglie-Schrödinger wave was a measure of the probability of finding the particle at each point in space. In other words, a measurement would always find a whole particle, rather than a fraction of one, but in regions where the wave intensity was low, the particle would rarely be found, whereas in regions of high intensity, the particle would often be found.

Heisenberg's Uncertainty Relation. An important contribution to the interpretation of quantum mechanics was given in 1927 by Heisenberg. He analyzed various "thought experiments" that were designed to suggest information about the location and velocity of a particle. An example would be the use of a microscope to image an electron. It is known that, because of the wave properties of light, a precise electron image requires the use of light of very short wavelength, and therefore high frequency. However, the Planck-Einstein relation implies that for such light, the photons must carry a large amount of energy and momentum. In the collisions between such photons and electrons, the electron momentum will be changed uncontrollably from what it was before the collision. As a result, the increased precision with which the electron's position is known is unavoidably accompanied by a loss of accuracy in the knowledge of its momentum. On the basis of this and related analyses, Heisenberg was led to formulate his UNCERTAINTY PRINCIPLE, which in its simplest form, states a reciprocal relation between the uncertainty Δx, with which one can know the position of any object, and simultaneously, the uncertainty Δp, with which one can know its momentum. The mathematical statement of the uncertainty relation is given by $\Delta x \Delta p > h/4\pi$. For an object of everyday size this limitation on simultaneous measurements is very unimportant, when compared to ordinary experimental uncertainties. For this reason, there is rarely any significant difference between the predictions of Newtonian and quantum mechanics for such objects. However, for an electron in an atom, the uncertainty restrictions are so significant that they essentially determine the atom's size and minimum energy.

The Copenhagen Interpretation. With Born's probability interpretation of the wave intensity and Heisenberg's uncertainty principle, the elements of the standard indeterministic interpretation of quantum mechanics were in place by 1930. This interpretation is often known as the Copenhagen interpretation, because Niels Bohr, who made

important contributions to its formulation, ran an influential physics institute there during this period. However, many physicists, including Einstein and Schrödinger, who accepted the mathematical formulation of quantum mechanics, were uncomfortable with the Copenhagen interpretation, and criticized it. The question of the correct interpretation of the mathematical formalism has remained something of a problem up to the present, and is discussed further below.

Applications of Quantum Mechanics

Directly after its discovery quantum mechanics was applied to many problems in atomic physics and chemistry, such as the structure of many-electron atoms and of molecules. These applications were generally successful in explaining old observations and in predicting newer ones. An example of the latter case was the successful prediction that hydrogen molecules could exist in two types, depending on the relative orientation of the angular momentum of the nucleus. This type of success led Paul Dirac, in 1928, to describe quantum mechanics as "including all of chemistry and most of physics." Although the second half of this statement has not proven to be perfectly accurate, extensions of quantum mechanics have been successful in explaining an ever-growing number of physical phenomena. For example, in the 1930s and 1940s, George GAMOW used quantum mechanics to explain radioactive alpha decay of atomic nuclei.

For some applications to atomic nuclei, and for accurate calculations in atomic physics, it became necessary to extend the original form of quantum mechanics to make it consistent with Einstein's special theory of RELATIVITY. This was first done by Dirac in 1927, with an equation bearing his name. Dirac's equation proved immediately successful in accounting for a property of electrons known as spin. Spin is angular momentum of rotation about an axis through the electron, somewhat like that of the Earth rotating about its own axis. It was previously known that all electrons carry a spin of $h/4\pi$, but the reason was not clear. The Dirac equation explained this and accurately accounted for some magnetic properties of spinning electrons. It also made a novel prediction of the existence of particles similar in mass and spin to electrons, but with opposite electric charge. These particles, which have come to be known as positrons, were discovered by Carl Anderson in 1932. There were the first example of antiparticles, whose existence is predicted by any theory that satisfies the requirements both of quantum mechanics and special relativity (see ANTIMATTER).

Quantum Field Theory

The study of antiparticles and their properties highlighted a new aspect of relativistic quantum theories, the creation and annihilation of matter. Dirac had predicted, and it was soon observed, that electrons and positrons could be created together in pairs, when high-energy photons passed through matter. Furthermore, a positron that comes near to an electron quickly disappears together with the electron, converting into several photons. In order to describe trans-

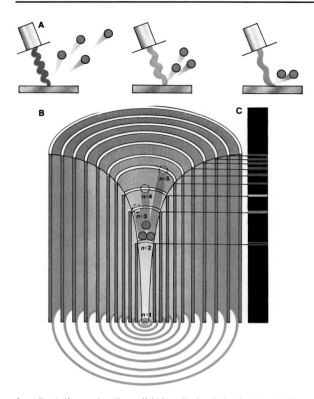

According to the quantum theory, light is emitted and absorbed by matter in quanta, or discrete amounts of energy that are related to the frequency of the light. In the photoelectric effect (A), electrons are ejected when light quanta fall on certain metals. More electrons are expelled as the light intensity increases because the number of quanta increase, but the electron velocities depend only on the light's frequency and decrease from a high value for violet light to a lower value for red light. When the electrons in an excited atom (B) drop from an orbit of high energy to one of lower energy, they emit light and produce the bright lines in the element's spectrum (C).

formations in which the number of particles changes, it was necessary to apply quantum mechanics to a new area, that of fields.

In Newtonian physics, a field represents a physical quantity, such as electric force, which varies from point to point in space and time according to precise mathematical equations. Such classical fields can have any numerical value at any point. The general version of quantum theory was first applied to the electromagnetic field by Dirac, who showed that this combination automatically implied the existence of photons with the properties assumed by Planck and Einstein. Furthermore, Dirac was able to use this quantum-field-theory formalism, which came to be known as QED, or QUANTUM ELECTRODYNAMICS, to describe how photons are emitted and absorbed by charged particles, as when an electron in an atom radiates. An important practical application of QED in the late 1950s was the invention of the laser.

A number of physicists applied similar ideas to other, previously unknown fields in order to describe processes in which the numbers of other types of particles change. For example, Enrico Fermi, in 1933, used quantum field theory to explain the emission of electrons from a nucleus, the process known as BETA DECAY. The general lesson learned from this is that fields satisfying the laws of quantum mechanics and relativity automatically describe particles that can be created or destroyed.

Virtual Particles. Quantum field theory had some unforeseen consequences. One aspect of Heisenberg's uncertainty principle is that the law of conservation of energy is not strictly observed for short periods of time. Because of this, a particle such as an electron can briefly emit and then reabsorb other particles, such as photons. These transients, called virtual particles, influence the properties that we measure for the electron. In particular, they change its mass from what it would have been if they did not exist. The extra mass due to virtual particles is called the self mass. Unfortunately, when physicists in the 1930s tried to calculate the self mass due to virtual photons, they got an infinite result. For some time, this result paralyzed progress in quantum field theory. However, in the 1940s, a method was found for dealing with infinite self mass, and certain related infinities. This procedure, known as renormalization, has dominated quantum field theory since.

Renormalization. The idea behind renormalization is that the self mass is not directly measurable. Only the combination of self mass and any intrinsic mass that the electron might have can be observed. It was suggested, first by Hendrik Kramers, that an infinite self mass might combine with an infinite intrinsic mass to give the finite observed mass. It should then be possible to express all other observable quantities in terms of this sum, avoiding the problem of infinities. Calculations involving this procedure, known as mass renormalization, are quite delicate to carry out. Indeed, they were only done successfully after new techniques were introduced in the late 1940s by Julian Schwinger and Richard FEYNMAN. These methods are designed to be consistent with relativity theory at all stages, unlike earlier methods, which made sharp distinctions between space and time. Feynman's methods involve the use of suggestive pictures, now called Feynman diagrams, which are correlated with any process to be calculated. For example, the emission of a photon by an electron is pictured as a solid line of indefinite length, representing the electron, with a wavy line, representing the photon, originating in the middle of the electron line. Feynman described a set of rules by which the probability of occurrence of any process could be calculated directly from the associated diagram.

In the late 1940s, using the methods of Feynman and Schwinger, scientists calculated small corrections, due to emission and absorption of virtual photons, for the energies of electrons in hydrogen atoms, and for the magnetic properties of electrons. These calculations, which have continued to ever higher levels of accuracy, in some cases agree with observation to the incredible accuracy of one part in a billion. This is probably the greatest triumph that theoretical physics has yet achieved.

Gauge Field Theories. The success of QED led many physicists to believe that other renormalizable quantum field theories could be found to describe properties of subatomic particles that are not included in QED, such as the strong forces that bind neutrons and protons into nuclei, and the weak forces responsible for beta decay. For many years this hope was not realized, because not enough was known either about types of renormalizable theories or about the particles to which such theories should be applied. This situation changed in the 1960s and 1970s, following the invention, by Chen-Ning Yang and Robert Mills, of a particular kind of renormalizable quantum field theory known as a gauge field theory. It was shown that one type of gauge field theory, named QUANTUM CHROMODYNAMICS, or QCD, was capable of describing the strong interactions provided that it was applied not to protons and neutrons, but to quarks, hypothetical particles that compose protons and neutrons and other particles affected by strong interactions. A second gauge field theory was shown by Sheldon GLASHOW, Steven WEINBERG, and Abdus Salam, to be capable of describing electromagnetic and weak interactions together, thus unifying in a single theory two important aspects of nature.

In spite of the success of renormalizable quantum field theories, some prominent theoretical physicists, such as Dirac, have expressed misgivings about them. Although observable quantities are finite in these theories, this is achieved through manipulations with infinite quantities that are mathematically suspect and aesthetically unpleasant.

The Interpretation of Quantum Mechanics

Although quantum mechanics is now over 60 years old, and has been very successful in providing explanations for physical phenomena, there remains a dissatisfaction among some physicists both with the theory itself and with the prevailing Copenhagen interpretation. Much of this criticism derives from the radical change from earlier theories that quantum mechanics represents, but some of it involves problems that arise within quantum mechanics itself.

Hidden Variable Theories. One criticism of quantum mechanics relates to its indeterminacy. This was Einstein's original objection, although he later developed others. Because an individual radioactive nucleus will eventually decay at a specific time, Einstein and others believed that a complete physical theory should allow this time to be predicted exactly, rather than just statistically. While Einstein did not specify what type of theory he had in mind to replace quantum mechanics, others have suggested that the solution be sought in some type of "hidden variable" theory. In hidden variable theories, physical properties other than those we can yet measure would determine those events about which quantum mechanics can only make probability predictions. The mathematician John von Neumann proved long ago that no hidden variable theory can agree exactly with the predictions of quantum mechanics, but the predictions have not all been examined, so there exists some possibility that a hidden variable theory could be formulated which agrees with all observations that have been made. However, none has yet been produced which physicists find satisfactory.

Reduction of the Wave Function. A second problem with the interpretation of quantum mechanics, which troubles even those who accept the theory, involves the idea of measurement. Schrödinger's wave equation can be used to describe how any system changes from one time to another. If the wave is known everywhere in space at one time, it can be predicted everywhere at a later time. However, knowing the wave intensity only allows for probability predictions of the results of measurements. When a measurement is actually made, the observer suddenly obtains exact information about at least one property of the system, such as its energy. This change from probabilistic to exact information has come to be called the reduction of the wave function. It has been proven that even if the interaction between the measuring instrument and the system being observed is taken into account, this reduction cannot be properly described by the Schrödinger equation. Various scientists have taken different attitudes toward this result. Some have championed the view that the consciousness of an observer plays a fundamental role in reduction of the wave function. Others have argued that because quantum mechanics cannot account for reduction, it is incomplete. Perhaps the most widely accepted view is that reduction of the wave function always involves the interaction of a microscopic object, such as an electron, with a macroscopic system, the measuring instrument. When this interaction takes place, there is an irreversible change in the macroscopic measuring instrument, and it is this change that results in the reduction of the electron's wave function. While there may be some truth to this view, it only solves part of the problem, because irreversibility itself is not completely understood.

Bell's Theorem. An argument given by John Bell, in 1964, dealt with the fact that Einstein's conclusion contradicts quantum mechanics. His finding, known as BELL'S THEOREM, derives from statistical measurements of spin values of many correlated electrons and protons. It states that any theory satisfying Einstein's reality condition—that reality is a localized phenomenon, and particles have determined properties—necessarily implies a relation among the results of a series of measurements. A series of experiments to test Einstein's reality condition, and Bell's theorem, have been carried out. The results do not support Einstein's reality condition, but instead support quantum mechanics.

Quantum Mechanics Today

Research that employs quantum mechanics remains at the center of contemporary physics. One aspect of this research involves the search for approximate methods that can be applied with the basic principles of quantum mechanics in studies of situations that are so complex that they cannot be dealt with exactly. Much of the research in condensed-matter physics is of this nature. An important discovery in this area is that in some situations, the discreteness of physical quantities that usually occurs on the subatomic level can also occur on the macroscopic level. The quantized HALL EFFECT, a property of electrical resistance of certain substances under the influence of electric and magnetic forces, is a recently discovered example of this.

Another important area of research involves the attempt to include gravity among the phenomena that can be described by quantum mechanics. Although there are no observations yet which require the use of a quantum theory of gravity, physicists believe that such phenomena may occur inside black holes, and may have occurred everywhere in the earliest moments of the universe. It has not yet been possible to formulate a consistent quantum theory of gravity, either by beginning with Einstein's non-quantum general theory of relativity, or by applying the usual ideas of quantum field theory. Currently, some physicists are pursuing an approach based on a quantum theory of strings, objects extended in one spatial dimension, as opposed to conventional particles, which are extensionless points (see SUPERSTRING THEORY). String theories may succeed in uniting gravity with the other forces of nature in a unified quantum-mechanical description of nature. Meanwhile, there is no doubt that quantum mechanics is the most successful theory of physical phenomena yet invented by the human mind.

Quapaw [kwah'-paw]   The Quapaw, or Arkansas, are a tribe of North American Indians who originated in the Ohio Valley. They separated from the OSAGE and OMAHA at the confluence of the Ohio and Mississippi to go downstream (Quapaw means "downstream") to the Arkansas River. They spoke a Siouan language, built bark-covered earth lodges in fortified villages, and cultivated maize and beans and occasionally hunted bison. Hernando DE SOTO made contact with them about 1540, and Jacques MARQUETTE and Louis JOLLIET visited them in the next century.

Before 1720 smallpox killed many of the Quapaw. Only 1,000 remained in 1818, when they ceded 30 million acres (12 million ha) to the United States for $4,000 and annuities. A remaining million acres (0.4 million ha) for a reservation were ceded in 1824. The following year the Quapaw moved to the Caddo Reservation in Louisiana, where diseases and floods struck them. They scattered during the Civil War, but in the late 1800s survivors gathered on the reservation to reestablish tribal life. Zinc was discovered on the reservation in the 1920s, and the Quapaw prospered. Reduced to a population of 400 in 1900, the Quapaw on or near the reservation increased to 995 (1991 est.), including some Osage and Ottawa. Some Quapaw still maintain features of their traditional life.

quark [kwahrk]   In nuclear physics, a quark is a hypothetical entity representing a basic constituent of matter—even more fundamental than the proton and neutron, which were once thought to be "elementary" particles. Quarks have not been observed, and it is conjectured that they have properties that render them unobservable. Even so, there is sufficient indirect evidence for most scientists to accept their existence.

PROPERTIES OF QUARKS

Quark	Mass (GeV)*	Charge	Charm	Strangeness
Up	0.378	$+\frac{2}{3}$	0	0
Down	0.336	$-\frac{1}{3}$	0	0
Strange	0.540	$-\frac{1}{3}$	0	−1
Charmed	1.5	$+\frac{2}{3}$	+1	0
Bottom	4.72	$-\frac{1}{3}$	0	0
Top	30–50	$+\frac{2}{3}$	0	0

*GeV = Gigaelectron volts.

The quark theory was independently proposed in 1963 by two physicists, Murray GELL-MANN and George Zweig of the California Institute of Technology. The theory was advanced in an attempt to establish order from the bewildering array of known subatomic particles (about 200) and to find some underlying simplicity. Noting that all strongly interacting particles could be grouped into families according to mathematical principles, Gell-Mann and Zweig showed that all their properties could be understood if it were assumed that they were built up from other, more elementary, particles. The latter have come to be called "quarks," the name originating from an arcane line in James Joyce's *Finnegan's Wake:* "Three quarks for Muster Mark."

Not all particles are affected by quark theory. The LEPTONS, a class of particles that includes the electron, muon, and neutrino, do not participate in the strong nuclear interaction and are thought not to be composed of quarks. Quarks combine to form HADRONS. A large subgroup of the hadrons is the BARYONS, a class that includes the proton and all heavier particles that ultimately decay into a proton and something else. Baryons are assumed to be made of three quarks. Another subgroup, the MESONS, are assumed to be made of one quark and one antiquark (see ANTIMATTER), each quark having an antiquark analogue. The differences among the various mesons and baryons result from different quark types and combinations.

The original quark theory called for three types, or "flavors," of quarks called up, down, and strange (u, d, and s). All ordinary matter can be constructed from just the up and down quarks. The s quark is needed to explain certain particles created by high-energy events that have the "strangeness" property of existing for longer periods of time (10^{-12} sec) than predicted (10^{-24} sec). One of the remarkable features of quarks is that they carry an electric charge that is a fraction of e, the charge of the electron, which was considered the fundamental unit of charge. The u quark bears a charge of $+\frac{2}{3}$ and the d quark a charge of $-\frac{1}{3}$. The proton is made of two u quarks and one d quark; its total charge is $\frac{2}{3} + \frac{2}{3} - \frac{1}{3} = 1$. Similarly, the uncharged neutron is composed of one u quark and two d quarks. An additional nuclear property given the whimsical name "charm" was experimentally verified in 1974 when Burton Richter and Samuel Ting simultaneously discovered the J/psi particle. This required the postulation of a fourth quark, the "charmed," or c, quark. Later theoretical work called for a symmetry between leptons and quarks, leading physicists to postulate two more quarks: the "bottom," "beauty," or b, quark; and the "top," "truth," or t, quark. The existence of the latter is not yet proved.

As if this proliferation of quarks were not enough, theorists assume that each "flavor" of quark can exhibit one of three forms of a further property, indistinguishable to an observer, so that the Pauli EXCLUSION PRINCIPLE is not violated. This further property is called "color." It is believed that the strong interaction may be an indirect manifestation of a more basic "color force," which is carried by GLUONS and is responsible for the permanent entrapment of quarks. Each of the six postulated quarks can have any one of three colors, usually called red, blue, and green. It is thought that quarks can exist only in certain color groupings (of 2 or 3 quarks) that produce a so-called color-neutral state. The theory behind the color force is called QUANTUM CHROMODYNAMICS (QCD).

No experiment has yet detected a single, isolated quark. Most attempts have involved searching for a particle with a charge that is a fraction of the electron charge. No matter how hard nuclear physicists collide hadrons, though, they only succeed in creating quark-antiquark pairs. The difficulty of separating quarks may be due to an increase in the nuclear force at larger (on a nuclear scale) distances. The inability to isolate a quark represents the unsolved problem of "quark confinement."

See also: FUNDAMENTAL INTERACTIONS; FUNDAMENTAL PARTICLES.

quarter horse   The quarter horse is thought to have originated in the mid- to late 1600s in the American colonies of Virginia and the Carolinas. It was used for racing on straight quarter-mile (400-m) tracks, from which it de-

The quarter horse is capable of extremely fast starts and can often beat the Thoroughbred over short distances. An American light horse with great endurance, it is used as a cattle horse and a polo pony.

rives its name. At such a short distance, equal to 2 furlongs, fast starts and the ability to reach top speed quickly are of great advantage, and the first quarter horses were bred with these points in mind. Bred probably from local native stock, and Thoroughbred as well, the quarter horse was developed with a relatively short body; broad, muscular hindquarters; strong, sloping shoulders; and sturdy feet. The breed or breed type appeared in the southwestern United States on cattle ranches, where its quick starting, stopping, and turning made it valuable as a cow pony.

Quarter horses may be any solid color, as well as buckskin, smoky, and palomino, but paints or pintos are not permissible. Quarter horses generally range in size from 14-2 to 15-2 hands high (147 to 157 cm/58 to 62 in).

quartz [kwohrts]   Quartz, which is the most abundant SILICA MINERAL and which occurs in most igneous and practically all metamorphic and sedimentary rocks, is nearly pure silicon dioxide (SiO_2). It has also been found in some lunar rocks and meteorites. The name *quartz* is believed to have originated in the early 1500s from the Saxon word *querklufterz* (cross-vein ore), which was corrupted to *quererz* and then to *quartz*. Quartz was well known to the ancients, who called it crystal or rock crystal.

Quartz is colorless and transparent when pure. Its hardness is 7 on the Mohs scale, and its specific gravity is 2.651. Quartz has no cleavage and fails by brittle fracture; the fracture surfaces have vitreous luster. Quartz is diamagnetic but does not conduct electricity. PIEZOELECTRICITY makes quartz valuable in pressure gauges, electronic frequency-control devices, and radio equipment.

Crystallography. Quartz occurs in a wide range of crystal sizes, from single crystals weighing many tons to cryptocrystalline varieties whose crystallinity may be seen only with the aid of an electron microscope. Quartz crystallizes in the trigonal trapezohedral class of the rhombohedral subsystem of hexagonal symmetry.

Varieties. Although coarsely crystalline quartz occurs in colorless or white (milky) masses, colored varieties are numerous and popular. AMETHYST (violet); smoky quartz; cairngorm, or morion (black); citrine (yellow); and rose quartz are common and arise by the incorporation of a tiny fraction of elements that substitute for silicon atoms, such as iron, aluminum, manganese, and titanium.

Very fine grained and cryptocrystalline varieties of quartz are numerous. Collectively called chalcedonic quartz, these varieties form slowly from evaporating or cooling solutions as crusts and fillings of veins and open spaces. When color banding is conspicuous, the variety is called AGATE. Agate with numerous flat bands of white, black, or dark brown is called ONYX. Translucent red or brown chalcedonic quartz colored by iron oxides; green varieties colored by chlorite, amphiboles, or nickel minerals; and mottled moss agates are used as semiprecious stones. BLOODSTONE is a green variety of chalcedonic quartz with red spots. Chalcedonic quartz is often colored by chemical processes. Finely crystallized quartz called CHERT AND FLINT occurs within calcareous or silty sedimen-

Quartz, the most abundant mineral on Earth, is found in a variety of forms and colors in nearly all rock types. Rock crystal, normally a colorless, transparent, long, prismatic crystalline form, shown embedded in marble, is sometimes colored by impurities.

tary rock as gray or black layers or nodules. JASPER is very fine grained quartz with abundant iron oxides—it may be red, brown, yellow, dark gray, or black.

When heated above 573° C (1,063° F) at 1 bar (14.50 lb/in^2) of pressure, quartz assumes higher symmetry as the threefold *c* axis becomes sixfold. This hexagonal form is known as high quartz or β-quartz. The transformation temperature is pressure-dependent, increasing by approximately 25 C degrees (45 F degrees) per kilobar. When high quartz is cooled below the inversion temperature, inversion to low quartz occurs rapidly. The first mild heating of quartz commonly will be accompanied by the emission of light (thermoluminescence), and irreversible color changes may occur in colored varieties. For example, amethyst may be transformed to citrine at 250° C (482° F) or higher. Vigorous rubbing of one quartz crystal by another may also produce visible light (triboluminescence).

Formation. Quartz forms in rocks of igneous origin only after other silicates have incorporated the other available cations. Thus only compositions that are more than approximately 47 percent (by weight) SiO_2 contain quartz. As the content of SiO_2 in the bulk composition of magma increases, increasing amounts of free SiO_2 appear as quartz or other silica minerals. Quartz can be dissolved in hot water or steam and is thus transported from place to place in the Earth, being deposited by the cooling of the transporting fluid or by the release of pressure. Because quartz is relatively resistant to mechanical abrasion, it is abundant in stream sediments, on beaches, and in wind-blown sands. SANDSTONE and its metamorphic equivalent, quartzite, are mostly quartz, and many other sedimentary and metamorphic rocks contain substantial amounts of quartz.

Uses. Quartz has various electronic applications. It is also used as a component of glass, ceramics, refractories, cements, and mortar; as an abrasive; as a chemical raw material for the manufacture of sodium silicate, silicon carbide, silicon metals, organic silicates, and silicones; and for components in optical and scientific apparatuses.

quartzite   see QUARTZ

quasar   Quasars are the most luminous known objects in the universe, some of them having luminosities more than 100 times greater than that of the brightest known galaxy. Some quasars are markedly and erratically variable in their light in a period of minutes; their diameters must therefore be less than 100 light-minutes across, or about the size of the solar system. These small sizes have been roughly corroborated by special radio techniques involving two widely separated radio telescopes operating together as a very long baseline interferometer. Thus more than 100 times the luminosity of the entire Galaxy is emitted from a volume 10^{17} times smaller than that of the Galaxy—an incredible outpouring of energy from a relatively small volume of space.

Quasars detected as radio sources are called radio quasars, quasi-stellar radio sources, or quasi-stellar sources (QSSs); radio-quiet quasars detected by other means are called quasi-stellar objects (QSOs) or quasi-stellar galaxies (QSGs).

The astronomer Maarten Schmidt was the first to recognize, in 1963, that quasars were objects with large values of *z*, or RED SHIFT, for their spectra, presumably due to their large velocities of recession. Some quasars discovered since the mid-1980s have a *z* of more than 4, making them the most distant objects yet found in the universe. A *z* of more than 4 means that spectral lines are shifted to wavelengths more than 4 times greater than normal, implying that the objects are moving away from Earth at 93 percent of the velocity of light or higher.

Strenuous efforts are under way to find distances to quasars independently of their red shifts. Some quasars appear to be located within clusters of galaxies and show the same red shift as the galaxies. These quasar distances are almost certainly cosmological and presumably correct. Some conflicting observations have been made, however, of quasars that lie almost in the same line of sight with galaxies having different red shifts, marginal evidence being claimed for interactions between the quasars and these galaxies. Should such interactions exist, they would imply that the quasars in question are not as far away as had been thought. Some patterns in the values of observed red shifts also do not seem to be accounted for in terms of standard cosmologies. Most astronomers, however, accept the concept that quasars do lie at their apparent cosmological distances and that they are violently active nuclei of distant galaxies. Quasars are generally assumed to be a relatively temporary phase in the early evolution of most larger galaxies, closely related to the massive BLACK HOLES widely thought to lie at the centers of the larger galaxies.

Quasimodo, Salvatore   [kwah-zee-moh'-doh]   Salvatore Quasimodo, b. Aug. 20, 1901, d. June 14, 1968, was a prominent Italian poet whose verse ranged from lyrical celebrations of his native Sicily reminiscent of the Greek classics to moving poems about human suffering and the ravages of war. His poems are remarkable for the beauty of their lyricism and their profound, often obscure imagery. Major collections include *Ed è subito sera* (And It Is Suddenly Evening, 1942), *Il falso e vero verde* (The False and the True Green, 1956), and *La terra impareggiabile* (The Incomparable Land, 1958). Also a fine translator of the Greek and Latin classics, Quasimodo was awarded the Nobel Prize for literature in 1959.

Quaternary Period   see EARTH, GEOLOGICAL HISTORY OF; GEOLOGIC TIME

◼

Quayle, Dan   James Danforth Quayle III, b. Indianapolis, Ind., Feb. 4, 1947, was elected vice-president of the United States on Nov. 8, 1988, on the Republican ticket headed by George BUSH. Quayle graduated (1969) from De Pauw University and received (1974) a law degree from Indiana University. Elected to the U.S. House of Representatives in 1976, he served two terms there before winning election to the U.S. Senate in 1980. He easily won reelection in 1986. A fiscal and social conservative, he focused in large part in the Senate on national security issues. Bush's choice of Quayle as his running mate drew some criticism from those who questioned Quayle's qualifications to serve as president, should the need arise.

◼

Quebec (city) [kwi-bek']   Quebec, at the confluence of the St. Lawrence and Saint Charles rivers in southeastern Canada, is the capital of the province of Quebec, the oldest city in Canada, and one of the most distinctive of all North American metropolises. The name is thought to be derived from an Algonquian Indian word that means "abrupt narrowing of the river," a reference to Quebec's location at the head of the St. Lawrence River estuary. The population of the city is 164,580, and that of the metropolitan area, 603,267 (1986). Most of Quebec's population is French-speaking and Roman Catholic.

Contemporary City. The city contains two major sections—Upper Town and Lower Town. The smaller Upper Town is clustered on the tableland west of Cape Diamond, the 101-m-high (333-ft) promontory overlooking the St. Lawrence. A completely walled section is the core of the Upper Town. It is primarily a governmental and cultural center of narrow, cobbled streets reminiscent of European cities. Upper Town is also the site of the once-fortified Citadel and a castlelike hotel, the Château Frontenac. Lower Town, at the base of Cape Diamond, extends over the valley of the Saint Charles River to the north and into the Laurentian foothills beyond. It encompasses residential, commercial, and industrial districts.

Quebec is a busy seaport and industrial center. Its major functions, however, are administrative, commercial, and ecclesiastical. Tourism is another important segment of the economy. Quebec is the seat of Laval University (1852). Historic landmarks include the Church of Notre Dame des Victoires (1688) and the Anglican cathedral (1810).

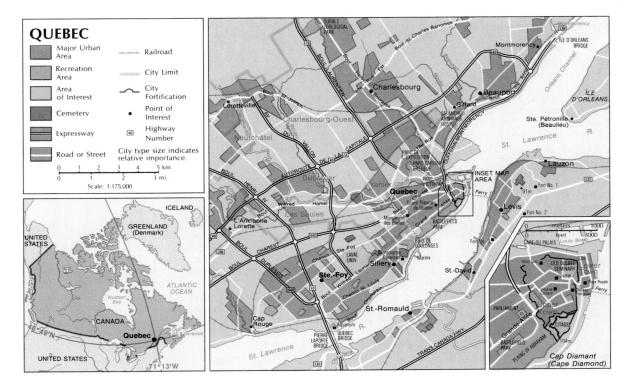

Dufferin Terrace, a broad promenade in Quebec City, overlooks the St. Lawrence River. Situated on the river's north bank, Quebec City is a seaport and the provincial capital. The immense Château Frontenac, a hotel, is in the background.

History. The initial settlement of Quebec was established in 1608 by Samuel de CHAMPLAIN as a combined fort and trading post. Quebec was the scene of frequent battles between British and French forces until finally captured by the British under James WOLFE in 1759 in the Battle of the Plains of Abraham. When the Province of Lower Canada (now Quebec) was created in 1791, Quebec was chosen its capital.

Quebec (province) Quebec (French: Québec) is the largest of the Canadian provinces, with an area of 1,540,680 km² (594,860 mi²). It stretches from the U.S. border and the Gulf of St. Lawrence north to Hudson Strait and from Hudson Bay east to Labrador and the Atlantic coast. It is bounded on the west and southwest by the province of Ontario. Quebec is nicknamed *la belle province* ("the beautiful province") because of its variety of lakes, forests, and open country, its commercial centers, and its French culture.

Quebec was first settled in 1608 by the French. Today 80% of the province's population is French-speaking; it is the only such province in Canada. The demand for greater provincial autonomy has increased, with some Quebecers advocating complete independence from Canada. Quebec remains a major focus of the Canadian debate on federal-provincial relations.

Land and Resources

More than 80% of the province is made up of the CANADIAN SHIELD, a vast, lake-studded plateau extending from the far north to the LAURENTIAN MOUNTAINS in the south and sloping westward to Hudson Bay. An extension of the APPA-LACHIAN MOUNTAINS, including the Shickshock Mountains, reaches from the east coast of the United States to the GASPÉ Peninsula of southeastern Quebec. In a fault zone between the Canadian Shield and the Appalachians lie the St. Lawrence lowlands formed by the St. Lawrence River.

Soils. In the southern part of the shield, podzol soils have developed, whereas in the north tundra soils are underlain by permanently frozen ground called permafrost. Bog soils are extensive around James Bay. The Appalachians have shallow, brown podzols, and the St. Lawrence lowlands have gray brown podzols, the best agricultural soils in the province.

Climate. Temperatures range from a January average of –9° C (16° F) at Montreal to –25° C (–13° F) at Inocdjouac (formerly Port Harrison) in the Arctic zone. July temperatures average 22° C (71° F) at Montreal and 11° C (52° F) at Port Hamson. Precipitation ranges from an annual average of about 1,000 mm (40 in) at Montreal to 356 mm (14 in) in the Arctic; at least one-third of the precipitation is snow.

Rivers and Lakes. Of Quebec's two major drainage systems, one flows eastward to the Atlantic by way of the ST. LAWRENCE RIVER, and another drains north and westward to Hudson and James bays. The major lakes include Mistassini, Gouin Reservoir, Manicouagan Reservoir, Eau Claire, Bienville, and Saint Jean.

Vegetation and Animal Life. Low shrubs and lichens dominate the tundra in the north. The subarctic climate of the central and southern shield supports coniferous forests. Hardwoods predominate in the St. Lawrence lowlands. A mixture of hardwoods and fir, spruce, and pine cover the Appalachians. Wildlife is varied: polar bear, seal, arctic fox, and hare in the far north; wolf, black bear, caribou, deer, and moose in the coniferous forests. Partridge, ducks, and geese, and trout, pike, pickerel, bass, and salmon attract sports enthusiasts.

Resources. Quebec's mineral resources include iron ore, gold, copper, and zinc from the Canadian Shield; asbestos and copper from the Appalachians; and limestone from the Montreal plain. Quebec imports all of its petroleum, gas, and coal, but many of its rivers have been harnessed for water power. Productive forests cover one-third of Quebec.

People

Although much of the total area of Quebec is unsettled, nearly 80% of the population are urban and are concentrated in the southwest. Approximately 45% of the population live in the MONTREAL census metropolitan area. Other major cities are TROIS-RIVIÈRES, Quebec City, Chicoutimi, and Sherbrooke. About 45,000 Indians and Eskimo (Inuit) live in widely scattered fishing and hunting villages. The population is 82% French-speaking and 11% English-speaking. Roman Catholics account for 87% of the population; 7% are Protestant, 2% are Jewish, and 4% practice other religions.

Education and Cultural Activity. Quebec has two parallel but independent systems of education: French Catholic and English Protestant, reflecting the dual nature of the population. The province's seven universities include

AT A GLANCE

QUEBEC

Land: Area: 1,540,680 km^2 (594,860 mi^2); rank: 1st. Capital: Quebec City (1986 pop., 164,580). Largest city: Montreal (1986 pop., 1,015,420). Municipalities: 1,614. Elevations: highest—1,652 m (5,420 ft), at Mont D'Iberville; lowest—sea level, along the Atlantic coast.

People: Population (1989 est.): 6,668,400; rank: 2d; density: 4.3 persons per km^2 (11.2 per mi^2). Distribution (1986): 77.9% urban, 22.1% rural. Average annual change (1981–86): +0.32%.

Government (1991): Lieutenant Governor: Martial Asselin. Premier: Robert Bourassa, Liberal. Parliament: Senate—24 members; House of Commons—9 Liberals; 57 Progressive Conservatives; 8 Bloc Québécois; 1 New Democratic party. Provincial legislature: 125 members. Admitted to Confederation: July 1, 1867, one of four original provinces.

Economy (monetary figures in Canadian dollars): Total personal income (1987): $113.7 billion; rank: 2d. Median family income (1987): $35,493. Agriculture: net income (1986): $1.1 billion. Fishing: value (1986)—$85.9 million. Forestry: lumber production (1985)—4.2 billion board feet. Mineral production: value (1986)—$2.3 billion. Manufacturing: value added (1986)—$26.2 billion.

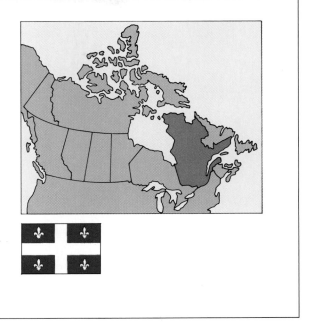

McGILL UNIVERSITY (English language), Laval University and the University of Quebec (both French language), and the University of Montreal. Quebec's cultural institutions include the Montreal and Quebec symphony orchestras; the Montreal opera; the Museum of Fine Arts, the Place des Arts (Concert Hall), and the National Library, all in Montreal; and, in Quebec City, the National Archives and Museum of Quebec.

Historic Sites and Recreation. Among the preserved historic sites in Quebec City are the Plains of Abraham battlefield, where the English under James WOLFE defeated the French under the marquis de MONTCALM; the fortified French city; and several Catholic churches, including Notre Dame (1688). In the Montreal area are the Saint Sulpice Seminary; the old Lachine canals; and Notre Dame Church (begun 1820).

Quebec City's winter carnival (in February before the Lenten season) and Montreal's Expo '67 World's Fair site are popular tourist attractions. Professional hockey, baseball, and football teams from Montreal compete in North American leagues.

Communications. The majority of Quebec's radio and television stations broadcast in French. Montreal has English- and French-language daily newspapers. *Le Journal de Montréal* has the largest daily circulation in the province. Quebec City's major daily newspapers are in the French language.

Economic Activity

Fur trading and fishing were early economic endeavors in Quebec, and by 1860 the province also had a developing manufacturing sector. Mining began to develop in the early 20th century. Today the services sector contributes the greatest part of Quebec's gross domestic product.

Forestry and Mining. Forest products—wood pulp, paper (especially newsprint), lumber, and plywood—are important to the economy. More than 40% of Canada's pulp and paper come from Quebec.

The province has about 40% of Canada's iron-ore reserves and nearly a quarter of the gold reserves. Other valuable metals are copper and zinc. Quebec also provides about 90% of Canada's asbestos.

Manufacturing and Energy. Quebec ranks second among Canadian provinces in the value of manufacturing shipments. The province's mineral wealth is the basis for much smelting and refining and for the manufacturing of automobiles, aircraft, and machinery. Food and beverage processing is the leading industry in Quebec. Industries based on timber and pulp are also of major importance. Brass and copper products, electrical machinery and equipment, chemicals, petroleum products, and textiles and apparel are also valuable.

Major energy sources in Quebec are petroleum, coal, natural gas, and hydropower. The province is a leading

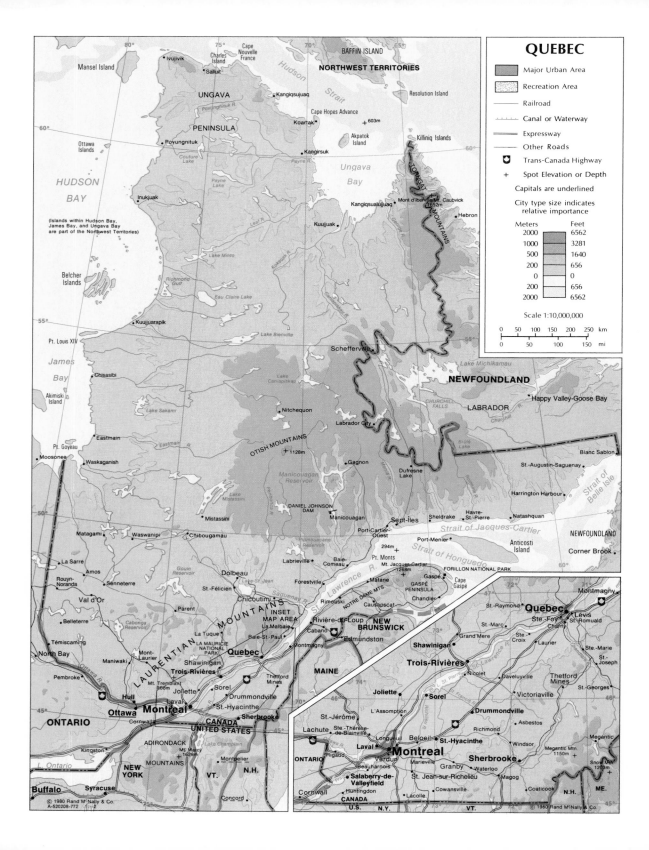

QUEBEC

Major Urban Area
Recreation Area
Railroad
Canal or Waterway
Expressway
Other Roads
Trans-Canada Highway
Spot Elevation or Depth

Capitals are underlined

City type size indicates
relative importance

Meters	Feet
2000	6562
1000	3281
500	1640
200	656
0	0
200	656
2000	6562

Scale 1:10,000,000

0 50 100 150 200 250 km
0   50   100   150 mi

NORTHWEST TERRITORIES

BAFFIN ISLAND

Mansel Island

Ivujivik
Charles Island
Cape Nouvelle France

Salluit

UNGAVA

Kangiqsujuaq

Povungnituk R.

PENINSULA

Cape Hopes Advance
Koartak
+603m

Resolution Island

Killiniq Islands

Ottawa Islands

Povungnituk

Kangirsuk

Payne R.

Ungava Bay

HUDSON BAY

Couture Lake

Payne Lake

Inukjuak

Leaf R.

Kangiqsualujjuaq
Mont d'Iberville/Mt. Caubvick 1652m

Hebron

(Islands within Hudson Bay,
James Bay, and Ungava Bay
are part of the Northwest Territories)

Lake Minto

Kuujjuak

Belcher Islands

Richmond Gulf

Eau Claire Lake

Lake Bienville

Pt. Louis XIV

Kuujjuarapik

James Bay

Chisasibi

Lake Sakami

Lake Caniapiscau

NEWFOUNDLAND

Lake Michikamau

Happy Valley-Goose Bay

CHURCHILL FALLS

LABRADOR

Churchill R.

Akimiski Island

Richmond Gulf

Nitchequon

Labrador City

Brûlé Lake

Eastmain

Pt. Goyeau

Eastmain R.

OTISH MOUNTAINS
+1128m

Gagnon

St.-Augustin-Saguenay

Blanc Sablon

Moosonee

Waskaganish

Lake Mistassini

Manicouagan Reservoir

DANIEL JOHNSON DAM

Dufresne Lake

Harrington Harbour

Strait of Belle Isle

Mistassini

Manicouagan

Sept-Îles

Sheldrake

Havre-St-Pierre

Natashquan

Port-Cartier-Ouest

Strait of Jacques-Cartier

NEWFOUNDLAND

Peribonca R.

Pipmuacan Reservoir

Port-Menier

294m

Anticosti Island

Corner Brook

Matagami

Waswanipi

Chibougamau

Labrieville

Baie-Comeau

Pt. Monts
Mt. Jacques-Cartier 1268m

Strait of Honguedo

La Sarre

Gouin Reservoir

Dolbeau

St-Félicien

Forestville

Gaspé

FORILLON NATIONAL PARK

Cape Gaspé

Amos

Senneterre

Lake St. Jean

Rimouski

NOTRE DAME MTS

Matane

GASPÉ PENINSULA

Chandler

Rouyn-Noranda

Val d'Or

Parent

Chicoutimi

INSET MAP AREA

Causapscal

Belleterre

Cabonga Reservoir

La Tuque

Saguenay R.

La Malbaie

Rivière-du-Loup

Cabano

NEW BRUNSWICK

Témiscaming

LA MAURICE NATIONAL PARK

Baie-St-Paul

Montmagny

Edmundston

North Bay

Maniwaki

Mont-Laurier

Quebec

MAINE

LAURENTIAN MOUNTAINS

Shawinigan

Thetford Mines

Pembroke

Mt. Tremblant 968m

Trois-Rivières

Joliette

Sorel

Drummondville

St-Hyacinthe

Hull

Ottawa

Laval

Montreal

Sherbrooke

ONTARIO

Cornwall

CANADA

UNITED STATES

Kingston

ADIRONDACK

Lake Champlain

Mt. Marcy 1629m

MOUNTAINS

Montpelier

N.H.

NEW YORK

VT.

Buffalo

Syracuse

L. Ontario

Concord

© 1980 Rand McNally & Co.
A-520208-772

Inset Map

Montmagny

Quebec

Lévis

St-Raymond

Ste-Foy
Charny
St-Romuald

St-Marc

Grand'Mère

Ste-Croix

Laurier

Ste-Marie

St-Joseph

Shawinigan

Trois-Rivières

Nicolet

Daveluyville

Thetford Mines

St-Georges

Joliette

St-Pierre

Victoriaville

L'Assomption

Sorel

Drummondville

Asbestos

St-Jérôme

Richmond

St-Hyacinthe

Windsor

Ste-Thérèse-de-Blainville

Beloeil

Megantic Mtn. 1150m

Megantic

Lachute

Longueuil

Laval

Montreal

Sherbrooke

ONTARIO

Rigaud

Verdun

Marieville

Granby

Waterloo

Snow Mtn. 1203m

Beauharnois

St. Jean-sur-Richelieu

Magog

Coaticook

Salaberry-de-Valleyfield

Cowansville

N.H.

ME.

Cornwall

Huntingdon

Lacolle

CANADA

U.S.

N.Y.

VT.

© 1980 Rand McNally & Co.

producer and exporter of hydroelectric power in North America. Quebec also has nuclear power resources.

Agriculture and Fishing. Dairy farming is Quebec's predominant agricultural activity. Principal crops are corn, mixed grains, barley, oats, tobacco, wheat, potatoes, and apples. Quebec is also the world's foremost producer of maple sugar and syrup.

The Gulf of St. Lawrence and the estuary of the St. Lawrence River are the centers of the fishing industry. Cod, snow crab, and perch provide about 75% of the fish catch.

Tourism and Transportation. Quebec has a thriving tourist industry, supported by thousands of kilometers of roads and rail tracks. Main routes connect Ontario, Quebec City, New Brunswick, and New York. Montreal, one of the hubs of the Canadian and U.S. transportation network, has two international airports and serves as an ocean and inland port.

Government

Constitutional government is based on the BRITISH NORTH AMERICA ACT (1867), which at Confederation in 1867 divided powers between the federal and provincial governments. The province exercises more control and seeks more autonomy than most other provinces over many socioeconomic and cultural affairs. The parliamentary system provides an elected provincial assembly consisting of 125 members. A federally appointed lieutenant governor has no real powers; most power rests with the premier, the leader of the majority provincial party. The Court of Appeals is Quebec's highest court. It and the Superior Court are made up of federally appointed judges.

History

The territory around the Gulf of St. Lawrence and the lands drained by the St. Lawrence River were claimed by Jacques CARTIER for France after his expeditions in 1534 to the Gaspé Peninsula and in 1535 to present-day Montreal. He encountered native Algonquian peoples and Es-

kimo. European settlement followed with the establishment of the first habitation in 1608 by Samuel de CHAMPLAIN at Quebec City. The colony of NEW FRANCE grew slowly. Encouraged by King Louis XIV of France, and welcomed by such administrators as Jean TALON and the comte de FRONTENAC (governor from 1672 to 1682), more than 10,000 immigrants arrived in the 150 years of the French regime, 7,000 of whom stayed. By about 1750 the population had reached 65,000. British-French rivalries resulted in the FRENCH AND INDIAN WARS. In 1759 the British general James Wolfe captured Quebec City, ending the hostilities. In the 1763 Treaty of Paris (see PARIS, TREATIES OF) France ceded all of New France to Britain.

New colonists arrived from Britain, and, after the American Declaration of Independence in 1776, Loyalists from America arrived. Through the QUEBEC ACT of 1774, the Constitutional Act of 1791, and the British North America Act of 1867 (when Quebec joined Ontario, Nova Scotia, and New Brunswick to form the Confederation of Canada), the French-speaking inhabitants were allowed to retain their language and religious and civil administrative systems.

The French remained dominant in agriculture. In the early 1800s the English-speaking inhabitants had begun to develop lumber, paper, mining, textile, and other industries and to establish commercial, financial, and trading companies, many centered in Montreal, which grew rapidly. Thus the English controlled the economic structures of the province, although the French, who formed 80% of the population, dominated the political scene. French Quebecers resented their position, and Louis PAPINEAU led (1837) an unsuccessful revolt (see REBELLIONS OF 1837).

Industrialization and urbanization, accelerated by World War I, continued. As Canada expanded westward and northward, more of the economic control of Quebec passed out of the province to Ontario, Great Britain, and the United States.

The fairgrounds of Expo '67, which occupy two islands in the St. Lawrence River, are marked by the enormous geodesic dome covering the U.S. pavilion. Expo '67, an international exposition hosted by Montreal in 1967, celebrated the centennial of Canada's confederation.

World War II hastened the modernization process and the questioning of traditional patterns, including the role of the church in society and government. Successive Quebec governments enacted legislation to achieve greater provincial control of socioeconomic policies. Most sought to do this within the existing Canadian Confederation, but they encountered rising sentiment in favor of the complete independence of Quebec from the rest of Canada. In 1976 the Parti Québécois, led by René LÉVESQUE, which advocated the formation of a separate sovereign state, was elected. In 1980, however, Quebec voters soundly defeated a referendum proposal that would have mandated federal-provincial negotiations of terms of sovereignty. The separatist issue, officially ended in 1987 after Quebec officials signed the 1982 CONSTITUTION ACT, was renewed in 1990 when the agreed-upon amendments failed to gain ratification. Another area of conflict between the province and the rest of Canada concerned language laws—most recently, a 1988 Quebec law mandating the exclusive use of French on outdoor signs.

Quebec Act   The Quebec Act, passed by the British Parliament in 1774, created a government for the French Roman Catholic colony of Quebec, which had been ceded to Great Britain by the Treaty of Paris (1763). Quebec's governor, Guy CARLETON, was largely responsible for the terms, which officially recognized the Roman Catholic church, French civil law, and the seigneurial land-tenure system in Canada. The act also set up an appointed council to assist the governor and extended Quebec's boundaries south to the Ohio River and west to the Mississippi. Some historians argue that the act was inspired by liberalism; others say that it was designed to preserve the loyalty of the French Canadians in the event of an American revolt. To Americans in the 13 colonies to the south it was one of the INTOLERABLE ACTS.

Quechua   [kech'-oo-uh]   The Quechua are a South American Indian people who from earliest times have occupied the central Andean highlands of Peru and Bolivia. Like the INCA who occupied the highlands from the 11th to the 15th century, they speak the Quechuan language, a branch of the Andean-Equatorial stock. They show other remnants of an Inca heritage in their pre-Columbian-style stone houses, pan-pipe music, religion, and mythology.

Together with the AYMARA, the Quechua constitute most of the rural population of highland Peru. Using traditional agricultural techniques, they grow crops of potatoes and maize in addition to keeping herds of llamas, alpacas, and sheep and raising pigs. Villages consist of kin groups, and marriage partners are chosen from within the village. Until the agrarian reform in the 1960s most Quechua were sharecroppers and wage laborers on the big inland plantations. Quechuan, which Peru has named an official language, was spoken by about 11 million Indians in the late 1980s.

queen   A queen is a woman ruler of a monarchy. The title may also be held by the wife of a king. A woman who occupies the throne in her own right is known as a queen regnant; the wife and widow of a king are known, respectively, as a queen consort and a dowager queen. Marriage to a king does not automatically make a woman a queen, although becoming one in this manner is more common than the awarding of a kingship to the husband (prince consort) of a queen regnant. The right of a woman to succeed to the throne is a relatively modern phenomenon in European history. In the 16th century, Mary Tudor, who ruled as Mary I, was the first accepted woman on the English throne. In France and several other European countries, the so-called SALIC LAW prohibited a woman from inheriting the crown.

Queen, Ellery   Writing under the pseudonym of Ellery Queen, two cousins, Frederic Dannay, b. Brooklyn, N.Y., Jan. 11, 1905, d. Sept. 3, 1982, and Manfred Bennington Lee, b. Brooklyn, N.Y., Oct. 20, 1905, d. Apr. 3, 1971, coauthored a popular mystery series featuring a likable, intelligent detective. Among the best of the Queen novels are *Calamity Town* (1942) and *And on the Eighth Day* (1964). Dannay and Lee wrote scripts for the long-running Ellery Queen radio show that began in 1939, and in 1941 they founded *Ellery Queen's Mystery Magazine*. Ellery Queen has inspired several films and television series.

Queen Anne style   Regarded as quintessentially English, the style of decorative arts named for Queen Anne developed from the assimilation of Dutch influence brought to England in the reign (1689–1702) of William III. By the time Queen Anne (r. 1702–14) came to the throne, a marked trend toward simplicity of form had emerged. In domestic architecture the Queen Anne style was often characterized by the use of red brick, sash windows, and hipped roofs. (The international baroque, practiced by Sir Christopher Wren and Sir John Vanbrugh during Anne's reign, has never been regarded as "Queen Anne style.") Furniture, generally of walnut and sometimes inlaid with marquetry, was often graced by the cabriole leg. The unadorned perfection of Queen Anne silver is famous. The style persisted well into the 18th century, and a Queen Anne revival occurred in late-19th-century England.

Queen Anne's lace   Queen Anne's lace, *Daucus carota,* of the carrot family, Umbelliferae, is a widely distributed herb native to Eurasia. Also called the wild carrot, it grows to about 1 m (3 ft) high and has hairy stems and usually flat-topped, circular flower clusters (umbels), which are white or pink. At one time it was used as a stimulant and a diuretic.

Queen Anne's War   see FRENCH AND INDIAN WARS

Queen Charlotte Islands   The Queen Charlotte Islands are a group of about 150 islands paralleling the western coast of Canada about 160 km (100 mi) from the mainland. The islands have an area of about 9,583 km² (3,700 mi²), and the population of 5,621 (1981) is mostly HAIDA Indians. Graham and Moresby are the two largest islands, with mountain ranges that rise to nearly 1,220 m (4,000 ft). The main towns are Masset, Skidegate, and Rose Harbour. The economy depends on the mining of copper, coal, and iron ore as well as lumbering and fishing. Sighted by the Spaniard Juan Pérez in 1774, the islands were named by the Englishman Capt. George Dixon in 1787.

Queen Elizabeth   The *Queen Elizabeth* was a British OCEAN LINER. It was driven by steam turbines and, weighing 75,909 metric tons (83,675 U.S. tons) and having a length of 312 m (1,031 ft), was slightly larger than its sister ship, the *Queen Mary*. The *Queen Elizabeth* was launched in 1938 and along with the *Queen Mary* operated as a troop ship during World War II. The *Queen Elizabeth* went into commercial transatlantic service in 1946. In 1969 the ship was sold to American investors, who planned to have it anchored and used as a tourist attraction; in 1972, however, the liner was destroyed by fire while anchored in Hong Kong. The *Queen Elizabeth II*, a replacement for the ship, made its maiden voyage in 1969. The new liner weighs 62,471 metric tons (68,863 U.S. tons) and is 294 m (963 ft) long.

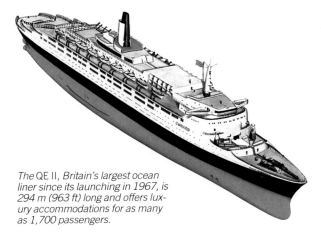

The QE II, Britain's largest ocean liner since its launching in 1967, is 294 m (963 ft) long and offers luxury accommodations for as many as 1,700 passengers.

Queens   The largest borough of NEW YORK City in area, Queens lies at the western end of Long Island and is coextensive with Queens County. The population is 1,951,598 (1990). The borough is primarily residential, but industries located there process foods and cut lumber. Kennedy and La Guardia airports are located there. Settled by the Dutch in 1635, Queens became a borough of New York City in 1898. The 1939 and 1964 WORLD'S FAIRS were held in Queens.

Queensland   Queensland, Australia's giant northeastern state, covers 1,727,200 km² (666,900 mi²), almost one-quarter of the continent. Four times the size of California, it is the country's third most populous state, with a population of 2,742,900 (1988 est.). BRISBANE is the capital.

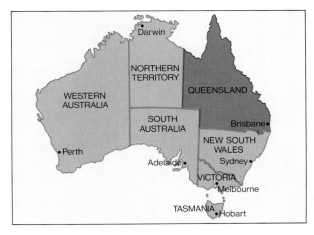

Dividing the eastern third of the state from the western portion is the GREAT DIVIDING RANGE. A vast plain with occasional subdued ranges characterizes the western two-thirds. Generally, summer temperatures are hot, averaging 31° C (88° F) in January; winters are mild with a July average of 11° C (52° F). Precipitation averages between 1,000 and 1,300 mm (40 and 50 in) along the east coast but decreases rapidly toward the arid interior. There are dense rain forests along the coasts.

Queensland's Caucasian population is largely of British ancestry and is about 80% urban. Almost half of all city dwellers live in Brisbane. A string of secondary cities, stretching along the coast, includes Townsville, Gold Coast, Rockhampton, and Cairns. Queensland has the largest aboriginal population in Australia.

Sheep are of historic importance, but in recent years the beef industry has grown more rapidly. Major crops include sugarcane, cotton, and wheat. Mineral products include bauxite, copper, lead, zinc, silver, and coal.

Originally part of New South Wales, Queensland became a separate colony in 1859 and a state of the Commonwealth of Australia in 1901. Since 1922 the state has had a unicameral legislature, the only one in Australia.

Quemoy [ki-moy']   Quemoy (or Chinmen) is a small island group off the Chinese coast in the Taiwan Strait. Both Quemoy and the neighboring Matsu island group served as fortified outposts for the Nationalist government on Taiwan.

The Quemoy group consists of 1 main island and 11 smaller islands with a total area of 147 km^2 (57 mi^2) and a population of 50,272 (1982 est.). The Matsu group lies 211 km (131 mi) to the north and consists of 19 islets with a total area of 28.8 km^2 (11.1 mi^2) and a population of 8,199 (1982 est.). Heavy bombardment of the islands by the mainland Chinese in 1958 forced a diplomatic confrontation between the United States and China.

Queneau, Raymond [ken-oh', ray-mohn']   Raymond Queneau, b. Feb. 21, 1903, d. Oct. 25, 1976, was a French poet and novelist, best known as a humorist and experimenter in literary forms. Rejecting traditional differences between prose and poetry, Queneau, in such fanciful novels as *The Bark Tree* (1933; Eng. trans., 1968) and *Zazie* (1959; Eng. trans., 1960), combined popular speech, unorthodox spelling and syntax, and enigmatic subject matter to create what he termed "natural" works. His novels *Pierrot* (1942; Eng. trans., 1950) and *The Sunday of Life* (1952; Eng. trans., 1976) show the influence of surrealism. A master of parody and irony and the possessor of an enormous vocabulary, Queneau produced a tour de force in *Exercises in Style* (1947; Eng. trans., 1958), in which the same story is recounted in 99 different styles.

Querétaro (city) [kay-ray'-tah-roh]   Querétaro, the capital of the state of Querétaro in central Mexico, lies about 175 km (110 mi) northwest of Mexico City. The city has a population of 293,586 (1982 est.), and its economy is based on cotton-textile manufacturing and food processing. Querétaro came under Spanish control in 1531. The 1810 revolt of Hildalgo y Costilla was planned there, and Emperor Maximilian surrendered there in 1867.

Querétaro (state)   Querétaro, a state of Mexico, is located on the central plain. It has an area of 11,449 km^2 (4,420 mi^2) and a population of 1,044,227 (1990). Most of the inhabitants are descendants of Otomí-Chichimec Indians. The capital is Querétaro. Agriculture, mining, and livestock are important in this area of high mountains and fertile valleys. Rich in mercury, silver, and gold, Querétaro is also known for opals. Conquered by the Spanish in 1531 and colonized from 1550, Querétaro became a state of independent Mexico in 1824.

Quételet, Lambert Adolphe [kay-tuh-lay']   The Belgian mathematician, astronomer, and statistician Lambert Adolphe (Jacques) Quételet, b. Feb. 22, 1796, d. Feb. 17, 1874, laid the foundation for modern-day statistics and social physics with a paper he wrote. Influenced by Pierre Laplace and Joseph Fourier, Quételet discovered the NORMAL DISTRIBUTION and developed methods for the computation of probabilities, which he applied to population statistics.

quetzal [ket-sahl']   One of the most beautiful birds in the world, the quetzal, *Pharomachrus mocino*, lives in humid mountain forests of southern Mexico and Central America. It is a member of the trogon family, Trogonidae.

The male is bright metallic green with golden highlights above and scarlet below, with the underside of the tail being white. Males measure about 38 cm (15 in) in length and beyond the end of the tail have a magnificent train of long green feathers that extends another 38 to 76 cm (15 to 30 in). These are not tail feathers; rather, they are elongated upper tail coverts. In the duller-

The quetzal, a Central American bird of great beauty, is the national bird of Guatemala. Aztecs and Mayans regarded the quetzal as sacred, plucking tail plumes from living male birds for ceremonial purposes.

colored female, this train of feathers is short. The quetzal figured prominently in the art and mythology of cultures of the region.

Quetzalcóatl

Quetzalcóatl [ket-sahl-koh-aht'-ul] The feathered serpent god, Quetzalcóatl, is one of the oldest and most important deities of ancient Mesoamerica. He is known to have been worshiped as early as AD 300 in highland Mexico and perhaps much earlier on the Gulf coast. At the time of the Spanish conquest (16th century) he was worshiped all over AZTEC and MAYA territory.

Quetzalcóatl was a creator god, and in one story he journeyed to the underworld to collect the bones from which he fashioned the human race after he sprinkled them with his own blood. In this aspect he was the god of self-sacrifice, wisdom, and science. As Ehecatl, he was god of the wind. He was also god of the planet Venus, which is both morning and evening star—the morning aspect represented by the feathered serpent, the evening aspect by Xolotl, a dog-headed monster. This duality made him the patron deity of twins, the god to whom barren women prayed for children.

The title *Quetzalcóatl* was taken by several historical rulers and heroes from Mexico to Guatemala, so that confusion often arises between historical and mythological events.

Quetzalcóatl, one of the oldest and most prominent deities of the ancient Mexican pantheon, is portrayed in this Aztec codex in his aspect as the wind god, Ehecatl. Revered as the god of learning, Quetzalcóatl is most commonly depicted as a plumed serpent.

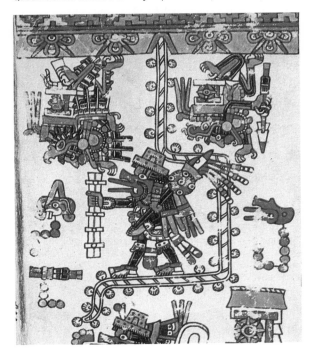

queuing theory

queuing theory [kue'-ing] Queuing theory is the branch of PROBABILITY theory that studies the behavior of queues, or waiting lines. Queues typically arise in arrival-service-departure settings, such as automobiles at a toll plaza, telephone calls coming into an exchange, and repair jobs submitted to a central repair shop. If the capacity to service the arrivals is not adequate, the waiting time will be long. On the other hand, extra service capacity is expensive. Queuing theory seeks to predict the behavior of the waiting lines so that informed decisions can be made regarding how much service capacity should be made available.

The first element of a queuing model is an "input process," which describes the pattern of arrivals over time. The arrivals are not regular, but rather are random, so that the input process is a STOCHASTIC PROCESS. The second element is a description of the service mechanism. Are there one or several servers? Do all arrivals wait in a single line, or does each server have a separate waiting line? These are nonrandom aspects of the service mechanism, which can be changed to cut costs or reduce the waiting times. The service mechanism also has random aspects.

Once a model is given, the behavior of the waiting line can be studied. Interest usually centers on the length of the waiting line (or lines) and the length of time between arrival and service. These quantities are RANDOM VARIABLES rather than fixed quantities.

Quezon, Manuel Luis

Quezon, Manuel Luis [kay'-sohn] A leading Philippine nationalist and statesman, Manuel Luis Quezon, b. Aug. 19, 1878, d. Aug. 4, 1944, helped pave the way for Philippine independence during the final period of U.S. colonial rule. He was president of the commonwealth from 1935 to 1944.

Quezon fought in the 1901 insurrection against U.S. rule, but after its failure he cooperated with the U.S. territorial government. He became majority leader of the first Philippine assembly under U.S. rule in 1907 and served as Filipino resident commissioner in Washington from 1909 to 1916. Subsequently he was president of the Philippine senate. Quezon led the successful protest against the Hare-Hawes-Cutting Act (passed by the U.S. Congress in 1933), because, although it promised independence, it also retained U.S. military bases in the Philippines. He then worked for passage of the Tydings-McDuffie Act of 1934, which pledged complete Filipino independence on July 4, 1946, and was elected president of the new Philippine Commonwealth.

Following the overrunning of the Philippines by the Japanese late in 1941, Quezon was evacuated by submarine; he governed in exile until his death.

Quezon City

Quezon City Quezon City, the former capital and the second largest city of the Philippines, is located on Luzon

Island, adjacent to Manila. The population is 1,587,140 (1990 est.). Quezon City is mostly residential but has a major textile industry. Planned in 1937 as the new capital of the Philippines, Quezon City officially replaced Manila in 1948. New government buildings were constructed, and the transfer was still in progress when the seat of government was returned to Manila in 1976.

quick clay

Quick clay is a natural aggregate made up of very fine mineral particles—more than half of them less than 2 micrometers in diameter—and water. It may change suddenly from a solid to a rapidly flowing liquid when subjected to shock, as from an earthquake, an explosion, or the jarring of a pile driver, and can slide over land with a slope of less than 1°, carrying along heavy structures in its path. Quick clays, loosely consolidated and usually dark blue gray when wet, were formed during the most recent advance of the continental glaciers.

quicksand

Quicksand is not a type of sand but rather a flow condition within the sand. A saturated sand becomes quick—quick meaning alive—when upward flow of water through the sand applies seepage forces equal to or exceeding the buoyant weight of the sand. Hence, any sand and even gravel can be made quick provided sufficient quantities of water are made to flow upward through it. Because the rate of flow required to make sands quick decreases with particle size, quick conditions in nature occur most commonly in fine sands. Contrary to popular belief, a human or an animal can easily float in such material.

quietism

[kwy'-et-izm] *Quietism* is the name usually given to a form of late-17th-century Christian mysticism whose chief proponent was the Spanish priest Miguel de MOLINOS. The quietists believed that the soul could have direct communion with God without any active religious practices and that this communion was best attainable through a state of absolute passivity and annihilation of the will. In 1687, Molinos was imprisoned in Rome, and 68 of his propositions were condemned by the pope. Later quietism achieved brief influence at the French court of Louis XIV through the cautious sympathy of Archbishop FÉNELON. It virtually disappeared, however, after the movement was condemned in the Conference of Issy (1695) and Fénelon was censored by the pope (1699).

Quileute-Hoh and Chemakum

[kwil'-uh-yoot, chem'-uh-kuhm] The Quileute-Hoh and Chemakum are tribes of North American Indians of the Pacific Northwest. The Quileute and Hoh are divisions of one group, traditionally residing on the Soleduck and Hoh rivers on the west coast of Washington State. They and the Chemakum, on the west shores of Admiralty Inlet below Hood Canal, are the only speakers of Chemakuan languages. The Chemakum, reputedly warlike at one time but outnumbered by equally warlike Coast SALISH neighbors, were dwindling in numbers during historic times and early in this century became extinct. Little is known of their lifeway except that it was similar to that of their Salishan-speaking neighbors. The Quileute-Hoh, in earlier times whalers and sea-hunters, also exploited the salmon-runs in their rivers. Their houses were large multifamily structures of cedar planks. Most descendants of the Quileute live on their reservation at La Push, Wash., the Hoh on theirs near Forks, Wash.; their combined estimated population was 691 in 1989.

quilting

Quilting is a needlework technique used to hold a layer of insulating or padding material between two outer layers of fabric. To prevent the interior layer from shifting, numerous runs of stitches are worked across the sandwiched layers. Long ago, people in China, Egypt, and elsewhere wore quilted garments for warmth and for protection in battle. Quilting is still used for making garments and bedcovers.

There are several types of quilting. Wadded quilting is evenly filled with thick padding, whereas flat quilting has little or no padding. In trapunto, parts of the design are raised by being heavily padded; in corded, or Italian, quilting, heavy yarn is threaded between double rows of stitching. The making of pieced, or patchwork, quilts was an especially popular form of FOLK ART in preindustrial America. The top of a pieced quilt consists of small scraps of fabric pieced together to create a complicated pattern; the quilting stitches follow the seams between the elements of the design.

Quimby, Phineas Parkhurst

Phineas Parkhurst Quimby, b. Lebanon, N.H., Feb. 16, 1802, d. Jan. 16, 1866, developed a philosophy of mental healing that laid the foundation for NEW THOUGHT. At first a hypnotist, he turned to mental healing in the belief that he had rediscovered the secret of Jesus' healing ministry. He held that all disease is an error of the mind and could be cured by a proper understanding of the relation between the divine and the human. One of Quimby's patients was Mary Baker EDDY, who may have derived from him the inspiration for CHRISTIAN SCIENCE; she denied this, however.

quince

[kwins] Quince is the common name for various shrubs and small trees in the rose family, Rosaceae. The common quince, *Cydonia oblonga*, is a slow-growing, wide-spreading shrub or small tree that yields greenish yellow or golden yellow fruit. The fruit is bitter and not palatable when raw; it is eaten cooked in fruit compotes, preserves, and jams. Of little commercial importance in the United States, the common quince is more widely cultivated in the temperate zones of Europe and Argentina. The flowering, or Japanese, quince, *Chaenomeles speciosa*, bears flowers in

The common quince, a small tree of the rose family, has been cultivated since ancient times for its fragrant fruit. It is inedible when raw, but when thoroughly cooked it makes excellent preserves.

shades ranging from creamy white to scarlet and is a favorite ornamental in home gardens.

Quincy [kwin'-zee]   Quincy is a city in eastern Massachusetts, about 13 km (8 mi) south of Boston on Quincy Bay, an arm of Boston Bay. Its population is 84,985 (1990). A commercial and major shipbuilding center within the Boston metropolitan area, Quincy has industries that manufacture electronic and soap products. Quincy was the birthplace of two U.S. presidents, John Adams and John Quincy Adams, and of John Hancock. The Adams National Historic Site includes the Adams family house (1685–18th century), birthplaces of both Adamses, and their burial sites at United First Parish Church (1828). Settled in 1625 by Thomas Morton, the town was originally the northern part of Braintree. It was incorporated in 1792 and named for Col. John Quincy, a local resident. Quincy was a farming community until the development of granite quarries in 1750. The shipbuilding industry developed after 1894.

Quincy, Josiah   Josiah Quincy, b. Boston, Feb. 4, 1772, d. July 1, 1864, was a member of the U.S. House of Representatives, a reform mayor of Boston, and president of Harvard University. Representing Boston in Congress from 1805 to 1813, he was an ardent Federalist and a die-hard opponent of the War of 1812. As mayor of Boston in the 1820s, he did much to modernize the city. While president of Harvard (1829–45) he professionalized the Law School and wrote a two-volume history of the university. He also wrote a biography of his father, Josiah Quincy (1744–75), a political leader prior to the American Revolution.

Quine, Willard Van Orman [kwyn]   Willard Van Orman Quine, b. Akron, Ohio, June 25, 1908, is an American philosopher and logician. His work is mainly in symbolic logic and the logic of ordinary language, but he also writes on ontology. Quine was influenced by such positivists as Rudolf CARNAP, but his denial of the distinction between analytic and synthetic statements marks a major deviation from LOGICAL POSITIVISM, as does his view on the logical status of the problem of what exists. The pragmatism of Clarence Irving LEWIS is evident in Quine's view that logic and language evolve as tools of inquiry.

quinine [kwy'-nyn]   Quinine is an alkaloid drug obtained by extraction of the bark of the cinchona tree of South America and Indonesia. The drug was once the only one available for MALARIA treatment, and it is still used as a muscle relaxant. It has largely been replaced by synthetic drugs, however, because of the serious hypersensitivity reactions it can produce.

quinone [kwi-nohn']   The quinone group of organic compounds are present in many plants and in some animals. They are cyclic hydrocarbons with one or more ring structures and two carbonyl groups ($C = O$). They are usually high colored—yellow, orange, or red—and most are toxic. Widely distributed in nature, they play diverse roles—as pigments in plants, growth factors, antibiotics, catalysts, and respiratory inhibitors. Synthetic quinones are used in medicine, in dyes and fungicides, and as antioxidants and stabilizers in varnishes, paints, fats, and oils.

Quintana Roo [keen-tah'-nah roh'-oh]   Quintana Roo, a state in southeastern Mexico on the Yucatán Peninsula, has an area of 50,212 km^2 (19,387 mi^2) and a population of 493,605 (1990). The capital is CHETUMAL. The state is dominated by tropical lowlands inhabited by scattered communities of MAYA. Henequen, chicle, and cotton are the main agricultural products. Fish, sponges, and turtles are taken from offshore waters. Three islands off the coast—Cancún, Cozumel, and Isla Mujeres—are centers of tourism. The Spanish landed in Quintana Roo in 1517; it became a Mexican territory in 1902 and a state in 1974.

Quintilian [kwin-til'-yun]   Quintilian is the anglicized name of Marcus Fabius Quintilianus, AD c.35–c.100, a Roman of Spanish origin whose *Institutio Oratoria* (c.95) is the most thorough textbook on the art of oratory that has come down from ancient times. A 12-book work that shows the influence of Cicero, the *Institutio Oratoria* touches on all aspects of Roman education and public speaking, including the organization of a speech, the use of argument, stylistic devices, the technique of memorization, and the art of delivery. Quintilian also stresses the importance to the speaker of a good character, some knowledge of philosophy, and a thorough familiarity with literature.

Quiriguá [kee-ree-gwah'] Quiriguá, a lowland MAYA center on the Motagua River in eastern Guatemala, is best known for its large stelae, upright stone shafts carved with hieroglyphic texts and rulers' portraits. Quiriguá flourished as a civic-ceremonial center during the Classic period (AD 250–950). During most of its history, it was politically subordinate to COPÁN, 50 km (31 mi) to the south. The stelae of Quiriguá, the tallest in the Maya world, are in the style of Copán, as is its architecture.

Quirino, Elpidio [kee-ree'-noh, el-pee'-dee-oh] Elpidio Quirino, b. Nov. 16, 1890, d. Feb. 29, 1956, was the second president (1948–53) of the Republic of the Philippines. In 1946 Quirino became his country's first vice-president. Succeeding to the presidency at the death of Manuel Roxas y Acuna in 1948, he was elected to the office in 1949. Quirino broke with the Roxas policy of crushing the insurgent Communist Hukbalahaps (Huks), persuading Huk leader Luis Taruc to accept an amnesty. A renewed Huk uprising in August 1948, however, forced Quirino's defense minister, Ramón MAGSAYSAY, to put down the rebellion. Magsaysay defeated Quirino in the 1953 presidential election.

Quisling, Vidkun [kvis'-ling, vid'-kuhn] Vidkun Abraham Lauritz Jonsson Quisling, b. July 18, 1887, d. Oct. 24, 1945, was a Norwegian fascist in World War II whose name became a synonym for traitor. Norwegian minister of defense from 1931 to 1933, he founded (1933) the National Unity party, modeled on the German Nazi party. In 1940 he aided the Germans in their conquest of Norway and was their puppet ruler throughout the war. After the war the Norwegians convicted him of high treason and shot him.

quiteron [kwit'-uh-rahn] The quiteron is an electronic device under study for its power-dissipation advantages over the transistors now used for digital switching in computers and other integrated-circuit arrays. Its name derives from "heavy-quasiparticle-injection tunneling effect" (see TUNNEL EFFECT). Developed in the early 1980s by Sadeg M. Faris of IBM, the quiteron employs the phenomenon of SUPERCONDUCTIVITY. It contains three layers of superconducting material separated by insulation. When it is not operating, the layers are in thermal equilibrium; but when a voltage is applied to one of its junctions, many quasiparticles are produced in the middle layer. (A quasiparticle is an electron, under superconducting conditions, that has a smaller effective charge than an ordinary electron.) Thermal equilibrium is lost, and quasiparticles can tunnel through to the second junction. This change in resistance, which takes place in less than a bil-

lionth of a second, is equivalent to the "on-off" switching function of an ordinary transistor.

Quito [kee'-toh] Quito, the capital and second largest city of Ecuador, has a population of 1,223,865 (1989 est.). Located in the Andean highlands, 24 km (15 mi) south of the equator, it lies on a fertile plateau. The nearby volcano Pichincha is dormant, but the city is subject to earthquakes. Leather goods, cotton and woolen fabrics, and jewelry are manufactured in Quito. The city retains much 16th-century Spanish architecture. In the city are many churches, as well as Central University (1586) and Catholic University of Ecuador (1946). Inhabited by Quitu Indians before the 11th century, the city became the northern capital of the Inca Empire in 1487 and was taken by Sebastián de Benalcázar in 1536. A local uprising against Spanish rule was defeated in 1809, but Ecuadorian independence was won after the Battle of Pichincha in 1822.

Qum Qum (also Qom or Kum) is a city in northwestern Iran located about 120 km (75 mi) southwest of Tehran. The population is 424,408 (1982 est.). A trade and rail center for the surrounding agricultural region, Qum also has textile factories. The city is best known, however, as a pilgrimage site for Shiite Muslims. The principal landmark is the gold-domed Shrine of Fatimah; more than 400 other saints and kings, including Shah Abbas II, are interred in Qum.

Established during the 9th century AD, the city was sacked (1380s) by Timur, revived under the Safavids during the 16th century, and destroyed (1722) by Afghans. Following Iran's Islamic revolution of 1979, Ayatollah Ruhollah KHOMEINI ruled the country from Qum, his native city.

Qumran [koom-rahn'] Khirbet Qumran, meaning the ruin of Qumran, stands on a rocky projection of the high cliffs overlooking the northwest corner of the Dead Sea, in the Israeli-occupied West Bank region. A few foundations date from the 8th to the 7th century BC. Most of the ruins are a walled complex of buildings built by a community of ESSENES who had withdrawn from Jerusalem and who produced the DEAD SEA SCROLLS, which were found in caves nearby. Building began about 150 BC and flourished from late in that century until an earthquake in 31 BC.

quota [kwoh'-tuh] A quota, in international trade, is a type of trade barrier that nations place on the physical amount of imports or exports of specific kinds of goods. A quota differs from a TARIFF, which is a schedule of taxes or duties placed on imports that does not categorically place limitations on the amount of the goods that may be imported. Both tariffs and quotas are regarded as detrimental to the concept of FREE TRADE, and the GENERAL AGREEMENT ON TARIFFS AND TRADE (GATT) works to reduce such trade barriers.

Rr

GERMAN-GOTHIC	RUSSIAN-CYRILLIC	CLASSICAL LATIN	EARLY LATIN	ETRUSCAN	CLASSICAL GREEK	EARLY GREEK	EARLY ARAMAIC	EARLY HEBREW	PHOENICIAN

R R/r is the 18th letter of the English alphabet. Both the letter and its position in the alphabet were derived from the Latin, which in turn derived it from the Greek by way of the Etruscan. The Greeks took the letter, which they called *rho*, from the Semitic sign *resh*. Both the Greek and Etruscan alphabets used a sign similar to modern *P/p* for *r*; when the Latin alphabet began using the modern form of *p*, however, a variant of the Etruscan *p* with a tail under the loop was used for *r*. The modern *R* developed from this form.

R/r is a liquid consonant like *L/l*. It is made with the tip of the tongue raised while allowing the voiced breath to vibrate it. The sound heard is a combination of the voicing and the tongue vibrations. The position of the tip of the tongue and the amount of vibration allowed determine the exact nature of the *r* sound. Before a vowel, *R/r* is normally pronounced as in *rise, rapid, forest*; before a consonant, except *h* or in final position, however, it is often much attenuated or dropped completely, especially in the dialects of certain geographical areas.

Ra see AMON-RE

Ra expeditions [rah] The Ra expeditions of 1969 and 1970 were two attempts by international crews led by Thor HEYERDAHL to cross the Atlantic Ocean in reed boats, to demonstrate that mariners from ancient Egypt could have reached the New World. The boats were named *Ra*, after the sun-god of ancient Egypt. Two years of research and $200,000 were invested to make the voyages authentically Egyptian. The second attempt was a success, but it has not convinced most archaeologists that trans-Atlantic migrations were made from ancient Egypt to the New World.

Rabat [rah-baht'] Rabat, the capital of Morocco, is located at the mouth of the Bou Regreg on the northwestern coast. Its population is 518,616 (1982). Rabat has textile, food-processing, and asbestos industries. The site of the king's main residence and an administrative and cultural center, it has been the capital since 1913. In the city are the Kasbah des Oudaïa, a 17th-century fortress, and Muhammad V University (1957).

The city was founded in the 10th century as a military camp and was taken by the Almoravids in 1140 and by the Almohads in 1146. The settlement at Rabat was soon eclipsed by neighboring Salé. The arrival of the French in 1912 gave Rabat new importance, however, and now Salé is a suburb of Rabat, linked to it by the Hassan II Bridge.

Ra II, *a papyrus boat designed by Norwegian anthropologist Thor Heyerdahl, crossed the Atlantic from Morocco to Barbados in 1970. The expedition's goal was to prove Heyerdahl's hypothesis of cultural contact between the ancient Egyptians and the New World.*

rabbi Rabbi (Hebrew for "my master") is the title given recognized Jewish religious teachers, sages, and leaders. Originally a form of respectful address, it became a formal title in the 1st century AD for those authorized by their teachers—after an examination on Scripture and the law—to interpret and expound the Jewish law. This "ordination" (in Hebrew, *simichah,* literally "laying on of hands") did not confer sacramental power, for laymen could perform all religious rites of the SYNAGOGUE.

Only in the late 14th century was a salaried rabbinate established. The rabbi functioned as a judge in civil cases, gave direction in matters of religious observance, supervised education and taught advanced students, and, in general, served as community leader. In the 19th century, rabbinical seminaries were established in Europe and North America; the seminary increasingly took over responsibility for conferring ordination.

In modern times the rabbi in Western countries has tended to become less of a scholar and more of a congregational minister in the Protestant style.

rabbit   Rabbits are members of the order Lagomorpha, which also contains the HARES and the short-legged pikas. They were once considered rodents but differ from them in many ways. For example, they have two pairs of upper incisors (front teeth), one small pair immediately behind a larger; rodents have only one. Rabbits can be distinguished from hares by their young, which are born hairless, blind, and helpless; young hares are born furred, with the eyes open, and can hop minutes after birth. Such distinctions, however, are not always followed in popular names: jackrabbits, for example, are actually hares, and the domestic breed known as the Belgian hare is a rabbit.

The rabbit and hare family, Leporidae, contains 18 species of rabbits grouped into 6 or 7 genera, the best known being the cottontails, *Sylvilagus,* and the Old World rabbit, *Oryctolagus.* Coat colors are usually uniform shades of browns or grays, but the Sumatran short-eared rabbit, *Nesolagus netscheri,* has a striped pattern of brown on gray, and a reddish rump. Female rabbits, or does, are generally larger than the males, or bucks. The smallest species are the North American pygmy rabbit, *S. idahoensis,* which may be as small as 25 cm (10 in) long and 400 g (14 oz) in weight; and the similar-sized dwarf Old World rabbit found on the Madeiran island of Santo Porto, near the northwest coast of Africa. The largest is the North American swamp rabbit, *S. aquaticus,* which may be 53 cm (21 in) long and 2.7 kg (6 lb) in weight. Some of the 60 or more domestic varieties may be considerably larger; the Flemish giant may exceed 7 kg (15 lb).

Rabbits are generally nocturnal or twilight-active and are native to all the continents except Antarctica and Australia; introduced into Australia, they increased to great numbers and destroyed much grazing land. The Old World rabbit, *O. cuniculus,* is gregarious, living in large colonial burrows, or warrens. Gestation lasts 28 to 31 days, with mostly four to six young to a litter; females may have seven litters per year.

The North American eastern cottontail, *S. floridanus,* does not dig its own burrows but uses surface resting places or the burrows of other animals. Eastern cottontails tend to be solitary, although they may gather into groups when feeding or mating. Gestation is 28 days, and litter size is usually one to eight young. A female may have five litters per year.

rabbit fever   see TULAREMIA

Rabe, David [rayb]   An American playwright, David Rabe, b. Dubuque, Iowa, Mar. 10, 1940, is the author of *The Basic Training of Pavlo Hummel* (1971) and *Sticks and Bones* (1971), dramas about the aftereffects of war. Drawn from his own experience in Vietnam, these works are notable for their brutal realism and moving characterizations. Rabe received an Obie Award in 1971 and a Tony Award in 1972. His other plays include *In the Boom Boom Room* (1973), *Streamers* (1976; film, 1983), *Hurlyburly* (1984), and *Goose and Tom-Tom* (1987).

Rabelais, François [rahb-lay']   Reflecting in his life and works the humanistic concerns of the French Renaissance, François Rabelais, b. Chinon, Touraine, 1483 or 1494, d. Apr. 9, 1553, was a French scholar and cleric who is remembered today for his satirical prose masterpiece *Gargantua and Pantagruel* (1532–64; Eng. trans., 1653–94), a vast, rambling compendium that gave currency to the adjectives "gargantuan" and "Rabelaisian"; the excesses of the body celebrated here together with the exercise of the intellect are a joyous affirmation of life.

Cottontail rabbits are named for their white tails, which resemble balls of cotton. The eastern cottontail has the widest distribution, ranging from southern Canada to the northern tip of South America. All domestic rabbits are descended from the Old World rabbit. Some, like the angora and chinchilla breeds, are raised for their fur or meat. Others are bred for use as laboratory animals.

chinchilla rabbit   **angora rabbit**   **eastern cottontail rabbit**

François Rabelais painted a satiric portrait of 16th-century French society in his five-volume comic masterpiece, Gargantua and Pantagruel *(1532–64), an earthy and erudite collection of tales about a family of giants.*

Comparatively little is known of Rabelais's career. In 1520 he was studying Greek in the Franciscan monastery at Fontenay-le-Comte. Five years later he was authorized by the pope to transfer to the Benedictine order. Subsequently he qualified as a doctor (1530) and practiced medicine in Lyon, where he is credited with performing one of the first public dissections in France; he also published several scientific treatises in Latin.

The first book of his great work, *Pantagruel* (1532), is a humanist's attack on prejudice and old-fashioned scholastic learning. Rabelais makes fun of linguistic affectation and legal jargon and proselytizes on behalf of humanist education and the Reformers' religious views: the Catholic church should be purified and simplified until it again resembles the church of the early Christians. In *Gargantua* (1534) the emphasis is more positive; Rabelais illustrates the content of an ideal education, the behavior of an ideal humanist prince, especially in war, and reveals a Utopia in the abbey of Thélème. Both these books were condemned by the Sorbonne as obscene.

The bulk of the third book (1546) concerns the dilemma of Pantagruel's companion Panurge: should he or should he not get married? He consults a wide variety of specialists and nonspecialists, most of whom tell him that he will be cuckolded. In large part an intellectual encyclopedia, this book reflects the contemporary debate on the status of women known as the *Querelle des Femmes* and the religious issue of marriage versus celibacy.

In the fourth book (1552), in search of an answer to Panurge's question, the companions set sail for the Oracle of the Divine Bottle. They visit strange islands inhabited by extraordinary people and things and are caught in a storm and in a battle with an army of sausages. The book contains some ferocious antipapal satire and many statements on intellectual issues. The oracle is finally reached only at the end of the fifth book (1564), which is of doubtful authenticity.

rabies   Rabies is a viral disease of humans and other mammals, especially carnivores. The virus is transmitted in saliva, either by the bite of an infected animal or by contact through the mucous membranes or breaks in the skin. Once within the body, the virus attacks the central nervous system. Symptoms develop 10 to 50 days after exposure; in humans they usually begin with depression, restlessness, fatigue, and fever. These are soon followed by a period of great excitability, excessive salivation, and convulsions, especially in the form of throat spasms. As a result the victim is unable to drink even though extremely thirsty—hence the old name for the disease, hydrophobia, meaning "fear of water." Death from paralysis and suffocation generally follows within 10 days. Once the symptoms of rabies appear, no treatment of the disease is possible.

A vaccine against rabies was first developed in France in the 1880s by Louis Pasteur. Since then, human rabies cases have become rare in developed countries because of effective vaccination programs for domestic animals. People in high-risk occupations, such as veterinarians and forestry-service agents, are also often immunized against the disease.

The few U.S. cases reported each year are mostly from contact with rabid wild animals such as skunks, foxes, coyotes, raccoons, rabbits, and rodents. Treatment consists of an injection of rabies immune globulin, followed by five injections of antirabies serum over the following month.

Rabin, Yitzhak [rah-been', yit-shahk']   Yitzhak Rabin, b. Mar. 1, 1922, Israel's prime minister from 1974 to 1977, was named defense minister in the national unity cabinet headed by Shimon Peres in 1984. He previously served as Israel's ambassador to the United States (1968–73) and as chief of staff of the armed forces (1964–68) and planned the 1967 Israeli victory in the Six-Day War. Rabin resigned as prime minister after he was found to have violated Israeli currency regulations by depositing $21,000 in a U.S. bank. As defense minister, he directed the Israeli handling of the 1988 Palestinian uprising in the occupied territories.

raccoon   Raccoons are stocky-bodied, usually solitary, and nocturnal mammals of the genus *Procyon* in the family Procyonidae. They are generally regarded as consisting of seven species: the North American raccoon, *P. lotor*; the South American crab-eating raccoon, *P. cancrivorus*; and five other species, each confined to one or more small islands off Florida and Mexico and in the West Indies. The North American species is from 40 to 60 cm (15.5 to 23 in) long, plus a 24- to 26.5-cm (9.5- to 10.5-in) tail. Its weight is usually between 5.5 and 7.25 kg (12 and 16 lb). The long, coarse fur of the North American raccoon is commonly yellowish gray to grayish brown, with markings of dark rings on the tail and a black mask across the face.

Raccoons prefer swampy areas or woods near water and are absent from very high elevations, very arid regions, and purely coniferous forests. Found throughout the United

The North American raccoon uses its hands to hold food while eating. In captivity a raccoon will often "wash" its food in water, behavior related to catching aquatic prey in the wild.

States except for large parts of some of the western states, they are omnivorous. In the North, if the temperature drops consistently below −4° C (25° F), or if the snows are heavy, the raccoon may spend weeks in a deep sleep but not in true hibernation. Gestation averages 63 days, and a litter commonly contains one to seven young. Raccoons seldom survive beyond 7 years in the wild.

Two related species are the cacomistles, or ring-tailed cats, genus *Bassariscus*. *B. astutus* lives in the western United States and south to southern Mexico. *B. sumichrasti* is found in tropical forests from southern Mexico to Peru.

---

race A race is a population group or subspecies within the living human species, *Homo sapiens,* set apart from other subspecies on the basis of arbitrarily selected, commonly visible, or phenotypic criteria. The criteria most often selected are skin color, hair quantity and form, and the shape and form of the body, head, and facial features. A problem is presented, however, by the high variability of such characteristics within any group. Not all genes that transmit all phenotypic characteristics ascribed to a subspecies are transmitted in a cluster (see GENETIC CODE). As a result, only some members of a particular "race" will have all the criteria for that race, although every member will probably have at least one.

Many scientists today reject the concept of race. Other scientists use the race concept as an expedient shorthand expression for variants in anatomical traits exhibited by the populations of broad geographic homelands—zoographic regions with characteristic resident animals that shared the terrain with developing human populations.

Even in this geographic sense, however, the term *race* must be understood to have value only as a general term without precise definition, because it does not take into account hybridization and movement of populations with the consequent "gene flow" from one area to another, nor does it allow for continuing evolution. Human beings do, however, partially reflect their geographic origin in the physical traits that have been mentioned, and in some physiological characteristics such as tolerance of cold, heat, and altitude. The idea of geographic races was explored by scientists as early as the 18th century, notably by Johann BLUMENBACH, who distinguished five divisions of humankind, and from whose classification later ones developed.

Geographic Races. Classifying races by geographic regions can result in distinguishing more than 30 subdivisions of lands and peoples across the world; or, homeland regions in the Old World can be combined and reduced to three—the Ethiopian, the Palaearctic, and the Oriental.

The Ethiopian region includes the southern third of Arabia and sub-Saharan Africa. Before the end of the Pleistocene Epoch the Ethiopian region probably included the whole of Africa, but when the Sahara developed and divided the continent, Palaearctic forms invaded North Africa. The Ethiopian region gave rise to the African subspecies, with these distinguishing characteristics: yellow brown to brown or black skin; dark and tightly spiraled hair on head and body; moderately abundant body hair; generally heavy bones; teeth of medium to large size; noses broad with flaring nostrils; turned-out lips; and prominent buttocks.

The Palaearctic region comprises Africa north of the Sahara, Europe, and Asia except southern Arabia, India, Southeast Asia, and southern China. The western Palaearctic was probably the homeland of the Caucasoid, or Caucasian, subspecies, and the eastern Palaearctic was the homeland of the Mongoloid, or Mongolian, subspecies. Caucasian physical traits are the following: ivory to medium-brown skin; variable hair and eye color; wavy or curly hair; plentiful body hair; small teeth; prominent noses; and bones of medium weight. Mongolian physical traits are as follows: ivory to medium-brown skin; dark eyes and dark, straight hair; large front teeth; prominent cheek bones; and short limbs and long trunks, with lightweight bones.

The Oriental region encompasses India, southern China, Southeast Asia, and the northerly islands of Indonesia. It was probably the homeland of the Australoid, or Australasian, race, although few live there today. Australasian people tend to have medium-brown to black skin; wavy to tightly spiraled hair of variable color; moderate to abundant body hair; large teeth; broad noses; and heavy bones.

As is evident from these descriptions, a significant similarity exists in many of these traits in all three regions. The original racial homelands in Eurasia and Africa probably were never wholly isolated from each other. Instead, human groups migrated and interbred enough so that physically intermediate populations may have existed for thousands of years in the spaces between the homelands. The fossil evidence suggests that in the Pleistocene Epoch, smaller-brained species of *Homo* gave rise to the large-brained *Homo sapiens* (see PREHISTORIC HUMANS). Gene flow among the homelands was great enough to preserve an essential biochemical and intellectual equality between the emerging human races, and evolutionary improvements such as speech, intelligence, and manual dexterity were spread throughout the species. This gene flow has been so pervasive that our species has never developed "pure" races in any meaningful genetic sense.

Migration and Gene Flow. The human species has migrated and hybridized dramatically in the past 40,000 years. As a result, some of the human subspecies have been drastically relocated. Late in the Pleistocene the Caucasians probably moved into northern Africa along with animals from the Palaearctic zone. From that time, if not earlier, a zone of racial intermediates has extended from the Sahara to Somalia. A similar zone of racial mixture is found in India between the more northerly Caucasians and the more southerly Australasians. Since the 16th century, Caucasians have spread into Siberia, the Americas, Australia, New Zealand, and southern Africa. Black Africans at the same time displaced the SAN (Bushmen) in South Africa, and millions of black Africans entered the New World as slaves.

The Australasian population group very early began movements south and east from their southern Asian homeland. Australia was occupied more than 30,000 years ago. At present, the Australasian subspecies is represented by the Australian ABORIGINES, the peoples of MELANESIA and NEW GUINEA in the Pacific, and remnants nearer Asia. Ab-

original tribes of Australasian appearance are found in the ANDAMAN ISLANDS in the Bay of Bengal, SRI LANKA, parts of southern India, Malaysia, and the Philippines. Most of the Australasian homeland, however, is now occupied by racially Mongolian invaders from the north.

The Mongolians moved into the Americas about 30,000 years ago (see NORTH AMERICAN ARCHAEOLOGY). After the end of the Pleistocene, they probably displaced and hybridized with the Australasians in Southeast Asia. These mixed groups became master seafarers and spread the Austronesian languages into Melanesia, MICRONESIA, and POLYNESIA. Speakers of one of these languages even reached Madagascar.

Both gene flow and reproductive isolation have been at work in the formation of the human races. The human species has split into innumerable, often temporary, populations, undergoing local microevolution and subject to the pressures of NATURAL SELECTION by disease, nutrition, and climate. One way to measure this evolutionary trend is by means of "marker genes," which define the biochemical structure of certain molecules in the blood, such as the familiar A, B, and O blood types (see BLOOD). Blood groups show a striking split into eastern and western branches. The western group includes nearly all of the

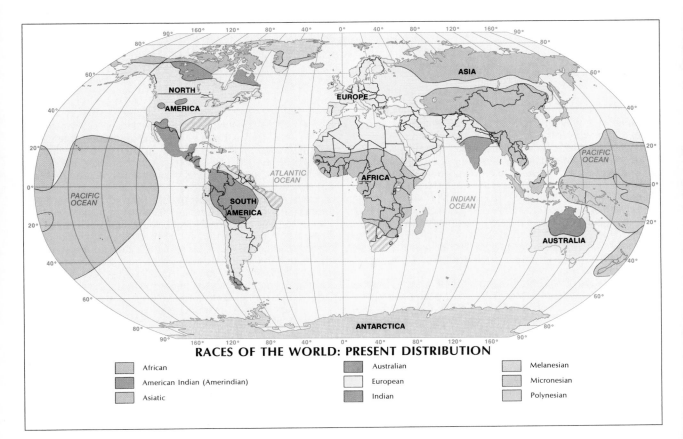

RACES OF THE WORLD: PRESENT DISTRIBUTION

African	Australian	Melanesian
American Indian (Amerindian)	European	Micronesian
Asiatic	Indian	Polynesian

Some anthropologists have subdivided the human species into population groups largely on the basis of geographic region. These groups may include Northwest European (1); Northeast European (2); Alpine (3); Mediterranean (4); Indian (5); Turkic (6); Tibetan (7); North Chinese (8); Mongoloid (9); Eskimo (10); Southeast Asiatic (11); Ainu (12), of northern Japan; Lapp (13), of northern Scandinavia; North American Indian (14); Central American Indian (15); South American Indian (16); Fuegian (17), of southern South America; East African (18); Sudanese (19); Forest African (20); Bantu (21); San (Bushman) and Khoikhoi (Hottentot) (22); African Pygmy (23); Dravidian (24), of southern India; Pacific Negrito (25); Melanesian-Papuan (26); Murrayian Australian (27); Carpenterian Australian (28); Micronesian (29); Polynesian (30); Neo-Hawaiian (31); Ladino (32), of Central and South America; American Black (33); and Cape Coloured (34), of South Africa. Various classification schemes based on arbitrarily selected visible traits have distinguished from 3 to more than 200 geographical "races." The minimal biological significance of such visible traits, as well as problems of classification and definition, have, however, led a growing number of scientists to question the value of human racial categories.

Africans and the Caucasians. Australasians and Mongolians, including the aboriginal peoples of the Americas and the Pacific Islands, comprise the eastern group.

Environmental Factors. In terms of physiological and genetic adaptations, all human beings are fundamentally tropical animals. Nevertheless, the peoples with the least exposure to severe climates, the Australasians and Africans, are dark skinned. This kind of skin is resistant to sunburn and skin cancer, but it is susceptible to frostbite. Not all population groups seem to be equally well adapted to high altitudes. Most of the really successful populations in this respect are racially Mongolian; they thrive and reproduce quite well in such regions as Tibet, and in the high Andes.

Migration of early human groups to temperate climates seems to have led to lighter skins, less massive bones, and straighter hair. The skeleton, especially in Caucasians, matures slowly. Light skin is better protected than dark skin against frostbite. Another Caucasian peculiarity, shared elsewhere mainly by cattle-raising and milk-drinking tribes in Africa, is the ability to digest milk sugar (lactose) as adults. All other young mammals digest lactose before weaning but lose this capacity at older ages. The ability to digest this carbohydrate throughout life provides the calories of milk sugar in cold climates; also, the minerals in milk, coupled with efficient Vitamin D production by the skin, may protect young Caucasians against rickets.

Recent work on microevolution has repeatedly uncovered evidence of local inherited resistance to disease. MALARIA has been a major killer of exposed populations, mainly through parasitization and destruction of the red blood cells. Genetic resistance implies changes in the chemistry of these cells, which inconvenience the parasite at stages in its life cycle.

Eastern and Western peoples in the Old World have developed somewhat different genetic adaptations to malaria. Most typical of the Africans is the sickle-cell gene. Those who have one normal hemoglobin gene and one sickle-cell gene are less likely to acquire malaria. Africans who inherit abnormal sickle cells from both parents suffer serious health impairment (see SICKLE-CELL DISEASE). Western populations in malarial regions often show another gene, which gives rise to an ineffective or deficient ENZYME in the red cells, a feature believed to inhibit increase of the malaria parasite. Another such Western gene, beta thalassemia, produces benefits if inherited from only one parent but produces a severe ANEMIA if inherited from both parents. The Australasian and Southeast Asian adaptations to malaria are genetically different. Groups in Southeast Asia and New Guinea lack the sickle-cell gene and show a different thalassemia system. Therefore, malaria resistance—and also blood groups—divide the human species into East and West. (See GENETIC DISEASES.)

Work is being done today on certain genes present

throughout the world in many populations, rather than in only one population, to investigate genetic adaptation to the conditions and requirements of various environments. Such studies show race as a constantly evolving process, rather than as static, immutable division of *Homo sapiens* into rigidly bounded groups.

race riots (in U.S. history)   Throughout most of U.S. history race riots have been outbreaks of mob action in which groups of different racial and ethnic backgrounds fight each other. In most instances these riots have been between blacks and whites; the few exceptions include the riots between Mexican Americans and whites in Los Angeles during World War II.

Mob action against blacks occurred as early as the 18th century, when whites attacked black enclaves in the cities of the North, burning and plundering homes and assaulting blacks. During the Civil War, white workers who feared job competition attacked freed black workers in northern cities. In the New York City DRAFT RIOTS of 1863, working-class whites, subject to a new conscription law, turned their hostility toward blacks, many of whom were murdered. In the early 20th century, race riots usually represented white reaction against the influx of Southern blacks into Northern cities, particularly during World War I. In East Saint Louis, Ill., violence erupted in 1917 over the issue of the employment of blacks in a factory that held government contracts.

By the 1960s a new kind of racial violence had evolved. Outbreaks usually occurred in black neighborhoods where black citizens took to the streets in what began as social protest but often degenerated into rioting, looting, and arson. These disorders differed from earlier race riots in that few whites—except for police officers and fire fighters—were directly involved. Newark, N.J., Watts (Los Angeles), and Detroit are examples of cities that experienced rioting in the mid-1960s. Rioting in black neighborhoods reached its height in 1968, when, after the assassination of Martin Luther KING, Jr., rioting occurred in approximately 150 cities. Later that year a special advisory commission established by President Lyndon B. Johnson—called the Kerner Commission after its first chairperson, Otto Kerner—issued a report placing much of the blame for the unrest on chronic high unemployment in black neighborhoods.

race runner   At least 3 species of lizards in the genus *Cnemidophorus,* of the family Teiidae, are called race runners for their great speed, clocked at 29 km/h (18 mph). (The other 18 to 42 species in the genus are more commonly called whiptails.) They are slender and long-tailed, with large scales on the head, small granular scales on the back, and a pattern of stripes or spots. The six-lined race runner, *C. sexlineatus,* found mostly in open, dry areas of the southern and central United States, reaches 8.6 cm (3⅜ in) in length plus an 18-cm (7-in) tail and has six (sometimes seven or eight) light-colored stripes of white, yellow, gray, or blue.

Rachel   In the Bible, Rachel was the second wife of JACOB and the mother of JOSEPH and Benjamin (Gen. 29–35). When she died, Jacob erected a monument over her tomb at Ephrath, traditionally identified with Bethlehem. She is regarded as one of the four Jewish matriarchs.

Rachmaninoff, Sergei   [rahk-mah'-neen-awf, sir-gay']   The composer, pianist, and conductor Sergei Vasilievich Rachmaninoff, b. Apr. 1 (N.S.), 1873, d. Mar. 28, 1943, is considered the last in the great tradition of Russian romantic composers. He was born at his family's estate, Semyonovo, in the Russian province of Novgorod. He attended the Saint Petersburg Conservatory, graduating in piano in 1891 and in composition with the Great Gold Medal in 1892. At just 19 years of age, he sold some pieces outright to a publisher who failed to secure an international copyright. Among them was the C-sharp Minor Prelude (1892), which would bring publishers a fortune and the composer world fame. The failure of his First Symphony in 1897 stifled his inspiration for three years. Following treatment by hypnosis he produced the Second Piano Concerto in 1901. It inspired a period of creativeness that lasted until 1917, yielding 22 of his total production of 45 opus numbers. Apprehensive about the Bolshevik revolution, he left Russia, making the United States his base of operations and, after 1939, his home. At first he composed nothing. Then between 1926 and 1940, five final works appeared, including the *Rhapsody on a Theme of Paganini* (1934) and the Third Symphony (1936). His international concert career intensified in exile. He toured until a month before his death, which occurred in Beverly Hills, Calif.

The Russian virtuoso pianist, conductor, and composer Sergei Rachmaninoff made his home in Europe and the United States after the Russian Revolution of 1917. As both performer and composer he excelled in a romantic style characterized by flowing melody and massive chords.

Racine   [ruh-seen']   Racine, a city in southeastern Wisconsin on Lake Michigan at the mouth of the Root River, is the seat of Racine County. The city's population is 84,298 (1990). Racine is an industrial city and a port of entry; its diversified manufactures include wax products and machinery. In 1834 settlers occupied a site on the river claimed by Capt. Gilbert Knapp, and they named the settlement Port Gilbert in his honor; the present name was adopted in 1837. Harbor improvements and the construction of a bridge across the Root in the 1840s, followed by the railroad's arrival (1855), brought rapid growth.

Jean Racine, one of the outstanding dramatists of the 17th-century French theater, proved himself the master of classical tragedy in such plays as Andromache *(1667),* Britannicus *(1669), and* Phèdre *(1677).*

Racine, Jean [rah-seen'] The rival of Pierre Corneille for the title of the greatest French tragic dramatist, Jean Racine, b. Dec. 22, 1639, d. Apr. 21, 1699, infused the high style of neoclassicism with the tension of human passion. Often set in ancient times, his plays combine the Greek concept of inexorable fate with a 17th-century metaphysics and an acute sense of human nature.

Orphaned in early childhood, Racine was raised by a grandmother who subscribed to the extreme doctrine of original sin as taught by JANSENISM, a Reform movement within Roman Catholicism. Sent (1655) to the Jansenist school at Port-Royal, Racine was profoundly influenced by Jansenist tenets while receiving a thorough classical education.

When Racine left Port-Royal in 1658 to pursue the study of philosophy in Paris, he subordinated his spiritual interests to the intellectual delights and ambitions of the secular world. Having already composed religious and pastoral poetry, he now adopted the contemporary custom of dedicating poems to potential patrons, and his marriage ode for King Louis XIV, *La Nymphe de la Seine* (The Nymph of the Seine, 1660), gained him recognition. Molière, already a noted man of the theater, produced Racine's first plays, *The Thebiad* (1664; Eng. trans., 1723) and *Alexander the Great* (1665; Eng. trans., 1714).

Beginning with *Andromache* (1667; Eng. trans., 1675) and ending with his masterpiece, *Phèdre* (1677; Eng. trans., 1707), the plays of this decade of Racine's life established him as France's leading dramatist. As great a success as Corneille's *Le Cid* had been three decades earlier, *Andromache* occasioned a great rivalry between the two dramatists that was intensified by Racine's treatment of the Corneillean theme of political strife in *Britannicus* (1669; Eng. trans., 1714) and came to a climax with *Bérénice* (1670; Eng. trans., 1922). Appearing at virtually the same time as a tragedy on the identical subject by Corneille, the latter play established Racine's preeminence. Encouraged by his triumph, Racine experimented with a contemporary setting in *Bajazet* (1672; Eng. trans., 1855) and with an almost exclusively inner, psychological action in *Mithridates* (1673; Eng. trans., 1926).

Although his success, symbolized by his election (1672) to the Académie Française, continued, Racine came under increasing attack from other playwrights. His *Iphigénie* (1674; Eng. trans., 1861), a return to Greek material, prevailed over a rival version; but the savagery of partisan attacks on *Phèdre,* combined with a personal moral crisis, led Racine to retire from theatrical activity in

1677. Marrying the same year, he reconciled his differences with Port-Royal and, devoting himself to his new duties as royal historiographer, abandoned secular drama. His last two plays, *Esther* (1689; Eng. trans., 1715) and *Athalie* (1691; Eng. trans., 1722), were on biblical themes, written for performance by students at a school for the sacred and secular education of young women.

racism Racism refers to any theory or doctrine stating that inherited physical characteristics, such as skin color, facial features, hair texture, and the like, determine behavior patterns, personality traits, or intellectual abilities. In practice, racism typically takes the form of a claim that some human races are superior to others. An abuse of the concept of differences among peoples, it has contributed to the practices of DISCRIMINATION and prejudice among groups in many parts of the world.

Racism was a prevalent ideology in Europe and America in the late 19th and early 20th centuries. Racist theories about supposed physical or intellectual superiority were advanced by Arthur de GOBINEAU and Houston Stewart CHAMBERLAIN, both of whom insisted that supreme among the races were members of the mythical Nordic, or Aryan, race. Nazi Germany under Adolf Hitler based its extermination of millions of Jews and other "non-Aryans" on this theory of race supremacy and the corollary concept of racial purity.

As an ideology, racism has been on the wane since the 1940s, although in a few countries, such as South Africa (see APARTHEID), it has had the support of the political leadership. In other countries it lingers on as a folk mythology. The overwhelming bulk of scientific opinion in both the social and the biological sciences, however, now rejects the notion that large human populations, such as the so-called white, black, and yellow races, behave differently because of their physical appearance, or that they can be said to be genetically superior or inferior to one another. Genetic differences between population groups do exist, of course. None of these group differences, however, has yet been shown to affect personality, intelligence, or, indeed, any ability that significantly relates to social behavior.

In recent years the term *racism* has been at times misapplied to various related but distinct social attitudes and occurrences. For example, feelings of cultural superiority based on language, religion, morality, manners, or some other aspect of culture are sometimes labeled *racist*, but the proper term for such feelings is ETHNOCENTRISM. Another loose usage of the term is the notion of institutional racism—meaning any practice that results, intentionally or otherwise, in differential representation of different human groups. For example, a college entrance examination is sometimes said to be institutionally racist if it results in a low admission rate of certain minority groups, irrespective of its intention. A more appropriate usage would be to say that such a test is discriminatory in its results.

The causes of racism are complex and cannot be reduced to a single factor. Its rise and fall are often linked with real conflicts of interest and competition for scarce resources. Historically, racism has commonly accompanied slavery, colonialism, and other forms of exploitation and gross inequality. In other cases relatively powerless groups that have felt threatened by social and economic instability have blamed other powerless groups for their predicament. The insecure white working class and lower middle class of industrial societies, for example, have often expressed racist attitudes toward defenseless minorities, such as blacks in the United States or Commonwealth immigrants in Great Britain. Racism, in short, is frequently an irrational reaction to a real or perceived threat to the status quo.

Rackham, Arthur [rak'-uhm] Arthur Rackham, b. Sept. 19, 1867, d. Sept. 6, 1939, was a British illustrator noted for his imaginative and fantastic drawings. He first achieved fame with his illustrations for Grimm's *Fairy Tales* (1900); thereafter he illustrated many kinds of books, such as special Christmas volumes and sumptuous limited edi-

Arthur Rackham's illustration of the Pool of Tears, a scene from the 1907 edition of Lewis Carroll's Alice's Adventures in Wonderland, *displays the sensitive, fanciful characterization and sinuous line typical of his work. Rackham was one of the leading illustrators of the late 19th and the early 20th century.*

tions of Germanic legends. His works included Washington Irving's *Rip Van Winkle* (1905), R. H. Barham's *Ingoldsby Legends* (1907), Charles Dickens's *A Christmas Carol* (1915), Izaak Walton's *The Compleat Angler* (1931), and Edgar Allan Poe's *Tales of Mystery* (1935).

racquetball Racquetball is a relatively new racquet-and-ball sport that is played indoors by either 2 or 4 players on a standard 4-wall HANDBALL court. Certain aspects of the game resemble squash, paddleball, and handball, but the origins of the sport are obscure. Joe Sobek, a former squash and tennis teacher from Greenwich, Conn., is unofficially recognized as the inventor of racquetball. In 1950 he started working on a game that would be less intricate than squash but more interesting than paddleball. Rules and regulations were first codified in North America in 1968. Racquetball is played with basically the same rules that govern handball except that games are to 15 points. The short racquet, lively ball—it may reach speeds of 265 km/h (165 mph)—and enclosed court add to the game's tremendous popularity in North America. A standard racquet is 18 in (45.7 cm) long and has a wrist strap. Racquet frames are made of wood, steel, aluminum, or fiberglass (which top players prefer). The racquets are strung with nylon.

rad Rad is an acronym for radiation absorbed dose. It is a special unit used for measuring the absorption by matter of all types of ionizing radiation (see RADIATION INJURY). One rad is equal to 100 ergs of energy per gram of matter. In terms of SI units (see UNITS, PHYSICAL), one rad is equal to 0.01 gray, a unit used to indicate an absorbed dose of ionizing radiation equal to one joule of energy imparted to one kilogram. In terms of the exposure unit called the roentgen, one roentgen equals about 0.9 rad.

See also: REM.

radar Radar was the name given during World War II to an electronic system by which radio waves were bounced off an aircraft in order to locate its position. The term is an acronym made from the fuller term *radio detection and ranging*. Development of the earliest practical radar system is usually credited to Sir Robert WATSON-WATT.

Operation

A radio TRANSMITTER generates radio waves, which are then radiated from an ANTENNA, "illuminating" the airspace with radio waves. A target, such as an aircraft, that enters this space scatters a small portion of this radio energy back to a receiving antenna. This weak signal is amplified by an electronic amplifier and displayed on a CATHODE-RAY TUBE (CRT). Thus the presence of the aircraft has been detected, but to determine its position the aircraft's distance (range) and bearing must be measured. Because radio waves travel at a known constant velocity—the speed of light, which is 300,000 km/sec, or 186,000 mi/sec—the range may be found by measuring the time taken for a radio wave to travel from transmitter to aircraft and back to the receiver. For example, if the range were 186 miles, the time for the round trip would be $(2 \times 186) \div 186,000$ = two-thousandths of a second, or 2,000 microseconds. In pulse radar the radiation is not continuous but is emitted as a succession of short bursts, each lasting a few microseconds. This radio-frequency pulse is emitted on receipt of a firing signal from a trigger unit that simultaneously initiates the time-base sweep on the CRT. Thus the electronic clock is started, and when the echo signal is seen on the tube the time delay can be measured, giving the range; the pulses are emitted at the rate of a few hundred per second so that the operator sees a steady signal.

Advances in Radar

The great operational advantage of microwave radars during World War II was that they were relatively free from electronic counter measures (ECM) by the enemy. The necessary high-power microwave pulses were generated by the cavity MAGNETRON. Electronic warfare has now become a major threat to military radar systems, and modern radars have to be designed to reduce the effects of ECM. For example, antennas have been developed with increased resolving power but with very low side lobes so that active jamming cannot penetrate into the receiver as readily as with earlier systems. Simultaneously, the effect of passive jamming is reduced: the observation of false targets because of backscatter from "chaff"—falling clouds of scattered tinfoil strips—is reduced.

This radar screen is one of many at the Kansas City Air Route Traffic Control Center, responsible for maintaining safe distances between aircraft over a multistate area. Electronic signals emitted by the craft are picked up by radar antennas and relayed to the center.

Modern radar also provides excellent moving-target indication (MTI) by use of the Doppler shift in frequency that a radio wave undergoes when it is reflected from a moving target (see DOPPLER EFFECT). Target detection is hindered by "clutter" echoes arising from backscatter from the ground or raindrops. The modern radar, with its higher transmitter power and more sensitive receiver, causes clutter to be even more pronounced so that even flocks of birds may show up on the screen. Antenna design can reduce these effects, and the use of circularly polarized waves reduces rain echoes.

The wartime radar operator interpreted the mass of data displayed on his PPI. The tracing of the histories of many targets simultaneously, however, which is what is needed in modern civil or military air-traffic control, requires that the incoming radar data be electronically processed to make it more accessible to the controller for the task of airspace management (see TRAFFIC CONTROL). Progress toward satisfying this need had to await the arrival of large-scale integrated circuits and charge-coupled devices and the development of the technology for processing digital signals. Another important advance has been the development of computerized handling of video data, as in automatic plot extraction and track formation.

Radar engineers recognize that detection of a target still remains a matter of statistical probability, rather than certainty, in spite of all the great advances in components made since World War II.

Applications

Although radar was first developed as a military aid, it has proved to be a very effective sensing and measuring device for use in many civil systems and in many fields of scientific research. It is employed for the blind landing of aircraft and for airport surface surveillance, and it is used in aircraft for cloud and collision warning. Other civil uses include merchant-ship navigation and docking radar, highway traffic control, and security systems. Scientific applications include lunar and planetary studies; METEOROLOGICAL INSTRUMENTATION for studying clouds and precipitation; measurement of the thickness of ice sheets from aircraft; satellite surveys of the Earth's surface; and ionospheric and magnetospheric investigations. Radar is now also making a major contribution to certain behavioral studies in biology, for example, the migration and flight behavior of birds, observations of the swarming of insects, crop protection, and investigations relating to the acoustic ECHOLOCATION system of bats.

radar astronomy   Radar astronomy is a relatively short-range astronomical technique limited to the study of objects in the solar system. It has had a key role in establishing exact distances and orbital dimensions for the planets and the rotation rates of Venus and Mercury and in determining the nature of the surfaces of the Moon and the planets.

In radar astronomy a powerful radio transmission is emitted in the direction of the object of interest. This transmission has a precise frequency that is generally

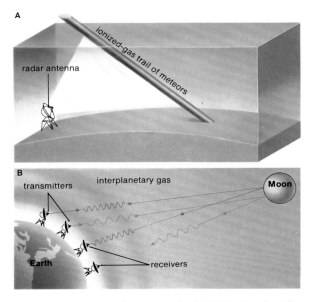

The altitudes and velocities of meteors entering the Earth's atmosphere (A) *are determined from measurements of radar signals reflected back from the ionized gas trails produced by the meteors. The density of ionized gas in interplanetary space* (B) *can be determined from measurements of the time required for radio waves of different wavelengths to be reflected from the Moon. The speed and signal strength of the reflected waves are changed by passage through the gas. Long-wavelength radio waves are affected most.*

controlled by an atomic clock and adjusted continuously to compensate for the changing DOPPLER EFFECT caused by the Earth's rotation and orbital motion. The transmission is in the form of pulses or is otherwise "modulated" (time scales are sometimes of the order of millionths of a second) to allow precise timing of the time-of-flight of the signal to the object of interest and back to Earth. A small fraction of the transmitted power is reflected back to Earth, where some very small part of this power is captured by the radar telescope and received and analyzed by the radar receiver and its associated electronics. Typically, the signal is reflected from a large number of different places on the Moon, satellite, or planet. The radar echoes from the various places arrive at the telescope at different times. The echoes have a radio frequency different from the transmitted signal because of the Doppler effect introduced by the motion and rotation of both the echoing object and the Earth. The precise time-of-flight of an echo and its Doppler-shifted frequency may be used to establish where on a planet or satellite the echo came from, thus allowing the mapping of echoing regions on the object and the determination of its rotation. It has been possible to make radar pictures of planets by using the time-of-flight and Doppler information.

The most powerful radar observatories have been the Haystack Observatory of the Lincoln Laboratory near Chelmsford, Mass. (no longer used as a radar observatory); the Goldstone Tracking Station of the Jet Propulsion Laboratory in Pasadena, Calif., sponsored by NASA, and the ARECIBO OBSERVATORY in Puerto Rico.

Radcliffe, Ann [rad'-klif]   An English writer of GOTHIC ROMANCE, Ann Ward Radcliffe, b. July 9, 1764, d. Feb. 7, 1823, gained an international reputation from her variations on one successful formula—tales of terror and suspense in which apparently supernatural occurrences are explained in the last chapters by natural and rational causes. *A Sicilian Romance* (1790), *The Romance of the Forest* (1791), and her most famous work, *The Mysteries of Udolpho* (1794), demonstrate her talent for picturesque descriptions of romantic locales and her ability to create psychological atmospheres of horror.

Radcliffe College   Established in 1879, Radcliffe College, a private 4-year liberal arts school for women, is a coordinate college of HARVARD UNIVERSITY in Cambridge, Mass. Although Radcliffe has its own administration, it shares classes, faculty, and facilities with Harvard College. Radcliffe graduates receive Harvard degrees.

Radek, Karl [rah'-dyik]   Karl Radek, b. 1885, d. 1939?, was a leading international Communist publicist in the early part of the 20th century. He was originally named Karl Sobelsohn. While a student at the universities of Kraków and Bern he joined the Polish Social Democratic party. In early 1917, he accompanied V. I. LENIN as far as Sweden in the famous sealed train that carried Lenin back to Russia.

After the Bolshevik revolution of November 1917, Radek joined the Russian Bolshevik party and in 1919 was elected to the executive committee of the Comintern. In 1927 he was expelled from the party as a Trotskyite but was readmitted three years later. Radek was an editor of *Izvestia* from 1931 to 1936. In 1937 he fell victim to the GREAT PURGE and was convicted of treason, dying in prison some time thereafter. In 1988, Radek was exonerated by the Gorbachev regime.

radial keratotomy   see EYE DISEASES

radian   A radian is a unit used for measuring angles. One radian is defined as the central angle, in a circle, that intercepts an arc of the circle equal in length to the circle's radius—that is, half its diameter. Thus to measure an angle in radians is to determine the number of times that the radius of the circle for which it is the central angle is contained in the arc it intercepts on that circle. Since the circumference of a circle is 2π times as long as its radius, 2π radians = 360° = 1 revolution, and 1 radian = 57°17'45", or about 57.2958°.

radiation   The term *radiation* refers both to the transmission of energy in the form of waves, and to the trans-

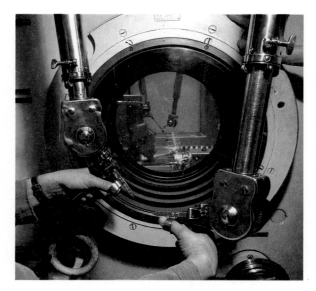

Highly radioactive substances, too dangerous to be handled directly, are manipulated with a hydraulic rod and lever device. Thick lead or concrete walls and lead-treated windows absorb the radioactive emissions and protect the worker from contamination.

mission of streams of atomic particles through space.

Any ENERGY that is transmitted in the form of waves is some kind of ELECTROMAGNETIC RADIATION. Each kind is distinguished by its wavelength, or frequency (see WAVES AND WAVE MOTION). All kinds of electromagnetic radiation obey the same physical laws (see BLACKBODY RADIATION), they all travel at the speed of LIGHT, and when they fall on a surface they exert a pressure proportional to the net flux of energy divided by the speed of light. Roughly in the order of decreasing wavelength, the kinds of electromagnetic radiation are RADIO waves, radiant heat energy (see HEAT AND HEAT TRANSFER) and MICROWAVES, INFRARED RADIATION, light, ultraviolet radiation, X RAYS, and GAMMA RAYS.

Many forms of particulate radiation are possible. In the phenomenon of RADIOACTIVITY, alpha radiation (helium nuclei) and beta radiation (ELECTRONS) are observed, along with gamma rays. Very energetic particles from outer space are called COSMIC RAYS. Any particulate or electromagnetic radiation that can dissociate atoms into ions (see ION AND IONIZATION) is called ionizing radiation. Such radiation can produce harmful effects in organisms, and it is of concern in matters dealing with NUCLEAR ENERGY (see FALLOUT; POLLUTION, ENVIRONMENTAL; RADIATION INJURY; RADON). It is also widely used in medicine, however, for both diagnosis and therapy (see NUCLEAR MEDICINE; RADIATION THERAPY; RADIOGRAPHY; RADIOLOGY), as well as being widely employed in scientific research (see ACCELERATOR, PARTICLE; SYNCHROTRON RADIATION).

radiation injury   When living tissue is irradiated, the tissue's molecular structure is disrupted, triggering a chain of events that can destroy living cells or produce chromosomal damage or other injury. The biological effects on the human body of large amounts of radiation are well known, due in large part to studies of the 76,000 survivors of the atomic bombings in Japan who have been closely monitored for more than 40 years. The possible deleterious effects of low-level radiation are still unclear, but a variety of studies suggest that low-level radiation exposure may be more dangerous than previously thought. Furthermore, recent studies have shown a statistically significant link between cancer and low-level electromagnetic fields generated by common appliances and power lines, although no causal relationship has yet been found.

Types of Radiation Exposure. Some radiation comes from natural sources, such as cosmic and solar rays and the decay of radium (which produces RADON). Sources of human-made radiation include medical X rays, NUCLEAR WASTES from nuclear reactors and weapons plants, nuclear-power-plant accidents (see NUCLEAR ENERGY), and FALLOUT from nuclear explosions.

The amount of radiation absorbed per gram of body tissue is expressed in RAD (radiation absorbed dose). The unit of measurement used to describe the expected biological effects from radiation exposure in human soft tissue is REM, an acronym for roentgen equivalent man. A dose of 300 rem delivered to the whole body is lethal 50 percent of the time. Radiation injury is probable at doses of 100 rem or more.

Radiation Effects. The effects of radiation may be divided into four types: acute somatic effects, developmental effects, genetic effects, and late somatic effects. Acute somatic effects occur in individuals within days or weeks of their exposure. Injuries to the brain cause delirium and convulsions; damage of the eye lens results in cataracts; nausea and vomiting occur if the gastrointestinal tract is injured; damage to the ovaries or testes may cause sterility; and damage to the bone marrow affects the body's ability to fight infection. Depending on the degree of irradiation, certain tissues, such as the bone marrow, the intestinal lining, or the skin, may be able to replace cells killed by radiation within a few days.

Developmental effects occur to unborn children of mothers exposed to radiation. A common consequence is brain damage or mental retardation. Radiation exposure also may cause genetic mutations in adults that are carried through to children or later descendants.

Late somatic effects are injuries produced in an individual many years after exposure to radiation. The major late somatic effect is the development of various forms of cancer. The estimated cancer risks for children exposed to radiation are about twice as large as those for adults.

radiation therapy   Radiation therapy, or radiotherapy, is a branch of RADIOLOGY used to treat CANCER. A patient is exposed to ionizing radiation in doses designed to kill a malignancy. Malignant tissues are more sensitive than normal tissues to radiation exposure and can be treated if they have not spread throughout the body and are not surrounded by normal tissue that is especially sensitive to radiation, such as the spinal cord. Sophisticated physical and biological techniques are used for radiation therapy, often accompanied by computer analyses (see NUCLEAR MEDICINE). A radiation therapist develops a treatment plan that permits the absorption of a fatal amount of radiation by all tumor cells but causes relatively minor damage to normal tissue. The usual mode of therapy is an external high-energy beam directed at the tumor site for a few minutes a day for 2 to 6 weeks, depending on the type of malignancy. X RAYS, gamma rays, and such isotopes as cobalt-60 and iodine-131 are often used.

radical (chemistry) In chemistry, a radical is an ionized (electrically charged) group of atoms that behaves as a single unit; the group is derived from the dissociation of organic compounds. Some of the more common radicals are ammonium (NH_4^+), carbonate (CO_3^{2-}), hydroxyl (OH^-), nitrate (NO_3^-), and sulfate (SO_4^{2-}). The term is also used, but less correctly, in organic chemistry to designate certain uncharged units, such as alkyl and aryl groups. A specialized meaning is extended to active molecular fragments known as FREE RADICALS.

radical (mathematics) A radical is the indicated ROOT of a quantity. (The root, when it is multiplied by itself a specified number of times, yields the given quantity.) The symbolic notation $\sqrt[n]{x}$ includes the radical sign $\sqrt{}$, an index number n, and a radicand x. The radical sign is derived from the letter r. The index number specifies which root is desired, and the radicand identifies the quantity whose root is being sought. The bar of the radical sign should extend over the entire radicand. It is also common to omit the index number for the second root, or SQUARE ROOT, writing $\sqrt{4}$ instead of $\sqrt[2]{4}$.

radicalism Radicalism is a political stance advocating fundamental changes in the existing political, economic, and social order. The radical posture tends to be rooted in what are perceived to be fundamental values, and its driving purpose is to force the status quo to conform to those principles. Often radicals' principles are based on tenets laid down by an authoritative philosopher or political leader.

Although traditionally radicalism has been primarily a movement of the left, not surprisingly the passionate appeals of the left produced various forms of radicalism of the right. Thus, while the doctrines of the radical left were based on notions of equality, the radicalism of the right espoused elitism.

radio Radio is a form of communication in which intelligence is transmitted without wires from one point to another by means of electromagnetic waves. Early forms of communication over great distances were the telephone and the telegraph. They required wires between the sender and receiver. Radio, on the other hand, requires no such physical connection because it relies on the radiation of energy from a transmitting antenna in the form of radio waves. These radio waves, traveling at the speed of light (300,000 km/sec; 186,000 mi/sec), carry the information. When the waves arrive at a receiving antenna, the original information contained in the radio waves is retrieved and presented in an understandable form, such as sound from a loudspeaker.

History

Early Experimenters. The principles of radio had been demonstrated in the early 1800s by such scientists as Michael FARADAY and Joseph HENRY. They had individually developed the theory that a current flowing in one wire could induce (produce) a current in another wire that was not physically connected to the first.

Hans Christian Oersted had shown in 1820 that a current flowing in a wire sets up a magnetic field around the wire. If the current is made to change and, in particular, made to alternate (flow back and forth), the building up and collapsing of the associated magnetic field induces a current in another conductor placed in this changing magnetic field. This is the principle of ELECTROMAGNETIC INDUCTION, which is applied in the operation of TRANSFORMERS.

In 1864, James Clerk Maxwell published his first paper that showed by theoretical reasoning that an electrical disturbance that results from a change in an electrical quantity such as voltage or current should propagate (travel) through space at the speed of light. He postulated that light waves were electromagnetic waves consisting of electric and magnetic fields. In fact, scientists now know that visible light is just a small portion of what is called the electromagnetic spectrum, which includes radio waves, X rays, and gamma rays (see ELECTROMAGNETIC RADIATION).

Heinrich Hertz, in the late 1880s, actually produced electromagnetic waves. He used oscillating circuits (combinations of capacitors and inductors) to transmit and receive radio waves. By measuring the wavelength (λ) of the waves and knowing the frequency of oscillation (f), he was able to calculate the velocity (v) of the waves using the equation $v = f\lambda$.

Guglielmo Marconi, a pioneer of radio, in 1895 produced the first practical wireless telegraph.

He thus verified Maxwell's theoretical prediction that electromagnetic waves travel at the speed of light.

Marconi's Contribution. The use of electromagnetic waves for long-distance communication was pursued by Guglielmo MARCONI; in 1895, he produced the first practical wireless telegraph system. In 1896 he received from the British government the first wireless patent.

The first wireless telegraph message across the English Channel was sent by Marconi in March 1899. The first transatlantic communication, which involved sending the Morse-code signal for the letter *s*, was sent, on Dec. 12, 1901, from Cornwall, England, to Saint John's, Newfoundland, where Marconi had set up receiving equipment.

The Electron Tube. Further advancement of radio was made possible by the development of the ELECTRON TUBE. The DIODE, or valve, produced by Sir Ambrose FLEMING in 1905, permitted the detection of high-frequency radio waves. In 1907, Lee DE FOREST invented the audion, or TRIODE, which was able to amplify radio and sound waves.

Radiotelephone and Radiotelegraph. Up through this time, radio communication was in the form of radio telegraphy; that is, individual letters in a message were sent by a dash-dot system called MORSE CODE. Communication of human speech first took place in 1906. Reginald Aubrey FESSENDEN, a physicist, spoke by radio from Brant Rock, Mass., to ships in the Atlantic Ocean.

Armstrong's Contributions. Much of the improvement of radio receivers is the result of work done by the American inventor Edwin ARMSTRONG. In 1918 he developed the superheterodyne circuit. Prior to this time, each stage of amplification in the receiver had to be adjusted to the frequency of the desired broadcast station. This was an awkward operation, and it was difficult to achieve perfect tuning over a wide range of frequencies. Using the HETERODYNE PRINCIPLE, the incoming signal is converted to a fixed frequency, which contains the information of the particular station to which the receiver is tuned. This type of receiver is much more stable than its prede-

Users of the first radio sets had to listen in on headphones.

cessor, the tuned-radio-frequency (TRF) receiver.

In order to transmit speech the radio waves had to be modulated by audio sound waves (see MODULATION). Prior to 1937 this modulation was done by varying the amplitude, or magnitude, of the radio waves, a process known as AMPLITUDE MODULATION (AM). In 1933, Armstrong discovered how to convey the sound on the radio waves by changing or modulating the frequency of the carrier radio waves, a process known as FREQUENCY MODULATION (FM). This system reduces the effects of artificial NOISE and natural interference caused by atmospheric disturbances such as lightning.

Radiobroadcasting. (This subject is treated in more detail under RADIO AND TELEVISION BROADCASTING.) The first regular commercial radio broadcasts began in 1920, but the golden age of broadcasting is generally considered to be from 1925 to 1950.

The development of the TRANSISTOR in the 1950s increased the availability of portable radios, and the number of car radios soared. Stereophonic FM broadcasts (see SOUND RECORDING AND REPRODUCTION) were initiated in the early 1960s, and stereo AM service became available in the 1980s.

Operation

Frequency Allocations. In the United States the FEDERAL COMMUNICATIONS COMMISSION (FCC) allocates the frequencies of the radio spectrum that may be used by various segments of society (see FREQUENCY ALLOCATION). Each user is assigned a specific frequency within the appropriate frequency range.

The Transmitter. The heart of every TRANSMITTER is an OSCILLATOR. The oscillator is used to produce an electrical signal having a frequency equal to that assigned to the user. In many cases the frequency of oscillation is accurately controlled by a quartz crystal. By means of the piezoelectric effect (see PIEZOELECTRICITY), the vibrations are transformed into a small alternating voltage having the same frequency. After being amplified several thousand times, this voltage becomes the radio-frequency carrier. The manner in which this carrier is used depends upon the type of transmitter.

Continuous Wave. If applied directly to the antenna, the energy of the carrier is radiated in the form of radio waves. In early radiotelegraph communications the transmitter was keyed on and off in a coded fashion using a telegraph key or switch. The intelligence was transmitted by short and long bursts of radio waves that represented letters of the alphabet by the Morse code's dots and dashes. This system, also known as interrupted continuous wave (ICW) or, simply, continuous wave, is used in modified form today in high-speed teletype, facsimile, missile-guidance telemetry, and space-satellite communication. In these cases, the carrier is not switched off but shifted slightly in frequency. These shifts in frequency are made in a coded fashion and are decoded in the receiver. This method keeps the receiver quiet between the dots and dashes and produces an audible sound in the receiver corresponding to the coded information.

Amplitude Modulation. In radio-telephone communication or standard broadcast transmissions the speech and music are used to modulate the carrier. This process means that the intelligence to be transmitted is used to vary some property of the carrier. One method is to super-impose the intelligence on the carrier by varying the am-plitude of the carrier, hence the term amplitude modula-tion (AM). The modulating audio signal (speech or music) is applied to a MICROPHONE. This produces electrical sig-nals that alternate, positively and negatively. After ampli-fication, these signals are applied to a modulator. When the audio signals go positive, they increase the amplitude of the carrier; when they go negative, they decrease the amplitude of the carrier. The amplitude of the carrier now has superimposed on it the variation of the audio signal, with peaks and valleys dependent on the volume of the audio input to the microphone. The carrier has been mod-ulated and, after further amplification, is sent by means of a transmission line to the transmitting antenna.

The maximum modulating frequency permitted by AM broadcast stations is 5 kHz at carrier frequencies between 535 and 1,605 kHz. The strongest AM stations have a power output of 50,000 watts.

Frequency Modulation. Another method of modulating the carrier is to vary its frequency. In frequency modula-tion (FM), on the positive half-cycle of the audio signal the frequency of the carrier gradually increases. On the negative half-cycle the carrier frequency is decreased. The louder the sound being used for modulation, the higher will be the change in frequency. A maximum devi-ation of 75 kHz above and below the carrier frequency is permitted at maximum volume in FM broadcasts. The rate at which the carrier frequency is varied is determined by the frequency of the audio signal. The maximum mod-ulating frequency permitted by FM broadcast stations is 15 kHz at carrier frequencies between 88 and 108 MHz. This wider carrier frequency (15 kHz for FM as opposed to 5 kHz for standard AM broadcasts) accounts for the high fidelity of FM receivers. FM stations range in power from 100 watts to 100,000 watts.

It should be noted that television transmitters use both AM and FM. The video, or picture, signals are trans-mitted by AM and the sound by FM.

The Antenna. An ANTENNA is a wire or metal conductor used either to radiate energy from a transmitter or to pick up energy at a receiver. It is insulated from the ground and may be situated vertically or horizontally.

The radio waves emitted from an antenna consist of electric and magnetic fields, mutually perpendicular to each other and to the direction of propagation. A vertical antenna is said to be vertically polarized because its elec-tric field has a vertical orientation. An AM broadcast an-tenna is vertically polarized, requiring the receiving an-tenna to be located vertically also, as in an automobile installation. Television and FM broadcast transmitters use a horizontal polarization antenna.

For efficient transmission (or reception) the required length of a dipole antenna must be half a wavelength or some multiple of a half-wavelength. Thus an FM station that broadcasts at 100 MHz, which has a wavelength of 3 m (9.8 ft), should have a horizontally polarized antenna

1½ m (4.9 ft) in length. Receiving antennas should be approximately the same length and placed horizontally.

For an AM station broadcasting at 1,000 kHz, the op-timal length would be 150 m (492 ft). This is an imprac-tical length, especially when it must be mounted vertical-ly. In this case, a quarter-wavelength Marconi antenna is often used, with the ground (earth), serving as the other quarter wavelength.

The Receiver. When the modulated carrier reaches the receiving antenna, a small voltage is induced. This may be as small as 0.1 μV (microvolt) in some commercial communication receivers but is typically 50 μV in a stan-dard AM broadcast receiver. This voltage is coupled to a tunable circuit, which consists of a coil and a variable CA-PACITOR. By adjusting the capacitance, the listener makes the circuit sensitive to a different, narrow frequency range, tuning the receiver to a particular station.

The Crystal Receiver. One of the earliest methods of de-tecting radio waves was the crystal receiver. A crystal of ga-lena or carborundum along with a movable pointed wire called a cat whisker provided a simple RECTIFIER. This com-ponent allows current to flow in one direction only, so that only the upper half of the modulated wave is allowed to pass. A capacitor is then used to filter out the unwanted high-frequency carrier, leaving the audio to operate the ear-phones. Since no external electrical power or amplifiers are used, the only source of power in the earphones is the in-coming signal. Only strong signals are audible, but with a long antenna and a good ground, reception of a signal from 1,600 km (1,000 mi) away is sometimes possible.

The TRF Receiver. Following the development of the triode, increasing selectivity, sensitivity, and audio output power in tuned-radio-frequency (TRF) receivers was possi-ble. This process involved a number of stages of radio-fre-quency amplification prior to the detection stage. In early receivers each of these stages had to be separately tuned to the incoming frequency, which was a difficult task.

The Superheterodyne Receiver. Practically all modern radio receivers use the heterodyne principle. The incom-ing modulated signal is combined with the output of a tunable local oscillator whose frequency is always a fixed amount above the incoming signal. This process, called frequency conversion or heterodyning, takes place in a mixer circuit. The output of the mixer is a radio frequency that contains the original information at the antenna. This frequency, called the intermediate frequency (IF), is typi-cally 455 kHz in AM broadcast receivers. No matter what the frequency that the receiver is tuned to, the intermedi-ate frequency is always the same; it contains the informa-tion of the desired station. As a result, all further stages of radio-frequency amplification can be designed to operate at this fixed intermediate frequency.

After detection, audio amplifiers boost the signal to a level capable of driving a loudspeaker.

Comparison of AM and FM. Although the method of de-tection differs in AM and FM receivers, the same hetero-dyne principle is used in each. An FM receiver, however, generally includes automatic frequency control (AFC). If the frequency of the local oscillator drifts from its correct value the station will fade. To avoid this problem, a DC voltage is developed at the detector and fed back to the local oscillator. This voltage is used to change automatically the frequency output of the local oscillator to maintain the proper intermediate frequency. Both AM and FM receivers incorporate automatic gain control (AGC), sometimes called automatic volume control (AVC). If a strong station is tuned in, the volume of the sound would tend to be overwhelming if the volume control had previously been set for a weak station. This drawback is overcome by the use of negative feedback—a DC voltage is developed at the detector and used to reduce automatically the gain, or amplification, of the IF amplifiers.

The prime advantage of FM, in addition to its fidelity, is its immunity to electrical noise. Lightning storms superimpose noise on an AM signal by increasing the amplitude of the signal. This effect shows up in a receiver as a crackling noise. Because it decodes only the frequency variations, an FM receiver is provided with a limiter circuit that restricts any amplitude variations that may result from added noise.

Single Sideband Systems. When an audio signal of 5 kHz is used to amplitude-modulate a carrier, the output of the transmitter contains sideband frequencies in addition to the carrier frequency. The upper sideband frequencies extend to 5 kHz higher than the carrier, and the lower sideband frequencies extend to 5 kHz lower than the carrier. In normal AM broadcasts both sidebands are transmitted, requiring a bandwidth in the frequency spectrum of 10 kHz, centered on the carrier frequency. The audio signal, however, is contained in and may be retrieved from either the upper or lower sideband. Furthermore, the carrier itself contains no useful information. Therefore, the only part that needs to be transmitted is one of the sidebands. A system designed to do this is called a single sideband suppressed carrier (abbreviated SSBSC, or SSB for short). This is an important system because it requires only half of the bandwidth needed for ordinary AM, thus allowing more channels to be assigned in any given portion of the frequency spectrum. Also, because of the reduced power requirements, a 110-watt SSB transmitter may have a range as great as that of a 1,000-watt conventional AM transmitter. Almost all HAM RADIOS, commercial radiotelephones, and marine-band radios, as well as CITIZENS BAND RADIOS, use SSB systems. Receivers for such systems are more complex, however, than those for other systems. The receiver must reinsert the nontransmitted carrier before successful heterodyning can take place.

—

radio astronomy   Radio astronomy is the study of the universe through observations of the radio waves emitted by cosmic objects. Everything in the universe radiates radio waves, and modern radio telescopes are capable of detecting these waves from almost all known objects.

Because the physical processes giving rise to radio emission are sometimes different from or more powerful than the processes giving rise to other types of radiations, objects can often be detected more easily by radio observations. In addition, important aspects of objects, such as the strength of magnetic fields, can often be determined only by radio observations. As a result, radio astronomy complements optical, X-ray, gamma-ray, infrared, and ultraviolet astronomy. All of these studies combine to reveal the true nature of celestial objects. (See ASTRONOMY AND ASTROPHYSICS; GAMMA-RAY ASTRONOMY; INFRARED ASTRONOMY; ULTRAVIOLET ASTRONOMY; X-RAY ASTRONOMY.)

Radio astronomy was born in 1931 with the discovery by Karl JANSKY at the Bell Telephone Laboratories in New Jersey that radio waves were coming from the sky. His discovery was followed by the work of Grote Reber, a radio engineer at Wheaton, Ill., who in 1937 constructed a steerable parabola radio telescope and used it to map the distribution of radio emission in the sky. This study was followed by work in many countries during and immediately after World War II; radar technology, originally developed for military purposes, was used for pioneering radio astronomy observations as well as for making radar observations of neighboring planets (see RADAR ASTRONOMY). The radio emission from the Sun was discovered in this way, and radio telescopes in Australia established the existence of discrete sources of radio emission.

These discoveries led to the construction throughout the world of ever bigger and more sensitive radio telescopes during the 1950s and 1960s. Particularly active countries were England, Australia, the Netherlands, and the United States. By the mid-1960s radio astronomy had become the cutting edge of modern astronomy, leading the way to the majority of major new discoveries, such as the existence of radio galaxies, QUASARS, PULSARS, BACKGROUND RADIATION from the primordial fireball, and a host of complex molecules in interstellar space (see ASTROCHEMISTRY).

Causes of Radio Emission

As late as 1950 some astronomers thought that radio observations would play no important role in the study of the universe. They believed that the only significant source of radio waves was thermal radiation caused by the heat of a body. Calculations indicated that the thermal radiation at radio wavelengths would be so faint that no useful radio measurements could be made of anything except perhaps the Sun and planets. The radio intensities observed by Jansky and Reber were, however, approximately 10 million million times brighter than might have been expected from the thermal emission of the stars and galaxies. This result implied that far more powerful mechanisms for the production of radio waves existed in the universe.

Nonthermal Radiation. The only important nonthermal mechanism of radio emission, and the one that almost always produces the observed radiation, is known as SYNCHROTRON RADIATION. This is radio emission from very energetic nuclear particles orbiting in a magnetic field. Scientists believe that these are, in every case, electrons orbiting in the magnetic field of, for example, a galaxy. With their very high energies the synchrotron mechanism causes the electrons to radiate primarily at radio frequencies and with very great intensity.

Because of the large release of energy, the overall radiation from celestial objects is likely to be relatively great,

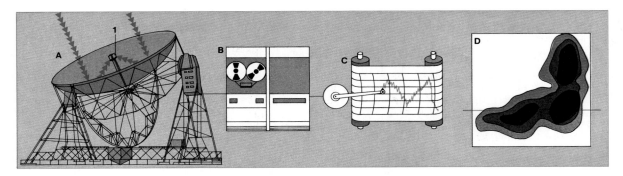

The intensity of radiation emanating from a radio source such as Centaurus A is mapped through use of a steerable dish reflector (A). The radio waves from a narrow region of the sky are focused onto the centrally mounted antenna (1), which transmits the signals to amplifying and recording equipment (B). As the telescope sweeps across the sky, the signal-intensity output is graphed on a pen recorder (C). After several sweeps a contour map (D) is built up, with the areas of more-intense radio flux represented by a darker shade.

allowing astronomers to detect and study many of the objects and to observe them at very great distances. Thus radio astronomy has given the astronomer a means to trace the history of the universe, even perhaps back to the creation of the universe.

Thermal Radiation. Although the nonthermal radio emission and the objects associated with it have been of the greatest interest, thermal radiation has also turned out to be a valuable source of information. With it astronomers have studied the gas clouds of our galaxy (see GALAXY, THE) and other galaxies (see EXTRAGALACTIC SYSTEMS), the emission nebulae, and the planets in our SOLAR SYSTEM.

Radio Sources within the Galaxy

When the sky is scanned with a radio telescope, a very bright band of radio emission is found that coincides with the Milky Way. The brightness of this band relative to the other cosmic sources of radio emission is much greater than the relative brightness of the Milky Way as compared to the ordinary stars as seen with the unaided eye. This radiation from the disk of our galaxy is, at most radio frequencies, synchrotron radiation from cosmic-ray electrons spiraling in the magnetic fields of our galaxy (see COSMIC RAYS).

In addition to the bright radiation of the Milky Way the sky is filled with distinct sources of radio emission. Some of these come from solar system objects, while others arise in more distant parts of the galaxy or outside of the galaxy. None of the bright radio sources is associated with any of the bright, well-known optical stars; instead, these sources of radio emission are associated with objects that in all cases are rather faint optically but radiate large amounts of radio energy due to synchrotron radiation or very high temperature. Aside from the solar system, the most prominent sources of radio emission within the galaxy are supernova remnants, pulsars, most ionized emission nebulae, and interstellar atoms and molecules (see INTERSTELLAR MATTER).

The Solar System. The SUN is an interesting and complex source of radio waves. It radiates a steady level of thermal radio emission because of its high temperature. When observed at long radio wavelengths, however, the

radio emission observed is very intense and is typical of a hot object whose temperature is 1,000,000 K rather than the 5,800 K temperature of the solar surface. This high-temperature radiation comes from the solar corona, which becomes the visible "surface" of the Sun when observed at long radio wavelengths. In addition to this steady emission, the Sun exhibits at least six other kinds of complicated, time-variable radio emissions. All of these seem to be associated with SUNSPOT activity and the solar flares that accompany this activity.

Radio observations of the Moon and all of the planets except Pluto have been used to determine their temperatures. The biggest surprises in solar-system research have been provided by Jupiter, which exhibits three different types of radio emission. First, radio emissions are caused by thermal emission from the body of the planet. A second type of radio emission, called decimeter emission, is synchrotron emission from a vast system of radiation belts that are held within the magnetic field of the planet. The third type of radio emission, called decameter emission, is a sporadic, very intense radio emission that is observed only at low frequencies of about 20 MHz.

The radio emissions of asteroids, comets, and Pluto are too faint for detection by contemporary radio telescopes, except for faint radio emission from several comet molecules.

Supernova Remnants and Pulsars. Supernova remnants are the clouds of gas that have been expelled in the violent nuclear explosion of a star known as a SUPERNOVA. These clouds, which often appear as hollow spherical shells, contain large quantities of electrons of relativistic energy, that is, electrons moving at speeds approaching the speed of light. Radiating through the synchrotron process, the electrons were evidently created in the supernova explosion; in some cases, however, this explosion has left behind a spinning NEUTRON STAR, which is both a pulsar and a continuous producer of new relativistic electrons and cosmic rays. The pulsars are radio sources in the Milky Way that are very unusual because, rather than producing a continuous radio intensity at the Earth, they produce short, regularly spaced bursts of radio emission.

Ionized Emission Nebulae. The other bright sources of radiation in the Milky Way are the ionized emission NEBU-LAE. In these objects, a very hot star has produced ultraviolet radiation that has ionized and heated the interstellar gas around it. This hot, charged gas is an excellent emitter of radio waves produced by thermal processes. These sources of radio emission—one of the brightest is the Great Nebula in Orion—are more prominent at the higher radio frequencies because the spectrum of synchrotron radiation is most intense at low frequencies, even though thermal emission has about the same intensity over a broad frequency range.

Stars. Several dozen normal stars have been detected as faint radio sources in our galaxy. The detectable radiation appears to come from hot shells or coronae, like that of the Sun, surrounding these stars.

Interstellar Atoms and Molecules. A very important feature of the galactic radio emission is the strong radiation on specific wavelengths, or so-called spectral lines, that are emitted by atoms and molecules in the interstellar gas. The most prominent of these is the radiation of neutral atomic hydrogen, the most abundant element in the universe, at the wavelength of 21 cm. The atoms in this case and others radiate at a specific frequency but may arrive at Earth at a different frequency due to the Doppler effect associated with the motion of the atoms toward or away from the Earth. By studying this Doppler shift in the frequencies of the observed spectral lines, the astronomer can deduce the temperatures and motions of the gas clouds that the radiation comes from. In this way the velocities and arrangements of gas clouds in our galaxy and others have been determined. In addition to atomic hydrogen, spectral lines have been discovered, surprisingly, from more than 40 different molecules.

(Right) *In this radio contour map, here superimposed over an optical photograph, of M 51 (the Whirlpool Galaxy) and its companion galaxy NGC 5195, the white lines are lines of constant radio intensity. These lines converge rapidly at such regions of maximal radio intensity as the nuclei of both galaxies and the spiral arms of M 51.*

(Below) *The distribution and velocity of neutral hydrogen in M 81 is revealed in this false-color image of the radiation emanating from that nearby spiral galaxy. The brightness indicates the intensity, whereas the colors represent the velocities, or Doppler shift: red to yellow, recession; green, no shift; blue to violet, approach. The rotation of this galaxy is clearly evident.*

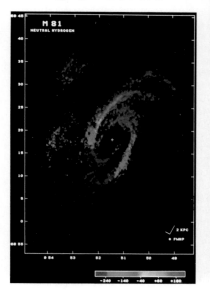

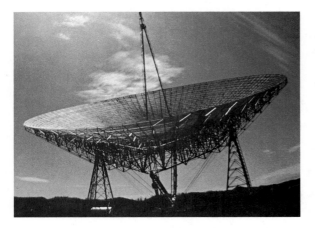

(Above) *One of the world's major radio telescopes was the 91.4-m-diameter (300-ft) meridional transit dish at the National Radio Astronomy Observatory in Green Bank, W. Va.; the telescope collapsed in November 1988.* (Below) *The 305-m-diameter (1,000-ft) spherical reflecting dish set near the town of Arecibo, in western Puerto Rico.*

Extraterrestrial Civilizations. At several observatories in the United States, Canada, and the Soviet Union, astronomers are searching for radio signals from other civilizations. Much more elaborate coverage over long time periods is called for, however, before such searches could in any way be considered statistically meaningful (see LIFE, EXTRATERRESTRIAL).

Extragalactic Radio Sources

Most of the bright objects in the radio sky are outside our galaxy. At least two distinct classes of objects exist—radio galaxies and quasars—but radio surveys of the sky also reveal a variety of less classifiable objects.

Radio Galaxies. Although all galaxies, including the Milky Way, emit some radio waves because they contain energetic electrons and magnetic field, some galaxies emit from a thousand to ten million times more radio energy than normal galaxies. These radio galaxies are very often peculiar in their optical appearance. A common type has a bright central region; other cases are elliptical galaxies with dust clouds. In a majority of cases the intense radio emission comes not from the optical body of the galaxy but from two very large regions placed symmetrically about the center of the galaxy, several galactic diameters away from the center.

In other cases a radio galaxy may have a very intense region of radio emission near the center of the galaxy, sometimes accompanied by a halo of bright radio emission extending throughout the galaxy. Many hundreds of such galaxies are known. The radio emission from radio galaxies is very highly polarized, indicating that its origin is the radio radiation of very energetic electrons moving at nearly the speed of light and spiraling in the weak magnetic field of the galaxy. These energetic electrons are the result of some very violent event, still not understood, in which an amount of energy equivalent to the total annihilation of up to ten million stars is released. Calculations indicate that the typical radio galaxy will be a brilliant radio emitter for anywhere from 100 million to 1 billion years.

Quasars. Quasars are far more extreme examples of radio galaxies and are the brightest objects in the universe. Even if situated near the bounds of the observable universe, they are easily detected by small radio telescopes. Their radio emission is typically 1 million to 100 million times greater than that of a normal galaxy, and they are as bright as or brighter than the brightest radio galaxies. In every case a quasar appears to be a galaxy with a very bright small region in its center, as seen optically. Because they create optical images that are indistinguishable from stars, they are called "quasi-stellar radio sources," or "quasars" for short. Spectral analysis of the objects, however, shows that they are indeed distant galaxies, in many cases receding from the Earth with a velocity that is a large fraction of the velocity of light. Their radio and optical emission changes with time, sometimes increasing or decreasing substantially in only a few months. This rapid change indicates that the main source of their energy is at most only a few light-months in size.

Background Radiation. A profound aspect of the radio sky is the uniform glow of radio emission found in all parts of the sky. Careful study shows that it has the same spectra as a thermally radiating body whose temperature is only 2.7 K. Surprisingly, such a spectrum is the same as the spectrum that has been predicted theoretically (see BLACKBODY RADIATION) to result from the big-bang cosmology (see BIG BANG THEORY).

Radio Telescopes

The first radio telescope, built by Karl Jansky in 1929, was originally intended for the purpose of studying the causes of short-wave interference. It was an ensemble of simple dipole antennas that could be rotated on a track. Most modern instruments are large parabolic reflector radio antennas that focus the radio emission from a small region of the sky to a focal point, where a small antenna captures the radio energy and delivers it to a very sensitive radio receiver. Other types of radio telescopes include the Mills Cross and the Very Large Array (see NATIONAL RADIO ASTRONOMY OBSERVATORY).

Resolution Sensitivity. The resolution of a radio telescope is the size of the region in the sky from which the telescope collects radiation. Sometimes called the beamwidth, the area is usually a circular region whose angular size is approximately 57° times the ratio of the observed wavelength to the diameter of the telescope. The largest single paraboloidal telescopes have a beamwidth, or resolution, of about one arc-minute—about the same as that of the human eye. Much greater resolution can be obtained with INTERFEROMETERS in which two or more radio telescopes are connected together to simulate the performance of a much larger telescope. In this case the resolution is 57° times the ratio of the wavelength to the maximum separation of the telescopes used in the interferometer. This separation may be thousands of meters or even an intercontinental distance, leading to resolutions as small as a few ten-thousandths of an arc-second.

The sensitivity of a radio telescope refers to the faintness of the signals that can be detected. It depends on both the energy-collecting area of the telescope and on the radio noise added to the incoming radio signals, primarily by the radio receiver but also to a lesser extent by the antenna itself. Special circuits have been constructed to minimize the effects of this noise, but physical laws prevent its complete elimination. In a high-quality receiver the minimum detectable signal becomes fainter in proportion to the reciprocal of the square root of the bandwidth used and in proportion to the reciprocal of the square root of the time over which the received signal is averaged. Both these qualities are utilized in modern radio telescopes to improve sensitivity. In some cases bandwidths of hundreds of Megahertz are used. In such cases, signal averaging times may be as much as 30 hours.

Astronomers prefer to build their radio telescopes on as large an area as possible, in order to capture the maximum amount of energy, and with energy-collecting elements that are constructed to precise geometric configurations that allow operation at higher radio frequencies and provide better resolution. They have found that it is particularly important to design structures that preserve their precise geometry in the presence of the changing force of gravity as the structure moves, the force of the wind, and the thermal deflections due to uneven heating of the telescope structure.

Steerable Paraboloid. In 1937, Grote Reber built the first steerable paraboloid antenna as an amateur project at Wheaton, Ill. This antenna became the prototype of most modern large radio telescopes. During and immediately after World War II the large radar instruments built for military purposes were used as radio telescopes. In the 1950s the main thrust of radio telescope construction was to build ever larger steerable paraboloids, a process that culminated in the 91.4-m (300-ft) paraboloid at Green Bank, W.Va., built in 1963, and the 100-m (328-ft) telescope near Bonn, Germany, constructed in the late 1960s. The development of more-precise antennas allowed operation at higher radio frequencies, which is im-

portant to the study of interstellar molecules. The most powerful for the study of such molecules is the 11-m (36-ft) radio telescope operated by the National Radio Astronomy Observatory at Kitt Peak, Ariz. An important variation of the paraboloidal antenna is the use of a fixed spherical antenna, as in the world's largest radio telescope, 305 m (1,000 ft) in diameter, constructed in 1963 near Arecibo, Puerto Rico. Another such antenna is the Soviet RATAN-600—an acronym for Radio Astronomy Telescope of the Academy of Sciences (Nauk)—in the northwestern Caucasus; it has about ¼ the reflecting area of the Arecibo antenna.

The operation of the paraboloid radio telescope is identical in concept to that of large optical telescopes. A reflector consisting of a paraboloid is oriented so that its axis is pointed at the place in the sky whose radio emission is to be measured. The paraboloid reflects all rays coming to it from the place of interest to the focus of the paraboloid. The electrical signal is carried from the antenna through a waveguide or wires to a high-sensitivity radio receiver. This receiver has electronic or waveguide filters that allow only those radio frequencies to pass that the astronomer wishes to observe. The signals, which may be at a very low power level such as 10^{-20} watt, are then amplified in a special amplifier, detected by a special circuit, recorded on magnetic tape, and analyzed.

Mills Cross. The quest for good resolution and large energy-collecting area has led to the development of several ingenious radio telescope systems. One of the earliest was the Mills Cross, invented in 1953 by Bernard Mills of the University of Sydney, Australia. In the Mills Cross two antennas are used, each long and thin and fixed to the ground. Because of their shapes each antenna has good resolution in one direction, the direction parallel to its long dimension, and poor resolution in the other direction. In a Mills Cross, the two antennas are arranged at right angles to one another, usually so that they look like a cross from above (hence the name), and the signals from the two antennas are multiplied together. The result is an overall response that gives good resolution in both directions. The largest Mills Cross is at Molonglo, Australia, where the antennas are each one mile long. Other large Mills Crosses are at Bologna, Italy, and Penticton, British Columbia. The configuration of a Mills Cross makes pointing the telescope's response pattern difficult and following objects as the Earth moves impossible; the telescope is also·difficult to operate at different radio frequencies. As a result new Mills Crosses are not being built.

Radio Interferometers. A very important development of the early 1960s and subsequent years was the application of groups of radio antennas as radio interferometers. In this approach, several antennas are connected together simultaneously, usually by an ordinary electrical cable connection but sometimes via radio links over distances of more than 80 km (50 mi). Alternatively, the signals received at various antennas can be tape-recorded and subsequently played into a common radio receiver simultaneously. The radio interferometer permits extremely high resolution and a very large equivalent antenna collecting area at much less cost than would be called for if these were achieved with a single large antenna. This procedure is the basis of most of the major instruments recently constructed or planned.

One of the most important developments to grow out of the successful application of interferometers was the process of aperture synthesis, pioneered by Sir Martin Ryle. When two parabolic antennas are connected as an interferometer, the pair gives the same information to the radio receiver as two points on a much larger paraboloid.

One large operating aperture synthesis is located at Westerbork, the Netherlands, where antennas are spaced along a line one kilometer long. Another powerful system is operated by Cambridge University. The largest system now in existence is the Very Large Array, which the National Radio Astronomy Observatory has built on the Plains of San Augustin near Socorro, N.Mex. This system, which was finished in 1981, possesses 27 steerable paraboloids, each 25 m (82 ft) in diameter, arranged along three railroad tracks. The three rail lines form an equiangular "Y" shape, and each is 20 km (12 mi) long. The resolution that is achieved by this instrument is a few tenths of an arc-second, about the same as that of the largest optical telescopes under the best atmospheric conditions. The entire array provides astronomers with the equivalent performance of a fully steerable radio dish 27 km (17 mi) in diameter. While it was under construction, the array already produced magnificent results.

Another powerful application of interferometry is called Very Long Baseline Interferometry. In this technique, two or more radio telescopes at different locations observe the same region simultaneously, and observations are combined in a very precise way.

Future of Radio Astronomy

Work began in the mid-1980s on the construction of a radio installation that is to stretch across the United States and its territories. Called the Very Long Baseline Array, it will consist of ten parabolic antennas, each 25 m (82 ft) in diameter. Scheduled to be completed in the early 1990s, the Very Long Baseline Array will have a resolution 1,000 times that of any currently existing optical or radio telescope. Canada is planning a similar array, called the Canadian Long-Baseline Array, which will consist of eight telescopes, each 32 m (105 ft) in diameter, arranged in a line across the southern part of the country. In the Southern Hemisphere, Australia is also planning a continent-wide array of radio telescopes. Another idea being explored is the development of an interferometer using a telescope aboard a spacecraft to observe simultaneously with another telescope on Earth or also in orbit.

Radio telescopes are also being constructed to explore the last remaining untapped region of the electromagnetic spectrum: the submillimeter region that lies between the very shortest radio wavelengths and the very longest wavelengths of infrared radiation. Because waves in this region of the spectrum are strongly absorbed by atmospheric water vapor, the submillimeter radio antennas to receive them must be built in arid regions, preferably at high altitudes.

See also: OBSERVATORY, ASTRONOMICAL.

Radio Free Europe and Radio Liberty Radio Free Europe and Radio Liberty, a U.S.-government–financed nonprofit corporation with headquarters in Munich, Germany, broadcasts more than 1,000 hours of programming weekly from 51 transmitters into Eastern Europe, the Soviet Union, and Afghanistan. These two radio stations were founded in 1950 and 1951, respectively, as separate stations and were merged into one corporation, RFE/RL, Inc., in 1976.

RFE broadcasts to five East European countries (Bulgaria, Czechoslovakia, Hungary, Poland, and Romania) and to the three Soviet Baltic republics (Latvia, Lithuania, and Estonia); RL broadcasts into other republics of the Soviet Union and into Afghanistan. The stations provide their listeners with news, commentary, sports, music, and religion.

Until 1971 the two stations were financed by U.S. government funds covertly channeled through the Central Intelligence Agency. In 1973 a semiautonomous agency, the Board for International Broadcasting, was created to oversee the operations of RFE/RL.

radio telescope see OBSERVATORY, ASTRONOMICAL; RADIO ASTRONOMY

radio and television broadcasting Radio and television broadcasting is a firmly established element of American life. The A. C. Nielsen Company, which measures audience size, reported in 1985 that 98.1% of U.S. homes contained at least one television set and that the average set is turned on for seven hours per day. More than 60% of television viewers receive their news from their sets rather than from newspapers, and over half that number trust television more than newspapers. According to the Radio Advertising Bureau, in 1985 only 1% of U.S. homes had no radio, and the average household owned at least five radios.

The Origins of Broadcasting—Radio

Early Years: 1920–29. Before World War I the inventors Guglielmo MARCONI, Lee DE FOREST, Reginald Aubrey FESSENDEN, and Edwin ARMSTRONG had laid the technological foundations of RADIO, but a wartime ban on nonmilitary broadcasting delayed radio's acceptance until the ban was lifted in 1919. Thereafter, hundreds of amateur stations sprang up. In 1922 more than 500 stations were licensed by the government. Most listeners employed homemade sets built around a galena or silicon crystal to receive signals from the "ether."

The U.S. Department of Commerce was in charge of regulating stations on the basis of the Radio Act of 1912 and assigned three- and then four-letter codes to stations. The act also confined most domestic broadcasting to the same wavelength, 360 m, thus creating an aerial traffic jam of overlapping signals. In 1922 the Commerce Department permitted more powerful stations to use the 400-m wavelength on condition that they play only live music. This two-tier structure encouraged large and small broadcasting

On July 2, 1921, one of the first radio broadcasts, of Jack Dempsey's heavyweight title defense against Georges Carpentier, was transmitted by RCA from New Jersey. These people on the Atlantic City boardwalk could listen to the broadcast at a radio-equipped cart for 25 cents per round.

systems to form associations to share costs and bring popular entertainment from cities to rural areas.

In 1920 the Westinghouse engineer Frank Conrad received a license for what is regarded as the nation's first true radio station, KDKA in Pittsburgh, Pa. KDKA broadcast scheduled music programs, sports, and the 1920 presidential election. During the following year Westinghouse began to sell radio sets. The least expensive model cost $25. By 1924 the radio-listening audience numbered 20 million.

American Telephone and Telegraph (AT&T) inaugurated its radio station, WEAF, in New York City in 1922. Soon after, WEAF broadcast the first paid commercial announcement, a 10-minute speech on behalf of the Queensborough Corporation, a real-estate concern. The advertisement cost $50. AT&T then licensed out-of-town stations to carry its programs. On the strength of its "toll," or sponsored approach to broadcasting, WEAF made a $150,000 profit in 1923.

American Marconi, the U.S. subsidiary of Marconi's highly successful British company, was bought by a newly formed Radio Corporation of America (RCA) in 1919, in large part to keep some of the new technology of radio in American hands. In 1920, Westinghouse, General Electric, and AT&T agreed to share the important broadcasting patents each had developed. RCA entered the patent pool in 1921. In return, the three original patent holders acquired an interest in the new company.

David SARNOFF, a onetime telegraph operator and American Marconi employee had suggested that music could be brought into American households via wireless receiver. As commercial manager of RCA, Sarnoff began to manufacture radios, and their sale became the chief source of RCA profits. In 1926, RCA purchased WEAF from AT&T for $1 million as the nucleus of a broadcasting network. AT&T retained a financial interest in broadcasting by supplying land lines to link the network's sta-

tions. During the same year, RCA established its broadcasting subsidiary, the National Broadcasting Company.

In 1927, Congress passed the Radio Act, which created a Federal Radio Commission empowered to license and regulate stations. Networks, whose influence was largely unforeseen, were free from direct FRC regulation.

The Columbia Broadcasting System, organized as a rival network to NBC, was founded in 1927, and rapidly passed through a number of owners—including the Columbia Phonograph Company, which gave the network its name. In 1928, William S. PALEY bought the network and negotiated new affiliate contracts. Whereas NBC charged affiliates to carry sustaining (nonsponsored) programs, CBS supplied them free in return for 5 hours of affiliates' time. The favorable terms helped CBS attract 47 stations to its roster by the end of 1929. Paley's entrepreneurial acumen now offered a significant challenge to NBC's dominance of domestic broadcasting.

Programming and Advertising. Although live music served as the staple of most early radio programming, networks soon realized that vaudeville-trained comedians lured larger audiences and served as effective on-the-air speakers for sponsors' products. AMOS 'N' ANDY made its NBC debut in 1929 and eventually attracted an audience estimated at 40 million. Other popular comedians of the Depression era included Fred ALLEN, Jack BENNY, and BURNS AND ALLEN. Networks did not produce these popular, sponsored programs themselves. They leased facilities to advertising agencies who in turn hired the performers.

Because advertising time was sold according to the estimated popularity of a given program, networks and sponsors relied on ratings as the arbiter of a performer's success. In 1930, Crossley, Inc., tabulated the first formal ratings, showing that NBC's "Amos 'n' Andy" was four times more popular than any CBS show. To fill hours dominated by popular NBC programming, CBS turned to prestigious but inexpensive dramas broadcast on a sustaining basis. Under the direction of William B. Lewis, the "Columbia Workshop" introduced the writers Archibald MacLeish and Norman Corwin, the actor-director Orson WELLES, and the composer Bernard Hermann to radio au-

Guglielmo Marconi, the inventor of the wireless radio, and David Sarnoff, president of the Radio Corporation of America (RCA), are seen in this photograph taken in 1933 at the RCA transmitting center on Long Island. The Marconi Wireless Company was taken over by RCA in 1919.

diences. In response to the CBS sustaining programming, NBC broadcast adaptations of Shakespeare starring John Barrymore and scored a significant coup by inducing Arturo Toscanini to leave Italy and take up the direction of the newly formed NBC Symphony Orchestra, beginning in late 1937.

The threat of world war spurred the development of network news departments. The coverage offered by a young CBS correspondent, Edward R. MURROW, of Hitler's march to Vienna in 1938 brought a new sophistication and immediacy to radio reporting. CBS that year inaugurated the world news roundup, and Murrow helped recruit for CBS such outstanding correspondents as Walter CRONKITE, Winston Burdett, Richard C. Hottelet, Larry Le Sueur, Eric Sevareid, William L. Shirer, and Howard K. Smith. Murrow's live reports of the Battle of Britain brought the far-off war into American living rooms in 1940. From within the United States the radio commentators Elmer Davis, Quincy Howe, H. V. Kaltenborn, and Raymond Swing offered analyses of world events. The "Columbia Workshop" also joined the war effort as it became part of the Office of War Information, and CBS dramatists turned to propaganda.

The Coming of Television

Early Years: 1935–44. In 1929, David Sarnoff had learned of the television experiments of Vladimir Kosma ZWORYKIN, a Soviet immigrant then working at Westinghouse. Whereas many other television inventors relied on mechanical devices to reproduce visual images, Zworykin emphasized the importance of an all-electronic system. Sarnoff eventually invested $50 million in Zworykin's inventions, and in 1939 demonstrated a television system at the New York World's Fair. Franklin D. Roosevelt spoke before the camera, becoming the first president to appear on television.

Despite Sarnoff's bold moves, several factors converged to delay the coming of television. The war forced RCA to suspend television development in favor of military production. A struggle over wavelength allocations, combined with a running battle over government regulation, further slowed television's progress. In 1933 the in-

Orson Welles's adaptation of H. G. Wells's War of the Worlds *became a landmark in radio history when it was presented (1938) as part of his "Mercury Theatre" drama series. Welles's realistic broadcast convinced millions of U.S. listeners that a Martian invasion was actually occurring and precipitated widespread panic.*

Edward R. Murrow, regarded as the finest of all radio and television journalists, broadcast from London during World War II and was primarily responsible for discrediting the anti-Communist propaganda of Sen. Joseph McCarthy in 1954.

ventor Edwin Armstrong demonstrated a new static-free method of transmission, FREQUENCY MODULATION (FM), far superior to the AMPLITUDE MODULATION (AM) then in use. Armstrong's advocacy of FM, which caught the ear of the government, threatened to block the introduction of Sarnoff's television, which required some of the same hotly contested frequencies. In 1940 the FEDERAL COMMUNICATIONS COMMISSION, successor to the FRC, approved FM for radio broadcasting, but required that it also be used for television transmission. In 1944 the FCC determined frequencies for both FM and television: 12 very high frequency (VHF) and 70 ultra-high frequency (UHF) television channels, with FM broadcasting located just above channel 6 on the VHF spectrum.

In 1941 the FCC issued its *Report on Chain Broadcasting,* which in effect ordered NBC to sell one of the two networks it operated. The report noted that RCA exercised a "practical monopoly of network broadcasting" since 25% of all radio stations were affiliated with NBC. A Supreme Court decision of 1943 confirmed the FCC's right to force NBC to divest itself of one of its networks. That year, NBC sold the Blue network to Edward J. Noble, a businessman who had made his fortune as a candy manufacturer. Renamed the American Broadcasting Company (ABC), the new network, after experimenting with inexpensive public-affairs programming, discovered that it would have to emphasize commercial programming if it were to survive in the marketplace. An FCC moratorium on construction of new television stations between 1948 and 1953 further hampered ABC's ability to enter new markets. In 1951, Noble agreed to sell his interest in ABC to Leonard Goldenson, head of United Paramount Theatres, and the FCC approved the ABC-UPT merger in 1953. With a background in movie promotion, Goldenson led ABC into thoroughly commercial programming designed to appeal to a youthful audience. Two early ABC successes, "Disneyland" (1954) and "The Mickey Mouse Club" (1955), gave the network its first profit, $6 million. ABC was also the first to buy the products of Hollywood film studios, which had

The comedian Milton Berle was popular between 1948 and 1956, when he was known as "Uncle Miltie." He is shown here in pie face with guest stars Buffalo Bob, Howdy Doody, and Clarabell the clown in a skit from NBC's "Texaco Star Theater."

initially competed with television as their greatest rival for audiences.

McCarthyism and the Golden Age of Television: 1953–60.
In 1947 the House Un-American Activities Committee began an investigation of the film industry, and in 1950 a *Counterattack* pamphlet, "Red Channels," listed the supposedly Communist associations of 151 performing artists, including Corwin and Welles. Artists thus blacklisted found it nearly impossible to get work. CBS instituted a loyalty oath for its employees. When anti-Communist vigilantes applied pressure to advertisers—the source of network profits—it became imperative that the industry defend itself. The task fell to the man considered by many the industry's moral leader, Edward R. Murrow.

In partnership with the news producer Fred Friendly, Murrow began "See It Now," a television documentary series, in 1950. "See It Now" occasionally explored ex-

Lucille Ball and Desi Arnaz star in a scene from "I Love Lucy," which ran from 1951 to 1957 and won enduring popularity in reruns.

amples of intimidation. On Mar. 9, 1954, Murrow narrated a report on Joseph McCARTHY himself, exposing the senator's shoddy tactics. Murrow observed: "His mistake has been to confuse dissent with disloyalty." Offered free time by CBS, McCarthy replied on April 6, calling Murrow "the leader and the cleverest of the jackal pack which is always found at the throat of anyone who dares to expose Communist traitors." In this TV appearance McCarthy proved to be his own worst enemy, and it became apparent that Murrow had helped to break McCarthy's reign of fear. In 1954 the U.S. Senate censured McCarthy, and CBS's "security" office was closed down.

That the McCarthy denouement occurred on television rather than on radio indicated the new medium's importance. The number of television sets in use had risen from 6,000 in 1946 to some 12 million by 1951. As viewers shifted from radio to television, radio's popularity and profit declined. Jack Benny's New York–area rating fell from 26.5% in 1948 to less than 5% in 1951. In 1952, CBS's radio network showed a deficit for the first time since 1928.

Ambitious network programmers with a taste for the experimental scheduled unorthodox series, especially between 1953 and 1955. NBC television president Sylvester Weaver devised the "spectacular," a notable example of which was "Peter Pan" (1955), starring Mary Martin, which attracted 60 million viewers. Weaver also developed the magazine-format programs "Today," which made its debut in 1952 with Dave Garroway as host, and "Tonight," which began in 1953 with Steve ALLEN as host. NBC had been known since 1948 as the home of Milton BERLE on "The Texaco Star Theater." Weaver scheduled other comedy revues, including "Your Show of Shows," starring Sid Caesar and Imogene Coca.

Both NBC and CBS presented such noteworthy dramatic anthologies as "Kraft Television Theater," "Studio One," "Playhouse 90," and "The U.S. Steel Hour." The Radio-Television Workshop of the Ford Foundation added cultural variety to early television programming with "Omnibus" (1952–59), which explored almost every form of artistic endeavor.

The golden age of television programming came to an ignominious end with the sudden popularity of the game show. "The $64,000 Question" and "Twenty-One" shot to the top of the ratings in the mid-1950s. In 1959, however, the creator of "The $64,000 Question," Louis G. Cowan, by that time president of CBS television, was forced to resign from the network amid revelations of widespread fixing of game shows.

Filmed and Videotaped Television.
Cowan's successor at CBS, James Aubrey, doubled that company's profits between 1960 and 1965 by canceling costly, unpredictable live anthologies and scheduling filmed situation comedies, such as "The Beverly Hillbillies" and "Petticoat Junction." CBS's situation comedy "I Love Lucy" had been a favorite since the early 1950s, and the fact that it was on film allowed the network to rerun episodes at low cost. These developments were assisted by the introduction of videotape in 1956, which made it possible to record television signals on magnetic tape for later replay-

Ed Sullivan (left, center), *with his Sunday night variety show, and Walter Cronkite* (right), *anchor (1962–81) of "CBS Evening News," both left their mark on U.S. society. Here, Sullivan introduces the young Beatles to his vast audience. Cronkite's reputation for trustworthiness established America's habit of watching TV news.*

ing. By 1980 recorded programming had virtually replaced "live" television, except for sporting events.

In 1964 broadcasting began in color on prime-time television. The FCC initially had approved a CBS color system developed by Peter Goldmark, then swung in RCA's favor after Sarnoff had swamped the marketplace with black-and-white sets compatible with RCA color. (The CBS color system was not compatible with black-and-white sets, and its introduction would have required the public to purchase new sets.)

On Jan. 12, 1971, CBS introduced a new situation comedy, "All in the Family," that explored prejudice and family strife through its portrayal of a likable bigot, Archie Bunker, played by Carroll O'Connor. The series, the most influential of the 1970s, marked a trend in programming. Other socially conscious series of the era included "The Mary Tyler Moore Show" and "Maude," but daytime television continued to rely heavily on soap operas and quiz shows.

Fred Silverman, chief of ABC's entertainment division,

introduced the miniseries. "Roots" was seen on successive winter nights in 1977 by an estimated 80 million viewers. By 1985 the networks competed for more advertising money and against the attractions of CABLE TV and videocassette recorders.

The Growth of PBS. Prompted by the three commercial networks' abandonment of sustaining or public-service programming, a Carnegie Commission report (1967) recommended the creation of a fourth, noncommercial, public television network built around the educational nonprofit stations already in operation throughout the United States (see TELEVISION, NONCOMMERCIAL). Congress created the Public Broadcasting System that year. Unlike commercial networks, which are centered in New York City, PBS's key stations—all of which produce programs that are shown throughout the network—are spread across the country. PBS today comprises more than 300 stations, more than any commercial network.

Early PBS anti–Vietnam War programming incurred the wrath of the Nixon administration, but nonpolitical

(Left) *Reputedly television's highest-paid performer, Johnny Carson is known for his urbane, mildly indecent monologues and for the sharp repartée with guests on his long-running program, "The Tonight Show."* (Right) *The Public Broadcasting System has attracted enthusiastic audiences with "Masterpiece Theatre," a group of British TV productions. Shown here is a scene from the popular series "Upstairs, Downstairs" (1974).*

imports from British television proved extremely popular. In 1969, PBS broadcast the 26-part British Broadcasting Corporation adaptation of John Galsworthy's *The Forsyte Saga* and followed with other British series. Well-received PBS programming produced in the United States includes SESAME STREET, "The MacNeil-Lehrer Report," "Nova," and occasional shorter series like the 1990 "Civil War," a 5-part documentary that won some of the largest audiences ever achieved by public TV. PBS funds come from three major sources: congressional appropriations (which suffered substantial cuts beginning in 1982), viewer donations, and private corporate underwriters.

Broadcasting—Present and Future

The changes that have occurred in broadcasting over the past decade result in large part from the rapid growth of communications technology, which has caused a burgeoning of new techniques for sending, receiving, and preserving TV signals (see VIDEO). Cable TV and satellite transmission, along with the increasing use of videocassette recorders, have transformed the operations of the industry, as have deregulation and a financial climate that has encouraged mergers and takeovers of some of the oldest and most powerful broadcasting entities. In 1985–86 alone, Capital Cities Communication took over ABC; General Electric bought RCA; Time, Inc. bought Group W Cable; press mogul Rupert Murdoch bought the six stations owned by Metromedia; and WOR-TV (New York) was purchased by MCA, Inc. Many smaller radio stations and cable companies have also changed ownership.

Radio Broadcasting. When television became the major electronic entertainment in the 1950s, the demise of radio was predicted by many experts. Instead, the medium flourishes as strongly now as in its heyday. According to the FCC, in the mid-1980s there were over 3,800 FM stations and 4,800 AM stations—an increase of more than 1,500 in one decade.

There are no more national commercial networks, however. Even the stations controlled by what were once the major networks now have only a local reach. Each station narrowly targets its potential listeners, hoping to attract a specific type of audience.

The advent of satellite transmission has produced a new type of network, however. Radio producers now sell shows, via satellite link, to any station with the equipment to receive them. Many of these network shows are among the most popular on radio and feature such well-known personalities as late-night conversationalist Larry King, news commentator Paul Harvey, and sex therapist Dr. Ruth Westheimer.

Radio's most unexpected success story is the rise in popularity of the two public radio networks, National Public Radio and American Public Radio. Both supply programming to public radio stations across the country. NPR specializes in news and information shows, and its two lengthy news programs, "Morning Edition" and "All Things Considered," attract an audience that grows larger every year. APR produces primarily cultural and music programming. Its most notable success was the two-hour combination of nostalgia, old-time music, and parody,

"The Prairie Home Companion," with its now-famous creator, Garrison Keillor.

The Changing Structure of the Television Industry. From the early days of TV until the coming of cable and satellite broadcasting, the structure of the industry mirrored that of its predecessor, radio. There were the three big national networks, ABC, CBS, and NBC, with headquarters in New York City, and affiliated stations across the country who were fed programming by their networks. Smaller networks existed, but they were shut out of the nationally broadcast programs that the big networks either produced themselves or bought from a small group of independent producers. Advertising rates were based on the size of the national audience for each show, as estimated by a rating system devised by the A. C. Nielsen Co.

The three networks still exercise power in the world of television, but their influence is challenged by a growing system of smaller networks. By 1990, Murdoch's Fox group—7 stations plus 126 independent affiliates—presented a serious challenge to the old network hegemony. Fox now could reach over 90% of American television viewers, with offbeat programming designed to attract the younger audiences that had begun to desert the more staid Big Three network presentations.

Programming now originates from the smaller network groups, as well as from the traditional sources, independent producers and the three networks. Producers eventually sell their successful material—game shows and cartoons as well as "sitcoms" and specials—on a syndicated basis to any station willing to buy.

Cable and Satellite Transmission. In 1990 some 50 million American TV households were wired for CABLE TV and subscribed to one of the 8,700 cable systems that span the country. In 1975, RCA orbited the first COMMUNICATIONS SATELLITE designed for the relaying of TV signals, allowing producers and sellers of TV programs to market

Typical of the new, syndicated breed of animated programs, "The Transformers," a cartoon show for children, is based on a real toy. Such shows are no longer confined to Saturday mornings, but now appear—usually on independent stations—every weekday.

The mid-1980s renaissance of the game show may have been caused by the great success of "Wheel of Fortune," the most popular syndicated show ever.

their products to any cable company with a satellite receiving dish. Today, 65 satellite-transmitted cable networks offer an enormous range of program types, from all-sports systems to religious programs (see RELIGIOUS BROADCASTING) to programs designed for special audiences and various language groups. Most cable networks are supported primarily by advertisers; but the "pay" networks earn their revenues from those viewers who are willing to pay additional fees to their cable system for the privilege of watching special sports events, first-run movies, or programs produced by the pay networks themselves. Both network types also receive fees for each subscriber from the cable systems.

Because of the initial heavy expense of wiring a community with cable—an expense the cable company itself undertakes —most cable systems operate under exclusive franchises made with each municipality. The "must carry" rule that required cable systems to carry all local broadcast channels within a certain radius of their transmitter was struck down in 1985, although the ramifications of that case are still being argued.

To avoid paying the monthly subscription fee (or to gain signal reception in remote areas where cable had not penetrated), many people chose to buy backyard dish antennas, smaller versions of the "earth stations" used by cable operators to capture satellite signals. Considering the use of home dishes a theft of their product, several satellite programmers began to scramble their signals in 1986 so that only cable earth stations could receive them. Others see the home dishes as a positive omen, a sign of the time when every house will own a small receiving dish and, for a fee, receive programs directly off a satellite. Direct Broadcast Satellite systems (DBS) have the advantage—to the programmer—of cutting out the need for cable. All the fees involved would go directly to the broadcaster, increasing profits by at least 50%. DBS has been tried in the United States, but at a time when the most appropriate technology did not exist. Japan will soon have a four-channel DBS service, however, and media tycoon Rupert MURDOCH offers DBS through-

out Europe, via French communications satellites.

Broadcasting Deregulation. The FCC was created in 1934 not only to assign frequencies to radio and, later, television stations, but also to carry out the decision of Congress that—in return for giving broadcasters a license to profit from the use of the radio spectrum ("the public domain")—stations were required to provide some programs that served the public. In essence, they were to act as trustees of the public interest, and every three years television stations appeared before the FCC to receive their license renewals, with logbooks of their daily programming to prove that they were carrying out their trusteeship. The number of stations any one firm or individual could own was limited to 5 on VHF (the stations with the strongest signals, channels 2 through 13), along with 7 AM and 7 FM radio stations.

Within the past decade, however, the FCC has weakened or eliminated the rules that cut into stations' profitability. Broadcasters are no longer required to devote a small portion of their broadcasting day to public affairs and children's shows. In addition, the number of commercials a station may show per hour has been raised. A television station may now keep its license for five years (seven for a radio station) before it need apply for renewal, and it is no longer required to keep a logbook to prove that it has served the public in the ways outlined by Congress. One person or firm may now own up to 12 FM stations, 12 AM stations, and 12 TV stations.

In 1987 the FCC abolished the Fairness Doctrine, a rule that required radio and television stations to offer opposing views on issues of public interest. The FCC agreed with broadcasters, who claimed that, rather than adding to public knowledge, the doctrine discouraged issue-oriented programming.

Internationalization via Satellite. Until recently, television in Europe was a government monopoly, and although there were a few spectacularly successful stations—notably Britain's two BBC channels—by and large, European TV was a fairly dull affair, enlivened now and then by made-for-TV movies by such directors as Federico Fellini and Ingmar Bergman or by American imports. Advertising in most countries was either banned or strictly limited. Stations were maintained by taxes and licensing fees paid by television-set owners.

Direct satellite broadcasting and the coming of cable to Europe have both caused immense changes in European television. Rupert Murdoch's Sky Channel broadcasts 18 hours a day by satellite to some 5 million European homes. Murdoch joined forces with media baron Robert Maxwell to distribute Sky Channel in Britain via Murdoch-owned cable. British Satellite Broadcasting, a consortium of British, French, and Australian firms, plans to launch its own satellite. The French government has already launched one, and it plans to build another. In addition to a concentrated home-cabling program, Germany will loft its own satellite in the 1990s. Eutelstat, a satellite operator that is owned by 26 European telephone organizations, will launch four new satellites in the coming years.

The European Community has agreed to open all its borders to television broadcasts from any of its member nations, and it hopes that a majority of programs shown on EC channels will originate within EC countries. Moral standards have been specified, and the proportion of advertising to be carried has also been agreed upon.

Home dishes for receiving DBS are relatively rare in Europe, but as satellite programming improves and as the dishes themselves become less expensive, they will undoubtedly appear on rooftops throughout the EC. In Japan a state-owned TV network began direct satellite broadcasting in 1987, and within a year half a million home dishes had been bought for $750 each.

radioactive fallout   See FALLOUT

---

radioactivity   Radioactivity is the spontaneous emission of energy in the form of particles or waves (electromagnetic radiation), or both, from the atomic nucleus of certain elements.

History

The discovery of radioactivity occurred in 1896 when Antoine Henri BECQUEREL observed that uranium emitted penetrating rays continuously and without initiation. The term *radioactivity* was coined by Pierre and Marie CURIE to designate this phenomenon. They proved that the radioactivity of uranium was an atomic property and not a chemical one. Marie Curie later discovered the radioactive elements polonium and radium in uranium ore. These elements possess shorter half-lives (the time it takes for the radioactive decay of one-half of a radioactive sample) and are more highly radioactive than uranium.

Research into the radioactivity of pitchblende, an ore of uranium, led Marie and Pierre Curie to discover the radioactive elements polonium and radium in 1898.

The half-life is used because it is statistically the most useful such measure.

Ernest Rutherford showed that one of the components of this radiation was deflected upon passage through a thin sheet of metal. He concluded that this phenomenon was due to positive electric charge repulsion between the metal ions of the lattice and a positively charged particle emitted by the radioactive sample and later shown to be a helium ion (an alpha particle). This led to the postulation of the nucleus and was one of the foundations for the formulation of the structure of the ATOM.

Atomic Structure and Nuclear Transformations

An atom is composed of two major components, a positively charged nucleus surrounded by a cloud of negatively charged particles (electrons). The nucleus is composed of protons and neutrons, which are collectively called nucleons. Protons are positively charged nucleons, whereas neutrons are uncharged nucleons. The sum of protons and neutrons is the atom's mass number.

An atom is neutral with respect to charge, with the number of protons equaling the number of electrons. The number of protons is equivalent to the atomic number, whereas the number of neutrons may vary for a given atomic number; each variation is called an ISOTOPE. Therefore, isotopes of a given atomic number will vary in their mass numbers. Usually, the lighter elements have fewer isotopes than the heavier elements.

An isotope of a given element may be designated with the atomic symbol for the element either preceded or followed by a superscript number representing the mass number, as in ^{14}C or C^{14}. Another accepted designation is the element name followed by a hyphen and the mass number of the isotope, as in nitrogen-15.

Stable and Unstable Nuclei. In general, the proton-neutron ratio as well as their total number determines the stability of the nucleus. Unstable nuclei tend to adjust their proton-neutron ratio to a more stable form by means of the spontaneous disintegration via expulsion of one or more of the nucleons, that is, radioactivity.

Stable isotopes vary in number from element to element, with the naturally occurring element uranium having no stable isotopes. It is not clear why certain combinations of protons and neutrons are stable while others are not.

Unstable nuclei, or radioisotopes, undergo radioactive decay resulting in particle or electromagnetic radiation. Radioisotopes may occur naturally or be produced artificially. The vast majority of radioisotopes are artificially produced, since the only naturally occurring radionuclides (radioisotopes) surviving from the time of the creation of matter are those that decay very slowly, and members of a decay series (naturally produced continuously) are very scarce. Some radioisotopes are produced continually by COSMIC RAY bombardment of atmospheric atoms. Carbon-14 and hydrogen-3 are formed from nitrogen-14 in this manner.

Artificially produced radioisotopes were first synthesized more than 40 years ago when Curie and Joliot transformed aluminum-27 to phosphorus-30. Bombardment

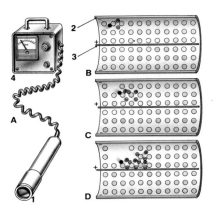

A Geiger-Müller counter (A) detects radioactive particles with a tube (1) containing (B) a negatively charged cylinder (2), neon gas (gray), and a positively charged wire (3). A particle (black) entering the tube knocks out an electron (blue) from a neon atom and forms a positive ion (red). (C) These collide with other atoms. (D) Electrons collect on the wire. A meter (4) records them as a pulse of current.

of stable nuclei with either charged or uncharged particles is the usual method for radioisotope production. This result may be achieved by nuclear reactors, which are the primary source of radioisotopes for biological purposes, by particle accelerators such as the cyclotron and linear accelerator, or by other neutron sources such as a neutron generator.

Types of Nuclear Transformations. In undergoing spontaneous nuclear changes, radioisotopes decay to more stable forms while giving off one or more of three types of emissions: alpha particles, beta particles, and gamma rays. The emission of alpha or beta particles converts one element into another via a nuclear charge change. Gamma radiation is a form of nuclear energy dissipation.

Alpha particle emission occurs only in elements of high atomic weight. An alpha particle is a helium nucleus consisting of two protons and two neutrons. Emission of an alpha particle from a radioisotope results in the formation of another element four mass units lighter and two atomic numbers lower. Examples of this type of radioactive decay include $^{226}Ra \rightarrow ^{222}Rn + \alpha$ and $^{209}Po \rightarrow ^{205}Pb + \alpha$.

Beta particles are of two types, negatrons (electrons) and positrons. Radioisotopes with excess neutrons may decay into a more stable form by the conversion of a neutron into a proton, with the concurrent emission of a negative beta particle (negatron, β^-). Negatron emission results in an increase in atomic number of one unit. Any excess energy in the nucleus is dissipated as gamma rays. Examples of negatron radioactive decay include $^{32}P \rightarrow ^{32}S + \beta^-$ and $^{60}Co \rightarrow ^{60}Ni + \beta^-$.

Radioisotopes with excess protons may become more energetically stable by positive beta particle (positron, β^+) emission. A nuclear proton is converted to a neutron with the concurrent emission of a positron. The atomic number decreases by one unit and any excess energy is emitted as gamma radiation. Examples of positron radioactive decay include $^{13}N \rightarrow ^{13}C + \beta^+$ and $^{15}O \rightarrow ^{15}N + \beta^+$. (See BETA DECAY.)

Gamma radiation, the emission of energetic PHOTONS, most often results in concurrence with beta emission; however, some nuclides decay by gamma ray emission alone. This means of decay does not change the mass number or the atomic number but provides a delayed means of disposing of excess energy from an energetic nucleus. Examples of gamma ray radioactive decay include $^{131}I \rightarrow ^{131}I + \gamma$.

Units and Standards

The rates of emission of radiation for different radioisotopes vary considerably. Each individual radioisotope, however, has its own intrinsic decay rate. The decay constant is defined as the given fraction of atoms disintegrating in a specific unit of time. A more useful way of expressing the decay constant is the half-life. The half-life of a radioisotope is the time it takes for its radioactivity to decrease by one-half. Half-lives vary from fractions of seconds to billions of years.

The standard unit of radioactivity is the curie, which is defined as the number of disintegrations occurring in one gram of radium per second. Radium was chosen because it was available in pure form and has a long half-life, 1,600 years. The curie is equivalent to 3.7×10^{10} disintegrations per second (dps). The curie is a rather large unit, so several fractions of this unit have found wide use. The millicurie (mC) is equal to one-thousandth of a curie, or 3.7×10^7 dps, while the microcurie (μC) is equal to one-millionth of a curie, or 3.7×10^4 dps, or 2.22×10^6 disintegrations per minute (dpm).

The usual state of a radioisotope is as a mixture with a large amount of the stable isotopes of the same element. Specific activity, defined as the amount of radioactivity per given weight or weight equivalent of a sample, expresses the relative abundance of a radioisotope in a sample. Specific activity is often expressed as dps or dpm, counting rates (counts per minute, cpm), or curies, mC, or μC per unit weight.

Measurement of Radioactivity

Radioactivity is quantitated in several ways. Absolute

The three types of rays (alpha, beta, and gamma) emitted by radioactive elements can be distinguished by their penetrating power. Alpha rays are unable to pass through a film of aluminum that is only 0.05 mm (0.002 in) thick, whereas a 1-mm-thick (0.039-in) aluminum foil is needed to stop beta rays. The thickness of material required to stop these rays depends on their energy and on the material. Gamma rays are scarcely affected by a 200-mm-thick (7.87-in) aluminum sheet. The best shielding for gamma rays is an element of high atomic number, such as lead.

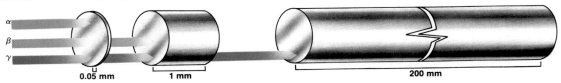

0.05 mm   1 mm   200 mm

counting measures every disintegration occurring in the sample (dps or dpm), whereas relative counting measures a given detected fraction of the true disintegrations occurring (cps or cpm). Relative counting is much easier and is the more frequently used approach.

Several different methods of relative counting are used successfully. These include gas ionization, scintillation, and autoradiography. Gas ionization techniques use the principle of ion pairs formed in gases upon exposure to radiation. An electric potential is applied between two electrodes in a gas-filled ion chamber. The negatively charged ions move to the anode while the positively charged ions move to the cathode. This creates a pulse, which is amplified and recorded. Gas-ionization counting with gas amplification may be achieved using proportional counters or the GEIGER COUNTER.

Scintillation in a solid fluor is a counting technique in which a fraction of the ionizing radiation is transferred to solid compounds that fluoresce. The absorbed energy in the fluor gives rise to visible or near ultraviolet energy emissions (scintillations) that are detected and amplified by a photomultiplier tube and recorded. Scintillation in a liquid fluor is a similar technique, except that the radioisotope and the fluor are dissolved in a liquid medium. Energy transfer goes through the solvent to the fluor and is finally detected as scintillations. Detection, amplification, and recording are similar.

Autoradiography is a photochemical detection method in which a radioactive sample is placed on a photographic emulsion on film. Radiation from the sample interacts with the silver halide in the emulsion. The resulting development of the film allows an estimate of the radioactivity in the sample to be taken.

Hazards and Safety

The effect of radiation on living matter can be quite devastating (see RADIATION INJURY). Therefore, radiation safety and monitoring is particularly important. Radiation safety problems fall into three categories: personnel protection, contamination control, and waste disposal (see NUCLEAR ENERGY).

Energy dissipation must be quantified to determine exposure levels. Biological effects of radiation are determined by the amount of energy absorbed. Therefore the time of exposure and rate of exposure must be defined. The roentgen (R) was defined as the quantity of gamma or X radiation required to produce one electrostatic unit of electricity of either sign per cubic centimeter of dry air. However, the roentgen is valid only for photon interaction with air and does not relate to tissue absorption or particulate radiation. Normally, exposure is expressed in roentgens/hour or milliroentgens/hour. A unit based on the energy dissipation of radiation in biological tissue was devised in 1953 and called the RAD. It was defined as 100 ergs of energy imparted by any ionizing radiation that is dissipated in one gram of irradiated material. The rad is the unit of choice when tissue irradiation is concerned.

Monitoring of radiation is essential to determining exposure. Area monitoring is usually accomplished with portable monitors such as Geiger-Müller survey meters or portable ionization chambers. Personnel monitoring is often achieved by film badges, which develop upon exposure to certain levels or total quantities of radiation.

Disposal of radioactive wastes may be accomplished by maximum dilution or maximum concentration. Disposal by concentration and storage is necessary for high levels of radioactivity.

radiocarbon dating   see RADIOMETRIC AGE-DATING

---

radiography   The technique known as radiography, in which X RAYS are passed through objects to produce photographic images called radiographs, is used for medical and industrial purposes. Because X rays have a short wavelength and high energy, they can easily penetrate most matter. Radiography is used medically to diagnose such disorders as tumors and bone fractures. Industrially, it is used to examine manufactured goods for internal flaws without damaging the product. (See also NUCLEAR MEDICINE; RADIOLOGY.)

---

radioimmunoassay   [ray'-dee-oh-im-yoo'-noh-as'-ay] Radioimmunoassay, an extremely sensitive medical technique, is used to measure the concentration of antigenic substances in the body. The antigen to be measured is injected into an animal, causing the animal to produce antibodies against it. The animal serum containing the antibodies is then treated with a radioactive sample of the same antigen. The reaction between the radioactive antigen molecules and those of their specific antibodies causes radioactive antigen-antibody complexes to be formed. When a solution containing an unknown concentration of the same antigen in nonradioactive form is then added to the solution, competition between the radioactive and nonradioactive forms of the antigen for the same binding sites on the antibodies causes some previously bound radioactive antigen to be displaced from the antibodies and go into solution. The amount displaced is determined by separating the antigen-antibody complexes and measuring the radioactivity remaining in the solution. This amount is proportional to the amount of nonradioactive antigen present in the unknown solution. The measurement of radioactivity can be made with great sensitivity and accuracy in an instrument called a scintillation counter.

Any substance capable of provoking antibody formation in an animal can be assayed by this technique. It is frequently used to measure hormones that are in such low concentration in body fluids that they cannot be measured by chemical methods. Before radioimmunoassay was invented, hormones had to be measured by bioassay, a laborious and inexact method that involved injecting a hormone into animals and measuring its biological effects.

---

radiolarian   [ray-dee-uh-lair'-ee-uhn]   Radiolarians represent a group of strikingly beautiful amoebalike shelled microorganisms in the protozoan class Sarcodina. Although the strong, opal, siliceous skeleton of many radiolarians appears heavy, for example, genus *Hexacontium*, these protozoans are highly adapted for floating. The many fine skeletal spines and thin capsules surrounded by living cytoplasm give a high ratio of surface to volume that retards sinking in the sea, where radiolarians are found exclusively. In addition, vacuoles containing fluid with a low specific gravity give the outer cytoplasm a frothy appearance and increase buoyancy. The siliceous skeleton is secreted by nearly all radiolarians, and needlelike pseudopods—extensions of the body mass for trapping food—project through the shell. The skeletons vary widely among the species, and many exhibit complex geometric designs. Some radiolarians are among the largest protozoans, measuring several millimeters in diameter.

Radiolarians reproduce by multiple division of cell nuclei, but the life cycle is poorly known. In some the preexisting skeleton breaks apart, and each daughter nucleus controls a portion and regenerates the rest to form an entire skeleton. (The outer cytoplasm lacks nuclei but may contain symbiotic smaller protozoans, which may possess chlorophyll, giving the entire radiolarian a greenish appearance.) After death the skeletons of radiolarians sink to the sea bottom. In the central ocean basins, where water depth exceeds 4,500 m (14,800 ft) and calcareous shells of other planktonic organisms dissolve, radiolarian skeletons constitute the primary sedimentary material of the deep sea.

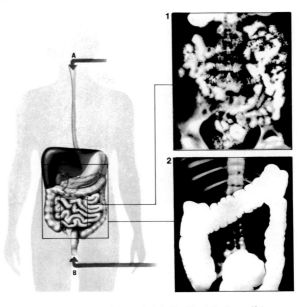

To photograph the organs of the gastrointestinal tract, barium sulfate, a radiopaque fluid, is introduced in the mouth (A) or rectum (B). X rays are absorbed by the fluid, producing a white image on treated film. A trained radiographer can follow the progress of the fluid through the small intestine (1) or large intestine (2), noting the presence of abnormalities.

radiology   Radiology is the branch of medicine specializing in the use of X RAYS, high-strength magnetic fields, high-frequency sound waves, and various radioactive compounds to diagnose and treat disease. A radiologist is a medical doctor and in the United States is required to take a minimum of 4–7 years of radiology specialty training following medical school.

X-Ray Imaging. The field of radiology dates back to 1895. Wilhelm Conrad ROENTGEN was experimenting with light when he unexpectedly discovered a new form of electromagnetic energy that he called X rays. Roentgen found that the rays could penetrate a person's hand, and the outline of bones could be seen on a chemically coated fluorescent screen behind the hand. Roentgen then replaced the screen with photographic film to make lasting pictures of the images. Today X-ray film or RADIOGRAPHY studies are the most common diagnostic radiology procedures. In recent years improved techniques and machines have greatly minimized the risk of RADIATION INJURY due to exposure from X rays.

X-ray studies are often performed as the initial examination to diagnose a wide variety of diseases and injuries. Chest X rays of the lungs can show a variety of respiratory diseases including cancer and tuberculosis. MAMMOGRAPHY, the X-ray examination of the breasts, is frequently used to detect breast cancer at its earliest, most curable stage.

Fluoroscopy, another type of X-ray procedure, produces images of internal body movements on a video screen in real time, that is, while the movement is occurring. Thus, images of the heart expanding and contracting, or intestinal motility, can be recorded on videotape or disk

to be reviewed and evaluated at a later time.

X rays make visible the contrast between tissue of different densities. Some internal body structures, however, have densities so similar that they are difficult to distinguish on conventional X-ray film and fluoroscopic studies. Contrast media (compounds that are opaque to X rays) can be used to highlight these organs. For example, a barium compound taken orally is monitored on a fluoroscopic screen as it moves through the esophagus, stomach, and intestine.

X-ray studies show the size and location of a structure using front, side, or back views of the organ. A highly advanced X-ray procedure, computerized axial tomography, or CAT scan, combines X-ray radiation with computers to produce cross-sectional images of the body. The CAT scan examines a part of the body from many different angles. A detector records the many X rays taken and sends these data to a computer, which produces a composite picture. A CAT scan is useful in examining the brain, spinal cord, bones, lungs, abdomen, and pelvis to determine the site, type, and extent of disease or injury. CAT scans, available since the early 1970s, have revolutionized diagnosis. For example, in head-injury cases, they can determine if there is bleeding inside the skull.

Other Imaging Techniques. In addition to X rays, radiology involves the use of a variety of other newly developed imaging techniques using different types of energy. MAGNETIC RESONANCE IMAGING (MRI) produces two-dimensional visual images of internal structures in any plane using strong electromagnetic fields. In MRI, the patient is

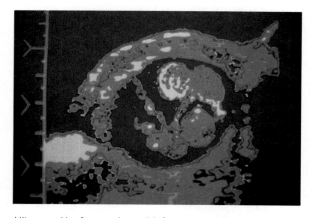

Ultrasound is often used as a risk-free prenatal diagnostic test. It uses sound waves to show the position and viability of a fetus as well as to detect multiple pregnancies, as in the case of the twins shown here.

placed inside a powerful magnet that aligns the hydrogen atoms in the body tissues. A radio signal is directed to the body part being examined, temporarily disrupting this alignment. When the radio signal stops, the hydrogen atoms return to alignment, but not all at the same time, because different body tissues align at different rates. A computer measures the change in realignment and converts the data into an image. MRI is used to evaluate bone, joint, and soft-tissue abnormalities, as well as injuries or tumors in the chest, abdomen, pelvis, brain, and spinal cord.

Ultrasound (see ULTRASONICS) produces images using high-frequency sound waves. When these sound waves come into contact with structures within the body, part of the sound energy is reflected back to the body surface, where it is converted electronically into a picture. This technique is commonly used during pregnancy to deter-

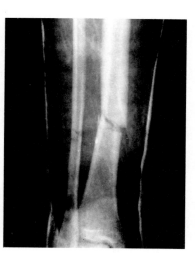

X rays are still the most commonly used diagnostic procedures to detect disease or injury. The ability of X rays to pass through matter depends on the density of the material. Bones, for example, are very dense and block most radiation, causing their X-ray image to appear white, as in this picture of a fractured tibia and fibula in the leg.

mine if multiple fetuses are present, or the position and age of a fetus. An echocardiogram is a useful ultrasonic technique to examine patients with congenital or acquired heart conditions, and Doppler ultrasound detects blood flow in the veins and arteries in the body.

The field of radiology also includes the subspecialty NUCLEAR MEDICINE, in which radioisotopes are introduced into the body. The isotopes are monitored as they travel through the veins and arteries to determine if specific organs are functioning properly. Special cameras measure the intensity of the radiation released by the isotope and allow visualization of parts of organs not usually seen by normal X rays. This method is also used to send a therapeutic dose of radiation to a specific site to kill cancer cells.

POSITRON EMISSION TOMOGRAPHY (PET) uses an isotope that emits a radioactive particle called a positron. These isotopes attach to a variety of chemicals, such as glucose, that are found in the body's metabolism. This procedure not only detects the anatomy of an organ but also the status of its metabolic function, such as brain function and blood flow. It is also useful in diagnosing cancer and Alzheimer's disease.

Single photon emission computed tomography (SPECT), like PET, tracks a radioactive isotope and a computer translates the data into an image showing details about metabolic function. SPECT is proving particularly successful in monitoring heart function.

Radiation Therapy. Interventional radiology uses imaging techniques to guide thin tubes called catheters through veins, arteries, and organs of the body to diagnose and treat a variety of conditions. These techniques are often outpatient procedures and are generally less invasive, safer, and less costly than surgical procedures. Balloon ANGIOPLASTY is a common interventional technique designed to open blocked or narrowed arteries. Guided by fluoroscopy, a balloon-tipped catheter is inserted into the blocked or narrowed blood vessel. The balloon is inflated to open the blocked or narrowed section of the vessel. Other procedures are used to block the arteries to stop them from bleeding or from supplying nutrients to cancerous tumors. Abscesses deep inside the body can be drained and biopsies of internal organs can be obtained using interventional techniques. High doses of anticancer drugs may be supplied directly to tumors via their blood supply.

Radiation oncology is a standard treatment for cancer using X rays, gamma rays, and other forms of energy. A radiation oncologist defines the known and probable extent of a tumor and selects the best type of radiation treatment for the situation—treatment that kills tumor cells while preventing major injury to any surrounding healthy cells. Depending on the treatment plan, radiation may be administered for a few minutes a day 5 days a week for 2 to 6 weeks. Radiation is often used in conjunction with surgery or chemotherapy to treat cancer.

Most cancer patients who are treated with radiation undergo external beam therapy, in which the radiation comes from a linear accelerator, betatron, or cobalt machine and is targeted to destroy the cancer inside the patient. In brachytherapy, radioactive sources such as iodine, cesium, and iridium are put directly into or along-

Mammography, X-ray exams of the breast, can detect cancers too small to be felt. Early detection of breast cancer before it has spread can result in a survival rate of over 90 percent.

side the tumor. One advantage of radiation therapy is that it is usually less traumatic than surgery for the patient. For example, a breast-cancer patient may be able to undergo a lumpectomy, in which only the tumor tissue is removed from the breast, followed by radiation. The alternative treatment would most likely be a mastectomy, in which the entire breast is surgically removed. Some patients with larynx cancer may be successfully treated with radiation, therefore avoiding the surgical removal of the voice box.

radiometric age-dating
Radiometric age-dating, or radiometric dating, is the determination of the age of natural materials such as rock by means of their radioactive contents. RADIOACTIVITY has provided scientists with a powerful new tool for the dating of past Earth events (see GEOLOGIC TIME). Called radiometric age-dating, it is based on the fact that every radioactive element decays. That is, the so-called "parent" element emits radiation and particles until it eventually is transformed by the loss into a stable "daughter" element, sometimes passing through a series of transformations into other radioactive elements before reaching this stability. Each radioactive element also has its own rate of decay, or half-life—the time needed for half of the mass of a radionuclide to be transformed.

Most rocks and minerals contain atoms of one or more radioactive elements. These elements arise from various sources. Some derive from stellar materials from even before the solar system was formed or from materials produced during the early moments of that formation. Their decay rates are so slow and their half-lives so long that some of their atoms have not yet decayed completely. Other radioactive atoms in the Earth are the unstable products of these longer-lived elements. Some radioactive elements are continually being produced, as well, by nuclear reactions caused by the interaction of cosmic rays with molecules in the atmosphere.

The decay of radioactive atoms and the resulting for-

mation of their stable daughters are described by the law of radioactivity. Suppose all the daughter atoms that form by decay of a radioactive parent in a mineral are allowed to accumulate in the mineral. A simple mathematical formula that incorporates the decay rate of the parent element then yields the ratio of daughter to parent atoms after a given period of time. Such equations are used for dating minerals by the potassium-argon (K-Ar), rubidium-strontium (Rb-Sr), and uranium (U) or thorium-lead (Th-Pb) methods. Other methods are also described below. In general, the concentrations of the chemical elements of the parent and daughter must be measured, as well as the isotopic composition (see ISOTOPE) of the element containing the daughter. The isotopic composition—that is, the relative abundances of all naturally occurring isotopes of an element—is measured by MASS SPECTROMETRY.

K-Ar Method. Naturally occurring radioactive potassium-40 decays to argon-40. The minerals datable by the K-Ar method, and variations on the method that also make use of this decay sequence, include the micas and hornblende in igneous and metamorphic rocks, certain kinds of feldspar and unaltered glass in volcanic rocks, and the clay mineral glauconite in sedimentary rocks. K-Ar dates have been used to construct the geologic time scale, to map structural provinces in North America and other continents, and to establish a chronology for reversals of Earth's magnetic field (see PALEOMAGNETISM).

Rb-Sr Method. Approximately one-third of all rubidium atoms are radioactive rubidium-87, which decays to sta-

HALF-LIVES OF SOME RADIOACTIVE ATOMS OCCURRING IN NATURE

Parent	Daughter	Half-Life of Parent* (Years)
Long-lived Parents		
$^{40}_{19}K$	$\rightarrow^{40}_{18}Ar$	11.93×10^9
	$\rightarrow^{40}_{20}Ca$	1.396×10^9
	$\rightarrow^{40}_{18}Ar + ^{40}_{20}Ca$	12.50×10^9
$^{87}_{37}Rb$	$\rightarrow^{87}_{38}Sr$	48.81×10^9
$^{238}_{92}U$	$\rightarrow^{206}_{82}Pb$	4.468×10^9
$^{235}_{92}U$	$\rightarrow^{207}_{82}Pb$	0.7038×10^9
$^{232}_{90}Th$	$\rightarrow^{208}_{82}Pb$	14.01×10^9
Short-lived Daughters of $^{238}_{92}U$		
$^{234}_{92}U$	$\rightarrow^{230}_{90}Th$	2.48×10^5
$^{230}_{90}Th$	$\rightarrow^{226}_{88}Ra$	7.52×10^4
$^{210}_{82}Pb$	$\rightarrow^{206}_{80}Hg$	22.26
Products of Nuclear Reactions by Cosmic Rays		
$^{3}_{1}H$	$\rightarrow^{3}_{2}He$	12.33
$^{10}_{4}Be$	$\rightarrow^{10}_{5}B$	1.6×10^6
$^{14}_{6}C$	$\rightarrow^{14}_{7}N$	5,730

*The half-life (t½) of a radioactive atom is the time required for half of a given number of these atoms to decay. It is related to the decay constant by t½ = ln 2/λ.

ble strontium-87 by emission of a beta particle. The abundance of the strontium isotope relative to radioactive and nonradioactive rubidium isotopes in a rock increases as a function of time according to a well-established mathematical relationship. Most rubidium-bearing minerals, such as the micas, the feldspars, and glauconite, can be dated in this way. In fact, this procedure has been used to date some of the oldest known terrestrial rocks, from Greenland, as well as rocks obtained from the Moon. Stony meteorites have also yielded a date, in this way, that is accepted as a reliable estimate of the age of the Earth: 4.6 billion years.

U or Th-Pb Methods. All the isotopes of uranium and thorium are radioactive and decay to stable isotopes of lead by the emission of alpha and beta particles. Because uranium and thorium commonly occur together, their minerals can be dated by three independent methods involving different decay sequences. (The dates obtained by these methods are often in disagreement, but a graphing technique resolves these difficulties.) Most minerals containing uranium and thorium in relatively large amounts are not suitable for dating, either because they lose the daughter lead or because they are too rare to be useful. The minerals zircon, monazite, sphene, and apatite, in which uranium and thorium occur as trace elements, are used instead. The U and Th-Pb methods have been widely used to date the granitic gneisses of Precambrian age that occur on all of the continents.

Fission-Track Method. When an atom of uranium-238 undergoes spontaneous fission (see FISSION, NUCLEAR), the fragments leave damage trails in crystals that can be made visible under the microscope by etching. The number of such tracks per unit area on a mineral surface is related to its uranium concentration and its age. The observed density of tracks is used to date uranium-bearing minerals and glasses. This method is sensitive to the temperature history of minerals, because of the fading of fission tracks at elevated temperatures.

Common-Lead Method. The isotopic composition of lead in its principal ore mineral, galena, can be treated as a mixture of primordial lead (inherited by the Earth from the solar nebula) and varying amounts of radioactivity-produced lead, depending on the age of the ore deposit. Young deposits contain more radioactivity-produced lead than do older ones, because they had less time for the uranium and thorium to decay. The common-lead method can be used to date the deposits and may reveal the age of the granitic basement rocks that form the continental crust.

Ionium-Thorium Method. Ionium (thorium-230) is a radioactive daughter of uranium-238. It enters the oceans by the discharge of rivers or by decay of uranium-234, its immediate parent. All of the isotopes of thorium in the oceans are rapidly removed to the sediment, whereas uranium tends to remain in solution. This process separates ionium from its parent, and its radioactivity in the sediment therefore decreases with time as it decays to radium-236. The radioactivity contributed by the common thorium isotope thorium-232, however, remains practically constant because of its slow rate of decay. A simple mathematical treatment of the ratio observed between ionium and thorium-232 provides a method of dating sediment recovered from the ocean bottom and determining the rate of sediment accumulation. The method is suitable for dating sediment deposits during the past 150,000 years, which includes the most recent ice age. Other radioactive daughters of uranium-238 may also be used.

Carbon-14 Method. Carbon-14 is a relatively short-lived radioisotope of carbon that is produced in the upper levels of the atmosphere by the interaction of energetic neutrons, produced by cosmic rays, with the nuclei of stable nitrogen-14. The carbon-14 atoms are rapidly incorporated into molecules of carbon dioxide, which is taken up by green plants in the course of photosynthesis. As long as the plants, or animals that feed on them, are alive, the level of radioactivity from carbon-14 in their tissues is constant, because the loss by decay is compensated by the addition of carbon-14 from the atmosphere. When the organism dies, however, the radioactivity decreases with time at a well-established rate. Dating by this method, which was developed by Willard LIBBY, is applicable primarily to materials such as wood, seeds, and bones. It has been used by archaeologists, anthropologists, and geologists to date samples as old as 35,000 years, although 10,000 years has been the more practical limit. Using accelerator-augmented techniques, scientists hope to push this limit back toward 100,000 years.

Tritium Method. Tritium is a naturally occurring radioisotope of hydrogen that is produced in the upper atmosphere by nuclear reactions involving cosmic rays. The natural tritium content of water on the Earth's surface is very low, but significant increases have occurred as a result of the testing of nuclear weapons in the atmosphere. The episodic input of tritium from the atmosphere into the oceans and groundwater has been used to measure the rate of movement of water masses.

radiosonde [ray'-dee-oh-sahnd] A radiosonde is an instrument, carried by an unpiloted balloon, that measures temperature, pressure, and humidity of the atmosphere and transmits the information by radio. Radiosondes were developed independently in France, the USSR, and Germany in the 1920s. Early versions were equipped with a clock or windmill, both of which had a horizontal axis to sequence data into the radio signal for instant recording on the ground. Later types had aneroid barometers, whose motion in response to atmospheric pressure allowed the temperature and humidity data to be sequenced into the radio signal; thermometers; and hygrometers. A giant balloon usually carries many different radiosondes so that they can be calibrated against each other. The United States has a network of about 70 radiosonde stations, and other countries have about 400 more; data from these stations are compiled twice daily (noon and midnight, Greenwich mean time) to provide maps of weather conditions worldwide.

radiotherapy   SEE NUCLEAR MEDICINE; RADIATION THERAPY

radish   The radish, *Raphanus sativus*, is an annual herb that belongs to the mustard family, Crucifereae. It is grown for its fleshy roots, which vary in size from the few grams of the popular red American and European varieties to the one or more kilograms of the Japanese white radish, or daikon. The radish was developed from a wild plant that grew in the cooler regions of Asia. There are three broad categories of radish roots: small, round, spring varieties that mature in 3 to 5 weeks; somewhat larger and more slender varieties that grow into summer; and larger, "winter" varieties that are grown in cooler weather. Some winter types may reach 60 cm (2 ft) in length and are used like turnips. The first two radish categories are generally eaten raw; the winter varieties are cooked.

The edible root of the radish ranges in color from red to red and white to the pure white of the daikon (upper right).

Radisson, Pierre Esprit [rah-dee-sohn']   Pierre Esprit Radisson, *c.*1640–1710, a French fur trader and explorer, played an important role in establishing trade in the Hudson Bay drainage basin of Canada. He went to Canada during childhood and spent more than two years as a captive of Mohawk Indians. In 1659–60 he traded furs and explored in the area west of Lake Superior with his brother-in-law, Médard Chouart des Groseilliers. The French authorities prosecuted them for illegal trading, however, and the partners persuaded the British to establish posts at the mouths of rivers flowing into Hudson Bay. The explorations of Radisson and Groseilliers in 1668–69 encouraged the British to form (1670) the HUDSON'S BAY COMPANY; the partners worked for the new company until 1675.

In 1681, Radisson began work for the Compagnie du Nord, a French rival of the Hudson's Bay Company, but he returned to the Hudson's Bay Company in 1684.

radium [ray'-dee-uhm]   Radium is a radioactive metallic chemical element, the sixth and final member of the ALKALINE EARTH METALS in Group IIA of the periodic table. Its chemical symbol is Ra, its atomic number is 88, and its atomic weight is 226.025. The name is derived from the Latin word *radius*, meaning "ray."

Discovery. In 1896 the French physicist Antoine Henri Becquerel discovered radioactivity in the form of penetrating radiation given off by the element uranium. Polish physicist Marie CURIE continued Becquerel's work. She discovered that the mineral pitchblende showed considerably more activity than could be ascribed to its uranium content. Marie and Pierre Curie carried out laborious fractionations of several tons of uranium residues. While doing so they isolated a new element, radium, in the form of the salt, radium chloride.

Occurrence. Radium is present in all URANIUM minerals, because it is a member of the radioactive disintegration series initiated by the decay of uranium. Pitchblende is the most important of these uranium minerals. It was originally mined in Czechoslovakia, but extensive deposits were later found in Zaire and near Great Bear Lake and Beaverlodge Lake in Canada. About 1 gram of radium can be isolated from about 7 tons of pitchblende. The second most important radium-bearing uranium ore is carnotite, found as a yellowish impregnation of sandstone in the western United States.

Isotopes. The radioactive disintegration of uranium gives rise to the following series, where the half-lives of the isotopes are shown in parentheses: ^{238}U (4.5 billion years) $\rightarrow$ ^{234}U (248,000 years) $\rightarrow$ ^{230}Th (80,000 years) $\rightarrow$ ^{226}Ra (1,620 years) $\rightarrow$ ^{208}Pb (stable). The very short-lived elements of the series have been omitted. In such a system the components are in a steady state, so that each element, apart from the first and last, disintegrates at a rate equal to that at which it is formed. This means that any undisturbed sample of uranium contains a quantity of radium in proportion to the uranium content. The observed ratio is about 1:3,000,000.

Physical and Chemical Properties. The element was first isolated as a pure metal in 1911 by Marie Curie and André Debierne by the electrolysis of a solution of pure radium chloride using a mercury cathode. The resulting amalgam yielded metallic radium upon distillation in an atmosphere of hydrogen. The metal is brilliant white when freshly prepared but blackens on exposure to air, presumably because of the formation of the nitride. The metal and its salts are luminescent, and the element imparts a carmine red color to a flame. Radium metal has a melting point of 700° C, an estimated boiling point of 1,700° C, and a density of 5.5 g/cm³ at 20° C.

The chemical properties of radium are similar to those of other members of the alkaline earth metals, particularly barium. All radium compounds are isomorphous with (have crystal structures similar to) the corresponding barium compounds, and consequently the elements are difficult to separate. Radium exhibits a valency of 2 exclusively.

Compounds. Radium sulfate, $RaSO_4$, is the least soluble of all known sulfates and is useful in the separation of the element from its ores. The nitrate, $Ra(NO_3)_2$, the chloride, $RaCl_2$, and the bromide, $RaBr_2$, are soluble in water but not in concentrated solutions of the corresponding acids. Again, this insolubility is used in purification of the element, especially in separating out the last traces of barium. Radium hydroxide, $Ra(OH)_2$, is the most soluble of the alkaline earth hydroxides.

Uses. Radium is mainly of historic interest now. In its medical and technological uses it has been supplanted by more readily accessible sources. At one time it was extensively employed in the treatment of cancer and for testing metal castings in industrial radiography. Radium salts mixed with zinc sulfide formed a paste once used in luminescent paints for watch and meter dials, but in this application radium has been replaced by the element PROMETHIUM, which emits less hazardous radiation.

radon [ray'-dahn] Radon is the sixth and last member of the INERT GAS series, Group 0 of the periodic table. Discovered in 1900 by F. E. Dorn, this element was called radium emanation, but when isolated by William Ramsay and Robert Whytlaw-Gray in 1908 the name was changed to niton, from the Latin *nitens*, meaning "shining." It has been known as radon (from radium) since 1923 and is given the symbol Rn. The atomic weight of radon is about 222 and the atomic number is 86. An approximate calculation indicates that every 2.6 km^2 (1 mi^2) of soil to a depth of 15 cm (6 in) contains about 1 gram (0.036 oz) of radon-emitting radium, and that radon makes up more than half of normal background radioactivity in the environment.

Radon is a radioactive gas of which 20 isotopes are known, including radon-222 from radium, with a half-life of 3.823 days, and radon-220, also called *thoron*, from thorium, with a half-life of 54.5 seconds. Both isotopes emit alpha particles. The melting point of the element is −71° C, the boiling point is −61.8° C, and the gas density is 9.73 g/l at 0° C. Recent reports have indicated a reaction may occur between radon and fluorine, forming radon fluoride. At room temperature radon is a colorless gas, but when cooled below its freezing point the solid exhibits a brilliant phosphorescence that becomes yellow as the temperature is lowered, and orange red at cryogenic temperatures. Radon has been used therapeutically as an alpha-particle source in the treatment of cancer.

Unsafe levels of radon gas have been discovered in a number of homes throughout the United States. Apparently, radon-222, produced by natural radium in the ground, can enter a house through small fissures or in well water, and remain in the air if unventilated. The radon then decays to radioactive products that can be absorbed in the lungs and can lead, over a long period of time and exposure, to lung cancer. The U.S. Environmental Protection Agency has estimated that from 5,000 to 20,000 lung-cancer deaths each year may be attributed to radon products. It recommends remedial action if radon levels in homes exceed 4 trillionths of a curie of radon per liter of air. So far, proposed remedies for indoor radon pollution, from ventilating houses to releasing air pressure in soil with suction, are extremely expensive.

Raeburn, Sir Henry [ray'-burn] The painter Sir Henry Raeburn, b. Mar. 4, 1756, d. July 8, 1823, was one of Scotland's celebrated masters of portraiture. Raeburn's portraits became fashionable in the 1780s and '90s. His works, painted broadly and rapidly in strong, pleasing colors, have an unmistakably romantic quality, an effect heightened by the often spacious and atmospheric backgrounds. Among Raeburn's approximately 600 canvases are portraits of many famous contemporary Scots. One of the finest collections of his works is in the National Gallery of Scotland, Edinburgh.

Raffles, Sir Thomas Stamford [raf'-ulz] Sir Thomas Stamford Raffles, known as Raffles of Singapore, b. at sea, July 6, 1781, d. July 5, 1826, played a key role in the founding of Britain's East Asian empire. He became an employee of the British East India Company at an early age. During the British rule of Java (in present-day Indonesia), Raffles served (1811–16) as the island's lieutenant governor-general, introducing major administrative reforms.

After Java returned to Dutch control in 1816, Raffles sought a British alternative. He directed the acquisition of the small island of Singapore for the East India Company in 1819 and founded the modern city of Singapore. Pursuing the liberal economic policies proposed by Raffles, Singapore became a thriving free port in the heart of colonial Southeast Asia. In 1824 he returned to London, helping to found the London Zoo and serving as first president of the London Zoological Society. Raffles was knighted in 1817.

Rafsanjani, Hashemi [rahf'-sahn-jah-nee, hash'-mee] Hojatolislam Ali Akbar Hashemi Rafsanjani, b. 1934, succeeded Ali Khameinei as president of Iran on Aug. 3, 1989. From a wealthy merchant family, he was a longtime favorite of Ayatollah KHOMEINI. After the 1979 Iranian revolution, he was speaker of parliament (1980–89), a member of the Assembly of Experts (1982–), and armed-forces commander in chief (1988–89). After being elected to a much-enhanced presidency in July 1989, he named a cabinet that excluded extremists and turned his attention to rebuilding the economy.

rag worm Rag worm is a common name for polychaete annelid worms of the genus *Nereis*. They are also known as mussel worms, pile worms, and sand worms and are found primarily in marine environments, burrowing in mud or sand. Rag worms range from 2.5 to 90 cm (1 to 35 in) in length. The initial head segments bear two palpi, four eyes, several tentacles, and sharp, retractable jaws. These annelids feed on other worms and small marine organisms.

raga see INDIAN MUSIC

Ragnarok [rag'-nuh-rahk] In Norse mythology Ragnarok is the final destruction of the world, when the gods and the giants will slaughter one another and in the process destroy all creation. According to the Icelandic Eddas, the giants will be led by the traitor-god LOKI and will attack ASGARD, the dwelling place of ODIN and the other major divinities. Their coming will be signaled by Heimdall, who will sound a mighty blast on his horn. After the destruction, creation will begin anew.

ragtime Ragtime was the most popular music idiom in the United States from 1896 to 1917. The style originated on the blackface minstrel stage (see MUSIC HALL, VAUDEVILLE, AND BURLESQUE), and the term means "ragged time," referring to the music's syncopated, offbeat rhythm. The most popular rags were such songs as "Hello! Ma Baby" (1899), "Under the Bamboo Tree" (1902), and "Alexander's Ragtime Band" (1911); of the many thousands of instrumental rags, the most famous was Scott JOPLIN's "Maple Leaf Rag" (1899). Thousands of rags reached the public in the form of sheet music, piano rolls, and recordings, but ragtime was also an improvised art and in this latter practice was a direct predecessor of JAZZ. Rags were designed both for listening and for dancing the cakewalk, two-step, one-step, fox-trot, and turkey trot.

Current interest in ragtime is focused primarily on the piano music, especially the "classic rags" of Joplin, James Scott, Joseph F. Lamb, and Eubie BLAKE. During the early 1970s, republication of Joplin's music and a succession of recordings stimulated new interest in ragtime. Joplin's rag "The Entertainer" (1902) was used in the award-winning film *The Sting* (1973) and created an even broader public for ragtime.

ragweed Ragweed is any of about 35 species of widely distributed, annual or perennial plants of the genus *Ambrosia* in the daisy family, Compositae. The common ragweed, *A. artemisiifolia,* is a coarse, typically hairy-stemmed annual growing to about 1.5 m (5 ft) high, with usually deeply divided leaves. Its minute, greenish flowers with yellow stamens are borne in tiny clusters spaced along a slender, erect stalk. The giant ragweed, *A. trifida,* an annual with three-lobed leaves, reaches a height of 4.5 m (15 ft). Ragweed pollen is the most prevalent cause of autumn hay fever in the United States. The seedlike fruits form an important part of the winter diet of birds.

Rahner, Karl [rah'-nur] Karl Rahner, b. Freiburg im Breisgau, Germany, Mar. 5, 1904, d. Mar. 30, 1984, is regarded by many as the foremost Roman Catholic theologian of the 20th century. He is perhaps best known for the work he did on the fundamental relationship between the order of nature and the order of grace, specifically on the possibility of self-transcendence. Although not avoiding controversial questions, Rahner always stressed the continuity between modern interpretations of Catholic doctrine and their original formulations.

rail Birds of the family Rallidae are called rails. The birds' bodies are usually narrow enough to enable them to slip through dense vegetation, such as that found in the marshes they typically inhabit. Rails ordinarily remain on the ground and are difficult to flush, secretive, and sometimes nocturnal in habit. Some rails forage at dawn and dusk. Commonly heard rather than seen, they emit certain calls, often clicking or ticking sounds, characteristic of the species.

These small to medium-sized birds have moderate to long legs and long toes, which are advantageous for walking or running over soft ground. They are usually but not always gray, brown, and dull red; the sexes look alike. Bills range from stubby to elongate, depending on the species. Rails are omnivorous, but many species feed mainly on small animals. Nests generally are well hidden. Clutches generally contain 6 to 12 eggs, and both sexes usually take part in incubation.

Rails are distributed throughout the world except in polar regions. About 132 species are recognized. Despite the fact that they have stubby wings, a high ratio of weight to wing area, and apparently weak flight when flushed, some species migrate long distances, often flying at night. Species of various islands have independently evolved flightlessness. Rails on islands have proved vulnerable to human-caused disturbances, and at least 12

The king rail (top), *a chicken-sized bird, usually inhabits freshwater marshes. The smaller Virginia rail* (right) *lives in fresh and brackish water. The sparrow-sized black rail* (bottom) *prefers coastal salt marshes.*

species and subspecies have become extinct within the past 300 years.

The rail family also includes gallinules and coots. Gallinules typically are marsh dwellers, and some have brightly colored bony shields covering the forehead and iridescent plumage. The coots have lobed toes specialized for swimming and diving.

---

railgun　A railgun is a device that uses electromagnetic forces to accelerate projectiles to high velocities. A strong pulse of electricity is sent through a pair of parallel rails, generating a magnetic field that accelerates a conducting projectile to speeds that have reached 10 km/sec (6.2 mi/sec) in tests. Possible applications include inexpensive launching of payloads into space and creation of thermonuclear fusion reactions by collisions between high-speed projectiles.

---

railroad　A railroad, called railway in Great Britain, is a form of land transportation in which a permanent roadway with parallel rails provides a track for cars drawn by locomotives or for self-propelled motor units. The principle of the flanged wheel (one having a projecting rim to guide it along a track) rolling on iron or steel rails furnishes a low-cost, high-volume, reliable mode of transport.

When railroads appeared in the early 19th century, they soon gained a major role in the Industrial Revolution, and the first successful lines were those built in the developing industrial nations. By the mid-19th century railroads had proven superior in several ways to earlier forms of transportation, such as turnpikes, canals, and steamboats. (See the article TRANSPORTATION for a discussion of the various modes of transport.) Later, railroads followed industrial development to the other continents.

Railroad History

As early as the 16th century, crude railways—horse-drawn wagons with wooden wheels and rails—were used in mining operations in England and western Europe. By the 18th century their use was improved with the introduction of cast-iron wheels and rails.

In England horse power began to be replaced by the power of the STEAM ENGINE when Richard TREVITHICK, John Blenkinsop, and William Hedley successfully invented, built, and operated several steam locomotives between 1797 and 1813. George STEPHENSON built and equipped the Stockton & Darlington Railway between 1823 and 1825.

Railroads in the United States. Following the pioneer work of British inventor-engineers, the first railroads appeared in the United States during the late 1820s. In 1827 the merchants of Baltimore, Md., chartered the Baltimore & Ohio Railroad. In 1830 the South Carolina Railroad began passenger service on a 9.6-km (6-mi) stretch of track with the U.S.-built *Best Friend of Charleston*, becoming the first railroad in the nation to use steam power in regular service.

In the 1830s the new form of transport gained acceptance, although there was some opposition, especially from canal owners and stagecoach operators worried about the competition to their businesses.

In 1850, 60% of the nation's rail mileage was located in New England and mid-Atlantic states. By that time, U.S. railroads were clearly superior to turnpikes, canals, and steamboats.

Perhaps no decade of rail growth in the United States was more important than the 1850s. What had been a scattering of short lines from Maine to Georgia then grew into a rail network serving all the states east of the Mississippi River.

The period between the Civil War and World War I was a golden age for U.S. railroads. For nearly 50 years after 1865 no new modes of transport seriously challenged this developing mode of transportation. The completion (May 10, 1869) of the first TRANSCONTINENTAL RAILROAD lines—the Union Pacific–Central Pacific line—which covered 2,848 km (1,780 mi) from the Missouri River to the Pacific Ocean, was one of the first major building efforts after the Civil War. Four of the five Pacific railroads, along with dozens of other western lines,

A locomotive of the Canadian Pacific Railway, one of Canada's two largest railroad companies, winds through the Rocky Mountains of western Canada. Today this privately owned railroad is increasingly used for efficient overland freight transportation.

Officials of the Union Pacific and Central Pacific railroads shake hands to mark the completion of the transcontinental railroad. As part of the ceremonies, a golden spike was driven to join the two rail lines on May 10, 1869, at Promontory Point, Utah.

were aided in these years by land grants from the federal government.

During the decades after the Civil War a host of technical advances made possible a new integration and uniformity of railroad service. These innovations included the introduction of more powerful locomotives, the use of larger and more varied types of cars, the general adoption of a track gauge (the distance between the inside faces of the rails) known as standard track gauge (1.44 m/4 ft 8½ in), and the general acceptance of the air BRAKE invented by George WESTINGHOUSE, improved couplers, and standard TIME ZONES.

The decades prior to World War I were also years of corruption and various forms of discrimination. False-front construction companies used in building western lines gave extra profits to builders such as Thomas Clark DURANT, who helped organize the CRÉDIT MOBILIER OF AMERICA for building the Union Pacific. Cornelius Vanderbilt (see VANDERBILT family), James FISK, and Jay GOULD were all masters at inflating and manipulating the securities of their lines. The evils of railroad pools, rebates, discriminatory freight rates, and charging "all the traffic will bear" contributed to agitation by western farmers for Granger laws, which regulated railroads and their freight rates in the 1870s (see GRANGER MOVEMENT). After the U.S. Supreme Court ruled that interstate commerce could be regulated only by the federal government, the U.S. Congress in 1887 approved federal regulation of railroads with the Interstate Commerce Act, which provided for establishment of the INTERSTATE COMMERCE COMMISSION (ICC).

Early in the 20th century a number of new modes of transport were developed: electric interurbans (lines that connected neighboring towns); private automobiles; intercity buses; larger trucks; airplanes carrying mail, passengers, and high-priority freight; and a growing network of pipelines.

The heavy wartime traffic from 1941 through 1945 helped the railways recover from the hard times of the Depression. Following World War II the railroads replaced the steam locomotive with more efficient diesel-electric locomotives (see DIESEL ENGINE) and introduced new, more efficient freight services. Nevertheless, by the mid-1970s, ten railroads in the Northeast and Midwest were in bankruptcy.

During the years after World War II the federal government tended to favor competing modes of transport with more generous subsidy programs and with less stringent regulation than those covering railroads. However, the 1971 introduction of the federally subsidized passenger service known as AMTRAK helped to relieve railroads of the annual passenger-service deficits they had known for many years. In addition, the Staggers Rail Act of 1980 substantially reduced the Interstate Commerce Commission's jurisdiction over railroads, permitting rail operators greater freedom to set rates, abandon or sell unprofitable lines, and offer service innovations.

Other Railroads in the Western Hemisphere. The total rail mileage in Canada, Mexico, and Central America amounts to about a third of that in the United States. In Canada the first rail service started in 1836, and by 1880 the network had expanded to about 11,200 km (6,960 mi). The CANADIAN PACIFIC RAILWAY was completed across the Rockies to the Pacific by 1885. In Mexico the majority of the 20,200 km (12,550 mi) of track is built in standard gauge, and the government-owned National Railways of Mexico operates nearly two-thirds of the total mileage.

More than 96,000 km (59,065 mi) of railway are in operation in South America, with much built in narrow gauge. Today the major mileage in the continent is located in three countries: Argentina, Brazil, and Chile.

Alfred de Glehn's compound, four-cylinder steam engine was invented in the 1890s for the Northern Railway of France. It could exceed 120 km/h (75 mph).

The Dunalastair class of locomotive, used by the Caledonian Railway, was one of the most successful engines in Scottish railway history.

The giant Beyer-Garratt articulated steam locomotive has drawn freight trains in South and East Africa since the early 1900s.

The Flying Hamburger of the German State Railways, introduced in 1932, was the first high-speed diesel-electric locomotive.

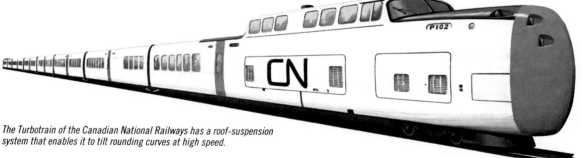

The Turbotrain of the Canadian National Railways has a roof-suspension system that enables it to tilt rounding curves at high speed.

British Railways' High Speed Train broke the world record for diesel trains at 230 km/h (143 mph) when it was introduced in 1973. Railway companies are now investigating new designs, including magnetic levitation trains and linear electric motors, which may reach speeds of up to 480 km/h (300 mph).

The Railroads of Europe. After the United States, the greatest concentration of rail mileage is found in Europe. Subsequent to the success of the Stockton & Darlington Railway, others quickly followed. The Liverpool & Manchester, which opened in 1830, used steam power for both passenger and freight service. Quite early the government insisted upon the uniform use of standard (1.44 m/4 ft 8½ in) gauge.

France had its first railway line by 1828, and Belgium, Germany, Italy, the Netherlands, and Russia all had some railroads in operation by the 1830s. Countries that were slower to industrialize were building railways by 1850. Most of the European countries followed the English in using standard gauge. Aside from the USSR, the European nations with the greatest mileage today are Germany and France.

Unlike some industrial states, the USSR has continued to build railroads in recent years. In 1891, Russia started the TRANS-SIBERIAN RAILROAD; upon its completion, from Moscow to Vladivostok in 1916, it was the longest continuous rail line in the world (9,259 km/5,787 mi). Because of the great size of the USSR, its large population, and its limited highway transport, Soviet railroads lead the world in freight service (ton-miles per year).

Railroads of Asia, Africa, and Australia. Other than the Soviet Union, the major Asiatic nations with extensive railroad systems are India, China, and Japan. Indian lines were built extensively in the 1.66 m (5 ft 6 in) gauge and also in the meter (3 ft 3 in) gauge. China built its first lines in the 1870s. Japan built its first lines in the 1870s and today has nearly 27,200 km (17,000 mi) in operation, most of it in 1.05 m (3 ft 6 in) gauge. The development of railroads in Africa accompanied the European colonization of the 19th century. The first railroad in Australia was opened in 1854 and now includes 40,000-km (25,000-mi) of track.

Railroad Operations

The three essential elements of a railroad are: (1) the roadbed and track, including necessary fills, cuts, bridges, and tunnels; (2) the LOCOMOTIVE, which may be steam, electric, or diesel-electric; and (3) the rolling stock.

Roadbed and Track. In the planning and construction of a new railroad, the first step is for surveyors and civil engineers to seek out and survey a route, then establish standards relative to grade (inclination of a track), curvature, gauge, and quality of construction. Builders of railroads must make an early decision concerning track gauge. Because the English were the pioneer builders of railroads and locomotives, their adoption of a standard gauge of 1.44 m (4 ft 8½ in) was to be widely followed. There are some economies of construction that result from using narrow gauge in mountain or frontier lines. Today standard gauge is universally used in North America and Europe and is found on about 60% of the world's total mileage.

Once the roadbed is fully graded, wooden ties, or sleepers, are distributed, and the rails are laid and spiked. Later a ballast of crushed rock or slag is applied, the track is aligned, and the ballast is tamped, or com-

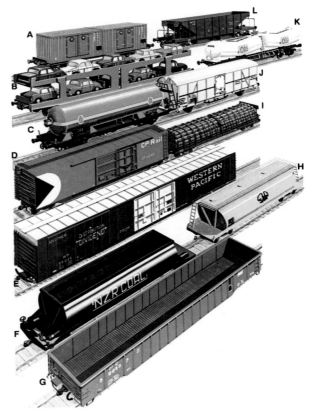

Freight cars of varying functions used by railroads around the world include a flatcar (A) bearing storage containers used by Coras Lompair Eireann of Ireland, a car carrier (B) of the French National Railways, a tank car (C) used by the Austrian Federal Railway to haul liquid gas, boxcars of the Canadian Pacific (D) and Western Pacific (E) railways, a coal-hopper car (F) of the New Zealand Railways, an open gondola car (G) of the Penn Central Railway, a grain-hopper car (H) of the South Australian Railway, a flatcar (I) of the Finnish State Railway, a refrigerated car (J) of the Italian State Railway, a cement car (K) used by British Rail, and a hopper car (L) of Indian Railways.

pacted, around the ties. The earliest rails were made of wood; later track often consisted of iron-strap rails fastened to long wooden stringers. In the 1830s, Robert L. Stevens of the Camden & Amboy Railroad designed the iron T-rail, which was fastened to ties with spikes. This type of rail soon became standard. Welded rail, in lengths of 0.8 km (0.5 mi) or more, is used on most U.S. mainline track today.

Locomotives. The first motive power on many railroads was horses or mules, but most lines quickly adopted steam locomotives. As trains grew longer and heavier during the 19th century, so did the locomotives. By the 1950s most railroads were shifting to diesel-electric motive power.

Cars and Rolling Stock. The early railroad passenger and freight cars were little more than stagecoaches and wagons fitted with flanged wheels. In the United States it did not take long for passenger cars and freight cars to be lengthened, with rigid axles being replaced by four-wheel swivel, or bogie, trucks at each end to improve the turning characteristics. European cars generally were shorter and frequently had only four wheels instead of the eight common in the United States.

Sleeping cars were introduced in the United States by the time of the Civil War, or before, but they appeared in England only after 1870. In the late 1860s, George M. PULLMAN was building dining cars and sleeping cars for some American lines. In the mid-20th century, streamlining, lightweight cars, domed observation cars, and economy slumber coaches were introduced by some U.S. lines as they sought to halt a decline in railroad passenger traffic. Since taking over the management of intercity rail passenger services in 1971, Amtrak has begun to revitalize the American passenger car fleet.

Changes in both size and type have appeared in freight equipment. In the mid-19th century, U.S. freight cars tended to be of three types: the open-top car, the boxcar, and the flatcar, each having a capacity of no more than 10 tons. European freight cars have increased only modestly in size, while the capacity of American cars has expanded greatly. The average capacity of freight cars in the United States in 1988 was 78 metric tons (86 U.S. tons). Among the types of freight cars most commonly used in the United States are open hopper cars (primarily used for hauling coal), covered hopper cars (for grain and other bulk commodities), tank cars used for hauling chemicals and other liquids, and flat cars, which can carry containers or highway truck-trailers "piggyback," or on which can be mounted multilevel racks for carrying automobiles. Piggyback freight traffic is the fastest-growing segment of the U.S. rail industry.

Traffic Control. As railroads expanded and developed, one area of high priority was internal communication and the necessary control and direction of all train movement. Because the telegraph was invented at about the same time that railroads were appearing in the United States and western Europe, this new mode of communication was soon adopted and widely used by most railroads. By the turn of the century the telephone began to supplement the telegraph. Various types of trackside signals and SEMAPHORES were improved in the 1860s when a manual block signal system was introduced. Soon after World War I, a system of automatic train control was introduced. Today, centralized traffic control permits a single operator to control all train movements over distances up to several hundred kilometers.

Labor. The wide variety of railroad occupations in the United States provided jobs for 299,000 people in 1988, most of them members of unions. Engineers had established their union in 1863, conductors in 1868, firemen and enginemen in 1873, and trainmen in 1883. The largest railroad union, the United Transportation Union, had about 100,000 active members in 1990.

Over the past decades, the unions have been forced to change work rules (see FEATHERBEDDING) and to offer labor concessions. In part these concessions have been granted because new technologies have made it possible to run railroads more efficiently and safely with smaller crews of operators and maintenance personnel.

Problems for Today's Railroads

Almost all railroads today face serious and continuing financial problems. The United States has heavily subsidized a highway system and in effect subsidizes the trucks that use it. Water and air carriers are also subsidized. Most of the world's railways are now state owned. Today the only substantial rail mileage still privately owned is in Canada and the United States. Although large railway systems like those in France, Italy, Germany, and Great Britain have a volume of rail travel at least twice that of the United States (and Japan's is 15 times as large), none of these nationalized rail systems is profitable.

In the United States, however, the Staggers Rail Act of 1980, which partially deregulated many aspects of rail freight operations, has allowed U.S. railroads to compete more effectively for traffic. New technology has allowed employment levels to be reduced. Mergers, consolidations, and reorganizations have resulted in fewer but larger Class I systems, and less total mileage. Concurrently, hundreds of regional and local short-line railroads have sprung up as major systems have sold off trackage they could not operate profitably. Today, railroads move nearly as much freight as trucks, barges, and airlines combined, and do it with an improved technology that has allowed them to operate with fewer employees and less equipment.

High-Speed Trains

In 1964 the Japanese began to operate their famous "bullet" train, the Shinkansen, which runs from Tokyo to Nagoya, a 338-km (210-mi) trip that the train is capable of completing in 1⅓ hours, at an average speed of about 258 km/h (160 mph). It runs on a specially constructed "dedicated" track, and each car is separately powered by four electric motors.

The French completed their *train à grand vitesse* (TGV)

A Japanese high-speed, or "bullet," train travels along an elevated track through Tokyo. This train has been successful in Japan, where rail-passenger volume is the heaviest in the world.

The German-designed Maglev (Magnetic Levitation train) rides 1.27 cm (0.5 in) above its track, lifted and guided by powerful magnets in its undercarriage.

in 1981. It makes the Paris-Lyon trip—much of which requires climbing extremely steep gradients—at speeds of up to 274 km/h (170 mph). It, too, uses "dedicated track" over much of its route; however, it employs electric-powered locomotives.

British High Speed Trains roll on rehabilitated track, which is also shared by freight trains. "Tilt" trains, used successfully by Canada, travel at high speeds on conventional tracks, but compensate for the sharp curves that freight trains travel at low speed by using coaches that tilt, or "bank," as they negotiate the turns.

In the most revolutionary new train design, the Maglev (Magnetic Levitation train), the train glides over a raised track, or guideway, lifted a few inches above the guideway surface by a magnetic field. Both Germany and Japan have worked on Maglev prototypes for several years. The Japanese are experimenting with a system whereby the train is raised off the track by repulsive magnets within the guideway. The Germans' attractive system uses electromagnets set on the bottom of the train's undercarriage wings that encircle the edges of the guideway. When current flows through the magnets they are drawn toward a steel rail on the underside of the guideway, and the train rises. Various other magnetic systems guide the train within the guideway walls, and brake or add speed.

Railway Brotherhoods *Railway Brotherhoods* is a collective term for the several railroad labor organizations; most of them were founded as brotherhoods or orders rather than unions because they were originally conceived of as mutual-benefit insurance associations and professional or fraternal societies.

When these organizations were founded (the first in 1863) in the second half of the 19th century, railroad operating employees usually were skilled and highly trained, leading to strong feelings of professional kinship in their organizations. Eventually, however, all brotherhoods were pushed from their original fraternalism toward trade-union militancy and then toward industrial unionism. By the

1920s all were functioning as trade unions as well as brotherhoods. The term *the Brotherhoods* eventually came to mean all railroad labor unions, although one, the Switchmen's Union of North America (SUNA; founded 1894), does not trace itself back to an actual brotherhood.

Rail employment has declined since World War II and so has brotherhood membership. In 1969 the principal brotherhoods—the Brotherhood of Railway Trainmen, the Brotherhood of Locomotive Firemen and Engineers, the Order of Railway Conductors, and the SUNA—merged into the United Transportation Union.

rain see PRECIPITATION (weather)

rain forest see JUNGLE AND RAIN FOREST

rainbow A rainbow is a colored arc in the sky, occurring when the Sun's rays shine upon falling rain. Every rainbow is a full circle; the full circle of arc cannot be seen from the ground but may be observed from an airplane. The center of the circle is always at a point in the sky opposite the Sun. The size of the visible portion of the rainbow depends on the altitude of the Sun, being largest when the Sun is at the horizon. Because the radius of a rainbow is 42°, it cannot be seen when the altitude of the Sun is greater than 42°; no part of the rainbow would be above the horizon. A rainbow exhibits the colors of the spectrum—the inner part is always violet and the outer red. Occasionally a second, larger arc (50° radius) is seen with the colors reversed.

A rainbow is a result of internal reflections of the Sun's rays by the individual drops of water. The second rainbow is caused by rays that undergo a second internal

A rainbow is created when rays of sunlight are bent by atmospheric water particles acting as prisms. Each color within the ray of white light is refracted at a different angle, forming successively wider bands of color (A). Together these bands produce a full spectrum (B). Spectra from many raindrops combine to form a circular pattern, the rainbow (C). Ony a short segment of the circle is visible to an earthbound observer. The position of this arc in the sky varies according to the viewer's position, but its angular size is always the same (D). A cross section (E) shows that all bands of a given color refract in the same direction relative to the source of light, the Sun.

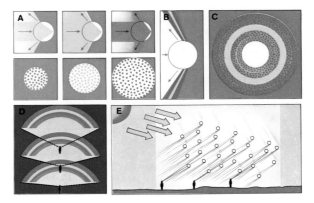

reflection. The coloring of the rainbow is a result of the dispersion of the Sun's rays into its component colors by the water drops.

See also: DISPERSION; REFRACTION.

Rainier, Mount [ruh-neer'] Mount Rainier (4,392 m/ 14,410 ft) forms the heart of Mount Rainier National Park, Washington. A dormant volcano in the Cascade Range, it has been carved by many glaciers. George Vancouver sighted the mountain in 1792 and named it for fellow navigator Peter Rainier.

Rainier III, Prince of Monaco [ren-yay'] Prince Rainier, b. May 31, 1923, succeeded his grandfather, Prince Louis II Goyon de Matignon-Grimaldi, as ruler of Monaco on May 5, 1949. On Apr. 18, 1956, he married Grace KELLY, the U.S. film actress. She died in 1982.

rainmaking SEE WEATHER MODIFICATION

raisin Raisins are grapes that have been dried, usually in sunlight. Grapes used for raisins must be densely fleshed and have a high sugar content. The most important varieties are Thompson seedless, a white grape that produces the raisin known as Sultanina and Oval Kishmish; the ancient grape variety Muscat of Alexandria, a white, seeded grape producing raisins that are large and meaty and are often sold in clusters; and Black Corinth, which yields the small raisins that are marketed as Zante Currants. Among the world's largest producers of raisins are Turkey, the United States (particularly the state of California), Greece, Australia, and Iran.

rajah [rah'-jah] Rajah, or raj (from the Sanskrit *rajan,* "king"), is a Hindu title once given to Indian kings and princes but also used later by lesser rulers and by tribal chiefs. The appellation is frequently assumed by rulers and chiefs in Malaysia. The title *maharajah* ("great king") was often taken by Indian princes under the British rule.

Rajasthan [rahj'-uh-stahn] Rajasthan, a state in northwestern India, covers an area of 342,214 km^2 (132,130 mi^2) and has a population of 34,261,862 (1981). The capital is JAIPUR. The Aravalli Hills cross Rajasthan from southwest to northeast, and the THAR DESERT covers most of the northwest. The principal rivers are the Chambal, the Banas, and the Luni. Cotton, grains, and vegetables are grown in the southeast. Industry is based on petroleum, wool, minerals, chemicals, and handicrafts.

Most of the state consists of the former historic region of Rajputana. The Rajputs ruled the area from the 7th century until it came under Mogul control in the 16th century. After 1817, Rajputana gradually came under British protection. In 1947 it was reorganized as the independent Union of Rajasthan, which became part of India in 1950.

Rajput [rahj'-poot] The Rajputs are one of the largest CASTES in northwest India, mostly concentrated in the state of Rajasthan. They claim *Kshatriya* or warrior status—unlike other high caste groups, the Rajputs freely indulge in meat-eating and the consumption of alcohol. Historically, the Rajputs came to the fore during the 8th century, when they founded a number of princely states. Later, they came under the control of the MARATHAS, and after 1818 under British rule.

Despite their claims to warrior status, most Rajputs are peasant cultivators today. They are organized in status-ranked groups that trace ancestry through the male line. Most marriages are between women from lower-status groups and higher-status men. Status claims of Rajputs are made clear through marriage alliances, and therefore marriages involve large dowries and heavy expenditures on ceremonials. Although most Rajputs are Hindus, some are Muslim. In the 1980s the Rajputs numbered more than 14 million.

Rákosi, Mátyás [rah'-koh-shee, maht'-yahs] Mátyás Rákosi, b. Mar. 14, 1892, d. Feb. 5, 1971, dominated the Communist regime of Hungary after World War II. A Stalinist, Rákosi was exiled in the USSR during World War II. He returned to Hungary in 1944 with the victorious Soviet troops. Becoming secretary of the Communist party, Rákosi gained complete control of Hungary by 1949 and was premier from 1952 to 1953. His regime was characterized by police terror, collectivization of agriculture, and nationalization of the economy. After the death of Joseph Stalin, Rákosi was replaced as premier by the reformer Imre NAGY. When the Hungarian Revolution broke out in 1956, Rákosi fled to the USSR.

Raleigh [rah'-lee] Raleigh is the capital of North Carolina and the seat of Wake County. Located in the east central part of the state, it has a population of 207,951 (1990). The city's industries manufacture food products, textiles, and electrical machinery. Raleigh is part of the Research Triangle complex, devoted to cultural, scientific, and educational research. Notable historical buildings include the Greek Revival capitol and U.S. president Andrew Johnson's birthplace. The city is the seat of North Carolina State University (1887) and Shaw University. The North Carolina Museum of Art is also located there.

Raleigh was named for Sir Walter Raleigh. The area was chosen as the site of the state capital in 1788, and a town was laid out in 1792. The first capitol (1792–94) burned in 1831, and the present building was completed in 1840. During the Civil War the city was occupied by Gen. William Tecumseh Sherman's Union troops on Apr. 14, 1865.

Raleigh, Sir Walter [raw'-lee] Sir Walter Raleigh, or Ralegh, b. *c.*1552, d. Oct. 29, 1618, English military commander, writer, and favorite of Queen ELIZABETH I, or-

Sir Walter Raleigh, English courtier, military adventurer, and poet, was a favorite of Queen Elizabeth I. He organized the first English colonizing venture in the New World, the ill-fated settlement on Roanoke Island, Va. Imprisoned by James I in 1603, Raleigh was finally released (1616) to lead an expedition to find gold in South America.

ganized an early and unsuccessful attempt to found a settlement in North America—the so-called lost colony of Roanoke. Raleigh was educated at Oxford and took part in military operations in France as early as 1569. In 1578 he sailed on a voyage of exploration under command of his half brother, Sir Humphrey Gilbert.

In 1584, Raleigh was knighted by Elizabeth and awarded a patent authorizing colonization of lands in North America; he christened these lands Virginia in honor of the Virgin Queen. Raleigh never visited Virginia himself, and the attempt at settlement on Roanoke Island (in present North Carolina) failed. For a time in the 1590s, Raleigh was out of Elizabeth's favor because of her displeasure over his marriage to one of her maids of honor, Elizabeth Throckmorton. He was imprisoned briefly in 1592 but was later restored to the queen's good graces. He distinguished himself as a naval commander in expeditions to the Guiana coast of northeastern South America (1595), Spain (1596), and the Azores (1597). He was governor of the Isle of Jersey (1600–03).

Raleigh fell into serious disfavor when JAMES I succeeded to the throne; his political enemies had convinced the new king that Raleigh had conspired against James's succession. Raleigh was found guilty of conspiracy in 1603, then imprisoned in the Tower of London for 13 years. In 1616 he persuaded James to allow him to undertake another expedition to search for gold in South America. When this expedition failed, he was sent back to the Tower, partly because Spain demanded his punishment for sacking a Spanish settlement in Guiana. He was then executed, under the original sentence.

Raleigh was active as a member of Parliament under Elizabeth and was a great patron of writers, especially Edmund SPENSER. His most famous work is probably his unfinished *History of the World* (1614).

Ramadan [rah-mah-dahn']

The ninth month of the Muslim year, Ramadan is a period during which all the faithful must fast between dawn and dusk. Observance of the fast is one of the five "pillars" of ISLAM. Because a lunar calendar is used, Ramadan falls at different times each year. It is sacred as the month in which the Koran was revealed to Muhammad.

Ramakrishna [rah-mah-krish'-nuh]

Ramakrishna, or Paramahansa Sri Ramakrishna, b. Feb. 20, 1836, d. Aug. 16, 1886, is perhaps the most famous Indian holy man of recent times. A Bengali Brahmin originally named Gadadhar Chatterji, he experienced ecstatic mystic visions as a child. He became a priest at the temple of Kali in Dakshineswar near Calcutta and experimented with many different religious practices, including Tantra, Vedanta, Vaishnava cults, Islam, and Christianity. He pronounced that all religions were directed toward the same God along different paths. His pupil VIVEKANANDA founded (1897) the Ramakrishna Mission, which is committed to social service in India and the teaching of Ramakrishna's ideas.

Raman, Sir Chandrasekhara Venkata [rah'-muhn, chuhn'-druh-sek-ah-ruh veng'-kuh-tuh]

The Indian physicist Sir Chandrasekhara Venkata Raman, b. Nov. 7, 1888, d. Nov. 21, 1970, worked mainly in optics and acoustics, fields to which he was drawn by a deep, almost mystical fascination for everything related to sight and sound. His most memorable achievement, honored by the 1930 Nobel Prize for physics, was the discovery (1928) that when visible light is scattered, the scattered light undergoes shifts in wavelength. The Raman effect lent support to the photon theory of light and furnished a valuable tool for probing the nature of matter.

Ramapithecus   SEE PREHISTORIC HUMANS

Ramayana [rah-mah'-yuh-nuh]

Unlike the *Mahabharata*, the other great Sanskrit epic of India, the *Ramayana* appears to be the work of one person—the sage Valmiki, who probably composed it in the 3d century BC. Its best-known recension (by Tulsi Das, 1532–1623) consists of 24,000 rhymed couplets of 16-syllable lines, organized into 7 books. The poem incorporates many ancient legends and draws on the sacred books of the Vedas. It describes the efforts of Kosala's heir, Rama, to regain his throne and rescue his wife, Sita, from the demon King of Lanka.

Rameau, Jean Philippe [rah-moh']

The most important French composer and theorist of the 18th century, Jean Philippe Rameau, baptized Sept. 25, 1683, d. Sept. 12, 1764, is best known for his stage works and keyboard music. After studying under his father and, briefly, in Milan, Rameau held several important posts as organist before settling permanently in Paris in 1722. During his last six years, Rameau engaged in bitter polemics about musical style with the philosophers D'Alembert and Rousseau.

Rameau's preeminence as a music theorist is based on 12 treatises and many articles written from 1722 (the year of his groundbreaking *Treatise on Harmony*) to 1762. From 1733 to 1757, Rameau composed his most important stage works, including the tragic operas *Hippolyte et Aricie* (1733), *Castor et Pollux* (1737), *Dardanus* (1739), and *Zoroastre* (1749); the opera-ballets *Les Indes galantes* (1735) and *Les Fêtes d'Hébé* (1739); and the lyric comedy *Platée* (1745). In Rameau's dramatic music, complex harmony and the expanded role of the orchestra point directly to high-classic opera. Rameau also composed three collections of harpsichord pieces (1706, 1724, *c.*1728), four motets, six cantatas, and a set of chamber works.

ramjet   Also called the stato-reactor or athodyd (a shortened form of aerothermodynamic duct), the ramjet is in principle one of the simplest possible propulsion units. It is essentially a duct open at front and rear (an early nickname was "the flying stovepipe"). At high speed, air is rammed into the front of the duct and is highly compressed by the varying profile of the interior, the profile depending on whether the airflow is to be subsonic or supersonic. At the region of peak pressure and minimum velocity, the fuel is injected into the airflow in a combustion section, where it is ignited. Temperatures can be higher than in gas-turbine engines because there is no turbine to impose such a limitation. The intensely hot gas then expands to highly supersonic speed through the divergent propelling nozzle. Unlike gas-turbine jet engines, the ramjet can be used only to propel moving atmospheric vehicles; its main drawbacks are that it cannot start from rest by itself and that its efficiency is poor except at supersonic speeds.

Although its promise seemed great at the end of World War II, the ramjet has been employed in few aircraft. Ramjet missiles have rarely been used, but various types, especially combined with solid-fuel rockets in so-called ram-rockets, are under development for missile propulsion.

Rampal, Jean Pierre   The French flutist and musicologist Jean Pierre Rampal, b. Jan. 7, 1922, whose delicate phrasing and powerful breathing produce luscious and sonorous tones, is equally at ease interpreting music of the 18th, 19th, and 20th centuries. After stints as solo flutist first with the Vichy (1946–50) and Paris (1956–62) Operas, Rampal has combined concert performances, recitals, and a vigorous recording schedule.

Ramsay, Sir William   The British physical chemist Sir William Ramsay, b. Oct. 2, 1852, d. July 23, 1916, received the 1904 Nobel Prize for chemistry for his discovery of the INERT GASES. From a conversation with Lord RAYLEIGH in 1894, Ramsay learned that nitrogen prepared chemically is always lighter than nitrogen prepared from air. Ramsay hypothesized that this results from the existence of some heavier gas in atmospheric nitrogen, and he isolated this new gas, argon, at the same time as Rayleigh. A lighter inert gas, helium, had been observed earlier in the Sun, but in 1895, Ramsay announced the existence of terrestrial helium. Beginning in April 1895, Ramsay worked with Morris W. Travers in a search for other inert gases. By evaporating liquid air and removing oxygen and nitrogen, they found krypton in 1898. From liquid argon they separated a fraction in which they observed spectroscopically the red presence of neon. Later in 1898 they obtained another inert gas, xenon, from the krypton residue. When F. E. Dorn discovered the last inert gas, radon, its atomic weight was determined (1904) by Ramsay.

Ramses II, King of Egypt   An Egyptian king (pharaoh) of the 19th dynasty, Ramses II (r. 1304–1237 BC) is remembered for his military campaigns and his extensive building program, the remains of which are still conspicuous. Succeeding his father, SETI I, Ramses pursued a vigorous foreign policy by attacking the HITTITES, the chief opponents of the Egyptian empire in the East. His first campaigns against them (1300–1299 BC) ended in an Egyptian retreat after a violent battle at Kadesh in Syria, during which Ramses narrowly escaped capture. The consequent loss of prestige sparked revolts within the empire, and Ramses could not resume direct hostilities against the Hittites until 1294; the conflicts were finally concluded by a peace treaty in 1283. He also fought in Trans-Jordan and Nubia and fortified the western coast road of Egypt against Libyan invaders.

Ramses was responsible for building many large temples, most notably that at ABU SIMBEL in Nubia. He also founded a new royal capital at Per-Ramesse ("the house of Ramses") in the Nile's eastern delta, where Israelites

Ramses II, the third king of the Egyptian 19th dynasty, is depicted in this stone sculpture. His 67-year reign was a time of great prosperity and marked the height of Egyptian military power, culminating in a peace treaty (1283 BC) with the neighboring Hittites.

may have labored before the Exodus. During his long reign, Ramses had more than 100 children, and by his death in 1237, he had outlived 11 sons. He was succeeded by the 12th, Merneptah.

Ramses III, King of Egypt   Ramses III, a pharaoh of the 20th dynasty, saved Egypt from foreign invasion but failed to solve internal problems that led to the collapse of the Egyptian state 80 years after his death. Succeeding his father, Sethnakhte, c.1198 BC, Ramses fought off Libyan invasions in 1194 and 1188 and in 1191 held back a horde of invading SEA PEOPLES of Aegean and west Anatolian origins. Despite external successes, royal power declined: the temples became richer and Ramses poorer; government was corrupt and inefficient; and Ramses himself was nearly assassinated before being succeeded by his son Ramses IV about 1166 BC. He was buried in the Valley of the Kings.

Ramus, Petrus [ray'-muhs]   Petrus Ramus (Pierre de la Ramée), b. 1515, d. Aug. 26, 1576, was an influential French anti-Aristotelian logician. His master of arts thesis (1536) was entitled *Quaecumque ab Aristotele dicta essent commentitia esse* (Whatever Aristotle Has Said Is a Fabrication). He created a new two-part logic to replace Aristotle's *Organon*. The orthodox Aristotelians at the University of Paris responded by securing a royal decree (1544) that suppressed Ramus's books and forbade him to teach logic. In 1547 this ban was lifted, and Ramus was appointed (1551) professor of rhetoric and philosophy at the Collège Royal. In 1562 he embraced Calvinism; he was killed during the Saint Bartholomew's Day Massacre.

Rand, Ayn [rand, yn]   A Russian-born American writer who originated a philosophy known as Objectivism, Ayn Rand, b. Feb. 2, 1905, d. Mar. 6, 1982, advocated capitalism in economics and individualism in ethics. Two novels, *The Fountainhead* (1943) and *Atlas Shrugged* (1957), contain the heart of her philosophy: that rational self-interest should be the basis of action and that self-fulfillment is an individual's moral responsibility, with productive achievement the noblest activity. She saw altruism as both a personal and a political weakness.

Randolph (family)   The Randolphs rank among the most eminent and influential families in the history of Virginia. The founder of the Virginia Randolphs, **William Randolph**, b. c.1651, d. Apr. 11, 1711, immigrated to the colony of Virginia from Warwickshire, England, about 1673. There he amassed large landholdings and was twice Speaker of the House of Burgesses (1696 and 1698). Through the marriages of his children, the Randolphs became allied with most of the other notable families of Virginia. Both Thomas Jefferson and John Marshall were related, through their mothers, to the Randolphs.

Edmund Randolph was the first U.S. attorney general and later succeeded Thomas Jefferson as secretary of state. Earlier in his career, as governor of Virginia and a delegate to the Constitutional Convention, Randolph had played an important role in drafting the U.S. Constitution.

Peyton Randolph, b. Williamsburg, Va., September 1721, d. Oct. 22, 1775, grandson of William, also served as Speaker of the House of Burgesses—during most of the crucial years prior to the American Revolution. He was the first president of the Continental Congress and chairperson of the Virginia Committee of Correspondence. His nephew, **Edmund Randolph**, b. Williamsburg, Va., Aug. 10, 1753, d. Sept. 12, 1813, was appointed aide-de-camp to Gen. George Washington in 1775. After the American Revolution he was prominent in Virginia politics and was the state's governor (1786–88). In 1787 he attended the CONSTITUTIONAL CONVENTION and introduced the influential Virginia Plan—also called the Randolph Plan. He later served (1789–94) as first attorney general in the new federal government and then as secretary of state (1794–95).

Randolph, A. Philip   Labor leader Asa Philip Randolph, b. Crescent City, Fla., Apr. 15, 1889, d. May 16, 1979, organized (1925) the Brotherhood of Sleeping Car Porters, which helped carry American blacks into the

A. Philip Randolph organized the Brotherhood of Sleeping Car Porters in an era when black workers were often excluded from unions. He became a leader in the U.S. labor movement and a spokesman for civil rights.

mainstream of the U.S. labor movement. As a student in New York City, he became involved in labor and socialist movements. He began (1917) a monthly magazine, *The Messenger,* which was later an important source of communications for the railway union and which encouraged greater black militancy. Randolph also worked for civil rights and influenced the organizing of President Franklin D. Roosevelt's Fair Employment Practices Committee to protect blacks in industry and government. In 1955, Randolph became vice-president of the newly merged AFL-CIO. He directed the 1963 March on Washington for Jobs and Freedom.

Randolph, Edward   Edward Randolph, baptized July 9, 1632, d. April 1703, was a controversial and unpopular British colonial official in America. Sent (1676) by the Lords of Trade to investigate Massachusetts, he submitted a critical report of the colony's government that led to the revocation (1684) of its charter. Appointed (1678) surveyor of customs for New England, Randolph antagonized the colonies by his attempts to enforce the British trade laws. In 1685 he was named secretary of the newly created Dominion of New England, a union that incensed many colonists. After the GLORIOUS REVOLUTION (1688–89), the Dominion was overthrown, and Randolph was jailed and returned to England. He soon gained favor there, however, and served (1691–1703) as surveyor general of all the American colonies.

random variable   A random variable is a numerical quantity associated with a chance-influenced experiment or phenomenon. The value it takes is not known with certainty before the experiment is performed or the phenomenon is observed, although the probabilities of all its possible values or outcomes are assumed to be fixed by some PROBABILITY law. Thus, if an experiment involved tossing a coin six times, the number of heads observed would be a random variable; it would not be known in advance exactly how many heads would be observed.

random walk   see STOCHASTIC PROCESS

range finder   A range finder, often used in military and photographic equipment, is an instrument that determines the distance from a home reference point to a distant object by optical and trigonometric means. Light from the object passes directly through a fixed, semitransparent mirror so that a person can see and keep the image of the object in view. Light from the object also travels to another mirror, which reflects the image to the semitransparent mirror. The viewer sees two images superimposed on one another, and the angle of the second mirror is adjusted until the direct image and the indirect one coincide. The distance between the two mirrors is fixed by the equipment so that the angle to which the second mirror is adjusted can be determined. The distance between the object and the instrument is then calculated by dividing the distance between the two mirrors by the tangent of that angle.

Ranger   Ranger was a series of U.S. spacecraft that were designed to provide, in the 20 minutes before impact on the Moon, about 300 close-up photos per minute of the lunar surface that could be used for increased accuracy in mapping, for studies of small-scale structure, and for the initial stage of selecting landing sites (see also LUNAR ORBITER; SURVEYOR) for the manned APOLLO PROGRAM missions to follow. The best Earth-based photos of the Moon up to 1963, taken with the 120-in (305-cm) telescope at the Lick Observatory, had a resolution of about 270 m (890 ft). By comparison, the best Ranger photos, taken by *Ranger 9* just before impact, had a resolution of approximately 0.25 m (10 in).

The Spacecraft. All of the Ranger spacecraft, which weighed about 365 kg (810 lb), were launched by an Atlas-Agena rocket from Kennedy Space Center. After Earth orbit was attained, the Agena second stage was briefly restarted (prior to separation from the spacecraft) in order to inject Ranger into a lunar trajectory. After midcourse corrections, the spacecraft crashed into the Moon at approximately 9,700 km/h (6,000 mph) about 66 hours after launch.

The Missions. The early missions, beginning in 1961, failed to meet their objectives but were followed by three successes. *Ranger 7,* launched on July 28, 1964, made impact 3 days later on the Sea of Clouds. It sent back 4,316 photos, the best of which had a resolution of 0.41 m (16 in). *Ranger 8* left the Earth on Feb. 17, 1965, and

In 1964, Ranger 7 transmitted close-up pictures of the Moon for about 13 minutes before striking the lunar surface. Numbers indicate: omnidirectional antenna (1); aperture (2), 33 cm (13 in), for camera lenses; solar panel latches (3); solar panels (4), capable of supplying 200 watts of power; battery (5); attitude-control gas storage (6); high-gain dish antenna (7); attitude-control electronics (8); conical camera shroud (9), 1.5 m (5 ft) high, housing six television cameras.

impacted on the Sea of Tranquility. It took 7,137 photos, showing a wide variety of features, including the first close-up views of the lunar highlands. *Ranger 9,* last of its line, was launched on Mar. 21, 1965, and impacted on the Moon inside the crater Alphonsus. The 5,814 photos provided the first close-up views of a lunar-crater interior.

The improved resolution of the Ranger photos over their Earth-based counterparts revealed several previously unknown aspects of the Moon, such as the small-scale topography. The photos showed striking similarities between mare and crater floors, a smoothed appearance in numerous shallow depressions, and a relative absence of rubble over substantial portions of the surface. *Ranger 9's* target, the crater Alphonsus, gave signs of a complex history influenced by both internal and external forces. The mare in the photos showed an absence of large mountain ranges as well as of impact-saturated areas containing numerous overlapping craters. This discovery influenced the selection of mare regions as preferred sites for the Surveyor and Apollo landings.

See also: SPACE EXPLORATION.

Rangoon [ran-goon']   Rangoon (renamed Yangon in 1989), the capital and largest city of Burma (Myanmar), is located on the Rangoon River in southern Burma, approximately 40 km (25 mi) inland from the Gulf of Martaban at the center of a rice-growing region. The city has a population of 2,458,712 (1983 est.).

The city's focal point—the ancient Buddhist Shwe Dagon Pagoda—is the center of Burmese religious life. Rangoon is the industrial center and chief port of Burma,

The Sule Pagoda, surrounded by smaller, similarly shaped stupas, rises from the central business district of Rangoon. Long a center of the Buddhist religion, Rangoon is today the political and economic capital of Burma.

although its once-flourishing economy has stagnated since the 1960s. River, road, and rail facilities connect the city with the rest of the country; a canal links it with the Irrawaddy River. The University of Rangoon was established in 1920.

During the mid-18th century the founder of the last Burman royal dynasty, Alaungpaya, established a port at the small coastal town of Dagon and renamed it Yangon (Rangoon), meaning "end of strife." The city became the capital of Lower Burma. The British first occupied the city between 1824 and 1826 and returned in 1852 following a second Anglo-Burmese War. Rangoon became the capital of all Burma following British annexation of the entire territory. With independence in 1948, Rangoon became the nation's capital.

rank, military   Military rank is the system of titles that forms the hierarchy of the armed services.

Army Rank.   Modern army rank traces its origins to the mercenary companies of Renaissance Italy, at the time when professional soldiers began to replace part-time feudal warriors. At the head of the company stood the headman (Latin *caput,* "head"), from which is derived the title captain, or later, in Germany, *Hauptmann.* The captain was assisted by a deputy, or lieutenant (Latin, *locum tenens,* "place holder"). Both depended on a number of trustworthy soldiers who carried the title of sergeant, which was derived from that of the feudal warrior's personal attendants (Latin, *servientem,* "serving"). All modern ranks, with minor exceptions, are derived from these three. As armies grew larger, companies were organized into columns. The modern rank of colonel is derived from the head of each column (Old Italian, *colonnello*). When armies grew larger still in the 17th century, superior officers were generally appointed to command the whole army; for them general was added to the original company titles. In this way evolved the ranks of lieutenant general, captain general, and colonel general. At the same time the title major was attached to some of the lower ranks to indicate special responsibility. The ranks of captain major (now major) and sergeant major developed in this way. The latter could also be a general rank (sergeant major general), but that title was abbreviated to major general.

The rank of marshal is derived from two Old High German words, *marah,* "horse," and *scalc,* "caretaker" or "servant." In the Teutonic tribes that overran the Roman Empire, the tribal chief's principal servant was his horse master (*Marah Scalc*). When the chiefs became kings of their conquered territories, the master of horse became a high court officer and, in wartime, the head of the cavalry. Later, in some countries, the courtly and military offices were divided; in Britain, for example, the earl marshal became, effectively, a civilian, and field marshals were appointed to command armies in the field.

When armies became permanent state organizations during the 17th century, the grant of rank became a royal prerogative, usually conferred by a commission from the king to a trusted subject. These commissioned officers in

MILITARY RANK IN U.S. ARMED FORCES*

Army	Navy	Air Force	Marine Corps
Officers			
General of the Army	Fleet Admiral	General of the Air Force	
General	Admiral	General	General
Lieutenant General	Vice Admiral	Lieutenant General	Lieutenant General
Major General	Rear Admiral (upper half)	Major General	Major General
Brigadier General	Commodore (wartime only)	Brigadier General	Brigadier General
	Rear Admiral (lower half)		
Colonel	Captain	Colonel	Colonel
Lieutenant Colonel	Commander	Lieutenant Colonel	Lieutenant Colonel
Major	Lieutenant Commander	Major	Major
Captain	Lieutenant	Captain	Captain
First Lieutenant	Lieutenant (junior grade)	First Lieutenant	First Lieutenant
Second Lieutenant	Ensign	Second Lieutenant	Second Lieutenant
Warrant Officers			
Chief Warrant Officer (W-4)	Same as Army	Same as Army	Same as Army
Chief Warrant Officer (W-3)	Same as Army	Same as Army	Same as Army
Chief Warrant Officer (W-2)	Same as Army	Same as Army	Same as Army
Warrant Officer (W-1)	Same as Army	Same as Army	Same as Army
Enlisted Personnel			
Sergeant Major of the Army (only one)	Master Chief Petty Officer of the Navy (only one)	Chief Master Sergeant of the Air Force (only one)	Sergeant Major of the Marine Corps (only one)
Command Sergeant Major or Sergeant Major	Master Chief Petty Officer	Chief Master Sergeant	Sergeant Major or Master Gunnery Sergeant
First Sergeant or Master Sergeant	Senior Chief Petty Officer	Senior Master Sergeant	First Sergeant or Master Sergeant
Sergeant First Class	Chief Petty Officer	Master Sergeant	Gunnery Sergeant
Staff Sergeant/Specialist 6	Petty Officer First Class	Technical Sergeant	Staff Sergeant
Sergeant/Specialist 5	Petty Officer Second Class	Staff Sergeant	Sergeant
Corporal/Specialist 4	Petty Officer Third Class	Sergeant or Senior Airman	Corporal
Private First Class	Seaman	Airman First Class	Lance Corporal
Private	Seaman Apprentice	Airman	Private First Class
	Seaman Recruit	Airman Basic	Private

*Coast Guard rank is the same as the Navy.

turn appointed suitable soldiers in their regiments to hold the minor ranks, which thus became known as noncommissioned. During the 19th century, officers of outstanding ability for whom a superior rank could not be immediately found were sometimes awarded a brevet to the next rank, which guaranteed them promotion when a vacancy occurred. It also became common practice to issue a warrant to the most senior of the noncommissioned officers, henceforth called warrant officers, which ensured that they could not arbitrarily be demoted. In most countries warrant officers now constitute an intermediate rank between commissioned and noncommissioned officers.

By 1900 the system of officer ranks was standard throughout the major armies, although some national variations existed. In the French army, for example, the major is known as commandant. The U.S. Army created for World War I hero Gen. John J. Pershing the field-marshal equivalent of general of the armies (subsequently army), whereas the USSR, which originally scorned rank titles, now has a more elaborate hierarchy than does any other country. Air force titles in most countries are similar to ranks in the army.

Navy Rank. The first naval title to acquire general currency was that of admiral, which was derived from the Arabic *amir-al-bahr,* "prince of the sea." The term was brought back to Europe by the Crusaders, who spelled it by analogy with the Latin *admirabilis,* "admirable." As late as the 16th century, however, the word was applied as often to the commander's ship as to the man, who was more often called general, captain, or captain general. In the British Royal Navy of the 17th century a man held title only while in post and on a ship of the line. He therefore came to be called a post captain, and vessels smaller than a sixth-rate ship were commanded by a master and commander, the common merchant title (abbreviated in 1794 to commander). Not until 1860 did Britain officially accord titles of rank to naval officers who were not actually in post. Custom, however, had long done so—to include also the captain's deputy, the lieutenant, and the apprentice officers, the midshipmen. During the 19th century the extra rank of lieutenant commander was invented to distinguish senior lieutenants in larger ships. In

1861 the rank sublieutenant was added. In the French and German navies the names of types of ships were attached to officers' ranks. *Capitaine de frégate,* for example, outranked *capitaine de corvette.*

In the higher naval ranks the old divisions of the line of battle—rear and van, the latter always commanded by the admiral's deputy, or vice admiral—had become attached to flag (admiral's) rank to give the titles in use today. In the Royal Navy the most senior officer had also long been known as admiral of the fleet, a title that became a rank in 1863. Its equivalent was *Grossadmiral* in the German Navy, which also used the unusual next rank of *Generaladmiral.* The U.S. Navy, which had generally followed British usage in these forms, adopted the title of fleet admiral in World War II.

Rank, Otto Otto Rank, b. Apr. 22, 1884, d. Oct. 31, 1939, was an Austrian psychoanalyst and associate of Sigmund Freud's. He was adept at applying analytical concepts to mythology and the arts. In stressing birth trauma—separation anxiety at birth—as the prototype of all subsequent anxiety, Rank both made his main contribution to psychoanalytic theory and necessitated his separation from Freud.

Ranke, Leopold von [rahn'-ke] The German historian Leopold von Ranke, b. Dec. 21, 1795, d. May 23, 1886, is considered a pioneer in the development of critical historical scholarship. Trained as a classical philologist, Ranke applied critical methods of text analysis to the study of modern history. Ranke insisted that history be written on the basis of the careful examination of primary sources. Teaching at the University of Berlin from 1825, he organized research seminars in which he trained several generations of historians in historical method. In his great works—*History of the Latin and Teutonic Nations from 1494 to 1514* (1824; Eng. trans., 1846), *The History of the Popes* (3 vols., 1834–36; Eng. trans., 1908), *History of the Reformation in Germany* (6 vols., 1839–

47; Eng. trans., 3 vols., 1845–47), *Civil Wars and Monarchy in France in the Sixteenth and Seventeenth Centuries* (5 vols., 1852–61; incomplete Eng. trans., 2 vols., 1852), and *A History of England, Principally in the Seventeenth Century* (7 vols., 1859–69; Eng. trans., 6 vols., 1875)—Ranke traced the development of the modern European world. His heavy reliance on documents contributed to a history that focused on the foreign affairs of the great powers and on military events and gave considerable emphasis to religious ideas.

Rankin, Jeannette [rang'-kin] Jeannette Rankin, b. Missoula, Mont., June 11, 1880, d. May 18, 1973, was an American feminist and pacifist and the first female member of the U.S. House of Representatives. She was elected to the House in 1916 as a Republican from Montana and served one term, during which she voted against U.S. entry into World War I. Elected to a second term in 1940, Rankin was the only representative to vote against war with Japan the following year. In the late 1960s she was active in opposing the Vietnam War.

Ransom, John Crowe [ran'-suhm] John Crowe Ransom, b. Pulaski, Tenn., Apr. 30, 1888, d. July 3, 1974, promoted the NEW CRITICISM in a book of that title (1941). One of the group of Vanderbilt University poets known as The Fugitives, Ransom contributed to their magazine and to their manifesto *I'll Take My Stand* (1930). From 1937 to 1938 he taught at Kenyon College and for 21 years edited the *Kenyon Review.* One of his best-known poems is "Bells for John Whiteside's Daughter," a graceful, deeply ironic lament for a child's death. Ransom's *Selected Poems* (1963) won the 1964 National Book Award for poetry.

rap music Rap music is not music so much as a unique combination of street-smart African-American ghetto rhyming talk, cannibalized recorded sound, and—in its initial years—break dancing. An extremely difficult acrobatics using head spins, rump spins, hand walking, and flips of all kinds, break dancing appeared on the streets of New York City in the mid-1970s, about the same time that black disc jockeys began to manipulate their offerings by mixing sounds from several records, playing them backward or replaying short sections repeatedly, all against a steady beat supplied by a synthesizer or yet another recording. Rapping to this musical collage soon followed. Rap was at first a swaggering, slangy language heavy with references to drugs, sex, and The Man (whites), but by the late 1980s it had become sanitized, comprehensible to whites, and popular. (In honor of break dancing, rap is often called "hip hop music.")

rape (crime) Rape is usually defined as the act of forcing sexual intercourse upon an unwilling victim. In the

Leopold von Ranke, a 19th-century German historian, appears in a portrait by Julius Schrader. Ranke applied analytic methods to the study of history, particularly to the evaluation of source materials.

United States, rape was traditionally considered an act that occurred only against females and only outside marriage. In recent decades, however, some states have broadened the legal definition to include other forms of sexual contact and to include spouses and males as possible victims.

Legally, there are two kinds of rape, forcible and statutory, and both are treated as felonies in the United States. Forcible rape is defined as sexual intercourse with a nonconsenting victim through the use or the threat of force. Statutory rape is defined as sexual intercourse with a person under a specified age. This age varies from state to state and country to country but usually ranges from 12 to 18 years. Sexual intercourse with a person who is mentally deficient or unconscious and therefore incapable of giving consent is also sometimes considered statutory rape.

Rape and Criminal Justice. The origin of rape laws can be traced to the widespread belief that women were the property of men. A female was considered first the property of her father. Because her virginity was valued as her principal asset, rape was considered a theft. Once a woman was married, she belonged to her husband. Rape then was treated as a crime against the husband's exclusive sexual rights to her. Because marriage gave these rights to the husband, legally, it was not possible for him to rape his own wife.

Because penalties for rape were severe, rape laws came to include elements that protected men against false accusation. The consent of the victim was often at issue, and the defense frequently argued that the woman had not resisted her alleged attacker. By the 20th century it had become increasingly difficult in U.S. courts for the victim to legally prove that she had been raped. She had to establish, often with a corroborating eyewitness, that intercourse had taken place, that it had not been provoked, and that violence had been threatened.

Rape is considered the most underreported of the violent crimes. It has been variously estimated that 50 to 90 percent of rapes occurring in the United States are not reported—because of shame, threat of retribution, or the victim's fear that she will not be believed. Convictions are difficult to obtain, and, even when convicted, the average rapist spends less than four years in jail for the offense. Reported incidents of rape have increased dramatically since the 1970s, although it is unclear whether this is the result of a growing willingness to report the crime.

Impact of the Women's Movement. During the 1970s the women's movement helped to redefine rape as a crime of violence. In many Western countries legal definitions of rape have been expanded to differentiate degrees of sexual assault and to adjust the penalty according to the extent to which aggressive force is used. The aim of such changes is to allow more active prosecution.

Women's groups have developed rape-crisis and counseling centers to help victims and to inform both professionals and the public. These centers aid victims in coping with their feelings after a rape and support them as necessary in dealing with the medical, police,

and legal systems. Additionally, some hospitals and police departments have implemented similar programs to help the victim. Preventive measures taken to deter the incidence of rape, particularly on college campuses in the United States, include improved street and corridor lighting, protective escort services, and self-defense training.

---

rape (plant)   Rape, or colza, is a hardy annual herbaceous variety of the plant species *Brassica napus* of the mustard family, Cruciferae. In North America rape is raised primarily as a forage and cover crop; in Eurasia rape is grown for its oil-containing seeds. Rape is about 90 cm (3 ft) tall with smooth, blue green foliage and clusters of yellow, four-petaled flowers. Its fruits are elongate pods that contain many oil-rich seeds. Oil pressed from rapeseed is used in cooking, as a fuel, as an ingredient in soaps and synthetic rubber, and as an industrial lubricant (see VEGETABLE OILS). China, India, Canada, and France are the chief producers.

Other cultivars of *B. napus* include the RUTABAGA, a plant with a large, edible, turniplike root, and Siberian KALE, a leafy green vegetable similar to cabbage.

Raphael [rah-fah-el']   Raphael (Raffaello Sanzio, or Santi), b. Urbino, Italy, Apr. 6, 1483, was one of the greatest painters of the High Renaissance in Rome. His early works, many of them painted for churches in or near Perugia, include a *Crucifixion* (1503; National Gallery, London) and a *Coronation of the Virgin* (1502; Pinacoteca Vaticana, Rome). In Florence (1504–08), Raphael painted *Saint George and the Dragon* (1506; National Gallery of Art, Washington, D.C.), as a gift from Duke Guidobaldo of Urbino to King Henry VII of England, as well as a large group of Madonnas and Holy Families,

Raphael's splendid portrait (c.1515) of Baldassare Castiglione, author of The Book of the Courtier, *not only conveys the sitter's subtle personality but also makes him, appropriately, the personification of the ideal High Renaissance scholar and gentleman. (Louvre, Paris.)*

Raphael painted The Marriage of the Virgin *(1504) shortly after completing an apprenticeship with Perugino, whose simplicity of style he emulated in this work. (Brera, Milan.)*

many still extant, among them the *Madonna of the Goldfinch* (1505–06; Uffizi, Florence) and the *Belle Jardinière* (1507; Louvre, Paris).

Around 1508–09, Raphael, although only 25 years old, was called to Rome by Pope Julius II to direct the decoration of the state rooms (Stanze) in the Vatican Palace. Here the painter found an opportunity to apply his classical vocabulary on a grand scale. A major impetus toward both classicism and monumentality was the art of Michelangelo, who was painting the ceiling of the Sistine Chapel, also in the Vatican Palace, at the very time of Raphael's arrival. On the four walls of the first room he decorated—the Stanza della Segnatura, completed in 1511—Raphael celebrated four aspects of human, and especially papal, accomplishment: theology (*Disputation over the Sacrament* or *Disputà*), philosophy (*School of Athens*, in which Raphael included portraits of both himself and Michelangelo among the philosophers), the arts (*Parnassus*), and law (*Cardinal Virtues* and *Giving of the Law*). Raphael next frescoed the Stanza d'Eliodoro, completed by mid-1514, where he depicted four historical events illustrating salvation of the church through divine intervention. About 1515 he painted part of a third room, the Stanza dell'Incendio, named after its main fresco, the *Fire in the Borgo.*

At the Villa Farnesina in Rome Raphael produced two works classical in theme as well as style: a wall fresco of the sea nymph Galatea (1513) and an entire ceiling with stories of Cupid and Psyche (1518–19). A famous papal portrait of this period is his *Pope Leo X with Cardinals Giulio de'Medici and Luigi de'Rossi* (Uffizi, Florence). Among the great religious works painted by Raphael on canvas or panel during his Roman years are the *Alba Madonna* (National Gallery, Washington, D.C.), the *Sistine Madonna* (Gemäldegalerie, Dresden), the *Madonna of the Chair* (Pitti Palace, Florence), and the *Transfiguration* (Pinacoteca Vaticana, Rome).

In 1514, Raphael succeeded Donato Bramante as chief architect of SAINT PETER'S BASILICA. At Saint Peter's, Raphael seems to have accomplished the substitution of a longitudinal for a central design, but nothing on his plan was actually built.

In 1515–16 he painted ten large watercolor cartoons (see CARTOON, art) illustrating the Acts of the Apostles as designs for tapestries to be hung in the Sistine Chapel. Seven cartoons survive in the Victoria and Albert Museum, London; the surviving tapestries are in the Vatican Museum.

Raphael died in Rome at the age of 37 and was buried in the Pantheon.

Rapid City   Rapid City is the seat of Pennington County in southwestern South Dakota, on Rapid Creek at the eastern edge of the Black Hills. It has a population of 54,523 (1990). Rapid City is a gold, silver, and uranium mining center. The South Dakota School of Mines and Technology (1885) is there. The city also serves the trade and industrial needs of the farming and lumbering enterprises in the area. Rapid City is a tourist mecca, as the gateway to nearby Mount Rushmore National Memorial, Crazy Horse Mountain, and Custer State Park. It is also the site of Ellsworth Air Force Base, a Strategic Air Command complex. Rapid City was settled in 1876 after the discovery of gold in the Black Hills.

Rapid Eye Movement sleep   see SLEEP

Rappahannock River [rap-uh-han'-uhk]   The Rappahannock River, in Virginia, rises in the Blue Ridge Mountains east of Front Royal and flows generally southeast for about 320 km (200 mi), passing Fredericksburg and finally emptying into Chesapeake Bay. Its main tributary is the Rapidan River. Several important Civil War battles were fought in the vicinity of the Rappahannock, notably the Fredericksburg and Chancellorsville campaigns.

rare earths   see LANTHANIDE SERIES

Rashi [rah'-shee]   Rabbi Solomon ben Isaac (or Yitzha-ki, abbreviated as Rashi), b. 1040, d. July 13, 1105, a famed scholar who wrote definitive commentaries on the Hebrew Bible and most of the Babylonian Talmud, is considered one of the greatest authorities on Jewish law. Rashi, who had studied at Mainz and Worms, established a Talmudic academy at Troyes and was a much-sought-after teacher and religious guide.

His biblical commentary, printed in Hebrew in 1475, was translated into Latin and studied by those preparing the first German translation of the Bible.

Rasmussen, Knud [rahs'-mu-suhn]   Knud Johan Victor Rasmussen, b. June 7, 1879, d. Dec. 21, 1933, was an explorer of Danish and Eskimo descent who devoted his life to ethnological studies throughout Arctic North America and tried to visit every known Eskimo group. To benefit local Eskimo and to serve as a base for explorations, he established station Thule in 1910. During his most famous trek (1921–24), he became the first to cross the NORTHWEST PASSAGE by dogsled. During his travels he collected Eskimo legends and songs.

raspberry   The raspberry plant, a member of the genus *Rubus*, family Rosaceae, is widely cultivated for its fruit. Together with the BLACKBERRY, it comprises the group of plants commonly called brambles. The crowns and roots of brambles are perennial; the thorned canes, or fruiting portions of the plants, however, are biennial, bearing in their second year and then dying. Native to many parts of the world, the raspberry is exceptionally hardy and flourishes even in the northern United States and southern Canada. Varieties include red, purple, and black raspberries and "everbearing" cultivars that produce two crops in a season.

The red raspberry is a biennial that bears fruit on canes. It is easily cultivated and is one of the hardiest of berries.

Rasputin, Grigory Yefimovich [ruhs-poo'-tin, gri-gohr'-ee yi-fee'-muh-vich]   The scandalous behavior of Grigory Yefimovich Rasputin, b. c.1865, d. Dec. 30

Rasputin was a Russian priest and faith healer who gained immense influence at the court of Nicholas II and Alexandra because of his apparent power to relieve the crown prince's sickness. His political influence and personal debauchery eventually provoked a group of nobles to murder him.

(N.S.), 1916, and the influence he wielded over the Russian imperial family served to erode its prestige and contributed directly to the collapse of the Romanov dynasty shortly after his own death. Originally surnamed Novykh, he was born into a peasant family in Siberia and spent much of his youth in debauchery, receiving the name Rasputin ("debaucher"). He entered the church, however, and gained a reputation as a faith healer.

Appearing at the imperial court about 1907, Rasputin soon became a favorite of Empress ALEXANDRA FYODOROVNA and through her influenced NICHOLAS II. Rasputin's hold over Alexandra stemmed from his hypnotic power to alleviate the suffering of the hemophiliac crown prince, Aleksei, and from her belief that this rude priest was a genuine representative of the Russian people. Rasputin's conduct became increasingly licentious and shocking to the Russian public, however.

When Nicholas took personal command of Russian troops in 1915, Alexandra and Rasputin were virtually in charge of the government. Several conservative noblemen, recognizing Rasputin's destructive influence on an already deteriorating government, assassinated him. They first poisoned and then shot him; when these efforts failed, they drowned Rasputin in the Neva River.

Rastafarians   [rah-stuh-far'-ee-uhnz]   Rastafarians are members of a Jamaican messianic movement dating back to the 1930s. According to Rastafarian belief the only true God is the late Ethiopian emperor HAILE SELASSIE (originally known as Ras Tafari), and Ethiopia is the true Zion. Rastafarians claim that white Christian preachers and missionaries have perverted the Scriptures to conceal the fact that Adam and Jesus were black. Their rituals include the use of marijuana and the chanting of revivalist hymns. REGGAE music is the popular music of the movement.

Rastrelli, Bartolommeo Francesco [rahs-trel'-lee]   The favorite architect of Empress Elizabeth of Russia and the creator of the Russian rococo style, Bartolommeo Francesco Rastrelli, 1700–71, was an Italian; his architectural background was purely French. His buildings in and around Saint Petersburg (now Leningrad) included the Summer Palace (1741–44; destroyed), the Anichkov Palace (c.1744), the Peterhof (1747–52), and Smolny Cathedral (1748–55). His major projects were the Great Palace at Tsarskoe-Selo (1749–56; now Pushkin) and the Winter Palace (1754–62).

rat   Rat is the common name for about 1,000 species of rodents in 70 genera and 8 families. These species include the kangaroo rats, *Dipodomys*, family Heteromyidae; wood rats, *Neotoma*, family Cricetidae; spiny rats, *Proechimys*, family Echimyidae; and the typical rats, *Rattus*, family Muridae. Most rodents called rats have an elongated body, a moderately pointed snout, approximately equal-length legs, and a long, sparsely haired or hairless tail. Rats are generally distinguished from mice by their larger size.

In the narrow sense, *rat* refers to members of the genus *Rattus*, which contains from 137 to 570 species, depending on which classification is followed. The genus *Rattus* is of special interest because two of its species, the black rat, *R. rattus*, and the Norway rat, *R. norvegicus*, have profoundly affected human history.

The black rat, also called the roof rat, is the primary host for bubonic plague, which is transmitted to humans by direct contact or through the bites of fleas that have fed on infected rats. The black rat is believed to have come originally from southern or southeastern Asia.

The black rat is found in the United States along both coasts and throughout most of the southeastern states. It is 16 to 22 cm (6.3 to 8.6 in) long, with a 17- to 24-cm (6.7- to 9.3-in) tail (always longer than the head and body combined), and weighs 115 to 350 g (4 to 12 oz). Black rats are usually grayish black with lighter gray underparts, but brown varieties exist. Breeding occurs throughout the year. Gestation is about 24 days, with 6 to 12 young per litter.

The Norway rat, also called the brown rat, probably originated in eastern Asia and is found throughout the United States. It is usually grayish brown above and pale gray or brown on its underparts, but blackish varieties also occur. Norway rats are 22 to 26 cm (8.6 to 10.2 in) long, with an 18- to 22-cm (7- to 8.6-in) tail (always shorter than the head and body combined); they weigh 200 to 485 g (7 to 17 oz). They breed throughout the year. Gestation varies from 21 to 24 days, with 6 to 12 young per litter.

Their preference for different habitats usually keeps the black and Norway rats apart, but where they do meet the larger and more aggressive Norway rat either forces the black rat to different portions of the habitat, such as

(Left) *The Australian water rat has such aquatic adaptations as partially webbed feet and seallike fur.*

(Right) *The Australian stick-nest rat uses sticks to build a shelter that may be 1 m (about 3 ft) tall.*

(Below) *The Luzon striped rat lives in the mountains of northern Luzon, in the Philippines.*

(Left) *Long, thick hair characterizes the bushy-tailed cloud rat, a tree-dwelling species found in the Philippines.*

(Right) *The mole rat, or zokor, of northeastern Asia, has strong, clawed forefeet adapted to underground life.*

(Right) *The maned rat, of eastern Africa, has along its back hair that becomes erect when the animal is irritated.*

the upper levels of buildings, or drives it completely out of the area. Both black and Norway rats will eat almost anything, but black rats show a preference for plant material, and Norway rats for animal food. Norway rats even become predators, and they often associate in packs of 60 or more animals, usually all closely related and often all descended from a single pair.

The Norway rat, in the form of the usually albino laboratory rat, has enabled researchers to make significant contributions in studies of nutrition, genetics, and disease. Domestic rats also make excellent pets.

ratel [rayt'-ul]   The ratel, or honey badger, *Mellivora capensis*, in the weasel family, Mustelidae, is a carnivore

A ratel, or honey badger, follows the call of a bird, the African honey guide, to a beehive the bird has located. The ratel breaks open the hive and feeds on honey, while the bird searches for bee grubs and wax.

that lives in brushlands and forests of Africa, India, and the Middle East. Its thick coat is gray above and black below. The skin is loose but very tough. The animal is about 60 cm (2 ft) long, excluding its tail, and is a good climber, living in trees as well as in burrows. It likes honey, and the HONEY GUIDE, or indicator bird, leads it to the nests of wild bees. The ratel also feeds on rodents and reptiles, even the cobra.

Rathenau, Walther [raht'-en-ow]   Walther Rathenau, b. Sept. 29, 1867, d. June 24, 1922, a German industrialist and social theorist, served (1922) as foreign minister in the Weimar Republic. During World War I he had organized and directed Germany's War Raw Materials Department, and in 1921 he was minister of reconstruction. As foreign minister, Rathenau sought reconciliation with the victorious powers and signed the Treaty of Rapallo between Germany and the USSR. This treaty canceled Germany's war debt to the USSR, extended to the Soviet government its first diplomatic recognition, and enabled Germany to build and test new weapons secretly in the USSR. Nationalist elements in Germany detested Rathenau both as a Jew and as a representative of the Weimar government. He was assassinated by one such extremist group in Berlin.

rational number   A rational number is defined to be the quotient of an integer and a nonzero integer; that is, it is a number that can be written in the form of a FRACTION. For example, $3/2$, $-2/3$, and $1,072/83$ are all rational numbers, as are $0 = 1/0$, $1 = 1/1$, $2 = 2/1$, and so forth. Every integer n is equal to $n/1$ and so is a rational number. Given a rational number a/b, the integer a is called the numerator and b is called the denominator. Every rational number has many representations as a quotient of two integers:

$2/3 = 6/9 = 8/12 = 18/27$. The fraction a/b is called reduced or in lowest terms if the integers a and b have no common factors (in the above example, $2/3$ is the reduced fraction). Two rational numbers a/b and c/d are equal provided $ad = bc$. All numerical calculations performed by people (or by computers) are actually done with rational numbers. All the IRRATIONAL NUMBERS that must be dealt with are in the end approximated by rational numbers for numerical computations.

rationalism   Rationalism is a theory that contends that the most fundamental knowledge is based on reason and that truth is found by rational analysis of ideas independent of empirical data, emotive attitudes, or authoritative pronouncements. Empiricists (see EMPIRICISM) claim that knowledge can be based only on information gained from the senses. Such information, the rationalists contend, is always open to question. They point to mathematics and logic as realms where unquestionable truths can be discovered by the use of reason alone. Baruch SPINOZA, perhaps the supreme rationalist of Western philosophy, presented his philosophical views in geometrical form and deduced theorems about the world based on axioms that he held to be rational truths.

The leading modern rationalists—the 17th-century philosophers Spinoza, René DESCARTES, and Gottfried Wilhelm von LEIBNIZ—sought to develop science in terms of basic concepts and the mathematical relationships between them. Empirical information, they conceded, might help in suggesting certain ideas, but the fundamental framework of science must be a mathematical schema of concepts and the laws logically deduced from them. The rationalist viewpoint led to applying mathematics in the sciences and to eliminating concepts—the notion of purpose, for example—that could not be expressed mathematically.

In religion, rationalism has been critical of accepted beliefs that cannot be logically justified. After the Reformation, rationalists questioned certain basic claims of Christianity; some insisted that reason alone should be the only guide in interpreting Scripture. Religious rationalism—especially as embodied in the works of such 18th-century thinkers as VOLTAIRE, Jean Jacques ROUSSEAU, and the American Thomas PAINE—accompanied the development of DEISM and AGNOSTICISM and led to some modern forms of ATHEISM.

Rationalist philosophers have not necessarily been religious rationalists. Descartes and Leibniz, for example, accepted orthodox Christianity, whereas many religious rationalists have been empiricists.

Rattigan, Terence [rat'-uh-guhn]   A master of the well-made play, the British playwright Terence Mervyn Rattigan, b. June 10, 1911, d. Nov. 30, 1977, enjoyed enormous success with *The Winslow Boy* (1946), which appeals to the audience's sense of humanity. Rattigan later explored the themes of loneliness and misunderstanding in *The Deep Blue Sea* (1952) and *Separate Tables* (1954) and based *Ross* (1960) on the life of Lawrence of Arabia. Much of his work has been filmed. Rattigan was knighted in 1971.

rattlesnake   Rattlesnakes are heavy-bodied, venomous snakes with movable front fangs, a heat-sensing pit on each side of the face, and, with rare exception, rattles on the tail. Venomous snakes with movable fangs make up the VIPER family, Viperidae. Rattlesnakes and other vipers with heat-sensing pits are placed in the subfamily Crotalinae of PIT VIPERS, although some classifications instead place them in a separate family, Crotalidae.

Rattlesnakes comprise two genera: *Crotalus*, which ranges from Canada into Argentina and contains about 28 species with many varieties, or subspecies; and *Sistrurus*, which includes the 2 species of pygmy rattlesnakes and the massasauga, found in the United States and Mexico. Rattlesnakes range in size from the eastern diamondback, *C. adamanteus*, which averages between 0.9 and 1.8 m (3 and 6 ft) long, to a number of small species, such as the sidewinder, *C. cerastes*, which is usually less than 60 cm (2 ft) long.

The two pit organs are located between the nostril and eye on either side of the lower face. Sensitive to infrared radiation and capable of detecting temperature differences of mere thousandths of a degree, the front-facing organs enable a snake to determine the location and size of a prey animal. Evidence further indicates that the nerve impulses from the organs cross to opposite sides of the brain, producing a stereoscoping heat image that precisely locates the prey and allows the snake to strike accurately in total darkness.

At the very front of the mouth on either side of the upper jaw is a short, deep bone called the maxilla; each bone bears a large, venom-injecting fang, normally carried folded back along the roof of the mouth. When pulled by a muscle, however, two bones called the

The timber, or prairie, or banded, rattlesnake is found from the eastern coast of the United States (as far north as New Hampshire) to Kansas and Oklahoma.

pterygoid and the ectopterygoid push against the loosely attached maxilla, rotating it forward and erecting the fang. Each maxilla has two fang sockets, and—normally two to four times a year—a fang is replaced by the first in a series of developing fangs directly behind it, moving into the empty socket. The old fang does not always drop out immediately, so a rattlesnake may have up to four working fangs in its mouth at one time. In general, the venom is largely blood-tissue-destroying (hemotoxic), but the tropical rattlesnake, or casabel, *C. durissus*, has venom that is largely nerve-destroying (neurotoxic). The hemotoxic-neurotoxic balance can vary greatly, even within a species, according to geographic location or the individual snake.

Rattlesnakes are generally characterized by the presence of rattles, but one species, the Santa Catalina rattlesnake, *C. catalinensis*, lacks them. Each rattle segment is a modified horny scale that once capped the tip of the tail. Other snakes shed these scales at each molt; the rattlesnake sheds it but once, at the first molt after birth. Thereafter, the caps are retained. Rattlesnakes molt an average of three times a year and often break off and lose their end rattles, so the number of rattles is not an indication of a snake's age.

Rattlesnakes mate in the spring in warmer climates or in the fall in colder regions. Females may retain sperm within their oviducts for a considerable time and bear successive litters without additional matings. Gestation is generally between 140 and 200 days and is apparently greatly influenced by climate. All rattlesnakes are live-bearing, with females producing an average of 8 to 15 young at a time.

Ratzinger, Joseph   German churchman Joseph Alois Ratzinger, b. Apr. 16, 1927, is a prominent member of the Roman Curia. He was a professor of theology before becoming archbishop of Munich-Freising and a cardinal in 1977. In 1981, Cardinal Ratzinger was named by Pope John Paul II to head the Vatican's Congregation for the Doctrine of the Faith, a body charged with safeguarding Catholic orthodoxy. Known as an opponent of church progressives, he aroused controversy when, in a 1985 interview published as *The Ratzinger Report*, he expressed disillusion with the results of the Second Vatican Council.

Rauschenberg, Robert   [row'-shen-burg]   The American artist Robert Rauschenberg, b. Port Arthur, Tex., Oct. 22, 1925, has been a leading figure in pop art, "happenings," environmental art, and experimental theater. Rauschenberg's early works include the "combine" paintings of the late 1950s, which grew from modest collages of newspaper fragments and photographs into complex, three-dimensional creations. The most spectacular, *Monogram* (1959; Moderna Museet, Stockholm), consists of a stuffed ram encircled by an automobile tire; the base is splashed with paint and collage elements. Since the 1960s Rauschenberg has produced

Reserve *(1961)* is one of the "combine" paintings that Robert Rauschenberg began to produce during the 1950s. Combine painting, like collage, incorporates mundane objects, but Rauschenberg extended the form by using the canvas as a mirror of the incoherent profusion of modern life. (National Gallery of Art, Washington, D.C.)

silk-screened kaleidoscopic works based on media culture, including the transfer of photographs to silk screen. He has also experimented with motors, plexiglas, and sound.

Rauschenbusch, Walter [row'-shen-bush]

The Baptist clergyman and theologian Walter Rauschenbusch, b. Rochester, N.Y., Oct. 4, 1861, d. July 25, 1918, was a leading advocate of the SOCIAL GOSPEL movement. As pastor to the Second German Baptist Church in New York City's notorious Hell's Kitchen, in the face of complex urban social problems, he came to believe that Jesus preached social as well as individual salvation and began to place new emphasis on the Kingdom of God. While in New York, Rauschenbusch coedited (1889–91) a workers' paper, *For the Right*, and helped found (1892) the Brotherhood of the Kingdom, a Baptist group dedicated to social action. In 1897 he began to teach in the German school of Rochester Theological Seminary, becoming professor of church history there in 1902. His writings include *Christianity and the Social Crisis* (1907) and *A Theology for the Social Gospel* (1917).

Ravel, Maurice [rah-vel']

Maurice Ravel, b. Mar. 7, 1875, d. Dec. 28, 1937, was one of France's great composers and an important master of early-20th-century music. He entered the Paris Conservatory in 1889, and soon became identified with the musical avant-garde. Following military service in World War I, he retired from Paris to a villa at Montfort-l'Amaury. Recognized as France's leading contemporary composer following the death of Debussy in 1918, Ravel made visits abroad, touring England and, in 1928, the United States. In his later years he suffered from a neurological disorder, which caused his death.

Often named with Debussy as an impressionist, Ravel was essentially a classicist in the French tradition of clarity, polish, and disciplined artistry. His imaginative piano music—such as the *Sonatine* (1905), *Miroirs* (1905), the stunning *Gaspard de la nuit* (1908), and *Le Tombeau de Couperin* (1917)—was particularly influential. His subtly crafted chamber works include his String Quartet (1902), the *Introduction and Allegro* for harp and ensemble (1905–06), the Trio for Piano and Strings (1914), the Sonata for Violin and Cello (1920–22), and the jazz-influenced Violin Sonata (1923–27). Jazz was also assimilated in his Piano Concerto in G (1930–31), composed simultaneously with his Piano Concerto for the Left Hand. Brilliant as a composer of songs, he showed great flair for the stage in his two operas, the witty *L'Heure espagnole* (The Spanish Hour, 1911) and the phantasmagoric *L'Enfant et les sortilèges* (The Child and the Spells, 1925). His ballet for Diaghilev, *Daphnis et Chloé* (1909–12), was followed by *Ma Mère l'Oye* (1915), *La Valse* (1919–20), and the popular *Boléro* (1928). These compositions, like his famous transcription (1922) of Mussorgsky's *Pictures at an Exhibition* and his own orchestral works that originated as piano pieces, display both Ravel's wizardry as an orchestrator and his capacity to rethink the same music idiomatically in different media.

Maurice Ravel, one of the greatest French composers of the early 20th century, was renowned for such works as Gaspard de la nuit *(1908) and* Boléro *(1928). His masterpiece, the ballet* Daphnis et Chloé *(1909–12), exhibits the skillful orchestration and superb craftsmanship characteristic of his work.*

The common raven, generally regarded as a pest, is rarely seen outside of rural areas because it has been driven off by guns and poison. Its diet is quite varied; in addition to frequenting garbage dumps, it eats the eggs and young of other birds.

raven   The larger members of the bird genus *Corvus* in the crow family, Corvidae, are referred to as ravens. The common raven, *C. corax*, of the Northern Hemisphere and the white-necked raven, *C. cryptoleucus*, of the southwestern United States to central Mexico are typical.

The common raven, found in a wide range of habitats, is deep, glossy black, as are other ravens. The largest SONGBIRD (order Passeriformes), it weighs almost 1.25 kg (3 lb) and reaches up to 66 cm (26 in) in length. This raven has long wings, a strong bill and feet, a wedge-shaped tail, and nostrils shielded by stiff feathers. Nests are usually large, made of sticks. Common ravens eat a variety of animal and plant material, including carrion. The smaller white-necked raven, 48 cm (19 in) in length, confined to arid habitats, has white only at the base of the neck feathers.

Ravenna [rah-ven'-nah]   Ravenna is a city located in the Emilia-Romagna region of northern Italy and connected to the Adriatic Sea, 8 km (5 mi) to the east, by canal. Ravenna has a population of 136,324 (1988 est.). The city is an agricultural market, railroad junction, and industrial center. Chief manufactures are fertilizers, furniture, cement, chemicals, and plastics. Landmarks include the Byzantine Church of SAN VITALE, the mausoleum of Empress Galla Placidia, the Church of Sant' Apollinare Nuovo, and the Church of Sant' Apollinare in Classe.

The city was probably occupied by northern Italic tribes as early as 1400 BC. It came under Rome in 191 BC. ODOACER of the Heruli and THEODORIC the Ostrogoth ruled Italy from Ravenna during the 5th and 6th centuries. The city served (c.585–751) as the capital of the Exarchate of Ravenna, the seat of Byzantine rule in Italy, before falling to the Lombards and later the Franks. A free commune during the 12th and 13th centuries, Ravenna was subsequently ruled by the Da Polenta family until Venice took control in 1441. The city was annexed to the Papal States in 1509 and joined the new unified kingdom of Italy in 1860.

Rawalpindi [rah-wul-pin'-dee]   Rawalpindi is a city in northeastern Pakistan 14 km (9 mi) southwest of the capital, Islamabad. An industrial center and grain market, it has a population of 928,000 (1981). Industries include petroleum refining, textiles, and ironworks.

Settled about 1756 on the site of an old village inhabited by Rawals, Rawalpindi controlled the route into Kashmir. When the British arrived in the 19th century, they made the city headquarters of their northern army. Rawalpindi retains many evidences of British colonial rule. From 1959 to 1960 it was the capital of Pakistan.

Rawlings, Jerry [raw'-lingz]   Jerry Rawlings, b. June 22, 1947, served as chief of state of Ghana in 1979 and again beginning in 1981. An almost unknown flight lieutenant before his May 1979 attempt to overthrow Lt.-Gen. Frederick W. K. Akuffo, he staged a successful coup in June. Akuffo and two other former heads of state were then charged with squandering public funds and executed. Although the popular Rawlings turned power over to an elected civilian regime in September, he staged another coup in December 1981, declaring that President Hilla Limann had failed to eliminate corruption. He instituted a variety of economic reforms and pledged to restore Ghana to prosperity.

Rawlings, Marjorie Kinnan   An American novelist and essayist, Marjorie Kinnan Rawlings, b. Washington, D.C., Aug. 8, 1896, d. Dec. 14, 1953, won the 1939 Pulitzer Prize for her best-selling novel *The Yearling* (1938). A classic story of growing up in the backwoods of Florida, it also achieved great popularity and critical success as a film (1946). Rawlings did her best work at her farm near Cross Creek, Fla., where she wrote six novels, a volume of short stories, and a collection of essays (1942).

Rawlinson, Sir Henry Creswicke   see CUNEIFORM; MESOPOTAMIA

Rawls, John [rawlz]   John Rawls, b. Baltimore, Md., Feb. 21, 1921, is an American philosopher and educator. He has taught at Princeton and Cornell universities and at the Massachusetts Institute of Technology and, since 1959, at Harvard University. His *A Theory of Justice* (1971) develops a contract theory in opposition to intuitionism and utilitarianism and posits two principles: that the individual has a right to as much liberty as is compatible with the liberty of others, and that social and economic inequalities are to be set up for everyone's advantage and under conditions of equal opportunity.

ray Rays are cartilagenous fishes represented by several families in the order Rajiformes, which includes SKATES, guitarfishes, and SAWFISHES. Rays, like skates, have flattened bodies and enlarged pectoral fins that join the head; unlike skates, they usually lack caudal fins and are ovoviviparous. Most species are marine. The electric rays, family Torpedinidae, have electric organs (modified muscles) on each side of the head capable of delivering up to 200 volts. Stingrays, family Dasyatidae, have saw-toothed spines located at the base of the tail. Associated with the spine or spines is a venom gland, and the apparatus can cause severe injury. Eagle rays, family Myliobatidae, are distinguished by having a distinct head region and a fleshy pad extending in front of the head; some also have a venomous spine. Cow-nose rays, family Rhinobatidae, are distinguished by two fleshy folds that look like split upper lips. The manta rays, family Mobulidae, are the largest and most pelagic of the rays. The Atlantic manta, *Manta borustris*, reaches 6.1 m (20 ft) across the pectorals and weighs more than 1,360 kg (3,000 lb). Mantas are harmless unless harpooned.

Ray, Man Man Ray, b. Philadelphia, Aug. 27, 1890, d. Nov. 18, 1976, was a pioneering painter and photographer in the Dada, surrealist, and abstract movements of the 1920s and '30s. After participating in radical art activities in New York, he moved (1921) to Paris, where he supported himself as a portrait photographer. In 1922 he published *Les Champs délicieux* (Delightful Fields), an album of abstract photographs made without use of a camera that he called rayographs. Later he experimented with solarization techniques and negative prints. He turned to filmmaking in 1923, producing *Le Retour à la Raison* (Return to Reason, 1923), *Anemic Cinema* (1925–26) with Marcel Duchamp, and *L'Étoile de Mer* (Star of the Sea, 1928). He exhibited frequently from the 1920s to the 1940s and continued to synthesize painting and photography.

Man Ray juxtaposed his model, Kiki, with one of his masks in this eerie photograph (1926). Ray, also an acclaimed surrealist painter, sculptor, and filmmaker, was instrumental in the evolution of photography as a modern art form.

Ray, Satyajit [ry, suht'-yuh-jit] Satyajit Ray, b. May 2, 1922, is India's foremost film director. A versatile craftsman who has worked in several film genres, Ray is known best outside India for his moving depictions of Indian family life. His acknowledged masterpiece, the neorealist trilogy made up of *Pather Panchali* (1955), *Aparajito* (1956), and *The World of Apu* (1959), lyrically chronicles the day-to-day activities of a rural Bengali family and the coming of age of the boy Apu. Two other outstanding Ray films, *The Music Room* (1958) and *The Big City* (1963), deal with the changing nature of contemporary Indian life, whereas *Charulata* (1964) is a graceful adaptation of Rabindranath Tagore's classic portrait of the Indian middle classes in the Victorian era. In later films such as *Days and Nights in the Forest* (1970), *Company Ltd.* (1971), *Distant Thunder* (1973), and *The Chess Players* (1977), Ray focused on political and social themes without losing his humanistic perspective.

Rayburn, Sam Samuel Taliaferro Rayburn, b. near Kingston, Tenn., Jan. 6, 1882, d. Nov. 16, 1961, served as Speaker of the U.S. House of Representatives for 17 years, longer than any other person in history. Having moved to Texas as a child, Rayburn, a Democrat, served (1907–13) in the Texas legislature. Elected to the U.S. House of Representatives in 1912, he served there continuously for 48 years, a congressional record. A strong supporter of the New Deal, he became majority leader in 1937. Elected House Speaker in 1940, Rayburn held that post until his death, except for four years (1947–49, 1953–55) when the Republicans were in power.

Rayleigh, Lord [ray'-lee] The Englishman John William Strutt, 3d Baron Rayleigh, b. Nov. 12, 1842, d. June 30, 1919, made numerous contributions spanning every field of classical physics. His dramatic discovery—with Sir William Ramsay—of a new element, the inert gas argon, received much publicity, but his other achievements were more significant. Early in his career (1871) he solved the problem of the blue color of the sky by deriving the formula specifying how light scattering varies with the wavelength of the incident light. Drawn particularly to wave phenomena, he produced a classic two-volume work on sound and laid the foundations for the Rayleigh-Jeans law (1900), formulated to account for the distribution of energy in BLACKBODY RADIATION. Lord Rayleigh was awarded the Nobel Prize for physics in 1904.

Raynaud's disease [ray-nohz'] Raynaud's disease is a disorder of unknown cause (idiopathic) that is characterized by episodes of sudden spasms, or constriction, of small arteries in the hands and feet, resulting in greatly reduced blood supply. Raynaud's disease is more common in women than men, and its onset usually occurs in young adulthood. The affected areas will show a color change, going from pallor to blue or red. Intermittent constriction is triggered by cold or emotional upset. The right and left digits are affected simultaneously; in about half the cases, only the hands are involved. The disease may improve quickly, remain mild, or grow progressively worse. More rarely, blood clots and gangrene may complicate progressive cases. Pain is uncommon, but numbness and tingling sensations frequently occur. Drugs that dilate arteries may be used long term. Attacks may be terminated by keeping the hands and feet warm. The use of tobacco aggravates the problem, because it causes arteries to constrict.

When the condition is secondary to another disorder, it is called Raynaud's phenomenon. Treatment then depends on the cause of the disorders.

rayon   The synthetic fiber known as rayon is produced from regenerated cellulose (wood pulp) that has been chemically treated. Fabrics made of rayon are strong, highly absorbent, and soft; they drape well and can be dyed in brilliant, long-lasting colors. Rayon fibers are also used as reinforcing cords in motor tires, and their excellent absorbency makes them useful in medical and surgical materials.

The first successful commercial process for producing rayon was developed in 1884 by the French inventor Hilaire de Chardonnet. Various methods are now used to produce three types of regenerated cellulose fibers: viscose, cuprammonium, and cellulose acetate. Viscose rayon, used for wearing apparel and heavy fabrics, is made

Cellulose, the major ingredient in both acetate and rayon fibers, is obtained from wood chips (1) by a sulfite process. Acetate fibers are formed from a diacetate reaction product of cellulose, mixed acid (2), and alkali (3). The diacetate is dissolved in acetone (4) and extruded through tiny holes in a spinneret into a hot-air tower. As acetone evaporates from the thin liquid streams, solid acetate filaments form and are wound on tubes (5). Viscose rayon is made from cellulose reacted (6) with aqueous alkali and carbon disulfide. A solution of viscose is produced that is pigmented (7) and pumped through holes into an acid bath (8). Rayon filaments are formed and wound up (9).

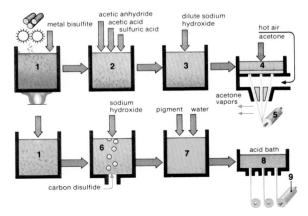

by treating cellulose (now derived from wood pulp) with caustic soda and carbon disulfide, and then forcing the solution through metal nozzles (spinnerets) so that filaments emerge into a bath of dilute sulfuric acid. Rayon can be prepared as a continuous filament yarn or cut into specified lengths and then spun like cotton or wool.

The cuprammonium process is used to make fine filaments to be used in silklike fabrics and sheer hosiery. The cellulose pulp, dissolved in caustic soda, is treated with copper oxide and ammonia. The filaments are forced out of the spinnerets into a spinning funnel and then stretched to the required fineness by the action of a jetstream of water.

In both the viscose and cuprammonium processes, cellulose is treated chemically and is then regenerated. Acetate and triacetate, however, are rayon fibers that are chemical derivatives (esters) of cellulose. They are considered a separate class of fiber. Acetate fabrics are known for their brilliance of color and ability to drape well, properties that have made them particularly successful as apparel fabrics. Triacetate yarns have many of the same properties as acetate but are particularly well known for their ability to provide pleat retention in apparel. Short fibers of acetate are used as filling materials in pillows, mattress pads, and quilts and also as filtering agents in cigarettes.

See also: SYNTHETIC FIBERS; TEXTILE INDUSTRY.

Rayonnant style   see GOTHIC ART AND ARCHITECTURE

Razin, Stenka [rah'-zeen, steng'-kah]   Stenka Razin, actually Stephan Timofeyevich Razin, d. June 16 (N.S.), 1671, an ataman, or chief, of the DON COSSACKS, led a large-scale peasant revolt in Russia. During 1667–69 he raided the lower Volga valley and trans-Caspian region with his Cossack band. In 1670 he organized peasants who had fled Moscow to seek freedom with the Cossacks. The rebels, eventually about 20,000 strong, captured several cities before they were defeated by tsarist troops. Razin was taken to Moscow and executed. He became a folk hero whose exploits are still celebrated in songs and legends.

RDX   see EXPLOSIVES

Re   see AMON-RE

reactance   In electrical circuits, reactance is a property of the circuit that arises from the presence of capacitative and inductive elements. Reactance (X) depends on the applied frequency (f) and is measured in ohms. If inductance (L) is measured in henrys, and capacitance (C) in farads, then the inductive reactance is equal to 2π times the product of the frequency and the inductance, and the capacitative reactance is inversely proportional to the product of the frequency and the capacitance. These quantities are important for determining the resonant frequency of a circuit.

reaction, chemical   The reaction is the heart of the study of chemistry. All chemical reactions involve the breakage and reformation of CHEMICAL BONDS to form different substances. Chemistry, then, can be defined as the science of substances—their composition, structure, and properties and the reactions that change one substance into another.

A simple chemical reaction occurs when hydrogen gas combines with oxygen gas to form the compound water. On the molecular level, two molecules of hydrogen (H_2) react with one molecule of oxygen (O_2) to produce two molecules of water (H_2O). The equation for this reaction is:

$$2H_2 + O_2 \rightarrow 2H_2O + energy$$

Chemical bonds actually are the result of the overlap of ELECTRON clouds (see ATOM), but for diagrammatic purposes they are represented by straight lines. The above reaction can then be shown as follows, with the two lines in the oxygen molecule representing a double bond (see CHEMICAL SYMBOLISM AND NOTATION):

$$\begin{array}{c} H-H \\ \\ H-H \end{array} + O=O \rightarrow \begin{array}{c} H-O-H \\ \\ H-O-H \end{array}$$

Reactions do not occur between heated solids such as aluminum sulfate (1) and potassium sulfate (2). If the solids are dissolved in water (3), however, and heating is continued until the water evaporates, the compounds combine to form alum (4). Dry copper sulfate crystals (5) will not conduct electricity, but when water is added (6) electrolysis occurs. Solids may react with liquids; sodium metal (7) reacts violently with water and liberates hydrogen. Reactions between liquids are common. Clear solutions of phenolphthalein (8) and alkali (9) produce a red solution (10), which is converted back to the colorless state by adding it to a colorless acid solution (11).

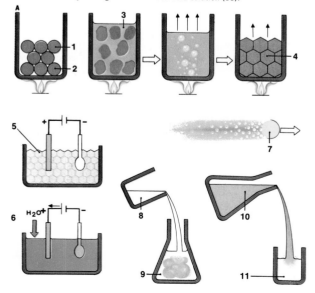

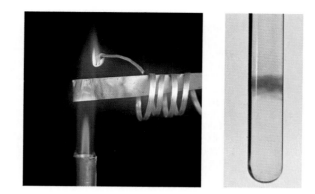

(Left) *The reaction rates of different materials vary considerably. Iron, for example, reacts so slowly with oxygen that it can be heated red hot without showing any appreciable change. A heated strip of magnesium, however, burns rapidly to form an oxide.* (Right) *The brown ring reaction is a simple method for detecting nitrate ions. A solution of potassium sulfate is carefully poured on top of an acidic nitrate solution so that the fluids do not mix. A characteristic brown color forms between the layers if nitrate ion is present.*

Chemical Reaction versus Physical Change. Care must be taken not to confuse a chemical reaction with a physical change, such as a change in state. Water, like all types of matter, can exist in either the solid, liquid, or gaseous state depending on the conditions of temperature and pressure. When the pressure is 1 atmosphere, the change from ice to water to steam occurs as shown:

$$H_2O\ (solid) \xrightarrow[0°C]{energy} H_2O\ (liquid) \xrightarrow[100°C]{energy} H_2O\ (gas)$$

In these changes no chemical reaction is involved because no chemical bonds are broken and no new ones formed.

Energy. The reaction between hydrogen and oxygen releases a large quantity of energy, most of it as heat. Such an energy-releasing reaction is said to be exothermic. Once the water molecules are formed, however, they cannot again be converted to hydrogen or oxygen merely by cooling (withdrawing the energy from) the newly formed water. The reverse chemical reaction to convert water back to hydrogen and oxygen can be accomplished only if an equal quantity of energy (possibly in the form of electrical energy) is returned to the water molecules to break the bonds that hold the hydrogen and oxygen atoms together. Such a reaction, which requires energy, is said to be endothermic (see CHEMICAL ENERGY; THERMOCHEMISTRY).

Property Changes. Chemical reactions are identified by the changes in the chemical properties of the substances during the course of the reaction. For example, table salt (sodium chloride, NaCl), when melted, can be decomposed to its elements by a passage of an electrical current through the melt. At the negative electrode the silvery molten metal sodium (Na) is formed, and at the positive electrode the poisonous, greenish yellow gas chlorine

(Cl_2) is released. This ELECTROLYSIS reaction can be represented by the following equation:

$$2NaCl \text{ (liquid)} \xrightarrow{\text{electrical current}} 2Na \text{ (liquid)} + Cl_2 \text{ (gas)}$$

In this equation the same number of sodium and chlorine atoms appear on both sides of the arrow because no atoms of matter can be destroyed during a chemical reaction (see CONSERVATION, LAWS OF). The only change can be in how they are bonded with each other.

See also: CATALYST; CHEMICAL COMBINATION, LAWS OF; CHEMICAL KINETICS AND EQUILIBRIUM; CHEMICAL NOMENCLATURE; OXIDATION AND REDUCTION.

reactor   see NUCLEAR REACTOR

Read, Sir Herbert   Sir Herbert Edward Read, b. Dec. 4, 1893, d. June 12, 1968, an English poet and critic, is remembered especially for his defense of modern art and culture. He was assistant keeper at the Victoria and Albert Museum, London (1922–31); professor of fine arts at the University of Edinburgh (1931–33); and editor of the *Burlington Magazine* (1933–38). His critical writings include *Wordsworth* (1930), *The Meaning of Art* (rev. ed., 1931), *Art and Industry* (1934; rev. ed., 1945), *Art and Society* (1936), *Icon and Idea: The Function of Art in the Development of Human Consciousness* (1955), *The Art of Sculpture* (1956), and *Henry Moore* (1965). Among his other works are a novel, *The Green Child* (1935), and an autobiography, *The Contrary Experience* (1963).

Reade, Charles [reed]   An English writer, Charles Reade, b. June 8, 1814, d. Apr. 11, 1884, was the author of a celebrated historical novel, *The Cloister and the Hearth* (1861). After studying law, he began to write for the theater. He then turned to carefully documented novels of contemporary life, dealing with such subjects as prisons and lunatic asylums. A similar concern for accuracy, but with greater detachment, characterized the depiction of the Middle Ages in his most famous novel.

Reading (England) [red′-ing]   Reading is the county town of Berkshire, England, on the River Kennet, 58 km (36 mi) west of London. The population of the city is 132,037 (1981). Reading, located on rail, highway, and air routes, is an industrial and market center. Its university was founded in 1892. The site of a Danish settlement (871), Reading was chartered as a county borough in 1253 and made a city in 1639. It was virtually destroyed (1640s) during the English Civil War.

Reading (Pennsylvania) Reading (1990 pop., 78,380), the seat of Berks County, is a city in southeastern Pennsylvania 72 km (45 mi) northwest of Philadelphia. Located in the center of the fertile Pennsylvania

Dutch region, Reading, a rail and manufacturing center, produces hosiery, textiles, steel, and metal products. Reading was settled in 1748 by Thomas Penn, the son of William Penn, the state's founder. During the late 18th century the city was a prosperous iron and steel center. Its growth was further stimulated by the construction (1820s) of canals on the Schuylkill and Susquehanna rivers and the arrival (1884) of the Philadelphia and Reading Railroad.

reading disability   see DYSLEXIA

reading education   The ability to read enables a person to satisfy both personal and functional needs and to participate fully in contemporary society. It is a basic skill necessary for success in other areas of study, and it can lead to a lifetime pursuit of learning, critical thinking, and enjoyment. The ability to read, therefore, is a fundamental goal—as well as a basic tool—of education.

Beginning Reading. The first learning experiences in school should create a foundation for successful reading by fostering favorable impressions of what is to be derived from books and language use. Programs should also accommodate children's varied stages of social and intellectual development. Research has shown that children with rich experiential and language backgrounds are better prepared for beginning reading than children who lack such backgrounds.

As children become acquainted with the materials that prepare them for formal reading, they begin to master auditory perception, visual discrimination, visual and auditory memory, and fine and gross motor skills that aid in reading development. Children should be able to discern likenesses and differences among sounds, letters, and words. Speaking, writing, and listening skills are also integral parts of a total reading program and should be introduced early.

Because primary language competence directly affects reading competence, it is important to provide young children with many and varied opportunities to develop facility with both oral and written language. Activities involving narrative communication, reasoning, dramatic play, and the appreciation of art, music, and literature are aimed at extending children's vocabularies, improving their ability to express themselves, and developing a concept of symbols.

Learning to Read. The first step in learning to read usually consists of learning the alphabet and the letters and combinations of letters that symbolize distinctive sounds of the language. Children learn sounds and then blend them to form words. Mere word calling, however, is not reading, in which meaning is derived from words appearing in a certain context.

Most schools use eclectic basal reading programs, which cover a wide range of reading skills through sequential instruction. In such programs learning materials usually progress from readiness books to preprimers, primers, first readers, and then to a series of books for each succeeding year. Supplementary materials include filmstrips and workbooks. Most of the reading materials deal with activities and experiences familiar to a child and incorporate language patterns, concepts, and interests appropriate to the student's age level.

In another method of instruction, based solely on language-experience activities, students learn to relate their experiences through storytelling. Their stories are written down and become the source of reading material.

In another procedure, students select their own reading materials and progress at their own rates. Frequent student-teacher conferences are required to monitor student progress.

Comprehension and Reading Rate. The ability to read for meaning develops gradually, and should be taught at each stage of reading development. As the structural elements of written communication develop, children recognize relationships among ideas and patterns of organization based on topic, details, sequence, classification, comparison and contrast, and cause and effect.

There are three main strands of reading comprehension. Literal reading captures the surface meaning of the information explicitly supplied by the author. Inferential reading requires the reader to draw a conclusion or to predict an outcome based not only on the information explicitly provided but on what the author implies. Critical reading involves evaluation and judgment and may require the reader to distinguish between fact and opinion or to question the accuracy of information.

See also: BILINGUAL EDUCATION; LITERACY AND ILLITERACY.

—

Reagan, Ronald [ray'-guhn] Ronald Wilson Reagan was elected the 40th president of the United States on Nov. 4, 1980, and was inaugurated on Jan. 20, 1981. At the age of 69, he was the oldest man and the first movie actor ever sworn into that office. During his two terms in office the popular president helped raise the nation's spirits. He also oversaw the creation of large budget and trade deficits and ultimately effected a historic arms-control agreement with the Soviet Union.

Early Life and Career. Born on Feb. 6, 1911, in Tampico, Ill., Reagan worked his way through Eureka College (B.A., 1932), had some success as a sportscaster, and began an acting career in 1937. He was to appear in about 53 films, with an interlude (1942–45) in the U.S. Army. Reagan married the actress Jane Wyman in 1940 (divorced 1948) and in 1952 wed Nancy Davis. He moved into television in the 1950s and became the popular host of "Death Valley Days" (1962–65) and spokesman for the General Electric Company. Beginning in the 1950s, Reagan spoke out against "big government" and communism, and by the 1960s he was a favorite conservative speaker.

With the shattering defeat of the Republicans under Barry Goldwater in 1964, Reagan was widely regarded as an ex–movie actor with simplistic views, no constituency of any size, and no future. In 1966, however, he easily defeated the incumbent governor of California, Democrat Edmund "Pat" Brown, and began two 4-year terms that made him a national figure.

Republican rivals thought Reagan too old to be a presidential contender in 1980, but with well-financed, loyal support, he swept the primaries to nomination. He selected George BUSH as his running mate.

Presidential Campaign. During the campaign, Reagan promised prosperity by "getting the government off our backs." Burdened by his failure to free the Americans held hostage by Iran and by a deteriorating economy, President Jimmy Carter saw his support erode as the voters concluded that Reagan was a safe choice to replace an ineffective regime. Reagan's margin of victory was sizable, the Californian carrying 44 states against Carter's 6, the popular vote 43 million to 36 million.

First Presidential Term. Immediately after his inauguration, Reagan launched a bold conservative program for economic "revitalization" that included sharp budget cutting to shrink the public sector; tax cutting, especially in the higher and business brackets, to unleash investment; and a broad retreat from business and social regulation. This policy was "supply-side economics," and Reagan promised a surge of noninflationary growth.

Reagan jammed his program through Congress in 1981—a major tax cut, $43 billion in budget cuts in domestic programs, and cutbacks in environmental and business regulation. House Democrats resisted this reversal in tax and spending policies, but Reagan's successful appeals to the public, combined with the assassination attempt in which he was wounded by shots fired by John W. Hinckley, Jr., on March 30, generated irresistible support.

Reagan's economic policy was cast into serious doubt by the fall, when economic recession deepened. In 1982 inflation dropped out of double figures, but interest rates remained high until the fall, and unemployment in 1982 was the highest in 40 years.

Reagan's defense buildup commenced, while foreign relations saw a stronger anti-Soviet stance but no major departures. The Israeli invasion of Lebanon in the summer of 1982 prompted the dispatch of U.S. and other peacekeeping forces to that beleaguered country. The congressional elections of November 1982 gave the Democrats a larger-than-normal, 26-seat gain in the House, while the Senate was unchanged in party totals.

Heavy casualties suffered by the Marines in Beirut in 1983 raised anxieties about the administration's Lebanese intervention (and early in 1984 the Marines were withdrawn). In late October 1983 the president ordered an invasion of the Caribbean island of Grenada and overthrew the country's anti-American dictatorship. The CIA worked openly to overturn the Sandinista regime in Nicaragua. Arms-control talks with the Soviet Union were frozen in mutual distrust as a new deployment of U.S. nuclear missiles began in Europe in November 1983.

In 1983 the economic picture brightened, with a resurgent stock market, low inflation, and rising production. Recovery was menaced by enormous deficits, but the jobless rate continued to inch downward.

Second Term. Early in 1984, Ronald Reagan announced his decision to run for a second term. The Democrats nominated former Vice-President Walter F. MONDALE, who made history by selecting N.Y. Rep. Geraldine FERRARO as his running mate. The president's radiant optimism, plus the con-

AT A GLANCE

RONALD WILSON REAGAN
40th President of the United States (1981–89)

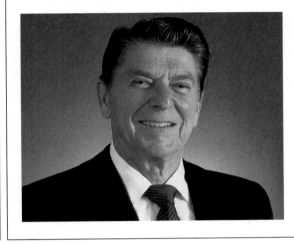

Born: Feb. 6, 1911, Tampico, Ill.

Education: Eureka College (graduated 1932)

Profession: Actor, Public Official

Religious Affiliation: Christian Church

Marriage: Jan. 25, 1940, to Jane Wyman (1914–)
—divorced, 1948; Mar. 4, 1952, to Nancy Davis
(1923–)

Children: Maureen Elizabeth Reagan (1941–); Michael Edward Reagan (1945–); Patricia Ann Reagan (1952–); Ronald Prescott Reagan (1958–)

Political Affiliation: Republican

Writings: *Where's the Rest of Me?* (1965)

Vice-President: George Bush

tinued economic recovery, produced a stunning victory. Reagan won 59% of the vote and carried 49 states.

Reagan and Bush were inaugurated for second terms in January 1985. That year, despite job expansion and steady economic growth, the country experienced huge trade deficits, a shaky farm sector, and a 1985 budget deficit of $211 billion. Reagan signed a tax reform bill in October 1986 that reduced and somewhat simplified taxes, but the Democrats claimed equal credit. In November the Democrats took control of the Senate by the unexpectedly wide margin of 55 to 45 seats.

During this period the White House was preoccupied with the Nicaraguan revolutionary government and the effort to overthrow the Sandinistas in Managua by aiding the rebel "contra" forces. Congress had prohibited aid to the contras from 1983 to 1986, but Reagan's determination to continue the struggle led members of his administration, notably the National Security Council staff, into a variety of activities including the secret sale of arms to Iran and the clandestine diversion of profits to the contras. The damaging IRAN-CONTRA AFFAIR became public in late 1986. With the administration already on the defensive, a stock-market collapse late in 1987 raised questions about Reagan's economic policies.

Reagan's fumbling performance at a second summit conference with Soviet leader Mikhail Gorbachev in Iceland during October 1986 (the first meeting had been in Geneva in November 1985) deepened doubts about the 75-year-old president. Reagan's persistent advocacy of his costly STRATEGIC DEFENSE INITIATIVE ("Star Wars") appeared to block an agreement to reduce nuclear missiles. In December 1987, however, Reagan signed an arms-control agreement with Gorbachev that eliminated intermediate-range missiles in Europe. Reagan visited Moscow in the spring of 1988.

His popularity rating again high, Reagan contributed to George Bush's election as president on Nov. 8, 1988.

Legacy. As Reagan retired his poll ratings were the highest of any president since World War II. Yet Reagan's place in history was unclear. His economic policies had been built upon deficit spending, pushing the national debt during his tenure from approximately $900 billion to over $2 trillion and transforming the United States from the world's leading creditor (as late as 1983) to the number-one debtor by 1986, with $400 billion owed abroad when Reagan left office.

Reagan's popularity survived concern over economic and other policy matters, for he possessed a leadership style that stressed inspiration over management. He had helped to alter the mood of the country from a brooding pessimism to a more confident outlook and had decisively changed the political agenda.

Reagan appointed three conservatives to the Supreme Court—Sandra D. O'Connor (the first woman justice), Antonin Scalia, and Anthony Kennedy. Observers expected these appointees to shift the court to the right in future years.

The government was no smaller at the end of Reagan's tenure than at the start, but its priorities had shifted. Social services and environmental protection had yielded priority to an arms buildup. Reagan claimed to have pursued policies that made possible Gorbachev's radical reforms of Soviet society and foreign policy, and thus to be the American president who ended the cold war.

real estate   SEE PROPERTY

---

real number   The set of all RATIONAL NUMBERS together with the set of all IRRATIONAL NUMBERS forms the set of real numbers. Any rational number a/b, where a and b are integers and $b \neq 0$, can be written as either a terminating decimal or as a repeating decimal. For example, $2 = 2.0$, $-3 = -3.0$, $\frac{5}{2} = 2.5$, and $-\frac{1}{4} = -0.25$ are all rational numbers that can be written as terminating decimals. On the other hand, $\frac{1}{3} = 0.333\ldots$ and $\frac{2}{7} = 0.285714285714\ldots$ are examples of repeating decimals. It is also possible to describe decimals that are not terminating or repeating. Numbers that are represented by nonterminating, nonrepeating decimals are called irrational numbers; examples of such numbers are $\sqrt{2}$, $\sqrt[3]{5}$, and π. Thus the set of real numbers can be described as the set of all decimals—terminating, repeating, or nonrepeating. Not all numbers, however, are real numbers (see COMPLEX NUMBER).

---

realism (art)   The art historical definition of *realism* originated in the movement that was dominant primarily in France from about 1840 to 1870–80 and that is identified particularly with the work of Gustave COURBET. The main precedents for 19th-century French realism are found in the work of artists painting in the tradition of Caravaggio. Realism, however, was decidedly an outgrowth of its particular time—one of great political and social upheaval. This unrest stirred the realists to reject prevailing canons of academic and romantic art and to undertake instead a nonescapist, democratic, empirical investigation of life as it existed around them. They painted ordinary people leading their everyday lives. Although other artists had depicted similar subjects in earlier times, the realists took a fresh and unemotional view.

Realism was most emphatically proclaimed in 1855, when Courbet, having been rejected for the Paris Exposition, arranged a private showing of his paintings that centered on his huge *The Artist's Studio* (1855; Louvre, Paris). He also distributed a manifesto of realism outlining his program. Among the other realists were Honoré DAUMIER, most noted for his incisive mockery of the petty bourgeoisie, and Jean François MILLET, whose scenes of workers in the countryside are more low-keyed and reflective in tone than those of Courbet. The works of Édouard MANET and Edgar DEGAS during the 1860s and '70s are also realist, which demonstrates the connection between realism and impressionism. The work of the PRE-RAPHAELITES in England is also related to the realist movement.

---

realism (literature)   The term *realism* as applied to a literary mode first appeared in France in the 1820s. By mid-century it was beginning to be used to denote a new kind of writing in France, Russia, and England, mainly as a reaction against literary ROMANTICISM. This new literary creed emerged primarily in the form of the NOVEL, which could closely approximate the speech and detail of everyday life better than poetry or even drama. In France, realism's first major exponent was Honoré de BALZAC, in a wide-ranging series of novels entitled *La Comédie Humaine* (1829–47). Balzac was followed by Gustave FLAUBERT, whose *Madame Bovary* (1857) is considered the foremost French realist novel. Later in the century, Émile ZOLA formulated a branch of literary realism called NATURALISM, which carried realism to extremes in its emphasis on the grosser aspects of human behavior. The French realist tradition presented objectively, without authorial intrusion, a cause-and-effect

Gustave Courbet's The Artist's Studio *(1855), subtitled* A True Allegory Concerning Seven Years of My Artistic Life, *portrays the artist at work amid an inattentive assembly of undistinguished figures. Courbet's emphasis on the familiar so offended accepted aesthetic precepts that he was forbidden to display his work at the Paris Exposition of 1855. (Louvre, Paris.)*

material universe that eschewed the far away and long ago of the romantics and repudiated exaggerated heroes in favor of ordinary people.

In Russia, realism's chief practitioners were Leo TOLSTOI, Fyodor DOSTOYEVSKY, and Anton CHEKHOV, who developed their own strain of realism. Many critics see the Russian form as more hopeful and compassionate than the French.

In England the realist movement was not so pervasive, for Victorian writers objected to its manner, and moralists deplored its content. Realism nevertheless attained new heights in England with George ELIOT, whose *Middlemarch* (1871–72) is often deemed the greatest 19th-century English novel. Fully conscious of her role as sociological reflector of English provincial life, Eliot extended realism into the complexities of the psychological, and her methods would find their extreme elaboration in the suprarealist novels and stories of the American Henry JAMES. George MOORE (Irish novelist, poet, and playwright), cited as a naturalist, and George GISSING (*New Grub Street*, 1891) also wrote about the common folk. Arnold BENNETT depicted with dexterity the life of the Five Towns, a pottery-making district in the Midlands, about 1900.

In the United States the banner for realism was carried by William Dean HOWELLS as critic and for a time as novelist (*The Rise of Silas Lapham*, 1885). Although Sinclair LEWIS (*Main Street*, 1920) followed in that tradition, the battle was carried on more vigorously by the naturalists Frank NORRIS, Jack LONDON, Theodore DREISER, James T. FARRELL, and, in dramaturgy, Eugene O'NEILL.

For about a century realism was the vital and increasingly dominant literary mode in the entire Western world. When in the 20th century theoretical physicists began to question the realists' tightly causal model of the universe and to allow the random and the relative, realism as a literary doctrine lost some of its compelling force. Having spawned many of the world's finest novels, the movement still surfaces occasionally in contemporary literature, as in the novels of manners written by the American Louis AUCHINCLOSS.

realism (philosophy) Realism denotes two distinct sets of philosophical theories, one regarding the nature of universal concepts and the other dealing with knowledge of objects in the world.

In late-classical and medieval philosophy, realism was a development of the Platonic theory of Forms and held, generally, that universals such as "red" or "man" have an independent, objective existence, either in a realm of their own or in the mind of God. Medieval realism is usually contrasted with NOMINALISM, and the classic critiques from this viewpoint were provided by Peter Abelard and William of Occam.

In modern philosophy realism is a broad term, encompassing several movements whose unity lies in a common rejection of philosophical IDEALISM and PRAGMATISM. In its most general form realism asserts that objects in the external world exist independently of what is thought about them and that concepts get their meaning by referring to them. The most straightforward of such theories is usually known as naive realism. It contends that in perception humans are made directly aware of objects and their attributes and thus have immediate access to the external world. This view fails, however, to explain perceptual mistakes and illusions, and most realists argue that causal processes in the mind mediate, or interpret, directly perceived appearances.

reaper The reaper is a device used for harvesting grains. It has revolving bars or teeth, which press the sheaves of grain against a cutting apparatus. The development of the mechanical reaper enabled farmers to grow crops on a large scale.

The first recorded English patent for a mechanical reaper was issued to Joseph Boyce in 1799. Soon after, many reapers were developed employing either revolving cutters or vibrating knives. None gained widespread use. Two Americans, Obed Hussey and Cyrus H. McCORMICK, are usually given credit for inventing the modern reaper. Hussey's reaper was patented in 1833, McCormick's in 1834. In 1850, McCormick purchased the patent rights to Hussey's cutting bar. The McCormick-Hussey reaper cut grain with a reciprocating cutting bar and had a reel that put the cut grain onto a conveyer, where it was manually bound. This model dominated the farm-implement market until the advent, in the 1870s, of wire and then twine binders, which cut and bundled the sheaves of grain mechanically. In the 20th century the reaper was replaced by the COMBINE.

Reason, Age of   see ENLIGHTENMENT

reasoning Reasoning is the process of drawing conclusions from a set of premises. Whereas LOGIC is concerned with the relations of legitimate inference among statements, studies of reasoning are concerned with how human beings change some of their beliefs because of other beliefs.

When reasoning is not logically correct, it provides particular insights into human thought processes. For example, in a famous reasoning experiment, subjects are shown four cards, each of which has a letter on one side and a number on the other. The sides they see show E, K, 4, and 7. When subjects are asked which cards they would have to turn over to determine whether the rule "*If there's a vowel on one side, there's an even number on the other*" is true, more than 80 percent make a mistake. (The correct answer is E and 7.) People generally have more trouble reasoning about abstract symbols than about concrete objects.

Reasoning can be classified into deductive and inductive reasoning, for which there are formal models in logic, and reasoning by analogy. Reasoning by analogy is usually classified as a type of inductive reasoning.

Thinking that is directed at reaching a goal is called PROBLEM SOLVING, and it can include the various types of reasoning.

See also: ARTIFICIAL INTELLIGENCE; COGNITIVE PSYCHOLOGY; INTELLIGENCE.

Rebecca

Rebecca [ree-bek'-uh] In the Bible, Rebecca (or Rebekah) was the wife of the patriarch ISAAC and the mother of ESAU and JACOB. After years of childlessness, she finally conceived the twins, whose struggle in her womb was taken as a sign of their impending hostility. Rebecca sided with Jacob, the younger son, and helped him cheat Esau out of Isaac's final blessing (Gen. 24–27).

Rebellions of 1837

Rebellions of 1837 The Rebellions of 1837 in Upper and Lower Canada (now Ontario and Quebec) were spurred by Britain's refusal to grant greater home rule. The locally elected legislative assembly in each province was dominated by the crown-appointed governor, executive council, and legislative council.

The rebellion in Upper Canada, led by William Lyon MACKENZIE, died almost before it began. In December a small group of rebels planning to attack Toronto were dispersed by militia north of that city. In Lower Canada, French Canadians led by Louis J. PAPINEAU staged a more substantial uprising in November–December 1837, mainly in the Richelieu River valley, east of Montreal. Papineau fled to New York State, and the rebellion was severely repressed.

In the wake of the rebellions, the British government sent Lord DURHAM to Canada. His report recommended a union of the two provinces—which was accomplished in 1841—and responsible government, that is, a cabinet type of executive accountable to an elected legislature. The latter suggestion was finally implemented in 1848.

Reber, Grote

Reber, Grote [ree'-bur] The American radio engineer Grote Reber, b. Wheaton, Ill., Dec. 22, 1911, designed and constructed (1937) in his own backyard the first radio telescope, a 31-ft (9.4-m) bowl-shaped antenna, with which he discovered the first discrete radio sources in the sky. Reber alone did research in RADIO ASTRONOMY in the period before World War II.

receiver

receiver (communications) In wireless communication, such as radar, radio, and television, intelligence is transmitted through space in the form of radio waves by means of a TRANSMITTER. The equipment necessary to pick up, amplify, and convert these radio-frequency (rf) signals back into their original form, usually speech or music, is called a receiver. For brevity, only RADIO receivers will be discussed here. The basic receiver consists of six parts: (1) the receiving antenna, which accepts carrier frequencies from all stations within range of the receiver; (2) a tuning stage, or tuner, which picks out the desired modulated carrier wave; (3) one or more amplification stages

that increase the weakly received signal to usable levels (see AMPLIFIER); (4) a detector, or demodulator, that extracts the modulation signal from the carrier wave; (5) an audio amplifier that brings the still-weak signal up to a level that is powerful enough to operate the sound producer; and (6) the actual sound producer, which may be a LOUDSPEAKER, a headset, or some other device that converts the radio signal into sound.

The sensitivity of a radio receiver—its ability to pick up and use weak signals—is largely determined by the number of amplification states that precede the sound-production device. The signal-to-noise ratio indicates how much amplification of the signal the receiver can provide as compared to the amount of NOISE that it introduces during the process. Selectivity is the ability of a receiver to select only the desired signal, rejecting all other signals. This process is accomplished by use of tuned or resonant circuits; the quality of these circuits determines selectivity. The stability of a receiver is its ability to remain on a certain frequency once the receiver has been tuned to that frequency. The better radio receivers have circuits for automatic frequency control (AFC) to accomplish this. Fidelity refers to the ability of the set to reproduce faithfully the original signal (see HIGH FIDELITY).

Recent Epoch

Recent Epoch The Recent, or Holocene, Epoch is the younger major subdivision of the Quaternary Period. After the last Pleistocene Epoch glaciation, an interglacial interval of warming followed, causing the glaciers to withdraw (see GLACIER AND GLACIATION; ICE AGES). This marked the beginning of the Recent Epoch. The rate of decay shown by radiocarbon (carbon-14) occurring in early Recent wood, peat, shells, and bones indicates that the Recent Epoch began approximately 10,000 years ago.

See also: EARTH, GEOLOGICAL HISTORY OF; GEOLOGIC TIME.

recession

recession Recession is a condition in which a nation's economic activity—the production and consumption of goods and services—declines. Recession is also defined as a period when the growth of a nation's economy slows to a halt or even declines slightly. It is the second phase of the classic BUSINESS CYCLE of expansion, or prosperity; recession; contraction, or depression; and recovery. Economists disagree about the cause of recessions. Some think that they are set off by declines in consumer spending; others point to decreases in capital investment; still others blame government budget policy. In any event, both capital investment and consumer spending do decline during recessions, as do wholesale sales, employment, personal income, and construction.

Since World War II no recession in the United States (1945–46, 1949, 1954, 1956, 1960–61, 1970, 1973–75, 1980–83, 1991) has worsened into a depression—as did those in 1807, 1837, 1873, 1882, 1893, 1920, 1933, and 1937—perhaps because of the success of government economic intervention. In times of recession the federal government has usually acted to create jobs by increasing its spending (see FISCAL POLICY) and the supply of money in circulation (see MONETARY POLICY). As employment picks up, consumer spending increases and the economy is usually on the way to recovery. In 1991 the Federal Reserve Board lowered the rates it charges memeber banks in order to bolster investment and spending.

Recife [ray-see'-fay]   Recife (formerly Pernambuco), the capital of the Pernambuco state in northeastern Brazil, lies on the Atlantic coast. The population is 1,287,623 (1985). Sometimes called the "Venice of Brazil," Recife lies on the banks of the Capibaribe and Beberibe rivers and on an island near the mouths of the rivers; bridges link its three main sections.

Recife is an important industrial and agricultural center. It is also one of Brazil's leading ports and is connected by air, highway, and rail to the hinterland. Exports include cotton, sugar, rum, hides, and cereals. The city is the seat of SUDENE, a federal government agency responsible since 1959 for the economic development of northeastern Brazil. Recife has many fine public buildings, colonial churches, and museums. The state university (1946) is there. Carnivals draw many tourists.

The site was first settled in the 1520s by the Portuguese, who cut and shipped brazilwood. The city was founded in 1548 and then occupied by the Dutch from 1630 until 1654. Brazil's first printing press was brought to Recife in 1706. South America's oldest daily newspaper, *Diário de Pernambuco,* has been published in Recife since 1825.

recitative [res-i-tuh-teev']   Recitative is a manner of reciting or declaiming words in musical works, usually but not exclusively in Latin, Italian, German, French, or English. Such declamation serves to carry forward a narrative in poetry or prose and generally leads to a balance between text and melody as, for example, in an ARIA. As an aspect of PLAINSONG, it is used for the singing of psalms, lessons, tones for the Passions, and other parts of the liturgy calling for rapid and simple declamation. It also appears in liturgical music dramas and oratorios. The arioso recitative came into favor during the 17th century and was described as a style "gracefully embellished with ornaments appropriate to the thought," which refers to the recitative soliloquy exploited in Italy by Monteverdi, Cavalli, and others.

On the operatic stage, recitative ranged from rapid speech-style declamation to a melodious arioso, which was sometimes in the form of an expressive lament. In the 18th century, the *secco* (continuo only) type was popular because of its speed of narrative; *stromentato* (with orchestra) tended to be more dramatic. Many later operas, including those by Wagner and Richard Strauss, lean heavily on a modified recitative style. Instrumental recitatives are by no means uncommon and are found in works by Bach, Beethoven, Johann Kuhnau, Schoenberg, Ludwig Spohr, and others.

recoilless rifle   A recoilless rifle is a lightweight portable gun with a rifled barrel. Such weapons do not have

The Carl-Gustav M2 recoilless gun, developed in Sweden, is a modern antitank weapon designed for use by the infantry. It fires an 84-mm (6.7-in) shell and has an effective range of 500 m (1,600 ft). The M2 employs the Krupp system (detail) to absorb recoil caused by firing. Gas from the burning propellant escapes through a venturi nozzle in the rear of the gun; the constriction increases the velocity of the gas to counterbalance the backward motion caused by the forward acceleration and weight of the shell. Part of the NATO arsenal, the 16-kg (36-lb) M2 is carried, aimed, and fired by one person, but an additional person must carry and load the ammunition.

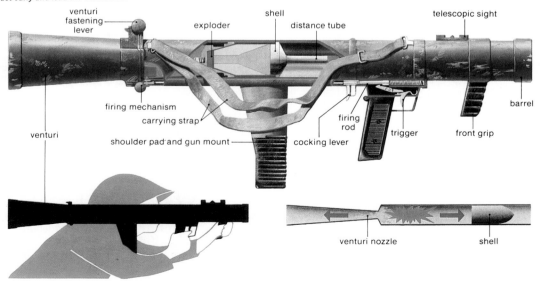

venturi
fastening lever
firing mechanism
carrying strap
venturi
shoulder pad and gun mount
exploder
shell
distance tube
telescopic sight
barrel
firing rod
cocking lever
trigger
front grip
venturi nozzle
shell

the sophisticated recoil system of conventional artillery, but offset recoil by allowing some of the propellant gases to escape through a nozzle at the back of the gun.

The simplest way to eliminate recoil would be to put two identical guns back to back and fire them at exactly the same time; the recoil of one would exactly balance the other. This principle was used by an American industrialist, Gregory Davison, in 1910 to develop a system that became the forerunner of present-day recoilless rifles. His arrangement was tried on a few aircraft in World War I. Such aircraft were too flimsy to carry a large gun, and the recoil-free Davison gun placed no strain on the airframe when it was fired. The largest Davison fired a 4.5-kg (12-lb) shell. It was discontinued after 1918.

The concept was revived in Germany in the 1930s when a portable field gun was required. This weapon is the basis of systems in use today. The principle requires the velocity of the gas escaping to the rear to be increased so as to balance the weight of a heavy shell. To achieve this, however, the amount of propellant must be about five times the normal charge, and a much larger and heavier cartridge case is required. Another difficulty is the backblast, which limits the range of the gun and is difficult to conceal. Because of these limitations, recoilless guns are now used primarily for short-range antitank defense when the barrel can be pointed directly at the target.

recombinant DNA   see GENETIC ENGINEERING

Reconstruction   In U.S. history Reconstruction refers to the period (1865–77) following the Civil War and to the process by which the states of the Confederacy were readmitted to full membership in the Union. The period was marked by struggles between political parties about how Reconstruction should proceed and between the president and Congress over who should direct it.

Differing Views of Reconstruction. Reconstruction aroused violent controversy, and political affiliations were a key determinant of where one stood on it. Northern Democrats believed the Constitution strictly limited federal power, anticipated that most Southern whites would vote Democratic, and had little sympathy for black aspirations. They favored a rapid Reconstruction that would make few demands on the ex-Confederates. Republicans believed that the secessionist states had forfeited their status and could be treated by Congress as territories or conquered provinces. In addition, most felt that blacks were entitled to fundamental human rights, and many hoped Southern Republicanism could be built with the help of black support.

Initial Plans of Reconstruction. President Abraham LINCOLN had hoped to set up loyal governments in the Southern states just as soon as a group of the state's citizens equaling 10 percent of the voters in the 1860 presidential election had signed oaths of loyalty to the Union. Republicans in Congress did not want a quick restoration, however, and in 1864 they passed the Wade-Davis Re-

construction Bill. This measure would have delayed the process of readmission until 50 percent of a state's 1860 voters had signed loyalty oaths, but Lincoln pocket-vetoed the bill.

Presidential Reconstruction. As president following Lincoln's assassination, Andrew JOHNSON adopted the Wade-Davis plan with some modifications. Allowing for few exceptions, he issued an amnesty to anyone who would take an oath to be loyal to the Union in the future. He required only that the secessionist states ratify the 13th Amendment freeing the slaves, abolish slavery in their own constitutions, repudiate debts incurred while in rebellion, and declare secession null and void. By the end of 1865, all but Texas had complied.

Congressional Reconstruction. The Republican majority in Congress, however, was unsatisfied with Johnson's program. It also noted that the program did nothing to protect the rights of the freedmen and that the Southern states were passing BLACK CODES to keep the former slaves

Thomas Nast's cartoon attacks Andrew Johnson's mild Reconstruction plan, seen as a betrayal of what the Union soldier fought for. Radical Republicans in Congress replaced Johnson's proposals with a more stringent plan, embodied initially in the 14th Amendment.

"The Solid South," which voted solidly for the Democratic party, emerged at the end of the Reconstruction period. The Republican party, identified here with Ulysses Grant, "Bayonet Rule", and carpetbag government, was long regarded as the oppressor.

in subservient positions. In 1866, Congress passed, over Johnson's veto, the FREEDMEN'S BUREAU Act and the Civil Rights Act (see CIVIL RIGHTS ACTS) to help freedmen shift from slavery to freedom and to assure them equality before the law. In June 1866, Republicans also proposed the 14TH AMENDMENT to the Constitution, which declared blacks to be citizens, prohibited states from discriminating against any class of citizens or denying any citizen fundamental rights, and banned Confederate leaders from holding federal or state office until Congress removed the disqualification.

The Southern state governments created under Johnson's plan refused to ratify this amendment, and in 1867, Congress passed a series of Reconstruction Acts. These laws placed the South under temporary military occupation. Reluctant to make the national government permanently responsible for the protection of the ex-slaves, Republicans decided to enfranchise African Americans so that Southern politicians would have to treat them fairly to get their votes. Congress agreed to recognize new state governments only after they had guaranteed equal civil and political rights regardless of race and had ratified the 14th Amendment. Moreover, Confederate leaders were not allowed to vote in the process that created the new state governments. This program became known as Radical Reconstruction.

As commander in chief of the armed forces, Johnson was able to interfere with the enforcement of these laws. Several efforts to restrain him failed, but when he fired Secretary of War Edwin M. STANTON in an effort to gain complete control of the army, House Republicans claimed he had violated the TENURE OF OFFICE ACT (1867) and impeached him. In the trial that followed, the Senate narrowly acquitted Johnson (May 1868). By that summer all ex-Confederate states except Mississippi, Texas, and Virginia had accepted the terms of Radical Reconstruction. To round out their program, the Republicans in 1869 proposed the 15th Amendment to the Constitution forbidding racial discrimination in voting qualifications and required ratification of it for readmission.

Radical Reconstruction in the South. Supported by an almost unanimous African-American vote and, in some states, by a sizable minority of whites, Republican governments were elected to office all over the South. They legislated many reforms—free public schools, labor laws fairer to employees, more equitable tax laws, and antidiscrimination measures. In the process, the Republicans raised taxes much higher than Southerners were used to; fell prey to the corruption that plagued all the states in the 1870s; and alienated many Southern whites who resented a system of racial equality. Unable to erode African-American support for Republicans with promises, many white Southerners resorted to force through the KU KLUX KLAN and other organizations, and they refined their own political organization. By 1875 all but three Southern states—South Carolina, Louisiana, and Florida—were back in the hands of Southern Democrats, who discontinued most of the Republican reforms and began to circumscribe the freedom of African Americans.

The Election of 1876 and the End of Reconstruction. During the early 1870s violence became so bad in the South that President Ulysses S. GRANT often sent troops there to protect Republicans during election campaigns. Northerners were tiring of the turmoil by the time of the 1876 presidential election and wanted a restoration of peace. The result of the 1876 presidential contest hinged on the disputed electoral votes of the three remaining Republican states in the South. Both sides agreed to send the votes to a special commission, which ruled Republican Rutherford B. HAYES the winner. Before the decision, Hayes had apparently let Southern Democrats know that he would not use federal troops to protect the Republicans in those states. Soon after taking office, he withdrew the troops to their barracks, and the last Southern Republican governments fell.

record player   see PHONOGRAPH

----

recorder   The principal type of European flute from the 16th to the mid-18th century was the end-blown fipple FLUTE called the recorder (German: *Blockflöte*; French: *flûte à bec*). It was usually built of wood and had eight finger holes. Its whistle mouthpiece made it easier to play than the transverse flute. Eight sizes were described in Michael Praetorius's *Syntagma musicum* (1615), but the largest and smallest were rarely used. Recorders were played together in consorts, were used in

The four recorders commonly used today are (left to right) *the soprano, alto, tenor, and bass, with the playing position shown* (left). *A simple recorder was known in 10th-century Europe, and by the 16th century a family of various-sized instruments had been developed. The recorder has remained a relatively simple instrument and is currently enjoying a revival of popular interest.*

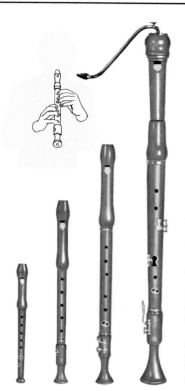

chamber music and orchestras, and—treble recorders especially—were used in solo sonatas.

The instrument fell into disuse before the end of the 18th century, probably because its tone lacked sufficient strength to compete with other, newer instruments. Its 20th-century revival derives from the interest of amateurs and performers of old music. Four sizes are now in common use: soprano and alto (called descant and treble in England), tenor, and bass. The bass has a crook like a bassoon to bring the finger holes within reach. Some modern recorders are made of plastic, but serious performers prefer wooden instruments.

recording   See SOUND RECORDING AND REPRODUCTION; VIDEO RECORDING

rectangle   A rectangle is a four-sided plane figure (a QUADRILATERAL), all of whose angles are right angles. Alternatively, a rectangle may be defined as a PARALLELOGRAM having one right angle; this implies that all the angles are right angles. A line segment connecting opposite (nonadjacent) vertices of a rectangle is called a diagonal and divides the rectangle into two congruent triangles. If adjacent sides have lengths a and b, then the perimeter of the rectangle, that is, the distance around the sides, is given by $P = 2a + 2b$. The area of the rectangle is given by the product of two adjacent sides (area $= ab$). If adjacent sides of a rectangle have the same length ($a = b$), then the figure is a SQUARE and has perimeter $4a$ and area a^2.

rectifier   A rectifier is an electronic component that permits passage of only the positive or negative portion of an alternating electrical current. Modern rectifiers are usually made from a pn junction formed in a SEMICONDUCTOR, usually silicon. Before the development of semiconductors, DIODES (two-electrode electron tubes) were commonly used as rectifiers.

All rectifiers perform the same basic function of rectifying an electronic current, that is, transforming an alternating current (AC) containing both positive and negative components into a fluctuating current having only a positive or negative component—a direct current (DC). Their physical construction and operating specifications, however, are diverse.

Rectifiers intended for low-power applications such as the detection of a modulated radio or microwave signal are generally small, often being composed of a small chip of an appropriate semiconductor installed in one end of a cylindrical package made from metal, glass, or ceramic.

Medium-power rectifiers designed to rectify electrical current supplied to various kinds of electronic equipment are usually installed in a metal case to permit excess heat to be radiated into the surrounding air and may also be attached to a heat sink, to increase radiation of heat.

High-power rectifiers are used in applications such as the power supply of heavy-duty motors. They are installed in metal packages, are almost always attached to a heat sink, and often are provided with additional cooling.

Rectifiers may be interconnected in various ways to efficiently use the voltage being rectified. A single rectifier blocks half of an AC voltage applied to it while allowing the other half to pass; it is therefore referred to as a half-wave rectifier. Two or four separate rectifiers, however, can be arranged in such a way that they will rectify both halves of an AC signal into direct current, making a full-wave rectifier. The output voltage has a ripple, but it can be smoothed by electronic filtering (see FILTER, ELECTRONIC).

Specialized rectifiers in common use include various kinds of pn-junction diodes, such as the ZENER DIODE, a component with the ability to regulate a voltage at a specified level.

rectum   See DIGESTION, HUMAN; DIGESTIVE SYSTEM; INTESTINE

recycling of materials   Recycling waste and used materials for some useful purpose is an effective means of conserving resources, of reducing waste disposal, and, often, of cutting costs.

Recycling Approaches.   Some materials can be reused for their original purpose. The most obvious example is the beverage container. Used only once and discarded, a bottle adds to the solid waste flow and requires costly replacement. A returnable beverage bottle, on the other hand, can be used up to 20 times.

Utilizing residual wastes is another recycling technique. For example, incineration ashes can be used in making concrete; organic wastes can be composted to make soil conditioners; combustible wastes can be burned to produce steam or electricity (see WASTE DISPOSAL SYSTEMS). Waste materials can also be reused in the manufacture of new products. The recovery and reforming of paper, glass, and metals are prominent examples of such recycling.

Recycling Methods. The most effective way of recycling wastes is to separate materials before they become part of the waste stream. This is especially true for municipal wastes. In an attempt to slow the rapid filling of LANDFILLS, increasing numbers of localities have instituted refuse-collection programs that require householders to segregate glass, metal, paper, and plastic for recycling.

Recycling techniques for the first three have been available for many years. Methods have recently also been developed to recycle several major types of plastics. Plastic foam containers can be melted and extruded, to make such plastic materials as plastic "lumber" and garbage cans. Certain kinds of plastic soda bottles can be shredded and reformed as a fiber, to be used as fiberfill.

The Economics of Recycling. The energy used to reprocess waste materials is far less than that required for making virgin materials. Rising energy costs, therefore, increase the economic incentives to recycle.

As more localities require household separation and curbside collection of recyclables, and as more states pass legislation to encourage the return of beverage containers, the flow of recyclable materials will increase. However, markets for many of these materials need to be expanded to absorb the supply that these programs will create.

Red Badge of Courage, The   Stephen CRANE's novel *The Red Badge of Courage* (1895), which appeared when the U.S. Civil War was still treated primarily as the subject for romance, was the first realistic fictional work on that subject to attain widespread popularity and critical acclaim. Its realism is all the more remarkable because Crane had no experience of war when he wrote the book. He was, however, able to describe it from the viewpoint of the protagonist, Henry Fleming—from his initial dreams of heroics through his internal struggle against cowardice, his acceptance of his place among the troops, and his first encounter with death.

red blood cell   see BLOOD

Red Cloud   Red Cloud, or Makhpiya Luta, 1822–1909, head chief of the Oglala Lakota, a SIOUX Indian group, for years frustrated efforts of the U.S. government to open up the West. By 1865 he was effectively discouraging white intrusion by way of the BOZEMAN TRAIL. A peace treaty of 1868, which Red Cloud signed, seems to have been a turning point for the war chief. After visiting Washington, D.C., where he perhaps was impressed by the numbers and power of white people, he agreed to settle down as a reservation chief. According to some of his contemporaries, such as SITTING BULL and CRAZY HORSE, he sold out to the whites, permitting corrupt and deplorable conditions on Sioux reservations. He lost his status as head chief in 1881. After the WOUNDED KNEE massacre (1890) he lived quietly on Pine Ridge Reservation.

Red Cross   The Red Cross, officially known since 1986 as the International Movement of the Red Cross and Red Crescent, is an international humanitarian organization with independent affiliates in most countries of the world. With the aim of voluntary service to others, the Red Cross was established to provide welfare service for victims of war and to help carry out the terms of the GENEVA CONVENTIONS of war. Its work has been extended to include such peacetime services as maintaining blood banks, offering training in first aid and water safety, and caring for victims of such disasters as floods, fires, and famines. It also aids refugees.

The Swiss humanitarian Jean Henri DUNANT established and brought recognition to the Red Cross. The first voluntary relief services that he proposed were organized in 1863. The present organization is centered on its international committee, whose work mainly involves providing legal protection and material assistance to military and civilian victims of both international and internal wars, and a second body, the League of Red Cross and Red Crescent Societies (founded 1919), which aids in disaster relief and promotes cooperation among the national societies. The International Red Cross comprises these two bodies, with administrative offices located in Geneva, Switzerland. It has received the Nobel Peace Prize three times—in 1917, 1944, and 1963.

The American Red Cross, founded in 1881 by Clara BARTON, is authorized by congressional charter requiring the society to assist in wartime and to provide disaster relief. Local offices may also provide services needed in their communities. The Red Cross is funded privately. The national headquarters is in Washington, D.C.

Red Jacket   Red Jacket, c.1758–1830, also known as Sagoyewatha, was a fiery SENECA chief known for his flamboyant personality, oratory, and political shrewdness. Although he publicly opposed land sales to settlers in order to gain his people's support, he secretly yielded land to maintain esteem among whites.

After the Seneca were drawn into the Revolutionary War on the side of the British, Red Jacket reputedly proved to be an unenthusiastic warrior, although he wore the British uniform coat, which earned him the English name Red Jacket. After the war, he worked to maintain peace between his people and the United States. During the War of 1812 he fought on the American side against the British. He later became well known as an advocate of the maintenance of separate Iroquois jurisdiction and customs.

Red River (China) see Yuan River

▬
Red River (United States) The Red River (or Red River of the South) is a 1,639-km-long (1,018-mi) tributary of the Mississippi River. It rises in eastern New Mexico, follows part of the Texas-Oklahoma border, and flows southeast through Arkansas to Shreveport, La. About 11 km (7 mi) upstream of its Mississippi River confluence, the Red divides into the Old River, which continues to the Mississippi, and the Atchafalaya, which flows south to enter the Gulf of Mexico west of the Mississippi delta. It drains an area of 236,700 km^2 (91,400 mi^2). Fulton, Ark., 632 km (455 mi) upstream, is at the head of navigation.

Flood-control and development projects include Denison Dam (1944), which impounds Lake Texoma. Cotton, cattle, and winter wheat are raised in the river valley; industries include lumbering and petroleum. The river was the site of a Confederate victory at Mansfield, La., during the Civil War.

Red River Rebellion see Riel, Louis

▬
Red River Settlement The Red River Settlement was a colony located in the valley of the Red River of the North in present-day Manitoba, Canada. Its founder, Thomas Douglas, 5th earl of Selkirk, obtained an extensive grant of land there from the Hudson's Bay Company in 1811. The same year he sent a group of Scots to the area to establish an agricultural colony, and other settlers followed (1812–15). The colony, later known as Assiniboia, was opposed by the North West Company, a rival of the Hudson's Bay Company. The Nor'Westers tried to persuade the colonists to leave and then resorted to violence that culminated on June 19, 1816, in the massacre of Red River's governor and 19 of his men at Seven Oaks (near modern Winnipeg).

Lord Selkirk reestablished the colony in 1817, and it began to grow after the Hudson's Bay Company absorbed the North West Company in 1821. Many métis, buffalo hunters, and traders settled there. Originally administered by officials appointed by Lord Selkirk and his heirs, the colony was transferred to the Hudson's Bay Company in the 1830s. In 1869 the company surrendered to Canada its rights of jurisdiction. The following year, despite the Red River Rebellion (see Riel, Louis), the area was admitted to the Canadian Confederation as the province of Manitoba.

▬
Red Sea The Red Sea, a long, narrow body of water between northeastern Africa and the Arabian Peninsula,

serves as a connecting waterway between the Mediterranean Sea and the Indian Ocean. It covers an area of about 437,700 km^2 (169,000 mi^2) to a maximum depth of 2,190 m (7,200 ft). At its northern end the Red Sea forks into the Gulf of Aqaba (see Aqaba, Gulf of) and the Gulf of Suez. The former leads through the Straits of Tiran to the ports of Elat (Israel) and al-Aqaba (Jordan). The Gulf of Suez leads to the Mediterranean Sea via the Suez Canal. The strait of Bab el-Mandeb at the southern end connects the Red Sea with the Gulf of Aden, the Arabian Sea, and the Indian Ocean. In addition to Elat and Aqaba, major ports on the sea include Jidda in Saudi Arabia,

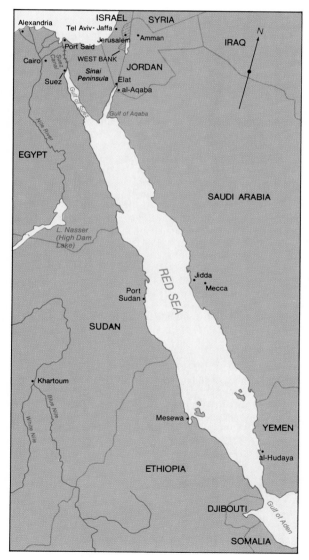

Port Sudan in Sudan, Suez in Egypt, Mesewa in Ethiopia, and al-Hudayda in Yemen.

The Red Sea became an important sea-lane after the opening of the Suez Canal in 1869. Since that time it has been the focus of many political and diplomatic confrontations. The 1967 ARAB-ISRAELI WAR was precipitated by the closing of the Straits of Tiran by Egypt and Saudi Arabia.

red shift   The phenomenon of the red shift is of central importance in modern COSMOLOGY, where it is commonly encountered. If the wavelength of light measured by a distant observer is longer than that which would be measured at the source of the light, the light is said to be red shifted—that is, shifted toward the red, or long-wavelength, end of the spectrum. Similarly, a blue shift is a displacement toward the blue, or short-wavelength, end of the spectrum. Red and blue shifts are most easily detected when the spectrum of a distant object contains identifiable features, such as absorption or emission lines of a particular element, and the positions of these lines are compared with those on a standard spectrum of the element obtained in a laboratory.

Two types of red shift are known. The first results from the line-of-sight relative motion between the source and the observer, explained by the DOPPLER EFFECT. If the shift z is small, the velocity v of the source relative to the observer may be obtained by the equation $z = \Delta\lambda/\lambda_0 = v/c$ where $\Delta\lambda$ is the change in wavelength, λ_0 is the rest wavelength (that which would be seen if the observer and the source were at rest relative to each other), and c is the velocity of light (300,000 km/sec, or 186,000 mi/sec). All stars in our Galaxy have slight Doppler red or blue shifts.

A normal spectrum (A) is for a star at rest with respect to the Earth. All spectral lines would be shifted (B) to the blue end of the spectrum if the star approached the Earth, whereas the lines would be moved (C) toward the red end if the star receded. The amount of blue or red shift depends on the star's relative speed.

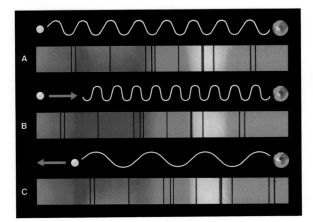

For larger Doppler shifts, the equation

$$z = \frac{\Delta\lambda}{\lambda_0} = \sqrt{\frac{c+v}{c-v}} - 1,$$

derived from the theory of special relativity, must be used to obtain the velocity of the object. All but the nearest galaxies (see EXTRAGALACTIC SYSTEMS) have substantial red shifts, indicating that nearly all galaxies are receding from our own. Such expansion of the universe confirms cosmological models based on the theory of general relativity.

In 1929, Edwin Hubble and Milton Humason discovered that the recessional velocity v and the distance d of galaxies are related linearly by the empirical relation $v = H_0 d$, where H_0 is a constant of proportionality now known as Hubble's constant. Thus if galactic red shifts are interpreted as effects of recessional velocity (and most astronomers are confident of such an interpretation), then the red shift of a galaxy can be used to determine its distance.

The second type of red shift results from the presence of a gravitational field. According to the theory of general relativity, the spectrum of light from a source located at a distance R from a mass M will suffer a gravitational red shift z when detected by a distant observer such that $z = GM/Rc^2$ where G is the gravitational constant.

red-spotted newt   The red-spotted newt, *Notophthalmus viridescens*, family Salamandridae, is found in the eastern United States and southern Canada. Growing to about 10 cm (4 in) long, it is commonly greenish with a series of large red spots on each side. Mating occurs in the early spring, and females lay from 200 to 400 eggs, which hatch in 20 to 35 days. Within 3 months the larvae transform into a terrestrial, immature stage called the red eft, remaining so for up to 3 years before returning to the water as adults; in some cases the larvae change directly into adults. (See SALAMANDER AND NEWT.)

The red-spotted newt, a small salamander adapted to cold habitats, can live in ice-covered ponds during winter.

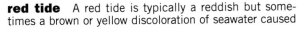

red tide   A red tide is typically a reddish but sometimes a brown or yellow discoloration of seawater caused by an enormous increase, or bloom, in the numbers of microscopic algae and protozoans. The discolored area may cover several square kilometers, and the density of occurrence of the microorganisms may reach many millions per liter, or quart, of seawater.

Toxic red tides, which vary in potency, generally occur in calm coastal waters during the summer months. Their appearance is often attributed to the coincidental occurrence of abundant food and optimal temperatures. Such tides are generally caused by several species of algae called DINOFLAGELLATES. The most common of these toxic dinoflagellates are *Gonyaulax polyedra, G. catenella, G. tamarensis,* and *Gymnodinium breve.* Their neurotoxins cause extensive mortality among invertebrates, fish, and birds. Clams, mussels, oysters, and other shellfish that feed on the dinoflagellates, however, appear to be immune and may concentrate the poisons within their bodies. Humans or other vertebrates that eat quantities of shellfish containing the toxins may suffer partial paralysis (paralytic shellfish poisoning) or, in some cases, death, because of paralysis of the heart and respiratory system.

redbud   Redbuds are seven species of small trees or shrubs of the genus *Cercis* in the pea family, Leguminosae, native to northern temperate regions. The eastern redbud, *C. canadensis,* of eastern North America, bears heart-shaped leaves and usually pinkish flowers. The western redbud, *C. occidentalis,* of the southwestern United States, commonly grows as a shrub with purplish flowers and rounded leaves. The Judas tree, *C. siliquastrum,* is native to Eurasia and grows to a height of 12 m (40 ft). Its name derives from the legend that Judas Iscariot hung himself from a redbud.

The eastern redbud tree, native to the northeastern United States and Canada, grows up to 7 m (15 ft) in height. It is used as a landscape tree because of its attractive leaves and spring flowers.

Redding, Otis   Singer and songwriter Otis Redding, b. Dawson, Ga., Sept. 9, 1941, d. Dec. 10, 1967, is considered one of the greatest exponents of SOUL MUSIC. He was killed in an airplane crash. Among his admirers were the Rolling Stones and Aretha Franklin, whose 1967 recording of his song "Respect" was an instant hit. Although he achieved considerable success during his lifetime, Redding's greatest fame came posthumously, with the 1968 release of his song "Sittin' on the Dock of the Bay."

Redford, Robert   One of Hollywood's most popular leading men, Charles Robert Redford, Jr., b. Santa Monica, Calif., Aug. 18, 1937, had his first success on Broadway in Neil Simon's *Barefoot in the Park* (1963; film, 1967). Redford's reputation soared with the films *Butch Cassidy and the Sundance Kid* (1969) and *The Sting* (1973), in which he played roguish but lovable crooks opposite Paul Newman. His other notable roles were in *Downhill Racer* (1969), *Jeremiah Johnson* and *The Candidate* (both 1972), *The Way We Were* (1973), *The Great Gatsby* (1974), *All the President's Men* (1976), *The Natural* (1984), *Out of Africa* (1985), and *Havana* (1990). Redford directed *Ordinary People* (1980; Academy Award) and *The Milagro Beanfield War* (1988). He has long been active in environmentalist causes.

Redgrave (family)   The combined careers of the Redgrave family span more than four decades of British theater and films. **Sir Michael Redgrave**, b. Mar. 20, 1908, d. Mar. 21, 1985, was knighted in 1959 for his distinguished contributions to the British stage. By contrast, his screen career was oddly disappointing despite an amiable beginning with *The Lady Vanishes* (1938) and occasional peaks such as *Kipps* (1941), *Dead of Night* (1945), *The Browning Version* (1951), and *The Go-Between* (1971). His extreme height made him difficult to cast. His elder daughter, **Vanessa Redgrave**, b. Jan. 30, 1937, although gaining notoriety for her radical politics, is an accomplished actress, highly praised for her roles in *Morgan* (1966), *Blow-up* (1967), *Isadora* (1968), *Julia* (1977; Academy Award), the television movie *Playing for Time* (1980; Emmy), *The Bostonians* (1984), and *Wetherby* (1985). A younger daughter, **Lynn Redgrave**, b. Mar. 8, 1943, playing more often in comedies, made a touchingly awkward heroine in *Georgy Girl* (1966), and turned to television in the 1970s and 1980s.

Redon, Odilon [ruh-dohn', oh-dee-lohn']   The French symbolist artist Odilon Redon, b. Apr. 20, 1840, d. July 6, 1916, peopled his works with imaginary beings. In his charcoal drawings and lithographs, such as *Death: "My Irony Surpasses All Others"* (1889), an illustration for Gustave Flaubert's *The Temptation of Saint Anthony*, he used chiaroscuro to convey subjective values.

Cyclops (c. 1898), by Odilon Redon, a portrayal of the one-eyed giant of classical Greek legend, exemplifies this painter's ability to represent hallucinations, often based on literary inspiration. (Rijksmuseum Kröller-Müller, Otterlo, the Netherlands.)

In 1889 radiant color harmonies replaced the dominance of black in Redon's works. *Evocation of Roussel* (1890; National Gallery of Art, Washington, D.C.) is not a traditional portrait of the composer. Instead the figure and the flowers emerge from amorphous colors symbolizing their evolution from the artist's imagination. The face, veiled with a brown tone, is a mystery. In his *Cyclops* (c.1898; Kröller-Müller Museum, Otterlo, Netherlands) the bizarre one-eyed creature depicted, and the improbable landscape, are underlined with a structural logic stemming from Redon's assiduous study of botany and osteology. The decorative effect associates Redon's pictorial attitude with the late-19th-century postimpressionist and Art Nouveau styles. The apparent naturalism of Redon's late bouquet paintings, like the *Vase of Flowers* (1914; Museum of Modern Art, New York City), is betrayed by the vague, dreamlike backgrounds and the cold blues within the flowers' general warmth.

redstart   The redstart is a small Old World bird, *Phoenicurus phoenicurus,* of the thrush family, Turdidae, widely distributed throughout Europe and western Asia. It is about 13 cm (5.5 in) long and has a rusty red rump and tail and, in the male, an orange breast and black bib. The name redstart is also applied to a number of other birds in the thrush family including the Eurasian black redstart, *P. ochruros,* and the Asiatic plumbeous redstart, *Rhyacornis fuliginosus.* In the New World the name redstart refers to a number of species in the wood warbler family, Parulidae. The American redstart, *Setophaga ruticilla,* is about 13 cm (5.5 in) long. Males are jet black with bright orange patches on the wings and tail; females and young have yellow patches on olive brown. The species nests from the southeastern United States into northwestern Canada and winters from Mexico into South America.

The American redstart is an accomplished flycatcher. The male's markings (left) are unlike those of any other warbler.

Redstone   Redstone was the rocket used to launch the first U.S. manned suborbital flights during the MERCURY PROGRAM. It was originally developed by the Army Ballistic Missile Agency (ABMA) at Redstone Arsenal in Huntsville, Ala., to satisfy a requirement for a ballistic missile with a range of 322 km (200 mi) for use in the field by the U.S. Army. The original Redstone stood 21 m (69 ft) tall, had a diameter of 178 cm (70 in), and a liftoff weight of 28,123 kg (62,000 lb). Redstone used much of the technology of the German A-4 (V-2) rocket. The propellants were liquid oxygen and ethyl alcohol, and guidance was obtained by an inertial system acting upon graphite exhaust vanes and small aerodynamic rudders.

Redstone was first test-launched at Cape Canaveral on Aug. 20, 1953, when it traveled just 7,315 m (24,000 ft). By the end of 1958, 36 more launchings had demonstrated the missile's great potential. Sixteen of them were built by Redstone Arsenal under the technical direction of Wernher von Braun; the others, by Chrysler Corporation.

The weapon entered service with the U.S. Army in West Germany in June 1958.

The Redstone became the basis for the JUPITER and Juno rockets, the first of which launched *Explorer 1*, the first U.S. satellite. With the motor and tank section lengthened and the 7.3-m (24-ft) Mercury capsule and escape tower substituted for the upper section and warhead, the Redstone used in the MERCURY PROGRAM had an overall height of 25 m (83 ft).

See also: ROCKETS AND MISSILES.

reduction   SEE OXIDATION AND REDUCTION

---

redwood   Once widespread in the Northern Hemisphere, the approximately 40 species of redwoods have dwindled to only 3: 2 in California and 1 in China. The redwoods, also called sequoias, are members of the family Taxodiaceae, variously called the redwood, bald-cypress, or swamp-cypress family.

The coast redwood, *Sequoia sempervirens*, is believed to be the tallest tree in the world; one specimen reportedly measured 117.3 m (385 ft) high. The coast redwood is a coniferous evergreen with a deeply furrowed, reddish brown bark up to 25 cm (10 in) thick. It has flat needles and tiny cones that mature in one season. The species is restricted to areas in which recurrent ocean fogs provide the trees with the required high humidity. This area forms an irregular coastal strip in California that varies in altitude from sea level to 900 m (3,000 ft). Coast redwoods are still extensively harvested for building lumber and other uses.

The giant redwood is now generally classified in a genus of its own as *Sequoiadendron giganteum*. Although not as tall as the coast redwood nor with the extensive

The redwood, a conifer native to the North American Pacific coast, is the tallest tree in the world.

trunk diameter of some baobabs, the tree's combination of immense height and trunk diameter make it the most massive living thing. Heights of about 99 m (325 ft) and diameters of 9 m (30 ft) have been reported. Immense size implies considerable age, and the big trees are among the oldest living things, some estimated to exceed 3,500 years in age. The giant redwood has a furrowed, reddish brown bark that may exceed 50 cm (20 in) in thickness. Its small, blue green needles appear to clothe the shoots; its cones take two seasons to mature. The trees are confined to altitudes of 1,500 to 2,560 m (5,000 to 8,400 ft) on the western slopes of the Sierra Nevada in central California. Once widely harvested for their wood, the big trees are now of insignificant commercial value because they are so few in number or are in protected areas.

The dawn redwood, *Metasequoia glyptostroboides*, native to south central China, was first known only from its fossil remains, which were scientifically described in 1941. It was not until several years later that botanists became aware that the tree still existed. The dawn redwood differs from the other redwoods in several ways, including the fact that it is deciduous.

Redwood National Park   SEE NATIONAL PARKS

---

reed   Reed is the common name for a variety of large, perennial plants of the grass family, Gramineae. The common reed, *Phragmites australis,* usually classified as *P. communis* or sometimes as *P. maximus,* is found in wetlands, most commonly brackish-water environments, throughout most of the world. It rarely produces fully developed seeds and usually spreads by means of its vigorous rootstock (rhizome).

The common reed, *Arundo donax,* also called the giant reed, has jointed, pithy stems (culms) that may reach 5.8 m (19 ft) in height. The stems bear long, narrow, blue green to gray green leaves that measure up to 60 cm (2 ft) long. Graceful, featherlike flower clusters are produced at the top of the stems in late summer. The flower clusters are purplish red when young but later become a silvery white. Long, silky hairs within a cluster accentuate its plumelike appearance. Native to southern Europe, the common reed has been introduced into the southern United States and tropical America as an ornamental and for erosion control. Its woody stems are used to produce reeds for certain musical instruments.

Reed, Sir Carol   An accomplished British film director who was knighted in 1952, Sir Carol Reed, b. Dec. 30, 1906, d. Apr. 25, 1976, had his first outstanding success with *The Stars Look Down* (1939). Two excellent war films, *The Way Ahead* (1944) and a documentary, *The True Glory* (1945), followed. Reed's postwar international reputation derived largely from such taut, highly literate suspense dramas as *The Fallen Idol* (1948) and *The Third Man* (1949), both scripted by novelist Graham Greene, and *The Man Between* (1953). Reed further distinguished himself with *The Key* (1958), *Our Man in Havana* (1959), and the musical *Oliver!* (1968), for which he won an Academy Award.

Reed, Ishmael   The American writer Ishmael Reed, b. Emmett Coleman in Chattanooga, Tenn., Feb. 22, 1938, is best known for his highly original fiction. Experimental in form, each of his novels is an exuberant, phantasmagoric satire on Western cultural values and a celebration of black survival against great odds. In *The Free-Lance Pallbearers* (1967), *Yellow Back Radio Broke-Down* (1969), *Mumbo-Jumbo* (1972), *The Last Days of Louisiana Red* (1974), *Flight to Canada* (1976), *The Terrible Twos* (1982), and *Reckless Eyeballing* (1986), Reed uses an array of cultural and historical references to rewrite history according to the values of "neo hoo-dooism," Reed's term for all that is culturally spontaneous and joyful. Neo hoo-dooism as an alternative to the traditions of whites also figures in his collections of poetry, among which are *Conjure: Selected Poems 1963–70* (1972) and *New and Collected Poetry* (1988).

Reed, John   John Reed, b. Portland, Oreg., Oct. 22, 1887, d. Oct. 19, 1920, American journalist, poet, and revolutionary, wrote the internationally famous *Ten Days That Shook the World* (1919), a sympathetic eyewitness account of the Bolshevik revolution of 1917. A graduate (1910) of Harvard University, Reed wrote poetry and began a career in journalism at *American Magazine.* Becoming interested in social problems, he joined the staff of Max Eastman's radical journal *Masses* in 1913. Reed's firsthand reports for the magazine *Metropolitan* on Pancho Villa's Mexican revolt in 1914 and on World War I in Eastern Europe in 1914–15 established his reputation as a war correspondent. Visiting Petrograd (now Leningrad), Russia, in 1917 during the Bolshevik revolution, Reed became a supporter and friend of V. I. Lenin before returning home. In 1919 he was expelled from the U.S. Socialist party and became head of the Communist Labor party. Indicted for sedition, Reed fled to the USSR in late 1919.

Reed, Thomas B.   Thomas Brackett Reed, b. Portland, Maine, Oct. 18, 1839, d. Dec. 7, 1902, was the U.S. legislator who formulated the "Reed Rules" of parliamentary procedure. He served in Congress from 1876 to 1899 as a Republican from Maine, including two terms (1889–91, 1895–99) as Speaker of the House. Called "czar" because of his arbitrary use of power, he brought the speakership to the peak of its political influence, notably by introducing (1890) rules designed to limit debate and ease the passage of legislation. "Czar" Reed wielded the Speaker's power of recognition to curb Democratic FILIBUSTERS. Under him the 51st Congress produced so much legislation that it was dubbed the billion-dollar congress.

Reed, Walter   The military surgeon Walter Reed, b. Belroi, Va., Sept. 13, 1851, d. Nov. 22, 1902, proved in 1901 that YELLOW FEVER is caused by a filterable virus transmitted by the bite of the *Aedes aegypti* mosquito. After working to improve sanitary conditions and prevent the spread of typhoid during the Spanish-American War, Reed was appointed (1900) to head a commission studying yellow fever in Cuba. He and his commission disproved the theory that yellow fever was caused by bacteria and found that it did not spread by contact. The subsequent clearing of mosquito-breeding areas in the southeastern United States and Latin America halted the disease. The Walter Reed Medical Center outside Washington, D.C., founded in 1909, is named for Reed.

reed instruments   SEE MUSICAL INSTRUMENTS

reed organ   The reed-organ family includes the ACCORDION, CONCERTINA, HARMONICA (or mouth organ), harmonium, and American organ. Those instruments, descended from the Chinese *sheng* (a mouth organ that played chords rather than melodies), came into existence early in the 19th century. They all employ the principle of the free reed, which beats to and fro in a slot. The harmonium and American organ are similar in their uses of free reeds, a keyboard, drawstops to alter the tonal qualities, and pedals that supply air to the bellows.

The application of a keyboard to reeds dates from the first decade of the 19th century; the first patents on the harmonium were taken out by A. F. Debain in 1840. Other manufacturers soon added devices that changed the sound and capabilities of the instrument: the most important include "percussion," in which a hammer strikes the end of the reed as the air activates it; a prolongation attachment that permits certain keys to continue sounding after they are released; a device to emphasize the top or bottom notes; and knee swells to suddenly add the full force of the instrument.

The American, or cottage, organ differs from the harmonium—it sucks air into the reeds rather than expelling it. American organs were popular for home use and were often found in small churches before the days of the electric organ.

reef   SEE CORAL REEF

Reeve, Tapping   The American jurist Tapping Reeve, b. Brookhaven, N.Y., October 1744, d. Dec. 13, 1823, established one of the first law schools in the United States. A graduate of the College of New Jersey (now Princeton University), Reeve began to practice (1772) law in Litchfield, Conn., and opened (1784) Litchfield Law School. He served (1798–1814) on the Connecticut superior court and was chief justice (1814–16) of the state supreme court of errors. Before Litchfield Law School closed in 1833, many later-eminent people studied there, including Aaron Burr and Horace Mann.

ILLUSTRATION CREDITS

5 Brown Brothers
6 The Hark Group Ltd./Slidemakers
8 Corcoran Gallery
14 Aldus Archives
22 Mirèille Vautier
23 Courtesy Library of Congress
24 New York Public Library Astor, Lenox, and Tilden Foundations, Rare Book Division; ABC Press/Seldow-Rona
26 Scala, Florence
31 The Bettmann Archive; The Bettmann Archive
33 UPI/Bettmann Newsphotos
36 The Bettmann Archive
38 NASA; NASA
39 Bruce Coleman Ltd./Oxford Scientific Films; Bruce Coleman Ltd./Oxford Scientific Films
40 Bruce Coleman Ltd./Oxford Scientific Films
41 Photo Researchers/Gregory G. Dimijian
62 National Gallery, London
65 Photographie Giraudon
73 Lowell Observatory
75 Smithsonian Institution, Washington D.C., National Collection of Fine Arts
76 National Portrait Gallery, Washington, D.C.
78 The Mansell Collection
88 Rand McNally & Company
89 Leo deWys Inc./J. Andrews
90 Woodfin Camp & Associates/Koni Nordmann
91 Lothar Roth and Associates
97 Santi Visalli
98 Sipa Press/Trippett
102 Corcoran Gallery of Art
103 Geocom BV; Geocom BV
108 AAE-Photo
109 Orion Press
110 Wheeler Pictures/Melford
111 Photo Researchers/Paolo Koch
113 Bodleian Library
119 Scala, Florence
120 Art Resource
121 Art Resource
125 National Portrait Gallery, London
141 Rand McNally & Company
142 Picture Point, London; Paul Pet
143 Sem Presser
144 Musea di Arte Antica, Lisbon
145 Douglas Dickins
147 Jacana/Joff
149 The Bettmann Archive

150 The Bettmann Archive
151 The Bettmann Archive
153 Norman McGrath
156 National Portrait Gallery, London
157 Royal Museum of Copenhagen; Metropolitan Museum of Art, New York, Gift of Robert E. Tod, 1937
158 Smithsonian Institution, Washington, D.C., Freer Gallery of Art; Metropolitan Museum of Art, New York, Bequest of Joseph H. Durkee, Gift of Darius Ogden Mills and Gift of C. Ruxton Love by Exchange, 1972; Metropolitan Museum of Art, New York/Rogers Fund
159 Cooper-Hewitt Museum, New York, The Smithsonian Institution's National Museum of Design; The Frick Collection, New York
160 Buten Museum of Wedgewood; Cooper-Hewitt Museum, New York, The Smithsonian Institution's National Museum of Design, Gift of Lionberger Davis, 1968
163 Wide World Photos
167 The Bettmann Archive
168 Mary Evans Picture Library
169 KEMA; Sem Presser
171 © Hank Morgan
173 Photo Researchers/D. W. Friedmann
176 Mirèille Vautier/Kodansha Ltd., Tokyo, Courtesy of National Museum of Anthropology, Mexico City
177 Lee Boltin; Peabody Museum, Harvard University
178 Kodansha Ltd., Tokyo, Courtesy of National Museum of Anthropology, Mexico City; The British Museum; Photo Researchers/George Holton
179 Photographie Giraudon; John F. Scott
180 Courtesy Museum of Fine Arts, Boston
181 The Stock Shop/Robert Matzkin
190 Monkmeyer Press Photo Service/ Douglas Mazonowicz
192 Sem Presser; Irish Tourist Board
195 Gino D'Achille, Courtesy Aldus Books
200 The Tate Gallery, London
203 UPI/Bettmann Newsphotos; UPI/ Bettmann Newsphotos
204 UPI/Bettmann Newsphotos; UPI/ Bettmann Newsphotos
205 UPI/Bettmann Newsphotos
206 The White House/David Valdez; Stefan Lorant: *The Glorious Burden* (author's edition)

207 Stefan Lorant: *The Glorious Burden* (author's edition)
208 UPI/Bettmann Newsphotos
209 Stefan Lorant: *The Glorious Burden* (author's edition); Stefan Lorant: *The Glorious Burden* (author's edition)
210 Harvard College Library, Theodore Roosevelt Collection; The Bettmann Archive
211 UPI/Bettmann Newsphotos; UPI/ Bettmann Newsphotos
215 The Bettmann Archive
222 Photo Researchers/Tomas D. W. Friedmann; Woodfin Camp and Associates/Kal Muller
223 Scala, Florence
227 Rand McNally & Company; George Hunter Photography
229 The British Museum
238 Courtesy of Allen Bradley Co., Inc.
241 Culver Pictures
242 Verlag Hans Huber, Bern
243 Harvard University Press
244 The Bettmann Archive
246 U.S. Army Photograph; Susan E. Meyer; Agence France Presse
257 Het Spectrum
259 UPI/Bettmann Newsphotos
260 Lothar Roth and Associates
262 Sem Presser
264 The Bettmann Archive
265 Courtesy Du-Atlantis, Zurich; Aldus Archives
271 The Bettmann Archive; The Bettmann Archive
272 Brown Brothers; Yale University Archives; Historical Picture Service; Life Nature Library—*Animal Behavior*, photograph by Nina Leen, © 1965 Time, Inc. Time-Life Books, Inc.
273 Brown Brothers; The Bettmann Archive
274 Wide World Photo
276 The British Museum
277 Agence De Presse Photographique Rapho
278 Photo Researchers/Will McIntyre; Photo Researchers/NIH/Science
283 George W. Goddard; The Bettmann Archive
287 The Bettmann Archive
288 Josef Muench
290 Rand McNally & Company; Servizio Editoriale Fotografico
293 Brown Brothers
299 The British Museum
301 Claus Hansmann; Mary Evans Picture Library; The Bettmann Archive
304 Novosti Press
305 Superstock/Shostal
307 Photo Researchers/John G. Ross; Photo Researchers/John G. Ross
308 Superstock/Shostal/August Upitis
309 Photo Reseachers/Charles Belinky
310 Art Resource

312 Gamma/Liaison
313 Rand McNally & Company
314 The Bettmann Archive
324 Photo Researchers/G. Tomsich
325 Lothar Roth and Associates
326 Picture Point, London
328 Rand McNally & Company
329 Peter Arnold
333 Opterreichische Nationalbibliothek
338 Greta Baars Jelgersma
339 Art Resource/Photographie Giraudon
343 The Bettmann Archive
344 Keystone Press Agency, Inc.
345 New York Public Library Astor, Lenox and Tilden Foundations
346 Aldus Archives
348 Zentrale Farbbild Agentur Zefa
349 The Bettmann Archive
350 RCA
354 Rijksuniversiteit Groningen/ Sterrenkundig Laboratorium "Kapteyn"; Sterrenwacht Leiden/ Huygens Laboratories
355 United States Information Service; United States Information Service
358 Aretê Archives; RCA
359 Brown Brothers; Culver Pictures
360 NBC; Wisconsin Center for Film
361 CBS; CBS; NBC; PBS
362 Courtesy Sunbow Productions, Inc., in association with Marvel Productions Ltd.
363 DOT/John Livzey
364 The Bettmann Archive
368 Medical Images/Howard Sochurek; Photo Researchers/Scott Camazine
369 Photo Researchers/ Will & Deni McIntyre
374 Courtesy Canadian Pacific Railroad
375 Culver Pictures
378 Bruce Coleman Inc.
379 Courtesy Transit America Inc.
381 National Portrait Gallery, London
382 Art Resource
383 The Bettmann Archive; NAACP
385 Photo Researchers/Van Bucher
387 Bildarchiv Preussicher Kulturbesitz
390 Brown Brothers
394 The Bettmann Archive
396 Sem Presser
398 Het Spectrum
401 Stefan Lorant: *The Glorious Burden* (author's edition)
406 Stefan Lorant: *The Glorious Burden* (author's edition)
407 Stefan Lorant: *The Glorious Burden* (author's edition)
411 Aldus Archives